# ספר בראשית

## THE BOOK OF GENESIS

## ספר בראשית

# THE BOOK OF GENESIS

The Hebrew name for the First Book of Moses was originally *Sefer Maaseh Bereshith*, 'Book of Creation.' This was rendered into Greek by *Genesis*, 'origin,' because it gives an account of the creation of the world and the beginnings of life and society. Its current Jewish name is בראשית *Bereshith* ('In the beginning'), which is the first Hebrew word in its opening sentence. *Bereshith* is also the name of Chap. I–VI, 8, the first of the fifty-four weekly Torah Readings (Sedrahs) on Sabbath mornings.

If the Pentateuch (which is a Greek word meaning the *five books* of Moses) were merely a code of civil and religious laws, it would have opened with the twelfth chapter of Exodus, which contains the earliest specific commandment given to Israel (Rashi). But it is far more than a code of law: it is the Torah, *i.e.* the Divine Teaching given to Israel, and the Message of Israel to mankind. Therefore, it describes the origins of the Jewish people; traces its kinship to the other portions of the human family—all being of one blood and offspring of one common stock; and goes back to the creation of the world, which it declares to be the work of One Almighty and Beneficent God. All this is told in the first eleven chapters of Genesis. The remaining thirty-nine chapters give the story of the Fathers of the Jewish people—Abraham, Isaac, Jacob and his children.

For the place of the tales of Genesis in human education, see p. 141.

## GENESIS I, 1

### CHAPTER I

1. In the beginning God created the heaven and the earth. 2. Now the earth was unformed and void, and darkness was upon the face of the deep; and the spirit of God hovered over the face of the waters. 3. And God said: 'Let there be light.' And there was light. 4. And God saw the light, that it was good; and God divided the light from the darkness. 5. And God called the light Day, and the darkness He called Night. And there was evening and there was morning, one day.

בראשית א

CAP. I. א

בְּרֵאשִׁ֖ית בָּרָ֣א אֱלֹהִ֑ים אֵ֥ת הַשָּׁמַ֖יִם וְאֵ֥ת הָאָֽרֶץ׃ וְהָאָ֗רֶץ הָיְתָ֥ה תֹ֙הוּ֙ וָבֹ֔הוּ וְחֹ֖שֶׁךְ עַל־פְּנֵ֣י תְה֑וֹם וְר֣וּחַ אֱלֹהִ֔ים מְרַחֶ֖פֶת עַל־פְּנֵ֥י הַמָּֽיִם׃ וַיֹּ֥אמֶר אֱלֹהִ֖ים יְהִ֣י א֑וֹר וַֽיְהִי־אֽוֹר׃ וַיַּ֧רְא אֱלֹהִ֛ים אֶת־הָא֖וֹר כִּי־ט֑וֹב וַיַּבְדֵּ֣ל אֱלֹהִ֔ים בֵּ֥ין הָא֖וֹר וּבֵ֥ין הַחֹֽשֶׁךְ׃ וַיִּקְרָ֨א אֱלֹהִ֤ים ׀ לָאוֹר֙ י֔וֹם וְלַחֹ֖שֶׁךְ קָ֣רָא לָ֑יְלָה וַֽיְהִי־עֶ֥רֶב וַֽיְהִי־בֹ֖קֶר י֥וֹם אֶחָֽד׃ פ

1. v. ב רבתי

## I. BERESHITH

### (CHAPTERS I–VI, 8)

### ORIGIN OF THE UNIVERSE AND THE BEGINNINGS OF THE HUMAN RACE

### CREATION OF THE WORLD. CHAPTER I–II, 3

**1.** *In the beginning.* Verse 1 is a majestic summary of the story of Creation: God is the beginning, nay, the Cause of all things. The remainder of the chapter gives details of the successive acts of creation. Ages untold may have elapsed between the calling of matter into being and the reduction of chaos to ordered arrangement.

*God.* Heb. *Elohim.* The existence of the Deity is throughout Scripture assumed: it is not a matter for argument or doubt. *Elohim* is the general designation of the Divine Being in the Bible, as the fountain and source of all things. *Elohim* is a plural form, which is often used in Hebrew to denote plenitude of might. Here it indicates that God comprehends and unifies all the forces of eternity and infinity.

*created.* The Heb. word is in the singular, thus precluding any idea that its subject, *Elohim*, is to be understood in a plural sense. The term ברא is used exclusively of Divine activity. Man is spoken of as 'making' or 'forming', but never as 'creating', *i.e.* producing something out of nothing.

*the heaven and the earth.* The visible world; that which is above (heaven), and that which is below (earth).

**2.** *the earth.* The material out of which the universe is formed.

*the deep.* Heb. *tehom*, the abyss.

*spirit of God.* The mysterious, unseen, and irresistible presence of the Divine Being.

*hovered.* The Heb. word occurs again only in Deut. XXXII, 11, where it is descriptive of the eagle hovering over the young to care for them and protect them. Matter in itself is lifeless. The Spirit of God quickens it and transforms it into material for a living world. The Jerusalem Targum translates this verse: 'And the earth was vacancy and desolation, solitary of the sons of men and void of every animal, and darkness was upon the face of the abyss; and the Spirit of Mercies from before the LORD breathed upon the face of the waters.'

3–5. FIRST DAY. CREATION OF LIGHT.

**3.** *And God said.* 'By the word of the LORD were the heavens made,' Psalm XXXIII, 6. One of the names for God in later Jewish literature is 'He who spake and the world came into existence' (Authorised Prayer Book, p. 16). 'The phrase *God said* must be taken as a figurative equivalent of "God willed" ' (Saadyah).

*let there be light.* A sublimely simple phrase to express a sublime fact. This light, which is distinct from that radiated later on from the sun, disperses the darkness that enshrouded the Deep (*v.* 2). The old question, Whence did the light issue before the sun was made, is answered by the nebular theory! The great astronomer Halley wrote: 'These nebulæ reply fully to the difficulty which has been raised against the Mosaic description of creation, in asserting that light could not be generated without the sun.'

**4.** *that it was good. i.e.* fulfils the will of the Creator. Repeated *v.* 10, 12, 18, 21, 25, 31. For the significance of this refrain, see Additional Note A, p. 193.

**5.** *called.* In calling the light Day, God defines the significance of light in human life. In the Bible account of Creation, everything centres round man and is viewed from his angle.

*And there was evening.* The day, according to the Scriptural reckoning of time, begins with the preceding evening. Thus, the observance of the Day of Atonement is to be 'from even unto even' (Lev. XXIII, 32); and similarly of the Sabbath and Festivals.

GENESIS I, 6 בראשית א

6 וַיֹּאמֶר אֱלֹהִים יְהִי רָקִיעַ בְּתוֹךְ הַמָּיִם וִיהִי מַבְדִּיל בֵּין
7 מַיִם לָמָיִם׃ וַיַּעַשׂ אֱלֹהִים אֶת־הָרָקִיעַ וַיַּבְדֵּל בֵּין הַמַּיִם
אֲשֶׁר מִתַּחַת לָרָקִיעַ וּבֵין הַמַּיִם אֲשֶׁר מֵעַל לָרָקִיעַ וַיְהִי־
8 כֵן׃ וַיִּקְרָא אֱלֹהִים לָרָקִיעַ שָׁמָיִם וַיְהִי־עֶרֶב וַיְהִי־בֹקֶר
יוֹם שֵׁנִי׃ פ
9 וַיֹּאמֶר אֱלֹהִים יִקָּווּ הַמַּיִם מִתַּחַת הַשָּׁמַיִם אֶל־מָקוֹם אֶחָד
10 וְתֵרָאֶה הַיַּבָּשָׁה וַיְהִי־כֵן׃ וַיִּקְרָא אֱלֹהִים ׀ לַיַּבָּשָׁה אֶרֶץ
11 וּלְמִקְוֵה הַמַּיִם קָרָא יַמִּים וַיַּרְא אֱלֹהִים כִּי־טוֹב׃ וַיֹּאמֶר
אֱלֹהִים תַּדְשֵׁא הָאָרֶץ דֶּשֶׁא עֵשֶׂב מַזְרִיעַ זֶרַע עֵץ פְּרִי
עֹשֶׂה פְּרִי לְמִינוֹ אֲשֶׁר זַרְעוֹ־בוֹ עַל־הָאָרֶץ וַיְהִי־כֵן׃
12 וַתּוֹצֵא הָאָרֶץ דֶּשֶׁא עֵשֶׂב מַזְרִיעַ זֶרַע לְמִינֵהוּ וְעֵץ עֹשֶׂה־
13 פְּרִי אֲשֶׁר זַרְעוֹ־בוֹ לְמִינֵהוּ וַיַּרְא אֱלֹהִים כִּי־טוֹב׃ וַיְהִי־
עֶרֶב וַיְהִי־בֹקֶר יוֹם שְׁלִישִׁי׃* פ
14 וַיֹּאמֶר אֱלֹהִים יְהִי מְאֹרֹת בִּרְקִיעַ הַשָּׁמַיִם לְהַבְדִּיל בֵּין
הַיּוֹם וּבֵין הַלָּיְלָה וְהָיוּ לְאֹתֹת וּלְמוֹעֲדִים וּלְיָמִים וְשָׁנִים׃

v. 11. הד׳ בז״ק ובספרי ספרד ברביע

¶ 6. And God said: 'Let there be a firmament in the midst of the waters, and let it divide the waters from the waters.' 7. And God made the firmament, and divided the waters which were under the firmament from the waters which were above the firmament; and it was so. 8. And God called the firmament Heaven. And there was evening and there was morning, a second day. ¶ 9. And God said: 'Let the waters under the heaven be gathered together unto one place, and let the dry land appear.' And it was so. 10. And God called the dry land Earth, and the gathering together of the waters called He Seas; and God saw that it was good. 11. And God said: 'Let the earth put forth grass, herb yielding seed, and fruit-tree bearing fruit after its kind, wherein is the seed thereof, upon the earth.' And it was so. 12. And the earth brought forth grass, herb yielding seed after its kind, and tree bearing fruit, wherein is the seed thereof, after its kind; and God saw that it was good. 13. And there was evening and there was morning, a third day.* ¶ 14. And God said: 'Let there be lights in the firmament of the heaven to divide the day from the night; and let them be for signs, and for seasons, and for days and

*one day*. Not an ordinary day but a Day of God (יומו של הקב״ה), an age. With Him a thousand years, nay a thousand thousand ages, are but as a day that is past; Psalm xc, 4. 'Earthly and human measurement of time, by a clock of human manufacture, cannot apply to the first three days, as the sun was not then in existence. The beginning of each period of creation is called morning; its close, evening' (Delitzsch); in the same way, we speak of the morning and evening of life.

6-8. SECOND DAY. THE FIRMAMENT

**6.** *firmament*. Sky, arch of heaven.

*waters from the waters*. i.e. the waters above the firmament (the mists and clouds that come down to earth in the shape of rain), from the waters on earth (rivers and seas).

**7.** *and it was so*. Fulfilment follows immediately upon the Divine fiat. 'For He spoke, and it was; He commanded, and it stood' (Psalm xxxiii, 9).

**8.** *Heaven*. In the Bible, Heaven (*shamayim*) is represented as the habitation of God, in the figurative sense in which the Temple is similarly described: 'Behold, heaven and the heaven of heavens cannot contain Thee; how much less this house that I have builded!' (I Kings viii, 27).

*and there was evening*. On the second day the usual formula, 'And God saw that it was good,' is omitted. The work begun on that day did not terminate until the middle of the third day. Hence, an uncompleted piece of work could not properly be pronounced 'good' (Rashi).

*a second day*. Or, 'the second day'; similarly, v. 13, 19, and 23.

9-13. THIRD DAY. SEA, LAND, AND VEGETATION

**9.** *be gathered together*. As long as the face of the earth was covered by the 'deep' (v. 2), life was impossible for man or beast. God therefore decreed boundaries for the waters; cf. Psalm civ, 6-8.

**10.** *Earth*. Here it signifies that part of the terrestrial surface which was to be the abode of man and the scene of his activity.

*that it was good*. i.e. a fitting stage for the drama of human history.

**11.** *put forth*. In creating the earth, God implanted in it the forces that at His command produced the vegetation.

**12.** *that it was good*. As food for man and beast (cf. v. 29 f).

14-19. FOURTH DAY. CREATION OF HEAVENLY BODIES

**14.** *lights*. The Heb. word signifies sources of light; hence, 'luminaries' would be a better translation.

Other ancient peoples ascribed to the sun, moon and stars a beneficent or malevolent potency over the lives of men and nations. Here,

# GENESIS I, 15

years; 15. and let them be for lights in the firmament of the heaven to give light upon the earth.' And it was so. 16. And God made the two great lights: the greater light to rule the day, and the lesser light to rule the night; and the stars. 17. And God set them in the firmament of the heaven to give light upon the earth, 18. and to rule over the day and over the night, and to divide the light from the darkness; and God saw that it was good. 19. And there was evening and there was morning, a fourth day. ¶ 20. And God said: 'Let the waters swarm with swarms of living creatures, and let fowl fly above the earth in the open firmament of heaven.' 21. And God created the great sea-monsters, and every living creature that creepeth, wherewith the waters swarmed, after its kind, and every winged fowl after its kind; and God saw that it was good. 22. And God blessed them, saying: 'Be fruitful, and multiply, and fill the waters in the seas, and let fowl multiply in the earth.' 23. And there was evening and there was morning, a fifth day.\* ¹¹¹ ᵃ· ¶ 24. And God said: 'Let the earth bring forth the living creature after its kind, cattle, and creeping thing, and beast of the earth after its kind.' And it was so. 25. And God made the beast of the earth after its kind, and the cattle after their kind, and every thing that creepeth upon the ground after its kind; and God saw that it was good. 26. And God said: 'Let us make man in our image, after our likeness; and let them have dominion over the fish of the sea, and over the fowl of the air, and over the

בראשית א

טו וְהָיוּ לִמְאוֹרֹת בִּרְקִיעַ הַשָּׁמַיִם לְהָאִיר עַל־הָאָרֶץ וַיְהִי־
16 כֵן: וַיַּעַשׂ אֱלֹהִים אֶת־שְׁנֵי הַמְּאֹרֹת הַגְּדֹלִים אֶת־הַמָּאוֹר
הַגָּדֹל לְמֶמְשֶׁלֶת הַיּוֹם וְאֶת־הַמָּאוֹר הַקָּטֹן לְמֶמְשֶׁלֶת
17 הַלַּיְלָה וְאֵת הַכּוֹכָבִים: וַיִּתֵּן אֹתָם אֱלֹהִים בִּרְקִיעַ
18 הַשָּׁמָיִם לְהָאִיר עַל־הָאָרֶץ: וְלִמְשֹׁל בַּיּוֹם וּבַלַּיְלָה
וּלֲהַבְדִּיל בֵּין הָאוֹר וּבֵין הַחֹשֶׁךְ וַיַּרְא אֱלֹהִים כִּי־טוֹב:
19 וַיְהִי־עֶרֶב וַיְהִי־בֹקֶר יוֹם רְבִיעִי: פ

כ וַיֹּאמֶר אֱלֹהִים יִשְׁרְצוּ הַמַּיִם שֶׁרֶץ נֶפֶשׁ חַיָּה וְעוֹף יְעוֹפֵף
21 עַל־הָאָרֶץ עַל־פְּנֵי רְקִיעַ הַשָּׁמָיִם: וַיִּבְרָא אֱלֹהִים אֶת־
הַתַּנִּינִם הַגְּדֹלִים וְאֵת כָּל־נֶפֶשׁ הַחַיָּה ׀ הָרֹמֶשֶׂת אֲשֶׁר
שָׁרְצוּ הַמַּיִם לְמִינֵהֶם וְאֵת כָּל־עוֹף כָּנָף לְמִינֵהוּ וַיַּרְא
22 אֱלֹהִים כִּי־טוֹב: וַיְבָרֶךְ אֹתָם אֱלֹהִים לֵאמֹר פְּרוּ וּרְבוּ
23 וּמִלְאוּ אֶת־הַמַּיִם בַּיַּמִּים וְהָעוֹף יִרֶב בָּאָרֶץ: וַיְהִי־עֶרֶב
וַיְהִי־בֹקֶר יוֹם חֲמִישִׁי:\* פ שלישי

24 וַיֹּאמֶר אֱלֹהִים תּוֹצֵא הָאָרֶץ נֶפֶשׁ חַיָּה לְמִינָהּ בְּהֵמָה
כה וָרֶמֶשׂ וְחַיְתוֹ־אֶרֶץ לְמִינָהּ וַיְהִי־כֵן: וַיַּעַשׂ אֱלֹהִים אֶת־
חַיַּת הָאָרֶץ לְמִינָהּ וְאֶת־הַבְּהֵמָה לְמִינָהּ וְאֵת כָּל־רֶמֶשׂ
26 הָאֲדָמָה לְמִינֵהוּ וַיַּרְא אֱלֹהִים כִּי־טוֹב: וַיֹּאמֶר אֱלֹהִים
נַעֲשֶׂה אָדָם בְּצַלְמֵנוּ כִּדְמוּתֵנוּ וְיִרְדּוּ בִדְגַת הַיָּם וּבְעוֹף

v. 18. נ״א ולהבדיל    v. 21. חסר י׳ בתראה

---

however, all idolatry and superstition are swept away. These lights are works of one Almighty God, and are created for His appointed purposes; see Jer. x, 2.

*for signs.* To help man locate his position when moving over the surface of the earth: they were primitive man's compass.

*for seasons.* To regulate the calendar. The 'seasons' are spring, summer, autumn, and winter; also seed-time and harvest. The Heb. word for 'seasons' later acquired the meaning of 'festivals', since these were fixed by the year's seasons.

**15.** *light upon the earth.* Without which life and growth are impossible.

**16.** *and the stars.* They are mentioned last and without explanation, because they play a subordinate part in the life of man, as compared with the sun and moon.

**20–23.** FIFTH DAY. FISHES AND BIRDS

**20.** *swarm.* Or, 'teem.' Heb. *sharatz*. Movement as well as fecundity is implied. It is used in connection with fishes and aquatic animals, rodents and insects.

*fowl.* Collective noun, meaning winged things.

*in the open firmament.* In mid-air; in the face of, or over against, the firmament.

**21.** *creature.* lit. 'soul.' In Hebrew, *soul* is used more widely than in English, often denoting, as here, merely a living being.

**22.** *God blessed them.* No blessing was bestowed upon the vegetation, as its growth is dependent upon sun and rain, and not upon its own volition.

**24–31.** SIXTH DAY. LAND ANIMALS AND MAN

**24.** *earth bring forth.* The seeds and possibility of life implanted within her on the first day of Creation (Rashi).

*cattle.* All domestic animals.

*creeping thing.* Reptiles.

*beast of the earth.* Wild animals.

**26.** *let us make man.* Mankind is described as in a special sense created by God Himself.

GENESIS I, 27

cattle, and over all the earth, and over every creeping thing that creepeth upon the earth.' 27. And God created man in His own image, in the image of God created He him; male and female created He them. 28. And God blessed them; and God said unto them: 'Be fruitful, and multiply, and replenish the earth, and subdue it; and have dominion over the fish of the sea, and over the fowl of the air, and over every living thing that creepeth upon the earth.' 29. And God said: 'Behold, I have given you every herb yielding seed, which is upon the face of all the earth, and every tree, in which is the fruit of a tree yielding seed—to you it shall be for food; 30. and to every beast of the earth, and to every fowl of the air, and to every thing that creepeth upon the earth, wherein there is a living soul, [I have given] every green herb for food.' And it was so. 31. And God saw every thing that He had made, and, behold, it was very good. And there was evening and there was morning, the sixth day.

בראשית א

הַשָּׁמַיִם וּבַבְּהֵמָה וּבְכָל־הָאָרֶץ וּבְכָל־הָרֶמֶשׂ הָרֹמֵשׂ עַל־הָאָרֶץ: 27 וַיִּבְרָא אֱלֹהִים ׀ אֶת־הָאָדָם בְּצַלְמוֹ בְּצֶלֶם אֱלֹהִים 28 בָּרָא אֹתוֹ זָכָר וּנְקֵבָה בָּרָא אֹתָם: וַיְבָרֶךְ אֹתָם אֱלֹהִים וַיֹּאמֶר לָהֶם אֱלֹהִים פְּרוּ וּרְבוּ וּמִלְאוּ אֶת־הָאָרֶץ וְכִבְשֻׁהָ וּרְדוּ בִּדְגַת הַיָּם וּבְעוֹף הַשָּׁמַיִם וּבְכָל־חַיָּה הָרֹמֶשֶׂת עַל־הָאָרֶץ: 29 וַיֹּאמֶר אֱלֹהִים הִנֵּה נָתַתִּי לָכֶם אֶת־כָּל־עֵשֶׂב ׀ זֹרֵעַ זֶרַע אֲשֶׁר עַל־פְּנֵי כָל־הָאָרֶץ וְאֶת־כָּל־הָעֵץ אֲשֶׁר־ ל בּוֹ פְרִי־עֵץ זֹרֵעַ זָרַע לָכֶם יִהְיֶה לְאָכְלָה: וּלְכָל־חַיַּת הָאָרֶץ וּלְכָל־עוֹף הַשָּׁמַיִם וּלְכֹל ׀ רוֹמֵשׂ עַל־הָאָרֶץ אֲשֶׁר־ 31 בּוֹ נֶפֶשׁ חַיָּה אֶת־כָּל־יֶרֶק עֵשֶׂב לְאָכְלָה וַיְהִי־כֵן: וַיַּרְא אֱלֹהִים אֶת־כָּל־אֲשֶׁר עָשָׂה וְהִנֵּה־טוֹב מְאֹד וַיְהִי־עֶרֶב פ וַיְהִי־בֹקֶר יוֹם הַשִּׁשִּׁי:

To enhance the dignity of this last work and to mark the fact that man differs in kind from the animals, Scripture represents God as deliberating over the making of the human species (Abarbanel). It is not 'let man be created' or 'let man be made', but 'let us make man'. The use of the plural, 'let *us* make man,' is the Heb. idiomatic way of expressing deliberation, as in XI, 7; or it is the plural of Majesty, royal commands being conveyed in the first person plural, as in Ezra IV, 18.

*man.* Heb. '*Adam.*' The word is used here, as frequently in the Bible, in the sense of 'human being'. It is derived from *adamah* 'earth', to signify that man is earth-born; see II, 7.

*in our image, after our likeness.* Man is made in the 'image' and 'likeness' of God: his character is potentially Divine. 'God created man to be immortal, and made him to be an image of His own eternity' (Wisdom of Solomon II, 23). Man alone among living creatures is gifted, like his Creator, with moral freedom and will. He is capable of knowing and loving God, and of holding spiritual communion with Him; and man alone can guide his actions in accordance with Reason. 'On this account he is said to have been made in the form and likeness of the Almighty' (Maimonides). Because man is endowed with Reason, he can subdue his impulses in the service of moral and religious ideals, and is born to bear rule over Nature. Psalm VIII says of man, 'O LORD . . . Thou hast made him but little lower than the angels, and hast crowned him with glory and honour. Thou hast made him to have dominion over the works of Thy hands.'

**27.** *male and female.* A general statement; man and woman, both alike, are in their spiritual nature akin to God.

**28.** *and God blessed them.* Cf. v. 22. Here the words, 'And God said unto them,' are added, indicating a more intimate relationship between Him and human beings.

*be fruitful and multiply.* This is the first precept (*mitzvah*) given to man. The duty of building a home and rearing a family figures in the rabbinic Codes as the first of the 613 *Mitzvoth* (commandments) of the Torah.

*and subdue it.* 'The secret of all modern science is in the first chapter of Genesis. Belief in the dominion of spirit over matter, of mind over nature, of man over the physical and the animal creation, was essential to the possession of that dominion' (Lyman Abbott). 'What we call the will or volition of Man . . . has become a power in nature, an imperium in imperio, which has profoundly modified not only Man's own history, but that of the whole living world, and the face of the planet on which he lives' (Ray Lankester).

**29.** In the primitive ideal age (as also in the Messianic future, see Isaiah XI, 7), the animals were not to prey on one another.

**31.** *very good.* Each created thing is 'good' in itself; but when combined and united, the totality is proclaimed 'very good'. Everything in the universe was as the Creator willed it— nothing superfluous, nothing lacking—a harmony. 'This harmony bears witness to the unity of God who planned this unity of Nature' (Luzzatto).

# GENESIS II, 1

## CHAPTER II

1. And the heaven and the earth were finished, and all the host of them. 2. And on the seventh day God finished His work which He had made; and He rested on the seventh day from all His work which He had made. 3. And God blessed the seventh day, and hallowed it; because that in it He rested from all His work which God in creating had made.* 1v a; 11 s.
¶ 4. These are the generations of the heaven and of the earth when they were created, in the day that the LORD God made earth

## בראשית ב

### CAP. II. ב

2 וַיְכֻלּוּ הַשָּׁמַיִם וְהָאָרֶץ וְכָל־צְבָאָם: וַיְכַל אֱלֹהִים בַּיּוֹם
הַשְּׁבִיעִי מְלַאכְתּוֹ אֲשֶׁר עָשָׂה וַיִּשְׁבֹּת בַּיּוֹם הַשְּׁבִיעִי
3 מִכָּל־מְלַאכְתּוֹ אֲשֶׁר עָשָׂה: וַיְבָרֶךְ אֱלֹהִים אֶת־יוֹם
הַשְּׁבִיעִי וַיְקַדֵּשׁ אֹתוֹ כִּי בוֹ שָׁבַת מִכָּל־מְלַאכְתּוֹ אֲשֶׁר־
בָּרָא אֱלֹהִים לַעֲשׂוֹת:* רביעי פ (שני לסיפ׳)
4 אֵלֶּה תוֹלְדוֹת הַשָּׁמַיִם וְהָאָרֶץ בְּהִבָּרְאָם בְּיוֹם עֲשׂוֹת יְהֹוָה

v. 4. ה׳ זעירא

### CHAPTER II, 1–3. THE SABBATH

The Torah was not originally divided into chapters. Such division originated in the Middle Ages; and, because of its convenience, found its way into the *printed* Hebrew text. Sometimes, as here, the division is misleading. Thus, the next three verses belong to the preceding chapter, and form its worthy and incomparable conclusion.

**1.** *were finished.* The Heb. verb implies not only completion but perfection.

*host.* lit. 'army'; the totality of the universe conceived as an organized whole, a cosmos.

**2.** *seventh day.* 'What did the world lack after the six days' toil? Rest. So God finished His labours on the seventh day by the creation of a day of rest, the Sabbath' (Midrash).

*finished.* Better, 'had finished' (Mendelssohn, M. Friedlander).

*rested.* Heb. 'desisted', from creating. In the fourth commandment (Exod. xx, 11) God is said to have 'rested' (*vayanach*) on the seventh day. This ascribing of human actions to God is called *anthropomorphism*, and is employed in the Bible to make intelligible to the finite, human mind that which relates to the Infinite. The Talmudic saying, דברה תורה כלשון בני אדם 'The Torah speaks the ordinary language of men,' became a leading principle in later Jewish interpretation of Scripture.

**3.** *God blessed.* The Creator endowed the Sabbath with a blessing which would be experienced by all who observed it. On the Sabbath, the Talmud says, the Jew receives an 'additional soul', נשמה יתרה; *i.e.* his spiritual nature is heightened through the influence of the holy day.

*hallowed.* lit. 'set apart' from profane usage. The Sabbath demands more than stoppage of work. It is specifically marked off as a day consecrated to God and the life of the spirit.

*in creating had made.* lit. 'which God created to make', *i.e.* to continue acting (Ibn Ezra, Abarbanel) throughout time by the unceasing operation of Divine laws. This thought is contained in the Prayer Book (p. 39): 'In His goodness He reneweth the creation every day continually.' Or, as the Rabbis say, the work of creation continues, and the world is still in the process of creation, as long as the conflict between good and evil remains undecided. Ethically the world is thus still 'unfinished', and it is man's glorious privilege to help finish it. He can by his life hasten the triumph of the forces of good in the universe.

See Additional Note A ('The Creation Chapter'), p. 193.

### THE BEGINNINGS OF THE HUMAN RACE

#### (a) THE GARDEN OF EDEN
#### CHAPTERS II, 4–III

Chapter II is *not* another account of Creation. No mention is made in it of the formation of the dry land, the sea, the sun, moon or stars. It is nothing else but the sequel of the preceding chapter. In Chap. I man is considered as part of the general scheme of created things. Chap. II *supplements* the brief mention of the creation of man in *v.* 27 of the last chapter, by describing the formation of man and woman and their first dwelling place, as preliminary to the Temptation, and the consequent expulsion from the Garden of Eden in Chap. III. Only such details as are indispensable for the understanding of that event are given.

**4.** *These are the generations of the heaven and of the earth.* Some consider these words as a summary of the preceding chapter (Rashi). Elsewhere, however, in ten different sections of the Book of Genesis, such opening words ('these are the generations') always refer to the things that *follow*: *e.g.* 'These are the generations of Adam' (VI, 9), means, these are the descendants of Adam. In the same way, 'the generations of the heaven and the earth' here begins the account of man, the offspring of heaven and earth; or, the history of Adam and his family.

*in the day that.* Heb. idiom for 'at the time when'.

*LORD God.* Heb. *Adonay Elohim*. The two most important Names of the Deity are here used. 'LORD' is the usual English translation of *Adonay*. *Adonay* is the prescribed traditional reading of the Divine Name expressed in the four Hebrew letters Y H W H—which is never

## GENESIS II, 5 — בראשית ב

and heaven. ¶ 5. No shrub of the field was yet in the earth, and no herb of the field had yet sprung up; for the LORD God had not caused it to rain upon the earth, and there was not a man to till the ground; 6. but there went up a mist from the earth, and watered the whole face of the ground. 7. Then the LORD God formed man of the dust of the ground, and breathed into his nostrils the breath of life; and man became a living soul. 8. And the LORD God planted a garden eastward, in Eden; and there He

5 אֱלֹהִ֖ים אֶ֥רֶץ וְשָׁמָֽיִם׃ וְכֹ֣ל ׀ שִׂ֣יחַ הַשָּׂדֶ֗ה טֶ֚רֶם יִֽהְיֶ֣ה בָאָ֔רֶץ וְכָל־עֵ֥שֶׂב הַשָּׂדֶ֖ה טֶ֣רֶם יִצְמָ֑ח כִּי֩ לֹ֨א הִמְטִ֜יר יְהוָ֤ה
6 אֱלֹהִים֙ עַל־הָאָ֔רֶץ וְאָדָ֣ם אַ֔יִן לַֽעֲבֹ֖ד אֶת־הָֽאֲדָמָֽה׃ וְאֵ֖ד
7 יַֽעֲלֶ֣ה מִן־הָאָ֑רֶץ וְהִשְׁקָ֖ה אֶֽת־כָּל־פְּנֵֽי־הָֽאֲדָמָֽה׃ וַיִּיצֶר֩ יְהוָ֨ה אֱלֹהִ֜ים אֶת־הָֽאָדָ֗ם עָפָר֙ מִן־הָ֣אֲדָמָ֔ה וַיִּפַּ֥ח בְּאַפָּ֖יו
8 נִשְׁמַ֣ת חַיִּ֑ים וַֽיְהִ֥י הָֽאָדָ֖ם לְנֶ֥פֶשׁ חַיָּֽה׃ וַיִּטַּ֞ע יְהוָ֧ה אֱלֹהִ֛ים

pronounced as written. This Divine Name is spoken of as the *Tetragrammaton*, which is a Greek word meaning 'the Name of four letters'. The High Priest of old pronounced it *as written*, on the Day of Atonement during the Temple Service; whereupon all the people fell on their faces and exclaimed, 'Blessed be His Name whose glorious Kingdom is for ever and ever.' The Heb. root of that Divine Name means 'to be'; *Adonay* thus expresses the eternal self-existence of Him who is the Author of all existence. A possible rendering, therefore, for *Adonay* is 'The Eternal', and this has been adopted in some Jewish versions of Scripture.

The other and more general Divine Name is *Elohim*. Whereas *Adonay* is used whenever the Divine is spoken of in close relationship with men or nations, *Elohim* denotes God as the Creator and Moral Governor of the Universe. The Rabbis find a clear distinction in the use of these two terms: *Adonay* (LORD) describes the Deity stressing His lovingkindness, His acts of mercy and condescension and revelation to mankind (מדת הרחמים); while *Elohim* (God) emphasizes His justice and rulership (מדת הדין). The Midrash says, 'Thus spake the Holy One, blessed be He: If I create the world by Mercy alone, sin will abound; if by Justice alone, how can the world endure? I will create it by both.' In the first chapter of Genesis, which treats of the Universe as a whole, *Elohim* ('God') is used; but in the second chapter, which begins the story of man, that Divine Name is no longer used alone, but together with *Adonay* ('LORD God'). There was soon need for the exercise of the Divine mercy. See Additional Note, p. 199.

*earth and heaven*. Since the centre of interest now turns to man, earth is mentioned before heaven.

**5.** *no shrub*. Vegetation remained in the same state as on the day of its creation (see I, 11), through lack of rain.

*not a man*. The edible fruits of the earth require not only God's gift of rain, but also man's cultivation. Man must be a co-worker with God in making this earth a garden.

**6.** *there went up*. 'There used to go up.' The Heb. verb expresses repeated action.

*a mist*. In Assyrian, the word means the 'overflow of a river', and it may here have the same significance.

*watered*. The vegetation did not therefore decay, though there was insufficient moisture for growth.

**7.** *formed*. The Heb. וייצר is from the same root, *yatzar*, as is used of the potter moulding clay into a vessel, possibly to remind us that man is 'as clay in the hands of the potter'. The Rabbis point to the fact that in this verse the word for 'formed' (*vayyitzer*) is written with two *yods*, whereas in v. 19, when relating the creation of animals, it has only one *yod* (ויצר). Man alone, they declare, is endowed with both a *Yetzer tob* (a good inclination) and a *Yetzer ra* (an evil inclination); whereas animals have no moral discrimination or moral conflict. Another explanation is: man alone is a citizen of two worlds; he is both of earth and of heaven.

*dust of the ground*. 'From which part of the earth's great surface did He gather the dust?' ask the Rabbis. Rabbi Meir answered, 'From every part of the habitable earth was the dust taken for the formation of Adam.' In a word, men of all lands and climes are brothers. Other Rabbis held that the dust was taken from the site on which the Holy Temple, with the altar of Atonement, was in later ages to be built. That means, though man comes from the dust, sin is not a permanent part of his nature. Man can overcome sin, and through repentance attain to at-one-ment with his Maker.

*a living soul*. The term may mean nothing more than 'living entity'. The Targum, however, renders it by 'a speaking spirit'; *viz*. a personality endowed with the faculty of thinking and expressing his thoughts in speech.

### 8–17. THE GARDEN

**8.** *garden*. The ancient Versions translate it by the Persian word 'Paradise', lit. enclosure or park.

*eastward*. Either, 'in the East,' the home of the earliest civilization; or, situated east of Eden. The Targum translates it, 'aforetime.'

*Eden*. The Heb. word means 'delight'; but it is probably the name of a country, *Edinu* (signifying 'plain, steppe'); and may denote the extensive plain watered by the rivers Tigris and Euphrates.

GENESIS II, 9        בראשית ב

put the man whom He had formed. 9. And out of the ground made the LORD God to grow every tree that is pleasant to the sight, and good for food; the tree of life also in the midst of the garden, and the tree of the knowledge of good and evil. 10. And a river went out of Eden to water the garden; and from thence it was parted, and became four heads. 11. The name of the first is Pishon; that is it which compasseth the whole land of Havilah, where there is gold; 12. and the gold of that land is good; there is bdellium and the onyx stone. 13. And the name of the second river is Gihon; the same is it that compasseth the whole land of Cush. 14. And the name of the third river is ¹Tigris; that is it which goeth toward the east of Asshur. And the fourth river is the Euphrates. 15. And the LORD God took the man, and put him into the garden of Eden to dress it and to keep it. 16. And the LORD God commanded the man, saying: 'Of every tree of the garden thou mayest freely eat; 17. but of the tree of the knowledge of good and evil, thou shalt not eat of it;

¹ Heb. *Hiddekel*.

9 גַּן־בְּעֵדֶן מִקֶּדֶם וַיָּשֶׂם שָׁם אֶת־הָאָדָם אֲשֶׁר יָצָר: וַיַּצְמַח יְהֹוָה אֱלֹהִים מִן־הָאֲדָמָה כָּל־עֵץ נֶחְמָד לְמַרְאֶה וְטוֹב לְמַאֲכָל וְעֵץ הַחַיִּים בְּתוֹךְ הַגָּן וְעֵץ הַדַּעַת טוֹב וָרָע:
10 וְנָהָר יֹצֵא מֵעֵדֶן לְהַשְׁקוֹת אֶת־הַגָּן וּמִשָּׁם יִפָּרֵד וְהָיָה
11 לְאַרְבָּעָה רָאשִׁים: שֵׁם הָאֶחָד פִּישׁוֹן הוּא הַסֹּבֵב אֵת
12 כָּל־אֶרֶץ הַחֲוִילָה אֲשֶׁר־שָׁם הַזָּהָב: וּזְהַב הָאָרֶץ הַהִוא
13 טוֹב שָׁם הַבְּדֹלַח וְאֶבֶן הַשֹּׁהַם: וְשֵׁם־הַנָּהָר הַשֵּׁנִי גִּיחוֹן
14 הוּא הַסּוֹבֵב אֵת כָּל־אֶרֶץ כּוּשׁ: וְשֵׁם־הַנָּהָר הַשְּׁלִישִׁי חִדֶּקֶל הוּא הַהֹלֵךְ קִדְמַת אַשּׁוּר וְהַנָּהָר הָרְבִיעִי הוּא
15 פְרָת: וַיִּקַּח יְהֹוָה אֱלֹהִים אֶת־הָאָדָם וַיַּנִּחֵהוּ בְגַן־עֵדֶן
16 לְעָבְדָהּ וּלְשָׁמְרָהּ: וַיְצַו יְהֹוָה אֱלֹהִים עַל־הָאָדָם לֵאמֹר
17 מִכֹּל עֵץ־הַגָּן אָכֹל תֹּאכֵל: וּמֵעֵץ הַדַּעַת טוֹב וָרָע לֹא

---

The phrase 'Garden of Eden' became in course of time descriptive of any place possessing beauty and fertility. In later Jewish literature, it signifies the Heavenly Paradise where the souls of the righteous repose in felicity.

**9.** *tree of life.* The fruit of which prolongs life, or renders immortal. The phrase also occurs in a purely figurative sense, *e.g.* Prov. III, 18.

*the knowledge of good and evil.* The Targum paraphrase is, 'the tree, the eaters of whose fruits know to distinguish between good and evil.' The expression 'good and evil' denotes the knowledge which infancy lacks and experience acquires ('Your children, that this day have no knowledge of good or evil', Deut. I, 39). 'Knowledge of good and evil' may also mean knowledge of all things, *i.e.* omniscience; see III, 5.

**10.** *it was parted.* After passing through the Garden, it divided into four separate streams.

**11.** *Pishon.* Nowhere else mentioned in the Bible.
*Havilah.* Cf. x, 29. N.E. of Arabia, on the Persian Gulf. Arabia was famed in antiquity for its gold.

**12.** *bdellium.* Possibly the pearl.

**13.** *Gihon.* Like the Pishon, the identity of this river is a matter of conjecture.
*Cush.* Usually rendered Ethiopia; but it may also denote some territory in Asia.

**14.** *Asshur.* Assyria; which lies some distance East of the Tigris and possibly includes Babylonia.
*Euphrates.* No further description is given, because it was universally known as 'the great River' (Deut. I, 7) and 'the River' (Exod. XXIII, 31, Isa. VII, 20).

**15–16.** *to dress it and to keep it. i.e.* to till it and guard it from running wild. Not indolence but congenial work is man's Divinely allotted portion. 'See what a great thing is work! The first man was not to taste of anything until he had done some work. Only after God told him to cultivate and keep the garden, did He give him permission to eat of its fruits' (Aboth di Rabbi Nathan).

**17.** *thou shalt not eat.* Man's most sacred privilege is freedom of will, the ability to obey or to disobey his Maker. This sharp limitation of self-gratification, this 'dietary law', was to test the use he would make of his freedom; and it thus begins the moral discipline of man. Unlike the beast, man has also a spiritual life, which demands the subordination of man's desires to the law of God. The will of God revealed in His Law is the one eternal and unfailing guide as to what constitutes good and evil—and not man's instincts, or even his Reason, which in the hour of temptation often call light darkness and darkness light.

*thou shalt surely die. i.e.* thou must inevitably become mortal (Symmachus). While this explanation removes the difficulty that Adam and Eve lived a long time after they had eaten of the forbidden fruit, it assumes that man was created to be a deathless being. A simpler explanation is that in view of all the circumstances of the temptation, the All-merciful God mercifully modified the penalty, and they did not die on the day of their sin.

## GENESIS II, 18

for in the day that thou eatest thereof thou shalt surely die.' ¶ 18. And the LORD God said: 'It is not good that the man should be alone; I will make him a help meet for him.' 19. And out of the ground the LORD God formed every beast of the field, and every fowl of the air; and brought them unto the man to see what he would call them; and whatsoever the man would call every living creature, that was to be the name thereof.* iii s. 20. And the man gave names to all cattle, and to the fowl of the air, and to every beast of the field; but for Adam there was not found a help meet for him. 21. And the LORD God caused a deep sleep to fall upon the man, and he slept; and He took one of his ribs, and closed up the place with flesh instead thereof. 22. And the rib, which the LORD God had taken from the man, made He a woman, and brought her unto the man. 23. And the man said: 'This is now bone of my bones, and flesh of my flesh; she shall be called ¹Woman, because she was taken out of ²Man.' 24. Therefore shall a man leave his father and

¹ Heb. *Ishshah*.   ² Heb. *Ish*.

### 18–25. CREATION OF WOMAN

**18.** *it is not good.* From this verse the Rabbis deduce that marriage is a Divine institution, a holy estate in which alone man lives his true and complete life. Celibacy is contrary to nature.

*a help.* A wife is not a man's shadow or subordinate, but his other self, his 'helper', in a sense which no other creature on earth can be.

*meet for him.* To match him. The Heb. term *k'negdo* may mean either 'at his side', *i.e.* fit to associate with; or, 'as over against him', *i.e.* corresponding to him.

**19.** Better, *The LORD God, having formed out of the ground every beast of the field, and every fowl of heaven, brought them unto the man* (S. R. Hirsch, Delitzsch, and W. H. Green). See I, 21, 25. The fishes are not alluded to because they are precluded from becoming man's companions.

*call them.* Man alone has language, and can give birth to languages. In giving names to earth's creatures, he would establish his dominion over them (I, 26, 28). The name would also reflect the impression produced on his mind by each creature, and indicate whether he regarded it as a fit companion for himself.

**20.** *but for Adam.* The dignity of human nature could not, in few words, be more beautifully expressed (Dillmann).

**21.** *a deep sleep.* As in xv, 12, the word implies that something mysterious and awe-inspiring was about to take place.

*one of his ribs.* Woman was not formed from the dust of the earth, but from man's own body.

'We have here a wonderfully conceived allegory designed to set forth the moral and social relation of the sexes to each other, the dependence of woman upon man, her close relationship to him, and the foundation existing in nature for the attachment springing up between them. The woman is formed out of the man's side; hence it is the wife's natural duty to be at hand, ready at all times to be a "help" to her husband; it is the husband's natural duty ever to cherish and defend his wife, as part of his own self' (Driver).

**22.** *made.* lit. 'builded'; the Rabbis connected this striking use of ויבן with the noun בינה, 'understanding,' intuition, and remarked, 'This teaches that God has endowed woman with greater intuition than He has man.'

**23.** *bone of my bones.* The phrase passed into popular speech (xxix, 14).

*woman.* The Hebr. word is *Ishshah;* that for man is *Ish.* The similarity in sound emphasizes the spiritual identity of man and woman.

**24.** *shall a man leave.* Or, 'therefore doth a man leave his father and his mother, and doth cleave . . . and they become one flesh.' Rashi says: 'These words are by the Holy Spirit (רוח הקודש)'; *i.e.* this verse is not spoken by Adam, but is the inspired comment of Moses in order to inculcate the Jewish ideal of marriage as a unique tie which binds a man to his wife even closer than to his parents.

The Biblical ideal is the monogamic marriage; a man shall cleave 'to his *wife*', not to his wives. The sacredness of marriage relations, according to Scripture, thus goes back to the very birth of human society; nay, it is part of the scheme of

GENESIS II, 25

his mother, and shall cleave unto his wife, and they shall be one flesh. 25. And they were both naked, the man and his wife, and were not ashamed.

## CHAPTER III

1. Now the serpent was more subtle than any beast of the field which the Lord God had made. And he said unto the woman: 'Yea, hath God said: Ye shall not eat of any tree of the garden?' 2. And the woman said unto the serpent: 'Of the fruit of the trees of the garden we may eat; 3. but of the fruit of the tree which is in the midst of the garden, God hath said: Ye shall not eat of it, neither shall ye touch it, lest ye die.' 4. And the serpent said unto the woman: 'Ye shall not surely die; 5. for God doth know that in the day ye eat thereof, then your eyes shall be opened, and ye shall be as God, knowing good and evil.' 6. And when the woman saw that

---

Creation. The Rabbinic term for marriage is קידושין, lit. 'the sanctities,' sanctification; the purpose of marriage being to preserve and sanctify that which had been made in the image of God; see *Marriage, Divorce, and the Position of Woman, in Judaism* (Additional Notes, Deut.).

*one flesh.* One entity, sharing the joys and burdens of life.

**25.** *not ashamed.* Before eating of the forbidden fruit (see on *v.* 9 above), they were like children in the Orient, who in the innocence and ignorance of childhood run about unclothed.

CHAPTER III, 1–8. THE TRIAL OF MAN'S FREEDOM

**1.** *the serpent.* According to the Rabbinic legend, the serpent in its original state had the power of speech, and its intellectual powers exceeded those of all other animals, and it was envy of man that made it plot his downfall.

*subtle.* The same Heb. root signifies both 'naked' and 'subtle, clever, mischievous'. Seeming simplicity is often the most dangerous weapon of cunning. The gliding stealthy movement of the serpent is a fitting symbol of the insidious progress of temptation.

*yea, hath God said.* lit. 'Is it really so, that God (*Elohim*) hath said'—a statement expressing surprise and incredulity with the object of creating doubt in the reasonableness of the Divine prohibition.

**2.** *the woman.* Guileless and unsuspecting, she falls into the trap—even enlarges on God's command.

**3.** *neither shall ye touch it.* There was no word concerning 'touching' in the original prohibition. This exaggeration on the part of the woman, says the Midrash, was the cause of her fall.

**4.** *ye shall not surely die.* The serpent boldly denies the validity of God's threat.

**5.** God assigned no reason for the command; the serpent suggests one; *viz.* when God gave His order, it was not for man's benefit, but because God was envious of what man would become, if he ate the forbidden fruit.

*opened.* To new sources of knowledge, hidden from ordinary sight—a strong appeal to the curiosity of the woman.

*as God.* i.e. you will become endowed with a power which is at present reserved exclusively to Himself, *viz.* omniscience (Sforno); and, having acquired omniscience, you will be in a position to repudiate His authority.

*good and evil.* A Heb. idiom for 'all things' (Cheyne, Ehrlich); cf. II Sam. XIV, 17. The same Heb. idiom occurs in a negative form in XXIV, 50 and XXXI, 24, 29, where it means 'nothing at all'. The ordinary explanation of the phrase 'good and evil' in the literal sense assumes that God would for any reason withhold from man the ability to discern between what is morally right and wrong—a view which contradicts the spirit of Scripture. Moreover, Adam would not have been made 'in the image of God' if he did not from the first possess the faculty of distinguishing between good and evil. And if he lacked such faculty, his obedience or disobedience to any command whatsoever could have no moral significance. None of these objections holds good in regard to the temporary withholding of ordinary knowledge from Adam, pending his decision to work with or against God.

**6.** *the woman saw.* Though the tempter did not tell the woman to eat the fruit, he had woven the spell. The woman looked upon the tree with a new longing—it was good to eat, a delight to the eyes, and it would give wisdom. She turns her

## GENESIS III, 7 — בראשית ג

the tree was good for food, and that it was a delight to the eyes, and that the tree was to be desired to make one wise, she took of the fruit thereof, and did eat; and she gave also unto her husband with her, and he did eat. 7. And the eyes of them both were opened, and they knew that they were naked; and they sewed fig-leaves together, and made themselves girdles. 8. And they heard the voice of the LORD God walking in the garden toward the cool of the day; and the man and his wife hid themselves from the presence of the LORD God amongst the trees of the garden. 9. And the LORD God called unto the man, and said unto him: 'Where art thou?' 10. And he said: 'I heard Thy voice in the garden, and I was afraid, because I was naked; and I hid myself.' 11. And He said: 'Who told thee that thou wast naked? Hast thou eaten of the tree, whereof I commanded thee that thou shouldest not eat?' 12. And the man said: 'The woman whom Thou gavest to be with me, she gave me of the tree, and I did eat.' 13. And the LORD God said unto the woman: 'What is this thou hast done?' And the woman said: 'The serpent beguiled me, and I did eat.' 14. And the LORD God said unto the serpent: 'Because thou hast done

---

back upon the impulses of gratitude, love, and duty to God. The story mirrors human experience.

*with her.* Either, 'who was with her,' or, 'to eat with her.' The desire for companionship in guilt is characteristic of sin.

**7.** *were opened.* The knowledge attained is neither of happiness, wisdom, or power, but of consciousness of sin and its conflict with the will of God (Ryle). Next come shame, fear, and the attempt to hide.

*naked.* They forfeited their innocence. Rashi gives a metaphorical interpretation to the words: 'They knew that they were naked'—naked of all sense of gratitude and obedience to the Divine will: one precept alone had they been asked to obey, and even this proved too much for them!

*fig-leaves.* Because they were the largest and best suited for a loin-covering.

**8.** *the voice.* Or, 'sound.'

*toward the cool of the day. i.e.* towards evening, when, in the Orient, a cooling breeze arises (Song of Songs II, 17). It was this evening wind that carried to Adam and Eve the sound which heralded the approach of God.

*hid themselves.* Conscience makes cowards of them.

### 9–21. THE SENTENCE

**9.** *where art thou?* The Midrash explains that this question was asked out of consideration for Adam, to afford him time to recover his self-possession. *'Where art thou?* is the call which, after every sin, resounds in the ears of the man who seeks to deceive himself and others concerning his sin' (Dillmann).

**10.** *because I was naked.* The Rabbis maintain that 'one sin leads to another sin'. Adam commits a further offence by attempting to conceal the truth by means of this excuse.

**11.** *hast thou eaten?* An opportunity is given Adam for full confession and expression of contrition. A sin unconfessed and unrepented is a sin constantly committed.

**12.** Finding his excuse useless, Adam throws the blame upon everybody but himself. First of all it is 'the woman'; then he insolently fixes a share of the responsibility upon God—'whom Thou gavest to be with me.'

**13.** Instead of a question, the words may be taken as an exclamation, 'What is this thou hast done!'

**14.** *the serpent.* As the tempter and instigator of the offence, sentence is passed upon it first; and as the tempter, the serpent is cursed, and not its dupes and victims.

*shalt thou go . . . shalt thou eat.* Better, *upon thy belly thou goest and dust thou eatest.* 'Till the eighteenth century it was the general belief that the serpent had been walking upright and was now reduced to crawling. This is quite un-Biblical.

## GENESIS III, 15

this, cursed art thou from among all cattle, and from among all beasts of the field; upon thy belly shalt thou go, and dust shalt thou eat all the days of thy life. 15. And I will put enmity between thee and the woman, and between thy seed and her seed; they shall bruise thy head, and thou shalt bruise their heel.' ¶ 16. Unto the woman He said: 'I will greatly multiply thy pain and thy travail; in pain thou shalt bring forth children; and thy desire shall be to thy husband, and he shall rule over thee.' ¶ 17. And unto Adam He said: 'Because thou hast hearkened unto the voice of thy wife, and hast eaten of the tree, of which I commanded thee, saying: Thou shalt not eat of it; cursed is the ground for thy sake; in toil shalt thou eat of it all the days of thy life. 18. Thorns also and thistles shall it bring forth to thee; and thou shalt eat the herb of the field. 19. In the sweat of thy face shalt thou eat bread, till thou return unto the ground; for out of it wast thou taken; for dust thou art, and unto dust shalt thou return.' 20. And the man called his wife's name ¹Eve; because she was the mother of all living. 21. And the LORD God made for

¹ Heb. *Havvah*, that is, *Life*.

---

The meaning is, Continue to crawl on thy belly and eat dust. Henceforth it will be regarded as a curse, recalling to men thy attempt to drag them to the dust' (B. Jacob).

*All the days of thy life.* As long as thy species lasts.

**15.** *enmity.* The sight of the serpent will create loathing in man, and fear of its deadly sting will call forth an instinctive desire to destroy it.

*bruise.* Because of its position on the ground, the serpent strikes at the heel of man; while the man deals the fatal blow by crushing its head. Therefore the victory will rest with man.

**16.** *greatly multiply . . . over thee.* Better, *Much, much will I make thy pain and thy travail; in pain wilt thou bring forth children, and thy desire is unto thy husband and he ruleth over thee* (B. Jacob). This is no sentence upon the woman. It does not contain the term 'cursed'. Moreover, God himself pronounced the fruitfulness of man a blessing (I, 28), and therewith woman's pain and travail are inextricably bound up, being part of woman's physical being. The words addressed to the woman are therefore parenthetical, and signify in effect: 'Thee I need not punish. A sufficiency of woe and suffering is thine because of thy physical being' (B. Jacob).

*thy desire.* In spite of the pangs of travail, the longing for motherhood remains the most powerful instinct in woman.

**17.** *cursed is the ground.* It was Adam's duty

from the beginning to till the ground (II, 15): but the work would now become much more laborious. The soil would henceforth yield its produce only as the result of hard and unceasing toil.

*for thy sake.* Only as long as Adam lived was the earth under a curse; see on V, 29 and VIII, 21.

**18.** *thou shalt eat the herb.* Render, '*whereas thou eatest the herb of the field.*' The spontaneous growth of the soil will be weeds, which are unsuitable for human consumption. Man's food is the herb, which he can only acquire by toil.

**19.** *in the sweat.* 'The necessity of labour has proved man's greatest blessing, and has been the cause of all progress and improvement' (Ryle).

**20.** *the mother of all living.* This translation is incorrect. Render, *the mother of all humankind.* Otherwise, some word must be supplied after 'living', so as to exclude animal life (Onkelos, Saadyah). W. Robertson Smith has shown that the word חי in the text, which is here wrongly translated 'living,' is the primitive Semitic word for 'clan'; Eve was the mother of every human clan, the mother of mankind. חי in this sense occurs also in I Sam. XVIII, 18 ('Who am I, and who are my kinsfolk, ומי חיי, or my father's family, etc.' RV Margin).

**21.** *The LORD God made.* Despite their sin, God had not withdrawn His care from them. Divine punishment is at once followed by Divine pity.

GENESIS III, 22

Adam and for his wife garments of skins, and clothed them.* v a; 1v s. ¶ 22. And the LORD God said: 'Behold, the man is become as one of us, to know good and evil; and now, lest he put forth his hand, and take also of the tree of life, and eat, and live for ever.' 23. Therefore the LORD God sent him forth from the garden of Eden, to till the ground from whence he was taken. 24. So He drove out the man; and He placed at the east of the garden of Eden the cherubim, and the flaming sword which turned every way, to keep the way to the tree of life.

## 4 CHAPTER IV

1. And the man knew Eve his wife; and she conceived and bore Cain, and said: 'I have ¹gotten a man with the help of the

---
¹ Heb. *kanah*, to get.

בראשית ג ד

21 חָי: וַיַּעַשׂ יְהוָה אֱלֹהִים לְאָדָם וּלְאִשְׁתּוֹ כָּתְנוֹת עוֹר וַיַּלְבִּשֵׁם:* חמישי פ (רביעי לסמ׳)
22 וַיֹּאמֶר ׀ יְהוָה אֱלֹהִים הֵן הָאָדָם הָיָה כְּאַחַד מִמֶּנּוּ לָדַעַת טוֹב וָרָע וְעַתָּה ׀ פֶּן־יִשְׁלַח יָדוֹ וְלָקַח גַּם מֵעֵץ הַחַיִּים
23 וְאָכַל וָחַי לְעֹלָם: וַיְשַׁלְּחֵהוּ יְהוָה אֱלֹהִים מִגַּן־עֵדֶן לַעֲבֹד
24 אֶת־הָאֲדָמָה אֲשֶׁר לֻקַּח מִשָּׁם: וַיְגָרֶשׁ אֶת־הָאָדָם וַיַּשְׁכֵּן מִקֶּדֶם לְגַן־עֵדֶן אֶת־הַכְּרֻבִים וְאֵת לַהַט הַחֶרֶב הַמִּתְהַפֶּכֶת לִשְׁמֹר אֶת־דֶּרֶךְ עֵץ־הַחַיִּים: ס

CAP. IV. ד ד

א וְהָאָדָם יָדַע אֶת־חַוָּה אִשְׁתּוֹ וַתַּהַר וַתֵּלֶד אֶת־קַיִן וַתֹּאמֶר

---

*garments of skin.* Better suited for the rough life in front of them than the apron of leaves they were wearing.

*and clothed them.* This is one of the passages on which the Rabbis base the Jewish ideal of *Imitatio Dei*, the duty of imitating God's ways of lovingkindness and pity. 'The beginning and the end of the Torah is the bestowal of lovingkindnesses,' they say; 'at the beginning of the Torah, God clothes Adam; and at its end, He buries Moses.'

### 22–24. THE EXPULSION FROM EDEN

**22.** *man is become as one of us.* As one of the angels; or, 'us' is a plural of Majesty (cf. I, 26), meaning, man is become as God—omniscient. Man having through disobedience secured the faculty of unlimited knowledge, there was real danger that his knowledge would outstrip his sense of obedience to Divine Law. In our own day, we see that deep insight into Nature's secrets, if unrestrained by considerations of humanity, may threaten the very existence of mankind; *e.g.* through chemical warfare.

*live for ever.* Through further disobedience he could secure deathlessness. Immortality, however, that had been secured through disobedience and lived in sin, an immortal life of Intellect without Conscience, would defeat the purpose of man's creation (Sforno). Therefore, not only for his punishment, but for his salvation, to bring him back from the sinister course on which he had entered, God sent man forth from the Garden. Man, having sunk into sin, must rise again through the spiritual purification of suffering and death (Strack).

**24.** *drove out.* Sin drives man from God's presence; and when man banishes God from his world, he dwells in a wilderness instead of a Garden of Eden.

*at the east.* Either because man dwelt to the east of the Garden, or because the entrance was on that side.

*cherubim.* What these really were is a matter of uncertainty. According to Rashi, they were 'angels of destruction'. The first man was forbidden to enter the Garden again, and the slightest attempt on his part to do so would bring down upon him instant destruction. In the Bible generally, the cherubim are symbols of God's presence (Exod. xxv, 18).

*to keep the way.* Though the entrance to Eden was guarded by the angels with the flaming sword, the gentler angel of mercy did not forsake them in their exile. Adam and Eve discovered Repentance—the Rabbis tell us—and thereby they came nearer to God outside of Eden than when in Eden.

### (b) CAIN, SETH, AND THEIR DESCENDANTS. CHAPTERS IV AND V

#### IV, 1–16. CAIN AND ABEL

This narrative describes the spread of sin, issuing in violence and death.

**1.** *gotten.* The derivation is based on the resemblance of sound between Cain and the Heb. root *kanah*—to acquire.

*with the help of the LORD.* The four Heb. words spoken by Eve are very obscure. The traditional interpretation makes 'a man' refer to Cain; and the words, an expression of thanksgiving for her child. Others refer 'man' to husband (cf. xxix, 32). The sequel to the act of disobedience in the Garden would have caused estrangement between husband and wife; and Eve rejoices in the birth of a child, because through Cain she wins back her husband.

## GENESIS IV, 2 — בראשית ד

LORD.' 2. And again she bore his brother Abel. And Abel was a keeper of sheep, but Cain was a tiller of the ground. 3. And in process of time it came to pass, that Cain brought of the fruit of the ground an offering unto the LORD. 4. And Abel, he also brought of the firstlings of his flock and of the fat thereof. And the LORD had respect unto Abel and to his offering; 5. but unto Cain and to his offering He had not respect. And Cain was very wroth, and his countenance fell. 6. And the LORD said unto Cain: 'Why art thou wroth? and why is thy countenance fallen? 7. If thou doest well, shall it not be lifted up? and if thou doest not well, sin coucheth at the door; and unto thee is its desire, but thou mayest rule over it.' 8. And Cain spoke unto Abel his brother. And it came to pass, when they were in the field, that Cain rose up against Abel his brother, and slew him. ¶ 9. And the LORD said unto Cain: 'Where is Abel thy brother?' And he said: 'I know not; am I my brother's keeper?' 10. And He said: 'What hast thou done? the voice of thy

2 קָנִ֛יתִי אִ֖ישׁ אֶת־יְהוָֽה׃ וַתֹּ֣סֶף לָלֶ֔דֶת אֶת־אָחִ֖יו אֶת־הָ֑בֶל
3 וַיְהִי־הֶ֙בֶל֙ רֹ֣עֵה צֹ֔אן וְקַ֕יִן הָיָ֖ה עֹבֵ֥ד אֲדָמָֽה׃ וַיְהִ֖י מִקֵּ֣ץ
4 יָמִ֑ים וַיָּבֵ֨א קַ֜יִן מִפְּרִ֧י הָֽאֲדָמָ֛ה מִנְחָ֖ה לַיהוָֽה׃ וְהֶ֨בֶל הֵבִ֥יא
   גַם־ה֛וּא מִבְּכֹר֥וֹת צֹאנ֖וֹ וּמֵֽחֶלְבֵהֶ֑ן וַיִּ֣שַׁע יְהוָ֔ה אֶל־הֶ֖בֶל
5 וְאֶל־מִנְחָתֽוֹ׃ וְאֶל־קַ֥יִן וְאֶל־מִנְחָת֖וֹ לֹ֣א שָׁעָ֑ה וַיִּ֤חַר לְקַ֙יִן֙
6 מְאֹ֔ד וַֽיִּפְּל֖וּ פָּנָֽיו׃ וַיֹּ֥אמֶר יְהוָ֖ה אֶל־קָ֑יִן לָ֚מָּה חָ֣רָה לָ֔ךְ
7 וְלָ֖מָּה נָפְל֥וּ פָנֶֽיךָ׃ הֲל֤וֹא אִם־תֵּיטִיב֙ שְׂאֵ֔ת וְאִם֙ לֹ֣א
   תֵיטִ֔יב לַפֶּ֖תַח חַטָּ֣את רֹבֵ֑ץ וְאֵלֶ֙יךָ֙ תְּשׁ֣וּקָת֔וֹ וְאַתָּ֖ה תִּמְשָׁל־
8 בּֽוֹ׃ וַיֹּ֥אמֶר קַ֖יִן אֶל־הֶ֣בֶל אָחִ֑יו וַֽיְהִי֙ בִּהְיוֹתָ֣ם בַּשָּׂדֶ֔ה וַיָּ֥קָם
9 קַ֛יִן אֶל־הֶ֥בֶל אָחִ֖יו וַיַּהַרְגֵֽהוּ׃ וַיֹּ֤אמֶר יְהוָה֙ אֶל־קַ֔יִן אֵ֖י
10 הֶ֣בֶל אָחִ֑יךָ וַיֹּ֙אמֶר֙ לֹ֣א יָדַ֔עְתִּי הֲשֹׁמֵ֥ר אָחִ֖י אָנֹֽכִי׃ וַיֹּ֖אמֶר

v. 3. מלרע   v. 4. ב' רפה   v. 8. בלא פסקא

---

**2.** *Abel.* In Assyrian, *ablu* means 'son'. The Heb. word signifies 'a breath', like his life, so tragically brief. As the younger brother, Abel is given the lighter task of caring for the flocks; while Cain assists his father in the cultivation of the soil.

**3.** *an offering.* This is the first mention of worship in Scripture. The religious instinct is part of man's nature, and sacrifice is the earliest outward expression of that worship. Its purpose was to express acknowledgment of His bounty to the Giver of all.

**4.** *firstlings.* The most highly-prized among the flocks.
*the fat.* The richest part of the animal.
*had respect unto.* i.e. accepted.

**5.** *but unto Cain.* Unlike Abel's, his sacrifice is rejected because of the difference of spirit in which it was offered. The Lord looks to the heart.
*his countenance fell.* In disappointment and dejection.

**7.** *shall it not be lifted up?* Alluding to the 'countenance' that had fallen. God mercifully intervenes to arrest the progress of evil thoughts. Another interpretation is, 'Shall there not be acceptance?'
*sin coucheth.* Sin is compared to a ravenous beast lying in wait for its prey. It crouches at the entrance of the house, to spring upon its victim as soon as the door is opened. By harbouring feelings of vexation, Cain opened the door of his heart to the evil passions of envy, anger, violence, which eventually ended in murder.

*and unto thee.* Passion and evil imagination are ever assaulting the heart of man; yet he can conquer them, if only he resist them with determination.

**8.** *and Cain spoke unto Abel.* What is said is not mentioned. The ancient Versions supply some such words as, 'let us go into the field.' This is unnecessary, as Scripture often omits words (see II Chron. I, 2) which are obvious, and can be gathered from the context (Ehrlich).
*in the field.* Far away from their parents' home, where Cain had his brother at his mercy; cf. Deut. XXII, 25.

**9.** *where is . . . brother?* As in III, 9, the object of the question is not information, but to elicit a confession of guilt (Rashi).
*am I my brother's keeper?* Cain's answer is both false and insolent. Only a murderer altogether renounces the obligations of brotherhood.

**10.** *what hast thou done?* The note of interrogation should be replaced by a note of exclamation. The meaning is: What a deed of horror hast thou wrought! This is further indicated by the fact that the word 'brother' is used no less than six times in verses 8–11.
*blood.* The Heb. word is in the plural. In slaying Abel, Cain slew also Abel's unborn descendants. 'He who destroys a single human life is as if he destroyed a whole world' (Talmud).
*crieth unto Me.* For vengeance. See Job XVI, 18, 'Oh, earth, cover not thou my blood, and let my cry have no resting-place.'

## GENESIS IV, 11     בראשית ד

brother's blood crieth unto Me from the ground. 11. And now cursed art thou from the ground, which hath opened her mouth to receive thy brother's blood from thy hand. 12. When thou tillest the ground, it shall not henceforth yield unto thee her strength; a fugitive and a wanderer shalt thou be in the earth.' 13. And Cain said unto the LORD: 'My punishment is greater than I can bear. 14. Behold, Thou hast driven me out this day from the face of the land; and from Thy face shall I be hid; and I shall be a fugitive and a wanderer in the earth; and it will come to pass, that whosoever findeth me will slay me.' 15. And the LORD said unto him: 'Therefore whosoever slayeth Cain, vengeance shall be taken on him sevenfold.' And the LORD set a sign for Cain, lest any finding him should smite him. ¶ 16. And Cain went out from the presence of the LORD, and dwelt in the land of ¹Nod, on the east of Eden. 17. And Cain knew his wife; and she conceived, and bore Enoch; and he builded a city, and called the name of the city after the name of his son Enoch. 18. And unto Enoch was born Irad; and Irad begot Mehujael; and ²Mehujael begot Methushael; and Methushael begot Lamech.*ᵛ ˢ· 19. And Lamech took unto him two wives;

¹ That is, *Wandering*.    ² Heb. *Mehijael*.

---

**11.** *from the ground.* Or, 'more than the ground,' upon which a curse had been pronounced (III, 17).

**12.** *when thou tillest.* Wherever he lives, the curse will follow him and the soil will be barren for him. The remainder of his existence will consequently be an unceasing vagabondage.

**13.** *my punishment.* The Heb. word עון means both the consequences of a sin, *i.e.* punishment, and the sin itself. The Targum renders 'mine iniquity is too great to be pardoned'. The Heb. word translated 'than I can bear' can also be rendered 'to be forgiven'. Rashi understands the phrase as a question, 'Is my iniquity too great to be forgiven?'

**14.** *land.* He complains that he is banished into the desert, to share the fate of an outlaw.

*and from Thy face.* To be 'hidden from the face of God' (Deut. XXXI, 18) is to forfeit Divine protection. 'This anguished cry of Cain reveals him as a man not wholly bad, one to whom banishment from the Divine presence is a distinct ingredient in his cup of misery' (Skinner).

*whosoever findeth me.* Cain feared death at the hands of some future 'avenger of blood'; cf. Num. XXXV, 10 f.

**15.** *sevenfold.* The number 'seven' is occasionally used in the Bible to express an indefinite large number; cf. Lev. XXVI, 27; Prov. XXIV, 16. Cain's murderer shall be visited with a punishment far greater than that exacted of Abel's, as God had now made manifest His abhorrence of bloodshed to all.

*set a sign for Cain.* According to the Rabbis, Cain was a repentant sinner. God, therefore, reassured him that he would not be regarded as a common, intentional murderer. God's mercy to the guilty who repents of his sin is infinitely greater than that of man. The popular expression, *the brand of Cain*, in the sense of the sign of the murderer, arises from a complete misunderstanding of the passage.

**16.** *from the presence of the* LORD. Having forfeited God's favour, Cain withdraws from the neighbourhood of Eden, which was the special abode of the Divine Presence.

### 17-24. DESCENDANTS OF CAIN

**17.** *his wife.* The marriage of brother and sister was quite common in primitive times, but the Hebrew people looked upon it with such abhorrence (cf. Lev. XVIII, 9) that Scripture makes no reference to the identity of the wife in this passage.

*he builded a city.* lit. 'he was building a city'; did not necessarily complete it. Cain said in his heart, 'If it is decreed upon me to be a wanderer on the earth, the decree shall not apply to my offspring' (Nachmanides).

**19.** *two wives.* This is especially mentioned, as it was a departure from the ideal expounded in II, 24.

## GENESIS IV, 20

the name of the one was Adah, and the name of the other Zillah. 20. And Adah bore Jabal; he was the father of such as dwell in tents and have cattle. 21. And his brother's name was Jubal; he was the father of all such as handle the harp and pipe. 22. And Zillah, she also bore Tubal-cain, the forger of every cutting instrument of brass and iron; and the sister of Tubal-cain was Naamah. 23. And Lamech said unto his wives:

> Adah and Zillah, hear my voice;
> Ye wives of Lamech, hearken unto my speech;
> For I have slain a man for wounding me,
> And a young man for bruising me;
> 24. If Cain shall be avenged sevenfold,
> Truly Lamech seventy and sevenfold.

25. And Adam knew his wife again; and she bore a son, and called his name ¹Seth: 'for God ²hath appointed me another seed instead of Abel; for Cain slew him.' 26. And to Seth, to him also there was born a son; and he called his name Enosh; then began men to call upon the name of the LORD.*ᵛⁱ.

## 5    CHAPTER V

1. This is the book of the generations of Adam. In the day that God created man, in the likeness of God made He him; 2. male and female created He them, and

---

¹ Heb. *Sheth*.   ² Heb. *shath*.

כ שְׁתֵּי נָשִׁים שֵׁם הָאַחַת עָדָה וְשֵׁם הַשֵּׁנִית צִלָּה: וַתֵּלֶד עָדָה
21 אֶת־יָבָל הוּא הָיָה אֲבִי יֹשֵׁב אֹהֶל וּמִקְנֶה: וְשֵׁם אָחִיו יוּבָל הוּא
22 הָיָה אֲבִי כָּל־תֹּפֵשׂ כִּנּוֹר וְעוּגָב: וְצִלָּה גַם־הִוא יָלְדָה אֶת־
תּוּבַל קַיִן לֹטֵשׁ כָּל־חֹרֵשׁ נְחֹשֶׁת וּבַרְזֶל וַאֲחוֹת תּוּבַל־קַיִן
23 נַעֲמָה: וַיֹּאמֶר לֶמֶךְ לְנָשָׁיו עָדָה וְצִלָּה שְׁמַעַן קוֹלִי נְשֵׁי
24 לֶמֶךְ הַאְזֵנָּה אִמְרָתִי כִּי אִישׁ הָרַגְתִּי לְפִצְעִי וְיֶלֶד
לְחַבֻּרָתִי: כִּי שִׁבְעָתַיִם יֻקַּם־קָיִן וְלֶמֶךְ שִׁבְעִים וְשִׁבְעָה:
כה וַיֵּדַע אָדָם עוֹד אֶת־אִשְׁתּוֹ וַתֵּלֶד בֵּן וַתִּקְרָא אֶת־שְׁמוֹ
שֵׁת כִּי שָׁת־לִי אֱלֹהִים זֶרַע אַחֵר תַּחַת הֶבֶל כִּי הֲרָגוֹ
26 קָיִן: וּלְשֵׁת גַּם־הוּא יֻלַּד־בֵּן וַיִּקְרָא אֶת־שְׁמוֹ אֱנוֹשׁ אָז
ששי    ס    הוּחַל לִקְרֹא בְּשֵׁם יְהוָה:*

## CAP. V. ה

א זֶה סֵפֶר תּוֹלְדֹת אָדָם בְּיוֹם בְּרֹא אֱלֹהִים אָדָם בִּדְמוּת
2 אֱלֹהִים עָשָׂה אֹתוֹ: זָכָר וּנְקֵבָה בְּרָאָם וַיְבָרֶךְ אֹתָם
3 וַיִּקְרָא אֶת־שְׁמָם אָדָם בְּיוֹם הִבָּרְאָם: וַיְחִי אָדָם שְׁלֹשִׁים
וּמְאַת שָׁנָה וַיּוֹלֶד בִּדְמוּתוֹ כְּצַלְמוֹ וַיִּקְרָא אֶת־שְׁמוֹ שֵׁת:

ד' v. 23. 'א נחח

---

**20.** *father*. i.e. the first, the originator of pastoral life. Abel had been the keeper of sheep (v. 2); but Jabal widened the class of animals which could be domesticated.

**21.** *harp and pipe*. Music, according to Hebrew tradition, is thus the most ancient art, dating from the beginnings of the human race.

**22.** *brass*. The Heb. is more accurately translated 'copper', since it was a metal dug from the earth (Deut. VIII, 9). Brass is an alloy. The discovery of the use of metals forms an important step in the progress of civilization.

*Naamah*. The word means, 'pleasant, gracious.' Jewish legend states she became the wife of Noah.

**23, 24.** A triumphal song on the invention of the weapons mentioned in the preceding verses. Lamech possibly committed an act of involuntary homicide on some young person. He turns to his wives and says boastfully, 'See! I have taken a man's life, though he only inflicted a bruise on me. Should the necessity arise, I feel able to lay low any assailant that crosses my path. If Cain, though unarmed, was promised a sevenfold vengeance on a foe, I, equipped with the weapons invented by Tubal-Cain, will be able to exact a vengeance very much greater!' This heathen song marks the growth of the spirit of Cain.

**26.** *Enosh*. In Heb. poetry, *enosh* means 'man'.
*to call upon*. Then men began to pray to God (Ibn Ezra); or, once more call upon God under the name *Adonay*, Lord, which seems to have been forgotten among the descendants of Cain (Hoffmann).

Chaps. II–IV record the sin of Adam and Eve, their expulsion from Eden, the murder of Abel, Cain's descendants reaching in Lamech the climax of boastful and unrestrained violence. Piety, however, does not perish with Abel, and it reaches a new development in the days of Enosh (W. H. Green).

### CHAPTER V. DESCENDANTS OF SETH

**1.** *this is the book*. Heb. *sefer* does not always mean a volume; it may be used of any written document. Rabbinic tradition states the Torah is not one continuous work, written at one definite moment. 'The Torah was given to Moses in separate scrolls' (תורה מגילה מגילה נתנה). The formula, 'These are the generations,' which

GENESIS V, 3                                                              בראשית ה

blessed them, and called their name Adam, in the day when they were created. 3. And Adam lived a hundred and thirty years, and begot a son in his own likeness, after his image; and called his name Seth. 4. And the days of Adam after he begot Seth were eight hundred years; and he begot sons and daughters. 5. And all the days that Adam lived were nine hundred and thirty years; and he died. ¶ 6. And Seth lived a hundred and five years, and begot Enosh. 7. And Seth lived after he begot Enosh eight hundred and seven years, and begot sons and daughters. 8. And all the days of Seth were nine hundred and twelve years; and he died. ¶ 9. And Enosh lived ninety years, and begot Kenan. 10. And Enosh lived after he begot Kenan eight hundred and fifteen years, and begot sons and daughters. 11. And all the days of Enosh were nine hundred and five years; and he died. ¶ 12. And Kenan lived seventy years, and begot Mahalalel. 13. And Kenan lived after he begot Mahalalel eight hundred and forty years, and begot sons and daughters. 14. And all the days of Kenan were nine hundred and ten years; and he died. ¶ 15. And Mahalalel lived sixty and five years, and begot Jared. 16. And Mahalalel lived after he begot Jared eight hundred and thirty years, and begot sons and daughters. 17. And all the days of Mahalalel were eight hundred ninety and five years; and he died. ¶ 18. And Jared lived a hundred sixty and two years, and begot Enoch. 19. And Jared lived after he begot Enoch eight hundred years, and begot sons and daughters. 20. And all the days of Jared were nine hundred sixty and two years; and he died. ¶ 21. And Enoch lived sixty and five years, and begot Methuselah. 22. And Enoch walked with

---

occurs ten times in Genesis, each time beginning a new section, would mark the beginning of such scroll or 'book'. This explains why some sections, as this Chapter, have introductory verses *which recall or summarize facts mentioned in earlier sections*.

*The book of the generations of Adam.* Heb. זה ספר תולדת אדם. One of the early Rabbis, Ben Azzai, translated these words, 'This is the book of the generations of *Man*,' and declared them to be 'a great, fundamental teaching of the Torah'. As all human beings are traced back to one parent, he taught, they must necessarily be brothers. These words, therefore, proclaim the vital truth of the Unity of the Human Race, and the consequent doctrine of the Brotherhood of Man. 'This is the book of the generations of Man'—not black, not white, not great, not small, but *Man*. In these Scriptural words we have a concept quite unknown in the ancient world—Humanity. And only the belief in One God could lead to such a clear affirmation of the unity of mankind.

*in the likeness.* A reminder of the dignity of man's nature.

5. Various theories have been propounded to explain the abnormally long lives of these antediluvians. Maimonides holds that only the distinguished individuals named in this chapter lived these long years, but others lived a more or less normal span. The idea that men in primeval times lived extraordinarily long lives is common to the traditions of most ancient peoples.

Two names in this series of descendants of Seth, Enoch and Lamech are identical with those among the children of Cain. In both cases, however, the connection makes it evident that they represent different characters.

## GENESIS V, 23

God after he begot Methuselah three hundred years, and begot sons and daughters. 23. And all the days of Enoch were three hundred sixty and five years. 24. And Enoch walked with God, and he was not; for God took him.*vii. ¶ 25. And Methuselah lived a hundred eighty and seven years, and begot Lamech. 26. And Methuselah lived after he begot Lamech seven hundred eighty and two years, and begot sons and daughters. 27. And all the days of Methuselah were nine hundred sixty and nine years; and he died. ¶ 28. And Lamech lived a hundred eighty and two years, and begot a son. 29. And he called his name Noah, saying: 'This same shall ¹comfort us in our work and in the toil of our hands, which cometh from the ground which the LORD hath cursed.' 30. And Lamech lived after he begot Noah five hundred ninety and five years, and begot sons and daughters. 31. And all the days of Lamech were seven hundred seventy and seven years; and he died. ¶ 32. And Noah was five hundred years old; and Noah begot Shem, Ham, and Japheth.

## 6 CHAPTER VI

1. And it came to pass, when men began to multiply on the face of the earth, and daughters were born unto them, 2. that the sons of God saw the daughters of men that they were fair; and they took them

---

¹ Heb. *naḥem*, to comfort.

---

**22.** *walked with God.* To avoid the anthropomorphism, Onkelos renders, 'Enoch walked in the fear of God,' and the Jerusalem Targum, 'served in truth before the Lord.' Whereas the other men enumerated merely existed and preserved the race physically, Enoch led a life of intimate companionship with God in that morally deteriorating age. The Heb. idiom 'to walk with God' is employed to express a righteous course of life, as though the man who is thus described walked with and was accompanied by his Maker. A similar phrase is used concerning Noah (VI, 9).

**24.** *and he was not.* These words may mean either that, as a reward for his piety, Enoch did not meet with the ordinary fate of mortals, but, like Elijah, was taken to Heaven without the agony of death; or, that Enoch died prematurely. Rashi explains that although Enoch was pious, he was weak and liable to go astray. To avert such a calamity, he was removed from earth.

*for God took him.* This description of death is profoundly significant. We come from God, and to Him do we return. To die is to be taken by God, in whose Presence there is life eternal.

Rabbinical legend was very busy with the story of Enoch. He was the repository of the mysteries of the universe; and even higher honours were later accorded to him in the circles of the Jewish mystics.

**29.** *comfort.* See on III, 17. Only as long as Adam lived was the earth under a curse; and as, according to the chronology of this chapter, Noah was the first man born after the death of Adam, his birth becomes the presage of a new age to mankind (B. Jacob). Instead of 'comfort us', Rashi translates 'shall give us rest'—referring to the invention of the plough, that was attributed to Noah, by which human labour was much lightened.

### CHAPTER VI, 1–8. THE GROWING CORRUPTION OF MANKIND

**2.** *sons of God.* Is the literal translation of the Heb. phrase *beney Elohim*.

Among several ancient peoples there was a belief that there once existed a race of men of gigantic strength and stature, who were the offspring of human mothers and celestial fathers, and we are supposed to have an echo of that legend in this Biblical passage. Philo, Josephus

GENESIS VI, 3

wives, whomsoever they chose. 3. And the LORD said: 'My spirit shall not abide in man for ever, for that he also is flesh; therefore shall his days be a hundred and twenty years.' 4. The Nephilim were in the earth in those days, and also after that, when the sons of God came in unto the daughters of men, and they bore children to them; the same were the mighty men that were of old, the men of renown.*ᵐ·
¶ 5. And the LORD saw that the wickedness of man was great in the earth, and that every imagination of the thoughts of his heart was only evil continually. 6. And it repented the LORD that He had

בראשית ו

3 וַיִּקְח֤וּ לָהֶם֙ נָשִׁ֔ים מִכֹּ֖ל אֲשֶׁ֥ר בָּחָֽרוּ׃ וַיֹּ֣אמֶר יְהֹוָ֗ה לֹֽא־יָד֨וֹן רוּחִ֤י בָֽאָדָם֙ לְעֹלָ֔ם בְּשַׁגַּ֖ם ה֣וּא בָשָׂ֑ר וְהָי֣וּ יָמָ֔יו מֵאָ֥ה
4 וְעֶשְׂרִ֖ים שָׁנָֽה׃ הַנְּפִלִ֞ים הָי֣וּ בָאָ֘רֶץ֮ בַּיָּמִ֣ים הָהֵם֒ וְגַ֣ם אַֽחֲרֵי־כֵ֗ן אֲשֶׁ֨ר יָבֹ֜אוּ בְּנֵ֤י הָֽאֱלֹהִים֙ אֶל־בְּנ֣וֹת הָֽאָדָ֔ם וְיָלְד֖וּ לָהֶ֑ם הֵ֧מָּה הַגִּבֹּרִ֛ים אֲשֶׁ֥ר מֵעוֹלָ֖ם אַנְשֵׁ֥י הַשֵּֽׁם׃ פ מפטיר
ה 5 וַיַּ֣רְא יְהֹוָ֔ה כִּ֥י רַבָּ֛ה רָעַ֥ת הָאָדָ֖ם בָּאָ֑רֶץ וְכָל־יֵ֙צֶר֙
6 מַחְשְׁבֹ֣ת לִבּ֔וֹ רַ֥ק רַ֖ע כָּל־הַיּֽוֹם׃ וַיִּנָּ֣חֶם יְהֹוָ֔ה כִּֽי־עָשָׂ֥ה

and the author of the Book of Jubilees were misled into this interpretation by the analogy of these heathen fables. There is, however, no trace in Genesis of 'fallen angels' or rebellious angels; and the idea of inter-marriage of angels and human beings is altogether foreign to Hebrew thought. The mythological explanation of this passage was in all ages repelled by a large body of Jewish and non-Jewish commentators, though it has been revived by many moderns.

Others render *beney Elohim* by 'sons of the great' (in poetic Hebrew, *elohim* often means 'mighty', cf. Ps XXIX, 1). This verse would thus state that the sons of the nobles took them wives of the daughters of the people, who were powerless to resist. These marriages were the result of mere unbridled passion, and are an indication of the licence and oppression in that time.

'Sons of God' may, however, also mean those who serve God and obey Him, those nourished and brought up in the love of Him as their Father and Benefactor (Exod. IV, 22; Deut. XIV, 1; XXXII, 5; Isa. I, 2; Hos. II, 1). It is quite in accord with Biblical usage that those who adhered to the true worship of God—the children of Seth—are called 'sons of God'; and that, in contrast to these, the daughters of the line of Cain should be spoken of as 'daughters of men' (Ibn Ezra, Mendelssohn, S. R. Hirsch, W. H. Green).

Verses 1–4 would then point out the calamitous consequences to mankind when the pious sons of Seth merged with those who had developed a Godless civilization and who, with all their progress in arts and inventions, had ended in depravity and despair. Through intermarriage, the sons of Seth sink to the level of the ungodly race; and likewise deserved the doom that, with the exception of one family, was to overtake mankind. These verses are thus the first warning in the Torah against intermarriage with idolaters.

**3.** *abide in.* The above interpretation is borne out by this verse. For, if 'fallen angels' were in question, and if it was wrong for them to marry human women, the angels surely were the chief offenders; and yet the sentence falls exclusively upon *man*. 'In God's judgments there is no unrighteousness, partiality, or even the appearance of partiality' (Keil).

*for that he also is flesh.* Another translation is, 'by reason of their going astray they are flesh.' Despite the fact that man is created in the Divine image, he has proved by his proneness to err that he is 'flesh'; *i.e.* the earthly side of his nature too readily overpowers the spiritual.

*a hundred and twenty years. i.e.* his days are numbered: but I will not at once destroy him. There shall yet be an interval of 120 years, before I bring the Deluge upon mankind (Targum); a respite to the human race to give them time for repentance (Ibn Ezra).

**4.** *Nephilim.* Or, 'giants.' They existed before the intermarriages took place. The mention of Nephilim in Num. XIII, 33 is no reason to assume that they survived the Flood. The excited imagination of the Spies expresses its terror at the men of great stature whom they saw at Hebron, by saying that they must be the old antediluvian giants (W. H. Green).

*men of renown.* By reason of their abnormal physical strength, they gained for themselves a reputation as heroes. But enduring fame does not rest upon such qualifications as these Nephilim possessed. Their fate was to disappear from the earth, and humanity was to continue through Noah, 'a righteous man, and blameless in his generation.'

**5.** *wickedness.* This verse and the two that follow form the climax to the previous four verses, in which the moral depravity of the age is depicted. Retribution is swiftly coming.

*imagination.* The desires; the whole bent of his thoughts.

*heart.* In Heb. the heart is the seat of mind, intellect, purpose.

**6.** *repented.* See note to Chap. II, 2. Here the feelings of a human being are ascribed to God. 'He who destroys his own work seems to repent of having made it' (Ibn Ezra).

*grieved Him.* A touching indication of the Divine love for His creation. God is grieved at

### GENESIS VI, 7

made man on the earth, and it grieved Him at His heart. 7. And the LORD said: 'I will blot out man whom I have created from the face of the earth; both man, and beast, and creeping thing, and fowl of the air; for it repenteth Me that I have made them.' 8. But Noah found grace in the eyes of the LORD.

7 אֶת־הָאָדָם בָּאָרֶץ וַיִּתְעַצֵּב אֶל־לִבּוֹ: וַיֹּאמֶר יְהֹוָה אֶמְחֶה אֶת־הָאָדָם אֲשֶׁר־בָּרָאתִי מֵעַל פְּנֵי הָאֲדָמָה מֵאָדָם עַד־בְּהֵמָה עַד־רֶמֶשׂ וְעַד־עוֹף הַשָּׁמָיִם כִּי נִחַמְתִּי כִּי עֲשִׂיתִם:
8 וְנֹחַ מָצָא חֵן בְּעֵינֵי יְהֹוָה:

the frustration of His purposes for the human race—the possibility of such frustration being the price of man's freedom of will. According to Biblical thought, God glories in the beauty of His handiwork; how great then must His grief be, when His handiwork is soiled through human wickedness!

**7.** *I will blot out man.* 'In the Divine economy of the universe, men or nations, or generations, that thwart God's purpose, have no permanent title to life' (Kent).

*and beast.* Rashi remarks: 'Beast and creeping thing and fowl were all created for man's sake. When, therefore, man disappears, what necessity is there for preserving the animals alive!' But a comparison with Jonah IV, 11, where the innocence of the animals, as well as of the little children, is invoked by the Prophet in his plea for Nineveh, suggests that in the Biblical view all life, whether human or animal, forms one organic whole; see *v.* 12 of this chapter.

**8.** *grace.* Favour. 'Righteousness delivereth from death.' On what grounds Noah won the Divine approval, is told in the next verse.

For Additional Notes on THE CREATION CHAPTER and THE GARDEN OF EDEN, see pp. 193–196.

## THE HAFTORAH

The Haftorah (the Heb. term is *haphtarah*, 'conclusion') is the Lesson from the Prophets recited immediately after the Reading of the Law. Long before the destruction of the Second Temple, the custom had grown up of *concluding* the Reading of the Torah on Sabbaths, Fasts and Festivals with a selection from the 'Earlier Prophets' (Joshua, Judges, Samuel and Kings) or from the 'Later Prophets' (Isaiah, Jeremiah, Ezekiel and the Book of the Twelve Prophets). We possess no historical data concerning the institution of these Lessons. A medieval author on the Liturgy states that a little more than two thousand years ago (168 B.C.E.), Antiochus Epiphanes, king of Syria and Palestine, forbade the reading of the Torah under penalty of death. The Scribes, thereupon, substituted a chapter of the Prophets cognate to the portion of the Law that ought to have been read. But whatever be the exact origin of the Haftorah, there is always some similarity between the Sedrah and the Prophetic selection. Even when the latter does not contain an explicit reference to the events of the Sedrah, it reinforces the teaching of the weekly Reading upon the mind of the worshipper by a Prophetic message of consolation and hope.

# HAFTORAH BERESHITH הפטרת בראשית

## ISAIAH XLII, 5–XLIII, 10

### Chapter XLII

### Cap. XLII. מב

5. Thus saith God the Lord,
He that created the heavens, and stretched them forth,
He that spread forth the earth and that which cometh out of it,
He that giveth breath unto the people upon it,
And spirit to them that walk therein:

6. I the Lord have called thee in righteousness,
And have taken hold of thy hand,
And kept thee, and set thee for a covenant of the people,
For a light of the nations;

7. To open the blind eyes,
To bring out the prisoners from the dungeon,
And them that sit in darkness out of the prison-house.

8. I am the Lord, that is My name;
And My glory will I not give to another,
Neither My praise to graven images.

9. Behold, the former things are come to pass,
And new things do I declare;
Before they spring forth I tell you of them.

---

### Isaiah XLII, 5–XLIII, 10. Israel's Destiny

The connection between the Sedrah and the Prophetical Lesson is found in the opening words of the Haftorah (*v.* 5), which speak of God as the Creator of Heaven and Earth. The first chapters of Genesis, after describing the Creation, recount the growth of sin and violence among the children of men. The Prophet, likewise, proclaims the omnipotence and sovereignty of the Creator of the Universe, and proceeds to declare unto Israel his mission to rescue the world from moral degeneracy.

These chapters are taken from the second portion of the Book of Isaiah. This part of the Book of Isaiah is sometimes called 'The Prophecy of Restoration'. It is addressed to the Jews in Babylon, who had been deported from Judea after the first destruction of Jerusalem in the year 586 B.C.E., and who were longing for the day when they would be free to return to the Holy Land and Holy City. During the years of weary waiting, the Prophet consoles his suffering brethren by setting before them the sublime mission of Israel: God had called Israel to be His witness before all peoples, to be 'a light unto the nations', and to point the way of righteousness and salvation to all the children of men.

**5–9.** God promises Israel, the 'Servant of the Lord', Divine aid in the achievement of his sacred task.

**6.** *in righteousness.* i.e. for My righteous purpose; I will strengthen thee ('hold thy hand') to accomplish thy destiny ('to be a light unto the nations').

*a covenant of the people.* Or, 'a covenant to mankind.' The knowledge of God and practice of righteousness which it is Israel's mission to spread will, when consummated, bind all peoples together in a covenant of peace (Kimchi). All the Prophets preach the moral unity of mankind.

*a light of the nations.* Better, '*unto the nations.*'

**7.** *to open the blind eyes.* To enlighten those who are blind to the truth, to free those who are in spiritual bondage.

**8.** *My name.* The name *Adonay* conveys the unique reality, and the power to confer reality, of the Divine Being. This 'glory' would be forfeited if His predictions should fail (Cheyne).

**9.** *former things are come to pass.* Former events, like the victories of Cyrus, have taken place in accordance with the utterances of the Prophets. Now, as surely, these new prophecies of the exaltation of the Servant of the Lord through these victories shall likewise come to pass.

## ISAIAH XLII, 10

10. Sing unto the LORD a new song,
And His praise from the end of the earth;
Ye that go down to the sea, and all that is therein,
The isles, and the inhabitants thereof.

11. Let the wilderness and the cities thereof lift up their voice,
The villages that Kedar doth inhabit;
Let the inhabitants of Sela exult,
Let them shout from the top of the mountains.

12. Let them give glory unto the LORD,
And declare His praise in the islands.

13. The LORD will go forth as a mighty man,
He will stir up jealousy like a man of war;
He will cry, yea, He will shout aloud,
He will prove Himself mighty against His enemies.

14. I have long time held My peace,
I have been still, and refrained Myself;
Now will I cry like a travailing woman,
Gasping and panting at once.

15. I will make waste mountains and hills,
And dry up all their herbs;
And I will make the rivers islands,
And will dry up the pools.

16. And I will bring the blind by a way that they knew not,
In paths that they knew not will I lead them;
I will make darkness light before them,
And rugged places plain.
These things will I do,
And I will not leave them undone.

---

Cyrus, the creator of the Persian Empire, is one of the great men in history. Whether as king, general or statesman, he has no superior among the rulers of the Orient. To the Greeks he appeared the ideal king; and in Israel the Prophets hailed him as God's Anointed, as the chosen Agent for the ending of idolatry and tyranny among the nations. In the year 549 before the Common Era he became king of the Medes, and when in 538 he conquered Babylon, he was master of Western Asia. Cyrus perceived the value of Jewish gratitude and loyalty, and one of his first acts was a proclamation to the Jewish exiles in Babylon, granting them the right to return to Jerusalem and rebuild the Temple. This 'Cyrus Declaration' is preserved in the last verse of the last book of the Hebrew Bible, II Chronicles xxxvi, 23.

**10–13.** Hymn of Praise to God, because of the restoration of Israel, which the Prophet foretells (Ibn Ezra); also because of the glad tidings that a Servant-People has been Divinely chosen to carry God's message to mankind. Therefore, all peoples will unite in this song—even all Nature is here figuratively represented as sharing in the rejoicing at the glorious news (Kimchi).

**10.** *new song.* 'A song of a kind which has not before been heard, concerning new events of a kind never before displayed' (R. Levy).

**13.** There are obstacles to the consummation of the great events foretold, but God will manifest His power to remove them.

*jealousy.* i.e. ardour of battle, against heathen gods after whom His people had gone astray.

*cry.* Shout aloud, according to the manner of warriors in battle (Kimchi).

**14–17.** Are a continuation of the verses 1–9. They are full of bold anthropomorphisms.

**14.** *I have long time held My peace.* Perhaps at Israel's sufferings, and the desolation of the Holy Land. Now shall God's power be manifest. The scales will fall from the eyes of those who are spiritually blind.

*cry.* Burst the bonds of restraint.

## ISAIAH XLII, 17

17. They shall be turned back, greatly ashamed,
That trust in graven images,
That say unto molten images:
'Ye are our gods.'

18. Hear, ye deaf,
And look, ye blind, that ye may see.

19. Who is blind, but My servant?
Or deaf, as My messenger that I send?
Who is blind as he that is whole-hearted,
And blind as the LORD's servant?

20. Seeing many things, thou observest not;
Opening the ears, he heareth not.

21. The LORD was pleased, for His righteousness' sake,
To make the teaching great and glorious.*

22. But this is a people robbed and spoiled,
They are all of them snared in holes,
And they are hid in prison-houses;
They are for a prey, and none delivereth,
For a spoil, and none saith: 'Restore.'

23. Who among you will give ear to this?
Who will hearken and hear for the time to come?

24. Who gave Jacob for a spoil, and Israel to the robbers?
Did not the LORD?
He against whom we have sinned,
And in whose ways they would not walk,
Neither were they obedient unto His law.

25. Therefore He poured upon him the fury of His anger,
And the strength of battle;
And it set him on fire round about, yet he knew not,
And it burned him, yet he laid it not to heart.

---
\* Sephardim conclude here.

### CHAPTER XLIII

1. But now thus saith the LORD that created thee, O Jacob,
And He that formed thee, O Israel:

---

**17.** *ashamed.* Put to shame.

**18–21.** The Restoration would offer Israel the opportunity of beginning his Divinely appointed work. But how great is the contrast between the ideal Israel and the real! Israel's mission should begin with Israel.

**19.** *Whole-hearted.* The meaning of the verse is, 'Who is blind but he who should be My servant ... who is deaf but he who should be whole-hearted with Me.'

**20.** So many wondrous happenings in Israel's history should have opened the eyes of the soul.

**21.** *the LORD was pleased.* God sent His messengers to proclaim His Teaching, and to render His Torah great and glorious, by making it effective amongst all nations.

**22–25.** How is the pitiable plight of Israel, the homelessness and bondage of the Exile, to be reconciled with the assertion of God's power? Israel's sufferings are due to disobedience and rebellion. He rebukes Israel's insensibility to God's message, and urges a better understanding of the significance of God's dealings with Israel. Israel's disasters are a moral discipline leading to the purification and deliverance of His chastened People.

### CHAPTER XLIII, 1–10. ISRAEL, GOD'S WITNESS

**1.** *I have redeemed.* The perfect tense of the verbs is used to express the certainty of this future event. This is called the 'Prophetic perfect': the Prophet is so confident that the Divine

23

## ISAIAH XLIII, 2

Fear not, for I have redeemed thee,
I have called thee by thy name, thou art Mine.

2. When thou passest through the waters, I will be with thee,
And through the rivers, they shall not overflow thee;
When thou walkest through the fire, thou shalt not be burned,
Neither shall the flame kindle upon thee.

3. For I am the LORD thy God,
The Holy One of Israel, thy Saviour;
I have given Egypt as thy ransom,
Ethiopia and Seba for thee.

4. Since thou art precious in My sight, and honourable,
And I have loved thee;
Therefore will I give men for thee,
And peoples for thy life.

5. Fear not, for I am with thee;
I will bring thy seed from the east,
And gather thee from the west;

6. I will say to the north: 'Give up,'
And to the south: 'Keep not back,
Bring My sons from far,
And My daughters from the end of the earth;

7. Every one that is called by My name,
And whom I have created for My glory,
I have formed him, yea, I have made him.'

8. The blind people that have eyes shall be brought forth,
And the deaf that have ears.

9. All the nations are gathered together,
And the peoples are assembled;
Who among them can declare this,
And announce to us former things?
Let them bring their witnesses, that they may be justified;
And let them hear, and say: 'It is truth.'

promise will be fulfilled, that he describes the future event as if it had already been seen or heard by him. Thus, the Prophet does not say, 'Babylon will fall,' but, 'Fallen is Babylon'—he sees it as a heap of ruins.

**2.** What a marvellous summary of Jewish history since the Exile!

**3.** *thy ransom.* The Prophet foresees the impending downfall of the Egyptian lands (*Seba* is identified by some as a place on the African side of the Red Sea) before the Persian arms (Cambyses, son of Cyrus, was the actual conqueror). Accordingly, the acquisition of these new territories is described as the equivalent (the 'ransom') to Persia for the emancipation of the exiled Jews (Ibn Ezra).

**4.** *men.* Israel's ransom is paid not in gold, but in whole nations.

**5–7.** The Jewish Dispersion is now known to have been more widespread than was formerly believed. Israel's scattered sons shall, however, not be lost, but shall be ingathered from all parts of the earth.

**8–10.** The nations and the Servant are summoned to God's judgment throne.

**8.** *brought forth.* Even if many are unaware of the full significance of their history, Israel is nevertheless a competent witness to the bare external facts; it has *heard* the predictions and *seen* them fulfilled (Skinner).

**9.** *former things.* i.e. past events in Israel's history which had been announced by Prophets before they occurred. If foreign nations can make such claims, let them bring forth their witnesses to support ('justify') them. They cannot; but Israel can testify to God's rule in history, and His sovereignty over the world. Therefore once again,

## ISAIAH XLIII, 10

10. Ye are My witnesses, saith the LORD,
And My servant whom I have chosen;
That ye may know and believe Me, and understand
That I am He;
Before Me there was no God formed,
Neither shall any be after Me.

י אֱמֶת: אַתֶּם עֵדַי נְאֻם־יְהֹוָה וְעַבְדִּי אֲשֶׁר בָּחָרְתִּי לְמַעַן
תֵּדְעוּ וְתַאֲמִינוּ לִי וְתָבִינוּ כִּי־אֲנִי הוּא לְפָנַי לֹא־נוֹצַר אֵל
וְאַחֲרַי לֹא יִהְיֶה:

**10.** *ye are My witnesses.* Israel's high vocation as God's witnesses, to the end that every succeeding generation shall 'know, understand and believe' in Him as the One Creator of the Universe and only Saviour of men and nations.

'Israel's "Heroic History", as Manasseh ben Israel called it, is in truth never-ending. Each Jew and each Jewess is making his or her mark, or his or her stain, upon the wonderful unfinished history of the Jews, the history which Herder called the greatest poem of all time. *Ye are my witnesses, saith the* LORD. Loyal and steadfast witnesses is it, or self-seeking and suborned ones? A witness of some sort every Jew born is bound to be. He must fulfil his mission, and through good report and through evil report, he must add his item of evidence to the record' (Katie Magnus).

# GENESIS VI, 9

**6** ¶9. These are the generations of Noah. Noah was in his generations a man righteous and whole-hearted; Noah walked with God. 10. And Noah begot three sons, Shem, Ham, and Japheth. 11. And the earth was corrupt before God, and the earth was filled with violence. 12. And God saw the earth, and, behold, it was corrupt; for all flesh had corrupted their way upon the earth. ¶ 13. And God said unto Noah: 'The end of all flesh is come before Me; for the earth is filled with violence through them; and, behold, I will destroy them with the earth. 14. Make thee an ark of gopher wood; with rooms shalt thou make the ark, and shalt pitch it within and without with pitch. 15. And this is how thou shalt make it: the length of the ark three hundred cubits, the breadth of it fifty cubits, and the height of it thirty cubits. 16. A light shalt thou make to the ark, and to a cubit

בראשית נח ו

פ פ פ ב 2

9 אֵלֶּה תּוֹלְדֹת נֹחַ נֹחַ אִישׁ צַדִּיק תָּמִים הָיָה בְּדֹרֹתָיו
10 אֶת־הָאֱלֹהִים הִתְהַלֶּךְ־נֹחַ: וַיּוֹלֶד נֹחַ שְׁלֹשָׁה בָנִים אֶת־
11 שֵׁם אֶת־חָם וְאֶת־יָפֶת: וַתִּשָּׁחֵת הָאָרֶץ לִפְנֵי הָאֱלֹהִים
12 וַתִּמָּלֵא הָאָרֶץ חָמָס: וַיַּרְא אֱלֹהִים אֶת־הָאָרֶץ וְהִנֵּה
נִשְׁחָתָה כִּי־הִשְׁחִית כָּל־בָּשָׂר אֶת־דַּרְכּוֹ עַל־הָאָרֶץ: ס
13 וַיֹּאמֶר אֱלֹהִים לְנֹחַ קֵץ כָּל־בָּשָׂר בָּא לְפָנַי כִּי־מָלְאָה
14 הָאָרֶץ חָמָס מִפְּנֵיהֶם וְהִנְנִי מַשְׁחִיתָם אֶת־הָאָרֶץ: עֲשֵׂה
לְךָ תֵּבַת עֲצֵי־גֹפֶר קִנִּים תַּעֲשֶׂה אֶת־הַתֵּבָה וְכָפַרְתָּ אֹתָהּ
15 מִבַּיִת וּמִחוּץ בַּכֹּפֶר: וְזֶה אֲשֶׁר תַּעֲשֶׂה אֹתָהּ שְׁלֹשׁ מֵאוֹת
אַמָּה אֹרֶךְ הַתֵּבָה חֲמִשִּׁים אַמָּה רָחְבָּהּ וּשְׁלֹשִׁים אַמָּה

## II. NOACH
### (Chapters VI, 9–XI, 32)

### THE FLOOD. Chapters VI, 9–IX
On the Flood and its parallels in Babylonian literature,
see Additional Notes C and E, pp. 196–198.

**Chapter VI, 9–22. The Building of the Ark**

**9.** *these are the generations.* *i.e.* this is the story of Noah. This phrase, as in II, 4, introduces a new section of the history.

*righteous.* In his actions, in his relationship with his fellows.

*whole-hearted.* 'Blameless' (RV); faultless.

*in his generations.* The Rabbis point out that these words may be understood as stating that, despite the depravity which raged around him, he remained unspotted and untainted by corruption. It may, however, also mean that in *his* generations, *i.e.* judged by the low standard of his age, Noah was righteous; but had he lived in the period of Abraham, he would not have been conspicuous for goodness.

*Noah walked with God.* But Abraham, Scripture later tells us, walked *before* God. A father takes his young child by the hand, so that the latter walks *with* him, but he allows an older, maturer child to walk *before* him. In moral strength, Abraham was the superior of Noah (Midrash).

**10.** A new section begins with *v.* 9. Hence the sons who had been enumerated in v, 32 are again referred to, because they figure in the story which forms the theme of this section.

**11.** *the earth.* *i.e.* the inhabitants of the earth. So again in XLI, 57.

*corrupt.* The Rabbis understand this as an allusion to gross immorality.

*before God.* Either in open and flagrant defiance of God, or what they did was an offence in the sight of God.

*violence.* Ruthless outrage of the rights of the weak by the strong.

**12.** *all flesh.* Including the animals. Their corruption manifested itself in the development of ferocity.

*way.* Manner of life, conduct.

**13.** *the end.* The destruction.

*is come before Me.* *i.e.* has come before God's mind, has been determined by Him.

*with the earth.* With the things that are upon the surface of the earth.

**14.** *make thee an ark.* *i.e.* a ship. The Rabbis say that the construction of the Ark occupied Noah for 120 years, in order to give his contemporaries an opportunity to repent. Their curiosity would naturally be aroused by what Noah was doing; and he would answer their enquiry by warning them of the judgment which God was bringing on mankind. They, however, scoffed at him and gave no heed to his words.

*gopher wood.* A resinous wood, which would not admit the water; probably the cypress.

*rooms.* lit. 'nests'; separate stalls for the different species of animals.

**15.** *this is how.* These are the measurements and directions.

*a cubit.* Roughly eighteen inches.

**16.** *a light.* The unusual word here used for light means in the plural (dual) 'noon'. Legend

GENESIS VI, 17

shalt thou finish it upward; and the door of the ark shalt thou set in the side thereof; with lower, second, and third stories shalt thou make it. 17. And I, behold, I do bring the flood of waters upon the earth, to destroy all flesh, wherein is the breath of life, from under heaven; every thing that is in the earth shall perish. 18. But I will establish My covenant with thee; and thou shalt come into the ark, thou, and thy sons, and thy wife, and thy sons' wives with thee. 19. And of every living thing of all flesh, two of every sort shalt thou bring into the ark, to keep them alive with thee; they shall be male and female. 20. Of the fowl after their kind, and of the cattle after their kind, of every creeping thing of the ground after its kind, two of every sort shall come unto thee, to keep them alive. 21. And take thou unto thee of all food that is eaten, and gather it to thee; and it shall be for food for thee, and for them.' 22. Thus did Noah; according to all that God commanded him, so did he.* 11.

## 7  CHAPTER VII

1. And the LORD said unto Noah: 'Come thou and all thy house into the ark; for thee have I seen righteous before Me in this generation. 2. Of every clean beast thou shalt take to thee seven and seven, each with his mate; and of the beasts that are not clean two [and two], each with

relates that it was a precious stone, which illuminated the whole interior of the Ark.

*to a cubit*. The precise meaning of these words is doubtful. The 'light' (which must be thought of as a kind of casement near to the roof) was to measure a cubit in height; or there was to be a space of a cubit between the roof and the top of the casement.

**17.** *and I, behold, I.* These emphatic words bring out the thought of the terrible necessity of the Flood.

**18.** *covenant.* A covenant means an agreement or compact between two parties, for the observance of which pledges are given. Here it is used in the simple sense of a promise. God will fulfil His promise to spare Noah and his family.

**22.** *thus did Noah.* i.e. he made the ark and collected provisions. The act of bringing the animals into the ark is described in the next chapter.

### CHAPTER VII, 1–9. ENTERING THE ARK

**1.** *righteous.* In VI, 9, Noah was described as 'righteous and blameless'. Since the present verse was addressed *to* Noah, whereas VI, 9 was spoken *of* him in his absence, the Rabbis deduced the rule: 'Utter only a part of a man's praise in his presence, but thou mayest speak the whole of a man's praise in his absence.' Most people unfortunately give utterance to the whole of a man's *blame* in his absence, graciously contenting themselves with only a portion of such blame in his presence.

**2.** *clean beast.* According to Rashi, this means 'of every beast which at a later period would be considered clean by the people of Israel' (Lev. XI and Deut. XIV). But more probably, the distinction between clean and unclean in this passage is based on the fitness of the ainmal to be used as a sacrifice to God; cf. VIII, 20, where it is narrated that Noah offered upon the altar 'of every clean beast, and of every clean fowl'.

*seven and seven.* i.e. seven pairs; seven males and seven females. The *general* direction in VI, 19 to take a pair of each kind of animal into the ark in order to preserve alive the various species, is here supplemented by the more *specific* injunction, when the time arrived for entering the ark, that *of the clean beasts* there shall be seven of each species. As Rashi points out, he required additional clean animals for sacrifice

27

## GENESIS VII, 3

his mate; 3. of the fowl also of the air, seven and seven, male and female; to keep seed alive upon the face of all the earth. 4. For yet seven days, and I will cause it to rain upon the earth forty days and forty nights; and every living substance that I have made will I blot out from off the face of the earth.' 5. And Noah did according unto all that the LORD commanded him. ¶ 6. And Noah was six hundred years old when the flood of waters was upon the earth. 7. And Noah went in, and his sons, and his wife, and his sons' wives with him, into the ark, because of the waters of the flood. 8. Of clean beasts, and of beasts that are not clean, and of fowls, and of every thing that creepeth upon the ground, 9. there went in two and two unto Noah into the ark, male and female, as God commanded Noah. 10. And it came to pass after the seven days, that the waters of the flood were upon the earth. 11. In the six hundredth year of Noah's life, in the second month, on the seventeenth day of the month, on the same day were all the fountains of the great deep broken up, and the windows of heaven were opened. 12. And the rain was upon the earth forty days and forty nights. ¶ 13. In the selfsame day entered Noah, and Shem, and Ham, and Japheth, the sons of Noah, and Noah's wife, and the three wives of his sons with them, into the ark; 14. they, and every beast after its kind, and all the cattle after their kind, and every creeping thing that creepeth upon

מֵע֣וֹף הַשָּׁמַ֗יִם שִׁבְעָ֤ה שִׁבְעָה֙ זָכָ֣ר וּנְקֵבָ֔ה לְחַיּ֥וֹת זֶ֖רַע עַל־
פְּנֵ֣י כָל־הָאָֽרֶץ׃ 4 כִּי֩ לְיָמִ֨ים ע֜וֹד שִׁבְעָ֗ה אָֽנֹכִי֙ מַמְטִ֣יר עַל־
הָאָ֔רֶץ אַרְבָּעִ֣ים י֔וֹם וְאַרְבָּעִ֖ים לָ֑יְלָה וּמָחִ֗יתִי אֶֽת־כָּל־
הַיְקוּם֙ אֲשֶׁ֣ר עָשִׂ֔יתִי מֵעַ֖ל פְּנֵ֥י הָֽאֲדָמָֽה׃ ה וַיַּ֖עַשׂ נֹ֑חַ כְּכֹ֛ל
אֲשֶׁר־צִוָּ֖הוּ יְהוָֽה׃ 6 וְנֹ֕חַ בֶּן־שֵׁ֥שׁ מֵא֖וֹת שָׁנָ֑ה וְהַמַּבּ֣וּל הָיָ֔ה
מַ֖יִם עַל־הָאָֽרֶץ׃ 7 וַיָּ֣בֹא נֹ֗חַ וּ֠בָנָיו וְאִשְׁתּ֧וֹ וּנְשֵֽׁי־בָנָ֛יו אִתּ֖וֹ אֶל־
הַתֵּבָ֑ה מִפְּנֵ֖י מֵ֥י הַמַּבּֽוּל׃ 8 מִן־הַבְּהֵמָה֙ הַטְּהוֹרָ֔ה וּמִן־
הַ֨בְּהֵמָ֔ה אֲשֶׁ֥ר אֵינֶ֖נָּה טְהֹרָ֑ה וּמִ֨ן־הָע֔וֹף וְכֹ֥ל אֲשֶׁר־רֹמֵ֖שׂ
עַל־הָֽאֲדָמָֽה׃ 9 שְׁנַ֨יִם שְׁנַ֜יִם בָּ֧אוּ אֶל־נֹ֛חַ אֶל־הַתֵּבָ֖ה זָכָ֣ר
וּנְקֵבָ֑ה כַּֽאֲשֶׁ֛ר צִוָּ֥ה אֱלֹהִ֖ים אֶת־נֹֽחַ׃ י וַיְהִ֖י לְשִׁבְעַ֣ת הַיָּמִ֑ים
וּמֵ֣י הַמַּבּ֔וּל הָי֖וּ עַל־הָאָֽרֶץ׃ 11 בִּשְׁנַ֨ת שֵׁשׁ־מֵא֤וֹת שָׁנָה֙ לְחַיֵּי־
נֹ֔חַ בַּחֹ֙דֶשׁ֙ הַשֵּׁנִ֔י בְּשִׁבְעָֽה־עָשָׂ֥ר י֖וֹם לַחֹ֑דֶשׁ בַּיּ֣וֹם הַזֶּ֗ה
נִבְקְעוּ֙ כָּל־מַעְיְנוֹת֙ תְּה֣וֹם רַבָּ֔ה וַאֲרֻבֹּ֥ת הַשָּׁמַ֖יִם נִפְתָּֽחוּ׃
12 וַֽיְהִ֥י הַגֶּ֖שֶׁם עַל־הָאָ֑רֶץ אַרְבָּעִ֣ים י֔וֹם וְאַרְבָּעִ֖ים לָֽיְלָה׃
13 בְּעֶ֨צֶם הַיּ֤וֹם הַזֶּה֙ בָּ֣א נֹ֔חַ וְשֵֽׁם־וְחָ֥ם וָיֶ֖פֶת בְּנֵי־נֹ֑חַ וְאֵ֣שֶׁת
נֹ֗חַ וּשְׁלֹ֧שֶׁת נְשֵֽׁי־בָנָ֛יו אִתָּ֖ם אֶל־הַתֵּבָֽה׃ 14 הֵ֜מָּה וְכָל־הַֽחַיָּ֣ה
לְמִינָ֗הּ וְכָל־הַבְּהֵמָה֙ לְמִינָ֔הּ וְכָל־הָרֶ֛מֶשׂ הָרֹמֵ֥שׂ עַל־

---

on leaving the ark. From the phrasing of the verse, Malbim shows that the command is concerning Noah's *domestic* animals. (Hence the phrase איש ואשתו instead of זכר ונקבה in vi, 19.)

*beasts that are not clean.* Of Noah's domestic animals—such as hares, asses, camels—he was to take two each. The phrase 'that are not clean' is itself noteworthy. It is a circumlocution which might have been avoided by the use of the simple word 'unclean'. The Talmud bases on this verse its admonition to avoid impure and unrefined language in conversation.

**4.** *for yet seven days.* To give Noah time to carry out the instructions which had been given him.

**5.** *according unto all.* Cf. vi, 22. There it refers to the construction of the ark; here it implies the strict fulfilment of the directions enumerated in the preceding verses.

**9.** *two and two.* In couples.

10–24. 'THE WINDOWS OF HEAVEN WERE OPENED'

**11.** *in the second month.* The Rabbis differ as to whether the year is here reckoned as beginning in Nisan or Tishri. On the view that the year commenced with Tishri, the Flood began about November, which is the time of the rainy season. More probably, the Flood began in May, which is the time of the inundation of the Babylonian plain.

*the great deep.* The *tehom* of I, 2. There was a seismic upheaval; the earth was swept by a gigantic tidal wave, and simultaneously there was a torrential downpour of rain.

*windows of heaven.* For the expression, cf. II Kings VII, 2, 19; Mal. III, 10; as if the vast reservoirs of water thought of as stored above the sky (I, 7) were coming down through special openings, constantly and in resistless strength.

**12.** *rain.* lit. 'heavy rain.' There was a continuous downpour for the period of time specified.

**13.** After a summary of the Flood-story (v. 6–12) we have a more detailed description of the event.

*selfsame day.* i.e. the day determined by God.

**14.** *every bird of every sort.* lit. 'every bird of every wing'; i.e. every species of winged creature.

## GENESIS VII, 15

the earth after its kind, and every fowl after its kind, every bird of every sort. 15. And they went in unto Noah into the ark, two and two of all flesh wherein is the breath of life. 16. And they that went in, went in male and female of all flesh, as God commanded him; and the LORD shut him in.* III. 17. And the flood was forty days upon the earth; and the waters increased, and bore up the ark, and it was lifted up above the earth. 18. And the waters prevailed, and increased greatly upon the earth; and the ark went upon the face of the waters. 19. And the waters prevailed exceedingly upon the earth; and all the high mountains that were under the whole heaven were covered. 20. Fifteen cubits upward did the waters prevail; and the mountains were covered. 21. And all flesh perished that moved upon the earth, both fowl, and cattle, and beast, and every swarming thing that swarmeth upon the earth, and every man; 22. all in whose nostrils was the breath of the spirit of life, whatsoever was in the dry land, died. 23. And He blotted out every living substance which was upon the face of the ground, both man, and cattle, and creeping thing, and fowl of the heaven; and they were blotted out from the earth; and Noah only was left, and they that were with him in the ark. 24. And the waters prevailed upon the earth a hundred and fifty days.

## 8     CHAPTER VIII

1. And God remembered Noah, and every living thing, and all the cattle that were with him in the ark; and God made a wind to pass over the earth, and the waters

---

**16.** *The* LORD *shut him in.* This means either literally that God fastened the door so that it withstood the violence of the storm; or it is a beautifully naïve figure of speech to denote the Divine protection which encompassed Noah. Hence the employment of the term Lord, *Adonay*, for this act of Divine mercy (cf. note on II, 4).

**17.** *the waters increased.* After it had rained for forty days, the waters were sufficiently deep to bear the ark, which, as Rashi remarks, had previously been like a heavily-laden ship stuck in shallow water and unable to move.

**18.** *the waters prevailed.* They covered the earth. It will be noted that there were three stages in the increase of the waters. The first was marked by the lifting of the ark (v. 17); the second by the floating of the ark (v. 18); the third by the total submergence of the mountains (v. 19).

**20.** *fifteen cubits upward.* This means that the waters rose twenty-two and a half feet above the top of the highest mountain.

**21.** What had been foretold in VI, 17 was literally fulfilled.

*every man.* i.e. the entire human race outside the ark.

**24.** *prevailed.* Dominated the earth. After forty days' downpour, the waters reached their highest point, and remained so for a period of one hundred and ten days. After 150 days had passed from the commencement of the Flood, the waters began to diminish.

CHAPTER VIII, 1–5. THE DIMINUTION OF WATERS

**1.** *God remembered.* His covenanted promise to Noah that He would preserve him, and all that were with him in the ark (Ibn Ezra). The animals are expressly included in the kindly

## GENESIS VIII, 2

assuaged; 2. the fountains also of the deep and the windows of heaven were stopped, and the rain from heaven was restrained. 3. And the waters returned from off the earth continually; and after the end of a hundred and fifty days the waters decreased. 4. And the ark rested in the seventh month, on the seventeenth day of the month, upon the mountains of Ararat. 5. And the waters decreased continually until the tenth month; in the tenth month, on the first day of the month, were the tops of the mountains seen. ¶ 6. And it came to pass at the end of forty days, that Noah opened the window of the ark which he had made. 7. And he sent forth a raven, and it went forth to and fro, until the waters were dried up from off the earth. 8. And he sent forth a dove from him, to see if the waters were abated from off the face of the ground. 9. But the dove found no rest for the sole of her foot, and she returned unto him to the ark, for the waters were on the face of the whole earth; and he put forth his hand, and took her, and brought her in unto him into the ark. 10. And he stayed yet other seven days; and again he sent forth the dove out of the ark. 11. And the dove came in to him at eventide; and lo in her mouth an olive-leaf freshly plucked; so Noah knew

2 הַמָּיִם: וַיִּסָּכְרוּ מַעְיְנֹת תְּהוֹם וַאֲרֻבֹּת הַשָּׁמָיִם וַיִּכָּלֵא
3 הַגֶּשֶׁם מִן־הַשָּׁמָיִם: וַיָּשֻׁבוּ הַמַּיִם מֵעַל הָאָרֶץ הָלוֹךְ וָשׁוֹב
4 וַיַּחְסְרוּ הַמַּיִם מִקְצֵה חֲמִשִּׁים וּמְאַת יוֹם: וַתָּנַח הַתֵּבָה
בַּחֹדֶשׁ הַשְּׁבִיעִי בְּשִׁבְעָה־עָשָׂר יוֹם לַחֹדֶשׁ עַל הָרֵי אֲרָרָט:
ה וְהַמַּיִם הָיוּ הָלוֹךְ וְחָסוֹר עַד הַחֹדֶשׁ הָעֲשִׂירִי בָּעֲשִׂירִי
6 בְּאֶחָד לַחֹדֶשׁ נִרְאוּ רָאשֵׁי הֶהָרִים: וַיְהִי מִקֵּץ אַרְבָּעִים
7 יוֹם וַיִּפְתַּח נֹחַ אֶת־חַלּוֹן הַתֵּבָה אֲשֶׁר עָשָׂה: וַיְשַׁלַּח אֶת־
הָעֹרֵב וַיֵּצֵא יָצוֹא וָשׁוֹב עַד־יְבֹשֶׁת הַמַּיִם מֵעַל הָאָרֶץ:
8 וַיְשַׁלַּח אֶת־הַיּוֹנָה מֵאִתּוֹ לִרְאוֹת הֲקַלּוּ הַמַּיִם מֵעַל פְּנֵי
9 הָאֲדָמָה: וְלֹא־מָצְאָה הַיּוֹנָה מָנוֹחַ לְכַף־רַגְלָהּ וַתָּשָׁב
אֵלָיו אֶל־הַתֵּבָה כִּי־מַיִם עַל־פְּנֵי כָל־הָאָרֶץ וַיִּשְׁלַח יָדוֹ
י וַיִּקָּחֶהָ וַיָּבֵא אֹתָהּ אֵלָיו אֶל־הַתֵּבָה: וַיָּחֶל עוֹד שִׁבְעַת
11 יָמִים אֲחֵרִים וַיֹּסֶף שַׁלַּח אֶת־הַיּוֹנָה מִן־הַתֵּבָה: וַתָּבֹא
אֵלָיו הַיּוֹנָה לְעֵת עֶרֶב וְהִנֵּה עֲלֵה־זַיִת טָרָף בְּפִיהָ וַיֵּדַע

thought of God. As there is no forgetfulness with God, so we cannot really apply the term remembrance to him (Kimchi). This phrase, which is in continual use in devotion, is only a human way of speaking of the Divine.

*assuaged*. The Heb. verb is used of anger being calmed down (Esther II, 1). The waters grew calm after the fury of the storm.

**3.** *returned .... continually*. i.e. kept gradually diminishing.

*an hundred and fifty days*. Cf. VII, 24. The Flood commenced on the 17th day of the second month (VII, 11); and 150 days later, on the 17th of the seventh month, the waters had decreased to such an extent that the ark grounded on the mountains of Ararat.

**4.** *the mountains of Ararat*. Ararat is the name of a country; see Isa. XXXVII, 38, where the Septuagint translates Ararat by Armenia. Assyrian inscriptions also speak of Armenia as 'Urartu'. Mount Ararat is 17,000 feet high.

**5.** The waters continued to decrease for a further period of 73 days, and then the tops of ordinary mountains, as contrasted with Ararat, became visible.

### 6–14. THE RAVEN AND THE DOVE

**6.** *at the end of forty days*. i.e. after the first day of the tenth month, referred to in the last verse.

*window*. lit. 'aperture.' The Heb. is a different word from that used in VI, 16.

**7.** *a raven*. He selected the raven because, as a bird of prey, the raven would sustain itself by feeding on carrion which would abound if the earth were dry.

**8.** *sent forth a dove*. Rashi explains that between the sending forth of the raven and the sending forth of the dove there was an interval of seven days, since in v. 10 it is stated 'he stayed *yet another seven days*'. Noah changed his scout, because the action of the dove would give more reliable information. The dove fed on vegetation; and should it find food, Noah would have the sign for which he was waiting.

**11.** *at eventide*. Noah had presumably let the dove out in the morning. It must therefore have flown a considerable distance if it did not return until the evening. The inference was that the earth all around was covered by water.

*olive-leaf*. Since the olive tree grew to no great height, Noah understood that the waters had almost disappeared, though not completely. He therefore waited another week. The Rabbis have a beautiful comment on the fact that the dove comes back to Noah with the bitter olive leaf in its mouth. 'Better,' it seemed to say, 'bitter food that comes from God than the sweetest food at the hands of man.'

GENESIS VIII, 12

that the waters were abated from off the earth. 12. And he stayed yet other seven days; and sent forth the dove; and she returned not again unto him any more. ¶ 13. And it came to pass in the six hundred and first year, in the first month, the first day of the month, the waters were dried up from off the earth; and Noah removed the covering of the ark, and looked, and, behold, the face of the ground was dried. 14. And in the second month, on the seven and twentieth day of the month, was the earth dry.* ¹ᵛ· ¶ 15. And God spoke unto Noah, saying: 16. 'Go forth from the ark, thou, and thy wife, and thy sons, and thy sons' wives with thee. 17. Bring forth with thee every living thing that is with thee of all flesh, both fowl, and cattle, and every creeping thing that creepeth upon the earth; that they may swarm in the earth, and be fruitful, and multiply upon the earth.' 18. And Noah went forth, and his sons, and his wife, and his sons' wives with him; 19. every beast, every creeping thing, and every fowl, whatsoever moveth upon the earth, after their families, went forth out of the ark. ¶ 20. And Noah builded an altar unto the LORD; and took of every clean beast, and of every clean fowl, and offered burnt-offerings on the altar. 21. And the LORD smelled the sweet savour; and the LORD said in His heart: 'I will not again curse the ground any more for man's sake; for the imagination of man's heart is evil from his youth; neither will I again smite any more every thing

בראשית נח ח

12 נֹחַ כִּי־קַלּוּ הַמַּיִם מֵעַל הָאָרֶץ׃ וַיָּחֶל עוֹד שִׁבְעַת יָמִים
13 אֲחֵרִים וַיֹּסֶף שַׁלַּח אֶת־הַיּוֹנָה וְלֹא־יָסְפָה שׁוּב־אֵלָיו עוֹד׃ וַיְהִי
בְּאַחַת וְשֵׁשׁ־מֵאוֹת שָׁנָה בָּרִאשׁוֹן בְּאֶחָד לַחֹדֶשׁ חָרְבוּ
הַמַּיִם מֵעַל הָאָרֶץ וַיָּסַר נֹחַ אֶת־מִכְסֵה הַתֵּבָה וַיַּרְא וְהִנֵּה
14 חָרְבוּ פְּנֵי הָאֲדָמָה׃ וּבַחֹדֶשׁ הַשֵּׁנִי בְּשִׁבְעָה וְעֶשְׂרִים יוֹם
טו לַחֹדֶשׁ יָבְשָׁה הָאָרֶץ׃∗ ס וַיְדַבֵּר אֱלֹהִים אֶל־נֹחַ לֵאמֹר׃
16 צֵא מִן־הַתֵּבָה אַתָּה וְאִשְׁתְּךָ וּבָנֶיךָ וּנְשֵׁי־בָנֶיךָ אִתָּךְ׃
17 כָּל־הַחַיָּה אֲשֶׁר־אִתְּךָ מִכָּל־בָּשָׂר בָּעוֹף וּבַבְּהֵמָה וּבְכָל־
הָרֶמֶשׂ הָרֹמֵשׂ עַל־הָאָרֶץ הוצא אִתָּךְ וְשָׁרְצוּ בָאָרֶץ וּפָרוּ
18 וְרָבוּ עַל־הָאָרֶץ׃ וַיֵּצֵא־נֹחַ וּבָנָיו וְאִשְׁתּוֹ וּנְשֵׁי־בָנָיו אִתּוֹ׃
19 כָּל־הַחַיָּה כָּל־הָרֶמֶשׂ וְכָל־הָעוֹף כֹּל רוֹמֵשׂ עַל־הָאָרֶץ
כ לְמִשְׁפְּחֹתֵיהֶם יָצְאוּ מִן־הַתֵּבָה׃ וַיִּבֶן נֹחַ מִזְבֵּחַ לַיהוָה
וַיִּקַּח מִכֹּל ׀ הַבְּהֵמָה הַטְּהֹרָה וּמִכֹּל הָעוֹף הַטָּהוֹר וַיַּעַל
21 עֹלֹת בַּמִּזְבֵּחַ׃ וַיָּרַח יְהוָה אֶת־רֵיחַ הַנִּיחֹחַ וַיֹּאמֶר יְהוָה
אֶל־לִבּוֹ לֹא אֹסִף לְקַלֵּל עוֹד אֶת־הָאֲדָמָה בַּעֲבוּר
הָאָדָם כִּי יֵצֶר לֵב הָאָדָם רַע מִנְּעֻרָיו וְלֹא־אֹסִף עוֹד

v. 17. חיצא קרי    v. 18. במקף ובנגינה

**13.** *first month.* Two months after the tops of the mountains had become visible (v. 5).
*removed the covering.* He took off part of the roof so as to get a view of what was outside.
*the ground was dried.* i.e. the water had drained away from the surface of the ground; but the surrounding earth must have been a mass of marsh and bog, and it was unsafe to step upon the ground.

**14.** *dry.* A different Heb. word from that used in the previous verse. It denotes that the ground had become hard, and could bear the weight of the inhabitants of the ark.

**15–22.** LEAVING THE ARK, AND BUILDING AN ALTAR

**17.** *swarm.* 'Breed abundantly' (RV). The Heb. word denotes a moving about from place to place.

**19.** *families.* i.e. species, as in Jer. xv, 3.

**20.** *builded an altar.* Noah feels moved to express his gratitude to God. He is the pioneer of all the altar-builders of the Bible.
*burnt-offerings.* A burnt-offering was entirely consumed by fire on the altar, and no part eaten by the priest or the bringer of the sacrifice.

**21.** *the sweet savour.* The sacrifice offered by Noah was as agreeable to the Deity, humanly speaking, as sweet odours are to a man. To avoid the anthropomorphism, the Targum renders 'And the Lord accepted with pleasure the sweet savour'.
*in His heart.* The Heb. is 'to His heart', i.e. to Himself. The phrase means simply, 'God resolved.'
*I will not again curse.* There will be no repetition of the curse pronounced in the days of Adam (see III, 17). In all probability, the 'curse' of the Flood is also implied. A world-catastrophe will in such measure never recur.
*for man's sake.* Better, *for Adam's sake.*
*of man's heart.* Better, *of Adam's heart.*
*imagination.* The Evil Inclination in man, *Yetzer hara*, which too often gains the mastery over the Good Inclination, *Yetzer tob*.
*from his youth.* i.e. from the dawn of his knowledge of good and evil.
*as I have done.* In the future, God will punish the individual sinners, and not the human family as a body.

## GENESIS VIII, 22

living, as I have done. 22. While the earth remaineth, seedtime and harvest, and cold and heat, and summer and winter, and day and night shall not cease.'

## 9 CHAPTER IX

1. And God blessed Noah and his sons, and said unto them: 'Be fruitful, and multiply, and replenish the earth. 2. And the fear of you and the dread of you shall be upon every beast of the earth, and upon every fowl of the air, and upon all wherewith the ground teemeth, and upon all the fishes of the sea: into your hand are they delivered. 3. Every moving thing that liveth shall be for food for you; as the green herb have I given you all. 4. Only flesh with the life thereof, which is the blood thereof, shall ye not eat. 5. And surely your blood of your lives will I require; at the hand of every beast will I require it; and at the hand of man, even at the hand of every man's brother, will I require the life of man. 6. Whoso sheddeth man's

בראשית נח ח ט

לְהַכּוֹת אֶת־כָּל־חַי כַּאֲשֶׁר עָשִׂיתִי: עֹד כָּל־יְמֵי הָאָרֶץ 22
זֶרַע וְקָצִיר וְקֹר וָחֹם וְקַיִץ וָחֹרֶף וְיוֹם וָלַיְלָה לֹא
יִשְׁבֹּתוּ:

CAP. IX. ט ס

וַיְבָרֶךְ אֱלֹהִים אֶת־נֹחַ וְאֶת־בָּנָיו וַיֹּאמֶר לָהֶם פְּרוּ וּרְבוּ א
וּמִלְאוּ אֶת־הָאָרֶץ: וּמוֹרַאֲכֶם וְחִתְּכֶם יִהְיֶה עַל כָּל־חַיַּת 2
הָאָרֶץ וְעַל כָּל־עוֹף הַשָּׁמָיִם בְּכֹל אֲשֶׁר תִּרְמֹשׂ הָאֲדָמָה
וּבְכָל־דְּגֵי הַיָּם בְּיֶדְכֶם נִתָּנוּ: כָּל־רֶמֶשׂ אֲשֶׁר הוּא־חַי לָכֶם 3
יִהְיֶה לְאָכְלָה כְּיֶרֶק עֵשֶׂב נָתַתִּי לָכֶם אֶת־כֹּל: אַךְ־בָּשָׂר 4
בְּנַפְשׁוֹ דָמוֹ לֹא תֹאכֵלוּ: וְאַךְ אֶת־דִּמְכֶם לְנַפְשֹׁתֵיכֶם ה
אֶדְרֹשׁ מִיַּד כָּל־חַיָּה אֶדְרְשֶׁנּוּ וּמִיַּד הָאָדָם מִיַּד אִישׁ אָחִיו
אֶדְרֹשׁ אֶת־נֶפֶשׁ הָאָדָם: שֹׁפֵךְ דַּם הָאָדָם בָּאָדָם דָּמוֹ 6

---

**22.** The regular change of the seasons will not again be suspended. According to the Talmud, these six terms here enumerated mark the actual divisions of the year, each being of two months.

CHAPTER IX, 1–17. THE COVENANT WITH NOAH. THE SEVEN COMMANDMENTS OF MAN

**1–2.** The blessing which was bestowed on Adam (I, 28) is repeated, since Noah and his sons were the heads of a new race. The Divine benediction would hearten them to undertake the task of rebuilding a ruined world.

**3.** *every moving thing.* The term is here used in a wide sense to include beast, fish and fowl.

*as the green herb.* The meaning is that just as the green herb was granted to man as food by God (I, 29), so now permission is given him to partake of the flesh of animals.

**4.** *blood.* In the Biblical conception, the blood is identified with life; cf. Deut. XII, 23, 'for the blood is the life.' This thought was the obvious deduction from the fact that as the blood is drained from the body, the vitality weakens until it ceases altogether. Life, in every form, has in it an element of holiness, since God is the source of all life. Therefore, although permission was given to eat the flesh of an animal, this was done with one special restriction; *viz.* life must altogether have departed from the animal before man partakes of its flesh. According to Rashi, the restriction was of a twofold nature. It, firstly, forbade אבר מן החי 'cutting a limb from a live animal'—a barbarous practice common among primitive races; and secondly, the blood must not on any account be eaten,

since it was the seat of life. This double prohibition, of cruelty to animals and the partaking of blood, is the basis of most of the rules of the Jewish slaughter of animals (Shechitah) and of the preparation (kashering) of meats, which have been observed by Jews from time immemorial.

**5.** *your blood of your lives.* lit. 'your blood, according to your own souls.' The Rabbis understood these words literally, *i.e. your* life-blood, and based on them the prohibition of suicide.

*will I require. i.e.* will I exact punishment for it.

*beast.* If an animal killed a man, it must be put to death; see Exod. XXI, 28–32 for the law concerning an ox which gored a man.

*at the hand of every man's brother.* Better, *at the hand of his brother-man* (M. Friedländer). This clause emphasizes the preceding phrase, 'and at the hand of man.' If God seeks the blood of a man at the hand of a beast which kills him, how much more will He exact vengeance from a human being who murders his brother-man!

**6.** *by man.* This is usually understood, as the Targum has it, through the agency of man, *viz.* by judges or by an avenger.

*for in the image of God.* See I, 27. We have here a declaration of the native dignity of man, irrespective of his race or creed. Because man is created in the image of God, he can never be reduced to the level of a thing or chattel; he remains a *personality*, with inalienable human rights. To rob a man of these inalienable rights constitutes an outrage against God. It is upon this thought that the Jewish conception of Justice, as respect for human personality, rests; see on Deut. XVI, 20.

## GENESIS IX, 7

blood, by man shall his blood be shed; for in the image of God made He man. 7. And you, be ye fruitful, and multiply; swarm in the earth, and multiply therein.'*ᵛ·¶ 8. And God spoke unto Noah, and to his sons with him, saying: 9. 'As for Me, behold, I establish My covenant with you, and with your seed after you; 10. and with every living creature that is with you, the fowl, the cattle, and every beast of the earth with you; of all that go out of the ark, even every beast of the earth. 11. And I will establish My covenant with you; neither shall all flesh be cut off any more by the waters of the flood; neither shall there any more be a flood to destroy the earth.' 12. And God said: 'This is the token of the covenant which I make between Me and you and every living creature that is with you, for perpetual generations: 13. I have set My bow in the cloud, and it shall be for a token of a covenant between Me and the earth. 14. And it shall come to pass, when I bring clouds over the earth, and the bow is seen in the cloud, 15. that I will remember My covenant, which is between Me and you and every living creature of all flesh; and the waters shall no more become a flood to destroy all flesh. 16. And the bow shall be in the cloud; and I will look upon it, that I may remember the everlasting covenant between God and every living creature of all flesh that is upon the earth.' 17. And God said unto Noah: 'This is the token of the covenant which

---

**7.** This verse is not a superfluous repetition of v. 1. It gives a further reason why God holds bloodshed in such abhorrence. It is His desire that life should be multiplied, and not diminished through murder. The Talmud founded on this verse its strong condemnation of him who does not fulfil the command to found a family.

Rabbinic interpretation of these verses deduced seven fundamental laws from them: viz. (1) the establishment of courts of justice; (2) the prohibition of blasphemy; (3) of idolatry; (4) of incest; (5) of bloodshed; (6) of robbery; (7) of eating flesh cut from a living animal. The Rabbis called these seven laws the 'Seven Commandments given to the descendants of Noah'. These constitute what we might call Natural Religion, as they are vital to the existence of human society. Whereas an Israelite was to carry out all the precepts of the Torah, obedience to these Seven Commandments alone was in ancient times required of non-Jews living among Israelites, or attaching themselves to the Jewish community.

**9.** *as for Me.* If man, by avoiding homicide, will do his part not to destroy human life, God will never send another Flood.

*establish.* i.e. confirm. The covenant is that mentioned in VI, 18.

**12.** *token.* The visible sign of the permanence of the covenant.

**13.** *I have set My bow.* This does not imply that the rainbow was then for the first time instituted; it merely assumed a new role as a token of the Divine pledge that there would never again be a world-devastating Deluge. 'We must explain the verse as saying, The bow which I have set in the clouds from the day of creation shall henceforth be a token of the covenant between Me and you ... a covenant of peace' (Nachmanides). The same commentator further asserts, 'We must accept the view of the Greeks that the rainbow is the result of the reflection of the sun in the moist atmosphere,' i.e. the refraction and reflection of light.

**16.** *I will look upon it.* The Midrashic comment is: 'When the attribute of Justice comes to accuse you and hold you guilty of offending, then I will look upon the bow and remember the covenant.'

**17.** This concluding verse of the paragraph stresses the idea that the covenant was not only with Noah but with 'all flesh that is upon the earth'.

# GENESIS IX, 18

I have established between Me and all flesh that is upon the earth.'* vl. ¶ 18. And the sons of Noah, that went forth from the ark, were Shem, and Ham, and Japheth; and Ham is the father of Canaan. 19. These three were the sons of Noah, and of these was the whole earth overspread. ¶ 20. And Noah the husbandman began, and planted a vineyard. 21. And he drank of the wine, and was drunken; and he was uncovered within his tent. 22. And Ham, the father of Canaan, saw the nakedness of his father, and told his two brethen without. 23. And Shem and Japheth took a garment, and laid it upon both their shoulders, and went backward, and covered the nakedness of their father; and their faces were backward, and they saw not their father's nakedness. 24. And Noah

אֲשֶׁר הֲקִמֹּתִי בֵּינִי וּבֵין כָּל־בָּשָׂר אֲשֶׁר עַל־הָאָרֶץ:

18 וַיִּֽהְיוּ בְנֵי־נֹחַ הַיֹּצְאִים מִן־הַתֵּבָה שֵׁם וְחָם וָיָפֶת וְחָם הוּא

19 אֲבִי כְנָעַן: שְׁלֹשָׁה אֵלֶּה בְּנֵי־נֹחַ וּמֵאֵלֶּה נָפְצָה כָל־הָאָֽרֶץ:

21 וַיָּחֶל נֹחַ אִישׁ הָאֲדָמָה וַיִּטַּע כָּֽרֶם: וַיֵּשְׁתְּ מִן־הַיַּיִן וַיִּשְׁכָּר

22 וַיִּתְגַּל בְּתוֹךְ אָהֳלֹה: וַיַּרְא חָם אֲבִי כְנַעַן אֵת עֶרְוַת אָבִיו

23 וַיַּגֵּד לִשְׁנֵֽי־אֶחָיו בַּחֽוּץ: וַיִּקַּח שֵׁם וָיֶפֶת אֶת־הַשִּׂמְלָה

וַיָּשִׂימוּ עַל־שְׁכֶם שְׁנֵיהֶם וַיֵּלְכוּ אֲחֹרַנִּית וַיְכַסּוּ אֵת עֶרְוַת

24 אֲבִיהֶם וּפְנֵיהֶם אֲחֹרַנִּית וְעֶרְוַת אֲבִיהֶם לֹא רָאֽוּ: וַיִּיקֶץ

### 18–29. PLANTING A VINEYARD

**18.** The historical thread of the main narrative—which is the story of the Human Family—is now resumed, after the digression on the symbolic meaning of the rainbow. Shem, Ham and Japheth are the fathers of the races from which the whole of mankind has descended.

*Canaan.* This is mentioned because of the narrative which follows. From a father showing such a fundamental lack of moral sense as Ham, it is not surprising that a wicked people like the Canaanites sprang.

**19.** *overspread.* Heb. 'the whole earth was dispersed'; the word 'earth' here meaning 'the population of the earth' as in VI, 11 f; XI, 1.

**20.** *began.* The Heb. word has also the meaning of 'being profane'. Hence, Rashi's comment:— 'Noah made himself profane, degraded himself. He should have planted anything but the vine,' which is the source of so much sin and crime among the children of men.

**21.** *uncovered.* 'Scripture shows in this narrative what shame and evil can through drunkenness befall even a man like Noah, who was otherwise found righteous and blameless before God. Some commentators, however, explain that as Noah was the first to cultivate the vine, he was ignorant of the intoxicating effect of its fruit. What happened to him is therefore a warning to mankind' (Luzzatto).

**22.** *Ham, the father of Canaan.* This vague narrative refers to some abominable deed in which Canaan seems to have been implicated.

*told his two brethren.* Instead of showing filial respect and covering his father, Ham deemed the occasion food for laughter, and mockingly repeated the incident to his brothers.

**23.** *garment.* Heb. 'an outer cloak.'

Some Jewish and non-Jewish teachers omit this story in children's Bible classes. Yet, it is of deep significance in a child's moral training. An intelligent child cannot help now and then detecting a fault or something to laugh at in his parents; but instead of mockery or callous exposure, it is for him to throw the mantle of filial love over the fault and turn away his face. 'Am I the one to judge my parents?' a child should ask himself (F. Adler). Few Jewish children have parents who are drunkards, but there is a great number whose fathers and mothers do not, e.g., speak the language of the land as fluently as they do. Instead of laughing at them, Jewish children should be taught to feel: 'Have my parents had the opportunities in life that they have given *me?*'

**24.** *youngest son.* Heb. *beno hak-katan,* which might also mean 'grandson', like the French *petit fils* (Wogue). The reference is evidently to Canaan.

**25.** *cursed be Canaan.* It was firmly held in ancient times (cf. XLVIII and XLIX) that the blessing or curse which a father pronounced upon a child affected the latter's descendants. We, therefore, have here in effect a forecast of the future, that the Canaanites would be a servile and degraded race.

*servant of servants.* A Hebraism expressing the superlative degree; the meanest, most degraded, servant; cf. 'Song of Songs'; *i.e.* the most beautiful song.

GENESIS IX, 25

awoke from his wine, and knew what his youngest son had done unto him. 25. And he said: Cursed be Canaan;
  A servant of servants shall he be unto his brethren.
26. And he said:
  Blessed be the LORD, the God of Shem;
  And let Canaan be their servant.
27. God ¹enlarge Japheth,
  And he shall dwell in the tents of Shem;
  And let Canaan be their servant.
¶ 28. And Noah lived after the flood three hundred and fifty years. 29. And all the days of Noah were nine hundred and fifty years; and he died.

## 10    CHAPTER X

1. Now these are the generations of the sons of Noah: Shem, Ham, and Japheth; and unto them were sons born after the flood. ¶ 2. The sons of Japheth: Gomer, and Magog, and Madai, and Javan, and Tubal, and Meshech, and Tiras. 3. And the sons of Gomer: Ashkenaz, and Riphath, and Togarmah. 4. And the sons of Javan: Elishah, and Tarshish, Kittim, and

¹ Heb. *japhth*.

**26.** *the God of Shem.* The meaning is, Blessed be the God who will, in the days to come, keep His promise to the descendants of Shem—the Israelites—the promise to give unto them the land of Canaan for a possession, and to be their God and their Guide.

**27.** *God enlarge Japheth.* A play on the root-meaning of the name, which may mean 'enlargement'. Japheth, the progenitor of the Indo-European or Aryan peoples, receives the blessing of worldly prosperity and widespread dominion, but he was to dwell 'in the tents of Shem'. Friendly relations should subsist between the Semitic and Japhetic races. This is the first of the universalist forecasts in Scripture of the day when enmity between nations will be forgotten, and they will unite in acknowledgment of the God of Israel.

The word Japheth may also mean 'beauty'. The Rabbis conceived of beauty under the category of purity; and longed for Japheth, *i.e.* the beauty of Greece, to dwell in the tents of Shem.

### CHAPTER X. THE FAMILY OF THE NATIONS

This chapter traces the nations of the earth to the sons of Noah. The principal races and peoples known to the Israelites are arranged as if they were different branches of one great family. Thus, all the nations are represented as having sprung from the same ancestry. All men are therefore brothers. This sublime conception of the *Unity of the Human Race* logically follows from the belief in the Unity of God, and like it, forms one of the corner-stones of the edifice of Judaism. Polytheism could never rise to the idea of Humanity; heathen society 'was vitiated by failure to recognize the moral obligation involved in our common humanity' (Elmslie). There is, therefore, no parallel to this chapter in the literature of any other ancient people. It has been rightly called a Messianic document.

While the surpassing importance of this wonderful chapter is *religious*, 'the so-called table of the nations remains, according to all results of archæological exploration, an ethnographic original document of the first rank which nothing can replace' (Kautzsch). In all essential details, its trustworthiness has been strikingly vindicated by the new light from ancient monuments.

**2.** Contains the names of peoples in Asia Minor.

*Gomer.* The Cimmerians, on the shores of the Caspian Sea.

*Magog.* The Scythians, whose territory lay on the borders of the Caucasus.

*Madai.* The Medes.

*Javan.* The Greeks (Ionians: in the older language, Iawones).

**3.** *Ashkenaz.* They lived in the neighbourhood of Ararat, Armenia. In later Jewish literature, Ashkenaz is used to denote Germany; hence, *Ashkenazim,* Jews hailing from Germanic countries. For *Sephardim,* see p. 140.

*Riphath and Togarmah.* Peoples of Asia Minor.

## GENESIS X, 5 — בראשית נח י

Dodanim. 5. Of these were the isles of the nations divided in their lands, every one after his tongue, after their families, in their nations. ¶ 6. And the sons of Ham: Cush, and Mizraim, and Put, and Canaan. 7. And the sons of Cush: Seba, and Havilah, and Sabtah, and Raamah, and Sabteca; and the sons of Raamah: Sheba, and Dedan. 8. And Cush begot Nimrod; he began to be a mighty one in the earth. 9. He was a mighty hunter before the Lord; wherefore it is said: 'Like Nimrod a mighty hunter before the Lord.' 10. And the beginning of his kingdom was Babel, and Erech, and Accad, and Calneh, in the land of Shinar.

ה אֱלִישָׁה וְתַרְשִׁישׁ כִּתִּים וְדֹדָנִים: מֵאֵלֶּה נִפְרְדוּ אִיֵּי הַגּוֹיִם
6 בְּאַרְצֹתָם אִישׁ לִלְשֹׁנוֹ לְמִשְׁפְּחֹתָם בְּגוֹיֵהֶם: וּבְנֵי חָם
7 כּוּשׁ וּמִצְרַיִם וּפוּט וּכְנָעַן: וּבְנֵי כוּשׁ סְבָא וַחֲוִילָה וְסַבְתָּה
8 וְרַעְמָה וְסַבְתְּכָא וּבְנֵי רַעְמָה שְׁבָא וּדְדָן: וְכוּשׁ יָלַד אֶת־
9 נִמְרֹד הוּא הֵחֵל לִהְיוֹת גִּבֹּר בָּאָרֶץ: הוּא־הָיָה גִבֹּר־צַיִד לִפְנֵי יְהוָה עַל־כֵּן יֵאָמַר כְּנִמְרֹד גִּבּוֹר צַיִד לִפְנֵי יְהוָה:
10 וַתְּהִי רֵאשִׁית מַמְלַכְתּוֹ בָּבֶל וְאֶרֶךְ וְאַכַּד וְכַלְנֵה בְּאֶרֶץ

**4. Elishah.** Most scholars see the word 'Hellas' in the name. Others identify it with Southern Italy, Sicily or Cyprus.
*Tarshish.* Frequently mentioned in the Bible as a flourishing and wealthy seaport. It is generally identified with Tartessus in ancient Spain.
*Kittim.* A race inhabiting part of the island of Cyprus, of Phœnician extraction.
*Dodanim.* In 1 Chron. I, 4–25 (with which this chapter should be compared) it is written *Rodanim*, i.e. the inhabitants of the Rhodian islands in the Ægean Sea. Both forms, רודנים and דודנים, are shortened forms of דרדנים, as given in Targum Jonathan, and refer to Dardania in the region of Troy (Luzzatto).

**5. of these.** From these, i.e. the sons of Javan enumerated in the preceding verse.
*divided.* As separate countries, because of their distinctive populations.
*after his tongue.* The differentiation of language is accounted for in the next chapter. The Rabbis explain that the narratives in Scripture are not always in strict chronological order. Sometimes an event is anticipated, at other times it is told in connection with a later event. אין מוקדם ומאוחר בתורה.

**6. Ham.** The most ancient name for Egypt was 'Chem', meaning 'black', alluding no doubt to the dark colour of the Egyptian soil.
*Cush.* Ethiopia.
*Mizraim.* The most common name for Egypt. The Heb. form of the name is dual, and refers to the division into Upper and Lower Egypt.
*Put.* Lybia.
*Canaan.* The word is probably derived from a root meaning 'to be low'; and Canaan was the term originally applied to the lowland of the coast of Phœnicia and the land of the Philistines. The name was afterwards extended to the whole of Western Palestine. According to this verse, Mizraim and Canaan were 'brothers'; i.e. Palestine and Egypt were provinces of the same Empire. This was the case only in the time of the Nineteenth Dynasty, the age of Moses (Sayce). It was quite untrue of the time of the Exile, when the alleged author of 'P' (see p. 198) is said to have lived. The name 'Persians' does not occur in the chapter, because in the days of Moses these did not yet exist.

**7.** Tribes and places on the African coast of the Red Sea, or on the opposite shore of Arabia.
*Sheba.* A great commercial state in Southern Arabia. The Queen of Sheba visited King Solomon (1 Kings x).

**8. Nimrod.** Nimrod is a descendant of Ham. It is now established that the original founders of Babylonian civilization, the Sumerians, were a people of non-Semitic stock.
*a mighty one.* He acquired dominion and ascendancy by conquest and by the terror he inspired.

**9. a mighty hunter.** lit. 'a hero of the chase.' The Assyrian monuments often depict monarchs and nobles in the act of hunting.
*before the Lord.* This phrase is an expression of emphasis, 'a very great hunter'; cf. Jonah III, 3, 'Nineveh was a city great unto God,' meaning, Nineveh was an exceeding great city.
*wherefore it is said.* A formula introducing a proverb; cf. XXII, 14, Num. XXI, 14, etc. Nimrod's exploits became proverbial.

**10. beginning of his kingdom.** When he commenced to reign, his dominion extended over the cities here enumerated.
*Babel.* Babylon; its building is described in the next chapter. It was the centre of the ancient Orient, and for many centuries, the mistress of the world.
*Erech.* The Babylonian city 'Uruk', now called 'Warka', on the left bank of the lower Euphrates.
*Accad.* Name of a city, Agade; also of the land of Accad, Northern Babylonia.
*Shinar.* A Heb. name for Babylonia; cf. XIV, 1, 9; Joshua VII, 21, etc. Some identify Shinar with 'Sumir', the land of the Sumerians (Delitzsch, Jampel).

## GENESIS X, 11

11. Out of that land went forth Asshur, and builded Nineveh, and Rehoboth-ir, and Calah, 12. and Resen between Nineveh and Calah—the same is the great city. 13. And Mizraim begot Ludim, and Anamim, and Lehabim, and Naphtuhim, 14. and Pathrusim, and Casluhim—whence went forth the Philistines—and Caphtorim. ¶15. And Canaan begot Zidon his first-born, and Heth; 16. and the Jebusite, and the Amorite, and the Girgashite; 17. and the Hivite, and the Arkite, and the Sinite; 18. and the Arvadite, and the Zemarite, and the Hamathite; and afterward were the families of the Canaanite spread abroad. 19. And the border of the Canaanite was from Zidon, as thou goest toward Gerar, unto Gaza; as thou goest toward Sodom and Gomorrah and Admah and Zeboiim, unto Lasha. 20. These are the sons of Ham, after their families, after their tongues, in their lands, in their nations. ¶ 21. And unto Shem, the father of all the children of Eber, the elder brother of Japheth, to him also were children born. 22. The sons

בראשית נח י

11 שִׁנְעָר׃ מִן־הָאָרֶץ הַהִוא יָצָא אַשּׁוּר וַיִּבֶן אֶת־נִינְוֵה וְאֶת־
12 רְחֹבֹת עִיר וְאֶת־כָּלַח׃ וְאֶת־רֶסֶן בֵּין נִינְוֵה וּבֵין כָּלַח
13 הִוא הָעִיר הַגְּדֹלָה׃ וּמִצְרַיִם יָלַד אֶת־לוּדִים וְאֶת־עֲנָמִים
14 וְאֶת־לְהָבִים וְאֶת־נַפְתֻּחִים׃ וְאֶת־פַּתְרֻסִים וְאֶת־כַּסְלֻחִים
טו אֲשֶׁר יָצְאוּ מִשָּׁם פְּלִשְׁתִּים וְאֶת־כַּפְתֹּרִים׃ ס וּכְנַעַן
16 יָלַד אֶת־צִידֹן בְּכֹרוֹ וְאֶת־חֵת׃ וְאֶת־הַיְבוּסִי וְאֶת־הָאֱמֹרִי
17 וְאֵת הַגִּרְגָּשִׁי׃ וְאֶת־הַחִוִּי וְאֶת־הַעַרְקִי וְאֶת־הַסִּינִי׃ וְאֶת־
18 הָאַרְוָדִי וְאֶת־הַצְּמָרִי וְאֶת־הַחֲמָתִי וְאַחַר נָפֹצוּ מִשְׁפְּחוֹת
19 הַכְּנַעֲנִי׃ וַיְהִי גְּבוּל הַכְּנַעֲנִי מִצִּידֹן בֹּאֲכָה גְרָרָה עַד־עַזָּה
כ בֹּאֲכָה סְדֹמָה וַעֲמֹרָה וְאַדְמָה וּצְבֹיִם עַד־לָשַׁע׃ אֵלֶּה
בְנֵי־חָם לְמִשְׁפְּחֹתָם לִלְשֹׁנֹתָם בְּאַרְצֹתָם בְּגוֹיֵהֶם׃ ס
21 וּלְשֵׁם יֻלַּד גַּם־הוּא אֲבִי כָּל־בְּנֵי־עֵבֶר אֲחִי יֶפֶת הַגָּדוֹל׃

v. 17. חה״א בקמץ   v. 19. וצבוים קרי

---

**11.** *went forth Asshur*. Archæology confirms the Biblical statement that the cities of Assyria owed their existence to the development of Babylonian power by conquest and colonization.
*Nineveh.* The capital of Assyria.

**12.** *great city. i.e.* Nineveh together with the other three places constituted one great city (Jonah III, 3).

**13.** *Lehabim.* The Lybians.
*Naphtuhim.* The dwellers of the Nile Delta.

**14.** *Pathrusim.* The population of Upper Egypt, Pathros.
*whence went forth the Philistines.* A difficulty arises from the fact that in Deut. II, 23, Amos IX, 7, the Philistines are spoken of as coming from Caphtor, *i.e.* Crete. The explanation may be that there were two immigrations of Philistines, one by way of the Egyptian sea-coast and the other from Crete. They have given their name to the land, 'Palestine.'
*Caphtorim.* The inhabitants of Crete.

**15.** *Zidon his first-born.* 'First-born,' the oldest settlement of the Canaanites. Zidon, the capital of ancient Phœnicia, stands for the whole country.
*Heth.* The Hittites, a powerful and warlike nation who held sway in Syria and Asia Minor from 1800 to 900 B.C.E. Wonderful remains of their civilization have been unearthed since the beginning of this century, and their language is now deciphered.

**16.** *Jebusite.* This tribe dwelt in and around Jerusalem, which was originally known as Jebus.

*Amorite.* This term is sometimes used to denote all the inhabitants of Canaan before the coming of the Israelites, and sometimes one particular warlike tribe amongst the Canaanites.
*Girgashite.* One of the peoples driven from Canaan by the Israelites (xv, 21).

**17.** The tribes mentioned in this and in the following verse lived in greater or less proximity to Mt. Lebanon.

**18.** *Hamathite.* Hamath, in Syria, was at one time the capital of a strong kingdom (Is. XXXVII, 13).
*spread abroad.* They extended into the territory mentioned in the next verse.

**19.** The border of the Canaanites was originally within the limits stated in this verse—from Zidon in the North to Gaza in the South, and from Sodom and Gomorrah in the South-east to Lasha in the North-east of Palestine.

**22–24.** According to this genealogical table, Eber was the great-grandson of Shem; but he was the ancestor of Abram, who is called *Ha-ibri* (XIV, 13). From 'Eber' is formed the word 'Hebrew', the name by which the Israelites were known to foreign peoples. Special stress is here laid on Eber because he is, through Abram, the ancestor of the people of Israel.

**22.** *Elam.* The name of a land and people beyond Babylonia and the Persian Gulf—the easternmost people with which the descendants of Shem were brought into contact. As the Elam of history is Aryan, the correctness of

## GENESIS X, 23

of Shem: Elam, and Asshur, and Arpachshad, and Lud, and Aram. 23. And the sons of Aram: Uz, and Hul, and Gether, and Mash. 24. And Arpachshad begot Shelah; and Shelah begot Eber. 25. And unto Eber were born two sons; the name of the one was ¹Peleg; for in his days was the earth divided; and his brother's name was Joktan. 26. And Joktan begot Almodad, and Sheleph, and Hazarmaveth, and Jerah; 27. and Hadoram, and Uzal, and Diklah; 28. and Obal, and Abimael, and Sheba; 29. and Ophir, and Havilah, and Jobab; all these were the sons of Joktan. 30. And their dwelling was from Mesha, as thou goest toward Sephar, unto the mountain of the east. 31. These are the sons of Shem, after their families, after their tongues, in their lands, after their nations. ¶ 32. These are the families of the sons of Noah, after their generations, in their nations; and of these were the nations divided in the earth after the flood.* vii.

## 11  CHAPTER XI

1. And the whole earth was of one language and of one speech. 2. And it came to pass,

---
¹ That is, *Division*.

בראשית נח י יא

22 בְּנֵי שֵׁם עֵילָם וְאַשּׁוּר וְאַרְפַּכְשַׁד וְלוּד וַאֲרָם: וּבְנֵי אֲרָם
23
24 עוּץ וְחוּל וְגֶתֶר וָמַשׁ: וְאַרְפַּכְשַׁד יָלַד אֶת־שָׁלַח וְשֶׁלַח
כה יָלַד אֶת־עֵבֶר: וּלְעֵבֶר יֻלַּד שְׁנֵי בָנִים שֵׁם הָאֶחָד פֶּלֶג
26 כִּי בְיָמָיו נִפְלְגָה הָאָרֶץ וְשֵׁם אָחִיו יָקְטָן: וְיָקְטָן יָלַד אֶת־
27 אַלְמוֹדָד וְאֶת־שָׁלֶף וְאֶת־חֲצַרְמָוֶת וְאֶת־יָרַח: וְאֶת־הֲדוֹרָם
28 וְאֶת־אוּזָל וְאֶת־דִּקְלָה: וְאֶת־עוֹבָל וְאֶת־אֲבִימָאֵל וְאֶת־
29 שְׁבָא: וְאֶת־אוֹפִר וְאֶת־חֲוִילָה וְאֶת־יוֹבָב כָּל־אֵלֶּה בְּנֵי
ל יָקְטָן: וַיְהִי מוֹשָׁבָם מִמֵּשָׁא בֹּאֲכָה סְפָרָה הַר הַקֶּדֶם:
31 אֵלֶּה בְנֵי־שֵׁם לְמִשְׁפְּחֹתָם לִלְשֹׁנֹתָם בְּאַרְצֹתָם לְגוֹיֵהֶם:
32 אֵלֶּה מִשְׁפְּחֹת בְּנֵי־נֹחַ לְתוֹלְדֹתָם בְּגוֹיֵהֶם וּמֵאֵלֶּה נִפְרְדוּ
הַגּוֹיִם בָּאָרֶץ אַחַר הַמַּבּוּל: פ    שביעי

CAP. XI. יא    יא

2 וַיְהִי כָל־הָאָרֶץ שָׂפָה אֶחָת וּדְבָרִים אֲחָדִים: וַיְהִי בְּנָסְעָם
3 מִקֶּדֶם וַיִּמְצְאוּ בִקְעָה בְּאֶרֶץ שִׁנְעָר וַיֵּשְׁבוּ שָׁם: וַיֹּאמְרוּ

v. 23. פתח בס״פ

---

the Biblical view that Elam is a son of Shem was questioned. The French exploration at Susa, however, has shown that the oldest Elamite inscriptions are written in Babylonian, which proves that early Elam was peopled by Semites. Bible critics did not relish the idea of being robbed of one of their stock arguments against the trustworthiness of this chapter. But as they are forced to admit that the statement in regard to Elam is correct, they add: 'The fact [that his statement is correct] is not one which the writer of the verse is very likely to have known' (Driver). No clearer proof is needed of the negative dogmatism of Bible critics.

*Asshur.* Assyria, the most powerful of the Semitic peoples.

*Arpachshad.* Sayce explains the name as 'the territory of the Chasd' (cf. Ur of the Casdim, *i.e.* Chaldæans).

*Lud.* The Lydians of Asia Minor.

*Aram.* The Aramæan or Syrian people, whose territory included Mesopotamia ('Aram of the two Rivers'). Both the Aramæan people and language were destined to exert great influence in Jewish history.

**23.** *Uz.* The land where Job lived (Job, I). In Lam. IV, 21, the Edomites are mentioned as dwelling in the land of Uz.

*Hul, Gether, Mash.* Unidentified localities in Syria.

**25.** *divided.* By 'earth' is meant the population of the earth. The allusion is probably to the scattering of the peoples described in the next chapter.

*Peleg.* In Assyrian, *palgu* means 'canal'; and Sayce believes the 'division of the land' to refer to the introduction of a system of canals into Babylonia.

**26.** *Joktan.* Regarded as the progenitor of the Southern Arabs.

*Hazarmaveth.* The land of Hadramaut, in Southern Arabia.

**29.** *Ophir.* Famed for its gold (I Kings IX, 28 and XXII, 49).

**30.** The identification of these Arabian landmarks is uncertain.

CHAPTER XI, 1–9. THE BUILDING OF THE TOWER

For an explanation of this difficult Chapter, see p. 197.

**1.** *one speech.* Better, '*few words*.' *i.e.* they had but a small vocabulary (Malbim).

**2.** *plain.* The territory of Babylon consisted of an almost unbroken plain.

*Shinar.* Cf. x, 10. It is more and more coming to be regarded as the cradle of the earliest civilization.

## GENESIS XI, 3

as they journeyed east, that they found a plain in the land of Shinar; and they dwelt there. 3. And they said one to another: 'Come, let us make brick, and burn them thoroughly.' And they had brick for stone, and slime had they for mortar. 4. And they said: 'Come, let us build us a city, and a tower, with its top in heaven, and let us make us a name; lest we be scattered abroad upon the face of the whole earth.' 5. And the LORD came down to see the city and the tower, which the children of men builded. 6. And the LORD said: 'Behold, they are one people, and they have all one language; and this is what they begin to do; and now nothing will be withholden from them, which they purpose to do. 7. Come, let us go down, and there confound their language, that they may not understand one another's speech.' 8. So the LORD scattered them abroad from thence upon the face of all the earth; and they left off to build the city. 9. Therefore was the name of it called Babel; because the LORD did there [1]confound the language of all the earth; and from thence did the LORD scatter them abroad upon the face of all the earth. ¶ 10. These are the generations of Shem. Shem was a hundred years old, and begot Arpachshad two years after the flood. 11. And Shem lived after he begot Arpachshad five hundred years, and begot sons and daughters. ¶ 12. And Arpachshad lived five and thirty years, and begot Shelah. 13. And Arpachshad lived after he begot Shelah four hundred and three years, and begot sons and daughters. ¶ 14. And Shelah lived thirty years, and begot Eber. 15. And Shelah lived after he begot Eber four hundred and three years, and begot sons

[1] Heb. *balal*, to confound.

**3.** *brick*. In Babylon, clay-bricks were the material for building.

*burn them thoroughly.* Bricks were usually sun-dried; but in order to make these more durable, they were put through a process of burning by fire.

*slime.* Bitumen.

**4.** *with its top in heaven.* An exaggerated statement; cf. Deut. I, 28, 'the cities are great and fortified up to heaven.'

*a name.* If they all dwelt together, they would be powerful and become renowned.

**5.** *came down.* So again XVIII, 21. An anthropomorphic expression. The Rabbis deduce from this the rule that a judge should never condemn an offender without first seeing for himself both him and the nature of the offence.

**6.** *begin to do.* At this early stage in human history, men are led to combine by an unworthy motive. If their design is not frustrated, they might employ their united strength for outrageous purposes. All human effort is both futile and empty, if dictated by self-exaltation, and divorced from acknowledgement of God.

**7.** *let us go down.* The plural of Majesty, as in I, 26.

**9.** *Babel.* This is an instance of popular etymology based on resemblance of sound and is frequently found in Scripture. The Assyrian name for Babel means, 'Gate of God.'

### 10–32. FROM SHEM TO ABRAHAM

**10.** *these are the generations.* This new section, leaving Universal History behind, reverts to the main purpose of the First Book of the Torah, which is that of giving a complete account of the founders of the Hebrew race, *viz.* Abraham, Isaac, and Jacob and their children. Abram is traced back through ten successive generations to Shem, the son of Noah.

**16.** *Peleg.* See X, 25. The descendants of

# GENESIS XI, 16

and daughters. ¶ 16. And Eber lived four and thirty years, and begot Peleg. 17. And Eber lived after he begot Peleg four hundred and thirty years, and begot sons and daughters. ¶ 18. And Peleg lived thirty years, and begot Reu. 19. And Peleg lived after he begot Reu two hundred and nine years, and begot sons and daughters. ¶ 20. And Reu lived two and thirty years, and begot Serug. 21. And Reu lived after he begot Serug two hundred and seven years, and begot sons and daughters. ¶ 22. And Serug lived thirty years, and begot Nahor. 23. And Serug lived after he begot Nahor two hundred years, and begot sons and daughters. ¶ 24. And Nahor lived nine and twenty years, and begot Terah. 25. And Nahor lived after he begot Terah a hundred and nineteen years, and begot sons and daughters. ¶ 26. And Terah lived seventy years, and begot Abram, Nahor, and Haran. ¶ 27. Now these are the generations of Terah. Terah begot Abram, Nahor, and Haran; and Haran begot Lot. 28. And Haran died in the presence of his father Terah in the land of his nativity, in Ur of the Chaldees. *m. 29. And Abram and Nahor took them wives: the name of Abram's wife was Sarai; and the name of Nahor's wife, Milcah, the daughter of Haran, the father of Milcah, and the father of Iscah. 30. And Sarai was barren; she had no child. 31. And Terah took Abram his son, and Lot the son of Haran, his son's son, and Sarai his daughter-in-law, his son Abram's wife; and they went forth with them from Ur of the Chaldees, to go into the land of Canaan; and they came unto Haran, and dwelt there. 32. And the days of Terah were two hundred and five years; and Terah died in Haran.

Peleg were omitted from the former chapter because they were to be mentioned here.

**26.** *Abram.* The name was in common use at Babylon. 'Abi-rama' is a witness to a Babylonian deed long before the days of Abraham.

**28.** *in the presence of.* During his father's lifetime
*Ur of the Chaldees.* Usually identified with Mugheir, a town on the Euphrates some distance east of its junction with the Tigris. The name Ur occurs in the inscriptions in the form Uru, which was one of the old Babylonian royal towns and a centre of the moon-god worship. Astounding discoveries have in recent years been made, and are still being made, in its ruins. These enable us to have a vivid picture of contemporary life in the native city of Abraham; see *Abraham*, by C. Leonard Woolley, 1936.

*Chaldees.* Is often used in the Bible as a synonym for Babylonians.

**29.** *Sarai.* The personal names 'Sarai' and 'Nahor' also occur in Babylonian inscriptions.
*Milcah.* The importance of mentioning her lies in the fact that she was the ancestress of Rebekah, the mother of Isaac (XXII, 20; XXIV, 15).
*Iscah.* This name is the basis for the Shakespearian name Jessica.

**31.** *Haran.* A town on the highway from Mesopotamia to the West; the converging point of the commercial routes from Babylon in the South, Nineveh in the East, and Damascus in the West.

**32.** The death of Terah did not take place till sixty years after Abram had left Haran; but it is recorded here to complete the story of Terah and thus concentrate on the life of Abram.

For Additional Notes on THE FLOOD, THE DELUGE AND ITS BABYLONIAN PARALLEL, see pp. 196–198.

# HAFTORAH NOACH הפטרת נח

## ISAIAH LIV–LV, 5

### Chapter LIV

1. Sing, O barren, thou that didst not bear,
Break forth into singing, and cry aloud, thou that didst not travail;
For more are the children of the desolate
Than the children of the married wife, saith the Lord.

2. Enlarge the place of thy tent,
And let them stretch forth the curtains of thy habitations, spare not;
Lengthen thy cords, and strengthen thy stakes.

3. For thou shalt spread abroad on the right hand and on the left;
And thy seed shall possess the nations,
And make the desolate cities to be inhabited.

4. Fear not, for thou shalt not be ashamed.
Neither be thou confounded, for thou shalt not be put to shame;
For thou shalt forget the shame of thy youth,
And the reproach of thy widowhood shalt thou remember no more.

5. For thy Maker is thy husband,
The Lord of hosts is His name;
And the Holy One of Israel is thy Redeemer,
The God of the whole earth shall He be called.

---

### Isaiah LIV–LV, 5

The Haftorah, like the preceding one, forms a portion of the glowing prophetic Rhapsody, 'Israel Redeemed,' which is the main theme of the second half of the Book of Isaiah.

The reference in *v.* 9 to 'the waters of Noah' provides a literal connection with the Sedrah. But the connection is deeper. The Flood was apparently an act of destruction; yet, by wiping out a corrupt world, it paved the way for a new humanity. So Israel's Exile. From its suffering, declares the Prophet, Israel is issuing stronger in loyalty to God and in the conception of his vocation. Again, God's covenant with Noah ('I will establish My covenant with you ... neither shall there any more be a flood to destroy the earth') is paralleled by the 'Covenant of Peace' into which, in God's everlasting mercy, Israel now enters.

### Chapter LIV. Jerusalem Rebuilt

1. *more are the children.* Zion's cities shall be repopulated; Jerusalem desolate was like a woman forsaken. Now, with her exiles returned, she is like the wife reunited with husband and children.

2. *enlarge.* Because of the increase of her children, *i.e.* Zion's population.

*tent.* *i.e.* Jerusalem.

*thy habitations.* The other cities of Israel. All of Zion's children who have become estranged from her, wherever they may be dispersed, shall renew their allegiance and return to her leading.

3. *possess.* *i.e.* dispossess those of alien race who have occupied the desolate Jewish cities during the Exile.

4. *the shame of thy youth.* The defeats and humiliations in Israel's earlier history.

*thy widowhood.* *i.e.* the Exile, when God, 'Zion's husband,' seemed to have withdrawn from her. 'Widowhood' has a wider significance than in ordinary English, being used to denote a woman abandoned by her husband.

ISAIAH LIV, 6

6. For the Lord hath called thee
As a wife forsaken and grieved in spirit;
And a wife of youth, can she be rejected?
Saith thy God.

7. For a small moment have I forsaken thee;
But with great compassion will I gather thee.

8. In a little wrath I hid My face from thee for a moment;
But with everlasting kindness will I have compassion on thee,
Saith the Lord thy Redeemer.

9. For this is as the waters of Noah unto Me;
For as I have sworn that the waters of Noah
Should no more go over the earth,
So have I sworn that I would not be wroth with thee,
Nor rebuke thee.

10. For the mountains may depart,
And the hills be removed;
But My kindness shall not depart from thee,
Neither shall My covenant of peace be removed,
Saith the Lord that hath compassion on thee.*

11. O thou afflicted, tossed with tempest,
And not comforted,
Behold, I will set thy stones in fair colours,
And lay thy foundations with sapphires.

\* Sephardim conclude here.

12. And I will make thy pinnacles of rubies,
And thy gates of carbuncles,
And all thy border of precious stones.

13. And all thy children shall be taught of the Lord;
And great shall be the peace of thy children.

ישעיה נד

6 הָאָרֶץ יִקְרָא: כִּֽי־כְאִשָּׁ֤ה עֲזוּבָ֛ה וַעֲצ֥וּבַת ר֖וּחַ קְרָאָ֑ךְ
7 יְהוָ֑ה וְאֵ֥שֶׁת נְעוּרִ֖ים כִּ֣י תִמָּאֵ֑ס אָמַ֖ר אֱלֹהָֽיִךְ: בְּרֶ֥גַע קָטֹ֛ן
8 עֲזַבְתִּ֖יךְ וּבְרַחֲמִ֥ים גְּדֹלִ֖ים אֲקַבְּצֵֽךְ: בְּשֶׁ֣צֶף קֶ֗צֶף הִסְתַּ֨רְתִּי
פָנַ֥י רֶ֨גַע֙ מִמֵּ֔ךְ וּבְחֶ֥סֶד עוֹלָ֖ם רִֽחַמְתִּ֑יךְ אָמַ֥ר גֹּאֲלֵ֖ךְ יְהוָֽה:
9 כִּי־מֵ֥י נֹ֨חַ֙ זֹ֣את לִ֔י אֲשֶׁ֣ר נִשְׁבַּ֗עְתִּי מֵעֲבֹ֥ר מֵי־נֹ֛חַ ע֖וֹד
10 עַל־הָאָ֑רֶץ כֵּ֥ן נִשְׁבַּ֛עְתִּי מִקְּצֹ֥ף עָלַ֖יִךְ וּמִגְּעָר־בָּֽךְ: כִּ֤י הֶהָרִים֙
יָמ֔וּשׁוּ וְהַגְּבָע֖וֹת תְּמוּטֶ֑נָה וְחַסְדִּ֞י מֵאִתֵּ֣ךְ לֹֽא־יָמ֗וּשׁ וּבְרִ֤ית
11 שְׁלוֹמִי֙ לֹ֣א תָמ֔וּט אָמַ֥ר מְרַחֲמֵ֖ךְ יְהוָֽה: עֲנִיָּ֥ה סֹעֲרָ֖ה
לֹ֣א נֻחָ֑מָה הִנֵּ֨ה אָנֹכִ֜י מַרְבִּ֤יץ בַּפּוּךְ֙ אֲבָנַ֔יִךְ וִיסַדְתִּ֖יךְ
12 בַּסַּפִּירִֽים: וְשַׂמְתִּ֤י כַּֽדְכֹד֙ שִׁמְשֹׁתַ֔יִךְ וּשְׁעָרַ֖יִךְ לְאַבְנֵ֣י אֶקְדָּ֑ח
13 וְכָל־גְּבוּלֵ֖ךְ לְאַבְנֵי־חֵֽפֶץ: וְכָל־בָּנַ֖יִךְ לִמּוּדֵ֣י יְהוָ֑ה וְרַ֖ב

v. 9. * כאן מסיימין הספרדים * נ״א כימי

---

**7–8.** God's anger is but momentary; cf. Psalm xxx, 5. Although the years of the Exile seemed interminably long, they will prove but a brief space in the vast sweep of Israel's history.

**9–10.** Yet another utterance of comfort.

**9.** *for this.* i.e. the Exile and the comfort. The Exile is compared to the Flood; and the comfort, to the Divine promise that the Flood should never again occur.

**11–17.** OUTER AND INNER SPLENDOUR OF ZION

**13.** *taught of the LORD.* Or, 'disciples of the LORD.' Zion's peace will be based not on armed force, but on the God-fearing lives of all its inhabitants. In some ancient manuscripts, it seems, the second word for 'thy children' (*banayich*) in this verse was read as *bonayich*, 'thy builders.' In other words, the children of a nation are the builders of its future. And every Jewish child must be reared to become such a builder of his People's better future; every Jewish child must be fortified by a knowledge of Judaism and trained for a life of beneficence for Israel and humanity. This verse ('All thy children shall be taught of the LORD') is an important landmark in the history of civilization. In obedience to it, Israel led the way in universal education. Thus, in his *History of the World*, H. G. Wells records, 'The Jewish religion, because it was a literature-sustained religion, led to the first efforts to provide elementary instruction for all the children of the community.'

## ISAIAH LIV, 14

14. In righteousness shalt thou be established;
Be thou far from oppression, for thou shalt not fear,
And from ruin, for it shall not come near thee.

15. Behold, they may gather together, but not by Me;
Whosoever shall gather together against thee shall fall because of thee.

16. Behold, I have created the smith
That bloweth the fire of coals,
And bringeth forth a weapon for his work;
And I have created the waster to destroy.

17. No weapon that is formed against thee shall prosper;
And every tongue that shall rise against thee in judgment thou shalt condemn.
This is the heritage of the servants of the LORD,
And their due reward from Me, saith the LORD.

### CHAPTER LV

1. Ho, every one that thirsteth, come ye for water,
And he that hath no money;
Come ye, buy, and eat;
Yea, come, buy wine and milk
Without money and without price.

2. Wherefore do ye spend money for that which is not bread?
And your gain for that which satisfieth not?
Hearken diligently unto Me, and eat ye that which is good,
And let your soul delight itself in fatness.

---

**14.** *be thou far from oppression.* Be steadfast in righteousness, and panic ('terror') shall not touch thee. The discharge of duty is a great moral tonic.

**15.** *not by Me.* All those who now stir up strife with thee shall shatter themselves against thee.

**17.** Israel's vindication in history is assured: neither might nor malice can destroy the Servant of the Lord.

*condemn.* Overthrow in argument.

*this.* i.e. no weapon forged against Israel shall succeed.

*the servants.* The worshippers.

*their due reward from Me.* צדקה means both 'righteousness' (i.e. holiness of life in the individual) and 'victory' (i.e. the triumph of right in the world).

CHAPTER LV. THE RETURN TO ZION SHOULD ALSO BE A RETURN TO GOD

**1.** A call to rich and poor alike to participate in the blessings of the new era, by coming to the source whence the knowledge of duty springs—the word of God. The cry is like that of the water-carrier in Eastern cities, and blessings are expressed in Oriental imagery, in terms of quickening water, nourishing milk, and gladdening wine. 'One cannot fail to perceive the note of wistfulness in the appeal, suggestive of the dread of an unspeakable disappointment' (Elmslie and Skinner).

**2.** Why spend time and labour and money on material pursuits that cannot in the end satisfy the soul created for holiness and righteousness?

*fatness.* Spiritual well-being. Its contrast is 'leanness of soul,' Ps. CVI, 15.

## ISAIAH LV, 3

3. Incline your ear, and come unto Me;
Hear, and your soul shall live;
And I will make an everlasting covenant with you,
Even the sure mercies of David.
4. Behold, I have given him for a witness to the peoples,
A prince and commander to the peoples.
5. Behold, thou shalt call a nation that thou knowest not,
And a nation that knew not thee shall run unto thee;
Because of the Lord thy God,
And for the Holy One of Israel, for He hath glorified thee.

3 הַטּוּ אָזְנְכֶם וּלְכוּ אֵלַי שִׁמְעוּ וּתְחִי נַפְשְׁכֶם וְאֶכְרְתָה
4 לָכֶם בְּרִית עוֹלָם חַסְדֵי דָוִד הַנֶּאֱמָנִים: הֵן עֵד לְאוּמִּים
5 נְתַתִּיו נָגִיד וּמְצַוֵּה לְאֻמִּים: הֵן גּוֹי לֹא־תֵדַע תִּקְרָא וְגוֹי
לֹא־יְדָעוּךָ אֵלֶיךָ יָרוּצוּ לְמַעַן יְהוָה אֱלֹהֶיךָ וְלִקְדוֹשׁ יִשְׂרָאֵל
כִּי פֵאֲרָךְ:

---

v. 4. דגש אחר שורק

**3.** *the sure mercies of David.* The new covenant shall be the fulfilment of the promise that the Davidic Kingdom would endure (II Sam. VII, 8–16).

**4.** *I have given him.* David or the representative of David's family. Zerubbabel, the leader of the returning exiles, was a descendant of David.

**5.** *thou shalt call.* A return to the description of the unconscious influence which Israel's loyalty to his Divinely-appointed mission is sure to effect.

# GENESIS XII, 1

בראשית לך לך יב

CAP. XII. יב

פ פ פ ג

א וַיֹּאמֶר יְהֹוָה אֶל־אַבְרָם לֶךְ־לְךָ מֵאַרְצְךָ וּמִמּוֹלַדְתְּךָ וּמִבֵּית
2 אָבִיךָ אֶל־הָאָרֶץ אֲשֶׁר אַרְאֶךָּ: וְאֶעֶשְׂךָ לְגוֹי גָּדוֹל וַאֲבָרֶכְךָ
3 וַאֲגַדְּלָה שְׁמֶךָ וֶהְיֵה בְּרָכָה: וַאֲבָרֲכָה מְבָרְכֶיךָ וּמְקַלֶּלְךָ
4 אָאֹר וְנִבְרְכוּ בְךָ כֹּל מִשְׁפְּחֹת הָאֲדָמָה: וַיֵּלֶךְ אַבְרָם כַּאֲשֶׁר

1. Now the LORD said unto Abram: 'Get thee out of thy country, and from thy kindred, and from thy father's house, unto the land that I will show thee. 2. And I will make of thee a great nation, and I will bless thee, and make thy name great; and be thou a blessing. 3. And I will bless them that bless thee, and him that curseth thee will I curse; and in thee shall all the families of the earth be blessed.' 4. So Abram went, as the LORD had spoken unto

## III. LECH LECHA

(CHAPTERS XII–XVII)

### HISTORY OF THE PATRIARCHS

#### (a) ABRAHAM (CHAPTERS XII, 1–XXV, 18)

CHAPTER XII. THE CALL OF ABRAHAM, v. 1–9

**1.** *out of thy country.* 'In this land of idol worship thou art not worthy to rear sons to the service of God' (Rashi)—the evil surroundings would contaminate them. The Midrash explains that the command was issued for the benefit of his fellow-men. 'When a flask of balsam is sealed and stored away, its fragrance is not perceptible; but, opened and moved about, its sweet odour is widely diffused.'

*thy country . . . thy kindred . . . thy father's house.* These are the main influences which mould a person's thoughts and actions. The words also indicate the severity of the trial which was being imposed upon him. He was to cut himself completely adrift from all associations that could possibly hinder his mission. A similar 'call' comes to Abraham's descendants in every age and clime, to separate themselves from all associations and influences that are inimical to their Faith and Destiny.

*thy country.* Babylonia, which was then the most powerful empire in the world, with a highly developed city-civilization, commercial society, and literary culture.

*land that I will show thee.* The destination of the journey is not specified, to increase the test of Abram's faith in the Divine call. He was to follow whithersoever the will of God would direct him.

**2.** *I will bless thee.* With all good.

*make thy name great.* Although at first he would be unknown, a stranger in a strange land.

*be thou a blessing.* These words contain the ideal which Abram was to set himself, to become a blessing to humanity by the beneficent influence of his godly life and by turning others to a knowledge of God. With the change of one vowel, says the Midrash, the Hebrew word for 'blessing' means 'spring of water'. Even as a spring purifies the defiled, so do thou attract those who are far from the knowledge of God and purify them for their Heavenly Father. And such has indeed been the role played by the children of Abraham on the stage of human history. 'The Jew is that sacred being,' says Tolstoy, 'who has brought down from heaven the everlasting fire, and has illumined with it the entire world. He is the religious source, spring, and fountain out of which all the rest of the peoples have drawn their beliefs and their religions.'

**3.** *I will bless.* They who follow Abram's teachings will, like him, enjoy God's favour.

*him that curseth thee.* 'The story of European history during the past centuries teaches one uniform lesson. That the nations which have received and in any way dealt fairly and mercifully with the Jew have prospered—and that the nations that have tortured and oppressed him have written out their own curse' (Olive Schreiner).

*all the families of the earth be blessed.* Israel shall be 'a light of the nations' (Isa. XLII, 6). Through him, all men were to be taught the existence of the Most High God, and the love of righteousness, thereby opening for themselves the same treasury of blessings which he enjoyed. 'The germ of the idea underlying the fuller conception of a Messianic Age was in existence from the time of the founders of the race of Israel. *In thy seed shall all the families of the earth be blessed*, was the promise given both to Abraham and Isaac. It was a promise that reached far beyond the lifetime of each, farther than the limits of the temporal kingdom their descendants founded; that has obtained but partial fulfilment up to our time, and looks for fullest realization to that future towards which each of us in his measure may contribute his share' (S. Singer).

**4.** *as the* LORD *had spoken.* In obedience to the Heavenly voice, he leaves the land of his birth

GENESIS XII, 5

him; and Lot went with him; and Abram was seventy and five years old when he departed out of Haran. 5. And Abram took Sarai his wife, and Lot his brother's son, and all their substance that they had gathered, and the souls that they had gotten in Haran; and they went forth to go into the land of Canaan; and into the land of Canaan they came. 6. And Abram passed through the land unto the place of Shechem, unto the terebinth of Moreh. And the Canaanite was then in the land. 7. And the LORD appeared unto Abram, and said: 'Unto thy seed will I give this land'; and he builded there an altar unto the LORD, who appeared unto him. 8. And he removed from thence unto the mountain on the east of Beth-el, and pitched his tent, having Beth-el on the west, and Ai on the east; and he builded there an altar unto the LORD, and called upon the name of the LORD. 9. And Abram journeyed, going on still toward the South. ¶ 10. And there was a famine in the land; and Abram went

and all the glamour and worldly prosperity of his native place; he becomes a pilgrim for life, enduring trials, famines, privations; wandering into Canaan as a sojourner, into Egypt as a refugee, and back again into Canaan—all for the sake of humanity, that it might share the blessing of his knowledge of God and Righteousness.

*Lot went with him.* Lot was a mere follower, and does not seem to have been inspired with the same ideals as prompted Abram's departure.

**5.** *their substance.* Their worldy goods, movable property.

*the souls.* i.e. their slaves and dependants. The Rabbis take the word 'souls' to mean the proselytes whom Abram made among the men, and Sarai among the women. These converts became subservient to God's law and followed their master in his spiritual adventure.

*gotten.* lit. 'made'; for, declare the Rabbis, he who wins over an idolater to the service of God is as though he had created him anew.

**6.** *Shechem.* The modern Nablus, 30 miles N. of Jerusalem. It is one of the oldest cities of Palestine.

*terebinth of Moreh.* Some translate, 'the directing terebinth,' i.e. the oracular tree held sacred by the tree-worshipping Canaanites. Such trees were attended by priests, who interpreted the answers of the oracle to those who came to consult it. The terebinth (or turpentine-tree) grows to a height of from twenty to forty feet, and may therefore well have served as a landmark.

*the Canaanite was then in the land.* i.e. was already in the land. 'Before the age of Abraham, the Canaanites had already settled in the lowlands of Palestine—Canaan, be it noted, signified Lowlands' (Sayce). The interpretation of this verse as meaning that the Canaanites were *at that time* in the land, but were no longer so at the time when Genesis was written (an interpretation which misled even Ibn Ezra), is quite impossible. The Canaanites formed part of the population down to the days of the later Kings.

**7.** *unto thy seed.* In spite of its possession by the warlike and racially alien Canaanites (x, 6).

**8.** *Beth-el.* In Central Palestine, the modern Beitin, 10 miles N. of Jerusalem. The place is here called by the name given to it by Jacob, XXVIII, 19.

*Ai.* Probably the modern Haiyan, about two miles E. of Bethel.

*called upon the name of the* LORD. The Targum renders, 'and prayed in the name of the LORD.' He proclaimed the knowledge of the true God (Talmud). He had the moral courage to preach his conception of God and duty in the very face of the soul-degrading ideas of divine worship and human duty held by the peoples then inhabiting Canaan.

**9.** *going on still.* The Hebrew indicates travelling by stages, after the manner of nomads.

*the South.* Or, 'the Negeb,' the name by which the Southern district of Judah is known. The Midrash explains that Abram was being drawn towards the city of Jerusalem, which is in the south of Palestine.

10–20. ABRAM IN EGYPT

**10.** *a famine in the land.* Owing to the scarcity of rivers and lack of irrigation, the country was

GENESIS XII, 11

down into Egypt to sojourn there; for the famine was sore in the land. 11. And it came to pass, when he was come near to enter into Egypt, that he said unto Sarai his wife: 'Behold now, I know that thou art a fair woman to look upon. 12. And it will come to pass, when the Egyptians shall see thee, that they will say: This is his wife; and they will kill me, but thee they will keep alive. 13. Say, I pray thee, thou art my sister; that it may be well with me for thy sake, and that my soul may live because of thee.'\*ii. 14. And it came to pass, that, when Abram was come into Egypt, the Egyptians beheld the woman that she was very fair. 15. And the princes of Pharaoh saw her, and praised her to Pharaoh; and the woman was taken into Pharaoh's house. 16. And he dealt well with Abram for her sake; and he had sheep, and oxen, and he-asses, and menservants, and maid-servants, and she-asses, and camels. 17. And the LORD plagued Pharaoh and his house with great plagues because of Sarai Abram's wife. 18. And Pharaoh called Abram, and said: 'What is

11 הָרָעָב בָּאָרֶץ: וַיְהִי כַּאֲשֶׁר הִקְרִיב לָבוֹא מִצְרָיְמָה וַיֹּאמֶר
אֶל־שָׂרַי אִשְׁתּוֹ הִנֵּה־נָא יָדַעְתִּי כִּי אִשָּׁה יְפַת־מַרְאֶה אָתְּ:
12 וְהָיָה כִּי־יִרְאוּ אֹתָךְ הַמִּצְרִים וְאָמְרוּ אִשְׁתּוֹ זֹאת וְהָרְגוּ
13 אֹתִי וְאֹתָךְ יְחַיּוּ: אִמְרִי־נָא אֲחֹתִי אָתְּ לְמַעַן יִיטַב־לִי
בַעֲבוּרֵךְ וְחָיְתָה נַפְשִׁי בִּגְלָלֵךְ: וַיְהִי כְּבוֹא אַבְרָם מִצְרָיְמָה 14
וַיִּרְאוּ הַמִּצְרִים אֶת־הָאִשָּׁה כִּי־יָפָה הִוא מְאֹד: וַיִּרְאוּ טו
אֹתָהּ שָׂרֵי פַרְעֹה וַיְהַלְלוּ אֹתָהּ אֶל־פַּרְעֹה וַתֻּקַּח הָאִשָּׁה
16 בֵּית פַּרְעֹה: וּלְאַבְרָם הֵיטִיב בַּעֲבוּרָהּ וַיְהִי־לוֹ צֹאן־וּבָקָר
17 וַחֲמֹרִים וַעֲבָדִים וּשְׁפָחֹת וַאֲתֹנֹת וּגְמַלִּים: וַיְנַגַּע יְהֹוָה ׀
אֶת־פַּרְעֹה נְגָעִים גְּדֹלִים וְאֶת־בֵּיתוֹ עַל־דְּבַר שָׂרַי אֵשֶׁת
18 אַבְרָם: וַיִּקְרָא פַרְעֹה לְאַבְרָם וַיֹּאמֶר מַה־זֹּאת עָשִׂיתָ לִּי
19 לָמָּה לֹא־הִגַּדְתָּ לִּי כִּי אִשְׁתְּךָ הִוא: לָמָה אָמַרְתָּ אֲחֹתִי

---

subject to famine if the rainy seasons failed. Palestine nomads would then seek safety in Egypt. A famine drove Abram to Egypt, and the same cause was again to bring his descendants to that land. As the Rabbis say, 'The lives of the Patriarchs foreshadow the story of their descendants.'

*to sojourn there*. For a temporary stay only.

**12.** *they will kill me*. To kill the husband in order to possess himself of his wife seems to have been a common royal custom in those days. A papyrus tells of a Pharaoh who, acting on the advice of one of his princes, sent armed men to fetch a beautiful woman and make away with her husband. Another Pharaoh is promised by his priest on his tombstone that even after death he will kill Palestinian sheiks and include their wives in his harem.

**13.** Once or twice Abram falls a prey to fear and plays with the truth in order to preserve his life. Though merely an episode with him, natural enough in an ordinary man, it is quite unworthy of his majestic soul. It is the glory of the Bible that it shows no partiality towards its heroes; they are *not* superhuman, sinless beings. And when they err—for 'there is no man on earth who doeth good always and sinneth never'—Scripture does not gloss over their faults. The great Jewish commentator Nachmanides refers to Abram's action as 'a great sin'.

*my sister*. The statement was partly true; see on xx, 12.

*that it may be well with me*. He would escape death. The same thought is repeated in the following clause.

*my soul may live*. The Heb. idiomatic way of saying, 'I may live.'

**14.** *very fair*. Sarai was then in middle age, and apparently had retained her youthful beauty.

**15.** *Pharaoh*. The Heb. transcription of *Pr-'o*, the Egyptian title of the king of the country. It signifies 'Great House'. The statement of some writers that the title did not come into use till much later is inaccurate. In the days of the Nineteenth Dynasty, the age of Moses, the word is the usual reverential designation of the King.

**16.** *and he had*. And he came to have. In this verse we have enumerated what was then considered true wealth. Note the omission of silver and gold; cf. Job I, 3.

**17.** *plagued*. A mysterious sickness fell upon Pharaoh and his house, which aroused suspicion and led to enquiries that resulted in the discovery of the truth (Driver). According to the Rabbis, the nature of the plague was such as to constitute a safeguard to Sarai's honour.

*and his house*. *i.e.* his household.

**18.** *what is this that thou hast done unto me?* 'Pharaoh, justly incensed with Abram, sternly reproves him and dismisses him with abruptness.' This is the usual non-Jewish comment on

## GENESIS XII, 19

this that thou hast done unto me? why didst thou not tell me that she was thy wife? 19. Why saidst thou: She is my sister? so that I took her to be my wife; now therefore behold thy wife, take her, and go thy way.' 20. And Pharaoh gave men charge concerning him; and they brought him on the way, and his wife, and all that he had.

## 13 CHAPTER XIII

1. And Abram went up out of Egypt, he, and his wife, and all that he had, and Lot with him, into the South. 2. And Abram was very rich in cattle, in silver, and in gold. 3. And he went on his journeys from the South even to Beth-el, unto the place where his tent had been at the beginning, between Beth-el and Ai; 4. unto the place of the altar, which he had made there at the first; and Abram called there on the name of the Lord.* ᴵᴵᴵ· 5. And Lot also, who went with Abram, had flocks, and herds, and tents. 6. And the land was not able to bear them, that they might dwell together; for their substance was great, so that they could not dwell together. 7. And there was a strife between the herdmen of Abram's cattle and the herdmen of Lot's cattle. And the Canaanite and the Perizzite dwelt then in the land. 8. And Abram said unto Lot: 'Let there be no strife, I pray thee, between me and thee, and between my herdmen and thy herdmen; for we are brethen. 9. Is not the whole land before thee? separate thyself, I pray thee, from me; if thou wilt take the left hand, then I will go to the right; or if thou take the right hand, then I will go to the left.' 10. And

this verse. Yet Pharaoh, in whose land the husband of a beautiful wife was in danger of being murdered so that the wife might be taken into the royal harem, was hardly justified in his moral indignation towards Abraham. Pharaoh's was largely the blame for the shortcoming on the part of the Patriarch.

### CHAPTER XIII. ABRAM AND LOT

**1.** *Lot with him.* Lot is here explicitly named because of the incident which follows.

**2.** *rich.* Lit. 'heavy,' *i.e.* laden with possessions.

**3.** *and he went on his journeys.* The Heb. implies that he travelled by stages, covering much the same ground as on the outward journey.

**4.** *at the first.* Rashi renders: 'Unto the place of the altar which he had made there at the first, and where Abram had called on the name of the Lord.' See XII, 8.

**6.** *not able to bear them.* i.e. there was insufficient pasturage and water for their numerous herds.

**7.** *the Canaanite and the Perizzite dwelt then in the land.* This seemingly superfluous clause explains how so large a tract of country could not supply sufficient pasturage for the flocks of Abram and Lot. The older inhabitants would naturally have taken possession of the fertile districts.

**8.** *no strife.* Abram's conduct is both self-denying and peace-loving.

*for we are brethen.* i.e. kinsmen. Strife would be especially unseemly among relations.

**9.** *the whole land before thee.* Although the Canaanites and the Perizzites inhabit the country, there are several unoccupied sites available. In the interests of peace, Abram waives his right, as the elder, to make the selection, and allows Lot to choose in which direction he will go.

**10.** *the plain of the Jordan.* Lit. 'the circle of the Jordan,' is the specific name for the land on both sides of the lower Jordan valley. 'A large part of this valley is of exuberant fertility... Wherever water comes, the flowers rise to the

48

## GENESIS XIII, 11

Lot lifted up his eyes, and beheld all the plain of the Jordan, that it was well watered every where, before the LORD destroyed Sodom and Gomorrah, like the garden of the LORD, like the land of Egypt, as thou goest unto Zoar. 11. So Lot chose him all the plain of the Jordan; and Lot journeyed east; and they separated themselves the one from the other. 12. Abram dwelt in the land of Canaan, and Lot dwelt in the cities of the Plain, and moved his tent as far as Sodom. 13. Now the men of Sodom were wicked and sinners against the LORD exceedingly. 14. And the LORD said unto Abram, after that Lot was separated from him: 'Lift up now thine eyes, and look from the place where thou art, northward and southward and eastward and westward; 15. for all the land which thou seest, to thee will I give it, and to thy seed for ever. 16. And I will make thy seed as the dust of the earth; so that if a man can number the dust of the earth, then shall thy seed also be numbered. 17. Arise, walk through the land in the length of it and in the breadth of it; for unto thee

knee, and the herbage to the shoulder' (G. A. Smith).

*well watered.* By the Jordan and its tributaries.

*like the garden of the* LORD. i.e. Eden and its river (II, 10).

*like the land of Egypt.* Watered by the Nile.

*as thou goest unto Zoar.* Better, *as thou camest unto Zoar.* This is one of the Mosaic 'touches' in Genesis (Naville). Zoar is *not* the town near Sodom. It is the name of an ancient Egyptian frontier fortress. *Speaking to men who had come out of Egypt,* Scripture compares the fertility of the Plain of Jordan to the verdure and richness of Egypt 'as thou camest unto Zoar', on the edge of the barren desert and sands.

**11.** *Lot chose him all the plain of the Jordan.* 'He chose the rich soil, and with it the corrupt civilization which had grown up in the rank climate of that deep descent; ... and left to Abraham the hardship, the glory, and the virtues of the rugged hills, the sea-breezes, and the inexhaustible future of Western Palestine' (Stanley).

**12.** *in the land of Canaan.* i.e. the remainder of the land.

**13.** *men of Sodom.* The fertility of the soil, with the luxurious and enervating character of the climate, rapidly developed the sensual vices of this early civilized but depraved race; cf. Ezek. XVI, 49 f. For all that, Lot was willing to dwell amongst them. The material attractions of the locality overbore his fear of moral contamination. This statement also prepares us for their destruction narrated in Chap. XIX.

*wicked and sinners.* Wicked—heartless and inhuman in their dealings with their fellowmen; and sinners—abandoning themselves to nameless abominations and depravities.

*against the* LORD. Their immoral conduct was an offence to God.

**14.** *Lot was separated from him.* God chose that moment to renew His assurance to Abram, because he may then have been depressed by the departure of his nephew, whom, in default of a son, he had regarded as his probable heir, through whom the Divine promise was to be fulfilled.

*from the place where thou art.* The spot near Bethel where he was standing commands a wonderful view of the whole country. Travellers speak in glowing terms of the panorama which this holy place affords.

**15.** *for ever.* 'It will be theirs for ever, even though they may not always be in possession of it; even as it was given to Abraham, without his being in actual possession of it' (S. R. Hirsch).

**16.** *as the dust.* 'As the dust of the earth extends from one end of the world to the other, so will thy seed be dispersed throughout all lands. And as the dust causes even metals to decay but itself endures, so will all worshippers of idolatry perish, but Israel will continue forever' (Midrash).

**17.** *arise, walk through the land.* The act of walking through the land was a legal formality denoting acquisition.

## GENESIS XIII, 18

will I give it.' 18. And Abram moved his tent, and came and dwelt by the terebinths of Mamre, which are in Hebron, and built there an altar unto the Lord.* iv.

## 14   CHAPTER XIV

1. And it came to pass in the days of Amraphel king of Shinar, Arioch king of Ellasar, Chedorlaomer king of Elam, and Tidal king of Goiim, 2. that they made war with Bera king of Sodom, and with Birsha king of Gomorrah, Shinab king of Admah, and Shemeber king of Zeboiim, and the king of Bela—the same is Zoar. 3. All these came as allies unto the vale of Siddim—the same is the Salt Sea. 4. Twelve years they served Chedorlaomer, and in the thirteenth year they rebelled. 5. And in the fourteenth year came Chedorlaomer and the kings that were with him, and smote the Rephaim in Ashteroth-karnaim, and the Zuzim in Ham, and the Emim in

---

**18.** *Hebron.* Josephus speaks of it as a 'more ancient city than Memphis in Egypt'. Of the oak-tree he says, 'Report goes, that this tree has continued since the creation of the world.'

CHAPTER XIV. THE WAR OF THE KINGS

Much has been written on this chapter during the last century. This chapter does not fit in with any of the so-called 'sources' of the Bible critics; hence their determined attacks on its veracity. Its historical accuracy has, however, been strikingly confirmed by recent discoveries, which conclusively show that the age of Abraham was a literary age with a developed historic sense (Sayce).

1–17. ABRAM RESCUES LOT

**1.** *Amraphel.* Usually identified with Hammurabi, a great and enlightened king of Babylon. He finally united all the city-states of North and South Babylonia into one strong centralized empire, defeated the Elamites, and extended his rule to the shores of the Mediterranean. He undertook the codification of Babylonian law, and his Code was rediscovered at the beginning of this century. The date of his reign is 1945–1902 before the Christian era. The final consonant in the Heb. form of the name probably corresponds to the ending *el*, 'God,' in Biblical names.

*Shinar.* The Targum reads 'Babylon'; it seems to have been one of the Egyptian names for Babylonia. The word may possibly be identical with Sumir; see on x, 10.

*Arioch king of Ellasar.* i.e. Eriaku, king of Larsa, midway between Babylon and the mouth of the Euphrates.

*Chedorlaomer.* A Hebraized form of Kudur-'servant of,' and Lagamar, the name of an Elamite deity.

*Elam.* See on x, 22. It was at this time in possession of Babylonia, and therefore also of Canaan, which was under Babylonian supremacy.

*Tidal king of Goiim.* Tudghula of the cuneiform texts, who was king of the 'hordes' of Northern Kurdish nations mentioned from time to time in the inscriptions as invading Assyria (Sayce). Some explain Goiim as the Heb. form of Gutium, Kurdistan.

**2.** *Bera*, etc. The names of these kings (like the 'kings' in Joshua, petty princes of Canaanite towns) are discussed in W. T. Pilter's monumental work on Genesis XIV, 'The Pentateuch, a Historical Record, 1928,' chap. x.

**3.** *vale of Siddim.* The name does not occur elsewhere.

*Salt Sea.* Deservedly so called. Whereas ordinary seawater contains six per cent of salt, its waters have four times that quantity. The Church Fathers named it 'the Dead Sea'.

**4.** *they served.* i.e. they paid tribute; withholding the annual payment was the act of rebellion.

**5.** The peoples named in this verse—Rephaim, Zuzim, Emim, Horites—are the aboriginal inhabitants of the regions afterwards occupied by Edom, Moab and Ammon; see Deut. II, 9 f.

*Ashteroth-karnaim.* A hill 21 miles E. of the Sea of Galilee. The name means 'Astarte of the two horns', derived in all probability from a local Sanctuary of that goddess, whose symbol was the crescent or two-horned moon.

*Ham.* The primitive name of the Ammonite capital, Rabbah, 25 miles N.E. of the upper end of the Dead Sea.

GENESIS XIV, 6

בראשית לך לך יד

6 בְּהַרְרָם: וְאֶת־הַחֹרִי בְּהַרְרָם בְּשָׁוֵה קִרְיָתָיִם: וְאֶת־הָאֵימִים
7 שֵׂעִיר עַד אֵיל פָּארָן אֲשֶׁר עַל־הַמִּדְבָּר: וַיָּשֻׁבוּ וַיָּבֹאוּ
אֶל־עֵין מִשְׁפָּט הִוא קָדֵשׁ וַיַּכּוּ אֶת־כָּל־שְׂדֵה הָעֲמָלֵקִי וְגַם
8 אֶת־הָאֱמֹרִי הַיֹּשֵׁב בְּחַצְצֹן תָּמָר: וַיֵּצֵא מֶלֶךְ־סְדֹם וּמֶלֶךְ
עֲמֹרָה וּמֶלֶךְ אַדְמָה וּמֶלֶךְ צְבֹיִים וּמֶלֶךְ בֶּלַע הִוא־צֹעַר
9 וַיַּעַרְכוּ אִתָּם מִלְחָמָה בְּעֵמֶק הַשִּׂדִּים: אֵת כְּדָרְלָעֹמֶר
מֶלֶךְ עֵילָם וְתִדְעָל מֶלֶךְ גּוֹיִם וְאַמְרָפֶל מֶלֶךְ שִׁנְעָר וְאַרְיוֹךְ
10 מֶלֶךְ אֶלָּסָר אַרְבָּעָה מְלָכִים אֶת־הַחֲמִשָּׁה: וְעֵמֶק הַשִּׂדִּים
בֶּאֱרֹת בֶּאֱרֹת חֵמָר וַיָּנֻסוּ מֶלֶךְ־סְדֹם וַעֲמֹרָה וַיִּפְּלוּ־שָׁמָּה
11 וְהַנִּשְׁאָרִים הֶרָה נָּסוּ: וַיִּקְחוּ אֶת־כָּל־רְכֻשׁ סְדֹם וַעֲמֹרָה
12 וְאֶת־כָּל־אָכְלָם וַיֵּלֵכוּ: וַיִּקְחוּ אֶת־לוֹט וְאֶת־רְכֻשׁוֹ בֶּן־אֲחִי
13 אַבְרָם וַיֵּלֵכוּ וְהוּא יֹשֵׁב בִּסְדֹם: וַיָּבֹא הַפָּלִיט וַיַּגֵּד

v. 8. צבוים ק׳

*Shaveh-kiriathaim.* Lit. 'the plain of the two towns'. Usually identified with the modern Kureyat, 10 miles E. of the Dead Sea.

**6.** *Seir.* The mountainous district S.E. of the Dead Sea.
*El-paran.* Probably the port at the Northern extremity of the Gulf of Akaba, Red Sea.
*the wilderness.* The bare plateau of limestone between Canaan and Egypt.

**7.** *they turned back.* Their march had hitherto been towards the South; but they now turned to the N.W.
*En-mishpat.* That is, 'the well of judgment,' probably the seat of an oracle to which disputants resorted for the settlement of their claims.
*the same is Kadesh.* Usually 'Kadesh-Barnea' (cf. Deut. I, 2, 46). It is situated on the S.E. frontier of Judah.
*all the country of the Amalekites.* More accurately, 'the field of the Amalekites,' a nomad people living between Palestine and Egypt, and later on attempting to prevent the Israelites from entering the peninsula of Sinai (Exod. XVII, 8 ff.). The phrase, 'all the country of the Amalekites,' must be understood to mean, 'the country afterwards inhabited by the Amalekites' (Midrash, Rashi). Esau's grandson was named after a chieftain, Amalek, who had founded the Amalekite people (Nachmanides).
*the Amorites.* Denoting generally the pre-Israelite population of Canaan.
*Hazazon-tamar.* At the mouth of the deep gorge which runs into the Dead Sea, about half-way down the western shore.

**10.** *full of slime pits.* i.e. wells of bitumen. These pits hampered the flight of the defeated army.
*and they fell there, etc.* The subject of the verb is vaguely expressed. The kings of Sodom and Gomorrah fell into the pits, whereas the remainder (*i.e.* the other three kings) made good their escape. From *v.* 17 we learn that the king of Sodom must have been rescued from the slime pits.
*to the mountain.* Of Moab, to the E. of the Dead Sea.

**12.** *who dwelt in Sodom.* It was because of Lot's willingness to live with evil-doers that this misfortune befell him (Rashi).

**13.** *the Hebrew.* This is the first time this word occurs in the Bible, where it is a title used of Israelites either by foreigners or in speaking of them to foreigners, or in contrast to foreigners. After the exile of the Ten Tribes, when the tribe of Judah (Yehudah) remained the principal branch of Israel, the name *Yehudim* (translated Judaioi, Judaei, Juden, Jews) came into general use. The Rabbis, also modern scholars, are divided as to the origin of the name Hebrew. Either the word is to be connected with Eber (see X, 21; XI, 16 f) and signifies 'a descendant of Eber'; or it means 'one from the other side', in accordance with the statement, 'And I took your father Abraham from the other side of the River (Euphrates)' (Josh. XXIV, 3). It is also claimed that the name is identical with that of the *Habiri*, a nomad people mentioned in the Tell-el-Amarna Tablets (see on *v.* 18 below), as making war upon the Canaanite towns and population.

# GENESIS XIV, 14

And there came one that had escaped, and told Abram the Hebrew—now he dwelt by the terebinths of Mamre the Amorite, brother of Eshcol, and brother of Aner; and these were confederate with Abram. 14. And when Abram heard that his brother was taken captive, he led forth his trained men, born in his house, three hundred and eighteen, and pursued as far as Dan. 15. And he divided himself against them by night, he and his servants, and smote them, and pursued them unto Hobah, which is on the left hand of Damascus. 16. And he brought back all the goods, and also brought back his brother Lot, and his goods, and the women also, and the people. 17. And the king of Sodom went out to meet him, after his return from the slaughter of Chedorlaomer and the kings that were with him, at the vale of Shaveh—the same is the King's Vale. 18. And Melchizedek king of Salem brought forth bread and

לְאַבְרָם הָעִבְרִי וְהוּא שֹׁכֵן בְּאֵלֹנֵי מַמְרֵא הָאֱמֹרִי אֲחִי
14 אֶשְׁכֹּל וַאֲחִי עָנֵר וְהֵם בַּעֲלֵי בְרִית־אַבְרָם: וַיִּשְׁמַע אַבְרָם
כִּי נִשְׁבָּה אָחִיו וַיָּרֶק אֶת־חֲנִיכָיו יְלִידֵי בֵיתוֹ שְׁמֹנָה עָשָׂר
טו וּשְׁלֹשׁ מֵאוֹת וַיִּרְדֹּף עַד־דָּן: וַיֵּחָלֵק עֲלֵיהֶם ׀ לַיְלָה הוּא
וַעֲבָדָיו וַיַּכֵּם וַיִּרְדְּפֵם עַד־חוֹבָה אֲשֶׁר מִשְּׂמֹאל לְדַמָּשֶׂק:
16 וַיָּשֶׁב אֵת כָּל־הָרְכֻשׁ וְגַם אֶת־לוֹט אָחִיו וּרְכֻשׁוֹ הֵשִׁיב
17 וְגַם אֶת־הַנָּשִׁים וְאֶת־הָעָם: וַיֵּצֵא מֶלֶךְ־סְדֹם לִקְרָאתוֹ
אַחֲרֵי שׁוּבוֹ מֵהַכּוֹת אֶת־כְּדָר־לָעֹמֶר וְאֶת־הַמְּלָכִים אֲשֶׁר
18 אִתּוֹ אֶל־עֵמֶק שָׁוֵה הוּא עֵמֶק הַמֶּלֶךְ: וּמַלְכִּי־צֶדֶק מֶלֶךְ
19 שָׁלֵם הוֹצִיא לֶחֶם וָיָיִן וְהוּא כֹהֵן לְאֵל עֶלְיוֹן: וַיְבָרְכֵהוּ

---

**14.** *when Abram heard.* The Midrash describes his emotions on hearing the news, in the words of Psalm CXII, 7, 'He shall not be afraid of evil tidings; his heart is stedfast, trusting in the LORD.' With gentleness and reasonableness of disposition, there were united in Abraham the most conspicuous courage and decision.

*his brother.* i.e. his kinsman, as in XIII, 8.

*he led forth.* 'He emptied': it therefore signifies that he called upon every one of his dependants to aid him in the attempt to rescue Lot.

*born in his house.* i.e. slaves reared in the Patriarch's home; and, therefore, feeling a greater attachment to their master.

*Dan.* The name is given to the place by anticipation. Formerly it was called Leshem (Josh. XIX, 47) or Laish (Judg. XVIII, 29). It is in the extreme North of Palestine.

**15.** *divided himself.* He formed his men into several bodies, which attacked the enemy in the dark from different directions. The suddenness of the onslaught, and the assault in several places simultaneously, would enable small bands of men to throw a far larger force into panic. The same strategy was used by Gideon (Judg. VII, 16 f).

*Hobah.* 50 miles N. of Damascus.

*Damascus.* An important political and commercial city from the earliest times; mentioned in Egyptian inscriptions of the sixteenth century B.C.E.

**16.** *all the goods.* As the captor, Abram could have taken undisputed possession of the spoils. The manner of their disposal affords fresh illustration of his magnanimous nature.

**17.** *the king of Sodom.* See on v. 10.

*from the slaughter of.* Better, 'from the smiting of.' The Heb. only signifies the defeat of the enemy.

*King's Vale.* Mentioned in II Sam. XVIII, 18, in connection with Absalom.

### 18–20. ABRAM AND MELCHIZEDEK

**18.** This name (which may mean 'My King is righteousness') is mentioned elsewhere in the Bible only in Psalm CX, 4, 'Thou art a priest for ever after the manner of Melchizedek,' the reference being to the offices of king and priest combined in one man. In the light of recent excavations, every reasonable doubt as to the authenticity of the account of Melchizedek is removed. Among the Tell-el-Amarna tablets are letters to the Egyptian government, written in the fifteenth pre-Christian century by the vassal king of Jerusalem, or 'Urusalim'. Like Melchizedek, he was a priest-king. For the name, cf. 'Adoni-zedek, king of Jerusalem' (Josh. X, 1). (As repeated reference is made to the Tell-el-Amarna tablets or letters, a few words must be said of this most remarkable archæological find. The last Pharaoh of the powerful and mighty 18th Dynasty was Amenophis IV or Ikhnaten, the so-called Heretic King, who undertook to replace the Egyptian religion by a monotheism in which the sun was to be worshipped as the sole god. He moved his capital from Thebes to the modern Tell-el-Amarna in Middle Egypt. His reformation was a failure; he died *circa* 1350 B.C.E. amidst the curses of his subjects. The capital returned to Thebes, and the place where he dwelt was abandoned because it was regarded as haunted by evil demons. And as a result of this belief, the complete royal archives, his own and his father's diplomatic correspondence, were preserved in the ruins of Tell-el-Amarna, where they were found 3,200 years later in 1887).

## GENESIS XIV, 19

wine; and he was priest of God the Most High. 19. And he blessed him, and said: 'Blessed be Abram of God Most High, Maker of heaven and earth; 20. and blessed be God the Most High, who hath delivered thine enemies into thy hand.' And he gave him a tenth of all.* 21. And the king of Sodom said unto Abram: 'Give me the persons, and take the goods to thyself.' 22. And Abram said to the king of Sodom: 'I have lifted up my hand unto the LORD, God Most High, Maker of heaven and earth, 23. that I will not take a thread nor a shoe-latchet nor aught that is thine, lest thou shouldest say: I have made Abram rich; 24. save only that which the young men have eaten, and the portion of the men which went with me, Aner, Eshcol, and Mamre, let them take their portion.'

## 15 CHAPTER XV

1. After these things the word of the LORD came unto Abram in a vision, saying: 'Fear not, Abram, I am thy shield, thy reward shall be exceeding great.' 2. And Abram said: 'O Lord GOD, what wilt Thou give me, seeing I go hence childless, and

---

*Salem.* An earlier, or poetic, designation for Jerusalem.

*bread and wine.* A token of friendship and hospitality.

*God the Most High.* Heb. *El Elyon.* The phrase occurs again in Scripture only in Psalm LXXVIII, 35, but the Ras Shamra tablets show that it was quite a familiar appellation of Deity in pre-Mosaic Canaan. Melchizedek was evidently a convert of Abraham's. A Talmudic tradition makes Melchizedek the head of a school for the propagation of the knowledge of God.

*maker.* lit. 'possessor'. The word combines the ideas of making, creating, and owning. The phrase 'Maker of heaven and earth' has been embodied in the Liturgy.

**19.** *and he blessed him.* In his capacity as priest, Melchizedek invokes the Divine blessing upon Abram for his chivalrous action.

**20.** *and he gave him a tenth.* Abram acknowledges Melchizedek as priest of the Most High, and gives him tithe of the spoil as a thanksgiving offering.

**21.** *give me the persons.* As the victor, Abram had the right to dispose of the people he had rescued in any manner he desired. He could have retained them as his slaves, sold them into bondage, or demanded a ransom. But he spurns the doctrine, To the victor belong the spoils.

**22.** *I have lifted up my hand unto the LORD.* Malbim explains that the purpose of this act was to declare that 'the victory is His, and the spoil therefore does not belong to me, ... and *it* (my hand) shall not say: I have made Abraham rich'; cf. Deut. VIII, 17, 'and thou say in thy heart: My power and the might of my hand hath gotten me this wealth.'

**23.** *nor a shoe-latchet.* His fine sense of independence would not permit him to benefit in the slightest degree by the rescue of his kinsmen.

**24.** He felt, however, that he had no right to penalize those who had shared the dangers of the campaign with him. His followers should receive their rations, and an equitable share of the spoil should go to his confederates.

CHAPTER XV. PROMISE OF AN HEIR TO ABRAM

**1.** *after these things.* This phrase commonly joins a new chapter with the preceding. It does not necessarily imply an immediate sequence.

*in a vision.* A frequent medium through which God communicated with man. Nachmanides points out that the vision happened during the day time.

*fear not.* The possibility of reprisals, because of his intervention in the war. Or, it may refer to the Patriarch's anxiety with regard to his childlessness.

*thy shield.* A symbol of defence and protection, often used in the Psalms.

*thy reward.* For obedience to God's call and for uprightness of life.

**2.** *what wilt Thou give me?* This agonizing cry

# GENESIS XV, 3

he that shall be possessor of my house is Eliezer of Damascus?' 3. And Abram said: 'Behold, to me Thou hast given no seed, and, lo, one born in my house is to be mine heir.' 4. And, behold, the word of the LORD came unto him, saying: 'This man shall not be thine heir; but he that shall come forth out of thine own bowels shall be thine heir.' 5. And He brought him forth abroad, and said: 'Look now toward heaven, and count the stars, if thou be able to count them'; and He said unto him: 'So shall thy seed be.' 6. And he believed in the LORD; and He counted it to him for righteousness.* vi. 7. And He said unto him: 'I am the LORD that brought thee out of Ur of the Chaldees, to give thee this land to inherit it.' 8. And he said: 'O Lord GOD, whereby shall I know that I shall inherit it?' 9. And He said unto him: 'Take Me a heifer of three years old, and a she-goat of three years old, and a ram of three years old, and a turtle-dove, and a young pigeon.' 10. And he took

בראשית לך לך טו

3 הוֹלֵךְ עֲרִירִי וּבֶן־מֶשֶׁק בֵּיתִי הוּא דַּמֶּשֶׂק אֱלִיעֶזֶר: וַיֹּאמֶר אַבְרָם הֵן לִי לֹא נָתַתָּה זָרַע וְהִנֵּה בֶן־בֵּיתִי יוֹרֵשׁ אֹתִי:
4 וְהִנֵּה דְבַר־יְהֹוָה אֵלָיו לֵאמֹר לֹא יִירָשְׁךָ זֶה כִּי־אִם אֲשֶׁר
ה יֵצֵא מִמֵּעֶיךָ הוּא יִירָשֶׁךָ: וַיּוֹצֵא אֹתוֹ הַחוּצָה וַיֹּאמֶר הַבֶּט־נָא הַשָּׁמַיְמָה וּסְפֹר הַכּוֹכָבִים אִם־תּוּכַל לִסְפֹּר
6 אֹתָם וַיֹּאמֶר לוֹ כֹּה יִהְיֶה זַרְעֶךָ: וְהֶאֱמִן בַּיהֹוָה וַיַּחְשְׁבֶהָ
ששי 7 לּוֹ צְדָקָה:* וַיֹּאמֶר אֵלָיו אֲנִי יְהֹוָה אֲשֶׁר הוֹצֵאתִיךָ מֵאוּר
8 כַּשְׂדִּים לָתֶת לְךָ אֶת־הָאָרֶץ הַזֹּאת לְרִשְׁתָּהּ: וַיֹּאמַר
9 אֲדֹנָי יֱהֹוִה בַּמָּה אֵדַע כִּי אִירָשֶׁנָּה: וַיֹּאמֶר אֵלָיו קְחָה לִי עֶגְלָה מְשֻׁלֶּשֶׁת וְעֵז מְשֻׁלֶּשֶׁת וְאַיִל מְשֻׁלָּשׁ וְתֹר וְגוֹזָל:
י וַיִּקַּח־לוֹ אֶת־כָּל־אֵלֶּה וַיְבַתֵּר אֹתָם בַּתָּוֶךְ וַיִּתֵּן אִישׁ־בִּתְרוֹ

---

enables us to look into the soul of the Patriarch. Of what value were earthly possessions to him if a worthy child who would continue his work after him was denied him? This attitude of the Father of the Jewish people towards the child, that it is the highest of human treasures, has remained that of his descendants to the present day. Among the most enlightened nations of antiquity, the child had no rights, no protection, no dignity of any sort. In Greece, for example, weak children were generally *exposed* on a lonely mountain to perish. The Roman historian (Tacitus) deemed it a contemptible prejudice of the Jews that 'it is a crime among them to kill any child!' The Rabbis, on the other hand, spoke of little children as 'the Messiahs of mankind', *i.e.* the child is the perennial regenerative force in humanity because in the child God continually gives mankind a chance to make good its mistakes.

*of Damascus.* Chap. XXIV shows the important position which he occupied in Abram's household. But, if he was to be Abram's heir, what of the great mission that was the motive of Abram's call from Ur of the Chaldees? The incident which follows allays these anxieties.

**3.** *one born in my house.* i.e. my servant. It is noteworthy that Abram does not think of Lot as his possible heir; *he* had returned to Sodom.

**5.** Since the words which follow, 'Look now toward heaven, etc.,' are part of the vision, we are not to suppose that Abram was actually led into the open. He imagined himself as gazing up at the stars.

**6.** *believed.* i.e. trusted. The childless Abram had faith in God's promise that his descendants would be countless like the stars of heaven. He was ready to wait God's time, without doubting God's truth. That is the mark of true faith—*steadfast trust* in God, despite darkness and disappointment, and despite the fact that circumstances all point in the opposite direction. True faith 'discovers through the mists of the present the sunshine of the future; and recognizes in the discordant strife of the world the traces of the Eternal Mind that leads it to an unceasing harmony' (Kalisch).

*and He counted it to him for righteousness.* 'Counted his trust as real religion' (Moffatt). Trustful surrender to the loving Will and Wisdom of God is the proof, as it is the basis, of true religion. Such spiritual faithfulness is a great spiritual virtue, and cannot be found where there is unrighteousness.

**8.** *whereby shall I know?* He does not doubt God, but desires confirmation of the vision that had been granted him.

**9.** *three years old.* Possibly because the number three has a sacred signification.

**10.** *and he took him.* 'Him' means, to himself.
*and divided them in the midst.* The ancient method of making a covenant was to cut an animal in half, and the contracting parties to pass through the portions of the slain animal. Thereby the parties were thought to be united by the bond of a common blood.

*but the birds divided he not.* Cf. Lev. I, 17.

## GENESIS XV, 11

him all these, and divided them in the midst, and laid each half over against the other; but the birds divided he not. 11. And the birds of prey came down upon the carcasses, and Abram drove them away. 12. And it came to pass, that, when the sun was going down, a deep sleep fell upon Abram, and, lo, a dread, even a great darkness, fell upon him. 13. And He said unto Abram: 'Know of a surety that thy seed shall be a stranger in a land that is not theirs, and shall serve them; and they shall afflict them four hundred years; 14. and also that nation, whom they shall serve, will I judge; and afterward shall they come out with great substance. 15. But thou shalt go to thy fathers in peace; thou shalt be buried in a good old age. 16. And in the fourth generation they shall come back hither; for the iniquity of the Amorite is not yet full.' 17. And it came to pass, that, when the sun went down, and there was thick darkness, behold a smoking furnace, and a flaming torch that passed between these pieces. 18. In that day the LORD made a covenant with Abram,

בראשית לך לך טו

11 לִקְרַאת רֵעֵהוּ וְאֶת־הַצִּפֹּר לֹא בָתָר׃ וַיֵּרֶד הָעַיִט עַל־
12 הַפְּגָרִים וַיַּשֵּׁב אֹתָם אַבְרָם׃ וַיְהִי הַשֶּׁמֶשׁ לָבוֹא וְתַרְדֵּמָה
נָפְלָה עַל־אַבְרָם וְהִנֵּה אֵימָה חֲשֵׁכָה גְדֹלָה נֹפֶלֶת עָלָיו׃
13 וַיֹּאמֶר לְאַבְרָם יָדֹעַ תֵּדַע כִּי־גֵר ׀ יִהְיֶה זַרְעֲךָ בְּאֶרֶץ לֹא
14 לָהֶם וַעֲבָדוּם וְעִנּוּ אֹתָם אַרְבַּע מֵאוֹת שָׁנָה׃ וְגַם אֶת־
הַגּוֹי אֲשֶׁר יַעֲבֹדוּ דָּן אָנֹכִי וְאַחֲרֵי־כֵן יֵצְאוּ בִּרְכֻשׁ גָּדוֹל׃
15 וְאַתָּה תָּבוֹא אֶל־אֲבֹתֶיךָ בְּשָׁלוֹם תִּקָּבֵר בְּשֵׂיבָה טוֹבָה׃
16 וְדוֹר רְבִיעִי יָשׁוּבוּ הֵנָּה כִּי לֹא־שָׁלֵם עֲוֹן הָאֱמֹרִי עַד־
17 הֵנָּה׃ וַיְהִי הַשֶּׁמֶשׁ בָּאָה וַעֲלָטָה הָיָה וְהִנֵּה תַנּוּר עָשָׁן
18 וְלַפִּיד אֵשׁ אֲשֶׁר עָבַר בֵּין הַגְּזָרִים הָאֵלֶּה׃ בַּיּוֹם הַהוּא
כָּרַת יְהוָה אֶת־אַבְרָם בְּרִית לֵאמֹר לְזַרְעֲךָ נָתַתִּי אֶת־
הָאָרֶץ הַזֹּאת מִנְּהַר מִצְרַיִם עַד־הַנָּהָר הַגָּדֹל נְהַר־פְּרָת׃

**11.** *and the birds of prey came down.* Symbolically foreshadowing the obstacles in the way of the taking possession of the land.

*Abram drove them away.* The attempts to frustrate God's design would not succeed.

**12.** *a deep sleep.* The same word is used of Adam in II, 21.

*a dread, even a great darkness.* The nation which was to issue from him would have to pass through bitter times of oppression.

**13.** *a stranger.* Better, 'a sojourner.' The word means a temporary resident. The reference is, of course, to the stay of the Israelites in Egypt.

*four hundred years.* A round number; Exod. XII, 40, gives the more precise number, 430 years.

**14.** *with great substance.* Referring to the gifts of the Egyptians, Exod. XII, 35 f.

**15.** *shalt go to thy fathers.* 'The death of Abram is predicted in one of those remarkable phrases which seem to prove that the Hebrews were not unacquainted with the doctrine of immortality. Here the return of the soul to the eternal abodes of the fathers is, with some distinctness, separated from the interment of the body. That both cannot be identical is evident; for while Abraham was entombed in Canaan, all his forefathers died and were buried in Mesopotamia' (Kalisch).

*in peace.* Thou wilt not witness any of the tribulations that will befall thy children (Kimchi).

**16.** *and in the fourth generation.* 'The Arabic *dahr* (corresponding to the Hebrew דור) is also used for a hundred years and over' (Burckhardt); thus, the 400 years mentioned in *v.* 13 are referred to here as four generations. Or, these four generations are not to be computed from the time of the vision of Abram, but from the time when his posterity first came into Egypt (Rashi).

*the iniquity of the Amorite.* 'Amorite' denotes the inhabitants of Canaan generally. Some of their abominations are enumerated in Leviticus XVIII, 21-30. The postponement of the penalty indicates Divine forbearance. God would give the Canaanites full time to repent. Hence he sent Abraham, who 'proclaimed the Lord', and, with his disciples and descendants, taught by precept and example 'the way of the Lord to do justice and mercy'. Meanwhile, the gradually accumulating guilt of the Amorites rendered dire punishment inevitable. God's prescience was certain that their hearts were forever turned from Him.

**17.** *a smoking furnace, and a flaming torch.* This symbol of the Godhead was seen to pass between the pieces, to ratify the covenant which was being made.

**18.** *have I given.* The perfect tense is used, although it refers to the future, in order to denote the certainty of the event.

*river of Egypt.* 'Brook of Egypt' (Num. XXXIV, 5), the Wady-el-Arish, which is the boundary between Egypt and Palestine.

*Euphrates.* The ideal limit of Israelite territory, reached in the days of Solomon (I Kings V, 1).

## GENESIS XV, 19

saying: 'Unto thy seed have I given this land, from the river of Egypt unto the great river, the river Euphrates; 19. the Kenite, and the Kenizzite, and the Kadmonite, 20. and the Hittite, and the Perizzite, and the Rephaim, 21. and the Amorite, and the Canaanite, and the Girgashite, and the Jebusite.'

## CHAPTER XVI

1. Now Sarai Abram's wife bore him no children; and she had a handmaid, an Egyptian, whose name was Hagar. 2. And Sarai said unto Abram: 'Behold now, the LORD hath restrained me from bearing; go in, I pray thee, unto my handmaid; it may be that I shall be builded up through her.' And Abram hearkened to the voice of Sarai. 3. And Sarai Abram's wife took Hagar the Egyptian, her handmaid, after Abram had dwelt ten years in the land of Canaan, and gave her to Abram her husband to be his wife. 4. And he went in unto Hagar, and she conceived; and when she saw that she had conceived, her mistress was despised in her eyes. 5. And Sarai said unto Abram: 'My wrong be upon thee: I gave my handmaid into thy bosom; and when she saw that she had conceived, I was despised in her eyes: the LORD judge between me and thee.' 6. But Abram said unto Sarai: 'Behold, thy maid is in thy hand; do to her that which is good in thine eyes.' And Sarai dealt harshly with her, and she fled from her face. 7. And the angel of the LORD found her by a fountain of water

---

**19.** *Kenite, and the Kenizzite.* Friendly tribes inhabiting the S. of Palestine, which merged with the Israelites.

*Kadmonite.* Not mentioned elsewhere.

**20.** *Perizzite.* See on XIII, 7.

*Rephaim.* See on XIV, 5.

**21.** For the peoples enumerated in this verse, see on X, 16.

### CHAPTER XVI. HAGAR AND ISHMAEL

**1.** *no children.* In the ancient Orient, childlessness was a calamity and a disgrace to a woman.

*an Egyptian.* Sarai probably acquired her during the stay in Egypt described in Chap. XII. Such female slaves remained the property of the wife solely.

**2.** *the LORD hath restrained me.* In Scripture the hand of God is traced in every occurrence of life. Even what we should call 'natural phenomena' are ascribed to Divine agency.

*unto my handmaid.* It was the legalized custom in Babylon, the home-land of Abram and Sarai, that if a man's wife was childless, he was allowed to take a concubine, but he was not to place her upon an equal footing with his first wife.

*be builded up through her.* By the adoption of Hagar's children as her own. The literal translation of the phrase is, 'be builded by her.' The family was pictured by the Hebrews under the image of a house; and the Rabbis speak of the wife as the husband's 'house'.

**4.** *her mistress was despised in her eyes.* Hagar, who was still a slave, behaved in a disrespectful and ungrateful manner towards her mistress.

**5.** *my wrong be upon thee.* i.e. thine is the responsibility for the wrong done to me by Hagar. Sarai's reproach is that he did not check Hagar's haughtiness towards her.

**6.** *in thy hand.* In thy power. From his knowledge of Sarai, he thought she would aim merely to bring Hagar back to proper behaviour.

*harshly.* Sarai probably imposed heavy tasks upon her. 'Sarah our Mother acted sinfully in thus ill-treating Hagar, and also Abram in permitting it; therefore, God heard her affliction and gave her a son who became the ancestor of a ferocious race that was destined to deal harshly with the descendants of Abram and Sarai' (Nachmanides). Some modern commentators, however, admit that 'few women would have borne the insolence of Hagar'.

## GENESIS XVI, 8

in the wilderness, by the fountain in the way to Shur. 8. And he said: 'Hagar, Sarai's handmaid, whence camest thou? and whither goest thou?' And she said: 'I flee from the face of my mistress Sarai.' 9. And the angel of the LORD said unto her: 'Return to thy mistress, and submit thyself under her hands.' 10. And the angel of the LORD said unto her: 'I will greatly multiply thy seed, that it shall not be numbered for multitude.' 11. And the angel of the LORD said unto her: 'Behold, thou art with child, and shalt bear a son; and thou shalt call his name ¹Ishmael, because the LORD hath heard thy affliction. 12. And he shall be a wild ass of a man: his hand shall be against every man, and every man's hand against him; and he shall dwell in the face of all his brethen.' 13. And she called the name of the LORD that spoke unto her, Thou art ²a God of seeing; for she said: 'Have I even here seen Him that seeth me?' 14. Wherefore the well was called ³Beer-lahai-roi; behold, it is between Kadesh and Bered. 15. And Hagar bore Abram a son; and Abram called the name of his son, whom Hagar bore, Ishmael. 16. And Abram was fourscore and six years old, when Hagar bore Ishmael to Abram.

## 17     CHAPTER XVII

1. And when Abram was ninety years old and nine, the LORD appeared to Abram,

---

¹ That is, *God heareth*.    ² Heb. *El roi*.    ³ That is, *The well of the Living One who seeth me*.

---

**7.** *the angel of the LORD found her.* 'The narrative, like XXI, 16–19, illustrates beautifully the Divine regard for the forlorn and desolate soul' (Driver). This is the first time that an 'angel' is mentioned in the Bible. The Hebrew word, like the English 'angel', originally means 'messenger', and is applied to any agent or missioner of God. The phrase 'angel of the Lord', however, is sometimes used to denote God Himself.

*Shur.* lit. 'the wall', or fortification which protected Egypt on the East from the incursion of raiding Bedouins. Hagar, in her flight through the wilderness, wanders in the direction of her native land.

**8.** *Hagar, Sarai's handmaid.* Reminding Hagar of the duty she owed her mistress.

*whence camest thou?* A leading question, not seeking for information, but giving Hagar an opportunity of unburdening her heart.

**11.** *affliction.* The use of this word clearly indicates the Divine disapproval of Sarah's treatment of Hagar. In ancient Israel, the servant is quite other than the 'helot' in Greece, or the 'slave' in Rome. Underlying the Hagar narrative is the assumption that fair and friendly treatment should be shown even to an alien bondwoman; cf. the position of Eliezer in Abraham's household.

**12.** *a wild ass of a man.* A vivid description of 'the sons of the desert, owning no authority save that of their own chief, reckless of life, treacherous towards strangers, ever ready for war or pillage' (Driver).

**13.** *a God of seeing.* i.e. a God who deigns to take notice of the plight of His creatures, and sends them succour in the hour of their need.

*even here.* In the desert, a 'God-forsaken place'!

**15.** *and Abram called.* On Hagar's return to her mistress, Abram learned all that had occurred; and he accordingly gave the child the name ordained for him.

### CHAPTER XVII. THE COVENANT OF ABRAHAM

**1.** *I am God Almighty.* Heb. *El Shaddai*; cf. Exod. VI, 3, 'and I appeared unto Abraham, unto Isaac, and unto Jacob, as God Almighty.' The derivation of the Divine Name, *Shaddai*, is

GENESIS XVII, 2

and said unto him: 'I am God Almighty; walk before Me, and be thou whole-hearted. 2. And I will make My covenant between Me and thee, and will multiply thee exceedingly.' 3. And Abram fell on his face; and God talked with him, saying: 4. 'As for Me, behold, My covenant is with thee, and thou shalt be ¹the father of a multitude of nations. 5. Neither shall thy name any more be called Abram, but thy name shall be Abraham; for the father of a multitude of nations have I made thee. 6. And I will make thee exceeding fruitful, and I will make nations of thee, and kings shall come out of thee.* ᵛⁱⁱ· 7. And I will establish My covenant between Me and thee and thy seed after thee throughout their generations for an everlasting covenant, to be a God unto thee and to thy seed after thee. 8. And I will give unto thee, and to thy seed after thee, the land of thy sojournings, all the land of Canaan, for an everlasting possession; and I will be their God.' 9. And God said unto Abraham: 'And as for thee, thou shalt keep My covenant, thou and thy seed after thee throughout their generations. 10. This is

¹ Heb. *Ab hamon*.

אֶל־אַבְרָם וַיֹּאמֶר אֵלָיו אֲנִי־אֵל שַׁדַּי הִתְהַלֵּךְ לְפָנַי וֶהְיֵה 
תָמִים: וְאֶתְּנָה בְרִיתִי בֵּינִי וּבֵינֶךָ וְאַרְבֶּה אוֹתְךָ בִּמְאֹד 2
מְאֹד: וַיִּפֹּל אַבְרָם עַל־פָּנָיו וַיְדַבֵּר אִתּוֹ אֱלֹהִים לֵאמֹר: 3
אֲנִי הִנֵּה בְרִיתִי אִתָּךְ וְהָיִיתָ לְאַב הֲמוֹן גּוֹיִם: וְלֹא־יִקָּרֵא 4 ה
עוֹד אֶת־שִׁמְךָ אַבְרָם וְהָיָה שִׁמְךָ אַבְרָהָם כִּי אַב־הֲמוֹן
גּוֹיִם נְתַתִּיךָ: וְהִפְרֵתִי אֹתְךָ בִּמְאֹד מְאֹד וּנְתַתִּיךָ לְגוֹיִם 6 שביעי
וּמְלָכִים מִמְּךָ יֵצֵאוּ: וַהֲקִמֹתִי אֶת־בְּרִיתִי בֵּינִי וּבֵינֶךָ 7
וּבֵין זַרְעֲךָ אַחֲרֶיךָ לְדֹרֹתָם לִבְרִית עוֹלָם לִהְיוֹת לְךָ
לֵאלֹהִים וּלְזַרְעֲךָ אַחֲרֶיךָ: וְנָתַתִּי לְךָ וּלְזַרְעֲךָ אַחֲרֶיךָ 8
אֵת ׀ אֶרֶץ מְגֻרֶיךָ אֵת כָּל־אֶרֶץ כְּנַעַן לַאֲחֻזַּת עוֹלָם וְהָיִיתִי
לָהֶם לֵאלֹהִים: וַיֹּאמֶר אֱלֹהִים אֶל־אַבְרָהָם וְאַתָּה אֶת־ 9
בְּרִיתִי תִשְׁמֹר אַתָּה וְזַרְעֲךָ אַחֲרֶיךָ לְדֹרֹתָם: זֹאת בְּרִיתִי

uncertain. The usual translation, 'Almighty,' is due to the Vulgate (the Latin version of the Bible). The realization of Abram's hopes must often have appeared dim and distant to him. Here he is reassured: nothing is impossible to God Almighty. *Shaddai* has also been derived from a root meaning 'to heap benefits'; and it would then mean 'Dispenser of benefits', the Friend who shepherds the Patriarchs and preserves them from all harm; see on Numbers I, 5.

*whole-hearted.* i.e. place implicit and undivided confidence in God alone. The Rabbis connect this exhortation with the Covenant of Circumcision, which was about to be instituted, and thus indicate the moral ideal which underlies the ritual act.

*make My covenant.* lit. 'I will give (*i.e.* grant) My covenant.' What follows is not a compact between God and the Patriarch, but a statement of the plans which He had designed for Abram and his descendants.

**3.** *and Abram fell on his face.* The Oriental mode of expressing gratitude.

**4.** *as for Me.* Introducing God's part of the covenant, as contrasted with 'And as for thee' in v. 9.

*a multitude of nations.* The Israelites; the Arabs, descended from Ishmael; and the tribes enumerated in xxv, 1 f.

**5.** *Abraham . . . multitude of nations. Ab* means 'father'; and *raham*, the second half of the new name, is an Arabic word for 'multitude'. The change of name emphasizes the mission of Abraham, which is 'To bring all the peoples under the wings of the Shechinah'.

**8.** *the land of thy sojournings.* The land in which Abraham dwelt only as 'a sojourner'.

**10.** *this is My covenant which ye shall keep.* The meaning is not that the Covenant is to consist in the rite of circumcision, but that circumcision is to be the external sign of the Covenant. As the following verse declares, 'it shall be a token of a covenant,' just as the rainbow was the token of the covenant with Noah. And even as the rainbow had existed before Noah, this rite had been practised among other peoples before Israel. To whatever origin and purpose it might be traced—whether as a measure safeguarding cleanliness and health (Philo), or to counteract excessive lust (Maimonides), or as a sacrificial symbol—for Abraham and his descendants all these conceptions are supplanted, and the rite is the abiding symbol of the consecration of the Children of Abraham to the God of Abraham. It is the *rite of the covenant;* and unbounded has been the loyalty and devotion with which this vital and fundamental institution of the Jewish Faith has been and is being observed. Jewish men and women have in all ages been ready to lay down their lives in its defence. The Maccabean martyrs died for it. The officers of King Antiochus put to death the mothers who initiated their children into the Covenant—'and they hanged their babes about their necks' (I Maccabees I, 61). The same readiness for self-immolation in defence of this sacred rite

## GENESIS XVII, 11

My covenant, which ye shall keep, between Me and you and thy seed after thee: every male among you shall be circumcised. 11. And ye shall be circumcised in the flesh of your foreskin; and it shall be a token of a covenant betwixt Me and you. 12. And he that is eight days old shall be circumcised among you, every male throughout your generations, he that is born in the house, or bought with money of any foreigner, that is not of thy seed. 13. He that is born in thy house, and he that is bought with thy money, must needs be circumcised; and My covenant shall be in your flesh for an everlasting covenant. 14. And the uncircumcised male who is not circumcised in the flesh of his foreskin, that soul shall be cut off from his people; he hath broken My covenant.' ¶ 15. And God said unto Abraham: 'As for Sarai thy wife, thou shalt not call her name Sarai, but ¹Sarah shall her name be. 16. And I will bless her, and moreover I will give thee a son of her; yea, I will bless her, and she shall be a mother of nations; kings of peoples shall be of her.' 17. Then Abraham fell upon his face, and laughed, and said in his heart: 'Shall a child be born unto him that is a hundred years old? and shall Sarah, that is ninety years old, bear?' 18. And Abraham said unto God: 'Oh that Ishmael might live before Thee!' 19. And God said: 'Nay, but Sarah thy wife shall bear thee a son; and thou shalt call his name ²Isaac; and I will establish My covenant with him for an everlasting covenant for his seed after him. 20. And as for Ishmael, I have heard thee; behold, I have blessed him, and will make him fruitful, and will multiply him exceedingly; twelve princes shall he beget, and I will make him a great nation. 21. But My covenant will I establish with Isaac, whom

¹ That is, *Princess*.   ² From the Heb. root meaning *to laugh*.

we find in the times of the Hadrianic persecution, in the dread days of the Inquisition, yea, whenever and wherever tyrants undertook to uproot the Jewish Faith.  Even an excommunicated semi-apostate like Benedict Spinoza declares: 'Such great importance do I attach to the sign of the Covenant, that I am persuaded that it is sufficient by itself to maintain the separate existence of the nation for ever.'

**12.** *he that is born in the house.* i.e. the child of a slave; see on XIV, 14. Slaves were regarded as part of the household.

**14.** *cut off from his people.* Either through punishment at the hands of God; or through expulsion from the community.

**15.** *Sarah.* Brings out more forcibly the meaning 'Princess' than the archaic form *Sarai*.

**17.** *and laughed.* The Targum renders 'and rejoiced', to imply that he laughed for joy, not from incredulity. What follows would accordingly not be a question, but an exclamation of surprise.

**18.** *Ishmael might live.* Abraham, despairing of the possibility of having issue by Sarah, expresses the hope that Ishmael 'might live before Thee', in order that the promises made to Abraham might be fulfilled through him. It is also possible to understand it as a prayer that, though Ishmael is excluded from the spiritual heritage, he may yet live under the Divine care and blessing.

**20.** *twelve princes.* They are enumerated in XXV, 13–16.

## GENESIS XVII, 22      בראשית לך לך יז

Sarah shall bear unto thee at this set time in the next year.' 22. And He left off talking with him, and God went up from Abraham. 23. And Abraham took Ishmael his son, and all that were born in his house, and all that were bought with his money, every male among the men of Abraham's house, and circumcised the flesh of their foreskin in the selfsame day, as God had said unto him.\* ᵐ· 24. And Abraham was ninety years old and nine, when he was circumcised in the flesh of his foreskin. 25. And Ishmael his son was thirteen years old, when he was circumcised in the flesh of his foreskin. 26. In the selfsame day was Abraham circumcised, and Ishmael his son. 27. And all the men of his house, those born in the house, and those bought with money of a foreigner, were circumcised with him.

22 בַּשָּׁנָה הָאַחֶרֶת: וַיְכַל לְדַבֵּר אִתּוֹ וַיַּעַל אֱלֹהִים מֵעַל
23 אַבְרָהָם: וַיִּקַּח אַבְרָהָם אֶת־יִשְׁמָעֵאל בְּנוֹ וְאֵת כָּל־יְלִידֵי
בֵיתוֹ וְאֵת כָּל־מִקְנַת כַּסְפּוֹ כָּל־זָכָר בְּאַנְשֵׁי בֵּית אַבְרָהָם
וַיָּמָל אֶת־בְּשַׂר עָרְלָתָם בְּעֶצֶם הַיּוֹם הַזֶּה כַּאֲשֶׁר דִּבֶּר   מפטיר
24 אִתּוֹ אֱלֹהִים: וְאַבְרָהָם בֶּן־תִּשְׁעִים וָתֵשַׁע שָׁנָה בְּהִמֹּלוֹ
כה בִּשַׂר עָרְלָתוֹ: וְיִשְׁמָעֵאל בְּנוֹ בֶּן־שְׁלֹשׁ עֶשְׂרֵה שָׁנָה בְּהִמֹּלוֹ
26 אֵת בְּשַׂר עָרְלָתוֹ: בְּעֶצֶם הַיּוֹם הַזֶּה נִמּוֹל אַבְרָהָם
27 וְיִשְׁמָעֵאל בְּנוֹ: וְכָל־אַנְשֵׁי בֵיתוֹ יְלִיד בָּיִת וּמִקְנַת־כֶּסֶף
מֵאֵת בֶּן־נֵכָר נִמֹּלוּ אִתּוֹ:

**23.** *in the selfsame day.* An indication of Abraham's readiness to perform his obligations without delay.

---

## HAFTORAH LECH LECHA     הפטרת לך לך

### ISAIAH XL, 27–XLI, 16

**CHAPTER XL**

27. Why sayest thou, O Jacob,
And speakest, O Israel:
'My way is hid from the LORD,
And my right is passed over from my God'?
28. Hast thou not known? hast thou not heard
That the everlasting God, the LORD,
The Creator of the ends of the earth,
Fainteth not, neither is weary?
His discernment is past searching out.

**CAP. XL.** מ

27 לָמָּה תֹאמַר יַעֲקֹב וּתְדַבֵּר יִשְׂרָאֵל נִסְתְּרָה
28 דַרְכִּי מֵיְהֹוָה וּמֵאֱלֹהַי מִשְׁפָּטִי יַעֲבוֹר: הֲלוֹא יָדַעְתָּ אִם־
לֹא שָׁמַעְתָּ אֱלֹהֵי עוֹלָם ׀ יְהֹוָה בּוֹרֵא קְצוֹת הָאָרֶץ לֹא

29. He giveth power to the faint;
And to him that hath no might He increaseth strength.

### ISAIAH XL, 27–XLI, 16

The Sedrah opens with the call of Abraham, and the Divine bidding, 'Be thou a blessing' unto all the families of the earth. Such, likewise declares the great Prophet of Consolation, is the Divine charge to the Children of Abraham. Israel, suffering in Exile, might well despair of the fulfilment of that Divine promise, nay, even of God's remembrance of that promise. The Prophet here stills such questionings. In God, Israel has the source of inexhaustible strength. The everlasting God will not fail to carry through His great purposes for mankind through Israel His servant, the child of 'Abraham, My friend'.

**27.** *my way is hid.* 'My lot is unnoticed by God. He passes over my right to be protected from intolerable oppression,' such is the despairing complaint of many in the Exile. Israel fears that it is forgotten by God.

**28.** Gives the answer of the Prophet.
*everlasting God.* The God of eternity.
*His discernment is past searching out.* He therefore must have good reason for delaying the Redemption.

# ISAIAH XL, 30

30. Even the youths shall faint and be weary,
And the young men shall utterly fall;
31. But they that wait for the LORD shall renew their strength;
They shall mount up with wings as eagles;
They shall run, and not be weary;
They shall walk, and not faint.

## CHAPTER XLI

1. Keep silence before Me, O islands,
And let the peoples renew their strength;
Let them draw near, then let them speak;
Let us come near together to judgment.
2. Who hath raised up one from the east,
At whose steps victory attendeth?
He giveth nations before him,
And maketh him rule over kings;
His sword maketh them as the dust,
His bow as the driven stubble.
3. He pursueth them, and passeth on safely;
The way with his feet he treadeth not.
4. Who hath wrought and done it?
He that called the generations from the beginning.
I, the Lord, who am the first,
And with the last am the same.
5. The isles saw, and feared;
The ends of the earth trembled;
They drew near, and came.
6. They helped every one his neighbour;
And every one said to his brother:
'Be of good courage.'

7. So the carpenter encouraged the goldsmith,
And he that smootheth with the hammer him that smiteth the anvil,

---

**31.** *they that wait.* They who hope in the Lord are borne aloft on wings of faith above all earthly cares. The phrases 'mount up with wings as eagles,' 'run,' and 'walk' do not form an anticlimax. Under a wave of enthusiasm we are all capable of an isolated act of heroism, i.e. to 'soar' or 'to run' for a time. It is far harder to follow the monotonous round of everyday duty when the vision has faded and the splendour seems gone, undeterred by trials and hindrances, meeting them in the spirit of faith and conquering them by steadfastness. This is the achievement of those who 'wait for the LORD'. Day by day, they shall renew their strength.

## CHAPTER XLI. GOD, ISRAEL AND THE HEATHENS

**1–5.** A summons to the nations to assemble for a process at law before the tribunal of the Almighty.

**1.** *islands.* Habitable lands.
*renew their strength.* Pluck up courage to speak.

**2.** *who hath raised up one from the east.* Since Ibn Ezra, it has been recognized that this refers to Cyrus. In the victorious career of this magnanimous conqueror and Liberator, which had at that time commenced, the Prophet beheld the instrument of God for the release of Israel from Exile.

**3.** *the way with his feet he treadeth not.* i.e. so swift is his victorious progress that he seems scarcely to touch the ground, but to fly over it.

**4.** *called generations from the beginning.* i.e. He who from the first knew all future times and events, and summons each to appear at its right moment. This verse is one of the sublimest in the Bible: 'Human history is the thought of God,' the 'counsel' of the Almighty. God is 'the First and the Last', initiating all movements—calling the generations from the beginning—and bringing them to a close. Prediction and fulfilment are thus manifestations of His universal Wisdom and Power (Davidson).

**5.** *the isles saw.* These victories of Cyrus.

**6–7.** The nations thereupon frantically set

## ISAIAH XLI, 8

Saying of the soldering: 'It is good';
And he fastened it with nails, that it
should not be moved.

8. But thou, Israel, My servant,
Jacob whom I have chosen,
The seed of Abraham My friend;
9. Thou whom I have taken hold of from
the ends of the earth,
And called thee from the uttermost
parts thereof,
And said unto thee: 'Thou art My
servant,
I have chosen thee and not cast thee
away';
10. Fear thou not, for I am with thee,
Be not dismayed, for I am thy God;
I strengthen thee, yea, I help thee;
Yea, I uphold thee with My victorious
right hand.
11. Behold, all they that were incensed
against thee
Shall be ashamed and confounded;
They that strove with thee
Shall be as nothing, and shall perish.
12. Thou shalt seek them, and shalt not
find them,
Even them that contended with thee;
They that warred against thee
Shall be as nothing, and as a thing of
nought.
13. For I the LORD thy God
Hold thy right hand,
Who say unto thee: 'Fear not,
I help thee.'
14. Fear not, thou worm Jacob,
And ye men of Israel;
I help thee, saith the LORD,
And thy Redeemer, the Holy One of
Israel.
15. Behold, I make thee a new threshing-
sledge
Having sharp teeth;

ישעיה מא

8 וְאַתָּה יִשְׂרָאֵל עַבְדִּי יַעֲקֹב אֲשֶׁר בְּחַרְתִּיךָ זֶרַע
9 אַבְרָהָם אֹהֲבִי: אֲשֶׁר הֶחֱזַקְתִּיךָ מִקְצוֹת הָאָרֶץ וּמֵאֲצִילֶיהָ
קְרָאתִיךָ וָאֹמַר לְךָ עַבְדִּי־אַתָּה בְּחַרְתִּיךָ וְלֹא מְאַסְתִּיךָ:
10 אַל־תִּירָא כִּי עִמְּךָ־אָנִי אַל־תִּשְׁתָּע כִּי־אֲנִי אֱלֹהֶיךָ אִמַּצְתִּיךָ
11 אַף־עֲזַרְתִּיךָ אַף־תְּמַכְתִּיךָ בִּימִין צִדְקִי: הֵן יֵבֹשׁוּ וְיִכָּלְמוּ
כֹּל הַנֶּחֱרִים בָּךְ יִהְיוּ כְאַיִן וְיֹאבְדוּ אַנְשֵׁי רִיבֶךָ:
12 תְּבַקְשֵׁם וְלֹא תִמְצָאֵם אַנְשֵׁי מַצֻּתֶךָ יִהְיוּ כְאַיִן וּכְאֶפֶס
13 אַנְשֵׁי מִלְחַמְתֶּךָ: כִּי אֲנִי יְהוָה אֱלֹהֶיךָ מַחֲזִיק יְמִינֶךָ
14 הָאֹמֵר לְךָ אַל־תִּירָא אֲנִי עֲזַרְתִּיךָ: אַל־תִּירְאִי תּוֹלַעַת
יַעֲקֹב מְתֵי יִשְׂרָאֵל אֲנִי עֲזַרְתִּיךְ נְאֻם־יְהוָה וְגֹאֲלֵךְ קְדוֹשׁ
15 יִשְׂרָאֵל: הִנֵּה שַׂמְתִּיךְ לְמוֹרַג חָרוּץ חָדָשׁ בַּעַל פִּיפִיּוֹת
16 תָּדוּשׁ הָרִים וְתָדֹק וּגְבָעוֹת כַּמֹּץ תָּשִׂים: תִּזְרֵם וְרוּחַ
תִּשָּׂאֵם וּסְעָרָה תָּפִיץ אֹתָם וְאַתָּה תָּגִיל בַּיהוָה בִּקְדוֹשׁ
יִשְׂרָאֵל תִּתְהַלָּל:

Thou shalt thresh the mountains, and
beat them small,
And shalt make the hills as chaff.
16. Thou shalt fan them, and the wind
shall carry them away,
And the whirlwind shall scatter them;
And thou shalt rejoice in the LORD,
Thou shalt glory in the Holy One of
Israel.

---

themselves to the fashioning of new and strong idols to deliver them from the conqueror.

**8–14.** In contrast to these other nations, Israel is the Servant of God, and need not fear.

**8.** *My servant.* My worshipper.
*My friend.* Or, 'who loved me.' Abraham was not merely passively but actively the 'friend of God'. His love was obedience. This striking title recurs in II Chron. xx, 7.

**9.** *ends of the earth.* Ur of the Chaldees.

**10.** *dismayed.* lit. 'gaze not anxiously around you.'

**11–16.** ISRAEL'S ENEMIES WILL BE CONFOUNDED

**14.** *worm Jacob.* Worm as a symbol of weakness, and of Israel's condition in captivity.
*Redeemer.* Heb. 'Goel', the technical term for the relative whose duty it was to redeem the person or property of a kinsman, or to avenge him if murdered. It is a favourite title of God in Isaiah.

**15–16.** *a new threshing-sledge.* The mountains and the hills represent the powerful, worldly forces that seek to block the spiritual and ethical ideals in Israel's message and work. These shall be reduced to powder and scattered by the whirlwind, and Israel shall rejoice in the vindication of his faith in God.

## GENESIS XVIII, 1

### CHAPTER XVIII

1. And the LORD appeared unto him by the terebinths of Mamre, as he sat in the tent door in the heat of the day; 2. and he lifted up his eyes and looked, and, lo, three men stood over against him; and when he saw them, he ran to meet them from the tent door, and bowed down to the earth, 3. and said: 'My lord, if now I have found favour in thy sight, pass not away, I pray thee, from thy servant. 4. Let now a little water be fetched, and wash your feet, and recline yourselves under the tree. 5. And I will fetch a morsel of bread, and stay ye your heart; after that ye shall pass on; forasmuch as ye are come to your servant.' And they said: 'So do, as thou hast said.' 6. And Abraham hastened into the tent unto Sarah, and said: 'Make ready quickly three measures of fine meal, knead it, and make cakes.' 7. And Abraham ran unto the herd, and fetched a calf tender and good, and gave it unto the servant; and he hastened to dress it. 8. And he took curd, and milk, and the calf which he had dressed, and set it before them; and he

בראשית וירא יח

CAP. XVIII. יח

פ פ פ ד 4

א וַיֵּרָא אֵלָיו יְהֹוָה בְּאֵלֹנֵי מַמְרֵא וְהוּא יֹשֵׁב פֶּתַח־הָאֹהֶל
2 כְּחֹם הַיּוֹם: וַיִּשָּׂא עֵינָיו וַיַּרְא וְהִנֵּה שְׁלֹשָׁה אֲנָשִׁים נִצָּבִים
עָלָיו וַיַּרְא וַיָּרָץ לִקְרָאתָם מִפֶּתַח הָאֹהֶל וַיִּשְׁתַּחוּ אָרְצָה:
3 וַיֹּאמַר אֲדֹנָי אִם־נָא מָצָאתִי חֵן בְּעֵינֶיךָ אַל־נָא תַעֲבֹר מֵעַל
4 עַבְדֶּךָ: יֻקַּח־נָא מְעַט־מַיִם וְרַחֲצוּ רַגְלֵיכֶם וְהִשָּׁעֲנוּ תַּחַת
ה הָעֵץ: וְאֶקְחָה פַת־לֶחֶם וְסַעֲדוּ לִבְּכֶם אַחַר תַּעֲבֹרוּ כִּי־
עַל־כֵּן עֲבַרְתֶּם עַל־עַבְדְּכֶם וַיֹּאמְרוּ כֵּן תַּעֲשֶׂה כַּאֲשֶׁר
6 דִּבַּרְתָּ: וַיְמַהֵר אַבְרָהָם הָאֹהֱלָה אֶל־שָׂרָה וַיֹּאמֶר מַהֲרִי
7 שְׁלֹשׁ סְאִים קֶמַח סֹלֶת לוּשִׁי וַעֲשִׂי עֻגוֹת: וְאֶל־הַבָּקָר
רָץ אַבְרָהָם וַיִּקַּח בֶּן־בָּקָר רַךְ וָטוֹב וַיִּתֵּן אֶל־הַנַּעַר וַיְמַהֵר
8 לַעֲשׂוֹת אֹתוֹ: וַיִּקַּח חֶמְאָה וְחָלָב וּבֶן־הַבָּקָר אֲשֶׁר עָשָׂה

v. 3. קדש   v. 6. חג' רפה

## IV. VAYYERA

(CHAPTERS XVIII–XXII)

### THE DESTRUCTION OF SODOM AND GOMORRAH (CHAPTERS XVIII–XIX)

CHAPTER XVIII, 1–16. VISIT OF THE ANGELS

**1.** *and the LORD appeared unto him.* The Rabbis connect this chapter with the preceding, and declare that God visited the Patriarch during the indisposition which resulted from his circumcision. From this passage they deduce the duty of visiting the sick.

*in the tent door.* Abraham was watching for passers-by to offer them hospitality, an occupation in which he delighted.

**2.** *three men.* One to announce the tidings of the birth of Isaac; the second to destroy Sodom; and the third to rescue Lot. 'An angel is never sent on more than one errand at a time' (Midrash).

**3.** *my lord.* Abraham speaks to the one who appeared to be the chief of the three men.

**4.** *wash your feet.* A refreshing comfort to travellers who wore sandals; cf. XIX, 2; XXIV, 32; XLIII, 24.

*recline yourselves.* While the meal was being prepared for them, they could enjoy the shade of the tree in front of his tent (see v. 1).

**5.** *and I will fetch a morsel of bread.* It is a mark of the good man, declare the Rabbis, to perform more than he promises. The Patriarch belittles the fare he offers to provide for his guests, but gives them of his best.

*stay ye your heart.* Refresh your strength.

*forasmuch as.* Seeing that you are in haste, for otherwise you would not be passing my tent in the heat of the day.

**6.** *and Abraham hastened.* Note also the instruction to Sarah, 'make ready *quickly*.'

**7.** *unto the servant.* lit. 'the lad', Ishmael, whom Abraham was thus instructing in the duties of hospitality (Midrash). Such instruction in the duty of hospitality to strangers may appear superfluous in the eyes of some parents and teachers to-day. They are in error. In Western countries, the old Bible command, *Love ye the stranger* (Deut. x, 19), is honoured more in the breach than in the observance. The vulgar, high and low, deem it 'patriotic' to despise aliens, and find their foreign manners and language contemptible.

**8.** The verse may be understood as meaning that the guests were given curd and milk to slake their thirst and refresh them (cf. Judges IV, 19), and then followed the meal proper, which consisted of the calf. This procedure would be quite in accord with the dietary laws.

*and he stood by them.* In the East, the host does not sit with his guests, but stands and attends to their needs.

*and they did eat.* This is the only place in the

GENESIS XVIII, 9

stood by them under the tree, and they did eat. 9. And they said unto him: 'Where is Sarah thy wife?' And he said: 'Behold, in the tent.' 10. And He said: 'I will certainly return unto thee when the season cometh round; and, lo, Sarah thy wife shall have a son.' And Sarah heard in the tent door, which was behind him.—11. Now Abraham and Sarah were old, and well stricken in age; it had ceased to be with Sarah after the manner of women.—12. And Sarah laughed within herself, saying: 'After I am waxed old shall I have pleasure, my lord being old also?' 13. And the LORD said unto Abraham: 'Wherefore did Sarah laugh, saying: Shall I of a surety bear a child, whom am old? 14. Is any thing too hard for the LORD? At the set time I will return unto thee, when the season cometh round, and Sarah shall have a son.' * 11. 15. Then Sarah denied, saying: 'I laughed not'; for she was afraid. And He said: 'Nay; but thou didst laugh.' ¶ 16. And the men rose up from thence, and looked out toward Sodom; and Abraham went with them to bring them on the way. 17. And the LORD said: 'Shall I hide from Abraham that which I am doing; 18. seeing that Abraham shall surely become a great and mighty nation, and all the nations of the earth shall be blessed in him? 19. For I have known him, to the end that he may command his children and his household after him, that they may keep the way of

---

Bible where celestial beings are mentioned as partaking of food, or as appearing to do so (see Tobit XII, 19). The Rabbis deduced from this, that it is necessary to conform to the social habits of the people in whose midst one lives.

**9.** *in the tent.* The Talmud sees herein praise of Sarah, the highest excellence of a wife being her domesticity.

**10.** *and He said.* One of the angels.

*cometh round.* lit. 'reviveth'—this time next year.

*and Sarah heard in the tent door.* More accurately, 'now Sarah was listening at the entrance of the tent.'

**11.** *well stricken.* 'Advanced.'

**12.** *and Sarah laughed.* Incredulous at the news.

*waxed old.* lit. 'withered'.

**13.** *shall I ... who am old?* Sarah had referred both to her and to Abraham's extreme age. God only mentioned the reference to herself. This was done so as not to give cause for quarrel between husband and wife, say the Rabbis.

**14.** *is anything too hard for the LORD?* Or, 'Is anything too wonderful for the LORD?'

**16.** *to bring them on the way.* The final act of courtesy of a gracious host.

**17–33. ABRAHAM'S INTERCESSION FOR SODOM**

**17.** *the LORD said.* Equivalent to 'the Lord thought'—a usage often found in the Bible.

**18.** *blessed in him.* See on XII, 3.

**19.** *for I have known him.* i.e. regarded and chosen him; cf. Amos III, 2, 'You only have I known of all the families of the earth'; Psalm I, 6, 'The Lord regardeth the way of the righteous.' God's choice of Abraham is no arbitrary election.

*command his children.* Or, 'charge his children.' An important doctrine is here taught in connection with the word 'command' צוה, which has played a conspicuous part in Jewish life. It is the sacred duty of the Israelite to transmit the Jewish heritage to his children after him. The last injunction of the true Jewish father to his children is that they walk in 'the way of the LORD' and live lives of probity and goodness. These injunctions were often put in writing; and this custom has given rise to a distinct type of literary production, the Jewish Ethical Will (צוואה).

GENESIS XVIII, 20

the LORD, to do righteousness and justice; to the end that the LORD may bring upon Abraham that which He hath spoken of him.' 20. And the LORD said: 'Verily, the cry of Sodom and Gomorrah is great, and, verily, their sin is exceeding grievous. 21. I will go down now, and see whether they have done altogether according to the cry of it, which is come unto Me; and if not, I will know.' 22. And the men turned from thence, and went toward Sodom; but Abraham stood yet before the LORD. 23. And Abraham drew near, and said: 'Wilt Thou indeed sweep away the righteous with the wicked? 24. Peradventure there are fifty righteous within the city; wilt Thou indeed sweep away and not forgive the place for the fifty righteous that are therein? 25. That be far from Thee to do after this manner, to slay the righteous with the wicked, that so the righteous should be as the wicked; that be far from

אַחֲרָיו וְשָׁמְרוּ דֶּרֶךְ יְהֹוָה לַעֲשׂוֹת צְדָקָה וּמִשְׁפָּט לְמַעַן
הָבִיא יְהֹוָה עַל־אַבְרָהָם אֵת אֲשֶׁר־דִּבֶּר עָלָיו: וַיֹּאמֶר 20
יְהֹוָה זַעֲקַת סְדֹם וַעֲמֹרָה כִּי־רָבָּה וְחַטָּאתָם כִּי כָבְדָה
מְאֹד: אֵרֲדָה־נָּא וְאֶרְאֶה הַכְּצַעֲקָתָהּ הַבָּאָה אֵלַי עָשׂוּ 21
כָּלָה וְאִם־לֹא אֵדָעָה: וַיִּפְנוּ מִשָּׁם הָאֲנָשִׁים וַיֵּלְכוּ סְדֹמָה 22
וְאַבְרָהָם עוֹדֶנּוּ עֹמֵד לִפְנֵי יְהֹוָה: וַיִּגַּשׁ אַבְרָהָם וַיֹּאמַר 23
הַאַף תִּסְפֶּה צַדִּיק עִם־רָשָׁע: אוּלַי יֵשׁ חֲמִשִּׁים צַדִּיקִם 24
בְּתוֹךְ הָעִיר הַאַף תִּסְפֶּה וְלֹא־תִשָּׂא לַמָּקוֹם לְמַעַן חֲמִשִּׁים
הַצַּדִּיקִם אֲשֶׁר בְּקִרְבָּהּ: חָלִלָה לְּךָ מֵעֲשֹׂת ׀ כַּדָּבָר 25
הַזֶּה לְהָמִית צַדִּיק עִם־רָשָׁע וְהָיָה כַצַּדִּיק כָּרָשָׁע חָלִלָה

v. 21. מֹעֵיל

---

**20.** *the cry of Sodom.* The cries of those who suffered from the atrocious wickedness of the inhabitants of Sodom and who implored Heaven's vengeance against their cruel oppressors (Ezek. XVI, 49). The following legend graphically describes their hatred of all strangers and their fiendish punishment of all who departed from their ways. A girl, overcome by pity, supplied food to a poor stranger. On detection, she was stripped, bound, daubed with honey and placed on the roof under the burning sun to be devoured by the bees.

*their sin.* Exemplified in the narrative of the next chapter.

**21.** *I will go down now.* An anthropomorphic expression, as in XI, 7, to convey the idea that before God decided to punish the dwellers of the cities, 'He descended,' as it were, to obtain ocular proof of, or extenuating circumstances for, their crimes.

**22.** *from thence.* From the place to which Abraham had accompanied them.

**23.** The remainder of the chapter forms one of the sublimest passages in the Bible or out of the Bible. Abraham's plea for Sodom is a signal illustration of his nobility of character. Amid the hatreds and feuds of primitive tribes who glorified brute force and despised pity, Abraham proves true to his new name and embraces in his sympathy all the children of men. Even the wicked inhabitants of Sodom were his brothers, and his heart overflows with sorrow over their doom. The unique dialogue between God and Abraham teaches two vital lessons: first, the supreme value of righteousness: and, secondly, God's readiness to pardon (Ezek. XXXIII, 11), if only He can do so consistently with justice.

*drew near.* By the act of prayer (Abarbanel).

*righteous ... wicked.* i.e. 'innocent ... guilty.' Abraham rests his case on the conviction that the action of God cannot be arbitrary but only in accordance with perfect justice. In an indiscriminate destruction, however, all the inhabitants, whether good or wicked, would share the same fate. Abraham pleads that as it would not be just to destroy the righteous, therefore, in order to save the righteous, the judgment which had been pronounced over the cities should be stayed (Ryle). This intercession on behalf of Sodom and Gomorrah—Abraham arguing with God, yea, bargaining with Him, to save their depraved inhabitants from merited destruction—is the highest spiritual pinnacle reached by the Patriarch. Its grandeur exceeds even the willingness to sacrifice his son at the Divine bidding. Within his breast there was a conflict between his sense of justice that the wicked must pay the penalty of their misdeeds, and his anguish at the thought that human beings were about to perish.

**25.** *far from Thee.* i.e. it would be unworthy of Thee (Mendelssohn).

*shall not the Judge of all the earth do justly?* These words have been well described as an 'epochal sentence in the Bible' (Zangwill). They make Justice the main pillar of God's Throne: without it, the whole idea of the Divine totters. Justice, it is true, is not the only ethical quality in God or man, nor is it the highest quality: but it is the basis for all the others. 'That which is

## GENESIS XVIII, 26

Thee; shall not the Judge of all the earth do justly?' 26. And the LORD said: 'If I find in Sodom fifty righteous within the city, then I will forgive all the place for their sake.' 27. And Abraham answered and said: 'Behold now, I have taken upon me to speak unto the LORD, who am but dust and ashes. 28. Peradventure there shall lack five of the fifty righteous; wilt Thou destroy all the city for lack of five?' And He said: 'I will not destroy it, if I find there forty and five.' 29. And he spoke unto Him yet again, and said: 'Peradventure there shall be forty found there.' And He said: 'I will not do it for the forty's sake.' 30. And he said: 'Oh, let not the LORD be angry, and I will speak. Peradventure there shall thirty be found there.' And He said: 'I will not do it if I find thirty there.' 31. And he said: 'Behold now, I have taken upon me to speak unto the LORD. Peradventure there shall be twenty found there.' And He said: 'I will not destroy it for the twenty's sake.' 32. And he said: 'Oh, let not the LORD be angry, and I will speak yet but this once. Peradventure ten shall be found there.' And He said: 'I will not destroy it for the ten's sake.' 33. And the LORD went His way, as soon as He had left off speaking to Abraham; and Abraham returned unto his place. * iii.

## 19 CHAPTER XIX

1. And the two angels came to Sodom at even; and Lot sat in the gate of Sodom; and Lot saw them, and rose up to meet them; and he fell down on his face to the earth; 2. and he said: 'Behold now, my lords, turn aside, I pray you, into your servant's house, and tarry all night, and wash your feet, and ye shall rise up early, and go on your way.' And they said:

---

above justice must be based on justice, and include justice, and be reached through justice' (Henry George). Only Israel, the Justice-intoxicated people, in time became בני רחמנים, 'merciful children of merciful ancestors.' The boldness of the Patriarch's ringing challenge, the universality of the phrase 'all the earth', and the absolute conviction that the infinite might of God must be controlled by the decrees of Justice—that, in fact, an unjust God would be a contradiction in terms—are truly extraordinary. Despite the lapse of thousands of years, mankind has not yet fully grasped this lofty conception of God and its ethical consequences in human society. 'When Abraham could not find fifty righteous men in Sodom, and pleaded on behalf of forty, thirty, twenty, ten, that the great city might be spared, do you think God did not know all the time that there were not even ten righteous men in Sodom? But God wanted our father Abraham to show whether he was a man or no; and didn't he show himself a man!' (Arnold Zweig).

**33.** *returned unto his place.* From where he prayed, unto his own abode, Mamre; see *v.* 1.

CHAPTER XIX. THE ANGELS, SODOM AND LOT

**1.** *angels.* This is the first time the visitors are referred to by this term.

*in the gate of Sodom.* i.e. the passage beneath the city-wall, where people congregate in the East to converse, transact business, or have their disputes adjudicated.

**2.** *your servant's house.* Being a resident of a

## GENESIS, XIX, 3

'Nay; but we will abide in the broad place all night.' 3. And he urged them greatly; and they turned in unto him, and entered into his house; and he made them a feast, and did bake unleavened bread, and they did eat. 4. But before they lay down, the men of the city, even the men of Sodom, compassed the house round, both young and old, all the people from every quarter. 5. And they called unto Lot, and said unto him: 'Where are the men that came in to thee this night? bring them out unto us, that we may know them.' 6. And Lot went out unto them to the door, and shut the door after him. 7. And he said: 'I pray you, my brethren, do not so wickedly. 8. Behold now, I have two daughters that have not known man; let me, I pray you, bring them out unto you, and do ye to them as is good in your eyes; only unto these men do nothing; forasmuch as they are come under the shadow of my roof.' 9. And they said: 'Stand back.' And they said: 'This one fellow came in to sojourn, and he will needs play the judge; now will we deal worse with thee, than with them.' And they pressed sore upon the man, even Lot, and drew near to break the door. 10. But the men put forth their hand, and brought Lot into the house to them, and the door they shut. 11. And they smote the men that were at the door of the house with blindness, both small and great; so that they wearied themselves to find the door. 12. And the men said unto Lot: 'Hast thou here any besides? son-in-law, and thy sons, and thy daughters, and whomsoever thou hast in the city; bring them out of the place; 13. for we will destroy this place, because the cry of them is waxed great before the LORD; and the LORD hath sent us to destroy it.' 14. And Lot went out, and spoke unto his sons-in-law, who married his daughters, and said: 'Up, get you out of this place; for the LORD will destroy the city.' But he seemed unto his sons-in-law as one that jested. 15. And

city, Lot dwelt in a 'house', whereas Abraham's abode was a 'tent'.

**broad place.** The 'square' of the city; and the climate being warm, it would be a natural place where a homeless visitor would spend the night.

**3.** *unleavened bread.* Which could be baked rapidly.

**4.** *all the people.* Emphasis is here laid on the fact that the inhabitants were all addicted to unnatural depravity. The rejection of Abraham's plea was, therefore, justified.

**8.** *my roof.* The duty of protecting a guest is sacred in the East. As soon as a stranger had touched the tent-rope, he could claim guest-right. But the price which Lot was prepared to pay is unthinkable in our eyes, though a different view would present itself to the Oriental in those times.

**9.** *this one fellow.* An expression of contempt.
*to sojourn.* i.e. this newcomer presumes to judge our actions, and interfere with our customs!

**11.** *blindness.* The Heb. word occurs again only in II Kings VI, 18, and denotes a temporary loss of vision.

**12.** *any besides.* Lot's household is to be saved with him.

**15.** *iniquity.* As in IV, 13, the Heb. word for

## GENESIS XIX, 16

when the morning arose, then the angels hastened Lot, saying: 'Arise, take thy wife, and thy two daughters that are here; lest thou be swept away in the iniquity of the city.' 16. But he lingered; and the men laid hold upon his hand, and upon the hand of his wife, and upon the hand of his two daughters; the LORD being merciful unto him. And they brought him forth, and set him without the city. 17. And it came to pass, when they had brought them forth abroad, that he said: 'Escape for thy life; look not behind thee, neither stay thou in all the Plain; escape to the mountain, lest thou be swept away.' 18. And Lot said unto them: 'Oh, not so, my lord; 19. behold now, thy servant hath found grace in thy sight, and thou hast magnified thy mercy, which thou hast shown unto me in saving my life; and I cannot escape to the mountain, lest the evil overtake me, and I die. 20. Behold now, this city is near to flee unto, and it is a little one; oh, let me escape thither—is it not a little one?—and my soul shall live.'*[iv.] 21. And he said unto him: 'See, I have accepted thee concerning this thing also, that I will not overthrow the city of which thou hast spoken. 22. Hasten thou, escape thither; for I cannot do anything till thou be come thither.'—Therefore the name of the city was called ¹Zoar.—23. The sun was risen upon the earth when Lot came unto Zoar. 24. Then the LORD caused to rain upon Sodom and upon Gomorrah brimstone and fire from the LORD out of heaven; 25. and He overthrew those cities, and all the Plain, and all the inhabitants of the cities, and that which grew upon the ground. 26. But his wife looked back from behind him, and she became a pillar of salt. 27. And Abraham got up early in the morning to the place where he had stood before the LORD. 28. And he looked out toward

---

¹ That is, *Little*, see verse 20.

---

'iniquity' means also its consequence, 'punishment.'

**16.** *but he lingered.* Either to collect his valuables, or he was reluctant to leave. All that Scripture tells of Lot is characteristic of a weak, irresolute character.

**17.** *that he said.* The angel whose mission it was to rescue Lot.

*the Plain.* See on XIII, 10.

*the mountain.* See on XIV, 10.

**19.** *the evil.* The disaster.

**20.** *a little one.* It is so insignificant in size: and, therefore, it is a small favour he is asking for, when pleading that it be spared.

*and my soul shall live.* i.e. my life be spared.

**26.** *a pillar of salt.* She looked back and lingered behind, to be overtaken by the brimstone and fire from which the others escaped. A similar fate befell lingering refugees at Pompeii. 'Her body became encrusted and saturated with a nitrous and saline substance, that very likely preserved it for some time from decay' (De Sola). Ancient writers refer to this pillar as being still in existence. Josephus claims to have seen it.

**27.** *Abraham.* After a restless night, his heart heavy with the knowledge of what was about to befall the five cities, he rises early in the morning to gaze with compassionate eyes upon the fulfilment of the Divine decree.

**28.** Archæological exploration has established the existence of an early Canaanite civilization in

## GENESIS XIX, 29

Sodom and Gomorrah, and toward all the land of the Plain, and beheld, and, lo, the smoke of the land went up as the smoke of a furnace. ¶ 29. And it came to pass, when God destroyed the cities of the Plain, that God remembered Abraham, and sent Lot out of the midst of the overthrow, when He overthrew the cities in which Lot dwelt. ¶ 30. And Lot went up out of Zoar, and dwelt in the mountain, and his two daughters with him; for he feared to dwell in Zoar; and he dwelt in a cave, he and his two daughters. 31. And the first-born said unto the younger: 'Our father is old, and there is not a man in the earth to come in unto us after the manner of all the earth. 32. Come, let us make our father drink wine, and we will lie with him, that we may preserve seed of our father.' 33. And they made their father drink wine that night. And the first-born went in, and lay with her father; and he knew not when she lay down, nor when she arose. 34. And it came to pass on the morrow, that the first-born said unto the younger: 'Behold, I lay yesternight with my father. Let us make him drink wine this night also; and go thou in, and lie with him, that we may preserve seed of our father.' 35. And they made their father drink wine that night also. And the younger arose, and lay with him; and he knew not when she lay down, nor when she arose. 36. Thus were both the daughters of Lot with child by their father. 37. And the first-born bore a son, and called his name Moab—the same is the father of the Moabites unto this day. 38. And the younger, she also bore a son, and called his name Ben-ammi—the same is the father of the children of Ammon unto this day.

## 20 CHAPTER XX

1. And Abraham journeyed from thence toward the land of the South, and dwelt between Kadesh and Shur; and he

the Plain. Many scholars to-day locate Sodom four miles north-east of the Dead Sea: formerly they located it to the south of the Dead Sea (Albright).

**29.** *remembered Abraham.* Gives the reason why Lot had been spared.

**30.** *he feared.* That God might yet include Zoar in the general destruction originally intended for all the five cities: and it seems that after his departure it was likewise destroyed by fire.

**31.** *there is not a man.* Some commentators state that Lot's daughters believed that the destruction had been universal, and that but for them the world would be completely depopulated. This explanation is untenable, seeing that they had just left Zoar. Their conduct does not admit of any extenuation; they were true children of Sodom.

**32.** *wine.* The mountainous country of Moab is full of caves; and the Midrash states that the inhabitants used to store their wines in such caves.

**37.** *Moab.* The name is explained as though it were the equivalent of *me-ab*, 'from a father.'

**38.** *Ben-ammi.* 'The son of my people,' or, 'the son of my father's kin.'

## GENESIS XX, 2

sojourned in Gerar. 2. And Abraham said of Sarah his wife: 'She is my sister.' And Abimelech king of Gerar sent, and took Sarah. 3. But God came to Abimelech in a dream of the night, and said to him: 'Behold, thou shalt die, because of the woman whom thou hast taken; for she is a man's wife.' 4. Now Abimelech had not come near her; and he said: 'Lord, wilt Thou slay even a righteous nation? 5. Said he not himself unto me: She is my sister? and she, even she herself said: He is my brother. In the simplicity of my heart and the innocency of my hands have I done this.' 6. And God said unto him in the dream: 'Yea, I know that in the simplicity of thy heart thou hast done this, and I also withheld thee from sinning against Me. Therefore suffered I thee not to touch her. 7. Now therefore restore the man's wife; for he is a prophet, and he shall pray for thee, and thou shalt live; and if thou restore her not, know thou that thou shalt surely die, thou, and all that are thine.' 8. And Abimelech rose early in the morning, and called all his servants, and told all these things in their ears; and the men were sore afraid. 9. Then Abimelech called Abraham, and said unto him: 'What hast thou done unto us? and wherein have I sinned against thee, that thou hast brought on me and on my kingdom a great sin? thou hast done deeds unto me that ought not to be done.' 10. And Abimelech said unto Abraham: 'What sawest thou, that thou hast done this thing?' 11. And Abraham said: 'Because I thought: Surely the fear of God is not in this place; and they will slay me for my wife's sake. 12. And moreover she is indeed my sister, the daughter of my father, but not the daughter of my mother;

### CHAPTER XX. ABIMELECH

The promise and hope of a son seems to have rejuvenated Sarah. She is taken into the harem of the king of Gerar.

**1.** *from thence.* From the terebinths of Mamre: see XVIII, 1.

*South.* The Negeb: see on XII, 9.

*Kadesh and Shur.* See on XIV, 7 and XVI, 7.

*Gerar.* Probably the Wady Jerur, 13 miles S.W. of Kadesh.

**2.** *my sister.* Abraham adopts the same precautions as when he was in Egypt: cf. XII, 13 f.

*Abimelech.* Abimilki is the name of the Egyptian governor of Tyre in the Tell-el-Amarna tablets.

*and took Sarah.* Had her brought to his harem.

**4.** *A righteous nation.* 'Innocent folk' (Moffatt).

**7.** *a prophet.* This is the first time the word occurs in the Bible. It is here used to denote a man who stands in a specially near relationship to God, and is consequently under the Divine protection.

**10.** *what sawest thou?* i.e. what hadst thou in view?

**12.** *daughter of my father.* The Bible sometimes uses 'son' and 'daughter' to denote a grandson or granddaughter (cf. IX, 24). Sarah may well have been Terah's granddaughter and Abraham's niece. Nachmanides, in his Commentary, severely denounces the Patriarch's conduct on the ground that it again imperilled his wife: and he adds that it makes no difference whether Abraham told Abimelech the truth in calling Sarah his 'sister', inasmuch as he suppressed the all-important fact that she was also his wife. Scripture impartially relates both the failings and the virtues of its heroes.

## GENESIS XX, 13

and so she became my wife. 13. And it came to pass, when God caused me to wander from my father's house, that I said unto her: This is thy kindness which thou shalt show unto me; at every place whither we shall come, say of me: He is my brother.' 14. And Abimelech took sheep and oxen, and men-servants and women-servants, and gave them unto Abraham, and restored him Sarah his wife. 15. And Abimelech said: 'Behold, my land is before thee: dwell where it pleaseth thee.' 16. And unto Sarah he said: 'Behold, I have given thy brother a thousand pieces of silver; behold, it is for thee a covering of the eyes to all that are with thee; and before all men thou art righted.' 17. And Abraham prayed unto God; and God healed Abimelech, and his wife, and his maid-servants; and they bore children. 18. For the LORD had fast closed up all the wombs of the house of Abimelech, because of Sarah Abraham's wife.

## 21 CHAPTER XXI

1. And the LORD remembered Sarah as He had said, and the LORD did unto Sarah as He had spoken. 2. And Sarah conceived, and bore Abraham a son in his old age, at the set time of which God had spoken to him. 3. And Abraham called the name of his son that was born unto him, whom Sarah bore to him, Isaac. 4. And Abraham circumcised his son Isaac when he was eight days old, as God had commanded him.\*v. 5. And Abraham was a hundred years old, when his son Isaac was born unto him. 6. And Sarah said: 'God hath made laughter for me; every one that heareth will laugh on account of me.' 7. And she said: 'Who would have said unto Abraham, that Sarah should give children suck? for I have borne him a son in his old age.' ¶ 8. And the child grew, and was weaned. And Abraham made a great feast on the day that Isaac was weaned. 9. And Sarah saw the son of Hagar the

---

**13.** *God caused me to wander.* The verb is in the plural, which is sometimes used when an Israelite speaks to a heathen; cf. also XXXI, 53. It may also be the 'plural of Majesty', cf. I, 26.

**15.** *my land.* This offer is to be contrasted with the action of Pharaoh in XII, 19 f.

**16.** *a thousand pieces of silver.* This is not mentioned in v. 14; probably an additional personal gift.

*a covering of the eyes.* Figurative for 'justification'; to make them blind to the wrong which had been done her.

CHAPTER XXI, 1–21. ISAAC AND ISHMAEL

**1.** *as He had said.* See XV, 4; XVIII, 10.

**2.** *at the set time.* See XVIII, 14.

**3.** *Isaac.* See XVII, 19.

**6.** *laughter.* i.e. joy; an additional reason why the name Isaac was appropriate for the child.
*laugh...me.* i.e. rejoice with me.

**8.** *the child...was weaned.* Usually at two or even three years; cf. II Maccabees, VII, 26. Weaning a child is in the East still made the occasion of a family feast.

GENESIS XXI, 10     בראשית וירא כא

Egyptian, whom she had borne unto Abraham, making sport. 10. Wherefore she said unto Abraham: 'Cast out this bondwoman and her son; for the son of this bondwoman shall not be heir with my son, even with Isaac.' 11. And the thing was very grievous in Abraham's sight on account of his son. 12. And God said unto Abraham: 'Let it not be grievous in thy sight because of the lad, and because of thy bondwoman; in all that Sarah saith unto thee, hearken unto her voice; for in Isaac shall seed be called to thee. 13. And also of the son of the bondwoman will I make a nation, because he is thy seed.' 14. And Abraham rose up early in the morning, and took bread and a bottle of water, and gave it unto Hagar, putting it on her shoulder, and the child, and sent her away; and she departed, and strayed in the wilderness of Beer-sheba. 15. And the water in the bottle was spent, and she cast the child under one of the shrubs. 16. And she went, and sat her down over against him a good way off, as it were a bowshot; for she said: 'Let me not look upon the death of the child.' And she sat over against him, and lifted up her voice, and wept. 17. And God heard the voice of the lad; and the angel of God called to Hagar out of heaven, and said unto her: 'What aileth thee, Hagar? fear not; for God hath heard the voice of the lad where he is. 18. Arise, lift up the lad, and hold him fast by thy hand; for I will make him a great nation.' 19. And God opened her eyes, and she saw a well of water; and she went, and filled the bottle with water, and gave the lad drink. 20. And God was with the lad, and he grew; and he dwelt in the wilderness, and became an archer. 21. And he dwelt

---

**9.** *making sport.* 'Mocking' (RV). The Heb. term usually refers to an act of impurity or idolatry. Or, 'Ishmael laughed derisively at the feasting and rejoicing over the child Isaac, inasmuch as he was the elder son and the heir to his father's estate. Hence Sarah's natural desire to drive him out of the house' (Ehrlich).

**11.** *the thing was very grievous.* For Abraham was attached to Ishmael; see XVII, 18.

**12.** *God said unto Abraham.* Probably in a dream during the night; cf. v. 14.

*in Isaac shall seed be called to thee.* Isaac was to be the Patriarch's heir; and consequently Abraham might act upon Sarah's wish, and send Ishmael away, thus avoiding any dispute later on concerning the inheritance.

**14.** *Bottle of water.* Still used in the East.
*and the child.* Abarbanel shows that the Heb. text can be translated to mean that both Hagar and the lad carried the food and water.

*wilderness of Beer-sheba.* The town Beer-sheba, in the extreme South of Palestine, is situated on the border of the desert.

**15.** *one of the shrubs.* To protect him from the fierce sun.

**16.** *as it were a bowshot.* i.e. within hearing.

**17.** *heard the voice of the lad.* God has pity on the anguish of the alien slave mother, and hears her prayer no less than that of an Abraham.
*where he is.* lit. 'as he now is'. The Rabbis deduce from this the doctrine that God, in answering prayer, judges the penitent worshipper *as he is at that moment of his penitence.*

**19.** *and God opened her eyes.* i.e. she now perceived the well of water which was quite near her,

## GENESIS XXI, 22    בראשית וירא כא

in the wilderness of Paran; and his mother took him a wife out of the land of Egypt.*vi.
¶ 22. And it came to pass at that time, that Abimelech and Phicol the captain of his host spoke unto Abraham, saying: 'God is with thee in all that thou doest. 23. Now therefore swear unto me here by God that thou wilt not deal falsely with me, nor with my son, nor with my son's son; but according to the kindness that I have done unto thee, thou shalt do unto me, and to the land wherein thou hast sojourned.' 24. And Abraham said: 'I will swear.' 25. And Abraham reproved Abimelech because of the well of water, which Abimelech's servants had violently taken away. 26. And Abimelech said: 'I know not who hath done this thing; neither didst thou tell me, neither yet heard I of it, but to-day.' 27. And Abraham took sheep and oxen, and gave them unto Abimelech; and they two made a covenant. 28. And Abraham set seven ewe-lambs of the flock by themselves. 29. And Abimelech said unto Abraham: 'What mean these seven ewe-lambs which thou hast set by themselves?' 30. And he said: 'Verily, these seven ewe-lambs shalt thou take of my hand, that it may be a witness unto me, that I have digged this well.' 31. Wherefore that place was called Beer-sheba; because there they swore both of them. 32. So they made a covenant at Beer-sheba; and Abimelech rose up, and Phicol the captain of his host, and they returned into the land of the Philistines. 33. And Abraham planted

but which in her anguish of mind she had overlooked. 'The Hebrew phrase *to open the eyes* is exclusively employed in the figurative sense of receiving new sources of knowledge, not in that of regaining the sense of sight' (Maimonides).

**21.** *wilderness of Paran.* See on XIV, 6.
*his mother took him a wife.* It was usually the concern of the parent to find a wife for the son, cf. XXIV, 3 f; XXXIV, 4.
*out of the land of Egypt.* Her native land.

v. 22-34. ALLIANCE BETWEEN ABRAHAM AND ABIMELECH

**22.** *God is with thee.* Evidenced by the birth of a son to the Patriarch in his old age.

**23.** *here.* In this place, *i.e.* Beer-sheba.
*kindness.* Referring to gifts and permission to dwell in the land, see XX, 14 f.

**25.** *reproved.* While agreeing to the suggested alliance, Abraham stated a grievance; cf. Lev. XIX, 17, 'Thou shalt not hate thy brother in thy heart; thou shalt surely rebuke thy neighbour.'

**27.** *sheep and oxen.* The exchange of gifts on making a treaty.

**30.** *witness.* The acceptance of the lambs would be equivalent to acknowledging Abraham's right to the possession of the well.

**31.** *Beer-sheba.* The name is given a double etymology; 'the well of seven (lambs)' and 'the well of swearing'.

**33.** *and called there on the name of the* LORD. See on XII, 8.
It is noteworthy that the story of Hagar and Ishmael is the Reading for the First Day of Rosh Hashanah; while the next chapter, the intended Sacrifice of Isaac, is read on the Second Day. The highest manifestation of the Divine is not to be found in the calling into existence of Nature's elemental forces; far higher are God's ways manifest in the hearts and souls of men, in the home life of those who do justice, love mercy, and walk humbly with their God.

GENESIS XXI, 34

a tamarisk-tree in Beer-sheba, and called there on the name of the LORD, the Everlasting God. 34. And Abraham sojourned in the land of the Philistines many days.*ᵛⁱⁱ

## CHAPTER XXII

1. And it came to pass after these things, that God did prove Abraham, and said unto him: 'Abraham'; and he said: 'Here am I.' 2. And He said: 'Take now thy son, thine only son, whom thou lovest, even Isaac, and get thee into the land of Moriah; and offer him there for a burnt-offering upon one of the mountains which I will tell thee of.' 3. And Abraham rose early in the morning, and saddled his ass, and took two of his young men with him, and Isaac his son; and he cleaved the wood for the burnt-offering, and rose up, and went unto the place of which God had told him. 4. On the third day Abraham lifted up his eyes, and saw the place afar off. 5. And Abraham said unto his young men: 'Abide ye here with the ass, and I and the lad will go yonder; and we will worship, and come back to you.' 6. And Abraham took the wood of the burnt-offering, and laid it upon Isaac his son; and he took in his hand the fire and the knife; and they went both of them together. 7. And Isaac spoke unto Abraham his father, and said: 'My father.' And he said:

### CHAPTER XXII
#### THE BINDING OF ISAAC

On the great importance of this chapter, see "THE AKEDAH", p. 201.

**1.** *prove.* The Authorised Version has the older English 'tempt', *i.e.* test; a trial (in older English, 'a temptation') is that which puts to the test. A test is never employed for the purpose of injury, but to certify the power of resistance. All his other trials of faith were to be crowned by Abraham's willingness to sacrifice his dearest hope to the will of God. The Rabbis speak of it as the tenth and the greatest of the trials to which he was exposed.

*and said unto him.* From v. 3 we may deduce that God communicated with Abraham during the night, perhaps in a vision.

**2.** *take now.* The Heb. is peculiar: the imperative 'take' is followed by the Heb. particle נא which means, 'I pray thee'—God was speaking to Abraham 'as friend to friend'.

*thy son, thine only son, whom thou lovest, even Isaac.* The repetition indicates the intense strain that was being placed upon Abraham's faith, and the greatness of the sacrifice demanded.

*the land of Moriah.* Jewish Tradition identifies the locality with the Temple Mount (II Chron. III, 1).

*and offer him there.* lit. 'lift him up' (upon the altar). God, in His command, did not use the word which signifies the *slaying* of the sacrificial victim. From the outset, therefore, there was no intention of accepting a human sacrifice, although Abraham was at first not aware of this.

**3.** *and Abraham rose early in the morning.* There is no response in words on the part of Abraham. His answer is in deeds. He lost no time in obeying the will of God.

*cleaved the wood.* This task, usually left to a servant to perform, he now did himself.

**5.** *abide ye here.* Desiring to be alone with Isaac at the dread moment of sacrifice.

*and come back.* Was there an undercurrent of conviction that God would not exact His demand of him? The Rabbis declare that at the moment the Spirit of Prophecy entered into him, and he spoke more truly than he knew.

**6.** *the fire.* i.e. the vessel containing glowing embers, by means of which the wood on the altar was to be kindled.

**7.** *the lamb for a burnt offering.* This simple expression of boyish curiosity heightens the intense pathos of the situation.

## GENESIS XXII, 8

בראשית וירא כב

'Here am I, my son.' And he said: 'Behold the fire and the wood; but where is the lamb for a burnt-offering?" 8. And Abraham said: 'God will ¹provide Himself the lamb for a burnt-offering, my son.' So they went both of them together. 9. And they came to the place which God had told him of; and Abraham built the altar there, and laid the wood in order, and bound Isaac his son, and laid him on the altar, upon the wood. 10. And Abraham stretched forth his hand, and took the knife to slay his son. 11. And the angel of the LORD called unto him out of heaven, and said: 'Abraham, Abraham.' And he said: 'Here am I.' 12. And he said: 'Lay not thy hand upon the lad, neither do thou any thing unto him; for now I know that thou art a God-fearing man, seeing thou hast not withheld thy son, thine only son, from Me.' 13. And Abraham lifted up his eyes, and looked, and behold behind him a ram caught in the thicket by his horns. And Abraham went and took the ram, and offered him up for a burnt-offering in the stead of his son. 14. And Abraham called the name of that place ²Adonaijireh; as it is said to this day: 'In the mount where the LORD is seen.' 15. And the angel of the LORD called unto Abraham a second time out of heaven, 16. and said: 'By Myself have I sworn, saith the LORD, because thou hast done this thing, and hast not withheld thy son, thine only son, 17. that in blessing I will bless thee, and in multiplying I will multiply thy seed as the stars of the heaven, and as the sand which is upon the sea-shore; and thy seed shall possess the gate of his enemies; 18. and in thy seed shall all the nations of the earth be blessed; because thou hast hearkened to My voice.' 19. So Abraham returned

8 הָאֵשׁ וְהָעֵצִים וְאַיֵּה הַשֶּׂה לְעֹלָה: וַיֹּאמֶר אַבְרָהָם אֱלֹהִים
9 יִרְאֶה־לּוֹ הַשֶּׂה לְעֹלָה בְּנִי וַיֵּלְכוּ שְׁנֵיהֶם יַחְדָּו: וַיָּבֹאוּ
אֶל־הַמָּקוֹם אֲשֶׁר אָמַר־לוֹ הָאֱלֹהִים וַיִּבֶן שָׁם אַבְרָהָם
אֶת־הַמִּזְבֵּחַ וַיַּעֲרֹךְ אֶת־הָעֵצִים וַיַּעֲקֹד אֶת־יִצְחָק בְּנוֹ וַיָּשֶׂם
י אֹתוֹ עַל־הַמִּזְבֵּחַ מִמַּעַל לָעֵצִים: וַיִּשְׁלַח אַבְרָהָם אֶת־
11 יָדוֹ וַיִּקַּח אֶת־הַמַּאֲכֶלֶת לִשְׁחֹט אֶת־בְּנוֹ: וַיִּקְרָא אֵלָיו
מַלְאַךְ יְהֹוָה מִן־הַשָּׁמַיִם וַיֹּאמֶר אַבְרָהָם | אַבְרָהָם וַיֹּאמֶר
12 הִנֵּנִי: וַיֹּאמֶר אַל־תִּשְׁלַח יָדְךָ אֶל־הַנַּעַר וְאַל־תַּעַשׂ לוֹ
מְאוּמָה כִּי | עַתָּה יָדַעְתִּי כִּי־יְרֵא אֱלֹהִים אַתָּה וְלֹא חָשַׂכְתָּ
13 אֶת־בִּנְךָ אֶת־יְחִידְךָ מִמֶּנִּי: וַיִּשָּׂא אַבְרָהָם אֶת־עֵינָיו וַיַּרְא
וְהִנֵּה־אַיִל אַחַר נֶאֱחַז בַּסְּבַךְ בְּקַרְנָיו וַיֵּלֶךְ אַבְרָהָם וַיִּקַּח
14 אֶת־הָאַיִל וַיַּעֲלֵהוּ לְעֹלָה תַּחַת בְּנוֹ: וַיִּקְרָא אַבְרָהָם שֵׁם־
הַמָּקוֹם הַהוּא יְהֹוָה | יִרְאֶה אֲשֶׁר יֵאָמֵר הַיּוֹם בְּהַר יְהֹוָה
טו יֵרָאֶה: וַיִּקְרָא מַלְאַךְ יְהֹוָה אֶל־אַבְרָהָם שֵׁנִית מִן־הַשָּׁמָיִם:
16 וַיֹּאמֶר בִּי נִשְׁבַּעְתִּי נְאֻם־יְהֹוָה כִּי יַעַן אֲשֶׁר עָשִׂיתָ אֶת־
17 הַדָּבָר הַזֶּה וְלֹא חָשַׂכְתָּ אֶת־בִּנְךָ אֶת־יְחִידֶךָ: כִּי־בָרֵךְ
אֲבָרֶכְךָ וְהַרְבָּה אַרְבֶּה אֶת־זַרְעֲךָ כְּכוֹכְבֵי הַשָּׁמַיִם וְכַחוֹל
אֲשֶׁר עַל־שְׂפַת הַיָּם וְיִרַשׁ זַרְעֲךָ אֵת שַׁעַר אֹיְבָיו: וְהִתְבָּרְכוּ
18
19 בְזַרְעֲךָ כֹּל גּוֹיֵי הָאָרֶץ עֵקֶב אֲשֶׁר שָׁמַעְתָּ בְּקֹלִי: וַיָּשָׁב
אַבְרָהָם אֶל־נְעָרָיו וַיָּקֻמוּ וַיֵּלְכוּ יַחְדָּו אֶל־בְּאֵר שָׁבַע

v. 10. סגול באתנח

---

¹ Heb. *jireh*; that is, *see for Himself.* ² That is, *The LORD seeth.*

---

**8.** *so they went both of them together.* This phrase is repeated from *v.* 6. Abraham's answer caused the truth to dawn upon Isaac's mind that *he* was to be the offering.

**9.** *bound.* Tied together the limbs.

**11.** *Abraham, Abraham.* This exclamation (Abraham, Abraham!) shows the anxiety of the angel of the Lord to hold Abraham back at the very last moment.

**12.** *now I know.* All that God desired was proof of Abraham's *willingness* to obey His command; and the moral surrender had been complete.

**14.** *to this day.* i.e. it has become a proverbial expression.

*where the* LORD *is seen.* i.e. where He reveals himself—referring to the Temple, which was afterwards erected on this mount.

**16.** *by Myself have I sworn.* Moses referred to this oath when he pleaded for Israel; see Exod. XXXII, 13. The expression is the equivalent of, 'as I live, saith the Lord,' Num. XIV, 28, and elsewhere.

**17.** *as the sand which is upon the sea-shore.* 'As the sand has been placed as a boundary for the sea, and though the waves thereof roar and toss themselves, yet can they not prevail (Jer. V, 22), so would multitudes of enemies strive in vain to destroy Abraham's descendants; *but thy seed shall possess, etc.*' (Malbim); cf. XXXII, 13.

*possess the gate of his enemies.* Cf. XXIV, 60. The 'gate' of the city was its most important site (see on XIX, 1), and its capture gave one command of the city.

**18.** *be blessed.* See on XII, 2.

## GENESIS XXII, 20 — בראשית וירא כב

מפטיר

כ וַיֵּ֥שֶׁב אַבְרָהָ֖ם בִּבְאֵ֥ר שָֽׁבַע׃ פ וַיְהִ֗י אַחֲרֵי֙ הַדְּבָרִ֣ים הָאֵ֔לֶּה וַיֻּגַּ֥ד לְאַבְרָהָ֖ם לֵאמֹ֑ר הִנֵּ֨ה

כא יָלְדָ֤ה מִלְכָּה֙ גַם־הִ֔וא בָּנִ֖ים לְנָח֥וֹר אָחִֽיךָ׃ אֶת־ע֥וּץ בְּכֹר֖וֹ

כב וְאֶת־בּ֣וּז אָחִ֑יו וְאֶת־קְמוּאֵ֖ל אֲבִ֥י אֲרָֽם׃ וְאֶת־כֶּ֣שֶׂד וְאֶת־חֲז֔וֹ

כג וְאֶת־פִּלְדָּ֖שׁ וְאֶת־יִדְלָ֑ף וְאֵ֖ת בְּתוּאֵֽל׃ וּבְתוּאֵ֖ל יָלַ֣ד אֶת־ רִבְקָ֑ה שְׁמֹנָ֥ה אֵ֙לֶּה֙ יָלְדָ֣ה מִלְכָּ֔ה לְנָח֖וֹר אֲחִ֥י אַבְרָהָֽם׃

כד וּפִֽילַגְשׁ֖וֹ וּשְׁמָ֣הּ רְאוּמָ֑ה וַתֵּ֤לֶד גַּם־הִוא֙ אֶת־טֶ֣בַח וְאֶת־ גַּ֔חַם וְאֶת־תַּ֖חַשׁ וְאֶת־מַעֲכָֽה׃

unto his young men, and they rose up and went together to Beer-sheba; and Abraham dwelt at Beer-sheba.*m· ¶ 20. And it came to pass after these things, that it was told Abraham, saying: 'Behold, Milcah, she also hath borne children unto thy brother Nahor: 21. Uz his first-born, and Buz his brother, and Kemuel the father of Aram; 22. and Chesed, and Hazo, and Pildash, and Jidlaph, and Bethuel.' 23. And Bethuel begot Rebekah; these eight did Milcah bear to Nahor, Abraham's brother. 24. And his concubine, whose name was Reumah, she also bore Tebah, and Gaham, and Tahash, and Maacah.

**20–24.** These verses are inserted to give the genealogy of Rebekah, whose life was to be linked with Isaac's.

**20.** *Milcah* and *Nahor*. See XI, 29.

**22.** *Bethuel*. Mentioned again in Chap. XXIV.

## HAFTORAH VAYYERA — הפטרת וירא

### II KINGS IV, 1–37

CAP. IV. ד

#### CHAPTER IV

א וְאִשָּׁ֣ה אַחַ֣ת מִנְּשֵׁ֣י בְנֵֽי־הַ֠נְּבִיאִים צָעֲקָ֨ה אֶל־אֱלִישָׁ֜ע לֵאמֹ֗ר עַבְדְּךָ֤ אִישִׁי֙ מֵ֔ת וְאַתָּ֣ה יָדַ֔עְתָּ כִּ֣י עַבְדְּךָ֔ הָיָ֥ה יָרֵ֖א אֶת־יְהוָ֑ה וְהַ֨נֹּשֶׁ֔ה בָּ֗א לָקַ֜חַת אֶת־שְׁנֵ֧י יְלָדַ֛י ל֖וֹ לַעֲבָדִֽים׃

ב וַיֹּ֨אמֶר אֵלֶ֤יהָ אֱלִישָׁע֙ מָ֣ה אֶֽעֱשֶׂה־לָּ֔ךְ הַגִּ֣ידִי לִ֔י מַה־יֶּשׁ־ לכי בַּבָּ֑יִת וַתֹּ֗אמֶר אֵ֣ין לְשִׁפְחָתְךָ֥ כֹל֙ בַּבַּ֔יִת כִּ֖י אִם־אָס֥וּךְ

ג שָֽׁמֶן׃ וַיֹּ֗אמֶר לְכִ֨י שַׁאֲלִי־לָ֤ךְ כֵּלִים֙ מִן־הַח֔וּץ מֵאֵ֖ת כָּל־

ד v. 2. לך קרי

1. Now there cried a certain woman of the wives of the sons of the prophets unto Elisha, saying: 'Thy servant my husband is dead; and thou knowest that thy servant did fear the LORD; and the creditor is come to take unto him my two children to be bondmen.' 2. And Elisha said unto her: 'What shall I do for thee? tell me; what hast thou in the house?' And she said: 'Thy handmaid hath not any thing in the house, save a pot of oil.' 3. Then he said: 'Go,

### II KINGS IV, 1–37

The parallel between the Sedrah and Haftorah is clear. The Prophet Elisha, like Abraham, seeks every opportunity to practise lovingkindness and bring relief and blessing wherever he goes in the course of his ministrations. Even more does the story of the Shunammite and her child recall the story of Sarah. Both occurrences were 'Providential' happenings. The Haftorah teaches that there is Divine control of human conditions, and that many humanly unaccountable things happen in life.

#### 1–7. THE WIDOW'S POT OF OIL

This story is one of a cycle of miraculous tales that relate the activities of Elisha, the disciple of the great Prophet Elijah.

**1.** *a certain woman.* According to tradition, she was the widow of Obadiah (I Kings XVIII, 3) the god-fearing minister of king Ahab, who fed and sheltered the Prophets when Jezebel persecuted them. Was her poverty due to the burden of debt with which Obadiah had loaded himself in order to save the Prophets of the LORD from the hands of the murderous Jezebel?

*sons of the prophets.* i.e. members of a guild, or company, of disciples of the Prophets.

*creditor.* Throughout antiquity the children of the debtor could be 'collected' instead of the debt.

## II KINGS IV, 4

borrow thee vessels abroad of all thy neighbours, even empty vessels; borrow not a few. 4. And thou shalt go in, and shut the door upon thee and upon thy sons, and pour out into all those vessels; and thou shalt set aside that which is full.' 5. So she went from him, and shut the door upon her and upon her sons; they brought the vessels to her, and she poured out. 6. And it came to pass, when the vessels were full, that she said unto her son: 'Bring me yet a vessel.' And he said unto her: 'There is not a vessel more.' And the oil stayed. 7. Then she came and told the man of God. And he said: 'Go, sell the oil, and pay thy debt, and live thou and thy sons of the rest.' ¶ 8. And it fell on a day, that Elisha passed to Shunem, where was a great woman; and she constrained him to eat bread. And so it was, that as oft as he passed by, he turned in thither to eat bread. 9. And she said unto her husband: 'Behold now, I perceive that this is a holy man of God, that passeth by us continually. 10. Let us make, I pray thee, a little chamber on the roof; and let us set for him there a bed, and a table, and a stool, and a candlestick; and it shall be, when he cometh to us, that he shall turn in thither.' 11. And it fell on a day, that he came thither, and he turned into the upper chamber and lay there. 12. And he said to Gehazi his servant: 'Call this Shunammite.' And when he had called her, she stood before him. 13. And he said unto him: 'Say now unto her: Behold, thou hast been careful for us with all this care; what is to be done for thee? wouldest thou be spoken for to the king, or to the captain of the host?' And she answered: 'I dwell among mine own people.' 14. And he said: 'What then is to be done for her?' And Gehazi answered: 'Verily she hath no son, and her husband is old.' 15. And he said: 'Call her.' And when he had called her, she stood in the door. 16. And he said: 'At this season, when the time cometh round, thou shalt embrace a son.' And she said: 'Nay, my lord, thou man of God, do not lie unto thy handmaid.' 17. And the woman conceived, and bore a son at that season, when the time came round, as Elisha had said unto her. ¶ 18. And when the child was grown, it fell on

4 שְׁכֵנַיִכְ֙י כֵּלִ֤ים רֵקִים֙ אַל־תַּמְעִ֔יטִי׃ וּבָ֗את וְסָגַ֤רְתְּ הַדֶּ֙לֶת֙
בַּעֲדֵ֣ךְ וּבְעַד־בָּנַ֔יִךְ וְיָצַ֕קְתְּ עַ֥ל כָּל־הַכֵּלִ֖ים הָאֵ֑לֶּה וְהַמָּלֵ֖א
5 תַּסִּֽיעִי׃ וַתֵּ֣לֶךְ מֵֽאִתּ֔וֹ וַתִּסְגֹּ֣ר הַדֶּ֔לֶת בַּעֲדָ֖הּ וּבְעַ֣ד בָּנֶ֑יהָ
6 הֵ֣ם מַגִּישִׁ֣ים אֵלֶ֔יהָ וְהִ֖יא מוֹצָֽקֶת׃ וַיְהִ֣י ׀ כִּמְלֹ֣את הַכֵּלִ֗ים
וַתֹּ֤אמֶר אֶל־בְּנָהּ֙ הַגִּ֤ישָׁה אֵלַי֙ ע֣וֹד כֶּ֔לִי וַיֹּ֣אמֶר אֵלֶ֔יהָ אֵ֥ין
7 ע֛וֹד כֶּ֖לִי וַֽיַּעֲמֹ֥ד הַשָּֽׁמֶן׃ וַתָּבֹ֗א וַתַּגֵּד֙ לְאִ֣ישׁ הָאֱלֹהִ֔ים
וַיֹּ֗אמֶר לְכִי֙ מִכְרִ֣י אֶת־הַשֶּׁ֔מֶן וְשַׁלְּמִ֖י אֶת־נִשְׁיֵ֑ךְ וְאַ֣תְּ
8 בָּנַ֔יִךְ תִּֽחְיִ֖י בַּנּוֹתָֽר׃ ¶ וַיְהִ֨י הַיּ֜וֹם וַיַּעֲבֹ֧ר אֱלִישָׁ֣ע
אֶל־שׁוּנֵ֗ם וְשָׁם֙ אִשָּׁ֣ה גְדוֹלָ֔ה וַתַּחֲזֶק־בּ֖וֹ לֶאֱכָל־לָ֑חֶם וַיְהִ֣י
9 מִדֵּ֣י עָבְר֔וֹ יָסֻ֥ר שָׁ֖מָּה לֶאֱכָל־לָֽחֶם׃ וַתֹּ֙אמֶר֙ אֶל־אִישָׁ֔הּ
הִנֵּה־נָ֣א יָדַ֔עְתִּי כִּ֛י אִ֥ישׁ אֱלֹהִ֖ים קָד֑וֹשׁ ה֥וּא עֹבֵ֛ר עָלֵ֖ינוּ
10 תָּמִֽיד׃ נַֽעֲשֶׂה־נָּ֤א עֲלִיַּת־קִיר֙ קְטַנָּ֔ה וְנָשִׂ֨ים ל֥וֹ שָׁ֖ם מִטָּ֥ה
וְשֻׁלְחָ֣ן וְכִסֵּ֣א וּמְנוֹרָ֑ה וְהָיָ֛ה בְּבֹא֥וֹ אֵלֵ֖ינוּ יָס֥וּר שָֽׁמָּה׃
11 וַיְהִ֥י הַיּ֖וֹם וַיָּ֣בֹא שָׁ֑מָּה וַיָּ֥סַר אֶל־הָעֲלִיָּ֖ה וַיִּשְׁכַּב־שָֽׁמָּה׃
12 וַיֹּ֙אמֶר֙ אֶל־גֵּחֲזִ֣י נַעֲר֔וֹ קְרָ֖א לַשּׁוּנַמִּ֣ית הַזֹּ֑את וַיִּקְרָא־
13 לָ֔הּ וַֽתַּעֲמֹ֖ד לְפָנָֽיו׃ וַיֹּ֣אמֶר ל֗וֹ אֱמָר־נָ֣א אֵלֶיהָ֮ הִנֵּ֣ה
חָרַ֣דְתְּ ׀ אֵלֵינוּ֮ אֶת־כָּל־הַחֲרָדָ֣ה הַזֹּאת֒ מֶ֚ה לַעֲשׂ֣וֹת לָ֔ךְ
הֲיֵ֤שׁ לְדַבֶּר־לָךְ֙ אֶל־הַמֶּ֔לֶךְ א֖וֹ אֶל־שַׂ֣ר הַצָּבָ֑א וַתֹּ֕אמֶר
14 בְּת֥וֹךְ עַמִּ֖י אָנֹכִ֥י יֹשָֽׁבֶת׃ וַיֹּ֕אמֶר וּמֶ֖ה לַעֲשׂ֣וֹת לָ֑הּ וַיֹּ֣אמֶר
15 גֵּיחֲזִ֗י אֲבָ֛ל בֵּ֥ן אֵֽין־לָ֖הּ וְאִישָׁ֥הּ זָקֵֽן׃ וַיֹּ֖אמֶר קְרָא־לָ֑הּ
16 וַיִּקְרָא־לָ֔הּ וַֽתַּעֲמֹ֖ד בַּפָּֽתַח׃ וַיֹּ֗אמֶר לַמּוֹעֵ֤ד הַזֶּה֙ כָּעֵ֣ת
חַיָּ֔ה אַ֖תְּ חֹבֶ֣קֶת בֵּ֑ן וַתֹּ֗אמֶר אַל־אֲדֹנִי֙ אִ֣ישׁ הָאֱלֹהִ֔ים
17 אַל־תְּכַזֵּ֖ב בְּשִׁפְחָתֶֽךָ׃ וַתַּ֥הַר הָאִשָּׁ֖ה וַתֵּ֣לֶד בֵּ֑ן לַמּוֹעֵ֣ד
18 הַזֶּ֞ה כָּעֵ֤ת חַיָּה֙ אֲשֶׁר־דִּבֶּ֣ר אֵלֶ֔יהָ אֱלִישָֽׁע׃ וַיִּגְדַּ֖ל הַיָּ֑לֶד

v. 3. שכניך ק'. v. 5. מוצקת קרי. v. 7. נשיך ק'. ibid. ובניך ק'. v. 16. את ק'.

**7.** *man of God.* Popular term for 'Prophet'.
*go, sell the oil, and pay thy debt.* An ethical rule of Jewish conduct: first pay thy debts, afterwards minister to thine own needs.

### 8-37. THE SHUNAMMITE'S SON

**8.** *a great woman.* i.e. a woman of substance and worth. She joyfully extended hospitality to the Prophet on his frequent journeys through that district.

**13.** *careful for us with all this care.* 'Showed us all this reverence' (RV Margin).
*I dwell among mine own people.* Among her own relatives; and she wished so to continue. She had no need for influence to be used on her behalf with the king or his officers (Rashi).

II KINGS IV, 19

a day, that he went out to his father to the reapers. 19. And he said unto his father: 'My head, my head.' And he said to his servant: 'Carry him to his mother.' 20. And when he had taken him, and brought him to his mother, he sat on her knees till noon, and then died. 21. And she went up, and laid him on the bed of the man of God, and shut the door upon him, and went out. 22. And she called unto her husband, and said: 'Send me, I pray thee, one of the servants, and one of the asses, that I may run to the man of God, and come back.' 23. And he said: 'Wherefore wilt thou go to him to-day? it is neither new moon nor sabbath.' And she said: 'It shall be well.'¹ 24. Then she saddled an ass, and said to her servant: 'Drive, and go forward; slacken me not the riding, except I bid thee.' 25. So she went, and came unto the man of God to mount Carmel. ¶ And it came to pass, when the man of God saw her afar off, that he said to Gehazi his servant: 'Behold, yonder is that Shunammite. 26. Run, I pray thee, now to meet her, and say unto her: Is it well with thee? is it well with thy husband? is it well with the child?' And she answered: 'It is well.' 27. And when she came to the man of God to the hill, she caught hold of his feet. And Gehazi came near to thrust her away; but the man of God said: 'Let her alone; for her soul is bitter within her; and the LORD hath hid it from me, and hath not told me.' 28. Then she said: 'Did I desire a son of my lord? did I not say: Do not deceive me?' 29. Then he said to Gehazi: 'Gird up thy loins, and take my staff in thy hand, and go thy way; if thou meet any man, salute him not; and if any salute thee, answer him not; and lay my staff upon the face of the child.' 30. And the

---

¹ Sephardim conclude here.

**19.** *my head, my head.* Heb. *roshi, roshi.* A marvellously vivid description of the child's sunstroke, and in two Heb. words!

**23.** *new moon.* This points to a custom of the time to make pilgrimages to the Prophet or to the sanctuary on Sabbaths and New Moons.
*it shall be well.* Expressed in one Heb. word, 'Shalom.' We have no sound of wailing: with perfect self-control and vivid faith the Shunammite woman hastens to the Prophet.

**25.** *yonder is that Shunammite.* He is surprised at her unexpected visit.

**26.** *Is it well with thee?* All mothers and fathers might well ask themselves these three soul-searching questions. השלום לך *Is it well with thee?* lit. 'Is peace thine?' Are you at peace with yourself, your conscience, your God? *Is it well with thy husband?* i.e. is it well with your home? Is it still a Jewish home, a sanctuary? *Is it well with the child?* In the Sedrah, Abraham and Isaac are called upon to tread the path of supreme sacrifice; yet Scripture records of father and son, 'And they walked both of them together.' Is there similar unity of heart and soul between you and *your* child? Education is the shibboleth of the hour; but in Judaism the word for 'education' (חינוך) is the same as for 'consecration'. Is your child being *consecrated* for a life of beneficence for Israel and humanity?

'The object of education is not merely to enable our children to gain their daily bread and to acquire pleasant means of recreation, but that they should know God and serve Him with earnestness and devotion. Are you thus training your children? Is it your care that they be

## II KINGS IV, 31

mother of the child said: 'As the Lord liveth, and as thy soul liveth, I will not leave thee.' And he arose, and followed her. 31. And Gehazi passed on before them, and laid the staff upon the face of the child; but there was neither voice, nor hearing. Wherefore he returned to meet him, and told him, saying: 'The child is not awaked.' ¶ 32. And when Elisha was come into the house, behold, the child was dead, and laid upon his bed. 33. He went in therefore, and shut the door upon them twain, and prayed unto the Lord. 34. And he went up, and lay upon the child, and put his mouth upon his mouth, and his eyes upon his eyes, and his hands upon his hands; and he stretched himself upon him; and the flesh of the child waxed warm. 35. Then he returned, and walked in the house once to and fro; and went up, and stretched himself upon him; and the child sneezed seven times, and the child opened his eyes. 36. And he called Gehazi, and said: 'Call this Shunammite.' So he called her. And when she was come in unto him, he said: 'Take up thy son.' 37. Then she went in, and fell at his feet, and bowed down to the ground; and she took up her son, and went out.

---

educated as Jews and Jewesses?' (Hermann Adler).

*it is well.* A mere affirmative; she will lay bare her grief only when she is alone with the Prophet.

**29.** *salute him not.* To avoid waste of time.

**31.** *voice, nor hearing.* No sign of life.

**35.** We may find deep suggestion in the restoration of the Shunammite's child to life. The child was revived by contact with the living warmth of the Prophet's body. Thus has Israel throughout the ages survived a thousand deaths, because his soul was ever quickened into life by direct contact with the Divine teaching of Israel's Lawgiver, Prophets, and Sages.

## GENESIS XXIII, 1 — בראשית חיי שרה כג

### CHAPTER XXIII / CAP. XXIII. כג

פ פ פ ה ס 5

1. And the life of Sarah was a hundred and seven and twenty years; these were the years of the life of Sarah. 2. And Sarah died in Kiriath-arba—the same is Hebron—in the land of Canaan; and Abraham came to mourn for Sarah, and to weep for her. 3. And Abraham rose up from before his dead, and spoke unto the children of Heth, saying: 4. 'I am a stranger and a sojourner with you; give me a possession of a burying-place with you, that I may bury my dead out of my sight.' 5. And the children of Heth answered Abraham, saying unto him: 6. 'Hear us, my lord: thou art a mighty prince among us; in the choice of our sepulchres bury thy dead; none of us shall withhold from thee his sepulchre, but that thou mayest bury thy dead.' 7. And Abraham rose up, and bowed down to the people of the land, even to the children of Heth. 8. And he spoke with them, saying: 'If it be your mind that I should bury my dead out of my sight,

א וַיִּהְיוּ֙ חַיֵּ֣י שָׂרָ֔ה מֵאָ֥ה שָׁנָ֛ה וְעֶשְׂרִ֥ים שָׁנָ֖ה וְשֶׁ֣בַע שָׁנִ֑ים
2 שְׁנֵ֖י חַיֵּ֥י שָׂרָֽה: וַתָּ֣מָת שָׂרָ֗ה בְּקִרְיַ֥ת אַרְבַּ֛ע הִ֥וא חֶבְר֖וֹן
בְּאֶ֣רֶץ כְּנָ֑עַן וַיָּבֹא֙ אַבְרָהָ֔ם לִסְפֹּ֥ד לְשָׂרָ֖ה וְלִבְכֹּתָֽהּ:
3 וַיָּ֨קָם֙ אַבְרָהָ֔ם מֵעַ֖ל פְּנֵ֣י מֵת֑וֹ וַיְדַבֵּ֥ר אֶל־בְּנֵי־חֵ֖ת לֵאמֹֽר:
4 גֵּר־וְתוֹשָׁ֥ב אָנֹכִ֖י עִמָּכֶ֑ם תְּנ֨וּ לִ֤י אֲחֻזַּת־קֶ֙בֶר֙ עִמָּכֶ֔ם וְאֶקְבְּרָ֥ה
ה מֵתִ֖י מִלְּפָנָֽי: וַיַּעֲנ֧וּ בְנֵי־חֵ֛ת אֶת־אַבְרָהָ֖ם לֵאמֹ֥ר ל֑וֹ: שְׁמָעֵ֣נוּ ׀
6 אֲדֹנִ֗י נְשִׂ֨יא אֱלֹהִ֤ים ׀ אַתָּה֙ בְּתוֹכֵ֔נוּ בְּמִבְחַ֣ר קְבָרֵ֔ינוּ קְבֹ֖ר
אֶת־מֵתֶ֑ךָ אִ֣ישׁ מִמֶּ֔נּוּ אֶת־קִבְר֛וֹ לֹֽא־יִכְלֶ֥ה מִמְּךָ֖ מִקְּבֹ֥ר
7 מֵתֶֽךָ: וַיָּ֧קָם אַבְרָהָ֛ם וַיִּשְׁתַּ֥חוּ לְעַם־הָאָ֖רֶץ לִבְנֵי־חֵֽת:
8 וַיְדַבֵּ֥ר אִתָּ֖ם לֵאמֹ֑ר אִם־יֵ֣שׁ אֶת־נַפְשְׁכֶ֗ם לִקְבֹּ֤ר אֶת־מֵתִי֙

v. 2. כ״ף זעירא

## V. CHAYYE SARAH

(CHAPTERS XXIII–XXV, 18)

### CHAPTER XXIII. DEATH AND BURIAL OF SARAH

**1.** *a hundred and seven and twenty years.* lit. 'a hundred years, and twenty years, and seven years'; and since the word 'year' is inserted after every figure, the Rabbis comment: 'She was as handsome at one hundred as at the age of twenty; and as sinless at twenty as at seven.' (This, according to Luzzatto and Berliner, was the original form of the saying.)

**2.** *Kiriath-arba.* lit. 'the city of four'. In Judges I, 10, it is stated that Kiriath-arba was the old name of Hebron, and in that city the Israelites slew three giant chieftains, the sons of a man named Arba (see Josh. xv, 13). Hence the city was named after Arba: or it signified the city of these *four* giants.

*Hebron.* See on XIII, 18.

*to mourn.* The Hebrew word indicates the loud wailing still usual in the East as a manifestation of grief.

**3.** *rose up.* This verb is used because the mourner sat and slept on the ground; see II Sam. XII, 16; Lam. II, 10.

*children of Heth.* i.e. the Hittites; see on x, 15.

**4.** *stranger and a sojourner.* A proverbial phrase describing one whose origin is foreign, and whose period of residence is uncertain (Ryle).

*out of my sight.* Better, 'from before me.'

This is the first reference in the Bible to burial; and the reverential concern which the Patriarch shows to give honourable sepulchre to his dead has been a distinguishing feature among his descendants. *Meth mitzvah*, care of the unburied body of a friendless man, takes precedence over all other commandments. Burial is the Jewish method of disposal of the dead. Tacitus (Hist. v, 5) remarked upon the fact that the Jews buried their dead, instead of burning them. Cremation has always been repugnant to Jewish feeling, and is at total variance with the law and custom of Israel.

**6–18.** The bargaining which follows, with grandiloquent phrases and lavish offers, not to be taken too seriously by the person addressed, is still typically Oriental.

**6.** *a mighty prince.* lit. 'a prince of God'; similarly, 'mountains of God' means 'great mountains'.

*in the choice of our sepulchres.* Family or tribal vaults were common in ancient times, and the Hittites gave Abraham permission to select any one of these vaults; but the Patriarch insists on a separate resting-place for his wife. He probably had the intention of being buried there himself. If such was his intention, it was fulfilled; see XLIX, 29 f.

**7.** *people of the land.* Heb. *Am ha-aretz*, which elsewhere means 'the people of the land', and in later Hebrew, 'an ignorant person,' here means the Council of the Hittites in session. Abraham desired to secure a burial place that should for ever

## GENESIS XXIII, 9

בראשית חיי שרה כג

9 מִלְּפָנַי שְׁמָעֹ֫ונִי וּפִגְעוּ־לִ֣י בְּעֶפְר֑וֹן בֶּן־צֹֽחַר: וְיִתֶּן־לִ֗י אֶת־
מְעָרַ֣ת הַמַּכְפֵּלָ֗ה אֲשֶׁר־לוֹ֙ אֲשֶׁ֣ר בִּקְצֵ֣ה שָׂדֵ֑הוּ בְּכֶ֨סֶף
מָלֵ֜א יִתְּנֶ֥נָּה לִ֛י בְּתוֹכְכֶ֖ם לַאֲחֻזַּת־קָֽבֶר: וְעֶפְר֥וֹן יֹשֵׁ֖ב בְּת֣וֹךְ
בְּנֵי־חֵ֑ת וַיַּעַן֩ עֶפְר֨וֹן הַחִתִּ֤י אֶת־אַבְרָהָם֙ בְּאָזְנֵ֣י בְנֵי־חֵ֔ת
11 לְכֹ֛ל בָּאֵ֥י שַֽׁעַר־עִיר֖וֹ לֵאמֹֽר: לֹֽא־אֲדֹנִ֣י שְׁמָעֵ֔נִי הַשָּׂדֶה֙
נָתַ֣תִּי לָ֔ךְ וְהַמְּעָרָ֥ה אֲשֶׁר־בּ֖וֹ לְךָ֣ נְתַתִּ֑יהָ לְעֵינֵ֧י בְנֵי־עַמִּ֛י
12 נְתַתִּ֥יהָ לָּ֖ךְ קְבֹ֥ר מֵתֶֽךָ: וַיִּשְׁתַּ֨חוּ֙ אַבְרָהָ֔ם לִפְנֵ֖י עַם־הָאָֽרֶץ:
13 וַיְדַבֵּ֨ר אֶל־עֶפְר֜וֹן בְּאָזְנֵ֤י עַם־הָאָ֨רֶץ֙ לֵאמֹ֔ר אַ֛ךְ אִם־אַתָּ֥ה
ל֖וּ שְׁמָעֵ֑נִי נָתַ֜תִּי כֶּ֤סֶף הַשָּׂדֶה֙ קַ֣ח מִמֶּ֔נִּי וְאֶקְבְּרָ֥ה אֶת־
14 מֵתִ֖י שָֽׁמָּה: וַיַּ֧עַן עֶפְר֛וֹן אֶת־אַבְרָהָ֖ם לֵאמֹ֥ר לֽוֹ: אֲדֹנִ֣י
15 שְׁמָעֵ֔נִי אֶרֶץ֩ אַרְבַּ֨ע מֵאֹ֧ת שֶֽׁקֶל־כֶּ֛סֶף בֵּינִ֥י וּבֵֽינְךָ֖ מַה־
16 הִ֑וא וְאֶת־מֵתְךָ֖ קְבֹֽר: וַיִּשְׁמַ֣ע אַבְרָהָם֮ אֶל־עֶפְרוֹן֒ וַיִּשְׁקֹ֤ל
אַבְרָהָם֙ לְעֶפְרֹ֔ן אֶת־הַכֶּ֕סֶף אֲשֶׁ֥ר דִּבֶּ֖ר בְּאָזְנֵ֣י בְנֵי־חֵ֑ת
17 אַרְבַּ֤ע מֵאוֹת֙ שֶׁ֣קֶל כֶּ֔סֶף עֹבֵ֖ר לַסֹּחֵֽר: וַיָּ֣קָם ׀ שְׂדֵ֣ה עֶפְר֗וֹן
אֲשֶׁר֙ בַּמַּכְפֵּלָ֔ה אֲשֶׁ֖ר לִפְנֵ֣י מַמְרֵ֑א הַשָּׂדֶה֙ וְהַמְּעָרָ֣ה אֲשֶׁר־

hear me, and entreat for me to Ephron the son of Zohar, 9. that he may give me the cave of Machpelah, which he hath, which is in the end of his field; for the full price let him give it to me in the midst of you for a possession of a burying-place.' 10. Now Ephron was sitting in the midst of the children of Heth; and Ephron the Hittite answered Abraham in the hearing of the children of Heth, even of all that went in at the gate of his city, saying: 11. 'Nay, my lord, hear me: the field give I thee, and the cave that is therein, I give it thee; in the presence of the sons of my people give I it thee; bury thy dead.' 12. And Abraham bowed down before the people of the land. 13. And he spoke unto Ephron in the hearing of the people of the land, saying: 'But if thou wilt, I pray thee, hear me: I will give the price of the field; take it of me, and I will bury my dead there.' 14. And Ephron answered Abraham, saying unto him: 15. 'My lord, hearken unto me: a piece of land worth four shekels of silver, what is that betwixt me and thee? bury therefore thy dead.' 16. And Abraham hearkened unto Ephron; and Abraham weighed to Ephron the silver, which he had named in the hearing of the children of Heth, four hundred shekels of silver, current money with the merchant.*  17. So the field of Ephron, which was in Machpelah, which was before Mamre, the field, and the cave

remain a possession of his family. Such 'freehold' purchase was impossible without the assent of the local Hittite national Council. 'The expression *am ha-aretz* occurs 49 times in Scripture. In 42 of these instances it means neither the nation nor an individual boor, but is simply a technical term of Hebrew Politics and signifies what we would call Parliament.' Judge Mayer Sulzberger, *The Am ha-aretz, the Ancient Hebrew Parliament*, Philadelphia, 1910.

**9.** *the cave of Machpelah.* It was a common practice to bury in caves. The word which is the name of the cave and of the locality denotes 'double': possibly because it consisted of two storeys.

*full price.* lit. 'full silver'; Abraham wished to establish an unassailable right to the land by the payment of its value.

**10.** *Ephron was sitting.* Presiding over the session of the Assembly.

*in the hearing.* i.e. publicly; cf. 'all that went out of the gate of his city,' xxxiv, 24.

**11.** *give I thee.* An expression of conventional politeness, neither intended nor taken literally.

**15.** *what is that betwixt me and thee?* What can such a sum as that just mentioned matter to persons such as we? In this apparently unconcerned tone, the seller indicates the price he wants. The sum demanded, four hundred shekels of silver, is a very substantial sum, perhaps equivalent in purchasing power to from £1,000 to £2,000 in our time. In the contemporary Code of Hammurabi (see on xiv, 1) the wages of a working-man for a year are fixed at six or eight shekels (Bennett).

**16.** *weighed.* There were no coins of standard size and shape; therefore the pieces of silver had to be weighed before their value could be ascertained.

*current money with the merchant.* The phrase probably denotes that the silver was in convenient-sized pieces, readily usable in business transactions.

**17.** *were made sure.* i.e. were assured to Abraham. This verse and the following may well be a citation from the deed of assignment which was drawn up at the purchase. Contracts of this kind, dating from very early Semitic times, have been discovered in large numbers.

81

## GENESIS XXIII, 18

which was therein, and all the trees that were in the field, that were in all the border thereof round about, were made sure 18. unto Abraham for a possession in the presence of the children of Heth, before all that went in at the gate of his city. 19. And after this, Abraham buried Sarah his wife in the cave of the field of Machpelah before Mamre—the same is Hebron—in the land of Canaan. 20. And the field, and the cave that is therein, were made sure unto Abraham for a possession of a burying-place by the children of Heth.

## CHAPTER XXIV

1. And Abraham was old, well stricken in age; and the LORD had blessed Abraham in all things. 2. And Abraham said unto his servant, the elder of his house, that ruled over all that he had: 'Put, I pray thee, thy hand under my thigh. 3. And I will make thee swear by the LORD, the God of heaven and the God of the earth, that thou shalt not take a wife for my son of the daughters of the Canaanites, among whom I dwell. 4. But thou shalt go unto my country, and to my kindred, and take a wife for my son, even for Isaac.' 5. And the servant said unto him: 'Peradventure the woman will not be willing to follow me unto this land; must I needs bring thy son back unto the land from whence thou camest?' 6. And Abraham said unto him: 'Beware thou that thou bring not my son back thither. 7. The LORD, the God of heaven, who took me from my father's house, and from the land of my nativity, and who spoke unto me, and who swore

---

**18.** *in the presence of.* The sale was duly witnessed; cf. Jer. XXXII, 12.

For generations, nay centuries, the children of Israel were to have no point of fixity save the sepulchre of the Patriarchs. The Cave of Machpelah is regarded with immense veneration by the Mohammedans, who built a large mosque over it, and until recently altogether excluded both Jews and Christians from viewing it. A visit is still fraught with considerable difficulty for a Jew.

### CHAPTER XXIV. REBEKAH

**1.** *well stricken in age.* See on XVIII, 11.

**2.** *the elder of his house.* The one who possessed the greatest authority. Although the servant is not named here, it is clear from what was stated in XV, 2 that Eliezer is intended.

*put thy hand under my thigh.* According to the Biblical idiom, children are said to issue from the 'thigh' or 'loins' of their father (cf. XLVI, 26). Therefore the formality of placing the hand upon the thigh was taken to signify that if the oath were violated, the children who have issued, or might issue, from the 'thigh' would avenge the act of disloyalty.

**3.** *God of heaven.* Abraham makes his servant swear in the name of the God he himself worshipped; he had converted his servant to the true Faith (see on XII, 5), evidenced by Eliezer's devout conduct throughout the narrative which follows.

*daughters of the Canaanites.* Who might divert Isaac from the path which his father had mapped out for him; cf. XXVIII, 1. This fear of the evil consequences which would result from intermarriage with heathens is frequently expressed in the Bible; e.g. Deut. VII, 3 f.

**4.** *my country ... kindred.* Here the reference is to Haran and to the family of his brother Nahor.

**5.** The meaning is, If I find a suitable wife for Isaac in Haran but the woman is not willing to leave her home, am I to take Isaac to Haran?

**6.** On no account is Isaac to return to Haran, lest he abandon the Land of Promise.

**7.** Abraham felt strongly that Isaac's marriage would be an important factor in the fulfilment of the Divine promise. Hence God would help

## GENESIS XXIV, 8

unto me, saying: Unto thy seed will I give this land; He will send His angel before thee, and thou shalt take a wife for my son from thence. 8. And if the woman be not willing to follow thee, then thou shalt be clear from this my oath; only thou shalt not bring my son back thither.' 9. And the servant put his hand under the thigh of Abraham his master, and swore to him concerning this matter.* III. 10. And the servant took ten camels, of the camels of his master, and departed; having all goodly things of his master's in his hand; and he arose, and went to ¹Aram-naharaim, unto the city of Nahor. 11. And he made the camels to kneel down without the city by the well of water at the time of evening, the time that women go out to draw water. 12. And he said: 'O LORD, the God of my master Abraham, send me, I pray Thee, good speed this day, and show kindness unto my master Abraham. 13. Behold, I stand by the fountain of water; and the daughters of the men of the city come out to draw water. 14. So let it come to pass, that the damsel to whom I shall say: Let down thy pitcher, I pray thee, that I may drink; and she shall say: Drink, and I will give thy camels drink also; let the same be she that Thou hast appointed for Thy servant, even for Isaac; and thereby shall I know that Thou hast shown kindness unto my master.' 15. And it came to pass, before he had done speaking, that, behold, Rebekah came out, who was born to Bethuel the son of Milcah, the wife of Nahor, Abraham's brother, with her pitcher upon her shoulder. 16. And the damsel was very fair to look upon, a virgin, neither had any man known her;

¹ That is, *Mesopotamia*.

---

Eliezer in his mission to find a worthy wife for Isaac.

*He will send His angel before thee.* An expression denoting that God's protection and aid would be given him; cf. Exod. XXIII, 20.

**9.** *concerning this matter.* lit. 'in accordance with this word,' i.e. on the terms just laid down; namely, if the woman declines to follow him, Eliezer should be free from his obligation.

**10.** *and the servant took.* Gifts for the bride and her family.

*Aram-naharaim.* i.e. Aram of the two rivers, Euphrates and Tigris, Mesopotamia.

*the city of Nahor.* i.e. the city in which Nahor and his family dwelt, Haran.

**11.** *by the well of water.* The place where a stranger would naturally wait who required information concerning an inhabitant of the city.

**12.** *send me good speed.* lit. 'make it happen before me' (as I desire).

**14.** *camels drink also.* Eliezer would only ask a drink of water for himself. The maiden on her own initiative was to suggest water for the camels. Her doing so would be evidence of a tender heart. Kindness to animals is a virtue upon which Judaism lays stress. The Talmud declares that a man must not sit down to his meal before giving food to his animals. It is noteworthy that Eliezer decided to make beauty of character the criterion in his selection of a wife for Isaac. He anticipated the writer of Prov. XXXI, 30, who declared, 'Grace is deceitful, and beauty is vain; but a woman that feareth the LORD, she shall be praised.'

**15.** *Bethuel.* See XXII, 20 f.

**16.** *very fair to look upon.* Rebekah possessed physical beauty as well as goodness of heart.

## GENESIS XXIV, 17

and she went down to the fountain, and filled her pitcher, and came up. 17. And the servant ran to meet her, and said: 'Give me to drink, I pray thee, a little water of thy pitcher.' 18. And she said: 'Drink, my lord'; and she hastened, and let down her pitcher upon her hand, and gave him drink. 19. And when she had done giving him drink, she said: 'I will draw for thy camels also, until they have done drinking.' 20. And she hastened, and emptied her pitcher into the trough, and ran again unto the well to draw, and drew for all his camels. 21. And the man looked stedfastly on her; holding his peace, to know whether the LORD had made his journey prosperous or not. 22. And it came to pass, as the camels had done drinking, that the man took a golden ring of half a shekel weight, and two bracelets for her hands of ten shekels weight of gold; 23. and said: 'Whose daughter art thou? tell me, I pray thee. Is there room in thy father's house for us to lodge in?' 24. And she said unto him: 'I am the daughter of Bethuel the son of Milcah, whom she bore unto Nahor.' 25. She said moreover unto him: 'We have both straw and provender enough, and room to lodge in.' 26. And the man bowed his head, and prostrated himself before the LORD.* 27. And he said: 'Blessed be the LORD, the God of my master Abraham, who hath not forsaken His mercy and His truth toward my master; as for me, the LORD hath led me in the way to the house of my master's brethren.' 28. And the damsel ran, and told her mother's house according to these words. 29. And Rebekah had a brother, and his name was Laban; and Laban ran out unto the man, unto the fountain. 30. And it came to pass, when he saw the ring, and the bracelets upon his sister's hands, and when he heard the words of Rebekah his sister, saying: 'Thus spoke the man unto me,' that he came unto the man; and, behold, he stood by the camels at the fountain. 31. And he said: 'Come

---

**21.** *holding his peace. i.e.* wondering in silence.
**22.** *ring. i.e.* nose-ring; see *v.* 47.
*half a shekel weight.* The shekel weighed about half an ounce. These gifts were both a token of gratitude and a means of obtaining the maiden's favourable opinion.
**27.** *mercy.* Better, 'kindness.' The phrase 'kindness and truth' is the Heb. idiom for 'true kindness'.
*brethren. i.e.* kinsfolk.
**28.** *her mother's house. i.e.* the part of Bethuel's house reserved for the women.

**30.** *he saw the ring.* Laban lacked the true spirit of hospitality, and was actuated solely by sordid motives.
**31.** *blessed of the LORD.* An expression denoting profound respect. So again XXVI, 29. Rebekah had heard Eliezer use the Divine Name (see *v.* 27), and had probably repeated it in her narrative (*v.* 28).
**32.** *he gave straw.* The pronouns, as often in Hebrew, are vaguely used. It was probably Laban who ungirded the camels; and it was certainly he who provided the water.

## GENESIS XXIV, 32

in, thou blessed of the LORD; wherefore standest thou without? for I have cleared the house, and made room for the camels.' 32. And the man came into the house, and he ungirded the camels; and he gave straw and provender for the camels, and water to wash his feet and the feet of the men that were with him. 33. And there was set food before him to eat; but he said: 'I will not eat, until I have told mine errand.' And he said: 'Speak on.' 34. And he said: 'I am Abraham's servant. 35. And the LORD hath blessed my master greatly; and he is become great; and He hath given him flocks and herds, and silver and gold, and men-servants and maid-servants, and camels and asses. 36. And Sarah my master's wife bore a son to my master when she was old; and unto him hath he given all that he hath. 37. And my master made me swear, saying: Thou shalt not take a wife for my son of the daughters of the Canaanites, in whose land I dwell. 38. But thou shalt go unto my father's house, and to my kindred, and take a wife for my son. 39. And I said unto my master: Peradventure the woman will not follow me. 40. And he said unto me: The LORD, before whom I walk, will send His angel with thee, and prosper thy way; and thou shalt take a wife for my son of my kindred, and of my father's house; 41. then shalt thou be clear from my oath, when thou comest to my kindred; and if they give her not to thee, thou shalt be clear from my oath. 42. And I came this day unto the fountain, and said: O LORD, the God of my master Abraham, if now Thou do prosper my way which I go: 43. behold, I stand by the fountain of water; and let it come to pass, that the maiden that cometh forth to draw, to whom I shall say: Give me, I pray thee, a little water from thy pitcher to drink; 44. and she shall say to me: Both drink thou, and I will also draw for thy camels; let the same be the woman whom the LORD hath appointed for my master's son. 45. And before I had done speaking to my heart, behold, Rebekah came forth with her pitcher on her shoulder; and she went down unto the fountain, and drew. And I said unto her: Let me drink, I pray thee.

**34.** *I am Abraham's servant.* The Arab host does not ask his guest's name, at any rate till the latter has eaten of his food, lest there should prove to be a blood-feud between them or their tribes. After the guest has eaten with his host, he is safe (Bennett).

**39.** *peradventure the woman will not follow me.* From this and *v.* 57 below, it is evident that whatever the preliminary negotiations in the 'arrangement' of the marriage, the whole matter was contingent on the consent of the maiden.

**40.** *my kindred.* lit. 'my family'.

**43.** *maiden.* A different Hebrew word from that rendered 'damsel' in *v.* 14. It denotes a girl of marriageable age, and is the word which occurs in Isaiah VII, 14.

## GENESIS XXIV, 46

46. And she made haste, and let down her pitcher from her shoulder, and said: Drink, and I will give thy camels drink also. So I drank, and she made the camels drink also. 47. And I asked her, and said: Whose daughter art thou? And she said: The daughter of Bethuel. Nahor's son, whom Milcah bore unto him. And I put the ring upon her nose, and the bracelets upon her hands. 48. And I bowed my head, and prostrated myself before the LORD, and blessed the LORD, the God of my master Abraham, who had led me in the right way to take my master's brother's daughter for his son. 49. And now if ye will deal kindly and truly with my master, tell me; and if not, tell me; that I may turn to the right hand, or to the left.' 50. Then Laban and Bethuel answered and said: 'The thing proceedeth from the LORD; we cannot speak unto thee bad or good. 51. Behold, Rebekah is before thee, take her, and go, and let her be thy master's son's wife, as the LORD hath spoken.' 52. And it came to pass, that, when Abraham's servant heard their words, he bowed himself down to the earth unto the LORD.* 53. And the servant brought forth jewels of silver, and jewels of gold, and raiment, and gave them to Rebekah; he gave also to her brother and to her mother precious things. 54. And they did eat and drink, he and the men that were with him, and tarried all night; and they rose up in the morning, and he said: 'Send me away unto my master.' 55. And her brother and her mother said: 'Let the damsel abide with us a few days, at the least ten; after that she shall go.' 56. And he said unto them: 'Delay me not, seeing the LORD hath prospered my way; send me away that

---

**47.** In point of fact, he had given her the presents before asking who she was; see *v.* 22 f.

**48.** *brother's daughter.* *i.e.* kinsman's daughter. 'Brother' is used here, as in XIV, 14, 16; XXIX, 12, to denote 'nephew'.

**49.** *that I may turn.* *i.e.* that he may consider what course he is next to pursue.

**50.** *Laban and Bethuel answered.* It is to be noted that Laban is mentioned first. He disrespectfully answered before his father.
*bad or good.* An idiomatic expression meaning 'anything at all'; cf. III, 22. They cannot act against the manifest decree of God.

**51.** *take her, and go.* As is usual in the Orient, the preliminary negotiations in regard to the marriage take place without consultation with the maiden; but see *v.* 39, 57.

**53.** Eliezer hands her mother and brother the *mohar*, or compensation for her loss to the family.

**54.** Only after he has discharged his duty to his master does Eliezer think of himself and partake of the food offered to him.

**55.** *her brother and her mother.* Again Laban interposes before his parent; see *v.* 50. We might have expected mention of the father instead of the mother. He was in all probability quite satisfied to let Rebekah go immediately.
*a few days, at the least ten.* Or, 'a full year or ten months.' This is the rendering of Onkelos and other ancient Jewish versions and is quite justified by Heb. idiom. Rebekah's mother and relatives were loth suddenly to part from her, as they might never see her again.

**57.** *inquire at her mouth.* *i.e.* consult her, as to

86

## GENESIS XXIV, 57

I may go to my master.' 57. And they said: 'We will call the damsel, and inquire at her mouth.' 58. And they called Rebekah, and said unto her: 'Wilt thou go with this man?' And she said: 'I will go.' 59. And they sent away Rebekah their sister, and her nurse, and Abraham's servant, and his men. 60. And they blessed Rebekah, and said unto her: 'Our sister, be thou the mother of thousands of ten thousands, and let thy seed possess the gate of those that hate them.' 61. And Rebekah arose, and her damsels, and they rode upon the camels, and followed the man. And the servant took Rebekah, and went his way. 62. And Isaac came from the way of Beer-lahai-roi; for he dwelt in the land of the South. 63. And Isaac went out to meditate in the field at the eventide; and he lifted up his eyes, and saw, and, behold, there were camels coming. 64. And Rebekah lifted up her eyes, and when she saw Isaac, she alighted from the camel. 65. And she said unto the servant: 'What man is this that walketh in the field to meet us?' And the servant said: 'It is my master.' And she took her veil, and covered herself. 66. And the servant told Isaac all the things that he had done. 67. And Isaac brought her into his mother Sarah's tent, and took Rebekah, and she became his wife; and he loved her. And Isaac was comforted for his mother.* vi.

---

the time of her going. The Rabbis take it to mean, as to whether she wishes to follow Eliezer, and deduce from this text the rule that a woman cannot legally be given away in marriage without her consent.

**59.** *their sister.* Laban had throughout been most prominent in the negotiations.

*her nurse.* Her name was Deborah: see xxxv, 8.

**60.** *be thou the mother of.* The Heb. is simply 'become', as in xvII, 16.

*let thy seed possess.* See on xxII, 17.

**61.** *and followed the man.* In the East it is still the custom for the woman to walk or ride in the rear.

**62.** *Beer-lahai-roi.* The well associated with the story of Hagar.

*the South.* i.e. the Negeb; see on xII, 9.

**63.** *to meditate.* The Targums and the Rabbis understood the word to mean 'pray', and declared that Isaac instituted the Afternoon Service (מנחה), as Abraham had instituted the Morning Service (derived from xix, 27), and Jacob later on instituted the Evening Service (deduced from xxvIII, 11).

**64.** *alighted from.* A mark of respect; cf. Joshua, xv, 18; I Sam. xxv, 23. In the East men and women dismount on the approach of a person of importance.

**65.** *took her veil.* Rebekah again acted in accordance with Eastern etiquette. It was not necessary for her to have her face veiled in the presence of Eliezer, since he was only a servant.

**67.** *into his mother Sarah's tent.* He installed her as mistress of the household.

The order of the words, *He took Rebekah, she became his wife, and he loved her,* calls for comment. In modern life we would place 'he loved her' first, and write: 'He loved Rebekah, he took her, and she became his wife.' But, however important it is that love shall precede marriage, it is far more important that it shall continue *after* marriage. The modern attitude lays all the stress on the romance before marriage; the olden Jewish view emphasizes the life-long devotion and affection after marriage (S. R. Hirsch).

*comforted.* Rebekah filled the gap caused in Isaac's life by the death of his mother. The Rabbis explain that on the death of Sarah the blessings which had attended the household of the Patriarch, and the pious customs which distinguished it, came to an end; but when Rebekah was brought to the tent, they were restored. 'The Sabbath lamp once more illumined the home of the Patriarch,' and Rebekah continued as well all the other religious rites which Sarah had initiated.

# GENESIS XXV, 1

בראשית חיי שרה כה

## Chapter XXV

CAP. XXV. כה

כה

1. And Abraham took another wife, and her name was Keturah. 2. And she bore him Zimram, and Jokshan, and Medan, and Midian, and Ishbak, and Shuah. 3. And Jokshan begot Sheba, and Dedan. And the sons of Dedan were Asshurim, and Letushim, and Leummim. 4. And the sons of Midian: Ephah, and Epher, and Hanoch, and Abida, and Eldaah. All these were the children of Keturah. 5. And Abraham gave all that he had unto Isaac. 6. But unto the sons of the concubines, that Abraham had, Abraham gave gifts; and he sent them away from Isaac his son, while he yet lived, eastward, unto the east country. 7. And these are the days of the years of Abraham's life which he lived, a hundred threescore and fifteen years. 8. And Abraham expired, and died in a good old age, an old man, and full of years; and was gathered to his people. 9. And Isaac and Ishmael his sons buried him in the cave of Machpelah, in the field of Ephron the son of Zohar the Hittite, which is before Mamre; 10. the field which Abraham purchased of the children of Heth; there was Abraham buried, and Sarah his wife. 11. And it came to pass after the death of Abraham, that God blessed Isaac his son; and Isaac dwelt by Beer-lahai-roi.* vii. ¶ 12. Now these

2 וַיֹּסֶף אַבְרָהָם וַיִּקַּח אִשָּׁה וּשְׁמָהּ קְטוּרָה: וַתֵּלֶד לוֹ אֶת־
זִמְרָן וְאֶת־יָקְשָׁן וְאֶת־מְדָן וְאֶת־מִדְיָן וְאֶת־יִשְׁבָּק וְאֶת־
3 שׁוּחַ: וְיָקְשָׁן יָלַד אֶת־שְׁבָא וְאֶת־דְּדָן וּבְנֵי דְדָן הָיוּ
4 אַשּׁוּרִם וּלְטוּשִׁם וּלְאֻמִּים: וּבְנֵי מִדְיָן עֵיפָה וָעֵפֶר וַחֲנֹךְ
5 וַאֲבִידָע וְאֶלְדָּעָה כָּל־אֵלֶּה בְּנֵי קְטוּרָה: וַיִּתֵּן אַבְרָהָם
6 אֶת־כָּל־אֲשֶׁר־לוֹ לְיִצְחָק: וְלִבְנֵי הַפִּילַגְשִׁים אֲשֶׁר
לְאַבְרָהָם נָתַן אַבְרָהָם מַתָּנֹת וַיְשַׁלְּחֵם מֵעַל יִצְחָק בְּנוֹ
7 בְּעוֹדֶנּוּ חַי קֵדְמָה אֶל־אֶרֶץ קֶדֶם: וְאֵלֶּה יְמֵי שְׁנֵי־חַיֵּי
אַבְרָהָם אֲשֶׁר־חָי מְאַת שָׁנָה וְשִׁבְעִים שָׁנָה וְחָמֵשׁ שָׁנִים:
8 וַיִּגְוַע וַיָּמָת אַבְרָהָם בְּשֵׂיבָה טוֹבָה זָקֵן וְשָׂבֵעַ וַיֵּאָסֶף אֶל־
9 עַמָּיו: וַיִּקְבְּרוּ אֹתוֹ יִצְחָק וְיִשְׁמָעֵאל בָּנָיו אֶל־מְעָרַת הַמַּכְפֵּלָה
אֶל־שְׂדֵה עֶפְרֹן בֶּן־צֹחַר הַחִתִּי אֲשֶׁר עַל־פְּנֵי מַמְרֵא:
10 הַשָּׂדֶה אֲשֶׁר־קָנָה אַבְרָהָם מֵאֵת בְּנֵי־חֵת שָׁמָּה קֻבַּר
11 אַבְרָהָם וְשָׂרָה אִשְׁתּוֹ: וַיְהִי אַחֲרֵי מוֹת אַבְרָהָם וַיְבָרֶךְ

---

### Chapter XXV. Death of Abraham and Descendants of Ishmael

**1.** *and Abraham took another wife.* It does not necessarily mean that it was not until after the death of Sarah that he married again. It is quite possible that he took his secondary wife (in I Chron. I, 32 Keturah is called a 'concubine') during her lifetime; and it is only mentioned here in connection with the disposal of the Patriarch's property.

**2.** The domestic tradition in these verses preserves the recollection of the early relationship between the ancestors of Israel and the tribes of the North Arabian desert (Ryle).
*Medan.* The 'Medanites' are referred to in XXXVII as traders with Egypt.
*Midian.* The name of a nomad tribe frequently occurring in the Bible.
*Shuah.* One of Job's friends is described as a Shuhite (Job II, 11).

**3.** *Sheba and Dedan.* Mentioned in X, 7. The other names are found on Arabian inscriptions.

**5.** Cf. XXIV, 36.

**6.** *concubines. i.e.* Hagar and Keturah.
*while he yet lived. i.e.* in his lifetime, a wise precaution to ensure the safety of Isaac and prevent disputes amongst the members of the family.
*eastward. i.e.* to Arabia. The Arabs are sometimes described as 'children of the East'; see Judges VI, 3; Job I, 3.

**7.** *a hundred threescore and fifteen years.* Abraham must have lived to see his grandchildren. Isaac was born when his father was a hundred (XXI, 5), and was sixty at the birth of Esau and Jacob (see *v.* 26); hence they were fifteen when the Patriarch died.

**8.** *was gathered to his people.* Not to be understood literally, as his people were buried in Mesopotamia. It is a parallel phrase to 'thou shalt go to thy fathers' in XV, 15; and, like it, is an intimation of immortality.

**9.** *Isaac and Ishmael.* At the graveside of their father, the half-brothers were reconciled (Midrash).
*Machpelah.* See XXIII, 9 f.

**11.** *God blessed Isaac. i.e.* the promises made to Abraham were now transferred to him.

### 12–18. Descendants of Ishmael

**12.** *generations.* Descendants. Some of the names that follow are found in Assyrian and Arabian inscriptions.

# GENESIS XXV, 13

בראשית חיי שרה כה

שביעי אֱלֹהִים אֶת־יִצְחָק בְּנוֹ וַיֵּשֶׁב יִצְחָק עִם־בְּאֵר לַחַי רֹאִי׃ פ

12 וְאֵלֶּה תֹּלְדֹת יִשְׁמָעֵאל בֶּן־אַבְרָהָם אֲשֶׁר יָלְדָה הָגָר
13 הַמִּצְרִית שִׁפְחַת שָׂרָה לְאַבְרָהָם׃ וְאֵלֶּה שְׁמוֹת בְּנֵי
יִשְׁמָעֵאל בִּשְׁמֹתָם לְתוֹלְדֹתָם בְּכֹר יִשְׁמָעֵאל נְבָיֹת וְקֵדָר
14 וְאַדְבְּאֵל וּמִבְשָׂם׃ וּמִשְׁמָע וְדוּמָה וּמַשָּׂא׃ חֲדַד וְתֵימָא
מפטיר
16 יְטוּר נָפִישׁ וָקֵדְמָה׃ אֵלֶּה הֵם בְּנֵי יִשְׁמָעֵאל וְאֵלֶּה שְׁמֹתָם
17 בְּחַצְרֵיהֶם וּבְטִירֹתָם שְׁנֵים־עָשָׂר נְשִׂיאִם לְאֻמֹּתָם׃ וְאֵלֶּה
שְׁנֵי חַיֵּי יִשְׁמָעֵאל מְאַת שָׁנָה וּשְׁלֹשִׁים שָׁנָה וְשֶׁבַע שָׁנִים
18 וַיִּגְוַע וַיָּמָת וַיֵּאָסֶף אֶל־עַמָּיו׃ וַיִּשְׁכְּנוּ מֵחֲוִילָה עַד־שׁוּר
אֲשֶׁר עַל־פְּנֵי מִצְרַיִם בֹּאֲכָה אַשּׁוּרָה עַל־פְּנֵי כָל־אֶחָיו נָפָל׃

are the generations of Ishmael, Abraham's son, whom Hagar the Egyptian, Sarah's handmaid, bore unto Abraham. 13. And these are the names of the sons of Ishmael, by their names, according to their generations: the first-born of Ishmael, Nebaioth; and Kedar, and Adbeel, and Mibsam, 14. and Mishma, and Dumah, and Massa; 15. Hadad, and Tema, Jetur, Naphish, and Kedem; *ᵐ· 16. these are the sons of Ishmael, and these are their names, by their villages, and by their encampments; twelve princes according to their nations. 17. And these are the years of the life of Ishmael, a hundred and thirty and seven years; and he expired and died; and was gathered unto his people. 18. And they dwelt from Havilah unto Shur, that is before Egypt, as thou goest toward Asshur: over against all his brethren he did settle.

**13.** *Nebaioth.* Later known as Nabatæans.
*Kedar.* In Ps. CXX, 5, they are taken as a type of hostile neighbours.

**15.** *Tema.* An important station on the trade-route from Yemen to Syria.

**16.** *encampments.* Probably a technical term to denote the circular enclosure used by a nomad people.
*princes.* Sheiks of clans.

**17.** *was gathered.* See on *v.* 8.

**18.** *Havilah.* See II, 11; situated in N.E. Arabia.
*Shur.* See on XVI, 7; cf. also I Sam. XV, 7.
*Asshur.* The reference is probably to the land of Asshurim mentioned in *v.* 3.
*did settle.* lit. 'fell.' For this sense of the word, cf. Judges VII, 12.

This chapter concludes the Biblical account of the first of the Patriarchs. It is difficult, indeed, because of our lifelong familiarity with the story, rightly to estimate the nobility and grandeur of the personality revealed in these chapters.

He was the pioneer of the monotheistic faith. Undazzled by the heathen splendour of a Nimrod or a Hammurabi, he broke away from the debasing idol-worship of his contemporaries, and devoted his life to the spread of the world-redeeming truth of the One God of Justice and Mercy. He forsook home and family to brave unknown dangers because the voice of God bade him do so; and, throughout his days, he showed that faith in God must manifest itself in implicit and joyful surrender to the Divine will. He set an example to his children to sacrifice the dearest things in life, and, if need be, life itself, in defence of the spiritual heritage entrusted to their care. While he preached renunciation in the service of God, he practised lovingkindess and truth towards his fellow men. Witness his magnanimity in his treatment of Lot; his fine independence in the refusal to accept any of the spoils won by the men of his household; his benevolence in the reception of strangers; his stand for justice, when pleading for the doomed cities; and his all-embracing human pity, which extended even to those who had forfeited all claim to human pity. Finally, the closing stage of his life shows his anxiety that the spiritual treasures he has acquired should be transmitted unimpaired through his son to future generations. Verily, he is the prototype of what the Jew should aim at being. 'Look unto the rock whence ye were hewn, ... look unto Abraham your father,' is the Divine exhortation addressed to Israel (Isaiah LI, 1–2).

# HAFTORAH CHAYYE SARAH הפטרת חיי שרה

## I KINGS I, 1–31

### CHAPTER I

1. Now king David was old and stricken in years; and they covered him with clothes, but he could get no heat. 2. Wherefore his servants said unto him: 'Let there be sought for my lord the king a young virgin; and let her stand before the king, and be a companion unto him; and let her lie in thy bosom, that my lord the king may get heat.' 3. So they sought for a fair damsel throughout all the borders of Israel, and found Abishag the Shunammite, and brought her to the king. 4. And the damsel was very fair; and she became a companion unto the king, and ministered to him; but the king knew her not. ¶ 5. Now Adonijah the son of Haggith exalted himself, saying: 'I will be king'; and he prepared him chariots and horsemen, and fifty men to run before him. 6. And his father had not grieved him all his life in saying: 'Why hast thou done so?' and he was also a very goodly man; and he was born after Absalom. 7. And he conferred with Joab the son of Zeruiah, and with Abiathar the priest; and they following Adonijah helped him. 8. But Zadok the priest, and Benaiah

---

### I KINGS I, 1–31

The Book of Kings (the division into two books occurs only in *printed* Hebrew Bibles) gives the history of the Monarchy from the last days of David to the Babylonian exile.

This opening chapter portrays the struggle for the Crown among David's surviving sons.

The connection between Sedrah and Haftorah is readily seen. The one portrays Abraham's old age, and the other David's; the one depicts Abraham's solicitude for the piety of his house, and the other, David's for the right succession in his.

There is contrast in the character of the two sons. Isaac allows himself to be guided by his father in a great decision, in spite of his forty years; Adonijah in the Haftorah cannot wait for the death of his father to proclaim himself king. In violent contrast to the simple life in Abraham's tent, we have, in David's palace, conspiracy and all the intrigues of an Oriental Court, 'told with a convincing realism which conveys the impression of first-hand information derived from the evidence of eye-witnesses' (Skinner).

**1.** *old.* Seventy years.

*clothes.* Bed-clothes.

**2.** *stand before the king.* Serve him.

**3.** *the Shunammite.* Shunem, 3 miles N. of Jezreel, not far from Mt. Carmel.

**5.** *Adonijah.* The fourth son of David, see II Sam. III, 4. Two of his elder brothers (Amnon and Absalom) being dead, he regards himself as heir.

*fifty men.* A royal bodyguard.

**6.** *also a very goodly man.* It gives the reason of Adonijah's disobedience—his father's reluctance to rebuke the handsome, self-willed boy. See, on Absalom, II Sam. XIV, 25. What warnings to

# I KINGS I, 9

the son of Jehoiada, and Nathan the prophet, and Shimei, and Rei, and the mighty men that belonged to David, were not with Adonijah. 9. And Adonijah slew sheep and oxen and fatlings by the stone of Zoheleth, which is beside En-rogel; and he called all his brethren the king's sons, and all the men of Judah the king's servants; 10. but Nathan the prophet, and Benaiah, and the mighty men, and Solomon his brother, he called not. ¶ 11. Then Nathan spoke unto Bath-sheba the mother of Solomon, saying: 'Hast thou not heard that Adonijah the son of Haggith doth reign, and David our lord knoweth it not? 12. Now therefore come, let me, I pray thee, give thee counsel, that thou mayest save thine own life, and the life of thy son Solomon. 13. Go and get thee in unto king David, and say unto him: Didst not thou, my lord, O king, swear unto thy handmaid, saying: Assuredly Solomon thy son shall reign after me, and he shall sit upon my throne? why then doth Adonijah reign? 14. Behold, while thou yet talkest there with the king, I also will come in after thee, and confirm thy words.' ¶ 15. And Bath-sheba went in unto the king into the chamber.—Now the king was very old; and Abishag the Shunammite ministered unto the king.—16. And Bath-sheba bowed, and prostrated herself unto the king. And the king said: 'What wouldest thou?' 17. And she said unto him: 'My lord, thou didst swear by the LORD thy God unto thy handmaid: Assuredly Solomon thy son shall reign after me, and he shall sit upon my throne. 18. And now, behold, Adonijah reigneth; and thou, my lord the king, knowest it not. 19. And he hath slain oxen and fatlings and sheep in abundance, and hath called all the sons of the king, and

---

parents against favouritism and indulgence to children! It is the road to unhappiness for themselves, and ruin for their children.

**7.** *Joab.* David's commander-in-chief.

*Abiathar.* A descendant of Aaron's youngest son, Ithamar.

**8.** *Zadok.* A descendant of Aaron's son Eleazar.

*Benaiah.* Succeeded Joab as commander-in-chief.

*Nathan.* The fearless Prophet: see II Sam. XII, 1–12.

*the mighty men.* Heb. *Gibborim.* David's army of picked warriors: II Sam. X, 7.

**9.** *En-rogel.* 'The Fuller's spring,' near Siloam, close to Jerusalem.

**11.** *Bath-sheba.* The note on Gen. XXVI, 33, throws light on the meaning of this name, which is 'Fortune's daughter', Fortunata, Glueckel. She was apparently the favourite wife of David.

**12.** Unless Adonijah's plot is defeated, his first act after the death of David would be to remove opposition by slaying Solomon, his rival to the throne, and Bath-sheba. Thus the successor to Alexander the Great put to death his widow, in addition to slaying his young son.

**14.** *confirm.* Supplement.

## I KINGS I, 20

Abiathar the priest, and Joab the captain of the host; but Solomon thy servant hath he not called. 20. And thou, my lord the king, the eyes of all Israel are upon thee, that thou shouldest tell them who shall sit on the throne of my lord the king after him. 21. Otherwise it will come to pass, when my lord the king shall sleep with his fathers, that I and my son Solomon shall be counted offenders.' ¶ 22. And, lo, while she yet talked with the king, Nathan the prophet came in. 23. And they told the king, saying: 'Behold Nathan the prophet.' And when he was come in before the king, he bowed down before the king with his face to the ground. 24. And Nathan said: 'My lord, O king, hast thou said: Adonijah shall reign after me, and he shall sit upon my throne? 25. For he is gone down this day, and hath slain oxen and fatlings and sheep in abundance, and hath called all the king's sons, and the captains of the host, and Abiathar the priest; and, behold, they eat and drink before him, and say: Long live king Adonijah. 26. But me, even me thy servant, and Zadok the priest, and Benaiah the son of Jehoiada, and thy servant Solomon, hath he not called. 27. Is this thing done by my lord the king, and thou hast not declared unto thy servant who should sit on the throne of my lord the king after him?' ¶ 28. Then king David answered and said: 'Call me Bath-sheba.' And she came into the king's presence, and stood before the king. 29. And the king swore and said: 'As the Lord liveth, who hath redeemed my soul out of all adversity, 30. verily as I swore unto thee by the Lord, the God of Israel, saying: Assuredly Solomon thy son shall reign after me, and he shall sit upon my throne in my stead; verily so will I do this day.' 31. Then Bath-sheba bowed with her face to the earth, and prostrated herself to the king, and said: 'Let my lord king David live for ever.'

**20. tell them.** She presses for a public pronouncement as to the succession.

**21. counted offenders.** *i.e.* shall be put to death.

**25. eat and drink before him.** Thus sealing their allegiance to him.

*long live king Adonijah.* 'God save king Adonijah' (RV).

**26. not called.** Because standing outside the conspiracy.

**29.** With a firm hand, David now safeguards the destinies of his House.

GENESIS XXV, 19

בראשית תולדת כה

פ פ פ ו 6

19. And these are the generations of Isaac, Abraham's son: Abraham begot Isaac. 20. And Isaac was forty years old when he took Rebekah, the daughter of Bethuel the Aramean, of Paddan-aram, the sister of Laban the Aramean, to be his wife. 21. And Isaac entreated the LORD for his wife, because she was barren; and the LORD let Himself be entreated of him, and Rebekah his wife conceived. 22. And the children struggled together within her; and she said: 'If it be so, wherefore do I live?' And she went to inquire of the LORD. 23. And the LORD said unto her:

Two nations are in thy womb,
And two peoples shall be separated from thy bowels;
And the one people shall be stronger than the other people;
And the elder shall serve the younger.

24. And when her days to be delivered were fulfilled, behold, there were twins in her womb. 25. And the first came forth ruddy, all over like a hairy mantle; and they called his name Esau. 26. And after that came forth his brother, and his hand had

19 וְאֵ֛לֶּה תּוֹלְדֹ֥ת יִצְחָ֖ק בֶּן־אַבְרָהָ֑ם אַבְרָהָ֖ם הוֹלִ֥יד אֶת־
כ יִצְחָֽק׃ וַיְהִ֤י יִצְחָק֙ בֶּן־אַרְבָּעִ֣ים שָׁנָ֔ה בְּקַחְתּ֣וֹ אֶת־רִבְקָ֗ה
בַּת־בְּתוּאֵל֙ הָֽאֲרַמִּ֔י מִפַּדַּ֖ן אֲרָ֑ם אֲח֛וֹת לָבָ֥ן הָאֲרַמִּ֖י ל֥וֹ
21 לְאִשָּֽׁה׃ וַיֶּעְתַּ֨ר יִצְחָ֤ק לַֽיהוָה֙ לְנֹ֣כַח אִשְׁתּ֔וֹ כִּ֥י עֲקָרָ֖ה
22 הִ֑וא וַיֵּעָ֤תֶר לוֹ֙ יְהוָ֔ה וַתַּ֖הַר רִבְקָ֥ה אִשְׁתּֽוֹ׃ וַיִּתְרֹֽצֲצ֤וּ
הַבָּנִים֙ בְּקִרְבָּ֔הּ וַתֹּ֣אמֶר אִם־כֵּ֔ן לָ֥מָּה זֶּ֖ה אָנֹ֑כִי וַתֵּ֖לֶךְ לִדְרֹ֥שׁ
23 אֶת־יְהוָֽה׃ וַיֹּ֨אמֶר יְהוָ֜ה לָ֗הּ שְׁנֵ֤י גוֹיִם֙ בְּבִטְנֵ֔ךְ וּשְׁנֵ֣י
לְאֻמִּ֔ים מִמֵּעַ֖יִךְ יִפָּרֵ֑דוּ וּלְאֹם֙ מִלְאֹ֣ם יֶֽאֱמָ֔ץ וְרַ֖ב יַעֲבֹ֥ד
24 צָעִֽיר׃ וַיִּמְלְא֥וּ יָמֶ֖יהָ לָלֶ֑דֶת וְהִנֵּ֥ה תוֹמִ֖ם בְּבִטְנָֽהּ׃ וַיֵּצֵ֤א
כה הָרִאשׁוֹן֙ אַדְמוֹנִ֔י כֻּלּ֖וֹ כְּאַדֶּ֣רֶת שֵׂעָ֑ר וַיִּקְרְא֥וּ שְׁמ֖וֹ עֵשָֽׂו׃
26 וְאַֽחֲרֵי־כֵ֞ן יָצָ֣א אָחִ֗יו וְיָד֤וֹ אֹחֶ֨זֶת֙ בַּעֲקֵ֣ב עֵשָׂ֔ו וַיִּקְרָ֥א

v. 23. גוים ק׳ ibid. קמץ בז״ק v. 24. חסר

## VI. TOLEDOTH

### (CHAPTERS XXV, 19–XXVIII, 9)

#### (b) JACOB (CHAPTERS XXV–XXXVI)

CHAPTER XXV, 19–34. THE BIRTHRIGHT

**19.** With this verse, a new section of the Book of Genesis commences, which extends to the end of Chapter XXXVI. Therefore, we are given a brief summary of what has gone before, to prepare us for the new events to be described.

*Abraham's son.* i.e. his son and heir, to distinguish him from the children of Hagar and Keturah.

*Abraham begot Isaac.* It was not until the Patriarch's name was altered from Abram to Abraham, 'father of a multitude of nations' (XVII, 5), that Isaac was born.

**20.** *Paddan-aram.* Identical with Aram-Naharaim, or Mesopotamia: cf. XXIV, 10.

**21.** *she was barren.* Like Sarah before her (XVI, 1) and Rachel after her (XXIX, 31). This sterility may have been intended to emphasize that the children who were eventually born were a gift of grace from God for the fulfilment of His purpose.

**22.** *struggled together.* A premonition of the rivalry which was to exist between the brothers and their descendants.

*if it be so, wherefore do I live?* Life was unbearable for her, and she wished to die (Nachmanides).

*to inquire of the LORD.* A technical term for seeking an answer from a Divine source. According to the Midrash, she went to the School of Shem, where the knowledge of God was taught. It is very probable that she went to 'inquire of the Lord' through Abraham, who was still alive at this time (see on v. 7 above).

**23.** *two nations.* i.e. the founders of two nations. The oracular answer is in four poetic lines.

*shall be separated.* Shall be mutually antagonistic from birth.

*the elder shall serve the younger.* This prophecy was fulfilled when David defeated Edom. See II Sam. VIII, 14.

**25.** *ruddy.* Heb. *admoni*. The Midrash explains the ruddiness as a premonition of his love for hunting and the shedding of blood.

*Esau.* Some authorities derive it from a Semitic root meaning 'thick-haired'.

**26.** *his hand had hold on Esau's heel.* As it were to pull him back and prevent him from being the firstborn: cf. Hosea XII, 4.

93

## GENESIS XXV, 27

hold on Esau's heel; and his name was called ¹Jacob. And Isaac was threescore years old when she bore them. 27. And the boys grew; and Esau was a cunning hunter, a man of the field; and Jacob was a quiet man, dwelling in tents. 28. Now Isaac loved Esau, because he did eat of his venison; and Rebekah loved Jacob. 29. And Jacob sod pottage; and Esau came in from the field, and he was faint. 30. And Esau said to Jacob: 'Let me swallow, I pray thee, some of this red, red pottage; for I am faint.' Therefore was his name called ²Edom. 31. And Jacob said: 'Sell me first thy birthright.' 32. And Esau said: 'Behold, I am at the point to die; and what profit shall the birthright do to me?' 33. And Jacob said: 'Swear to me first'; and he swore unto him; and he sold his birthright unto Jacob. 34. And Jacob gave Esau bread and pottage of lentils; and he did eat and drink, and rose up, and went his way. So Esau despised his birthright.

## 26 CHAPTER XXVI

1. And there was a famine in the land, beside the first famine that was in the days of

---
¹ That is, *One that takes by the heel*, or, *supplants*. ² That is, *Red*.

**27.** *a cunning hunter.* lit. 'knowing hunting. The word 'cunning' is used in its old meaning, 'skilful.'

*quiet.* lit. 'perfect'; *i.e.* harmless.

*dwelling in tents. i.e.* a shepherd. The Midrash explains 'tents' to mean 'schools of religious study'; cf. on *v.* 22.

**28.** *now Isaac loved Esau.* Although in Rabbinic literature Esau the roving huntsman is, like Nimrod, depicted as a bad character because of the bloodshed and cruelty to animals that the hunter's life entails, yet he is praised for his devotion to Isaac. To have merited his father's love is regarded as the consequence of Esau's filial piety.

*and Rebekah loved Jacob.* Each parent had a favourite child, which was to lead to the break-up of the household. 'Love thy children with an impartial love,' is the wise admonition of a medieval Jewish teacher.

**30.** *swallow.* The Heb. word, which does not occur elsewhere in the Bible, implies animal-like voracity.

*Edom.* 'The Hebrews saw in the name of the rival nation a standing reminder of the impulsive shortsightedness of its ancestor' (Driver). The term 'mess of pottage', used proverbially of this transaction, does not occur in the Authorised Version of the Bible.

**31.** *sell me first thy birthright.* At first sight, Jacob's conduct appears indeed reprehensible. On closer examination, however, we learn that the privileges of the birthright so coveted by Jacob were purely spiritual. In primitive times, the head of the clan or the firstborn acted as the priest. Esau's general behaviour hardly accorded with what was due from one who was to serve the Supreme God; and Jacob suspected that his brother did not value the dignity and privilege of being the firstborn as they should be valued. When, therefore, an opportunity suggested itself, Jacob determined to put his brother to the test. He knew full well that the withholding of the pottage would not have fatal consequences. He would, however, find out what Esau really thought of his birthright. 'As to power and command, Jacob never exercised any over Esau; but on the contrary, humbly and submissively addresses him as "my Lord" ' (Abarbanel).

**32.** *I am at the point to die.* The exaggeration of a hungry man of uncontrolled appetite.

**34.** *So Esau despised his birthright.* Which he would not have done had it carried with it material advantages. The spiritual inheritance of Abraham, which would normally have passed into the hands of Esau, was not worth to him as much as a dish of pottage. Like the true sensualist, this fickle and impulsive hunter readily sacrifices to the gratification of the moment that which to a man of nobler build would be of transcendent worth.

CHAPTER XXVI. ISAAC AND THE PHILISTINES

**1.** *the first famine.* Mentioned in XII, 10.

*Abimelech.* See on xx, 2. Possibly the dynastic name of the Philistine rulers.

*Gerar.* See on xx, 1.

## GENESIS XXVI, 2

Abraham. And Isaac went unto Abimelech king of the Philistines unto Gerar. 2. And the LORD appeared unto him, and said: 'Go not down into Egypt; dwell in the land which I shall tell thee of. 3. Sojourn in this land, and I will be with thee, and will bless thee; for unto thee, and unto thy seed, I will give all these lands, and I will establish the oath which I swore unto Abraham thy father; 4. and I will multiply thy seed as the stars of heaven, and will give unto thy seed all these lands; and by thy seed shall all the nations of the earth bless themselves; 5. because that Abraham hearkened to My voice, and kept My charge, My commandments, My statutes, and My laws.'* ii. 6. And Isaac dwelt in Gerar. 7. And the men of the place asked him of his wife; and he said: 'She is my sister'; for he feared to say: 'My wife'; 'lest the men of the place should kill me for Rebekah, because she is fair to look upon.' 8. And it came to pass, when he had been there a long time, that Abimelech king of the Philistines looked out at a window, and saw, and, behold, Isaac was sporting with Rebekah his wife. 9. And Abimelech called Isaac, and said: 'Behold, of a surety she is thy wife; and how saidst thou: She is my sister?' And Isaac said unto him: 'Because I said: Lest I die because of her.' 10. And Abimelech said: 'What is this thou hast done unto us? one of the people might easily have lain with thy wife, and thou wouldest have brought guiltiness upon us.' 11. And Abimelech charged all the people, saying: 'He that toucheth this man or his wife shall surely be put to death.' 12. And Isaac sowed in that land, and found in the same year a hundredfold; and the LORD blessed him.* iii.

**2.** *go not down into Egypt.* Isaac would naturally resolve to do what his father had done in similar circumstances, as described in XII, 10.

**3.** *sojourn.* Stay for the time being; cf. on XII, 10.

**4.** *as the stars of heaven.* Cf. XV, 5.
*bless themselves.* See on XII, 3.

**5.** *because that Abraham.* Emphasizing the unity and continuity of Abraham and his descendants.
*commandments.* Laws dictated by the moral sense, *e.g.* against the crimes of robbery, bloodshed, etc. (מצות).
*statutes.* Laws ordained by God which we are to observe although reason cannot assign an explanation, *e.g.* the prohibition of swine's flesh (חוקים).
*laws.* Customs and traditional ordinances orally transmitted from generation to generation (תורות). These definitions are given in the Midrash.

**7.** Isaac meets with the same experience as his father (XII, 13; XX, 5), and unwisely adopts the same plan for safeguarding his person.

**8.** Abimelech has not taken Rebekah into his household as had been done with Sarah.
*at a window.* Or, 'through the window.'
*sporting.* The same word as used in XXI, 9, but having here a different meaning. Their conduct was such that Abimelech suspected they were husband and wife.

**12.** *in the same year. i.e.* in the year of famine. That is why his prosperity was regarded as not a natural thing but a Divine blessing.
*a hundredfold.* 'In the rich lava-soil of Hauran, wheat is said to yield on an average 80 fold, and barley, 100 fold' (Wetzstein).

## GENESIS XXVI, 13

13. And the man waxed great, and grew more and more until he became very great. 14. And he had possessions of flocks, and possessions of herds, and a great household; and the Philistines envied him. 15. Now all the wells which his father's servants had digged in the days of Abraham his father, the Philistines had stopped them, and filled them with earth. 16. And Abimelech said unto Isaac: 'Go from us; for thou art much mightier than we.' 17. And Isaac departed thence, and encamped in the valley of Gerar, and dwelt there. 18. And Isaac digged again the wells of water, which they had digged in the days of Abraham his father; for the Philistines had stopped them after the death of Abraham; and he called their names after the names by which his father had called them. 19. And Isaac's servants digged in the valley, and found there a well of living water. 20. And the herdmen of Gerar strove with Isaac's herdmen, saying: 'The water is ours.' And he called the name of the well ¹Esek; because they contended with him. 21. And they digged another well, and they strove for that also. And he called the name of it ²Sitnah. 22. And he removed from thence, and digged another well; and for that they strove not. And he called the name of it ³Rehoboth; and he said: 'For now the LORD hath made room for us, and we shall be fruitful in the land.'* ᶦᵛ· 23. And he went up from thence to Beer-sheba. 24. And the LORD appeared unto him the same night, and said: 'I am the God of Abraham thy father. Fear not, for I am with thee, and will bless thee, and multiply thy seed for My servant Abraham's sake.' 25. And he builded an altar there, and called upon the name of the LORD, and pitched his tent there; and there Isaac's servants digged a well. 26. Then Abimelech went to him from Gerar, and Ahuzzath his friend, and Phicol the captain of his host. 27. And Isaac said unto them: 'Wherefore are ye come unto me, seeing ye hate me, and have

---

¹ That is, *Contention*. ² That is, *Enmity*. ³ That is, *Room*.

---

**16.** The prosperity of the Patriarch creates envy among his neighbours. Modern anti-Semitism is, likewise, largely dictated by envy, thus illustrating the Rabbinic saying, 'What happened to the Patriarchs, repeats itself in the life of their descendants.'

**17.** *valley*. The Heb. word *nahal* means a *wady* or river-bed, which in the winter, or even after a storm, is a rushing stream, but in summer is usually reduced to a mere thread of water, or may even be entirely dry. In the bed of such wadys, water may often be found by digging (Driver).

**19.** *living water*. Or, 'springing water'; the opposite of stagnant water.

**22.** *Rehoboth*. i.e. 'Room', latitude; lit. 'broad places'. In Heb. the word denoting 'spaciousness' is used to express comfort and security. Twenty miles S.W. of Beer-sheba there is a well known as *Ruhaibeh*.

**24.** *fear not*. In view of the hostility recently shown him.

**25.** *called upon the name of the* LORD. See on XII, 8.

**26.** *his friend*. i.e. his intimate counsellor.
*Phicol*. The same as in XXI, 22. If the Abimelech and Phicol are identical with those mentioned in Chap. XXI, they must have been old men in the time of Isaac.

## GENESIS XXVI, 28

sent me away from you?' 28. And they said: 'We saw plainly that the LORD was with thee; and we said: Let there now be an oath betwixt us, even betwixt us and thee, and let us make a covenant with thee; 29. that thou wilt do us no hurt, as we have not touched thee, and as we have done unto thee nothing but good, and have sent thee away in peace; thou art now the blessed of the LORD.'* ᵛ· 30. And he made them a feast, and they did eat and drink. 31. And they rose up betimes in the morning, and swore one to another; and Isaac sent them away, and they departed from him in peace. 32. And it came to pass the same day, that Isaac's servants came, and told him concerning the well which they had digged, and said unto him: 'We have found water.' 33. And he called it Shibah. Therefore the name of the city is Beer-sheba unto this day. ¶ 34. And when Esau was forty years old, he took to wife Judith the daughter of Beeri the Hittite, and Basemath the daughter of Elon the Hittite. 35. And they were a bitterness of spirit unto Isaac and to Rebekah.

## CHAPTER XXVII

1. And it came to pass, that when Isaac was old, and his eyes were dim, so that he could not see, he called Esau his elder son, and said unto him: 'My son'; and he said unto him: 'Here am I.' 2. And he said: 'Behold now, I am old, I know not the day of my death. 3. Now therefore take, I pray thee, thy weapons, thy quiver and thy bow, and go out to the field, and take me venison; 4. and make me savoury food, such as I love, and bring it to me, that I may eat; that my soul may bless thee before I die.' 5. And Rebekah heard when Isaac

---

**28.** *the LORD was with thee.* The same motive for seeking friendship as in XXI, 22.

*oath.* A compact sealed by an oath.

**29.** *we have not touched thee.* Cf. *v.* 11.

**33.** *Shibah.* Better, *Good Fortune.* The Semitic root שבע—in addition to its other meanings and because of those other meanings—denotes 'to be fortunate'. Thus the Samaritan Targum for באשרי in Gen. XXX, 13 is במשבעי (Oppenheim in Berliner's *Magazin*, 1875).

*Beer-sheba.* i.e. Fortune's Well.

**34.** *Judith.* It is not found again in the Bible, but is the name of the heroine of one of the books of the Apocrypha.

*Basemath.* In XXXVI, 2 f, we are given the names of more wives of Esau.

**35.** *a bitterness of spirit.* Or, 'a grief of mind.' It was against the family tradition to intermarry with these races; see XXIV, 3; XXVII, 46. The mention of Esau's wives is introduced here to show how faithless he was to the teachings and example of Abraham and Isaac, and therefore unworthy to be regarded as their spiritual heir and to receive his father's blessing.

CHAPTER XXVII. THE BLESSING OF ISAAC

**2.** *I know not the day of my death.* 'I know not how soon I may die' (Moffatt).

**4.** *my soul may bless thee.* Only an emphatic form of 'I may bless thee'; see on XII, 13. The dying utterance was deemed prophetic.

**5.** *heard.* More accurately, 'was listening.' To understand Rebekah's action, it is necessary to bear in mind what had been stated in XXV, 23. When she had inquired of the LORD about her unborn children, she had been told, 'the elder

## GENESIS XXVII, 6

spoke to Esau his son. And Esau went to the field to hunt for venison, and to bring it. 6. And Rebekah spoke unto Jacob her son, saying: 'Behold, I heard thy father speak unto Esau thy brother, saying: 7. Bring me venison, and make me savoury food, that I may eat, and bless thee before the LORD before my death. 8. Now therefore, my son, hearken to my voice according to that which I command thee. 9. Go now to the flock, and fetch me from thence two good kids of the goats; and I will make them savoury food for thy father, such as he loveth; 10. and thou shalt bring it to thy father, that he may eat, so that he may bless thee before his death.' 11. And Jacob said to Rebekah his mother: 'Behold, Esau my brother is a hairy man, and I am a smooth man. 12. My father peradventure will feel me, and I shall seem to him as a mocker; and I shall bring a curse upon me, and not a blessing.' 13. And his mother said unto him: 'Upon me be thy curse, my son; only hearken to my voice, and go fetch me them.' 14. And he went, and fetched, and brought them to his mother; and his mother made savoury food, such as his father loved. 15. And Rebekah took the choicest garments of Esau her elder son, which were with her in the house, and put them upon Jacob her younger son. 16. And she put the skins of the kids of the goats upon his hands, and upon the smooth of his neck. 17. And she gave the savoury food and the bread, which she had prepared, into the hand of her son Jacob. 18. And he came unto his father, and said: 'My father'; and he said: 'Here am I; who art thou, my son?' 19. And Jacob said unto his father: 'I am Esau thy first-born; I have done according as thou badest me. Arise, I pray thee, sit and eat of my venison, that thy soul may bless me.' 20. And Isaac said unto his son: 'How is it that thou hast found it so quickly, my son?' And he said: 'Because the LORD thy God sent me good

shall serve the younger.' This prophecy appeared on the point of being falsified by Isaac's intention to bestow his chief blessing upon Esau. Knowing how attached Isaac was to the elder son, she must have felt that it would be useless to try and dissuade her husband from his intention. She, therefore, in desperation, decided to circumvent him.

**12.** *mocker.* Or, 'deceiver.'

**15.** *choicest garments.* As distinct from the rough and blood-stained garments he wore when hunting.

*which were with her in the house.* Though Esau was married and presumably had a home of his own, he would keep some of his clothes at his father's house, which he would don during his visits from hunting, after removing his soiled garments.

**19.** *I am Esau thy first-born.* These words misled Isaac, and were spoken with the intention of inducing his father to believe that it was Esau who stood before him. Jacob, having been persuaded to adopt his mother's plan, is forced to play his part to the end (Ibn Ezra).

**20.** *so quickly.* This was not an oversight of Rebekah's. She was obliged to hurry lest Esau should return and upset the plot.

*the LORD thy God sent me good speed.* Such words were not of the kind likely to have been spoken by the rough Esau. The name of God was probably rare on his lips. Hence Jacob's

## GENESIS XXVII, 21

speed.' 21. And Isaac said unto Jacob: 'Come near, I pray thee, that I may feel thee, my son, whether thou be my very son Esau or not.' 22. And Jacob went near unto Isaac his father; and he felt him, and said: 'The voice is the voice of Jacob, but the hands are the hands of Esau.' 23. And he discerned him not, because his hands were hairy, as his brother Esau's hands; so he blessed him. 24. And he said: 'Art thou my very son Esau?' And he said: 'I am.' 25. And he said: 'Bring it near to me, and I will eat of my son's venison, that my soul may bless thee.' And he brought it near to him, and he did eat; and he brought him wine, and he drank. 26. And his father Isaac said unto him: 'Come near now, and kiss me, my son.' 27. And he came near, and kissed him. And he smelled the smell of his raiment, and blessed him, and said:

> See, the smell of my son
> Is as the smell of a field which the Lord hath blessed.* vi.
> 28. So God give thee of the dew of heaven,
> And of the fat places of the earth,
> And plenty of corn and wine.
> 29. Let peoples serve thee,
> And nations bow down to thee.
> Be lord over thy brethren,
> And let thy mother's sons bow down to thee.
> Cursed be every one that curseth thee,
> And blessed be every one that blesseth thee.

30. And it came to pass, as soon as Isaac had made an end of blessing Jacob, and Jacob was yet scarce gone out from the presence of Isaac his father, that Esau his brother came in from his hunting. 31. And he also made savoury food, and brought it unto his father; and he said unto his father: 'Let my father arise, and eat of his son's venison, that my soul may bless me.' 32. And Isaac his father said unto him: 'Who art thou?' And he said: 'I am thy son, thy first-born, Esau.' 33. And

statement arouses his father's suspicions, who requires to be assured by the very test which Jacob dreaded, in *v.* 12.

**23.** *so he blessed him.* If that be the meaning of the Hebrew, we should expect the wording of the blessing to follow immediately. We do not, however, have that until *v.* 28. It is therefore possible that the Hebrew should here be rendered: 'he greeted him.'

**28.** *the dew of heaven.* In those countries where the days are hot and the nights are cold, the dew is very abundant and drenches the ground. It is essential to vegetation during the rainless summer, and was therefore regarded as a Divine blessing.

**29.** *peoples.* Refers to foreign nations, like the Canaanites.

*brethren.* Kindred peoples.

*thy mother's sons.* 'Sons' is here used in the sense of descendants.

*cursed . . . blessed.* Jacob was thus to inherit the Divine promise made to Abraham in XII, 3.

**33.** *yea, and he shall be blessed.* The benediction, having been uttered, was irrevocable. It may also imply that Isaac saw in what had happened the will of God.

## GENESIS XXVII, 34

Isaac trembled very exceedingly, and said: 'Who then is he that hath taken venison, and brought it me, and I have eaten of all before thou camest, and have blessed him? yea, and he shall be blessed.' 34. When Esau heard the words of his father, he cried with an exceeding great and bitter cry, and said unto his father: 'Bless me, even me also, O my father.' 35. And he said: 'Thy brother came with guile, and hath taken away thy blessing.' 36. And he said: 'Is not he rightly named Jacob? for he hath supplanted me these two times: he took away my birthright; and, behold, now he hath taken away my blessing.' And he said: 'Hast thou not reserved a blessing for me?' 37. And Isaac answered and said unto Esau: 'Behold, I have made him thy lord, and all his brethren have I given to him for servants; and with corn and wine have I sustained him; and what then shall I do for thee, my son?' 38. And Esau said unto his father: 'Hast thou but one blessing, my father? bless me, even me also, O my father.' And Esau lifted up his voice, and wept. 39. And Isaac his father answered and said unto him:

Behold, of the fat places of the earth shall be thy dwelling,
And of the dew of heaven from above;
40. And by thy sword shalt thou live, and thou shalt serve thy brother;
And it shall come to pass when thou shalt break loose,
That thou shalt shake his yoke from off thy neck.

41. And Esau hated Jacob because of the blessing wherewith his father blessed him. And Esau said in his heart: 'Let the days of mourning for my father be at hand; then will I slay my brother Jacob.' 42. And the words of Esau her elder son were told to Rebekah; and she sent and called Jacob her younger son, and said unto him:

---

**36.** *supplanted. i.e.* outwitted.

*my birthright.* In his passionate anger, he blames Jacob for 'taking away' that which he sold and ratified with an oath.

**38.** *wept.* 'Those tears of Esau, the sensuous, wild impulsive man, almost like the cry of some "trapped creature", are among the most pathetic in the Bible' (Davidson). The Rabbis declare that bitter retribution was in later years exacted from Jacob for having caused these tears of Esau.

**40.** *by the sword shalt thou live. i.e.* by campaigns of plunder. The life of marauders dwelling in mountain fastnesses will be his. He will raid his brother's borders, and cut off the merchants travelling with caravans (Ryle).

*thou shalt serve thy brother.* The promise of lordship made to Jacob could not be recalled; but Isaac foretells that it will be of limited duration. We read of revolts on the part of the Edomites in I Kings XI, 14 f, and II Kings VIII, 20 f.

**41.** *mourning for my father.* It is at least to Esau's credit that he decided to spare his father's feelings, and wait for his death before avenging himself on Jacob (Midrash).

## GENESIS XXVII, 43

'Behold, thy brother Esau, as touching thee, doth comfort himself, purposing to kill thee. 43. Now therefore, my son, hearken to my voice; and arise, flee thou to Laban my brother to Haran; 44. and tarry with him a few days, until thy brother's fury turn away; 45. until thy brother's anger turn away from thee, and he forget that which thou hast done to him; then I will send, and fetch thee from thence; why should I be bereaved of you both in one day?' ¶ 46. And Rebekah said to Isaac: 'I am weary of my life because of the daughters of Heth. If Jacob take a wife of the daughters of Heth, such as these, of the daughters of the land, what good shall my life do me?'

## 28

### CHAPTER XXVIII

1. And Isaac called Jacob, and blessed him, and charged him, and said unto him: 'Thou shalt not take a wife of the daughters of Canaan. 2. Arise, go to Paddan-aram, to the house of Bethuel thy mother's father; and take thee a wife from thence of the daughters of Laban thy mother's brother. 3. And God Almighty bless thee, and make thee fruitful, and multiply thee, that thou mayest be a congregation of peoples; 4. and give thee the blessing of Abraham, to thee, and to thy seed with thee; that thou mayest inherit the land of thy sojournings, which God gave unto Abraham.'* vii. 5. And Isaac sent away Jacob; and he went to Paddan-aram unto Laban, son of Bethuel the Aramean, the brother of Rebekah, Jacob's and Esau's mother. 6. Now Esau saw that Isaac had blessed Jacob and sent him away to Paddan-aram, to take him a wife from thence; and that as he blessed him he gave him a charge, saying: 'Thou shalt not take a wife of the daughters of Canaan';* m. 7. and that Jacob hearkened to his father and his mother, and was gone to Paddan-aram; 8. and Esau saw that the daughters of Canaan pleased not Isaac his father; 9. so Esau went unto Ishmael, and took unto the wives that he had Mahalath the daughter of Ishmael Abraham's son, the sister of Nebaioth, to be his wife.

**44.** *a few days.* It was the mother's hope that the difference between the brothers would soon be smoothed over, and the pain of separation be quickly succeeded by the joy of reunion. But she was fated never to see him again.

**45.** *bereaved of you both.* Isaac and Jacob; the death of the former being the signal for the murder of the latter.

**46.** *daughters of Heth.* See XXVI, 34 f. To save Isaac from the knowledge of the true reason why Jacob was leaving his home, Rebekah pretends that he is going to Haran in search of a wife.

### CHAPTER XXVIII

**2.** *Paddan-aram.* See on XXV, 20.
**3.** *God Almighty.* See on XVII, 1.
**4.** *the blessing of Abraham.* Cf. XXV, 20.
**9.** *unto the wives.* In addition to those mentioned in XXVI, 34. It seems that he married his cousin in order to propitiate his parents, who were grieved at his alien wives.

# HAFTORAH TOLEDOTH  הפטרת תולדת

## MALACHI I–II, 7

CHAPTER I

1. The burden of the word of the LORD to Israel by Malachi.

2. I have loved you, saith the LORD.
Yet ye say: 'Wherein hast Thou loved us?'
Was not Esau Jacob's brother?
Saith the LORD;
Yet I loved Jacob;

3. But Esau I hated,
And made his mountains a desolation,
And gave his heritage to the jackals of the wilderness.

4. Whereas Edom saith:
'We are beaten down,
But we will return and build the waste places';
Thus saith the LORD of hosts:
They shall build, but I will throw down;
And they shall be called The border of wickedness,
And The people whom the LORD execrateth for ever.

5. And your eyes shall see,
And ye shall say:
'The LORD is great beyond the border of Israel.'

---

MALACHI I–II, 7

Malachi was the last of the Prophets. Nothing is known of his life, except what can be gathered from his prophecies, which seem to have been spoken some time about the year 450 before the Common Era.

The Second Temple had been rebuilt, but the high hopes of the returned exiles had not been fulfilled. The lamp of religious enthusiasm burned but dimly in that age, and both priest and people treated sacred things with a weary indifference. Though from the rising of the sun until the going down of the same, God's name was revered among the nations, It was Israel that began to doubt whether there was a righteous Governor of the universe, and was losing Israel's belief in Israel. 'I have loved you, saith the LORD. Yet ye say, "Wherein hast Thou loved us?" Your words have been stout against Me. Ye have said, "it is vain to serve God, and what profit is it that we have kept His charge?"'

It is to such a generation that Malachi brings his 'burden', i.e. utterance, message. He reaffirms and boldly proclaims the Divine election and the deathlessness of Israel. Confronted by sordid irreligion and cruel selfishness, he preaches the reality of the Unseen, and gives eternal expression to the brotherhood of man. 'Have we not all one father? Hath not one God created us? Why do we deal treacherously every man against his brother?' he asks. These words alone should endear him to every human heart.

The connection with the Sedrah lies chiefly in the opening verses.

The difference in the treatment of the two nations descended from Jacob and Esau is due to the difference in the character and life of these nations. The Edomites were a fierce and cruel people, 'a turbulent and unruly race, always hovering on the verge of revolution, ... rushing to battle as if going to a feast' (Josephus). In the Rabbinical writings, Edom became the name, the veiled name for tyrannous Imperial Rome, and in later times for the persecuting Christian Church.

3. *Esau I hated.* 'Loved' and 'hated' in this and the preceding verse are relative terms only, denoting that one has been preferred to another; cf. the similar phraseology applied to Leah and Rachel, and used in Deut. XXI, 15.

4. Some disaster has recently befallen the Edomites; but for them there is no hope of restoration such as Israel has enjoyed.

# MALACHI I, 6

6. A son honoureth his father,
And a servant his master;
If then I be a father,
Where is My honour?
And If I be a master,
Where is My fear?
Saith the Lord of hosts
Unto you, O priests, that despise My name.
And ye say: 'Wherein have we despised Thy name?'

7. Ye offer polluted bread upon Mine altar.
And ye say: 'Wherein have we polluted Thee?'
In that ye say: 'The table of the Lord is contemptible.'

8. And when ye offer the blind for sacrifice, it is no evil!
And when ye offer the lame and sick, it is no evil!
Present it now unto thy governor;
Will he be pleased with thee?
Or will he accept thy person?
Saith the Lord of hosts.

9. And now, I pray you, entreat the favour of God
That He may be gracious unto us!—
This hath been of your doing.—
Will He accept any of your persons?
Saith the Lord of hosts.

10. Oh that there were even one among you that would shut the doors,
That ye might not kindle fire on Mine altar in vain!
I have no pleasure in you,
Saith the Lord of hosts,
Neither will I accept an offering at your hand.

11. For from the rising of the sun even unto the going down of the same
My name is great among the nations;

And in every place offerings are presented unto My name,
Even pure oblations;
For My name is great among the nations,
Saith the Lord of hosts.

12. But ye profane it,
In that ye say:

---

**6–8.** The Prophet rebukes the degenerate priests who are bringing the service of God into contempt.

**7.** *polluted bread.* In their indifference, they accepted blemished animals and did not rebuke the people who presented them.

**8.** *accept thy person. i.e.* receive thee favourably. Would you treat your earthly ruler as you treat God?

**9.** The office of the true priest was to supplicate God on behalf of the people: could He receive prayers at their hands when they were responsible for such wrong?

**10.** It were better that the altar fires go out altogether, than that sacrifices should be offered in such spirit.

**11.** *great among the nations. i.e.* even the heathen nations that worship the heavenly hosts pay tribute to a Supreme Being, and in this way honour My Name; and the offerings which they thus present (indirectly) unto Me are animated by a pure spirit, God looking to the heart of the worshipper. This wonderful thought was further developed by the Rabbis, and is characteristic of the universalism of Judaism; see on Deut. IV, 19.

**12.** *in that ye say.* Not literally—their actions speak.

# MALACHI I, 13

'The table of the LORD is polluted,
And the fruit thereof, even the food thereof, is contemptible.'

13. Ye say also:
'Behold, what a weariness is it!'
And ye have snuffed at it,
Saith the LORD of hosts;
And ye have brought that which was taken by violence,
And the lame, and the sick;
Thus ye bring the offering;
Should I accept this of your hand?
Saith the LORD.

14. But cursed be he that dealeth craftily,
Whereas he hath in his flock a male,
And voweth, and sacrificeth unto the LORD a blemished thing;
For I am a great King,
Saith the LORD of hosts,
And My name is feared among the nations.

### CHAPTER II

1. And now, this commandment
Is for you, O ye priests.

2. If ye will not hearken, and if ye will not lay it to heart,
To give glory unto My name,
Saith the LORD of hosts,
Then will I send the curse upon you,
And I will curse your blessings;
Yea, I curse them,
Because ye do not lay it to heart.

3. Behold, I will rebuke the seed for your hurt,
And will spread dung upon your faces,
Even the dung of your sacrifices;
And ye shall be taken away unto it.

4. Know then that I have sent
This commandment unto you,
That My covenant might be with Levi,
Saith the LORD of hosts.

5. My covenant was with him
Of life and peace, and I gave them to him,
And of fear, and he feared Me,
And was afraid of My name.

---

**13.** *that which was taken by violence.* Even 'wild animals' were not to be brought as sacrifices, because a person must not offer anything which costs nothing; how much the more heinous was it to offer a robbed thing as a sacrifice! It is adding blasphemy to crime.

#### CHAPTER II, 1-7

A charge to the priests to be worthy of their vocation, or dire suffering and indignity will be the result.

**2.** *curse your blessings.* Those to whom you should be a source of blessing will suffer grave injury through you and your example.

**3.** *rebuke the seed.* That it will not sprout and thrive—to your loss.

*upon your faces.* i.e. in your presence. An act of insult. Malachi means that the priests will be utterly despised by the people.

**4.** *Levi.* The tribe of Levi, as the priestly tribe.

**5.** *covenant of life and peace.* Life, in the highest sense, and peace would be the result of the priest's faithfulness to his vocation; but the fear of God, *i.e.* the reverential awe for the God of Holiness, is the first essential.

## MALACHI II, 6 — מלאכי ב

6. The law of truth was in his mouth,
And unrighteousness was not found in his lips;
He walked with Me in peace and uprightness,
And did turn many away from iniquity.
7. For the priest's lips should keep knowledge,
And they should seek the law at his mouth;
For he is the messenger of the LORD of hosts.

6 וּמִפְּנֵי שְׁמִי נִחַת הוּא: תּוֹרַת אֱמֶת הָיְתָה בְּפִיהוּ וְעַוְלָה לֹא־נִמְצָא בִשְׂפָתָיו בְּשָׁלוֹם וּבְמִישׁוֹר הָלַךְ אִתִּי וְרַבִּים
7 הֵשִׁיב מֵעָוֺן: כִּי־שִׂפְתֵי כֹהֵן יִשְׁמְרוּ־דַעַת וְתוֹרָה יְבַקְשׁוּ מִפִּיהוּ כִּי מַלְאַךְ יְהֹוָה־צְבָאוֹת הוּא:

**6.** The spiritual results that had been achieved through the faithful priests in whom this true fear of God was found.

*turn many away from iniquity.* His influence was seen in the lives of men; cf. Daniel XII, 3.

**7.** Completes with *v.* 6 the ideal of the true priest, as the spokesman of God, never more beautifully expressed.

*law.* lit. 'instruction', in God's commands.

## GENESIS XXVIII, 10

**28** 10. And Jacob went out from Beer-sheba, and went toward Haran. 11. And he lighted upon the place, and tarried there all night, because the sun was set; and he took one of the stones of the place, and put it under his head, and lay down in that place to sleep. 12. And he dreamed, and behold a ladder set up on the earth, and the top of it reached to heaven; and behold the angels of God ascending and descending on it. 13. And, behold, the LORD stood beside him, and said: 'I am the LORD, the God of Abraham thy father, and the God of Isaac. The land whereon thou liest, to thee will I give it, and to thy seed. 14. And thy seed shall be as the dust of the earth, and thou shalt spread abroad to the west, and to the east, and to the north, and to the south. And in thee and in thy seed shall all the families of the earth be blessed. 15. And behold, I am with thee, and will keep thee whithersoever thou goest, and will bring thee back into this land; for I will not leave thee, until I have done that which I have spoken to thee of.' 16. And Jacob awaked out of his sleep, and he said:

בראשית ויצא כח

כח ס ס ס 7

11 וַיֵּצֵא יַעֲקֹב מִבְּאֵר שָׁבַע וַיֵּלֶךְ חָרָנָה: וַיִּפְגַּע בַּמָּקוֹם וַיָּלֶן שָׁם כִּי־בָא הַשֶּׁמֶשׁ וַיִּקַּח מֵאַבְנֵי הַמָּקוֹם וַיָּשֶׂם מְרַאֲשֹׁתָיו

12 וַיִּשְׁכַּב בַּמָּקוֹם הַהוּא: וַיַּחֲלֹם וְהִנֵּה סֻלָּם מֻצָּב אַרְצָה וְרֹאשׁוֹ מַגִּיעַ הַשָּׁמָיְמָה וְהִנֵּה מַלְאֲכֵי אֱלֹהִים עֹלִים וְיֹרְדִים

13 בּוֹ: וְהִנֵּה יְהוָה נִצָּב עָלָיו וַיֹּאמַר אֲנִי יְהוָה אֱלֹהֵי אַבְרָהָם אָבִיךָ וֵאלֹהֵי יִצְחָק הָאָרֶץ אֲשֶׁר אַתָּה שֹׁכֵב עָלֶיהָ לְךָ

14 אֶתְּנֶנָּה וּלְזַרְעֶךָ: וְהָיָה זַרְעֲךָ כַּעֲפַר הָאָרֶץ וּפָרַצְתָּ יָמָּה וָקֵדְמָה וְצָפֹנָה וָנֶגְבָּה וְנִבְרְכוּ בְךָ כָּל־מִשְׁפְּחֹת הָאֲדָמָה

טו וּבְזַרְעֶךָ: וְהִנֵּה אָנֹכִי עִמָּךְ וּשְׁמַרְתִּיךָ בְּכֹל אֲשֶׁר־תֵּלֵךְ וַהֲשִׁבֹתִיךָ אֶל־הָאֲדָמָה הַזֹּאת כִּי לֹא אֶעֱזָבְךָ עַד אֲשֶׁר אִם־

16 עָשִׂיתִי אֵת אֲשֶׁר־דִּבַּרְתִּי לָךְ: וַיִּיקַץ יַעֲקֹב מִשְּׁנָתוֹ וַיֹּאמֶר

17 אָכֵן יֵשׁ יְהוָה בַּמָּקוֹם הַזֶּה וְאָנֹכִי לֹא יָדָעְתִּי: וַיִּירָא וַיֹּאמַר

## VII. VAYYETZE

### (CHAPTERS XXVIII, 10–XXXII, 3)

CHAPTER XXVIII, 10–22. JACOB'S DREAM

**10.** *went out from Beer-sheba.* Why is this mentioned—ask the Rabbis—since it would have been sufficient to state, 'Jacob went towards Haran'? They reply that the departure of a righteous man from any place diminishes its importance, and should be keenly felt by its inhabitants.

**11.** *and he lighted.* Since the same Heb. word signifies 'to entreat', the Talmud deduces from this passage that Jacob prayed there for Divine protection, and thus instituted the Evening Prayer (see on XXIV, 63).

*the place.* The Rabbis stress the definite article in the Heb. idiom, and state that it was Mount Moriah.

**12.** The description of Jacob's dream is among the most beautiful in literature (Hazlitt). We have here wonderful imagery which, in its symbolism, speaks to each man according to his mental and spiritual outlook. Its message to Jacob is its message to all men in all ages—that the earth is full of the glory of God, that He is not far off in His heavenly abode and heedless of what men do on earth. Every spot on earth may be for man 'the gate of heaven'.

*ascending and descending.* It is to be noted that the angels are first mentioned as ascending, as though they had been accompanying the Patriarch on his journey. He may have been without human friends; but, unseen, there had been angels by his side to protect and encourage him.

**13.** *beside him.* Or, 'above it,' *i.e.* the ladder. The translation, 'beside him,' is supported by many Jewish commentators and is to be preferred.

*thy father.* *i.e.* thy ancestor. Jacob's relationship with Abraham is referred to because it was to him that the original promise had been made which Jacob was now told he would inherit.

**14.** *spread abroad.* lit. 'break forth', *i.e.* burst the narrow boundaries.

*be blessed.* See on XII, 3.

**15.** *I am with thee.* Therefore Jacob need have no fear of the threats of Esau.

**16.** *I knew it not.* In popular belief the presence of God was restricted to 'sacred places'. Many people still confine religion to sacred occasions and the sacred locality which is their place of worship, instead of looking upon religion as a continuously active influence and regulative principle in their daily life.

# GENESIS XXVIII, 17

בְּרֵאשִׁית וַיֵּצֵא כח כט

'Surely the LORD is in this place; and I knew it not.' 17. And he was afraid, and said: 'How full of awe is this place! this is none other than the house of God, and this is the gate of heaven.' 18. And Jacob rose up early in the morning, and took the stone that he had put under his head, and set it up for a pillar, and poured oil upon the top of it. 19. And he called the name of that place ¹Beth-el, but the name of the city was Luz at the first. 20. And Jacob vowed a vow, saying: 'If God will be with me, and will keep me in this way that I go, and will give me bread to eat, and raiment to put on, 21. so that I come back to my father's house in peace, then shall the LORD be my God, 22. and this stone, which I have set up for a pillar, shall be God's house; and of all that Thou shalt give me I will surely give the tenth unto Thee.'* ᴵᴵ.

מַה־נּוֹרָא הַמָּקוֹם הַזֶּה אֵין זֶה כִּי אִם־בֵּית אֱלֹהִים וְזֶה
שַׁעַר הַשָּׁמָיִם: וַיַּשְׁכֵּם יַעֲקֹב בַּבֹּקֶר וַיִּקַּח אֶת־הָאֶבֶן אֲשֶׁר־
שָׂם מְרַאֲשֹׁתָיו וַיָּשֶׂם אֹתָהּ מַצֵּבָה וַיִּצֹק שֶׁמֶן עַל־רֹאשָׁהּ:
וַיִּקְרָא אֶת־שֵׁם־הַמָּקוֹם הַהוּא בֵּית־אֵל וְאוּלָם לוּז שֵׁם־
הָעִיר לָרִאשֹׁנָה: וַיִּדַּר יַעֲקֹב נֶדֶר לֵאמֹר אִם־יִהְיֶה
אֱלֹהִים עִמָּדִי וּשְׁמָרַנִי בַּדֶּרֶךְ הַזֶּה אֲשֶׁר אָנֹכִי הוֹלֵךְ וְנָתַן־
לִי לֶחֶם לֶאֱכֹל וּבֶגֶד לִלְבֹּשׁ: וְשַׁבְתִּי בְשָׁלוֹם אֶל־בֵּית אָבִי
וְהָיָה יְהוָה לִי לֵאלֹהִים: וְהָאֶבֶן הַזֹּאת אֲשֶׁר־שַׂמְתִּי מַצֵּבָה
יִהְיֶה בֵּית אֱלֹהִים וְכֹל אֲשֶׁר תִּתֶּן־לִי עַשֵּׂר אֲעַשְּׂרֶנּוּ לָךְ׃

18
19
כ
20
21
22
שני

## 29 CHAPTER XXIX

CAP. XXIX. כט

כט

1. Then Jacob went on his journey, and came to the land of the children of the east. 2. And he looked, and behold a well in the field, and lo three flocks of sheep lying there by it.—For out of that well they watered the flocks. And the stone upon the well's mouth was great. 3. And thither were all the flocks gathered; and they rolled the stone from the well's mouth, and watered the sheep, and put the stone back upon the well's mouth in its place.—4. And Jacob said unto them: 'My brethren, whence are ye?' And they said: 'Of Haran are we.' 5. And he said unto them: 'Know

וַיִּשָּׂא יַעֲקֹב רַגְלָיו וַיֵּלֶךְ אַרְצָה בְנֵי־קֶדֶם: וַיַּרְא וְהִנֵּה
בְאֵר בַּשָּׂדֶה וְהִנֵּה־שָׁם שְׁלֹשָׁה עֶדְרֵי־צֹאן רֹבְצִים עָלֶיהָ
כִּי מִן־הַבְּאֵר הַהִוא יַשְׁקוּ הָעֲדָרִים וְהָאֶבֶן גְּדֹלָה עַל־
פִּי הַבְּאֵר: וְנֶאֶסְפוּ־שָׁמָּה כָל־הָעֲדָרִים וְגָלֲלוּ אֶת־הָאֶבֶן
מֵעַל פִּי הַבְּאֵר וְהִשְׁקוּ אֶת־הַצֹּאן וְהֵשִׁיבוּ אֶת־הָאֶבֶן עַל־
פִּי הַבְּאֵר לִמְקֹמָהּ: וַיֹּאמֶר לָהֶם יַעֲקֹב אַחַי מֵאַיִן אַתֶּם
וַיֹּאמְרוּ מֵחָרָן אֲנָחְנוּ: וַיֹּאמֶר לָהֶם הַיְדַעְתֶּם אֶת־לָבָן

א 2

3

4

ה

---

¹ That is, *The house of God.*

כח׳ v. 18. צ׳ רפה

---

**17.** *full of awe.* The Heb. word *nora* signifies, inspiring reverential awe.

**18.** *for a pillar.* Not intended as an altar or as an act of worship, but to mark the spot where he had had the fateful dream-vision. He hopes, however, at a later time to erect a Sanctuary on the spot (see *v.* 22).

*poured oil.* To distinguish that stone from the rest, so that Jacob might recognize it on his return (Ibn Ezra).

**19.** *Luz.* The holy place Beth-el was outside the old city of Luz. Jacob did not spend the night in Luz but on its outskirts. We learn from Chap. XIX of the dangers which might attend a traveller who entered a strange town at night.

**20.** *vowed.* Jacob resolved to devote a part of the prosperity which God had promised him to His service. This is the first mention of a vow in the Bible.

**21.** *then shall the LORD be my God.* i.e. in gratitude for His care and protection, I will dedicate my life to Him.

**22.** *tenth.* Cf. XIV, 20. The tithe figures later in the laws of the Israelite people. To this day pious Jews spend a tenth of their earnings in charity.

### CHAPTER XXIX. JACOB AND LABAN

**1.** *children of the east.* A term to denote generally the Arab tribes located E. and N.E. of Palestine.

**2.** *the stone upon the well's mouth.* In the East, wells are still covered over with a large boulder to prevent the water from becoming polluted.

**3.** *gathered.* The verbs are 'frequentative', and should be rendered, 'All the flocks used to gather together ... used to roll ... and water' (Rashi).

**4.** *my brethren.* Evidently a common form of address.

**5.** *the son of Nahor.* Laban was Nahor's grandson; but see on XX, 12.

*we know him.* There is no word in Biblical Hebrew corresponding to our 'yes'; consequently the answer to a question is a repetition of the word or words in the affirmative or negative.

GENESIS XXIX, 6

ye Laban the son of Nahor?' And they said: 'We know him.' 6. And he said unto them: 'Is it well with him?' And they said: 'It is well; and, behold, Rachel his daughter cometh with the sheep.' 7. And he said: 'Lo, it is yet high day, neither is it time that the cattle should be gathered together; water ye the sheep, and go and feed them.' 8. And they said: 'We cannot, until all the flocks be gathered together, and they roll the stone from the well's mouth; then we water the sheep.' 9. While he was yet speaking with them, Rachel came with her father's sheep; for she tended them. 10. And it came to pass, when Jacob saw Rachel the daughter of Laban his mother's brother, and the sheep of Laban his mother's brother, that Jacob went near, and rolled the stone from the well's mouth, and watered the flock of Laban his mother's brother. 11. And Jacob kissed Rachel, and lifted up his voice, and wept. 12. And Jacob told Rachel that he was her father's brother, and that he was Rebekah's son; and she ran and told her father. 13. And it came to pass, when Laban heard the tidings of Jacob his sister's son, that he ran to meet him, and embraced him, and kissed him, and brought him to his house. And he told Laban all these things. 14. And Laban said to him: 'Surely thou art my bone and my flesh.' And he abode with him the space of a month. 15. And Laban said unto Jacob: 'Because thou art my brother, shouldest thou therefore serve me for nought? tell me, what shall thy wages be?' 16. Now Laban had two daughters: the name of the elder was Leah, and the name of the younger was Rachel. 17. And Leah's eyes were weak; but Rachel was of

---

**6.** *is it well with him?* lit. 'is there peace to him?'
*cometh.* lit. 'is coming'.

**8.** They wait for others to arrive, so that by their combined effort they remove the stone; or, possibly, because it would be unwise to remove the stone until all the flocks were there, lest in the interval the wind blew dust and sand into the well.

**9.** *tended them.* To this day it would not be considered derogatory for an Arab Sheik's daughter to be his shepherdess.

**10.** Jacob disregards the local custom, and by a feat of great personal strength removes the stone. The phrase 'his mother's brother' is used three times in this verse, to denote the joy Jacob felt in meeting and helping a member of his mother's family.

**11.** *kissed.* When the Heb. verb is, as here, not followed by the accusative case, it denotes kissing the hand as a respectful salutation (Ibn Ezra).
*and wept.* 'The demonstrative display of feeling is Homeric in its simplicity' (Ryle).

**12.** *her father's brother. i.e.* her relative.
*told her father.* Her mother having died (Midrash).

**13.** *embraced him.* The effusive welcome stands in sharp contrast to Laban's later treatment of Jacob. The Rabbis doubted its genuineness.
*all these things. i.e.* that Rebekah had sent him because of the wrath of Esau.

**14.** *my bone and my flesh.* As his near kinsman, he is welcome to his home.

**15.** *wages.* Jacob from the outset seems to have decided not to be indebted to his uncle but to earn his maintenance.

**17.** *weak.* Better, *tender*, which the Targum understands in the sense of 'beautiful'.

GENESIS XXIX, 18

בראשית ויצא כט

beautiful form and fair to look upon.* iii.
18. And Jacob loved Rachel; and he said:
'I will serve thee seven years for Rachel thy
younger daughter.' 19. And Laban said:
'It is better that I give her to thee, than that
I should give her to another man; abide
with me.' 20. And Jacob served seven
years for Rachel; and they seemed unto
him but a few days, for the love he had to
her. 21. And Jacob said unto Laban:
'Give me my wife, for my days are fulfilled,
that I may go in unto her.' 22. And Laban
gathered together all the men of the place,
and made a feast. 23. And it came to pass
in the evening, that he took Leah his
daughter and brought her to him; and
he went in unto her. 24. And Laban gave
Zilpah his handmaid unto his daughter
Leah for a handmaid. 25. And it came to
pass in the morning that, behold, it was
Leah; and he said to Laban: 'What is
this thou hast done unto me? did not I
serve with thee for Rachel? wherefore then
hast thou beguiled me?' 26. And Laban
said: 'It is not so done in our place, to give
the younger before the first-born. 27.
Fulfil the week of this one, and we will give
thee the other also for the service which
thou shalt serve with me yet seven other
years.' 28. And Jacob did so, and fulfilled
her week; and he gave him Rachel his
daughter to wife. 29. And Laban gave to
Rachel his daughter Bilhah his handmaid
to be her handmaid. 30. And he went in
also unto Rachel, and he loved Rachel more
than Leah, and served with him yet seven
other years. ¶ 31. And the LORD saw that
Leah was hated, and He opened her womb;

18 וַיֶּאֱהַב יַעֲקֹב אֶת־רָחֵל וַיֹּאמֶר אֶעֱבָדְךָ שֶׁבַע שָׁנִים בְּרָחֵל
19 בִּתְּךָ הַקְּטַנָּה: וַיֹּאמֶר לָבָן טוֹב תִּתִּי אֹתָהּ לָךְ מִתִּתִּי
כ אֹתָהּ לְאִישׁ אַחֵר שְׁבָה עִמָּדִי: וַיַּעֲבֹד יַעֲקֹב בְּרָחֵל שֶׁבַע
21 שָׁנִים וַיִּהְיוּ בְעֵינָיו כְּיָמִים אֲחָדִים בְּאַהֲבָתוֹ אֹתָהּ: וַיֹּאמֶר
יַעֲקֹב אֶל־לָבָן הָבָה אֶת־אִשְׁתִּי כִּי מָלְאוּ יָמָי וְאָבוֹאָה
22 אֵלֶיהָ: וַיֶּאֱסֹף לָבָן אֶת־כָּל־אַנְשֵׁי הַמָּקוֹם וַיַּעַשׂ מִשְׁתֶּה:
23 וַיְהִי בָעֶרֶב וַיִּקַּח אֶת־לֵאָה בִתּוֹ וַיָּבֵא אֹתָהּ אֵלָיו וַיָּבֹא
24 אֵלֶיהָ: וַיִּתֵּן לָבָן לָהּ אֶת־זִלְפָּה שִׁפְחָתוֹ לְלֵאָה בִתּוֹ שִׁפְחָה:
כה וַיְהִי בַבֹּקֶר וְהִנֵּה־הִוא לֵאָה וַיֹּאמֶר אֶל־לָבָן מַה־זֹּאת
26 עָשִׂיתָ לִּי הֲלֹא בְרָחֵל עָבַדְתִּי עִמָּךְ וְלָמָּה רִמִּיתָנִי: וַיֹּאמֶר
לָבָן לֹא־יֵעָשֶׂה כֵן בִּמְקוֹמֵנוּ לָתֵת הַצְּעִירָה לִפְנֵי הַבְּכִירָה:
27 מַלֵּא שְׁבֻעַ זֹאת וְנִתְּנָה לְךָ גַּם־אֶת־זֹאת בַּעֲבֹדָה אֲשֶׁר
28 תַּעֲבֹד עִמָּדִי עוֹד שֶׁבַע־שָׁנִים אֲחֵרוֹת: וַיַּעַשׂ יַעֲקֹב כֵּן
29 וַיְמַלֵּא שְׁבֻעַ זֹאת וַיִּתֶּן־לוֹ אֶת־רָחֵל בִּתּוֹ לוֹ לְאִשָּׁה: וַיִּתֵּן
ל לָבָן לְרָחֵל בִּתּוֹ אֶת־בִּלְהָה שִׁפְחָתוֹ לָהּ לְשִׁפְחָה: וַיָּבֹא
גַּם אֶל־רָחֵל וַיֶּאֱהַב גַּם־אֶת־רָחֵל מִלֵּאָה וַיַּעֲבֹד עִמּוֹ עוֹד
31 שֶׁבַע־שָׁנִים אֲחֵרוֹת: וַיַּרְא יְהֹוָה כִּי־שְׂנוּאָה לֵאָה וַיִּפְתַּח

v. 28. במקצת ספרים אין מלת לו

**18.** *for Rachel.* See on XXIV, 53. It is still the custom in the East for a man who cannot provide money or cattle to offer his labour as a substitute for such compensation.

**19.** *to thee.* A relative; it was considered preferable for husband and wife to belong to the same family.

**20.** *and they seemed unto him but a few days, for the love he had to her.* The six Heb. words of which this is the translation condense a world of affection and tenderest love. They are unsurpassed in the whole literature of romantic love.

**21.** *my wife.* i.e. the woman who was betrothed to him as his wife.

**23.** *he took Leah.* Heavily veiled and in the dark. This fraud may be regarded as a retribution for the deception which Jacob himself practised upon his father.

**26.** *give the younger.* A feigned excuse, since the feast was for the maiden for whom Jacob had served.

**27.** *fulfil the week of this one.* i.e. do not repudiate the marriage with Leah. The wedding celebrations usually lasted a week; cf. Judges XIV, 12.

*we will give thee.* i.e. Laban and his family will give; cf. XXIV, 50.

**28.** *and he gave him Rachel.* Eight days after Leah, on the understanding that Jacob was to serve Laban for another seven years. After the Giving of the Law at Sinai, the marrying of two sisters was forbidden.

**30.** *seven other years.* The Midrash comments that Jacob served the second term as conscientiously as the first, although he was labouring under a sense of grievance against his uncle.

CHAPTER XXIX, 31—XXX, 24. THE BIRTH OF
JACOB'S CHILDREN

**31.** *hated.* The word here only means 'less loved'—not that Jacob had an aversion to her, but that he preferred Rachel; cf. Deut. XXI, 15.

## GENESIS XXIX, 32

but Rachel was barren. 32. And Leah conceived, and bore a son, and she called his name Reuben; for she said: 'Because the LORD ¹hath looked upon my affliction; for now my husband will love me.' 33. And she conceived again, and bore a son; and said: 'Because the LORD ²hath heard that I am hated, He hath therefore given me this son also.' And she called his name ³Simeon. 34. And she conceived again, and bore a son; and said: 'Now this time will my husband be ⁴joined unto me, because I have borne him three sons.' Therefore was his name called Levi. 35. And she conceived again, and bore a son; and she said: 'This time will I ⁵praise the LORD.' Therefore she called his name ⁶Judah; and she left off bearing.

## 30 CHAPTER XXX

1. And when Rachel saw that she bore Jacob no children, Rachel envied her sister; and she said unto Jacob: 'Give me children, or else I die.' 2. And Jacob's anger was kindled against Rachel; and he said: 'Am I in God's stead, who hath withheld from thee the fruit of the womb?' 3. And she said: 'Behold my maid Bilhah, go in unto her; that she may bear upon my knees, and I also may be builded up through her.' 4. And she gave him Bilhah her handmaid to wife; and Jacob went in unto her. 5. And Bilhah conceived, and bore Jacob a son. 6. And Rachel said: 'God hath ⁷judged me, and hath also heard my voice, and hath given me a son.' Therefore called she his name Dan. 7. And Bilhah Rachel's handmaid conceived again, and bore Jacob a second son. 8. And Rachel said: 'With mighty wrestlings have I ⁸wrestled with my sister, and have prevailed.' And she called his name Naphtali. 9. When Leah saw that she had left off bearing, she took Zilpah her handmaid, and gave her to Jacob to wife. 10. And Zilpah Leah's handmaid bore Jacob

בראשית ויצא כט ל

32 אֶת־רַחְמָהּ וְרָחֵל עֲקָרָה: וַתַּהַר לֵאָה וַתֵּלֶד בֵּן וַתִּקְרָא
שְׁמוֹ רְאוּבֵן כִּי אָמְרָה כִּי־רָאָה יְהֹוָה בְּעָנְיִי כִּי עַתָּה
33 יֶאֱהָבַנִי אִישִׁי: וַתַּהַר עוֹד וַתֵּלֶד בֵּן וַתֹּאמֶר כִּי־שָׁמַע
יְהֹוָה כִּי־שְׂנוּאָה אָנֹכִי וַיִּתֶּן־לִי גַּם־אֶת־זֶה וַתִּקְרָא שְׁמוֹ
34 שִׁמְעוֹן: וַתַּהַר עוֹד וַתֵּלֶד בֵּן וַתֹּאמֶר עַתָּה הַפַּעַם יִלָּוֶה
אִישִׁי אֵלַי כִּי־יָלַדְתִּי לוֹ שְׁלֹשָׁה בָנִים עַל־כֵּן קָרָא־שְׁמוֹ
לה לֵוִי: וַתַּהַר עוֹד וַתֵּלֶד בֵּן וַתֹּאמֶר הַפַּעַם אוֹדֶה אֶת־
יְהֹוָה עַל־כֵּן קָרְאָה שְׁמוֹ יְהוּדָה וַתַּעֲמֹד מִלֶּדֶת:

CAP. XXX. ל ל

א וַתֵּרֶא רָחֵל כִּי לֹא יָלְדָה לְיַעֲקֹב וַתְּקַנֵּא רָחֵל בַּאֲחֹתָהּ
וַתֹּאמֶר אֶל־יַעֲקֹב הָבָה־לִּי בָנִים וְאִם־אַיִן מֵתָה אָנֹכִי:
2 וַיִּחַר־אַף יַעֲקֹב בְּרָחֵל וַיֹּאמֶר הֲתַחַת אֱלֹהִים אָנֹכִי אֲשֶׁר
3 מָנַע מִמֵּךְ פְּרִי־בָטֶן: וַתֹּאמֶר הִנֵּה אֲמָתִי בִלְהָה בֹּא אֵלֶיהָ
4 וְתֵלֵד עַל־בִּרְכַּי וְאִבָּנֶה גַם־אָנֹכִי מִמֶּנָּה: וַתִּתֶּן־לוֹ אֶת־
ה בִּלְהָה שִׁפְחָתָהּ לְאִשָּׁה וַיָּבֹא אֵלֶיהָ יַעֲקֹב: וַתַּהַר בִּלְהָה
6 וַתֵּלֶד לְיַעֲקֹב בֵּן: וַתֹּאמֶר רָחֵל דָּנַנִּי אֱלֹהִים וְגַם שָׁמַע
7 בְּקֹלִי וַיִּתֶּן־לִי בֵּן עַל־כֵּן קָרְאָה שְׁמוֹ דָּן: וַתַּהַר עוֹד
8 וַתֵּלֶד בִּלְהָה שִׁפְחַת רָחֵל בֵּן שֵׁנִי לְיַעֲקֹב: וַתֹּאמֶר רָחֵל
נַפְתּוּלֵי אֱלֹהִים ׀ נִפְתַּלְתִּי עִם־אֲחֹתִי גַּם־יָכֹלְתִּי וַתִּקְרָא
9 שְׁמוֹ נַפְתָּלִי: וַתֵּרֶא לֵאָה כִּי עָמְדָה מִלֶּדֶת וַתִּקַּח אֶת־
י זִלְפָּה שִׁפְחָתָהּ וַתִּתֵּן אֹתָהּ לְיַעֲקֹב לְאִשָּׁה: וַתֵּלֶד זִלְפָּה

---

¹ Heb. *raah beonji*.  ² Heb. *shama*.  ³ Heb. *Shimeon*.  ⁴ From the Heb. root *lavah*.  ⁵ From the Heb. *hodah*.  ⁶ Heb. *Jehudah*.
⁷ Heb. *dan*, he judged.  ⁸ Heb. *niphtal*, he wrestled.

---

**32.** *Reuben*. In this and the following names, the meaning is derived by the resemblance of the name in sound to the words which explain it.

*will love me.* The birth of a son raised the wife in the esteem of her husband.

**33.** *hath heard.* Better, *knows*.

**35.** *Judah.* Heb. *Yehudah*. The name of the members of his tribe was later extended to all the descendants of Jacob, *Yehudim*.

### CHAPTER XXX

**1.** *else I die.* Of grief and shame.

**2.** *am I in God's stead?* In His hands alone are the issues of life and death.

**3.** *behold my maid.* Rachel resorts to the same expedient as Sarah.

*upon my knees.* A figurative expression denoting the adoption of a child.

*be builded up.* As in xvi, 2. She can thus have 'sons whom I may nurse and rear as my own' (Targum).

**6.** *judged me.* God has decided in her favour.

**8.** *mighty wrestlings.* lit. 'wrestlings of God', where 'of God' is merely the Heb. idiom for the superlative.

## GENESIS XXX, 11

a son. 11. And Leah said: 'Fortune is come!' And she called his name ¹Gad. 12. And Zilpah Leah's handmaid bore Jacob a second son. 13. And Leah said: 'Happy am I! for the daughters will call me happy.' And she called his name ²Asher.* ⁱᵛ· 14. And Reuben went in the days of wheat harvest, and found mandrakes in the field, and brought them unto his mother Leah. Then Rachel said to Leah: 'Give me, I pray thee, of thy son's mandrakes.' 15. And she said unto her: 'Is it a small matter that thou hast taken away my husband? and wouldest thou take away my son's mandrakes also?' And Rachel said: 'Therefore he shall lie with thee to-night for thy son's mandrakes.' 16. And Jacob came from the field in the evening, and Leah went out to meet him, and said: 'Thou must come in unto me; for I have surely hired thee with my son's mandrakes.' And he lay with her that night. 17. And God hearkened unto Leah, and she conceived, and bore Jacob a fifth son. 18. And Leah said: 'God hath given me my ³hire, because I gave my handmaid to my husband.' And she called his name Issachar. 19. And Leah conceived again, and bore a sixth son to Jacob. 20. And Leah said: 'God hath endowed me with a good dowry; now will my husband ⁴dwell with me, because I have borne him six sons.' And she called his name Zebulun. 21. And afterwards she bore a daughter, and called her name Dinah. 22. And God remembered Rachel, and God hearkened to her, and opened her womb. 23. And she conceived, and bore a son, and said: 'God ⁵hath taken away my reproach.' 24. And she called his name Joseph, saying: 'The LORD ⁶add to me another son.' ¶ 25. And it came to pass, when Rachel had borne Joseph, that Jacob said unto Laban: 'Send me away, that I may go unto mine own place, and to my country. 26. Give me my wives and my children for whom I have served thee, and let me go; for thou knowest my service

---

¹ That is, *Fortune*.  ² That is, *Happy*.  ³ Heb. *sachar*.
⁴ Heb. *zabal*, he dwelt.  ⁵ Heb. *asaph*.  ⁶ Heb. *Joseph*.

---

**11.** *Fortune is come.* This translation is according to the traditional Reading, the *Kre*.

**14.** *mandrakes.* Or, as the RV Margin translates, 'love-apples.' The fruit is of the size of a large plum, quite round, yellow and full of soft pulp. The fruit is still considered in the East as a love-charm. This explains Rachel's anxiety to obtain it.

**15.** *thou hast taken away.* By holding first place in his affections.

**22.** *God hearkened.* To her prayers.

**23.** *my reproach.* Of being left childless. The Heb. name has the double sense of 'taking away' (the reproach) and of 'adding' (to her another son).

### 25–43. JACOB'S WAGES

**25.** *send me away.* It would thus seem that the fourteen years' service terminated shortly after Joseph's birth.

**26.** *give me my wives.* In spite of Jacob's completed years of service the wives and children were in the *legal* power of Laban, who could refuse to hand them over to Jacob; see XXXI, 43.

## GENESIS XXX, 27

wherewith I have served thee.' 27. And Laban said unto him: 'If now I have found favour in thine eyes—I have observed the signs, and the LORD hath blessed me for thy sake.* 28. And he said: 'Appoint me thy wages, and I will give it.' 29. And he said unto him: 'Thou knowest how I have served thee, and how thy cattle have fared with me. 30. For it was little which thou hadst before I came, and it hath increased abundantly; and the LORD hath blessed thee whithersoever I turned. And now when shall I provide for mine own house also?' 31. And he said: 'What shall I give thee?' And Jacob said: 'Thou shalt not give me aught; if thou wilt do this thing for me, I will again feed thy flock and keep it. 32. I will pass through all thy flock to-day, removing from thence every speckled and spotted one, and every dark one among the sheep, and the spotted and speckled among the goats; and of such shall be my hire. 33. So shall my righteousness witness against me hereafter, when thou shalt come to look over my hire that is before thee: every one that is not speckled and spotted among the goats, and dark among the sheep, that if found with me shall be counted stolen.' 34. And Laban said: 'Behold, would it might be according to thy word.' 35. And he removed that day the he-goats that were streaked and spotted, and all the she-goats that were speckled and spotted, every one that had white in it, and all the dark ones among the sheep, and gave them into the hand of his sons. 36.

---

**27.** *found favour in thine eyes.* Laban wishes to retain Jacob.

**29.** *with me.* Under my care.

**30.** *whithersoever I turned.* lit. 'at my foot', *i.e.* either 'at every step I took'; or (so the Midrash), 'at my coming' into thy house.
*provide for mine own house.* His wives and children now belong to him, and he feels the responsibility of making provision for their future.

**31.** Jacob, still feeling sore at the way he had been outwitted by Laban over the matter of Rachel, determines to put to good use his exceptional knowledge and skill as a shepherd.

**32.** The sheep in Syria are white and the goats black. Jacob asks as his wages the sheep which are not white and the goats which are not black. Laban considers the request fair and, to him, profitable.
*of such shall be my hire.* These, and the lambs and kids subsequently born with the same peculiarity, should belong to him.

**33.** *righteousness.* 'In this way my honesty will tell, when you come to cast your eye over my share; any goat in my lot that is not speckled or spotted, any sheep that is not black, you may consider to have been stolen' (Moffatt).
The compact is all in Laban's favour; but, crafty, selfish and grasping, he starts to circumvent Jacob, by preventing the increase of any speckled or brown cattle.

**36.** *three days' journey.* A phrase denoting a considerable distance; cf. Exod. III, 18.

**37.** *streaks.* Jacob devises three plans for the purpose of frustrating Laban. He placed streaked rods over against the ewes. The sight of these rods would affect the colouring of the young about to be born. 'He did not resort to this device the first year, and thereafter only in connection with his own flock; otherwise it would have been flagrant dishonesty' (Kimchi).

112

## GENESIS XXX, 37

And he set three days' journey betwixt himself and Jacob. And Jacob fed the rest of Laban's flocks. 37. And Jacob took him rods of fresh poplar, and of the almond and of the plane-tree; and peeled white streaks in them, making the white appear which was in the rods. 38. And he set the rods which he had peeled over against the flocks in the gutters in the watering-troughs where the flocks came to drink; and they conceived when they came to drink. 39. And the flocks conceived at the sight of the rods, and the flocks brought forth streaked, speckled, and spotted. 40. And Jacob separated the lambs—he also set the faces of the flocks toward the streaked and all the dark in the flock of Laban—and put his own droves apart, and put them not unto Laban's flock. 41. And it came to pass, whensoever the stronger of the flock did conceive, that Jacob laid the rods before the eyes of the flock in the gutters, that they might conceive among the rods; 42. but when the flock were feeble, he put them not in; so the feebler were Laban's, and the stronger Jacob's. 43. And the man increased exceedingly, and had large flocks, and maidservants and men-servants, and camels and asses.

## 31 CHAPTER XXXI

1. And he heard the words of Laban's sons, saying: 'Jacob hath taken away all that was our father's; and of that which was our father's hath he gotten all this wealth.' 2. And Jacob beheld the countenance of Laban, and, behold, it was not toward him as beforetime. 3. And the LORD said unto Jacob: 'Return unto the land of thy fathers, and to thy kindred; and I will be with thee.' 4. And Jacob sent and called Rachel and Leah to the field unto his flock, 5. and said unto them: 'I see your father's countenance, that it is not toward me as beforetime; but the God of my father hath been with me. 6. And ye

---

**40.** The second plan was, Jacob separates the newly-born spotted lambs and kids from the rest of the flock, but so arranges them that there should be a further tendency to bear spotted young.

**41.** He arranges to secure for his own share the young of the strongest animals.

CHAPTER XXXI, 1–21. THE FLIGHT OF JACOB

**1.** *Laban's sons.* See xxx, 35. Jacob's prosperity bred jealousy among his relatives.

**3.** *said unto Jacob.* In a dream, see v. 11.

*the land of thy fathers.* Canaan.

**4.** *Rachel and Leah.* Another instance of the dignified position of woman in ancient Israel. The Patriarchs do nothing without consulting their wives, whom they regard as their equals.

*to the field.* To speak with them in private. As the Midrash states, 'Walls have ears.'

**5.** *hath been with me.* Hence my great increase in wealth.

**7.** *my wages.* See on xxix, 15.

*ten times.* The phrase only means 'several times'. Laban would naturally make attempt after attempt to alter the conditions in his favour when he found they were against him. The story here supplements what was related in the last chapter.

## GENESIS XXXI, 7

know that with all my power I have served your father. 7. And your father hath mocked me, and changed my wages ten times; but God suffered him not to hurt me. 8. If he said thus: The speckled shall be thy wages; then all the flock bore speckled; and if he said thus: The streaked shall be thy wages; then bore all the flock streaked. 9. Thus God hath taken away the cattle of your father and given them to me. 10. And it came to pass at the time that the flock conceived, that I lifted up mine eyes and saw in a dream, and, behold, the he-goats which leaped upon the flock were streaked, speckled, and grizzled. 11. And the angel of God said unto me in the dream: Jacob; and I said: Here am I. 12. And he said: Lift up now thine eyes, and see, all the he-goats which leap upon the flock are streaked, speckled, and grizzled; for I have seen all that Laban doeth unto thee. 13. I am the God of Beth-el, where thou didst anoint a pillar, where thou didst vow a vow unto Me. Now arise, get thee out from this land, and return unto the land of thy nativity.' 14. And Rachel and Leah answered and said unto him: 'Is there yet any portion or inheritance for us in our father's house? 15. Are we not accounted by him strangers? for he hath sold us, and hath also quite devoured our price. 16. For all the riches which God hath taken away from our father, that is ours and our children's. Now then, whatsoever God hath said unto thee, do.'* ⱽᴵ· 17. Then Jacob rose up, and set his sons and his wives upon the camels; 18. and he carried away all his cattle, and all his substance which he had gathered, the cattle of his getting, which he had gathered in Paddan-aram, to go to Isaac his father unto the land of Canaan. 19. Now Laban was gone to shear his sheep. And Rachel stole the teraphim that were her father's. 20. And Jacob outwitted Laban the Aramean, in that he told him not that he fled. 21. So he fled with all that he had; and he rose up, and passed over the ¹River,

---

¹ That is, the Euphrates.

**11.** *angel of God.* In *v.* 3 it is 'The Lᴏʀᴅ said'. The interchange of 'God' and 'angel of God' is frequent.

**13.** *The God of Beth-el.* The God who appeared unto thee at Beth-el, see xxvIII.

**15.** *strangers.* He has not allowed us and our children to enjoy some of the prosperity which accrued during Jacob's fourteen years of labour for us. And now he begrudges what our husband has gained by his toil.

**17.** *his sons.* The word should be rendered here, '*his children.*'

**18.** *the cattle of his getting.* *i.e.* which he had purchased; viz. camels and asses, xxx, 43.

**19.** *gone to shear his sheep.* The occasion of sheep-shearing was a time of feasting, and lasted several days.

*teraphim.* Images kept in the house, perhaps corresponding to the Roman *penates*, to bring protection and good fortune. Laban calls them 'my gods' (*v.* 30). Why did Rachel carry them off? The Midrash answers, to prevent her father from worshipping them.

**21.** *passed over the River.* Euphrates.

## GENESIS XXXI, 22

and set his face toward the mountain of Gilead. ¶ 22. And it was told Laban on the third day that Jacob was fled. 23. And he took his brethren with him, and pursued after him seven days' journey; and he overtook him in the mountain of Gilead. 24. And God came to Laban the Aramean in a dream of the night, and said unto him: 'Take heed to thyself that thou speak not to Jacob either good or bad.' 25. And Laban came up with Jacob. Now Jacob had pitched his tent in the mountain; and Laban with his brethren pitched in the mountain of Gilead. 26. And Laban said to Jacob: 'What hast thou done, that thou hast outwitted me, and carried away my daughters as though captives of the sword? 27. Wherefore didst thou flee secretly, and outwit me; and didst not tell me, that I might have sent thee away with mirth and with songs, with tabret and with harp; 28. and didst not suffer me to kiss my sons and my daughters? now hast thou done foolishly. 29. It is in the power of my hand to do you hurt; but the God of your father spoke unto me yesternight, saying: Take heed to thyself that thou speak not to Jacob either good or bad. 30. And now that thou art surely gone, because thou sore longest after thy father's house, wherefore hast thou stolen my gods?' 31. And Jacob answered and said to Laban: 'Because I was afraid; for I said: Lest thou shouldest take thy daughters from me by force. 32. With whomsoever thou findest thy gods, he shall not live; before our brethren discern thou what is thine with me, and take it to thee.'—For Jacob knew not that Rachel had stolen them.—33. And Laban went into Jacob's tent, and into Leah's tent, and into the tent of the two maid-servants; but he found them not. And he went out of Leah's tent, and entered into Rachel's tent. 34. Now Rachel had taken the teraphim, and put

---

*the mountain of Gilead.* Or, 'the hill-country of Gilead,' the region E. of Jordan.

**23.** *brethren.* Men of his clan.

22–54. LABAN'S PURSUIT

**24.** *either good or bad. i.e.* anything, as in XXIV, 50. The phrase is the same Heb. phrase and idiom as in II, 17, III, 5 and 22, where it means, 'all things.' Here it is in negative form and means, 'not anything.' Laban was neither to entice him by offers of kindness, nor force him to return by threats.

**26.** *as though captives of the sword.* Without allowing them an opportunity of taking farewell of their father and brothers. Laban strikes the note of injured innocence.

**28.** *sons. i.e.* grandsons (see on XX, 12), and *daughters* may include Rachel, Leah and Laban's granddaughters.

**29.** *to do you hurt.* It would thus seem that Laban was accompanied by a large band, which outnumbered Jacob and his servants.

**31.** This verse answers the first point mentioned by Laban, viz. the secrecy with which Jacob left him.

**32.** *shall not live.* The Patriarch does not mean that he will himself kill the culprit, but the wrongdoer's life will be placed in Laban's hands; cf. XLIV, 9.

**33.** Nachmanides explains that Laban's search was in the following order: Jacob, Leah, Rachel, and lastly the handmaids. The narrative, however, reserves the mention of Rachel for the last, because it is upon her that interest is centred.

## GENESIS XXXI, 35

them in the saddle of the camel, and sat upon them. And Laban felt about all the tent, but found them not. 35. And she said to her father: 'Let not my lord be angry that I cannot rise up before thee; for the manner of women is upon me.' And he searched, but found not the teraphim. 36. And Jacob was wroth, and strove with Laban. And Jacob answered and said to Laban: 'What is my trespass? what is my sin, that thou hast hotly pursued after me? 37. Whereas thou hast felt about all my stuff, what hast thou found of all thy household stuff? Set it here before my brethren and thy brethren, that they may judge betwixt us two. 38. These twenty years have I been with thee; thy ewes and thy she-goats have not cast their young, and the rams of thy flocks have I not eaten. 39. That which was torn of beasts I brought not unto thee; I bore the loss of it; of my hand didst thou require it, whether stolen by day or stolen by night. 40. Thus I was: in the day the drought consumed me, and the frost by night; and my sleep fled from mine eyes. 41. These twenty years have I been in thy house: I served thee fourteen years for thy two daughters, and six years for thy flock; and thou hast changed my wages ten times. 42. Except the God of my father, the God of Abraham, and the Fear of Isaac, had been on my side, surely now hadst thou sent me away empty. God hath seen mine affliction and the labour of my hands, and gave judgment yesternight.' *vii. 43. And Laban answered and said unto Jacob: 'The daughters are my

---

**34.** *saddle.* The word is better translated 'palanquin'—a sort of compartment, tied on to the saddle, covered with an awning, and surrounded with curtains, in which Oriental women travel.

**35.** *rise.* A child had to stand up when the father entered the room.

**36.** *wroth.* The Patriarch's indignation is aroused when his innocence is established; and he accuses Laban of fabricating the charge of stealing the teraphim as a pretext to search his possessions.

*answered.* i.e. replied to Laban's accusations.

**38.** *have not cast their young.* Due to the skill and assiduity of the shepherd.

**39.** *or by night.* In these words lies the bitterness of reproach. A shepherd was entitled to his rest at night, and he could not in justice be held responsible if damage was then done by prowling beasts, provided reasonable precautions had been taken.

According to the Code of Hammurabi, which was the Common Law in Mesopotamia at the time, the shepherd gave a receipt for the animals entrusted to him, and was bound to return them with reasonable increase. He was allowed to use a certain number for food, and was not responsible for those killed by lion or lightning. Any loss due to his carelessness he had to repay tenfold. All this throws wonderful light on the relations between Jacob and Laban.

**42.** *Fear of Isaac.* Or, 'Awe of Isaac'; *i.e.* He whom Isaac feared. The noun, in this special use as a Divine appellation, occurs again in *v.* 53. See Isaiah VIII, 13, where a synonymous word is used.

*gave judgment.* See *v.* 29.

**43.** Laban is unable to answer Jacob's reproaches, and therefore repeats the claim based on primitive usage, whereby the head of the family is the nominal possessor of all that belonged to its members. He then pretends to be solicitous for the welfare of his daughters and grandchildren.

## GENESIS XXXI, 44

daughters, and the children are my children, and the flocks are my flocks, and all that thou seest is mine; and what can I do this day for these my daughters, or for their children whom they have borne? 44. And now come, let us make a covenant, I and thou; and let it be for a witness between me and thee.' 45. And Jacob took a stone, and set it up for a pillar. 46. And Jacob said unto his brethren: 'Gather stones'; and they took stones, and made a heap. And they did eat there by the heap. 47. And Laban called it ¹Jegar-sahadutha; but Jacob called it ²Galeed. 48. And Laban said: 'This heap is witness between me and thee this day.' Therefore was the name of it called Galeed; 49. and ³Mizpah, for he said: 'The LORD watch between me and thee, when we are absent one from another. 50. If thou shalt afflict my daughters, and if thou shalt take wives beside my daughters, no man being with us; see, God is witness betwixt me and thee.' 51. And Laban said to Jacob: 'Behold this heap, and behold the pillar, which I have set up betwixt me and thee. 52. This heap be witness, and the pillar be witness, that I will not pass over this heap to thee, and that thou shalt not pass over this heap and this pillar unto me, for harm. 53. The God of Abraham, and the God of Nahor, the God of their father, judge betwixt us.' And Jacob swore by the Fear of his father Isaac. 54. And Jacob offered a sacrifice in the mountain, and called his brethren to eat bread; and they did eat bread, and tarried all night in the mountain * ᵐ·

## 32  CHAPTER XXXII

1. And early in the morning Laban rose up, and kissed his sons and his daughters, and blessed them. And Laban departed, and returned unto his place. 2. And Jacob went on his way, and the angels of God met him. 3. And Jacob said when he saw them: 'This is God's camp.' And he called the name of that place ⁴Mahanaim.

---

¹ That is, *The heap of witness*, in Aramaic.   ² That is, *The heap of witness*, in Hebrew.   ³ *The watch-post*.   ⁴ *Two camps*.

**46.** heap. Or, 'cairn.'
*they did eat.* The meal was part of the ceremony of the covenant of friendship.

**50.** Laban still keeps up the pretext that the pact made between him and Jacob is for the protection of his daughters; but he immediately proceeds to set up another heap and pillar to safeguard himself from any aggression on Jacob's part in the future.

**53.** Laban, being a descendant of Nahor (XXII, 20 f), calls upon the deity worshipped by his family as well as upon the God worshipped by Jacob's family to witness the covenant; but Jacob, who refuses to acknowledge the 'god of Nahor', swears only by the 'Fear' of Isaac.

*God of their father.* Each one swears by the God of his father (Nachmanides).

**54.** *offered a sacrifice.* Of thanksgiving to God.

### CHAPTER XXXII

**1.** *his sons. i.e.* his grandchildren.

**2.** *went on his way.* To Beth-el, whither God had sent him to fulfil his vow. This vision assured him that God was mindful of His promises.

**3.** *Mahanaim. i.e.* two camps; the company of the angels and Laban's camp.

# HAFTORAH VAYYETZE—(For Ashkenazim) הפטרת ויצא

## HOSEA XII, 13–XIV, 10

### Chapter XII

13. And Jacob fled into the field of Aram,
And Israel served for a wife,
And for a wife he kept sheep.
14. And by a prophet the Lord brought Israel up out of Egypt,
And by a prophet was he kept.
15. Ephraim hath provoked most bitterly;
Therefore shall his blood be cast upon him,
And his reproach shall his Lord return unto him.

### Chapter XIII

1. When Ephraim spoke, there was trembling,
He exalted himself in Israel;
But when he became guilty through Baal, he died.
2. And now they sin more and more,
And have made them molten images of their silver,
According to their own understanding, even idols,
All of them the work of the craftsmen;
Of them they say:
'They that sacrifice men kiss calves.'

---

Like his older contemporary, Amos, Hosea is the Prophet of the Decline and Fall of the Northern Kingdom.

The reign of Jeroboam II—a time of prosperity, luxury and idolatry in the Northern Kingdom—closed in the year 740 before the Common Era. And very soon thereafter came 'the beginning of the end'. A succession of usurpers and adventurers occupied the throne, and the land was swiftly drifting towards social and political disintegration. Instead of obeying the law of God, Israel amused itself with international intrigues, and imitated the morals and idolatries of her allies. But the world-power of Assyria had appeared on the horizon, and was soon destined to engulf everything. 'Let Israel come back to God, and call upon Him in their anguish. Let Israel seek the Lord, it is still time,' such is the burden of Hosea. 'His sensitive soul is full of sympathy and love for his people; and his keen perception of the destruction towards which they are hastening produces a conflict of emotions which is reflected in the pathos, and force, and artless rhythm of sighs and sobs which characterize his prophecy' (Driver).

**13.** *Jacob fled.* The Prophet takes the people back to their beginnings, to their ancestor Jacob. (This connects the Sedrah with the Haftorah.) Did not the Patriarch, in his hard life, find God his support, guide and Redeemer? And Israel in Egypt was freed by Divine power, just as later he was 'guarded' (and guided) by God's chosen Prophet (Moses), whose successors the people were now disregarding and despising. Hosea bids the people remember that God is their only Saviour, even as His hand is manifest in all their history.

**15.** *Ephraim.* The Northern Kingdom is so called from the name of its most prominent tribe.

### Chapter XIII. The Last Judgment of Ephraim

**1.** *when Ephraim spoke.* A rapid résumé of the history of the Northern Kingdom. At first Ephraim's power was great, and he was feared by surrounding tribes. Jeroboam, the first king of the Ten Tribes, was an Ephraimite. 'He sinned and led Israel to sin,' through the calf-worship which he had set up at Dan and Beersheba.

*Baal.* See I Kings XVI, 31.

*died.* Spiritually; yet literally too, for Baal-worship was a cause of the national decay and final downfall. 'It could no more inspire courage than love of goodness' (Cheyne).

**2.** *kiss calves.* See I Kings XIX, 18. Kissing a calf as an act of religious homage!

# HOSEA XIII, 3

3. Therefore they shall be as the morning cloud,
And as the dew that early passeth away,
As the chaff that is driven with the wind out of the threshing-floor,
And as the smoke out of the window.

4. Yet I am the LORD thy God
From the land of Egypt;
And thou knowest no God but Me,
And beside Me there is no saviour.

5. I did know thee in the wilderness,
In the land of great drought.

6. When they were fed, they became full,
They were filled, and their heart was exalted;
Therefore have they forgotten Me.

7. Therefore am I become unto them as a lion;
As a leopard will I watch by the way;

8. I will meet them as a bear that is bereaved of her whelps,
And will rend the enclosure of their heart;
And there will I devour them like a lioness,
The wild beast shall tear them.

9. It is thy destruction, O Israel,
That thou art against Me, against thy help.

10. Ho, now, thy king,
That he may save thee in all thy cities!
And thy judges, of whom thou saidst:
'Give me a king and princes!'

11. I give thee a king in Mine anger,
And take him away in My wrath.

12. The iniquity of Ephraim is bound up;
His sin is laid up in store.

13. The throes of a travailing woman shall come upon him;
He is an unwise son;
For it is time he should not tarry
In the place of the breaking forth of children.

14. Shall I ransom them from the power of the nether-world?

---

**3.** *morning cloud.* Figures of speech to represent the swift and complete extinction of the Northern Kingdom. The morning cloud which passes as one observes it, the chaff scattered by the whirlwind, the smoke of the chimney—all leave no trace behind. So shall it be with the Kingdom of Israel. The prophecy was fulfilled within 20 years.

**7–9.** God, who is and would be their help, they have turned to be their destroyer; and they have brought ruin on themselves.

**11.** *a king in Mine anger.* Jeroboam I, who became king of Israel when the Ten Tribes broke away from Solomon's incompetent son.

*take him away in my wrath.* Refers to the list of usurping kings on the eve of the destruction of the kingdom by Assyria.

**12.** *bound up.* It is not forgotten; it is tied up as in a bag.

**13.** Israel is compared to a travailing woman, and also to the child imperilled by its weak will.

## HOSEA XIII, 15

Shall I redeem them from death?
Ho, thy plagues, O death!
Ho, thy destruction, O nether-world!
Repentance be hid from Mine eyes!

15. For though he be fruitful among the
reed-plants,
An east wind shall come, the wind of the
LORD coming up from the wilderness,
And his spring shall become dry, and
his fountain shall be dried up;
He shall spoil the treasure of all precious
vessels.

### CHAPTER XIV

1. Samaria shall bear her guilt,
For she hath rebelled against her God;
They shall fall by the sword;
Their infants shall be dashed in pieces,
And their women with child shall be
ripped up.

2. Return, O Israel, unto the LORD thy
God;
For thou hast stumbled in thine iniquity.

3. Take with you words,
And return unto the LORD;
Say unto Him; 'Forgive all iniquity,
And accept that which is good;
So will we render for bullocks the offering
of our lips.

4. Asshur shall not save us;
We will not ride upon horses;
Neither will we call any more the work
of our hands our gods;
For in Thee the fatherless findeth mercy.'

5. I will heal their backsliding,
I will love them freely;
For Mine anger is turned away from him.

6. I will be as the dew unto Israel;
He shall blossom as the lily,
And cast forth his roots as Lebanon.

7. His branches shall spread,
And his beauty shall be as the olive-tree,
And his fragrance as Lebanon.

---

**15.** *he shall spoil.* i.e. the enemy who is to destroy Israel, symbolized here by the evil wind.

### CHAPTER XIV

**1.** *Samaria.* The capital of the Northern Kingdom, standing here for the whole land. The savage inhumanities of ancient barbaric warfare recall the atrocities of modern pogroms.

### 2–10. A DESPERATE CALL TO REPENTANCE

**2.** *return unto the LORD.* God's love and mercy are unending. Even after the pronouncement of doom, there is Hope and Forgiveness to repentant Israel.

**3.** *take with you words.* God does not require gifts or sacrifices, but sincere confession and penitent words expressing the resolve to amend (Midrash).

**4.** *Asshur shall not save us.* The people will no longer put their trust in alliances with foreign idol-worshipping nations—Assyria or Egypt.

*will not ride upon horses.* A reference to the help looked for from Egypt. (See I Kings X, 28; Isaiah XXX and XXXI).

**5–7.** God's gracious and loving reply to those words of repentance and faith. The blessings that will follow Israel's spiritual regeneration.

**6.** *blossom as the lily.* Israel shall be as the lily, a symbol of beauty and fruitfulness; but his roots shall be deep and immovable as Lebanon.

**7.** *his fragrance as Lebanon.* See Song of Songs IV, 11. On the lower slopes of Lebanon are aromatic shrubs, lavender and myrtle.

# HOSEA XIV, 8

הושע יד

8 יָנֻקוֹתָיו וִיהִי כַזַּיִת הוֹדוֹ וְרֵיחַ לוֹ כַּלְּבָנוֹן: יָשֻׁבוּ יֹשְׁבֵי
9 בְצִלּוֹ יְחַיּוּ דָגָן וְיִפְרְחוּ כַגָּפֶן זִכְרוֹ כְּיֵין לְבָנוֹן: אֶפְרַיִם
מַה־לִּי עוֹד לָעֲצַבִּים אֲנִי עָנִיתִי וַאֲשׁוּרֶנּוּ אֲנִי כִּבְרוֹשׁ רַעֲנָן
י מִמֶּנִּי פֶּרְיְךָ נִמְצָא: מִי חָכָם וְיָבֵן אֵלֶּה נָבוֹן וְיֵדָעֵם כִּי־
יְשָׁרִים דַּרְכֵי יְהוָֹה וְצַדִּקִים יֵלְכוּ בָם וּפֹשְׁעִים יִכָּשְׁלוּ בָם:

8. They that dwell under his shadow shall again
Make corn to grow,
And shall blossom as the vine;
The scent thereof shall be as the wine of Lebanon.

9. Ephraim [shall say]:
'What have I to do any more with idols?'
As for Me, I respond and look on him;
I am like a leafy cypress-tree;
From Me is thy fruit found.

10. Whoso is wise, let him understand these things,
Whoso is prudent, let him know them.

For the ways of the LORD are right,
And the just do walk in them;
But transgressors do stumble therein.

כצ״ל v. 10.

**9.** *from Me is thy fruit found.* 'From Me all thy good cometh.'

**10.** *stumble therein.* They stumble as if the ways were actually crooked, because their wrong thoughts and desires pervert the meaning of the Divine commands. Thus they do wrong and stumble, even when they would claim to be walking in the ways of the LORD.

Chapter XIV, 2–10, is appropriately enough the Haftorah for the Sabbath of Penitence, שבת שובה, lit. 'The Sabbath of *O Israel, return unto the* LORD'. The very term, *Teshubah*, i.e. 'a turning away from sin and turning towards God', is taken from the word שובה in its opening verse. The doctrine of Repentance, which is founded on it, is of fundamental importance in Judaism.

## GENESIS XXXII, 4 — בראשית וישלח לב

**32** 4. And Jacob sent messengers before him to Esau his brother unto the land of Seir, the field of Edom. 5. And he commanded them, saying: 'Thus shall ye say unto my lord Esau: Thus saith thy servant Jacob: I have sojourned with Laban, and stayed until now. 6. And I have oxen, and asses and flocks, and men-servants and maid-servants; and I have sent to tell my lord, that I may find favour in thy sight.' 7. And the messengers returned to Jacob, saying: 'We came to thy brother Esau, and moreover he cometh to meet thee, and four hundred men with him.' 8. Then Jacob was greatly afraid and was distressed. And he divided the people that was with him, and the flocks, and the herds, and the camels, into two camps. 9. And he said: 'If Esau come to the one camp, and smite it, then the camp which is left shall escape.' 10. And Jacob said: 'O God of my father Abraham, and God of my father Isaac, O LORD, who saidst unto me: Return unto thy country, and to thy kindred, and I will do thee good; 11. I am not worthy of all the mercies, and of all the truth, which

פ פ פ פ ח 8 ס

4 וַיִּשְׁלַח יַעֲקֹב מַלְאָכִים לְפָנָיו אֶל־עֵשָׂו אָחִיו אַרְצָה שֵׂעִיר
5 שְׂדֵה אֱדוֹם: וַיְצַו אֹתָם לֵאמֹר כֹּה תֹאמְרוּן לַאדֹנִי לְעֵשָׂו כֹּה אָמַר עַבְדְּךָ יַעֲקֹב עִם־לָבָן גַּרְתִּי וָאֵחַר עַד־עָתָּה:
6 וַיְהִי־לִי שׁוֹר וַחֲמוֹר צֹאן וְעֶבֶד וְשִׁפְחָה וָאֶשְׁלְחָה לְהַגִּיד
7 לַאדֹנִי לִמְצֹא־חֵן בְּעֵינֶיךָ: וַיָּשֻׁבוּ הַמַּלְאָכִים אֶל־יַעֲקֹב לֵאמֹר בָּאנוּ אֶל־אָחִיךָ אֶל־עֵשָׂו וְגַם הֹלֵךְ לִקְרָאתְךָ וְאַרְבַּע
8 מֵאוֹת אִישׁ עִמּוֹ: וַיִּירָא יַעֲקֹב מְאֹד וַיֵּצֶר לוֹ וַיַּחַץ אֶת־הָעָם אֲשֶׁר־אִתּוֹ וְאֶת־הַצֹּאן וְאֶת־הַבָּקָר וְהַגְּמַלִּים לִשְׁנֵי
9 מַחֲנוֹת: וַיֹּאמֶר אִם־יָבוֹא עֵשָׂו אֶל־הַמַּחֲנֶה הָאַחַת וְהִכָּהוּ
10 וְהָיָה הַמַּחֲנֶה הַנִּשְׁאָר לִפְלֵיטָה: וַיֹּאמֶר יַעֲקֹב אֱלֹהֵי אָבִי אַבְרָהָם וֵאלֹהֵי אָבִי יִצְחָק יְהוָה הָאֹמֵר אֵלַי שׁוּב
11 לְאַרְצְךָ וּלְמוֹלַדְתְּךָ וְאֵיטִיבָה עִמָּךְ: קָטֹנְתִּי מִכֹּל הַחֲסָדִים

## VIII. VAYYISHLACH

### (CHAPTERS XXXII, 4–XXXVI)

CHAPTERS XXXII, 4–XXXIII, 17. THE FEAR OF ESAU

**4.** As Jacob approaches his home land, the fear of his brother revives in him. Twenty years had passed, but Esau might still wreak vengeance on Jacob and his dependants. Jacob well knew that some men nurse their anger, so that it should not die down or out.

*field.* i.e. territory.

**5.** Jacob frames his message in the most humble and conciliatory words.

*I have sojourned.* Rashi takes these words to mean: 'I have not become a prince but am only a "sojourner"; therefore thou hast no cause to hate me because of my father's blessing, in which I was promised to be made greater than thou. It has not been fulfilled.' Since the letters of the Hebrew word גרתי 'I have sojourned' correspond to the numerals denoting 'six hundred and thirteen', the number of Pentateuch commandments (תרי"ג מצוות), the Midrash comments: 'With Laban I sojourned, but the 613 Commandments I observed'—an exhortation to Jacob's descendants to be faithful to the Torah even when living in a non-Jewish environment.

**6.** *to tell my lord.* That I am on my way home, and am desirous of finding 'favour in thy sight'.

**7.** *to thy brother Esau.* lit. 'to thy brother, to Esau'; which the Rabbis explain to mean, 'We came to him whom thou hast called "brother", but we found that we had come to "Esau", to one who still hates thee.'

*four hundred men.* A considerable following; which naturally alarmed Jacob as to his brother's intentions.

**8.** *greatly afraid.* Lest he and his be slain.

*and was distressed.* Even greater anguish possessed him at the thought that he might be compelled *to slay* (Midrash). He does not, however, give way to despair, but takes all possible steps to safeguard himself and those with him. He adopted three methods for overcoming the evil intentions of his brother. His first defence was prayer to God for His protection (v. 10–13); the second was to turn Esau's hate into goodwill by gifts (v. 14–22); his third and last resource was to stand his ground and fight (XXXIII, 1–3).

**10.** Jacob's prayer, showing his humility and gratitude, is proof that misfortune had developed the nobler impulses of his heart. Twenty years of fixed principle, steadfast purpose, and resolute sacrifice of present for future, purify and ennoble. It proves that even from the first, though he may appear self-centred, Jacob is yet delicately sensitive to spiritual realities and capable of genuine reformation. And the truly penitent—declare the Rabbis—come nearer unto God than even those who have never stumbled or fallen into sin.

*who saidst unto me.* See XXXI, 3.

# GENESIS XXXII, 12

בראשית וישלח לב

וּמִכָּל־הָאֱמֶת אֲשֶׁר עָשִׂיתָ אֶת־עַבְדֶּךָ כִּי בְמַקְלִי עָבַרְתִּי
אֶת־הַיַּרְדֵּן הַזֶּה וְעַתָּה הָיִיתִי לִשְׁנֵי מַחֲנוֹת: הַצִּילֵנִי נָא 12
מִיַּד אָחִי מִיַּד עֵשָׂו כִּי־יָרֵא אָנֹכִי אֹתוֹ פֶּן־יָבוֹא וְהִכַּנִי אֵם
עַל־בָּנִים: וְאַתָּה אָמַרְתָּ הֵיטֵב אֵיטִיב עִמָּךְ וְשַׂמְתִּי אֶת־ 13
זַרְעֲךָ כְּחוֹל הַיָּם אֲשֶׁר לֹא־יִסָּפֵר מֵרֹב: וַיָּלֶן שָׁם בַּלַּיְלָה 14
הַהוּא וַיִּקַּח מִן־הַבָּא בְיָדוֹ מִנְחָה לְעֵשָׂו אָחִיו: עִזִּים 15
מָאתַיִם וּתְיָשִׁים עֶשְׂרִים רְחֵלִים מָאתַיִם וְאֵילִים עֶשְׂרִים:
גְּמַלִּים מֵינִיקוֹת וּבְנֵיהֶם שְׁלֹשִׁים פָּרוֹת אַרְבָּעִים וּפָרִים 16
עֲשָׂרָה אֲתֹנֹת עֶשְׂרִים וַעְיָרִם עֲשָׂרָה: וַיִּתֵּן בְּיַד־עֲבָדָיו 17
עֵדֶר עֵדֶר לְבַדּוֹ וַיֹּאמֶר אֶל־עֲבָדָיו עִבְרוּ לְפָנַי וְרֶוַח
תָּשִׂימוּ בֵּין עֵדֶר וּבֵין עֵדֶר: וַיְצַו אֶת־הָרִאשׁוֹן לֵאמֹר כִּי 18
יִפְגָשְׁךָ עֵשָׂו אָחִי וּשְׁאֵלְךָ לֵאמֹר לְמִי־אַתָּה וְאָנָה תֵלֵךְ
וּלְמִי אֵלֶּה לְפָנֶיךָ: וְאָמַרְתָּ לְעַבְדְּךָ לְיַעֲקֹב מִנְחָה הִוא 19
שְׁלוּחָה לַאדֹנִי לְעֵשָׂו וְהִנֵּה גַם־הוּא אַחֲרֵינוּ: וַיְצַו גַּם כ
אֶת־הַשֵּׁנִי גַּם אֶת־הַשְּׁלִישִׁי גַּם אֶת־כָּל־הַהֹלְכִים אַחֲרֵי
הָעֲדָרִים לֵאמֹר כַּדָּבָר הַזֶּה תְּדַבְּרוּן אֶל־עֵשָׂו בְּמֹצַאֲכֶם
אֹתוֹ: וַאֲמַרְתֶּם גַּם הִנֵּה עַבְדְּךָ יַעֲקֹב אַחֲרֵינוּ כִּי־אָמַר 21
אֲכַפְּרָה פָנָיו בַּמִּנְחָה הַהֹלֶכֶת לְפָנָי וְאַחֲרֵי־כֵן אֶרְאֶה
פָנָיו אוּלַי יִשָּׂא פָנָי: וַתַּעֲבֹר הַמִּנְחָה עַל־פָּנָיו וְהוּא לָן 22

v. 21 קמץ בז"ק

Thou hast shown unto Thy servant; for with my staff I passed over this Jordan; and now I am become two camps. 12. Deliver me, I pray Thee, from the hand of my brother, from the hand of Esau; for I fear him, lest he come and smite me, the mother with the children. 13. And Thou saidst: I will surely do thee good, and make thy seed as the sand of the sea, which cannot be numbered for multitude.'* 14. And he lodged there that night; and took of that which he had with him a present for Esau his brother: 15. two hundred she-goats and twenty he-goats, two hundred ewes and twenty rams, 16. thirty milch camels and their colts, forty kine and ten bulls, twenty she-asses and ten foals. 17. And he delivered them into the hand of his servants, every drove by itself; and said unto his servants: 'Pass over before me, and put a space betwixt drove and drove.' 18. And he commanded the foremost, saying: 'When Esau my brother meeteth thee, and asketh thee, saying: Whose art thou? and whither goest thou? and whose are these before thee? 19. then thou shalt say: They are thy servant Jacob's; it is a present sent unto my lord, even unto Esau; and, behold, he also is behind us.' 20. And he commanded also the second, and the third, and all that followed the droves, saying: 'In this manner shall ye speak unto Esau, when ye find him; 21. and ye shall say: Moreover, behold, thy servant Jacob is behind us.' For he said: 'I will appease him with the present that goeth before me, and afterward I will see his face; peradventure he will accept me.' 22. So the present passed over before him; and he himself lodged that night in the

**11.** *truth.* i.e. faithfulness.

*staff.* Such as a lonely wanderer would use on his journey.

**12.** *the mother with the children.* lit. 'the mother *upon* the children'—a vivid picture of the mother placing herself in front of her children to shield them, so that she is slain *upon* them. The phrase is apparently a proverbial expression to describe a pitiless massacre; like a pogrom in our own times, not sparing the weak and helpless.

**13.** *as the sand of the sea.* Jacob was thinking of the promise to his forefathers (XXII, 17).

**15-21.** Jacob hopes by the succession of gifts to pacify Esau's wrath against him.

**21.** *appease him.* lit. 'cover his face'; so that he no longer sees any cause for being angry with me; cf. the phrase used in XX, 16.

*accept me.* lit. 'lift up my face', *i.e.* receive me favourably.

### 23-33. JACOB BECOMES ISRAEL

This passage represents the crisis in Jacob's spiritual history. It records his meeting with a Heavenly Being, the change of his name to Israel, the blessing of the Being that wrestled with him, and the consequent transformation of his character. Maimonides is of opinion that the whole incident was a 'prophetic vision'; and other commentators likewise have in all ages regarded the contest as symbolic, the outward manifestation of the struggle within the Patriarch, as in every mortal, between his baser passions and his nobler ideals. In the dead of night he had sent his wives and sons and all that he had across the river. Jacob was left alone—with God. There, in the darkness, given over to anxious fears, God's

## GENESIS XXXII, 23      בראשית וישלח לב

camp. ¶ 23. And he rose up that night, and took his two wives, and his two handmaids, and his eleven children, and passed over the ford of the Jabbok. 24. And he took them, and sent them over the stream, and sent over that which he had. 25. And Jacob was left alone; and there wrestled a man with him until the breaking of the day. 26. And when he saw that he prevailed not against him, he touched the hollow of his thigh; and the hollow of Jacob's thigh was strained, as he wrestled with him. 27. And he said: 'Let me go, for the day breaketh.' And he said: 'I will not let thee go, except thou bless me.' 28. And he said unto him: 'What is thy name?' And he said: 'Jacob.' 29. And he said: 'Thy name shall be called no more Jacob, but ¹Israel; for thou hast striven with God and with men, and hast prevailed.' 30. And Jacob asked him, and said: 'Tell me, I pray thee, thy name.' And he said: 'Wherefore is it that thou dost ask after my name?' And he blessed him there. * ¹¹¹· 31. And Jacob called the name of the place ²Peniel: 'for I have seen God face to face, and my life is preserved.' 32. And the sun rose upon him as he passed over ³Peniel, and he limped upon his thigh. 33. Therefore the children of Israel eat not the sinew of the thigh-vein which is

¹ That is, *He who striveth with God*.    ² That is, *The face of God*.    ³ Heb. Penuel.

---

Messenger was wrestling with him who had so often wrestled with men and had won by sheer energy, persistency and superior wit. In the words of the Prophet chosen as the Haftorah for this Sedrah, 'He (Jacob) strove with an angel, and prevailed: he (Jacob) wept, and made supplication unto him.' That supplication for mercy, forgiveness and Divine protection is heard. Jacob, the Supplanter, becomes Israel, Prince of God. 'This mysterious encounter of the Patriarch has become the universal human allegory of the struggles and wrestlings on the eve of some dreadful crisis, in the solitude and darkness of some overhanging trial' (Stanley).

**23.** *Jabbok*. A tributary of the Jordan, halfway between the Dead Sea and the Sea of Galilee.

**26.** *touched the hollow of his thigh*. This is usually interpreted as a final effort of the assailant to overcome Jacob.

**27.** The opponent's anxiety to escape before 'the day breaketh' suggested to the Patriarch's mind that he was a supernatural Being. Jacob, therefore, demanded a blessing as the price of release.

**28.** *what is thy name?* A rhetorical question, not seeking information. As indicated on XVII, 5, a name in Scripture is more than a label; it possesses significance.

**29.** *no more Jacob*. That is, 'the Supplanter,' prevailing over opponents by deceit.

*Israel*. The name is clearly a title of victory; probably 'a champion of God'. The children of the Patriarch are *Israelites*, Champions of God, Contenders for the Divine, conquering by strength from Above.

*striven*. The Septuagint and Vulgate translate, 'Thou didst prevail with God, and thou shalt prevail against men.'

*with God*. Cf. Hosea XII, 4. We have here another instance of 'God' interchanging with 'angel of God', as in XVI, 7, XXXI, 11.

*with men*. Laban and Esau.

**30.** As in Judg. XIII, 17 f, the angel refuses to disclose his name, because it was something mysterious.

**31.** *I have seen God face to face*. The Targum translates, 'I have seen angels of God face to face.'

*my life is preserved*. Jacob had seen an angel, A Divine Being, and yet lives; cf. Exod. XXXIII, 20.

**32.** *limped*. The struggle left its mark, but Jacob issued from the contest victor, redeemed and transformed by the contest. So it has ever been with the People called by his name.

**33.** *thigh-vein*. The sciatic nerve. This, together with other arteries and tendons, must be removed from the slaughtered animal, before

GENESIS XXXIII, 1

upon the hollow of the thigh, unto this day; because he touched the hollow of Jacob's thigh, even in the sinew of the thigh-vein.

## CHAPTER XXXIII

1. And Jacob lifted up his eyes, and looked, and, behold, Esau came, and with him four hundred men. And he divided the children unto Leah, and unto Rachel, and unto the two handmaids. 2. And he put the handmaids and their children foremost, and Leah and her children after, and Rachel and Joseph hindermost. 3. And he himself passed over before them, and bowed himself to the ground seven times, until he came near to his brother. 4. And Esau ran to meet him, and embraced him, and fell on his neck, and kissed him; and they wept. 5. And he lifted up his eyes, and saw the women and the children; and said: 'Who are these with thee?' And he said: 'The children whom God hath graciously given thy servant,'* ⁱᵛ· 6. Then the handmaids came near, they and their children, and they bowed down. 7. And Leah also and her children came near, and bowed down; and after came Joseph near and Rachel, and they bowed down. 8. And he said: 'What meanest thou by all this camp which I met?' And he said: 'To find favour in the sight of my lord.' 9. And Esau said: 'I have enough; my brother, let that which thou hast be thine.' 10. And Jacob said: 'Nay, I pray thee, if now I have found favour in

---

CHAPTER XXXIII. THE MEETING OF JACOB AND ESAU

**1.** *came.* Or, 'was coming.'

**2.** *hindermost.* Placing those he loved best in as secure a position as possible.

**3.** *passed over before them.* To conciliate his brother if possible, or to bear the brunt of the attack, and thus help his wives and children to escape.

*seven times.* In ancient inscriptions, the phrase, 'at the feet of my lord, seven times and seven times I fall,' frequently occurs.

**4.** *kissed him.* Esau proved both good-natured and forgiving. He fell on Jacob's neck, kissed Jacob, and they wept with the strong emotion of Orientals. Yet, the word for 'and kissed him' וישקהו is marked in the Heb. text with dots on every letter. The Rabbis doubted whether the kiss of Esau was genuine or not. Esau's conduct is certainly strange. If his intentions were friendly

that portion of the animal can be ritually prepared for Jewish consumption. This precept is a constant reminder of the Divine Providence to Israel as exemplified in the experience of the Patriarch.

from the first, why was he accompanied by so considerable a force as four hundred armed men? And if he had started out with a resolve to injure his brother, how account for the warm greeting immediately on coming face to face with him? This was in answer to Jacob's prayer, the Rabbis say. God had turned Esau's hate to love. Be that as it may, we have here another instance of the splendid impartiality of Scripture. The ancestor of Israel's hereditary enemy, the Edomites, is presented as chivalrous and dignified, full of magnanimity and generosity.

**8.** *camp.* i.e. the droves sent ahead as a gift to Esau. See XXXII, 17.

**9.** *I have enough.* lit. 'I have much.' Esau's reluctance to accept the gift was probably only another illustration of Oriental courtesy; see Chap. XXIII.

**10.** *seen thy face.* The phrase 'to see the face' expresses the idea of being favourably received. Jacob accordingly meant, 'I have been graciously pardoned by you, as I would have received forgiveness from God, had I appeared before Him in the humble spirit and with the tokens of contrition wherewith I approach you. Regard, then, my gift as a *minchah*, an offering.'

125

# GENESIS XXXIII, 11

thy sight, then receive my present at my hand; forasmuch as I have seen thy face, as one seeth the face of God, and thou wast pleased with me. 11. Take, I pray thee, my gift that is brought to thee; because God hath dealt graciously with me, and because I have enough.' And he urged him, and he took it. 12. And he said: Let us take our journey, and let us go, and I will go before thee.' 13. And he said unto him: 'My lord knoweth that the children are tender, and that the flocks and herds giving suck are a care to me; and if they overdrive them one day, all the flocks will die. 14. Let my lord, I pray thee, pass over before his servant; and I will journey on gently, according to the pace of the cattle that are before me and according to the pace of the children, until I come unto my lord unto Seir.' 15. And Esau said: 'Let me now leave with thee some of the folk that are with me.' And he said: 'What needeth it? let me find favour in the sight of my lord.' 16. So Esau returned that day on his way unto Seir. 17. And Jacob journeyed to Succoth, and built him a house, and made booths for his cattle. Therefore the name of the place is called ¹Succoth. ¶ 18. And Jacob came in peace

¹ That is, *Booths*.

---

**11.** *my gift*. lit. 'my blessing', the gift being the outward manifestation of the goodwill in the giver's heart.

*I have enough*. Lit. 'all'. Jacob has 'all' now that the danger of being slain by a brother, *or of slaying a brother*, is over; (see on XXXII, 8). Whereas Esau has 'much'; therefore, he is quite willing to have 'more'.

**12.** *I will go before thee*. Esau offers him his armed men.

**13.** Jacob, knowing the unstable character of Esau, is anxious that they should part company as quickly as possible.

*tender*. i.e. unequal to the fatigues of travel.

**14.** *the cattle*. lit. 'the work'; cf. the use of the word in Gen. II, 2, where it refers to, among other things, the creatures that God had made. The Heb. word for 'work' might here also mean 'property', as in Exod. XXII, 7, 10.

*unto Seir*. There is no record that Jacob went to Seir to see his brother. But, add the Rabbis, Jacob will yet visit Esau in the day of the Messiah, when the reconciliation between Israel and Edom will be complete.

**15.** Jacob prudently declines the offer.

**17.** *Succoth*. The exact site is unknown. It was part of the territory of the tribe of Gad, West of the Jordan (Josh. XIII, 27). Jacob must have stayed some years in Succoth.

### 18–20. AT SHECHEM

**18.** *in peace*. i.e. peaceably, with peaceable intentions. Since the word also has the meaning 'complete, whole' we have various Midrashic interpretations; such as, *recovered* from his lameness; and *perfect* in his knowledge of Torah, which he had not forgotten during his stay with Laban.

*Shechem*. See on XII, 6.

*before the city*. i.e. to the east of the city. About a mile from the city there is still shown Jacob's well.

**19.** *he brought*. The Patriarchs display their independent spirit by establishing an inalienable right to their land by means of purchase. See Chap. XXIII.

*children of Hamor*. People of the clan of Hamor.

*Shechem's father*. The founder, or chieftain, of the city of Shechem.

**20.** *altar*. In gratitude to God, who had permitted him to return in safety to the land of his fathers.

*El-elohe-Israel*. A profession of faith in the one true God, made at the moment when Jacob comes to dwell among the heathen Canaanites (Ryle).

## GENESIS XXXIII, 19

to the city of Shechem, which is in the land of Canaan, when he came from Paddan-aram; and encamped before the city. 19. And he bought the parcel of ground, where he had spread his tent, at the hand of the children of Hamor, Shechem's father, for a hundred pieces of money. 20. And he erected there an altar, and called it ¹El-elohe-Israel.*ᵛ·

## 34 CHAPTER XXXIV

1. And Dinah the daughter of Leah, whom she had borne unto Jacob, went out to see the daughters of the land. 2. And Shechem the son of Hamor the Hivite, the prince of the land, saw her; and he took her, and lay with her, and humbled her. 3. And his soul did cleave unto Dinah the daughter of Jacob, and he loved the damsel, and spoke comfortingly unto the damsel. 4. And Shechem spoke unto his father Hamor, saying: 'Get me this damsel to wife.' 5. Now Jacob heard that he had defiled Dinah his daughter; and his sons were with his cattle in the field; and Jacob held his peace until they came. 6. And Hamor the father of Shechem went out unto Jacob to speak with him. 7. And the sons of Jacob came in from the field when they heard it; and the men were grieved, and they were very wroth, because he had wrought a vile deed in Israel in lying with Jacob's daughter; which thing ought not to be done. 8. And Hamor spoke with them, saying: 'The soul of my son Shechem longeth for your daughter. I pray you give her unto him to wife. 9. And make ye marriages with us; give your daughters unto us, and take our daughters unto you. 10. And ye shall dwell with us; and the land shall be before you; dwell and trade ye therein, and get you

¹ That is, *God, the God of Israel.*

---

### CHAPTER XXXIV. DINAH

This chapter is an exception to the series of peaceful scenes from Patriarchal life and character—a tale of dishonour, wild revenge, and indiscriminate slaughter.

**1.** *to see.* 'and be seen,' is added in the Samaritan text. The Heb. idiom 'to see, to look upon' means 'to make friendship with'. It was wrong of Jacob to suffer his daughter alone and unprotected to visit the daughters of the land (Adam Clarke).

**2.** *humbled.* i.e. dishonoured; the Heb. implies by force.

**3.** *comfortingly.* lit. 'spoke to the heart' of the damsel; cf. Isaiah XL, 2. He tried to console her by his words of love, and his declared wish to make her his wife.

**4.** *get me this damsel.* It was the parent's duty to secure a wife for the son; cf. XXI, 21.

**7.** *vile deed.* Or, 'folly' (RV). The Heb. word translated by 'folly' means senseless wickedness, total insensibility to moral distinctions.

*in Israel.* Since the word means 'the people of Israel', it is strictly an anachronism, because the nation was not yet in existence. The latter part of this sentence must therefore be regarded not as spoken by Jacob's sons, but as the reflection of Scripture on the incident, wherein it points out that in the homes of the Patriarchs high conceptions of morality were entertained, and the defilement of a daughter was looked upon as an outrage against family honour and morality that demanded stern retribution.

**10.** The cordiality of Hamor's invitation is to be contrasted with what he told his townsmen in *v.* 23. To induce them to adopt his suggestion, he promises that it would be profitable to them, and they would gradually absorb the rich possessions of Jacob's household.

## GENESIS XXIV, 11

possessions therein.' 11. And Shechem said unto her father and unto her brethren: 'Let me find favour in your eyes, and what ye shall say unto me I will give. 12. Ask me never so much dowry and gift, and I will give according as ye shall say unto me; but give me the damsel to wife.' 13. And the sons of Jacob answered Shechem and Hamor his father with guile, and spoke, because he had defiled Dinah, their sister, 14. and said unto them: 'We cannot do this thing, to give our sister to one that is uncircumcised; for that were a reproach unto us. 15. Only on this condition will we consent unto you: if ye will be as we are, that every male of you be circumcised; 16. then will we give our daughters unto you, and we will take your daughters to us, and we will dwell with you, and we will become one people. 17. But if ye will not hearken unto us, to be circumcised; then will we take our daughter, and we will be gone.' 18. And their words pleased Hamor, and Shechem Hamor's son. 19. And the young man deferred not to do the thing, because he had delight in Jacob's daughter. And he was honoured above all the house of his father. 20. And Hamor and Shechem his son came unto the gate of their city, and spoke with the men of their city, saying: 21. 'These men are peaceable with us; therefore let them dwell in the land, and trade therein; for, behold, the land is large enough for them; let us take their daughters to us for wives, and let us give them our daughters. 22. Only on this condition will the men consent unto us to dwell with us, to become one people, if every male among us be circumcised, as they are circumcised. 23. Shall not their cattle and their substance and all their beasts be ours? only let us consent unto them, and they will dwell with us.' 24. And unto Hamor and unto Shechem his son hearkened all that went out of the gate of his city; and every male was circumcised, all that went out of the gate

**12.** *dowry*. The purchase price, *mohar*, given to the father and brothers of the bride; see on XXIV, 53, XXIX, 18.

*gift*. Personal presents to the bride.

**13.** *with guile*. Knowing that they were outnumbered by the citizens of Shechem, Jacob's sons resort to devious methods to carry out their determination to avenge their sister's dishonour. Their proposal would, if adopted, render the male population weak and helpless for a time; and this would give them the opportunity of making a successful attack. But why should all the men of the city suffer for the misdeed of one of their number? The sons of Jacob certainly acted in a treacherous and godless manner. Jacob did not forgive them to his dying day; see XLIX, 7.

**14.** *reproach*. Cf. Josh. v, 9.

**20.** *unto the gate*. The usual place of assembly. See on XIX, 1.

**23.** *be ours*. This argument proves Hamor's disingenuousness.

**24.** *all that went out of the gate* Cf. on XXIII, 10. Probably the able-bodied men, to the exclusion of the old men and boys, who would not be affected by the proposal of inter-marriage.

## GENESIS XXXIV, 25

of his city. 25. And it came to pass on the third day, when they were in pain, that two of the sons of Jacob, Simeon and Levi, Dinah's brethren, took each man his sword, and came upon the city unawares, and slew all the males. 26. And they slew Hamor and Shechem his son with the edge of the sword, and took Dinah out of Shechem's house, and went forth. 27. The sons of Jacob came upon the slain, and spoiled the city, because they had defiled their sister. 28. They took their flocks and their herds and their asses, and that which was in the city and that which was in the field; 29. and all their wealth, and all their little ones and their wives, took they captive and spoiled, even all that was in the house. 30. And Jacob said to Simeon and Levi: 'Ye have troubled me, to make me odious unto the inhabitants of the land, even unto the Canaanites and the Perizzites; and, I being few in number, they will gather themselves together against me and smite me; and I shall be destroyed, I and my house.' 31. And they said: 'Should one deal with our sister as with a harlot?'

## 35 CHAPTER XXXV

1. And God said unto Jacob: 'Arise, go up to Beth-el, and dwell there; and make there an altar unto God, who appeared unto thee when thou didst flee from the face of Esau thy brother.' 2. Then Jacob said unto his household, and to all that were with him: 'Put away the strange gods that are among you, and purify yourselves, and change your garments; 3. and let us arise, and go up to Beth-el; and I will make there an altar unto God, who answered me in the day of my distress, and was with me in the way

---

**25.** *Dinah's brethren.* These words are added to emphasize that Simeon, Levi and Dinah were children of the same mother, and therefore they felt the more acutely the insult and the desire for revenge.

**30.** Jacob has been criticized for merely rebuking his sons because their action might cause him personal danger, and not pointing out the heinous crime they had done in taking advantage of the helplessness of men with whom they had made a pact of friendship. Scripture, however, often lets facts speak for themselves, and does not always append the moral or the warning to a tale. Moreover, this chapter is supplemented by Jacob's Blessing in XLIX, 5 f. In reference to Simeon and Levi, the dying Patriarch there exclaims: 'Simeon and Levi are brethren; weapons of violence their kinship... Cursed be their anger, for it was fierce, and their wrath, for it was cruel.'

**31.** Jacob's sons reply that the dishonour of their sister had to be avenged, and there was only one course of action to follow. High-spirited and martial men have among all nations and throughout history often yielded to blind cruelty when dealing with an outrage of this nature.

### CHAPTER XXXV. THE RETURN TO BETH-EL. DEATH OF ISAAC

**1.** *go up to Beth-el.* Shechem is situated 1,880 ft. above sea-level, and Beth-el 2,890 ft. From the former place to the latter is a continuous ascent.

*an altar.* Alluding to the Patriarch's vow in XXVIII, 22.

**2.** *the strange gods.* i.e. gods worshipped by foreign tribes. According to Rashi, the reference is to the images which were included in the spoil of Shechem.

*purify yourselves.* By bathing, and abstaining from any act that would render them ceremonially unclean; cf. Exod. XIX, 10 ff.

## GENESIS XXXV, 4

which I went.' 4. And they gave unto Jacob all the foreign gods which were in their hand, and the rings which were in their ears; and Jacob hid them under the terebinth which was by Shechem. 5. And they journeyed; and a terror of God was upon the cities that were round about them, and they did not pursue after the sons of Jacob. 6. So Jacob came to Luz, which is in the land of Canaan—the same is Beth-el—he and all the people that were with him. 7. And he built there an altar, and called the place ¹El-beth-el, because there God was revealed unto him, when he fled from the face of his brother. 8. And Deborah Rebekah's nurse died, and she was buried below Beth-el under the oak; and the name of it was called ²Allon-bacuth. ¶9. And God appeared unto Jacob again, when he came from Paddan-aram, and blessed him. 10. And God said unto him: 'Thy name is Jacob; thy name shall not be called any more Jacob, but Israel shall be thy name'; and He called his name Israel. 11. And God said unto him: 'I am God Almighty. Be fruitful and multiply; a nation and a company of nations shall be of thee, and kings shall come out of thy loins;\* ᵛⁱ ᵃ· 12. and the land which I gave unto Abraham and Isaac, to thee I will give it, and to thy seed after thee will I give the land.' 13. And God went up from him in the place where He spoke with him. \* ᵛⁱ ˢ· 14. And Jacob set up a pillar in the place where He spoke with him, a pillar of stone, and he poured out a drink-offering thereon, and poured oil thereon. 15. And Jacob called the name of the place where God spoke with him, Beth-el. 16. And they journeyed from Beth-el; and there was still some way to come to Ephrath; and Rachel travailed, and she had hard labour. 17. And

---

¹ That is, *The God of Beth-el*.   ² That is, *The oak of weeping*.

---

**4.** *rings.* In their ears. They were more than ornaments; they were also amulets and charms (Targum Jonathan).

*terebinth.* See on XII, 6.

**5.** *a terror of God.* A fear inspired by God.

**6.** *Luz.* See on XXVIII, 19.

**7.** *El-beth-el.* Rashi explains, 'God who manifested Himself in Beth-el.'

**8.** *Deborah Rebekah's nurse died.* Cf. XXIV, 59. She had accompanied Jacob all this while.

**9.** *again.* As God had appeared to him on the outward journey, He once more manifested Himself on the return journey, to renew the promises.

*Paddan-aram.* See on XXV, 20.

**10.** God confirms the change of name made by the Angel in the heat of the contest (XXXII, 29).

**11.** *God Almighty.* Heb. 'El Shaddai'. For the promise which follows, cf. Isaac's blessing to Jacob in XXVIII, 3.

**13.** *and God went up from him.* The same phrase in XVII, 22.

**14.** *poured oil thereon.* Cf. on XXVIII, 18.

**16.** *some way to come.* i.e. a distance of no great length.

*Ephrath.* A place south of Beth-el.

**17.** *also is a son.* 'So the nurse cheers the dying woman by recalling her prayer at the birth of Joseph, xxx, 24' (Skinner).

GENESIS XXXV, 18

it came to pass, when she was in hard labour, that the midwife said unto her: 'Fear not; for this also is a son for thee.' 18. And it came to pass, as her soul was in departing—for she died—that she called his name ¹Ben-oni; but his father called him ²Benjamin. 19. And Rachel died, and was buried in the way to Ephrath—the same is Beth-lehem. 20. And Jacob set up a pillar upon her grave; the same is the pillar of Rachel's grave unto this day. 21. And Israel journeyed, and spread his tent beyond Migdal-eder. 22. And it came to pass, while Israel dwelt in that land, that Reuben went and lay with Bilhah his father's concubine; and Israel heard of it. ¶ Now the sons of Jacob were twelve: 23. the sons of Leah: Reuben, Jacob's first-born, and Simeon, and Levi, and Judah, and Issachar, and Zebulun; 24. the sons of Rachel: Joseph and Benjamin; 25, and the sons of Bilhah, Rachel's handmaid: Dan and Naphtali; 26. and the sons of Zilpah, Leah's handmaid: Gad and Asher. These are the sons of Jacob, that were born to him in Paddan-aram. 27. And Jacob came unto Isaac his father to Mamre, to Kiriath-arba—the same is Hebron—where Abraham and Isaac sojourned. 28, And the days of Isaac were a hundred and fourscore years. 29. And Isaac expired, and died, and was gathered unto his people, old and full of days; and Esau and Jacob his sons buried him.

---

¹ That is, *The son of my sorrow*.   ² That is, *The son of the right hand*.

**18.** Benjamin. The correct translation is, 'the son of my old age' (Hoffmann). The Samaritan Targum rightly transliterates בנימין by בן ימים.

**19.** Rachel died. Nothing is said of Jacob's grief. Another instance of the marvellous reserve of the Scriptural narrative. His grief for her, on whose behalf he rendered patient service for fourteen years, is indicated by a pathetic reference in XLVIII, 7.

**20.** pillar. The Heb. word מצבה is that which was in later use for 'tombstone'. Rachel's Tomb is one of the Jewish 'Holy Places' in Palestine.

**21.** Migdal-eder. The site has not been identified.

**22.** Reuben. It was the practice among Eastern heirs-apparent to take possession of their father's wives, as an assertion of their right to the succession; cf. on Lev. XVIII, 8. But whatever the reason, the memory of this repulsive incident lingered in the Patriarch's mind; it influenced the 'blessing' which on his death-bed he imparted to his eldest son (XLIX, 4).

*and Israel heard of it.* 'Of it' is not represented in the Hebrew. The ancient editors of the Hebrew text, the Massoretes, indicated 'A pause in the middle of a verse'. This means that the subject is abruptly dropped; it being too distasteful to continue so revolting a theme.

**26.** born to him in Paddan-aram. A generalization, disregarding the one exception, Benjamin, who was born in Canaan.

**27.** Mamre. See on XIII, 18.

*Kiriath-arba.* See on XXIII, 2. Since Rebekah is not mentioned here, we may infer that she died before Jacob's return.

**29.** expired. As Rashi points out, the Bible does not follow the chronological order here. It is only for the sake of convenience that his death is recorded at this point.

*was gathered unto his people.* See on XXV, 8.

*Esau and Jacob.* Similarly Isaac and Ishmael had jointly performed the last rites for Abraham (XXV, 9). Isaac is a less active character than either Abraham or Jacob. 'Abraham was an epoch-maker; his life, therefore, was an eventful one. Jacob closes the Patriarchal period, and his life was both rough and eventful. Not so Isaac. He inherits the true belief in God; his is merely the task of loyally transmitting it. No wonder that we hear little of him, and that he repeats some of his father's experiences' (Hoffmann). 'Isaac, a

## GENESIS XXXVI, 1

### CHAPTER XXXVI

1. Now these are the generations of Esau—the same is Edom. 2. Esau took his wives of the daughters of Canaan; Adah the daughter of Elon the Hittite, and Oholibamah the daughter of Anah, the daughter of Zibeon the Hivite. 3. and Basemath Ishmael's daughter, sister of Nebaioth. 4. And Adah bore to Esau Eliphaz; and Basemath bore Reuel; 5. and Oholibamah bore Jeush, and Jalam, and Korah. These are the sons of Esau, that were born unto him in the land of Canaan. 6. And Esau took his wives, and his sons, and his daughters, and all the souls of his house, and his cattle, and all his beasts, and all his possessions, which he had gathered in the land of Canaan; and went into a land away from his brother Jacob. 7. For their substance was too great for them to dwell together; and the land of their sojournings could not bear them because of their cattle. 8. And Esau dwelt in the mountain-land of Seir—Esau is Edom. 9. And these are the generations of Esau the father of ¹the Edomites in the mountain-land of Seir. 10. These are the names of Esau's sons: Eliphaz the son of Adah the wife of Esau, Reuel the son of Basemath the wife of Esau. 11. And the sons of Eliphaz were Teman, Omar, Zepho, and Gatam, and Kenaz. 12. And Timna was concubine to Eliphaz Esau's son; and she bore to Eliphaz Amalek. These are the sons of Adah Esau's wife. 13. And these are the sons of Reuel: Nahath, and Zerah, Shammah, and Mizzah. Thsee were the sons of Basemath Esau's wife. 14. And these were the sons of Oholibamah the daughter of Anah, the daughter of Zibeon, Esau's wife; and she bore to Esau Jeush, and Jalam, and Korah. 15. These are the chiefs of the sons of Esau: the sons of Eliphaz the first-born of Esau: the chief of Teman, the chief of Omar, the chief of Zepho, the chief of Kenaz, 16. the chief of Korah, the chief of Gatam, the chief of Amalek. These are the chiefs that came of Eliphaz in the land of Edom. These

¹ Heb. *Edom*.

patient, meditative man, strong in affection and love, typical of the domestic virtues for which his descendants have throughout the ages been remarkable. He stands as a type of the passive virtues, which have a strength of their own.' (The Study Bible.)

CHAPTER XXXVI. THE GENERATIONS OF ESAU

**1.** *the same is Edom.* Cf. xxv, 30.
**2.** *Esau took.* More accurately, 'had taken.' On the names of Esau's wives, see on xxvi, 34.
**6.** *into a land.* 'Unto another land' (Targum) as distinct from 'the land of Canaan'.

**7.** The same cause induced Abraham to separate from his nephew Lot (xiii, 6).

**8.** *Seir.* See on xiv, 6.

**10.** *Eliphaz.* In Rabbinic legend he is the worthiest of Esau's descendants; he was trained to pious living under the eyes of Isaac; the Lord had even endowed him with the spirit of prophecy, for he was none other than Eliphaz the friend of Job.

**12.** *Amalek.* Cf. on xiv, 7.

## GENESIS XXXVI, 17

are the sons of Adah. 17. And these are the sons of Reuel Esau's son: the chief of Nahath, the chief of Zerah, the chief of Shammah, the chief of Mizzah. These are the chiefs that came of Reuel in the land of Edom. These are the sons of Basemath Esau's wife. 18. And these are the sons of Oholibamah Esau's wife: the chief of Jeush, the chief of Jalam, the chief of Korah. These are the chiefs that came of Oholibamah the daughter of Anah, Esau's wife. 19. These are the sons of Esau, and these are their chiefs; the same is Edom.  *vii.
¶ 20. These are the sons of Seir the Horite, the inhabitants of the land: Lotan and Shobal and Zibeon and Anah, 21. and Dishon and Ezer and Dishan. These are the chiefs that came of the Horites, the children of Seir in the land of Edom. 22. And the children of Lotan were Hori and Hemam; and Lotan's sister was Timna. 23. And these are the children of Shobal: Alvan and Manahath and Ebal, Shepho and Onam. 24. And these are the children of Zibeon: Aiah and Anah—this is Anah who found the hot springs in the wilderness, as he fed the asses of Zibeon his father. 25. And these are the children of Anah: Dishon and Oholibamah the daughter of Anah. 26. And these are the children of [1]Dishon: Hemdan and Eshban and Ithran and Cheran. 27. These are the children of Ezer: Bilhan and Zaavan and Akan. 28. These are the children of Dishan: Uz and Aran. 29. These are the chiefs that came of the Horites: the chief of Lotan, the chief of Shobal, the chief of Zibeon, the chief of Anah, 30, the chief of Dishon, the chief of Ezer, the chief of Dishan. These are the chiefs that came of the Horites, according to their chiefs in the land of Seir. ¶ 31. And these are the kings that

---

[1] Heb. *Dishan*.

---

**20.** *the inhabitants of the land.* The original settlers before the arrival of Esau's clans. The Horites seem to have been cave-dwellers. Some consider them to have been the cultural ancestors of the Hittites; see on Deut. II, 12.

**24.** *hot springs.* The Heb. word occurs only here. The older Jewish commentators understood it to mean 'mules'.

**31.** This verse raises an obvious difficulty. Ibn Ezra understands the 'king' to refer to Moses, the ruler of the Children of Israel. A more satisfactory explanation of the verse is the following. In the last chapter (xxxv, 11) there had been an emphatic promise from God Almighty to Jacob that 'kings shall come out of thy loins'. The Israelites, no doubt, cherished a constant hope of such a kingdom and such a kingly race. Moses himself (Deut. xxviii, 36) prophesied concerning the king whom the Israelites would set over them; and hence it was not unnatural that, when recording the eight kings who had reigned in the family of Esau up to his own time, Scripture should go out of its way to reassure the Israelites that their history was not yet complete. The words in the Hebrew are, 'before the reigning of a king to the sons of Israel'; and might be rendered 'whilst as yet the Children of Israel have no king'; there being nothing in the words expressive of past tense, or indicating that, before they were written, a king had reigned in Israel.

## GENESIS XXXVI, 32

reigned in the land of Edom, before there reigned any king over the children of Israel. 32. And Bela the son of Beor reigned D Edom; and the name of his city was ininhabah. 33. And Bela died, and Jobab the son of Zerah of Bozrah reigned in his stead. 34. And Jobab died, and Husham of the land of the Temanites reigned in his stead. 35. And Husham died, and Hadad the son of Bedad, who smote Midian in the field of Moab, reigned in his stead; and the name of his city was Avith. 36. And Hadad died, and Samlah of Masrekah reigned in his stead. 37. And Samlah died, and Shaul of Rehoboth by the River reigned in his stead. 38. And Shaul died, and Baal-hanan the son of Achbor reigned in his stead. 39. And Baal-hanan the son of Achbor died, and Hadar reigned in his stead; and the name of his city was Pau; and his wife's name was Mehetabel, the daughter of Matred, the daughter of Mezahab.*  ᵐ· 40. And these are the names of the chiefs that came of Esau, according to their families, after their places, by their names: the chief of Timna, the chief of Alvah, the chief of Jetheth; 41. the chief of Oholibamah, the chief of Elah, the chief of Pinon; 42. the chief of Kenaz, the chief of Teman, the chief of Mibzar; 43. the chief of Magdiel, the chief of Iram. These are the chiefs of Edom, according to their habitations in the land of their possession. This is Esau the father of the Edomites.

בראשית וישלח לו

31 וְאֵ֣לֶּה הַמְּלָכִ֗ים אֲשֶׁ֤ר מָלְכוּ֙ בְּאֶ֣רֶץ אֱד֔וֹם לִפְנֵ֥י מְלָךְ־מֶ֖לֶךְ
32 לִבְנֵ֣י יִשְׂרָאֵ֑ל וַיִּמְלֹ֣ךְ בֶּֽאֱד֗וֹם בֶּ֚לַע בֶּן־בְּע֔וֹר וְשֵׁ֥ם עִיר֖וֹ
33 דִּנְהָֽבָה: וַיָּ֖מָת בָּ֑לַע וַיִּמְלֹ֣ךְ תַּחְתָּ֔יו יוֹבָ֥ב בֶּן־זֶ֖רַח מִבָּצְרָֽה:
34 וַיָּ֖מָת יוֹבָ֑ב וַיִּמְלֹ֣ךְ תַּחְתָּ֔יו חֻשָׁ֖ם מֵאֶ֥רֶץ הַתֵּימָנִֽי: וַיָּ֖מָת
לה
   חֻשָׁ֑ם וַיִּמְלֹ֣ךְ תַּחְתָּ֗יו הֲדַ֤ד בֶּן־בְּדַד֙ הַמַּכֶּ֣ה אֶת־מִדְיָ֔ן
36 בִּשְׂדֵ֣ה מוֹאָ֔ב וְשֵׁ֥ם עִיר֖וֹ עֲוִֽית: וַיָּ֖מָת הֲדָ֑ד וַיִּמְלֹ֣ךְ תַּחְתָּ֔יו
37 שַׂמְלָ֖ה מִמַּשְׂרֵקָֽה: וַיָּ֖מָת שַׂמְלָ֑ה וַיִּמְלֹ֣ךְ תַּחְתָּ֔יו שָׁא֖וּל
38 מֵרְחֹב֣וֹת הַנָּהָֽר: וַיָּ֖מָת שָׁא֑וּל וַיִּמְלֹ֣ךְ תַּחְתָּ֔יו בַּ֥עַל חָנָ֖ן
39 בֶּן־עַכְבּֽוֹר: וַיָּ֖מָת בַּ֣עַל חָנָ֣ן בֶּן־עַכְבּ֔וֹר וַיִּמְלֹ֣ךְ תַּחְתָּ֗יו
   הֲדַ֔ר וְשֵׁ֥ם עִיר֖וֹ פָּ֑עוּ וְשֵׁ֨ם אִשְׁתּ֤וֹ מְהֵֽיטַבְאֵל֙ בַּת־מַטְרֵ֔ד
מפטיר
מ  בַּת־מֵ֥י זָהָֽב: אֵ֠לֶּה שְׁמ֞וֹת אַלּוּפֵ֤י עֵשָׂו֙ לְמִשְׁפְּחֹתָ֔ם
   לִמְקֹמֹתָ֖ם בִּשְׁמֹתָ֑ם אַלּ֥וּף תִּמְנָ֛ע אַלּ֥וּף עַלְוָ֖ה אַלּ֥וּף יְתֵֽת:
41 אַלּ֧וּף אָהֳלִיבָמָ֛ה אַלּ֥וּף אֵלָ֖ה אַלּ֥וּף פִּינֹֽן: אַלּ֥וּף קְנַ֛ז
42
43 אַלּ֥וּף תֵּימָ֖ן אַלּ֥וּף מִבְצָֽר: אַלּ֥וּף מַגְדִּיאֵ֖ל אַלּ֣וּף עִירָ֑ם
   אֵ֣לֶּה ׀ אַלּוּפֵ֣י אֱד֗וֹם לְמֹֽשְׁבֹתָם֙ בְּאֶ֣רֶץ אֲחֻזָּתָ֔ם ה֥וּא עֵשָׂ֖ו
   אֲבִ֥י אֱדֽוֹם:

---

**35.** *Hadad.* The name of the Syrian storm-god, and common in Edomite names.

**38.** *Baal-hanan.* The same name as Hannibal, *i.e.* 'Baal is favourable'.

**40.** *chiefs.* The clan-chiefs (as their title indicates) were not sovereigns of the whole of Edom, but rulers of tribes or provinces. The RV (following AV) calls them 'dukes'.

# HAFTORAH VAYYETZE (For Sephardim)
# HAFTORAH VAYYISHLACH (For Ashkenazim)

הפטרת ויצא לספרדים
הפטרת וישלח לאשכנזים

## HOSEA XI, 7–XII, 12

### Chapter XI

7. And My people are in suspense about returning to Me;
And though they call them upwards,
None at all will lift himself up.

8. How shall I give thee up, Ephraim?
How shall I surrender thee, Israel?
How shall I make thee as Admah?
How shall I set thee as Zeboim?
My heart is turned within Me,
My compassions are kindled together.

9. I will not execute the fierceness of Mine anger,
I will not return to destroy Ephraim;
For I am God, and not man,
The Holy One in the midst of thee,
And I will not come in fury.

10. They shall walk after the Lord,
Who shall roar like a lion;
For He shall roar,
And the children shall come trembling from the west.

11. They shall come trembling as a bird out of Egypt,
And as a dove out of the land of Assyria;
And I will make them to dwell in their houses,
Saith the Lord.

### Chapter XII

1. Ephraim compasseth Me about with lies,
And the house of Israel with deceit;
And Judah is yet wayward towards God,
And towards the Holy One who is faithful.

---

Hosea's is the message of God's unwearying love to Israel, a message which reached its fullest expression in the cry 'O Israel, return unto the Lord thy God'. In this Haftorah, he interweaves incidents from the life of Jacob in the Sedrah, in order to recall what Israel was intended to be, in contrast with the degeneracy of his contemporaries. The Prophet's whole soul goes out in sympathy for his People; he would give his all to reclaim it, if only it were possible. Hosea's is a deeply affectionate nature; and his sentences of doom against his people read like short, disconnected sobs. The connection between the parts of his discourse, or even between his sentences, is not always distinct. But 'ever and anon, the tossing restless discourse begins again, like the wild cry of an anguish that can hardly be mastered' (Ewald).

**7.** *in suspense about returning to Me.* Uncertain, swaying to and fro like a door on its hinges.
*And though they call them.* 'They,' i.e. the Prophets.

**8.** Hosea portrays God's yearning, unending love for His people.
*Admah, Zeboim.* Cities of the Plain, destroyed together with Sodom and Gomorrah (Gen. xix).

**9.** *for I am God.* Therefore, merciful and gracious, slow to anger, and abounding in mercy.

**10.** God's message shall stir the hearts of Israel. The figure of the lion, roaring to call his young, represents God calling His people out of captivity.
*trembling.* With contrition and joy.

**11.** *as a dove.* Noted for its swiftness, which shall characterize Israel's return.

### Chapter XII

From this vision of a happier future the Prophet returns to the sad conditions of the present.

135

# HOSEA XII, 2 הושע יב

2. Ephraim striveth after wind, and
followeth after the east wind;
All the day he multiplieth lies and
desolation;
And they make a covenant with Assyria,
And oil is carried into Egypt.

3. The Lord hath also a controversy with
Judah,
And will punish Jacob according to his
ways,
According to his doings will He recompense him.

4. In the womb he took his brother by
the heel,
And by his strength he strove with a
godlike being;

5. So he strove with an angel, and prevailed;
He wept, and made supplication unto
him;
At Beth-el he would find him,
And there he would speak with us.

6. But the Lord, the God of hosts,
The Lord is His name.

7. Therefore turn thou to thy God;
Keep mercy and justice,
And wait for thy God continually.

8. As for the trafficker, the balances of
deceit are in his hand,
He loveth to oppress.

9. And Ephraim said: 'Surely I am become rich,
I have found me wealth;
In all my labours they shall find in me
No iniquity that were sin.'

---

**2.** *striveth after wind.* Vain and fruitless efforts, resulting in 'lies and desolation'; a telling summary of the results of the foreign alliances.

*oil.* Representing the wealth which the last king, Hoshea, sent to Egypt for help against Assyria.

**4.** In order to move them to repentance, the Prophet reminds the people of the wrestling in prayer of their ancestor Jacob, and of God's acceptance of him.

*with a godlike being.* An angel, as is evident from the very next verse.

**5.** *he wept.* The subject is Jacob.

*he would find him.* God found Jacob at Beth-el.

*would speak with us.* In speaking to Jacob, God as it were spake also to his descendants.

**6.** *the Lord is His name.* The same now as then. As He received Jacob, so will He receive Israel; therefore, 'turn to thy God'.

**7.** *keep mercy and justice.* This sums up the teaching of Hosea. 'Justice' (judgement) alone is not sufficient. Mercy, loving sympathy towards our fellowmen, must go with it; *and mercy must precede it.*

**8.** *trafficker.* lit. 'Canaanite'. From the call to repentance, the Prophet again returns to the evil-doing of his day. Israel's ideal is now Canaan's—to get rich. 'Canaanite' had become a synonym for 'trafficker', from the low repute of the Phœnician (Canaanitish) merchant for honesty.

**9.** *Ephraim's answer.* He boasts of his wealth, and callously maintains it has been obtained honestly—and that any trifling lapses in his methods cannot be accounted as sins. He does not perceive that, apart from his methods of acquisition, his reliance on material possessions and absorption in amassing them have blinded the moral and spiritual sense within him. Israel had become Canaan, and yet was quite unconscious of it!

## HOSEA XII, 10

10. But I am the LORD thy God
   From the land of Egypt;
   I will yet again make thee to dwell in tents,
   As in the days of the appointed season.
11. I have also spoken unto the prophets,
   And I have multiplied visions;
   And by the ministry of the prophets have I used similitudes.
12. If Gilead be given to iniquity
   Becoming altogether vanity,
   In Gilgal they sacrifice unto bullocks;
   Yea, their altars shall be as heaps
   In the furrows of the field.

הושע יב

י אָן לִי בָּל־יְגִיעַי לֹא יִמְצְאוּ־לִי עָוֹן אֲשֶׁר־חֵטְא: וְאָנֹכִי יְהֹוָה אֱלֹהֶיךָ מֵאֶרֶץ מִצְרָיִם עֹד אוֹשִׁיבְךָ בָאֳהָלִים כִּימֵי מוֹעֵד: וְדִבַּרְתִּי עַל־הַנְּבִיאִים וְאָנֹכִי חָזוֹן הִרְבֵּיתִי וּבְיַד 11
הַנְּבִיאִים אֲדַמֶּה: אִם־גִּלְעָד אָוֶן אַךְ־שָׁוְא הָיוּ בַּגִּלְגָּל 12
שְׁוָרִים זִבֵּחוּ גַּם מִזְבְּחוֹתָם כְּגַלִּים עַל תַּלְמֵי שָׂדָי:

10. *to dwell in tents.* 'The tent-life of the wilderness was a trial and pain for which the settlement in the Promised Land was readily exchanged. But it was also a blessing and a revelation, a walking in mystery and wonder, the Divine Presence always felt and often manifest. The Feast of Tabernacles was the yearly remembrance of this wonderful pilgrim experience' (Horton). Israel must go back to captivity and begin his discipline over again, as when he came out of Egypt.

11. In vain did the Prophets convey the Divine will in visions and similitudes. They failed to bring Israel to repentance.

12. References to the heathen practices at Gilgal following the ill example of neighbouring Gilead on the other side of the Jordan. The meaning seems to be: 'In Gilead there are iniquity and falsehood; they sacrifice to demons in Gilgal; their altars shall become stone-heaps in the furrows of the fields.' They that make the idols become like unto them.

# HAFTORAH VAYYISHLACH (FOR SEPHARDIM)

הפטרת וישלח לספרדים

## THE BOOK OF OBADIAH

1. The vision of Obadiah.
   Thus saith the LORD God concerning Edom:
   We have heard a message from the LORD,
   And an ambassador is sent among the nations:
   'Arise ye, and let us rise up against her in battle.'
2. Behold, I make thee small among the nations;
   Thou art greatly despised.

א חֲזוֹן עֹבַדְיָה כֹּה־אָמַר אֲדֹנָי יְהֹוִה לֶאֱדוֹם שְׁמוּעָה שָׁמַעְנוּ מֵאֵת יְהֹוָה וְצִיר בַּגּוֹיִם שֻׁלָּח קוּמוּ וְנָקוּמָה עָלֶיהָ 2 לַמִּלְחָמָה: הִנֵּה קָטֹן נְתַתִּיךָ בַּגּוֹיִם בָּזוּי אַתָּה מְאֹד:

קמץ בז״ק ibid. v. 1.

The prophecy of Obadiah is directed against Edom, the nation descended from Esau. It thus connects with the Sedrah, reflecting the opposition between the two brothers in the story of Jacob and Esau. The bitter enmity of the Edomites to Israel was particularly inexcusable, because of their common descent. The Prophet instances the cruelty of the Edomites in the day of Israel's ruin. Apart, however, from the denunciation of unbrotherliness wherever exhibited, the book has a wider application. Other nations in later times played the cruel role of Edom towards Israel. Against these too, according to our commentators, Obadiah prophetically inveighs and predicts Israel's triumph over them. The forces of evil will never destroy Israel, because Israel's Faith, and the Truth enshrined in it, are eternal.

1. *we have heard.* 'We,' i.e. other Prophets, who also denounced Edom; see especially Jer. XLIX, 7-12.

## OBADIAH, 3

3. The pride of thy heart hath beguiled thee,
O thou that dwellest in the clefts of the rock,
Thy habitation on high;
That sayest in thy heart:
'Who shall bring me down to the ground?'

4. Though thou make thy nest as high as the eagle,
And though thou set it among the stars,
I will bring thee down from thence, saith the LORD.

5. If thieves came to thee, if robbers by night—
How art thou cut off!—
Would they not steal till they had enough?
If grape-gatherers came to thee,
Would they not leave some gleaning grapes?

6. How is Esau searched out!
How are his hidden places sought out!

7. All the men of thy confederacy
Have conducted thee to the border;
The men that were at peace with thee
Have beguiled thee, and prevailed against thee;
They that eat thy bread lay a snare under thee,
In whom there is no discernment.

8. Shall I not in that day, saith the LORD,
Destroy the wise men out of Edom,
And discernment out of the mount of Esau?

9. And thy mighty men, O Teman, shall be dismayed,
To the end that every one may be cut off from the mount of Esau by slaughter.

10. For the violence done to thy brother Jacob shame shall cover thee,
And thou shalt be cut off for ever.

11. In the day that thou didst stand aloof,
In the day that strangers carried away his substance,
And foreigners entered into his gates,
And cast lots upon Jerusalem,
Even thou wast as one of them.

---

**3.** *pride of thy heart.* Their previous successes, and their belief that they could not be dislodged from their impregnable position.

*clefts of the rock.* Edom occupied a mountainous strip to the South of Palestine. Its rocky valleys were fertile and difficult of access to outsiders. The ruins of its capital, Petra, the mysterious, secluded city with its thousand caves, have come down to our day.

**4.** Their pride defies God. So does all pride.

**5.** The meaning is that ordinary thieves and grape-gleaners will leave something behind. Not so those who will fall upon Edom. They will destroy everything.

**7.** Not merely enemies—but their own familiar friends shall be against them.

**8.** *wise men out of Edom.* Edom's reputation for wisdom and shrewdness was proverbial. The story of Job was enacted in Edom.

**9.** *Teman.* Probably the north part of Edom; used for Edom as a whole.

**10–15.** The crowning cruelty of Edom to his brother Jacob, his malice when Jerusalem fell. Instead of helping his brother, or at least standing aside, Edom took part in the looting, and in the slaughter of the inhabitants (Ps. CXXXVII, 7).

**11.** *thou wast as one of them.* As one of the pitiless enemies. A brief but biting indictment.

## OBADIAH, 12

12. But thou shouldst not have gazed on the day of thy brother
In the day of his disaster,
Neither shouldst thou have rejoiced over the children of Judah
In the day of their destruction;
Neither shouldst thou have spoken proudly
In the day of distress.

13. Thou shouldest not have entered into the gate of My people
In the day of their calamity;
Yea, thou shouldest not have gazed on their affliction
In the day of their calamity,
Nor have laid hands on their substance
In the day of their calamity.

14. Neither shouldest thou have stood in the crossway,
To cut off those of his that escape;
Neither shouldest thou have delivered up those of his
That did remain in the day of distress.

15. For the day of the LORD is near upon all the nations;
As thou hast done, it shall be done unto thee;
Thy dealing shall return upon thine own head.

16. For as ye have drunk upon My holy mountain,
So shall all the nations drink continually,
Yea, they shall drink, and swallow down,
And shall be as though they had not been.

17. But in mount Zion there shall be those that escape,
And it shall be holy;
And the house of Jacob shall possess their possessions.

18. And the house of Jacob shall be a fire,
And the house of Joseph a flame,
And the house of Esau for stubble,
And they shall kindle in them, and devour them;
And there shall not be any remaining of the house of Esau;
For the LORD hath spoken.

19. And they of the South shall possess the mount of Esau,
And they of the Lowland the Philistines;
And they shall possess the field of Ephraim,
And the field of Samaria;
And Benjamin shall possess Gilead.

12 גוֹרָל גַּם־אַתָּה כְּאַחַד מֵהֶם: וְאַל־תֵּרֶא בְיוֹם־אָחִיךָ בְּיוֹם
נָכְרוֹ וְאַל־תִּשְׂמַח לִבְנֵי־יְהוּדָה בְּיוֹם אָבְדָם וְאַל־תַּגְדֵּל
13 פִּיךָ בְּיוֹם צָרָה: אַל־תָּבוֹא בְשַׁעַר־עַמִּי בְּיוֹם אֵידָם אַל־
תֵּרֶא גַם־אַתָּה בְּרָעָתוֹ בְּיוֹם אֵידוֹ וְאַל־תִּשְׁלַחְנָה בְחֵילוֹ
14 בְּיוֹם אֵידוֹ: וְאַל־תַּעֲמֹד עַל־הַפֶּרֶק לְהַכְרִית אֶת־פְּלִיטָיו
טו וְאַל־תַּסְגֵּר שְׂרִידָיו בְּיוֹם צָרָה: כִּי־קָרוֹב יוֹם־יְהוָה עַל־
כָּל־הַגּוֹיִם כַּאֲשֶׁר עָשִׂיתָ יֵעָשֶׂה לָּךְ גְּמֻלְךָ יָשׁוּב בְּרֹאשֶׁךָ:
16 כִּי כַּאֲשֶׁר שְׁתִיתֶם עַל־הַר קָדְשִׁי יִשְׁתּוּ כָל־הַגּוֹיִם תָּמִיד
17 וְשָׁתוּ וְלָעוּ וְהָיוּ כְּלוֹא הָיוּ: וּבְהַר צִיּוֹן תִּהְיֶה פְלֵיטָה
18 וְהָיָה קֹדֶשׁ וְיָרְשׁוּ בֵּית יַעֲקֹב אֵת מוֹרָשֵׁיהֶם: וְהָיָה בֵית־
יַעֲקֹב אֵשׁ וּבֵית יוֹסֵף לֶהָבָה וּבֵית עֵשָׂו לְקַשׁ וְדָלְקוּ בָהֶם
וַאֲכָלוּם וְלֹא־יִהְיֶה שָׂרִיד לְבֵית עֵשָׂו כִּי יְהוָה דִּבֵּר:
19 וְיָרְשׁוּ הַנֶּגֶב אֶת־הַר עֵשָׂו וְהַשְּׁפֵלָה אֶת־פְּלִשְׁתִּים וְיָרְשׁוּ
אֶת־שְׂדֵה אֶפְרַיִם וְאֵת שְׂדֵה שֹׁמְרוֹן וּבִנְיָמִן אֶת־הַגִּלְעָד:

**12.** *Thou shouldest not have gazed.* With malicious pleasure, with *Schadenfreude.*
*disaster.* lit. 'strange, unwonted fortune.'

**15.** *day of the LORD.* God's triumphant vindication of His people against their cruel enemies.

**16.** *ye have drunk. i.e.* the Israelites, have drunk of the cup of suffering.
*shall be as though they had not been.* This verse is an indictment of the 'gospel of hate' wherever held, whether by nations or individuals. They who nourish and practise it are, in the end, self-destroyers.

**17.** *possess their possessions.* The house of Jacob shall not finally lack anything which is rightly theirs. The Heb. word for 'possessions' is rare; the national and religious values of Israel are singularly precious.

**19-20.** Generally meaning that the returning exiles shall occupy a territory enlarged on all sides.

## OBADIAH, 20

20. And the captivity of this host of the children of Israel,
That are among the Canaanites, even unto Zarephath,
And the captivity of Jerusalem, that is in Sepharad,
Shall possess the cities of the South.
21. And saviours shall come up on mount Zion
To judge the mount of Esau;
And the kingdom shall be the LORD's.

כ וְגָלֻת הַחֵל־הַזֶּה לִבְנֵי יִשְׂרָאֵל אֲשֶׁר־כְּנַעֲנִים עַד־צָרְפַת
21 וְגָלֻת יְרוּשָׁלִַם אֲשֶׁר בִּסְפָרַד יִרְשׁוּ אֵת עָרֵי הַנֶּגֶב: וְעָלוּ
מוֹשִׁעִים בְּהַר צִיּוֹן לִשְׁפֹּט אֶת־הַר עֵשָׂו וְהָיְתָה לַיהוָה
הַמְּלוּכָה:

v. 20. הר׳ בפתח

**20.** *Sepharad.* Some locality in Babylonia or Asia Minor. Targum Jonathan, however, and all subsequent Jewish writers, understand by that name, Spain; hence Jews hailing from the Iberian Peninsula are called *Sephardim.*

**21.** *saviours.* A wider sweep here than even Israel's triumphant vindication. For it is not merely Israel's supremacy that the Prophet sees in his vision of saviours climbing Mount Zion but the supremacy of God. There shall be no more causeless enmity (שנאת חנם) between nation and nation, between man and man. Such causeless enmity Edom stands for. It shall cease. And then humanity will be nearer the time when 'the kingdom shall be the LORD's'.

# GENESIS XXXVII, 1

## CHAPTER XXXVII

1. And Jacob dwelt in the land of his father's sojournings, in the land of Canaan. 2. These are the generations of Jacob. Joseph, being seventeen years old, was feeding the flock with his brethren, being still a lad, even with the sons of Bilhah, and with the sons of Zilpah, his father's wives; and Joseph brought evil report of them unto their father. 3. Now Israel loved Joseph more than all his children, because he was the son of his old age; and he made him a coat of many colours. 4. And when his brethren saw that their father loved him more than all his brethren, they hated him, and could not speak peaceably unto him. 5. And Joseph dreamed a dream, and he told it to his brethren; and they hated him yet the more. 6. And he said unto them: 'Hear, I pray you, this dream which I have

## CAP. XXXVII. לז

פ פ פ ס 9

וַיֵּ֣שֶׁב יַעֲקֹ֔ב בְּאֶ֖רֶץ מְגוּרֵ֣י אָבִ֑יו בְּאֶ֖רֶץ כְּנָֽעַן: אֵ֣לֶּה ׀ תֹּלְד֣וֹת
יַעֲקֹ֗ב יוֹסֵ֞ף בֶּן־שְׁבַֽע־עֶשְׂרֵ֤ה שָׁנָה֙ הָיָ֨ה רֹעֶ֤ה אֶת־אֶחָיו֙
בַּצֹּ֔אן וְה֣וּא נַ֗עַר אֶת־בְּנֵ֥י בִלְהָ֛ה וְאֶת־בְּנֵ֥י זִלְפָּ֖ה נְשֵׁ֣י אָבִ֑יו
3 וַיָּבֵ֥א יוֹסֵ֛ף אֶת־דִּבָּתָ֥ם רָעָ֖ה אֶל־אֲבִיהֶֽם: וְיִשְׂרָאֵ֗ל אָהַ֤ב
אֶת־יוֹסֵף֙ מִכָּל־בָּנָ֔יו כִּֽי־בֶן־זְקֻנִ֥ים ה֖וּא ל֑וֹ וְעָ֥שָׂה ל֖וֹ כְּתֹ֥נֶת
4 פַּסִּֽים: וַיִּרְא֣וּ אֶחָ֗יו כִּֽי־אֹת֞וֹ אָהַ֤ב אֲבִיהֶם֙ מִכָּל־אֶחָ֔יו
5 וַֽיִּשְׂנְא֖וּ אֹת֑וֹ וְלֹ֥א יָכְל֖וּ דַּבְּר֥וֹ לְשָׁלֹֽם: וַיַּחֲלֹ֤ם יוֹסֵף֙ חֲל֔וֹם
6 וַיַּגֵּ֖ד לְאֶחָ֑יו וַיּוֹסִ֥פוּ ע֖וֹד שְׂנֹ֥א אֹתֽוֹ: וַיֹּ֖אמֶר אֲלֵיהֶ֑ם שִׁמְעוּ־

## IX. VAYYESHEV

### (CHAPTERS XXXVII–XL)

#### (c) JOSEPH AND HIS BRETHREN

**CHAPTER XXXVII. JOSEPH'S DREAMS**

**1.** After a brief enumeration of Esau's descendants, without giving their history, Scripture resumes the account of the fortunes of Jacob and his sons.

**2.** *the generations.* Joseph alone is mentioned because he is the centre of the narrative which fills the remainder of Genesis, and forms its notable climax.

The stories of Genesis, and especially the story of Joseph, have at all times called forth the admiration of mankind. Dealing with the profoundest thoughts in terms of everyday life, yet a child is thrilled by the story; and at the same time the greatest thinkers are continually finding in it fresh depths of unexpected meaning (Ryle). Like summer and the starry skies, like joy and childhood, these stories touch and enthral the human soul with their sublime simplicity, high seriousness and marvellous beauty. And they are absolutely irreplaceable in the moral and religious training of children. The fact that, after having been repeated for three thousand years and longer, these stories still possess an eternal freshness to children of all races and climes, proves that there is in them something of imperishable worth. There is no other literature in the world which offers that something. This is recognized even in educational circles that are far removed not only from the Traditional attitude towards the Bible, but even from the religious outlook. The uniqueness of these stories consists in the fact that there is in them a sense of overruling Divine Providence realizing its purpose through the complex interaction of human motives. They are saturated with the moral spirit. Duty, guilt and its punishment, the conflict of conscience with inclination, the triumph of moral and spiritual forces amidst the vicissitudes of human affairs—are the leading themes. And what is pre-eminently true of Genesis applies to the whole of Bible history. Not by means of abstract formulae does it bring God and duty to the soul of man, but by means of *lives* of human beings who feel and fail, who stumble and sin as we do; yet who, in their darkest groping, remain conscious of the one true way—and rise again. Witness the conduct of the brothers of Joseph when they had fully grasped the enormity of their crime. 'By the study of what other book,' asked the agnostic T. H. Huxley, 'could children be so much humanized and made to feel that each figure in the vast procession of history fills, like themselves, but a momentary space in the interval between the eternities; and earns the blessings or the curses of all time according to its effort to do good and hate evil?'

*feeding.* Or, 'supervising.' The picture of Joseph doing the same work as his brothers is out of accord with what is told in the next verse. Ehrlich therefore translates: 'Joseph, being seventeen years old, used to supervise—although only a lad—his brethren, *viz.*, the sons of Bilhah and the sons of Zilpah (when they were) with the sheep.' Joseph would thus be placed in charge of only the sons of the handmaids.

*evil report of them.* Probably, their inattention to duty.

**3.** *he was the son of his old age.* At this time

## GENESIS XXXVII, 7

dreamed: 7. for, behold, we were binding sheaves in the field, and, lo, my sheaf arose, and also stood upright; and, behold, your sheaves came round about, and bowed down to my sheaf.' 8. And his brethren said to him: 'Shalt thou indeed reign over us? or shalt thou indeed have dominion over us?' And they hated him yet the more for his dreams, and for his words. 9. And he dreamed yet another dream, and told it to his brethren, and said: 'Behold, I have dreamed yet a dream: and, behold, the sun and the moon and eleven stars bowed down to me.' 10. And he told it to his father, and to his brethren; and his father rebuked him, and said unto him: 'What is this dream that thou hast dreamed? Shall I and thy mother and thy brethren indeed come to bow down to thee to the earth?' 11. And his brethren envied him; but his father kept the saying in mind. *11. ¶ 12. And his brethren went to feed their father's flock in Shechem. 13. And Israel said unto Joseph: 'Do not thy brethren feed the flock in Shechem? come, and I will send thee unto them.' And he said to him: 'Here am I.' 14. And he said to him: 'Go now, see whether it is well with thy brethren, and well with the flock; and bring me back word.' So he sent him out of the vale of Hebron, and he came to Shechem. 15. And a certain man found him, and, behold, he

7 נָא הַחֲלוֹם הַזֶּה אֲשֶׁר חָלָמְתִּי: וְהִנֵּה אֲנַחְנוּ מְאַלְּמִים אֲלֻמִּים בְּתוֹךְ הַשָּׂדֶה וְהִנֵּה קָמָה אֲלֻמָּתִי וְגַם־נִצָּבָה וְהִנֵּה
8 תְסֻבֶּינָה אֲלֻמֹּתֵיכֶם וַתִּשְׁתַּחֲוֶיןָ לַאֲלֻמָּתִי: וַיֹּאמְרוּ לוֹ אֶחָיו הֲמָלֹךְ תִּמְלֹךְ עָלֵינוּ אִם־מָשׁוֹל תִּמְשֹׁל בָּנוּ וַיּוֹסִפוּ עוֹד
9 שְׂנֹא אֹתוֹ עַל־חֲלֹמֹתָיו וְעַל־דְּבָרָיו: וַיַּחֲלֹם עוֹד חֲלוֹם אַחֵר וַיְסַפֵּר אֹתוֹ לְאֶחָיו וַיֹּאמֶר הִנֵּה חָלַמְתִּי חֲלוֹם עוֹד וְהִנֵּה הַשֶּׁמֶשׁ וְהַיָּרֵחַ וְאַחַד עָשָׂר כּוֹכָבִים מִשְׁתַּחֲוִים לִי:
10 וַיְסַפֵּר אֶל־אָבִיו וְאֶל־אֶחָיו וַיִּגְעַר־בּוֹ אָבִיו וַיֹּאמֶר לוֹ מָה הַחֲלוֹם הַזֶּה אֲשֶׁר חָלָמְתָּ הֲבוֹא נָבוֹא אֲנִי וְאִמְּךָ וְאַחֶיךָ
11 לְהִשְׁתַּחֲוֹת לְךָ אָרְצָה: וַיְקַנְאוּ־בוֹ אֶחָיו וְאָבִיו שָׁמַר אֶת־
12 הַדָּבָר:* וַיֵּלְכוּ אֶחָיו לִרְעוֹת אֶת־צֹאן אֲבִיהֶם בִּשְׁכֶם:
13 וַיֹּאמֶר יִשְׂרָאֵל אֶל־יוֹסֵף הֲלוֹא אַחֶיךָ רֹעִים בִּשְׁכֶם לְכָה
14 וְאֶשְׁלָחֲךָ אֲלֵיהֶם וַיֹּאמֶר לוֹ הִנֵּנִי: וַיֹּאמֶר לוֹ לֶךְ־נָא רְאֵה אֶת־שְׁלוֹם אַחֶיךָ וְאֶת־שְׁלוֹם הַצֹּאן וַהֲשִׁבֵנִי דָּבָר וַיִּשְׁלָחֵהוּ
15 מֵעֵמֶק חֶבְרוֹן וַיָּבֹא שְׁכֶמָה: וַיִּמְצָאֵהוּ אִישׁ וְהִנֵּה תֹעֶה

v. 12. נקוד על את

---

Benjamin was but an infant, and the father's affections were centred in Joseph. However, when the latter was sold, Jacob's whole life was bound up with Benjamin (XLIV, 20).

*coat of many colours.* This translation is based on the Septuagint, Targum Jonathan and Kimchi. People have often wondered why a trifle like this gaudy garment should have provoked the murderous hatred of all the brethren. We now know from the painted Tombs of the Bene Hassein in Egypt that, in the Patriarchal age, Semitic chiefs wore coats of many colours as insignia of rulership. Joseph had made himself disliked by his brothers for reporting on them; and Jacob, in giving him a coat of many colours, *marked him for the chieftainship of the tribes at his father's death.* Add to this the lad's vanity in telling his dreams, and the rage of the brethren becomes intelligible. This sign of rulership and royalty was still in use in the household of King David, as is seen from II Sam. XIII, 18, though the chronicler must explain this strange fashion in dress. The fact that in the Joseph story no such explanatory gloss is given is proof of the antiquity of the narrative. When it was first written its implications were perfectly intelligible (M. G. Kyle).

**10.** *to his father.* Joseph is at first the clever child of a large family, too untutored in life to veil his superiority (Moulton).

*rebuked him.* Because his words were deepening the ill-will against him among his brothers.

*thy mother.* Who was dead.

**11.** *envied.* The repetition of the dream was a sign to them that it was more than a dream. They envied him his assured greatness. And now that envy was added to hatred, they were in a mental state to do him violence. One of the hardest things to learn is to recognize without envy the superiority of a younger brother.

*kept the saying in mind.* He noted with satisfaction that his designation of Joseph as the future ruler of the family seemed to have the Divine approval.

**12.** *in Shechem.* Meaning in the region of Shechem, which was a fertile plain. It would appear hazardous for Jacob's sons to venture thither after what is narrated in Chap. XXXIV. But we are expressly told in XXXV, 5, that God inspired fear in the peoples, which caused Jacob to be unmolested.

**14.** *Hebron.* The residence of Jacob, XXXV, 27. The city lies low down on the sloping sides of a narrow valley of its mountainous setting.

GENESIS XXXVII, 16

was wandering in the field. And the man asked him, saying: 'What seekest thou?' 16. And he said: 'I seek my brethren. Tell me, I pray thee, where they are feeding the flock.' 17. And the man said: 'They are departed hence; for I heard them say: Let us go to Dothan.' And Joseph went after his brethren, and found them in Dothan. 18. And they saw him afar off, and before he came near unto them, they conspired against him to slay him. 19. And they said one to another: 'Behold, this dreamer cometh. 20. Come now therefore, and let us slay him, and cast him into one of the pits, and we will say: An evil beast hath devoured him; and we shall see what will become of his dreams.' 21. And Reuben heard it, and delivered him out of their hand; and said: 'Let us not take his life.' 22. And Reuben said unto them: 'Shed no blood; cast him into this pit that is in the wilderness, but lay no hand upon him'— that he might deliver him out of their hand, to restore him to his father.* III. 23. And it came to pass, when Joseph was come unto his brethren, that they stripped Joseph of his coat, the coat of many colours that was on him; 24. and they took him, and cast him into the pit—and the pit was empty, there was no water in it. 25. And they sat down to eat bread; and they lifted up their eyes and looked, and, behold, a caravan of Ishmaelites came from Gilead, with their camels bearing spicery and balm and

בראשית וישב לז

16 בַּשָּׂדֶה וַיִּשְׁאָלֵהוּ הָאִישׁ לֵאמֹר מַה־תְּבַקֵּשׁ׃ וַיֹּאמֶר אֶת־
17 אַחַי אָנֹכִי מְבַקֵּשׁ הַגִּידָה־נָּא לִי אֵיפֹה הֵם רֹעִים׃ וַיֹּאמֶר
הָאִישׁ נָסְעוּ מִזֶּה כִּי שָׁמַעְתִּי אֹמְרִים נֵלְכָה דֹּתָיְנָה וַיֵּלֶךְ
18 יוֹסֵף אַחַר אֶחָיו וַיִּמְצָאֵם בְּדֹתָן׃ וַיִּרְאוּ אֹתוֹ מֵרָחֹק
19 וּבְטֶרֶם יִקְרַב אֲלֵיהֶם וַיִּתְנַכְּלוּ אֹתוֹ לַהֲמִיתוֹ׃ וַיֹּאמְרוּ
כ אִישׁ אֶל־אָחִיו הִנֵּה בַּעַל הַחֲלֹמוֹת הַלָּזֶה בָּא׃ וְעַתָּה ׀
לְכוּ וְנַהַרְגֵהוּ וְנַשְׁלִכֵהוּ בְּאַחַד הַבֹּרוֹת וְאָמַרְנוּ חַיָּה רָעָה
21 אֲכָלָתְהוּ וְנִרְאֶה מַה־יִּהְיוּ חֲלֹמֹתָיו׃ וַיִּשְׁמַע רְאוּבֵן וַיַּצִּלֵהוּ
22 מִיָּדָם וַיֹּאמֶר לֹא נַכֶּנּוּ נָפֶשׁ׃ וַיֹּאמֶר אֲלֵהֶם ׀ רְאוּבֵן אַל־
תִּשְׁפְּכוּ־דָם הַשְׁלִיכוּ אֹתוֹ אֶל־הַבּוֹר הַזֶּה אֲשֶׁר בַּמִּדְבָּר
וְיָד אַל־תִּשְׁלְחוּ־בוֹ לְמַעַן הַצִּיל אֹתוֹ מִיָּדָם לַהֲשִׁיבוֹ שלישי
23 אֶל־אָבִיו׃ וַיְהִי כַּאֲשֶׁר־בָּא יוֹסֵף אֶל־אֶחָיו וַיַּפְשִׁיטוּ אֶת־
24 יוֹסֵף אֶת־כֻּתָּנְתּוֹ אֶת־כְּתֹנֶת הַפַּסִּים אֲשֶׁר עָלָיו׃ וַיִּקָּחֻהוּ
כה וַיַּשְׁלִכוּ אֹתוֹ הַבֹּרָה וְהַבּוֹר רֵק אֵין בּוֹ מָיִם׃ וַיֵּשְׁבוּ
לֶאֱכָל־לֶחֶם וַיִּשְׂאוּ עֵינֵיהֶם וַיִּרְאוּ וְהִנֵּה אֹרְחַת יִשְׁמְעֵאלִים
בָּאָה מִגִּלְעָד וּגְמַלֵּיהֶם נֹשְׂאִים נְכֹאת וּצְרִי וָלֹט הוֹלְכִים

**17.** *Dothan.* The modern name is Tel-Dothan. It has a rich pasturage.

**19.** *dreamer.* lit. 'master of dreams'; this is only the Heb. idiom for 'dreamer'.
The brothers speak of him with a bitter derision which bodes ill for him.

**20.** *pits.* Or, 'cisterns,' where water was stored; these are still in common use in the East. The opening is narrow, so that any one imprisoned in them could not get out unassisted.
*and we shall see.* The Midrash regards these words as the comment of God upon the brother's declaration, 'let us slay him.' The Divine reply is to the effect: We shall see whose counsel will stand, Mine or theirs. The Midrash furthermore states that it was Simeon who first made the fratricidal proposal. This explains Joseph's procedure later in XLII, 24.

**22.** *shed no blood.* Reuben's first appeal of 'No murder' fell on deaf ears (see XLII, 22); he then hopes to outwit them by a stratagem. He appeals to them that at least they need not shed any blood, hoping later to rescue Joseph and bring him back to Jacob, against whom he had previously so grievously sinned (Nachmanides, Abarbanel).

**23.** *stripped.* Tore off with violence. What Joseph's words were in connection with this unnatural conduct of his brethren, we only indirectly know from XLII, 21; just as we are left to gather Jacob's feelings at the death of Rachel from the pathetic references in XLVIII, 7. The reserve of the Scripture narrative in this chapter, as in XXII, represents the acme of literary art (Steinthal).

**24.** *no water in it.* But it did contain serpents and scorpions (Rashi).

**25.** *to eat bread.* While the piercing cries of their doomed brother were still ringing in their ears. Nothing can more forcibly paint the callousness to all human feeling which comes from slavery to hate.
*caravan.* Such a caravan would in the clear air of Palestine be seen many miles away. It might take two or three hours before it came up to the brothers. Dothan lay on the trade-route from Gilead, the country east of the Jordan, across the Valley of Jezreel, along the Philistine coast to Egypt.
*balm.* For which Gilead was proverbially famous.

## GENESIS XXXVII, 26

ladanum, going to carry it down to Egypt. 26. And Judah said unto his brethren: 'What profit is it if we slay our brother and conceal his blood? 27. Come, and let us sell him to the Ishmaelites, and let not our hand be upon him; for he is our brother, our flesh.' And his brethren hearkened unto him. 28. And there passed by Midianites, merchantmen; and they drew and lifted up Joseph out of the pit, and sold Joseph to the Ishmaelites for twenty shekels of silver. And they brought Joseph into Egypt. 29. And Reuben returned unto the pit; and, behold, Joseph was not in the pit; and he rent his clothes. 30. And he returned unto his brethren, and said: 'The child is not; and as for me, whither shall I go?' 31. And they took Joseph's coat, and killed a he-goat, and dipped the coat in the blood; 32. and they sent the coat of many colours, and they brought it to their father; and said: 'This have we found. Know now whether it is thy son's coat or not.' 33. And he knew it, and said: 'It is my son's coat; an evil beast hath devoured him; Joseph is without doubt torn in pieces.' 34. And Jacob rent his garments, and put sackcloth upon his loins, and mourned for his son many days. 35. And all his sons and all his daughters rose up to comfort him; but he refused to be comforted; and he said: 'Nay, but I will go down to the grave to my son mourning.' And his father wept for him. 36. And the

**27.** *hearkened unto him*. The horror of their contemplated murder by starvation dawns upon them; they agree to a less violent scheme. Reuben keeps his counsel.

**28.** *Midianites*. In the meantime, while the brethren were at the meal, some Midianite merchants, casually passing by and hearing human cries from the pit near the roadside, carry off Joseph and sell him to the caravan going to Egypt. The brothers did not thus actually sell Joseph. He was 'stolen away', as he himself says in XL, 15 (Rashbam, Luzzatto).

**29.** Reuben, who, it seems, did not participate in the meal, v. 25, had intended to remove Joseph from the pit and bring him back to his father. He finds the pit empty and no trace of Joseph. Some wild beast, he thinks, has carried him off.

**30.** *whither shall I go?* As the first-born, the father would hold him morally responsible. 'Whither shall I flee from my father's grief?' (Rashi).

**31.** *they took*. The brothers, however, were not displeased to be rid of Joseph.

**32.** *they sent*. Through others; *i.e.* they arranged that people should bring the coat to Jacob (Rashbam).
*they said*. Those who brought the coat.

**33.** The lit. translation of the Heb. is 'My son's coat! a wild beast hath eaten him! torn, torn is Joseph!'—a reproduction of the father's anguish that is as natural as nature.

**34.** *rent his garments*. The traditional mourning rite on the loss of a near relative, *Keriah*.
*many days*. A long time; two and twenty years.

**35.** *daughters*. Includes granddaughters and daughters-in-law, as 'sons' may include grandsons.
*grave*. Heb. '*Sheol*', the name of the abode of the dead. Jacob's words mean either that he will mourn his son all his life, or that even in the grave he will continue to mourn him.

**36.** *into Egypt*. Through the Ishmaelite caravan.
*Potiphar*. The name means, 'The gift of Ra,' the sun-god.
*officer*. The Heb. word came to have the general significance of 'court official'.

GENESIS XXXVIII, 1

¹Midianites sold him into Egypt unto Potiphar, an officer of Pharaoh's, the captain of the guard.*¹ᵛ

## 38

CHAPTER XXXVIII

1. And it came to pass at that time, that Judah went down from his brethren, and turned in to a certain Adullamite, whose name was Hirah. 2. And Judah saw there a daughter of a certain Canaanite whose name was Shua; and he took her, and went in unto her. 3. And she conceived, and bore a son; and he called his name Er. 4. And she conceived again, and bore a son; and she called his name Onan. 5. And she yet again bore a son, and called his name Shelah; and he was at Chezib, when she bore him. 6. And Judah took a wife for Er his first-born, and her name was Tamar. 7. And Er, Judah's first-born, was wicked in the sight of the LORD; and the LORD slew him. 8. And Judah said unto Onan: 'Go in unto thy brother's wife, and perform the duty of a husband's brother unto her, and raise up seed to thy brother.' 9. And Onan knew that the seed would not be his; and it came to pass, when he went in unto his brother's wife, that he spilled it on the ground, lest he should give seed to his brother. 10. And the thing which he did was evil in the sight of the LORD; and He slew him also. 11. Then said Judah to Tamar his daughter-in-law: 'Remain a widow in thy father's house, till Shelah my son be grown up'; for he said: 'Lest he also die, like his brethren.' And Tamar

---
¹ Heb. *Medanites*.

בראשית וישב לז לח

36 וְהַמְּדָנִ֗ים מָכְר֤וּ אֹתוֹ֙ אֶל־מִצְרָ֔יִם לְפֽוֹטִיפַר֙ סְרִ֣יס פַּרְעֹ֔ה שַׂ֖ר הַטַּבָּחִֽים׃ פ

רביעי

CAP. XXXVIII. לח    לח

א וַֽיְהִי֙ בָּעֵ֣ת הַהִ֔וא וַיֵּ֥רֶד יְהוּדָ֖ה מֵאֵ֣ת אֶחָ֑יו וַיֵּ֛ט עַד־אִ֥ישׁ
2 עֲדֻלָּמִ֖י וּשְׁמ֥וֹ חִירָֽה׃ וַיַּרְא־שָׁ֧ם יְהוּדָ֛ה בַּת־אִ֥ישׁ כְּנַעֲנִ֖י
3 וּשְׁמ֣וֹ שׁ֑וּעַ וַיִּקָּחֶ֖הָ וַיָּבֹ֥א אֵלֶֽיהָ׃ וַתַּ֖הַר וַתֵּ֣לֶד בֵּ֑ן וַיִּקְרָ֥א
4 אֶת־שְׁמ֖וֹ עֵֽר׃ וַתַּ֥הַר ע֖וֹד וַתֵּ֣לֶד בֵּ֑ן וַתִּקְרָ֥א אֶת־שְׁמ֖וֹ אוֹנָֽן׃
ה וַתֹּ֤סֶף עוֹד֙ וַתֵּ֣לֶד בֵּ֔ן וַתִּקְרָ֥א אֶת־שְׁמ֖וֹ שֵׁלָ֑ה וְהָיָ֥ה בִכְזִ֖יב
6 בְּלִדְתָּ֥הּ אֹתֽוֹ׃ וַיִּקַּ֧ח יְהוּדָ֛ה אִשָּׁ֖ה לְעֵ֣ר בְּכוֹר֑וֹ וּשְׁמָ֖הּ
7 תָּמָֽר׃ וַיְהִ֗י עֵ֚ר בְּכ֣וֹר יְהוּדָ֔ה רַ֖ע בְּעֵינֵ֣י יְהוָ֑ה וַיְמִתֵ֖הוּ
8 יְהוָֽה׃ וַיֹּ֤אמֶר יְהוּדָה֙ לְאוֹנָ֔ן בֹּ֛א אֶל־אֵ֥שֶׁת אָחִ֖יךָ וְיַבֵּ֣ם
9 אֹתָ֑הּ וְהָקֵ֥ם זֶ֖רַע לְאָחִֽיךָ׃ וַיֵּ֣דַע אוֹנָ֔ן כִּ֛י לֹּ֥א ל֖וֹ יִהְיֶ֣ה
הַזָּ֑רַע וְהָיָ֞ה אִם־בָּ֨א אֶל־אֵ֤שֶׁת אָחִיו֙ וְשִׁחֵ֣ת אַ֔רְצָה לְבִלְתִּ֥י
י נְתָן־זֶ֖רַע לְאָחִֽיו׃ וַיֵּ֛רַע בְּעֵינֵ֥י יְהוָ֖ה אֲשֶׁ֣ר עָשָׂ֑ה וַיָּ֖מֶת גַּם־
11 אֹתֽוֹ׃ וַיֹּ֣אמֶר יְהוּדָה֩ לְתָמָ֨ר כַּלָּת֜וֹ שְׁבִ֧י אַלְמָנָ֣ה בֵית־
אָבִ֗יךְ עַד־יִגְדַּל֙ שֵׁלָ֣ה בְנִ֔י כִּ֣י אָמַ֔ר פֶּן־יָמ֥וּת גַּם־ה֖וּא

---

*Pharaoh.* The *title* of the Egyptian Sovereign.
*captain of the guard.* Or, 'chief of the executioners'.

### CHAPTER XXXVIII. JUDAH AND TAMAR

In the history of Jacob's family the two central persons are Judah and Joseph. The former became the leader of his brethren and the ancestor of David; the latter, from his noble character and personal influence on the future destinies of Jacob's children, is regarded as next in importance. Before recounting Joseph's fortunes in Egypt, Scripture records the following incident in the life of Judah, so as to draw a contrast between his conduct and that of Joseph in the hour of temptation.

**1.** *at that time.* An indefinite phrase used sometimes of events which occurred several years earlier or later. In this instance, the marriage took place prior to the sale of Joseph (Ibn Ezra).

*went down.* From the rocky hills around Hebron to Adullam, in the Lowland, 17 miles S.W. of Jerusalem.

**2.** *Canaanite.* Following Esau's evil example (cf. xxvi, 34 f), and reaping an abundant harvest of sin and shame. Many commentators, however, take the word in the sense used in Zech. xiv, 21, and translate 'merchant' (Targum, Rashi, Mendelssohn).

**6.** *Judah took.* Such was the custom, for the parent to select the son's bride.

*Tamar.* lit. 'a date palm'. The name occurs later in the family of David.

**7.** *slew him.* lit. 'caused him to die'.

**8.** *perform the duty of a husband's brother.* This refers to the custom of the levirate marriage, by which a surviving brother-in-law (in Latin, *levir*) marries the childless widow, see Deut. xxv, 5 and cf. Ruth iv, 5 f. The eldest son of such a marriage inherited the name and property of the deceased.

**9.** *would not be his.* i.e. would not bear his name.

**11.** *daughter-in-law.* Tamar. The childless widow went back to her father's house. Judah believed that the deaths of Er and Onan were due to Tamar. He, therefore, fears to have Shelah perform the levirate duty.

GENESIS XXXVIII, 12 — בראשית וישב לח

12 בְּאֶחָיו וַתֵּלֶךְ תָּמָר וַתֵּשֶׁב בֵּית אָבִיהָ׃ וַיִּרְבּוּ הַיָּמִים וַתָּמָת בַּת־שׁוּעַ אֵשֶׁת־יְהוּדָה וַיִּנָּחֶם יְהוּדָה וַיַּעַל עַל־גֹּזְזֵי צֹאנוֹ
13 הוּא וְחִירָה רֵעֵהוּ הָעֲדֻלָּמִי תִּמְנָתָה׃ וַיֻּגַּד לְתָמָר לֵאמֹר
14 הִנֵּה חָמִיךְ עֹלֶה תִמְנָתָה לָגֹז צֹאנוֹ׃ וַתָּסַר בִּגְדֵי אַלְמְנוּתָהּ מֵעָלֶיהָ וַתְּכַס בַּצָּעִיף וַתִּתְעַלָּף וַתֵּשֶׁב בְּפֶתַח עֵינַיִם אֲשֶׁר עַל־דֶּרֶךְ תִּמְנָתָה כִּי רָאֲתָה כִּי־גָדַל שֵׁלָה וְהִוא לֹא־נִתְּנָה
15 לוֹ לְאִשָּׁה׃ וַיִּרְאֶהָ יְהוּדָה וַיַּחְשְׁבֶהָ לְזוֹנָה כִּי כִסְּתָה
16 פָּנֶיהָ׃ וַיֵּט אֵלֶיהָ אֶל־הַדֶּרֶךְ וַיֹּאמֶר הָבָה־נָּא אָבוֹא אֵלַיִךְ כִּי לֹא יָדַע כִּי כַלָּתוֹ הִוא וַתֹּאמֶר מַה־תִּתֶּן־לִי כִּי תָבוֹא
17 אֵלָי׃ וַיֹּאמֶר אָנֹכִי אֲשַׁלַּח גְּדִי־עִזִּים מִן־הַצֹּאן וַתֹּאמֶר
18 אִם־תִּתֵּן עֵרָבוֹן עַד שָׁלְחֶךָ׃ וַיֹּאמֶר מָה הָעֵרָבוֹן אֲשֶׁר אֶתֶּן־לָךְ וַתֹּאמֶר חֹתָמְךָ וּפְתִילֶךָ וּמַטְּךָ אֲשֶׁר בְּיָדֶךָ וַיִּתֶּן־
19 לָהּ וַיָּבֹא אֵלֶיהָ וַתַּהַר לוֹ׃ וַתָּקָם וַתֵּלֶךְ וַתָּסַר צְעִיפָהּ
כ מֵעָלֶיהָ וַתִּלְבַּשׁ בִּגְדֵי אַלְמְנוּתָהּ׃ וַיִּשְׁלַח יְהוּדָה אֶת־גְּדִי הָעִזִּים בְּיַד רֵעֵהוּ הָעֲדֻלָּמִי לָקַחַת הָעֵרָבוֹן מִיַּד הָאִשָּׁה
21 וְלֹא מְצָאָהּ׃ וַיִּשְׁאַל אֶת־אַנְשֵׁי מְקֹמָהּ לֵאמֹר אַיֵּה הַקְּדֵשָׁה הִוא בָעֵינַיִם עַל־הַדָּרֶךְ וַיֹּאמְרוּ לֹא־הָיְתָה בָזֶה קְדֵשָׁה׃
22 וַיָּשָׁב אֶל־יְהוּדָה וַיֹּאמֶר לֹא מְצָאתִיהָ וְגַם אַנְשֵׁי הַמָּקוֹם
23 אָמְרוּ לֹא־הָיְתָה בָזֶה קְדֵשָׁה׃ וַיֹּאמֶר יְהוּדָה תִּקַּח־לָהּ פֶּן נִהְיֶה לָבוּז הִנֵּה שָׁלַחְתִּי הַגְּדִי הַזֶּה וְאַתָּה לֹא מְצָאתָהּ׃

---

went and dwelt in her father's house. 12. And in process of time Shua's daughter, the wife of Judah, died; and Judah was comforted, and went up unto his sheep-shearers to Timnah, he and his friend Hirah the Adullamite. 13. And it was told Tamar, saying: 'Behold, thy father-in-law goeth up to Timnah to shear his sheep.' 14. And she put off from her the garments of her widowhood, and covered herself with her veil, and wrapped herself, and sat in the entrance of Enaim, which is by the way to Timnah; for she saw that Shelah was grown up, and she was not given unto him to wife. 15. When Judah saw her, he thought her to be a harlot; for she had covered her face. 16. And he turned unto her by the way, and said: 'Come I pray thee, let me come in unto thee;' for he knew not that she was his daughter-in-law. And she said: 'What wilt thou give me, that thou mayest come in unto me?' 17. And he said: 'I will send thee a kid of the goats from the flock.' And she said: 'Wilt thou give me a pledge, till thou send it?' 18. And he said: 'What pledge shall I give thee?' And she said: 'Thy signet and thy cord, and thy staff that is in thy hand.' And he gave them to her, and came in unto her, and she conceived by him. 19. And she arose, and went away, and put off her veil from her, and put on the garments of her widowhood. 20. And Judah sent the kid of the goats by the hand of his friend the Adullamite, to receive the pledge from the woman's hand; but he found her not. 21. Then he asked the men of her place, saying: 'Where is the harlot, that was at Enaim by the wayside?' And they said: 'There hath been no harlot here.' 22. And he returned to Judah, and said: 'I have not found her; and also the men of the place said: There hath been no harlot here.' 23. And Judah said: 'Let her take it, lest we be put to shame; behold, I sent this kid, and thou hast not found her.' 24. And it came to pass about three months after, that it was told Judah, saying: 'Tamar thy daughter-in-law hath played the harlot;

---

**12.** *Shua's daughter.* Her own name is not known. Some time after the death, Judah found it becoming to attend the Canaanite festivities in connection with the sheep-shearing.

*Timnah.* A few miles S. of Hebron.

**14.** *garments of her widowhood.* To prevent detection by Judah. She resorts to a disguise and stratagem that must have appeared quite honourable in her Canaanite eyes. She assumes the veil of a votary of Astarte. Her intention was to force Judah himself to perform the levirate duty. In pre-Mosaic times, it seems, every member of the late husband's family was under that obligation.

**15.** *harlot.* In v. 21 she is described as a *kedeshah*; that is, a woman dedicated to impure heathen worship. This repulsive custom was common in ancient Phœnicia and Babylonia and survives in many forms of Hindu worship. No *kedeshah* was permitted in Israel; see Deut. XXIII, 18.

**16.** *and he turned unto her.* He left his path to go to her (Rashi).

**18.** Tamar thus secured a pledge which rendered the identification of the owner absolutely certain. Signet, cord and staff were the insignia of a sheik in Canaan, as of a man of rank among the Babylonians and Egyptians.

*cord.* Used to suspend the seal.

## GENESIS XXXVIII, 25

and moreover, behold, she is with child by harlotry.' And Judah said: 'Bring her forth, and let her be burnt.' 25. When she was brought forth, she sent to her father-in-law, saying: 'By the man, whose these are, am I with child'; and she said: 'Discern, I pray thee, whose are these, the signet, and the cords, and the staff.' 26. And Judah acknowledged them, and said: 'She is more righteous than I; forasmuch as I gave her not to Shelah my son.' And he knew her again no more. 27. And it came to pass in the time of her travail, that, behold, twins were in her womb. 28. And it came to pass, when she travailed, that one put out a hand; and the midwife took and bound upon his hand a scarlet thread, saying: 'This came out first.' 29. And it came to pass, as he drew back his hand, that, behold, his brother came out; and she said: 'Wherefore hast thou made a breach for thyself?' Therefore his name was called ¹Perez. 30. And afterward came out his brother, that had the scarlet thread upon his hand; and his name was called Zerah.*ᵛ⋅

## 39 CHAPTER XXXIX

1. And Joseph was brought down to Egypt; and Potiphar, an officer of Pharaoh's, the captain of the guard, an Egyptian, bought him of the hand of the Ishmaelites, that had brought him down thither. 2. And the LORD was with Joseph, and he was a prosperous man; and he was in the house of his master the Egyptian. 3. And his master saw that the LORD was with him, and that the LORD made all that he did to prosper

---
¹ That is, *A breach.*

---

**23.** *let her take it.* Let her keep the pledges, lest, if they search further, he be exposed to shame. Even before מתן תורה, the revelation of a higher ideal of personal conduct at Sinai and the promulgation of the Holiness code (Lev. XIX), some moral turpitude attached to such conduct.
*sent this kid.* He feels he could do no more.

**24.** *let her be burnt.* Judah, as head of the family, has power of life and death; cf. xxxi, 32. Tamar was the betrothed of Shelah, and betrothal was considered to be as binding as marriage.

**25.** *by the man.* Tamar acts nobly in withholding the name of the betrayer. Judah also shows his better side by confessing his sin. The Rabbis dwell on this act of contrition.

**26.** Scripture does not hide the sins of its heroes and heroines.

**28.** *a scarlet thread.* To secure his right as the first-born.

CHAPTER XXXIX. POTIPHAR'S WIFE

The story of Joseph is resumed in this chapter. Amid the new and trying circumstances of his new existence, Joseph's winsome personality and innate nobility of character are revealed. He gains the confidence of his master and emerges unscathed from sinful temptation.

**1.** *was brought down.* Better, 'had been brought down.'
*an Egyptian.* The story of Joseph took place during the reign of the Hyksos kings, the Bedouin conquerors of Egypt. Exceptionally, 'an Egyptian' was entrusted with a high Government post.

**2.** *prosperous man.* All that he did prospered.

## GENESIS XXXIX, 4

in his hand. 4. And Joseph found favour in his sight, and he ministered unto him. And he appointed him overseer over his house, and all that he had he put into his hand. 5. And it came to pass from the time that he appointed him overseer in his house, and over all that he had, that the LORD blessed the Egyptian's house for Joseph's sake; and the blessing of the LORD was upon all that he had, in the house and in the field. 6. And he left all that he had in Joseph's hand; and, having him, he knew not aught save the bread which he did eat. And Joseph was of beautiful form, and fair to look upon.\*vi ¶ 7. And it came to pass after these things, that his master's wife cast her eyes upon Joseph; and she said: 'Lie with me.' 8. But he refused, and said unto his master's wife: 'Behold, my master, having me, knoweth not what is in the house, and he hath put all that he hath into my hand; 9. he is not greater in this house than I; neither hath he kept back any thing from me but thee, because thou art his wife. How then can I do this great wickedness, and sin against God?' 10. And it came to pass, as she spoke to Joseph day by day, that he hearkened not unto her, to lie by her, or to be with her. 11. And it came to pass on a certain day, when he went into the house to do his work, and there was none of the men of the house there within, 12. that she caught him by his garment, saying: 'Lie with me.' And he left his garment in her hand, and fled, and got him out. 13. And it came to pass, when she saw that he had left his garment in her hand, and was fled forth, 14. that she called unto the men of her house, and spoke unto them, saying: 'See, he hath brought

---

**4.** *ministered unto him.* As his personal attendant. Then he is advanced to the position of overseer, or controller of the household and estate generally.

**6.** *having him, he knew not aught.* i.e. having him, he troubled himself about nothing, and left all his affairs to the care of Joseph, except his food. This could not be left to a non-Egyptian; see XLIII, 32.

*of beautiful form.* Like his mother Rachel (Ibn Ezra).

**7.** *after these things.* i.e. after the twofold advancement of Joseph, when he was no longer a slave, but had become overseer and trusted confidant, his master's wife makes advances to him. The immorality of the ancient Egyptians, both men and women, was notorious.

**9.** *and sin against God.* Joseph would not betray his master's confidence, neither would he sin against God. As a God-fearing man, he knows that the thing is wrong in the sight of God; and that is enough for him. Potiphar might never know of the sin, but God would know.

**12.** *and fled.* Some sins can only be avoided by flight. Ecclesiasticus XXI, 2. 'Flee from sin, as from the face of a serpent; for if thou come too near it will bite thee: the teeth thereof are as the teeth of a lion, slaying the souls of men.' The Rabbis say, 'At the moment of temptation, his father's image appeared to him and gave him strength to resist.'

**14.** *she called.* Filled with vindictive malice because of thwarted desire, she calls aloud to the men of the house, who would be envious of their master's favour towards Joseph.

*a Hebrew.* See v. 17 and XLIII, 32. Being of ancient Egyptian stock (see v. 1), she appeals to Egyptian racial prejudice. The admission of this Asiatic alien into her home is an insult to her and to every race-pure Egyptian!

*to mock us.* To attempt the greatest outrage against us.

## GENESIS XXXIX, 15

in a Hebrew unto us to mock us; he came in unto me to lie with me, and I cried with a loud voice. 15. And it came to pass, when he heard that I lifted up my voice and cried, that he left his garment by me, and fled, and got him out.' 16. And she laid up his garment by her, until his master came home. 17. And she spoke unto him according to these words, saying: 'The Hebrew servant, whom thou hast brought unto us, came in unto me to mock me. 18. And it came to pass, as I lifted up my voice and cried, that he left his garment by me, and fled out.' 19. And it came to pass, when his master heard the words of his wife, which she spoke unto him, saying: 'After this manner did thy servant to me'; that his wrath was kindled. 20. And Joseph's master took him, and put him into the prison, the place where the king's prisoners were bound; and he was there in the prison. 21. But the LORD was with Joseph, and showed kindness unto him, and gave him favour in the sight of the keeper of the prison. 22. And the keeper of the prison committed to Joseph's hand all the prisoners that were in the prison; and whatsoever they did there, he was the doer of it. 23. The keeper of the prison looked not to any thing that was under his hand, because the LORD was with him; and that which he did, the LORD made it to prosper.*ᵛⁱⁱ

## 40 CHAPTER XL

1. And it came to pass after these things, that the butler of the king of Egypt and his baker offended their lord the king of Egypt. 2. And Pharaoh was wroth against his two officers, against the chief of the butlers, and against the chief of the bakers.

---

**16.** *laid up.* i.e. put by.

*his garment.* As evidence to convict Joseph, and convince Potiphar of her own innocence.

**20.** *the prison.* The Heb. word occurs only here, and seems to be Egyptian. The Midrash explains that Potiphar had some doubt as to the truth of the accusation against Joseph; otherwise he would have put him to death, instead of putting him in prison. To this episode in Joseph's life, there is an interesting parallel in the Egyptian 'Tale of the Two Brothers'. In the Tale, the wicked wife is slain by her husband.

**21.** *but the LORD was with Joseph.* In the prison, giving him comfort and strength to endure the suffering and the shame. He wins the confidence of the keeper, as he did of his master. The light of a superior mind and soul cannot be hidden even in a prison.

**22.** *committed to Joseph's hand.* i.e. he is made superintendent of the other prisoners.

*he was the doer of it.* All was done at the suggestion of Joseph.

**23.** *looked not to any thing.* Just as Potiphar had done. Joseph enjoyed full confidence.

CHAPTER XL. JOSEPH AND THE PRISONERS

Joseph interprets the dreams of Pharaoh's two officers. The scene faithfully reflects Egyptian conditions in the age of Joseph.

**1.** *after these things.* Recounted in the preceding chapter.

**2.** *the butlers . . . the bakers.* The Egyptian court had a 'scribe of the sideboard' and a 'superintendent of the bakehouse' (Erman).

# GENESIS XL, 3

3. And he put them in ward in the house of the captain of the guard, into the prison, the place where Joseph was bound. 4. And the captain of the guard charged Joseph to be with them, and he ministered unto them; and they continued a season in ward. 5. And they dreamed a dream both of them, each man his dream, in one night, each man according to the interpretation of his dream, the butler and the baker of the king of Egypt, who were bound in the prison. 6. And Joseph came in unto them in the morning, and saw them, and, behold, they were sad. 7. And he asked Pharaoh's officers that were with him in the ward of his master's house, saying: 'Wherefore look ye so sad to-day?' 8. And they said unto him: 'We have dreamed a dream, and there is none that can interpret it.' And Joseph said unto them: 'Do not interpretations belong to God? tell it me, I pray you.' 9. And the chief butler told his dream to Joseph, and said to him: 'In my dream, behold, a vine was before me; 10. and in the vine were three branches; and as it was budding, its blossoms shot forth, and the clusters thereof brought forth ripe grapes; 11. and Pharaoh's cup was in my hand; and I took the grapes, and pressed them into Pharaoh's cup, and I gave the cup into Pharaoh's hand.' 12. And Joseph said unto him: 'This is the interpretation of it: the three branches are three days; 13. within yet three days shall Pharaoh lift up thy head, and restore thee unto thine office; and thou shalt give Pharaoh's cup

בראשית וישב מ

3 סָרִיסָיו עַל שַׂר הַמַּשְׁקִים וְעַל שַׂר הָאוֹפִים: וַיִּתֵּן אֹתָם בְּמִשְׁמַר בֵּית שַׂר הַטַּבָּחִים אֶל־בֵּית הַסֹּהַר מְקוֹם אֲשֶׁר
4 יוֹסֵף אָסוּר שָׁם: וַיִּפְקֹד שַׂר הַטַּבָּחִים אֶת־יוֹסֵף אִתָּם
ה וַיְשָׁרֶת אֹתָם וַיִּהְיוּ יָמִים בְּמִשְׁמָר: וַיַּחַלְמוּ חֲלוֹם שְׁנֵיהֶם אִישׁ חֲלֹמוֹ בְּלַיְלָה אֶחָד אִישׁ כְּפִתְרוֹן חֲלֹמוֹ הַמַּשְׁקֶה וְהָאֹפֶה אֲשֶׁר לְמֶלֶךְ מִצְרַיִם אֲשֶׁר אֲסוּרִים בְּבֵית הַסֹּהַר:
6 וַיָּבֹא אֲלֵיהֶם יוֹסֵף בַּבֹּקֶר וַיַּרְא אֹתָם וְהִנָּם זֹעֲפִים:
7 וַיִּשְׁאַל אֶת־סְרִיסֵי פַרְעֹה אֲשֶׁר אִתּוֹ בְמִשְׁמַר בֵּית אֲדֹנָיו
8 לֵאמֹר מַדּוּעַ פְּנֵיכֶם רָעִים הַיּוֹם: וַיֹּאמְרוּ אֵלָיו חֲלוֹם חָלַמְנוּ וּפֹתֵר אֵין אֹתוֹ וַיֹּאמֶר אֲלֵהֶם יוֹסֵף הֲלוֹא לֵאלֹהִים
9 פִּתְרֹנִים סַפְּרוּ־נָא לִי: וַיְסַפֵּר שַׂר־הַמַּשְׁקִים אֶת־חֲלֹמוֹ לְיוֹסֵף וַיֹּאמֶר לוֹ בַּחֲלוֹמִי וְהִנֵּה־גֶפֶן לְפָנָי: וּבַגֶּפֶן שְׁלֹשָׁה
י שָׂרִיגִם וְהִוא כְפֹרַחַת עָלְתָה נִצָּהּ הִבְשִׁילוּ אַשְׁכְּלֹתֶיהָ
11 עֲנָבִים: וְכוֹס פַּרְעֹה בְּיָדִי וָאֶקַּח אֶת־הָעֲנָבִים וָאֶשְׂחַט אֹתָם אֶל־כּוֹס פַּרְעֹה וָאֶתֵּן אֶת־הַכּוֹס עַל־כַּף פַּרְעֹה:
12 וַיֹּאמֶר לוֹ יוֹסֵף זֶה פִּתְרֹנוֹ שְׁלֹשֶׁת הַשָּׂרִגִים שְׁלֹשֶׁת יָמִים
13 הֵם: בְּעוֹד שְׁלֹשֶׁת יָמִים יִשָּׂא פַרְעֹה אֶת־רֹאשֶׁךָ וַהֲשִׁיבְךָ

---

These officers had to taste the food for the king before the royal meal began. The word for butler may also be rendered, 'cup-bearer.' It is conjectured that these officials were accused of plotting to poison Pharaoh.

**3.** *in ward.* In confinement, pending their trial.

*captain of the guard.* i.e. Potiphar. In the prison, the keeper was in charge and was responsible to Potiphar.

**4.** Potiphar appoints Joseph to be with the imprisoned officers. He is not appointed over them, but he is deputed to be their attendant— a mark of courtesy on the part of Potiphar to his unfortunate colleagues.

*a season.* lit. 'days'; implying a considerable time.

**5.** *according to the interpretation.* As the future verified.

**8.** *none that can interpret it.* No professional interpreter was available, and they had in vain consulted others in the prison as to the possible meaning of their dreams. The interpreter was a professional man of importance in Egypt and Babylon, belonging to the class of soothsayers, magicians and 'wise men'.

*do not interpretations belong to God?* i.e. it may be that God who sent the dreams will give me the interpretation of them. 'Man cannot by his own wisdom interpret dreams. God alone can reveal their true meaning. Pray tell me the dream, perhaps He will favour me with wisdom to explain its import' (Chizkuni).

**11.** *pressed them.* Grape juice mixed with water is mentioned as a refreshing drink on the Egyptian inscriptions.

**13.** *lift up thy head.* In honour, by restoring thee to thy post.

**14.** *have me in thy remembrance.* All he asks is that the chief butler should not forget him, but try to secure his freedom.

# GENESIS XL, 14 — בראשית וישב מ

עַל־כַּנֶּךָ וְנָתַתָּ כוֹס־פַּרְעֹה בְּיָדוֹ כַּמִּשְׁפָּט הָרִאשׁוֹן אֲשֶׁר
הָיִיתָ מַשְׁקֵהוּ: כִּי אִם־זְכַרְתַּנִי אִתְּךָ כַּאֲשֶׁר יִיטַב לָךְ 14
וְעָשִׂיתָ־נָּא עִמָּדִי חָסֶד וְהִזְכַּרְתַּנִי אֶל־פַּרְעֹה וְהוֹצֵאתַנִי
מִן־הַבַּיִת הַזֶּה: כִּי־גֻנֹּב גֻּנַּבְתִּי מֵאֶרֶץ הָעִבְרִים וְגַם־פֹּה טו
לֹא־עָשִׂיתִי מְאוּמָה כִּי־שָׂמוּ אֹתִי בַּבּוֹר: וַיַּרְא שַׂר־הָאֹפִים 16
כִּי טוֹב פָּתָר וַיֹּאמֶר אֶל־יוֹסֵף אַף־אֲנִי בַּחֲלוֹמִי וְהִנֵּה
שְׁלֹשָׁה סַלֵּי חֹרִי עַל־רֹאשִׁי: וּבַסַּל הָעֶלְיוֹן מִכֹּל מַאֲכַל 17
פַּרְעֹה מַעֲשֵׂה אֹפֶה וְהָעוֹף אֹכֵל אֹתָם מִן־הַסַּל מֵעַל
רֹאשִׁי: וַיַּעַן יוֹסֵף וַיֹּאמֶר זֶה פִּתְרֹנוֹ שְׁלֹשֶׁת הַסַּלִּים 18
שְׁלֹשֶׁת יָמִים הֵם: בְּעוֹד ׀ שְׁלֹשֶׁת יָמִים יִשָּׂא פַרְעֹה אֶת־ 19
רֹאשְׁךָ מֵעָלֶיךָ וְתָלָה אוֹתְךָ עַל־עֵץ וְאָכַל הָעוֹף אֶת־
בְּשָׂרְךָ מֵעָלֶיךָ: וַיְהִי ׀ בַּיּוֹם הַשְּׁלִישִׁי יוֹם הֻלֶּדֶת אֶת־ מפטיר כ
פַּרְעֹה וַיַּעַשׂ מִשְׁתֶּה לְכָל־עֲבָדָיו וַיִּשָּׂא אֶת־רֹאשׁ ׀ שַׂר
הַמַּשְׁקִים וְאֶת־רֹאשׁ שַׂר הָאֹפִים בְּתוֹךְ עֲבָדָיו: וַיָּשֶׁב 21
אֶת־שַׂר הַמַּשְׁקִים עַל־מַשְׁקֵהוּ וַיִּתֵּן הַכּוֹס עַל־כַּף פַּרְעֹה:
וְאֵת שַׂר הָאֹפִים תָּלָה כַּאֲשֶׁר פָּתַר לָהֶם יוֹסֵף: וְלֹא־זָכַר 22 23
שַׂר־הַמַּשְׁקִים אֶת־יוֹסֵף וַיִּשְׁכָּחֵהוּ:

v. 15. מלרע

---

into his hand, after the former manner when thou wast his butler. 14. But have me in thy remembrance when it shall be well with thee, and show kindness, I pray thee, unto me, and make mention of me unto Pharaoh, and bring me out of this house. 15. For indeed I was stolen away out of the land of the Hebrews; and here also have I done nothing that they should put me into the dungeon.' 16. When the chief baker saw that the interpretation was good, he said unto Joseph: 'I also saw in my dream, and, behold, three baskets of white bread were on my head; 17. and in the uppermost basket there was of all manner of baked food for Pharaoh; and the birds did eat them out of the basket upon my head.' 18. And Joseph answered and said: 'This is the interpretation thereof: the three baskets are three days; 19. within yet three days shall Pharaoh lift up thy head from off thee, and shall hang thee on a tree; and the birds shall eat thy flesh from off thee.'* ᵐ· 20. And it came to pass the third day, which was Pharaoh's birthday, that he madê a feast unto all his servants; and he lifted up the head of the chief butler and the head of the chief baker among his servants. 21. And he restored the chief butler back unto his butlership; and he gave the cup into Pharaoh's hand. 22. But he hanged the chief baker, as Joseph had interpreted to them. 23. Yet did not the chief butler remember Joseph, but forgot him.

---

**15.** *stolen away.* See XXXVII, 28, implying that he was not a slave by birth.

*land of the Hebrews.* The land where Jacob was dwelling. Some identify the word 'Hebrews' in this verse with the *Habiri*, the invaders of Palestine in the 14th pre-Christian century, who are mentioned in the Tell-el-Amarna tablets.

**16.** *that the interpretation was good.* i.e. favourable. This encourages him to relate his dream.

*baskets of white bread.* For the king (cf. Neh. v, 18); or, 'baskets of open wicker-work,' enabling the birds to peck at the contents (Rashbam).

**17.** *baked food.* Confectionery.

*and the birds.* The butler dreamed that he actually performed the duties of his office, whereas the baker only sought to do so, but was prevented. The further ominous circumstance was the birds darting down upon the food, he being powerless to drive them away.

**19.** *hang thee.* Impale thee. The decapitated corpse of a malefactor was allowed to hang exposed to the public view, and to become the prey of the birds. In Israel, this barbarous custom was prohibited (Deut. XXI, 23).

**20.** *Pharaoh's birthday.* On that day he reviewed the prisoners or considered their petitions.

**23.** *not . . . remember Joseph.* On that day.

*but forgot him.* Afterwards (Rashi). As Joseph had put his trust in the butler, God caused him to wait two years for his freedom (Midrash). The chief butler's forgetfulness, in the enjoyment of his own good fortune, is sadly natural. Nothing alas is more common than ingratitude. Man forgets; but God does not forget his own. And when the night is darkest, the dawn is near.

# HAFTORAH VAYYESHEV    הפטרת וישב

### AMOS II, 6–III, 8

#### CHAPTER II

6. Thus saith the Lord:
For three transgressions of Israel,
Yea, for four, I will not reverse it:
Because they sell the righteous for silver,
And the needy for a pair of shoes;
7. That pant after the dust of the earth
  on the head of the poor,
And turn aside the way of the humble;
And a man and his father go unto the
  same maid,
To profane My holy name;
8. And they lay themselves down beside
  every altar
Upon clothes taken in pledge,
And in the house of their God they drink
The wine of them that have been fined.

#### CAP. II. ב

6 כֹּה אָמַר יְהֹוָה עַל־שְׁלֹשָׁה
פִּשְׁעֵי יִשְׂרָאֵל וְעַל־אַרְבָּעָה לֹא אֲשִׁיבֶנּוּ עַל־מִכְרָם בַּכֶּסֶף
7 צַדִּיק וְאֶבְיוֹן בַּעֲבוּר נַעֲלָיִם: הַשֹּׁאֲפִים עַל־עֲפַר־אֶרֶץ
בְּרֹאשׁ דַּלִּים וְדֶרֶךְ עֲנָוִים יַטּוּ וְאִישׁ וְאָבִיו יֵלְכוּ אֶל־
8 הַנַּעֲרָה לְמַעַן חַלֵּל אֶת־שֵׁם קָדְשִׁי: וְעַל־בְּגָדִים חֲבֻלִים
יַטּוּ אֵצֶל כָּל־מִזְבֵּחַ וְיֵין עֲנוּשִׁים יִשְׁתּוּ בֵּית אֱלֹהֵיהֶם:

Amos, a herdsman and dresser of sycamore trees, felt the stirring of the spirit of the Lord while pursuing his lonely calling amid the hills of Judea. He is an older contemporary of Hosea, and is the first of the literary Prophets. The master-word of existence to Amos is Righteousness—which to him, as to his successors, means holiness of life in the individual and the triumph of right in the world. Righteousness is the basis of national as of individual life. Without it, all else crumbles to ruin. For God is righteousness. He is the God of all families of the earth; and all of them alike He judges according to their humane dealings towards their fellowmen. Man's inhumanity to man, Amos proclaims to be *the* cardinal sin. As to Israel, it is God's chosen people; but this great privilege carried no immunity against Divine punishment for wrong-doing. On the contrary. Just because Israel is God's people, the higher must be its standard of life; and the greater its guilt and punishment, if and when it falls away from righteousness.

After pronouncing judgment on the surrounding peoples for their violation of the dictates of universal morality and their participation in barbarous practices, Amos turns to the Northern Kingdom of Israel, judging its inhabitants with the same standard and in the very same words as he did the heathens.

**6-8.** Israel's crimes are no less heinous. It sins against justice, mercy and purity.

**6.** *For three transgressions of Israel, yea, for four, I will not reverse it.* i.e. turn away the punishment. Three or four—a phrase signifying an indefinite number, and illustrating the mercy of God. For the first, second, and even third transgression, He holds His hand, waiting for the transgressor to cease wrong-doing. It is not till the fourth sin, that His long-suffering is at an end (Kimchi).

*sell the righteous.* The innocent are declared guilty for a bribe; and rich men sell into slavery poor honest people whose only crime was that they were in debt to them, sometimes only to the value of a pair of shoes. This sale of the innocent man (צדיק) gives the connection with the story of Joseph, spoken of by the Rabbis as הצדיק, the innocent victim of hatred and slander.

**7.** *that pant.* So great is the cupidity of the rich and powerful that they covet the most insignificant possession still left to the poor, even the dust on the poor man's head sprinkled there as a sign of mourning—ironically adds the Prophet.

*turn aside the way of the humble.* 'Humble souls they harry' (Moffatt). The word 'way' here means the right. They pervert the justice of those who are too weak to defend themselves against their cunning.

*the same maid.* With callousness to human suffering goes lust. And their unchastity is abominable, devoid of all human shame.

*profane My holy name.* Their life and actions constitute a *chillul hashem*, a profanation of the Name of God and Israel—an unpardonable sin; cf. Lev. XXII, 2; Ezek. XX, 9, 14.

**8.** *clothes taken in pledge.* They make the necessities of the poor serve their heartless luxury during their religious feasts. For the sin against the poor, see Exod. XXII, 25, and Deut. XXIV, 12–13.

# AMOS II, 9

9. Yet destroyed I the Amorite before them,
Whose height was like the height of the cedars,
And he was strong as the oaks;
Yet I destroyed his fruit from above,
And his roots from beneath.
10. Also I brought you up out of the land of Egypt,
And led you forty years in the wilderness,
To possess the land of the Amorite.
11. And I raised up of your sons for prophets,
And of your young men for Nazirites.
Is it not even thus, O ye children of Israel?
Saith the Lord.
12. But ye gave the Nazirites wine to drink;
And commanded the prophets, saying:
'Prophesy not.'
13. Behold, I will make it creak under you,
As a cart creaketh that is full of sheaves.
14. And flight shall fail the swift,
And the strong shall not exert his strength,
Neither shall the mighty deliver himself;
15. Neither shall he stand that handleth the bow;
And he that is swift of foot shall not deliver himself;
Neither shall he that rideth the horse deliver himself;
16. And he that is courageous among the mighty
Shall flee away naked in that day,
Saith the Lord.

### CHAPTER III

1. Hear this word that the Lord hath spoken against you, O children of Israel, against the whole family which I brought up out of the land of Egypt, saying:

2. You only have I known of all the families of the earth;
Therefore I will visit upon you all your iniquities.

---

**9. the Amorite.** Representing the previous inhabitants of Palestine, as the Amorite was the most powerful tribe. The Prophet points to the monstrous ingratitude of Israel.

**11. Nazirites.** True and inspired men are among a nation's most precious possessions. The Nazirite, who vowed to refrain from wine (Numbers VI, 2–21), stood for self-control, and by his very existence rebuked the intemperance of the day. So he was basely urged to break his vow.

**12. prophesy not.** The experience of Amos himself, VII, 13.

**13.** As a cart overloaded with its harvest creaks under the weight; so a people overladen with sin cannot escape the consequences of its sins. The prophecy was fulfilled by the invasion of the Assyrians.

### CHAPTER III

**2. therefore.** The most famous 'therefore' in history. Israel is the chosen of God. *Therefore*, God demands higher, not lower, standards of goodness from Israel, and will punish lapses more severely. The higher the privilege, the graver the responsibility. The greater the opportunity, the more inexcusable the failure to use it.

**3–8.** These verses give the ground on which Amos claims to be heard.

AMOS III, 3

3. Will two walk together,
Except they have agreed?

4. Will a lion roar in the forest,
When he hath no prey?
Will a young lion give forth his voice out of his den,
If he have taken nothing?

5. Will a bird fall in a snare upon the earth,
Where there is no lure for it?
Will a snare spring up from the ground,
And have taken nothing at all?

6. Shall the horn be blown in a city,
And the people not tremble?
Shall evil befall a city,
And the LORD hath not done it?

7. For the Lord GOD will do nothing,
But He revealeth His counsel unto His servants the prophets.

8. The lion hath roared,
Who will not fear?
The Lord GOD hath spoken,
Who can but prophesy?

**3.** A declaration of the Prophet's Divine authority. The Prophet has spoken, only because God has inspired him. God and the Prophet are met on this sad task.

**4–6.** Figures of speech illustrating the cause and effect stated in the previous verse, drawn from experiences in the Prophet's earlier calling as herdsman. If the roar of the lion is heard in the desert, it is because he has seized his prey. The bird has fallen, because the snare has caught it. The tocsin is sounded in the city, because the enemy is at the gate. So likewise disaster does not overwhelm a people without a cause.

**7.** *He revealeth His counsel.* The watcher on the tower at the entrance of the city who sees attacking troops advancing will sound the alarm that arouses and terrifies the people. Israel cannot plead lack of warning. The Prophet is the true Watcher on the tower, who would deliver from threatening evils by his summons to repentance. And he speaks because God is acting within, and irresistibly compels him.

**8.** *who can but prophesy?* To us the voice of God speaks through the pages of Scripture; and, if we would listen and understand and perform its precepts, surely would 'all the LORD's people be prophets'.

GENESIS XLI, 1      בראשית מקץ מא

## CHAPTER XLI      CAP. XLI. מא

1. And it came to pass at the end of two full years, that Pharaoh dreamed: and, behold, he stood by the ¹river. 2. And, behold, there came up out of the river seven kine, well-favoured and fat-fleshed; and they fed in the reed-grass. 3. And, behold, seven other kine came up after them out of the river, ill-favoured and lean-fleshed; and stood by the other kine upon the brink of the river. 4. And the ill-favoured and lean-fleshed kine did eat up the seven well-favoured and fat kine. So Pharaoh awoke. 5. And he slept and dreamed a second time: and, behold, seven ears of corn came up upon one stalk, rank and good. 6. And, behold, seven ears, thin and blasted with the east wind, sprung up after them. 7. And the thin ears swallowed up the seven rank and full ears. And Pharaoh awoke, and, behold, it was a dream. 8. And it came to pass in the morning that his spirit was troubled; and he sent and called for all the magicians of Egypt, and all the wise men thereof; and Pharaoh told them his dream; but there was none that could interpret them unto Pharaoh. 9. Then spoke the chief butler unto Pharaoh, saying: 'I make mention of my faults this day: 10. Pharaoh was wroth with his servants, and put me in the ward of the house of the captain of the guard, me and the chief baker. 11. And we dreamed a dream in one night, I and he; we dreamed each man according to the interpretation of his dream. 12. And there was with us there a young man, a Hebrew, servant to the captain of the guard; and we told him, and he interpreted to us our dreams; to each man according to his dream he did interpret. 13. And it came to pass, as he interpreted to us, so it was: I was restored unto mine office,

¹ *That is, the Nile.*

---

# X. MIKKETZ

(CHAPTERS XLI–XLIV, 17)

### CHAPTER XLI. JOSEPH AND PHARAOH

**1.** *two full years.* After the events recounted in the previous chapter.

**2.** *reed-grass.* Heb. *achu*, another Egyptian loan-word. The Nile-grass is meant here.

**5.** *rank.* Heb. 'fat'. *i.e.* rich.

**6.** *east wind.* The dreaded sirocco coming from Arabia. It lasts at times fifty days and destroys the vegetation.

**8.** *his spirit was troubled.* The double dream convinced him of its significance. The Heb. verb for 'was troubled' suggests the violent beating of the heart in excitement.

*magicians.* Or, 'sacred scribes'; Heb. *chartumim*—probably an Egyptian word.

*none that could interpret.* The complete failure of heathen magic is here contrasted with the perfect wisdom of the God-inspired Hebrew slave; cf. Exod. VII, 12, and Daniel II and V.

**9.** *I make mention of my faults.* Not only his offence against the king, but also his sin against Joseph in forgetting him.

**12.** *to each man according to his dream.* The dream was appropriate to each one, and the interpretation was equally appropriate.

## GENESIS XLI, 14

and he was hanged.' 14. Then Pharaoh sent and called Joseph, and they brought him hastily out of the dungeon. And he shaved himself, and changed his raiment, and came in unto Pharaoh.* ¹¹ᵃ· 15. And Pharaoh said unto Joseph: 'I have dreamed a dream, and there is none that can interpret it; and I have heard say of thee, that when thou hearest a dream thou canst interpret it.' 16. And Joseph answered Pharaoh, saying: 'It is not in me; God will give Pharaoh an answer of peace.'* ¹¹ᴮ· 17. And Pharaoh spoke unto Joseph: 'In my dream, behold, I stood upon the brink of the river. 18. And, behold, there came up out of the river seven kine, fat-fleshed and well-favoured; and they fed in the reed-grass. 19. And, behold, seven other kine came up after them, poor and very ill-favoured and lean-fleshed, such as I never saw in all the land of Egypt for badness. 20. And the lean and ill-favoured kine did eat up the first seven fat kine. 21. And when they had eaten them up, it could not be known that they had eaten them; but they were still ill-favoured as at the beginning. So I awoke. 22. And I saw in my dream, and, behold, seven ears came up upon one stalk, full and good. 23. And, behold, seven ears, withered, thin, and blasted with the east wind, sprung up after them. 24. And the thin ears swallowed up the seven good ears. And I told it unto the magicians; but there was none that could declare it to me.' 25. And Joseph said unto Pharaoh: 'The dream of Pharaoh is one; what God is about to do He hath declared unto Pharaoh. 26. The seven good kine are seven years; and the seven good ears are seven years: the dream is one. 27. And the seven lean and ill-favoured kine that came up after them are seven years, and also the seven empty ears blasted with the east wind; they shall be seven years of famine. 28. That is the thing which I spoke unto Pharaoh: what God is about to do He hath shown unto Pharaoh. 29. Behold, there come seven years of great plenty throughout all

---

**16.** *it is not in me.* Pharaoh assumed that Joseph was a professional interpreter of dreams. Joseph's answer is a fine combination of religious sincerity and courtly deference.

*an answer of peace.* i.e. an answer that will correspond to the needs of Pharaoh and his people.

**19.** *such as I never saw.* Pharaoh colours the recital by giving expression to the feelings which the dream excited.

**25.** *is one.* The two dreams have the same meaning. They are a foreboding of what God is about to do.

**30.** *shall consume the land.* i.e. the people of the land (Onkelos).

**33-36.** Joseph explains how God gives Pharaoh the answer of peace (v. 16). The interpretation of the dream is supplemented by the practical advice as to how the coming crisis should be met. Joseph the dreamer and saint proves himself in an eminent degree a man of practical affairs.

## GENESIS XLI, 30

the land of Egypt. 30. And there shall arise after them seven years of famine; and all the plenty shall be forgotten in the land of Egypt; and the famine shall consume the land; 31. and the plenty shall not be known in the land by reason of that famine which followeth; for it shall be very grievous. 32. And for that the dream was doubled unto Pharaoh twice, it is because the thing is established by God, and God will shortly bring it to pass. 33. Now therefore let Pharaoh look out a man discreet and wise, and set him over the land of Egypt. 34. Let Pharaoh do this, and let him appoint overseers over the land, and take up the fifth part of the land of Egypt in the seven years of plenty. 35. And let them gather all the food of these good years that come, and lay up corn under the hand of Pharaoh for food in the cities, and let them keep it. 36. And the food shall be for a store to the land against the seven years of famine, which shall be in the land of Egypt; that the land perish not through the famine.' 37. And the thing was good in the eyes of Pharaoh, and in the eyes of all his servants. 38. And Pharaoh said unto his servants: 'Can we find such a one as this, a man in whom the spirit of God is?'* 111. 39. And Pharaoh said unto Joseph: 'Forasmuch as God hath shown thee all this, there is none so discreet and wise as thou. 40. Thou shalt be over my house, and according unto thy word shall all my people be ruled; only in the throne will I be greater than thou.' 41. And Pharaoh said unto Joseph: 'See, I have set thee over all the land of Egypt.' 42. And Pharaoh took off his signet ring from his hand, and put it upon Joseph's hand, and arrayed him in vestures of fine linen, and put a gold chain about his neck. 43. And he made him to ride in the second chariot which he had; and they cried before

**35.** *the hand of Pharaoh.* *i.e.* in the royal granaries.

*in the cities.* Where the royal granaries were.

**36.** *store.* A reserve.

**38.** *in whom the spirit of God is.* *i.e.* combining the supernatural power of interpreting dreams with the practical sagacity of a statesman.

**40.** *over my house.* He makes him Grand Vizier.
*be ruled.* Or, 'do homage.'

**42.** *signet ring.* Thereby symbolically endowing him with royal authority.

*fine linen.* The Heb. word comes from the Egyptian. It is the material worn by the royal family and the highest officials of the kingdom.

*a gold chain.* The gold collar appertaining to the office of Grand Vizier. This is another instance of the remarkable historical exactness of the Joseph narrative. 'No ancient civilization was more distinct and unique than that of Egypt. Her customs, her language, and her system of writing were shared by no other people; and yet, at every point, the narrative reveals a thorough familiarity with Egyptian life. Peculiar Egyptian customs are also reflected in the stories; as, for example, the giving of the much-prized golden collar, which was bestowed upon a public servant for distinguished achievement' (F. C. Kent).

**43.** *second chariot.* Next to Pharaoh's. Horses and chariots were introduced into Egypt during the Hyksos period.

*abrech.* 'Probably an Egyptian word similar in sound to the Hebrew word meaning "to kneel"' (RV Margin).

## GENESIS XLI, 44

him: 'Abrech'; and he set him over all the land of Egypt. 44. And Pharaoh said unto Joseph: 'I am Pharaoh, and without thee shall no man lift up his hand or his foot in all the land of Egypt.' 45. And Pharaoh called Joseph's name Zaphenath-paneah; and he gave him to wife Asenath the daughter of Poti-phera priest of On. And Joseph went out over the land of Egypt.—46. And Joseph was thirty years old when he stood before Pharaoh king of Egypt.—And Joseph went out from the presence of Pharaoh, and went throughout all the land of Egypt. 47. And in the seven years of plenty the earth brought forth in heaps. 48. And he gathered up all the food of the seven years which were in the land of Egypt, and laid up the food in the cities; the food of the field, which was round about every city, laid he up in the same. 49. And Joseph laid up corn as the sand of the sea, very much, until they left off numbering; for it was without number. 50. And unto Joseph were born two sons before the year of famine came, whom Asenath the daughter of Poti-phera priest of On bore unto him. 51. And Joseph called the name of the first-born [1]Manasseh: 'for God hath made me forget all my toil, and all my father's house.' 52. And the name of the second called he [2]Ephraim: 'for God hath made me fruitful in the land of my affliction.'\* iv. 53. And the seven years of plenty, that was in the land of Egypt, came to an end. 54. And the seven years of famine began to come, according as Joseph had said; and there was famine in all lands; but in all the land of Egypt there was bread. 55. And when all the land of Egypt was famished, the people cried to Pharaoh for bread; and Pharaoh said unto all the Egyptians: 'Go unto Joseph; what he saith to you, do.' 56. And the famine was over all the face of

---

[1] That is, *Making to forget*.   [2] From a Hebrew word signifying *to be fruitful*.

**44.** *lift up his hand or his foot.* i.e. do anything.

**45.** *Zaphenath-paneah.* Joseph receives a new name on his state appointment. This is both an Egyptian and a Hebrew custom; e.g. Num. XIII, 16. Egyptologists explain that *Zaphenath* means 'food-man', and *paneah*, 'of the life,' i.e. the Chief Steward in the realm in face of Famine (Kyle). The importance of the change of name in the story lies in the fact that it helps to conceal the identity of Joseph when his brethren come to Egypt.

*Asenath.* i.e. belonging to the goddess Neith.

*Poti-phera.* To be distinguished from Potiphar, the former master of Joseph.

*On.* Later known as Heliopolis, near Cairo. On was the centre of Sun worship in Egypt. Cleopatra's Needle on the Thames Embankment originally stood in On.

**46.** *thirty years old.* He had spent about twelve years in prison.

**47.** *in heaps.* The produce was most abundant. Some Jewish commentators render, 'for the storehouses.'

**51.** *all my toil, and all my father's house.* His position had made him forget his toil as a bondman, and the ill-will of his brethren that was the cause of that bondage. Or, the phrase can be viewed as the Heb. idiom for 'all the suffering caused to me by my father's house', i.e. my brethren (Wogue).

**54.** *all lands.* All the neighbouring lands.

**56.** *the storehouses.* The granaries.

# GENESIS XLI, 57

the earth; and Joseph opened all the storehouses, and sold unto the Egyptians; and the famine was sore in the land of Egypt. 57. And all countries came into Egypt to Joseph to buy corn; because the famine was sore in all the earth.

## 42 CHAPTER XLII

1. Now Jacob saw that there was corn in Egypt, and Jacob said unto his sons: 'Why do ye look one upon another?' 2. And he said: 'Behold, I have heard that there is corn in Egypt. Get you down thither, and buy for us from thence; that we may live, and not die.' 3. And Joseph's ten brethren went down to buy corn from Egypt. 4. But Benjamin, Joseph's brother, Jacob sent not with his brethren; for he said: 'Lest peradventure harm befall him.' 5. And the sons of Israel came to buy among those that came; for the famine was in the land of Canaan. 6. And Joseph was the governor over the land; he it was that sold to all the people of the land. And Joseph's brethren came, and bowed down to him with their faces to the earth. 7. And Joseph saw his brethren, and he knew them, but made himself strange unto them, and spoke roughly with them; and he said unto them: 'Whence come ye?' And they said: 'From the land of Canaan to buy food.' 8. And Joseph knew his brethren, but they knew not him. 9. And Joseph remembered the dreams which he dreamed of them, and said unto them: 'Ye are spies; to see the nakedness of the land ye are come.' 10. And they said unto him: 'Nay, my lord, but to buy food are thy servants come. 11. We are all one man's sons; we are upright men, thy

## בראשית מקץ מא מב

פְּנֵי הָאָרֶץ וַיִּפְתַּח יוֹסֵף אֶת־כָּל־אֲשֶׁר בָּהֶם וַיִּשְׁבֹּר לְמִצְרַיִם 57 וַיֶּחֱזַק הָרָעָב בְּאֶרֶץ מִצְרָיִם: וְכָל־הָאָרֶץ בָּאוּ מִצְרַיְמָה לִשְׁבֹּר אֶל־יוֹסֵף כִּי־חָזַק הָרָעָב בְּכָל־הָאָרֶץ:

### CAP. XLII. מב

א וַיַּרְא יַעֲקֹב כִּי יֶשׁ־שֶׁבֶר בְּמִצְרָיִם וַיֹּאמֶר יַעֲקֹב לְבָנָיו
2 לָמָּה תִּתְרָאוּ: וַיֹּאמֶר הִנֵּה שָׁמַעְתִּי כִּי יֶשׁ־שֶׁבֶר בְּמִצְרָיִם
3 רְדוּ־שָׁמָּה וְשִׁבְרוּ־לָנוּ מִשָּׁם וְנִחְיֶה וְלֹא נָמוּת: וַיֵּרְדוּ
4 אֲחֵי־יוֹסֵף עֲשָׂרָה לִשְׁבֹּר בָּר מִמִּצְרָיִם: וְאֶת־בִּנְיָמִין אֲחִי
יוֹסֵף לֹא־שָׁלַח יַעֲקֹב אֶת־אֶחָיו כִּי אָמַר פֶּן־יִקְרָאֶנּוּ אָסוֹן:
ה וַיָּבֹאוּ בְּנֵי יִשְׂרָאֵל לִשְׁבֹּר בְּתוֹךְ הַבָּאִים כִּי־הָיָה הָרָעָב
6 בְּאֶרֶץ כְּנָעַן: וְיוֹסֵף הוּא הַשַּׁלִּיט עַל־הָאָרֶץ הוּא הַמַּשְׁבִּיר
לְכָל־עַם הָאָרֶץ וַיָּבֹאוּ אֲחֵי יוֹסֵף וַיִּשְׁתַּחֲווּ־לוֹ אַפַּיִם
7 אָרְצָה: וַיַּרְא יוֹסֵף אֶת־אֶחָיו וַיַּכִּרֵם וַיִּתְנַכֵּר אֲלֵיהֶם
וַיְדַבֵּר אִתָּם קָשׁוֹת וַיֹּאמֶר אֲלֵהֶם מֵאַיִן בָּאתֶם וַיֹּאמְרוּ
8 מֵאֶרֶץ כְּנַעַן לִשְׁבָּר־אֹכֶל: וַיַּכֵּר יוֹסֵף אֶת־אֶחָיו וְהֵם
9 לֹא הִכִּרֻהוּ: וַיִּזְכֹּר יוֹסֵף אֵת הַחֲלֹמוֹת אֲשֶׁר חָלַם לָהֶם
וַיֹּאמֶר אֲלֵהֶם מְרַגְּלִים אַתֶּם לִרְאוֹת אֶת־עֶרְוַת הָאָרֶץ
י בָּאתֶם: וַיֹּאמְרוּ אֵלָיו לֹא אֲדֹנִי וַעֲבָדֶיךָ בָּאוּ לִשְׁבָּר־אֹכֶל:
11 כֻּלָּנוּ בְּנֵי אִישׁ־אֶחָד נָחְנוּ כֵּנִים אֲנַחְנוּ לֹא־הָיוּ עֲבָדֶיךָ

---

**57.** *all countries.* i.e. 'the whole world', everybody. This verse prepares for the next scene of the drama (chap. XLII).

CHAPTER XLII. JOSEPH'S BRETHREN IN EGYPT

**1.** *saw.* He had probably seen the corn brought by caravans.

*why do ye look one upon another?* Paralysed by doubt and helplessness (Luzzatto).

**2.** *get you down.* Cf. XII, 10.

**6.** *he it was that sold.* He superintended the sales, and foreign purchasers would be brought to him to be interrogated. His dreams were being fulfilled, see XXXVII, 7-10. The brothers 'bowed themselves down before him'.

**7.** *spoke roughly with them.* The brother who had been shamefully and pitilessly sold into slavery now had his opportunity for revenge. The greatness of Joseph lies in the fact that for all time he showed men a better way. He tests his brethren, holding his own natural feelings in check until convinced of their filial piety to their father, their love for Benjamin, and their sincere contrition for their crime towards him. Then he forgives them freely, fully, and lovingly.

**8.** *his brethren.* Recognized, but not recognizing the Grand Vizier, who in dress, name, language, and bearing was an Egyptian, as their brother.

**9.** *and Joseph remembered the dreams.* Not in a spirit of pride and hatred, but as the revealed will of the good God whose ways are inscrutable.

*ye are spies.* The most natural accusation to bring against strangers in Egypt, or anywhere.

*nakedness of the land.* The weak spots in the line of defence along the border. The North-East of Egypt was its weak side, and strangers entering from this direction were jealously watched.

**11.** *one man's sons.* A sufficient answer to the charge of being spies, for no man would risk the lives of ten sons in so dangerous an undertaking.

## GENESIS XLII, 12

servants are no spies.' 12. And he said unto them: 'Nay, but to see the nakedness of the land ye are come.' 13. And they said: 'We thy servants are twelve brethren, the sons of one man in the land of Canaan; and, behold, the youngest is this day with our father, and one is not.' 14. And Joseph said unto them: 'That is it that I spoke unto you, saying: Ye are spies. 15. Hereby ye shall be proved: as Pharaoh liveth, ye shall not go forth hence, except your youngest brother come hither. 16. Send one of you, and let him fetch your brother, and ye shall be bound, that your words may be proved, whether there be truth in you; or else, as Pharaoh liveth, surely ye are spies.' 17. And he put them all together into ward three days. 18. And Joseph said unto them the third day: 'This do, and live; for I fear God:\*v. 19. if ye be upright men, let one of your brethren be bound in your prison-house; but go ye, carry corn for the famine of your houses; 20. and bring your youngest brother unto me; so shall your words be verified, and ye shall not die.' And they did so. 21. And they said one to another: 'We are verily guilty concerning our brother, in that we saw the distress of his soul, when he besought us, and we would not hear; therefore is this distress come upon us.' 22. And Reuben answered them, saying: 'Spoke I not unto you, saying: Do not sin against the child; and ye would not hear? therefore also, behold, his blood is required.' 23. And they knew not that Joseph understood them; for the interpreter was between them. 24. And he turned himself about from them, and wept; and he returned to them, and spoke to them,

בראשית מקץ מב

12 מְרַגְּלִים: וַיֹּאמֶר אֲלֵהֶם לֹא כִּי־עֶרְוַת הָאָרֶץ בָּאתֶם
13 לִרְאוֹת: וַיֹּאמְרוּ שְׁנֵים עָשָׂר עֲבָדֶיךָ אַחִים ׀ אֲנַחְנוּ בְּנֵי
אִישׁ־אֶחָד בְּאֶרֶץ כְּנָעַן וְהִנֵּה הַקָּטֹן אֶת־אָבִינוּ הַיּוֹם
14 וְהָאֶחָד אֵינֶנּוּ: וַיֹּאמֶר אֲלֵהֶם יוֹסֵף הוּא אֲשֶׁר דִּבַּרְתִּי
טו אֲלֵכֶם לֵאמֹר מְרַגְּלִים אַתֶּם: בְּזֹאת תִּבָּחֵנוּ חֵי פַרְעֹה אִם־
16 תֵּצְאוּ מִזֶּה כִּי אִם־בְּבוֹא אֲחִיכֶם הַקָּטֹן הֵנָּה: שִׁלְחוּ
מִכֶּם אֶחָד וְיִקַּח אֶת־אֲחִיכֶם וְאַתֶּם הֵאָסְרוּ וְיִבָּחֲנוּ דִבְרֵיכֶם
הַאֱמֶת אִתְּכֶם וְאִם־לֹא חֵי פַרְעֹה כִּי מְרַגְּלִים אַתֶּם:
17 וַיֶּאֱסֹף אֹתָם אֶל־מִשְׁמָר שְׁלֹשֶׁת יָמִים: וַיֹּאמֶר אֲלֵהֶם
18
חמישי יוֹסֵף בַּיּוֹם הַשְּׁלִישִׁי זֹאת עֲשׂוּ וִחְיוּ אֶת־הָאֱלֹהִים אֲנִי
19 יָרֵא: אִם־כֵּנִים אַתֶּם אֲחִיכֶם אֶחָד יֵאָסֵר בְּבֵית מִשְׁמַרְכֶם
כ וְאַתֶּם לְכוּ הָבִיאוּ שֶׁבֶר רַעֲבוֹן בָּתֵּיכֶם: וְאֶת־אֲחִיכֶם
הַקָּטֹן תָּבִיאוּ אֵלַי וְיֵאָמְנוּ דִבְרֵיכֶם וְלֹא תָמוּתוּ וַיַּעֲשׂוּ־כֵן:
21 וַיֹּאמְרוּ אִישׁ אֶל־אָחִיו אֲבָל אֲשֵׁמִים ׀ אֲנַחְנוּ עַל־אָחִינוּ
אֲשֶׁר רָאִינוּ צָרַת נַפְשׁוֹ בְּהִתְחַנְנוֹ אֵלֵינוּ וְלֹא שָׁמָעְנוּ עַל־
22 כֵּן בָּאָה אֵלֵינוּ הַצָּרָה הַזֹּאת: וַיַּעַן רְאוּבֵן אֹתָם לֵאמֹר
הֲלוֹא אָמַרְתִּי אֲלֵיכֶם ׀ לֵאמֹר אַל־תֶּחֶטְאוּ בַיֶּלֶד וְלֹא
23 שְׁמַעְתֶּם וְגַם־דָּמוֹ הִנֵּה נִדְרָשׁ: וְהֵם לֹא יָדְעוּ כִּי שֹׁמֵעַ
24 יוֹסֵף כִּי הַמֵּלִיץ בֵּינֹתָם: וַיִּסֹּב מֵעֲלֵיהֶם וַיֵּבְךְּ וַיָּשָׁב

**12.** *nay.* Joseph repeats his accusation. This throws them off their guard, and they seek to disarm his suspicions by volunteering information about their father and youngest brother, of which Joseph at once takes advantage.

**13.** *one is not.* Refers of course to Joseph. They did not say that he was dead, because they did not really know what became of him.

**15.** *ye shall be proved.* Their story is improbable. It must be verified. Let them bring Benjamin down to Egypt. In this way, Joseph would test their loyalty to their youngest brother. Did they also hate Benjamin as they had hated him? He delicately refrains from cross-questioning them about the brother who 'is not'.

*as Pharaoh liveth.* A form of oath, or strong asseveration. The oath by the life of the king is found in an Egyptian inscription of the twentieth pre-Christian century.

**18.** *this do, and live.* Better, '*this do in order that ye may live.*' The brethren claimed to be upright, honest men. Profession was not enough. Let them bring the youngest brother, 'so shall your words be verified, and ye shall not die' (v. 20).

*for I fear God.* And so am unwilling to treat you with unnecessary severity on mere suspicion. I will keep one of you as a hostage, the rest shall convey food for your families. 'Fear of God is the universal element in religion which humanizes our dealings with "foreigners", even when national interests are involved' (Procksch); cf. xx, 11.

**21.** *we are verily guilty.* Joseph had at last awakened remorse in their hearts. They had been blind to the distress of their brother, and deaf to his entreaties. They were guilty, and their misfortune was a just retribution for their cruelty. It is only now, in the mirror of their repentance, that we see reflected the agonizing scene when the lad was thrown into the pit many years before.

GENESIS XLII, 25

and took Simeon from among them, and bound him before their eyes. 25. Then Joseph commanded to fill their vessels with corn, and to restore every man's money into his sack, and to give them provision for the way; and thus was it done unto them. 26. And they laded their asses with their corn, and departed thence. 27. And as one of them opened his sack to give his ass provender in the lodging-place, he espied his money; and, behold, it was in the mouth of his sack. 28. And he said unto his brethren: 'My money is restored; and, lo, it is even in my sack.' And their heart failed them, and they turned trembling one to another, saying: 'What is this that God hath done unto us?' 29. And they came unto Jacob their father unto the land of Canaan, and told him all that had befallen them, saying: 30. 'The man, the lord of the land, spoke roughly with us and took us for spies of the country. 31. And we said unto him: We are upright men; we are no spies. 32. We are twelve brethren, sons of our father; one is not, and the youngest is this day with our father in the land of Canaan. 33. And the man, the lord of the land, said unto us: Hereby shall I know that ye are upright men: leave one of your brethren with me, and take corn for the famine of your houses, and go your way. 34. And bring your youngest brother unto me; then shall I know that ye are no spies, but that ye are upright men; so will I deliver you your brother, and ye shall traffic in the land.' 35. And it came to pass as they emptied their sacks, that, behold,

See on XXXVII, 23. With broken and contrite hearts, they now recall their inhuman callousness —all in the hearing of Joseph.

**22.** *his blood is required.* Reuben assumes that Joseph's death, whatever form it took, was due to them. They were morally guilty of his death. His blood is 'required', *i.e.* is now being avenged (see IX, 5).

**23.** *interpreter.* Joseph throughout spoke to them as the Viceroy, in Egyptian.

**24.** *and wept.* He is touched to tears by their penitence and contrition.
*Simeon.* As the next in age to Reuben, who as the eldest was to report to Jacob. According to Rabbinic tradition, it was Simeon who had counselled that Joseph be slain.

**27.** *lodging-place.* Wayside shelter.

**28.** *they turned trembling.* They wonder what such an unusual occurrence may portend. Will they be accused of theft?

**29–34.** They recount their experience to their father.

**30.** *the lord of.* The Heb. is in the plural, often used to express power or greatness.

**33.** *corn for the famine.* The words 'corn for' are supplied from the context.

**34.** *traffic in the land.* Joseph did not say this, but 'and ye shall not die' (v. 20). This could only be by allowing the brethren to come to Egypt and buy corn.

**35.** *they were afraid. i.e.* Jacob and his sons. They looked upon it as a deliberate act on the part of the Egyptian lord to bring a charge of theft against them.

**36.** *upon me are all these things come.* The point of the reproach is that it is his children, not their own, that they are endangering: to which Reuben's offer is the rejoinder.

## GENESIS XLII, 36

every man's bundle of money was in his sack; and when they and their father saw their bundles of money, they were afraid. 36. And Jacob their father said unto them: 'Me have ye bereaved of my children: Joseph is not, and Simeon is not, and ye will take Benjamin away; upon me are all these things come.' 37. And Reuben spoke unto his father, saying: 'Thou shalt slay my two sons, if I bring him not to thee; deliver him into my hand, and I will bring him back to thee.' 38. And he said: 'My son shall not go down with you; for his brother is dead, and he only is left; if harm befall him by the way in which ye go, then will ye bring down my gray hairs with sorrow to the grave.'

## 43    CHAPTER XLIII

1. And the famine was sore in the land. 2. And it came to pass, when they had eaten up the corn which they had brought out of Egypt, that their father said unto them: 'Go again, buy us a little food.' 3. And Judah spoke unto him, saying: 'The man did earnestly forewarn us, saying: Ye shall not see my face, except your brother be with you. 4. If thou wilt send our brother with us, we will go down and buy thee food; 5. but if thou wilt not send him, we will not go down, for the man said unto us: Ye shall not see my face, except your brother be with you.' 6. And Israel said: 'Wherefore dealt ye so ill with me, as to tell the man whether ye had yet a brother?' 7. And they said: 'The man asked straitly concerning ourselves, and concerning our kindred, saying: Is your father yet alive? have ye another brother? and we told him according to the tenor of these words; could we in any wise know that he would say: Bring your brother down?' 8. And Judah said unto Israel his father: 'Send the lad with me, and we will arise and go, that we may live, and not die, both we, and thou, and also our little ones. 9. I will be surety for him; of my hand shalt thou require him; if

---

**37.** *slay my two sons.* The impetuous nature of Reuben is seen here. 'Two sons,' one for Benjamin and one for Joseph—of whose death he *feels* that he shares the guilt with his brothers.

### CHAPTER XLIII. THE SECOND VISIT OF JOSEPH'S BRETHREN TO EGYPT

**1-14.** Judah prevails upon Jacob to allow Benjamin to accompany the brethren. Judah now takes the lead in the place of Reuben, in whom his father had little confidence.

**2.** *eaten up the corn.* Not in its entirety; they must have left sufficient for their father and the household during their absence in Egypt.

**5.** *we will not go down.* Judah's decisive language has the desired effect with Jacob.

**6.** *dealt ye so ill with me.* This is not a question, but a reproach. He blames them for volunteering statements.

**7.** *straitly.* Closely, particularly.
*according to the tenor of these words.* i.e. we gave the answers which his questions called for.

**9.** *I will be surety for him.* I guarantee to bring him back. Jacob is more impressed by his words than by Reuben's wild offer.
*bear the blame.* lit. 'I shall have sinned against thee for ever'.

GENESIS XLIII, 10

I bring him not unto thee, and set him before thee, then let me bear the blame for ever. 10. For except we had lingered, surely we had now returned a second time.' 11. And their father Israel said unto them: 'If it be so now, do this: take of the choice fruits of the land in your vessels, and carry down the man a present, a little balm and a little honey, spicery and ladanum, nuts, and almonds; 12. and take double money in your hand; and the money that was returned in the mouth of your sacks carry back in your hand; peradventure it was an oversight; 13. take also your brother, and arise, go again unto the man; 14. and God Almighty give you mercy before the man, that he may release unto you your other brother and Benjamin. And as for me, if I be bereaved of my children, I am bereaved.' ¶ 15. And the men took that present, and they took double money in their hand, and Benjamin; and rose up, and went down to Egypt, and stood before Joseph.* vi. 16. And when Joseph saw Benjamin with them, he said to the steward of his house: 'Bring the men into the house, and kill the beasts, and prepare the meat; for the men shall dine with me at noon.' 17. And the man did as Joseph bade; and the man brought the men into Joseph's house. 18. And the men were afraid, because they were brought into Joseph's house; and they said: 'Because of the money that was returned in our sacks at the first time are we brought in; that he may seek occasion against us, and fall upon us, and take us for bondmen, and our asses.' 19. And they came near to the steward of Joseph's house, and they spoke unto him at the door of the house,

בראשית מקץ מג

אִם־לֹא הֲבִיאֹתִיו אֵלֶיךָ וְהִצַּגְתִּיו לְפָנֶיךָ וְחָטָאתִי לְךָ
כָּל־הַיָּמִים: כִּי לוּלֵא הִתְמַהְמָהְנוּ כִּי־עַתָּה שַׁבְנוּ זֶה 10
פַעֲמָיִם: וַיֹּאמֶר אֲלֵהֶם יִשְׂרָאֵל אֲבִיהֶם אִם־כֵּן ׀ אֵפוֹא 11
זֹאת עֲשׂוּ קְחוּ מִזִּמְרַת הָאָרֶץ בִּכְלֵיכֶם וְהוֹרִידוּ לָאִישׁ
מִנְחָה מְעַט צֳרִי וּמְעַט דְּבַשׁ נְכֹאת וָלֹט בָּטְנִים וּשְׁקֵדִים:
וְכֶסֶף מִשְׁנֶה קְחוּ בְיֶדְכֶם וְאֶת־הַכֶּסֶף הַמּוּשָׁב בְּפִי 12
אַמְתְּחֹתֵיכֶם תָּשִׁיבוּ בְיֶדְכֶם אוּלַי מִשְׁגֶּה הוּא: וְאֶת־ 13
אֲחִיכֶם קָחוּ וְקוּמוּ שׁוּבוּ אֶל־הָאִישׁ: וְאֵל שַׁדַּי יִתֵּן לָכֶם 14
רַחֲמִים לִפְנֵי הָאִישׁ וְשִׁלַּח לָכֶם אֶת־אֲחִיכֶם אַחֵר וְאֶת־
בִּנְיָמִין וַאֲנִי כַּאֲשֶׁר שָׁכֹלְתִּי שָׁכָלְתִּי: וַיִּקְחוּ הָאֲנָשִׁים אֶת־ 15
הַמִּנְחָה הַזֹּאת וּמִשְׁנֶה־כֶּסֶף לָקְחוּ בְיָדָם וְאֶת־בִּנְיָמִן
וַיָּקֻמוּ וַיֵּרְדוּ מִצְרַיִם וַיַּעַמְדוּ לִפְנֵי יוֹסֵף: ששי וַיַּרְא יוֹסֵף 16
אִתָּם אֶת־בִּנְיָמִין וַיֹּאמֶר לַאֲשֶׁר עַל־בֵּיתוֹ הָבֵא אֶת־הָאֲנָשִׁים
הַבָּיְתָה וּטְבֹחַ טֶבַח וְהָכֵן כִּי אִתִּי יֹאכְלוּ הָאֲנָשִׁים
בַּצָּהֳרָיִם: וַיַּעַשׂ הָאִישׁ כַּאֲשֶׁר אָמַר יוֹסֵף וַיָּבֵא הָאִישׁ 17
אֶת־הָאֲנָשִׁים בֵּיתָה יוֹסֵף: וַיִּירְאוּ הָאֲנָשִׁים כִּי הוּבְאוּ 18
בֵּית יוֹסֵף וַיֹּאמְרוּ עַל־דְּבַר הַכֶּסֶף הַשָּׁב בְּאַמְתְּחֹתֵינוּ
בַּתְּחִלָּה אֲנַחְנוּ מוּבָאִים לְהִתְגֹּלֵל עָלֵינוּ וּלְהִתְנַפֵּל עָלֵינוּ
וְלָקַחַת אֹתָנוּ לַעֲבָדִים וְאֶת־חֲמֹרֵינוּ: וַיִּגְּשׁוּ אֶל־הָאִישׁ 19

v. 21. חש׳ בפתח

**10.** *except we had lingered.* And wasted time in discussion.

**11.** *if it be so now, do this.* 'Since it must be so, do this.' Jacob yields to the inevitable, and offers his children prudent counsel.

*honey.* i.e. the date-honey, rarely found in Egypt.

*nuts.* i.e. pistachio nuts. Still considered a delicacy in the East.

**12.** *double money ... and the money.* They were now to take double money, as they were returning the money that had been placed in their sacks.

**14.** *God Almighty.* Heb. *El Shaddai.* 'The God of Abraham can alone now help him, an old man trembling for the life of his two children' (Procksch).

*mercy.* Divine pity for the helpless misery of the weak and the defenceless.

*if I be bereaved.* An expression of mournful acquiescence in the Divine will, like the exclamation of Esther IV, 16, 'and if I perish, I perish.'

**15-34.** The brethren in Joseph's palace.

**15.** *before Joseph.* At his government office, where the people came to purchase corn.

**16.** *the steward of his house.* lit. 'him that was over his house'.

*bring the men into the house.* i.e. Joseph's private residence.

*dine with me at noon.* This is interesting as indicating the time when meat was eaten in the house of the upper classes in ancient Egypt.

**18.** *money that was returned.* The brethren fear that they are entrapped and about to be punished.

*take us for bondmen.* As detected thieves; cf. Ex. XXII, 2.

**19.** *at the door of the house.* Before crossing the threshold, they would clear themselves of the suspicion against them.

## GENESIS XLIII, 20

20. and said: 'Oh my lord, we came indeed down at the first time to buy food. 21. And it came to pass, when we came to the lodging-place, that we opened our sacks, and, behold, every man's money was in the mouth of his sack, our money in full weight; and we have brought it back in our hand. 22. And other money have we brought down in our hand to buy food. We know not who put our money in our sacks.' 23. And he said: 'Peace be to you, fear not; your God, and the God of your father, hath given you treasure in your sacks; I had your money.' And he brought Simeon out unto them. 24. And the man brought the men into Joseph's house, and gave them water, and they washed their feet; and he gave their asses provender. 25. And they made ready the present against Joseph's coming at noon; for they heard that they should eat bread there. 26. And when Joseph came home, they brought him the present which was in their hand into the house, and bowed down to him to the earth. 27. And he asked them of their welfare, and said: 'Is your father well, the old man of whom ye spoke? Is he yet alive?' 28. And they said: 'Thy servant our father is well, he is yet alive.' And they bowed the head, and made obeisance. 29. And he lifted up his eyes, and saw Benjamin his brother, his mother's son, and said: 'Is this your youngest brother of whom ye spoke unto me?' And he said: 'God be gracious unto thee, my son.'\*vii. 30. And Joseph made haste; for his heart yearned towards his brother; and he sought where to weep; and he entered into his chamber, and wept there. 31. And he washed his face, and came out; and he refrained himself, and said: 'Set on bread.' 32. And they set on for him by himself, and for them by themselves, and for the Egyptians, that did eat with him, by themselves; because the Egyptians might not eat bread with the Hebrews; for that is an abomination

**21.** *we have brought it back.* They say this to forestall the suspicion of theft.

**22.** *we know not who put.* They emphasize their ignorance of the entire transaction.

**23.** *I had your money.* Doubtless on the instruction of Joseph, the steward reassures them that what they found in their sacks was God's gift.

**25.** *against Joseph's coming.* Here means, 'so as to be ready when Joseph arrived.' This is the old use of 'against', in the sense of 'in readiness for the time when'.

**27.** *of whom ye spoke.* Joseph carefully avoids betraying himself to his brethren.

**29.** *his mother's son.* These words augment the pathos of the situation.

**30.** *Joseph made haste.* To close the interview and to retire.

*his heart yearned toward.* Seeing his own mother's son, he felt unable to restrain his tears.

**31.** *set on bread. i.e.* let the food be served.

**32.** *for him by himself.* As an Egyptian noble he would have his food apart from his retinue, and, of course, apart from the Hebrews, who were foreigners in the eyes of the Egyptians. The Hyksos conquerors soon adopted the old Egyptian exclusiveness in intercourse with foreigners.

GENESIS XLIII, 33

unto the Egyptians. 33. And they sat before him, the first-born according to his birthright, and the youngest according to his youth; and the men marvelled one with another. 34. And portions were taken unto them from before him; but Benjamin's portion was five times so much as any of theirs. And they drank, and were merry with them.

## 44          CHAPTER XLIV

1. And he commanded the steward of his house, saying: 'Fill the men's sacks with food, as much as they can carry, and put every man's money in his sack's mouth. 2. And put my goblet, the silver goblet, in the sack's mouth of the youngest, and his corn money.' And he did according to the word that Joseph had spoken. 3. As soon as the morning was light, the men were sent away, they and their asses. 4. And when they were gone out of the city, and were not yet far off, Joseph said unto his steward: 'Up, follow after the men; and when thou dost overtake them, say unto them: Wherefore have ye rewarded evil for good? 5. Is not this it in which my lord drinketh, and whereby he indeed divineth? ye have done evil in so doing.' 6. And he overtook them, and he spoke unto them these words. 7. And they said unto him: 'Wherefore speaketh my lord such words as these? Far be it from thy servants that they should do such a thing. 8. Behold, the money, which we found in our sacks' mouths, we brought back unto thee out of the land of Canaan; how then should we steal out of thy lord's house silver

---

**33.** *the men marvelled.* How could the Egyptian know their ages? They looked at one another in astonishment.

**34.** *were merry.* lit. 'drank largely'. Joseph wishes to divert their attention from his table, whence his goblet was about to be removed. The extra portion given to Benjamin was a special mark of respect.

### CHAPTER XLIV

The chapter sets forth Joseph's device to test still further the sincerity and loyalty of his brethren.

#### 1–17. THE DIVINING CUP

**1.** *as much as they can carry.* More than they were entitled to by their purchase. This act of kindness on Joseph's part was intentional, so as to increase the apparent baseness of their conduct; see v. 4.

*put every man's money.* This was done to prevent the brethren from suspecting Benjamin of having really stolen the goblet. When they again found their money returned, they could not but believe that the goblet had in the selfsame unaccountable manner come into Benjamin's sack (Abarbanel).

**2.** *the silver goblet.* Diving goblets were much used in Egypt. Pieces of gold or silver were thrown into the water or liquid in the goblet and caused movements, which were supposed to represent coming events.

**4.** *rewarded evil for good.* Joseph's steward assumes that they are aware of the theft of this valuable and wonderful goblet.

**5.** *whereby he indeed divineth.* The cup is a sacred one, by which their host obtains oracles.

**8.** *how then should we steal?* Their argument is sound. They had brought back from Canaan the money which they had found in their sacks. Would they then think of robbing the Egyptian lord, who had treated them with so much consideration?

## GENESIS XLIV, 9

or gold? 9. With whomsoever of thy servants it be found, let him die, and we also will be my lord's bondmen.' 10. And he said: 'Now also let it be according unto your words: he with whom it is found shall be my bondman; and ye shall be blameless.' 11. Then they hastened, and took down every man his sack to the ground. and opened every man his sack. 12. And he searched, beginning at the eldest, and leaving off at the youngest; and the goblet was found in Benjamin's sack. 13. Then they rent their clothes, and laded every man his ass, and returned to the city.\*m a. 14. And Judah and his brethren came to Joseph's house, and he was yet there; and they fell before him on the ground.\*m s. 15. And Joseph said unto them: 'What deed is this that ye have done? know ye not that such a man as I will indeed divine?' 16. And Judah said: 'What shall we say unto my lord? what shall we speak? or how shall we clear ourselves? God hath found out the iniquity of thy servants; behold, we are my lord's bondmen, both we, and he also in whose hand the cup is found.' 17. And he said: 'Far be it from me that I should do so; the man in whose hand the goblet is found, he shall be my bondman; but as for you, get you up in peace unto your father.'

**9.** *let him die.* Convinced of their absolute innocence, they propose the penalty of death as the punishment to be inflicted on the thief. They add to this, slavery for all the other brothers.

**10.** The steward asks only for the guilty one to be his bondman. According to Rashi the verse means: 'Verily it should be as ye have said (for ye are all accessories, and, therefore, all guilty; but I will be more lenient) he alone with whom it is found shall be my bondman.'

**11.** *Then they hastened.* This agitated zeal wonderfully depicts their confident innocence (Procksch).

**12.** *beginning at the eldest.* To prevent suspicion of his knowledge of the affair. It is also a dramatic touch adding to the excitement of the scene described.

**13.** *then they rent their clothes.* In their grief at the thought of the loss of Benjamin, mourning him as if he were dead.

**14.** *and Judah.* Who assumes the leadership, having undertaken the responsibility of bringing Benjamin home again.

*and they fell.* The Heb. word denotes a prostration in utter despair.

**15.** *will indeed divine.* And thereby discover the thief.

**16.** *or how shall we clear ourselves? i.e.* prove our innocence; the goblet condemns us.

*God hath found out the iniquity.* The exclamation does not imply admission of that particular sin: it is the wrong done to their father and to Joseph in the olden days which is behind Judah's confession. The work of the moral regeneration of the brothers is complete.

# HAFTORAH MIKKETZ הפטרת מקץ

## I KINGS III, 15–IV, 1

### CHAPTER III

15. And Solomon awoke, and, behold, it was a dream; and he came to Jerusalem, and stood before the ark of the covenant of the Lord, and offered up burnt-offerings, and offered peace-offerings, and made a feast to all his servants. ¶ 16. Then came there two women, that were harlots, unto the king, and stood before him. 17. And the one woman said: 'Oh, my lord, I and this woman dwell in one house; and I was delivered of a child with her in the house. 18. And it came to pass the third day after I was delivered, that this woman was delivered also; and we were together; there was no stranger with us in the house, save we two in the house. 19. And this woman's child died in the night; because she overlay it. 20. And she arose at midnight, and took my son from beside me, while thy handmaid slept, and laid it in her bosom, and laid her dead child in my bosom. 21. And when I rose in the morning to give my child suck, behold, it was dead; but when I had looked well at it in the morning, behold, it was not my son, whom I did bear.' 22. And the other woman said: 'Nay; but the living is my son, and the dead is thy son.' And this said: 'No; but the dead is thy son, and the living is my son.' Thus they spoke before the king. ¶ 23. Then said the king: 'The one saith: This is my son that liveth, and thy son is the dead; and the other saith: Nay; but thy son is the dead, and my son is the living.' 24. And the king said: 'Fetch me a sword.' And they brought a sword before the king. 25. And the king said: 'Divide the living child in two, and give half to the one, and half to the other.' 26. Then spoke the woman

### CAP. III. ג

טו וַיִּקַץ שְׁלֹמֹה וְהִנֵּה חֲלוֹם וַיָּבוֹא יְרוּשָׁלַםִ וַיַּעֲמֹד ׀ לִפְנֵי ׀ אֲרוֹן בְּרִית־אֲדֹנָי וַיַּעַל עֹלוֹת וַיַּעַשׂ שְׁלָמִים וַיַּעַשׂ מִשְׁתֶּה לְכָל־עֲבָדָיו: 16 אָז תָּבֹאנָה שְׁתַּיִם נָשִׁים זֹנוֹת אֶל־הַמֶּלֶךְ וַתַּעֲמֹדְנָה לְפָנָיו: 17 וַתֹּאמֶר הָאִשָּׁה הָאַחַת בִּי אֲדֹנִי אֲנִי וְהָאִשָּׁה הַזֹּאת יֹשְׁבֹת בְּבַיִת אֶחָד וָאֵלֵד עִמָּהּ בַּבָּיִת: 18 וַיְהִי בַּיּוֹם הַשְּׁלִישִׁי לְלִדְתִּי וַתֵּלֶד גַּם־הָאִשָּׁה הַזֹּאת וַאֲנַחְנוּ יַחְדָּו 19 אֵין־זָר אִתָּנוּ בַּבַּיִת זוּלָתִי שְׁתַּיִם־אֲנַחְנוּ בַּבָּיִת: וַיָּמָת בֶּן־ כ הָאִשָּׁה הַזֹּאת לָיְלָה אֲשֶׁר שָׁכְבָה עָלָיו: וַתָּקָם בְּתוֹךְ הַלַּיְלָה וַתִּקַּח אֶת־בְּנִי מֵאֶצְלִי וַאֲמָתְךָ יְשֵׁנָה וַתַּשְׁכִּיבֵהוּ 21 בְּחֵיקָהּ וְאֶת־בְּנָהּ הַמֵּת הִשְׁכִּיבָה בְחֵיקִי: וָאָקֻם בַּבֹּקֶר לְהֵינִיק אֶת־בְּנִי וְהִנֵּה־מֵת וָאֶתְבּוֹנֵן אֵלָיו בַּבֹּקֶר וְהִנֵּה 22 לֹא־הָיָה בְנִי אֲשֶׁר יָלָדְתִּי: וַתֹּאמֶר הָאִשָּׁה הָאַחֶרֶת לֹא כִי בְּנִי הַחַי וּבְנֵךְ הַמֵּת וְזֹאת אֹמֶרֶת לֹא כִי בְּנֵךְ הַמֵּת 23 וּבְנִי הֶחָי וַתְּדַבֵּרְנָה לִפְנֵי הַמֶּלֶךְ: וַיֹּאמֶר הַמֶּלֶךְ זֹאת אֹמֶרֶת זֶה־בְּנִי הַחַי וּבְנֵךְ הַמֵּת וְזֹאת אֹמֶרֶת לֹא כִי בְּנֵךְ 24 הַמֵּת וּבְנִי הֶחָי: וַיֹּאמֶר הַמֶּלֶךְ קְחוּ לִי־חָרֶב וַיָּבִאוּ הַחֶרֶב כה לִפְנֵי הַמֶּלֶךְ: וַיֹּאמֶר הַמֶּלֶךְ גִּזְרוּ אֶת־הַיֶּלֶד הַחַי לִשְׁנָיִם 26 וּתְנוּ אֶת־הַחֲצִי לְאַחַת וְאֶת־הַחֲצִי לְאֶחָת: וַתֹּאמֶר הָאִשָּׁה

---

In both Sedrah and Haftorah, kings have dreams which are more than dreams. In the Sedrah, Joseph unravels the mystery to the Egyptian sovereign, first humbly ascribing his power of understanding to God, the Source of all wisdom. In the Haftorah, all Israel join the king in acknowledging that the wisdom which the youthful monarch possesses is of God. In the spirit of reverence, Solomon had asked not for long life or riches or honour, but for power to serve others, for an understanding heart to discharge the duties and responsibilities of his position, and to advance the welfare of the great people entrusted to him while so young and inexperienced.

**16–28.** Solomon the wise judge.

**16.** *two women*. The meanest of his subjects had access to the king for justice.

*harlots*. The word may also be translated 'innkeepers' (Ralbag).

**18.** *no stranger*. None but they could ever know the truth. Observation on the part of a judge must in a case of this nature be supplemented by extraordinary intuition.

# I KINGS III, 27

whose the living child was unto the king, for her heart yearned upon her son, and she said: 'Oh, my lord, give her the living child, and in no wise slay it.' But the other said: 'It shall be neither mine nor thine; divide it.' 27. Then the king answered and said: 'Give her the living child, and in no wise slay it: she is the mother thereof.' 28. And all Israel heard of the judgment which the king had judged; and they feared the king; for they saw that the wisdom of God was in him, to do justice.

## CHAPTER IV

1. And king Solomon was king over all Israel.

---

**27.** *she is the mother.* A Heavenly Voice (בַּת קוֹל) resounded in his ears, and told him, '*She is the mother thereof*' (Targum Jonathan, Talmud).

**28.** *heard of the judgment.* His decision arrived at by his keen-sighted appeal to the instincts of human nature, his shrewd insight into the workings of the human heart.

*they feared the king.* Revered him; or, fear possessed evil-doers because of the certainty of punishment.

## CHAPTER IV

**1.** *over all Israel.* The display of such a Divine gift of Wisdom establishes his sway over all Israel.

'To be the successor of David was a great inheritance, but a much greater responsibility. Solomon was eighteen years old when he ascended the throne. The fact that, in spite of this, he maintained his dominion for forty years under the most trying conditions, is of itself evidence of his great qualities. If David created an Israelitish nation, Solomon created an Israelitish state. He extended immensely the intellectual horizon of Israel. He placed Israel in the rank of the great nations' (Cornill).

## GENESIS XLIV, 18

**44** 18. Then Judah came near unto him, and said: Oh my lord, let thy servant, I pray thee, speak a word in my lord's ears, and let not thine anger burn against thy servant; for thou art even as Pharaoh. 19. My lord asked his servants, saying: Have ye a father, or a brother? 20. And we said unto my lord: We have a father, an old man, and a child of his old age, a little one; and his brother is dead, and he alone is left of his mother, and his father loveth him. 21. And thou saidst unto thy servants: Bring him down unto me, that I may set mine eyes upon him. 22. And we said unto my lord: The lad cannot leave his father; for if he should leave his father, his father would die. 23. And thou saidst unto thy servants: Except your youngest brother come down with you, ye shall see my face no more. 24. And it came to pass when we came up unto thy servant my father, we told him the words of my lord. 25. And our father said: Go again, buy us a little food. 26. And we said: We cannot go down; if our youngest brother be with us, then will we go down; for we may not see the man's face, except our youngest brother be with us. 27. And thy servant my father said unto us: Ye know that my wife bore me two sons; 28. and the one went out from me, and I said: Surely he is torn in pieces; and I have not seen him since; 29, and if ye take this one also from me, and harm befall him, ye

מד ס ס ס יא 11 בראשית ויגש מד

18 וַיִּגַּשׁ אֵלָיו יְהוּדָה וַיֹּאמֶר בִּי אֲדֹנִי יְדַבֶּר־נָא עַבְדְּךָ דָבָר בְּאָזְנֵי אֲדֹנִי וְאַל־יִחַר אַפְּךָ בְּעַבְדֶּךָ כִּי כָמוֹךָ כְּפַרְעֹה:
19 אֲדֹנִי שָׁאַל אֶת־עֲבָדָיו לֵאמֹר הֲיֵשׁ־לָכֶם אָב אוֹ־אָח:
כ וַנֹּאמֶר אֶל־אֲדֹנִי יֶשׁ־לָנוּ אָב זָקֵן וְיֶלֶד זְקֻנִים קָטָן וְאָחִיו
21 מֵת וַיִּוָּתֵר הוּא לְבַדּוֹ לְאִמּוֹ וְאָבִיו אֲהֵבוֹ: וַתֹּאמֶר אֶל־
22 עֲבָדֶיךָ הוֹרִדֻהוּ אֵלָי וְאָשִׂימָה עֵינִי עָלָיו: וַנֹּאמֶר אֶל־
אֲדֹנִי לֹא־יוּכַל הַנַּעַר לַעֲזֹב אֶת־אָבִיו וְעָזַב אֶת־אָבִיו וָמֵת:
23 וַתֹּאמֶר אֶל־עֲבָדֶיךָ אִם־לֹא יֵרֵד אֲחִיכֶם הַקָּטֹן אִתְּכֶם לֹא
24 תֹסִפוּן לִרְאוֹת פָּנָי: וַיְהִי כִּי עָלִינוּ אֶל־עַבְדְּךָ אָבִי וַנַּגֶּד־
כה לוֹ אֵת דִּבְרֵי אֲדֹנִי: וַיֹּאמֶר אָבִינוּ שֻׁבוּ שִׁבְרוּ־לָנוּ מְעַט־
26 אֹכֶל: וַנֹּאמֶר לֹא נוּכַל לָרֶדֶת אִם־יֵשׁ אָחִינוּ הַקָּטֹן אִתָּנוּ
וְיָרַדְנוּ כִּי־לֹא נוּכַל לִרְאוֹת פְּנֵי הָאִישׁ וְאָחִינוּ הַקָּטֹן
27 אֵינֶנּוּ אִתָּנוּ: וַיֹּאמֶר עַבְדְּךָ אָבִי אֵלֵינוּ אַתֶּם יְדַעְתֶּם כִּי
28 שְׁנַיִם יָלְדָה־לִּי אִשְׁתִּי: וַיֵּצֵא הָאֶחָד מֵאִתִּי וָאֹמַר אַךְ
29 טָרֹף טֹרָף וְלֹא רְאִיתִיו עַד־הֵנָּה: וּלְקַחְתֶּם גַּם־אֶת־זֶה

## XI. VAYYIGGASH

(CHAPTERS XLIV, 18–XLVII, 27)

### CHAPTER XLIV

**18–34.** The pathos and beauty of Judah's plea on behalf of Benjamin have retained their appeal to man's heart throughout the ages. Sir Walter Scott called it 'the most complete pattern of genuine natural eloquence extant in any language. When we read this generous speech, we forgive Judah all the past, and cannot refuse to say "Thou art he whom thy brethren shall praise"'. The spirit of self-sacrifice which Judah's speech reveals, offering to remain as a slave in Benjamin's place, has its parallel in the life-story of Moses, who besought God to blot out his name from the Book of Life, unless his people, Israel, is saved with him (Exod. XXXII, 32).

**18.** *came near.* Not in fear, but conscious of the vital issues at stake. Benjamin's servitude would involve the death of Jacob and the shame of Judah.

*speak a word.* He asks pardon for venturing to continue the conversation after Joseph had decided their case. Just because Joseph is like Pharaoh in authority, it behoves him to listen to the appeal which Judah is about the make.

**19.** *my lord asked.* See XLIII, 7. Judah wishes to divert the sympathy of Joseph towards the unhappy position of the old father bereft of his youngest son, whom Judah refers to as 'a child of his old age, a little one'.

**20.** *his brother is dead.* Joseph is now spoken of before his eleven brethren as dead. Dead, but still remembered by father and brothers.

**28.** *torn in pieces; and I have not seen him since.* Joseph now learns the manner of his supposed death. Do these last words imply a lurking disbelief in Jacob's mind as to the story of Joseph's death? Perhaps they give expression to Jacob's unquenchable longing for his beloved Joseph. The words must have touched the very core of Joseph's heart.

## GENESIS XLIV, 30

will bring down my gray hairs with sorrow to the grave. 30. Now therefore when I come to thy servant my father, and the lad is not with us; seeing that his soul is bound up with the lad's soul;* 11· 31. it will come to pass, when he seeth that the lad is not with us, that he will die; and thy servants will bring down the gray hairs of thy servant our father with sorrow to the grave. 32. For thy servant became surety for the lad unto my father, saying: If I bring him not unto thee, then shall I bear the blame to my father for ever. 33. Now therefore, let thy servant, I pray thee, abide instead of the lad a bondman to my lord; and let the lad go up with his brethren. 34. For how shall I go up to my father, if the lad be not with me? lest I look upon the evil that shall come on my father.'

## 45    CHAPTER XLV

1. Then Joseph could not refrain himself before all them that stood by him; and he cried: 'Cause every man to go out from me.' And there stood no man with him, while Joseph made himself known unto his brethren. 2. And he wept aloud; and the Egyptians heard, and the house of Pharaoh heard. 3. And Joseph said unto his brethren: 'I am Joseph; doth my father yet live?' And his brethren could not answer him; for they were affrighted at his presence. 4. And Joseph said unto his brethren: 'Come near to me, I pray you.' And they came near. And he said: 'I am Joseph your brother, whom ye sold into Egypt. 5. And now be not grieved, nor angry with yourselves, that ye sold

---

**30.** *his soul is bound up with the lad's soul.* The same phrase is used of the intertwined souls of David and Jonathan, I Sam. XVIII, 1. The beauty and conciseness of the three Hebrew words cannot be reproduced in translation.

**31.** *with sorrow to the grave.* The skilful repetition of the phrase by Judah is poignantly pathetic.

**33.** *abide instead of the lad a bondman.* Judah became surety (*v.* 32) and now offers himself as a substitute. He prefers bondage to freedom, so as to save his brother. He once saw the anguish of his old father when Joseph was gone; he cannot endure to see a repetition.

### CHAPTER XLV. JOSEPH REVEALS HIMSELF

**1.** *could not refrain himself.* The repeated references to the misfortune of his aged father overwhelm him; and as he does not wish his retinue to hear of the old crime of his brethren, he orders every man to depart. He is now alone with his eleven brothers. There is no interpreter present, and Joseph uses the language of his brethren.

**2.** *wept aloud.* lit. 'gave forth his voice in weeping'.

*the house of Pharaoh heard.* From the retinue of Joseph. The news of the coming of Joseph's brethren travelled fast.

**3.** *doth my father yet live?* The question seems to ask, 'Is it really true that our father, so old, so sorely tried, is still alive?' The wonder of it seems to urge the question from Joseph's lips as the first word in revealing himself to his brethren. The thought of his father is uppermost in his mind. He does not wait for an answer.

*they were affrighted.* Consternation made them dumb. They do not believe their eyes and ears.

**4.** *come near to me.* The better to convince themselves.

**5.** *be not grieved.* 'With singular generosity Joseph reassures them by pointing out the Providential purpose which had overruled their crime for good' (Skinner).

# GENESIS XLV, 6

בראשית ויגש מה

6 אֱלֹהִים לִפְנֵיכֶם: כִּי־זֶה שְׁנָתַיִם הָרָעָב בְּקֶרֶב הָאָרֶץ וֹחַר בְּעֵינֵיכֶם כִּי־מְכַרְתֶּם אֹתִי הֵנָּה כִּי לְמִחְיָה שְׁלָחַנִי

7 וְעוֹד חָמֵשׁ שָׁנִים אֲשֶׁר אֵין־חָרִישׁ וְקָצִיר: וַיִּשְׁלָחֵנִי אֱלֹהִים לִפְנֵיכֶם לָשׂוּם לָכֶם שְׁאֵרִית בָּאָרֶץ וּלְהַחֲיוֹת לָכֶם שלישי

8 לִפְלֵיטָה גְּדֹלָה: וְעַתָּה לֹא־אַתֶּם שְׁלַחְתֶּם אֹתִי הֵנָּה כִּי הָאֱלֹהִים וַיְשִׂימֵנִי לְאָב לְפַרְעֹה וּלְאָדוֹן לְכָל־בֵּיתוֹ וּמֹשֵׁל

9 בְּכָל־אֶרֶץ מִצְרָיִם: מַהֲרוּ וַעֲלוּ אֶל־אָבִי וַאֲמַרְתֶּם אֵלָיו כֹּה אָמַר בִּנְךָ יוֹסֵף שָׂמַנִי אֱלֹהִים לְאָדוֹן לְכָל־מִצְרָיִם

10 רְדָה אֵלַי אַל־תַּעֲמֹד: וְיָשַׁבְתָּ בְאֶרֶץ־גֹּשֶׁן וְהָיִיתָ קָרוֹב אֵלַי אַתָּה וּבָנֶיךָ וּבְנֵי בָנֶיךָ וְצֹאנְךָ וּבְקָרְךָ וְכָל־אֲשֶׁר־לָךְ:

11 וְכִלְכַּלְתִּי אֹתְךָ שָׁם כִּי־עוֹד חָמֵשׁ שָׁנִים רָעָב פֶּן־תִּוָּרֵשׁ

12 אַתָּה וּבֵיתְךָ וְכָל־אֲשֶׁר־לָךְ: וְהִנֵּה עֵינֵיכֶם רֹאוֹת וְעֵינֵי

13 אָחִי בִנְיָמִין כִּי־פִי הַמְדַבֵּר אֲלֵיכֶם: וְהִגַּדְתֶּם לְאָבִי אֶת־כָּל־כְּבוֹדִי בְּמִצְרַיִם וְאֵת כָּל־אֲשֶׁר רְאִיתֶם וּמִהַרְתֶּם

14 וְהוֹרַדְתֶּם אֶת־אָבִי הֵנָּה: וַיִּפֹּל עַל־צַוְּארֵי בִנְיָמִן־אָחִיו וַיֵּבְךְּ

15 וּבִנְיָמִן בָּכָה עַל־צַוָּארָיו: וַיְנַשֵּׁק לְכָל־אֶחָיו וַיֵּבְךְּ עֲלֵהֶם

16 וְאַחֲרֵי כֵן דִּבְּרוּ אֶחָיו אִתּוֹ: וְהַקֹּל נִשְׁמַע בֵּית פַּרְעֹה לֵאמֹר בָּאוּ אֲחֵי יוֹסֵף וַיִּיטַב בְּעֵינֵי פַרְעֹה וּבְעֵינֵי עֲבָדָיו:

17 וַיֹּאמֶר פַּרְעֹה אֶל־יוֹסֵף אֱמֹר אֶל־אַחֶיךָ זֹאת עֲשׂוּ טַעֲנוּ

18 אֶת־בְּעִירְכֶם וּלְכוּ־בֹאוּ אַרְצָה כְּנָעַן: וּקְחוּ אֶת־אֲבִיכֶם

---

me hither; for God did send me before you to preserve life. 6. For these two years hath the famine been in the land; and there are yet five years, in which there shall be neither plowing nor harvest. 7. And God sent me before you to give you a remnant on the earth, and to save you alive for a great deliverance.*iii. 8. So now it was not you that sent me hither, but God; and He hath made me a father to Pharaoh, and lord of all his house, and ruler over all the land of Egypt. 9. Hasten ye, and go up to my father, and say unto him: Thus saith thy son Joseph: God hath made me lord of all Egypt; come down unto me, tarry not. 10. And thou shalt dwell in the land of Goshen, and thou shalt be near unto me, thou, and thy children, and thy children's children, and thy flocks, and thy herds, and all that thou hast; 11. and there will I sustain thee; for there are yet five years of famine; lest thou come to poverty, thou, and thy household, and all that thou hast. 12. And, behold, your eyes see, and the eyes of my brother Benjamin, that it is my mouth that speaketh unto you. 13. And ye shall tell my father of all my glory in Egypt, and of all that ye have seen; and ye shall hasten and bring down my father hither.' 14. And he fell upon his brother Benjamin's neck, and wept; and Benjamin wept upon his neck. 15. And he kissed all his brethren, and wept upon them; and after that his brethren talked with him. ¶ 16. And the report thereof was heard in Pharaoh's house, saying: 'Joseph's brethren are come'; and it pleased Pharaoh well, and his servants. 17. And Pharaoh said unto Joseph: 'Say unto thy brethren: This do ye: lade your beasts, and go, get you unto the land of Canaan; 18. and take your father and your households, and come unto me; and I will give you the good of

---

*sold me hither.* i.e. caused me to be sold hither.

**7.** *a remnant.* Offspring, descendants.

**8.** *but God.* Joseph again ascribes his presence in Egypt to the intervention of God.

*a father.* Heb. *Ab*, which is the exact transliteration of an Egyptian title of state rank, corresponding to 'vizier'.

**9.** *tarry not.* The anxiety to see his father is revealed by this request.

**10.** *Goshen.* The railway from Alexandria to Suez now runs through the district where Joseph's father and family settled. It was the best pasture-land in Egypt.

*thou shalt be near unto me.* This was possibly spoken with a view of inducing Jacob to come to Egypt.

**12.** *your eyes see.* This is spoken to his dazed and still incredulous brethren.

**15.** *after that.* The brethren did not talk with him until he had shown the same fraternal love to them as he had done to Benjamin. Then they knew 'that his heart was with them' (Kimchi).

**16-20.** Pharaoh seconds Joseph's invitation and orders wagons to be sent for the conveyance of Jacob and his family.

**17.** *beasts.* Of burden.

**18.** *the good of the land.* Seems to be parallel to the next phrase, 'the fat of the land'; wherever the word *fat* is used, it means the best, the most desirable part of anything (Rashi).

GENESIS XLV, 19

the land of Egypt, and ye shall eat the fat of the land.*iv· 19. Now thou art commanded, this do ye: take your wagons out of the land of Egypt for your little ones, and for your wives, and bring your father, and come. 20. Also regard not your stuff; for the good things of all the land of Egypt are yours.' 21. And the sons of Israel did so; and Joseph gave them wagons, according to the commandment of Pharaoh, and gave them provision for the way. 22. To all of them he gave each man changes of raiment; but to Benjamin he gave three hundred shekels of silver, and five changes of raiment. 23. And to his father he sent in like manner ten asses laden with the good things of Egypt, and ten she-asses laden with corn and bread and victual for his father by the way. 24. So he sent his brethren away, and they departed; and he said unto them: 'See that ye fall not out by the way.' 25. And they went up out of Egypt, and came into the land of Canaan unto Jacob their father. 26. And they told him, saying: 'Joseph is yet alive, and he is ruler over all the land of Egypt.' And his heart fainted, for he believed them not. 27. And they told him all the words of Joseph, which he had said unto them; and when he saw the wagons which Joseph had sent to carry him, the spirit of Jacob their father revived.*v· 28. And Israel said: 'It is enough; Joseph my son is yet alive; I will go and see him before I die.'

## 46   CHAPTER XLVI

1. And Israel took his journey with all that he had, and came to Beer-sheba, and offered sacrifices unto the God of his father Isaac. 2. And God spoke unto Israel in the visions of the night, and said:

בראשית וינש מה מו

רביעי וְאֶת־בָּתֵּיכֶם וּבֹאוּ אֵלָי וְאֶתְּנָה לָכֶם אֶת־טוּב אֶרֶץ מִצְרַיִם
19 וְאִכְלוּ אֶת־חֵלֶב הָאָרֶץ: וְאַתָּה צֻוֵּיתָה זֹאת עֲשׂוּ קְחוּ־
לָכֶם מֵאֶרֶץ מִצְרַיִם עֲגָלוֹת לְטַפְּכֶם וְלִנְשֵׁיכֶם וּנְשָׂאתֶם
כ אֶת־אֲבִיכֶם וּבָאתֶם: וְעֵינְכֶם אַל־תָּחֹס עַל־כְּלֵיכֶם כִּי־
21 טוּב כָּל־אֶרֶץ מִצְרַיִם לָכֶם הוּא: וַיַּעֲשׂוּ־כֵן בְּנֵי יִשְׂרָאֵל
וַיִּתֵּן לָהֶם יוֹסֵף עֲגָלוֹת עַל־פִּי פַרְעֹה וַיִּתֵּן לָהֶם צֵדָה
22 לַדָּרֶךְ: לְכֻלָּם נָתַן לָאִישׁ חֲלִפוֹת שְׂמָלֹת וּלְבִנְיָמִן נָתַן
23 שְׁלֹשׁ מֵאוֹת כֶּסֶף וְחָמֵשׁ חֲלִפֹת שְׂמָלֹת: וּלְאָבִיו שָׁלַח
כְּזֹאת עֲשָׂרָה חֲמֹרִים נֹשְׂאִים מִטּוּב מִצְרָיִם וְעֶשֶׂר אֲתֹנֹת
24 נֹשְׂאֹת בָּר וָלֶחֶם וּמָזוֹן לְאָבִיו לַדָּרֶךְ: וַיְשַׁלַּח אֶת־אֶחָיו
כה וַיֵּלֵכוּ וַיֹּאמֶר אֲלֵהֶם אַל־תִּרְגְּזוּ בַּדָּרֶךְ: וַיַּעֲלוּ מִמִּצְרָיִם
26 וַיָּבֹאוּ אֶרֶץ כְּנַעַן אֶל־יַעֲקֹב אֲבִיהֶם: וַיַּגִּדוּ לוֹ לֵאמֹר עוֹד
יוֹסֵף חַי וְכִי־הוּא מֹשֵׁל בְּכָל־אֶרֶץ מִצְרָיִם וַיָּפָג לִבּוֹ כִּי לֹא־
27 הֶאֱמִין לָהֶם: וַיְדַבְּרוּ אֵלָיו אֵת כָּל־דִּבְרֵי יוֹסֵף אֲשֶׁר דִּבֶּר
חמישי אֲלֵהֶם וַיַּרְא אֶת־הָעֲגָלוֹת אֲשֶׁר־שָׁלַח יוֹסֵף לָשֵׂאת אֹתוֹ
28 וַתְּחִי רוּחַ יַעֲקֹב אֲבִיהֶם: וַיֹּאמֶר יִשְׂרָאֵל רַב עוֹד־יוֹסֵף
בְּנִי חָי אֵלְכָה וְאֶרְאֶנּוּ בְּטֶרֶם אָמוּת:

CAP. XLVI. מו מו

א וַיִּסַּע יִשְׂרָאֵל וְכָל־אֲשֶׁר־לוֹ וַיָּבֹא בְּאֵרָה שָּׁבַע וַיִּזְבַּח זְבָחִים

---
מח׳ v. 25. סבירין ארצה

---

**19.** *now thou art commanded, this do ye.* The phrase is elliptical, it means: 'Now thou art commanded by me to tell them, this do ye' (Rashi).

**20.** *also regard not your stuff.* They would have to leave much of their property in the land of Canaan, and would be able to transport only part of their movable property, but they should pay no regard to this.
*for the good things of all the land of Egypt are yours.* Thus Jacob and his family came to Egypt at the express invitation of the king. There was even a promise of good treatment to the immigrants as guests of the State, which one of their family had saved. As free men they were subsequently entitled to return at their pleasure to their old home in Canaan.

**21.** *according to the commandment of Pharaoh.* i.e. provided by the king.

**24.** *fall not out by the way.* This is usually interpreted as meaning, 'Do not quarrel owing to mutual recriminations.'

**26.** *his heart fainted.* i.e. his heart stood still, unable to beat for astonishment.
*for he believed them not.* The news was too good to be true.

**28.** *it is enough.* 'What care I for all his glory? Joseph, my son, is still alive!'

CHAPTER XLVI. JACOB'S JOURNEY TO EGYPT

**1.** *came to Beer-sheba.* From Hebron, to offer sacrifice where God had appeared to Abraham. Jacob desired God's sanction, prior to his leaving the land of Promise.
*his father Isaac.* Who had built the altar and fixed his home at Beer-sheba.

172

GENESIS XLVI, 3

'Jacob, Jacob.' And he said: 'Here am I.'
3. And He said: 'I am God, the God of thy father; fear not to go down into Egypt; for I will there make of thee a great nation. 4. I will go down with thee into Egypt; and I will also surely bring thee up again; and Joseph shall put his hand upon thine eyes.' 5. And Jacob rose up from Beer-sheba; and the sons of Israel carried Jacob their father, and their little ones, and their wives, in the wagons which Pharaoh had sent to carry him. 6. And they took their cattle, and their goods, which they had gotten in the land of Canaan, and came into Egypt, Jacob, and all his seed with him; 7. his sons, and his sons' sons with him, his daughters, and his sons' daughters, and all his seed brought he with him into Egypt. ¶ 8. And these are the names of the children of Israel, who came into Egypt, Jacob and his sons: Reuben, Jacob's first-born. 9. And the sons of Reuben: Hanoch, and Pallu, and Hezron, and Carmi. 10. And the sons of Simeon: Jemuel, and Jamin, and Ohad, and Jachin, and Zohar, and Shaul the son of a Canaanitish woman. 11. And the sons of Levi: Gershon, Kohath, and Merari. 12. And the sons of Judah: Er, and Onan, and Shelah, and Perez, and Zerah; but Er and Onan died in the land of Canaan. And the sons of Perez were Hezron and Hamul. 13. And the sons of Issachar: Tola, and Puvah, and Iob, and Shimron. 14. And the sons of Zebulun: Sered, and Elon, and Jahleel. 15. These are the son of Leah, whom she bore unto

בראשית ויגש מו

2 לֵאלֹהֵי אָבִיו יִצְחָק: וַיֹּאמֶר אֱלֹהִים ׀ לְיִשְׂרָאֵל בְּמַרְאֹת
3 הַלַּיְלָה וַיֹּאמֶר יַעֲקֹב ׀ יַעֲקֹב וַיֹּאמֶר הִנֵּנִי: וַיֹּאמֶר אָנֹכִי
הָאֵל אֱלֹהֵי אָבִיךָ אַל־תִּירָא מֵרְדָה מִצְרַיְמָה כִּי־לְגוֹי גָּדוֹל
4 אֲשִֽׂימְךָ שָֽׁם: אָנֹכִי אֵרֵד עִמְּךָ מִצְרַיְמָה וְאָנֹכִי אַעַלְךָ
ה גַם־עָלֹה וְיוֹסֵף יָשִׁית יָדוֹ עַל־עֵינֶיךָ: וַיָּקָם יַעֲקֹב מִבְּאֵר
שָׁבַע וַיִּשְׂאוּ בְנֵי־יִשְׂרָאֵל אֶת־יַעֲקֹב אֲבִיהֶם וְאֶת־טַפָּם
וְאֶת־נְשֵׁיהֶם בָּעֲגָלוֹת אֲשֶׁר־שָׁלַח פַּרְעֹה לָשֵׂאת אֹתוֹ:
6 וַיִּקְחוּ אֶת־מִקְנֵיהֶם וְאֶת־רְכוּשָׁם אֲשֶׁר רָכְשׁוּ בְּאֶרֶץ כְּנַעַן
7 וַיָּבֹאוּ מִצְרָיְמָה יַעֲקֹב וְכָל־זַרְעוֹ אִתּוֹ: בָּנָיו וּבְנֵי בָנָיו אִתּוֹ
בְּנֹתָיו וּבְנוֹת בָּנָיו וְכָל־זַרְעוֹ הֵבִיא אִתּוֹ מִצְרָיְמָה: ס
8 וְאֵלֶּה שְׁמוֹת בְּנֵי־יִשְׂרָאֵל הַבָּאִים מִצְרַיְמָה יַעֲקֹב וּבָנָיו
9 בְּכֹר יַעֲקֹב רְאוּבֵן: וּבְנֵי רְאוּבֵן חֲנוֹךְ וּפַלּוּא וְחֶצְרֹן וְכַרְמִי:
י וּבְנֵי שִׁמְעוֹן יְמוּאֵל וְיָמִין וְאֹהַד וְיָכִין וְצֹחַר וְשָׁאוּל בֶּן־
11 הַכְּנַעֲנִית: וּבְנֵי לֵוִי גֵּרְשׁוֹן קְהָת וּמְרָרִי: וּבְנֵי יְהוּדָה עֵר
12 וְאוֹנָן וְשֵׁלָה וָפֶרֶץ וָזָרַח וַיָּמָת עֵר וְאוֹנָן בְּאֶרֶץ כְּנַעַן וַיִּהְיוּ בְנֵי־
13 פֶרֶץ חֶצְרֹן וְחָמוּל: וּבְנֵי יִשָּׂשכָר תּוֹלָע וּפֻוָּה וְיוֹב וְשִׁמְרֹן:
14 וּבְנֵי זְבֻלוּן סֶרֶד וְאֵלוֹן וְיַחְלְאֵל: אֵלֶּה ׀ בְּנֵי לֵאָה אֲשֶׁר יָלְדָה
טו

---

**2.** *in the visions of the night.* In a dream.

**3.** *fear not to go down.* Isaac had intended to migrate to Egypt, but God had forbidden it. Now permission is granted to Jacob. 'It was a sleepless night in which God brought the peace of certainty to the aged man whose being had been stirred to its foundations. We should feel with the Patriarch that we are at the turning-point of his history, which we to-day may well call a turning-point in the history of mankind. It was in Egypt that Israel's greatest religious genius was to arise' (Procksch).

**4.** *I will go down with thee.* God's words here imply His promise to protect Jacob in Egypt and to achieve the Divine will concerning him and his offspring (cf. XXVIII, 15).

*bring thee up again.* i.e. thy descendants. Some commentators explain the phrase as referring to the burial of Jacob, L, 13 (Rashi and Kimchi).

*put his hand upon thine eyes.* At thy death; it is customary that the living do this to the dead (Ibn Ezra).

**5.** *Pharaoh had sent to carry him.* This is repeated with a view of showing how Pharaoh had invited the family of Jacob to come to Egypt.

**7.** *his daughters.* Includes the daughters-in-law.
*all his seed.* i.e. his great-grandchildren.

**8–27.** The list of Jacob's descendants who came into Egypt. Compare the lists in Num. XXVI and I Chron. II–VIII, which show slight variations in the forms of the names.

**10.** *Jachin.* For this name in Solomon's Temple, see I Kings VII, 21.
*a Canaanitish woman.* Luzzatto explains that she was the daughter of Dinah, and because of her father, Shechem, she is called a 'Canaanite woman'.

**15.** *thirty and three.* This number included Jacob, see v. 8. The actual number of the descendants of Jacob in v. 9–14 is thirty-two. The Rabbis add Jochebed, the daughter of Levi, who was born exactly at the time of the entrance into Egypt.

173

## GENESIS XLVI, 16

Jacob in Paddan-aram, with his daughter Dinah; all the souls of his sons and his daughters were thirty and three. 16. And the sons of Gad: Ziphion, and Haggi, Shuni, and Ezbon, Eri, and Arodi, and Areli. 17. And the sons of Asher: Imnah, and Ishvah, and Ishvi, and Beriah, and Serah their sister; and the sons of Beriah: Heber, and Malchiel. 18. These are the sons of Zilpah, whom Laban gave to Leah his daughter, and these she bore unto Jacob, even sixteen souls. 19. The sons of Rachel Jacob's wife; Joseph and Benjamin. 20. And unto Joseph in the land of Egypt were born Manasseh and Ephraim, whom Asenath the daughter of Poti-phera priest of On bore unto him. 21. And the sons of Benjamin: Bela, and Becher, and Ashbel, Gera, and Naaman, Ehi, and Rosh, Muppim, and Huppim, and Ard. 22. These are the sons of Rachel, who were born to Jacob; all the souls were fourteen. 23. And the sons of Dan: Hushim. 24. And the sons of Naphtali: Jahzeel, and Guni, and Jezer, and Shillem. 25. These are the sons of Bilhah, whom Laban gave unto Rachel his daughter, and these she bore unto Jacob; all the souls were seven. 26. All the souls belonging to Jacob that came into Egypt, that came out of his loins, besides Jacob's sons' wives, all the souls were threescore and six. 27. And the sons of Joseph, who were born to him in Egypt, were two souls; all the souls of the house of Jacob, that came into Egypt, were threescore and ten*vi. ¶ 28. And he sent Judah before him unto Joseph, to show the way before him unto Goshen; and they came into the land of Goshen. 29. And Joseph made ready his chariot, and went up to meet Israel his father, to Goshen; and he presented himself unto him, and fell on his neck, and wept on his neck a good while. 30. And Israel said unto Joseph: 'Now let me die, since I have seen thy face, that thou art yet alive.'

---

**21.** *Naaman.* Is here one of the sons of Benjamin, but in Num. XXVI, 40, the same name occurs as that of a grandson. Ibn Ezra suggests that the same name is applied to two different persons. The supposed difficulty of Benjamin having sons and grandsons when coming to Egypt, and at the same time being referred to as 'a little one' (XLIV, 20), is to be explained by comparing Jacob's age with that of Benjamin, his youngest son.

**26.** *threescore and six.* The descendants of Leah numbered 33, of Zilpah 16, of Rachel 14, and of Bilhah 7. The sum of these figures gives a total of 70; but if Jacob, Joseph, and his two sons be excluded, the result is 66.

**28.** *to show the way.* For Joseph to direct Judah as to the place where Jacob should dwell. The Midrash explains the Heb. phrase literally, 'to establish a house of teaching.' Such has remained the first care of Jews whenever migrating to a new land—to provide for the religious teaching of their children.

**29.** *a good while.* i.e. at first neither of them can speak, being overpowered by emotion.

**30.** *now let me die.* Having once more seen Joseph, there was nothing more for him to live for. He had attained the highest joy in life.

## GENESIS XLVI, 31

31. And Joseph said unto his brethren, and unto his father's house: 'I will go up, and tell Pharaoh, and will say unto him: My brethren, and my father's house, who were in the land of Canaan, are come unto me; 32. and the men are shepherds, for they have been keepers of cattle; and they have brought their flocks, and their herds, and all that they have. 33. And it shall come to pass, when Pharaoh shall call you, and shall say: What is your occupation? 34. that ye shall say: Thy servants have been keepers of cattle from our youth even until now, both we, and our fathers; that ye may dwell in the land of Goshen; for every shepherd is an abomination unto the Egyptians.'

## 47 CHAPTER XLVII

1. Then Joseph went in and told Pharaoh, and said: 'My father and my brethren, and their flocks, and their herds, and all that they have, are come out of the land of Canaan; and, behold, they are in the land of Goshen.' 2. And from among his brethren he took five men, and presented them unto Pharaoh. 3. And Pharaoh said unto his brethren: 'What is your occupation?' And they said unto Pharaoh: 'Thy servants are shepherds, both we, and our fathers.' 4. And they said unto Pharaoh: 'To sojourn in the land are we come; for there is no pasture for thy servants' flocks; for the famine is sore in the land of Canaan. Now therefore, we pray thee, let thy servants dwell in the land of Goshen.' 5. And Pharaoh spoke unto Joseph, saying: 'Thy father and thy brethren are come unto thee; 6. the land of Egypt is before thee; in the best of the land make thy father and thy brethren to dwell; in the land of Goshen let them dwell. And if thou knowest any able men among them, then make them rulers over my cattle.' 7. And Joseph brought in Jacob his father, and set him before Pharaoh. And Jacob blessed

**34.** *every shepherd*. The Hyksos, or alien Shepherd-kings, thus seem to have acquired the native Egyptian dislike of foreigners in general and herdsmen in particular.

### CHAPTER XLVII, 1-10. JACOB AND HIS SONS BEFORE PHARAOH

This is the crucial test of Joseph's character. For the Viceroy of Egypt to acknowledge as his own brothers the rude Canaanite shepherds, who had besides given him every reason for repudiating them, called for the highest loyalty and devotion. 'Many men resist the temptations of youth, and attain to positions of eminence, and then fail to pay the debt which they owe to their own humble kinsmen who have helped them to success. With Joseph the debt, if any, was small. There was also no absolute necessity of revealing his identity, much less of inviting his uncouth kinsmen to the land of Egypt. His action, therefore, shows a simple nobility of character rarely equalled in the past or present' (C. F. Kent).

**6.** *the best of the land*. Is to be placed at their disposal. This was Pharaoh's gratitude to Joseph for his eminent services to Egypt.

*make them rulers over my cattle*. A further sign of the king's gratitude. Joseph's relatives are to be appointed royal officers, superintendents of the king's herdsmen.

**7-11.** Joseph presents his father to the king.

## GENESIS XLVII, 8

Pharaoh. 8. And Pharaoh said unto Jacob: 'How many are the days of the years of thy life?' 9. And Jacob said unto Pharaoh: 'The days of the years of my sojournings are a hundred and thirty years; few and evil have been the days of the years of my life, and they have not attained unto the days of the years of the life of my fathers in the days of their sojournings.' 10. And Jacob blessed Pharaoh, and went out from the presence of Pharaoh.* ⁷ⁱⁱ· 11. And Joseph placed his father and his brethren, and gave them a possession in the land of Egypt, in the best of the land, in the land of Rameses, as Pharaoh had commanded. 12. And Joseph sustained his father, and his brethren, and all his father's household, with bread, according to the want of their little ones. ¶ 13. And there was no bread in all the land; for the famine was very sore, so that the land of Egypt and the land of Canaan languished by reason of the famine. 14. And Joseph gathered up all the money that was found in the land of Egypt, and in the land of Canaan, for the corn which they bought; and Joseph brought the money into Pharaoh's house. 15. And when the money was all spent in the land of Egypt, and in the land of Canaan, all the Egyptians came unto Joseph, and said: 'Give us bread; for why should we die in thy presence? for our money faileth.' 16. And Joseph said: 'Give your cattle, and I will give you [bread] for your cattle, if money fail.' 17. And they brought their cattle unto Joseph. And Joseph gave them bread in exchange for the horses, and for the flocks. and for the herds, and for the asses; and he fed them with bread in exchange for all

---

**7.** *set him.* Or, 'presented him.'

*Jacob blessed Pharaoh.* The aged Patriarch asks the blessing of God for the king who had befriended his beloved son.

**9.** *sojournings.* Jacob does not say 'my life'. 'All the days of my life I have been a sojourner' (Rashi). To the Patriarch this earthly life is but a pilgrimage, the real life is Beyond. ; cf. Ps. xxxix, 13.

*few and evil.* 'Few', as compared with the long life of his father and grandfather; 'evil,' sad or unhappy.

**11.** *and Joseph placed.* Or, 'settled.'

*in the land of Rameses.* i.e. the district round the town Rameses. This town is mentioned in Ex. I, 11. Its name was given to it in the reign of Rameses II, who is held by some to be the Pharaoh of the Oppression.

**12.** *sustained.* Supported.

**13–27.** The famine in Egypt.

**13.** *in all the land.* lit. 'in all the earth'.

*languished.* Dean Stanley recalls the descriptions of similar famines in Egypt, which enable us to realize the calamity from which Joseph delivered the country. 'The eating of human flesh became so common as to excite no surprise,' writes a medieval eye-witness of one of these famines; 'the road between Syria and Egypt was like a vast field sown with human bodies.'

**14.** *Pharaoh's house.* i.e. the royal treasury.

**15.** *faileth.* lit. 'is at an end.'

**16.** *for your cattle.* In exchange for your cattle.

**17.** *horses.* As articles of luxury, the horses are mentioned first.

**18.** *the second year.* The year following the year after the five years, *i.e.* the seventh year (Luzzatto).

## GENESIS XLVII, 18

their cattle for that year. 18. And when that year was ended, they came unto him the second year, and said unto him: 'We will not hide from my lord, how that our money is all spent; and the herds of cattle are my lord's; there is nought left in the sight of my lord, but our bodies, and our lands. 19. Wherefore should we die before thine eyes, both we and our land? buy us and our land for bread, and we and our land will be bondmen unto Pharaoh; and give us seed, that we may live, and not die, and that the land be not desolate.' 20. So Joseph bought all the land of Egypt for Pharaoh; for the Egyptians sold every man his field, because the famine was sore upon them; and the land became Pharaoh's. 21. And as for the people, he removed them city by city, from one end of the border of Egypt even to the other end thereof. 22. Only the land of the priests bought he not, for the priests had a portion from Pharaoh, and did eat their portion which Pharaoh gave them; wherefore they sold not their land. 23. Then Joseph said unto the people: 'Behold, I have bought you this day and your land for Pharaoh. Lo, here is seed for you, and ye shall sow the land. 24. And it shall come to pass at the ingatherings, that ye shall give a fifth unto Pharaoh, and four parts shall be your own, for seed of the field, and for your food, and for them of your households, and for food for your little ones.'* m. 25. And they said: 'Thou hast saved our lives. Let us find favour in the sight of my lord, and we will be Pharaoh's bondmen.' 26. And Joseph made it a statute concerning the land of Egypt unto this day, that Pharaoh should have the fifth; only the land of the priests alone became not Pharaoh's. 27. And Israel dwelt in the land of Egypt, in the land of Goshen; and they got them possessions therein, and were fruitful, and multiplied exceedingly.

---

*our bodies, and our lands.* Which they offer in exchange for bread.

**19.** *both we and our land.* 'The old feudal nobility of Egypt disappeared in the Hyksos period, and from the time of the eighteenth Dynasty onward we find the land, which had formerly been held by local proprietors, belonging either to the Pharaoh or to the temples. At the same time public granaries make their appearance, the superintendent of which became one of the most important of Egyptian officials' (Sayce).

*seed.* See v. 23.

**20.** *bought all the land of Egypt.* In this manner Pharaoh became the feudal lord of all Egypt.

**21.** *city by city.* The cities became depots for facilitating the distribution of food.

**22.** *only the land of the priests.* The priests had a fixed portion from the royal granaries; so there was no occasion for them to sell their lands.

**24.** *a fifth.* This tax was not excessive. The Jews, in the time of the Maccabees, paid the Syrian government one-third of the seed (I Macc. x, 30).

**25.** *Pharaoh's bondmen.* To pay the tax as ordained (Rashi).

**26.** *unto this day.* In the days of Moses, the arrangement described was still in force.

**27.** *got them possessions.* Acquired property by purchase (Kimchi).

# HAFTORAH VAYYIGGASH   הפטרת ויגש

### EZEKIEL XXXVII, 15–28

#### CHAPTER XXXVII

15. And the word of the LORD came unto me, saying: 16. 'And thou, son of man, take thee one stick, and write upon it: For Judah, and for the children of Israel his companions; then take another stick, and write upon it: For Joseph, the stick of Ephraim, and of all the house of Israel his companions; 17. and join them for thee one to another into one stick, that they may become one in thy hand. 18. And when the children of thy people shall speak unto thee, saying: Wilt thou not tell us what thou meanest by these? 19. say unto them: Thus saith the Lord GOD: Behold, I will take the stick of Joseph, which is in the hand of Ephraim, and the tribes of Israel his companions; and I will put them unto him together with the stick of Judah, and make them one stick, and they shall be one in My hand. 20. And the sticks whereon thou writest shall be in thy hand before their eyes. 21. And say unto them: Thus saith the Lord GOD: Behold, I will take the children of Israel from among the nations, whither they are gone, and will gather them on every side, and bring them into their own land; 22. and I will make them one nation in the land, upon the mountains of Israel, and one king shall be king to them all; and they shall be no more two nations, neither shall they be divided into two kingdoms any more at all; 23. neither shall

---

Ezekiel, the son of a priest, was among those who were carried off into exile in Babylon. He became one of the spiritual agencies that kept Israel's soul alive in those years of despair. He is at once priest and prophet, preacher and writer, inspirer of the nation and pastor of individual souls. A characteristic feature of his teaching is his insistence on *individual responsibility*. He is the great preacher of Repentance, and of the Divine Forgiveness to those who in sincerity seek God's pardon. 'When the wicked man turneth away from his wickedness that he hath committed, and doeth that which is lawful and right, he shall save his soul alive.' When the members of the House of Israel shall thus be purified, Israel would be restored, and become a Holy People amid whom God would be seen to dwell.

More than any other Prophet, Ezekiel makes vivid use of allegory, symbol and parable to illustrate his message. The first half of this chapter (*v*. 1–14) is his Vision of the Valley of Dry Bones. The Prophet sees the nation dead, as it were, with all fires extinct in the dreary winter of Exile; and then beholds Israel revived through the Spirit of Prophecy, rising to renewed life and glory. In the second half of the chapter, *v*, 15–28, which constitutes our Haftorah, the Prophet pictures the continuation of this national resurrection by the definite announcement of the reunion of the two kingdoms of Judah and Joseph (the Northern Kingdom of Israel). This is symbolized by the union of the two sticks and is a reflex of the picture given in the Sedrah, of Joseph and his Brethren united after long years of estrangement.

**16.** The symbolic action of the Prophet is intended to secure attention to his message. One stick, to represent the Kingdom of Judah (two tribes); the other, to represent the Kingdom of Israel (ten tribes). As here, the latter kingdom is often called Ephraim (the name of one of the two sons of Joseph).

**18–22.** The people ask the meaning of Ezekiel's action, which is the reunion of the two kingdoms into one, as they were under Saul, David and Solomon.

## EZEKIEL XXXVII, 24

they defile themselves any more with their idols, nor with their detestable things, nor with any of their transgressions; but I will save them out of all their dwelling-places, wherein they have sinned, and will cleanse them; so shall they be My people, and I will be their God. 24. And My servant David shall be king over them, and they all shall have one shepherd; they shall also walk in Mine ordinances, and observe My statutes, and do them. 25. And they shall dwell in the land that I have given unto Jacob My servant, wherein your fathers dwelt; and they shall dwell therein, they, and their children, and their children's children, for ever; and David My servant shall be their prince for ever. 26. Moreover I will make a covenant of peace with them— it shall be an everlasting covenant with them; and I will establish them, and multiply them, and will set My sanctuary in the midst of them for ever. 27. My dwelling-place also shall be over them; and I will be their God, and they shall be My people. 28. And the nations shall know that I am the LORD that sanctify Israel, when My sanctuary shall be in the midst of them for ever.'

יחזקאל לז

23 עוֹד: וְלֹא יִטַּמְּאוּ עוֹד בְּגִלּוּלֵיהֶם וּבְשִׁקּוּצֵיהֶם וּבְכֹל פִּשְׁעֵיהֶם וְהוֹשַׁעְתִּי אֹתָם מִכֹּל מוֹשְׁבֹתֵיהֶם אֲשֶׁר חָטְאוּ בָהֶם וְטִהַרְתִּי אוֹתָם וְהָיוּ־לִי לְעָם וַאֲנִי אֶהְיֶה לָהֶם
24 לֵאלֹהִים: וְעַבְדִּי דָוִד מֶלֶךְ עֲלֵיהֶם וְרוֹעֶה אֶחָד יִהְיֶה
25 לְכֻלָּם וּבְמִשְׁפָּטַי יֵלֵכוּ וְחֻקּוֹתַי יִשְׁמְרוּ וְעָשׂוּ אוֹתָם: וְיָשְׁבוּ עַל־הָאָרֶץ אֲשֶׁר נָתַתִּי לְעַבְדִּי לְיַעֲקֹב אֲשֶׁר יָשְׁבוּ־בָהּ אֲבוֹתֵיכֶם וְיָשְׁבוּ עָלֶיהָ הֵמָּה וּבְנֵיהֶם וּבְנֵי בְנֵיהֶם עַד־
26 עוֹלָם וְדָוִד עַבְדִּי נָשִׂיא לָהֶם לְעוֹלָם: וְכָרַתִּי לָהֶם בְּרִית שָׁלוֹם בְּרִית עוֹלָם יִהְיֶה אוֹתָם וּנְתַתִּים וְהִרְבֵּיתִי אוֹתָם
27 וְנָתַתִּי אֶת־מִקְדָּשִׁי בְּתוֹכָם לְעוֹלָם: וְהָיָה מִשְׁכָּנִי עֲלֵיהֶם
28 וְהָיִיתִי לָהֶם לֵאלֹהִים וְהֵמָּה יִהְיוּ־לִי לְעָם: וְיָדְעוּ הַגּוֹיִם כִּי אֲנִי יְהֹוָה מְקַדֵּשׁ אֶת־יִשְׂרָאֵל בִּהְיוֹת מִקְדָּשִׁי בְּתוֹכָם לְעוֹלָם:

**23.** The result is not merely political reunion, but spiritual regeneration. Israel united—but united in a return to God and in faithful performance of His Law. Then would they deserve the name of 'God's People'.

**24.** *David. i.e.* the ideal ruler in the future kingdom; one who, like David, would be the leader in the Messianic time.

**27.** The Shechinah (שכינה). God's Divine Presence will be clearly among them when they are true to their vocation as a Holy People. And thus too will Israel be the means of revealing God to the nations.

## GENESIS XLVII, 28

**47** 28. And Jacob lived in the land of Egypt seventeen years; so the days of Jacob, the years of his life, were a hundred forty and seven years. 29. And the time drew near that Israel must die; and he called his son Joseph, and said unto him: 'If now I have found favour in thy sight, put, I pray thee, thy hand under my thigh, and deal kindly and truly with me; bury me not, I pray thee, in Egypt. 30. But when I sleep with my fathers, thou shalt carry me out of Egypt, and bury me in their burying-place.' And he said: 'I will do as thou hast said.' 31. And he said: 'Swear unto me.' And he swore unto him. And Israel bowed down upon the bed's head.

**48** CHAPTER XLVIII

1. And it came to pass after these things, that one said to Joseph: 'Behold, thy father is sick.' And he took with him his two sons, Manasseh and Ephraim. 2. And one told Jacob, and said: 'Behold, thy son

## XII. VAYYECHI
(CHAPTERS XLVII, 28–L, 26)

### CHAPTER XLVII

In this concluding Sedrah of Genesis, we see the sunset of Jacob's career. We behold this storm-tossed soul on his death-bed, blessing his children. He is not afraid to die: 'I will sleep with my fathers,' he says. He is at peace with God. 'I wait for Thy salvation O LORD,' are among the last words he utters. He knows that he can never travel beyond God's care. He is at peace with man. Esau, Dinah, Joseph—what a world of strife and suffering and anguish did each of these tragedies bring him—and yet he dies blessing. Though starting as 'a plain man dwelling in tents', his is no cloistered virtue, and he certainly is no sinless being. But he possesses the rare art of extracting good from every buffeting of Destiny. He errs and he stumbles, but he ever rises again; and on the anvil of affliction his soul is forged.

**28.** *And Jacob lived.* Heb. ויחי יעקב. Of how few men, asks a famous modern Jewish preacher, can we repeat a phrase like, 'And Jacob *lived*'? When many a man dies, a death-notice appears in the Press. In reality, it is a life-notice; because but for it, the world would never have known that that man had ever been alive. Only he who has been a force for human goodness, and abides in hearts and souls made better by his presence during his pilgrimage on earth, can be said to have *lived*, only such a one is heir to immortality.

**29.** *and the time drew near.* lit. 'and the days of Israel drew near to die'. The 'days' play an important part in the story of Jacob. He lived every day; every moment counted.

*thy hand under my thigh.* See on XXIV, 2.

*kindly and truly.* Heb. ' *chesed ve-emess*'. 'Deal in true kindness with me even after my death by carrying out my wishes as regards my burial.' 'Which is the highest form of loving-kindness?' ask the Rabbis. 'The kindness shown to one who is dead,' חסד של אמת.

*bury me not, I pray thee, in Egypt.* His one thought, oftentimes repeated, was that his bones should not rest in that strange land; not in pyramid or painted chamber, but in the cell that he had digged for himself in the primitive sepulchre of his fathers (Stanley).

**30.** *but when I sleep with my fathers.* Better, *so that I sleep with my fathers.* His burial in Canaan would keep alive the wish of his descendants to return to the Promised Land.

**31.** *swear unto me.* The actual oath seems to be independent of the ceremony of placing the hand under the thigh, in *v.* 29. The oath was to enable Joseph to overcome any objections that might be raised by Pharaoh.

*bowed down upon the bed's head.* i.e. he worshipped God on the pillow of the bed. During the taking of the oath, Jacob was sitting up in bed. He now lies down again in his bed, and thanks God for the assurance given by Joseph to bury him in Canaan (Ibn Ezra, Sforno).

### CHAPTER XLVIII. EPHRAIM AND MANASSEH

**1.** *took with him his two sons.* That Jacob might bless them before his death.

Joseph cometh unto thee.' And Israel strengthened himself, and sat upon the bed. 3. And Jacob said unto Joseph: 'God Almighty appeared unto me at Luz in the land of Canaan, and blessed me, 4. and said unto me: Behold, I will make thee fruitful, and multiply thee, and I will make of thee a company of peoples; and will give this land to thy seed after thee for an everlasting possession. 5. And now thy two sons, who were born unto thee in the land of Egypt before I came unto thee into Egypt, are mine; Ephraim and Manasseh, even as Reuben and Simeon, shall be mine. 6. And thy issue, that thou begettest after them, shall be thine; they shall be called after the name of their brethren in their inheritance. 7. And as for me, when I came from Paddan, Rachel died unto me in the land of Canaan in the way, when there was still some way to come unto Ephrath; and I buried her there in the way to Ephrath—the same is Beth-lehem.' 8. And Israel beheld Joseph's sons, and said: 'Who are these?' 9. And Joseph said unto his father: 'They are my sons, whom God hath given me here.' And he said: 'Bring them, I pray thee, unto me, and I will bless them.'* 10. Now the eyes of Israel were dim for age, so that he could not see. And he brought them near unto him; and he kissed them, and embraced them. 11. And Israel said unto Joseph: 'I had not thought to see thy face; and, lo, God hath let me see thy seed also.' 12. And Joseph brought

**2.** *Israel strengthened himself.* He exerted himself and sat up, with his feet on the ground.

**3.** *God Almighty.* Heb. '*El Shaddai*'.
*Luz.* i.e. Beth-el, see XXVIII, 19.

**4.** *an everlasting possession.* In spite of temporary loss, the children of Israel have an inalienable right to the Land of Promise.

**5.** *and now.* Jacob adopts the two sons of Joseph, Ephraim and Manasseh, born before he came to Egypt, thus making them equal to any of his other sons. By giving him a double portion of his inheritance, he transferred to Joseph the rights of the true firstborn.

**6.** *called after the name of their brethren.* They will be included in the tribe of Ephraim or in the tribe of Manasseh.

**7.** *Rachel.* These words, it seems, Jacob spoke to himself; otherwise he would have said, 'thy mother.' It is to honour Rachel, the sorrow of whose loss haunts him all his life, that Jacob adopts her grandchildren as his own sons. Instead of being the mother of only two tribes, she will now be accounted the ancestress of three, her honour and esteem increasing accordingly (Herxheimer, S. R. Hirsch).

*unto me.* Or, 'to my sorrow' (RV); cf. XXXIII, 13.

**8.** *beheld.* He is on his death-bed with eyes dimmed by the mist that would soon close them for ever. He does not know his grandchildren who accompany their father. He discerned faintly the figures of the young men, but could not distinguish their features; see v. 10.

**10.** *could not see.* Clearly; hence his question when seeing Joseph's sons, 'Who are these?'

**12.** *from between his knees.* To place a child upon the knees was the symbol of adoption. Joseph's sons had thus been placed upon or between the knees of Jacob. This having been done, Joseph removes them.

*fell down on his face.* In gratitude to his father.

## GENESIS XLVIII, 13

them out from between his knees; and he fell down on his face to the earth. 13. And Joseph took them both, Ephraim in his right hand towards Israel's left hand, and Manasseh in his left hand towards Israel's right hand, and brought them near unto him. 14. And Israel stretched out his right hand, and laid it upon Ephraim's head, who was the younger, and his left hand upon Manasseh's head, guiding his hands wittingly; for Manasseh was the first-born. 15. And he blessed Joseph, and said: 'The God before whom my fathers Abraham and Isaac did walk, the God who hath been my shepherd all my life long unto this day, 16. the angel who hath redeemed me from all evil, bless the lads; and let my name be named in them, and the name of my fathers Abraham and Isaac; and let them grow into a multitude in the midst of the earth.'* 17. And when Joseph saw that his father was laying his right hand upon the head of Ephraim, it displeased him, and he held up his father's hand, to remove it from Ephraim's head unto Manasseh's head. 18. And Joseph said unto his father: 'Not so, my father, for this is the first-born; put thy right hand upon his head.' 19. And his father refused, and said: 'I know it, my son, I know it; he also shall become a people, and he also shall be great; howbeit his younger brother shall be greater than he, and his seed shall become a multitude of nations.' 20. And

---

**13.** Jacob was now to bless the lads. Joseph places Manasseh, the first-born, opposite to Jacob's right hand. This position was the station of honour.

**14.** *guiding his hands wittingly*. Jacob, against Joseph's wish, places the younger above the elder. This is the first instance in Scripture of the laying on of the hands in blessing.

**15.** *blessed Joseph*. By blessing his children (Rashbam).

**16.** *the angel*. This verse is connected with the preceding verse. The Jonathan Targum paraphrases: 'The God whom my fathers Abraham and Isaac worshipped, the God who hath nourished me all my life long unto this day—may it be Thy will that the angel whom Thou didst appoint to redeem me from all evil, bless the lads.'

*let my name be named in them*. i.e. 'may they be worthy of having their names coupled with my own, and those of my ancestors Abraham and Isaac' (Sforno).

**17.** *it displeased him*. Seeing his father place the younger son above the older. What is narrated in *v*. 17–19 happened before the blessing was given (Rashbam).

*he held up*. He grasped.

**19.** *I know it*. 'That Manasseh is the firstborn' (Rashi).

*his younger brother shall be greater*. Just as if he had been endowed with his birthright. The younger brother in Scripture is at times preferred to the elder. Abel, Abraham, Isaac, Moses and David afford striking instances of this fact.

*a multitude*. lit. 'fullness'.

**20.** *By thee shall Israel bless*. To this day, every pious Jewish father on Sabbath eve places his hands on the head of his son, and blesses him in the words: 'God make thee as Ephraim and Manasseh' (Authorised Prayer Book, p. 122). Ephraim and Manasseh would not barter away their 'Jewishness' for the most exalted social position, or the most enviable political career, in the Egyptian state. They voluntarily gave up their place in the higher Egyptian aristocracy, and openly identified themselves with their 'alien' kinsmen, the despised shepherd-immigrants. Every Jewish parent may well pray that his children show the same loyalty to their father and their father's God as did Ephraim and Manasseh.

## GENESIS XLVIII, 21

he blessed them that day, saying: 'By thee shall Israel bless, saying: God make thee as Ephraim and as Manasseh.' And he set Ephraim before Manasseh. 21. And Israel said unto Joseph: 'Behold, I die; but God will be with you, and bring you back unto the land of your fathers. 22. Moreover I have given to thee one ¹portion above thy brethren, which I took out of the hand of the Amorite with my sword and with my bow.'* ⁱᵛ·

## CHAPTER XLIX

1. And Jacob called unto his sons, and said: 'Gather yourselves together, that I may tell you that which shall befall you in the end of days.

2. Assemble yourselves, and hear, ye sons of Jacob;
And hearken unto Israel your father.

3. Reuben, thou art my first-born,
My might, and the first-fruits of my strength;
The excellency of dignity, and the excellency of power.

¹ Heb. *schechem*, shoulder.

---

**22.** This verse is the blessing addressed to Joseph personally.

*portion*. Heb. *shechem*. The reference is to the plot of ground purchased by Jacob from Hamor at Shechem; see XXXIII, 19. It seems from the context that this plot of land had fallen into the hands of the Amorites, and had been retaken from them by force of arms. Jacob's military exploit is not elsewhere mentioned.

*above thy brethren*. i.e. more than thy brethren. Some commentators explain the extra portion bestowed upon Joseph as referring to the privilege accorded to his two sons in being accounted equals of the other tribes.

CHAPTER XLIX. THE BLESSING OF JACOB

**1.** *Jacob called unto his sons.* His other sons, who were not present when Jacob blessed Ephraim and Manasseh.

*shall befall you.* Jacob's words are prophetic anticipations of the future destinies of his children. The counsel and benediction which Israel imparts to them are such that their descendants have remained 'Children of Israel' for all time.

*in the end of days.* i.e. in the distant future. In the Prophets, this phrase is used to express the Messianic age.

**2.** The Blessing is in poetic form, and therefore marked by *parallelism*, or 'thought rhythm', which is a characteristic of all Heb. poetry. This verse forms an introduction to the main theme of the chapter. Jacob demands their earnest attention because of the fateful message he has to convey to them.

### 3-4. REUBEN

**3.** *my first-born.* Reuben's natural rights have been forfeited. He has birth, dignity, opportunity; but no strength of character. In the Scripture narrative, he appears as a man who begins good actions, but does not complete them. Thus, he plans to save Joseph, and he actually prevents the murder, but Joseph is sold nevertheless. Reuben's descendants in Jewish history remain true to ancestral type. When Deborah unfurled the banner of Israelitish independence in the days of the Judges, the tribes rallied round her. In the camp of Reuben, however, there were great deliberations and mighty searchings of heart, but no action; see Judges v, 15. Subsequently, the tribe of Reuben is rarely mentioned in Israel's history.

*my might.* 'As the first-born, Reuben is endowed with a superabundant vitality, which is the cause at once of his pre-eminence and his undoing' (Skinner).

*the excellency of dignity.* A Hebraism for 'superior in dignity'. Superiority in dignity and power belonged to the first-born. Onkelos renders, 'For thee it was provided to receive three portions, the right of first-born, the priesthood, and the kingdom.' The first of these was given to Joseph, I Chron. v, 1; the priesthood was given to Levi, Num. III, 41; the kingly power or headship was allotted to Judah, see v. 8.

**4.** *unstable as water.* Any breeze can ruffle its surface. Or, 'bubbling over like water,' in uncontrolled vehemence of passion. Reuben's cardinal sin, says Jacob, was weakness of will, lack of self-control and firmness of purpose.

## GENESIS XLIX, 4

4. Unstable as water, have not thou the excellency;
Because thou wentest up to thy father's bed;
Then defilest thou it—he went up to my couch.

5. Simeon and Levi are brethren;
Weapons of violence their kinship.

6. Let my soul not come into their council;
Unto their assembly let my glory not be united;
For in their anger they slew men,
And in their self-will they houghed oxen.

7. Cursed be their anger, for it was fierce,
And their wrath, for it was cruel;
I will divide them in Jacob,
And scatter them in Israel.

4 וְרָאשִׁית אוֹנִי יֶתֶר שְׂאֵת וְיֶתֶר עָז: פַּחַז כַּמַּיִם אַל־תּוֹתַר
כִּי עָלִיתָ מִשְׁכְּבֵי אָבִיךָ אָז חִלַּלְתָּ יְצוּעִי עָלָה: פ

5 שִׁמְעוֹן וְלֵוִי אַחִים כְּלֵי חָמָס מְכֵרֹתֵיהֶם: בְּסֹדָם אַל־תָּבֹא
6 נַפְשִׁי בִּקְהָלָם אַל־תֵּחַד כְּבֹדִי כִּי בְאַפָּם הָרְגוּ אִישׁ וּבִרְצֹנָם
7 עִקְּרוּ־שׁוֹר: אָרוּר אַפָּם כִּי עָז וְעֶבְרָתָם כִּי קָשָׁתָה אֲחַלְּקֵם
בְּיַעֲקֹב וַאֲפִיצֵם בְּיִשְׂרָאֵל: פ

8 יְהוּדָה אַתָּה יוֹדוּךָ אַחֶיךָ יָדְךָ בְּעֹרֶף אֹיְבֶיךָ יִשְׁתַּחֲווּ לְךָ

8. Judah, thee shall thy brethren praise;
Thy hand shall be on the neck of thine enemies;
Thy father's sons shall bow down before thee.

v. 8. בראש עמוד סימן בי״ח שמ״ו

---

The Heb. word for 'unstable', *pachaz*, means recklessness; the same root in Aramaic means 'to be lascivious'.

*have not thou the excellency.* i.e. 'thou shalt forfeit thy privileges' as the first-born. None of the descendants of Reuben ever became Judge, Prophet, or leader. Here Scripture stresses the idea that moral character is a more important factor than hereditary right.

*he went up to my couch.* The sudden change from the second to the third person is due to Jacob's loathing at the mere memory of Reuben's offence; see on XXXV, 22.

### 5–7. SIMEON AND LEVI

**5.** *Simeon and Levi are brethren.* In violence. See XXXIV, 26 f. Moffatt translates: 'Simeon and Levi are a pair.'

*weapons of violence their kinship.* The phrase is also rendered, 'instruments of cruelty are in their habitations' (Onkelos, Kimchi, and AV). The reference is evidently to their dealings in Shechem; see XXXIV.

**6.** *council.* Or, 'secret'; i.e. secret confederacy.

*my glory.* i.e. my soul; as in Psalm XVI, 9. What lofty conception of both glory and soul, to make them synonymous as the Heb. language does!

*men.* The Heb. is in the singular, the word being used collectively.

*they houghed oxen.* A figure of vindictive destructiveness, such as is recounted in XXXIV, 28, 29. To 'hough' is to sever certain sinews and so render the animal helpless. The mutilation of animals is not recorded in that chapter. Many Versions therefore render, 'they digged down a wall', referring to the destruction of Shechem. The Heb. words for 'ox' and 'wall' differ only in one dot—שׁוֹר and שׁוּר.

**7.** *cursed be their anger.* Jacob does not curse them but their sin, of which he could not have given a stronger condemnation. It is characteristic of the untrustworthiness of the Samaritan Text that instead of the reading אָרוּר, 'Cursed be their anger,' it has אדיר, 'How splendid is their anger!'

*I will divide them in Jacob.* Fulfilled by the intermingling of the Simeonites in the inheritance of Judah (see Josh. XIX, 1), and by the dispersion of the tribe of Levi among the other tribes of Israel.

### 8–12. JUDAH

Contrast the characterization of Reuben with Jacob's jubilant praise of Judah. Unlike Reuben, Judah has neither birthright nor the dignity or opportunity of the first-born, but he has both strength and consistency of purpose. He knows his enemy, and—whether it be a person, an evil, or a cause—his hand is upon that enemy's neck. Capable indeed of falling into grievous error and sin, he is yet true at heart. Judah's character fits him to take the lead and rule. He is the worthy ancestor of David, Isaiah and Nehemiah, the father of the royal tribe that led in the conquest of the Promised Land.

**8.** *Judah, thee shall thy brethren praise.* Foretells Judah's military glory in subduing the enemies of his brethren, the Philistines and Edomites, resulting in the acknowledgment of Judah as the national leader, or king.

## GENESIS XLIX, 9

9. Judah is a lion's whelp;
From the prey, my son, thou art gone up.
He stooped down, he couched as a lion,
And as a lioness; who shall rouse him up?

10. The sceptre shall not depart from Judah,
Nor the ruler's staff from between his feet,
As long as men come to Shiloh;
And unto him shall the obedience of the peoples be.

11. Binding his foal unto the vine,
And his ass's colt unto the choice vine;
He washeth his garments in wine,
And his vesture in the blood of grapes;

12. His eyes shall be red with wine,
And his teeth white with milk.

13. Zebulun shall dwell at the shore of the sea,
And he shall be a shore for ships,
And his flank shall be upon Zidon.

14. Issachar is a large-boned ass,
Couching down between the sheepfolds.

9 בְּנֵי אָבִיךָ: גּוּר אַרְיֵה יְהוּדָה מִטֶּרֶף בְּנִי עָלִיתָ כָּרַע רָבַץ
10 כְּאַרְיֵה וּכְלָבִיא מִי יְקִימֶנּוּ: לֹא־יָסוּר שֵׁבֶט מִיהוּדָה וּמְחֹקֵק
11 מִבֵּין רַגְלָיו עַד כִּי־יָבֹא שִׁילֹה וְלוֹ יִקְּהַת עַמִּים: אֹסְרִי
לַגֶּפֶן עִירֹה וְלַשֹּׂרֵקָה בְּנִי אֲתֹנוֹ כִּבֵּס בַּיַּיִן לְבֻשׁוֹ וּבְדַם־
12 עֲנָבִים סוּתֹה: חַכְלִילִי עֵינַיִם מִיָּיִן וּלְבֶן־שִׁנַּיִם מֵחָלָב: פ
13 זְבוּלֻן לְחוֹף יַמִּים יִשְׁכֹּן וְהוּא לְחוֹף אֳנִיּוֹת וְיַרְכָתוֹ עַל־צִידֹן: פ
14 יִשָּׂשכָר חֲמֹר גָּרֶם רֹבֵץ בֵּין הַמִּשְׁפְּתָיִם: וַיַּרְא מְנֻחָה

v. 10. ק׳ בותו ibid. ק׳ עירו v. 11. ק׳ רגושה

---

**9.** *lion's whelp*. According to the Midrash, the emblem of the tribe of Judah was a lion. The metaphor suggests the vigour and nobility of Judah and his offspring; and the habitual swiftness and force of their military movements.

*thou art gone up*. To the security of the Judean hills, after the victorious conflicts in the Plain below.

**10.** *the sceptre*. The emblem of kingship.

*from between his feet*. The figure is that of an Oriental king sitting, with the ruler's staff between his knees; as can be seen on Assyrian and Persian monuments.

*as long as men come to Shiloh*. Heb. *ad ki yabo shiloh*; lit. 'until Shiloh come'; or, 'until that which is his shall come'; *i.e.* Judah's rule shall continue till he comes to his own, and the obedience of all the tribes is his. This translation may also mean that when the tribe of Judah has come into its own, the sceptre shall be taken out of its hands.

The explanation of this verse, especially of the Hebrew words עד כי יבא שילה, is very difficult. Some Jewish commentators have given it a Messianic meaning. For the interpretation that it has been given in the Church, see the Additional Note, p. 201.

*the peoples*. *i.e.* the tribes of Israel, as in Deut. XXXIII, 3, 19.

**11.** Instead of the translation, 'Binding his foal unto the vine' (also AV and RV), which would make Judah out to be a fool, render:

'*Harnessing his foal for* (the produce of) *one vine*,
'*And his ass's colt for* (the produce of) *one choice vine*'—

which brings out in a striking figure the fruitfulness of Judah's land: one ass is required to carry away the produce of one vine; and even one choice vine yields enough fruit for the load of an ass's colt. This translation, founded on the interpretation of the Rabbis, is plainly indicated in Rashi and Rashbam; yet it has been overlooked by subsequent commentators (Marcus Jastrow).

*choice vine*. Heb. *sorek*, produced sweet grapes of superior quality. Grapes are to be abundant that the people of Judah might wash their garments in them.

**12.** *his eyes shall be red with wine*. This rendering is absurd. According to it, Judah's eyes are red from excessive drinking, and Jacob's blessing is that Judah should be a drunkard! The word rendered 'red', however, means 'sparkling' (Septuagint, Gunkel, Gressmann); and the correct translation of the verse is: '*his eyes are more sparkling than wine.*'

*his teeth white with milk*' Does drinking milk produce white teeth? The correct translation (Septuagint, Vulgate, Saadyah, Jastrow) is, '*his teeth are whiter than milk.*'

### 13. ZEBULUN

**13.** The favourable geographical position of Zebulun's territory is described.

*a shore for ships*. To which they may come in safety.

*Zidon*. The actual territory of Zebulun stretched from the Sea of Galilee to Mt. Carmel, close under Tyre and Zidon.

### 14–15. ISSACHAR

**14.** *large-boned ass*. Indicating great physical power.

GENESIS XLIX, 22

15. For he saw a resting-place that it was good,
And the land that it was pleasant;
And he bowed his shoulder to bear,
And became a servant under taskwork.

16. Dan shall judge his people,
As one of the tribes of Israel.

17. Dan shall be a serpent in the way,
A horned snake in the path,
That biteth the horse's heels,
So that his rider falleth backward.

18. I wait for Thy salvation, O LORD.* v.

19. Gad, ¹a troop ²shall troop upon him;
But he shall troop upon their heel.

20. As for Asher, his bread shall be fat,
And he shall yield royal dainties.

21. Naphtali is a hind let loose:
He giveth goodly words.

¹ Heb. *gedud*.   ² From the Heb. root *gadad*.

---

**15.** *A resting-place.* As opposed to the wandering life of nomads (Ryle).

*taskwork.* Or, 'tribute.' Issachar, possessed of rich territory, preferred rather to submit to tribute than to leave his ploughshare and take up the sword. See Deut. XXXIII, 18. Zunz translates, 'and yieldeth himself to the service of the labourer.'

### 16-18. DAN

**16.** *shall judge.* Or, 'shall defend,' or, 'avenge.' Onkelos understood this to refer to the tribe of Dan in the days of Samson (Judg. xv, 20).

*his people.* The tribe of Dan.

**17.** *a horned snake.* Is small, but highly venomous; it coils itself in the sand and, if disturbed, darts out upon any passing animal. Dan will prove dangerous to his foes by ambuscades and guerilla warfare.

**18.** *I wait for Thy salvation.* Is probably intended as part of the blessing bestowed upon Dan, who was in the most exposed position among all the tribes of Israel.

*Thy salvation.* i.e. deliverance wrought by Thee.

### 19. GAD

**19.** *a troop shall troop.* There is here, as in previous verses, a play upon the name. Perhaps the translation should be 'a raiding band raids him, but he will band himself against their heel'.

Gad succeeded in repelling the Ammonites, Moabites and Aramæans, who were constantly raiding his borders. Jephthah was of this tribe.

### 20. ASHER

**20.** *Asher.* The name Asher means, 'happy' or 'fortunate' (see XXX, 13); and this meaning is reflected in the blessing bestowed upon him. The land of Asher was prosperous or happy; cf. Arabia Felix.

*royal dainties.* Delicacies fit for the table of kings. The allusion is probably to an export trade carried on by the men of Asher.

### 21. NAPHTALI

**21.** *hind let loose.* An image of swiftness and grace in movement.

*he giveth goodly words.* Refers to the tribe's reputation for eloquence, and the great victory of Barak, a Naphtalite, which was followed by the glorious Song of Deborah (Kimchi). Another translation is, 'Naphtali is a slender terebinth, which putteth forth goodly branches.' Joseph, too (next verse), is compared to a vine.

### 22-26. JOSEPH

Jacob reserves his softest and most loving accents for Joseph, who united whatever is best and noblest in both Reuben and Judah. He is the man of vision, the man of dreams; but to this he joins moral and spiritual strength in all the vicissitudes of life. He is the ideal son, the ideal brother, the ideal servant, the ideal administrator. His character and story have from of old been held to be typical of the character and story of Israel. Like Joseph, the Jew has been the dreamer of the ages, dreaming Israel's dream of universal justice and peace and brotherhood. Like Joseph, he has everywhere been the helpless victim of the hatred of his step-brethren, hatred that drove him from home and doomed him to Exile. In that Exile, he has, like Joseph, times without number resisted the Great Temptation of disloyalty to the God of his fathers. In the dreams of Joseph, the sun, moon and eleven stars bowed down to him. It is the stars that bow to *him*, and not he to the stars. This is characteristic of both Joseph and Israel. אין מזל לישראל, says

## GENESIS, XLIX, 22

22. Joseph is a fruitful vine,
A fruitful vine by a fountain;
Its branches run over the wall.

23. The archers have dealt bitterly with him,
And shot at him, and hated him;

24. But his bow abode firm,
And the arms of his hands were made supple,
By the hands of the Mighty One of Jacob,
From thence, from the Shepherd, the Stone of Israel,

25. Even by the God of thy father, who shall help thee,
And by the Almighty, who shall bless thee,
With blessings of heaven above,
Blessings of the deep that coucheth beneath,
Blessings of the breasts, and of the womb.

26. The blessings of thy father
Are mighty beyond the blessings of my progenitors
Unto the utmost bound of the everlasting hills;
They shall be on the head of Joseph,
And on the crown of the head of the prince among his brethren.*vi.

27. Benjamin is a wolf that raveneth;
In the morning he devoureth the prey,
And at even he divideth the spoil.'

28. All these are the twelve tribes of Israel,

---

Rabbi Yochanan. An Israelite should be ashamed to blame his star, his environment, or any outward circumstance for his moral downfall or his religious apostasy. Man is captain of his own soul; and wherever there is a will to Judaism, there is a way to lead the Jewish life.

**22.** *by a fountain.* Cf. Psalm I, 3; the proximity of water is a necessary condition, if the tree is to grow and bear fruit.

**23.** *the archers.* His brethren.
*dealt bitterly.* Harassed by hostile action. In spite of attack, the strength of Joseph and his descendants is unimpaired, because the Almighty is with him.

**24.** *abode firm.* i.e. continued strong.
*made supple.* Or, 'active.' This verse suggests a fine picture: the bow held steadily in position, while the hand that discharges the arrows in quick succession moves nimbly to and fro (Gunkel).
*by the hands.* Indicating the source of Joseph's salvation.
*the Mighty One of Jacob.* A title of God, see Is. I, 24.
*from thence.* From the Mighty One of Jacob.
*the Stone of Israel.* A rare parallel to the better known 'Rock of Israel'.

**25.** Three blessings are mentioned.
*blessings of heaven.* Rain and dew, sunshine and wind.
*the deep.* The subterranean reservoir of waters beneath, from which springs the fertility to soil.
*the breasts.* The fruitfulness of the family.

**26.** *are mighty beyond.* The verse states that the blessings received by Jacob surpass the blessings vouchsafed to Jacob's fathers. Jacob now bestows these enhanced blessings upon Joseph, thereby making him the heir both of himself and of his ancestors.
*unto the utmost bound of the everlasting hills.* As high above the blessings bestowed on Jacob's father as the hills are above the plains.
*prince.* lit. 'that is separate from his brethren', i.e. apart from, eminent, among his brethren.

### 27. BENJAMIN

**27.** *a wolf that raveneth.* Or, 'that teareth,' referring to the warlike character of the tribe; see Judg. v, 14 and xx, 16.

**28.** *twelve tribes.* Joseph, and not his sons, receives the blessings. Jacob in blessing his sons was at the same time blessing the future tribes.
*every one.* Received his appropriate blessing. The future would prove the prophetic nature of their father's benediction.

## GENESIS XLIX, 29

בראשית ויחי מט נ

and this is it that their father spoke unto them and blessed them; every one according to his blessing he blessed them. 29. And he charged them, and said unto them: 'I am to be gathered unto my people; bury me with my fathers in the cave that is in the field of Ephron the Hittite, 30. in the cave that is in the field of Machpelah, which is before Mamre, in the land of Canaan, which Abraham bought with the field from Ephron the Hittite for a possession of a burying-place. 31. There they buried Abraham and Sarah his wife; there they buried Isaac and Rebekah his wife; and there I buried Leah. 32. The field and the cave that is therein, which was purchased from the children of Heth.' 33. And when Jacob made an end of charging his sons, he gathered up his feet into the bed, and expired, and was gathered unto his people.

לָהֶ֖ם אֲבִיהֶ֑ם וַיְבָ֣רֶךְ אוֹתָ֔ם אִ֛ישׁ אֲשֶׁ֥ר כְּבִרְכָת֖וֹ בֵּרַ֥ךְ
אֹתָֽם׃ 29 וַיְצַ֣ו אוֹתָ֗ם וַיֹּ֤אמֶר אֲלֵהֶם֙ אֲנִי֙ נֶאֱסָ֣ף אֶל־עַמִּ֔י קִבְר֥וּ
אֹתִ֖י אֶל־אֲבֹתָ֑י אֶל־הַ֨מְּעָרָ֔ה אֲשֶׁ֥ר בִּשְׂדֵ֖ה עֶפְר֥וֹן הַחִתִּֽי׃
ל בַּמְּעָרָ֞ה אֲשֶׁ֨ר בִּשְׂדֵ֧ה הַמַּכְפֵּלָ֛ה אֲשֶׁר־עַל־פְּנֵי־מַמְרֵ֖א
בְּאֶ֣רֶץ כְּנָ֑עַן אֲשֶׁר֩ קָנָ֨ה אַבְרָהָ֜ם אֶת־הַשָּׂדֶ֗ה מֵאֵ֛ת עֶפְרֹ֥ן
הַחִתִּ֖י לַאֲחֻזַּת־קָֽבֶר׃ 31 שָׁ֣מָּה קָֽבְר֞וּ אֶת־אַבְרָהָ֗ם וְאֵת֙ שָׂרָ֣ה
אִשְׁתּ֔וֹ שָׁ֚מָּה קָבְר֣וּ אֶת־יִצְחָ֔ק וְאֵ֖ת רִבְקָ֣ה אִשְׁתּ֑וֹ וְשָׁ֥מָּה
32 קָבַ֖רְתִּי אֶת־לֵאָֽה׃ מִקְנֵ֧ה הַשָּׂדֶ֛ה וְהַמְּעָרָ֥ה אֲשֶׁר־בּ֖וֹ מֵאֵ֥ת
33 בְּנֵי־חֵֽת׃ וַיְכַ֤ל יַעֲקֹב֙ לְצַוֺּ֣ת אֶת־בָּנָ֔יו וַיֶּאֱסֹ֥ף רַגְלָ֖יו אֶל־
הַמִּטָּ֑ה וַיִּגְוַ֖ע וַיֵּאָ֥סֶף אֶל־עַמָּֽיו׃

## 50 CHAPTER L

CAP. L. נ  נ

1. And Joseph fell upon his father's face and wept upon him, and kissed him. 2. And Joseph commanded his servants the physicians to embalm his father. And the physicians embalmed Israel. 3. And forty days were fulfilled for him; for so are fulfilled the days of embalming. And the Egyptians wept for him threescore and ten days. ¶ 4. And when the days of weeping for him were past, Joseph spoke unto the house of Pharaoh, saying: 'If now I have found favour in your eyes, speak, I pray you, in the ears of Pharaoh, saying: 5. My father made me swear, saying: Lo, I die; in my grave which I have digged for me in the land of Canaan, there shalt thou bury me. Now therefore let me go up, I pray thee, and bury my father, and I will come back.' 6. And Pharaoh said: 'Go up, and bury thy father, according as he

א 2 וַיִּפֹּ֥ל יוֹסֵ֖ף עַל־פְּנֵ֣י אָבִ֑יו וַיֵּ֥בְךְּ עָלָ֖יו וַיִּשַּׁק־לֽוֹ׃ וַיְצַ֨ו יוֹסֵ֤ף
אֶת־עֲבָדָיו֙ אֶת־הָרֹ֣פְאִ֔ים לַחֲנֹ֖ט אֶת־אָבִ֑יו וַיַּחַנְט֥וּ הָרֹפְאִ֖ים
3 אֶת־יִשְׂרָאֵֽל׃ וַיִּמְלְאוּ־לוֹ֙ אַרְבָּעִ֣ים י֔וֹם כִּ֛י כֵּ֥ן יִמְלְא֖וּ יְמֵ֣י
4 הַחֲנֻטִ֑ים וַיִּבְכּ֥וּ אֹת֛וֹ מִצְרַ֖יִם שִׁבְעִ֥ים יֽוֹם׃ וַיַּֽעַבְרוּ֙ יְמֵ֣י
בְכִית֔וֹ וַיְדַבֵּ֣ר יוֹסֵ֔ף אֶל־בֵּ֥ית פַּרְעֹ֖ה לֵאמֹ֑ר אִם־נָ֨א מָצָ֤אתִי
ה חֵן֙ בְּעֵ֣ינֵיכֶ֔ם דַּבְּרוּ־נָ֕א בְּאָזְנֵ֥י פַרְעֹ֖ה לֵאמֹֽר׃ אָבִ֞י הִשְׁבִּיעַ֣נִי
לֵאמֹ֗ר הִנֵּ֣ה אָנֹכִי֮ מֵת֒ בְּקִבְרִ֗י אֲשֶׁ֨ר כָּרִ֤יתִי לִי֙ בְּאֶ֣רֶץ כְּנַ֔עַן
שָׁ֖מָּה תִּקְבְּרֵ֑נִי וְעַתָּ֗ה אֶֽעֱלֶה־נָּ֛א וְאֶקְבְּרָ֥ה אֶת־אָבִ֖י וְאָשֽׁוּבָה׃

---

**32.** *purchased from the children of Heth.* With their knowledge and consent (Abarbanel). Joseph, having been away from Canaan for so many years, receives explicit directions as to the spot where his father is to be buried. This verse implies a deed of purchase.

**33.** *gathered up his feet.* He had been sitting; he now lay down in bed.

*and was gathered unto his people.* This passage shows that not burial of the body is meant, but the soul's departure to join the souls of those who had gone before.

CHAPTER L. JACOB'S BURIAL. THE DEATH OF JOSEPH

**1.** *and Joseph.* This does not imply that the other children of Jacob did not do even as Joseph did.

**2.** *to embalm his father.* Not in imitation of the custom of the Egyptians, who took care to preserve the body after death and keep it ready for occupation by the soul. Joseph's purpose was merely to preserve it from dissolution before it reached the Cave of Machpelah.

**3.** *the Egyptians wept for him.* Out of respect for Joseph. Probably the forty days of embalming formed part of the seventy days (Rashi).

**4.** *unto the house of Pharaoh.* Joseph, as a mourner, would not approach the king in person.

**5.** *which I have digged.* 'Which I have prepared' (Onkelos). It is quite likely that Jacob had prepared the grave for his own interment, next to the grave of Leah in the Cave of Machpelah.

*and I will come back.* Joseph assures Pharaoh that he intends to return to Egypt.

## GENESIS L, 7

made thee swear.' 7. And Joseph went up to bury his father; and with him went up all the servants of Pharaoh, the elders of his house, and all the elders of the land of Egypt, 8. and all the house of Joseph, and his brethren, and his father's house; only their little ones, and their flocks, and their herds, they left in the land of Goshen. 9. And there went up with him both chariots and horsemen; and it was a very great company. 10. And they came to the threshing-floor of Atad, which is beyond the Jordan, and there they wailed with a very great and sore wailing; and he made a mourning for his father seven days. 11. And when the inhabitants of the land, the Canaanites, saw the mourning in the floor of Atad, they said: 'This is a grievous ¹mourning to the Egyptians.' Wherefore the name of it was called Abel-mizraim, which is beyond the Jordan. 12. And his sons did unto him according as he commanded them. 13. For his sons carried him into the land of Canaan, and buried him in the cave of the field of Machpelah, which Abraham bought with the, field for a possession of a burying-place, of Ephron the Hittite, in front of Mamre. ¶ 14. And Joseph returned into Egypt, he, and his brethren, and all that went up with him to bury his father, after he had buried his father. 15. And when Joseph's brethren saw that their father was dead, they said: 'It may be that Joseph will hate us, and will fully requite us all the evil which we did unto him.' 16. And they sent a message unto Joseph, saying: 'Thy father did command before he died, saying: 17. So shall ye say unto Joseph: Forgive, I pray thee now, the transgression of thy brethren,

¹ Heb. *ebel*.

בראשית ויחי נ

6 וַיֹּאמֶר פַּרְעֹה עֲלֵה וּקְבֹר אֶת־אָבִיךָ כַּאֲשֶׁר הִשְׁבִּיעֶךָ׃
7 וַיַּעַל יוֹסֵף לִקְבֹּר אֶת־אָבִיו וַיַּעֲלוּ אִתּוֹ כָּל־עַבְדֵי פַרְעֹה
8 זִקְנֵי בֵיתוֹ וְכֹל זִקְנֵי אֶרֶץ־מִצְרָיִם׃ וְכֹל בֵּית יוֹסֵף וְאֶחָיו וּבֵית אָבִיו רַק טַפָּם וְצֹאנָם וּבְקָרָם עָזְבוּ בְּאֶרֶץ גֹּשֶׁן׃
9 וַיַּעַל עִמּוֹ גַּם־רֶכֶב גַּם־פָּרָשִׁים וַיְהִי הַמַּחֲנֶה כָּבֵד מְאֹד׃
10 וַיָּבֹאוּ עַד־גֹּרֶן הָאָטָד אֲשֶׁר בְּעֵבֶר הַיַּרְדֵּן וַיִּסְפְּדוּ־שָׁם מִסְפֵּד גָּדוֹל וְכָבֵד מְאֹד וַיַּעַשׂ לְאָבִיו אֵבֶל שִׁבְעַת יָמִים׃
11 וַיַּרְא יוֹשֵׁב הָאָרֶץ הַכְּנַעֲנִי אֶת־הָאֵבֶל בְּגֹרֶן הָאָטָד וַיֹּאמְרוּ אֵבֶל־כָּבֵד זֶה לְמִצְרָיִם עַל־כֵּן קָרָא שְׁמָהּ אָבֵל מִצְרַיִם
12 אֲשֶׁר בְּעֵבֶר הַיַּרְדֵּן׃ וַיַּעֲשׂוּ בָנָיו לוֹ כֵּן כַּאֲשֶׁר צִוָּם׃
13 וַיִּשְׂאוּ אֹתוֹ בָנָיו אַרְצָה כְּנַעַן וַיִּקְבְּרוּ אֹתוֹ בִּמְעָרַת שְׂדֵה הַמַּכְפֵּלָה אֲשֶׁר קָנָה אַבְרָהָם אֶת־הַשָּׂדֶה לַאֲחֻזַּת־קֶבֶר מֵאֵת עֶפְרֹן הַחִתִּי עַל־פְּנֵי מַמְרֵא׃
14 וַיָּשָׁב יוֹסֵף מִצְרַיְמָה הוּא וְאֶחָיו וְכָל־הָעֹלִים אִתּוֹ לִקְבֹּר אֶת־אָבִיו אַחֲרֵי קָבְרוֹ אֶת־אָבִיו׃
15 וַיִּרְאוּ אֲחֵי־יוֹסֵף כִּי־מֵת אֲבִיהֶם וַיֹּאמְרוּ לוּ יִשְׂטְמֵנוּ יוֹסֵף וְהָשֵׁב יָשִׁיב לָנוּ אֵת כָּל־הָרָעָה אֲשֶׁר גָּמַלְנוּ
16 אֹתוֹ׃ וַיְצַוּוּ אֶל־יוֹסֵף לֵאמֹר אָבִיךָ צִוָּה לִפְנֵי מוֹתוֹ לֵאמֹר׃
17 כֹּה־תֹאמְרוּ לְיוֹסֵף אָנָּא שָׂא נָא פֶּשַׁע אַחֶיךָ וְחַטָּאתָם

v. 17 ב׳ טעמים

---

**7.** *the elders*. The respect shown to Jacob is evidently due to the great position occupied by Joseph in Egypt. Such processions as described in our text are frequently represented on Egyptian tombs.

**8.** *only their little ones . . . they left in the land of Goshen*. Because unable to endure the fatigue of travel to Canaan.

**9.** *chariots and horsemen*. To protect the procession.

**10.** *the threshing-floor of Atad*. The place Atad has not been identified.

*beyond the Jordan*. This cannot mean east of the Jordan, as it is unthinkable that in going to the cave of Machpelah at Hebron the company would take the circuitous route round the Dead Sea. All difficulties disappear when we remember that to Moses and the Israelites in the land of Moab, the words 'beyond Jordan' meant *west* of Jordan. This phrase therefore is another incidental confirmation of the Mosaic authorship of Genesis (W. H. Green).

*seven days*. This is still the Jewish period of mourning for the dead. The sacred institution of *Shivah* in its essence thus goes back to Patriarchal times.

**11.** *a grievous mourning*. Or, 'an honourable mourning.'

**15.** *Joseph will hate us*. A notable example of the never-to-be-silenced voice of the guilty conscience.

**16.** *thy father did command*. An unrecorded message.

**17.** *servants of the God of thy father*. Though thy father is dead, the God of thy father liveth (Rashi). They ask for his forgiveness, basing their plea on the claims of brotherhood of Faith. A fine religious appeal.

*Joseph wept*. Because of their want of confidence in him.

GENESIS L, 18

and their sin, for that they did unto thee evil. And now, we pray thee, forgive the transgression of the servants of the God of thy father.' And Joseph wept when they spoke unto him. 18. And his brethren also went and fell down before his face; and they said: 'Behold, we are thy bondmen.' 19. And Joseph said unto them: 'Fear not; for am I in the place of God? 20. And as for you, ye meant evil against me; but God meant it for good, to bring to pass, as it is this day, to save much people alive. * ᵛⁱⁱ· 21. Now therefore fear ye not; I will sustain you, and your little ones.' And he comforted them, and spoke kindly unto them. ¶ 22. And Joseph dwelt in Egypt, he, and his father's house; and Joseph lived a hundred and ten years.* ᵐ· 23. And Joseph saw Ephraim's children of the third generation; the children also of Machir the son of Manasseh were born upon Joseph's knees. 24. And Joseph said unto his brethren: 'I die; but God will surely remember you, and bring you up out of this land unto the land which He swore to Abraham, to Isaac, and to Jacob.' 25.

כִּֽי־רָעָ֥ה גְמָל֖וּךָ וְעַתָּ֗ה שָׂ֥א נָ֛א לְפֶ֥שַׁע עַבְדֵ֖י אֱלֹהֵ֣י אָבִ֑יךָ 18 וַיֵּ֥בְךְּ יוֹסֵ֖ף בְּדַבְּרָ֥ם אֵלָֽיו׃ וַיֵּֽלְכוּ֙ גַּם־אֶחָ֔יו וַֽיִּפְּל֖וּ לְפָנָ֑יו 19 וַיֹּ֣אמְר֔וּ הִנֶּ֥נּֽוּ לְךָ֖ לַעֲבָדִֽים׃ וַיֹּ֧אמֶר אֲלֵהֶ֛ם יוֹסֵ֖ף אַל־ כ תִּירָ֑אוּ כִּ֛י הֲתַ֥חַת אֱלֹהִ֖ים אָֽנִי׃ וְאַתֶּ֕ם חֲשַׁבְתֶּ֥ם עָלַ֖י רָעָ֑ה
אֱלֹהִים֙ חֲשָׁבָ֣הּ לְטֹבָ֔ה לְמַ֗עַן עֲשֹׂ֛ה כַּיּ֥וֹם הַזֶּ֖ה לְהַחֲיֹ֥ת שביעי
21 עַם־רָֽב׃ וְעַתָּה֙ אַל־תִּירָ֔אוּ אָנֹכִ֛י אֲכַלְכֵּ֥ל אֶתְכֶ֖ם וְאֶֽת־ 22 טַפְּכֶ֑ם וַיְנַחֵ֣ם אוֹתָ֔ם וַיְדַבֵּ֖ר עַל־לִבָּֽם׃ וַיֵּ֤שֶׁב יוֹסֵף֙ בְּמִצְרַ֔יִם מפטיר
23 ה֖וּא וּבֵ֣ית אָבִ֑יו וַיְחִ֣י יוֹסֵ֔ף מֵאָ֥ה וָעֶ֖שֶׂר שָׁנִֽים׃ וַיַּ֤רְא יוֹסֵף֙ לְאֶפְרַ֔יִם בְּנֵ֖י שִׁלֵּשִׁ֑ים גַּ֚ם בְּנֵ֣י מָכִ֔יר בֶּן־מְנַשֶּׁ֔ה יֻלְּד֖וּ
24 עַל־בִּרְכֵּ֥י יוֹסֵֽף׃ וַיֹּ֤אמֶר יוֹסֵף֙ אֶל־אֶחָ֔יו אָנֹכִ֖י מֵ֑ת וֵֽאלֹהִ֞ים פָּקֹ֨ד יִפְקֹ֤ד אֶתְכֶם֙ וְהֶעֱלָ֤ה אֶתְכֶם֙ מִן־הָאָ֣רֶץ הַזֹּ֔את אֶל־
כה הָאָ֕רֶץ אֲשֶׁ֥ר נִשְׁבַּ֛ע לְאַבְרָהָ֥ם לְיִצְחָ֖ק וּֽלְיַעֲקֹֽב׃ וַיַּשְׁבַּ֣ע

v. 23 מ׳ רבתי

---

**18.** *and his brethren also went.* Having originally sent others on their behalf, see v. 16, they now come in person to plead with Joseph.

*behold, we are thy bondmen.* Again fulfilling the old dreams, see XXXVII, 6 f.

**19.** It is quite impossible for any man to counteract the Divine plan.

**20.** *ye meant evil.* Man proposes, but God disposes. 'To me it appears that the sale of Joseph was the work of Providence, not only for him who was to be advanced to an exalted station, but also in the benign care that resulted from it for the whole people of Israel. Therefore, Joseph's brethren were not deserving punishment; on the contrary, Joseph repeatedly declares that in whatever they had done, they were unwittingly carrying out the design of Providence' (Abarbanel).

*save much people alive.* Not only the Egyptians and the children of Israel, but other people who came to Egypt to buy corn in the time of famine.

**21.** *spoke kindly unto them.* lit. 'and he spoke to their heart'.

**22.** *a hundred and ten years.* He survived his father fifty-four years. In Egyptian writings, the age of 110 years is spoken of as an ideal lifetime.

**23.** *Machir.* The most powerful of the clans of Manasseh; see Judg. v, 14.

*born upon Joseph's knees.* The symbolical act of adoption.

**24.** *brethren.* Not necessarily brothers; near relatives is the meaning in our context.

*which He swore.* See XXII, 16; XXVI, 3.

**25.** *and ye shall carry up my bones from hence.* He has faith in the Divine promise to redeem His people. Joseph's bones are to participate in the return to Canaan, and to rest there. The promise was fulfilled; see Exod. XIII, 19, and Josh. XXIV, 32.

**26.** *coffin.* Heb. *aron.* The same Heb. word is used of the receptacle of the Tables of the Law. This is significant. Judaism preaches respect for human personality as a duty, because man has it in his power to become a living embodiment of the Moral Law. The Rabbis tell: The nations wondered why the Children of Israel, in their wanderings through the desert, carried with them the bones of Joseph in a similar ark and in the same reverential manner as they did the Tables of the Covenant. 'He whose remains are preserved in the one ark,' they answered, 'loyally obeyed the Divine commands enshrined in the other.'

*in Egypt.* These last words prepare the mind for the new era that awaits Israel in Egypt, and for the eventful story of the Exodus.

According to Jewish custom, the completion of any of the Five Books of the Torah is marked in the Synagogue by the congregation exclaiming חֲזַק חֲזַק וְנִתְחַזֵּק, 'Be strong, be strong, and let us strengthen one another'—an echo of the words

GENESIS L, 26　　　　　　　　　　בראשית ויחי נ

And Joseph took an oath of the children of Israel, saying: 'God will surely remember you, and ye shall carry up my bones from hence.' 26. So Joseph died, being a hundred and ten years old. And they embalmed him, and he was put in a coffin in Egypt.

יוֹסֵף אֶת־בְּנֵי יִשְׂרָאֵל לֵאמֹר פָּקֹד יִפְקֹד אֱלֹהִים אֶתְכֶם 
26 וְהַעֲלִתֶם אֶת־עַצְמֹתַי מִזֶּה: וַיָּמָת יוֹסֵף בֶּן־מֵאָה וָעֶשֶׂר 
שָׁנִים וַיַּחַנְטוּ אֹתוֹ וַיִּישֶׂם בָּאָרוֹן בְּמִצְרָיִם:

חֲזַק

סכום פסוקי דספר בראשית אלף וחמש מאות ושלשים וארבעה.
אַ"ךְ לְ"דָ סימן: וחציו ועל חרבך תחיה: ופרשיותיו י"ב. זה
שמי לעלם סימן: וסדריו מ"ג. גם ברוך יהיה סימן: ופרקיו
נ'. יִ"י חננו לך קוינו סימן: מנין הפתוחות שלשה וארבעים
והסתומות שמנה וארבעים. הכל תשעים ואחת פרשיות.
צֵא אתה וכל העם אשר ברגליך סימן:

of the ancient warrior, 'Be of good courage, and let us prove strong for our people, and for the cities of our God' (II Sam. x, 12). *Be strong.* i.e. to carry out the teaching contained in the Book just completed.

The Massoretic Note states the number of verses in Genesis to be 1,534; its Sedrahs (*parshiyyoth*) 12; its Sedarim, smaller divisions according to the Triennial Cycle, 43; and its Chapters 50.

## HAFTORAH VAYYECHI　　　הפטרת ויחי
### I KINGS II, 1–12

CHAPTER II　　　　　　　　　　　　　　　CAP. II. ב

1. Now the days of David drew nigh that he should die; and he charged Solomon his son, saying: 2. 'I go the way of all the earth; be thou strong therefore, and show thyself a man; 3. and keep the charge of the LORD thy God, to walk in His ways, to keep His statutes, and His commandments, and His ordinances, and His testimonies, according to that which is written in the law of Moses, that thou mayest prosper in all that thou doest, and whithersoever thou turnest thyself; 4. that the LORD may establish His word which He spoke concerning me, saying: If thy children take heed to their way, to walk before Me in truth with all their heart and with all their soul, there shall not fail thee, said He, a man on the throne of Israel. 5. Moreover thou knowest also what Joab the son of Zeruiah did unto me, even what he did to the two captains of the hosts of Israel, unto Abner the son of Ner and unto Amasa the son of Jether, whom he slew, and shed the blood of war in peace, and put the blood of war upon his girdle that was about his loins,

א וַיִּקְרְבוּ יְמֵי־דָוִד לָמוּת וַיְצַו אֶת־שְׁלֹמֹה בְנוֹ לֵאמֹר:
2 אָנֹכִי הֹלֵךְ בְּדֶרֶךְ כָּל־הָאָרֶץ וְחָזַקְתָּ וְהָיִיתָ לְאִישׁ: וְשָׁמַרְתָּ
3 אֶת־מִשְׁמֶרֶת יְהֹוָה אֱלֹהֶיךָ לָלֶכֶת בִּדְרָכָיו לִשְׁמֹר חֻקֹּתָיו
מִצְוֹתָיו וּמִשְׁפָּטָיו וְעֵדְוֹתָיו כַּכָּתוּב בְּתוֹרַת מֹשֶׁה לְמַעַן
תַּשְׂכִּיל אֵת כָּל־אֲשֶׁר תַּעֲשֶׂה וְאֵת כָּל־אֲשֶׁר תִּפְנֶה שָׁם:
4 לְמַעַן יָקִים יְהֹוָה אֶת־דְּבָרוֹ אֲשֶׁר דִּבֶּר עָלַי לֵאמֹר אִם־
יִשְׁמְרוּ בָנֶיךָ אֶת־דַּרְכָּם לָלֶכֶת לְפָנַי בֶּאֱמֶת בְּכָל־לְבָבָם
וּבְכָל־נַפְשָׁם לֵאמֹר לֹא־יִכָּרֵת לְךָ אִישׁ מֵעַל כִּסֵּא יִשְׂרָאֵל:
ה וְגַם אַתָּה יָדַעְתָּ אֵת אֲשֶׁר־עָשָׂה לִי יוֹאָב בֶּן־צְרוּיָה אֲשֶׁר
עָשָׂה לִשְׁנֵי־שָׂרֵי צִבְאוֹת יִשְׂרָאֵל לְאַבְנֵר בֶּן־נֵר וְלַעֲמָשָׂא
בֶן־יֶתֶר וַיַּהַרְגֵם וַיָּשֶׂם דְּמֵי־מִלְחָמָה בְּשָׁלֹם וַיִּתֵּן דְּמֵי

**1–4.** In the Sedrah, the dying Patriarch, assembling his sons, speaks to them last words of guidance and admonition, and 'blesses them each one according to his blessing'. In the Haftorah, David, feeling his end near, gives his son the best of blessings in words which point the way of life for every son of Israel. 'Be thou strong, therefore, and show thyself a man; and keep the charge of the LORD thy God, to walk in His ways, to keep His statutes and His commandments.'

I KINGS II, 6

and in his shoes that were on his feet. 6. Do therefore according to thy wisdom, and let not his hoar head go down to the grave in peace. 7. But show kindness unto the sons of Barzillai the Gileadite, and let them be of those that eat at thy table; for so they drew nigh unto me when I fled from Absalom thy brother. 8. And, behold, there is with thee Shimei the son of Gera, the Benjamite, of Bahurim, who cursed me with a grievous curse in the day when I went to Mahanaim; but he came down to meet me at the Jordan, and I swore to him by the LORD, saying: I will not put thee to death with the sword. 9. Now therefore hold him not guiltless, for thou art a wise man; and thou wilt know what thou oughtest to do unto him, and thou shalt bring his hoar head down to the grave with blood.' ¶ 10. And David slept with his fathers, and was buried in the city of David. 11. And the days that David reigned over Israel were forty years: seven years reigned he in Hebron, and thirty and three years reigned he in Jerusalem. 12. And Solomon sat upon the throne of David his father; and his kingdom was established firmly.

---

**5.** *Abner.* He was treacherously slain by Joab; II Sam. III, 27.

*Amasa.* Similarly murdered, II Sam. XX, 10.

*shed the blood of war in peace.* Joab's unpardonable crime consisted in having avenged, in time of peace, blood justifiably shed in self-defence in time of war.

**6.** *do therefore according to thy wisdom.* Solomon need not act precipitately. Both men, true to their nature, would sooner or later commit themselves, and for that reason give Solomon just cause for dealing effectively with them.

**7.** The dying king cherishes tender gratitude for kindness shown him.

**5-9.** The difficulty created by these verses cannot be ignored. As part of a last charge, they shock one's finer feelings. No admirer of David's otherwise magnanimous character can read without a pang that he passes into eternity with vengeance in his heart and on his lips.

Is there any extenuation or explanation? David charges his son to carry out the Divine laws. The thought then flashes through his mind that, as the guardian of justice in the land, he had grievously failed inasmuch as he allowed the perpetration of treacherous murders committed by Joab to go unpunished. It was a blot on his government, and the thought weighed on him at this hour. Unless justice, even-handed and impartial, was seen to rule in the highest quarter, no kingdom could be established.

A note of warning must be uttered. Whatever *reasons of state* may be advanced in mitigation of David's action, it is not an act for imitation in the life of the ordinary individual. The temptation to take vengeance is never so insidious as when it comes cloaked under high-sounding names; as when, for example, we say that it is in the interests of justice that we satisfy those feelings of vindictiveness. The Divine command 'Thou shalt not take vengeance, nor bear any grudge' (Lev. XIX, 18) is the safest guiding principle for prince and people.

There is recorded another Farewell Speech of David (I Chron. XXVIII and XXIX), and we take our leave of him with a few verses from that nobler utterance. He lays the solemn charge upon his son to complete the Temple which *he* was not permitted to begin, and in a prayer of fine humility and faith he commends his son and his children to the eternal God of Israel. 'As for me, it was in my heart to build a house of rest for the ark of the covenant of the LORD . . . and I had made ready for the building. But God said unto me, Thou shalt not build a house for My name, because thou art a man of war, and hast shed blood. . . . Thine, O LORD, is the greatness, and the power, and the glory, and the victory, and the majesty . . . all things come of Thee, and of Thine own have we given Thee. For we are strangers before Thee, and sojourners, as all our fathers were: our days on the earth are as a shadow, and there is no abiding.'

# ADDITIONAL NOTES TO GENESIS

## A

### THE CREATION CHAPTER

Genesis I–II, 3, is a worthy opening of Israel's Sacred Scriptures, and ranks among the most important chapters of the Bible. Even in form it is pre-eminent in the literature of religion. No other ancient account of creation (cosmogony) will bear a second reading. Most of them not only describe the origin of the world, but begin by describing how the gods emerged out of pre-existent chaos (theogony). In contrast with the simplicity and sublimity of Genesis I, we find all ancient cosmogonies, whether it be the Babylonian or the Phœnician, the Greek or the Roman, alike unrelievedly wild, cruel, even foul.

Thus, the Assyro-Babylonian mythology tells how, before what we call earth or heaven had come into being, there existed a primeval watery chaos—Tiamat—out of which the gods were evolved:—

'When, in the height, heaven was not yet named,
And the earth beneath did not bear a name,
And the primeval Apsu (the Abyss), their begetter,
And Chaos (Tiamat), the mother of them both,
Their waters were mingled together,
Then were created the gods in the midst of heaven.'

Apsu, the Abyss, disturbed at finding his domain invaded by the new gods, induced Tiamat and Chaos to join him in contesting their supremacy; he was, however, subdued by the cunning of Ea; and Tiamat, left to carry on the struggle alone, provides herself with a brood of hideous allies. The alarmed gods thereupon appoint Marduk as their champion. With winds and lightnings, Marduk advances; he seizes Tiamat in a huge net, and 'with his merciless club he crushed her skull'. The carcase of the monster he split into two halves, one of which he fixed on high, to form a firmament supporting the waters above it. In the same grotesque way the story continues to describe the formation of sun, moon, plants, animals and man. Many moderns feign to believe that this is the source from which Genesis I is taken. But a thorough-going Bible critic like the late Dr. Driver admits, 'It is incredible that the monotheistic author of Genesis I could have borrowed any detail, however slight, from the polytheistic epic of the conflict of Marduk and Tiamat.'

The infinite importance, however, of the first page of the Bible consists in the fact that it enshrines some of the fundamental beliefs of Judaism. Among these are:—

I. GOD IS THE CREATOR OF THE UNIVERSE. Each religion has certain specific teachings, convictions, dogmas. Such a dogma of Judaism is its belief that the world was called into existence at the will of the One, Almighty and All-good God. And nowhere does this fundamental conviction of Israel's Faith find clearer expression than in Genesis I. When neighbouring peoples deified the sun, moon and stars, or worshipped stocks and stones and beasts, the sacred river Nile, the crocodile that swam in its waters, and the very beetles that crawled along its banks, the opening page of Scripture proclaimed in language of majestic simplicity that the universe, and all that therein is, are the product of one supreme directing Intelligence; of an eternal, spiritual Being, prior to them and independent of them.

Now, while the *fact* of creation has to this day remained the first of the articles of the Jewish Creed, there is no uniform and binding belief as to the *manner* of creation, *i.e.* as to the process whereby the universe came into existence. The manner of the Divine creative activity is presented in varying forms and under differing metaphors by Prophet, Psalmist and Sage; by the Rabbis in Talmudic times, as well as by our medieval Jewish thinkers. In the Bible itself we have at least three modes of representing the overwhelming fact of Divine Creation. Genesis I gives us the story of Creation in the form of a Divine drama set out in six acts of a day each, with a similar refrain (*And there was evening, and there was morning, etc.*) closing the creative work of each day. The Psalmist, to whom Nature was a continual witness of its Divine Author (Ps. XIX), gives in Psalm CIV a purely poetic representation of the Creation story:—

'O LORD my God, Thou art very great;
Thou art clothed with glory and majesty.
Who coverest Thyself with light as with a garment,
Who stretchest out the heavens like a curtain . . .
Who makest the clouds Thy chariot,
Who walkest upon the wings of the wind :
Who makest winds Thy messengers . . .'

Again, Proverbs VIII, 22–31, shows forth Divine Wisdom presiding at the birth of Nature.

The mode of creation continued to engage Jewish minds after the close of the Bible and throughout the Rabbinic period, even though the Mishnah warns against all speculation concerning the beginning of things. To some, the relation of God to the universe was that of a mason to his work, and they accordingly spoke of God's 'architect's plans'; others lost themselves in heretic fancies as to what constituted the raw material, so to speak, of Creation; while to Philo of Alexandria, Creation was altogether outside time. Several of the ancient Rabbis, followed by the later Mystics, believed in successive creations. Prior to the existence of the present universe, they held, certain formless worlds issued from the Fountain of Existence and then vanished, like sparks which fly from a red-hot iron beaten by a hammer, that are extinguished as they separate themselves from the burning mass. In contrast to these abortive creations, the medieval Jewish Mystics maintain, ours is the best of all possible worlds. It is the outcome of a series of emanations and eradiations from God, the Infinite, *En Sof*. Furthermore, Rashi, the greatest Jewish commentator of all times, taught that the purpose of Scripture was not to give a strict chronology of Creation; while no less an authority than Maimonides declared: 'The account given in Scripture of the Creation is not, as is generally believed, intended to be in all its parts literal.' Later Jewish philosophers (Levi ben Gerson, Crescas, Albalag) made dangerous concessions to the Aristotelian doctrine of the eternity of matter; which doctrine Yehudah Hallevi, among others, strongly opposed as both contrary to Reason and as limiting God's Omnipotence.

### Jewish Attitude towards Evolution

In face of this great diversity of views as to the *manner* of creation, there is, therefore, nothing inherently un-Jewish in the evolutionary conception of the origin and growth of forms of existence from the simple to the complex, and from the lowest to the highest. The Biblical account itself gives expression to the same general truth of gradual ascent from amorphous chaos to order, from inorganic to organic, from lifeless matter to vegetable, animal and man; *insisting, however, that each stage is no product of chance, but is an act of Divine will*, realizing the Divine purpose, and receiving the seal of the Divine approval. Such, likewise, is in effect the evolutionary position. Behind the orderly development of the universe there must be a Cause, at once controlling and permeating the process. Allowing for all the evidence in favour of interpreting existence in terms of the evolutionary doctrine, there still remain facts—tremendous facts—to be explained; *viz.* the origin of life, mind, conscience, human personality. For each of these, we must look back to the Creative Omnipotence of the Eternal Spirit. Nor is that all. Instead of evolution ousting design and purpose from nature, 'almost every detail is now found to have a purpose and a use' (A. R. Wallace). In brief, evolution is conceivable only as the activity of a creative Mind purposing, by means of physical and biological laws, that wonderful organic development which has reached its climax in a being endowed with rational and moral faculties and capable of high ethical and spiritual achievement; in other words, as the activity of a supreme, directing Intelligence that has planned out, far back in the recesses of time, the ultimate goal of creation—'last in production, first in thought' סוף מעשה במחשבה תחלה. Thus evolution, far from destroying the *religious* teaching of Gen. I, is its profound confirmation.

As a noted scientist well remarks:—

'Slowly and by degrees, Science is being brought to recognize in the universe the existence of One Power, which is of no beginning and no end; which existed before all things were formed, and will remain in its integrity when all is gone—the Source and Origin of all, in Itself beyond any conception or image that man can form and set up before his eye or mind. This sum total of the scientific discoveries of all lands and times is the approach of the world's thought to our *Adon Olam*, the sublime chant by means of which the Jew has wrought and will further work the most momentous changes in the world' (Haffkine).

II. The second teaching of this chapter is, MAN IS THE GOAL AND CROWN OF CREATION—he is fundamentally distinguished from the lower creation, and is akin to the Divine. Man, modern scientists declare, is cousin to the anthropoid ape. But it is not so much the descent, as the *ascent* of man, which is decisive. Furthermore, it is not the resemblance, but the *differences* between man and the ape, that are of infinite importance. It is the differences between them that constitute the humanity of man, the Godlikeness of man. The qualities that distinguish the lowest man from the highest brute make the differences between them differences in kind rather than in degree; so much so that, whatever man might have inherited from his animal ancestors, his advent can truly be spoken of as a specific Divine act, whereby a new being had arisen with God-like possibilities within him, and *conscious* of these God-like possibilities within him. Man is of God, declared Rabbi Akiba; and what is far more, he *knows* he is of God.

Nor is the Biblical account of the creation of man irreconcilable with the view that certain forms of organized being have been endowed with the capacity of developing, in God's good time and under the action of suitable environment, the attributes distinctive of man. 'God formed man of the dust of the ground' (Gen. II, 7). Whence that dust was taken is not, and cannot be, of fundamental importance. Science holds that man was formed from the lower animals; are they not too 'dust of the ground'? 'And God said, *Let the earth bring forth the living creature*'—this command, says the Midrash, includes Adam as well, תוצא הארץ נפש חיה, זו רוחו של אדם הראשון. The thing that eternally matters is the breath of Divine and everlasting life that He breathed into the being coming from the dust. By virtue of that Divine impact, a new and distinctive creature made its appearance—man, dowered with an immortal soul. The sublime revelation of the unique worth and dignity of man, contained in Gen. I, 27 ('And God created man in His own image, in the image of God created He him'), may well be called the Magna Charta of humanity. Its purpose is not to explain the biological origins of the human race, but *its spiritual kinship with God*. There is much force in the view expressed by a modern thinker: '(The Bible) neither provides, nor, in the nature of things, could provide, faultless anticipations of sciences still unborn. If by a miracle it had provided them, without a miracle they could not have been understood' (Balfour). And fully to grasp the eternal power and infinite beauty of these words—'And God created man in His own image'—we need but compare them with the genealogy of man, condensed from the pages of one of the leading biologists of the age (Haeckel):—

'Monera begat Amoeba, Amoeba begat Synamoebae, Synamoebae begat Ciliated Larva, Ciliated Larva begat Primeval Stomach Animals, Primeval Stomach Animals begat Gliding Worms, Gliding Worms begat Skull-less Animals, Skull-less Animals begat Single-nostrilled Animals, Single-nostrilled Animals begat Primeval Fish, Primeval Fish begat Mud-fish, Mud-fish begat Gilled Amphibians, Gilled Amphibians begat Tailed Amphibians, Tailed Amphibians begat Primary Mammals, Primary Mammals begat Pouched Animals, Pouched Animals begat Semi-Apes, Semi-Apes begat Tailed Apes, Tailed Apes begat Man-like Apes, Man-like Apes begat Ape-like Men, Ape-like Men begat Men.'

Let anyone who is disturbed by the fact that Scripture does not include the latest scientific doctrine, try to imagine such information provided in a Biblical chapter.

III. JUDAISM IS OPTIMISM, is the third teaching of this chapter. No less than five times is the refrain, 'And God saw that it was good' repeated in the Creation Chapter. The world is not something hostile to God or independent of Him. All comes from God and all is His handiwork; all is in its essence good, nor is there anything absolutely evil. Israel acclaims God as the sole 'King of the universe, who formest light and createst darkness, who makest peace and createst all things' (Authorised Prayer Book, p. 37). Though Nature seems to be indifferent to man's sense of compassion, the world is good, since goodness is its final aim: without struggle, there would be no natural selection or adaptation to changing surroundings, and therefore no progress from lower to higher. 'And God saw everything that He had made, and, behold it was *very good*'—even suffering, evil, nay death itself, have a rightful and beneficent place in the Divine scheme, is the Rabbinic comment on this verse.

IV. THE SABBATH CONSECRATES WORK AND HALLOWS MAN'S LIFE, is the culminating teaching of the Chapter. The institution of the Sabbath is part of the cosmic plan, and therefore intended for all humanity. The Sabbath is a specifically Jewish contribution to human civilization. 'The actual Jewish Sabbath as we know it is without any point of contact in Babylonian institutions' (Skinner). The ancient Babylonians had 'a day of cessation', which they called by a name somewhat similar to 'Sabbath', and it was observed on the 7th, 14th, 19th, 21st, and 28th days of the months Ellul and Marcheshvan. These were considered unlucky days, and on them the king was not to offer sacrifice, nor consult an oracle, nor invoke curses on his enemies. Quite other is the Jewish Sabbath. It is not merely a day of cessation from toil. On the one hand, it has its positive aspect as a day of spiritual recreation; and, on the other hand, it is a day of joy, and is greeted in the Synagogue in the words לכה דודי לקראת כלה ('Come, my Beloved, to meet the Bride, Queen Sabbath'). It banishes toil and sorrow—a symbol of immortality, of that Life which is wholly a Sabbath; see on Exod. xx, 9–11.

*God the Creator and Lord of the Universe, which is the work of His goodness and wisdom; and Man, made in His image, who is to hallow his week-day labours by the blessedness of Sabbath-rest*—such are the teachings of the Creation chapter. Its purpose is to reveal these teachings to the children of men—and not to serve as a textbook of astronomy, geology or anthropology. Its object is not to teach scientific facts; but to proclaim highest religious truths respecting God, Man, and the Universe. The 'conflict' between the fundamental realities of Religion and the established facts of Science is seen to be unreal as soon as Religion and Science each recognizes the true borders of its dominion.

B

THE GARDEN OF EDEN

Chapter III is one of the most beautiful in the Bible. It has been called the 'pearl of Genesis', and men read with wonder its profound psychology of temptation and conscience. With unsurpassable art, it shows the beginning, the progress and the culmination of temptation and the consequences of sin. It depicts the earliest tragedy in the life of each human soul—the loss of man's happy, natural relation with God through deliberate disobedience of the voice of conscience, the voice of God. 'Every man who knows his own heart, knows that the story is true; it is the story of his own fall. Adam אדם is man, and his story is ours' (McFadyen).

Is the narrative literal or figurative, and is the Serpent an animal, a demon or merely the symbolic representation of Sin? Various have been the answers to these questions; and none of them are of cardinal importance to the Faith of the Jew. There is nothing in Judaism against the belief that the Bible attempts to convey deep truths of life and conduct by means of allegory. The Rabbis often taught by parable; and such method of instruction is, as is well known, the

## GENESIS—ADDITIONAL NOTES

immemorial way among Oriental peoples. Eminent Jewish thinkers, like Maimonides and Nachmanides, have accordingly understood this chapter as a parable; and Saadyah regarded the Serpent as the personification of the sinful tendencies in man, the *Yetzer hara*, the Evil Imagination.

Two fundamental religious truths are reflected in this Chapter. One of them is, *the seriousness of sin*. There is an everlasting distinction between right and wrong, between good and evil. There have always been voices—Serpent voices—deriding all moral do's and dont's, proclaiming instinct and inclination to be the truest guides to human happiness, and bluntly denying that any evil consequences follow defiance of God's commands. This Chapter for all time warns mankind against these insidious and fateful voices. In the words of Isaiah it seems to say, 'Woe unto them that call evil good, and good evil; that put darkness for light, and light for darkness; that put bitter for sweet, and sweet for bitter! Woe unto them that are wise in their own eyes.'

The other vital teaching of this chapter is, *Free will has been given to man*, and it is in his power to work either with or against God. It is not the knowledge of evil, but the succumbing to it, which is deadly; man may see the forbidden fruit, he need not eat of it. Man himself can make or mar his destiny. In all ages and in all conditions, man has shown the power to resist the suggestions of sin and proved himself superior to the power of evil. And if a man stumble and fall on the pathway of life, Judaism bids him rise again and seek the face of his Heavenly Father in humility, contrition and repentance. 'If a man sin, what is his punishment?' ask the Rabbis. The answer of the Prophet is, 'The soul that sinneth, it shall die'—the wages of sin is death. The answer of the Sage is, 'Evil pursueth the evil-doer'—the wages of sin is sin. The answer of the Almighty is, 'Let a man repent, and his sin will be forgiven him'—*the wages of sin is repentance*.

### Jewish View of the 'Fall of Man'

Strange and sombre doctrines have been built on this chapter of the Garden of Eden, such as the Christian doctrine of Original Sin (*e.g.* 'In Adam's fall, we sinned all'—New England Primer. 'The condition of man after the fall of Adam is such that he cannot turn and prepare himself by his own natural strength and good works to faith and calling upon God'—Art x, Free Will, of the Thirty-nine Articles). This Christian dogma of Original Sin is throughout the Middle Ages accompanied by an unbelievable vilification of Woman, as the authoress of death and all our earthly woe. Judaism rejects these doctrines. Man was mortal from the first, and death did not enter the world through the transgression of Eve. Stray Rabbinic utterances to the contrary are merely homiletic, and possess no binding authority in Judaism. There is no loss of the God-likeness of man, nor of man's ability to do right in the eyes of God; and no such loss has been transmitted to his latest descendants. Although a few of the Rabbis occasionally lament Eve's share in the poisoning of the human race by the Serpent, even they declare that the antidote to such poison has been found at Sinai; rightly holding that the Law of God is the bulwark against the devastations of animalism and godlessness. The Psalmist oftens speak of sin and guilt; but never is there a reference to this chapter or to what Christian Theology calls 'The Fall'. One searches in vain the Prayer Book, of even the Days of Penitence, for the slightest echo of the doctrine of the Fall of man. 'My God, the soul which Thou hast given me is pure,' is the Jew's daily morning prayer. 'Even as the soul is pure when entering upon its earthly career, so can man return it pure to his Maker' (Midrash).

Instead of the Fall of man (in the sense of humanity as a whole), Judaism preaches the Rise of man; and instead of Original Sin, it stresses Original Virtue (זכות אבות), the beneficent hereditary influence of righteous ancestors upon their descendants. 'There is no generation without its Abraham, Moses or Samuel,' says the Midrash; *i.e.* each age is capable of realizing the highest potentialities of the moral and spiritual life. Judaism clings to the idea of Progress. The Golden Age of Humanity is not in the past, but in the future (Isaiah II and XI); and all the children of men are destined to help in the establishment of that Kingdom of God on earth.

### C

### THE FLOOD

The primeval traditions recorded in the early chapters of Genesis stretch away into prehistoric times, and enshrine, in outline, great universal truths that touch the origin and meaning of Life and Man. The Rabbis tell us that the Patriarch Jacob spent fourteen years in the centres of ancient Semitic learning, the 'academies of Shem and Eber' (בבית מדרשו של שם ועבר), acquiring the ancient traditions which he handed on to his descendants. Among these was the memory of a fearful upheaval with an all-destroying Flood that caused a complete breach in the continuity of civilization in the primitive dwelling-place of mankind. Striking evidence is now at hand that the Bible story of the Flood is an event in historic times, approximately about the year 3800 before the Common Era. 'New discoveries have brought history so close to the Flood period and have produced so many phenomena requiring for their explanation just such an event as the Flood is supposed to have been, that the *a priori* denial of the Flood becomes thoroughly unscientific. We are justified in asking for more evidence, but there can be little doubt which way that evidence will trend' (L. Woolley). As it was recounted in the families of the Patriarchs, the story of that Flood is of great ethical and religious value. The Deluge was a Divine judgment upon an age in which might was right, and depravity degraded and enslaved the children of men. There were giants on earth in those days; *they* were the 'men of renown'; and life to these super-men meant unscrupulous selfishness and the deification of power and pleasure.

Among these men of violence, one man alone was upright and blameless, Noah, who believed in justice and practised mercy. He preached to the men of his generation—the Rabbis tell us—and warned them that a Deluge was coming, peradventure they might desist from iniquity and turn to righteousness. In vain. He saw that entire generation swept away; but he also lived to see the Rainbow of Promise, and the beginnings of a better world that was eventually to gain in strength, and to find lasting expression in Abraham and his descendants.

## D

### THE TOWER OF BABEL AND THE DIVERSITY OF LANGUAGES

One explanation of Genesis, chapter XI, is that it continues the theme of the preceding section and indicates that the Divine ideal was One Humanity united by one universal language. In view of the division of mankind by diversity of tongue, which has ever been a source of misunderstanding, hostility and war, this chapter answers the question how the original Divinely-ordained unity of language, that indispensable link for the unity of mankind, was lost. Only a great transgression—an enterprise colossal in its insolent impiety and evidencing an open revolt against God—could account for such a moral catastrophe to humanity (Steinthal). Standing symbols of such heathen impiety to the Hebrew mind were the *ziggurats*, the Mesopotamian temple-towers, rising to an immense height as if intended to scale Heaven.

The building of the greatest of these towers was associated with Babylon, the centre of ancient luxury and power. The Rabbis assert that the builders of this Tower of Babel wished to storm the heavens in order to wage war against the Deity; and 'as the highest stage in an Assyrian or Babylon ziggurat was surmounted by a shrine of the Deity, there is perhaps less fancifulness in these words than is often suspected' (Ryle). Jewish legend tells of the godlessness and inhumanity of these tower-builders. If, in the course of the construction of the Tower, a man fell down and met his death, none paid heed to it; but if a brick fell down and broke into fragments, they were grieved and even shed tears—a graphic summing up of heathen civilization, ancient or modern. Such an enterprise provoked Divine punishment; and that insolence and power were broken by lasting division occasioned by diversity of language.

Quite a different interpretation of this chapter is given by Ibn Ezra: 'The purpose of the builders was simply to prevent their becoming separated, and to secure their dwelling together. But as this purpose was contrary to the design of Providence (IX, 1; I, 28) that the whole earth should be inhabited, it was frustrated. The expression 'with its top in heaven' must accordingly be interpreted that that tower was to be of very great height, so that it would be visible at a considerable distance and become a rallying point to all people.

## E

### THE DELUGE AND ITS BABYLONIAN PARALLEL

Flood stories are very numerous, and are found in every part of the world. But these are of little or no interest to the Bible student or to the modern reader. The Babylonian parallel to the Biblical account of the Deluge, however, stands in a class by itself. Both the resemblances and the differences of the two accounts are of great importance for the understanding and proper appreciation of the Bible narrative.

The Babylonian story is as follows: The gods in council decide to send a Flood upon the earth. One of the gods, Ea, who was present at the council, resolves to save his favourite Utnapishtim—this is the name of the Babylonian Noah. He warns him of the impending danger and at the same time commands him to build a ship. He also furnishes the 'superlatively clever one', Utnapishtim, with a misleading pretext to offer his contemporaries when questioned as to the reason for his building the ship. (In the Rabbinical legend, Noah, during the years of the ship's construction, is a preacher of repentance. 'Turn from your evil ways and live,' is his admonition to his fellow-men). When the ship is built, Utnapishtim fills it with his possessions, his family, dependants, including artisans, together with domestic and wild animals. He then enters it himself and closes the door behind him. The storm rages for six days and nights, till all mankind are destroyed, and the very gods 'cowered in terror like dogs'. On the seventh day, he sends out a dove, which comes back to him. And then he lets go a raven, which does not return. On this, Utnapishtim released all the animals; and leaving the ship, offered a sacrifice. 'The gods gathered like flies over the sacrifice.' The deities then began to quarrel; but eventually Utnapishtim is blessed, and is received into the society of the gods.

The resemblances between this Babylonian story and the Biblical account lie on the surface. To mention only a few features common to both: the whole human race is doomed to destruction; one man with his dependants and animals is saved in a ship; the episode of the dove and raven; and after leaving the ship, the man offers sacrifices and receives Divine blessings.

Of far greater significance, however, are the differences between the two accounts. The Babylonian story is unethical and polytheistic, devoid of any uniform or exalted purpose, and lacking in reverence and restraint. Not so the terse, direct, and simple Hebrew narrative. Instead of the quarrelsome, deceitful, vindictive pack of Babylonian deities, false to one another and false to men, we have in the Hebrew account the One and Supreme God—holy and righteous in His dealings with man. Unlike its Babylonian counterpart, the Hebrew Deluge is a proclamation of the eternal truth that the basis of human society is justice, and that any society which is devoid of justice deserves to perish, and will inevitably perish. Noah is saved, not through celestial caprice or favouritism, not because he was 'superlatively clever', but because he was righteous and blameless in a perverse generation; a man who was worthy of God's approval, as well as of inaugurating a new era for humanity. An impassable gulf separates the Biblical and the Babylonian Deluge stories. This infinite ethical *difference* between them is recognized even by those who are otherwise hostile to the Bible. 'The Biblical story of the Deluge possesses an intrinsic power to stir the conscience of the world, and it was written with this educational and moral end in view. Of this end there is no trace in the Deluge records outside the Bible' (A. Jeremias).

In its Babylonian form, Assyriologists tell us, the story seems to have been reduced to writing as early as the days of Abraham. It must have been known in substance to the children of Israel in Canaan and later in Egypt. But in the form in which, under God's Providence, the Patriarchs transmitted it to their descendants, it was free from all degrading elements, and became an assertion of the everlasting righteousness of the One God. 'The Babylonian parallel only serves to bring out the unique grandeur of Israel's God-idea, which could thus purify and transform the most uncongenial and repugnant features of the ancient Deluge tradition' (Gunkel).

F

ARE THERE TWO CONFLICTING ACCOUNTS OF CREATION AND THE DELUGE IN THE BIBLE?

All those scholars who are followers of what is called 'Higher Criticism' maintain that the account of the Flood in the Bible was written much later than Moses. In the face of all archæological evidence to the contrary, they maintain that the art of writing was not known in Israel before the days of David. Like all primitive nations, Israel had bards and singers who recited and composed legends and tales concerning the exploits of the ancestral heroes; and in the course of centuries, these early legends and tales of Israel assumed a fixed literary form in two distinct collections. They call one of these supposed 'collections' E, because the Divine Name used in it is *Elohim* (rendered in English by GOD), and allege that it arose in the Prophetic circles of Northern Israel in the ninth pre-Christian century. The other collection they call J, because, they say, it regularly employs the Divine Name which is read as *Adonay* (translated into English by the word LORD), and they declare it arose in the Prophetic circles of Judea in the eighth pre-Christian century. A third document (Deuteronomy), they tell us, arose in the reign of King Josiah; and on the return from Exile, a fourth portion of the Torah came into existence, the Priestly Document, which they call P. As these distinct documents, however, E, J, D, and P, do not exist separately or even side by side, we are asked to believe that at various stages in Israel's history, those different parts have been combined and edited by a succession of 'redactors'. We shall elsewhere in the course of this commentary show the utter baselessness of this revolutionary view of Israel's history and religion. At this point, we shall examine the principal reasons which the critics assign for the division of the text of the Torah into what they call its 'original elements'. These reasons are: (*a*) the alleged diversity in the use of Divine Names; and (*b*) supposed discrepancies in statement between the various 'sources'. And nowhere in the Pentateuch, they hold, are these differences in Divine Names and in details of statement more evident than in the chapters dealing with the Creation and the Deluge. These sections, therefore, should afford the best test to prove the tenability, or otherwise, of the claims of the Bible critics.

A. Genesis, chapters I and II are supposed to contain two distinct accounts of Creation. Genesis, chapter I–II, 3, is called P—the Priestly account, and is supposed to be post-exilic; whereas Genesis, chapter II, 4–25 is the Prophetic account, J, and is stated to be some two centuries earlier.

But, *are* there two accounts of Creation? Can Genesis II, 4–25, honestly be considered as such? Unlike chapter I, it does not describe the coming into existence of the sun, moon and stars, of the seas and their inhabitants. Even Heaven and earth are mentioned only indirectly, in an introductory phrase. Genesis II, 4–25, pre-supposes Gen. I, supplements it, and is unintelligible without it. The proposed distinguishing of the two sources by the use of the different Divine

Names fails at the very start. *Elohim* they declare to be exclusively used by the Priestly writer of Gen. I; and *Adonay* to be the Divine Name used only by the supposed Prophetic writer to whom they assign Gen. II, 4–15; *and yet Elohim occurs* 20 *times together with Adonay in Gen.* II, 4–25 and in Chap. III, which is also held by them to be Prophetic. The critics attempt to get over this difficulty by stating that Elohim has been here interpolated by the 'redactor' 20 times in one chapter. But then, in the conversation between Eve and the serpent, Elohim without Adonay is used! Is this, too, an interpolation?

As explained in the comment on II, 4, the alternate, or combined, use of Elohim and Adonay for the Name of God presents no difficulty whatsoever. Their employment varies according to the nature of the context. Thus, in connection with the creation of the Universe at large (Genesis I), the Divine Name employed is *Elohim*. In God's merciful relations with human beings, however (Gen. II, 4–25), He is spoken of as *Adonay*, Lord. There is nothing strange or out of the way in such usage. In English, we choose words like Deity, Supreme Being, Almighty, God, Lord, according as the subject and occasion demand. *One and the same writer* may at various times use any one of these English terms for the Divine Being. The nature of the context decides what Divine Name is employed. In the same way, different Divine Names in the Hebrew text do not argue a diversity of writers, but simply that the Divine Name has each time been selected in accordance with the idea to be expressed. David Hoffmann, W. H. Green, and B. Jacob have examined each and every instance of the use of these Names throughout Genesis, and have shown the exact appropriateness of each Name to the subject matter in which it occurs.

B. No more are there two distinct accounts of the Deluge than there are two accounts of Creation. Here, too, the Divine Name 'test' fails completely. One example will suffice. 'And they that went in, went in male and female of all flesh, as God (Elohim) commanded him; and the LORD (Adonay) shut him in' (VII, 16). As the Bible critics declare this verse to be written by P, it ought to contain only Elohim; and yet we have Elohim followed by *Adonay!* The critics are compelled by their theory to assign the 'offending' words to J, although the whole context belongs to P. Those who are not critics find, of course, no difficulty here: Adonay is used, because 'the LORD (Adonay) shut him in' describes a merciful action. In face of such a combined use of both Elohim and Adonay as we have here, and in Genesis II, the test of the Divine Name surely breaks down.

Equally baseless is the argument triumphantly brought forward that there is a striking discrepancy of statement in the directions given to Noah, which discrepancy compels the assumption of two distinct accounts. Noah is first told (VI, 19) to take into the ark two each of all animals; whereas, in the next chapter, he is told to take two of all animals, but *seven* of all clean beasts! The answer is plain: VI, 19 does not say that *only* two shall be taken from each kind. The first is a general command; whereas the second command at the moment of entering the ark is more specific, and directs that of the clean domestic animals of Noah that were to serve him for food and later for sacrifices, he was to take seven of each. Such general statements (כלל) followed by a statement giving specific details (פרט) are the rule in Scripture. Thus, the opening verse of Gen. I, 'In the beginning God created the heavens and the earth,' is a general statement. This is followed by a whole series of supplementary specific statements, giving the details of creation. Yet there certainly is no contradiction between the general statement that behind the whole Universe is a Creator, and the remainder of the chapter describing the various creative acts. The same rule of general and specific statement obtains in connection with the command to Noah.

But the utter falsity of the critical theory is proved by the Babylonian version itself. The Babylonian version is in agreement with the Bible account *as an undivided whole*. There are special points of agreement between it and the portions assigned to P; such as, the precise instructions for building the ark, and the statement that the ark rested on a mountain, etc. There are also special points of agreement between it and the portions assigned to J, such as, the sending forth of birds, and the later building of an altar and the offering of sacrifices. This is unanswerable testimony to the unity of the Scriptural Deluge account.

The procedure of the critics in connection with the Creation and Deluge chapters is typical of their method throughout. It justifies the protest of the late Lord Chancellor of England, the Earl of Halsbury—an excellent judge of evidence—who in 1915 found himself impelled to declare:— 'For my own part I consider the assignment of different fragments of Genesis to a number of wholly imaginary authors great rubbish. I do not understand the attitude of those men who base a whole theory of this kind on hypotheses for which there is no evidence whatsoever.' A generation before the Earl of Halsbury, the historian Lecky gave expression to a similar judgment, in the following words: 'I may be pardoned for expressing my belief that this kind of investigation is often pursued with an exaggerated confidence. Plausible conjecture is too easily mistaken for positive proof. Undue significance is attached to what may be mere casual coincidence, and a minuteness of accuracy is professed in discriminating between different elements in a narrative which cannot be attained by mere internal evidence.'

Whenever *external* evidence comes to light, as in the case of the Babylonian version of the

Deluge, or, as we shall see later, in the case of the discovery of the Babylonian Code of Laws—the arbitrary and purely fictitious nature of the critical theories becomes patent to all.

## G
## ABRAHAM

### I

Mankind descending from Adam became hopelessly corrupt and was swept away by the Deluge. Noah alone was spared. But before many generations pass away, mankind once again becomes arrogant and impious, and moral darkness overspreads the earth.' And God said *Let Abraham be*—and there was light,' is the profound saying of the Midrash. In many a beautiful legend, the Rabbis recount how Abraham refused to walk in the way of the Tower-builders, and broke away from the debasing heathenism of his contemporaries. In his early childhood one night, he looked at the stars under the clear Mesopotamian sky, and felt, 'These are the gods!' But the dawn came, and soon the stars could be seen no longer when the sun rose. 'This is my god, him will I adore!' he exclaimed. But then the sun set, and he hailed the moon as his deity. When in turn the moon was obscured, he cried out: 'This, too, is no god! There must be One who is the Maker of Sun, Moon and Stars.' Having gradually reached the momentous conviction that the Universe is the work of One Supreme Being who is the God of righteousness, he endeavours to open the eyes of others to the folly of idol-worship, and becomes the Preacher of the True Faith. In his father's house, the legend continues, there stood one great idol and a large number of smaller ones. Abraham broke all the smaller ones and then placed the hammer in the hand of the big idol. 'They quarrelled among themselves,' he later explained to his dumb-founded father, 'and the big one thereupon took a hammer and shattered them all. Behold, it is still in his hands!' 'But there is no life and power in them to do such things,' his father answered in rage. 'Why then dost thou serve them? Can they hear thy prayers when thou callest upon them?' was the reply. Abraham was thereupon haled before the ruler of Babylon, Nimrod, who cast him into a fiery furnace (whence the name of the city 'Ur', which means *fire*). An angel of God rescues him unhurt from its devouring flames (Midrash). Abraham the idol-wrecker is the father of that People which was to shatter all idolatries; which was to suffer all things, endure all things, and survive all things in its defiance of despotisms of the body and soul; which was to succeed in turning the course of history by the perpetuation of true religion for the children of men. The call of Abraham is the beginning of the higher spiritual life of humanity.

### II

With Abraham, the nature of the Book of Genesis changes. Hitherto, in its first eleven chapters, it has given an account of the dawn of the world and of human society. The remainder of the Book is the story of the founders of the People whose destiny, in the light of God's purpose, forms the main theme of Scripture. These founders of the Jewish People are not divine or semi-divine beings, as is the case with the mythical heroes of Greece, Rome or the Teutonic nations. They are purely human personalities, just normal men, of like passions with ourselves, having their faults and excellencies. 'Abraham is the "Friend of God". He is nothing more; but he is nothing less. In him was exemplified the fundamental truth of all religion, that God has not deserted the world; that His work is carried on by His own chosen instruments; that good men are not only His creatures and His servants, but His friends' (Stanley).

With the Patriarchs, we leave the dim, Primeval world and enter the full daylight of historical times. Even a generation ago, Bible critics looked upon the Patriarchal stories in Genesis as a tissue of fabrications, at best as legends, but in no case as authentic history. No theory was too fantastic, or too blasphemous, to be put forward as a serious explanation of the narrative. One critic declared Abraham to be a 'free creation of unconscious art'; another turned him into a 'fetish stone'; a third identified him with the 'starry heavens'; and a fourth made of him 'a sacred locality'. One of the greatest of these Bible critics (Dillmann), who at one time shared those preposterous views, eventually felt himself impelled to state 'we have no right to explain these Genesis narratives as pure fiction. They rest in essentials on sound historical recollection'. This view is now that of all responsible students of the Bible. 'The patriarchal period has been so illumined by recent discoveries,' says the author of the commentary on 'Genesis' in the *International Critical Series*, 'that it is no longer possible to doubt its substantial historicity. Contemporary documents reveal a set of conditions into which the patriarchal narratives fit perfectly, and which are so different from those prevailing under the monarchy that the situation could not possibly have been imagined by an Israelite of that age' (John Skinner). The words of the Psalmist, 'Truth shall spring out of the earth,' have become literally fulfilled, and the very stones of the Nile and the Euphrates valleys, of Palestine, and Asia Minor, have given their decisive testimony in vindication of the Torah. 'We have travelled far from the time when scholars attempted to turn the Patriarchs into mythical beings. To-day that attempt itself almost appears mythical' (Professor D. H. Müller).

# H

## THE BINDING OF ISAAC (AKEDAH)

This Chapter is of great importance both in the life of Abraham and in the life of Israel. The aged Patriarch, who had longed for a rightful heir ('O Lord God, what wilt Thou give me, seeing I go hence childless?'), and who had had his longing fulfilled in the birth of Isaac, is now bidden offer up this child as a burnt offering unto the Lord. The purpose of the command was to apply a supreme test to Abraham's faith, thus strengthening his faith by the heroic exercise of it. The proofs of a man's love of God are his willingness to serve Him with all his heart, all his soul and all his might; as well as his readiness to sacrifice unto Him what is even dearer than life. It was a test safe only in a Divine hand, capable of intervening as He did intervene, and as it was His purpose from the first to intervene, as soon as the spiritual end of the trial was accomplished.

So much for what may be called the *positive* lesson of the Akedah. We shall now examine another side, the great *negative* teaching of this trial of Abraham. The story of the Binding of Isaac opens the age-long warfare of Israel against the abominations of child sacrifice, which was rife among the Semitic peoples, as well as their Egyptian and Aryan neighbours. In that age, it was astounding that Abraham's God should have interposed *to prevent* the sacrifice, not that He should have asked for it. A primary purpose of this command, therefore, was to demonstrate to Abraham and his descendants after him that God abhorred human sacrifice with an infinite abhorrence. Unlike the cruel heathen deities, *it was the spiritual surrender alone that God required*. Moses warns his people not to serve God in the manner of the surrounding nations. 'For every abomination to the LORD, which He hateth, have they done unto their gods; for even their sons and their daughters do they burn in the fire to their gods' (Deuteronomy XII, 31). All the Prophets alike shudder at this hideous aberration of man's sense of worship, and they do not rest till all Israel shares their horror of this savage custom. It is due to the influence of their teaching that the name *Ge-Hinnom*, the valley where the wicked kings practised this horrible rite, became a synonym for 'Hell'.

A new meaning and influence begin for the Akedah, and its demand for man's unconditional surrender to God's will and the behests of God's law, with the Maccabean revolt, when Jews were first called upon to die for their Faith. Abraham's readiness to sacrifice his most sacred affections on the altar of his God evoked and developed a new ideal in Israel, *the ideal of martyrdom*. The story of Hannah and her seven sons, immortalized in the Second Book of Maccabees, has come down to us in many forms. In one of these, the martyr mother says to her youngest child, 'Go to Abraham our Father, and tell him that I have bettered his instruction. He offered one child to God; I offered seven. He merely bound the sacrifice; I performed it' (Midrash). As persecution deepened during later centuries, the Binding of Isaac was ever in the mind of men and women who might at any moment be given the dread alternative of apostasy or death. Allusions to the Akedah early found their way into the Liturgy; and in time a whole cycle of synagogue hymns (*piyyutim*) grew round it. In the Middle Ages, it gave fathers and mothers the superhuman courage to immolate themselves and their children, rather than see them fall away to idolatry or baptism. English Jews need but think of the soul-stirring tragedy enacted at York Castle in the year 1190 to understand the lines of the modern Jewish poet:—

'We have sacrificed all. We have given our wealth,
Our homes, our honours, our land, our health,
Our lives—like Hannah her children seven—
For the sake of the Torah that came from Heaven' (J. L. Gordon).

Many to-day have no understanding of martyrdom. They fail to see that it represents the highest moral triumph of humanity—unwavering steadfastness to principle, even at the cost of life. They equally fail to see the lasting influence of such martyrdoms upon the life and character of the nation whose history they adorn. Those who are thus blind to unconquerable courage and endurance naturally display hostility to the whole idea of the Akedah and its place and associations in Jewish thought. 'Only a Moloch requires human sacrifices' (Geiger), they exclaim. But in all human history, there is not a single noble cause, movement or achievement that did not call for sacrifice, nay sacrifice of life itself. Science, Liberty, Humanity, all took their toll of martyrs; and so did and does Judaism. Israel is the classical people of martyrdom. No other people has made similar sacrifices for Truth, Conscience, Human Honour and Human Freedom (Martin Schreiner). Even in our own day, Jewish parents in Eastern and Central European lands have refused, and refuse, fortune and honours for the sake of conscience. What is far harder, they sacrifice the careers of their children, whenever these involve disloyalty to the God of their Fathers. Few chapters of the Bible have had a more potent and more lasting influence on the lives and souls of men than the Akedah.

# I

## ALLEGED CHRISTOLOGICAL REFERENCES IN SCRIPTURE

The first of these references is alleged to be in the words often translated by 'Until Shiloh come', in Gen. XLIX, 10. Most of the ancient and modern explanations of this verse turn upon the Heb. word rendered by *Shiloh*.

## GENESIS—ADDITIONAL NOTES

I. It is a strange circumstance that the older Jewish Versions and commentators (Septuagint, Targums, Saadyah and Rashi) read this word without a *yod*, as if written שֶׁלֹּה, the archaic form for 'his'; or, as if it were a poetic form for 'peace'.

(*a*) The translation, 'until that which is his shall come,' is derived from the Septuagint. Its meaning is, The sceptre shall not depart from Judah till all that is reserved for him shall have been fulfilled.

(*b*) 'Till he come whose it (the kingdom) is' (Onkelos and Jerusalem Targum, Saadyah, Rashi and other Jewish commentators).

(*c*) 'Till peace cometh' (M. Friedlander).

II. Most commentators, however, take the word שילה as the name of a place or person.

(*a*) 'As long as men come to Shiloh' (to worship). Shiloh was the location of the sanctuary in the days of the Prophet Samuel, before Jerusalem became the centre of Jewish worship. As the outstanding superiority of the tribe of Judah only began after the Temple was built at Jerusalem, this interpretation is unsatisfactory.

(*b*) 'Till he of Shiloh cometh, and the obedience of the peoples be turned to him.' Mendelssohn and Zunz see in the verse a prediction of the event described in I Kings XI, 29 f. Ahijah, the Prophet of Shiloh, foretold to Jeroboam that a part of the Kingdom would be taken from Solomon and transferred to him; that ten tribes of Israel (here called 'peoples', see Gen. XLVIII, 4) would break away from the House of David, and submit to his rule. This ingenious explanation fails to satisfy for various reasons. 'He of Shiloh' would be in Heb. not שילה but השילוני; the tribes were not turned to the Prophet of Shiloh but to Jeroboam; and the utterance would have been quite unintelligible to Judah.

(*c*) 'Till Shiloh come.' This is the rendering of the Authorised Version, and assumes that *Shiloh* is a personal name or a Messianic title. Although this assumption finds support in Rabbinic literature, it is there only a homiletic comment without official and binding authority. Despite the fact that nowhere in Scripture is that term applied to the Messiah, Christian theologians assume that Shiloh is a name of the Founder of Christianity. In this sense, 'Till Shiloh come' is a favourite text of Christian missionaries in attempting to convert illiterate Jews or those ignorant of Scripture. It is noteworthy that this translation only dates from the year 1534, and is found for the first time in the German Bible of Sebastian Munster. Although it is retained in the text of the Revised Version, it is now rejected by all those who have a scholarly acquaintance with the subject. Even a loyal Bishop of the Church of England, the late Dean of Westminster, wrote, 'The improbability of this later interpretation is so great that it may be dismissed from consideration' (Ryle).

Such likewise is the judgment which must be passed on the translations of all the other alleged Christological passages which missionaries to the Jews are fond of quoting. Christian scholars of repute are gradually giving up such partisan interpretations. Thus Psalm II, 12 is translated in the Authorised Version as 'Kiss the Son,' with the obvious Christian reference. In the Revised Version text, however, this is softened to 'Kiss the son'; while the Margin gives, 'Worship in purity.' This latter is in agreement with Jewish authorities.

Similarly, in connection with Isaiah VII, 14, 'A virgin shall conceive,' Christian scholars today admit that 'virgin' is a mistranslation for the Heb. word *almah*, in that verse. A 'maid' or unmarried woman is expressed in Hebrew by *bethulah*. The word *almah* in Isaiah VII, 14 means no more than a young woman of age to be a mother, whether she be married or not.

The most famous passage of this class is the Fifty-third chapter of Isaiah. For eighteen hundred years Christian theologians have passionately maintained that it is a Prophetic anticipation of the life of the Founder of their Faith. An impartial examination of the chapter, however, shows that the Prophet is speaking of *a past historical fact*. and is describing one who had already been smitten to death. Consequently, a reference to an event which is said to have happened many centuries later is excluded.

These three instances may be taken as typical. Modern scholarship has shattered the arguments from the Scriptures which missionaries have tried, and are still trying, to impose upon ignorant Jews.

ספר שמות

# THE BOOK OF EXODUS

# ספר שמות

# THE BOOK OF EXODUS

NAME. The Second Book of Moses was originally called ספר יציאת מצרים, 'the Book of the Going out of Egypt.' At an early date, however, it came to be known as שמות, from its opening phrase, *Ve-eleh shemoth* ('And these are the names'). Its current designation in Western countries is Exodus—from the Greek term *exodos*, 'The Departure' (of the children of Israel out of Egypt), a name applied to it in the Septuagint, the ancient Greek translation of Scripture.

CONTENTS. The Book of Exodus is the natural continuation of Genesis. Genesis describes the lives of the Fathers of the Hebrew People: Exodus tells the beginning of the People itself. It records Israel's enslavement in Egypt, and the deliverance from the House of Bondage. It describes the institution of the Passover, the Covenant at Mount Sinai, and the organization of Public Worship that was to make Israel into 'a kingdom of priests and a holy nation'. It recounts the murmurings and backslidings of Israel, as well as the Divine guidance and instruction vouchsafed to it; the apostasy of the Golden Calf, as well as the supreme Revelation that followed it—the revelation of the Divine Being as a 'God, merciful and gracious, long-suffering, and abundant in goodness and truth ; keeping mercy unto the thousandth generation, forgiving iniquity and transgression and sin ; and that will by no means clear the guilty'.

IMPORTANCE. Nearly all the foundations on which Jewish life is built—the Ten Commandments, the historic Festivals, the leading principles of civil law—are contained in the Book of Exodus. And the importance of this Book is not confined to Israel. In its epic account of Israel's redemption from slavery, mankind learned that God is a God of Freedom; that, even as in Egypt He espoused the cause of brick-making slaves against the royal tyrant, Providence ever exalts righteousness and freedom, and humbles iniquity and oppression. And the Ten Commandments, spoken at Sinai, form the Magna Charta of religion and morality, linking them for the first time, and for all time, in indissoluble union.

DIVISIONS. The Book may be divided into five parts. The first part (chaps. I–XV) relates the story of the Oppression and Redemption. The second part (chaps. XVI–XXIV) describes the journey to Sinai, and embodies the Decalogue and the civil laws and judgments that were to have such a profound influence on human society. Then follow, in chaps. XXV–XXXI, the directions for the building of the Sanctuary. Chaps. XXXII–XXXIV detail Israel's apostasy in connection with the Golden Calf; and chaps. XXXV–XL describe the construction of the Sanctuary, and thus prepare the way for the Third Book of Moses, the Book of Leviticus.

# EXODUS I, 1

## CHAPTER I

1. Now these are the names of the sons of Israel, who came into Egypt with Jacob; every man came with his household: 2. Reuben, Simeon, Levi, and Judah; 3. Issachar, Zebulun, and Benjamin; 4. Dan and Naphtali, Gad and Asher. 5. And all the souls that came out of the loins of Jacob were seventy souls; and Joseph was in Egypt already. 6. And Joseph died, and all his brethren, and all that generation. 7. And the children of Israel were fruitful, and increased abundantly, and multiplied, and waxed exceeding mighty; and the land was filled with them. ¶ 8. Now there arose a new king over Egypt, who knew not Joseph. 9. And he said unto his people: 'Behold, the people of the children of Israel are too many and too

שמות א

CAP. I. א

א וְאֵ֗לֶּה שְׁמוֹת֙ בְּנֵ֣י יִשְׂרָאֵ֔ל הַבָּאִ֖ים מִצְרָ֑יְמָה אֵ֣ת יַעֲקֹ֔ב אִ֥ישׁ
2 וּבֵית֖וֹ בָּֽאוּ: רְאוּבֵ֣ן שִׁמְע֔וֹן לֵוִ֖י וִיהוּדָֽה: יִשָּׂשכָ֖ר זְבוּלֻ֥ן
3
4 וּבִנְיָמִֽן: דָּ֥ן וְנַפְתָּלִ֖י גָּ֥ד וְאָשֵֽׁר: וַֽיְהִ֗י כָּל־נֶ֛פֶשׁ יֹצְאֵ֥י יֶֽרֶךְ־
5
6 יַעֲקֹ֖ב שִׁבְעִ֣ים נָ֑פֶשׁ וְיוֹסֵ֖ף הָיָ֥ה בְמִצְרָֽיִם: וַיָּ֤מָת יוֹסֵף֙ וְכָל־
7 אֶחָ֔יו וְכֹ֖ל הַדּ֥וֹר הַהֽוּא: וּבְנֵ֣י יִשְׂרָאֵ֗ל פָּר֧וּ וַֽיִּשְׁרְצ֛וּ וַיִּרְבּ֥וּ
   וַיַּֽעַצְמ֖וּ בִּמְאֹ֣ד מְאֹ֑ד וַתִּמָּלֵ֥א הָאָ֖רֶץ אֹתָֽם: פ
8 וַיָּ֥קָם מֶֽלֶךְ־חָדָ֖שׁ עַל־מִצְרָ֑יִם אֲשֶׁ֥ר לֹֽא־יָדַ֖ע אֶת־יוֹסֵֽף:

## I. SHEMOTH

(CHAPTERS I–VI, 1)

### ISRAEL IN EGYPT: THE OPPRESSION AND THE REDEMPTION
### THE OPPRESSION OF THE ISRAELITES. CHAPTER I

**1.** *now these.* lit. 'and these', which better indicates the close connection between the first two books of the Pentateuch, since the whole Torah is one continuous narrative.

**5.** *seventy souls.* Jacob himself is included in the number; see Gen. XLVI, 8–27. Of the seventy, sixty-eight were males. If to these we add the wives of the sons and grandsons, and the husbands of the daughters and granddaughters, and all their servants and their families, the total number of those who entered Egypt must have been several hundreds, if not thousands.

**6.** *and Joseph died.* This verse resumes the thread of the narrative of the last verse of Gen. (L. 26) where we read, 'So Joseph died.'
*all that generation.* Both Israelites and Egyptians.

**7.** *increased abundantly.* lit. 'swarmed.' Note the accumulation of the synonyms—were fruitful, increased abundantly, multiplied, and waxed exceeding mighty. The extraordinary increase of the Israelites in Egypt presents a difficulty that is more apparent than real. As we have seen, the seventy souls who went down to Egypt did so accompanied by extensive households, whom they eventually incorporated into their families (cf. Gen. XVII, 12, 27). Prof. Orr recalls from personal knowledge the case of a golden wedding where the original couple had multiplied to 69. If, he says, one bears this in mind in connection with the descendants of Jacob in Egypt, and 'reckons the result of a similar rate of increase for 300 or 400 years, the figures may surprise him'.
*the land was filled.* Not only Goshen, the eastern Delta of the Nile, the abode originally assigned to the Israelites. In time, they were found everywhere in Egypt as well as outside Egypt, in territories under Egyptian control; see v. 12.

**8.** *a new king.* A monarch of a new dynasty, with a 'nationalist' policy; probably Rameses II. Joseph served one of the Hyksos (Shepherd) kings, an Asiatic dynasty whose rule in Egypt began some centuries before him; see note on Gen. XXXIX, 1. Their rule came to an end not long after the death of Joseph, when the Hyksos were driven back into Asia, and a descendant of the native dynasty regained the throne. See Additional Note A, 'Israel in Egypt,' p. 394.
*who knew not Joseph.* He feigned to know nothing of Joseph's merits (Rashi). The immemorial ingratitude of rulers and commonwealths is proverbial. Especially common is ingratitude to Israel—the People that has achieved so much of eternal worth, but has rarely succeeded in winning gratitude.

With the death of Joseph, a large portion of the Israelites in time forgot the religious traditions and the religious practices of the Fathers (Josh. XXIV, 14; Ezek. XX, 8). The greater portion of the people, however, must have kept alive in their hearts the memory and hope of Israel. Otherwise it is quite impossible to understand how they maintained their separate existence during generations of oppression, and still more during centuries of prosperity, in a highly civilized society like the Egyptian. Foremost among the loyalists were the tribe of Levi, who alone maintained the covenant of Abraham. Of those who had abandoned Israel's hope, many reverted to heathen Semitic practices; while others, the Midrash tells us, adopted the motto, 'Let us be Egyptians in all things.'

EXODUS I, 10

mighty for us; 10. come, let us deal wisely with them, lest they multiply, and it come to pass, that, when there befalleth us any war, they also join themselves unto our enemies, and fight against us, and get them up out of the land.' 11. Therefore they did set over them taskmasters to afflict them with their burdens. And they built for Pharaoh store-cities, Pithom and Raamses. 12. But the more they afflicted them, the more they multiplied and the

9 וַיֹּ֣אמֶר אֶל־עַמּ֑וֹ הִנֵּ֗ה עַ֚ם בְּנֵ֣י יִשְׂרָאֵ֔ל רַ֥ב וְעָצ֖וּם מִמֶּֽנּוּ׃
10 הָ֥בָה נִֽתְחַכְּמָ֖ה ל֑וֹ פֶּן־יִרְבֶּ֗ה וְהָיָ֞ה כִּֽי־תִקְרֶ֤אנָה מִלְחָמָה֙ וְנוֹסַ֤ף גַּם־הוּא֙ עַל־שֹׂ֣נְאֵ֔ינוּ וְנִלְחַם־בָּ֖נוּ וְעָלָ֥ה מִן־הָאָֽרֶץ׃
11 וַיָּשִׂ֤ימוּ עָלָיו֙ שָׂרֵ֣י מִסִּ֔ים לְמַ֥עַן עַנֹּת֖וֹ בְּסִבְלֹתָ֑ם וַיִּ֜בֶן עָרֵ֤י מִסְכְּנוֹת֙ לְפַרְעֹ֔ה אֶת־פִּתֹ֖ם וְאֶת־רַעַמְסֵֽס׃
12 וְכַאֲשֶׁר֙ יְעַנּ֣וּ

**9.** *too many and too mighty for us.* The exaggeration of hatred, jealousy and fear. The land, it seemed to them, was full of Israelites; they were *everywhere!* 'They filled the theatres and all the places of amusement,' is the comment of the Midrash. The fact that their increase is their only crime, and that no activity inimical to society could be charged against them, is striking testimony to the blameless civic life of our ancestors in Egypt.

**10.** *come, let us deal.* The king plans the means of crushing the Israelites in common deliberation with his counsellors. 'This first instance of *rishus* on a large scale is noteworthy also for the fact that it arises *not from the Egyptian people*, but from the ruling classes. It is the king who stirs it up, and assigns high reasons of state for making it a national policy. This has often repeated itself in history' (Hirsch).

*wisely. i.e.* craftily.

*join themselves.* Living in Goshen, the Israelites might assist the enemy and make common cause with the Hittites, whose power Rameses could not break; or with any Semitic invaders of Egypt from the East. It is at all times a common stratagem of 'patriots' to suspect the loyalty of the envied alien who is living peacefully and prosperously among them. One of the first laws the children of Israel were to learn on leaving Egypt was: 'And a stranger shalt thou not wrong, neither shalt thou oppress him; for ye were strangers in the land of Egypt' (XXII, 20; see p. 63, note on Gen. XVIII, 7).

*and get them.* Mendelssohn here translates the conjunction *vav* by *or* (as in XXI, 15); 'and fight against us'—in case of invasion; '*or* get them out of the land' and strengthen the enemy peoples who are threatening us. Hence the anxiety of the Egyptian rulers both to *retain* the Israelites, and at the same time to decimate, and eventually destroy, them through forced labour.

*up out of the land.* Heb. idiom speaks of 'going *down* to Egypt' and 'going *up* to Canaan', because Egypt lies lower than Palestine.

**11.** *taskmasters.* Or, 'gang-overseers.' This was the first move in the scheme of checking the increase of the Israelites. The free and independent settlers in Goshen, who had been invited to Egypt (Gen. XLV, 16–20), were now subjected to the corvée, *i.e.* compelled to labour on public works without pay. 'Their labour was a sort of tribal tax which they had to render, and for which their own head-men were responsible' (Petrie). The Egyptian and Assyrian monuments show us gangs of slaves working at brick-making, stone-breaking, and other severe labours, under the lash of their overseers.

*to afflict them. i.e.* to break their spirit.

*burdens.* Heavy burdens, carried out under compulsion.

*store-cities.* Fortresses to protect the kingdom against possible invasion from the Asiatic side; and, at the same time, arsenals and granaries for Egyptian armies about to cross into Asia.

*Pithom.* In Egyptian Pi-Tum, 'the dwelling of the God Tum'; was identified by Naville in 1883 with the ruins in the Wady Tumilat about 60 miles N.E. of Cairo. He found a number of thick-walled rectangular chambers not communicating with one another, but filled from above, as required in the case of granaries. A. H. Gardiner places it eight miles farther west, at the modern Tell-er-Retabeh.

*Raamses.* The site on which later the Roman city Pelusium stood, at the mouth of the ancient Eastern branch of the Nile Delta on the Mediterranean (Gardiner). It was the capital of the Hyksos kings, and was enlarged and renamed at this time. In an inscription of Rameses II, recently found at Beisan, Palestine, he boasts that he built the city called after his name with *Semitic* slaves (Naville).

**12.** Pharaoh's first plan to destroy Israel—the first, too, known to history—had failed.

*spread abroad.* lit. 'breaking over limits'. They spread not only beyond the confines of Goshen, but beyond the borders of Egypt itself, into S. Palestinian territory, which was then under Egyptian sovereignty; see p. 395.

*adread.* Or, 'had an horror of.' They loathed the Israelites.

EXODUS I, 13

more they spread abroad. And they were adread because of the children of Israel. 13. And the Egyptians made the children of Israel to serve with rigour. 14. And they made their lives bitter with hard service, in mortar and in brick, and in all manner of service in the field; in all their service, wherein they made them serve with rigour. ¶ 15. And the king of Egypt spoke to the Hebrew midwives, of whom the name of the one was Shiphrah, and the name of the other Puah; 16. and he said: 'When ye do the office of a midwife to the Hebrew women, ye shall look upon the birthstool: if it be a son, then ye shall kill him; but if it be a daughter, then she shall live.' 17. But the midwives feared God, and did not as the king of Egypt commanded them, but saved the men-children alive. 18. And the king of Egypt called for the midwives, and said unto them: 'Why have ye done this thing, and have saved the men-children alive?' 19. And the midwives said unto Pharaoh: 'Because the Hebrew women are not as the Egyptian women;

שמות א

13 אֹתוֹ כֵּן יִרְבֶּה וְכֵן יִפְרֹץ וַיָּקֻצוּ מִפְּנֵי בְּנֵי יִשְׂרָאֵל: וַיַּעֲבִדוּ
14 מִצְרַיִם אֶת־בְּנֵי יִשְׂרָאֵל בְּפָרֶךְ: וַיְמָרֲרוּ אֶת־חַיֵּיהֶם בַּעֲבֹדָה קָשָׁה בְּחֹמֶר וּבִלְבֵנִים וּבְכָל־עֲבֹדָה בַּשָּׂדֶה אֵת
טו כָּל־עֲבֹדָתָם אֲשֶׁר־עָבְדוּ בָהֶם בְּפָרֶךְ: וַיֹּאמֶר מֶלֶךְ מִצְרַיִם לַמְיַלְּדֹת הָעִבְרִיֹּת אֲשֶׁר שֵׁם הָאַחַת שִׁפְרָה וְשֵׁם
16 הַשֵּׁנִית פּוּעָה: וַיֹּאמֶר בְּיַלֶּדְכֶן אֶת־הָעִבְרִיּוֹת וּרְאִיתֶן עַל־הָאָבְנָיִם אִם־בֵּן הוּא וַהֲמִתֶּן אֹתוֹ וְאִם־בַּת הִוא וָחָיָה:
17 וַתִּירֶאןָ הַמְיַלְּדֹת אֶת־הָאֱלֹהִים וְלֹא עָשׂוּ כַּאֲשֶׁר דִּבֶּר אֲלֵיהֶן
שני 18 מֶלֶךְ מִצְרַיִם וַתְּחַיֶּיןָ אֶת־הַיְלָדִים: וַיִּקְרָא מֶלֶךְ־מִצְרַיִם לַמְיַלְּדֹת וַיֹּאמֶר לָהֶן מַדּוּעַ עֲשִׂיתֶן הַדָּבָר הַזֶּה וַתְּחַיֶּיןָ
19 אֶת־הַיְלָדִים: וַתֹּאמַרְןָ הַמְיַלְּדֹת אֶל־פַּרְעֹה כִּי לֹא כַנָּשִׁים הַמִּצְרִיֹּת הָעִבְרִיֹּת כִּי־חָיוֹת הֵנָּה בְּטֶרֶם תָּבוֹא אֲלֵהֶן

**13.** *with rigour.* Or, 'with crushing oppression,' to annihilate both the energies and the spirit of the labourer, and calculated to bring about the degeneration of the Hebrew race. Sir H. H. Johnston, in his account of slavery in Africa, has shown that the horrible traffic in human beings, as in fact all slavery, often created in the master a deliberate love of cruelty, even when it entailed considerable commercial loss.

**14.** *in brick.* Bricks, stamped with the name of Rameses II, are in the British Museum.

*in the field.* For the difficult works of irrigation (see Deut. XI, 10). The water had to be brought to the high-lying fields artificially, by a series of buckets attached to long poles, worked on axles. Nothing was, and still is, as tiring in the daily life of the Egyptian as this irrigation of the fields (Erman).

**15–22.** Failing to weaken the Israelites by the corvée, Pharaoh now proposes infanticide.

**15.** *Hebrew midwives.* i.e. the Egyptian women who served as midwives to the Hebrews (Septuagint, Josephus, Abarbanel). It is hardly probable that the king would have expected Hebrew women to slay the children of their own people.

*Shiphrah . . . Puah.* The names are probably Egyptian. They were the two midwives in the capital, where Hebrew women would seek the services of a midwife (Strack). In the capital, furthermore, dwelt the 'better classes' of the children of Israel—their natural leaders. If Pharaoh could only succeed in exterminating these, he would experience little difficulty in rendering the slave portion harmless.

**16.** *then ye shall kill him.* The purpose of the king is to make an end of the Israelites altogether.

*a daughter . . . shall live.* These could not prove dangerous in time of war, and would be serviceable as slaves. The remnant of the Israelite people would thus be absorbed in the native population.

**17.** *feared God.* And would not be parties to a monstrous crime. The expression *fearing God* in Scripture is used in connection with heathens to denote the feeling which humanizes man's dealings with foreigners, even where national interests are supposed to be at stake; see note on Gen. XLII, 18. Thus, when Amalek attacked Israel, not in open warfare but stealthily, from the rear, slaying the old and the feeble, showing himself devoid of this natural piety and fundamental humanity, Scripture says of him, 'and he feared not God' (Deut. xxv, 18). The midwives were required by their king to act barbarously towards 'aliens'. But they preferred to obey the voice of human kindliness, the voice of conscience: 'the midwives feared God.' See also Gen. xx, 11.

**19.** *lively.* Better, *vigorous* (Ibn Ezra); *i.e.* the Hebrew women had greater vitality than the Egyptian women, and—like most Arabian women, ancient and modern—did not require the services of midwives; it would therefore be impossible to slay the child unperceived by the mother. The Heb. word *chayoth* may, however, be taken as a noun, meaning 'animals' (Talmud). The midwives would then have said to the king, 'The Hebrew women are not human; they are *animals*, and do not need a midwife.' Their loathing of the Hebrew women would disarm the suspicions of the king (Ehrlich, Yahuda).

EXODUS I, 20

for they are lively, and are delivered ere the midwife come unto them.' 20. And God dealt well with the midwives; and the people multiplied, and waxed very mighty. 21. And it came to pass, because the midwives feared God, that He made them houses. 22. And Pharaoh charged all his people, saying: 'Every son that is born ye shall cast into the river, and every daughter ye shall save alive.'

## CHAPTER II

1. And there went a man of the house of Levi, and took to wife a daughter of Levi. 2. And the woman conceived, and bore a son; and when she saw him that he was a goodly child, she hid him three months.

---

**21.** *made them houses.* God built up their families or increased their prosperity. The verse may also be translated, 'And it came to pass, that because the midwives feared God, He made them (the Israelites) houses'; *i.e.* the people multiplied and increased abundantly.

**22.** *charged all his people.* In consequence of this continuous increase of the Israelites, and having failed in his measures with the midwives, Pharaoh now orders his people generally to drown the male children born to the Israelites. 'The whole people were now let loose against the Hebrews; spying and informing were made acts of loyalty, and compassion stamped as high treason' (Kalisch). While many would still, like the midwives, 'fear God,' others would now take a special delight in carrying out the command of the king.

*cast into the river.* The Spartans practised similar barbarities upon their helot population.

*the river. i.e.* the Nile. The longest river in the Old World, starting in the heart of Africa, and flowing northward, over 3,000 miles, into the Mediterranean. Egypt is by nature a rainless desert, which the Nile, and the Nile only, converts into a garden every year. As most of the Israelites, however, lived away from the Nile, such a savage decree could not have been strictly carried out, and must in time have become a dead letter. Rabbinic tradition states that the edict was in force some three years.

## CHAPTER II

### THE BIRTH AND EDUCATION OF MOSES

Providence overrules the despotic plans of men, and Israel's future deliverer is being prepared for his task in the very court of the merciless tyrant. The marvellous and unique emergence of a people from the midst of another land and people would be both impossible and inexplicable, apart from a great directing genius. This chapter opens the story of the Father of the Prophets, the Liberator and Teacher of Israel, the man who not only led the children of Israel from the Egyptian house of bondage, but brought them to Sinai and trained them to become a free people consecrated unto God and righteousness. 'Moses was a great artist, and possessed the true artistic spirit. But this spirit was directed by him, as by his Egyptian compatriots, to colossal and indestructible undertakings. He built human pyramids, carved human obelisks; he took a poor shepherd family and made a nation of it—a great, eternal, holy people: a people of God, destined to outlive the centuries, and to serve as a pattern to all other nations, a prototype to the whole of mankind. He created Israel' (Heine).

Even in its literary form this chapter is noteworthy. Few portions of Scripture condense so many dramatic incidents into a few verses. The power of the narrative only gains thereby.

**1.** *the house of Levi. i.e.* tribe of Levi. His name and that of his wife are given in VI, 20. Here the narrative *hastens* on to the story of the Redemption.

*took to wife.* The explicit language in these two verses brings out an important characteristic of Judaism. In other religions, the founders are represented as of supernatural birth. Not so in Judaism. Even Moses is human as to birth, as also in regard to death (Deut. XXXIV, 5).

**2.** *bore a son.* Two children had already been born to them—Miriam, the elder, was a young woman at the time of the birth of Moses; and Aaron, who was born three years before Moses. The king's order to drown the Israelite children must have been promulgated after the birth of Aaron, as his life had not been in peril.

*when she saw.* Better, *and she saw that he was a goodly child, and she hid,* etc.; because the mother would in any case have been anxious to preserve his life.

*a goodly child. i.e.* a 'good child'; not betraying his presence by crying, so that she could hide him for a space of three months (Luzzatto).

EXODUS II, 3

3. And when she could not longer hide him, she took for him an ark of bulrushes, and daubed it with slime and with pitch; and she put the child therein, and laid it in the flags by the river's brink. 4. And his sister stood afar off, to know what would be done to him. 5. And the daughter of Pharaoh came down to bathe in the river; and her maidens walked along by the river-side; and she saw the ark among the flags, and sent her handmaid to fetch it. 6. And she opened it, and saw it, even the child; and behold a boy that wept. And she had compassion on him, and said: 'This is one of the Hebrews' children.' 7. Then said his sister to Pharaoh's daughter: 'Shall I go and call thee a nurse of the Hebrew women, that she may nurse the child for thee?' 8. And Pharaoh's daughter said to her: 'Go.' And the maiden went and called the child's mother. 9. And Pharaoh's daughter said unto her: 'Take this child away, and nurse it for me, and I will give thee thy wages.' And the woman took the child, and nursed it. 10. And the child grew, and she brought him unto

3 וְלֹא־יָכְלָה עוֹד הַצְּפִינוֹ וַתִּקַּח־לוֹ תֵּבַת גֹּמֶא וַתַּחְמְרָה בַחֵמָר וּבַזָּפֶת וַתָּשֶׂם בָּהּ אֶת־הַיֶּלֶד וַתָּשֶׂם בַּסּוּף עַל־
4 שְׂפַת הַיְאֹר: וַתֵּתַצַּב אֲחֹתוֹ מֵרָחֹק לְדֵעָה מַה־יֵּעָשֶׂה
ה לוֹ: וַתֵּרֶד בַּת־פַּרְעֹה לִרְחֹץ עַל־הַיְאֹר וְנַעֲרֹתֶיהָ הֹלְכֹת עַל־יַד הַיְאֹר וַתֵּרֶא אֶת־הַתֵּבָה בְּתוֹךְ הַסּוּף וַתִּשְׁלַח אֶת־
6 אֲמָתָהּ וַתִּקָּחֶהָ: וַתִּפְתַּח וַתִּרְאֵהוּ אֶת־הַיֶּלֶד וְהִנֵּה־נַעַר
7 בֹּכֶה וַתַּחְמֹל עָלָיו וַתֹּאמֶר מִיַּלְדֵי הָעִבְרִים זֶה: וַתֹּאמֶר אֲחֹתוֹ אֶל־בַּת־פַּרְעֹה הַאֵלֵךְ וְקָרָאתִי לָךְ אִשָּׁה מֵינֶקֶת
8 מִן הָעִבְרִיֹּת וְתֵינִק לָךְ אֶת־הַיָּלֶד: וַתֹּאמֶר־לָהּ בַּת־פַּרְעֹה
9 לֵכִי וַתֵּלֶךְ הָעַלְמָה וַתִּקְרָא אֶת־אֵם הַיָּלֶד: וַתֹּאמֶר לָהּ בַּת־פַּרְעֹה הֵילִיכִי אֶת־הַיֶּלֶד הַזֶּה וְהֵינִקִהוּ לִי וַאֲנִי אֶתֵּן
י אֶת־שְׂכָרֵךְ וַתִּקַּח הָאִשָּׁה הַיֶּלֶד וַתְּנִיקֵהוּ: וַיִּגְדַּל הַיֶּלֶד

v. 3. ח׳ בלא מפיק

**3.** *an ark.* A chest. The Heb. for 'ark' is elsewhere used only for Noah's ark.
*bulrushes.* The Heb. is an Egyptian loan-word. It denotes the paper-reed (called papyrus), growing ten to twelve feet high. Its leaves were used for making boats, mats, ropes and paper.
*slime.* i.e. bitumen—to make it watertight.
*flags.* A kind of reed, of smaller growth than the papyrus.

**4.** *stood.* Better, '*took her stand*,' not far from the place reserved for bathing.

**5.** *came down.* From her palace, probably at Zoan (Tanis), one of the chief royal residences in the Delta.
*by the river-side.* To give warning of any intrusion upon the privacy of the princess.
*handmaid.* Her personal attendant at the moment of bathing.

**6.** *a boy that wept.* lit. 'a weeping boy'.
*she had compassion.* Despite Pharaoh's orders, she is moved to spare the child. She 'feared God'.
*one of the Hebrews' children.* Only a Hebrew mother, in desperation to save her child from destruction, would thus expose it on the River.

**7.** *sister.* When she saw that the ark was found, she ventured to join the princess's attendants to see what would happen to her brother.
*a nurse of the Hebrew women.* lit. 'a woman giving suck'. A native Egyptian woman would not have undertaken to nurse a Hebrew child (Driver).

**9.** *give thee thy wages.* Pharaoh's plans for the annihilation of the Israelite children are defeated by women—the human feelings of the midwives, the tender sympathy of a woman of royal birth, and a sister's watchfulness and resource in extremity. 'It was to the merit of pious women that Israel owed its redemption in Egypt,' say the Rabbis.

**10.** *the child grew.* He remained under his mother's care till he was quite a lad. During these most impressionable years of his life, his mother must have instilled into him the belief in one God, the Creator of heaven and earth, an Eternal Spirit without any shape or form that the mind of man could devise; and imparted to him the sacred traditions of Israel, the story of the Fathers in Canaan, of Joseph in Egypt, and of the Divine promise of deliverance from Egyptian bondage. When Moses returned to the Palace, he received, as the adopted child of the princess, the education of boys of the highest rank, probably at Heliopolis—'the Oxford of Ancient Egypt' (Stanley). There he 'must have learnt many things which from a Hebrew point of view would be extremely undesirable for him to know' (Driver). But whenever the priests undertook to initiate him into their fantastic idolatry, he remembered the teachings of his childhood; and he remained a Hebrew.
*he became her son.* He was adopted by the princess, and life at the Egyptian court gave him the training which was essential for a leader of men. 'Deep are the ways of Providence! It was His inscrutable intention that Moses should be reared in a Palace, that his spirit might remain

## EXODUS II, 11

Pharaoh's daughter, and he became her son. And she called his name ¹Moses, and said: 'Because I ²drew him out of the water.' *¹¹¹·¶ 11. And it came to pass in those days, when Moses was grown up, that he went out unto his brethren, and looked on their burdens; and he saw an Egyptian smiting a Hebrew, one of his brethren. 12. And he looked this way and that way, and when he saw that there was no man, he smote the Egyptian, and hid him in the sand. 13. And he went out the second day, and, behold, two men of the Hebrews were striving together; and he said to him that did the wrong: 'Wherefore smitest thou thy fellow?' 14. And he said: 'Who made thee a ruler and a judge over us? thinkest thou to kill me, as thou didst kill

---
¹ Heb. *Mosheh*.   ² Heb. *mashah*, to draw out.

שלישי 
11 וַתְּבִאֵ֙הוּ֙ לְבַת־פַּרְעֹ֔ה וַֽיְהִי־לָ֖הּ לְבֵ֑ן וַתִּקְרָ֤א שְׁמוֹ֙ מֹשֶׁ֔ה וַתֹּ֕אמֶר כִּ֥י מִן־הַמַּ֖יִם מְשִׁיתִֽהוּ׃ וַיְהִ֣י ׀ בַּיָּמִ֣ים הָהֵ֗ם וַיִּגְדַּ֤ל
12 מֹשֶׁה֙ וַיֵּצֵ֣א אֶל־אֶחָ֔יו וַיַּ֖רְא בְּסִבְלֹתָ֑ם וַיַּרְא֙ אִ֣ישׁ מִצְרִ֔י מַכֶּ֥ה אִישׁ־עִבְרִ֖י מֵאֶחָֽיו׃ וַיִּ֤פֶן כֹּה֙ וָכֹ֔ה וַיַּ֖רְא כִּ֣י אֵ֣ין אִ֑ישׁ
13 וַיַּךְ֙ אֶת־הַמִּצְרִ֔י וַֽיִּטְמְנֵ֖הוּ בַּחֽוֹל׃ וַיֵּצֵא֙ בַּיּ֣וֹם הַשֵּׁנִ֔י וְהִנֵּ֛ה שְׁנֵֽי־אֲנָשִׁ֥ים עִבְרִ֖ים נִצִּ֑ים וַיֹּ֙אמֶר֙ לָֽרָשָׁ֔ע לָ֥מָּה תַכֶּ֖ה רֵעֶֽךָ׃
14 וַ֠יֹּאמֶר מִ֣י שָֽׂמְךָ֞ לְאִ֨ישׁ שַׂ֤ר וְשֹׁפֵט֙ עָלֵ֔ינוּ הַלְהָרְגֵ֙נִי֙ אַתָּ֣ה אֹמֵ֔ר כַּאֲשֶׁ֥ר הָרַ֖גְתָּ אֶת־הַמִּצְרִ֑י וַיִּירָ֤א מֹשֶׁה֙ וַיֹּאמַ֔ר אָכֵ֕ן

---

uncurbed by the oppressive and enervating influence of slavery. Thus he slew the Egyptian because his heart could not see violence and injustice, and from the same generous motive he took the part of the daughters of Reuel against the shepherds. It served another purpose also. Had he always lived amongst his own people, they would not so readily have accepted him as their leader, nor would they have shown him the respect and deference which were essential for the accomplishment of his great mission' (Ibn Ezra).

*Moses.* Heb. *Mosheh*, the Hebraised reproduction of an Egyptian word which probably means 'child of the Nile' (Yahuda). The explanation of the name given in the text ('because I drew him out of the water') rests upon the similarity of sound, as is repeatedly seen in Genesis; the word *Mosheh* resembling the word for 'the one who is drawn out.'

**11.** *when Moses was grown up.* lit. 'when Moses became great', he went out *to* his brethren. In later ages it must alas be said of many a son of Israel who had become great, that he went away *from* his brethren. No so Moses. He went out of the Palace into the brick-fields where his brethren toiled and agonized in cruel bondage. It was lovingkindness to his people that impelled him to do so. There are ten strong things in the world, say the Rabbis: rock is strong but iron cleaves it; fire melts iron; water extinguishes fire; the clouds bear aloft the water; the wind drives away the clouds; man withstands the wind; fear unmans man; wine dispels fear: sleep overcomes wine; and death sweeps away even sleep. But strongest of all is lovingkindness, for it defies and survives death. Now Moses was filled with lovingkindness. Full of pity, he watched his brethren groaning beneath their burdens. 'What has Israel done to deserve such wretchedness?' he wondered.

*an Egyptian smiting.* Probably one of the taskmasters applying the lash to an Israelite. We know only too well from ancient writings and paintings what the flogging of slaves was like. Moses for the first time saw a poor Hebrew flogged, and it was more than he could bear. His loyalty to his kin had not been destroyed by his Egyptian upbringing.

**12.** *he smote.* Moses resembles 'the great patriots of the past and the present, who have taken the sword to deliver their people from the hands of tyrants. His act may be condemned as hasty. In its immediate results it was fruitless, as is every intemperate attempt to right a wrong by violence. However, it allied Moses definitely with his kinsmen' (Kent).

**13.** *to him that did the wrong. i.e.* to the man who was in the wrong.

**14.** *who made thee a ruler.* A typical attitude of a small but persistent Jewish minority towards anyone working for Israel. The Rabbis speak of it as the Dathan-and-Abiram type of mind (cf. Num. xvi).

*surely the thing is known.* Referring to the death of the Egyptian. The Midrash takes these words as an answer to his question why Israel should suffer such slavery. Now he knew the reason: they deserved it. 'It is characteristic of the faithfulness of the Sacred Record that his flight is occasioned rather by the malignity of his countrymen than by the enmity of the Egyptians' (Stanley).

The first action of Moses shows him swept away by fierce indignation against the oppressor; the second, anxious to restore harmony among the oppressed. In both these acts, Moses is seen burning with patriotic ardour. His nature, however, requires to be freed from impetuous passion. In the desert whither he is now fleeing, his spirit will be purified and deepened, and he will return as the destined Liberator of his brethren.

## EXODUS II, 15      שמות ב

the Egyptian?' And Moses feared, and said: 'Surely the thing is known.' 15. Now when Pharaoh heard this thing, he sought to slay Moses. But Moses fled from the face of Pharaoh, and dwelt in the land of Midian; and he sat down by a well. 16. Now the priest of Midian had seven daughters; and they came and drew water, and filled the troughs to water their father's flock. 17. And the shepherds came and drove them away; but Moses stood up and helped them, and watered their flock. 18. And when they came to Reuel their father, he said: 'How is it that ye are come so soon to-day?' 19. And they said: 'An Egyptian delivered us out of the hand of the shepherds, and moreover he drew water for us, and watered the flock.' 20. And he said unto his daughters: 'And where is he? why is it that ye have left the man? call him, that he may eat bread.' 21. And Moses was content to dwell with the man; and he gave Moses Zipporah his daughter. 22. And she bore a son, and he called his name Gershom; for he said: 'I have been a stranger[1] in a strange land.'
¶ 23. And it came to pass in the course of those many days that the king of Egypt died; and the children of Israel sighed by reason of the bondage, and they cried,

[1] Heb. *ger*.

### 15–22. MOSES IN MIDIAN

**15.** *Midian*. In the south-eastern part of the Sinai peninsula. Here he would be beyond Egyptian jurisdiction. The main home of the Midianites appears to have been on the east side of the Gulf of Akabah.

**16.** *priest of Midian*. Heb. *kohen*, which does not necessarily mean *priest*. It may also mean 'chief'. And so Onkelos and Rashi translate it here. The sons of David are likewise termed *kohanim* in II Sam. VIII, 18, where it only means nobles or officers.

*to water their father's flock*. Even to this day the young women tend the sheep among the Bedouin of the Sinai peninsula.

**17.** *drove them away*. These 'chivalrous' Arabs wished to water their own sheep first, although the women had already filled the troughs. Moses again takes the part of the injured side, but this time without violence.

**18.** *Reuel their father*. Reuel seems to have been their father, while Jethro was the father-in-law of Moses. The word Jethro means, 'His Excellency,' and may be regarded as a title borne by the priest or chief of Midian, whose proper name is given in Num. x, 29, as Hobab. Reuel, therefore, was the grandfather (often called 'father' in Scripture; see Gen. XXVIII, 13 and XXXII, 10) of the shepherdesses. If Jethro and Reuel are taken as one person, there is nothing unusual in one man having two names (*e.g.* Jacob, Israel); and South Arabian inscriptions show many chieftains having two names.

*ye are come so soon*. Reuel was familiar with the usual delay caused by the interference of the shepherds.

**19.** *an Egyptian*. Moses' dress and speech would be Egyptian.

*drew water for us*. lit. 'he actually drew water for us'; they are surprised at the kindness of his action in helping them to draw water.

**20.** *where is he?* Expresses displeasure that they had failed in hospitality towards the stranger who had befriended them.

**21.** *was content*. Or, 'agreed.' One cannot help contrasting the breadth with which the wooing of both Isaac and Jacob is recounted, with the extraordinary, nay irreducible, brevity with which the wooing of Moses is told. What we would call the 'romantic' element in the story of Moses disappears like a bubble; it is the woe of his People that engrosses his mind.

*Zipporah*. The meaning of this name is 'bird'. The Midianites spoke a language kindred to Hebrew.

**22.** *Gershom*. Heb. *ger*, 'a stranger', and *sham*, 'there,' in a strange land. His heart was with his suffering brethren in Egypt.

*strange land*. *i.e.* foreign land.

**23–25.** Transition to the Call and Commission of Moses.

## EXODUS II, 24

and their cry came up unto God by reason of the bondage. 24. And God heard their groaning, and God remembered His covenant with Abraham, with Isaac, and with Jacob. 25. And God saw the children of Israel, and God took cognizance of them.*iv.

## CHAPTER III

1. Now Moses was keeping the flock of Jethro his father-in-law, the priest of Midian; and he led the flock to the farthest end of the wilderness, and came to the mountain of God, unto Horeb. 2. And the angel of the LORD appeared unto him in a flame of fire out of the midst of a bush; and he looked, and, behold, the bush burned with fire, and the bush was not consumed. 3. And Moses said: 'I will turn aside now, and see this great sight, why the bush is not burnt.' 4. And when the LORD saw that he turned aside to see,

---

**23.** *many days.* Rabbinic tradition assigns 40 years to the period spent by Moses in exile from Egypt.

*the king of Egypt died.* Probably Rameses II, who reigned 67 years. The Israelites evidently hoped that his successor, Merneptah, might offer them some relief; but they were disappointed. The régime of ruthless oppression towards Israel would now become the *status quo.* They realize the hopelessness of their bondage. Therefore, 'they cried unto God.'

**24.** *remembered His covenant.* Not that He had forgotten it, but that now the opportunity had come for the fulfilment of His merciful purposes.

**25.** *took cognizance of them.* God did not close His eyes to their suffering (Rashi), but He chose His own time when to send deliverance and cause Israel to go forth from Egypt. See also Additional Note B, 'Israel and Egypt: the Spiritual Contrast,' p. 396.

CHAPTERS III AND IV. THE CALL OF MOSES

**1.** *keeping the flock.* God never gives an exalted office to a man unless He has first tested him in small things, say the Rabbis. When feeding the flocks of Jethro, they tell us, Moses saw a little lamb escape from the flock, and when he followed it, he overtook it at a brook quenching its thirst. 'Had I known that thou wast thirsty, I would have taken thee in my arms and carried thee thither,' he said. 'As thou livest,' a Heavenly Voice resounded, 'thou art fit to shepherd Israel' (Midrash).

*to the farthest end of the wilderness.* Behind or beyond the wilderness, as the scanty shrubs in the wilderness itself were insufficient for the flock. 'The solemn solitude of the dreary desert was to prepare his mind for the sublime commission for which Providence had selected him' (Kalisch).

*mountain of God.* So called because the Glory of God was later manifested there. The spot chosen by God to announce the physical redemption of Israel was also chosen by Him as the place of their spiritual redemption.

*Horeb.* Horeb is the mountain and district, Sinai the summit itself; or, the two names refer to two peaks of the same mountain range, which some identify with Jebel Musa (7,636 feet), others with Mount Serbal (6,734 feet), in the Sinai Peninsula. The aridity and dryness of this region have been much exaggerated. In the highest region, fertile valleys are found, with fruit trees and water in plenty.

**2.** *angel of the* LORD. The angel in Scripture is not to be identified with God. The angel is the messenger of God and speaks in His name, and is often called by the Name of Him who sent him (see *v.* 4). The speech and action are the work of the angel, but the thought or will is God's.

*in a flame of fire.* Or, 'in the heart of the fire'; *i.e.* in the midst of fire (Maimonides).

*bush. i.e.* the thorn-bush, the wild acacia, which is the characteristic shrub of that region.

*was not consumed.* The burning bush has often been taken as a symbol of Israel—small and lowly among the nations, and yet indestructible; because of the Divine Spirit that dwelleth within Israel.

**4.** *God called unto him. i.e.* the angel of God, mentioned in *v.* 2. The angel is here spoken of as

## EXODUS III, 5 — שמות ג

God called unto him out of the midst of the bush, and said: 'Moses, Moses.' And he said: 'Here am I.' 5. And He said: 'Draw not nigh hither; put off thy shoes from off thy feet, for the place whereon thou standest is holy ground.' 6. Moreover He said: 'I am the God of thy father, the God of Abraham, the God of Isaac, and the God of Jacob.' And Moses hid his face; for he was afraid to look upon God. 7. And the LORD said: 'I have surely seen the affliction of My people that are in Egypt, and have heard their cry by reason of their taskmasters; for I know their pains; 8. and I am come down to deliver them out of the hands of the Egyptians, and to bring them up out of that land unto a good land and a large, unto a land flowing with milk and honey; unto the place of the Canaanite, and the Hittite, and the Amorite, and the Perizzite, and the Hivite, and the Jebusite. 9. And now, behold, the cry of the children of Israel is come unto Me; moreover I have seen the oppression wherewith the Egyptians oppress them. 10. Come now therefore,

אֱלֹהִים מִתּוֹךְ הַסְּנֶה וַיֹּאמֶר מֹשֶׁה מֹשֶׁה וַיֹּאמֶר הִנֵּנִי:
ה וַיֹּאמֶר אַל־תִּקְרַב הֲלֹם שַׁל־נְעָלֶיךָ מֵעַל רַגְלֶיךָ כִּי הַמָּקוֹם
6 אֲשֶׁר אַתָּה עוֹמֵד עָלָיו אַדְמַת־קֹדֶשׁ הוּא: וַיֹּאמֶר אָנֹכִי
אֱלֹהֵי אָבִיךָ אֱלֹהֵי אַבְרָהָם אֱלֹהֵי יִצְחָק וֵאלֹהֵי יַעֲקֹב
7 וַיַּסְתֵּר מֹשֶׁה פָּנָיו כִּי יָרֵא מֵהַבִּיט אֶל־הָאֱלֹהִים: וַיֹּאמֶר
יְהֹוָה רָאֹה רָאִיתִי אֶת־עֳנִי עַמִּי אֲשֶׁר בְּמִצְרָיִם וְאֶת־
צַעֲקָתָם שָׁמַעְתִּי מִפְּנֵי נֹגְשָׂיו כִּי יָדַעְתִּי אֶת־מַכְאֹבָיו:
8 וָאֵרֵד לְהַצִּילוֹ ׀ מִיַּד מִצְרַיִם וּלְהַעֲלֹתוֹ מִן־הָאָרֶץ הַהִוא
אֶל־אֶרֶץ טוֹבָה וּרְחָבָה אֶל־אֶרֶץ זָבַת חָלָב וּדְבָשׁ אֶל־
מְקוֹם הַכְּנַעֲנִי וְהַחִתִּי וְהָאֱמֹרִי וְהַפְּרִזִּי וְהַחִוִּי וְהַיְבוּסִי:
9 וְעַתָּה הִנֵּה צַעֲקַת בְּנֵי־יִשְׂרָאֵל בָּאָה אֵלָי וְגַם־רָאִיתִי אֶת־
10 הַלַּחַץ אֲשֶׁר מִצְרַיִם לֹחֲצִים אֹתָם: וְעַתָּה לְכָה וְאֶשְׁלָחֲךָ

v. 4. משה משה בלא פסיק ביניהן

God, because he represents the Almighty (Ibn Ezra).

*Moses, Moses.* God here addresses Moses by his name. 'The repetition of the name is an expression of affection intended to encourage him' (Mechilta); cf. *Abraham, Abraham,* in Gen. XXII, 11; and *Jacob, Jacob,* in Gen. XLVI, 2. God's choice is never groundless or arbitrary. Moses' warm heart for his brethren, and his burning indignation against all injustice, made him worthy of God's love and choice.

5. *holy ground.* Every spot where God manifests Himself is holy ground.

6. *thy father.* i.e. thy fathers; the word is here used collectively (Onkelos), and is explained by the words, 'the God of Abraham, Isaac and Jacob'; see xv, 2. The Midrash, however, refers the word 'father' to Amram, the father of Moses. It was with his father's voice that the angel of God addressed him, 'I am the God of thy father, *i.e.* the God of whom thy father spake, the unchangeable God of eternity, who is now about to fulfil the promise given to Israel's ancestors.'

*hid his face,* Or, 'covered his face' (Jerusalem Targum) in reverence (cf. I Kings XIX, 13). In the presence of the All-holy, an instant and irresistible feeling of human nothingness overpowers him. In sacred awe before the majesty of the Godhead, he hides his face. No mortal eye is worthy of beholding God. Even the angels are not pure in His sight; and, therefore, in the vision of Isaiah VI, 2, they are spoken of as covering their faces and bodies; see p. 302.

7. *My people.* This is the first time Israel is so called: God had made their cause His own. 'God always takes the side of the persecuted,' say the Rabbis.

*heard their cry.* See II, 23–25. The cry of the Israelites was the cry of human beings who were being inhumanly treated, a cry of despair that ascends to the very throne of the Almighty.

*for I know their pains.* Better, *indeed, I know their sorrows.*

8. *I am come down.* A similar human way of speaking of the Divine (*anthropomorphism*) occurs in XIX, 11.

*flowing with milk and honey.* A proverbial expression, often applied to Canaan, see XIII, 5; Num. XIII, 27. The description of the Promised Land is here required, because Moses does not know it from personal observation.

*the Canaanite.* The general name for all the peoples inhabiting ancient Palestine. Originally Canaan, meaning *the Lowland,* was applied only to the coast of Phœnicia and the land of the Philistines; see Gen. x, 6.

*the Hittite.* A powerful and warlike nation whose seat was Asia Minor; an offshoot of this people lived in Southern Palestine; see Gen. XXIII.

*Amorite.* Originally a warlike tribe inhabiting the hill country, behind Phœnicia. Later, it was the name for all pre-Israelitish inhabitants of Canaan (Amos II, 9).

*Perizzite, Hivite.* Seem to have lived in Central Palestine.

*Jebusite.* This tribe inhabited Jerusalem.

and I will send thee unto Pharaoh, that thou mayest bring forth My people the children of Israel out of Egypt.' 11. And Moses said unto God: 'Who am I, that I should go unto Pharaoh, and that I should bring forth the children of Israel out of Egypt?' 12. And He said: 'Certainly I will be with thee; and this shall be the token unto thee, that I have sent thee: when thou hast brought forth the people out of Egypt, ye shall serve God upon this mountain.' 13. And Moses said unto God: 'Behold, when I come unto the children of Israel, and shall say unto them: The God of your fathers hath sent me unto you: and they shall say to me: What is His name? what shall I say unto them?' 14. And God said unto Moses: 'I AM THAT I AM'; and He said. 'Thus shalt thou say unto the children of Israel: I AM hath sent me unto you.' 15. And God said moreover unto Moses: 'Thus shalt thou say unto the children of Israel: The LORD, the God of your fathers, the God of Abraham, the

11 אֶל־פַּרְעֹה וְהוֹצֵא אֶת־עַמִּי בְנֵי־יִשְׂרָאֵל מִמִּצְרָיִם: וַיֹּאמֶר מֹשֶׁה אֶל־הָאֱלֹהִים מִי אָנֹכִי כִּי אֵלֵךְ אֶל־פַּרְעֹה וְכִי
12 אוֹצִיא אֶת־בְּנֵי יִשְׂרָאֵל מִמִּצְרָיִם: וַיֹּאמֶר כִּי־אֶהְיֶה עִמָּךְ וְזֶה־לְּךָ הָאוֹת כִּי אָנֹכִי שְׁלַחְתִּיךָ בְּהוֹצִיאֲךָ אֶת־הָעָם מִמִּצְרַיִם תַּעַבְדוּן אֶת־הָאֱלֹהִים עַל הָהָר הַזֶּה:
13 וַיֹּאמֶר מֹשֶׁה אֶל־הָאֱלֹהִים הִנֵּה אָנֹכִי בָא אֶל־בְּנֵי יִשְׂרָאֵל וְאָמַרְתִּי לָהֶם אֱלֹהֵי אֲבוֹתֵיכֶם שְׁלָחַנִי אֲלֵיכֶם וְאָמְרוּ־לִי
14 מַה־שְּׁמוֹ מָה אֹמַר אֲלֵהֶם: וַיֹּאמֶר אֱלֹהִים אֶל־מֹשֶׁה אֶהְיֶה אֲשֶׁר אֶהְיֶה וַיֹּאמֶר כֹּה תֹאמַר לִבְנֵי יִשְׂרָאֵל אֶהְיֶה שְׁלָחַנִי אֲלֵיכֶם:
15 וַיֹּאמֶר עוֹד אֱלֹהִים אֶל־מֹשֶׁה כֹּה תֹאמַר אֶל־בְּנֵי יִשְׂרָאֵל יְהוָה אֱלֹהֵי אֲבֹתֵיכֶם אֱלֹהֵי אַבְרָהָם אֱלֹהֵי

### 11-12. MOSES' FIRST DIFFICULTY: HE IS UNSUITED FOR HIS MISSION

**11.** *who am I.* How different was Moses' attitude in his youth! With age, Moses can only think of his own unfitness for the gigantic undertaking; cf. Jeremiah's diffidence to assume the Prophet's office, Jer. I, 6 f.; see p. 229.

**12.** *I will be with thee.* This tremendous fact of the reality of the Divine help would make it possible for Moses, an old man of eighty years, to face Pharaoh and demand the emancipation of his enslaved brethren. Moses' humility, therefore, is here out of place; and, when persisted in, earns him a Divine rebuke (IV, 14).

*this shall be the token.* i.e. the proof that thou art sent by God will be that in this very place, where thou art now doubting the possibility of redemption, the children of Israel will worship, in thanksgiving, the God who will have brought them out of the land of bondage.

*serve God upon this mountain.* See XIX, 3 f.

### 13-22. MOSES' SECOND DIFFICULTY: THE 'NAME' OF GOD

**13.** *when I come.* i.e. assuming that I come.

*what is His name?* Heb. מה שמו. Not an inquiry for information as to what God is *called*. Moses comes to Israel with the words, 'the God of your fathers hath sent me unto you.' It is, therefore, hardly conceivable that he should proclaim a God quite unknown unto them, as the God of their Fathers (G. B. Gray). They must have known what He was *called*, 'since nothing is more un-Biblical than the idea of an "Unknown God"' (B. Jacob). But since *name* means fame, 'record', and in IX, 16 is the synonym of 'power', *What is His name?* means 'What are the mighty deeds which thou canst recount of Him—what is His power—that we should listen to thy message from Him?'

**14.** I AM THAT I AM. Heb. *Ehyeh asher ehyeh*—the self-existent and eternal God; a declaration of the unity and spirituality of the Divine Nature, the exact opposite of all the forms of idolatry, human, animal, and celestial, that prevailed everywhere else. *I am that I am* is, however, not merely a philosophical phrase; the emphasis is on *the active manifestation* of the Divine existence; cf. the explanation of the Midrash, אהיה אשר אהיה אני נקרא לפי מעשי. To the Israelites in bondage, the meaning would be, 'Although He has not yet displayed His power towards you, He will do so; He is eternal and will certainly redeem you.'

Most moderns follow Rashi in rendering '*I will be what I will be*'; i.e. no words can sum up all that He will be to His people, but His everlasting faithfulness and unchanging mercy will more and more manifest themselves in the guidance of Israel. The answer which Moses receives in these words is thus equivalent to, 'I shall save in the way that I shall save.' It is to assure the Israelites of the *fact* of deliverance, but does not disclose the *manner*. It must suffice the Israelites to learn that, 'Ehyeh, I WILL BE (with you), hath sent me unto you.'

**15.** *the* LORD. This is the translation of the Divine Name written in the four Hebrew letters Y H W H and always pronounced 'Adonay' (see *Genesis*, p. 6). This Divine Name of four letters—the Tetragrammaton—comes from the same Heb. root (*hayah*) as *Ehyeh*; viz. 'to be'. It gives expression to the fact that He was, He

EXODUS III, 16

God of Isaac, and the God of Jacob, hath sent me unto you; this is My name for ever, and this is My memorial unto all generations.*¹. 16. Go, and gather the elders of Israel together, and say unto them: The LORD, the God of your fathers, the God of Abraham, of Isaac, and of Jacob, hath appeared unto me, saying: I have surely remembered you, and seen that which is done to you in Egypt. 17. And I have said: I will bring you up out of the affliction of Egypt unto the land of the Canaanite, and the Hittite, and the Amorite, and the Perizzite, and the Hivite, and the Jebusite, unto a land flowing with milk and honey. 18. And they shall hearken to thy voice. And thou shalt come, thou and the elders of Israel, unto the king of Egypt, and ye shall say unto him: The LORD, the God of the Hebrews, hath met with us. And now let us go, we pray thee, three days' journey into the wilderness, that we may sacrifice to the LORD our God. 19. And I know that the king of Egypt will not give you leave to go, except by a mighty hand. 20. And I will put forth My hand, and smite Egypt with all My wonders which I will do in the midst thereof. And after that he will let you go. 21. And

is, and He ever will be. Here, too, the words must not be understood in the philosophical sense of mere 'being', but as active manifestation of the Divine existence. According to the Rabbis, this Name stresses the lovingkindness and faithfulness of God in relation to His creatures: He who educates, punishes, and guides; He who hears the cry of the oppressed, and makes known His ways of righteousness unto the children of men. He is the great Living God who reveals Himself in the Providential care of His people.

*the LORD, the God of your fathers.* Not a deity discovered by Moses in Midian, but the same God who had revealed Himself to their fathers, the Creator of the world and the righteous Judge of all the earth—*Adonay*—the ever-living God of faithfulness and lovingkindness, hath sent him unto them.

*this is My memorial.* The designation by which I will be remembered. 'Memorial' is a synonym of 'Name'; Hos. XII, 6 (*Genesis*, p. 136).

**16.** *the elders of Israel.* It seems that the Israelites had a representative national organization consisting of the elders or leading men in each family; see v, 5.

*the LORD, the God of your fathers.* This shows that the elders, as well as the people, are acquainted with the Name of God. 'What impression could Moses have possibly hoped to make upon them with an altogether new Name?' (B. Jacob).

*Remembered you. i.e.* borne you in mind.

**18.** *shall hearken.* Better, *will hearken.*
*the God of the Hebrews.* As distinct from the gods of the Egyptians.
*hath met with us.* Through Moses, who represented the whole people.
*three days' journey.* A current expression for a considerable distance; Gen. xxx, 36; Num. x, 33. 'The Israelites were to ask what could not reasonably be refused, being a demand quite in accordance with Egyptian customs. . . . It is important to observe that the first request which Pharaoh rejected could have been granted without any damage to Egypt, or any risk of the Israelites passing the strongly fortified frontier' (Speaker's Bible). The request was *not* granted; and so it resolved itself in the end into a demand for the unconditional release of the people and their actual departure.

**20.** *with all My wonders. i.e.* the plagues.

**21.** *will give this people favour.* The Egyptian people are throughout far friendlier to the Israelites than the hard-hearted king. Not only will they let the Israelites go, but God will dispose them favourably towards the Israelites.

*when ye go, ye shall not go empty.* To understand this phrase and the promise it contains, we must recall Deut. xv, 12 f, which ordains that when a faithful servant leaves his master after many years' service, he is to be liberally equipped from his owner's property. 'When thou lettest

## EXODUS III, 22      שמות ג

I will give this people favour in the sight of the Egyptians. And it shall come to pass, that, when ye go, ye shall not go empty; 22. but every woman shall ask of her neighbour, and of her that sojourneth in her house, jewels of silver, and jewels of gold, and raiment; and ye shall put them upon your sons, and upon your daughters; and ye shall spoil the Egyptians.'

הֲוֶה בְּעֵינֵי מִצְרָיִם וְהָיָה כִּי תֵלֵכוּן לֹא תֵלְכוּ רֵיקָם: 22 וְשָׁאֲלָה אִשָּׁה מִשְּׁכֶנְתָּהּ וּמִגָּרַת בֵּיתָהּ כְּלֵי־כֶסֶף וּכְלֵי זָהָב וּשְׂמָלֹת וְשַׂמְתֶּם עַל־בְּנֵיכֶם וְעַל־בְּנֹתֵיכֶם וְנִצַּלְתֶּם אֶת־מִצְרָיִם:

him go free from thee, thou shalt not let him go empty; thou shalt furnish him liberally out of thy flock, and out of thy threshing-floor, and out of thy winepress.' The phrase, 'Thou shalt furnish him liberally,' is a paraphrase of the Heb. הַעֲנֵיק תַּעֲנִיק לוֹ, which means lit. 'make him a necklace'—the metaphor being that of ornamenting and embellishing, of giving some striking gift, as from a man who wishes to show his lasting regard for the servant who had served him faithfully through many years. Such—God announces unto Moses—will be the farewell which the Egyptian people will accord unto the departing Israelites.

**22.** *shall ask.* For the mere asking, they will be given in gladness and friendliness precious and valuable gifts. The Heb. שאל means to ask as a gift (see Ps. II, 8), with no idea of giving back the object thus received. AV translates, 'every woman shall borrow of her neighbour.' This translation is thoroughly mischievous and misleading. 'If there was any borrowing, it was on the part of the Egyptians, who had been taking the labour of the Israelites without recompense' (Dummelow).

*that sojourneth in her house.* It is most unlikely that the households of the oppressed Israelites included Egyptian dependants. Therefore, Ehrlich, following Rashi and in strict accordance with Semitic idiom, rightly translates, *in whose house she sojourneth.*

*jewels.* Heb. 'articles'. These articles were not asked for to be used for festive wear when worshipping God. Worship requires purification, sanctification on the part of the worshipper (cf. Gen. XXXV, 2), not ornamentation (B. Jacob); see following note.

*upon your sons, and upon your daughters.* The striking manifestation of kindliness and goodwill on the side of the Egyptian people is to be remembered by the Israelites throughout the generations; and, therefore, they are bidden to put these gifts and ornaments upon their children, who will ask concerning that great Day when the Lord saved Israel out of the hands of Pharaoh. These jewels, tokens of friendship and repentance, were fittingly employed later in the adornment and enrichment of the Sanctuary.

*ye shall spoil the Egyptians.* This rendering should be replaced by *ye shall save the Egyptians* (B. Jacob). 'Spoil the Egyptians' (or, 'strip Egypt') is an incorrect, nay impossible, rendering of the Heb. text. The root נצל, which is here translated 'spoil' or 'strip', occurs 212 times in Scripture; and in 210 instances its meaning is admitted by all to be, to snatch (from danger), to rescue (from a wild beast), to recover (property, also to plunder (booty). Its direct object is never the person or thing *from whom* the saving or the rescuing or the snatching has taken place, but always the person or thing rescued. The usual translation, both here and in XII, 36, 'ye shall spoil the Egyptians,' is, therefore, unwarranted, for two reasons. It takes the persons from whom things are snatched as the direct object; and, furthermore, it necessitates an entire reversal of the meaning of נצל from *save* into *despoil!* There is no justification for departing, in this verse, or in XII, 36, from the rendering which is absolutely unchallenged in the 210 other places where it occurs. The words וְנִצַּלְתֶּם אֶת מִצְרַיִם can only be translated, '*and ye shall save the Egyptians*,' i.e. clear the name, and vindicate the humanity, of the Egyptians. Bitter memories and associations would have clung to the word 'Egyptians' in the mind of the Israelites, as the hereditary enslavers and oppressors of Israel. A friendly parting, and generous gifts, however, would banish that feeling. The Israelites would come to see that the oppressors were Pharaoh and his courtiers, not the Egyptian people. They would be enabled thereby to carry out the command to be given to them forty years later, 'Thou shalt not abhor an Egyptian' (Deut. XXIII, 8). It is for such reasons that the Israelites are bidden to ask their neighbours for these gifts, in order to ensure such a parting in friendship and goodwill, with its consequent clearing of the name, and vindication of the honour, of the Egyptian people (B. Jacob).

*v.* 21 and 22 lend a poetic and unforgettable touch of beauty to the going out of Egypt; and yet these verses, as few others, have been misunderstood and been looked upon as a 'blot' on the moral teaching of Scripture. The Talmud records a formal claim for indemnity put forward by the Egyptians before Alexander the Great for the vessels of gold and silver which the Israelites had taken with them at the Exodus! The Jewish spokesman, however, had little difficulty in proving to Alexander that, if any indemnity was to be paid, it was the Egyptians who were the debtors, seeing that they had enslaved and exploited the Israelites for many centuries without any pay for their labours.

In modern times, enemies of the Bible vie with one another in finding terms strong enough in which to condemn the 'deceit' practised on the

# EXODUS IV, 1

## CHAPTER IV

1. And Moses answered and said: 'But, behold, they will not believe me, nor hearken unto my voice; for they will say: The LORD hath not appeared unto thee.' 2. And the LORD said unto him: 'What is that in thy hand?' And he said: 'A rod.' 3. And He said: 'Cast it on the ground.' And he cast it on the ground, and it became a serpent; and Moses fled from before it. 4. And the LORD said unto Moses: 'Put forth thy hand, and take it by the tail— and he put forth his hand, and laid hold of it, and it became a rod in his hand— 5. that they may believe that the LORD, the God of their fathers, the God of Abraham, the God of Isaac, and the God of Jacob, hath appeared unto thee.' 6. And the LORD said furthermore unto him: 'Put now thy hand into thy bosom.' And he put his hand into his bosom; and when he took it out, behold, his hand was leprous, as white as snow. 7. And He said: 'Put

Egyptians. Apologists, both Jewish and non-Jewish, usually reply that this silver and gold was in exchange for the property the Israelites left behind them (Malbim); or they repeat the reply of the Alexandrian Jews: 'Through God's providence, the Israelites were enriched at the expense of their oppressors, and gained as it were a prize of victory in compensation for their long oppression' (Dillmann). Far better than any of these current explanations is that given by Rabbiner Dr. B. Jacob, which we have adopted. It meets all the apparent difficulties, and brings out unexpected beauties in the Divine command. Thus, the phrase *spoiling the Egyptians*, which has become a proverbial expression, is, like the phrase *brand of Cain* (*Genesis*, p. 15), due to a complete misunderstanding of the text.

## CHAPTER IV

1–9. MOSES' THIRD DIFFICULTY: THE ISRAELITES MAY NOT BELIEVE HIS MESSAGE OF FREEDOM

**1.** *the LORD hath not appeared unto thee.* How could this be answered? Argument would be of little avail. Their unbelief must be swept aside by something that would carry conviction to men whose religious memories are dimmed and whose spirit is crushed.

**2–5.** The first sign.

**2.** *a rod.* Jewish legend has woven marvellous tales round the Rod of Moses. 'It was probably only a shepherd's crook. What a history, how-ever, awaited it! It was to be stretched out over the Red Sea, pointing a pathway through its depths; to smite the flinty rock; to win victory over the hosts of Amalek; to be known as the rod of God' (Meyer).

**3.** *a serpent.* Heb. *nachash*; the basilisk, the symbol of royal and divine power in the diadem worn by Pharaoh. 'The meaning of this miracle seems to be, Pharaoh's own power shall become an instrument of punishment, and his enslaved enemy shall triumph' (Hirsch).

**4.** *put forth thy hand.* Snake-charmers usually take hold of snakes by the neck to prevent them biting. It is much more dangerous to seize them by the tail. The living serpent becomes a staff by the will of God. Pharaoh can be overcome, like the serpent.

**6–8.** The second sign.

**6.** *his hand was leprous.* Moses' ability to produce, and to heal, that most malignant disease would be to them an even more convincing proof of his Divine commission.
*as white as snow.* Leprosy was common in Egypt. In its worst form, the whole skin becomes glossy white, dry and ulcerous.

**7.** *it was turned.* Old English for, 'it turned.'
*as his other flesh.* This miracle was the greater, as white leprosy, when fully developed, is rarely curable (Kalisch).

EXODUS IV, 8

thy hand back into thy bosom.—And he put his hand back into his bosom; and when he took it out of his bosom, behold, it was turned again as his other flesh.— 8. And it shall come to pass, if they will not believe thee, neither hearken to the voice of the first sign, that they will believe the voice of the latter sign. 9. And it shall come to pass, if they will not believe even these two signs, neither hearken unto thy voice, that thou shalt take of the water of the river, and pour it upon the dry land; and the water which thou takest out of the river shall become blood upon the dry land.' 10. And Moses said unto the LORD: 'Oh Lord, I am not a man of words, neither heretofore, nor since Thou hast spoken unto Thy servant; for I am slow of speech, and of a slow tongue.' 11. And the LORD said unto him: 'Who hath made man's mouth? or who maketh a man dumb, or deaf, or seeing, or blind? is it not I the LORD? 12. Now therefore go, and I will be with thy mouth, and teach thee what thou shalt speak.' 13. And he said: 'Oh Lord, send, I pray Thee, by the hand of him whom Thou wilt send.' 14. And the anger of the LORD was kindled against Moses, and He said: 'Is there not Aaron

שמות ד

8 בְּכְשָׂרוֹ: וְהָיָה אִם־לֹא יַאֲמִינוּ לָךְ וְלֹא יִשְׁמְעוּ לְקֹל הָאֹת
9 הָרִאשׁוֹן וְהֶאֱמִינוּ לְקֹל הָאֹת הָאַחֲרוֹן: וְהָיָה אִם־לֹא
יַאֲמִינוּ גַּם לִשְׁנֵי הָאֹתוֹת הָאֵלֶּה וְלֹא יִשְׁמְעוּן לְקֹלֶךָ
וְלָקַחְתָּ מִמֵּימֵי הַיְאֹר וְשָׁפַכְתָּ הַיַּבָּשָׁה וְהָיוּ הַמַּיִם אֲשֶׁר
10 תִּקַּח מִן־הַיְאֹר וְהָיוּ לְדָם בַּיַּבָּשֶׁת: וַיֹּאמֶר מֹשֶׁה אֶל־
יְהוָה בִּי אֲדֹנָי לֹא אִישׁ דְּבָרִים אָנֹכִי גַּם מִתְּמוֹל גַּם
מִשִּׁלְשֹׁם גַּם מֵאָז דַּבֶּרְךָ אֶל־עַבְדֶּךָ כִּי כְבַד־פֶּה וּכְבַד
11 לָשׁוֹן אָנֹכִי: וַיֹּאמֶר יְהוָה אֵלָיו מִי שָׂם פֶּה לָאָדָם אוֹ
מִי־יָשׂוּם אִלֵּם אוֹ חֵרֵשׁ אוֹ פִקֵּחַ אוֹ עִוֵּר הֲלֹא אָנֹכִי יְהוָה:
12 וְעַתָּה לֵךְ וְאָנֹכִי אֶהְיֶה עִם־פִּיךָ וְהוֹרֵיתִיךָ אֲשֶׁר תְּדַבֵּר:
13 וַיֹּאמֶר בִּי אֲדֹנָי שְׁלַח־נָא בְּיַד־תִּשְׁלָח: וַיִּחַר־אַף יְהוָה
14 בְּמֹשֶׁה וַיֹּאמֶר הֲלֹא אַהֲרֹן אָחִיךָ הַלֵּוִי יָדַעְתִּי כִּי־דַבֵּר
יְדַבֵּר הוּא וְגַם הִנֵּה־הוּא יֹצֵא לִקְרָאתֶךָ וְרָאֲךָ וְשָׂמַח

**8.** *if they will not believe.* God knows full well whether they will believe or not; but Moses is to be fortified by the information that if a portion of the people refuse to be convinced by the first miracle, they will be convinced by the second miracle (Ibn Ezra).

*the voice of the first sign.* The lesson or purport of the sign.

**9.** *the third sign.*

*take of the water.* Moses is thus given three signs to attest his Divine commission to the Israelites, the third being similar to the first of the ten plagues.

*the river.* i.e. the Nile.

**10-17.** MOSES STILL HESITATES: HE IS NOT ELOQUENT

**10.** *a man of words.* Or, 'eloquent.' He had spent the years of his manhood in the great silent spaces of the desert, and he could only stammer forth the message of freedom. Leadership, it seemed to him, was impossible to a man unskilled in forensic eloquence with which to win the Council of Elders to his way of thinking, or to state his case fluently and convincingly before Pharaoh.

*neither heretofore.* lit. 'neither from yesterday nor from before yesterday'.

*slow of speech, and of a slow tongue.* lit. 'heavy of speech and heavy of tongue'. He may have had an actual impediment in his speech. Rabbinic legend tells that Moses when a child was one day taken by Pharaoh on his knee. He thereupon grasped Pharaoh's crown and placed it on his head. The astrologers were horror-struck. 'Let two braziers be brought'—they counselled; 'one filled with gold, the other with glowing coals; and set them before him. If he grasps the gold, it will be safer for Pharaoh to put the possible usurper to death.' When the braziers were brought, the hand of Moses was stretching for the gold, but the angel Gabriel guided it to the coals. The child plucked out a burning coal and put it to his lips, and for life remained 'heavy of speech and heavy of tongue'.

**12.** *and teach thee.* The fluent expression of the right thought.

**13.** *of him whom Thou wilt send.* i.e. by anyone but myself (Rashbam). Discouraged by the failure of his first blow for freedom in his youth, he is unwilling to undertake the mission.

**14.** *was kindled.* Because of his obstinate reluctance in accepting the charge, despite the Divine promise of help. Another anthropomorphic phrase.

*is there not ... speak well.* Or, 'Do I not know that Aaron the Levite thy brother can speak well?' (Kalisch).

*the Levite.* This description is not superfluous. Heb. usage for indicating affection is by giving the full name of the person in question; cf. 'Take now thy son, thine only son, whom thou lovest, even Isaac,' Gen. XXII, 2.

EXODUS IV, 15      שמות ד

thy brother the Levite? I know that he can speak well. And also, behold, he cometh forth to meet thee; and when he seeth thee, he will be glad in his heart. 15. And thou shalt speak unto him, and put the words in his mouth; and I will be with thy mouth, and with his mouth, and will teach you what ye shall do. 16. And he shall be thy spokesman unto the people; and it shall come to pass, that he shall be to thee a mouth, and thou shalt be to him in God's stead. 17. And thou shalt take in thy hand this rod, wherewith thou shalt do the signs.'
*vi. ¶ 18. And Moses went and returned to ¹Jethro his father-in-law, and said unto him: 'Let me go, I pray thee, and return unto my brethren that are in Egypt, and see whether they be yet alive.' And Jethro said to Moses: 'Go in peace.' 19. And the Lord said unto Moses in Midian: 'Go, return into Egypt; for all the men are dead that sought thy life.' 20. And Moses took his wife and his sons, and set them upon an ass, and he returned to the land of Egypt; and Moses took the rod of God in his hand. 21. And the Lord said unto Moses: 'When thou

טו בְּלִבּוֹ: וְדִבַּרְתָּ אֵלָיו וְשַׂמְתָּ אֶת־הַדְּבָרִים בְּפִיו וְאָנֹכִי אֶהְיֶה עִם־פִּיךָ וְעִם־פִּיהוּ וְהוֹרֵיתִי אֶתְכֶם אֵת אֲשֶׁר תַּעֲשׂוּן:
16 וְדִבֶּר־הוּא לְךָ אֶל־הָעָם וְהָיָה הוּא יִהְיֶה־לְּךָ לְפֶה וְאַתָּה
17 תִּהְיֶה־לּוֹ לֵאלֹהִים: וְאֶת־הַמַּטֶּה הַזֶּה תִּקַּח בְּיָדֶךָ אֲשֶׁר תַּעֲשֶׂה־בּוֹ אֶת־הָאֹתֹת: פ ששי
18 וַיֵּלֶךְ מֹשֶׁה וַיָּשָׁב ׀ אֶל־יֶתֶר חֹתְנוֹ וַיֹּאמֶר לוֹ אֵלְכָה נָּא וְאָשׁוּבָה אֶל־אַחַי אֲשֶׁר־בְּמִצְרַיִם וְאֶרְאֶה הַעוֹדָם חַיִּים
19 וַיֹּאמֶר יִתְרוֹ לְמֹשֶׁה לֵךְ לְשָׁלוֹם: וַיֹּאמֶר יְהוָה אֶל־מֹשֶׁה בְּמִדְיָן לֵךְ שֻׁב מִצְרָיִם כִּי־מֵתוּ כָּל־הָאֲנָשִׁים הַמְבַקְשִׁים
כ אֶת־נַפְשֶׁךָ: וַיִּקַּח מֹשֶׁה אֶת־אִשְׁתּוֹ וְאֶת־בָּנָיו וַיַּרְכִּבֵם עַל־הַחֲמֹר וַיָּשָׁב אַרְצָה מִצְרָיִם וַיִּקַּח מֹשֶׁה אֶת־מַטֵּה
21 הָאֱלֹהִים בְּיָדוֹ: וַיֹּאמֶר יְהוָה אֶל־מֹשֶׁה בְּלֶכְתְּךָ לָשׁוּב

---
¹ Heb. *Jether.*

**16.** *in God's stead.* Moses receives his inspiration direct from God; and becomes the inspirer of his brother, who acts as his interpreter to Pharaoh and Israel.

    18–31. Moses returns to Egypt

**18.** *brethren.* To my kinsfolk; see Gen. XIII, 8.

**19.** *go, return into Egypt.* There were still some hesitancies and fears in the mind of Moses. Hence the distinct assurance that all his enemies were dead.

**20.** *sons.* The birth of the elder is mentioned in II, 22; the second seems to have been a mere infant.

*ass.* 'The animal is of a far superior quality in Arabia and Egypt than in Northern countries. It is livelier, quicker, more courageous and robust' (Kalisch).

*the rod of God.* Called thus by reason of the miracle performed in connection therewith; *v.* 2 and 3.

**21.** *harden his heart.* Or, *make his heart strong; i.e.* stubborn. This does not mean that God on purpose made Pharaoh sinful. For God to make it impossible for a man to obey Him, and then punish him for his disobedience, would be both unjust and contrary to the fundamental Jewish belief in Freedom of the Will.

The phrase most often translated 'hardening of the heart' occurs nineteen times; ten times it is said that Pharaoh hardened his heart; and nine times the hardening of Pharaoh's heart is ascribed to God. There thus seem to be two sides to this hardening. When the Divine command came to Pharaoh, 'Set the slaves free,' and his reply was, 'I will not,' each repetition of Pharaoh's persistent obstinacy made it less likely that he would eventually listen to the word of God. For such is the law of conscience: every time the voice of conscience is disobeyed, it becomes duller and feebler, and the heart grows harder. Man cannot remain 'neutral' in the presence of Duty or of any direct command of God. He either obeys the Divine command, and it becomes unto him a blessing; or he defies God, and such command then becomes unto him a curse. 'It is part of the Divinely ordered scheme of things that if a man deliberately chooses evil, it proceeds to enslave him; it blinds and stupefies him, making for him repentance well-nigh impossible' (Riehm). Thus, every successive refusal on the part of Pharaoh to listen to the message of Moses froze up his better nature more and more, until it seemed as if God had hardened his heart. But this is only so because Pharaoh had first hardened it himself, and continued doing so. The Omniscient God knew beforehand whither his obstinacy would lead Pharaoh, and prepared Moses for initial failure by warning him that Pharaoh's heart would become 'hardened'.

The modern mind, whilst agreeing that all things are ultimately controlled by God's will, does not attribute results to the *immediate* action of God. Not so the Biblical idiom. Events, whether physical or moral, which are the inevitable result of the Divine ordering of the universe, are spoken of as the direct work of God (Dillmann, Driver, Jacob). See also note on Isa. VI, 9, p. 303.

## EXODUS IV, 22     שמות ד

goest back into Egypt, see that thou do before Pharaoh all the wonders which I have put in thy hand; but I will harden his heart, and he will not let the people go. 22. And thou shalt say unto Pharaoh: Thus saith the Lord: Israel is My son, My first-born. 23. And I have said unto thee: Let My son go, that he may serve Me; and thou hast refused to let him go. Behold, I will slay thy son, thy first-born.'—24. And it came to pass on the way at the lodging-place, that the Lord met him, and sought to kill him. 25. Then Zipporah took a flint and cut off the foreskin of her son, and cast it at his feet; and she said: 'Surely a bridegroom of blood art thou to me.' 26. So He let him alone. Then she said: 'A bridegroom of blood in regard of the circumcision.' ¶ 27. And the Lord said to Aaron: 'Go into the wilderness to meet Moses.' And he went, and met him in the mountain of God, and kissed him. 28. And Moses told Aaron all the words of the Lord wherewith He had sent him, and all the signs wherewith He had charged him. 29. And Moses and Aaron went and

---

**22.** *Israel is My son.* This expression is here applied for the first time to Israel as a nation.

*first-born.* Implying the universal fatherhood of God. The other nations, too, are God's children; and in Abraham's seed, spiritually the first-born among them, all the families of the earth are to be blessed (Gen. XII, 3).

**23.** *thou hast refused.* Better, *'and if thou refusest . . . I shall slay.'*

**24.** *at the lodging-place.* The verse can also be translated: 'On the way, he tarried in a lodging-place.' Moses was still distrusting himself in regard to his mission, hesitating, tarrying in the inn. This brings down the Divine displeasure upon him (Wogue).

*sought to kill him.* An anthropomorphic way of saying that Moses fell suddenly into a serious illness. Many commentators connect this sudden illness of Moses with his postponing, for some reason, the circumcision of his son. Tradition ascribes the omission to the influence of Jethro and Zipporah, who may have desired the circumcision postponed to the 13th year, as was customary among the Bedouin tribes. However, in the previous verse Moses had warned Pharaoh that disobedience of God's will carried dire punishment with it; and he himself should, therefore, on no account have permitted any postponement of a duty incumbent upon him.

**25.** *Zipporah.* Moses being disabled by illness, Zipporah performed the ceremony.

*a flint.* A sharp stone instrument; see Josh. v. 2.

*cast it at his feet.* i.e. the feet of Moses—to connect him with what she had done.

*bridegroom of blood.* This is the literal translation of the Heb. *chathan damim.* Since circumcision is the symbol of the covenant between God and the child, the child was spoken of as the *bridegroom* of the covenant; in the same way as the 'hero' of *Simchath Torah*, the Festival of the Rejoicing of the Law, came in medieval times to be called *chathan Torah*, the 'bridegroom' of the Torah.

According to Ibn Ezra, the words, 'Surely a bridegroom of blood art thou to me,' were addressed to the child: 'Indeed, thee I might call literally a *bridegroom of blood*, because thou didst nearly cause the death of my husband.'

**26.** *So He let him alone.* The illness of Moses abated, and he was soon restored to health.

*then she said, A bridegroom, etc.* i.e. Zipporah was the first to use the term *chathan damim* in connection with circumcision (Rosin, Baentsch).

**27.** *the mountain of God.* i.e. Horeb, see III, 1. The 'wilderness' is the one between Horeb and Egypt.

**28.** *He had charged him.* To perform.

**29.** *elders.* See note on III, 16.

'Now after all these years comes a vague rumour through the brick-fields and along the great canal, about the two old men from far-off Midian with a most startling message. One, it was said, was that Moses whose exciting story their aged elders still talked about, the story that had so stirred the slave settlements long ago—

## EXODUS IV, 30

gathered together all the elders of the children of Israel. 30. And Aaron spoke all the words which the Lord had spoken unto Moses, and did the signs in the sight of the people. 31. And the people believed; and when they heard that the Lord had remembered the children of Israel, and that He had seen their affliction, then they bowed their heads and worshipped.*vii.

## 5

### CHAPTER V

1. And afterward Moses and Aaron came, and said unto Pharaoh: 'Thus saith the Lord, the God of Israel: Let My people go, that they may hold a feast unto Me in the wilderness.' 2. And Pharaoh said: 'Who is the Lord, that I should hearken unto His voice to let Israel go? I know not the Lord, and moreover I will not let Israel go.' 3. And they said: 'The God of the Hebrews hath met with us. Let us go, we pray thee, three days' journey into the wilderness

when a prince of Egypt, who was one of themselves, had, for their sakes, refused to be called the son of Pharaoh's daughter. Then came the secret messages from Moses and Aaron to the heads of families. Before going to Pharaoh, they must first be sure that their leadership will be accepted by the people. You can imagine the secret gatherings along the canals, the midnight meetings of desperate men assembling at risk of their lives, such as one reads of in *Uncle Tom's Cabin*—the old slaves, the elders of the tribes, with the first dawn of hope in their eyes. Ah, poor wretches, one needs to have suffered like them to understand the goodness of finding out that God cared after all' (Smyth).

**30.** *Aaron spoke.* Acting as the spokesman of Moses; see *v.* 15.

*and did the signs.* Jewish commentators assume that this means that Aaron performed the signs; others hold that it was Moses.

**31.** *the people.* As represented by the elders. It is also reasonable to assume that the elders called the people together to hear the message brought by Moses and Aaron. Already the word of God, 'They shall hearken to thy voice' (III, 18), was being fulfilled.

*worshipped.* lit. 'they prostrated themselves', in prayer and gratitude to God.

CHAPTER V-VI, 1. UNSUCCESSFUL APPEAL TO PHARAOH AND INCREASE OF THE OPPRESSION

**1.** *and afterward.* Only after the confidence of the Israelites had been assured by means of the signs, could Moses and Aaron approach Pharaoh.

*Pharaoh.* Probably Merneptah, see p. 395.

*a feast.* Heb. *hag*, the common Semitic word for a pilgrimage to a sanctuary, where pilgrims took part in religious processions and ritual dances. Sacrifice was an essential part of such a festival.

*in the wilderness.* The Israelites could not offer sacrifices in the presence of the Egyptians, in view of the fact that the animals to be sacrificed were held sacred by the Egyptians; just as Mohammedans in India cannot with impunity slaughter cows in sight of a Hindu mob. Hence the request to go to the wilderness to celebrate the feast.

**2.** *who is the LORD.* An expression of contempt; Pharaoh does not know *Adonay*, and does not acknowledge His right to command him. The Rabbis say that he turned to his seventy scribes, who knew all the tongues spoken on earth, and asked them: 'Know ye a god who is called *Adonay*, the God of Eternity?' They answered, 'We have sought in all the books of all the peoples among the names of all the gods; but we have not found *Adonay* among them.' They spoke the truth. It was a new revelation, a new conception of God that Moses brought to the children of men. None of the heathen empires or emperors of old knew the God of Freedom, Holiness and Righteousness. He was not in their pantheon.

**3.** *the God of the Hebrews hath met with us.* Moses and Aaron now use language which Pharaoh is more likely to understand. Instead of speaking of *Adonay*, they tell him that the God who had manifested Himself to Moses is the God of the Hebrews.

*three days' journey.* See III, 18.

*with the sword.* Even Pharaoh could understand that for a people to neglect the worship of its god rendered it liable to divine punishment by sword or pestilence.

## EXODUS V, 4

and sacrifice unto the Lord our God; lest He fall upon us with pestilence, or with the sword.' 4. And the king of Egypt said unto them: 'Wherefore do ye, Moses and Aaron, cause the people to break loose from their work? get you unto your burdens.' 5. And Pharaoh said: 'Behold, the people of the land are now many, and will ye make them rest from their burdens?' 6. And the same day Pharaoh commanded the taskmasters of the people, and their officers, saying: 7. 'Ye shall no more give the people straw to make brick, as heretofore. Let them go and gather straw for themselves. 8. And the tale of the bricks, which they did make heretofore, ye shall lay upon them; ye shall not diminish aught thereof; for they are idle; therefore they cry, saying: Let us go and sacrifice to our God. 9. Let heavier work be laid upon the men, that they may labour therein; and let them not regard lying words.' 10. And the taskmasters of the people went out, and their officers, and they spoke to the people, saying: 'Thus saith Pharaoh: I will not give you straw. 11. Go yourselves, get you straw where ye can find it; for nought of your work shall be diminished.' 12. So the people were scattered abroad throughout all the land of Egypt to gather stubble for straw. 13. And the taskmasters were urgent, saying: 'Fulfil your work, your daily task, as when there was straw.' 14. And the officers of the children of Israel,

4 בַּדֶּבֶר א֣וֹ בֶחָֽרֶב׃ וַיֹּ֤אמֶר אֲלֵהֶם֙ מֶ֣לֶךְ מִצְרַ֔יִם לָ֚מָּה מֹשֶׁ֣ה וְאַהֲרֹ֔ן תַּפְרִ֥יעוּ אֶת־הָעָ֖ם מִֽמַּעֲשָׂ֑יו לְכ֖וּ לְסִבְלֹתֵיכֶֽם׃
5 וַיֹּ֣אמֶר פַּרְעֹ֔ה הֵן־רַבִּ֥ים עַתָּ֖ה עַ֣ם הָאָ֑רֶץ וְהִשְׁבַּתֶּ֥ם אֹתָ֖ם מִסִּבְלֹתָֽם׃
6 וַיְצַ֥ו פַּרְעֹ֖ה בַּיּ֣וֹם הַה֑וּא אֶת־הַנֹּגְשִׂ֣ים בָּעָ֔ם
7 וְאֶת־שֹׁטְרָ֖יו לֵאמֹֽר׃ לֹ֣א תֹאסִפ֞וּן לָתֵ֨ת תֶּ֤בֶן לָעָם֙ לִלְבֹּ֣ן הַלְּבֵנִ֔ים כִּתְמ֥וֹל שִׁלְשֹׁ֖ם הֵ֣ם יֵֽלְכ֔וּ וְקֹשְׁשׁ֥וּ לָהֶ֖ם תֶּֽבֶן׃
8 וְאֶת־מַתְכֹּ֨נֶת הַלְּבֵנִ֜ים אֲשֶׁ֣ר הֵם֩ עֹשִׂ֨ים תְּמ֤וֹל שִׁלְשֹׁם֙ תָּשִׂ֣ימוּ עֲלֵיהֶ֔ם לֹ֥א תִגְרְע֖וּ מִמֶּ֑נּוּ כִּֽי־נִרְפִּ֣ים הֵ֔ם עַל־כֵּ֗ן
9 הֵ֤ם צֹֽעֲקִים֙ לֵאמֹ֔ר נֵלְכָ֖ה נִזְבְּחָ֥ה לֵאלֹהֵֽינוּ׃ תִּכְבַּ֧ד הָעֲבֹדָ֛ה עַל־הָאֲנָשִׁ֖ים וְיַעֲשׂוּ־בָ֑הּ וְאַל־יִשְׁע֖וּ בְּדִבְרֵי־שָֽׁקֶר׃
10 וַיֵּ֨צְא֜וּ נֹגְשֵׂ֤י הָעָם֙ וְשֹׁ֣טְרָ֔יו וַיֹּאמְר֥וּ אֶל־הָעָ֖ם לֵאמֹ֑ר כֹּ֚ה אָמַ֣ר
11 פַּרְעֹ֔ה אֵינֶ֛נִּי נֹתֵ֥ן לָכֶ֖ם תֶּֽבֶן׃ אַתֶּ֗ם לְכ֨וּ קְח֤וּ לָכֶם֙ תֶּ֔בֶן
12 מֵאֲשֶׁ֖ר תִּמְצָ֑אוּ כִּ֣י אֵ֥ין נִגְרָ֛ע מֵעֲבֹדַתְכֶ֖ם דָּבָֽר׃ וַיָּ֥פֶץ הָעָ֖ם
13 בְּכָל־אֶ֣רֶץ מִצְרָ֑יִם לְקֹשֵׁ֥שׁ קַ֖שׁ לַתֶּֽבֶן׃ וְהַנֹּגְשִׂ֖ים אָצִ֑ים לֵאמֹ֔ר כַּלּ֤וּ מַעֲשֵׂיכֶם֙ דְּבַר־י֣וֹם בְּיוֹמ֔וֹ כַּאֲשֶׁ֖ר בִּהְי֥וֹת
14 הַתֶּֽבֶן׃ וַיֻּכּ֗וּ שֹֽׁטְרֵי֙ בְּנֵ֣י יִשְׂרָאֵ֔ל אֲשֶׁר־שָׂ֣מוּ עֲלֵהֶ֔ם נֹגְשֵׂ֖י

---

**4.** *cause the people to break loose from the work.* Why do you unsettle the people in their work with all this talk of a pilgrimage, which is only an excuse for a holiday? Back, to your labours!

**5.** *people of the land.* Better, *Council of Elders* (see page 80, note on Gen. XXIII, 7), Heb. *am ha-aretz*, refers to the elders who, as representatives of the people, accompanied Moses (III, 18). 'Why, asked Pharaoh, should *all these elders*—and there are so many of them—rest from their labours, in order to listen to the talk of Moses and Aaron?'

**6.** *the same day.* Pharaoh lost no time in devising a plan by which to crush the aspirations of the Hebrew leaders.

*taskmasters.* Heb. *nogesim*, not the same word as in I, 11 (*sare missim*). The *nogesim* were probably subordinate to them.

*their officers.* Who were Hebrews; see v. 14.

**7.** *straw.* Necessary for holding the clay together and to prevent it from cracking.

*let them go and gather straw.* They would have to seek it in the fields of the Egyptians.

**8.** *tale.* Number; the same quantity was to be required of them under the new regulations as before. The demand was, as Pharaoh well knew, impossible, and increased the task of his Hebrew subjects beyond the point of human performance.

*they are idle.* In two papyrus documents found in Egyptian tombs of the time of the Exodus, one passage says: 'I have no one to help me in making bricks, no straw, etc.'; and another tells of twelve labourers punished for failing to make up their daily tale of bricks.

**9.** *let heavier work be laid.* He is determined to leave his slaves no time to think of freedom or worship.

*let them not regard lying words.* The 'lying words' refer to the promised redemption, which in his eyes is merely a pretext for seeking a holiday.

**10–12.** The taskmasters communicate Pharaoh's orders to the people.

**12.** *stubble.* All kinds of field rubbish, small twigs, stems, roots of withered plants. This had to be chopped and sorted.

*for straw.* i.e. to make into straw.

**14.** *yesterday and to-day.* Heb. idiom for *recently*.

EXODUS V, 15

whom Pharaoh's taskmasters had set over them, were beaten, saying: 'Wherefore have ye not fulfilled your appointed task in making brick both yesterday and to-day as heretofore?' 15. Then the officers of the children of Israel came and cried unto Pharaoh, saying: 'Wherefore dealest thou thus with thy servants? 16. There is no straw given unto thy servants, and they say to us: Make brick: and, behold, thy servants are beaten, but the fault is in thine own people.' 17. But he said: 'Ye are idle, ye are idle; therefore ye say: Let us go and sacrifice to the Lord. 18. Go therefore now, and work; for there shall no straw be given you, yet shall ye deliver the tale of bricks.' 19. And the officers of the children of Israel did see that they were set on mischief, when they said: 'Ye shall not diminish aught from your bricks, your daily task.' 20. And they met Moses and Aaron, who stood in the way, as they came forth from Pharaoh; 21. and they said unto them: 'The Lord look upon you, and judge; because ye have made our savour to be abhorred in the eyes of Pharaoh, and in the eyes of his servants, to put a sword in their hand to slay us.'*ᵐ· 22. And Moses returned unto the Lord, and said: 'Lord, wherefore hast Thou dealt ill with this people? why is it that Thou hast sent me? 23. For since I came to Pharaoh to speak in Thy name, he hath dealt ill with this people; neither hast Thou delivered Thy people at all.'

## 6  Chapter VI

1. And the Lord said unto Moses: 'Now shalt thou see what I will do to Pharaoh; for by a strong hand shall he let them go, and by a strong hand shall he drive them out of his land.'

---

**15–19.** The officers of the Israelites cry in vain to the king.

**15.** *unto Pharaoh.* 'Direct access to the ruler on the part of petitioners of humble rank is comparatively easy in the East' (Bennett).

**16.** *they say.* i.e. the Egyptian taskmasters.
*the fault is in thine own people.* lit. 'but thy people sins'. A hint that the tyrannical conduct of the overseers constitutes a sin, and will call down the punishment of Heaven (Kalisch).

**19.** *they were set on mischief.* The word *they* refers to the Egyptian taskmasters.

**20–21.** The Hebrew officers blame Moses and Aaron for the plight of the Hebrews.

**20.** *stood in the way.* lit. 'standing to meet them'. Moses and Aaron were waiting to learn the reply of the king (Luzzatto).

**21.** *the Lord look upon you, and judge.* May God requite you for the evil you have brought upon the Israelites!

*a sword.* A pretext to ruin us.

**22–23.** Moses complains to God that the bondage has become more cruel than ever.

**22.** *returned.* 'The expression is beautiful in its simplicity, implying his constant communion with God' (McNeile).

**23.** *neither hast Thou.* Fulfilled Thy promise of deliverance, III, 8. 'He could not understand this long-suffering delay of the Eternal Judge to afford time for the hardened tyrant to repent. The desponding complaint of Moses was the effort of a pious soul struggling after a deeper penetration into the mysteries of the Almighty' (Kalisch).

### Chapter VI

**1.** *now shalt thou see.* God calms Moses by renewing the promise of redemption.
*by a strong hand.* Compelled by the power of God.

# HAFTORAH SHEMOTH (FOR ASHKENAZIM)
## ISAIAH XXVII, 6–XXVIII, 13 AND XXIX, 22, 23

CHAPTER XXVII          CAP. XXVII. כז

6. In days to come shall Jacob take root, Israel shall blossom and bud; And the face of the world shall be filled with fruitage.

7. Hath He smitten him as He smote those that smote him? Or is he slain according to the slaughter of them that were slain by Him?

8. In full measure, when Thou sendest her away, Thou dost contend with her; He hath removed her with His rough blast in the day of the east wind.

9. Therefore by this shall the iniquity of Jacob be expiated, And this is all the fruit of taking away his sin:

---

Isaiah the son of Amoz was a native of Jerusalem. His family seems to have been one of rank, and he moved in royal circles. His Prophetic ministry extended for close upon 40 years, from 740–701 B.C.E. These years were the most stirring that the kingdom of Judah had yet passed through; and throughout that entire period he was the dominant figure in the land. The momentous event of his time was the rise of Assyria. From being a mere garrison province of Babylon in northern Mesopotamia, Assyria had become a world power. The kingdoms of Syria and Israel fell before the Assyrians in 721; and only as by a miracle was Jerusalem delivered from their grasp in 701.

With the downfall of the kingdom of Israel, Judah became the sole representative and repository of true Religion; and in the fate of that tiny land the moral destinies of the whole world were involved. In this time of upheaval and spiritual travail, Isaiah brought to King and People the message of the holiness, omnipotence, and sovereignty of God ('Holy, holy, holy, is the LORD of hosts: the whole earth is full of His glory'). With passionate fervour he sought to instil his own vital faith in God and Providence into the hearts of his brethren, and interpret for them the crises of history in the light of Divine guidance and Righteousness. His efforts brought him into violent conflict with the war party of his day; and throughout his life he remained an implacable enemy of shallow 'patriots' and opportunist politicians. According to one tradition, he perished in the heathen reaction under King Manasseh.

Great in thought and great in action, Isaiah united the profoundest religious insight with wide knowledge of men and affairs. The princely personality of the man is reflected in his style. His words are instinct with power, and he is the master of the sublime in universal literature. His moral passion, moreover, marks him as one of the world's greatest orators. See also p. 302.

The connection between the Sedrah and Haftorah is apparent. Israel had suffered in Egypt, but Israel's taskmasters had received adequate punishment; and Israel's affliction in Isaiah's day was as nothing compared with the fate that would befall its foes. Israel in Egypt chafed at Redemption's delay, tiring of the visits of Moses and Aaron; Israel of Isaiah's age gibed at the monotony of Prophetical teaching, and doubted the validity of Divine promise. The Egyptian Deliverance revealed that Justice triumphs in God's universe; so would the men of a later age see that the hand of God moves in the destinies of men.

**6.** *in days to come.* The word for 'days' must be supplied in the Heb. text.

*the face of the world shall be filled with fruitage.* Israel is saved, and saving the world. The prophet dreams for Israel the ascendancy of noble example to the other nations; as in Isa. II, 2 f.

**7.** *smitten him. i.e.* Israel. Severely as Israel had been punished, its punishment was mild in comparison to that meted out to Israel's enemies (Kimchi). The implied answer is No.

**8.** *in full measure.* According to their sins, but tempered with mercy.

*when Thou sendest her away.* The reference is to Samaria, representing Israel, *i.e.* the Northern Kingdom (Ibn Ezra).

*the east wind.* The Assyrians, who would lead the Kingdom into captivity.

**9.** *therefore.* God had only banished, not destroyed, Israel; hence repentance is still possible.

*Jacob.* The poetical name for Israel.

*the fruit of taking away his sin.* Penitence is at once the condition and the 'fruit' of Israel's forgiveness.

*when he maketh.* Better, *that he should make.*

*Asherim and the sun-images.* The Asherah was probably the sacred pole, or symbol of fertility, found in ancient shrines. The sun-images were pillars dedicated to the worship of the sun-god.

## ISAIAH XXVII, 10

When he maketh all the stones of the altar as chalkstones that are beaten in pieces,
So that the Asherim and the sun-images shall rise no more.

10. For the fortified city is solitary,
A habitation abandoned and forsaken, like the wilderness;
There shall the calf feed, and there shall he lie down,
And consume the branches thereof.

11. When the boughs thereof are withered, they shall be broken off;
The women shall come, and set them on fire;
For it is a people of no understanding;
Therefore He that made them will not have compassion upon them,
And He that formed them will not be gracious unto them.

12. And it shall come to pass in that day,
That the Lord will beat off [His fruit]
From the flood of the River unto the Brook of Egypt,
And ye shall be gathered one by one, O ye children of Israel.

13. And it shall come to pass in that day,
That a great horn shall be blown;
And they shall come that were lost in the land of Assyria,
And they that were dispersed in the land of Egypt;
And they shall worship the Lord in the holy mountain at Jerusalem.

## CHAPTER XXVIII

1. Woe to the crown of pride of the drunkards of Ephraim,
And to the fading flower of his glorious beauty,
Which is on the head of the fat valley of them that are smitten down with wine!

---

**10, 11.** Repentance can bring forgiveness, but it does not imply immunity from punishment. The 'solitary city' is Jerusalem, deserted and forsaken, with grass and boughs growing in the streets, food for calves and fuel for its needy inhabitants. They are 'a people of no understanding'. The time of punishment, in the shape of exile, must therefore inevitably come.

**12, 13.** But there will be a Return from that exile, and it will include even those who are scattered in distant lands.

**12.** *in that day.* The day of salvation; see the opening verse of the Haftorah and *v.* 1 of the chapter.

*beat off His fruit.* As one beats the olives from the leaves (or the grain from the chaff) and goes back again and again and collects all the fruit, so that all is gathered in (Rashi).

*one by one.* With such loving care for each individual Israelite, that not a single soul shall be lost.

**13.** *horn.* Heb. *shofar.* But even those who seem to be lost in distant Assyria, or the interior of Egypt, will be ingathered. This verse is employed with soul-stirring effect in the Mussaph Prayers for the New Year.

*lost.* To Israel.

## CHAPTER XXVIII

The date of this denunciation of the luxury and dissoluteness of the aristocracy of Samaria, the capital of Israel, the northern Kingdom, must be before the capture of Samaria by the Assyrians, which took place in 722. In Judah, an influential party favoured resistance to Assyria and an alliance with Egypt for that purpose—a course of action opposed by Isaiah as both foolish and fatal.

**1.** *Woe to.* Or, 'alas for.'

*crown of pride.* Samaria, a city of great strength and beauty, on a hill overlooking a rich valley, is likened to a chaplet of flowers on the head of a reveller. But the wearer is a drunkard, and the flowers are fading (Skinner).

# ISAIAH XXVIII, 2

2. Behold, the Lord hath a mighty and strong one,
As a storm of hail, a tempest of destruction,
As a storm of mighty waters overflowing,
That casteth down to the earth with violence.

3. The crown of pride of the drunkards of Ephraim
Shall be trodden under foot;

4. And the fading flower of his glorious beauty,
Which is on the head of the fat valley,
Shall be as the first-ripe fig before the summer,
Which when one looketh upon it,
While it is yet in his hand he eateth it up.

5. In that day shall the Lord of hosts be
For a crown of glory, and for a diadem of beauty,
Unto the residue of His people;

6. And for a spirit of judgment to him that sitteth in judgment,
And for strength to them that turn back the battle at the gate.

7. But these also reel through wine,
And stagger through strong drink;
The priest and the prophet reel through strong drink,
They are confused because of wine,
They stagger because of strong drink;
They reel in vision, they totter in judgment.

8. For all tables are full of filthy vomit,
And no place is clean.

9. Whom shall one teach knowledge?
And whom shall one make to understand the message?
Them that are weaned from the milk,
Them that are drawn from the breasts?

---

**2.** *a mighty and strong one.* i.e. the coming Assyrian invasion, compared to a devastating storm and flood.

**4.** *as the first-ripe fig.* A delicacy eagerly coveted and devoured. Thus would the enemy pounce upon Samaria with avidity (Kimchi).

**5.** *crown of glory.* Isaiah denounces, but never fails to bring a message of comfort. Samaria, 'the crown of pride,' will fall; but a faithful residue of Israel shall survive the storm, and to them God Himself will be 'the crown of glory'.

**6.** *spirit of judgment.* To the faithful remnant of Israel, God will be the source of justice within, and of strength to withstand the enemy already pouring in through the gate of the almost captured city.

**7.** *these also.* The prophet now turns from Samaria to Jerusalem, and finds the ruling classes in Jerusalem are those of Samaria over again. Why should Judah escape Samaria's fate, if she too remain deaf to the Divine Voice?

*they reel in vision...judgment.* Through intemperance the 'prophets' lack the capacity to discern the real significance of their own visions, or to understand and convey the teachings of their great predecessors. The priests, who were forbidden while on duty to take any wine or strong drink, from the same cause give feeble and irresolute guidance.

**8.** *all tables.* This verse is either a figurative description of the debasement of the national intelligence and conscience (Kay); or, 'of an actual banquet at which priests, prophets, and nobles were carousing. When the orgy is at its height, Isaiah enters and expresses his abhorrence of the scene' (Skinner).

**9.** *whom shall one teach.* The revellers, who resent the monotonous lessons of this Prophetic pedagogue, as they think him, are mocking Isaiah over their cups. 'Does he take us for mere children, that he gives us these platitudes and repetitions?'

## ISAIAH XXVIII, 10

10. For it is precept by precept, precept by precept,
Line by line, line by line;
Here a little, there a little.

11. For with stammering lips and with a strange tongue
Shall it be spoken to this people;

12. To whom it was said: 'This is the rest,
Give ye rest to the weary;
And this is the refreshing';
Yet they would not hear.

13. And so the word of the LORD is unto them
Precept by precept, precept by precept,
Line by line, line by line;
Here a little, there a little;
That they may go, and fall backward, and be broken,
And snared, and taken.

### CHAPTER XXIX

22. Therefore thus saith the LORD, who redeemed Abraham, concerning the house of Jacob:

Jacob shall not now be ashamed,
Neither shall his face now wax pale;

23. When he seeth his children, the work of My hands, in the midst of him
That they sanctify My name;

Yea, they shall sanctify the Holy One of Jacob,
And shall stand in awe of the God of Israel.

---

**10.** *precept... a little.* Heb. *tzav latzav... kav lakav.* The Heb. words are purposely of one syllable and made to rhyme, so as to convey the idea of childish instruction, what they deem the Prophet's unnecessary repetition of elementary truths.

**11.** *with strange tongue.* Isaiah's reply is, You stammer out mocking words; God will soon 'talk Assyrian' to you. Through the harsh, laconic speech of the merciless invader, you will be fittingly chastised.

**12.** *to whom it was said.* God had pointed out the way of peace and recovery for the nation; but the politicians in Judah were preparing further trouble for the suffering people by seeking alliance with Egypt (Dummelow).

*to the weary.* The plain man of the people, who would bear the brunt of the privation in any war.

**13.** *precept by precept.* Their contempt, even their caricature, of the Prophet's plain teachings will come bitterly home to them when God speaks to them through 'line upon line', in punishment upon punishment, for 'every precept upon precept' they have defied and broken (Rashi).

### CHAPTER XXIX, 22, 23

The Prophetic message must not end in despair. These verses hark back to Israel's early history; they look forward to the future as a time of restoration, when the people shall by their lives sanctify the Holy One of Jacob.

# HAFTORAH SHEMOTH (FOR SEPHARDIM)
## JEREMIAH I–II, 3

### Chapter I

1. The words of Jeremiah the son of Hilkiah, of the priests that were in Anathoth in the land of Benjamin, 2. to whom the word of the Lord came in the days of Josiah the son of Amon, king of Judah, in the thirteenth year of his reign. 3. It came also in the days of Jehoiakim the son of Josiah, king of Judah, unto the end of the eleventh year of Zedekiah the son of Josiah, king of Judah, unto the carrying away of Jerusalem captive in the fifth month. ¶ 4. And the word of the Lord came unto me, saying:

5. Before I formed thee in the belly I knew thee,
And before thou camest forth out of the womb I sanctified thee;
I have appointed thee a prophet unto the nations.

6. Then said I: 'Ah, Lord God! behold, I cannot speak; for I am a child.' 7. But the Lord said unto me:

Say not: I am a child;
For to whomsoever I shall send thee thou shalt go,
And whatsoever I shall command thee thou shalt speak.

8. Be not afraid of them;
For I am with thee to deliver thee,
Saith the Lord.

---

The call of Jeremiah has been aptly chosen by the Sephardim as the Haftorah for the Sedrah dealing with the call of Moses: diffidence and hesitancy, in assuming the well-nigh superhuman task that Heaven assigned to them, are common to both. The final verses of the Haftorah (II, 2, 3) poetically recalling the wanderings in the Wilderness, form another link with the Sedrah.

Jeremiah was born of a priestly family about the year 650 B.C.E. His Prophetic call came to him in the reign of Josiah, king of Judah, in the year 626. He witnessed the fall of Nineveh and the annihilation of the Assyrian Empire in 606; the death of Josiah, Judah's righteous king, in 605; and lived through the two sieges of Jerusalem in 597 and 586, with the attendant destruction of the Jewish state and the consequent transportation of the greater portion of his people to 'the rivers of Babylon'. We last hear of him in Egypt, carried thither by fugitive Judeans; and legend relates that he died a martyr's death at the hands of his brethren. Whatever basis there may be for this legend, it is but too true that Jeremiah the Prophet lived a martyr's life. For the greater part of his career, he was one man against the whole nation. By nature timid and shrinking, he proclaimed the Divine message fearlessly to ruler, noble, priest, and people alike.

Jeremiah is the spiritual heir of the great Prophets that preceded him. He combines the tenderness of Hosea, the fearlessness of Amos, and the stern majesty of Isaiah. Like them, he is first of all a preacher of repentance; threatening judgment and, at the same time, holding out the promise of restoration. But even in his darkest moments, when he utterly despairs of the future of the Jewish state, his faith and trust in God do not forsake him. 'Though all be lost,' he seems to say to Israel, 'turn to God in perfect trust, call Him your Father, and His love will regenerate you.' To Jeremiah, Religion is an inward thing, a personal relation between the individual and his Maker, a relation that is untouched by national prosperity and can only be deepened by national ruin. 'The history of Israel begins with the migration of Abraham from the Euphrates to the Jordan; its classical period closes with the compulsory migration of the exiles from the Jordan back to the Euphrates. If Israel had been merely a race like others, it would never have survived this fearful catastrophe, and would have disappeared in the Babylonian exile' (Cornill). That it did not so disappear was due to the activity of two men—Jeremiah and his disciple Ezekiel. Jeremiah's message to his despairing brethren in Babylon, 'Seek the welfare of the city wherein ye dwell, and pray unto the Lord for it: for in its welfare shall be your peace,' has been of incalculable influence in the civic life of all Jews throughout the world.

## JEREMIAH I, 9

9. Then the LORD put forth His hand, and touched my mouth; and the LORD said unto me:

> Behold, I have put My words in thy mouth;
> 10. See, I have this day set thee over the nations and over the kingdoms,
> To root out and to pull down,
> And to destroy and to overthrow;
> To build, and to plant.

11. Moreover the word of the LORD came unto me, saying: 'Jeremiah, what seest thou?' And I said: 'I see a rod of an ¹almond-tree.' 12. Then said the LORD unto me: 'Thou hast well seen; for I ²watch over My word to perform it.' ¶ 13. And the word of the LORD came unto me the second time, saying: 'What seest thou?' And I said: 'I see a seething pot; and the face thereof is from the north.' 14. Then the LORD said unto me: 'Out of the north the evil shall break forth upon all the inhabitants of the land. 15. For, lo, I will call all the families of the kingdoms of the north, saith the LORD; and they shall come, and they shall set every one his throne at the entrance of the gates of Jerusalem, and against all the walls thereof round about, and against all the cities of Judah. 16. And I will utter my judgments against them touching all their wickedness; in that they have forsaken Me, and have offered unto other gods, and worshipped the work of their own hands. 17. Thou therefore gird up thy loins, and arise, and speak unto them all that I com-

---
¹ Heb. *shaked*. ² Heb. *shoked*.

9 כִּי־אִתְּךָ אֲנִי לְהַצִּלֶךָ נְאֻם־יְהוָֹה: וַיִּשְׁלַח יְהוָֹה אֶת־יָדוֹ
וַיַּגַּע עַל־פִּי וַיֹּאמֶר יְהוָֹה אֵלַי הִנֵּה נָתַתִּי דְבָרַי בְּפִיךָ׃
10 רְאֵה הִפְקַדְתִּיךָ ׀ הַיּוֹם הַזֶּה עַל־הַגּוֹיִם וְעַל־הַמַּמְלָכוֹת
לִנְתוֹשׁ וְלִנְתוֹץ וּלְהַאֲבִיד וְלַהֲרוֹס לִבְנוֹת וְלִנְטוֹעַ׃
11 וַיְהִי דְבַר־יְהוָֹה אֵלַי לֵאמֹר מָה־אַתָּה רֹאֶה יִרְמְיָהוּ וָאֹמַר
12 מַקֵּל שָׁקֵד אֲנִי רֹאֶה: וַיֹּאמֶר יְהוָֹה אֵלַי הֵיטַבְתָּ לִרְאוֹת
13 כִּי־שֹׁקֵד אֲנִי עַל־דְּבָרִי לַעֲשֹׂתוֹ׃ וַיְהִי דְבַר־יְהוָֹה ׀
אֵלַי שֵׁנִית לֵאמֹר מָה אַתָּה רֹאֶה וָאֹמַר סִיר נָפוּחַ אֲנִי
14 רֹאֶה וּפָנָיו מִפְּנֵי צָפוֹנָה: וַיֹּאמֶר יְהוָֹה אֵלָי מִצָּפוֹן תִּפָּתַח
15 הָרָעָה עַל כָּל־יֹשְׁבֵי הָאָרֶץ: כִּי ׀ הִנְנִי קֹרֵא לְכָל־
מִשְׁפְּחוֹת מַמְלְכוֹת צָפוֹנָה נְאֻם־יְהוָֹה וּבָאוּ וְנָתְנוּ אִישׁ
כִּסְאוֹ פֶּתַח ׀ שַׁעֲרֵי יְרוּשָׁלַםִ וְעַל כָּל־חוֹמֹתֶיהָ סָבִיב וְעַל
16 כָּל־עָרֵי יְהוּדָה: וְדִבַּרְתִּי מִשְׁפָּטַי אוֹתָם עַל כָּל־רָעָתָם
אֲשֶׁר עֲזָבוּנִי וַיְקַטְּרוּ לֵאלֹהִים אֲחֵרִים וַיִּשְׁתַּחֲווּ לְמַעֲשֵׂי
17 יְדֵיהֶם: וְאַתָּה תֶּאְזֹר מָתְנֶיךָ וְקַמְתָּ וְדִבַּרְתָּ אֲלֵיהֶם אֵת

---

**1.** *Hilkiah.* Not the priest of that name.
*Anathoth.* Four miles north-east of Jerusalem.
*land of Benjamin.* This hilly territory was 26 miles by 12 miles, about the size of Middlesex.

**2.** *Josiah.* He reigned from 626–605. He put down the idolatries, abominations and immoralities that had been introduced by Manasseh, and led a great religious revival in Israel.

**3.** *Zedekiah.* The youngest son of Josiah, and the last king of Judah.

#### 4–10. JEREMIAH'S CALL

**5.** *knew thee.* i.e. chose thee; cf. Gen. XVIII, 19.
*sanctified thee.* Consecrated thee; i.e. set thee apart for My service. 'In the very moment of his call, Jeremiah learnt that he was a child of destiny. God had planned his life, even before he was born. The riddle and purpose of existence were thus solved for Jeremiah' (Duhm).
*unto the nations.* As Amos and Isaiah before him, but more so. Israel was now caught in the current of universal politics, and its career was inextricably bound up with Assyria, Babylon and Egypt (Peake).

**6.** *I am a child.* These words express the shrinking self-distrust of a sensitive nature, and the humility that characterizes truly great minds; cf. the reply of Moses in the Sedrah, IV, 10.

**7.** *say not.* Whatever his limitations may be, they matter not, for he is to be God's messenger; and whatever opposition or even persecution may be his lot, he would be Divinely supported.

**9.** *touched my mouth.* Symbolic of Divine inspiration.

**10.** *set thee.* lit. 'made thee My deputy'.
*to root out.* Because the Word of God, which the Prophet proclaims, determines the fate of nations and kingdoms.
*to plant.* Jeremiah's activity would also be to prepare the way for the work of restoration.

#### 11, 12. THE SYMBOL OF THE ALMOND-TREE

**11.** *an almond-tree.* Heb. *shaked*, and the Heb. for 'watching' is *shoked*. There is more than a play on words here. The almond-tree is so named in Hebrew because, blossoming early in January, it is the first to awake from winter's sleep. On seeing it, the thought flashes across

JEREMIAH I, 18

mand thee; be not dismayed at them, lest I dismay thee before them. 18. For, behold, I have made thee this day a fortified city, and an iron pillar, and brazen walls, against the whole land, against the kings of Judah, against the princes thereof, against the priests thereof, and against the people of the land. 19. And they shall fight against thee; but they shall not prevail against thee; For I am with thee, saith the LORD, to deliver thee.'

### CHAPTER II

1. And the word of the LORD came to me, saying: 2. Go, and cry in the ears of Jerusalem, saying: Thus saith the LORD:

I remember for thee the affection of thy youth,
The love of thine espousals;
How thou wentest after Me in the wilderness,
In a land that was not sown.

3. Israel is the LORD's hallowed portion,
His first-fruits of the increase;
All that devour him shall be held guilty,
Evil shall come upon them,
Saith the LORD.

the Prophet's mind that God is awake and watches over His word to fulfil it, without delay.

**13-16. THE SYMBOL OF THE CALDRON**

**14.** *out of the north.* From the North had come the Assyrian invasions, and into the North the Ten Tribes had been led captive. And Babylon, which was to take Judah into exile, also lay to the North.

*the evil.* Foretold by all the prophets as the result of the nation's sinning.

**15.** *shall set every one his throne.* The neighbourhood of the city gate was the place where trials were ordinarily held. Here the rulers of the invading army will sit in judgment on the conquered people. This was literally fulfilled; see Jer. XXXIX, 3.

**17-19. ENCOURAGEMENT TO JEREMIAH**

**17.** *gird up thy loins.* Prepare thyself for a strenuous task.

*lest I dismay thee before them.* If thou fearest them, thou wilt fail before them (Kimchi). Jeremiah can only conquer if he does not for one moment lose courage—a warning needed by the Prophet whose life would be full of anguish and martyrdom.

**18.** *the people of the land.* Heb. *am ha-aretz*; probably the National Assembly; see p. 80, note 7.

**19.** *shall not prevail. i.e.* shall not finally prevail (Streane). Before the Prophet's death,

his warnings would be justified, and his cause vindicated.

### CHAPTER II

**1-3.** The opening verses of the first prophecy of Jeremiah. God reminds Israel of her loyalty and affection in the Wilderness. Jeremiah pictures Israel's loyalty to God as that of an affectionate bride, who follows the chosen of her heart even into a wilderness.

**2.** *affection.* Heb. *chesed.* A very rich and beautiful word, here meaning unquestioned and whole-hearted devotion and total forgetfulness of self, a love more than filial, like that of a youthful, loving bride.

*how thou wentest after Me.* It was only such love, thought the Prophet, that could account for Israel's willingness to forget the grandeur of Egypt, and brave the terrors of the Wilderness—its hardships, perils and treacherous foes. It was only such love that could cause them gladly to follow the call of God into the Unknown, on a novel quest of the Divine, that was to fill man's earthly existence with new hopes; on an unheard-of adventure in Religion, that was to turn the current of history and humanize mankind.

**3.** *the LORD'S hallowed portion.* All the nations are the LORD'S harvest; but Israel is set apart for Him alone, even as the first-fruits are set apart for the use of the priest. In the Sedrah, IV, 22, Israel is called God's firstborn son.

*evil shall come upon them.* Woe to anyone who violates that sanctity, and assails Israel.

EXODUS VI, 2     שמות וארא ו

**6** 2. And God spoke unto Moses, and said unto him: 'I am the Lord; 3. and I appeared unto Abraham, unto Isaac, and unto Jacob, as God Almighty, but by My name ¹יהוה I made Me not known to them. 4. And I have also established My covenant with them, to give them the land of Canaan, the land of their sojournings, wherein they sojourned. 5. And moreover I have heard the groaning of the children of Israel, whom the Egyptians keep in bondage; and I have

ס ס ס 14 יד

ב וַיְדַבֵּר אֱלֹהִים אֶל־מֹשֶׁה וַיֹּאמֶר אֵלָיו אֲנִי יְהוָה: וָאֵרָא
ג אֶל־אַבְרָהָם אֶל־יִצְחָק וְאֶל־יַעֲקֹב בְּאֵל שַׁדָּי וּשְׁמִי יְהוָה
ד לֹא נוֹדַעְתִּי לָהֶם: וְגַם הֲקִמֹתִי אֶת־בְּרִיתִי אִתָּם לָתֵת
לָהֶם אֶת־אֶרֶץ כְּנָעַן אֵת אֶרֶץ מְגֻרֵיהֶם אֲשֶׁר־גָּרוּ בָהּ:
ה וְגַם ׀ אֲנִי שָׁמַעְתִּי אֶת־נַאֲקַת בְּנֵי יִשְׂרָאֵל אֲשֶׁר מִצְרַיִם

¹ The ineffable name, read *Adonai*, which means, *the Lord*.

## II. VA-AYRA

(Chapters VI, 2–IX)

### RENEWED PROMISE OF REDEMPTION. Chapter VI, 2–13

These verses are the concluding portion of the Call of Moses, and can only be understood in connection with Chaps. III–V.

In view of the despair and despondency of both Moses and the People recorded in the last chapter, and in reply to the reproach of Moses 'Thou hast not delivered Thy people,' God repeats the promises of redemption made at Horeb.

**2.** *I am the* Lord. Or, *I am* ADONAY.

The emphasis is on the words *I am the* Lord. They are not intended to inform Moses what God is *called*, but to impress upon him that *the guarantee of the fulfilment of the Divine promises lay in the nature of the Being who had given the promises*. Even as the phrase, 'I am Pharaoh' (Gen. XLI, 44) is merely an assertion of royal authority and power, in the same manner, 'I am Adonay,' means, 'I am He who has the power and the faithfulness to fulfil any promise vouchsafed by Me. I have promised Redemption, and I shall fulfil that promise; I will and can do it. Israel shall yet know that I am the Lord; and Pharaoh, who had contemptuously declared, I know not the Lord!—he too shall know it.' This is also the explanation given by Rashi: 'God says unto Moses, I have not sent thee in vain as thou complainest, but in order to fulfil My words to the Fathers. *I am the* Lord is often used as a reminder of Divine retribution in connection both with rewards and with punishments.'

**3.** *as God Almighty.* Heb. *El Shaddai*; see Gen. XVII, 1 (p. 57, note 1). Note that the text reads, 'as God Almighty' and not, '*with my name* God Almighty.' There is here no question of contrasting an old Name with any new Name about to be disclosed.

*but by My name* ADONAY *I made Me not known to them.* Better, '*but as to My name* ADONAY, *I was not known to them.*' Although the Patriarchs were familiar with, and freely used, the Name *Adonay*, its import *as the everlasting God of faithfulness whose promises, even though they extend over centuries and millennia, are invariably fulfilled*, was not fully understood by them. 'Scripture does not state, My Name Adonay *I did not make known* to them (הודעתי); but, By My Name Adonay *I was not known* to them (נודעתי); *i.e.* I was not recognized by them in my attribute of Faithfulness, which is the essential part of the Name *Adonay*, signifying One who is faithful to give reality of His word; seeing that I had promised them possession of Canaan, but had not in their day fulfilled that promise' (Rashi). God was now to make the full signification of that Name known to the children of Israel by redeeming them from slavery. Thus would He manifest Himself to the children in a manner that He had not done to the Fathers. See Additional Note C, p. 397.

**4.** *of their sojournings.* The land of their temporary abode, in which they resided as strangers, but which was promised to their descendants as a permanent possession.

**5.** *I have heard.* The pronoun is emphatic; *i.e.* the same Being who established the Covenant. The context of the passage implies: 'I am unchangeable and My plans are unalterable. I have promised to your ancestors the possession of Canaan after a certain time of trial and misery; this period of oppression is now drawing near its close; and I shall therefore fulfil My promise by rescuing you with great judgments from your oppressors' (Kalisch).

# EXODUS VI, 6

remembered My covenant. 6. Wherefore say unto the children of Israel: I am the Lord, and I will bring you out from under the burdens of the Egyptians, and I will deliver you from their bondage, and I will redeem you with an outstretched arm, and with great judgments; 7. and I will take you to Me for a people, and I will be to you a God; and ye shall know that I am the Lord your God, who brought you out from under the burdens of the Egyptians. 8. And I will bring you in unto the land concerning which I lifted up My hand to give it to Abraham, to Isaac, and to Jacob; and I will give it you for a heritage: I am the Lord.' 9. And Moses spoke so unto the children of Israel; but they hearkened not unto Moses for impatience of spirit, and for cruel bondage. ¶ 10. And the Lord spoke unto Moses, saying: 11. 'Go in, speak unto Pharaoh king of Egypt, that he let the children of Israel go out of his land.' 12. And Moses spoke before the Lord, saying: 'Behold, the children of Israel have not hearkened unto me; how then shall Pharaoh hear me, who am of uncircumcised lips?' ¶ 13. And the Lord spoke unto Moses and unto Aaron, and gave them a charge unto the children of Israel, and unto Pharaoh king of Egypt, to bring the children

---

**6.** *I will redeem you.* Heb. *gaal* means, 'to reclaim, redeem'; hence *goel*, the technical term for the kinsman whose duty it was to ransom or, if need be, avenge the person or property of his relative. God intervenes in order to ransom His helpless and suffering People from slavery; and in mercy and faithfulness, He becomes their Redeemer (*goel*).

*with an outstretched arm.* With manifestation of My power.

*judgments.* Wherewith to punish the oppressing tyrant.

**7.** *I will take you to Me for a people.* After the redemption from Egypt, God will take Israel to Mount Sinai to receive His revealed Teaching. The covenant at Mount Sinai was the higher spiritual purpose of Israel's deliverance.

*ye shall know.* Here again it is not a question of learning a new Name of God, but of feeling His power in actual experiences of life.

**8.** *lifted up My hand.* i.e. sware. The expression is taken from the custom of lifting up the hand to heaven when taking an oath.

*heritage.* Heb. *morashah*, the same word used in Deut. XXXIII, 4 of the Torah. This is significant. Israel has been offered two heritages: the one spiritual—the Torah—is unconditional and eternal. Not so the other heritage, the Land of Promise. Its possession depends upon Israel's appreciation of, and obedience to, its God-given Law (Hirsch).

*I am the LORD.* Or, 'I am ADONAY.' The message to Moses closes with the same Divine assertion with which it opens—God is a God of faithfulness, and His promises are unfailingly realized.

**9.** *impatience of spirit.* The people were utterly crushed by their disappointment, and they paid no heed to fresh promises of redemption.

*cruel bondage.* lit. 'hard labour'.

**12.** *who am.* i.e. especially since I am.

*of uncircumcised lips.* i.e. with lips closed or impeded, not properly prepared to deliver an all-important message; see IV, 10. The same metaphor is used of the heart (Lev. XXVI, 41) and of the ear (Jer. VI, 10). He believes that his effort had failed owing to his stammering and hesitating speech.

**13.** *unto Moses and unto Aaron.* God replies by charging Aaron to take part with Moses in the emancipation of Israel (Rashi).

## Chapter VI, 14–VII, 7

### The Genealogy of Moses and Aaron

**14-27.** At this point the narrative gives the genealogical tree of Moses and Aaron, who now assume leadership of the People. In giving the chiefs of the families of the tribe of Levi, the

233

EXODUS VI, 14

of Israel out of the land of Egypt.* ‖. ¶ 14. These are the heads of their fathers' houses: the sons of Reuben the first-born of Israel: Hanoch, and Pallu, Hezron, and Carmi. These are the families of Reuben. 15. And the sons of Simeon: Jemuel, and Jamin, and Ohad, and Jachin, and Zohar, and Shaul the son of a Canaanitish woman. These are the families of Simeon. 16. And these are the names of the sons of Levi according to their generations: Gershon and Kohath, and Merari. And the years of the life of Levi were a hundred thirty and seven years. 17. The sons of Gershon: Libni and Shimei, according to their families. 18. And the sons of Kohath: Amram, and Izhar, and Hebron, and Uzziel. And the years of the life of Kohath were a hundred thirty and three years. 19. And the sons of Merari: Mahli and Mushi. These are the families of the Levites according to their generations. 20. And Amram took him Jochebed his father's sister to wife; and she bore him Aaron and Moses. And the years of the life of Amram were a hundred and thirty and seven years. 21. And the sons of Izhar: Korah, and Nepheg, and Zichri. 22. And the sons of Uzziel: Mishael, and Elzaphan, and Sithri. 23. And

14 מִצְרָיִם: ס אֵלֶּה רָאשֵׁי בֵית־אֲבֹתָם בְּנֵי רְאוּבֵן
בְּכֹר יִשְׂרָאֵל חֲנוֹךְ וּפַלּוּא חֶצְרֹן וְכַרְמִי אֵלֶּה מִשְׁפְּחֹת
טו רְאוּבֵן: וּבְנֵי שִׁמְעוֹן יְמוּאֵל וְיָמִין וְאֹהַד וְיָכִין וְצֹחַר
16 וְשָׁאוּל בֶּן־הַכְּנַעֲנִית אֵלֶּה מִשְׁפְּחֹת שִׁמְעוֹן: וְאֵלֶּה שְׁמוֹת
בְּנֵי־לֵוִי לְתֹלְדֹתָם גֵּרְשׁוֹן וּקְהָת וּמְרָרִי וּשְׁנֵי חַיֵּי לֵוִי שֶׁבַע
17 וּשְׁלֹשִׁים וּמְאַת שָׁנָה: בְּנֵי גֵרְשׁוֹן לִבְנִי וְשִׁמְעִי לְמִשְׁפְּחֹתָם:
18 וּבְנֵי קְהָת עַמְרָם וְיִצְהָר וְחֶבְרוֹן וְעֻזִּיאֵל וּשְׁנֵי חַיֵּי קְהָת
19 שָׁלֹשׁ וּשְׁלֹשִׁים וּמְאַת שָׁנָה: וּבְנֵי מְרָרִי מַחְלִי וּמוּשִׁי אֵלֶּה
כ מִשְׁפְּחֹת הַלֵּוִי לְתֹלְדֹתָם: וַיִּקַּח עַמְרָם אֶת־יוֹכֶבֶד דֹּדָתוֹ
לוֹ לְאִשָּׁה וַתֵּלֶד לוֹ אֶת־אַהֲרֹן וְאֶת־מֹשֶׁה וּשְׁנֵי חַיֵּי עַמְרָם
21 שֶׁבַע וּשְׁלֹשִׁים וּמְאַת שָׁנָה: וּבְנֵי יִצְהָר קֹרַח וָנֶפֶג וְזִכְרִי:
22 וּבְנֵי עֻזִּיאֵל מִישָׁאֵל וְאֶלְצָפָן וְסִתְרִי: וַיִּקַּח אַהֲרֹן אֶת־
23 אֱלִישֶׁבַע בַּת־עַמִּינָדָב אֲחוֹת נַחְשׁוֹן לוֹ לְאִשָּׁה וַתֵּלֶד לוֹ

names of the families of the two elder tribes are included, possibly to show that even as Moses was not the eldest son of Amram, Kohath was not the eldest son of Levi. The firstborn according to nature is not always the 'first-born' in the sight of God. This thought is general in Scripture. Abel, Shem, Isaac, Jacob, Levi, Judah, Joseph, Ephraim, Moses, David, were none of them eldest sons in their families.

**14.** *fathers' houses.* A technical term for 'clans' or 'families'—the 'heads' are the acknowledged chiefs and founders of families. For the names enumerated, see Gen. XLVI, 9 and 1 Chron. v, 3.

**15.** *the sons of Simeon.* The list corresponds with that given in Gen. XLVI, 10.

**16.** *according to their generations.* This phrase is introduced here because in regard to Levi, the grandsons, great-grandsons, and other descendants are also given.

**20.** *Amram.* Referred to, but not mentioned, in II, 1.

*Jochebed.* As later in the case of royal persons, *e.g.* 1 Kings xv, 2, the names of the mothers of Moses and Aaron, Eleazar and Phinehas, are given. The name means, 'Adonay is my glory' (which shows that, contrary to the belief of Bible critics, even according to 'P' the name *Adonay* was used *before* the days of Moses. Some scholars maintain that it was known in Abraham's home, long before Abraham. There is nothing contrary to Jewish tradition in such a belief).

*his father's sister.* Marriage with an aunt is prohibited in Lev. XVIII, 12. Such marriages were not unlawful before the Giving of the Torah. That such a circumstance is not suppressed in regard to the family of the Lawgiver is eloquent testimony to the unsparing veracity of Scripture.

*Aaron and Moses.* Miriam is not mentioned, as the descent in the male line only is traced.

**21.** *Korah.* See Num. XVI, 1 and 1 Chron. VI, 22.

**23.** *Aaron took.* Aaron's children are enumerated because of their later prominence in Israel's history.

*Elisheba.* This name is better known under the form given in the Septuagint, 'Elizabeth.'

*Nadab and Abihu.* They died before the altar for offering 'strange fire'; see Lev. x, 1, 2.

**25.** *Eleazar.* Became high-priest upon the death of Aaron; see Num. xx, 23–28.

*Phinehas.* Became high-priest on the death of Eleazar; see Judg. xx, 28. The name Phinehas

EXODUS VI, 24

Aaron took him Elisheba, the daughter of Amminadab, the sister of Nahshon, to wife; and she bore him Nadab and Abihu, Eleazar and Ithamar. 24. And the sons of Korah: Assir, and Elkanah, and Abiasaph; these are the families of the Korahites. 25. And Eleazar Aaron's son took him one of the daughters of Putiel to wife; and she bore him Phinehas. These are the heads of the fathers' houses of the Levites according to their families. 26. These are that Aaron and Moses, to whom the LORD said: 'Bring out the children of Israel from the land of Egypt according to their hosts.' 27. These are they that spoke to Pharaoh king of Egypt, to bring out the children of Israel from Egypt. These are that Moses and Aaron. 28. And it came to pass on the day when the LORD spoke unto Moses in the land of Egypt,* III. 29. that the LORD spoke unto Moses, saying: 'I am the LORD; speak thou unto Pharaoh king of Egypt all that I speak unto thee.' 30. And Moses said before the LORD: 'Behold, I am of uncircumcised lips, and how shall Pharaoh hearken unto me?'

## 7    CHAPTER VII

1. And the LORD said unto Moses: 'See, I have set thee in God's stead to Pharaoh; and Aaron thy brother shall be thy prophet. 2. Thou shalt speak all that I command thee; and Aaron thy brother shall speak unto Pharaoh, that he let the children of Israel go out of his land. 3. And I will harden Pharaoh's heart, and multiply My signs and My wonders in the land of Egypt. 4. But Pharaoh will not hearken unto you, and I will lay My hand upon Egypt, and bring forth My hosts, My people the children of Israel, out of the land of

---

is common in Egyptian and signifies, 'the child of dark complexion.'

**26.** *Aaron and Moses.* Mentioned here in the order of age.

*according to their hosts.* Or, 'armies.' The Israelites did not leave Egypt as a disorderly mob; they were divided into tribes, clans and families, with leaders and elders.

VI, 28–VII, 7, are a continuation of VI, 2–12, at the point where the narrative gives place to the genealogical list.

**29 and 30.** These verses are, in effect, identical with *v.* 11 and 12, and the repetition serves merely to resume the story of the Redemption.

### CHAPTER VII

**1.** *I have set thee in God's stead to Pharaoh.* Moses would give the Divine message as the direct representative of God; see IV, 16.

*prophet.* Spokesman; this is the *original* meaning of the Semitic root of the Heb. *nabi*, prophet. Aaron would give utterance to the words communicated by God to Moses, or to the thoughts which God put into the mind of Moses, with reference to Pharaoh. The Prophets are inspired spokesmen of God's will. They warn the people of the consequences of disobedience, and they often foretell events; but the latter is not their primary function.

**3.** *I will harden.* See on IV, 21. The phrase predicts what is likely to be Pharaoh's attitude.

*signs, wonders, judgments.* Terms describing the same acts from different points of view.

**4.** *lay My hand. i.e.* display My almighty power.

*by great judgments. i.e.* punishments; see VI, 6.

235

EXODUS VII, 5

Egypt by great judgments. 5. And the Egyptians shall know that I am the LORD, when I stretch forth My hand upon Egypt and bring out the children of Israel from among them.' 6. And Moses and Aaron did so; as the LORD commanded them, so did they. 7. And Moses was fourscore years old, and Aaron fourscore and three years old, when they spoke unto Pharaoh.* iv. ¶ 8. And the LORD spoke unto Moses and unto Aaron, saying: 9. 'When Pharaoh shall speak unto you, saying: Show a wonder for you; then thou shalt say unto Aaron: Take thy rod, and cast it down before Pharaoh, that it become a serpent.' 10. And Moses and Aaron went in unto Pharaoh, and they did so, as the LORD had commanded; and Aaron cast down his rod before Pharaoh and before his servants, and it became a serpent. 11. Then Pharaoh also called for the wise men and the sorcerers; and they also, the magicians of Egypt, did in like manner with their secret arts. 12. For they cast down every man his rod, and they became serpents; but Aaron's rod swallowed up their rods. 13. And Pharaoh's heart was hardened, and he hearkened not unto them; as the LORD had

---

**5.** *I am the* LORD. Or, 'I am ADONAY'; see VI, 3. When God led His people forth from the brickfields of Egypt into freedom, there would be such a display of His mercy and power, that Egypt, and all the surrounding nations, would know that only a Being of such attributes as are implied in His holy Name (ADONAY) could have wrought that redemption.

**6.** *Moses and Aaron did so.* Henceforth all diffidence ceased, and they applied themselves in confidence and zeal to their charge (Kalisch).

**7.** *fourscore years old.* The age of Joseph is similarly indicated (Gen. XLI, 46) on his appointment as Viceroy by the king. That appointment is made with the formula, 'I am Pharaoh,' and is followed by the statement, 'and Joseph was thirty years old.' Then his official activity begins. The appointment of Moses to be 'in God's stead to Pharaoh' is announced with a similar formula, 'I am Adonay'; and his official activity, like that of Joseph, is prefaced by the statement of his age. This disposes of the belief that *I am Adonay* in VI, 2 is any revelation of a new Name of God.

**8-13.** Moses, Aaron and the Magicians.

**9.** *show a wonder.* Display some portent as the credential of being God's messengers; see IV, 21.
*serpent.* Heb. *tannin*, denotes any large reptile, sea or river monster, and more especially the crocodile, as the symbol of Egypt.

**10.** *Aaron cast down his rod. i.e.* the rod of Moses used by Aaron at the bidding of Moses.
*before his servants.* Pharaoh's ministers of state were present.

**11.** *wise men.* Wizards, who possessed a knowledge of many secrets of nature which were unknown to the people.
*sorcerers.* 'Men who are adept in altering the external appearance of things by their arts' (Ibn Ezra).
*magicians.* 'Sacred scribes,' versed in magic lore and practice; jugglers of marvellous skill; see Gen. XLI, 8.
*secret arts.* Their spells and sleight-of-hand. Snake-charming is widespread in the East, ancient and modern; and is to-day a professional secret with many families in Egypt. Dr. A. Macalister says that he has 'seen both a snake and a crocodile thrown by hypnotism into the condition of rigidity in which they could be held up as rods by the tip of the tail'.

**12.** *they became serpents.* Through their 'secret arts' they produced the illusion of converting them into serpents (Ibn Ezra, Maimonides and Abarbanel).

**13.** *Pharaoh's heart was hardened. i.e.* the sign failed to make any impression on him. The fact that Moses and Aaron had done so more easily than his own magicians only served to increase his stubbornness; see note on IV, 21.

## EXODUS VII, 14

spoken. ¶ 14. And the LORD said unto Moses: 'Pharaoh's heart is stubborn, he refuseth to let the people go. 15. Get thee unto Pharaoh in the morning; lo, he goeth out unto the water; and thou shalt stand by the river's brink to meet him; and the rod which was turned to a serpent shalt thou take in thy hand. 16. And thou shalt say unto him: The LORD, the God of the Hebrews, hath sent me unto thee, saying: Let My people go, that they may serve Me in the wilderness; and, behold, hitherto thou hast not hearkened; 17. thus saith the LORD: In this thou shalt know that I am the LORD—behold, I will smite with the rod that is in my hand upon the waters which are in the river, and they shall be turned to blood. 18. And the fish that are in the river shall die, and the river shall become foul; and the Egyptians shall loathe to drink water from the river.' ¶ 19. And the LORD said unto Moses: 'Say unto Aaron: Take thy rod and stretch out thy hand over the waters of Egypt, over their rivers, over their streams, and over their pools, and over all their ponds of water, that they may become blood; and there shall be blood throughout all the land of Egypt, both in vessels of wood and in vessels of stone.' 20. And Moses and Aaron did so, as the LORD commanded; and he lifted up the rod, and smote the waters that were in the river, in the sight of Pharaoh, and in the sight of his servants; and all the waters that were in the river were turned to blood. 21. And the fish that were in the river died, and the

14 וַיֹּ֣אמֶר יְהוָה֮ אֶל־מֹשֶׁה֒ כָּבֵ֖ד לֵ֣ב פַּרְעֹ֑ה מֵאֵ֖ן לְשַׁלַּ֥ח הָעָֽם׃
טו לֵ֣ךְ אֶל־פַּרְעֹ֞ה בַּבֹּ֗קֶר הִנֵּה֙ יֹצֵ֣א הַמַּ֔יְמָה וְנִצַּבְתָּ֥ לִקְרָאת֖וֹ עַל־שְׂפַ֣ת הַיְאֹ֑ר וְהַמַּטֶּ֛ה אֲשֶׁר־נֶהְפַּ֥ךְ לְנָחָ֖שׁ תִּקַּ֥ח בְּיָדֶֽךָ׃
16 וְאָמַרְתָּ֣ אֵלָ֗יו יְהוָ֞ה אֱלֹהֵ֤י הָֽעִבְרִים֙ שְׁלָחַ֤נִי אֵלֶ֙יךָ֙ לֵאמֹ֔ר שַׁלַּח֙ אֶת־עַמִּ֔י וְיַֽעַבְדֻ֖נִי בַּמִּדְבָּ֑ר וְהִנֵּ֥ה לֹא־שָׁמַ֖עְתָּ עַד־כֹּֽה׃
17 כֹּ֚ה אָמַ֣ר יְהוָ֔ה בְּזֹ֣את תֵּדַ֔ע כִּ֖י אֲנִ֣י יְהוָ֑ה הִנֵּ֨ה אָנֹכִ֜י מַכֶּ֣ה ׀ בַּמַּטֶּ֣ה אֲשֶׁר־בְּיָדִ֗י עַל־הַמַּ֛יִם אֲשֶׁ֥ר בַּיְאֹ֖ר וְנֶהֶפְכ֥וּ לְדָֽם׃
18 וְהַדָּגָ֧ה אֲשֶׁר־בַּיְאֹ֛ר תָּמ֖וּת וּבָאַ֣שׁ הַיְאֹ֑ר וְנִלְא֣וּ מִצְרַ֔יִם לִשְׁתּ֥וֹת מַ֖יִם מִן־הַיְאֹֽר׃
19 וַיֹּ֣אמֶר יְהוָה֮ אֶל־מֹשֶׁה֒ אֱמֹ֣ר אֶֽל־אַהֲרֹ֗ן קַ֤ח מַטְּךָ֙ וּנְטֵֽה־יָדְךָ֙ עַל־מֵימֵ֣י מִצְרַ֔יִם עַֽל־נַהֲרֹתָ֣ם ׀ עַל־יְאֹרֵיהֶ֣ם וְעַל־אַגְמֵיהֶ֗ם וְעַ֛ל כָּל־מִקְוֵ֥ה מֵימֵיהֶ֖ם וְיִֽהְיוּ־דָ֑ם וְהָ֤יָה דָם֙ בְּכָל־אֶ֣רֶץ מִצְרַ֔יִם וּבָעֵצִ֖ים וּבָאֲבָנִֽים׃
כ וַיַּֽעֲשׂוּ־כֵן֩ מֹשֶׁ֨ה וְאַהֲרֹ֜ן כַּאֲשֶׁ֣ר ׀ צִוָּ֣ה יְהוָ֗ה וַיָּ֤רֶם בַּמַּטֶּה֙ וַיַּ֤ךְ אֶת־הַמַּ֙יִם֙ אֲשֶׁ֣ר בַּיְאֹ֔ר לְעֵינֵ֥י פַרְעֹ֖ה וּלְעֵינֵ֣י עֲבָדָ֑יו וַיֵּהָ֥פְכ֛וּ כָּל־הַמַּ֥יִם אֲשֶׁר־בַּיְאֹ֖ר לְדָֽם׃
21 וְהַדָּגָ֨ה אֲשֶׁר־

---

CHAPTERS VII, 14–XII, 36. THE TEN PLAGUES

For a general explanation of the Ten Plagues, see Additional Note, p. 399.

14–25. THE FIRST PLAGUE: THE WATER TURNED INTO BLOOD

**15.** *unto the water.* To learn how many degrees it had risen (Ibn Ezra); or, to offer worship to the god of the River. The Nile, as the source of Egypt's 'fertility', was venerated under various names and symbols. In honour of the Nile-god, religious festivals were held, at which Pharaoh himself sometimes officiated. Hymns addressed to the Nile are extant.

**17.** *know that I am the LORD.* Pharaoh had boldly and wantonly said at his first interview with Moses, 'I know not the LORD' (v, 2). He is now told that he shall soon *know* the LORD.

*I will smite.* The speaker is Moses. Aaron performed the act at the bidding of Moses.

*be turned to blood.* They shall have the appearance of blood (cf. Joel III, 4. 'The sun shall be turned into darkness, and the moon into blood').

The plague spoke its own message: 'At the sight of the bloody Nile, the Egyptians were with horror reminded of Pharaoh's murderous command against the Hebrew children' (Wisdom of Solomon XI, 6, 7).

**18.** *the fish that are in the river.* The Nile possesses abundant fish, whose death would be a national calamity, as fish was one of the principal articles of food in ancient Egypt.

*loathe to drink water.* The word here translated 'loathe' may be rendered 'weary themselves'; see Gen. XIX, 11. 'They will exert themselves in vain to find a remedy to make the water of the Nile palatable' (Rashi).

**19.** *rivers.* The arms of the Nile flowing into the Mediterranean. The Nile has no tributary rivers.

*streams.* Dug by human hands from the Nile to fertilize the fields (Rashi).

*pools.* Caused by the inundation of the Nile (see Isa. XLII, 15).

*ponds.* Wells, cisterns and reservoirs.

**20.** *he lifted up.* i.e. Aaron.

EXODUS VII, 22

river became foul, and the Egyptians could not drink water from the river; and the blood was throughout all the land of Egypt. 22. And the magicians of Egypt did in like manner with their secret arts; and Pharaoh's heart was hardened, and he hearkened not unto them; as the LORD had spoken. 23. And Pharaoh turned and went into his house, neither did he lay even this to heart. 24. And all the Egyptians digged round about the river for water to drink; for they could not drink of the water of the river. 25. And seven days were fulfilled, after that the LORD had smitten the river. ¶ 26. And the LORD spoke unto Moses: 'Go in unto Pharaoh, and say unto him: Thus saith the LORD: Let My people go, that they may serve Me. 27. And if thou refuse to let them go, behold, I will smite all thy borders with frogs. 28. And the river shall swarm with frogs, which shall go up and come into thy house, and into thy bed-chamber, and upon thy bed, and into the house of thy servants, and upon thy people, and into thine ovens, and into thy kneading-troughs. 29. And the frogs shall come up both upon thee, and upon thy people, and upon all thy servants.'

## 8   CHAPTER VIII

1. And the LORD said unto Moses: 'Say unto Aaron: Stretch forth thy hand with thy rod over the rivers, over the canals, and over the pools, and cause frogs to come up upon the land of Egypt.' 2. And Aaron stretched out his hand over the waters of Egypt; and the frogs came up, and covered the land of Egypt. 3. And the magicians did in like manner with their secret arts, and brought up frogs upon the land of Egypt. 4. Then Pharaoh called for Moses and Aaron, and said: 'Entreat the

**22.** *in like manner.* From where did the magicians obtain water for their experiment, as *all* the water had been turned into blood? asks Ibn Ezra. They took rain (Midrash), or they obtained the water from Goshen, or they dug for it (v. 24).

**23.** *neither did he lay even this to heart.* Referring to the first miracle of Aaron's serpent, to which he paid no attention. To make an apparent change of small quantities of water into blood was one of the common tricks of Egyptian magic. Pharaoh, therefore, disregarding the universality and completeness of Moses' miracle, thought it nothing more than what he had often seen done by his magicians.

**25.** *seven days were fulfilled.* Evidently referring to the duration of the plague. Nothing is said about the restoration of the Nile to its natural state. The flow of fresh water from the Upper Nile would cleanse the Nile in Egypt.

CHAPTERS VII, 26–VIII, 11. THE SECOND PLAGUE: FROGS

**27.** *thy borders.* But not the land of Goshen.
*frogs.* This plague, like the preceding, was in general accordance with natural phenomena, but marvellous for both its extent and its intensity.

**28.** *upon thy bed.* The extreme cleanliness of the Egyptians rendered this plague peculiarly disagreeable to them.

CHAPTER VIII

**4–10.** At Pharaoh's request the plague ceases. He promises to let the Israelites go.

**4.** *entreat the LORD.* Pharaoh hereby acknow-

EXODUS VIII, 5

LORD, that He take away the frogs from me, and from my people; and I will let the people go, that they may sacrifice unto the LORD.' 5. And Moses said unto Pharaoh: 'Have thou this glory over me; against what time shall I entreat for thee, and for thy servants, and for thy people, that the frogs be destroyed from thee and thy houses, and remain in the river only?' 6. And he said: 'Against to-morrow.' And he said: 'Be it according to thy word; that thou mayest know that there is none like unto the LORD our God.* 7. And the frogs shall depart from thee, and from thy houses, and from thy servants, and from thy people; they shall remain in the river only.' 8. And Moses and Aaron went out from Pharaoh; and Moses cried unto the LORD concerning the frogs, which He had brought upon Pharaoh. 9. And the LORD did according to the word of Moses; and the frogs died out of the houses, out of the courts, and out of the fields. 10. And they gathered them together in heaps; and the land stank. 11. But when Pharaoh saw that there was respite, he hardened his heart, and hearkened not unto them; as the LORD had spoken. ¶ 12. And the LORD said unto Moses: 'Say unto Aaron: Stretch out thy rod, and smite the dust of the earth, that it may become gnats throughout all the land of Egypt.' 13. And they did so; and Aaron stretched out his hand with his rod, and smote the dust of the earth, and there were gnats upon man, and upon beast; all the dust of the earth became gnats throughout all the land of Egypt. 14. And the magicians did so with their secret arts to bring forth gnats, but they could not; and there were gnats upon man, and upon

ledges that this plague had been sent by the God of the Hebrews.

**5.** *have thou this glory over me.* i.e. 'assume the honour of deciding when the plague shall cease'; or, 'have this glory over me, in fixing the time when the plague shall cease at my entreaty' (Luzzatto). The words are a polite address to the king.

**6.** *against to-morrow.* 'To-morrow' (AV).
*none like unto the* LORD. The removal of the plague at a time fixed by Pharaoh himself should be conclusive evidence to him that it was sent by God (Driver).

**7.** *in the river only.* Where they would naturally be at any time.

**8.** *Moses cried.* The expression is a strong one. Moses had ventured to allow Pharaoh to fix a time for the removal of the plague without the Divine approval. Hence earnest prayer was necessary (Ibn Ezra).

**9.** *courts.* Belonging to the private houses.

**10.** *they gathered them.* Better, *they piled them.*

**11.** *respite.* Relief.
*he hardened his heart.* He again breaks his promise.
*hearkened not unto them.* When they demanded the promised freedom.

12–15. THE THIRD PLAGUE: GNATS

**12.** *gnats.* Heb. *kinnim.* RV Margin has 'sand flies', or, 'fleas.'

**13.** *dust of the earth became gnats.* Thus it appeared to the people, owing to the multitude of the insects (Luzzatto).

**14.** *to bring forth.* Or, 'to remove' the gnats (Chizkuni, Hirsch).

EXODUS VIII, 15     שמות וארא ח

beast. 15. Then the magicians said unto Pharaoh: 'This is the finger of God'; and Pharaoh's heart was hardened, and he hearkened not unto them; as the Lord had spoken. ¶ 16. And the Lord said unto Moses: 'Rise up early in the morning, and stand before Pharaoh; lo, he cometh forth to the water; and say unto him: Thus saith the Lord: Let My people go, that they may serve Me. 17. Else, if thou wilt not let My people go, behold, I will send swarms of flies upon thee, and upon thy servants, and upon thy people, and into thy houses; and the houses of the Egyptians shall be full of swarms of flies, and also the ground whereon they are. 18. And I will set apart in that day the land of Goshen, in which My people dwell, that no swarms of flies shall be there; to the end that thou mayest know that I am the Lord in the midst of the earth.\* ᵛⁱ· 19. And I will put a division between My people and thy people—by to-morrow shall this sign be.' 20. And the Lord did so; and there came grievous swarms of flies into the house of Pharaoh, and into his servants' houses; and in all the land of Egypt the land was ruined by reason of the swarms of flies. 21. And Pharaoh called for Moses and for Aaron, and said: 'Go ye, sacrifice to your God in the land.' 22. And Moses said: 'It is not meet so to do; for we shall sacrifice the abomination of the Egyptians to the Lord our God; lo, if we sacrifice the abomination of the Egyptians before their eyes, will they not

טו הַכִּנִּים וְלֹא יָכֹלוּ וַתְּהִי הַכִּנָּם בָּאָדָם וּבַבְּהֵמָה: וַיֹּאמְרוּ
הַחַרְטֻמִּם אֶל־פַּרְעֹה אֶצְבַּע אֱלֹהִים הִוא וַיֶּחֱזַק לֵב־פַּרְעֹה
16 וְלֹא־שָׁמַע אֲלֵהֶם כַּאֲשֶׁר דִּבֶּר יְהוָֹה: ס וַיֹּאמֶר יְהוָֹה
אֶל־מֹשֶׁה הַשְׁכֵּם בַּבֹּקֶר וְהִתְיַצֵּב לִפְנֵי פַרְעֹה הִנֵּה יוֹצֵא
הַמָּיְמָה וְאָמַרְתָּ אֵלָיו כֹּה אָמַר יְהוָֹה שַׁלַּח עַמִּי וְיַעַבְדֻנִי:
17 כִּי אִם־אֵינְךָ מְשַׁלֵּחַ אֶת־עַמִּי הִנְנִי מַשְׁלִיחַ בְּךָ וּבַעֲבָדֶיךָ
וּבְעַמְּךָ וּבְבָתֶּיךָ אֶת־הֶעָרֹב וּמָלְאוּ בָּתֵּי מִצְרַיִם אֶת־
18 הֶעָרֹב וְגַם הָאֲדָמָה אֲשֶׁר־הֵם עָלֶיהָ: וְהִפְלֵיתִי בַיּוֹם
הַהוּא אֶת־אֶרֶץ גֹּשֶׁן אֲשֶׁר עַמִּי עֹמֵד עָלֶיהָ לְבִלְתִּי הֱיוֹת־
19 שָׁם עָרֹב לְמַעַן תֵּדַע כִּי אֲנִי יְהוָֹה בְּקֶרֶב הָאָרֶץ:\* וְשַׂמְתִּי ששי
כ פְדֻת בֵּין עַמִּי וּבֵין עַמֶּךָ לְמָחָר יִהְיֶה הָאֹת הַזֶּה: וַיַּעַשׂ
יְהוָֹה כֵּן וַיָּבֹא עָרֹב כָּבֵד בֵּיתָה פַרְעֹה וּבֵית עֲבָדָיו וּבְכָל־
21 אֶרֶץ מִצְרַיִם תִּשָּׁחֵת הָאָרֶץ מִפְּנֵי הֶעָרֹב: וַיִּקְרָא פַרְעֹה
אֶל־מֹשֶׁה וּלְאַהֲרֹן וַיֹּאמֶר לְכוּ זִבְחוּ לֵאלֹהֵיכֶם בָּאָרֶץ:
22 וַיֹּאמֶר מֹשֶׁה לֹא נָכוֹן לַעֲשׂוֹת כֵּן כִּי תּוֹעֲבַת מִצְרַיִם
נִזְבַּח לַיהוָֹה אֱלֹהֵינוּ הֵן נִזְבַּח אֶת־תּוֹעֲבַת מִצְרַיִם לְעֵינֵיהֶם

v. 20. סבירין ובבית

---

**15.** *finger of God*. The magicians had encouraged Pharaoh in his defiance of the Divine will; hence their confessed failure now is the more complete. They discern the hand or work of God in the plague.

**16–28. THE FOURTH PLAGUE: BEETLES**

**17.** *swarms of flies*. Heb. *ha-arob*, a collective singular, from a root meaning 'to mix'. The authorities again differ as to the exact interpretation; some render, 'a mixture of noxious animals' (Rashi); others, 'beetles' (Kalisch). 'The beetle, or scarab, was sacred and was regarded as the emblem of the Sun-god. It was sculptured on monuments, painted on tombs, engraved on gems, worn round the neck as an amulet and honoured in ten thousand images' (Geikie).

**18.** *set apart*. Dividing and miraculously distinguishing Goshen from the rest of Egypt. 'Such swarms may advance along particular lines, and so spare a given district' (Dillmann).

*the LORD in the midst of the earth*. Although My glory is in Heaven, My will is omnipotent on earth (Rashi).

**19.** *I will put a division*. Or, 'set a sign of deliverance.'

*to-morrow*. Allowing time for repentance.

**20.** *grievous*. Burdensome, severe, numerous.
*the land was ruined*. Not only did the Egyptians and their cattle suffer, but the daily occupations of the people were interrupted.

**21.** *in the land*. But not in the wilderness, as demanded by Moses. At last the king begins to yield.

**22.** *abomination of the Egyptians*. The sacrifice of these animals, sacred to the Egyptians, would be an abominable crime in their eyes. The ancient historian Diodorus tells of a Roman ambassador who was put to death in Egypt for killing a cat. We need only think of Hindu riots at the slaughtering of cows by Moslems in our own days.

**23.** *three days' journey*. Idiomatic expression for a long distance; see III, 18.
*as He shall command us*. See x, 26. The manner of sacrificial worship had not yet been laid down to the Israelites.

## EXODUS VIII, 23

stone us? 23. We will go three days' journey into the wilderness, and sacrifice to the LORD our God, as He shall command us.' 24. And Pharaoh said: 'I will let you go, that ye may sacrifice to the LORD your God in the wilderness; only ye shall not go very far away; entreat for me.' 25. And Moses said: 'Behold, I go out from thee, and I will entreat the LORD that the swarms of flies may depart from Pharaoh, from his servants, and from his people, to-morrow; only let not Pharaoh deal deceitfully any more in not letting the people go to sacrifice to the LORD.' 26. And Moses went out from Pharaoh and entreated the LORD. 27. And the LORD did according to the word of Moses; and He removed the swarms of flies from Pharaoh, from his servants, and from his people; there remained not one. 28. And Pharaoh hardened his heart this time also, and he did not let the people go.

## 9 CHAPTER IX

1. Then the LORD said unto Moses: 'Go in unto Pharaoh, and tell him: Thus saith the LORD, the God of the Hebrews: Let My people go, that they may serve Me. 2. For if thou refuse to let them go, and wilt hold them still, 3. behold, the hand of the LORD is upon thy cattle which are in the field, upon the horses, upon the asses, upon the camels, upon the herds, and upon the flocks; there shall be a very grievous murrain. 4. And the LORD shall make a division between the cattle of Israel and the cattle of Egypt; and there shall nothing die of all that belongeth to the children of Israel.' 5. And the LORD appointed a set time, saying: 'To-morrow the LORD shall do this thing in the land.' 6. And the LORD did that thing on the morrow, and all the cattle of Egypt died; but of the cattle of the children of Israel died not one. 7. And

**25.** *deal deceitfully.* Or, 'mock.' Moses fears Pharaoh will once more prove faithless, as in v. 11 after the promise to let the people go.

**28.** *this time also.* As he had done before. On this occasion he had given a more definite promise (v. 24).

### CHAPTER IX, 1–7. THE FIFTH PLAGUE: THE MURRAIN ON CATTLE

**3.** *a very grievous murrain.* A 'rinderpest'; see v. 15.

*camels.* Traders who brought merchandise across the Arabian desert early introduced the camel into Egypt; see Gen. XXXVII, 25. Horses, which are said to have been unknown there prior to the Hyksos invasion, became common under the Eighteenth Dynasty, when they were used in war.

**4.** *shall make a division.* See VIII, 18; the land of Goshen is again to be immune from the plague.

**6.** *all the cattle.* In the field. The word 'all' need not be pressed, but understood (as often in Hebrew and other languages) merely to denote such a large number that those which remained may be disregarded (Keil); cf. the English phrase, 'all the world knows.'

**7.** *Pharaoh sent.* To see if it was even so; but the very knowledge embittered his heart the more.

## EXODUS IX, 8

Pharaoh sent, and, behold, there was not so much as one of the cattle of the Israelites dead. But the heart of Pharaoh was stubborn, and he did not let the people go. ¶ 8. And the LORD said unto Moses and unto Aaron: 'Take to you handfuls of soot of the furnace, and let Moses throw it heavenward in the sight of Pharaoh. 9. And it shall become small dust over all the land of Egypt, and shall be a boil breaking forth with blains upon man and upon beast, throughout all the land of Egypt.' 10. And they took soot of the furnace, and stood before Pharaoh; and Moses threw it up heavenward; and it became a boil breaking forth with blains upon man and upon beast. 11. And the magicians could not stand before Moses because of the boils; for the boils were upon the magicians, and upon all the Egyptians. 12. And the LORD hardened the heart of Pharaoh, and he hearkened not unto them; as the LORD had spoken unto Moses. ¶ 13. And the LORD said unto Moses: 'Rise up early in the morning, and stand before Pharaoh, and say unto him: Thus saith the LORD, the God of the Hebrews: Let My people go, that they may serve Me. 14. For I will this time send all My plagues upon thy person, and upon thy servants, and upon thy people; that thou mayest know that there is none like Me in all the earth. 15. Surely now I had put forth My hand, and smitten thee and thy people with pestilence, and thou hadst been cut off from the earth. 16. But in very deed for this cause have I made thee to stand, to show thee My power, and that My name may be declared throughout all the earth.* ᵛⁱⁱ· 17. As yet exaltest thou thyself against My people, that thou wilt not let them go? 18. Behold, to-morrow about this

---

### 8–12. SIXTH PLAGUE: BOILS

**9.** *small dust.* The disease would be carried through Egypt by the air.

**11.** *the magicians could not stand.* Not only were they unable to imitate it, but they were themselves included in the affliction.

**12.** *hardened the heart.* 'Pharaoh's sin preceded and provoked God's punishments, which, however, far from moving his stubborn heart, tended to harden it still more, and to bring him into a self-conscious opposition to the God of Israel' (Kalisch). See note on IV, 21.

**14** and **15.** These two verses are interdependent. Moffatt translates *v.* 15: 'Otherwise, I would have exerted my force and struck you and your people with pestilence, till you were swept off the earth.'

**14.** *this time.* i.e. at one time, and without delay.

*plagues.* Heb. *maggephah*; is not the word for the ten plagues, but means a fatal chastisement; cf. Num. XIV, 37.

**16.** *to show thee.* i.e. to make thee experience My power, which *might* have had the effect of softening Pharaoh's heart, and did in fact lead him more than once to give God the glory, *v.* 27; X, 16 (Driver).

### 17–35. THE SEVENTH PLAGUE: HAIL

**17.** *exaltest thou thyself.* lit. 'thou raisest thyself as an obstacle' against My people, and opposest their emancipation. Targum and Rashi translate: 'thou treadest down (i.e. oppressest) My people.'

**18.** *since the day it was founded.* i.e. since it was inhabited.

# EXODUS IX, 19　　　　　שמות וארא ט

time I will cause it to rain a very grievous hail, such as hath not been in Egypt since the day it was founded even until now. 19. Now therefore send, hasten in thy cattle and all that thou hast in the field; for every man and beast that shall be found in the field, and shall not be brought home, the hail shall come down upon them, and they shall die.' 20. He that feared the word of the LORD among the servants of Pharaoh made his servants and his cattle flee into the houses; 21. and he that regarded not the word of the LORD left his servants and his cattle in the field. ¶ 22. And the LORD said unto Moses: 'Stretch forth thy hand toward heaven, that there may be hail in all the land of Egypt, upon man, and upon beast, and upon every herb of the field, throughout the land of Egypt.' 23. And Moses stretched forth his rod toward heaven; and the LORD sent thunder and hail, and fire ran down unto the earth; and the LORD caused to hail upon the land of Egypt. 24. So there was hail, and fire flashing up amidst the hail, very grievous, such as had not been in all the land of Egypt since it became a nation. 25. And the hail smote throughout all the land of Egypt all that was in the field, both man and beast; and the hail smote every herb of the field, and broke every tree of the field. 26. Only in the land of Goshen, where the children of Israel were, was there no hail. 27. And Pharaoh sent, and called for Moses and Aaron, and said unto them: 'I have sinned this time; the LORD is righteous, and I and my people are wicked. 28. Entreat the LORD, and let there be enough of these mighty thunderings and hail; and I will let you go, and ye shall stay no longer.' 29. And Moses said unto him: 'As soon as I am gone out of the city, I will spread forth my hands unto the LORD; the thunders shall cease, neither shall there be any more hail;

**19.** *hasten in.* Or, 'bring in safety'.

*they shall die.* God had compassion on man and beast, in order to save the sinners and deliver them from death (Nachmanides).

**20.** *feared the word of the LORD.* This is the first indication that the warnings had a salutary effect upon the Egyptians.

**22.** *upon man, and upon beast.* Of those who disregarded the Divine warning; see the preceding verses.

**23.** *fire ran down unto the earth.* Probably lightning is implied. Luzzatto suggests thunderbolts.

**24.** *fire flashing up amidst the hail.* Perhaps forked or zigzag lightning is meant.

**25.** *every herb of the field.* lit. 'all the grass of the field'; *all*, according to the Heb. usage meaning *a great part*.

**26.** *only in the land of Goshen.* See VIII, 22; IX, 4, 7.

**27-33.** Pharaoh craves a third time for the cessation of the Plague (see VIII, 8, 28).

**27.** *sinned this time.* Pharaoh this time confesses his fault as he had never done before. His penitence, however, as the sequel shows, is not very deep (Driver).

*is righteous.* i.e. is the one in the right.

*are wicked.* Are in the wrong.

**29.** *gone out of the city.* Which was full of idols (Midrash).

*spread forth my hands.* i.e. in prayer.

243

## EXODUS IX, 30 — שמות וארא ט

that thou mayest know that the earth is the LORD's. 30. But as for thee and thy servants, I know that ye will not yet fear the LORD God.'—31. And the flax and the barley were smitten; for the barley was in the ear, and the flax was in bloom. 32. But the wheat and the spelt were not smitten; for they ripen late.\*ᵐ· 33. And Moses went out of the city from Pharaoh, and spread forth his hands unto the LORD; and the thunders and hail ceased, and the rain was not poured upon the earth. 34. And when Pharaoh saw that the rain and the hail and the thunders were ceased, he sinned yet more, and hardened his heart, he and his servants. 35. And the heart of Pharaoh was hardened, and he did not let the children of Israel go; as the LORD had spoken by Moses.

יְהֹוָה הַקֹּלוֹת יֶחְדָּל֖וּן וְהַבָּרָ֔ד לֹ֥א יִֽהְיֶה־ע֖וֹד לְמַ֣עַן תֵּדַ֔ע
ל כִּ֥י לַיהֹוָ֖ה הָאָֽרֶץ: וְאַתָּ֖ה וַעֲבָדֶ֑יךָ יָדַ֕עְתִּי כִּ֚י טֶ֣רֶם תִּֽירְא֔וּן
31 מִפְּנֵ֖י יְהוָ֥ה אֱלֹהִֽים: וְהַפִּשְׁתָּ֥ה וְהַשְּׂעֹרָ֖ה נֻכָּ֑תָה כִּ֤י הַשְּׂעֹרָה֙
32 אָבִ֔יב וְהַפִּשְׁתָּ֖ה גִּבְעֹֽל: וְהַחִטָּ֥ה וְהַכֻּסֶּ֖מֶת לֹ֣א נֻכּ֑וּ כִּ֥י
מפטיר 33 אֲפִילֹ֖ת הֵֽנָּה:\* וַיֵּצֵ֨א מֹשֶׁ֜ה מֵעִ֤ם פַּרְעֹה֙ אֶת־הָעִ֔יר וַיִּפְרֹ֥שׂ
כַּפָּ֖יו אֶל־יְהֹוָ֑ה וַֽיַּחְדְּל֤וּ הַקֹּלוֹת֙ וְהַבָּרָ֔ד וּמָטָ֖ר לֹא־נִתַּ֥ךְ
34 אָֽרְצָה: וַיַּ֣רְא פַּרְעֹ֗ה כִּֽי־חָדַ֨ל הַמָּטָ֧ר וְהַבָּרָ֛ד וְהַקֹּלֹ֖ת
לה וַיֹּ֣סֶף לַחֲטֹ֑א וַיַּכְבֵּ֥ד לִבּ֖וֹ ה֥וּא וַעֲבָדָֽיו: וַֽיֶּחֱזַק֙ לֵ֣ב פַּרְעֹ֔ה
וְלֹ֥א שִׁלַּ֖ח אֶת־בְּנֵ֣י יִשְׂרָאֵ֑ל כַּאֲשֶׁ֛ר דִּבֶּ֥ר יְהֹוָ֖ה בְּיַד־מֹשֶֽׁה:

*the earth is the LORD'S.* The imaginary sway of the idols was limited to a single land or part thereof. The God of the Hebrews is living Ruler of the whole earth.

**30.** *not yet fear.* i.e. you do not yet stand in awe of Him, so as to set Israel free.

**31.** *flax and the barley were smitten.* The time indicated is the end of January or the beginning of February. Flax was much esteemed by the Egyptians, and Egypt was the great linen market of the ancient world. Barley was used for making a coarse bread eaten by the poor.

**32.** *wheat and the spelt.* Wheat was the most cultivated grain in Egypt. Spelt, see Isa. XXVIII, 25 and Ezek. IV, 9, is a kind of wild wheat.

*for they ripen late.* And therefore, being then tender and flexible, they yielded to the stroke of the hail without any hurt.

**33.** *not poured upon the earth.* At the prayer of Moses, the lightning and the hail ceased.

**34.** *he sinned yet more.* Having acknowledged that God was righteous (*v.* 27), he continues to resist His commands. He now becomes a rebel. The ministers of state are associated with the king in the obstinate resistance to God.

**35.** *was hardened.* Repeating his sin by again breaking his promise.

## HAFTORAH VA-AYRA    הפטרת וארא

### EZEKIEL XXVIII, 25–XXIX, 21

CHAPTER XXVIII

25. Thus saith the Lord GOD: When I shall have gathered the house of Israel from the peoples among whom they are scattered, and shall be sanctified in them in the sight of the nations, then shall they dwell in their own land which I gave to My servant Jacob. 26. And they shall dwell safely therein, and shall build houses, and plant vineyards; yea, they shall dwell safely; when I have executed judgments

CAP. XXVIII. כח

כה כֹּֽה־אָמַר֮ אֲדֹנָ֣י
יֱהֹוִה֒ בְּקַבְּצִ֣י ׀ אֶת־בֵּ֣ית יִשְׂרָאֵ֗ל מִן־הָֽעַמִּים֙ אֲשֶׁ֣ר נָפֹ֣צוּ
בָ֔ם וְנִקְדַּ֥שְׁתִּי בָ֖ם לְעֵינֵ֣י הַגּוֹיִ֑ם וְיָֽשְׁבוּ֙ עַל־אַדְמָתָ֔ם אֲשֶׁ֥ר
26 נָתַ֖תִּי לְעַבְדִּ֣י לְיַעֲקֹֽב: וְיָשְׁב֣וּ עָלֶיהָ֮ לָבֶטַח֒ וּבָנ֤וּ בָתִּים֙

The section is chiefly a prophecy against Egypt, and this forms the link with the Sedrah.

For Ezekiel's life and message, see p. 178, as well as the introductory notes to the Haftorah of Tetzaveh, Parah and Hachodesh. He and the

flower of the nation were deported to Babylon in 597 B.C.E. He seems to have lived a peaceful and honoured life in Chaldea. The exiles had their own houses and lands, and their own government by Elders. They seem readily to have entered into the

EZEKIEL XXIX, 1

upon all those that have them in disdain round about them; and they shall know that I am the LORD their God.

CHAPTER XXIX

1. In the tenth year, in the tenth month, in the twelfth day of the month, the word of the LORD came unto me, saying: 2. 'Son of man, set thy face against Pharaoh king of Egypt, and prophesy against him, and against all Egypt; 3. speak, and say: Thus saith the Lord GOD:

Behold, I am against thee, Pharaoh
King of Egypt,
The great dragon that lieth
In the midst of his rivers,
That hath said: My river is mine own,
And I have made it for myself.

4. And I will put hooks in thy jaws, and I will cause the fish of thy rivers to stick unto thy scales; and I will bring thee up out of the midst of thy rivers, and all the fish of thy rivers shall stick unto thy scales. 5. And I will cast thee into the wilderness,

Thee and all the fish of thy rivers;
Thou shalt fall upon the open field;
Thou shalt not be brought together, nor gathered;

יחזקאל כח כט

וְנָטְעוּ כְרָמִים וְיָשְׁבוּ לָבֶטַח בַּעֲשׂוֹתִי שְׁפָטִים בְּכֹל הַשָּׁאטִים
אֹתָם מִסְּבִיבוֹתָם וְיָדְעוּ כִּי אֲנִי יְהוָה אֱלֹהֵיהֶם׃

CAP. XXIX. כט

א בַּשָּׁנָה הָעֲשִׂרִית בָּעֲשִׂרִי בִּשְׁנֵים עָשָׂר לַחֹדֶשׁ הָיָה דְבַר־
2 יְהוָה אֵלַי לֵאמֹר׃ בֶּן־אָדָם שִׂים פָּנֶיךָ עַל־פַּרְעֹה מֶלֶךְ
3 מִצְרַיִם וְהִנָּבֵא עָלָיו וְעַל־מִצְרַיִם כֻּלָּהּ׃ דַּבֵּר וְאָמַרְתָּ
כֹּה־אָמַר ׀ אֲדֹנָי יְהוִֹה הִנְנִי עָלֶיךָ פַּרְעֹה מֶלֶךְ־מִצְרַיִם
הַתַּנִּים הַגָּדוֹל הָרֹבֵץ בְּתוֹךְ יְאֹרָיו אֲשֶׁר אָמַר לִי יְאֹרִי
4 וַאֲנִי עֲשִׂיתִנִי׃ וְנָתַתִּי חחיים בִּלְחָיֶיךָ וְהִדְבַּקְתִּי דְגַת־
יְאֹרֶיךָ בְּקַשְׂקְשֹׂתֶיךָ וְהַעֲלִיתִיךָ מִתּוֹךְ יְאֹרֶיךָ וְאֵת כָּל־
ה דְּגַת יְאֹרֶיךָ בְּקַשְׂקְשֹׂתֶיךָ תִּדְבָּק׃ וּנְטַשְׁתִּיךָ הַמִּדְבָּרָה
אוֹתְךָ וְאֵת כָּל־דְּגַת יְאֹרֶיךָ עַל־פְּנֵי הַשָּׂדֶה תִּפּוֹל לֹא
תֵאָסֵף וְלֹא תִקָּבֵץ לְחַיַּת הָאָרֶץ וּלְעוֹף הַשָּׁמַיִם נְתַתִּיךָ

כ״ט v. 4. החיים קרי

---

'modern' life of Babylon, under the firm and not unjust rule of Nebuchadnezzar. In common with Jeremiah, he held that the future of the nation lay with the exiles, and he devoted his extraordinary genius to saving these exiles, as Israelites, for Israel. He follows events in the Holy Land with feverish anxiety, and warns his brethren against the alliance with Egypt.

**25.** *shall have gathered.* A leading doctrine in Ezekiel's message is that God will restore and purify His people.
*shall be sanctified. i.e.* be recognized as holy. Through Israel, God will be recognized as the God of Holiness by all the nations.

**26.** *they shall know that I am the LORD.* The result of such restoration and purification of Israel will vindicate the supreme power of the God of Israel. A repentant and restored Israel would reveal to all the nations the 'Name' of God; *i.e.* the real character and majesty of the God of Israel. On the meaning of this phrase, see p. 398.

CHAPTER XXIX. THE ORACLE AGAINST EGYPT

Egypt, the house of bondage and oppression for Israel in the days of its youth, was again the enemy during the last years of the Jewish state. It was 'a broken reed', and was as perfidious as it was decadent.

**1.** *in the tenth year.* Of the reign of Zedekiah, the last king of Judah; 587 B.C.E.
*tenth month. i.e.* Tebeth (January–February), about seven months before the destruction of Jerusalem.

**2.** *son of man.* A favourite expression of Ezekiel, and equivalent to *man* or *mortal*.
*Pharaoh.* Pharaoh Hophra.

**3.** *the great dragon.* The crocodile; which infested the Nile and was worshipped as a god. It is here the symbol of Egypt.
*his rivers.* The Nile and its branches.
*my river is mine own.* It is this insolent pride of Egypt in its land and River, this self-deification on the part of the Pharaohs, that was an assured forerunner of its fall.

**4.** *hooks in thy jaws.* The crocodile is really less formidable than he appears to be, and is an easy prey to such as assail him with skill; the same will be true of Egypt.
*fish of thy rivers.* The subjects or allies of Egypt will be involved in its ruin.

245

# EZEKIEL XXIX, 6

6. To the beasts of the earth and to the fowls of the heaven
Have I given thee for food.

6. And all the inhabitants of Egypt shall know
That I am the LORD,
Because they have been a staff of reed
To the house of Israel.

7. When they take hold of thee with the hand, thou dost break,
And rend all their shoulders;
And when they lean upon thee, thou breakest,
And makest all their loins to be at a stand.

8. Therefore thus saith the Lord GOD: Behold, I will bring a sword upon thee, and will cut off from thee man and beast. 9. And the land of Egypt shall be desolate and waste, and they shall know that I am the LORD; because he hath said: The river is mine, and I have made it. 10. Therefore, behold, I am against thee, and against thy rivers, and I will make the land of Egypt utterly waste and desolate, from Migdol to Syene even unto the border of Ethiopia. 11. No foot of man shall pass through it, nor foot of beast shall pass through it, neither shall it be inhabited forty years. 12. And I will make the land of Egypt desolate in the midst of the countries that are desolate, and her cities among the cities that are laid waste shall be desolate forty years; and I will scatter the Egyptians among the nations, and will disperse them through the countries. ¶ 13. For thus saith the Lord GOD: At the end of forty years will I gather the Egyptians from the peoples whither they were scattered; 14. and I will turn the captivity of Egypt, and will cause them to return into the land of Pathros, into the land of their origin; and they shall be there a lowly kingdom. 15. It shall be the lowliest of the kingdoms, neither shall it any more lift itself up above the nations; and I will

---

**6.** *a staff of reed to the house of Israel.* An exact picture of the deceptive character of Egypt's relationship with Israel. By promises of assistance she incited Israel to rebel against Assyria and Babylon, but always failed at the critical hour to redeem her promise.

**7.** *to be at a stand. i.e.* to stand alone, without the support on which the tired body could lean in time of strain.

**10.** *Migdol to Syene. i.e.* the whole of Egypt. Migdol is in the North, and Syene, the modern Assouan, in the South. (In 1904, a large quantity of Aramaic documents were found at Assouan, dating from the years 471–411 B.C.E. They reveal the existence of a large and prosperous Jewish community, probably the descendants of the Jewish refugees from Jerusalem; Jer. XLIV, 1.)

*Ethiopia.* The land and people of the southern Nile-valley, towards the Sudan and Abyssinia.

**11.** *forty years.* A round number, indicating a generation.

**13.** *will I gather.* Isaiah and Jeremiah also foretell a restored Egypt.

**14.** *Pathros.* In Upper (*i.e.* South) Egypt, the original seat of Egyptian rule.

## EZEKIEL XXIX, 16

16 וְלֹא יִהְיֶה־עוֹד לְבֵית יִשְׂרָאֵל לְמִבְטָח מַזְכִּיר עָוֹן בִּפְנוֹתָם
אַחֲרֵיהֶם וְיָדְעוּ כִּי אֲנִי אֲדֹנָי יֱהֹוִה: וַיְהִי בְּעֶשְׂרִים
וָשֶׁבַע שָׁנָה בָּרִאשׁוֹן בְּאֶחָד לַחֹדֶשׁ הָיָה דְבַר־יְהֹוָה אֵלַי
18 לֵאמֹר: בֶּן־אָדָם נְבוּכַדְרֶאצַּר מֶלֶךְ־בָּבֶל הֶעֱבִיד אֶת־חֵילוֹ
עֲבֹדָה גְדוֹלָה אֶל־צֹר כָּל־רֹאשׁ מֻקְרָח וְכָל־כָּתֵף מְרוּטָה
וְשָׂכָר לֹא־הָיָה לוֹ וּלְחֵילוֹ מִצֹּר עַל־הָעֲבֹדָה אֲשֶׁר־עָבַד
19 עָלֶיהָ: לָכֵן כֹּה אָמַר אֲדֹנָי יֱהֹוִה הִנְנִי נֹתֵן לִנְבוּכַדְרֶאצַּר
מֶלֶךְ־בָּבֶל אֶת־אֶרֶץ מִצְרָיִם וְנָשָׂא הֲמֹנָהּ וְשָׁלַל שְׁלָלָהּ
20 וּבָזַז בִּזָּהּ וְהָיְתָה שָׂכָר לְחֵילוֹ: פְּעֻלָּתוֹ אֲשֶׁר־עָבַד בָּהּ נָתַתִּי
21 לוֹ אֶת־אֶרֶץ מִצְרַיִם אֲשֶׁר עָשׂוּ לִי נְאֻם אֲדֹנָי יֱהֹוִה: בַּיּוֹם
הַהוּא אַצְמִיחַ קֶרֶן לְבֵית יִשְׂרָאֵל וּלְךָ אֶתֵּן פִּתְחוֹן־פֶּה
בְּתוֹכָם וְיָדְעוּ כִּי־אֲנִי יְהֹוָה:

16 diminish them, that they shall no more rule over the nations. 16. And it shall be no more the confidence of the house of Israel, bringing iniquity to remembrance, when they turn after them; and they shall know that I am the Lord GOD.' ¶ 17. And it came to pass in the seven and twentieth year, in the first month, in the first day of the month, the word of the LORD came unto me, saying: 18. 'Son of man, Nebuchadrezzar king of Babylon caused his army to serve a great service against Tyre; every head was made bald, and every shoulder was peeled; yet had he no wages, nor his army, from Tyre, for the service that he had served against it; 19. therefore thus saith the Lord GOD: Behold, I will give the land of Egypt unto Nebuchadrezzar king of Babylon; and he shall carry off her abundance, and take her spoil, and take her prey; and it shall be the wages for his army. 20. I have given him the land of Egypt as his hire for which he served, because they wrought for Me, saith the Lord GOD. ¶ 21. In that day will I cause a horn to shoot up unto the house of Israel, and I will give thee the opening of the mouth in the midst of them; and they shall know that I am the LORD.'

**16.** *no more the confidence.* Too weak to help, and no longer able either to harm or tempt Israel into trusting Egypt. After its conquest by the Babylonians, Egypt never again became really independent.

*bringing iniquity to remembrance.* 'Every alliance with Egypt brings the headstrong folly of Israel into fresh prominence' (Lofthouse).

### 17-20. THE CONQUEST OF EGYPT BY NEBUCHADNEZZAR

**17.** *the seven and twentieth year.* 570 B.C.E. This is Ezekiel's latest prophecy.

**18.** *Nebuchadrezzar.* The original and more correct form of the name.

*every shoulder was peeled.* From the constant carrying of burdens. As Nebuchadnezzar had no fleet, the arm of the sea between Tyre and the mainland had to be filled up. Hence the arduous toil of his army.

*no wages.* He was disappointed in the spoil he expected from Tyre.

**20.** *they wrought for Me.* Nebuchadnezzar and his army, who are God's instruments against Egypt, which is now given to the Babylonian king as compensation for Tyre.

**21.** *in that day.* The humiliation of Egypt would open the way for Israel's restoration. Israel would see 'the finger of God' in all this upheaval.

*horn.* Symbol of power and prosperity.

*opening of the mouth.* The Prophet's prediction having been fulfilled, the people would believe in the efficacy of his teaching and message.

EXODUS X, 1

שמות בא י

## CHAPTER X

1. And the Lord said unto Moses: 'Go in unto Pharaoh; for I have hardened his heart, and the heart of his servants, that I might show these My signs in the midst of them; 2. and that thou mayest tell in the ears of thy son, and of thy son's son, what I have wrought upon Egypt, and My signs which I have done among them; that ye may know that I am the Lord.' 3. And Moses and Aaron went in unto Pharaoh, and said unto him: 'Thus saith the Lord, the God of the Hebrews: How long wilt thou refuse to humble thyself before Me? let My people go, that they may serve Me. 4. Else, if thou refuse to let My people go, behold, to-morrow will I bring locusts into thy border; 5. and they shall cover the face of the earth, that one shall not be able to see the earth; and they shall eat the residue of that which is escaped, which remaineth unto you from the hail, and shall

CAP. X. י

פ פ פ טו 15

א וַיֹּאמֶר יְהֹוָה אֶל־מֹשֶׁה בֹּא אֶל־פַּרְעֹה כִּי־אֲנִי הִכְבַּדְתִּי אֶת־לִבּוֹ וְאֶת־לֵב עֲבָדָיו לְמַעַן שִׁתִי אֹתֹתַי אֵלֶּה בְּקִרְבּוֹ:
ב וּלְמַעַן תְּסַפֵּר בְּאָזְנֵי בִנְךָ וּבֶן־בִּנְךָ אֵת אֲשֶׁר הִתְעַלַּלְתִּי בְּמִצְרַיִם וְאֶת־אֹתֹתַי אֲשֶׁר־שַׂמְתִּי בָם וִידַעְתֶּם כִּי־אֲנִי יְהֹוָה:
ג וַיָּבֹא מֹשֶׁה וְאַהֲרֹן אֶל־פַּרְעֹה וַיֹּאמְרוּ אֵלָיו כֹּה־אָמַר יְהֹוָה אֱלֹהֵי הָעִבְרִים עַד־מָתַי מֵאַנְתָּ לֵעָנֹת מִפָּנָי שַׁלַּח עַמִּי וְיַעַבְדֻנִי:
ד כִּי אִם־מָאֵן אַתָּה לְשַׁלֵּחַ אֶת־עַמִּי הִנְנִי מֵבִיא מָחָר אַרְבֶּה בִּגְבֻלֶךָ:
ה וְכִסָּה אֶת־עֵין הָאָרֶץ וְלֹא יוּכַל לִרְאֹת אֶת־הָאָרֶץ וְאָכַל ׀ אֶת־יֶתֶר הַפְּלֵטָה

## III. BO

(CHAPTERS X–XIII, 16)

### CHAPTER X, 1–20

### THE EIGHTH PLAGUE: LOCUSTS

**1.** *go in unto Pharaoh.* And caution him (Rashi).

*hardened his heart.* See note on IV, 21.

**2.** *that thou.* i.e. Moses, as the representative of the Israelites.

*mayest tell.* 'This phrase is appropriate in regard to the plague of locusts, which constantly recurs in those lands; and men on such occasions would compare their visitation with preceding ones, and thus be reminded of the unparalleled visitation in the days of Moses' (Bechor Shor).

*wrought upon Egypt.* The Heb. verb is uncommon. It implies an action which brings shame and disgrace upon its objects, making them, so to speak, playthings of Divine power.

*know that I am the LORD.* See notes on VI, 3–7. The object of the plagues is the education of men in the knowledge of God. Ps. LXXVIII and CV are instances of the instruction of later generations in the meaning of the wonders wrought by God for the Israelites of old.

**3.** *refuse to humble thyself.* This was now the real cause of Pharaoh's sin after all these plagues—refusal to humble himself before God. And Pharaoh would not really humble himself, until he made God's will his own, and fulfilled his oft-given promise to permit the Israelites to leave Egypt. His heart was hardened, but his will was still free, and he could repent if he chose.

**4.** *to-morrow.* Again another opportunity is given to the king to submit himself to the Divine command.

**5.** *they shall cover the face of the earth.* This is literally true of locusts. Lord Bryce thus describes a swarm of locusts:—

'It is a strange sight, beautiful if you can forget the destruction it brings with it. The whole air, to twelve or even eighteen feet above the ground, is filled with the insects, reddish-brown in body, with bright, gauzy wings. When the sun's rays catch them, it is like the seas sparkling with light. When you see them against a cloud, they are like the dense flakes of a driving snowstorm. You feel as if you had never before realized immensity in number. ... They blot out the sun above, and cover the ground beneath, and fill the air whichever way one looks. The breeze carries them swiftly past, but they come on in fresh clouds, a host of which there is no end, each of them a harmless creature which you can catch and crush in your hand, but appalling in their power of collective devastation.'

*eat the residue.* Their voracity is incredible: see Joel II, 25 (Haftorah Sabbath Shuvah). Not only the leaves, but the branches and even the wood are attacked and devoured. The residue here refers to the wheat and the spelt (IX, 32), which escaped the havoc wrought by the hail (Malbim).

EXODUS X, 6

eat every tree which groweth for you out of the field; 6. and thy houses shall be filled, and the houses of all thy servants, and the houses of all the Egyptians; as neither thy fathers nor thy fathers' fathers have seen, since the day that they were upon the earth unto this day.' And he turned, and went out from Pharaoh. 7. And Pharaoh's servants said unto him: 'How long shall this man be a snare unto us? let the men go, that they may serve the Lord their God; knowest thou not yet that Egypt is destroyed?' 8. And Moses and Aaron were brought again unto Pharaoh; and he said unto them: 'Go, serve the Lord your God; but who are they that shall go?' 9. And Moses said: 'We will go with our young and with our old, with our sons and with our daughters, with our flocks and with our herds we will go; for we must hold a feast unto the Lord.' 10. And he said unto them: 'So be the Lord with you, as I will let you go, and your little ones; see ye that evil is before your face. 11. Not so; go now ye that are men, and serve the Lord; for that is what ye desire.' And they were driven out from Pharaoh's presence.*¹¹. ¶ 12. And the Lord said unto Moses: 'Stretch out thy hand over the land of Egypt for the

הַנִּשְׁאֶרֶת לָכֶם מִן־הַבָּרָד וְאָכַל אֶת־כָּל־הָעֵץ הַצֹּמֵחַ לָכֶם
מִן־הַשָּׂדֶה: וּמָלְאוּ בָתֶּיךָ וּבָתֵּי כָל־עֲבָדֶיךָ וּבָתֵּי כָל־ 6
מִצְרַיִם אֲשֶׁר לֹא־רָאוּ אֲבֹתֶיךָ וַאֲבוֹת אֲבֹתֶיךָ מִיּוֹם
הֱיוֹתָם עַל־הָאֲדָמָה עַד הַיּוֹם הַזֶּה וַיִּפֶן וַיֵּצֵא מֵעִם פַּרְעֹה:
וַיֹּאמְרוּ עַבְדֵי פַרְעֹה אֵלָיו עַד־מָתַי יִהְיֶה זֶה לָנוּ לְמוֹקֵשׁ 7
שַׁלַּח אֶת־הָאֲנָשִׁים וְיַעַבְדוּ אֶת־יְהֹוָה אֱלֹהֵיהֶם הֲטֶרֶם תֵּדַע
כִּי אָבְדָה מִצְרָיִם: וַיּוּשַׁב אֶת־מֹשֶׁה וְאֶת־אַהֲרֹן אֶל־ 8
פַּרְעֹה וַיֹּאמֶר אֲלֵהֶם לְכוּ עִבְדוּ אֶת־יְהֹוָה אֱלֹהֵיכֶם מִי וָמִי
הַהֹלְכִים: וַיֹּאמֶר מֹשֶׁה בִּנְעָרֵינוּ וּבִזְקֵנֵינוּ נֵלֵךְ בְּבָנֵינוּ 9
וּבִבְנוֹתֵנוּ בְּצֹאנֵנוּ וּבִבְקָרֵנוּ נֵלֵךְ כִּי חַג־יְהֹוָה לָנוּ: וַיֹּאמֶר י
אֲלֵהֶם יְהִי כֵן יְהֹוָה עִמָּכֶם כַּאֲשֶׁר אֲשַׁלַּח אֶתְכֶם וְאֶת־
טַפְּכֶם רְאוּ כִּי רָעָה נֶגֶד פְּנֵיכֶם: לֹא כֵן לְכוּ־נָא הַגְּבָרִים 11
וְעִבְדוּ אֶת־יְהֹוָה כִּי אֹתָהּ אַתֶּם מְבַקְשִׁים וַיְגָרֶשׁ אֹתָם מֵאֵת
שני
פְּנֵי פַרְעֹה: ס וַיֹּאמֶר יְהֹוָה אֶל־מֹשֶׁה נְטֵה יָדְךָ עַל־אֶרֶץ 12

**6.** *thy houses shall be filled.* If part of a swarm alights on a house, the locusts enter its innermost recesses, and fill every corner.

*since the day.* Cf. ix, 24.

*and he turned.* i.e. Moses, and Aaron followed; see v. 3.

**7–11.** For the first time the servants intervene before the plague is inflicted, showing at once their belief in Moses' threat and their dread of the affliction. They suggest that Pharaoh should come to terms with Moses, who demands that the entire people must go to worship God.

**7.** *Pharaoh's servants.* Their hearts were not so hard as their master's; see viii, 15, and ix, 20.

*this man.* i.e. Moses.

*a snare.* fig. for any cause of destruction.

*destroyed.* i.e. ruined through all the plagues.

**8.** *who are they that shall go.* lit. 'who and who are those who are going?' i.e. who exactly is to go?

**9.** *go with our young.* There was nothing extraordinary in Moses' demand, as great festivals in Egypt were kept by the whole population.

**10.** *so be the Lord with you.* Pharaoh replies ironically, 'May God be with you as assuredly as I will let you go.'

*evil is before your face.* Or, 'evil is what ye purpose.' The evil intention which you harbour, to leave Egypt for good with all your belongings, is standing plainly before your face; it is evident to all (Bechor Shor).

**11.** *not so.* As ye have said, to take your little ones with you (Rashi).

*ye that are men.* This policy of Pharaoh has more than once been imitated by Israel's oppressors. After the expulsion from Spain, 80,000 Jews took refuge in Portugal, 'relying on the promise of the king. Spanish priests lashed the Portuguese into fury, and the king was persuaded to issue an edict which threw even that of Isabella into the shade. All the adult Jews were banished from Portugal; but first of all their children below the age of fourteen were taken from them to be educated as Christians. Then, indeed, the serene fortitude with which the exiled people had borne so many and such grievous calamities gave way, and was replaced by the wildest paroxysms of despair' (Lecky). And in our own day, the Soviet rulers extend considerable religious freedom *to adults;* religious instruction *to children,* however, is rigorously suppressed.

*that is what ye desire.* This is what you asked for hitherto, to hold a sacrificial feast unto God; and for this men alone suffice. Moses, however, demanded from the first 'Let my people go'— the entire people, and not the men only.

## EXODUS X, 13

locusts, that they may come up upon the land of Egypt, and eat every herb of the land, even all that the hail hath left.' 13. And Moses stretched forth his rod over the land of Egypt, and the LORD brought an east wind upon the land all that day, and all the night; and when it was morning, the east wind brought the locusts. 14. And the locusts went up over all the land of Egypt, and rested in all the borders of Egypt; very grievous were they; before them there were no such locusts as they, neither after them shall be such. 15. For they covered the face of the whole earth, so that the land was darkened; and they did eat every herb of the land, and all the fruit of the trees which the hail had left; and there remained not any green thing, either tree or herb of the field, through all the land of Egypt. 16. Then Pharaoh called for Moses and Aaron in haste; and he said: 'I have sinned against the LORD your God, and against you. 17. Now therefore forgive, I pray thee, my sin only this once, and entreat the LORD your God, that He may take away from me this death only.' 18. And he went out from Pharaoh, and entreated the LORD. 19. And the LORD turned an exceeding strong west wind, which took up the locusts, and drove them into the Red Sea; there remained not one locust in all the border of Egypt. 20. But the LORD hardened Pharaoh's heart, and he did not let the children of Israel go. ¶ 21. And the

**14.** *the borders.* *i.e.* the territory.
*very grevious were they.* See VIII, 20. The reference here is to the tremendous quantities of the locusts.
*no such locusts.* In Egypt.
*neither after them shall be such.* In Egypt. The last two phrases are to be taken as proverbial, hyperbolical expressions (Luzzatto); cf. II Kings XVIII, 5 and XXIII, 25. See also IX, 24.

**15.** *was darkened.* The expression is exact and graphic. Afar off the locusts appear like a heavy cloud hanging over the land. As they approach, they completely hide the sun.
*not any green thing.* Where such a swarm appears, they eat the land bare and everything green vanishes from the fields.

**16.** *and against you.* See IX, 27. Here the king confesses his double sin against God and against Israel.

**17.** *this death.* *i.e.* this pestilence, destructive of all food and sustenance.

**19.** *into the Red Sea.* A swarm of locusts floats upon an easy breeze, but is beaten down by a storm; and if it touches water it perishes. Pliny also speaks of swarms of locusts carried away by the wind and cast into the sea.

*Red Sea.* lit. 'the sea of reeds.' It may also originally have been the name of the fresh-water lake lying immediately to the North of the Red Sea. The name, Red Sea (Septuagint), has been variously derived from the corals within its waters, the colour of the mountains bordering its coasts, or the glow of the sky reflected on it.

**20.** After the removal of the plague, Pharaoh once again breaks faith.

### 21–23. NINTH PLAGUE: DARKNESS

**21.** *darkness over the land.* 'Like the third and sixth plagues, it is inflicted unannounced; and the parleying, the driving of a bargain and then breaking it, by which the eighth was attended, is quite enough to account for this' (Chadwick).
This plague would especially affect the spirits of the Egyptians, whose chief object of worship was Ra, the sun-God. Merneptah is depicted in a sculptured effigy with the inscription, 'He adores the sun.'
*darkness which may be felt.* Explained as an aggravation of the *khamsin*, or 'wind of the desert', which is not uncommon in Egypt, and is accompanied by weird darkness, beyond that of our worst fogs (Rawlinson). The following

EXODUS X, 22                         שמות בא י

21 וַיֹּאמֶר יְהֹוָה אֶל־מֹשֶׁה נְטֵה יָדְךָ עַל־הַשָּׁמַיִם וִיהִי חֹשֶׁךְ עַל־
22 אֶרֶץ מִצְרָיִם וְיָמֵשׁ חֹשֶׁךְ: וַיֵּט מֹשֶׁה אֶת־יָדוֹ עַל־הַשָּׁמָיִם
23 וַיְהִי חֹשֶׁךְ־אֲפֵלָה בְּכָל־אֶרֶץ מִצְרַיִם שְׁלֹשֶׁת יָמִים: לֹא־רָאוּ
   אִישׁ אֶת־אָחִיו וְלֹא־קָמוּ אִישׁ מִתַּחְתָּיו שְׁלֹשֶׁת יָמִים וּלְכָל־      שלישי
24 בְּנֵי יִשְׂרָאֵל הָיָה אוֹר בְּמוֹשְׁבֹתָם: וַיִּקְרָא פַרְעֹה אֶל־מֹשֶׁה
   וַיֹּאמֶר לְכוּ עִבְדוּ אֶת־יְהֹוָה רַק צֹאנְכֶם וּבְקַרְכֶם יֻצָּג גַּם־
כה טַפְּכֶם יֵלֵךְ עִמָּכֶם: וַיֹּאמֶר מֹשֶׁה גַּם־אַתָּה תִּתֵּן בְּיָדֵנוּ זְבָחִים
26 וְעֹלֹת וְעָשִׂינוּ לַיהֹוָה אֱלֹהֵינוּ: וְגַם־מִקְנֵנוּ יֵלֵךְ עִמָּנוּ לֹא
   תִשָּׁאֵר פַּרְסָה כִּי מִמֶּנּוּ נִקַּח לַעֲבֹד אֶת־יְהֹוָה אֱלֹהֵינוּ
27 וַאֲנַחְנוּ לֹא־נֵדַע מַה־נַּעֲבֹד אֶת־יְהֹוָה עַד־בֹּאֵנוּ שָׁמָּה: וַיְחַזֵּק
28 יְהֹוָה אֶת־לֵב פַּרְעֹה וְלֹא אָבָה לְשַׁלְּחָם: וַיֹּאמֶר־לוֹ פַרְעֹה

LORD said unto Moses: 'Stretch out thy hand toward heaven, that there may be darkness over the land of Egypt, even darkness which may be felt.' 22. And Moses stretched forth his hand toward heaven; and there was a thick darkness in all the land of Egypt three days; 23. they saw not one another, neither rose any from his place for three days; but all the children of Israel had light in their dwellings.* iii. 24. And Pharaoh called unto Moses, and said: 'Go ye, serve the LORD; only let your flocks and your herds be stayed; let your little ones also go with you.' 25. And Moses said: 'Thou must also give into our hand sacrifices and burnt-offerings, that we may sacrifice unto the LORD our God. 26. Our cattle also shall go with us; there shall not a hoof be left behind; for thereof must we take to serve the LORD our God; and we know not with what we must serve the LORD, until we come thither.' 27. But the LORD hardened Pharaoh's heart, and he would not let them go. 28. And Pharaoh

verses are from the wonderful description of the plague of Darkness in Wisdom of Solomon XVII.

'No force of fire prevailed to give them light, neither were the bright flames of the stars strong enough to illumine that gloomy night;

'For wickedness, condemned by a witness within, is a coward thing; and being pressed hard by conscience, always forecasteth the worst lot;

'Whether there were a whistling wind, or a melodious noise of birds among the spreading branches, or a measured fall of water running violently;

'All these things paralysed them with terror; but for thy saints there was great light.'

**23.** *they saw not one another.* lit. 'man did not see his brother'.

*neither rose any from his place.* Too terrified to move.

*had light in their dwellings.* i.e. in the land of Goshen. Prof. Mahler identifies the ninth plague with the solar eclipse of March 13, 1335 B.C.E., which darkened Egypt proper but did not extend *as a total eclipse* to Goshen; hence, 'all the children of Israel had light in their habitations.' (Thus, the eclipse of the sun on January 24, 1925, was not visible in the lower half of New York City—96th Street marking the southern limit of the path of totality.) Tradition states that the darkness took place on the first of Nisan, which then fell on a Thursday. If Mahler's identification is correct, we would know the exact date—Thursday, March 27, 1335 B.C.E.—of the Exodus. Prof. Mahler, furthermore, takes the words 'three days' at the end of v. 22, and joins them to v. 23; thus, 'Three days they saw not one another, neither rose any from his place three days.' Accordingly, the eclipse was on one day only, but its terrifying effects—the blank, utter paralysis of dread—lasted three days. Greek writers have left us graphic descriptions of the effects of eclipses, 'when sore fear comes upon men.' Herodotus tells us that a total eclipse of the sun in 585 B.C.E., during a battle between the Lydians and Medes, so terrified the combatants that they ceased fighting and concluded peace. When the spectators are 'natives', a total eclipse of the sun is the occasion of remarkable scenes in which alarm and despair and anger are intermingled.

**24.** *called unto Moses.* After the darkness had passed away.

*your little ones also.* Pharaoh offers a greater concession than before, a step further on the way to complete capitulation. The entire people may now go. Their cattle, however, he desires them to leave behind as a security for their return. Moses refuses to listen to compromise.

**25.** *sacrifices.* Part of which was consumed on the altar, and part eaten by the worshippers.

*burnt-offerings.* Were wholly burnt on the altar.

**26.** *not a hoof be left behind.* Moses emphasizes his intention of not bringing Israel back to Egypt.

*with what we must serve the LORD.* We do not know what kind of animals are to be used for the sacrifice, neither do we know how many (Ibn Ezra).

**28.** *see my face no more.* Seek no more admittance to my presence; cf. II Sam. XIV, 24, 28; II Kings XXV, 19. When they once more met, it was the king that changed his purpose; and

251

## EXODUS X, 29

said unto him: 'Get thee from me, take heed to thyself, see my face no more; for in the day thou seest my face thou shalt die.' 29. And Moses said: 'Thou hast spoken well; I will see thy face again no more.'

## 11 CHAPTER XI

1. And the LORD said unto Moses: 'Yet one plague more will I bring upon Pharaoh, and upon Egypt; afterwards he will let you go hence; when he shall let you go, he shall surely thrust you out hence altogether. 2. Speak now in the ears of the people, and let them ask every man of his neighbour, and every woman of her neighbour, jewels of silver, and jewels of gold.' 3. And the LORD gave the people favour in the sight of the Egyptians. Moreover the man Moses was very great in the land of Egypt, in the sight of Pharaoh's servants, and in the sight of the people.* ¹ᵛ· ¶ 4. And Moses said: 'Thus saith the LORD: About midnight will I go out into the midst of Egypt; 5. and all the first-born in the land of Egypt shall die, from the first-born of Pharaoh that

---

on *his* face, not on that of Moses, was the pallor of impending death. In his negotiations with Pharaoh, Moses was ever ready to intercede; he never 'reviles the ruler', nor transgresses the limits of courtesy towards the king; yet he never falters nor compromises. Throughout, the dignified bearing is with Moses, the meanness and shame with Pharaoh, who begins by insulting him, goes on to impose on him, and ends by an ignominious surrender, to be followed by treachery and abject defeat on the shores of the Red Sea (Chadwick).

**29.** *spoken well.* Further interviews would be useless.

*see thy face again no more.* But before Moses leaves the king's presence, he announces to him the tenth plague (XI, 4), and then leaves him for the last time (XI, 8).

### CHAPTER XI. THE WARNING OF THE LAST PLAGUE

**1.** *the LORD said.* Or, 'had said' (Ibn Ezra). The tense is pluperfect and *v.* 1–3 are parenthetical, having been communicated to Moses on a previous occasion.

*thrust you out.* Moses thus learns that the last plague would be followed by an immediate departure; and this gave him time to devise measures of preparing the Israelites for the journey.

**2.** *let them ask.* They were, however, to leave Egypt, where they had lived for so many centuries, without any bitter memories of the Egyptian people. See note on III, 21.

**3.** *gave the people favour.* And therefore the Egyptians were most generous and friendly in the way they parted with the Israelites; see the explanation of Deut. xv, 14 in note on III, 21.

*was very great.* *i.e.* had gained a great reputation, because of the visitations; and especially by the care he had taken to warn them, and, so far as was possible, to save them from suffering. This conduct elicited their kindliest feelings towards the people of Moses.

**4.** *Moses said.* To Pharaoh, in answer to his ultimatum, x, 28.

*will I go out.* Onkelos renders, 'I will reveal Myself.'

**5.** *that sitteth upon his throne.* This phrase refers to Pharaoh, and not to the eldest son.

*first-born of the maidservant.* The meanest person in the kingdom is contrasted with the noblest. Grinding the corn, the lowest drudgery, was the work of women, slaves and captives. The hand-mill is still in daily use in practically every Eastern or East European village.

*first-born of cattle.* The plague of the cattle described in IX, 6 was limited to the 'cattle which are in the field'. The Heb. word for cattle in IX, 6 is *mikneh*, whereas here the word *behemah* is used. The Egyptians paid Divine honours to various animals; and the first-born of all these beasts were to be doomed.

## EXODUS XI, 6

sitteth upon his throne, even unto the first-born of the maid-servant that is behind the mill; and all the first-born of cattle. 6. And there shall be a great cry throughout all the land of Egypt, such as there hath been none like it, nor shall be like it any more. 7. But against any of the children of Israel shall not a dog whet his tongue, against man or beast; that ye may know how that the LORD doth put a difference between the Egyptians and Israel. 8. And all these thy servants shall come down unto me, and bow down unto me, saying: Get thee out, and all the people that follow thee; and after that I will go out.' And he went out from Pharaoh in hot anger. ¶ 9. And the LORD said unto Moses: 'Pharaoh will not hearken unto you; that My wonders may be multiplied in the land of Egypt.' 10. And Moses and Aaron did all these wonders before Pharaoh; and the LORD hardened Pharaoh's heart, and he did not let the children of Israel go out of his land.

## 12   CHAPTER XII

1. And the LORD spoke unto Moses and Aaron in the land of Egypt, saying: 2. 'This month shall be unto you the beginning of months; it shall be the first month of the

---

**6.** *a great cry.* The freedom with which Orientals give vent to their emotions is well known.

**7.** *a dog whet his tongue.* A proverbial expression indicating safety and peace.

**8.** *shall come down.* The courtiers will be sent in haste to Moses to grant all that he had demanded.

*in hot anger.* Because of the words 'see my face no more' that the king had addressed to him (x, 28).

**9.** *the LORD said.* All that had hitherto happened to Pharaoh, as well as the effect of the miracles upon him, is here briefly restated. This summary marks the close of one principal division of the Book of Exodus.

### CHAPTER XII

### THE INSTITUTION OF THE PASSOVER

The deliverance from Egypt is to be not only from physical but also from spiritual slavery. Israel is to be freed from all heathen influences and consecrated to the service of God. These commandments concerning the Passover open the religious legislation of the Torah. The occasion when they were given, and the manner in which they were enjoined, emphasize the basic importance of that Festival in the life and history of Israel. 'The Exodus from Egypt is not only one of the greatest events and epochs in the history of the Jews, but one of the greatest events and epochs in the history of the world. To that successful escape, Europe, America, and Australia are as much indebted as the Jews themselves. And the men of Europe, the men of America, and the men of Australia might join with us Jews in celebrating that feast of the Passover' (C. G. Montefiore).

**2.** *this month.* The month of 'Abib', or Nisan, in which the deliverance was about to take place.

*the beginning of months.* 'The first month of your Freedom shall be made the first in reckoning the months, so that you reckon your time from the hour of Freedom. In this way will ye remember the hour of Freedom, and also My beneficent dealings with you, and you will be heedful to fear, love, and serve Me' (Bechor Shor). The redemption from Egypt is to be both in deed and in word 'epoch-making'. The Exodus was to mark the beginning of a new era; and not only the years in the national history were to be counted from it (see XVI, 1; XIX, 1; Num. I, 1; I Kings VI, 1), but also the months of each year were to be counted from the first month of Israel's Freedom. Israel is now given a new Calendar, thus making the break with Egypt complete.

The ordinary Jewish year consists of twelve lunar months of a little more than $29\frac{1}{2}$ days each, with every new moon (Rosh Chodesh) a minor

EXODUS XII, 3

3 וַיְדַבֵּר יְהֹוָה אֶל־מֹשֶׁה וְאֶל־אַהֲרֹן בְּאֶרֶץ מִצְרַיִם לֵאמֹר׃ הַחֹדֶשׁ הַזֶּה לָכֶם רֹאשׁ חֳדָשִׁים רִאשׁוֹן הוּא לָכֶם לְחָדְשֵׁי הַשָּׁנָה׃ דַּבְּרוּ אֶל־כָּל־עֲדַת יִשְׂרָאֵל לֵאמֹר בֶּעָשֹׂר לַחֹדֶשׁ
4 הַזֶּה וְיִקְחוּ לָהֶם אִישׁ שֶׂה לְבֵית־אָבֹת שֶׂה לַבָּיִת׃ וְאִם־יִמְעַט הַבַּיִת מִהְיוֹת מִשֶּׂה וְלָקַח הוּא וּשְׁכֵנוֹ הַקָּרֹב אֶל־בֵּיתוֹ בְּמִכְסַת נְפָשֹׁת אִישׁ לְפִי אָכְלוֹ תָּכֹסּוּ עַל־הַשֶּׂה׃
5 שֶׂה תָמִים זָכָר בֶּן־שָׁנָה יִהְיֶה לָכֶם מִן־הַכְּבָשִׂים וּמִן־
6 הָעִזִּים תִּקָּחוּ׃ וְהָיָה לָכֶם לְמִשְׁמֶרֶת עַד אַרְבָּעָה עָשָׂר יוֹם לַחֹדֶשׁ הַזֶּה וְשָׁחֲטוּ אֹתוֹ כֹּל קְהַל עֲדַת־יִשְׂרָאֵל בֵּין

year to you. 3. Speak ye unto all the congregation of Israel, saying: In the tenth day of this month they shall take to them every man a lamb, according to their fathers' houses, a lamb for a household; 4. and if the household be too little for a lamb, then shall he and his neighbour next unto his house take one according to the number of the souls; according to every man's eating ye shall make your count for the lamb. 5. Your lamb shall be without blemish, a male of the first year; ye shall take it from the sheep, or from the goats; 6. and ye shall keep it until the fourteenth

festival. As, on the one hand, twelve lunar months total only a little more than 354¼ days, eleven days less than the solar year, which consists, roughly, of 365¼ days; and, on the other hand, the Festivals had to be celebrated in their seasons according to the solar year—Passover in spring, Pentecost in summer, and Tabernacles in autumn—it was essential to harmonize the lunar and solar years. This was done by the 'intercalation', or introduction, of an extra month Adar, which made that year a leap year. There are seven such leap years, of thirteen months each, in every cycle of nineteen years. But years, whether ordinary years or leap years, have not a uniform duration in the Jewish reckoning. According as the months of Kislev and Cheshvan have 29 or 30 days, ordinary years vary between 353, 354, and 355 days, and leap years between 383, 384, and 385 days. By these means the mathematical exactness of the Jewish Calendar was secured. A renowned non-Jewish scholar declared, 'There is nothing more perfect than the calculation of the Jewish year' (Scaliger).

*unto you.* Heb. לכם. The Rabbis emphasize this word, and deduce from it that the exact fixation of the Festivals is in the hands of Israel and his ancient religious guides. In Biblical and early Talmudic times, the Sanhedrin fixed the new moons by actual observation, and the dates were announced by messengers from Jerusalem to surrounding countries. Later, the dates were determined by astronomical calculation. Religious considerations decided which year was to be a leap year, and when the months of Kislev and Chesvan were to be 'long' (having 30 days) or 'short' (29 days). Furthermore, Rosh Hashanah could never be a Sunday, Wednesday, or Friday (לא אד״ו ראש השנה) which rule secured, among other things, that the Day of Atonement did not either immediately precede or immediately follow the Sabbath.

3. *all the congregation.* Hitherto Moses and Aaron had been God's ambassadors to Pharaoh; they now become God's ambassadors to Israel. The 'congregation of Israel', *adath Yisrael*, is the term for the community as a religious entity.

*tenth day of this month.* Only on this occasion was the paschal lamb to be chosen on the tenth of the month.

*according to their fathers' houses.* A 'father's house' is here synonymous with *mishpachah*, a family. The Passover is to be the specific *family* festival of Israel. And it is noteworthy that the first ordinance of the Jewish religion was a domestic service. A nation is strong in so far as it cherishes the domestic sanctities.

4. *too little for a lamb. i.e.* too few to consume it at a sitting. 'If, however, the men of the house are less than ten' (Jerusalem Targum). Had a family of two or three been compelled to take a lamb, a considerable quantity would have been wasted; see *v.* 10.

*souls.* Persons.

*according to every man's eating.* Small children and the very aged, who cannot eat even the small obligatory quantity (כזית), were not to be reckoned among the number.

5. *without blemish.* Faultless, like all animals for sacrifice; Lev. XXII, 19, 21.

*male.* As in the case of a burnt-offering; Lev. I, 3, 10.

*of the first year.* lit. 'the son of a year'. The Rabbis take this to mean, within the first year of its birth; Lev. IX, 3. 'This tender age, the type of innocence, made it peculiarly adapted for a sacrifice of the Covenant to be concluded between God and Israel as a nation' (Kalisch).

6. *at dusk.* Better, *towards even* (M. Friedlander); lit. 'between the two evenings'. According to the Talmud, the 'first evening' is the time in the afternoon when the heat of the sun begins to decrease, about 3 o'clock; and the 'second evening' commences with sunset. Josephus relates that the Passover sacrifice 'was offered from the ninth to the eleventh hour', *i.e.* between 3 and 5 p.m.

## EXODUS XII, 7

day of the same month; and the whole assembly of the congregation of Israel shall kill it at dusk. 7. And they shall take of the blood, and put it on the two side-posts and on the lintel, upon the houses wherein they shall eat it. 8. And they shall eat the flesh in that night, roast with fire, and unleavened bread; with bitter herbs they shall eat it. 9. Eat not of it raw, nor sodden at all with water, but roast with fire; its head with its legs and with the inwards thereof. 10. And ye shall let nothing of it remain until the morning; but that which remaineth of it until the morning ye shall burn with fire. 11. And thus shall ye eat it: with your loins girded, your shoes on your feet, and your staff in your hand; and ye shall eat it in haste—it is the LORD's passover. 12. For I will go through the land of Egypt in that night, and will smite all the first-born in the land of Egypt, both man and beast; and against all the gods of Egypt I will execute judgments: I am the LORD. 13. And the blood shall be to you for

הָעַרְבָּיִם: וְלָקְחוּ מִן־הַדָּם וְנָתְנוּ עַל־שְׁתֵּי הַמְּזוּזֹת וְעַל־ 7
הַמַּשְׁקוֹף עַל הַבָּתִּים אֲשֶׁר־יֹאכְלוּ אֹתוֹ בָּהֶם: וְאָכְלוּ 8
אֶת־הַבָּשָׂר בַּלַּיְלָה הַזֶּה צְלִי־אֵשׁ וּמַצּוֹת עַל־מְרֹרִים
יֹאכְלֻהוּ: אַל־תֹּאכְלוּ מִמֶּנּוּ נָא וּבָשֵׁל מְבֻשָּׁל בַּמָּיִם כִּי 9
אִם־צְלִי־אֵשׁ רֹאשׁוֹ עַל־כְּרָעָיו וְעַל־קִרְבּוֹ: וְלֹא־תוֹתִירוּ 10
מִמֶּנּוּ עַד־בֹּקֶר וְהַנֹּתָר מִמֶּנּוּ עַד־בֹּקֶר בָּאֵשׁ תִּשְׂרֹפוּ: וְכָכָה 11
תֹּאכְלוּ אֹתוֹ מָתְנֵיכֶם חֲגֻרִים נַעֲלֵיכֶם בְּרַגְלֵיכֶם וּמַקֶּלְכֶם
בְּיֶדְכֶם וַאֲכַלְתֶּם אֹתוֹ בְּחִפָּזוֹן פֶּסַח הוּא לַיהוָה: וְעָבַרְתִּי 12
בְאֶרֶץ־מִצְרַיִם בַּלַּיְלָה הַזֶּה וְהִכֵּיתִי כָל־בְּכוֹר בְּאֶרֶץ
מִצְרַיִם מֵאָדָם וְעַד־בְּהֵמָה וּבְכָל־אֱלֹהֵי מִצְרַיִם אֶעֱשֶׂה
שְׁפָטִים אֲנִי יְהוָה: וְהָיָה הַדָּם לָכֶם לְאֹת עַל הַבָּתִּים 13

v. 7. ב׳ טעמים v. 11. מלעיל

**7.** *lintel.* The beam across the top of the doorway; or possibly, the latticed window which was commonly placed over a doorway in an Egyptian house (Rawlinson).

**8.** *the flesh.* Of the paschal lamb.
*in that night.* Following the fourteenth day of Nisan.
*roast with fire.* Because of the haste when they would leave Egypt.
*unleavened bread.* 'Because they could prepare it hastily' (Maimonides); symbolic of the haste with which the Israelites left Egypt, when there was no time for their dough to leaven. In Deut. XVI, 3, the 'unleavened bread' (Heb. *matzoth*, plural of *matzah*) is called the 'bread of affliction'.
*bitter herbs.* Heb. *merorim*, plural of *maror*. To symbolize the bitterness of the Egyptian bondage; I, 14.

**9.** *eat not of it raw.* As was the custom of many heathen peoples at their sacrifices.
*nor sodden at all with water.* The lamb was not to be boiled, because this would make the dismemberment of the animal indispensable. It is not to be divided, but to be roasted whole. This rite was probably intended to represent the perfect unity of Israel as a nation. One meal, at one table, eaten whole and eaten entirely (nothing left till the morning).

**10.** *remaineth of it.* Was not to be used for an ordinary meal, and was not to be thrown away disrespectfully; it was to be burned instead.

**11.** *loins girded.* The long and loose robes worn by the people of the East were fastened up round the waist with a girdle when proceeding on a journey. These and the following instructions apply only to the Passover in Egypt, not to any succeeding Passover celebration.
*shoes on your feet.* Ready for travel. The shoe or sandal was not generally worn in the house.
*staff in your hand.* Essential for the traveller in the desert.
*eat it in haste.* As they might have to commence their journey at any moment.
*the* LORD'S *passover.* Better, *a passover unto the* LORD (M. Friedlander); *i.e.* a paschal sacrifice in honour of the LORD (Mendelssohn). The word *pesach*, 'passover,' here means the paschal lamb; and is derived from the verb *pasach*, 'to pass over,' to protect and deliver; see *v.* 13.

**12.** *go through the land of Egypt.* Cf. XI, 4. 'The power of God will fearfully manifest itself in the land; His majesty will create terror; His justice will produce awe and veneration—and *thus* He will pass through the land' (Kalisch).
*against all the gods of Egypt.* In smiting the firstborn of all living beings, man and beast, God smote objects of Egyptian worship. Not a single deity of Egypt was unrepresented by some beast.
*I am the* LORD. Further evidence that this phrase in VI, 2 means an assertion of power, and not the revelation of a new Name.

**13.** *to you.* For you, in your interest.
*a token.* A pledge of mercy. The sight of the blood will strengthen your hearts, when ye hear the cry of the Egyptians as their firstborn die by the hand of the angel of destruction (Ibn Ezra and Reggio).
*when I see the blood.* 'Everything is revealed before Him, but the Holy One, blessed be He,

EXODUS XII, 14

a token upon the houses where ye are; and when I see the blood, I will pass over you, and there shall no plague be upon you to destroy you, when I smite the land of Egypt. 14. And this day shall be unto you for a memorial, and ye shall keep it a feast to the LORD; throughout your generations ye shall keep it a feast by an ordinance for ever. 15. Seven days shall ye eat unleavened bread; howbeit the first day ye shall put away leaven out of your houses; for whosoever eateth leavened bread from the first day until the seventh day, that soul shall be cut off from Israel. 16. And in the first day there shall be to you a holy convocation, and in the seventh day a holy convocation; no manner of work shall be done in them, save that which every man must eat, that only may be done by you. 17. And ye shall observe the feast of unleavened bread; for in this selfsame day have I brought your hosts out of the land of Egypt; therefore shall ye observe this day throughout your generations by an ordinance for ever. 18. In the first month, on the fourteenth day of the month at even, ye shall eat unleavened bread, until the one and twentieth day of the month at even. 19. Seven days shall there be no leaven found in your houses; for whosoever eateth that which is leavened, that soul shall be cut off from the congregation of Israel,

said: I will direct My eye to see whether you are occupied in obeying My precepts, and then I will spare you' (Rashi).

*I will pass over you.* Or, 'I will spare you' (Targum); 'I will protect you' (Septuagint). The Heb. verb. פסח combines the idea of passing over and sparing.

*no plague be upon you.* The angel of destruction will not have permission to bring the plague upon you (Reggio).

14–20. REGULATIONS FOR THE PASSOVER FESTIVAL

**14.** *for a memorial.* In the future. The regulations so far concerned the Passover in Egypt (v. 1–13); now (v. 14–20) the precepts for its future celebration are given.

*ye shall keep it.* i.e. the anniversary of the paschal sacrifice as an annual festival of seven days marked by eating unleavened bread.

*for ever.* Israel still keeps it.

**15.** *howbeit the first day . . . leaven out of your houses.* Better, *Of a surety on the first day ye shall have removed the leaven from your houses* (Mendelssohn). The leaven is therefore removed and symbolically destroyed by fire (ביעור חמץ) on the forenoon of the day before Passover. The Rabbis have also instituted a search for leaven (בדיקת חמץ) on the preceding evening.

Leaven is the symbol of corruption, passion and sin.

*soul.* Person.

*cut off from Israel.* See Gen. XVII, 14. Not put to death, but cast out from the congregation of Israel, becoming like one of the heathen.

**16.** *holy convocation.* A holy festival. The term is no doubt derived from the fact that originally the worshippers were called together for the celebration of a festival.

*which every man must eat.* The preparation of food for man or beast is permitted on the Festival when it occurs on a week day. This constitutes the main difference between Sabbath and Festival.

**17.** *have I brought.* Better, *I shall have brought out* (Mendelssohn).

**18.** *at even.* The Jewish day begins with the preceding evening, and terminates at evening.

**19.** *that which is leavened.* Heb. *machmetzeth*; i.e. anything which leavens; not merely *chametz*, leavened food.

*sojourner.* Heb. *ger.* The resident alien. 'He was not directed or compelled to assume a religious duty of Israel, but he was prevented from interfering with the religious practices of

EXODUS XII, 20

whether he be a sojourner, or one that is born in the land. 20. Ye shall eat nothing leavened; in all your habitations shall ye eat unleavened bread.'* ¶ 21. Then Moses called for all the elders of Israel, and said unto them: 'Draw out, and take you lambs according to your families, and kill the passover lamb. 22. And ye shall take a bunch of hyssop, and dip it in the blood that is in the basin, and strike the lintel and the two side-posts with the blood that is in the basin; and none of you shall go out of the door of his house until the morning. 23. For the LORD will pass through to smite the Egyptians; and when He seeth the blood upon the lintel, and on the two side-posts, the LORD will pass over the door, and will not suffer the destroyer to come in unto your houses to smite you. 24. And ye shall observe this thing for an ordinance to thee and to thy sons for ever. 25. And it shall come to pass, when ye be come to the land which the LORD will give you, according as He hath promised, that ye shall keep this service. 26. And it shall come to pass,

---

Israel' (Sulzberger). In later Hebrew law, the resident alien is either a *ger tzedek*, a righteous proselyte, who has been received into the covenant of Abraham, and thereby enjoys the same privileges and obligations as the born Israelite; or *ger toshab* or *sha'ar*, 'the stranger of the gate,' the alien squatter who remains outside the religious life of Israel, but who has undertaken to adhere to the seven Noachic laws that are binding upon all men who desire to live in human society; see p. 33.

**20.** *in all your habitations.* Even out of Palestine, where there was no paschal lamb offered up, the observance of the Passover festival is obligatory.

**21–28.** Moses communicates the laws of Passover to the elders.

**21.** *draw out.* The elders should tell the people to draw the lamb out of the fold.
*take you.* If you have none, buy your lamb (Rashi).
*according to your families.* i.e. a lamb for a household; see v. 3 and 4.

**22.** *hyssop.* Heb. *ezob.* A few bunches of this plant could be used as a sponge to take up a liquid. It became a symbol for spiritual purification from sin (Ps. LI, 9).
*strike.* lit. 'make it touch'.
*none of you shall go out.* But ye shall all be ready to answer the call to Freedom.

**23.** *smite the Egyptians.* Their firstborn.
*will pass over the door.* Sparing those within; see v. 13.

*the destroyer.* The destroying angel; as in II Sam. XXIV, 16.

**24.** *observe this thing.* Cf. v. 17. The reference here is to the Passover celebration, and not to the sprinkling of the blood, which was restricted to the Passover in Egypt at the time of the Exodus.

**25.** *come to the land.* i.e. of Canaan. The sacrifice of the paschal lamb was to be a regular institution in the land of Canaan, after its conquest by Israel.
*as He hath promised.* To Abraham; Gen. XII, 7.
*keep this service.* In connection with the paschal lamb.

**26.** *your children shall say.* The children of successive generations are to be instructed at Passover as to the origin and significance of the Festival. In the Seder service on the first two nights of Passover, this command has found its solemn realization. In it we have history raised to religion. The youngest child present asks the Questions, which are answered by a recital of the events that culminated in the original institution of Passover. Education in the home is thus as old as the Hebrew people; see Gen. XVIII, 19.
*what mean ye by this service?* By the religious rites and ceremonies in connection with the Passover, intended to keep the memory of the wonderful deliverance alive in the hearts of the Israelites. Since the destruction of the Temple, the Questions of the child are concerned with the distinctive features of the Seder meal.

# EXODUS XII, 27

when your children shall say unto you: What mean ye by this service? 27. that ye shall say: It is the sacrifice of the LORD's passover, for that He passed over the houses of the children of Israel in Egypt, when He smote the Egyptians, and delivered our houses.' And the people bowed the head and worshipped. 28. And the children of Israel went and did so; as the LORD had commanded Moses and Aaron, so did they.*vi.
¶ 29. And it came to pass at midnight, that the LORD smote all the first-born in the land of Egypt, from the first-born of Pharaoh that sat on his throne unto the first-born of the captive that was in the dungeon; and all the first-born of cattle. 30. And Pharaoh rose up in the night, he, and all his servants, and all the Egyptians; and there was a great cry in Egypt; for there was not a house where there was not one dead. 31. And he called for Moses and Aaron by night, and said: 'Rise up, get you forth from among my people, both ye and the children of Israel; and go, serve the LORD, as ye have said. 32. Take both your flocks and your herds, as ye have said, and be gone; and bless me also.' 33. And the Egyptians were urgent upon the people, to send them out of the land in haste; for they said: 'We are all dead men.' 34. And the people took their dough before it was leavened, their kneading-troughs being bound up in their clothes upon their shoulders. 35. And the children of Israel did according to the word of Moses; and they asked of the Egyptians jewels of silver, and jewels of gold, and raiment. 36. And the LORD gave the people favour in the sight of the Egyptians, so that they let them have what they asked.

**27.** *delivered our houses.* The children of future generations are to consider that their freedom is associated with that of their ancestors in Egypt.

*the people bowed ... worshipped.* When they heard the promise of Redemption and of the future inheritance of Canaan (Rashi).

**28.** *went and did so.* They prepared for the Passover celebration.

### 29–36. THE LAST PLAGUE, AND ISRAEL'S DEPARTURE

**29.** *the captive that was in the dungeon.* In xi, 5, 'the maid-servant that is behind the mill.'

**30.** *a great cry.* A frantic wail of agony, the wild cry of Eastern bereavement, through the whole land.

*not a house.* Of the Egyptians.

**31.** *and he called.* i.e. Pharaoh; cf. x, 24.

*from among my people.* Even in Goshen the Israelites were in Pharaoh's land and among his people. Many Israelites, however, were doing slave-labour in various parts of Egypt.

**32.** *and bless me also.* Pray on my behalf that no further plague come upon me.

**33.** *were urgent upon the people.* Fearing that new plagues might follow, unless the Israelites were sent away without further delay.

**34.** *kneading-troughs.* These would soon be a necessity in the wilderness.

*clothes.* Or, 'mantles.'

**35.** *asked of the Egyptians.* See III, 22. The command had been given to the people some time before their departure.

**36.** *and they despoiled the Egyptians.* Render, 'and they *saved* the Egyptians,' from hatred and revengeful feelings. See, and read carefully, note on III, 22.

## EXODUS XII, 37

And they despoiled the Egyptians. ¶ 37. And the children of Israel journeyed from Rameses to Succoth, about six hundred thousand men on foot, beside children. 38. And a mixed multitude went up also with them; and flocks, and herds, even very much cattle. 39. And they baked unleavened cakes of the dough which they brought forth out of Egypt, for it was not leavened; because they were thrust out of Egypt, and could not tarry, neither had they prepared for themselves any victual. 40. Now the time that the children of Israel dwelt in Egypt was four hundred and thirty years. 41. And it came to pass at the end of four hundred and thirty years, even the selfsame day it came to pass, that all the hosts of the LORD went out from the land of Egypt. 42. It was a night of watching unto the LORD for bringing them out from the land of Egypt; this same night is a night of watching unto the LORD for all the children of Israel throughout their generations. ¶ 43. And the LORD said unto Moses and Aaron: 'This is the ordinance of the pass-

שמות בא יב

37 וַיִּסְעוּ בְנֵי־יִשְׂרָאֵל מֵרַעְמְסֵס סֻכֹּתָה כְּשֵׁשׁ־מֵאוֹת אֶלֶף
38 רַגְלִי הַגְּבָרִים לְבַד מִטָּף: וְגַם־עֵרֶב רַב עָלָה אִתָּם וְצֹאן
39 וּבָקָר מִקְנֶה כָּבֵד מְאֹד: וַיֹּאפוּ אֶת־הַבָּצֵק אֲשֶׁר הוֹצִיאוּ
מִמִּצְרַיִם עֻגֹת מַצּוֹת כִּי לֹא חָמֵץ כִּי־גֹרְשׁוּ מִמִּצְרַיִם וְלֹא
מ יָכְלוּ לְהִתְמַהְמֵהַּ וְגַם־צֵדָה לֹא־עָשׂוּ לָהֶם: וּמוֹשַׁב בְּנֵי
יִשְׂרָאֵל אֲשֶׁר יָשְׁבוּ בְּמִצְרָיִם שְׁלֹשִׁים שָׁנָה וְאַרְבַּע מֵאוֹת
41 שָׁנָה: וַיְהִי מִקֵּץ שְׁלֹשִׁים שָׁנָה וְאַרְבַּע מֵאוֹת שָׁנָה וַיְהִי
בְּעֶצֶם הַיּוֹם הַזֶּה יָצְאוּ כָּל־צִבְאוֹת יְהֹוָה מֵאֶרֶץ מִצְרָיִם:
42 לֵיל שִׁמֻּרִים הוּא לַיהֹוָה לְהוֹצִיאָם מֵאֶרֶץ מִצְרָיִם הוּא־
הַלַּיְלָה הַזֶּה לַיהֹוָה שִׁמֻּרִים לְכָל־בְּנֵי יִשְׂרָאֵל לְדֹרֹתָם: פ
43 וַיֹּאמֶר יְהֹוָה אֶל־מֹשֶׁה וְאַהֲרֹן זֹאת חֻקַּת הַפָּסַח כָּל־בֶּן־

v. 39. הג' רפה

### 37–51. OUT OF EGYPT

**37.** *Rameses.* See I, 11.

*Succoth.* The place has been identified with Thuku, either another name for Pithom or in its immediate neighbourhood.

*six hundred thousand.* A round number, representing the 603,550 of Num. I, 46. There are no doubt difficulties in conceiving the departure at one time and in one place of such a large body of men; but the event has its parallels in history. At the close of the 18th century, 400,000 Tartars started in a single night from the confines of Russia towards the Chinese borders.

*men on foot.* All the males who could march.

**38.** *a mixed multitude.* The mass of non-Israelite strangers, including slaves and prisoners of war, who took advantage of the panic to escape from Egypt. They were not a desirable class of associates, as appears from Num. XI, 4, 5.

*flocks, and herds.* The Israelites were not all slave-labourers, but also nomad tribes possessing cattle.

**39.** *any victual.* Other than the dough.

**40.** *four hundred and thirty years.* In Gen. XV, 13, the period of affliction is foretold, and was to be four hundred years, beginning—according to Rabbinic tradition—with the birth of Isaac. The thirty years not accounted for are supposed to refer to the years that elapsed between the vision when the affliction was foretold and the birth of Isaac (Luzzatto). Others refer these thirty years to the exploit of the Ephraimites, who, according to the Book of Chronicles, made a raid out of Egypt a generation before the Exodus. Of these four hundred and thirty years, the Rabbis state, the Israelites were in Egypt for a period of 210 years. This accords with the narrative of Exodus, and with the genealogies given in chap. VI.

**41.** *the selfsame day.* The fifteenth of Nisan.

**42.** *of watching.* i.e. of keeping in mind. Heb. *shimmurim;* 'of celebration,' and, 'of vigilance' are alternative translations. 'Because God shielded them, and did not suffer destruction to approach their houses, He ordered that the night be observed by all Israelites as a night of watching, a memorial of the night of redemption' (Ibn Ezra). It was the birthnight of the Israelite nation, and the whole history of Israel is stamped with its memory.

### 43–51. FURTHER REGULATIONS REGARDING THE PASSOVER

**43.** *ordinance of the passover.* Introduced here in consequence of what is said concerning the mixed multitude in *v.* 38 (Abarbanel).

*no alien eat thereof.* The non-Israelite, who has not chosen to enter the Covenant of Abraham, as well as the man whose deeds have alienated him from his Father in Heaven (Rashi), was not to partake of the paschal meal. It is to be a distinctly Israelitish observance.

## EXODUS XII, 44

over: there shall no alien eat thereof; 44. but every man's servant that is bought for money, when thou hast circumcised him, then shall he eat thereof. 45. A sojourner and a hired servant shall not eat thereof. 46. In one house shall it be eaten; thou shalt not carry forth aught of the flesh abroad out of the house; neither shall ye break a bone thereof. 47. All the congregation of Israel shall keep it. 48. And when a stranger shall sojourn with thee, and will keep the passover to the LORD, let all his males be circumcised, and then let him come near and keep it; and he shall be as one that is born in the land; but no uncircumcised person shall eat thereof. 49. One law shall be to him that is homeborn, and unto the stranger that sojourneth among you.' 50. Thus did all the children of Israel; as the LORD commanded Moses and Aaron, so did they.* ¶ 51. And it came to pass the selfsame day that the LORD did bring the children of Israel out of the land of Egypt by their hosts.

## 13  CHAPTER XIII

1. And the LORD spoke unto Moses, saying: 2. 'Sanctify unto Me all the first-born, whatsoever openeth the womb among the children of Israel, both of man and of beast, it

**44.** *servant.* However, a foreigner who as a bought servant permanently enters the family circle of an Israelite, may become a full member of the people of Israel, and therefore partake of the Passover.

*hast circumcised him.* 'With his consent' (Ibn Ezra). He cannot be forced to embrace the faith of Israel. Circumcision and Passover belong together; the former is the sign of Israel's election, and of God's covenant with His people; the latter is a sign of the fulfilment of the covenant on God's part (Talmud).

**45.** *a sojourner.* i.e. an alien, who is his own master; as distinguished from 'a hired servant,' who, as a rule, was also merely a temporary resident in Israel. The bought slave, however, who has consented to circumcision shares the religious privileges of the born Israelite.

**46.** *in one house.* i.e. in one company (Rashi).

**49.** *the stranger that sojourneth among you.* See v. 19. According to Ibn Ezra, the stranger referred to here is the *ger tzedek*, the 'righteous proselyte'. The principle of this injunction—*one law shall be to him that is homeborn, and unto the stranger that sojourneth among you*—has an application in Jewry beyond the sphere of ritual practice. (See especially Lev. XXIV, 22.) It is dominant not only in Jewish moral conduct, but also in the civil legislation of ancient Israel; and, in consequence, Jewish law recognizes no distinction in civil rights between native and alien. Only recently this verse was recommended for selection as the motto of the Congress for the Protection of Minority Populations in European Countries.

**50.** *thus did all the children of Israel.* A repetition of *v.* 28, because new precepts regarding the Passover have been introduced.

**51.** *the selfsame day.* The fifteenth of Nisan, after the night of the Passover.

### CHAPTER XIII. CONSECRATION OF THE FIRST-BORN

**2.** *sanctify unto Me.* Dedicate, devote unto Me; see Num. III, 13 and XVIII, 17, 18.

*all the first-born.* Just as the annual celebration of the Passover served to remind the Israelites of the great Redemption, so the sanctification of every male first-born would keep the memory fresh in every home blessed with a first-born son. The rite is still remembered in the ceremony of 'Redeeming the son' (*pidyon habben*) which is solemnized on the thirty-first day of the child's birth; see Authorised Prayer Book, p. 308. First-born Israelites keep the fourteenth day of Nisan as a fast, in commemoration of the miracle wrought for their ancestors.

**3–9.** Repeated exhortation concerning the Passover Festival.

# EXODUS XIII, 3

is Mine.' ¶ 3. And Moses said unto the people: 'Remember this day, in which ye came out from Egypt, out of the house of bondage; for by strength of hand the LORD brought you out from this place; there shall no leavened bread be eaten. 4. This day ye go forth in the month Abib. 5. And it shall be when the LORD shall bring thee into the land of the Canaanite, and the Hittite, and the Amorite, and the Hivite, and the Jebusite, which He swore unto thy fathers to give thee, a land flowing with milk and honey, that thou shalt keep this service in this month. 6. Seven days thou shalt eat unleavened bread, and in the seventh day shall be a feast to the LORD. 7. Unleavened bread shall be eaten throughout the seven days; and there shall no leavened bread be seen with thee, neither shall there be leaven seen with thee, in all thy borders. 8. And thou shalt tell thy son in that day, saying: It is because of that which the LORD did for me when I came forth out of Egypt. 9. And it shall be for a sign unto thee upon thy hand, and for a memorial between thine eyes, that the law of the LORD may be in thy mouth; for with a strong hand hath the LORD brought thee out of Egypt. 10. Thou shalt therefore keep this ordinance in its season from year to year. ¶ 11. And it shall be when the LORD shall bring thee into the land of the Canaanite, as He swore unto thee and to thy fathers, and shall give it thee, 12. that thou shalt set apart unto the LORD all that openeth the womb; every firstling that is a

---

**3.** *remember this day.* Every year.

*the house of bondage.* lit. 'the house of bondmen', *i.e.* the land where they were treated like slaves.

*from this place.* This phrase could only have been used at the exact stage when they were emancipated and as yet upon Egyptian soil.

**8.** *tell thy son.* The Rabbis derive from this verse the law that every father should relate on the evening of Passover the story of the Deliverance to his children. The story itself, as formulated for recitation during the domestic service on the eve of Passover, is called *Haggadah shel Pesach*.

**9.** *for a sign unto thee.* The Exodus is to be more than a mere annual celebration. Its eternal lessons are to be ever before the mind of the Israelite, by means of a 'sign' upon the hand, and of a 'memento' between the eyes. The reminders on arm and forehead are called *tephillin*, a late Heb. plural of תפלה, prayer. Four sections from the Torah (Ex. XIII, 1–10, 11–16; Deut. VI, 4–9 and XI, 13–21) are in the tephillin; and 'these four sections have been chosen in preference to all the other passages of the Torah, because they embrace the acceptance of the Kingdom of Heaven, the unity of the Creator, and the exodus from Egypt—fundamental doctrines of Judaism'. (Sefer ha-Chinuch.) The purpose of the tephillin is given in the Meditation recited before putting on the tephillin (Authorised Prayer Book, p. 15):—

'Within these Tephillin are placed four sections of the Law, that declare the absolute unity of God, and that remind us of the miracles and wonders which He wrought for us when He brought us forth from Egypt, even He who hath power over the highest and lowest to deal with them according to His will. He hath commanded us to lay the Tephillin on the hand as a memorial of His outstretched arm; opposite the heart, to indicate the duty of subjecting the longings and designs of our heart to His service, blessed be He; and upon the head over against the brain, thereby teaching that the mind, whose seat is in the brain, together with all senses and faculties, is to be subjected to His service, blessed be He.'

The tephillin are not worn at night, nor on

EXODUS XIII, 13        שמות בא יג

male, which thou hast coming of a beast, shall be the LORD's. 13. And every firstling of an ass thou shalt redeem with a lamb; and if thou wilt not redeem it, then thou shalt break its neck; and all the first-born of man among thy sons shalt thou redeem.* ᵐ· 14. And it shall be when thy son asketh thee in time to come, saying: What is this? that thou shalt say unto him: By strength of hand the LORD brought us out from Egypt, from the house of bondage; 15. and it came to pass, when Pharaoh would hardly let us go, that the LORD slew all the first-born in the land of Egypt, both the first-born of man, and the first-born of beast; therefore I sacrifice to the LORD all that openeth the womb, being males; but all the first-born of my sons I redeem. 16. And it shall be for a sign upon thy hand, and for frontlets between thine eyes; for by strength of hand the LORD brought us forth out of Egypt.'

13 וְכָל־פֶּטֶר ׀ שֶׁגֶר בְּהֵמָה אֲשֶׁר יִהְיֶה לְךָ הַזְּכָרִים לַיהוָה:
וְכָל־פֶּטֶר חֲמֹר תִּפְדֶּה בְשֶׂה וְאִם־לֹא תִפְדֶּה וַעֲרַפְתּוֹ וְכֹל
14 בְּכוֹר אָדָם בְּבָנֶיךָ תִּפְדֶּה: וְהָיָה כִּי־יִשְׁאָלְךָ בִנְךָ מָחָר מפטיר
לֵאמֹר מַה־זֹּאת וְאָמַרְתָּ אֵלָיו בְּחֹזֶק יָד הוֹצִיאָנוּ יְהוָה
15 מִמִּצְרַיִם מִבֵּית עֲבָדִים: וַיְהִי כִּי־הִקְשָׁה פַרְעֹה לְשַׁלְּחֵנוּ
וַיַּהֲרֹג יְהוָה כָּל־בְּכוֹר בְּאֶרֶץ מִצְרַיִם מִבְּכֹר אָדָם וְעַד־
בְּכוֹר בְּהֵמָה עַל־כֵּן אֲנִי זֹבֵחַ לַיהוָה כָּל־פֶּטֶר רֶחֶם
16 הַזְּכָרִים וְכָל־בְּכוֹר בָּנַי אֶפְדֶּה: וְהָיָה לְאוֹת עַל־יָדְכָה
וּלְטוֹטָפֹת בֵּין עֵינֶיךָ כִּי בְּחֹזֶק יָד הוֹצִיאָנוּ יְהוָה מִמִּצְרָיִם:

Sabbaths or Festivals, as these are themselves called 'a sign' of the great truths symbolized by the tephillin. The commandment of tephillin applies to all male persons from their thirteenth birthday, when they attain their religious majority (*Barmitzvah*). On the Sabbath following that birthday, the Barmitzvah is called to the Law, publicly to acknowledge God as the Giver of the Torah.

**10.** *this ordinance.* Of the Passover.
*in its season.* Or, 'appointed time,' *i.e.* at the full moon of the month of Nisan.
*from year to year.* lit. 'from days to days'. The same Heb. idiom is found in Judges XI, 40.

**11.** *land of the Canaanite.* The term is general, and includes all the tribes of the land. The law of the redemption of the firstborn was to be obligatory after the conquest of the Holy Land.

**12.** *thou shalt set apart.* Heb. 'cause to pass over', to the LORD; *i.e.* thou shalt put it aside for the LORD, lest it be mixed with other beasts (Ibn Ezra).

**13.** *firstling of an ass.* The ass is an unclean animal and could not be sacrificed.
*redeem with a lamb.* The priest received the lamb, and then the Israelite could retain the firstborn ass for his own use.
*break its neck.* This requirement ensured the scrupulous execution of the law of redemption in regard to unclean animals, as every one would prefer parting with a lamb to losing an ass.

*thy sons shalt thou redeem.* With 'five shekels apiece'; Num. III, 45–47. This law is in direct opposition to the practice of the heathen Semitic peoples of sacrificing their first-born. Even Wellhausen admits that of this abomination there is no trace in the religion of Israel. Driver writes: 'The instances of child-sacrifice which occur are either altogether abnormal, or, as in the reigns of Ahaz and Manasseh, due to the importation of Phœnician customs into Judah.'

**14.** *what is this?* *i.e.* what is the meaning of the precept concerning the first-born?

**15.** *would hardly let us go.* *i.e.* hardened himself *not* to let us go.
*slew all the first-born.* And spared our first-born.
*therefore I sacrifice.* In gratitude for sparing the first-born of our cattle.
*of my sons I redeem.* In memory of the preservation of those of the Israelites.

**16.** *frontlets.* Heb. '*totafoth*', phylacteries; see Deut. VI, 8.
This verse, with the preceding two verses, is to form the answer of the father to the question put by his son. The religious education of the children is a Divine command, and the future of religion depends upon this precept being loyally obeyed. In addition to these signs and observances, both the Sabbath, and even those Festivals that have other historic associations, are all spoken of in the Liturgy as זכר ליציאת מצרים 'memorials of the Going forth out of Egypt'.

# HAFTORAH BO הפטרת בא

## JEREMIAH XLVI, 13–28

### CHAPTER XLVI      CAP. XLVI. מו

13. The word that the LORD spoke to Jeremiah the prophet, how that Nebuchadrezzar king of Babylon should come and smite the land of Egypt.

14. Declare ye in Egypt, and announce in Migdol,
And announce in Noph and in Tahpanhes;
Say ye: 'Stand forth, and prepare thee,
For the sword hath devoured round about thee.'

15. Why is thy strong one overthrown?
He stood not, because the LORD did thrust him down.

16. He made many to stumble;
Yea, they fell one upon another,
And said: 'Arise, and let us return to our own people,
And to the land of our birth,
From the oppressing sword.'

17. They cried there: 'Pharaoh king of Egypt is but a noise;
He hath let the appointed time pass by.'

18. As I live, saith the King,
Whose name is the LORD of hosts,
Surely like Tabor among the mountains,
And like Carmel by the sea, so shall he come.

19. O thou daughter that dwellest in Egypt,
Furnish thyself to go into captivity;
For Noph shall become a desolation,
And shall be laid waste, without inhabitant.

---

For Jeremiah's life and message, see p. 229.

Like the previous Haftorah, this also is a prophecy against Egypt, and is thus connected with the Sedrah. Jeremiah was the older contemporary of Ezekiel; and during the last days of the Jewish state, both of them, the one in Jerusalem, and the other in Babylon, denounced the sin and folly of seeking help from Egypt. This is one of the last prophecies uttered by Jeremiah. It forms part of his Ode of Triumph upon the humiliating defeat of Pharaoh at the great battle of Charchemish in 605 B.C.E., and foretells the total collapse of Egypt before the power of Babylon.

**14.** *declare ye.* All Egypt is called upon to stand forth and prepare to repel the coming invader. Migdol is a frontier town in the north, also Tahpanhes; and Noph (Memphis) is the capital of Upper Egypt.

**15.** *why is thy strong one overthrown?* The Heb. for 'strong one' is in the plural, 'the plural of majesty,' and refers to the king, not to the people. The Septuagint divides the Heb. word for 'overthrown' into two, reading 'Why is Apis fled? The mighty one stood not, etc.' Apis was the sacred bull, the symbol of Osiris, the chief Egyptian deity worshipped at Memphis, and was called *the mighty one.*

**16.** *they fell one upon another.* The Egyptian armies in the panic of defeat.
*and said.* Either the mercenaries from other countries brought in to help Egypt; or, the foreign traders who prepare to flee to their several countries.

**17.** *they cried.* The mercenaries and traders.
*a noise ... pass by.* Pharaoh's name is but an empty noise; the time when he might have saved himself and them is past.

**18.** *like Tabor.* As surely as Tabor is among the mountains and Carmel is by the sea, so surely shall the conqueror come (Rashi and Kimchi). Others explain: just as Tabor stands out among mountains, and Carmel rises sheer out of the sea, so shall the coming foe—Nebuchadnezzar—overtop other conquerors.

**19.** *daughter.* Heb. poetical expression for 'population'; cf. *daughter of Zion.*

JEREMIAH XLVI, 20

20. Egypt is a very fair heifer;
But the gadfly out of the north is come,
  it is come.
21. Also her mercenaries in the midst of
  her
Are like calves of the stall,
For they also are turned back, they are
  fled away together,
They did not stand;
For the day of their calamity is come
  upon them,
The time of their visitation.
22. The sound thereof shall go like the
  serpent's;
For they march with an army,
And come against her with axes,
As hewers of wood.
23. They cut down her forest, saith the
  LORD,
Though it cannot be searched;
Because they are more than the locusts,
And are innumerable.
24. The daughter of Egypt is put to
  shame;
She is delivered into the hand of the
  people of the north.
25. The LORD of hosts, the God of Israel,
saith: Behold, I will punish Amon of No,
and Pharaoh, and Egypt, with her gods, and
her kings; even Pharaoh, and them that
trust in him; 26. and I will deliver them into
the hand of those that seek their lives, and
into the hand of Nebuchadrezzar king of
Babylon, and into the hand of his servants;
and afterwards it shall be inhabited, as in
the days of old, saith the LORD.
27. But fear not thou, O Jacob My
  servant,
Neither be dismayed, O Israel;
For, lo, I will save thee from afar,
And thy seed from the land of their
  captivity;
And Jacob shall again be quiet and at
  ease,
And none shall make him afraid.

28. Fear not thou, O Jacob My servant,
  saith the LORD,
For I am with thee;
For I will make a full end of all the
  nations whither I have driven thee,
But I will not make a full end of thee;
And I will correct thee in measure,
But will not utterly destroy thee.

20–26. THE OVERTHROW WOULD NOT BE FINAL

**20.** *fair heifer.* Well-nourished; the figure is chosen in allusion to her spouse, the bull Apis.
*the gadfly.* i.e. the foe, is stinging her to flight.
*out of the north.* Babylon was, of course, north of Egypt.

**21.** *like calves.* They were well-fed but cowardly, proving useless in the hour of danger.

**22.** *the sound.* The voice of Egypt as she flees from the enemy shall be like a serpent hissing impotently at the wood-cutters who attack her (Streane).

**25.** *Amon.* The god worshipped at No (Thebes, now Luxor, in South Egypt).

**26.** *and afterwards it shall be inhabited.* A promise of restoration to Egypt; cf. previous Haftorah, v. 13.

27–28. WORDS OF HOPE FOR ISRAEL

**27.** *fear not.* In contrast with all the foregoing, the Prophet closes with a message of hope and restoration, addressed to the Jewish exiles in Egypt and Chaldea.

**28.** *will not utterly destroy thee.* Other nations shall be blotted out of existence; not so shall it be with Israel.

**EXODUS XIII, 17**

**13** 17. And it came to pass, when Pharaoh had let the people go, that God led them not by the way of the land of the Philistines, although that was near; for God said: 'Lest peradventure the people repent when they see war, and they return to Egypt.' 18. But God led the people about, by the way of the wilderness by the Red Sea; and the children of Israel went up armed out of the land of Egypt. 19. And Moses took the bones of Joseph with him; for he had straitly sworn the children of Israel, saying: 'God will surely remember you; and ye shall carry up my bones hence with you.' 20. And they took their journey from Succoth, and encamped in Etham, in the edge of the wilderness. 21. And the LORD went before them by day

שמות בשלח יג

יג ס ס ס יו 16

17 וַיְהִ֗י בְּשַׁלַּ֣ח פַּרְעֹה֮ אֶת־הָעָם֒ וְלֹא־נָחָ֣ם אֱלֹהִ֗ים דֶּ֚רֶךְ אֶ֣רֶץ פְּלִשְׁתִּ֔ים כִּ֥י קָר֖וֹב ה֑וּא כִּ֣י ׀ אָמַ֣ר אֱלֹהִ֗ים פֶּן־יִנָּחֵ֥ם הָעָ֛ם
18 בִּרְאֹתָ֥ם מִלְחָמָ֖ה וְשָׁ֥בוּ מִצְרָֽיְמָה׃ וַיַּסֵּ֨ב אֱלֹהִ֧ים ׀ אֶת־הָעָ֛ם דֶּ֥רֶךְ הַמִּדְבָּ֖ר יַם־ס֑וּף וַחֲמֻשִׁ֛ים עָל֥וּ בְנֵי־יִשְׂרָאֵ֖ל מֵאֶ֥רֶץ
19 מִצְרָֽיִם׃ וַיִּקַּ֥ח מֹשֶׁ֛ה אֶת־עַצְמ֥וֹת יוֹסֵ֖ף עִמּ֑וֹ כִּי֩ הַשְׁבֵּ֨עַ הִשְׁבִּ֜יעַ אֶת־בְּנֵ֤י יִשְׂרָאֵל֙ לֵאמֹ֔ר פָּקֹ֨ד יִפְקֹ֤ד אֱלֹהִים֙ אֶתְכֶ֔ם
20 וְהַעֲלִיתֶ֧ם אֶת־עַצְמֹתַ֛י מִזֶּ֖ה אִתְּכֶֽם׃ וַיִּסְע֖וּ מִסֻּכֹּ֑ת וַיַּחֲנ֣וּ
21 בְאֵתָ֔ם בִּקְצֵ֖ה הַמִּדְבָּֽר׃ וַֽיהוָ֡ה הֹלֵךְ֩ לִפְנֵיהֶ֨ם יוֹמָ֜ם בְּעַמּ֤וּד

הש׳ רפה v. 18.

## IV. BESHALLACH

(CHAPTERS XIII, 17–XVII)

### THE REDEMPTION FROM EGYPT

XIII, 17–XIV, 31. THE PASSAGE OF THE RED SEA

**17.** *had let the people go.* God did not lead His people toward Canaan by the shorter way through the land of the Philistines, the direct caravan route to Canaan along the coast to Gaza, but by the opposite route towards the Red Sea.

*the Philistines.* A strongly intrenched and warlike people, who gave their name Philistia, *i.e.* Palestine, to all the land of Canaan; see p. 37, note 14. They are probably to be identified with the Purasati or Pulsata, one of a group of piratical tribes from the coast of Asia Minor or the Aegean Islands, who are known to have raided Egypt in the time of Rameses III, after the Exodus. There is no reason to assume that that was their first emergence from the place of their origin.

*although that was near.* It would have enabled them to reach the Land of Promise in about eleven days.

*repent.* 'Have regrets' (Moffatt), and change their mind and go back to Egypt. They required training and teaching and disciplining. 'It is like that king who wished to give his son his inheritance. He thought to himself, My son is young; he hardly knows how to read and write. If I give him all my possessions now, will he be able to keep them? I will wait until he has grown in strength and wisdom. In the same way God thought, The children of Israel are verily still children; first let Me teach them to understand and practise My precepts and commandments, then will I give them the Promised Land' (Talmud).

**18.** *by the way of the wilderness.* i.e. in the direction of the Egyptian wilderness, west of the northern end of the Gulf of Suez.

*Red Sea.* lit. 'the sea of reeds', see II, 3, 5. Denotes the northern part of our Red Sea; see on x, 19. Reeds have been found on spots N. of Suez, and they abound in Lake Timsah, exactly at the entrance of Goshen. In those days, there was a shallow extension of the Gulf of Suez, reaching to Lake Timsah; see note on *v.* 2 in next chapter.

*armed.* Better, *armed with lances.* Heb. *chamushim*, which probably comes from the Egyptian word *chams*, 'lance' (Yahuda).

**19.** *Moses took the bones of Joseph with him.* Joseph had caused his brethren to swear that they would carry his bones with them from Egypt. Moses, in performing this solemn duty, set an example of noble piety towards the dead; see on Gen. L, 26.

*straitly.* Strictly.

**20.** *Succoth.* See note on XII, 37.

*Etham, in the edge of the wilderness.* Where their route crossed the Egyptian frontier, *i.e.* in the neighbourhood of the modern Ismailia (Naville). At the frontier, the green land of Egypt would be cut off as with a knife from the hard desert tract on which they entered.

**21.** *a pillar of cloud.* The pillar of cloud by day and the pillar of fire by night were symbols of, and witnesses to, God's watching providence (Abarbanel). Sir Walter Scott has based on this

## EXODUS XIII, 22

in a pillar of cloud, to lead them the way; and by night in a pillar of fire, to give them light; that they might go by day and by night: 22. the pillar of cloud by day, and the pillar of fire by night, departed not from before the people.

# 14

### CHAPTER XIV

1. And the LORD spoke unto Moses, saying: 2. 'Speak unto the children of Israel, that they turn back and encamp before Pi-hahiroth, between Migdol and the sea, before Baal-zephon, over against it shall ye encamp by the sea. 3. And Pharaoh will say of the children of Israel: They are entangled in the land, the wilderness hath shut them in. 4. And I will harden Pharaoh's heart, and he shall follow after

שמות בשח יג יד

עָנָן לַנְחֹתָם הַדֶּרֶךְ וְלַיְלָה בְּעַמּוּד אֵשׁ לְהָאִיר לָהֶם
לָלֶכֶת יוֹמָם וָלָיְלָה: לֹא־יָמִישׁ עַמּוּד הֶעָנָן יוֹמָם וְעַמּוּד 22
הָאֵשׁ לָיְלָה לִפְנֵי הָעָם: פ

### CAP. XIV. יד

וַיְדַבֵּר יְהוָה אֶל־מֹשֶׁה לֵּאמֹר: דַּבֵּר אֶל־בְּנֵי יִשְׂרָאֵל וְיָשֻׁבוּ
וְיַחֲנוּ לִפְנֵי פִּי הַחִירֹת בֵּין מִגְדֹּל וּבֵין הַיָּם לִפְנֵי בַּעַל
צְפֹן נִכְחוֹ תַחֲנוּ עַל־הַיָּם: וְאָמַר פַּרְעֹה לִבְנֵי יִשְׂרָאֵל 3
נְבֻכִים הֵם בָּאָרֶץ סָגַר עֲלֵיהֶם הַמִּדְבָּר: וְחִזַּקְתִּי אֶת־לֵב־ 4

---

verse one of the most beautiful religious songs in English literature, *Rebecca's Hymn*.

Luzzatto and Kalisch refer to the Oriental custom of fire-signals in front of armies, or of a brazier filled with burning wood borne along at the head of a caravan, as the natural basis of the miracle. In that case, we should have in this narrative of the guiding Cloud and Pillar another instance of the interweaving of the supernatural and the natural in Scripture.

### CHAPTER XIV

**2.** *that they turn back.* The march was no sooner begun than it was checked. The people were ordered to return. They were now in great danger, in case the king of Egypt wished to pursue them. His chariots would soon have overtaken this multitude, and his host would have made a slaughter of the fugitives. This seemed to be the reason why they received a command which they must have considered as very extraordinary, and of a nature to shake their confidence in their leader (Naville). Instead of continuing to march to the north of the northern end of the Gulf of Suez, they were bidden to turn south or south-west, keeping the Sea, *i.e.* the Gulf of Suez, on their left. It is probable that the Gulf of Suez then extended much further north than it does now, and that the modern Lake Timsah and the Bitter Lakes were connected with each other and the Gulf of Suez by necks of shallow water, which would in a tornado be swept almost dry.

The landmarks mentioned in this verse have long ago disappeared, and cannot be identified with certainty. The precision, however, with which they are designated, guarantees that the spots were once well known. No portion of the world outside of Palestine was more familiar to the Israelites than the western border of Egypt; and no event in Bible history more perennially popular than the story of the Deliverance from Egypt.

*Pi-hahiroth.* Has been identified by Naville with Pi-kerehet, which he argues was on the S.W. edge of Lake Timsah. It was a sanctuary of Osiris. Cf. Num. XXXIII, 7.

*Baal-zephon.* The place of worship of a Semitic deity, on the opposite, Asiatic, side of the Sea which was in front of them.

**3.** *entangled.* Or, 'perplexed,' not knowing which way to turn in order to escape.

*in the land.* They are now back on Egyptian territory.

*the wilderness. i.e.* the Egyptian wilderness, a tract of desert land between the Nile and the Red Sea. The southern boundary of that wilderness was a high mountain range. With mountains to the south and the Sea to the west, they are 'shut in'.

**4.** *I will harden Pharaoh's heart.* After an interval of several days, during which the king gradually recovered from his panic, and reflected on his loss through the dismissal of so many scores of thousands of labourers, his innate obstinacy returned. His blindness to the right of the Israelites to their freedom became a malady of the mind with him, that was to drive him to destruction. His obdurate impiety was encouraged by the report that the Hebrew army was now between Migdol and the Sea, patently ignorant of the trap in which they now found themselves.

*follow after.* Pursue.

*I will get Me honour upon Pharaoh.* Better, *through Pharaoh.* By shielding the righteous and overthrowing the wicked, God manifests His justice and might. Thus, the Egyptians and all humanity come to know that there is a God of righteousness in the world.

*they did so.* The Israelites turned back and encamped before Pi-hahiroth.

EXODUS XIV, 5

them; and I will get Me honour upon Pharaoh, and upon all his host; and the Egyptians shall know that I am the LORD.' And they did so. 5. And it was told the king of Egypt that the people were fled; and the heart of Pharaoh and of his servants was turned towards the people, and they said: 'What is this we have done, that we have let Israel go from serving us?' 6. And he made ready his chariots, and took his people with him. 7. And he took six hundred chosen chariots, and all the chariots of Egypt, and captains over all of them. 8. And the LORD hardened the heart of Pharaoh king of Egypt, and he pursued after the children of Israel; for the children of Israel went out with a high hand.\* 11. 9. And the Egyptians pursued after them, all the horses and chariots of Pharaoh, and his horsemen, and his army, and overtook them encamping by the sea, beside Pi-hahiroth, in front of Baal-zephon. 10. And when Pharaoh drew nigh, the children of Israel lifted up their eyes, and, behold, the Egyptians were marching after them; and they were sore afraid; and the children of Israel cried out unto the LORD. 11. And they said unto Moses: 'Because there were no graves in Egypt, hast thou taken us away to die in the wilderness? wherefore hast thou dealt thus with us, to bring us forth out of Egypt? 12. Is not this the word that we spoke unto thee in Egypt, saying: Let us alone, that we may serve the

שמות בשלח יד

פַּרְעֹה וְרָדַף אַחֲרֵיהֶם וְאִכָּבְדָה בְּפַרְעֹה וּבְכָל־חֵילוֹ וְיָדְעוּ
מִצְרַיִם כִּי־אֲנִי יְהֹוָה וַיַּעֲשׂוּ־כֵן: וַיֻּגַּד לְמֶלֶךְ מִצְרַיִם כִּי
בָרַח הָעָם וַיֵּהָפֵךְ לְבַב פַּרְעֹה וַעֲבָדָיו אֶל־הָעָם וַיֹּאמְרוּ
מַה־זֹּאת עָשִׂינוּ כִּי־שִׁלַּחְנוּ אֶת־יִשְׂרָאֵל מֵעָבְדֵנוּ: וַיֶּאְסֹר
אֶת־רִכְבּוֹ וְאֶת־עַמּוֹ לָקַח עִמּוֹ: וַיִּקַּח שֵׁשׁ־מֵאוֹת רֶכֶב
בָּחוּר וְכֹל רֶכֶב מִצְרָיִם וְשָׁלִשִׁם עַל־כֻּלּוֹ: וַיְחַזֵּק יְהֹוָה
אֶת־לֵב פַּרְעֹה מֶלֶךְ מִצְרַיִם וַיִּרְדֹּף אַחֲרֵי בְּנֵי יִשְׂרָאֵל וּבְנֵי
יִשְׂרָאֵל יֹצְאִים בְּיָד רָמָה: וַיִּרְדְּפוּ מִצְרַיִם אַחֲרֵיהֶם וַיַּשִּׂיגוּ
אוֹתָם חֹנִים עַל־הַיָּם כָּל־סוּס רֶכֶב פַּרְעֹה וּפָרָשָׁיו וְחֵילוֹ
עַל־פִּי הַחִירֹת לִפְנֵי בַּעַל צְפֹן: וּפַרְעֹה הִקְרִיב וַיִּשְׂאוּ
בְנֵי־יִשְׂרָאֵל אֶת־עֵינֵיהֶם וְהִנֵּה מִצְרַיִם ׀ נֹסֵעַ אַחֲרֵיהֶם
וַיִּירְאוּ מְאֹד וַיִּצְעֲקוּ בְנֵי־יִשְׂרָאֵל אֶל־יְהֹוָה: וַיֹּאמְרוּ אֶל־
מֹשֶׁה הֲמִבְּלִי אֵין־קְבָרִים בְּמִצְרַיִם לְקַחְתָּנוּ לָמוּת בַּמִּדְבָּר
מַה־זֹּאת עָשִׂיתָ לָּנוּ לְהוֹצִיאָנוּ מִמִּצְרָיִם: הֲלֹא־זֶה הַדָּבָר
אֲשֶׁר דִּבַּרְנוּ אֵלֶיךָ בְמִצְרַיִם לֵאמֹר חֲדַל מִמֶּנּוּ וְנַעַבְדָה

**5–14.** The epic story of Israel's Redemption is now swiftly approaching its climax. The last chapters described Israel's final night in Egypt, with its panic for the Egyptians and rejoicing for the Israelites, when monarch and people alike hurried the children of Israel out of the land of bondage. But no sooner had Israel gone, than Pharaoh and his court regretted the act of emancipation. 'What have we done!' they exclaimed. There followed a swift marshalling of the cavalry and chariots of Egypt; and only a few days after being thrust out into freedom, the children of Israel beheld the hosts of Egypt in hot pursuit after them.

**5.** *turned toward the people.* They saw Goshen empty, the brickfields deserted, great works of Egypt stopped for want of slaves, and they regretted that the Israelites had been allowed to depart; see XII, 31 f.

**6.** *made ready.* lit. 'bound', *i.e.* attached the chariots to the horses; cf. Gen. XLVI, 29.

*his people with him. i.e.* his warriors; cf. Num. XXI, 23.

**8.** *with a high hand. i.e.* confidently and fearlessly.

**9.** *horsemen.* Probably charioteers. Rameses II is said to have had a force of 2,400 cavalry, independent of his chariots. Isaiah (XXXI, 1) makes the same distinction between the chariots and horsemen of Egypt.

**10.** *they were sore afraid.* 'It is very surprising that such a large host should be so terrified by an approaching enemy. But our astonishment ceases if we consider that the Egyptians had been the lords of the Hebrews, and that that generation had learned from their youth patiently to endure all insults which the Egyptians inflicted upon them. Thus had their minds become depressed and servile' (Ibn Ezra).

**11.** *because there were no graves in Egypt.* Is the bitter taunt of the Israelites. 'These words show the hand of the eye-witness of the events he relates' (Naville). Similar taunts were flung at their leader every time anything went wrong in regard to food, water or comfort.

**12.** *let us alone.* The Midrash indicates that not only were the people distracted by fear, but they were further demoralized by divided counsels. One group, frantic with despair, cried, Let us cast ourselves into the sea. Another group said, Let us go back to Egypt and submit to slavery. Other groups were for giving battle to the enemy.

EXODUS XIV, 13                      שמות בשלח יד

Egyptians? For it were better for us to serve the Egyptians, than that we should die in the wilderness.' 13. And Moses said unto the people: 'Fear ye not, stand still, and see the salvation of the LORD, which He will work for you to-day; for whereas ye have seen the Egyptians to-day, ye shall see them again no more for ever. 14. The LORD will fight for you, and ye shall hold your peace.'*¹¹¹ ᵃ· ¶ 15. And the LORD said unto Moses: 'Wherefore criest thou unto Me? speak unto the children of Israel, that they go forward. 16. And lift thou up thy rod, and stretch out thy hand over the sea, and divide it; and the children of Israel shall go into the midst of the sea on dry ground. 17. And I, behold, I will harden the hearts of the Egyptians, and they shall go in after them; and I will get Me honour upon Pharaoh, and upon all his host, upon his chariots, and upon his horsemen. 18. And the Egyptians shall know that I am the LORD when I have gotten Me honour upon Pharaoh, upon his chariots, and upon his horsemen.' 19. And the angel of God, who went before the camp of Israel, removed and went behind them; and the pillar of cloud removed from before them, and stood behind them; 20. and it came between the camp of Egypt and the camp of Israel; and there was the cloud and the darkness here, yet gave it light by night there; and the one came not near the other all the night. 21. And Moses stretched out his

אֶת־מִצְרַיִם כִּי טוֹב לָנוּ עֲבֹד אֶת־מִצְרַיִם מִמֻּתֵנוּ בַּמִּדְבָּר׃
13 וַיֹּאמֶר מֹשֶׁה אֶל־הָעָם אַל־תִּירָאוּ הִתְיַצְּבוּ וּרְאוּ אֶת־
יְשׁוּעַת יְהֹוָה אֲשֶׁר־יַעֲשֶׂה לָכֶם הַיּוֹם כִּי אֲשֶׁר רְאִיתֶם אֶת־
14 מִצְרַיִם הַיּוֹם לֹא תֹסִיפוּ לִרְאֹתָם עוֹד עַד־עוֹלָם׃ יְהֹוָה
יִלָּחֵם לָכֶם וְאַתֶּם תַּחֲרִישׁוּן׃      פ    שלישי
טו וַיֹּאמֶר יְהֹוָה אֶל־מֹשֶׁה מַה־תִּצְעַק אֵלָי דַּבֵּר אֶל־בְּנֵי־
16 יִשְׂרָאֵל וְיִסָּעוּ׃ וְאַתָּה הָרֵם אֶת־מַטְּךָ וּנְטֵה אֶת־יָדְךָ עַל־
הַיָּם וּבְקָעֵהוּ וְיָבֹאוּ בְנֵי־יִשְׂרָאֵל בְּתוֹךְ הַיָּם בַּיַּבָּשָׁה׃
17 וַאֲנִי הִנְנִי מְחַזֵּק אֶת־לֵב מִצְרַיִם וְיָבֹאוּ אַחֲרֵיהֶם וְאִכָּבְדָה
18 בְּפַרְעֹה וּבְכָל־חֵילוֹ בְּרִכְבּוֹ וּבְפָרָשָׁיו׃ וְיָדְעוּ מִצְרַיִם
19 כִּי־אֲנִי יְהֹוָה בְּהִכָּבְדִי בְּפַרְעֹה בְּרִכְבּוֹ וּבְפָרָשָׁיו׃ וַיִּסַּע
מַלְאַךְ הָאֱלֹהִים הַהֹלֵךְ לִפְנֵי מַחֲנֵה יִשְׂרָאֵל וַיֵּלֶךְ מֵאַחֲרֵיהֶם
כ וַיִּסַּע עַמּוּד הֶעָנָן מִפְּנֵיהֶם וַיַּעֲמֹד מֵאַחֲרֵיהֶם׃ וַיָּבֹא בֵּין ׀
מַחֲנֵה מִצְרַיִם וּבֵין מַחֲנֵה יִשְׂרָאֵל וַיְהִי הֶעָנָן וְהַחֹשֶׁךְ וַיָּאֶר
21 אֶת־הַלָּיְלָה וְלֹא־קָרַב זֶה אֶל־זֶה כָּל־הַלָּיְלָה׃ וַיֵּט מֹשֶׁה

v. 13. סבירין כאשר

**13.** *the salvation of the LORD.* A great expression, implying help, deliverance, welfare, and blessings Divine.

**14.** *ye shall hold your peace.* This was no time for giving wild expression to fear, but to await God's deliverance in quiet confidence.

**15.** *wherefore criest thou.* That moment of anguish called not for prayer but for action.
*go forward.* To the shore of the sea.

**16.** *and divide it.* 'We know that the rod did not divide the sea, but as soon as Moses stretched out his hand over the sea, God caused the sea to go back by a strong east wind' (Ibn Ezra).

**17.** *get Me honour.* See v. 4.

**18.** *Egyptians shall know.* The Egyptians who remain in Egypt will acknowledge Me as God, for I do not delight in the death of the sinner, but that he turn from his evil ways and live (Sforno).

**19.** *angel of God.* See note on XIII, 21.
*before the camp of Israel.* That is, the angel of God and the pillar of cloud, instead of being in front of the Israelites, as hitherto, now stand behind them. The pillar is the instrument of the angel. The second half of the verse, 'the pillar of cloud removed from before them, and stood behind them,' is synonymous with the first half of the verse.

**20.** *cloud and the darkness.* Heb. idiom for 'the dark cloud.'
*light by night.* To the Israelites. If there was a pillar of light and another of darkness, then the one enabled the Israelites to pass through the sea during that night, whilst the pillar of darkness stood before the Egyptians and hindered their movement. On the other hand, if we assume that there was only one pillar, then it was dark to the Egyptians and gave light to the Israelites.

**21.** *caused the sea to go back.* A strong east wind, blowing all night and acting with the ebbing tide, may have laid bare the neck of water joining the Bitter Lakes to the Red Sea, allowing the Israelites to cross in safety. 'As in all the wonders of Egypt, this also, the greatest of all, is based upon a natural cause; and in this the boundless power of God, who, by an insignificant change, knows how to convert the natural and common course of things into extraordinary and marvellous events, is sublimely manifest' (Kalisch).

EXODUS XIV, 22

hand over the sea; and the LORD caused the sea to go back by a strong east wind all the night, and made the sea dry land, and the waters were divided. 22. And the children of Israel went into the midst of the sea upon the dry ground; and the waters were a wall unto them on their right hand, and on their left. 23. And the Egyptians pursued, and went in after them into the midst of the sea, all Pharaoh's horses, his chariots, and his horsemen. 24. And it came to pass in the morning watch, that the LORD looked forth upon the host of the Egyptians through the pillar of fire and of cloud, and discomfited the host of the Egyptians. 25. And He took off their chariot wheels, and made them to drive heavily; so that the Egyptians said: 'Let us flee from the face of Israel; for the LORD fighteth for them against the Egyptians.'*¹¹¹ ˢ, ¹ᵛ ᵃ· ¶ 26. And the LORD said unto Moses: 'Stretch out thy hand over the sea, that the waters may come back upon the Egyptians, upon their chariots, and upon their horsemen.' 27. And Moses stretched forth his hand over the sea, and the sea returned to its strength when the morning appeared; and the Egyptians fled

שמות בשלח יד

אֶת־יָדוֹ עַל־הַיָּם וַיּוֹלֶךְ יְהוָה ׀ אֶת־הַיָּם בְּרוּחַ קָדִים עַזָּה
כָּל־הַלַּיְלָה וַיָּשֶׂם אֶת־הַיָּם לֶחָרָבָה וַיִּבָּקְעוּ הַמָּיִם: וַיָּבֹאוּ 22
בְנֵי־יִשְׂרָאֵל בְּתוֹךְ הַיָּם בַּיַּבָּשָׁה וְהַמַּיִם לָהֶם חוֹמָה מִימִינָם
וּמִשְּׂמֹאלָם: וַיִּרְדְּפוּ מִצְרַיִם וַיָּבֹאוּ אַחֲרֵיהֶם כֹּל סוּס 23
פַּרְעֹה רִכְבּוֹ וּפָרָשָׁיו אֶל־תּוֹךְ הַיָּם: וַיְהִי בְּאַשְׁמֹרֶת הַבֹּקֶר 24
וַיַּשְׁקֵף יְהוָה אֶל־מַחֲנֵה מִצְרַיִם בְּעַמּוּד אֵשׁ וְעָנָן וַיָּהָם אֶת
מַחֲנֵה מִצְרָיִם: וַיָּסַר אֵת אֹפַן מַרְכְּבֹתָיו וַיְנַהֲגֵהוּ בִּכְבֵדֻת כה
וַיֹּאמֶר מִצְרַיִם אָנוּסָה מִפְּנֵי יִשְׂרָאֵל כִּי יְהוָה נִלְחָם לָהֶם
בְּמִצְרָיִם: פ    רביעי (שלישי לספ׳)
וַיֹּאמֶר יְהוָה אֶל־מֹשֶׁה נְטֵה אֶת־יָדְךָ עַל־הַיָּם וְיָשֻׁבוּ הַמַּיִם 26
עַל־מִצְרַיִם עַל־רִכְבּוֹ וְעַל־פָּרָשָׁיו: וַיֵּט מֹשֶׁה אֶת־יָדוֹ 27
עַל־הַיָּם וַיָּשָׁב הַיָּם לִפְנוֹת בֹּקֶר לְאֵיתָנוֹ וּמִצְרַיִם נָסִים

---

**22.** *a wall unto them.* i.e. a protection and a defence. Pharaoh could not attack them on either flank, on account of the two bodies of water between which their march lay. He could only come at them by following after them (Rawlinson).

**24.** *in the morning watch.* From two to six in the morning. The night was divided into three 'watches'. The passage across the Red Sea was thus not effected in broad daylight but in the depth of the night.

*the LORD looked forth.* Metaphorical for lightning. One glance of God's eye sufficed to throw into hopeless confusion the enemies of His redeemed firstborn. An anthropomorphic expression, but most forcible. For a similar metaphor, see Amos IX, 4; Ps. CIV, 32.

*discomfited.* Threw into confusion. The text does not allude to the means whereby the panic of the Egyptians was produced. The Psalmist supplies this omission. 'The clouds flooded forth waters; the skies sent out a sound; Thine arrows also went abroad. The voice of Thy thunder was in the whirlwind; the lightnings lighted up the world; the earth trembled and shook... Thou didst lead Thy people like a flock, by the hand of Moses and Aaron' (LXXVII, 18–21). There was a hurricane raging with tornado force, causing the sea to go back, amidst a darkness lit up only by the glare of lightning, as 'the LORD looked out' from the black skies.

**25.** *and He took off.* The Egyptians were hindered in their pursuit, because the lightning struck the chariot-wheels, and slew the Egyptian warriors who commanded the chariots (Rashi).

*drive heavily.* The wheels stuck fast in the loose wet sand.

*the Egyptians said.* One to another. The Heb. is in the singular, 'And Egypt said.'

*the LORD fighteth for them.* At last the Egyptians realize against Whom they are fighting.

**26.** *may come back.* 'A sudden cessation of the wind, possibly coinciding with a spring tide (it was full moon), would immediately convert the low flat sandbanks first into a quicksand, and then into a mass of waters, in a time far less than would suffice for the escape of a single chariot' (F. C. Cook).

**27.** *its strength.* Or, 'its wonted flow.'

*fled against it.* Better, *were fleeing towards it* (Rashi). Terror maddened them, and instead of fleeing from the waters, they ran towards them.

**28.** *after them.* i.e. the Israelites.

*not so much as one of them.* Escape was impossible; see Ps. CXXXVI, 15. According to some Rabbis, Pharaoh alone escaped. Later Jewish legend adds that he never died, and never will die. He stands at the portals of

EXODUS XIV, 28

against it; and the LORD overthrew the Egyptians in the midst of the sea. 28. And the waters returned, and covered the chariots, and the horsemen, even all the host of Pharaoh that went in after them into the sea; there remained not so much as one of them. 29. But the children of Israel walked upon dry land in the midst of the sea; and the waters were a wall unto them on their right hand, and on their left. 30. Thus the LORD saved Israel that day out of the hand of the Egyptians; and Israel saw the Egyptians dead upon the sea-shore. 31. And Israel saw the great work which the LORD did upon the Egyptians, and the people feared the LORD; and they believed in the LORD, and in His servant Moses.

**15** CHAPTER XV

1. Then sang Moses and the children of Israel this song unto the LORD, and spoke, saying:

I will sing unto the LORD, for He is highly exalted;
The horse and his rider hath He thrown into the sea.

---

Gehinnom and, when heathen tyrants enter, he greets them with the words: 'Why have ye not profited by my example?'

**29.** *dry land.* Dry ground.

**30.** *the LORD saved Israel.* It was not a victory in which a feeling of pride or self-exaltation could enter. Unlike any other nation that has thrown off the yoke of slavery, neither Israel nor its leader claimed any merit of glory for the victory. In the *Haggadah shel Pesach*, the story of the Redemption is told without any reference to the Leader. Once only, indirectly in a quotation, does the name Moses occur at all in the whole Seder Service!

*Egyptians dead upon the sea-shore.* The fact that the Egyptians had to perish mars the completeness of Israel's victory. 'When the Egyptian hosts were drowning in the Red Sea,' say the Rabbis, 'the angels in heaven were about to break forth into songs of jubilation. But the Holy One, blessed be He, silenced them with the words, "My creatures are perishing, and ye are ready to sing!"' In the same spirit, a medieval rabbi explained why a drop of wine is poured out of the wine-cup on Seder eve at the mention of each of the plagues that were inflicted on the Egyptians. Israel's cup of joy, he said, cannot be full if Israel's triumph involves suffering even to its enemies.

**31.** *the great work.* lit. 'the great hand', i.e. power, achievement.

*believed in the LORD, and in His servant Moses.* 'An experience such as the Exodus, and the passage through the Red Sea, must have been reckoned by all who participated in them as a direct act of God. Moses was thereby authenticated in the eyes of his people' (Kittel). Their new-born faith in God, and their witnessing of His marvellous help, led to the wonderful outburst of song in the next chapter. Whenever Israel has faith in God and in the Divine Mission of Moses, Israel sings.

CHAPTER XV. THE SONG AT THE RED SEA

**1–21.** This Song, notable for poetic fire, vivid imagery and quick movement, gives remarkable expression to the mingled horror, triumph and gratitude that the hosts of Israel had lived through during the fateful hours when they were in sight of Pharaoh's pursuing hosts. In Jewish literature it is spoken of as the Song, שירה, and the Sabbath on which it is read in the Synagogue as שבת שירה.

**1.** *Moses and the children of Israel.* Moses composed the Song, and the Israelites joined their Leader in praising God. From *v.* 20 and 21, it appears that there was musical accompaniment, with male and female choruses. It is probably the oldest song of national triumph extant.

*unto the LORD.* In His honour.

*for He is highly exalted.* Or, 'for He hath triumphed gloriously.'

*the horse and his rider hath He thrown into the sea.* In four Heb. words is the complete ruin of the military power of Egypt described. 'Its chariots and horses, the mainstay of its strength, are, by Divine might, cast irretrievably into the sea' (Driver).

270

## EXODUS XV, 2

2. The Lord is my strength and song,
And He is become my salvation;
This is my God, and I will glorify Him;
My father's God, and I will exalt Him.

3. The Lord is a man of war,
The Lord is His name.

4. Pharaoh's chariots and his host hath He cast into the sea,
And his chosen captains are sunk in the Red Sea.

5. The deeps cover them—
They went down into the depths like a stone.

6. Thy right hand, O Lord, glorious in power,
Thy right hand, O Lord, dasheth in pieces the enemy.

7. And in the greatness of Thine excellency Thou overthrowest them that rise up against Thee;
Thou sendest forth Thy wrath, it consumeth them as stubble.

8. And with the blast of Thy nostrils the waters were piled up—
The floods stood upright as a heap;
The deeps were congealed in the heart of the sea.

9. The enemy said:
'I will pursue, I will overtake, I will divide the spoil;
My lust shall be satisfied upon them;
I will draw my sword, my hand shall destroy them.'

---

**2.** *the* LORD. Heb. *Yah*, the shortened form of the Tetragrammaton, as in *Hallelujah* (lit. 'praise ye Yah').

*my strength and song.* He is the source of my strength and the theme of my song.

*and He is become my salvation.* lit. 'and He is become to me a salvation', *i.e.* the source of deliverance.

*this is my God.* Who has saved me. The redeemed at the Red Sea had a unique realization of the Presence and of the present help of God. The Rabbis say, 'A maidservant at the Red Sea had a more vivid and vitalizing experience of the Divine than many a prophet.'

*and I will glorify Him.* The rendering, 'I will prepare him an habitation' (AV), follows Onkelos and the Rabbis, who translate, 'I shall build Thee a sanctuary.'

*my father's God.* The continuity of worship among the children of the Patriarchs is emphasized here. The God of tradition has justified Himself by redeeming Israel. The promises made to the forefathers have now been fulfilled. 'My father's God' stands here for 'the God of my fathers'; see III, 6.

**3.** *the* LORD *is a man of war.* God has fought the battle of His persecuted children and overthrown the cruel oppressor.

*the* LORD *is His name.* 'For He has wrought justice' (Rashbam); see note on VI, 3.

**4.** *his chosen captains.* lit. 'the choice of his captains', *i.e.* the flower of his warriors.

**5.** *cover them.* lit. 'are covering them.' The Heb. verb is in the imperfect tense, and graphically describes the event as if taking place before the eyes of the singers.

**6.** *Thy right hand. i.e.* the power of God.

**7.** *excellency.* Better, *majesty*.

**8.** *blast of Thy nostrils.* Is the poetical version of XIV, 22–23. Used figuratively for the wind.

*stood upright as a heap.* See XIV, 23. The fine poetic image is sustained throughout the verse. The effect of the wind was to pile up the waters into a wall-like formation.

**9.** *I will pursue, I will overtake, I will divide the spoil.* A magnificent specimen of Hebrew poetry. The short crisp words express the eagerness of the exultant foe, and his assurance of complete victory.

*my lust.* lit. 'my soul', which in Heb. psychology is the seat of *desire*, here for vengeance and plunder.

## EXODUS XV, 10

10. Thou didst blow with Thy wind, the sea covered them;
They sank as lead in the mighty waters.

11. Who is like unto Thee, O Lord, among the mighty?
Who is like unto Thee, glorious in holiness,
Fearful in praises, doing wonders?

12. Thou stretchedst out Thy right hand—
The earth swallowed them.

13. Thou in Thy love has led the people that Thou hast redeemed;
Thou hast guided them in Thy strength to Thy holy habitation.

14. The peoples have heard, they tremble;
Pangs have taken hold on the inhabitants of Philistia.

15. Then were the chiefs of Edom affrighted;
The mighty men of Moab, trembling taketh hold upon them;
All the inhabitants of Canaan are melted away.

16. Terror and dread falleth upon them;
By the greatness of Thine arm they are as still as a stone;
Till Thy people pass over, O Lord,
Till the people pass over that Thou hast gotten.

---

**11.** *glorious in holiness.* Exalted in the majesty of holiness, which is the essential distinguishing attribute of the God of Israel.

*fearful in praises.* Or, 'revered in praises,' i.e. praiseworthy acts; inspiring awe by the mighty deeds for which His people are to praise Him.

**12.** *Thou stretchedst out Thy right hand.* As a man puts forth his hand to indicate his will to his servants (Luzzatto).

**13.** *Thou in Thy love.* God at the same time shows his abounding love to those who had been persecuted by the Egyptians.

*hast led.* Better, *leadest*. The verbs of this and the following verses are, according to the sense, futures. In v. 16 the text itself passes over into the future tense.

*Thou hast guided.* Better, *thou guidest them*, gently as a shepherd leads his flock. 'The following part of the Song describes in prophetic images the providence of God for the Israelites, shielding them till they have overcome the dangers of the desert, conquered the nations of Canaan, and erected the sanctuary on Zion' (Kalisch).

*Thy holy habitation.* Mount Sinai, on which God's glory abode when Moses received the Torah (Ibn Ezra); or the Temple on Mount Moriah. Rashbam considers that Canaan is meant here, as it is sometimes called 'the habitation of God'; see Ps. CXXXII, 13.

**14.** *peoples have heard.* The story of God's miracles on behalf of Israel. The defeat of the Egyptians would be a source of terror to the heathens who hear the report; see Josh. II, 9–11.

*they tremble.* lit. 'are trembling'. The poet sees the nations trembling at the approach of God's people (Luzzatto).

*pangs.* As of childbirth.

*Philistia.* See XIII, 17.

**15.** *chiefs of Edom affrighted.* Edom embraced the ranges of Mount Seir on either side of the Arabah, the depression which runs southward from the Dead Sea to the head of the Gulf of Akabah.

*mighty men of Moab.* Moab was the high tableland east of the Dead Sea and the southernmost section of the Jordan.

*are melted away.* fig. for, 'are helpless through terror and despair'; cf. Josh. II, 9, 24.

**16.** *terror and dread falleth upon them.* Or, 'let terror and dread fall upon them . . . let them be still as a stone' (Septuagint).

*of Thine arm.* Of Thy power.

*pass over.* On their way to Canaan.

*hast gotten.* lit. 'hast purchased'; God acquired Israel by redeeming them from the power of Pharaoh.

EXODUS XV, 17

17. Thou bringest them in, and plantest them in the mountain of Thine inheritance,
The place, O LORD, which Thou hast made for Thee to dwell in,
The sanctuary, O LORD, which Thy hands have established.

18. The LORD shall reign for ever and ever.

19. For the horses of Pharaoh went in with his chariots and with his horsemen into the sea, and the LORD brought back the waters of the sea upon them; but the children of Israel walked on dry land in the midst of the sea. ¶ 20. And Miriam the prophetess, the sister of Aaron, took a timbrel in her hand; and all the women went out after her with timbrels and with dances. 21. And Miriam sang unto them:

Sing ye to the LORD, for He is highly exalted:
The horse and his rider hath He thrown into the sea.

¶ 22. And Moses led Israel onward from the Red Sea, and they went out into the wilderness of Shur; and they went three days in

שמות בשלח טו

16 כָּל־יֹשְׁבֵי כְנָעַן׃ תִּפֹּל עֲלֵיהֶם אֵימָתָה
וָפַחַד בִּגְדֹל זְרוֹעֲךָ יִדְּמוּ כָּאָבֶן עַד־
יַעֲבֹר עַמְּךָ יְהוָה עַד־יַעֲבֹר עַם־זוּ
17 קָנִיתָ׃ תְּבִאֵמוֹ וְתִטָּעֵמוֹ בְּהַר נַחֲלָתְךָ מָכוֹן
לְשִׁבְתְּךָ פָּעַלְתָּ יְהוָה מִקְּדָשׁ אֲדֹנָי כּוֹנְנוּ
18 יָדֶיךָ׃ יְהוָה ׀ יִמְלֹךְ לְעֹלָם וָעֶד׃ כִּי
19 בָא סוּס פַּרְעֹה בְּרִכְבּוֹ וּבְפָרָשָׁיו בַּיָּם וַיָּשֶׁב יְהוָה עֲלֵהֶם
אֶת־מֵי הַיָּם וּבְנֵי יִשְׂרָאֵל הָלְכוּ בַיַּבָּשָׁה בְּתוֹךְ הַיָּם׃ פ
כ וַתִּקַּח מִרְיָם הַנְּבִיאָה אֲחוֹת אַהֲרֹן אֶת־הַתֹּף בְּיָדָהּ וַתֵּצֶאןָ
21 כָל־הַנָּשִׁים אַחֲרֶיהָ בְּתֻפִּים וּבִמְחֹלֹת׃ וַתַּעַן לָהֶם מִרְיָם
שִׁירוּ לַיהוָה כִּי־גָאֹה גָּאָה סוּס וְרֹכְבוֹ רָמָה בַיָּם׃ ס
22 וַיַּסַּע מֹשֶׁה אֶת־יִשְׂרָאֵל מִיַּם־סוּף וַיֵּצְאוּ אֶל־מִדְבַּר־שׁוּר

v. 16. כ׳ דגושה v. 17. ק׳ דגושה v. 21. ג׳ דגושה

**17.** *Thou bringest them in.* The final goal of Israel's triumphant progress was to be the land of Canaan, promised to the forefathers.
*mountain of Thine inheritance.* i.e. Canaan, and thus spoken of owing to the mountainous character of many of its most important parts; cf. Deut. III, 25; Is. XI, 9; Ps. LXXVIII, 54 (with allusion to this passage).
*the sanctuary.* Mount Moriah is probably referred to here.
*have established.* To stand firm; see Ps. XLVIII, 9.

**18.** *the LORD shall reign for ever and ever.* The Song closes, not with the conquest of material domains, but with the promise of the Kingdom of God. This is the climax. The redemption from Egypt was to be followed by the Revelation on Mount Sinai, when God's Kingdom on earth was inaugurated. That Kingdom is eternal.

**19.** This verse does not belong to the Song. It is a summary of the great event culminating in the Song of victory, and forms the transition to the following narrative.
*for the horses of Pharaoh.* It is better to combine this and the following verse; thus, *when the horses of Pharaoh went in ... but the children of Israel walked on dry land in the midst of the sea, Miriam the prophetess ... took* (Rashi, Mendelssohn).

**20.** *the prophetess.* See Num. XII, 2, and cf. Judg. IV, 4.

*sister of Aaron.* Miriam being more closely associated with Aaron than with Moses; see Num. XII, 1 f.
*went out after her.* She led the women in the praise of God.
*dances.* See II Sam. VI, 14 and Ps. CXLIX, 3. In the East, dancing was, and is, part of the language of religion.

**21.** *sang unto them.* i.e. answered as a chorus; see I Sam. XVIII, 7. Miriam sang, and the women responded (Luzzatto).

THE JOURNEY TO SINAI

**22–27.** Israel at Marah and Elim.

**22.** *led Israel onward.* lit. 'made Israel to journey'.
*the wilderness of Shur.* The district of the N.E. frontier of Egypt, see Gen. XVI, 7 and XXV, 18. Along the coast of the Gulf of Suez is a strip of level country: the northern part is called the wilderness of Shur; the southern, the wilderness of Sin.
The station where Moses and the Israelites halted after their passage of the Red Sea is believed by the Arabs to be Ayun Musa, 'the springs of Moses,' 9 miles below Suez, on the east side of the Gulf, and 1½ miles from the coast.
*three days.* About 45 miles would thus be covered by a caravan, travelling with baggage.

EXODUS XV, 23

the wilderness, and found no water. 23. And when they came to Marah, they could not drink of the waters of Marah, for they were bitter. Therefore the name of it was called ¹Marah. 24. And the people murmured against Moses, saying: 'What shall we drink?' 25. And he cried unto the LORD; and the LORD showed him a tree, and he cast it into the waters, and the waters were made sweet. There He made for them a statute and an ordinance, and there He proved them; 26. and He said: 'If thou wilt diligently hearken to the voice of the LORD thy God, and wilt do that which is right in His eyes, and wilt give ear to His commandments, and keep all His statutes, I will put none of the diseases upon thee, which I have put upon the Egyptians; for I am the LORD that healeth thee.'* ⁱᵛ ˢ, ᵛ ᵃ· ¶ 27. And they came to Elim, where were twelve springs of water, and three score and ten palm-trees; and they encamped there by the waters.

## 16  CHAPTER XVI

1. And they took their journey from Elim, and all the congregation of the children of Israel came unto the wilderness of Sin, which is between Elim and Sinai, on the fifteenth day of the second month after their departing out of the land of Egypt. 2. And the whole congregation of the children of Israel murmured against Moses

¹ That is, *Bitterness*.

**23.** *Marah*. Has been identified by some with Bir Huwara, about 47 miles S.E. of Ayun Musa, and 7 miles from the coast, on the usual route to Mt. Sinai. Others identify Marah with 'Ain Naba' (also called el-Churkudeh), a fountain with a considerable supply of brackish water, about 10 miles S.E. of Suez, and 50 miles from Lake Timsah.

**25.** *the LORD showed him a tree*. There are certain shrubs that sweeten bitter water.
*a statute and an ordinance*. The moral and social basis of the Hebrew Law is here taught the people in connection with the sweetening of the bitter waters. God set before them the fundamental principle of implicit faith in His providence, to be shown by willing obedience to His will. The healing of the bitter waters was a symbol of the Divine deliverance from all evils.
*there He proved them*. Man is tried by the gifts of God, and also by the lack of them.

**26.** *diligently hearken*. At Marah the Israelites found themselves threatened with one of the plagues of Egypt, undrinkable water. God delivered them from this; and similarly, if they were obedient, He would protect them from the diseases which had afflicted the Egyptians.

*that healeth thee*. lit. 'thy physician'. 'A master demands obedience in order to assert his own authority. A physician likewise demands obedience, but only for the purpose of securing the patient's welfare. Such are the statutes of the Lord, our Physician' (Malbim).

**27.** *Elim*. lit. 'terebinths'. Often identified with Wady Gherandel, which is situated two and a half miles north of Tor, in a very beautiful valley, with excellent fountains and many palm trees.

### CHAPTER XVI, 1–36. THE MANNA

**1.** *the wilderness of Sin*. See on xv, 22.
*fifteenth day of the second month*. i.e. one month after the departure from Egypt.

**2.** *murmured*. The moment that the want of food was felt. The fact that these constant murmurings of the people are recorded is evidence for 'the historic truthfulness of the narratives of the wanderings. A purely ideal picture of the Chosen People would have omitted them. They also serve to display the wonderful personality of Moses, who could control, pacify, and lead such a collection of rude nomad tribes' (McNeile).

274

EXODUS XVI, 3

and against Aaron in the wilderness; 3. and the children of Israel said unto them: 'Would that we had died by the hand of the LORD in the land of Egypt, when we sat by the flesh-pots, when we did eat bread to the full; for ye have brought us forth into this wilderness, to kill this whole assembly with hunger.' ¶ 4. Then said the LORD unto Moses: 'Behold, I will cause to rain bread from heaven for you; and the people shall go out and gather a day's portion every day, that I may prove them, whether they will walk in My law or not. 5. And it shall come to pass on the sixth day that they shall prepare that which they bring in, and it shall be twice as much as they gather daily.' 6. And Moses and Aaron said unto all the children of Israel: 'At even, then ye shall know that the LORD hath brought you out from the land of Egypt; 7. and in the morning, then ye shall see the glory of the LORD; for that He hath heard your murmurings against the LORD; and what are we, that ye murmur against us?' 8. And Moses said: 'This shall be, when the LORD shall give you in the evening flesh to eat, and in the morning bread to the full; for that the LORD heareth your murmurings which ye murmur against Him; and what are we? your murmurings are not against us, but against the LORD.' 9. And Moses said unto Aaron: 'Say unto all the congregation of the children of Israel: Come near before the LORD; for He hath heard your murmurings.' 10. And it came to pass, as Aaron spoke unto the whole congregation of the children of Israel, that they looked toward the wilderness,

3. *sat by the flesh-pots.* They remembered the bread and the flesh-pots, but not the slavery. Some commentators infer from this that the Israelites in Egypt must have had a good and full diet. Such inference is quite unwarranted. The pangs of hunger cause them to look back upon their slave-fare, served to them from pots large enough to supply a whole gang, as the height of luxury.

4. *prove them.* The food that God will send will save them from hunger, but the manner in which it will be given will test their faith and obedience.

5. *the sixth day.* Of the week, *i.e.* Friday.
*they shall prepare.* As no cooking was to take place on the Sabbath.
*twice as much.* As the supply will be more abundant on the sixth day, every one will gather more, and when they come to prepare it, they will find that it is just twice as much as they gather usually.

6. *the LORD hath brought you out.* And not Moses and Aaron, as you have falsely said; see *v.* 3.
*at even.* The gift of the quails would take place; see *v.* 8.

7. *and in the morning.* They would have the bread from heaven.
*see the glory of the LORD.* Manifested by the wonderful gift of the manna (Rashi, Luzzatto).
*murmurings against the LORD.* Really against Moses and Aaron, but they were merely the servants of God.

8. *this shall be.* *i.e.* the fulfilment of the promise referred to in *v.* 6 and 7, is about to take place.

10. *toward the wilderness.* In the direction of the impending journey (Strack).
*the glory of the LORD.* Cf. XIII, 21 f. The Glory of God was 'a certain light', also called 'Divine light' (Maimonides). Perhaps the cloud shrouded the full brilliancy of the Divine Light.

## EXODUS XVI, 11

שמות בשלח טז

וְהִנֵּה כְּבוֹד יְהֹוָה נִרְאָה בֶּעָנָן: פ ששי (חמישי לסם׳)

11 וַיְדַבֵּר יְהֹוָה אֶל־מֹשֶׁה לֵּאמֹר: שָׁמַעְתִּי אֶת־תְּלוּנֹּת בְּנֵי
12 יִשְׂרָאֵל דַּבֵּר אֲלֵהֶם לֵאמֹר בֵּין הָעַרְבַּיִם תֹּאכְלוּ בָשָׂר
וּבַבֹּקֶר תִּשְׂבְּעוּ־לָחֶם וִידַעְתֶּם כִּי אֲנִי יְהֹוָה אֱלֹהֵיכֶם:

13 וַיְהִי בָעֶרֶב וַתַּעַל הַשְּׂלָו וַתְּכַס אֶת־הַמַּחֲנֶה וּבַבֹּקֶר הָיְתָה
14 שִׁכְבַת הַטָּל סָבִיב לַמַּחֲנֶה: וַתַּעַל שִׁכְבַת הַטָּל וְהִנֵּה
עַל־פְּנֵי הַמִּדְבָּר דַּק מְחֻסְפָּס דַּק כַּכְּפֹר עַל־הָאָרֶץ:

15 וַיִּרְאוּ בְנֵי־יִשְׂרָאֵל וַיֹּאמְרוּ אִישׁ אֶל־אָחִיו מָן הוּא כִּי לֹא
יָדְעוּ מַה־הוּא וַיֹּאמֶר מֹשֶׁה אֲלֵהֶם הוּא הַלֶּחֶם אֲשֶׁר נָתַן
16 יְהֹוָה לָכֶם לְאָכְלָה: זֶה הַדָּבָר אֲשֶׁר צִוָּה יְהֹוָה לִקְטוּ
מִמֶּנּוּ אִישׁ לְפִי אָכְלוֹ עֹמֶר לַגֻּלְגֹּלֶת מִסְפַּר נַפְשֹׁתֵיכֶם
17 אִישׁ לַאֲשֶׁר בְּאָהֳלוֹ תִּקָּחוּ: וַיַּעֲשׂוּ־כֵן בְּנֵי יִשְׂרָאֵל וַיִּלְקְטוּ
18 הַמַּרְבֶּה וְהַמַּמְעִיט: וַיָּמֹדּוּ בָעֹמֶר וְלֹא הֶעְדִּיף הַמַּרְבֶּה
19 וְהַמַּמְעִיט לֹא הֶחְסִיר אִישׁ לְפִי־אָכְלוֹ לָקָטוּ: וַיֹּאמֶר
כ מֹשֶׁה אֲלֵהֶם אִישׁ אַל־יוֹתֵר מִמֶּנּוּ עַד־בֹּקֶר: וְלֹא־שָׁמְעוּ

v. 12. ג׳ דגש אחר ת״ג v. 13. השליו ק׳

and, behold, the glory of the LORD appeared in the cloud.* v 8, vI a. 11. And the LORD spoke unto Moses, saying: 12. 'I have heard the murmurings of the children of Israel. Speak unto them, saying: At dusk ye shall eat flesh, and in the morning ye shall be filled with bread; and ye shall know that I am the LORD your God.' 13. And it came to pass at even, that the quails came up, and covered the camp; and in the morning there was a layer of dew round about the camp. 14. And when the layer of dew was gone up, behold upon the face of the wilderness a fine, scale-like thing, fine as the hoar-frost on the ground. 15. And when the children of Israel saw it, they said one to another: [1]"What is it?"—for they knew not what it was. And Moses said unto them: 'It is the bread which the LORD hath given you to eat. 16. This is the thing which the LORD hath commanded: Gather ye of it every man according to his eating; an omer a head, according to the number of your persons, shall ye take it, every man for them that are in his tent.' 17. And the children of Israel did so, and gathered some more, some less. 18. And when they did mete it with an omer, he that gathered much had nothing over, and he that gathered little had no lack; they gathered every man according to his eating. 19. And Moses said unto them: 'Let no man leave of it till the morning.' 20. Notwithstanding they

[1] Heb. *Man hu.*

---

**12.** *that I am the* LORD *your God.* Who not only hears your murmuring, but can supply all your wants.

**13.** *the quails came up.* Quails are migratory birds, coming in the spring in immense numbers from Arabia and other southern countries. They are nowhere more common than in the neighbourhood of the Red Sea. They always fly with the wind; and when exhausted after a long flight, they are easily captured even with the hand. 'The gift of quails, unlike the gift of manna, was limited to the one occasion here mentioned' (Abarbanel).

*in the morning.* Following the night when the quails appeared.

**14.** *was gone up.* Had risen or evaporated.

*a fine, scale-like thing. i.e.* the manna. According to Rashi, and other Jewish commentators, first dew had fallen, then manna over the dew, and then dew again over the manna. Consequently the manna was enclosed between two layers of dew.

**15.** *what is it?* Or, 'It is manna' (RV Margin). The Heb. word *man* may really be Egyptian (Rashbam, Ebers); the translation would then be, 'They said one to another, It is *man*, for they knew not what it was'; *i.e.* they called it by the name of the substance that resembled it most in appearance, and was well known to them in Egypt. The Arabs give the name *man* to a sweet, sticky, honey-like juice, exuding in heavy drops, in May or June, from a shrub found in the Sinai peninsula. This, however, is found only in small quantities and does not correspond to the description given in our text, where the manna is clearly a miraculous substance. God in His ever-sustaining providence fed Israel's hosts during the weary years of wandering in His own unsearchable way.

*the bread.* The food.

**16.** *this is the thing.* The commandment concerning the manna.

*an omer.* A measure, less than two quarts.

**18.** *when they did mete it.* However much or little the individual gathered, when he measured it in his tent, he found that there was just an *omer* apiece for his family.

**20.** *Moses was wroth.* Because of their disobedience and lack of faith in God's loving providence.

276

# EXODUS XVI, 21 שמות בשלח טז

hearkened not unto Moses; but some of them left of it until the morning, and it bred worms, and rotted; and Moses was wroth with them. 21. And they gathered it morning by morning, every man according to his eating; and as the sun waxed hot, it melted. 22. And it came to pass that on the sixth day they gathered twice as much bread, two omers for each one; and all the rulers of the congregation came and told Moses. 23. And he said unto them: 'This is that which the LORD hath spoken: To-morrow is a solemn rest, a holy sabbath unto the LORD. Bake that which ye will bake, and seethe that which ye will seethe; and all that remaineth over lay up for you to be kept until the morning.' 24. And they laid it up till the morning, as Moses bade; and it did not rot, neither was there any worm therein. 25. And Moses said: 'Eat that to-day; for to-day is a sabbath unto the LORD; to-day ye shall not find it in the field. 26. Six days ye shall gather it; but on the seventh day is the sabbath, in it there shall be none.' 27. And it came to pass on the seventh day, that there went out some of the people to gather, and they found none. 28. And the LORD said unto Moses: 'How long refuse ye to keep My commandments and My laws? 29. See that the LORD hath given you the sabbath; therefore He giveth you on the sixth day the bread of two days; abide ye every man in his place, let no man go out of his place on the seventh day.' 30. So the people rested on the seventh day.* ⱽᴵ ˢ· 31. And the house of Israel called the name thereof ¹Manna; and it was like coriander seed, white; and the

¹ Heb. *Man*.

**23.** *the* LORD *hath spoken*. With reference to the Sabbath.

*holy sabbath unto the* LORD. The seventh day must have been known to the people as a special day, distinct from the other days of the week. The children of the Patriarchs had brought with them to Egypt the tradition that God had completed His work of creation in six days, and that He had sanctified the seventh day. At Mt. Sinai, therefore, the children of Israel are bidden, 'Remember the Sabbath day.'

*bake that which ye will bake*. On the Friday. What was not eaten on the Friday was to be kept for the Sabbath day.

**27.** *there went out some of the people*. Not because they were lacking food, for they had gathered a double portion on the previous day; but because they doubted the word of Moses.

**28.** *how long refuse ye*. The rebuke is addressed to Moses as the representative of the people.

**29.** *abide ye*. i.e. do not go out in order to gather manna.

*go out of his place*. To gather manna on the Sabbath. Rabbinical tradition has deduced from this context the prohibition, that no Israelite shall go more than 2,000 yards from the place of his abode. This is called the תחום שבת 'the Sabbath journey'. Travelling interrupts the rest both of man and of his beast, and was therefore to be avoided on the Sabbath day.

**31.** *house of Israel*. An unusual expression for 'the children of Israel'; see XL, 38; Num. XX, 29.

*like coriander seed, white*. The coriander plant grows wild in Palestine and Egypt, producing small greyish-white seeds, with a pleasant spicy flavour.

*wafers made with honey*. Cf. Num. XI, 8, 'the taste of it was as the taste of a cake baked with oil.' Jewish tradition says that the manna contained the ingredients of every delicious food, and suited the taste of all who partook thereof.

**32-36.** Various commands relating to the manna.

## EXODUS XVI, 32

taste of it was like wafers made with honey. 32. And Moses said: 'This is the thing which the LORD hath commanded: Let an omerful of it be kept throughout your generations; that they may see the bread wherewith I fed you in the wilderness, when I brought you forth from the land of Egypt.' 33. And Moses said unto Aaron: 'Take a jar, and put an omerful of manna therein, and lay it up before the LORD, to be kept throughout your generations.' 34. As the LORD commanded Moses, so Aaron laid it up before the Testimony, to be kept. 35. And the children of Israel did eat the manna forty years, until they came to a land inhabited; they did eat the manna, until they came unto the borders of the land of Canaan. 36. Now an omer is the tenth part of an ephah.* vii.

## 17  CHAPTER XVII

1. And all the congregation of the children of Israel journeyed from the wilderness of Sin, by their stages, according to the commandment of the LORD, and encamped in Rephidim; and there was no water for the people to drink. 2. Wherefore the people strove with Moses, and said: 'Give us water

---

**32.** *throughout your generations.* i.e. for posterity.

*they may see the bread.* And derive the spiritual lessons connected therewith; e.g. trust in God, belief in the providence and mercy of God.

**33.** *take a jar.* Of earthenware (Rashi).

*lay it up before the LORD.* i.e. before the Ark of the Testimony, in the Tabernacle. Ibn Ezra says that this section should come after the story of the erection of the Tabernacle; and Luzzatto suggests that Moses wrote v. 33–35 in the fortieth year of the wandering in the wilderness. It is well to keep in mind the Rabbinical saying, that the events in Scripture are not always arranged in strict chronological order. אין מוקדם ומאוחר בתורה. Sometimes an *inner connection* causes events wide apart in time to be mentioned together in one chapter.

**34.** *the Testimony.* i.e. the Ark, so called because of the Tables on which the Ten Commandments (spoken of as 'the Testimony' in XXV, 22, XXXI, 18) were engraved.

**35.** *forty years.* This does not lead the narrative beyond the time of Moses, and there is no reason why Moses could not have written it just before his death.

*to a land inhabited.* Canaan, so called in contrast to the desert.

*unto the borders of the land of Canaan.* This was the limit of the wanderings under the leadership of Moses. Moses gives the complete history of the manna up to the end of his own life. He does not state that the manna ceased; because the manna was not withheld until after the death of Moses, when the Israelites had passed the Jordan under Joshua (Josh. v, 12).

**36.** *an ephah.* The name of a measure well known to the people, whereas the name *omer* was not known (Abarbanel). This seems to be supported by the fact that the Torah does not employ the name *omer* as a measure anywhere outside this chapter.

### CHAPTER XVII

#### 1–7. WATER FROM THE ROCK IN HOREB

**1.** *by their stages.* Or, 'journeys.' The route was as follows: the wilderness of Sin, Dophkah, Alush, Rephidim: see Num. XXXIII, 12–14. The various stages are omitted, as it is not the intention of Scripture here to enumerate the different places where the Israelites halted. Its purpose is to narrate the occasions when the people murmured (Biur).

*Rephidim.* Either the upper part of the broad and long oasis of Feiran, the most fertile part of the Peninsula of Sinai, or the narrow defile el-Watiyeh, 27 miles beyond Feiran.

**2.** *give us water.* The Heb. for 'give' is in the plural, and refers to Moses and Aaron.

*try the LORD.* Heb. *nissah* means to *test* or *prove* a person, to see *whether* he will act in a particular way, or *whether* the character he bears is well established (Driver).

EXODUS XVII, 3

that we may drink.' And Moses said unto them: 'Why strive ye with me? wherefore do ye try the LORD?' 3. And the people thirsted there for water; and the people murmured against Moses, and said: 'Wherefore hast thou brought us up out of Egypt, to kill us and our children and our cattle with thirst?' 4. And Moses cried unto the LORD, saying: 'What shall I do unto this people? they are almost ready to stone me.' 5. And the LORD said unto Moses: 'Pass on before the people, and take with thee of the elders of Israel; and thy rod, wherewith thou smotest the river, take in thy hand, and go. 6. Behold, I will stand before thee there upon the rock in Horeb; and thou shalt smite the rock, and there shall come water out of it, that the people may drink.' And Moses did so in the sight of the elders of Israel. 7. And the name of the place was called ¹Massah, and ²Meribah, because of the striving of the children of Israel, and because they tried the LORD, saying: 'Is the LORD among us, or not?' ¶ 8. Then came Amalek, and fought

שמות בשלח יז

הָעָם עִם־מֹשֶׁה וַיֹּאמְרוּ תְּנוּ־לָנוּ מַיִם וְנִשְׁתֶּה וַיֹּאמֶר לָהֶם
מֹשֶׁה מַה־תְּרִיבוּן עִמָּדִי מַה־תְּנַסּוּן אֶת־יְהוָה: וַיִּצְמָא שָׁם 3
הָעָם לַמַּיִם וַיָּלֶן הָעָם עַל־מֹשֶׁה וַיֹּאמֶר לָמָּה זֶּה הֶעֱלִיתָנוּ
מִמִּצְרַיִם לְהָמִית אֹתִי וְאֶת־בָּנַי וְאֶת־מִקְנַי בַּצָּמָא: וַיִּצְעַק 4
מֹשֶׁה אֶל־יְהוָה לֵאמֹר מָה אֶעֱשֶׂה לָעָם הַזֶּה עוֹד מְעַט
וּסְקָלֻנִי: וַיֹּאמֶר יְהוָה אֶל־מֹשֶׁה עֲבֹר לִפְנֵי הָעָם וְקַח ה
אִתְּךָ מִזִּקְנֵי יִשְׂרָאֵל וּמַטְּךָ אֲשֶׁר הִכִּיתָ בּוֹ אֶת־הַיְאֹר קַח
בְּיָדְךָ וְהָלָכְתָּ: הִנְנִי עֹמֵד לְפָנֶיךָ שָּׁם | עַל־הַצּוּר בְּחֹרֵב 6
וְהִכִּיתָ בַצּוּר וְיָצְאוּ מִמֶּנּוּ מַיִם וְשָׁתָה הָעָם וַיַּעַשׂ כֵּן מֹשֶׁה
לְעֵינֵי זִקְנֵי יִשְׂרָאֵל: וַיִּקְרָא שֵׁם הַמָּקוֹם מַסָּה וּמְרִיבָה 7
עַל־רִיב | בְּנֵי יִשְׂרָאֵל וְעַל נַסֹּתָם אֶת־יְהוָה לֵאמֹר הֲיֵשׁ
יְהוָה בְּקִרְבֵּנוּ אִם־אָיִן:                ס

---

¹ That is, *Trying*.   ² That is, *Strife*.

**3. to kill us ... with thirst.** lit. 'to kill me and my sons and my cattle with thirst', as if each one had cried out separately. The reaction from the mood of exultation at the Red Sea is complete. 'It is the nature of man,' says Macaulay, 'to overrate present evil. A hundred generations have passed away since the first great national emancipation of which an account has come down to us. We read in the most ancient of books that a people bowed to the dust under a cruel yoke, scourged to toil by hard taskmasters, not supplied with straw, yet compelled to furnish the daily tale of bricks, became sick of life, and raised such a cry of misery as pierced the heavens. The slaves were wonderfully set free; at the moment of their liberation they raised a song of gratitude and triumph; but in a few hours they began to regret their slavery, and to reproach the leader who had decoyed them away from the savoury fare of the house of bondage to the dreary waste which still separated them from the land flowing with milk and honey. Since that time the history of every great deliverer has been the history of Moses retold. Down to the present hour, rejoicings like those on the shore of the Red Sea have ever been speedily followed by murmurings like those at the Waters of Strife.'

**4. what shall I do unto this people?** To save them from despair and sin.

**5. take with thee of the elders.** To witness the wonder that was to be done. They were the people's representatives.

**thy rod.** The rod which could make the waters of the Nile undrinkable for the Egyptians (VII, 17), could produce water to satisfy the thirst of the Israelites. Although Aaron performed the symbolic action preceding the first plague, it is attributed to Moses, and therefore termed his rod. Aaron acted on his behalf.

**and go.** To the rock in Horeb.

**6. I will stand before thee.** I will be present with My omnipotence (Dillmann).

**upon the rock in Horeb.** The rock known to Moses, where he had already seen the Glory of God (Abarbanel).

**that the people may drink.** The people were at Rephidim, some distance away from Horeb. The water from the rock flowed down to them.

**7. Meribah.** There they had murmured against Moses; see Ps. XCV, 8.

**tried the LORD.** Better, 'put the LORD to the proof' (Driver).

**is the LORD among us, or not?** i.e. can He help us in our need or not?

### 8-16. THE BATTLE WITH THE AMALEKITES

The Amalekites were a predatory tribe, who are spoken of as having their home in the desert of Palestine. At the same time, a nomad tribe is quite capable of raids at a distance from its usual home (*e.g.* it was with some difficulty that the Transjordan Arabs were prevented from taking part in the loot and murder of Palestine Jews in August, 1929); or, the Amalekites may in the summer months have led their flocks up into the cooler and fresher pastures in the mountains of the Sinai Peninsula.

EXODUS XVII, 9     שמות בשלח יז

with Israel in Rephidim. 9. And Moses said unto Joshua: 'Choose us out men, and go out, fight with Amalek; to-morrow I will stand on the top of the hill with the rod of God in my hand.' 10. So Joshua did as Moses had said to him, and fought with Amalek; and Moses, Aaron, and Hur went up to the top of the hill. 11. And it came to pass, when Moses held up his hand, that Israel prevailed; and when he let down his hand, Amalek prevailed. 12. But Moses' hands were heavy; and they took a stone, and put it under him, and he sat thereon; and Aaron and Hur stayed up his hands, the one on the one side, and the other on the other side; and his hands were steady until the going down of the sun. 13. And Joshua discomfited Amalek and his people with the edge of the sword.*ᵐ· ¶ 14. And the LORD said unto Moses: 'Write this for a memorial in the book, and rehearse it in the ears of Joshua: for I will utterly blot out the remembrance of Amalek from under heaven.' 15. And Moses built an altar, and

8 וַיָּבֹא עֲמָלֵק וַיִּלָּחֶם עִם־יִשְׂרָאֵל בִּרְפִידִם: 9 וַיֹּאמֶר מֹשֶׁה אֶל־יְהוֹשֻׁעַ בְּחַר־לָנוּ אֲנָשִׁים וְצֵא הִלָּחֵם בַּעֲמָלֵק מָחָר אָנֹכִי נִצָּב עַל־רֹאשׁ הַגִּבְעָה וּמַטֵּה הָאֱלֹהִים בְּיָדִי: 10 וַיַּעַשׂ יְהוֹשֻׁעַ כַּאֲשֶׁר אָמַר־לוֹ מֹשֶׁה לְהִלָּחֵם בַּעֲמָלֵק וּמֹשֶׁה אַהֲרֹן וְחוּר עָלוּ רֹאשׁ הַגִּבְעָה: 11 וְהָיָה כַּאֲשֶׁר יָרִים מֹשֶׁה יָדוֹ וְגָבַר יִשְׂרָאֵל וְכַאֲשֶׁר יָנִיחַ יָדוֹ וְגָבַר עֲמָלֵק: 12 וִידֵי מֹשֶׁה כְּבֵדִים וַיִּקְחוּ־אֶבֶן וַיָּשִׂימוּ תַחְתָּיו וַיֵּשֶׁב עָלֶיהָ וְאַהֲרֹן וְחוּר תָּמְכוּ בְיָדָיו מִזֶּה אֶחָד וּמִזֶּה אֶחָד וַיְהִי יָדָיו אֱמוּנָה עַד־בֹּא הַשָּׁמֶשׁ: 13 וַיַּחֲלֹשׁ יְהוֹשֻׁעַ אֶת־עֲמָלֵק וְאֶת־עַמּוֹ לְפִי־חָרֶב: *
         פ    מפטיר
14 וַיֹּאמֶר יְהֹוָה אֶל־מֹשֶׁה כְּתֹב זֹאת זִכָּרוֹן בַּסֵּפֶר וְשִׂים בְּאָזְנֵי יְהוֹשֻׁעַ כִּי־מָחֹה אֶמְחֶה אֶת־זֵכֶר עֲמָלֵק מִתַּחַת הַשָּׁמָיִם:

**8.** *then came Amalek.* As an immediate sequence of the murmuring on the part of the Israelites, say the Rabbis. It is the invariable lesson of Jewish history that whenever Israel begins to doubt God and itself, asking, *Is the* LORD *among us or not?* an Amalek unexpectedly assails it.
*fought with Israel.* Deut. xxv, 18 records that Amalek cut off, at the rear of Israel, all that were feeble and weary.

**9.** *Joshua.* His name was originally Hoshea (Num. XIII, 8). This is the first mention of the great captain and successor of Moses. By anticipation, he is here called by his latter name.
*to-morrow.* When the battle is waged.
*with the rod of God.* The victory over their enemies was to be attributed altogether to God.

**10.** *Hur.* The son of Miriam and Caleb (Talmud).

**11.** *Moses held up his hand.* The Talmud remarks, 'Can the hands of Moses really cause victory, if they are raised; or defeat, if they are lowered? Scripture teaches here, that, when the Israelites looked up to God, and humbled themselves before their Father in Heaven, they were victorious; when they did not, they were defeated.' Some commentators explain that Moses raised his staff like a banner. When the Israelites saw this banner, they were courageous and victorious; when they did not see it, they were despondent and fled; and therefore the place was called Adonai-nissi, *i.e.* 'The LORD is my banner' (*v.* 15).

**12.** *heavy.* With weariness, after the exertion of holding them up a long time.

*they took. i.e.* Aaron and Hur.
*a stone.* 'Could they not have given him a chair or a cushion? But he said, Since the Israelites are in trouble, lo, I will bear my part with them; for he who bears his share in the troubles of Israel, will live to enjoy the hour of consolation' (Talmud).
*Aaron and Hur stayed up his hands.* This is another trait which no legend would have created for the first martial exploit of Israel. Moses plays but a secondary part; and even as intercessor his arms have to be held up! Everything is as prosaic as the *real course of events* in this poor world is wont to be (Chadwick).
*steady.* Heb. *emunah*; lit. steadiness, steadfastness, faithfulness, faith.
*until the going down of the sun.* It was no mere raid, but a fierce battle.

**13.** *discomfited.* lit. 'weakened'.
*Amalek and his people.* Heb. idiom for, 'the people of the Amalekites.'

**14.** *write this.* The attack of the Amalekites.
*in the book.* In the Torah, the Book written by Moses; cf. XXIV, 4, 7, and XXXIV, 27.
*rehearse it in the ears of. i.e.* impress it upon.
*Joshua.* Who would have to fight the kings of Canaan, and was destined to lead the Israelites into the Holy Land.
*I will utterly blot out.* On account of the unprovoked and inhuman attack on the people of God; see Deut. xxv, 17 f.

**15.** *built an altar.* On Horeb.
*Adonai-nissi.* God had again saved His people. He is Israel's victorious Banner.

EXODUS XVII, 16     שמות בשלח יז

called the name of it ¹Adonai-nissi. 16. And he said: 'The hand upon the throne of the LORD: the LORD will have war with Amalek from generation to generation.'

וַיִּ֤בֶן מֹשֶׁה֙ מִזְבֵּ֔חַ וַיִּקְרָ֥א שְׁמ֖וֹ יְהוָ֣ה ׀ נִסִּֽי: וַיֹּ֗אמֶר כִּי־יָד֙ עַל־כֵּ֣ס יָ֔הּ מִלְחָמָ֥ה לַיהוָ֖ה בַּעֲמָלֵ֑ק מִדֹּ֖ר דֹּֽר:

¹ That is, *The* LORD *is my banner.*

**16.** *the hand upon the throne of the* LORD. i.e. the hand of Amalek was against Israel, the host of God. The text is difficult, and can also be translated, 'The LORD hath sworn, the LORD will have war with Amalek from generation to generation' (Onkelos, Rashi, Ibn Ezra, Luzzatto, RV Text).

*war with Amalek.* See I Sam. xv, 2 f; Deut. xxv, 17–19. 'As Amalek was the first to attack Israel with the sword, Israel was commanded to blot out his name by means of the sword' (Maimonides). Amalek has disappeared from under heaven, but his spirit still walks the earth. In the battle of the LORD against the Amalekites in the realm of the Spirit, the only successful weapons are courage and conviction, truth and righteousness.

## HAFTORAH BESHALLACH     הפטרת בשלח

### JUDGES IV, 4–V, 31

**CHAPTER IV**     CAP. IV. ד

4. Now Deborah, a prophetess, the wife of Lappidoth, she judged Israel at that time. 5. And she sat under the palm-tree of Deborah between Ramah and Beth-el in the hill-country of Ephraim; and the children of Israel came up to her for judgment. 6. And she sent and called Barak the son of Abinoam out of Kedesh-naphtali,

וּדְבוֹרָה֙ אִשָּׁ֣ה נְבִיאָ֔ה אֵ֖שֶׁת לַפִּיד֑וֹת הִ֛יא שֹׁפְטָ֥ה אֶת־ יִשְׂרָאֵ֖ל בָּעֵ֥ת הַהִֽיא: וְ֠הִיא יוֹשֶׁ֨בֶת תַּֽחַת־תֹּ֜מֶר דְּבוֹרָ֗ה בֵּ֧ין הָרָמָ֛ה וּבֵ֥ין בֵּֽית־אֵ֖ל בְּהַ֣ר אֶפְרָ֑יִם וַיַּעֲל֥וּ אֵלֶ֛יהָ בְּנֵ֥י יִשְׂרָאֵ֖ל לַמִּשְׁפָּֽט: וַתִּשְׁלַ֗ח וַתִּקְרָא֙ לְבָרָ֣ק בֶּן־אֲבִינֹ֔עַם 4 ה 6

v. 4. יש מתחילין ותשר דבורה

In both Sedrah and Haftorah we have the story of a deliverance from oppression celebrated in a Song of triumph and praise.

These chapters of the Book of Judges take us back to an early period in Israel's history, the days after the death of Joshua, when the tribes were compelled to wage a hard and often desperate struggle against the remaining warlike Canaanites. It was a barbaric period, without national unity and devoid of religious authority. 'In those days there was no king of Israel: every man did that which was right in his own eyes.' But God does not utterly forsake His people. An overwhelming national calamity, or foreign oppression, would bring forth a Champion, who would repel or destroy the foe, or rescue the people from the threatened calamity. Such Champions, known as *Shofetim* ('Judges'), were Gideon, Jephthah, Samson, and the most remarkable of all, Deborah. The story of her achievement has come down to us in two versions, in prose and in verse. From them we can reconstruct the mortal danger from which her victory saved Israel. That victory was one of the 'decisive battles' of the world. It settled the destiny of Palestine, and a great many other things, for all time. Moreover, under the inspiration of Deborah's lofty patriotism, most of the tribes for the first time combined in face of a common danger. Those wild years forged the bonds of a nationality that has survived unprecedented shocks throughout the ages.

**4.** *prophetess.* Although she did not foretell the future, she is described as a prophetess, because she was inspired to grapple with the great difficulties of the hour (Kimchi).

**5.** *sat.* To decide disputes brought to her for judgment.

**6.** *Kedesh-naphtali.* About four miles from the north end of the 'waters of Merom'.

*mount Tabor.* The conical shaped hill commanding the Plain of Esdraelon. The Plain runs like a wedge from the coast to within 10 miles of the Jordan, and is dominated by hills on all sides. It is to-day known as 'the Emek'.

*of Naphtali...Zebulun.* These two tribes bordering on the Plain suffered most under the oppression of the heathens.

281

## JUDGES IV, 7

and said unto him: 'Hath not the LORD, the God of Israel, commanded, saying: Go and draw toward mount Tabor, and take with thee ten thousand men of the children of Naphtali and of the children of Zebulun? 7. And I will draw unto thee to the brook Kishon Sisera, the captain of Jabin's army, with his chariots and his multitude; and I will deliver him into thy hand.' 8. And Barak said unto her: 'If thou wilt go with me, then I will go; but if thou wilt not go with me, I will not go.' 9. And she said: 'I will surely go with thee; notwithstanding the journey that thou takest shall not be for thy honour; for the LORD will give Sisera over into the hand of a woman.' And Deborah arose, and went with Barak to Kedesh. 10. And Barak called Zebulun and Naphtali together to Kedesh; and there went up ten thousand men at his feet; and Deborah went up with him. ¶ 11. Now Heber the Kenite had severed himself from the Kenites, even from the children of Hobab the father-in-law of Moses, and had pitched his tent as far as Elon-bezaanannim, which is by Kedesh. ¶ 12. And they told Sisera that Barak the son of Abinoam was gone up to mount Tabor. 13. And Sisera gathered together all his chariots, even nine hundred chariots of iron, and all the people that were with him, from Harosheth-goiim, unto the brook Kishon. 14. And Deborah said unto Barak: 'Up; for this is the day in which the LORD hath delivered Sisera into thy hand; is not the LORD gone out before thee?' So Barak went down from mount Tabor, and ten thousand men after him. 15. And the LORD discomfited Sisera, and all his chariots, and all his host, with the edge of the sword before Barak; and Sisera alighted from his chariot, and fled away on his feet. 16. But Barak pursued after the chariots, and after the host, unto Harosheth-goiim; and all the host of Sisera fell by the edge of the

**7.** *Jabin.* The king of Canaan who oppressed Israel. He had 900 chariots of iron; and against these 'armoured cars', the Israelite peasants were powerless.

**8.** *if thou wilt go with me.* Indicates the remarkable confidence that Deborah's wisdom and work had inspired.

**9.** *for thy honour.* The word *thy* is emphatic: the chief glory of the victory shall not be his.
*give.* Deliver.

**10.** *went up.* i.e. to Mount Tabor.

**11.** *the Kenites.* A nomadic tribe in close league with Israel; see Num. XXIV, 22. Heber had branched off from the main clan, in Southern Palestine, and wandered as far north as Kedesh. This information is necessary for the understanding of v. 17.

**13.** *Harosheth-goiim.* Near Megiddo.
*Kishon.* The river rises in the S.E. of the Plain of Esdraelon, and flows through it into the sea near Haifa. It is the second river of Palestine.

**14.** *went down.* From Mt. Tabor; the Israelites dashed down, and drove the Canaanites back upon the banks of the river Kishon. Its overflowing waters, swollen by a rain-storm, had turned the Plain into a morass, rendering any use of the chariots impossible.

**15.** *discomfited.* Confused, threw into a panic; cf. the Sedrah, XIV, 24.

## JUDGES IV, 17

sword; there was not a man left. ¶ 17. Howbeit Sisera fled away on his feet to the tent of Jael the wife of Heber the Kenite; for there was peace between Jabin the king of Hazor and the house of Heber the Kenite. 18. And Jael went out to meet Sisera, and said unto him: 'Turn in, my lord, turn in to me; fear not.' And he turned in unto her into the tent, and she covered him with a rug. 19. And he said unto her: 'Give me, I pray thee, a little water to drink; for I am thirsty.' And she opened a bottle of milk, and gave him drink, and covered him. 20. And he said unto her: 'Stand in the door of the tent, and it shall be, when any man doth come and inquire of thee, and say: Is there any man here? that thou shalt say: No.' 21. Then Jael Heber's wife took a tent-pin, and took a hammer in her hand, and went softly unto him, and smote the pin into his temples, and it pierced through into the ground; for he was in a deep sleep; so he swooned and died. 22. And, behold, as Barak pursued Sisera, Jael came out to meet him, and said unto him: 'Come, and I will show thee the man whom thou seekest.' And he came unto her; and, behold, Sisera lay dead, and the tent-pin was in his temples. 23. So God subdued on that day Jabin the king of Canaan before the children of Israel. 24. And the hand of the children of Israel prevailed more and more against Jabin the king of Canaan, until they had destroyed Jabin king of Canaan.

### CHAPTER V

1. Then sang Deborah and Barak the son of Abinoam on that day, saying:

2. When men let grow their hair in Israel,
When the people offer themselves willingly,
Bless ye the LORD.

3. Hear, O ye kings; give ear, O ye princes;
I, unto the LORD will I sing;
I will sing praise to the LORD, the God of Israel.

**17.** *Jael the wife of Heber.* This family had taken no part in the battle.

**21.** *tent-pin.* On the morality of the action, see note on *v.* 24 of next chapter.

**24.** *prevailed more and more.* This staggering success was the beginning of a series of crushing victories over Jabin.

### CHAPTER V. DEBORAH'S SONG OF DELIVERANCE AND PRAISE

'The Song of Deborah holds a high place among Triumphal Odes in the literature of the world. It is a work of that highest art which is not studied and artificial, but spontaneous and inevitable. It shows a development and command of the resources of the language for ends of poetical expression, which prove that poetry had long been cultivated among the Hebrews' (Moore).

**2.** *when men let grow their hair in Israel.* i.e. when men took the vow and consecrated themselves to the war of liberation. 'Wearing the hair long was the mark of a vow not to do certain things until a specified object had been attained' (Cooke); cf. Num. VI, 5.

## JUDGES V, 4

4. LORD, when Thou didst go forth out of Seir,
When Thou didst march out of the field of Edom,
The earth trembled, the heavens also dropped,
Yea, the clouds dropped water.
5. The mountains quaked at the presence of the LORD,
Even yon Sinai at the presence of the LORD, the God of Israel.
6. In the days of Shamgar the son of Anath,
In the days of Jael, the highways ceased,
And the travellers walked through byways.
7. The rulers ceased in Israel, they ceased,
Until that thou didst arise, Deborah,
That thou didst arise a mother in Israel.
8. They chose new gods;
Then was war in the gates;
Was there a shield or spear seen
Among forty thousand in Israel?
9. My heart is toward the governors of Israel,
That offered themselves willingly among the people.
Bless ye the LORD.
10. Ye that ride on white asses,
Ye that sit on rich cloths,
And ye that walk by the way, tell of it;
11. Louder than the voice of archers, by the watering-troughs!
There shall they rehearse the righteous acts of the LORD,
Even the righteous acts of His rulers in Israel.
Then the people of the LORD went down to the gates.

4 לַיהֹוָה אֱלֹהֵי יִשְׂרָאֵל: יְהֹוָה בְּצֵאתְךָ
מִשֵּׂעִיר בְּצַעְדְּךָ מִשְּׂדֵה אֱדוֹם אֶרֶץ
רָעָשָׁה גַּם־שָׁמַיִם נָטָפוּ גַּם־עָבִים נָטְפוּ
ה מָיִם: הָרִים נָזְלוּ מִפְּנֵי יְהֹוָה זֶה
6 סִינַי מִפְּנֵי יְהֹוָה אֱלֹהֵי יִשְׂרָאֵל: בִּימֵי שַׁמְגַּר בֶּן־
עֲנָת בִּימֵי יָעֵל חָדְלוּ אֳרָחוֹת וְהֹלְכֵי
7 נְתִיבוֹת יֵלְכוּ אֳרָחוֹת עֲקַלְקַלּוֹת: חָדְלוּ פְרָזוֹן בְּיִשְׂרָאֵל
חָדֵלּוּ עַד שַׁקַּמְתִּי דְּבוֹרָה
8 שַׁקַּמְתִּי אֵם בְּיִשְׂרָאֵל: יִבְחַר אֱלֹהִים
חֲדָשִׁים אָז לָחֶם שְׁעָרִים מָגֵן
אִם־יֵרָאֶה וָרֹמַח בְּאַרְבָּעִים אֶלֶף
9 בְּיִשְׂרָאֵל: לִבִּי לְחוֹקְקֵי יִשְׂרָאֵל הַמִּתְנַדְּבִים
י בָּעָם בָּרְכוּ יְהֹוָה: רֹכְבֵי אֲתֹנוֹת
צְחֹרוֹת יֹשְׁבֵי עַל־מִדִּין וְהֹלְכֵי
11 עַל־דֶּרֶךְ שִׂיחוּ: מִקּוֹל מְחַצְצִים בֵּין
מַשְׁאַבִּים שָׁם יְתַנּוּ צִדְקוֹת יְהֹוָה צִדְקֹת
פִּרְזוֹנוֹ בְּיִשְׂרָאֵל אָז יָרְדוּ לַשְּׁעָרִים עַם־
12 יְהֹוָה: עוּרִי עוּרִי דְּבוֹרָה עוּרִי
עוּרִי דַבְּרִי־שִׁיר קוּם בָּרָק וּשֲׁבֵה שֶׁבְיְךָ בֶּן

12. Awake, awake, Deborah;
Awake, awake, utter a song;
Arise, Barak, and lead thy captivity captive, thou son of Abinoam.

---

**4.** LORD, *when Thou didst go forth*. A bringing to remembrance of God's might in the days of old, at the Revelation at Sinai, as an encouragement in the present distress.

#### 6–11. THE OPPRESSION

**6.** *Shamgar*. The previous judge; see Judges III, 31.

*highways ceased*. Israel was in hiding, and all travel on the highways was stopped. The people had to abandon their villages because of the harrying armed bands of Canaanites.

**7.** *thou didst arise a mother in Israel*. The Heb. is as an old grammatical form, and has also been translated, 'till I arose a mother in Israel.'

**8.** *was there a shield or spear*. The people had no proper weapons with which to defend themselves.

**9.** *governors*. Commanders; they are praised for this instant response to her clarion call.

**10.** *tell of it*. All should now join in praising God—the leaders and magistrates, the men of wealth as well as the plain people. They could now travel in safety on the high-roads, in contrast to *v*. 6.

**11.** *righteous*. With the additional meaning, 'victorious.'

*went down to the gates*. Prepared to assault the strongholds of the enemy.

#### 12–23. THE GATHERING OF THE TRIBES

**12.** *utter a song*. The war-song which roused the clans to battle.

*lead thy captivity captive*. An idiomatic phrase for *turn the tables* in war.

## JUDGES V, 13

13. Then made He a remnant to have dominion over the nobles and the people;
The LORD made me have dominion over the mighty.
14. Out of Ephraim came they whose root is in Amalek;
After thee, Benjamin, among thy peoples;
Out of Machir came down governors,
And out of Zebulun they that handle the marshal's staff.
15. And the princes of Issachar were with Deborah;
As was Issachar, so was Barak;
Into the valley they rushed forth at his feet.
Among the divisions of Reuben
There were great resolves of heart.
16. Why sattest thou among the sheep-folds,
To hear the pipings for the flocks?
At the divisions of Reuben
There were great searchings of heart.
17. Gilead abode beyond the Jordan;
And Dan, why doth he sojourn by the ships?
Asher dwelt at the shore of the sea,
And abideth by its bays.
18. Zebulun is a people that jeoparded their lives unto the death,
And Naphtali, upon the high places of the field.
19. The kings came, they fought;
Then fought the kings of Canaan,
In Taanach by the waters of Megiddo;
They took no gain of money.

20. They fought from heaven,
The stars in their courses fought against Sisera.

---

**14.** *root is in Amalek.* This suggests that Ephraim possessed land formerly held by Amalekites (see Judges XII, 15).

*after thee.* i.e. Ephraim. The largest and the smallest tribes are mentioned together. Others are included in the words, 'among thy peoples' (Kimchi).

*Machir.* On the other side of the Jordan.

*governors.* Commanders.

*the marshal's staff.* lit. 'the staff of the scribe', who enrols the muster of troops.

**15.** *great resolves of heart.* There was much discussion of the situation, but they did not join their brethren in their life-and-death struggle. Reuben remains true to his character as delineated in Jacob's blessing; see p. 183.

**16.** *searchings.* Mighty deliberations, but no action. They preferred to listen to the pipings of the shepherds.

**17.** Gilead, Dan and Asher are similarly branded. The latter had established themselves on the sea-coast with the Phœnicians.

*bays.* Landing-places at the mouth of a river.

**18.** The shining example of Zebulun and Naphtali contrasted with the cowardice or indifference of the above.

### 19–22. THE BATTLE

**19.** *the kings.* The rulers of the districts united under Sisera.

*no gain of money.* They got no booty from the Israelites: they themselves were vanquished.

**20.** *the stars in their courses.* One of the most beautiful figures in literature. The powers of heaven themselves were arrayed against the heathen, and the victory was not won by Israel unaided. The reference is to torrential rain which swept away the Canaanite chariots; cf. in the Sedrah, XIV, 25. 'In 1799, at the battle of Mt. Tabor between the army of Napoleon and the Turks, many of the latter were drowned when attempting to escape across the Plain inundated by the Kishon' (Cooke).

## JUDGES V, 21 — שופטים ה

21. The brook Kishon swept them away,
That ancient brook, the brook Kishon.
O my soul, tread them down with strength.

22. Then did the horsehoofs stamp
By reason of the prancings, the prancings of their mighty ones.

23. 'Curse ye Meroz,' said the angel of the LORD,
'Curse ye bitterly the inhabitants thereof,
Because they came not to the help of the LORD,
To the help of the LORD against the mighty.'

24. Blessed above women shall Jael be,
The wife of Heber the Kenite,
Above women in the tent shall she be blessed.

25. Water he asked, milk she gave him;
On a lordly bowl she brought him curd.

26. Her hand she put to the tent-pin,
And her right hand to the workmen's hammer;
And with the hammer she smote Sisera, she smote through his head,
Yea, she pierced and struck through his temples.

27. At her feet he sunk, he fell, he lay;
At her feet he sunk, he fell;
Where he sunk, there he fell down dead.

28. Through the window she looked forth, and peered,
The mother of Sisera, through the lattice:
'Why is his chariot so long in coming?
Why tarry the wheels of his chariots?'

29. The wisest of her princesses answer her,
Yea, she returneth answer to herself:

---

**22.** *horsehoofs stamp.* A picture of the confusion of flight.

### 23–31. THE DEFEAT OF THE ENEMY

**23.** *Meroz.* An Israelite town near the scene of the battle that refused to help in following up the victory.

*against the mighty.* Or, 'among the brave'; as brave men who rallied to the LORD's banner.

**24.** *Jael.* The resource and 'pro-Israelite' action of this heathen, Kenite woman is contrasted with the cowardice and perfidy of the inhabitants of Meroz. Jael's murder is viewed as an act of national deliverance, without which the victory might have been fruitless; it therefore receives high praise. Judged by standards of peace, her act was one of treacherous cruelty; but every nation glorifies similar, and worse, deeds in its history. Our own age, in which the most enlightened nations have, for reasons of policy or patriotism, committed or condoned crimes and inhumanities on an immeasurably greater scale, is not entitled to condemn the praise bestowed upon the fierce deed of this wild Bedouin woman.

*women in the tent.* Or, 'Bedouin women' (Moore), tenting women.

**25.** *lordly bowl.* A bowl fit for nobles.

**29.** *the wisest of her princesses.* Comfort her by their certainty that Sisera is bringing back rich booty. His delay, they tell her, is being caused by his collecting and apportioning this booty.

*she returneth answer to herself.* Or, 'keeps repeating to herself.' She silences her presentiments of evil by the same kind of anwer which her companions give her (Rashi).

## JUDGES V, 30     שופטים ה

30. 'Are they not finding, are they not dividing the spoil?
A damsel, two damsels to every man;
To Sisera a spoil of dyed garments,
A spoil of dyed garments of embroidery,
Two dyed garments of broidery for the neck of every spoiler?'

31. So perish all Thine enemies, O LORD;
But they that love Him be as the sun when he goeth forth in his might.
And the land had rest forty years.

ל הֲלֹא יִמְצְאוּ יְחַלְּקוּ שָׁלָל רַחַם רַחֲמָתַיִם לְרֹאשׁ גֶּבֶר שְׁלַל צְבָעִים לְסִיסְרָא שְׁלַל צְבָעִים רִקְמָה צֶבַע רִקְמָתַיִם לְצַוְּארֵי שָׁלָל׃
31 כֵּן יֹאבְדוּ כָל־אוֹיְבֶיךָ יְהוָה וְאֹהֲבָיו כְּצֵאת הַשֶּׁמֶשׁ בִּגְבֻרָתוֹ וַתִּשְׁקֹט הָאָרֶץ אַרְבָּעִים שָׁנָה׃

---

**30.** *are they not finding*. The Heb. phrase means, 'no doubt they are finding.'

*damsel*. The Heb. is a rare, and, it seems, an insulting word. It is intentionally used to show her contempt for the Israelite women.

*dyed garments of embroidery*. Or, 'embroidered garments of divers colours'—a picturesque touch that betrays the hand of the feminine author of this ode. Its climax 'is as weird as it is fantastic, the figure of Sisera's mother mumbling to herself of the "spoil of damsels, divers colours and embroidery", which her son is to bring home, and which we already know he never will' (George A. Smith).

**31.** *so*. 'With consummate art the poet breaks off, leaving to the imagination of the reader, who knows all, the terrible revelation of the truth' (Moore).

*as the sun when he goeth forth in his might*. Invincible, annihilating the darkness of the night —a marvellously effective ending to one of the most magnificent lyrical poems in any language. The Rabbis based the following teaching on this verse: 'Whosoever does not persecute them that persecute him, whosoever takes an offence in silence, he who does good for its own sake, he who is cheerful under his sufferings—they are the friends of God; and of them Scripture says, "They that love Him shall be as the sun, when he goeth forth in his might."'

*and the land had rest forty years*. 'These words are not by Deborah, but by the writer of the Book of Judges' (Rashi).

EXODUS XVIII, 1          שמות יתרו יח

## 18    Chapter XVIII

1. Now Jethro, the priest of Midian, Moses' father-in-law, heard of all that God had done for Moses, and for Israel His people, how that the Lord had brought Israel out of Egypt. 2. And Jethro, Moses' father-in-law, took Zipporah, Moses' wife, after he had sent her away, 3. and her two sons; of whom the name of the one was Gershom; for he said: 'I have been a stranger in a strange land'; 4. and the name of the other was [1]Eliezer: 'for the God of my father was my help, and delivered me from the sword of Pharaoh.' 5. And Jethro, Moses' father-in-law, came with his sons and his wife unto Moses into the wilderness where he was encamped, at the mount of God; 6. and he said unto Moses: 'I thy father-in-law Jethro am coming unto thee, and thy wife, and her two sons with her.' 7. And Moses went out to meet his father-in-law, and bowed down and kissed him; and they asked each other of their welfare; and they came into the tent. 8. And Moses told his father-in-law all that the Lord had done unto Pharaoh and to the Egyptians for Israel's sake, all the travail that had come upon them by the way, and how the Lord delivered them. 9. And Jethro rejoiced for all the goodness which the Lord had done to Israel, in that He had delivered them out of the hand of the Egyptians. 10. And Jethro said: 'Blessed

[1] Heb. *El*, God, and *ezer*, help.

---

## V. YITHRO

### (Chapters XVIII–XX)

Chapter XVIII. The Visit of Jethro

**1.** *Jethro.* See III, 1 and II, 16 f. This chapter is one of the few passages in Exodus that are reminiscent of Patriarchal scenes in Genesis.

**2.** *he had sent her.* Back to Jethro in Midian, after the incident related in IV, 24–26.

**3.** *Gershom.* See on II, 22.

**4.** *the God of my father.* See III, 6; xv, 2.
*from the sword of Pharaoh.* See II, 15. One may assume that when Moses named his second son, he said, 'For the God of my father was my help,' etc.

**5.** *at the mount of God.* Sinai, or Horeb. Moses had there struck the rock in order to procure water for the people, XVII, 6. Rephidim lies in the vicinity of Horeb.

**6.** *and he said unto Moses.* i.e. through a messenger.

**7.** *went out to meet.* And to pay respect to his father-in-law, his guest. This was the usual etiquette; see Gen. XVIII, 2.

**8.** *travail.* lit. 'weariness'; the pursuit of the Israelites on the part of the Egyptians, and the events associated with Marah, Massah, Meribah and Rephidim.

**9.** *Jethro rejoiced.* Not because the Egyptians had been punished, but because of all the goodness shown by God to Israel.

**10.** *delivered you.* i.e. Moses and Aaron.
*delivered the people.* By defeating the Egyptians at the crossing of the Red Sea.
*hand.* Power.

EXODUS XVIII, 11

be the LORD, who hath delivered you out of the hand of the Egyptians, and out of the hand of Pharaoh; who hath delivered the people from under the hand of the Egyptians. 11. Now I know that the LORD is greater than all gods; yea, for that they dealt proudly against them.' 12. And Jethro, Moses' father-in-law, took a burnt-offering and sacrifices for God; and Aaron came, and all the elders of Israel, to eat bread with Moses' father-in-law before God. *11. 13. And it came to pass on the morrow, that Moses sat to judge the people; and the people stood about Moses from the morning unto the evening. 14. And when Moses' father-in-law saw all that he did to the people, he said: 'What is this thing that thou doest to the people? why sittest thou thyself alone, and all the people stand about thee from morning unto even?' 15. And Moses said unto his father-in-law: 'Because the people come unto me to inquire of God; 16. when they have a matter, it cometh unto me; and I judge between a man and his neighbour, and I make them know the statutes of God, and His laws.' 17. And Moses' father-in-law said unto him: 'The thing that thou doest is not good. 18. Thou wilt surely wear away, both thou, and this people that is with thee; for the thing is too heavy for thee; thou art not able to perform it thyself alone. 19. Hearken now unto my voice, I will give thee counsel, and God be with thee: be thou for the people before God, and bring thou the causes unto God. 20. And thou

**11.** *they dealt proudly against them.* Because the Egyptians had dealt proudly and obstinately with Israel, God felt the need of using His power to humble the Egyptians (Rashbam). God made use of their very pride and defiance to bring about their doom, and, at the same time, the salvation of Israel. By this, Jethro realizes that God is 'greater than all other gods'. According to the Rabbis, Jethro thereupon forsook idolatry and became a proselyte.

**12.** *Aaron came, and all the elders.* Though Moses is not mentioned, he was naturally present, as the meeting took place in his tent (Ibn Ezra).
*to eat bread ... before God.* To take part in the sacrificial meal.
*before God.* Before the altar built by Moses in honour of God; see XVII, 15.

**13–23.** Jethro's advice to Moses. This section is of the greatest interest: it presents a picture of Moses legislating, and deciding cases as they arose.

**13.** *on the morrow.* After his arrival.
*judge the people.* In primitive Semitic society, the ruler was both leader in war and arbiter in disputes.

**14.** *all that he did.* Acting single-handed as leader and judge.

**15.** *to inquire of God.* See Gen. XXV, 22. The phrase may mean to obtain from God a legal decision; see Num. IX, 8. In Israel, justice was considered as belonging to God; see Deut. I, 17.

**16.** *a matter.* A cause of dispute.
*statutes of God.* Naturally, the Israelites, like every group constituting a human society, had such definite rules (*e.g.* against theft and violence) long before the promulgation of the Decalogue.
*His laws.* Heb. *toroth.* Directions delivered for special circumstances.

**18.** *this people that is with thee.* Because they will not all receive the attention they require.

**19.** *God be with thee.* God will help thee, if thou wilt follow this advice (Ibn Ezra).
*before God.* God's representative to the people.
*bring thou the causes.* The difficult cases. This refers to the occasions when the people come to Moses to inquire of God (see *v.* 15).

**20.** *they must do.* Their conduct in any given case. Jethro conceives the activity of Moses as that of instructor.

## EXODUS XVIII, 21

shalt teach them the statutes and the laws, and shalt show them the way wherein they must walk, and the work that they must do. 21. Moreover, thou shalt provide out of all the people able men, such as fear God, men of truth, hating unjust gain; and place such over them, to be rulers of thousands, rulers of hundreds, rulers of fifties, and rulers of tens. 22. And let them judge the people at all seasons; and it shall be, that every great matter they shall bring unto thee, but every small matter they shall judge themselves; so shall they make it easier for thee and bear the burden with thee. 23. If thou shalt do this thing, and God command thee so, then thou shalt be able to endure, and all this people also shall go to their place in peace.'*ⁱⁱⁱ· 24. So Moses hearkened to the voice of his father-in-law, and did all that he had said. 25. And Moses chose able men out of all Israel, and made them heads over the people, rulers of thousands, rulers of hundreds, rulers of fifties, and rulers of tens. 26. And they judged the people at all seasons: the hard causes they brought unto Moses, but every small matter they judged themselves. 27. And Moses let his father-in-law depart; and he went his way into his own land.*ⁱᵛ

## 19  CHAPTER XIX

1. In the third month after the children of Israel were gone forth out of the land of Egypt, the same day came they into the

---

**21.** *provide.* The Heb. is an unusual word for 'look out', select, appoint. It is used of prophetic vision; 'select by the prophetic insight which God has given thee' (Rashi).

*such as fear God.* And not man; men of fundamental piety and humanity; cf. I, 17.

*hating unjust gain.* Incorruptible and above the suspicion of bribery.

*rulers of thousands.* An elaborate system of judges and assistant judges is here indicated. Gersonides suggests that the ruler of tens controlled several such subdivisions, but less than a hundred; the ruler of hundreds, several hundreds, but less than a thousand; and so on.

**22.** *at all seasons.* i.e. as cases arise.
*every great matter.* Extraordinary cases.

**23.** *and God command thee so.* Jethro's suggestions required Divine sanction.

*go to their place in peace.* After having their cases settled quickly, the parties will return to their tents satisfied. No longer will the people have to stand all day waiting for their turn before Moses (see v. 14). Moreover, by the new institution the people would be able to obtain justice in their own part of the camp.

**27.** *his own land.* Midian, see II, 15 and cf. Num. x, 30.

'The wise plan devised by Jethro has never become antiquated. The statesman-like principle of decentralization—the delegation of responsibility—is as important to-day as in the time of Moses' (McNeile).

### CHAPTER XIX. PREPARATIONS FOR THE COVENANT AT SINAI

The arrival at the foot of Mt. Sinai marks the beginning of Israel's spiritual history. We reach what was the kernel and core of the nation's life, the Covenant by which all the tribes were united in allegiance to One God, the Covenant by which a priest-people was created, and a Kingdom of God on earth inaugurated among the children of men.

**1.** *in the third month.* The month of Sivan.
*the same day.* lit. 'in that day', i.e. the first of the month (Mechilta).
*into the wilderness of Sinai.* As foretold when God first revealed Himself to Moses at the Burning Bush (see III, 12). Moses is bringing his

EXODUS XIX, 2 שמות יתרו יט

wilderness of Sinai. 2. And when they were departed from Rephidim, and were come to the wilderness of Sinai, they encamped in the wilderness; and there Israel encamped before the mount. 3. And Moses went up unto God, and the LORD called unto him out of the mountain, saying: 'Thus shalt thou say to the house of Jacob, and tell the children of Israel: 4. Ye have seen what I did unto the Egyptians, and how I bore you on eagles' wings, and brought you unto Myself. 5. Now therefore, if ye will hearken unto My voice indeed, and keep My covenant, then ye shall be Mine own treasure from among all peoples; for all the earth is Mine; 6. and ye shall be unto Me a kingdom of priests, and a

2 הַזֶּה בָּאוּ מִדְבַּר סִינָי: וַיִּסְעוּ מֵרְפִידִים וַיָּבֹאוּ מִדְבַּר
3 סִינַי וַיַּחֲנוּ בַּמִּדְבָּר וַיִּחַן־שָׁם יִשְׂרָאֵל נֶגֶד הָהָר: וּמֹשֶׁה
עָלָה אֶל־הָאֱלֹהִים וַיִּקְרָא אֵלָיו יְהוָה מִן־הָהָר לֵאמֹר כֹּה
4 תֹאמַר לְבֵית יַעֲקֹב וְתַגֵּיד לִבְנֵי יִשְׂרָאֵל: אַתֶּם רְאִיתֶם
אֲשֶׁר עָשִׂיתִי לְמִצְרָיִם וָאֶשָּׂא אֶתְכֶם עַל־כַּנְפֵי נְשָׁרִים
5 וָאָבִא אֶתְכֶם אֵלָי: וְעַתָּה אִם־שָׁמוֹעַ תִּשְׁמְעוּ בְּקֹלִי וּשְׁמַרְתֶּם
אֶת־בְּרִיתִי וִהְיִיתֶם לִי סְגֻלָּה מִכָּל־הָעַמִּים כִּי־לִי כָּל־
6 הָאָרֶץ: וְאַתֶּם תִּהְיוּ־לִי מַמְלֶכֶת כֹּהֲנִים וְגוֹי קָדוֹשׁ אֵלֶּה

v. 5. מלעיל

People to acknowledge and worship the God of their Fathers at that Mount.

The *wilderness* is the wide plain in front of Mt. Sinai. This mountain is generally identified with Jebel Musa; and accordingly, the wilderness is in all probability the plain of Er-Rahah, situated 5,000 feet above the sea. By careful local investigation, Robinson arrived at the conviction that there was space enough in the plain Er-Rahah to satisfy all the requirements of the Scripture narrative, so far as it relates to the assembling of the people for the Divine revelation. The plain is one-and-half miles long and one mile broad; while the adjacent valleys afford ample space for tents, animals and baggage.

**2.** *departed from Rephidim.* Or, 'For they had journeyed from Rephidim' (Mendelssohn, Benisch); see XVII, 8 f. This supplies the link in the narrative, interrupted by the story of Jethro's visit in the preceding chapter.

*they encamped.* In the wilderness of Sinai.

**3.** *Moses went up unto God.* i.e. he ascended the mountain. On the day when the Israelites came to Mt. Sinai, the cloud of God's glory covered the mountain; see XXIV, 16.

*out of the mountain.* Out of the cloud on the summit; see v. 20.

*house of Jacob . . . children of Israel.* Israel has an exalted future in store for it; it is called to become the priest-people of the God of Holiness and Righteousness. *House of Jacob* occurs only here in the Pentateuch, and is a poetical synonym of 'house of Israel'. The Rabbis understood by the 'house of Jacob' the women of the nation. Moses is bidden to approach the women first, as it is they who rear the children in the ways of Religion. God asked Israel, 'What sureties have you to give that you will keep My Covenant?' They offered the Patriarchs, the Prophets and their righteous Rulers as their guarantors. But all of them were rejected. It was only when they offered their children as sureties for the permanence of the Covenant, that these were accepted.

**4.** *ye have seen.* They were eye-witnesses, and not listening merely to the recital of old traditions (Rashi).

*how I bore you.* 'As though I bare you' (Ibn Ezra, Luzzatto).

*on eagles' wings.* This verse is a magnificent and beautiful example of Heb. poetry, expressing God's relations with Israel. The Jewish commentators point out that the eagle carried its young upon its wings, offering its own body as a shield to protect the fledglings from the arrows of the archer. This strong tenderness of the eagle towards its young is a symbol of God's love in taking His people out of the reach of danger to His own abode.

*brought you unto Myself.* To Sinai, where My Kingdom is to be proclaimed.

**5.** *Mine own treasure.* 'A peculiar treasure' (RV). Heb. *segullah*, a term used to denote a precious object or treasure that is one's special possession; I Chron. XXIX, 3. 'These words, *a peculiar treasure*, sound more partial than they really are. If I have chosen an instrument for a peculiar purpose, that instrument may be to me a peculiar treasure, but the purpose is greater than the instrument. So with the Jews. They are God's instrument, and as such a peculiar treasure; but the work is far greater than the instrument' (C. G. Montefiore).

*for all the earth is Mine.* See VI, 7. God is the Creator of all things and the Father of all mankind. Israel, in common with every other nation, forms part of God's possession; but He has chosen Israel to be His in a special degree, to be 'a light unto the nations' and a blessing to all humanity. There is no thought of favouritism in God's choice. Israel's call has not been to privilege and rulership, but to martyrdom and service.

**6.** *a kingdom of priests.* Or, 'a priestly kingdom'; a kingdom whose citizens are all priests (cf. Isa. LXI, 6), living wholly in God's service and ever enjoying the right of access to Him. As it is the duty of the priest to bring man nearer

EXODUS XIX, 7 שמות יתרו יט

7 holy nation. These are the words which thou shalt speak unto the children of Israel.'* v. 7. And Moses came and called for the elders of the people, and set before them all these words which the LORD commanded him. 8. And all the people answered together, and said: 'All that the LORD hath spoken we will do.' And Moses reported the words of the people unto the LORD. 9. And the LORD said unto Moses: 'Lo, I come unto thee in a thick cloud, that the people may hear when I speak with thee, and may also believe thee for ever.' And Moses told the words of the people unto the LORD. 10. And the LORD said unto Moses: 'Go unto the people, and sanctify them to-day and to-morrow, and let them wash their garments, 11. and be ready against the third day; for the third day the LORD will come down in the sight of all the people upon mount Sinai. 12. And thou shalt set bounds unto the people

to God, so Israel has been called to play the part of a priest to other nations; *i.e.* to bring them closer to God and Righteousness. This spiritual Kingdom constitutes the highest mission of Israel.

*and a holy nation*. 'Holy' here means, 'separated' from the false beliefs and the idolatry of the other nations. Israel becomes holy by cleaving unto God and by obeying His Torah; see also on XXII, 30.

**7–9.** Moses informs the Israelites of God's purpose.

**7.** *Moses came*. From the mount to the elders.
*called for the elders*. Who reported to the people.
*set before them*. Giving the entire nation the choice of accepting or rejecting the Divine message; cf. Ex. XXIV, 3 and Deut. IV, 44. Religion in Israel was not to be a secret doctrine of one favoured class, not a body of 'mysteries' entrusted to the keeping of priests, as in Egypt. At Sinai, the Divine Message comes to rich and poor, old and young, learned and unlearned alike.

**8.** *all that the LORD hath spoken*. They gladly and freely expressed their willingness to enter God's Covenant; cf. XXIV, 3. They thereby become, in a special sense, God's People. The conviction of having entered upon such a Covenant—a conviction that henceforth remains imprinted for all time in the consciousness of Israel—cannot have arisen of itself. Its historicity is as unassailable as that of the sojourn in Egypt.

*Moses reported*. He returned to the mountain. God knew their reply, and immediately declared His intention of revealing Himself in the hearing of the people.

**9.** *that the people may hear*. Directly and not through a messenger or an intermediary; see XX, 16. The actual witnessing by the entire nation of the redemption from Egypt, and their direct perception of the Divine Manifestation at Sinai, these *religious experiences* form, according to Yehudah Hallevi, the Foundations of Belief in Israel.

*also believe thee*. The pronoun *thee* is emphatic. Having heard the Voice from the cloud and fire, the people would nevermore doubt the Divine mission of Moses. 'Henceforth the people knew that Moses held direct communication with God, that his words were not creations of his own mind' (Hallevi).

*for ever*. 'The Law of Moses will not be changed, and there will never be any other Torah from the Creator, blessed be His name' (IXth article of the Jewish Creed, as formulated by Maimonides).

**10–15.** The People were to be rendered fit for the approaching Revelation. These ceremonies and warnings were to impress God's holiness upon their untutored minds.

**10.** *sanctify them*. Bid them sanctify themselves. Prepare them to meet God. The exceptional solemnity of the Divine Manifestation demanded sanctification; cf. Gen. XXXV, 2.
*to-day and to-morrow*. The fourth and fifth of Sivan.
*let them wash their garments*. An outward symbol implying purification by bathing and abstention from bodily pleasure; cf. Isa. I, 16; Ps. LI, 9.

**11.** *against the third day*. Not of the month, but of 'the three days of preparation', and therefore the sixth of Sivan.
*will come down*. His glory will be revealed in fire.

# EXODUS XIX, 13      שמות יתרו יט

round about, saying: Take heed to yourselves, that ye go not up into the mount, or touch the border of it; whosoever toucheth the border shall be surely put to death; 13. no hand shall touch him, but he shall surely be stoned, or shot through; whether it be beast or man, it shall not live; when the ram's horn soundeth long, they shall come up to the mount.'\* ᵛⁱ ˢ· 14. And Moses went down from the mount unto the people, and sanctified the people; and they washed their garments. 15. And he said unto the people; 'Be ready against the third day; come not near a woman.' 16. And it came to pass on the third day, when it was morning, that there were thunders and lightnings and a thick cloud upon the mount, and the voice of a horn exceeding loud; and all the people that were in the camp trembled. 17. And Moses brought forth the people out of the camp to meet God; and they stood at the nether part of the mount. 18. Now mount Sinai was altogether on smoke, because the LORD

---

**12.** *set bounds unto the people.* *i.e.* confine them within certain marked limits (Rashi). The mount where God's glory was about to be revealed would for the time being be a Sanctuary, and endowed with the unapproachable sacredness of the Ark or the Holy of Holies in the later Tabernacle.

*the border.* *i.e.* even its border (Rashi).

**13.** *no hand shall touch him.* *i.e.* the trespasser; as this would necessitate another touching at least the edge of the mountain.

*soundeth long.* *i.e.* drawing out the same tone for a long time. This would be the signal that the Manifestation was at an end, and the mountain had resumed its ordinary character.

*they.* The people.

*shall come up.* Better, *may come up.*

**16–19.** NATURAL ACCOMPANIMENTS OF THE REVELATION

**16.** *thick cloud.* lit. 'heavy', *i.e.* dense cloud. No mortal can gaze on the unveiled majesty of God. The cloud is the symbol and vehicle of the Divine Presence; see XIII, 21. The Revelation takes place in a thunderstorm of exceptional impressiveness and grandeur, amid overwhelming natural phenomena—lightning, thunder, earthquake and fire; cf. the revelation to Elijah, I Kings XIX, 11–13.

*the voice of a horn.* Heb., *shofar* see *v.* 19 and XX, 15. The shofar was used to signalize, or accompany, important public events, such as the proclamation of a king. At Sinai, God's Kingdom was inaugurated by the voice of the shofar. On the New Year, the shofar is used to proclaim God's sovereignty; and at the conclusion of the Day of Atonement, it is sounded to announce Israel's emancipation from sin obtained through the Day of Atonement, just as, in ancient times, the blowing of the shofar on that Day proclaimed freedom for the slave (Lev. xxv, 9 and 10).

**17.** *to meet God.* Or, 'toward God.'

*they stood.* Or, 'they took their stand.'

*at the nether part of the mount.* i.e. within the bounds, see *v.* 12.

**18.** *on smoke.* *i.e.* in smoke.

*of a furnace.* Cf. Gen. xv, 17, and Isa. VI, 4.

**19.** *God answered him by a voice.* This does not refer to the Ten Commandments, but to what took place in *v.* 21–24; Moses spoke to God, and God answered with voice loud enough to surpass the ever increasing sound of the horn.

**20–25.** The final directions before the Revelation.

**20.** *the LORD came down.* 'The Torah employs the language of man,' so that the listener or reader may understand the narrative.

**21.** *charge.* *i.e.* warn them not to go up the mountain (Rashi).

*break through.* The barriers (*v.* 12).

*to gaze.* Beyond the barriers, to see more closely the Divine Manifestation.

## EXODUS XIX, 19

descended upon it in fire; and the smoke thereof ascended as the smoke of a furnace, and the whole mount quaked greatly. 19. And when the voice of the horn waxed louder and louder, Moses spoke, and God answered him by a voice.* ᵛⁱᵃ, ᵛⁱⁱˢ. 20. And the LORD came down upon mount Sinai, to the top of the mount; and the LORD called Moses to the top of the mount; and Moses went up. 21. And the LORD said unto Moses: 'Go down, charge the people, lest they break through unto the LORD to gaze, and many of them perish. 22. And let the priests also, that come near to the LORD, sanctify themselves, lest the LORD break forth upon them.' 23. And Moses said unto the LORD: 'The people cannot come up to mount Sinai; for thou didst charge us, saying: Set bounds about the mount, and sanctify it.' 24. And the LORD said unto him: 'Go, get thee down, and thou shalt come up, thou, and Aaron with thee; but let not the priests and the people break through to come up unto the LORD, lest He break forth upon them.' 25. So Moses went down unto the people, and told them.

## 20        CHAPTER XX

1. And God spake all these words, saying:
¶ 2. I am the LORD thy God, who brought thee out of the land of Egypt, out of the

---

**22.** *priests.* The first-born (Rashi, Ibn Ezra); cf. XIII, 2 and XXIV, 5. Even the 'priests', who are privileged to come nigh to God, require sanctification on this occasion.

*come near.* To the barrier of the Mount.
*break forth.* Or, 'make a breach in them.'

**23.** *the people cannot come.* Moses makes bold 'to question the need of such precaution, urging that the people are already debarred from trespassing by the bounds. God's answer in v. 24 shows a deeper knowledge of the human heart. His commands are never unnecessary' (H. F. Stewart).

**25.** *and told them.* He repeated the warning (Rashi).

In the next chapter, the Ten Commandments have a double accentuation in the Hebrew text—one for use in public reading in the Synagogue, and one for use in private devotion or study. The latter alone is given in the Authorized Prayer Book, p. 87.

### THE TEN COMMANDMENTS
#### CHAPTER XX, 1-14

The 'Ten Words' or Commandments, the עשרת הדברות or the Decalogue (from *deka*, ten, and *logos*, word), are supreme among the precepts of the Torah, both on account of their fundamental and far-reaching importance, and on account of the awe-inspiring manner in which they were revealed to the whole nation. Amid thunder and lightning and the sounding of the shofar, amid flames of fire that enveloped the smoking mountain, a Majestic Voice pronounced the Words which from that day to this have been the guide of conduct to mankind. That Revelation was the most remarkable event in the history of humanity. It was the birth-hour of the Religion of the Spirit, which was destined in time to illumine the souls, and order the lives, of all the children of men. The Decalogue is a sublime summary of human duties binding upon all mankind; a summary unequalled for simplicity, comprehensiveness and solemnity; a summary which bears divinity on its face, and cannot be antiquated as long as the world endures. It is at the same time a Divine epitome of the fundamentals of Israel's Creed and Life; and Jewish teachers, ancient and modern, have looked upon it as the fountain-head from which all Jewish truth and Jewish teaching could be derived. 'These Commandments are written on the walls of Synagogue and Church; they are the world's laws for all time. Never will their empire cease. The prophetic cry is true: the word of our God

EXODUS XX, 3 שמות יתרו כ

house of bondage. ¶ 3. Thou shalt have no other gods before Me. 4. Thou shalt not make unto thee a graven image, nor any manner of likeness, of any thing that is in heaven above, or that is in the earth beneath, or that is in the water under the earth; 5. thou shalt not bow down unto them, nor serve them; for I the LORD thy God am a jealous God, visiting the iniquity

יְהוָה אֱלֹהֶיךָ אֲשֶׁר הוֹצֵאתִיךָ מֵאֶרֶץ מִצְרַיִם מִבֵּית עֲבָדִים׃
3 לֹא־יִהְיֶה לְךָ אֱלֹהִים אֲחֵרִים עַל־פָּנָי׃ לֹא־תַעֲשֶׂה־לְךָ
4 פֶסֶל ׀ וְכָל־תְּמוּנָה אֲשֶׁר בַּשָּׁמַיִם ׀ מִמַּעַל וַאֲשֶׁר בָּאָרֶץ
5 מִתַּחַת וַאֲשֶׁר בַּמַּיִם ׀ מִתַּחַת לָאָרֶץ׃ לֹא־תִשְׁתַּחֲוֶה לָהֶם ה

shall stand for ever' (M. Joseph). See Additional Note E, 'The Decalogue,' p. 400.

The most natural division of the Ten Commandments is into *man's duties towards God* (בין אדם למקום), the opening five Commandments engraved on the First Table; and *man's duties to his fellow-man* (בין אדם לחברו), the five Commandments engraved on the Second Table.

## FIRST TABLE: DUTIES TOWARDS GOD

### FIRST COMMANDMENT: RECOGNITION OF THE SOVEREIGNTY OF GOD

**2.** *I am the LORD thy God.* Jewish Tradition considers this verse as the first of the Ten Words, and deduces from it the positive precept, *To believe in the existence of God.*

*I.* Heb. *anochi.* The God adored by Judaism is not an impersonal Force, an It, whether spoken of as 'Nature' or 'World-Reason'. The God of Israel is the Source not only of power and life, but of consciousness, personality, moral purpose and ethical action (M. Joël).

*thy God.* The emphasis is on *thy.* He is the God not merely of the past generations, but of every individual soul in each generation.

*who brought thee out of the land of Egypt.* God is not here designated, 'Creator of heaven and earth'. Israel's God is seen not merely in Nature, but in the destinies of man. He had revealed Himself to Israel in a great historic deed, the greatest in the life of any people: the God who saved Israel from slavery had a moral claim, as their Benefactor and Redeemer, on their gratitude and obedience. 'The foundation of Jewish life is not merely that there is only one God, but the conviction that this One, Only and True God is *my* God, my sole Ruler and Guide in all that I do' (Hirsch). The first Commandment is thus an exhortation to acknowledge the sovereignty of God (קבלת עול מלכות שמים, lit. 'the taking upon ourselves the yoke of the Kingdom of Heaven').

The reference to the redemption from Egypt is of deepest significance, not only to the Israelites, but to all mankind. The primal word of Israel's Divine Message is the proclamation of the One God as the God of Freedom. The recognition of God as the God of Freedom illumines the whole of human history for us. In the light of this truth, history becomes one continuous Divine revelation of the gradual growth of freedom and justice on earth.

### SECOND COMMANDMENT: THE UNITY AND SPIRITUALITY OF GOD

Jewish Tradition (based on Talmud, Midrash and Targum) makes *v.* 3 the beginning of the Second Commandment.

**3.** *thou shalt have no other gods.* Because there are no other gods besides God. The fundamental dogma of Israel's religion, as of all higher religion, is the Unity of God.

*before Me.* Or, 'besides Me'; or, 'to My face' (Koenig). Nothing shall receive the worship due to Him. Neither angels nor saintly men or women are to receive adoration as Divine beings; and the Jew is forbidden to pray to them. This Commandment also forbids belief in evil spirits, witchcraft, and similar evil superstition. Furthermore, he who believes in God will not put his trust in Chance or 'luck'.

**4.** *a graven image.* This verse forbids the worship of the One God in the wrong way. Judaism alone, from the very beginning, taught that God was a Spirit; and made it an unpardonable sin to worship God under any external form that human hands can fashion. No doubt this law hindered the free development of plastic arts in ancient Israel; but it was of incalculable importance for the purity of the conception of God.

*nor any manner of likeness.* Nor is He to be worshipped under any image, though such be not graven, which the human mind can conceive.

*in heaven above.* i.e. of the heavenly bodies; such as the ancestors of the Hebrews in Babylonia adored.

*in the earth beneath.* e.g. of animals, such as the Israelites saw the Egyptians worshipping.

*in the water under the earth.* The monsters of the deep.

**5.** *a jealous God.* The Heb. root for 'jealous', *kanna*, designates the just indignation of one injured; used here of the all-requiting righteousness of God. God desires to be all in all to His children, and claims an exclusive right to their love and obedience. He hates cruelty and unrighteousness, and loathes impurity and vice; and, even as a mother is jealous of all evil influences that rule her children, He is jealous

EXODUS XX, 6

of the fathers upon the children unto the third and fourth generation of them that hate Me; 6. and showing mercy unto the thousandth generation of them that love Me and keep My commandments. ¶ 7. Thou shalt not take the name of the LORD thy

וְלֹא תָעָבְדֵם כִּי אָנֹכִי יְהֹוָה אֱלֹהֶיךָ אֵל קַנָּא פֹּקֵד עֲוֺן
6 אָבֹת עַל־בָּנִים עַל־שִׁלֵּשִׁים וְעַל־רִבֵּעִים לְשֹׂנְאָי׃ וְעֹשֶׂה
7 חֶסֶד לַאֲלָפִים לְאֹהֲבַי וּלְשֹׁמְרֵי מִצְוֺתָי׃ ס לֹא תִשָּׂא

when, instead of purity and righteousness, it is idolatry and unholiness that command their heart-allegiance. It is, of course, evident that terms like 'jealousy' or 'zeal' are applied to God in an anthropomorphic sense. It is also evident that this jealousy of God is of the very essence of His holiness. Outside Israel, the ancients believed that the more gods the better; the richer the pantheon of a people, the greater its power. It is because the heathen deities were free from 'jealousy' and, therefore, tolerant of one another and all their abominations, that heathenism was spiritually so degrading and morally so devastating; see on Deut. IV, 24.

*visiting the iniquity of the fathers upon the children.* The Torah does not teach here or elsewhere that the sins of the guilty fathers shall be visited upon their innocent children. *The soul that sinneth it shall die* proclaims the Prophet Ezekiel. And in the administration of justice by the state, the Torah distinctly lays down, 'The fathers shall not be put to death for the children, neither shall the children be put to death for the fathers; every man shall be put to death for his own sin' (Deut. XXIV, 16). However, human experience all too plainly teaches the moral interdependence of parents and children. The bad example set by a father frequently corrupts those that come after him. His most dreadful bequest to his children is not a liability to punishment, but a liability to the commission of fresh offences. In every parent, therefore, the love of God, as a restraining power from evil actions, should be reinforced by love for his children; that they should not inherit the tendency to commit, and suffer the consequences of, *his* transgressions.

Another translation is, '*remembering* the sins of the fathers unto the children'; *i.e.* God *remembers* the sins of the fathers when about to punish the children. He distinguishes between the moral responsibility which falls exclusively upon the sinful parents, and the natural consequences and predisposition to sin, inherited by the descendants. He takes into account the evil environment and influence. He therefore tempers justice with mercy; and He does so to the third and fourth generation.

*of them that hate Me.* The Rabbis refer these words to the children. The sins of the fathers will be visited upon them, only if they too transgress God's commandments.

**6.** *unto the thousandth generation.* Contrast the narrow limits, three or four generations, within which the sin is visited, with the thousand generations that His mercy is shown to those who love God and keep His commandments. 'History and experience alike teach how often, and under what varied conditions, it happens that the misdeeds of a parent result in bitter consequence for the children. In His providence, the beneficent consequences of a life of goodness extend indefinitely further than the retribution which is the penalty of persistence in sin' (Driver)

*that love Me.* Note the verb 'love', used to designate the right attitude to God; cf. 'Thou shalt love the Lord thy God with all thy heart, with all thy soul, and with all thy might' (Deut. VI, 5). Love of God is the essence of Judaism, and from love of God springs obedience to His will.

THIRD COMMANDMENT: AGAINST PERJURY AND PROFANE SWEARING

The Second Commandment lays down the duty of worshipping God alone, and worshipping Him in spirit and not through images. The Third Commandment forbids us to dishonour God by invoking His name to attest what is untrue, or by joining His name to anything frivolous or insincere.

**7.** *take the name of the* LORD. Upon the lips; *i.e.* to utter.

*in vain.* lit. 'for vanity', or 'falsehood'; for anything that is unreal or groundless.

God is holy and His Name is holy. His Name, therefore, must not be used profanely to testify to anything that is untrue, insincere or empty. We are to swear by God's Name, only when we are fully convinced of the truth of our declaration, and then only when we are required to do so in a Court of law. This verse, according to the Rabbis, forbids using the Name of God in false oaths (*e.g.* that wood is stone); as well as using the Name of God in vain and flippant oaths (*e.g.* that stone is stone). God's Name is, moreover, not to be uttered unnecessarily in common conversation.

*will not hold him guiltless. i.e.* will not leave him unpunished. Perjury is an unpardonable offence, which, unless repressed by severest penalties, would destroy human society. The Rabbis ordained a special solemn warning to be administered to anyone about to take an oath in a Court of law. In various ages, saintly men have avoided swearing altogether. The Essenes, a Jewish Sect in the days of the Second Temple, held that 'he who cannot be believed without swearing is already condemned'. 'Let thy yea be yea, and thy nay, nay,' says the Talmud.

EXODUS XX, 8          שמות יתרו כ

God in vain; for the LORD will not hold him guiltless that taketh His name in vain. ¶ 8. Remember the sabbath day, to keep it holy. 9. Six days shalt thou labour, and do all thy work; 10. but the seventh day is a sabbath unto the LORD thy God, in it thou shalt not do any manner of work, thou, nor thy son, nor thy daughter, nor thy man-servant, nor thy maid-servant, nor thy cattle, nor thy stranger that is within

אֶת־שֵׁם־יְהֹוָה אֱלֹהֶיךָ לַשָּׁוְא כִּי לֹא יְנַקֶּה יְהֹוָה אֵת אֲשֶׁר־יִשָּׂא אֶת־שְׁמוֹ לַשָּׁוְא׃ פ

8 זָכוֹר אֶת־יוֹם הַשַּׁבָּת לְקַדְּשׁוֹ׃ שֵׁשֶׁת יָמִים תַּעֲבֹד וְעָשִׂיתָ
9 כָּל־מְלַאכְתֶּךָ׃ וְיוֹם הַשְּׁבִיעִי שַׁבָּת ׀ לַיהֹוָה אֱלֹהֶיךָ לֹא־
10 תַעֲשֶׂה כָל־מְלָאכָה אַתָּה ׀ וּבִנְךָ־וּבִתֶּךָ עַבְדְּךָ וַאֲמָתְךָ

### FOURTH COMMANDMENT: THE SABBATH

**8.** *remember.* The use of the word 'remember' may indicate that the institution was well known to the Israelites, long before their manna experiences; that it was a treasured and sacred institution inherited from the days of the Patriarchs; see also Note IV, p. 195. The Rabbis, however, explain 'Remember the Sabbath day' to mean, Bear it in mind and prepare for its advent; think of it day by day, and speak of its holiness and sanctifying influence. They instituted the Kiddush prayer, praising God for the gift of the Sabbath, to celebrate its coming in; and the Havdalah blessing, praising God for the distinction between the Sabbath and the six weekdays, to mark its going out.

*sabbath day.* Heb. *shabbath*, from a root meaning desisting from work.

*to keep it holy.* To treat it as a day unprofaned by workaday purposes. In addition to being a day of rest, the Sabbath is to be 'a holy day, set apart for the building up of the spiritual element in man' (Philo). Religious worship and religious instruction—the renewal of man's spiritual life in God—form an essential part of Sabbath observance. We therefore sanctify the Sabbath by a special Sabbath liturgy, by statutory Lessons from the Torah and the Prophets, and by attention to discourse and instruction by religious teachers. The Sabbath has thus proved the great educator of Israel in the highest education of all; namely the laws governing human conduct. The effect of these Sabbath prayers and Synagogue homilies upon the Jewish people has been incalculable. Leopold Zunz, the founder of the New Jewish Learning, has shown that almost the whole of Israel's inner history since the close of Bible times can be traced in following the development of these Sabbath discourses on the Torah. Sabbath worship is still the chief bond which unites Jews into a *religious* Brotherhood. Neglect of such worship injures the spiritual life of both the individual and the community.

**9.** *shalt thou labour.* Work during the six days of the week is as essential to man's welfare as is the rest on the seventh. No man or woman, howsoever rich, is freed from the obligation of doing some work, say the Rabbis, as idleness invariably leads to evil thoughts and evil deeds.

The proportion of one day's rest in seven has been justified by the experience of the last 3,000 years. Physical health suffers without such relief. The first French Republic rejected the one day in seven, and ordained a rest of one day in ten. The experiment was a complete failure.

*work.* Heb. מלאכה, that which man produces by his thought, effort and will.

**10.** *a sabbath unto the LORD.* A day specially devoted to God.

*thou shalt not do any manner of work.* Scripture does not give a list of labours forbidden on Sabbath; but it incidentally mentions field-labour, buying and selling, travelling, cooking, etc., as forbidden work. The Mishna enumerates under thirty-nine different heads all such acts as are in Jewish Law defined as 'work', and therefore not to be performed on the Sabbath day; such as ploughing, reaping, carrying loads, kindling a fire, writing, sewing, etc. Certain other things which cannot be brought under any of these 39 Categories are also prohibited, because they lead to a breach of Sabbath laws (שבות); as well as all acts that would tend to change the Sabbath into an ordinary day. Whatever we are not allowed to do ourselves, we must not have done for us by a fellow-Jew, even by one who is a Sabbath-breaker. All these Sabbath laws, however, are suspended as soon as there is the least danger to human life; פקוח נפש דוחה את השבת say the Rabbis. The Commandments of God are to promote life and well-being, a principle based on Lev. XVIII, 5, 'and these are the precepts of the LORD by which *ye shall live* וחי בהם.'

*thou.* The head of the house, responsible for all that dwell therein.

*manservant . . . maidservant.* Or, 'bondman' . . . 'bondmaid'; cf. Deut. v, 14. Not only the children but also the servants, whether Israelite or heathen, nay even the beasts of burden, are to share in the rest of the Sabbath day; see note on XXIII, 12. 'The Sabbath is a boundless boon for mankind and the greatest wonder of religion. Nothing can appear more simple than this institution, to rest on the seventh day after six days of work. And yet no legislator in the world hit upon this idea! To the Greeks and the Romans it was an object of derision, a super-

### EXODUS XX, 11

thy gates; 11. for in six days the LORD made heaven and earth, the sea, and all that in them is, and rested on the seventh day; wherefore the LORD blessed the sabbath day, and hallowed it. ¶ 12. Honour thy father and thy mother, that thy days may be

stitious usage. But it has removed with one stroke the contrast between slaves who must labour incessantly, and their masters who may celebrate continuously' (B. Jacob).

*thy cattle.* It is one of the glories of Judaism that, thousands of years before anyone else, it so fully recognized our duties to the dumb friends and helpers of man; see on Deut. v, 14.

*thy stranger.* The non-Israelite, who agrees to keep the seven Noachic precepts; see XII, 48. Though the Sabbath was not included in these precepts, he too is to enjoy the Sabbath rest for his own sake as a human being.

*within thy gates.* Within the borders of the town.

**11.** *rested.* See on Gen. II, 1–3.

By keeping the Sabbath, the Rabbis tell us, we testify to our belief in God as the Creator of the Universe; in a God who is not identical with Nature, but is a *free Personality*, the creator and ruler of Nature. The Talmudic mystics tell that when the heavens and earth were being called into existence, matter was getting out of hand, and the Divine Voice had to resound, 'Enough! So far and no further!' Man, made in the image of God, has been endowed by Him with the power of creating. But in his little universe, too, matter is constantly getting out of hand, threatening to overwhelm and crush out the soul. By means of the Sabbath, called זכרון למעשה בראשית, 'a memorial of Creation,' we are endowed with the Divine power of saying 'Enough!' to all rebellious claims of our environment, and are reminded of our potential victory over all material forces that would drag us down.

*blessed the sabbath.* Made it a day of blessing to those who observe it. See note on Gen. II, 3. The Sabbath was something quite new, which had never before existed in any nation or in any religion—a standing reminder that man can emancipate himself from the slavery of his worldly cares; that man was made for spiritual freedom, peace and joy (Ewald). 'The Sabbath is one of the glories of our humanity. For if to labour is noble, of our own free will to pause in that labour which may lead to success, to money, to fame is nobler still. To dedicate one day a week to rest and to God, this is the prerogative and the privilege of man alone' (C. G. Montefiore).

*and hallowed it.* Endowed it with sanctifying powers. The sanctity of the Sabbath is seen in its traces upon the Jewish soul. Isaiah speaks of the Sabbath as 'a delight'; and the Liturgy describes Sabbath rest as 'voluntary and congenial, happy and cheerful'. 'The Sabbath planted a heaven in every Jewish home, filling it with long-expected and blissfully-greeted peace; making each home a sanctuary, the father a priest, and the mother who lights the Sabbath candles an angel of light' (B. Jacob). The Sabbath banishes care and toil, grief and sorrow. All fasting (except on the Day of Atonement, which as the Sabbath of Sabbath transcends this rule of the ordinary Sabbath) is forbidden; and *all* mourning is suspended on the Sabbath day. Each of the three Sabbath-meals is an obligatory religious act (מצוה); and is in the olden Jewish home accompanied by זמירות, Table Songs. The spiritual effect of the Sabbath is termed by the Rabbis the 'extra soul', which the Israelite enjoys on that day.

Ignorant and unsympathetic critics condemn the Rabbinic Sabbath-laws with their numberless minutiæ as an intolerable 'burden'. These restrictions justify themselves in that the Jew who actually and strictly obeys these injunctions, *and only such a Jew*, has a Sabbath. And in regard to the alleged formalism of all these Sabbath laws, a German Protestant theologian of anti-Semitic tendencies has recently confessed: 'Anyone who has had the opportunity of knowing in our own day the inner life of Jewish families that observe the Law of the fathers with sincere piety and in all strictness, will have been astonished at the wealth of joyfulness, gratitude and sunshine, undreamt of by the outsider, which the Law animates in the Jewish home. The whole household rejoices on the Sabbath, which they celebrate with rare satisfaction not only as the day of rest, but rather as the day of rejoicing. Jewish prayers term the Sabbath a "joy of the soul" to him who hallows it; *he* "enjoys the abundance of Thy goodness". Such expressions are not mere words; they are the outcome of pure and genuine happiness and enthusiasm' (Kittel).

Without the observance of the Sabbath, of the olden Sabbath, of the Sabbath as perfected by the Rabbis, the whole of Jewish life would in time disappear.

FIFTH COMMANDMENT: HONOUR OF PARENTS

This Commandment follows the Sabbath command, because the Sabbath is the source and the guarantor of the family life; and it is among the Commandments engraved on the First Tablet, the laws of piety towards God, because parents stand in the place of God, so far as their children are concerned. Elsewhere in Scripture, the duty to one's parents stands likewise next to the duties towards God (Lev. XIX, 3).

EXODUS XX, 13

long upon the land which the LORD thy God giveth thee.

¶ 13. Thou shalt not murder.
Thou shalt not commit adultery.
Thou shalt not steal.
Thou shalt not bear false witness against thy neighbour.

שמות יתרו כ

12 וַיְקַדְּשֵׁהוּ׃ ס כַּבֵּד אֶת־אָבִיךָ וְאֶת־אִמֶּךָ לְמַעַן יַאֲרִכוּן
13 יָמֶיךָ עַל הָאֲדָמָה אֲשֶׁר־יְהֹוָה אֱלֹהֶיךָ נֹתֵן לָךְ׃ ס לֹא
תִּרְצָח׃ ס לֹא תִּנְאָף׃ ס לֹא תִּגְנֹב׃ ס לֹא־
14 תַעֲנֶה בְרֵעֲךָ עֵד שָׁקֶר׃ ס לֹא תַחְמֹד בֵּית רֵעֶךָ

**12.** *honour thy father and thy mother.* By showing them respect, obedience and love. Each parent alike is entitled to these. For although 'father' is here mentioned first, in Lev. XIX, 3 we read, 'each one shall fear (*i.e.* reverence) *his mother* and his father.' And this obligation extends beyond the grave. The child must revere the memory of the departed parent in act and feeling. Respect to parents is among the primary human duties; and no excellence can atone for the lack of such respect. Only in cases of extreme rarity (*e.g.* where godless parents would guide children towards crime) can disobedience be justified. Proper respect to parents may at times involve immeasurable hardship; yet the duty remains. Shem and Japhet throw the mantle of charity over their father's shame: only an unnatural child gloats over a parent's disgrace or dishonour. See note on Gen. IX, 23 (p. 34) and Prov. XXX, 17. The greatest achievement open to parents is to be ever fully worthy of their children's reverence and trust and love.

*that thy days may be long. i.e.* the honouring one's parents will be rewarded by happiness and blessing. This is not always seen in the life of the individual; but the Commandment is addressed to the individual as a member of society, as the child of a people. The home is infinitely more important to a people than the schools, the professions or its political life; and filial respect is the ground of national permanence and prosperity. If a nation thinks of its past with contempt, it may well contemplate its future with despair; it perishes through moral suicide.

### SECOND TABLE: DUTIES TOWARDS FELLOW-MEN

The first five Commandments have each an explanatory addition; the last five are brief and emphatic Thou shalt not's. Our relation to our neighbours requires no elucidation; since we feel the wrongs which others do to us, we have a clear guide how we ought to act towards others. These duties have their root in the principle 'Thou shalt love thy neighbour as thyself', applied to life, house, property and honour.

### THE SIXTH COMMANDMENT: THE SANCTITY OF HUMAN LIFE

**13.** *thou shalt not murder.* The infinite worth of human life is based on the fact that man is created 'in the image of God'. God alone gives life, and He alone may take it away. The intentional killing of any human being, apart from capital punishment legally imposed by a judicial tribunal, or in a war for the defence of national and human rights, is absolutely forbidden. Child life is as sacred as that of an adult. In Greece, weak children were *exposed*; that is, abandoned on a lonely mountain to perish. Jewish horror of child-murder was long looked upon as a contemptible prejudice. 'It is a crime among the Jews to kill any child,' sneered the Roman historian Tacitus.

Hebrew law carefully distinguishes homicide from wilful murder. It saves the involuntary slayer of his fellow-man from vendetta; and does not permit composition, or money-fine, for the life of the murderer. Jewish ethics enlarges the notion of murder so as to include both the doing of anything by which the health and well-being of a fellow-man is undermined, and the omission of any act by which a fellow-man could be saved in peril, distress or despair. For the prohibition of suicide, see note on Gen. IX, 5.

### SEVENTH COMMANDMENT: THE SANCTITY OF MARRIAGE

*adultery.* 'Is an execrable and God-detested wrong-doing' (Philo). This Commandment against infidelity warns husband and wife alike against profaning the sacred Covenant of Marriage. It involves the prohibition of immoral speech, immodest conduct, or association with persons who scoff at the sacredness of purity. Among no people has there been a purer home-life than among the Jewish people. No woman enjoyed greater respect than the Jewish woman; and she fully merited that respect.

### EIGHTH COMMANDMENT: THE SANCTITY OF PROPERTY

*thou shalt not steal.* Property represents the fruit of industry and intelligence. Any aggression on the property of our neighbour is, therefore, an assault on his human personality. This Commandment also has a wider application than theft and robbery; and it forbids every illegal acquisition of property by cheating, by embezzlement or forgery. 'There are transactions which are legal and do not involve any breach of law, which are yet base and disgraceful. Such are all transactions in which a person takes advantage of the ignorance or embarrassment of his neighbour for the purpose of increasing his own property' (M. Friedländer).

### EXODUS XX, 14

¶ 14. Thou shalt not covet thy neighbour's house; thou shalt not covet thy neighbour's wife, nor his man-servant, nor his maidservant, nor his ox, nor his ass, nor any thing that is thy neighbour's.*ᵛⁱⁱ ᵃ· ¶ 15. And all the people perceived the thunderings, and the lightnings, and the voice of the horn, and the mountain smoking; and when the people saw it, they trembled, and stood afar off. 16. And they said unto Moses: 'Speak thou with us, and we will hear; but let not God speak with us, lest we die.' 17. And Moses said unto the people: 'Fear not; for God is come to prove you, and that His fear may be before you, that ye

ס לֹא תַחְמֹד אֵשֶׁת רֵעֶךָ וְעַבְדּוֹ וַאֲמָתוֹ וְשׁוֹרוֹ וַחֲמֹרוֹ וְכֹל אֲשֶׁר לְרֵעֶךָ׃ פ
שביעי
טו וְכָל־הָעָם רֹאִים אֶת־הַקּוֹלֹת וְאֶת־הַלַּפִּידִם וְאֵת קוֹל הַשֹּׁפָר וְאֶת־הָהָר עָשֵׁן וַיַּרְא הָעָם וַיָּנֻעוּ וַיַּעַמְדוּ מֵרָחֹק׃
16 וַיֹּאמְרוּ אֶל־מֹשֶׁה דַּבֵּר־אַתָּה עִמָּנוּ וְנִשְׁמָעָה וְאַל־יְדַבֵּר
17 עִמָּנוּ אֱלֹהִים פֶּן־נָמוּת׃ וַיֹּאמֶר מֹשֶׁה אֶל־הָעָם אַל־תִּירָאוּ כִּי לְבַעֲבוּר נַסּוֹת אֶתְכֶם בָּא הָאֱלֹהִים וּבַעֲבוּר תִּהְיֶה
18 יִרְאָתוֹ עַל־פְּנֵיכֶם לְבִלְתִּי תֶחֱטָאוּ׃ וַיַּעֲמֹד הָעָם מֵרָחֹק

---

### NINTH COMMANDMENT: AGAINST BEARING FALSE WITNESS

The three preceding Commandments are concerned with wrongs inflicted upon our neighbour by actual deed: this Commandment is concerned with wrong inflicted by word of mouth.

*thou shalt not bear false witness.* The prohibition embraces all forms of slander, defamation and misrepresentation, whether of an individual, a group, a people, a race, or a Faith. None have suffered so much from slander, defamation and misrepresentation as the Jew and Judaism. Thus, modernist theologians still repeat that, according to this Commandment, the Israelite is prohibited only from slandering a fellow-Israelite; because, they allege, the Heb. word for 'neighbour' (רע) here, and in 'Thou shalt love *thy neighbour* as thyself' (Lev. XIX, 18), does not mean fellow-man, but only fellow-Israelite. This is a glaring instance of bearing false witness against Judaism; and is proved to be so by XI, 2 ('Let every man ask of his neighbour, jewels of silver, etc.'), where the word *neighbour* cannot possibly mean an Israelite, but distinctly refers to the Egyptian. In this Commandment, as in all moral precepts in the Torah, the Heb. word *neighbour* is equivalent to *fellowman*.

### TENTH COMMANDMENT: AGAINST COVETOUS DESIRES

**14.** *covet.* i.e. to long for the possession of anything that we cannot get in an honest and legal manner. This Commandment goes to the root of all evil actions—the unholy instincts and impulses of predatory desire, which are the spring of nearly every sin against a neighbour. The man who does not covet his neighbour's goods will not bear false witness against him; he will neither rob nor murder, nor will he commit adultery. It commands self-control; for every man has it in his power to determine whether his desires are to master him, or he is to master his desires. Without such self-control, there can be no worthy human life; it alone is the measure of true manhood or womanhood. 'Who is strong?' ask the Rabbis. 'He who controls his passions,' is their reply.

*thy neighbour's house.* i.e. his household. The examples enumerated are the objects most likely to be coveted.

This Commandment is somewhat differently worded in the Decalogue which is repeated by Moses in his Farewell Addresses to Israel. That difference, together with the other slight variations in that Decalogue from the original in this chapter of Exodus, is dealt with in the Commentary on *Deuteronomy*.

### 15–18. THE EFFECT OF THE REVELATION

**15.** *perceived the thunderings, and the lightnings.* An example of the rhetorical figure called *zeugma*, by which a verb is used with two or more objects, some of which should strictly be governed by another verb. As soon as the people heard the thunder and saw the lightning (XIX, 16, 19) they trembled, even before the Commandments were given; see Deut. v, 19–30.

*trembled.* Or, 'reeled,' fell in panic.

**16.** *we will hear.* And obey; see Deut. v, 24.
*but let not God speak with us.* Prior to the promulgation of the Decalogue.
*lest we die.* See Deut. v, 22.

**17.** *to prove you.* Moses pacifies the people. The object of the terrors of Sinai was to 'prove' them; i.e. to put them to the proof (XVI, 4) whether they were inclined to submit themselves to God. Luzzatto takes the expression in the sense of testing a person desiring to be initiated, with a view of determining his fitness.

*that His fear may be before you.* The fear of God means the fear or dread of offending God; and since this prevents sin, the 'fear of God' becomes the 'love of God'.

*that ye sin not.* God desires that righteousness shall be the rule of man's life.

EXODUS XX, 18

sin not.' 18. And the people stood afar off; but Moses drew near unto the thick darkness where God was.*ᵐ ᵃ· ¶ 19. And the LORD said unto Moses: Thus thou shalt say unto the children of Israel: Ye yourselves have seen that I have talked with you from heaven. 20. Ye shall not make with Me—gods of silver, or gods of gold, ye shall not make unto you.*ᵐ ˢ· 21. An altar of earth thou shalt make unto Me, and shalt sacrifice thereon thy burnt-offerings, and thy peace-offerings, thy sheep, and thine oxen; in every place where I cause My name to be mentioned I will come unto thee and bless thee. 22. And if thou make Me an altar of stone, thou shalt not build it of hewn stones; for if thou lift up thy tool upon it, thou hast profaned it. 23. Neither shalt thou go up by steps unto Mine altar, that thy nakedness be not uncovered thereon.

שמות יתרו כ

מפטיר וּמֹשֶׁה נִגַּשׁ אֶל־הָעֲרָפֶל אֲשֶׁר־שָׁם הָאֱלֹהִים׃ ס
19 וַיֹּאמֶר יְהֹוָה אֶל־מֹשֶׁה כֹּה תֹאמַר אֶל־בְּנֵי יִשְׂרָאֵל אַתֶּם
פטיר כ רְאִיתֶם כִּי מִן־הַשָּׁמַיִם דִּבַּרְתִּי עִמָּכֶם׃ לֹא תַעֲשׂוּן אִתִּי
לספ׳) 21 אֱלֹהֵי כֶסֶף וֵאלֹהֵי זָהָב לֹא תַעֲשׂוּ לָכֶם׃ מִזְבַּח אֲדָמָה
תַּעֲשֶׂה־לִּי וְזָבַחְתָּ עָלָיו אֶת־עֹלֹתֶיךָ וְאֶת־שְׁלָמֶיךָ אֶת־
צֹאנְךָ וְאֶת־בְּקָרֶךָ בְּכָל־הַמָּקוֹם אֲשֶׁר אַזְכִּיר אֶת־שְׁמִי
22 אָבוֹא אֵלֶיךָ וּבֵרַכְתִּיךָ׃ וְאִם־מִזְבַּח אֲבָנִים תַּעֲשֶׂה־לִּי
לֹא־תִבְנֶה אֶתְהֶן גָּזִית כִּי חַרְבְּךָ הֵנַפְתָּ עָלֶיהָ וַתְּחַלְלֶהָ׃
23 וְלֹא־תַעֲלֶה בְמַעֲלֹת עַל־מִזְבְּחִי אֲשֶׁר לֹא־תִגָּלֶה
עֶרְוָתְךָ עָלָיו׃

**18.** The people remained standing afar off (see *v.* 15), whilst Moses approached the thick darkness.

*where God was.* 'Where the Glory of God was' (Onkelos).

### THE BOOK OF THE COVENANT

#### CHAPTERS XX, 19–XXIII, 33

This section is a body of miscellaneous laws—civil, criminal, moral and religious. Nothing could be more appropriate for the opening of such a collection of laws than regulations for public worship.

#### 19–23. HOW GOD IS TO BE WORSHIPPED

**19.** *ye yourselves have seen.* You have been eye-witnesses, and know the reality of My revelation.

*from heaven.* In an overwhelming and incomparable manner (Strack).

**20.** *make with Me—gods.* The regulations concerning worship begin by repeating the prohibition of idol-worship, even if the idol be of silver or gold. The incident of the Golden Calf shows that such repetition was far from unnecessary.

**21.** *an altar of earth.* Not even an altar of stone is essential for worshipping God; see *v.* 22.

*thereon.* Better, '*thereby*,' for the animal was not to be slain on the altar.

*in every place.* Refers to the different places at which the Tabernacle rested, from the entry of the Israelites into Canaan to the erection of the Temple by Solomon (Hoffmann); see Additional Notes on Deuteronomy, *Centralization of Worship*.

*to be mentioned.* i.e. wherever I command thee to build an altar or sanctuary unto Me. To *mention* or *remember* the name of God means to worship Him; cf. Ps. xx, 8 and Isa. xxvi, 13.

**22.** *an altar of stone.* Is permissible; but the stones must be of unhewn natural rock, with the stamp of God's handiwork alone.

*tool.* lit. 'sword' or, 'iron instrument.' The Talmud explains this prohibition as follows: 'Iron shortens life, while the altar prolongs it. The sword, or weapon of iron, is the symbol of strife; whereas the altar is the symbol of reconciliation and peace between God and man, and between man and his fellow.'

**23.** *uncovered.* Lest the clothes of the priest be disturbed and his limbs uncovered. It is a warning not only against the frantic indecencies of pagan rituals, but against all infractions of propriety in worship.

# HAFTORAH YITHRO    הפטרת יתרו

### ISAIAH VI–VII, 6 AND IX, 5, 6

CHAPTER VI

1. In the year that king Uzziah died I saw the Lord sitting upon a throne high and lifted up, and His train filled the temple. 2. Above Him stood the seraphim; each one had six wings: with twain he covered his face, and with twain he covered his feet, and with twain he did fly. 3. And one called unto another, and said:

Holy, holy, holy, is the Lord of hosts;
The whole earth is full of His glory.

4. And the posts of the door were moved at the voice of them that called, and the house was filled with smoke 5. Then said I:

---

For the life and message of Isaiah, see p. 225.

The Sedrah describes the Revelation on Sinai that was to turn Israel into a Holy Nation, and guide the children of men in the paths of Reverence and Righteousness. The Haftorah records the revelation that came to Isaiah in his early manhood, when, one day in the Temple, he heard the Seraphim sing, 'Holy, holy, holy is the Lord of hosts, the whole earth is full of His glory.' This cry out of eternity, proclaiming the ineffable holiness, the supreme majesty, and universal sovereignty of God, has been called the quintessence of all the teachings of the Prophets. It is the quintessence of the teachings of all true Religion.

### 1–5. THE CALL OF ISAIAH

**1.** *in the year that king Uzziah died.* After a prosperous reign of over a half-century (790–740 B.C.E.). He had greatly increased the wealth and power of the kingdom of Judah (II Chron. XXVI, 1-15); and his death filled all minds with misgivings. 'What will become of Judah now that Uzziah is gone?' was on the lips of all. In that year Isaiah 'saw the Lord', and realized that though mortal rulers come and go, God is in His heaven. This vision marks the beginning of Isaiah's ministry.

*I saw the Lord.* In prophetic ecstasy (Kimchi). The unseen spiritual world opens to Isaiah's inner eye; the Temple walls seem to him to expand into a Heavenly Palace; and he beholds God enthroned as the Sovereign of every being on earth or in heaven. 'How God reveals Himself to His chosen messengers will scarcely ever be understood. It is the greatest of mysteries; although *that* He reveals Himself is the greatest of certainties' (Marti).

**2.** *above Him stood the seraphim.* Better, *seraphim were standing over Him; i.e.* angelic beings were in attendance upon Him.

*covered his face.* In reverence (Exod. III, 6).

*covered his feet.* In humility, as unworthy to meet directly the Divine glance.

*he did fly.* To perform the will of the Creator.

**3.** *holy, holy, holy.* Threefold repetition in Heb. poetry indicates the superlative degree: God is the highest Holiness. 'Holy—in the highest Heaven, the place of His Divine abode; holy—upon earth, the work of His might; holy —for ever and ever unto all eternity' (Targum Jonathan).

'The Holy One of Israel,' is the title of God in Isaiah's writings. In Rabbinical literature, the most frequent Name used for God is הקדוש ברוך הוא 'The Holy One, blessed be He.' *Holy* denotes the awe-ful and august ethical majesty of God (R. Otto), His moral perfectness and complete freedom from all that makes men imperfect and impure. It denotes 'more than goodness, more than purity, more than righteousness: it embraces all these in their ideal completeness, but it expresses besides the recoil from everything which is their opposite' (Driver). Holiness is the *essential* attribute of God. Because of this holiness, inherent in Himself, His power is absolute and infinite.

*the whole earth is full of His glory.* All that is sublime in nature and human history is the outward expression and eradiation of the Divine Spirit.

**4.** *posts.* Though the vision is seen with his inner eye, it is none the less actual. In the agitation of such a soul-experience, the pillars shake and the House becomes blurred before his physical eyes.

**5.** *I am undone.* God's holiness is, as it were, 'a devouring fire' of all impurity. The Prophet, therefore, is overwhelmed by the sense of his own unworthiness, and of the unworthiness of his people. Like Abraham of old, he feels that

ISAIAH VI, 6

Woe is me! for I am undone;
Because I am a man of unclean lips,
And I dwell in the midst of a people of unclean lips;
For mine eyes have seen the King,
The LORD of hosts.

6. Then flew unto me one of the seraphim, with a glowing stone in his hand, which he had taken with the tongs from off the altar;
7. and he touched my mouth with it, and said:

Lo, this hath touched thy lips;
And thine inquity is taken away,
And thy sin expiated.

8. And I heard the voice of the Lord, saying:

Whom shall I send,
And who will go for us?

Then I said: 'Here am I; send me.' 9. And He said: 'Go, and tell this people:

Hear ye indeed, but understand not;
And see ye indeed, but perceive not.

10. Make the heart of this people fat,
And make their ears heavy,
And shut their eyes;
Lest they, seeing with their eyes,
And hearing with their ears,
And understanding with their heart,
Return, and be healed.'

11. Then said I: 'Lord, how long?' And He answered:

'Until cities be waste without inhabitant,
And houses without man,
And the land become utterly waste,

v. 10. קמץ ברביע

he and his people and all existence are but 'dust and ashes' in the presence of the Divine Holiness (R. Otto).

*mine eyes have seen the King.* No vision of any form or appearance is meant, but a revelation of His transcendent holiness and might.

### 6–13. ISAIAH'S PURIFICATION AND MISSION

**6.** *from off the altar.* Where the fire is holy; and where there is no 'strange fire' (Ibn Ezra). Man must be sanctified, *i.e.* purged of impurity, before he can hear God. 'As earthly fire burns away the outward impurity, so the heavenly fire burns away the defilement of sin, first from the lips, but through them from the whole man' (Dillmann).

**8.** *who will go for us.* The plural is the so-called plural of majesty; as in Gen. I, 26.

*here am I; send me.* Isaiah answers the call not out of compulsion, but out of freedom. His eager response rushes from heart and lips cleansed of human impurity.

**9.** *hear ye indeed.* The great failing of the inhabitants of Judah and Jerusalem during the prosperous reign of Uzziah was an insensibility to God and Divine things; they did not *miss* God, and therefore they were not prepared to *seek* Him. To such a generation, the first effect of Isaiah's message of the holiness of God and His absolute sovereignty over their lives, would be to *increase* their blindness and obduracy. It would tend to 'harden their hearts'; see on Exod. IV, 21. Most of his hearers will stubbornly reject his message; they will harden their hearts; and the fuller the teachings imparted to them, the deeper will be the guilt of rejecting them. This tragic effect of his message Isaiah is clearly shown on the very threshold of his ministry; and the '*result* of the prophet's ministration is described as though it were its purpose' (Skinner).

**11.** *Lord, how long?* How long shall this spiritual blindness and unwillingness to repent endure? This question is wrung from the Prophet by his compassion for his people. The answer is given in *v.* 11–13. The perseverance in unbelief will continue until national disasters and exile have swept away the idolatrous majority and enabled the Remnant, the indestructible germ of spiritual Israel, to flourish and blossom under God's care.

## ISAIAH VI, 12

12. And the LORD have removed men far away,
And the forsaken places be many in the midst of the land.

13. And if there be yet a tenth in it, it shall again be eaten up; as a terebinth, and as an oak, whose stock remaineth, when they cast their leaves, so the holy seed shall be the stock thereof.'

### CHAPTER VII

1. And it came to pass in the days of Ahaz the son of Jotham, the son of Uzziah, king of Judah, that Rezin the king of Aram, and Pekah the son of Remaliah, king of Israel, went up to Jerusalem to war against it; but could not prevail against it. 2. And it was told the house of David, saying: 'Aram is confederate with Ephraim.' And his heart was moved, and the heart of his people, as the trees of the forest are moved with the wind. ¶3. Then said the LORD unto Isaiah: 'Go forth now to meet Ahaz, thou, and ¹Shear-jashub thy son, at the end of the conduit of the upper pool, in the highway of the fullers' field; 4. and say unto him: Keep calm, and be quiet; fear not, neither let thy heart be faint, because of these two tails of smoking firebrands, for the fierce anger of Rezin and Aram, and of the son of Remaliah. 5. Because Aram hath counselled evil against thee, Ephraim also, and the son of Remaliah, saying: 6. Let us go up against Judah, and vex it, and let us make a breach therein for us, and set up a king in the midst of it, even the son of Tabeel.

---

¹ That is, *A remnant shall return.*

ישעיה ו ז

12 אָדָם וְהָאֲדָמָה תִּשָּׁאֶה שְׁמָמָה: וְרִחַק יְהוָה אֶת־הָאָדָם
13 וְרַבָּה הָעֲזוּבָה בְּקֶרֶב הָאָרֶץ: וְעוֹד בָּהּ עֲשִׂרִיָּה וְשָׁבָה
וְהָיְתָה לְבָעֵר כָּאֵלָה וְכָאַלּוֹן אֲשֶׁר בְּשַׁלֶּכֶת מַצֶּבֶת בָּם
זֶרַע קֹדֶשׁ מַצַּבְתָּהּ:

### CAP. VII. ז

א וַיְהִי בִּימֵי אָחָז בֶּן־יוֹתָם בֶּן־עֻזִּיָּהוּ מֶלֶךְ יְהוּדָה עָלָה רְצִין
מֶלֶךְ־אֲרָם וּפֶקַח בֶּן־רְמַלְיָהוּ מֶלֶךְ־יִשְׂרָאֵל יְרוּשָׁלִַם
2 לַמִּלְחָמָה עָלֶיהָ וְלֹא יָכֹל לְהִלָּחֵם עָלֶיהָ: וַיֻּגַּד לְבֵית דָּוִד
לֵאמֹר נָחָה אֲרָם עַל־אֶפְרָיִם וַיָּנַע לְבָבוֹ וּלְבַב עַמּוֹ כְּנוֹעַ
3 עֲצֵי־יַעַר מִפְּנֵי־רוּחַ: וַיֹּאמֶר יְהוָה אֶל־יְשַׁעְיָהוּ צֵא־
נָא לִקְרַאת אָחָז אַתָּה וּשְׁאָר יָשׁוּב בְּנֶךָ אֶל־קְצֵה תְּעָלַת
4 הַבְּרֵכָה הָעֶלְיוֹנָה אֶל־מְסִלַּת שְׂדֵה כוֹבֵס: וְאָמַרְתָּ אֵלָיו
הִשָּׁמֵר וְהַשְׁקֵט אַל־תִּירָא וּלְבָבְךָ אַל־יֵרַךְ מִשְּׁנֵי זַנְבוֹת
הָאוּדִים הָעֲשֵׁנִים הָאֵלֶּה בָּחֳרִי־אַף רְצִין וַאֲרָם וּבֶן־
ה רְמַלְיָהוּ: יַעַן כִּי־יָעַץ עָלֶיךָ אֲרָם רָעָה אֶפְרַיִם וּבֶן־רְמַלְיָהוּ
6 לֵאמֹר: נַעֲלֶה בִיהוּדָה וּנְקִיצֶנָּה וְנַבְקִעֶנָּה אֵלֵינוּ וְנַמְלִיךְ
מֶלֶךְ בְּתוֹכָהּ אֵת בֶּן־טָבְאַל:

ז׳ v. 2. מלעיל

---

### CHAPTER VII

From the vision of the future, the prophet returns to events of his day. The kings of Israel, having failed to induce Ahaz, king of Judah, to join them in their alliance against Assyria, advanced upon Jerusalem, and were determined to dethrone Ahaz. Isaiah bids the despairing king have faith in God and fear nought.

**2.** *the house of David, i.e.* Ahaz.
*Ephraim.* The poetical name for the kingdom of Israel.

**13.** *if there be yet a tenth.* After the exile of the ten tribes of the Northern Kingdom, Judah maintained its existence for 134 years.
*it shall again be eaten up.* The kingdom of Judah too shall go into exile.
*whose stock remaineth.* As when a tree is cut down, the stump retains the vitality from which new shoots may grow, so there is a kernel of Israel, a Remnant of faithful and godly men, that form the indestructible 'stock' of the Tree of Judaism.

**3.** *Shear-jashub.* lit. 'A remnant shall return'. Isaiah gave significant and prophetic names to his sons, as did Hosea (I, 4, 9).
*conduit of the upper pool.* Identified with recently discovered reservoirs near to the pool of Siloam. Ahaz had gone there to assure himself of an adequate water supply in the event of a siege.

**4.** *tails of smoking firebrands.* Incapable of more mischief; the strength of the advance of the two allies is exhausted; they do not know that they are two dying nations already doomed. The Assyrian hordes were at that moment hastening on to descend upon Syria and Israel.
*son of Remaliah. i.e.* Pekah, king of Israel.

**6.** *a breach.* In its walls; *i.e.* capture its capital city.
*son of Tabeel.* One of their own puppets, amenable to their plans.
The Prophet assures Ahaz that the campaign against him will utterly fail, and exhorts him to have confidence in God's care and guidance.

ISAIAH IX, 5                                                                                  ישעיה ט

### Chapter IX                                                                                 Cap. IX. ט

5. For a child is born unto us,
A son is given unto us;
And the government is upon his shoulder;
And his name is called
¹Pele-joez-el-gibbor-
Abi-ad-sar-shalom;
6. That the government may be increased,
And of peace there be no end,
Upon the throne of David, and upon his kingdom,
To establish it, and to uphold it
Through justice and through righteousness
From henceforth even for ever.
The zeal of the LORD of hosts doth perform this.

כִּי־יֶלֶד יֻלַּד־לָנוּ                                                                          ה
בֵּן נִתַּן־לָנוּ וַתְּהִי הַמִּשְׂרָה עַל־שִׁכְמוֹ וַיִּקְרָא שְׁמוֹ פֶּלֶא
6 יוֹעֵץ אֵל גִּבּוֹר אֲבִי־עַד שַׂר־שָׁלוֹם: לְםַרְבֵּה הַמִּשְׂרָה
וּלְשָׁלוֹם אֵין־קֵץ עַל־כִּסֵּא דָוִד וְעַל־מַמְלַכְתּוֹ לְהָכִין אֹתָהּ
וּלְסַעֲדָהּ בְּמִשְׁפָּט וּבִצְדָקָה מֵעַתָּה וְעַד־עוֹלָם קִנְאַת יְהֹוָה
צְבָאוֹת תַּעֲשֶׂה־זֹּאת:

---

¹ That is, *Wonderful in counsel is God the mighty, the Everlasting Father, the Ruler of peace.*           מ' סתומה באמצע תיבה v. 6.

### Chapter IX, 5, 6

The Haftorah breaks off here and continues with two verses from a later prophecy, concerning Hezekiah, the son of Ahaz, then but a lad. His righteous reign will lift Judah from the degenerate condition into which it had sunk. Hezekiah will be the leader of the 'holy seed', the indestructible faithful Remnant in Israel.

**5. a child is born unto us.** The correct rendering of the Heb. is: unto us a child *has been* born —unto us a son *has been* given. The reference is not to any future Messiah, nor to any one yet unborn (see p. 202). Hezekiah had already given promise of the qualities of heart and mind that pointed to him as the future regenerator of his people.

*the government is upon his shoulder.* This clearly indicates that the 'crown prince' is the person referred to.

*pele-joez-el-gibbor-abi-ad-sar-shalom. i.e. Wonderful in counsel is God the mighty, the Everlasting Father, the Ruler of Peace* (Rashi and Luzzatto). This is the significant name by which the child will be known; it is, therefore, left untranslated; in the same way as *Shear-jashub* (v. 3), *Immanuel* (VII, 14) and *Maher-shalal-hash-baz* (VIII, 3) are all given in the Hebrew form.

The RV gives 'Wonderful, Counsellor, Mighty God, Everlasting Father, Prince of Peace'. This is quite impossible. No true Prophet—indeed, no true Israelite—would apply a term like 'Mighty God' or 'Everlasting Father' to any mortal prince. What is equally decisive against the RV rendering (which is followed by all Christian translators and, with some modifications, by many Jewish ones; *e.g.* Zunz, Leeser, Philippson) is the fact that the significant names of the children of the Prophets never describe the child, but in each case embody some religious message to the Prophet's contemporaries. Thus, *Shear-jashub* proclaimed that a faithful Remnant would survive the successive calamities that would befall Israel. This is true of all the other significant names in Isaiah; as well as of Hosea's names, like Lo-ruhammah and Lo-ammi.

**6.** *the throne of David.* The kingdom of Israel, devastated by the Assyrians in the days of Ahaz, fell into the hands of Hezekiah by reason of the weakening of Assyria in his days. For the first time since the days of Solomon, the national unity was re-established, and Hezekiah was the first ruler once more to occupy the throne of David; hence the Prophet speaks of the *increase of his government*.

*for ever. i.e.* during the days of Hezekiah (Rashi).

*through justice and through righteousness.* Characteristics of true government—and of Hezekiah's reign.

*the zeal of the LORD of hosts.* The love of God for His people, and His passion for Righteousness, guarantee the promised deliverance.

# EXODUS XXI, 1

## CHAPTER XXI

1. Now these are the ordinances which thou shalt set before them. ¶ 2. If thou buy a Hebrew servant, six years he shall serve; and in the seventh he shall go out free for nothing. 3. If he come in by himself, he shall go out by himself; if he be married, then his wife shall go out with him. 4. If his master give him a wife, and she bear him sons or daughters; the wife and her children shall be her master's, and he shall go out by himself. 5. But if the servant shall

## CAP. XXI. כא

שמות משפטים כא

פ פ פ יח 18

2 וְאֵ֙לֶּה֙ הַמִּשְׁפָּטִ֔ים אֲשֶׁ֥ר תָּשִׂ֖ים לִפְנֵיהֶֽם׃ כִּ֤י תִקְנֶה֙ עֶ֣בֶד
3 עִבְרִ֗י שֵׁ֤שׁ שָׁנִים֙ יַעֲבֹ֔ד וּבַ֨שְּׁבִעִ֔ת יֵצֵ֥א לַֽחָפְשִׁ֖י חִנָּֽם׃ אִם־
בְּגַפּ֥וֹ יָבֹ֖א בְּגַפּ֣וֹ יֵצֵ֑א אִם־בַּ֤עַל אִשָּׁה֙ ה֔וּא וְיָצְאָ֥ה אִשְׁתּ֖וֹ
4 עִמּֽוֹ׃ אִם־אֲדֹנָיו֙ יִתֶּן־ל֣וֹ אִשָּׁ֔ה וְיָלְדָה־ל֥וֹ בָנִ֖ים א֣וֹ בָנ֑וֹת

---

## VI. MISHPATIM

### (CHAPTERS XXI–XXIV)

### CIVIL LEGISLATION

**CHAPTER XXI, 1–32. THE RIGHTS OF PERSONS**

**1.** *now these are.* lit. 'and these are.' 'And links together the preceding commandments with those that follow. As the preceding commandments were revealed on Sinai, so were the succeeding regulations also communicated there' (Mechilta). The Torah recognizes no strong line of demarcation between the Decalogue and the civil laws in the chapters that follow it. All alike disclose the will of God. His Torah treats of every phase of human and national life—civil as well as religious, physical as well as spiritual.

*set before them.* Rehearse and explain to them.

### 2–11. THE HEBREW SERVANT

**2.** *servant.* Or, 'bondman.' The very first civil ordinance secures the personal rights of the lowliest in the social scale, the bondman.

The Rabbis limit this provision to the thief who is sold to make restitution for his theft. The case of the Hebrew who sells himself into bondage because of poverty is dealt with in Lev. xxv, 39.

*Hebrew servant.* Slavery as permitted by the Torah was quite different from Greek and Roman slavery, or even the cruel system in some modern countries down to our own times. In Hebrew law, the slave was not a thing, but a human being; he was not the chattel of a master who had unlimited power over him. In the Hebrew language, there is only one word for slave and servant. Brutal treatment of any slave, whether Hebrew or heathen, secured his immediate liberty; see on v. 26 f.

*in the seventh.* From the time that he was sold. If, however, the year of Jubilee occurs during the six years, the slave goes free without completing the time (Lev. xxv, 10).

*for nothing.* Without paying for his release.

**3.** *by himself.* And not with wife or children.

*go out by himself.* See v. 4.

*married.* To an Israelitish woman. The master is obliged to provide lodging and maintenance for the family of his bondman, the wife and older children doubtless paying for their keep by their labour. Both the wife and the children accompanied their father when he acquired his freedom.

**4.** *give him.* The slave had not the right of contracting a marriage for himself.

*a wife.* A non-Israelite slave. There was a saying current among ancient peoples to the effect that there was no morality among slaves. To prevent such promiscuity, the Torah makes a concession to human frailty and permits a temporary marriage.

*the wife and her children.* In Jewish law, the children share the status of the mother. If the Israelite had been permitted to take them into freedom with him, it would have impaired the purity of the race, and created a body of half-castes.

**5.** *plainly say.* Or, 'firmly say.' The master attempts to dissuade the Israelite slave from preferring bondage to freedom, but the latter is resolute in his intention.

*my wife, and my children.* Although it is natural for a man to become attached to his wife and offspring even in the circumstances here described, yet such conduct must have highly injurious results to the Hebrew state. It would tend to produce a class of dependent slaves; and, instead of the community consisting of free and equal citizens, it would be divided into a ruling and a servile class (Kalisch).

# EXODUS XXI, 6

## שמות משפטים כא

plainly say: I love my master, my wife, and my children; I will not go out free: 6. then his master shall bring him unto ¹God, and shall bring him to the door, or unto the door-post; and his master shall bore his ear through with an awl; and he shall serve him for ever. ¶ 7. And if a man sell his daughter to be a maid-servant, she shall not go out as the men-servants do. 8. If she please not her master, who hath espoused her to himself, then shall he let her be redeemed; to sell her unto a foreign people he shall have no power, seeing he hath dealt deceitfully with her. 9. And if he espouse her unto his son, he shall deal with her after the manner of daughters. 10. If he take him another wife, her food, her raiment, and her conjugal rights, shall he not diminish. 11. And if he do not these three unto her, then shall she go out for nothing, without money. ¶ 12. He that smiteth a man, so that he dieth, shall surely be put to death. 13. And if a man lie not

ה הָאִשָּׁ֤ה וִֽילָדֶ֙יהָ֙ תִּהְיֶ֣ה לַֽאדֹנֶ֔יהָ וְה֖וּא יֵצֵ֥א בְגַפּֽוֹ׃ וְאִם־
אָמֹ֤ר יֹאמַר֙ הָעֶ֔בֶד אָהַ֙בְתִּי֙ אֶת־אֲדֹנִ֔י אֶת־אִשְׁתִּ֖י וְאֶת־בָּנָ֑י
6 לֹ֥א אֵצֵ֖א חָפְשִֽׁי׃ וְהִגִּישׁ֤וֹ אֲדֹנָיו֙ אֶל־הָ֣אֱלֹהִ֔ים וְהִגִּישׁוֹ֙ אֶל־
הַדֶּ֔לֶת א֖וֹ אֶל־הַמְּזוּזָ֑ה וְרָצַ֨ע אֲדֹנָ֤יו אֶת־אָזְנוֹ֙ בַּמַּרְצֵ֔עַ
7 וַעֲבָד֖וֹ לְעֹלָֽם׃ ס וְכִֽי־יִמְכֹּ֥ר אִ֛ישׁ אֶת־בִּתּ֖וֹ לְאָמָ֑ה
8 לֹ֥א תֵצֵ֖א כְּצֵ֥את הָעֲבָדִֽים׃ אִם־רָעָ֞ה בְּעֵינֵ֧י אֲדֹנֶ֛יהָ אֲשֶׁר־
ל֥וֹ יְעָדָ֖הּ וְהֶפְדָּ֑הּ לְעַ֥ם נָכְרִ֛י לֹא־יִמְשֹׁ֥ל לְמָכְרָ֖הּ בְּבִגְדוֹ־
9 בָֽהּ׃ וְאִם־לִבְנ֖וֹ יִֽיעָדֶ֑נָּה כְּמִשְׁפַּ֥ט הַבָּנ֖וֹת יַעֲשֶׂה־לָּֽהּ׃ אִם־
11 אַחֶ֖רֶת יִֽקַּֽח־ל֑וֹ שְׁאֵרָ֛הּ כְּסוּתָ֥הּ וְעֹנָתָ֖הּ לֹ֥א יִגְרָֽע׃ וְאִם־
שְׁלָשׁ־אֵ֙לֶּה֙ לֹ֣א יַעֲשֶׂ֣ה לָ֔הּ וְיָצְאָ֥ה חִנָּ֖ם אֵ֥ין כָּֽסֶף׃ ס
12 מַכֵּ֥ה אִ֛ישׁ וָמֵ֖ת מ֥וֹת יוּמָֽת׃ וַאֲשֶׁר֙ לֹ֣א צָדָ֔ה וְהָ֣אֱלֹהִ֔ים
13

---
¹ That is, the judges.

לו ק׳ v. 8.

**6.** *unto God.* Or, 'unto the judges.' The judges pronounce sentence in the name of God (Deut. I, 17).

The slave's declaration had to be made publicly before the judges, in order to prevent the master from boring his servant's ear by force, and alleging that it was by the servant's desire.

*door.* Of the house belonging to the master.

*bore his ear.* 'Why was the ear, among all the organs of the body, selected for perforation?' asked the pupils of Rabban Yochanan ben Zakkai. He answered 'The ear that heard the Divine utterance, *for unto Me the children of Israel are servants* (Lev. xxv, 55), and yet preferred a human master, let that ear be bored.' The drilling of the ear to the door of the house may also have symbolized the attaching of the slave to the household, and may have served as permanent evidence that the slave had remained in service of his own free will. This boring of the ear was thus something altogether different from the inhuman custom in modern times of branding slaves by a red-hot iron, marked with certain letters, and then pouring ink into the furrows to make the inscription more conspicuous.

*for ever.* All the days of his life (Rashbam). The Rabbis, however, understood the Heb. word לעלם as signifying 'until the year of Jubilee' (Lev. xxv, 10). This Rabbinic interpretation is confirmed by Josephus.

**7.** *a maidservant.* Or, 'a bondwoman'; to be the secondary wife for the master or his son. In an age of polygamy, the position of concubine, or second wife, was not a degraded one. Her offspring had equal rights in matters of inheritance with the children of the first wife (Deut. XXI, 10-14).

*as the menservants.* i.e. not only after six years, but even earlier, according to the circumstances as given in the succeeding verse.

**8.** *espoused.* Or, 'designated.' The master had intended her for himself, not for his son (v. 9).; but finding her displeasing to himself, he must allow her father or relatives to buy her back.

*a foreign people.* The master must either allow her to be redeemed by her relatives, or he must keep her. The abominable practice against which this law is directed was not confined to Hebrew masters or to ancient times. Thus, William of Malmesbury, speaking of the days before the Norman Conquest, complains of the horrible custom of Saxon masters who, after associating with the maid servants on their estates, sold them to a life of shame or into foreign slavery.

*he shall have no power.* The Talmud refers 'he' to both the master and the father: the master has acted deceitfully in that he has not kept faith with her; the father in that he sold her at all.

*dealt deceitfully with her.* By not carrying out the purpose for which he had acquired her,

**9.** *deal with her after the manner of daughters.* 'Treat her as a daughter' (Moffatt). Whether as wife to the father or to the son, the bondwoman is to be treated like a freeborn girl who marries. The rights due to her are enumerated in the next verse.

**11.** *these three.* The three obligations mentioned in the preceding verse (Abarbanel).

## EXODUS XXI, 14

in wait, but God cause it to come to hand; then I will appoint thee a place whither he may flee. ¶ 14. And if a man come presumptuously upon his neighbour, to slay him with guile: thou shalt take him from Mine altar, that he may die. ¶ 15. And he that smiteth his father, or his mother, shall be surely put to death. ¶ 16. And he that stealeth a man, and selleth him, or if he be found in his hand, he shall surely be put to death. ¶ 17. And he that curseth his father or his mother, shall surely be put to death. ¶ 18. And if men contend, and one smite the other with a stone, or with his fist, and he die not, but keep his bed; 19, if he rise again, and walk abroad upon his staff, then shall he that smote him be quit; only he shall pay for the loss of his time, and shall cause him to be thoroughly healed. *11 ¶ 20. And if a man smite his bondman, or

14 וְכִי־יָנֻם שָׁמָּה׃ ס אֲשֶׁר לֹא צָדָה וְהָאֱלֹהִים אִנָּה לְיָדוֹ וְשַׂמְתִּי לְךָ מָקוֹם
יָזִד אִישׁ עַל־רֵעֵהוּ לְהָרְגוֹ בְעָרְמָה מֵעִם מִזְבְּחִי תִּקָּחֶנּוּ
15 לָמוּת׃ ס וּמַכֵּה אָבִיו וְאִמּוֹ מוֹת יוּמָת׃ ס וְגֹנֵב 16
17 אִישׁ וּמְכָרוֹ וְנִמְצָא בְיָדוֹ מוֹת יוּמָת׃ ס וּמְקַלֵּל אָבִיו
18 וְאִמּוֹ מוֹת יוּמָת׃ ס וְכִי־יְרִיבֻן אֲנָשִׁים וְהִכָּה־אִישׁ
אֶת־רֵעֵהוּ בְּאֶבֶן אוֹ בְאֶגְרֹף וְלֹא יָמוּת וְנָפַל לְמִשְׁכָּב׃
19 אִם־יָקוּם וְהִתְהַלֵּךְ בַּחוּץ עַל־מִשְׁעַנְתּוֹ וְנִקָּה הַמַּכֶּה רַק
שִׁבְתּוֹ יִתֵּן וְרַפֹּא יְרַפֵּא׃ * ס וְכִי־יַכֶּה אִישׁ אֶת־עַבְדּוֹ
21 אוֹ אֶת־אֲמָתוֹ בַּשֵּׁבֶט וּמֵת תַּחַת יָדוֹ נָקֹם יִנָּקֵם׃ אַךְ אִם־

### 12–14. Laws concerning Murder

**13.** *lie not in wait.* The Torah draws a distinction between intentional and accidental homicide.

*God cause it to come to hand.* The modern mind, whilst agreeing that all things are ultimately controlled by God's will, does not attribute results to the *immediate* action of God. Not so the Biblical idiom. Nothing happens except by God's will; so if the murderer had no intention of killing his victim, the death must be due to His decree. English law retains the same idea, and uses the term 'act of God'; cf. note on the hardening of Pharaoh's heart, p. 220.

*a place.* Of shelter from the vengeance of the next-of-kin. Special cities were to be set apart for this purpose when the Israelites had settled in Canaan (Num. XXXV, Deut. XIX).

**14.** *from Mine altar.* Even if it was a priest who officiated at the altar, he was not to escape his punishment, if his act was other than unintentional homicide (Talmud). Among the Greeks, an altar gave asylum to every murderer. In the Middle Ages, the Church offered 'sanctuary' to criminals of every description.

### 15–17. Crimes against Parents; Kidnapping

**15.** *smiteth.* The Rabbis rule that only when the blow left a bruise was the death penalty incurred.

**16.** *stealeth a man.* Kidnapping for the purpose of selling the victim into slavery in a foreign land (cf. the story of Joseph). It therefore meant both loss of liberty and spiritual death to the victim, if an Israelite. It was only towards the end of the eighteenth century that the slave trade, *i.e.* organized kidnapping on a vast scale, with the hideous cruelties attendant on it, began to be recognized in Western European countries as something unspeakably vile.

*or if he be found.* lit. 'and he be found.' Prompted by the desire to reduce capital punishment as much as possible, the Rabbis cling to the *literal* translation of these words. The victim must have been seen by witnesses in the hands of the kidnapper *and* also have been sold, before the crime was punishable by death.

**17.** *curseth.* The Rabbis declared that for capital punishment to be incurred, the son must have used the Divine Name itself in cursing his parents.

*put to death.* By a court of law, and after judicial trial not by the parents themselves. In Rome, a father was allowed to put to death a grown-up son, even for no reason whatsoever.

### 18–27. Personal Injuries

**18.** *he die not.* If the blow proved fatal, then v. 12 applied.

**19.** *be quit.* As soon as the injured person walks abroad, there can be no possibility of manslaughter.

*loss of his time.* lit. 'his ceasing' from work. However, the Rabbis permitted him to claim compensation also on other grounds; *viz.* for the pain he had suffered, the 'shame' he had incurred by his disfigurement, etc.

*to be thoroughly healed.* Pay the doctor's bill (Talmud).

**20.** *bondman.* i.e. a heathen slave, because he only could be described as 'his money' (see on v. 21).

*with a rod.* Better, *with the rod, i.e.* the

## EXODUS XXI, 21

his bondwoman, with a rod, and he die under his hand, he shall surely be punished. 21. Notwithstanding, if he continue a day or two, he shall not be punished; for he is his money. ¶ 22. And if men strive together, and hurt a woman with child, so that her fruit depart, and yet no harm follow, he shall be surely fined, according as the woman's husband shall lay upon him; and he shall pay as the judges determine. 23. But if any harm follow, then thou shalt give life for life, 24. eye for eye, tooth for tooth, hand for hand, foot for foot, 25. burning for burning, wound for wound, stripe for stripe. ¶ 26. And if a man smite the eye of his bondman, or the eye of his bondwoman, and destroy it, he shall let him go free for his eye's sake. 27. And if he smite out his bondman's tooth, or his bondwoman's tooth, he shall let him go free

---

instrument customarily used (Prov. x, 13; XIII, 24) and sufficient to secure obedience from the rebellious slave, but not to injure him severely. The master was allowed to chastise his slave, but not in a brutal manner so as to endanger his life.

*surely be punished.* There was no fixed penalty; the judges had to determine each case on its own merits. The Mechilta declares that the master was to be beheaded for such brutality.

**21.** *a day or two.* The master is not then punished, as it is clear that he had intended only to chastise the slave. Similar considerations have in all ages weighed in judging a parent whose child died in consequence of a correction. The death is then looked upon as an unfortunate accident, nothing more.

*he is his money.* 'This bare fact was presumptive evidence that the master had not intended to inflict serious injury, inasmuch as that would have involved pecuniary loss to himself' (H. Adler). In the circumstances, therefore, the financial loss was sufficient punishment for him.

**22.** *a woman.* Either she was near the men who were fighting, or she had endeavoured to separate them.

*no harm.* i.e. no fatal injury (Mechilta).

*as the judges determine.* If the husband makes an exorbitant claim, the sum to be paid is to be fixed by the court.

**23.** *life for life.* The Rabbis ruled that since no homicide was here intended, it was a case for monetary compensation. That the words 'life for life' are merely a *legal term* meaning 'fair compensation', is seen from the parallel passage in Lev. XXIV, 18, which says: 'He that smiteth a beast mortally shall make it good: life for life.' This only means 'fair compensation'; otherwise, any man who slew an animal would have to forfeit his own life in return! To remove all doubt as to the meaning of the legal term 'life for life', the same paragraph (Lev. XXIV, 21) states, 'He that killeth a beast shall make it good; and he that killeth a man shall be put to death.'

**24.** *eye for eye.* This law of retaliation—'measure for measure'—existed among ancient peoples, and persists to our own day in capital punishment. In the Torah, likewise, this law of 'measure for measure' is carried out literally only in the case of murder. 'Ye shall take no ransom for the life of a murderer, that is guilty of death: but he shall surely be put to death,' says Scripture (Num xxxv, 31). Hence, it is evident that other physical injuries which are not fatal are a matter of *monetary compensation* for the injured party. Such monetary compensation, however, had to be equitable, and as far as possible *equivalent*. This is the significance of the *legal technical terms*, 'life for life, eye for eye, and tooth for tooth.' See Additional Note, p. 405.

**25.** *wound.* When blood is drawn.

*stripe.* When there is only a bruise. In computing compensation, the actual damage, the loss of time, the cost of the cure, the pain and the disfigurement, are all taken into consideration.

**26.** *bondman.* The loss of any limb, from the most essential down to the least indispensable, gave the slave immediate freedom, if that loss was due to brutal treatment by the master. According to the Rabbinic interpretation, *v.* 26 and 27 apply only to a heathen slave. If the slave was a Hebrew, he was treated entirely like the free Hebrew citizen, and received the same indemnification, but could not *ipso facto* claim his release.

*eye.* The Rabbis regard 'eye' and 'tooth' as typical, and enumerate twenty-four organs of the body which come within the operation of this law.

## EXODUS XXI, 28

for his tooth's sake. ¶ 28. And if an ox gore a man or a woman, that they die, the ox shall be surely stoned, and its flesh shall not be eaten; but the owner of the ox shall be quit. 29. But if the ox was wont to gore in time past, and warning hath been given to its owner, and he hath not kept it in, but it hath killed a man or a woman; the ox shall be stoned, and its owner also shall be put to death. 30. If there be laid on him a ransom, then he shall give for the redemption of his life whatsoever is laid upon him. 31. Whether it have gored a son, or have gored a daughter, according to this judgment shall it be done unto him. 32. If the ox gore a bondman or a bondwoman, he shall give unto their master thirty shekels of silver, and the ox shall be stoned. ¶ 33. And if a man shall open a pit, or if a man shall dig a pit and not cover it, and an ox or an ass fall therein, 34. the owner of the pit shall make it good; he shall give money unto the owner of them, and the dead beast shall be his. ¶ 35. And if one man's ox hurt another's, so that it dieth; then they shall sell the live ox, and divide the price of it; and the dead also they shall divide. 36. Or if it be known that the ox was wont to gore in time past, and its owner hath not kept it in; he shall surely pay ox for ox, and the dead beast shall be his own. ¶ 37. If a man steal an ox, or a sheep, and kill it, or sell it, he shall pay five oxen for an ox, and four sheep for a sheep.

שמות משפטים כא

28 וְכִי־יִגַּח שׁוֹר אֶת־אִישׁ אוֹ אֶת־אִשָּׁה וָמֵת סָקוֹל יִסָּקֵל הַשּׁוֹר וְלֹא יֵאָכֵל אֶת־בְּשָׂרוֹ וּבַעַל הַשּׁוֹר נָקִי׃ 29 וְאִם שׁוֹר נַגָּח הוּא מִתְּמֹל שִׁלְשֹׁם וְהוּעַד בִּבְעָלָיו וְלֹא יִשְׁמְרֶנּוּ וְהֵמִית אִישׁ אוֹ אִשָּׁה הַשּׁוֹר יִסָּקֵל וְגַם־בְּעָלָיו יוּמָת׃ ל 30 אִם־כֹּפֶר יוּשַׁת עָלָיו וְנָתַן פִּדְיֹן נַפְשׁוֹ כְּכֹל אֲשֶׁר־יוּשַׁת עָלָיו׃ 31 אוֹ־בֵן יִגָּח אוֹ־בַת יִגָּח כַּמִּשְׁפָּט הַזֶּה יֵעָשֶׂה לּוֹ׃ 32 אִם־עֶבֶד יִגַּח הַשּׁוֹר אוֹ אָמָה כֶּסֶף שְׁלֹשִׁים שְׁקָלִים יִתֵּן לַאדֹנָיו וְהַשּׁוֹר יִסָּקֵל׃ ס 33 וְכִי־יִפְתַּח אִישׁ בּוֹר אוֹ כִּי־יִכְרֶה אִישׁ בֹּר וְלֹא יְכַסֶּנּוּ וְנָפַל־שָׁמָּה שּׁוֹר אוֹ חֲמוֹר׃ 34 בַּעַל הַבּוֹר יְשַׁלֵּם כֶּסֶף יָשִׁיב לִבְעָלָיו וְהַמֵּת יִהְיֶה־לּוֹ׃ לה 35 וְכִי־יִגֹּף שׁוֹר־אִישׁ אֶת־שׁוֹר רֵעֵהוּ וָמֵת וּמָכְרוּ אֶת־הַשּׁוֹר הַחַי וְחָצוּ אֶת־כַּסְפּוֹ וְגַם אֶת־הַמֵּת יֶחֱצוּן׃ 36 אוֹ נוֹדַע כִּי שׁוֹר נַגָּח הוּא מִתְּמוֹל שִׁלְשֹׁם וְלֹא יִשְׁמְרֶנּוּ בְּעָלָיו שַׁלֵּם יְשַׁלֵּם שׁוֹר תַּחַת הַשּׁוֹר וְהַמֵּת יִהְיֶה־לּוֹ׃ ס 37 כִּי יִגְנֹב־אִישׁ שׁוֹר אוֹ־שֶׂה וּטְבָחוֹ אוֹ מְכָרוֹ חֲמִשָּׁה בָקָר יְשַׁלֵּם תַּחַת הַשּׁוֹר וְאַרְבַּע־צֹאן תַּחַת הַשֶּׂה׃

### 28–32. INJURY CAUSED BY A BEAST

**28.** *ox*. Or any other animal.
*stoned*. In order to implant horror against murder, even the beast, although it had not a moral sense, was to be removed from existence, since it was the cause of the destruction of a human being, made in the image of God.

**29.** *put to death*. Not by the hand of a human tribunal, but 'death by the hand of God' (Mechilta). Nachmanides quotes as a parallel, 'And the common man that draweth nigh shall be put to death' (Num. I, 51), where the punishment for sacrilege is left to God.

**30.** *laid on him*. By a tribunal.
*ransom*. lit. 'covering'; a payment for the next of kin to forgive such intentional bloodshed.

**31.** *son . . . daughter*. For the explanation of this puzzling verse, and the light it throws on the true meaning of the *lex talionis* ('measure for measure'), as well as on the immeasurable moral difference between the civil legislation of the Torah and the Code of Hammurabi, see Additional Note F, p. 403.

**32.** *bondman*. A heathen slave (Mechilta). The valuation of an adult Israelite slave was fifty shekels (Lev. XXVII, 3).

### OFFENCES AGAINST PROPERTY
### XXI, 33–XXII, 14

#### 33–36. THROUGH NEGLECT OR THROUGH AN ANIMAL

**33.** *open a pit*. For the storage of water. Where rivers are few and the rain falls only at certain periods, water has to be stored and covered. To 'open' a pit, therefore, means to remove the covering and fail to replace it.
*ox or an ass*. i.e. any animal. The law excludes the human being, because it assumes that a human being looks where he is walking.

**34.** *owner of the pit*. The man concerned in connection with the pit. It need not be his property; if he left it open, he is liable for his heedlessness.
*shall be his*. i.e. the man's who incurred the loss (Mechilta).

**36.** *wont to gore*. See on *v*. 29.
*shall be his own*. The Heb. is identical with the wording in *v*. 34, where 'own' is omitted.

#### 37–XXII, 3. THEFT

**37.** *five oxen*. Multiple restitution, but in far heavier ratios, is the penalty prescribed in the Hammurabi Code. In most European countries

EXODUS XXII, 1

## CHAPTER XXII

1. If a thief be found breaking in, and be smitten so that he dieth, there shall be no bloodguiltiness for him. 2. If the sun be risen upon him, there shall be bloodguiltiness for him—he shall make restitution; if he have nothing, then he shall be sold for his theft. 3. If the theft be found in his hand alive, whether it be ox, or ass, or sheep, he shall pay double.*iii. ¶ 4. If a man cause a field or vineyard to be eaten, and shall let his beast loose, and it feed in another man's field; of the best of his own field, and of the best of his own vineyard, shall he make restitution. ¶ 5. If fire break out, and catch in thorns, so that the shocks of corn, or the standing corn, or the field are consumed; he that kindled the fire shall surely make restitution. ¶ 6. If a man deliver unto his neighbour money or stuff to keep, and it be stolen out of the man's house; if the thief be found, he shall pay double. 7. If the thief be not found, then the master of the house shall come near unto ¹God, to see whether he have not put his hand unto his neighbour's goods. 8. For every matter of trespass, whether it be for ox, for ass, for

---
¹ That is, the judges.

death was meted out for offences against property well into the nineteenth century. In Israel, however, the death penalty was not inflicted for an offence against property.

## CHAPTER XXII

**1.** *breaking in.* lit. 'digging through.' The houses were built of clay and cross-beams, and the thief dug a hole in the wall.

*no bloodguiltiness.* The thief would only do this in the dead of night, and it could not be considered murder if the owner killed the intruder who, it is assumed in both ancient and modern codes of law, would not hesitate to take life.

**2.** *be risen upon him.* i.e. upon the thief. If the burglary takes place after daybreak (Ibn Ezra, Nachmanides), the slaying of the thief is murder, because it is not absolutely necessary to take his life.

*for him.* The murdered thief.

*he shall make restitution.* He who steals in the daytime; likewise, the thief in the night who is caught in the act and not slain (Herxheimer).

*for his theft.* The Rabbis add that if the value of the stolen animal was less than the price of a slave, the thief may not be sold. If the thief is sold, it can only be for the 'theft'; i.e. the price of the stolen article, and not for the four-fold or five-fold fine which is imposed.

**3.** *double.* He must return the stolen animal and give the owner another as a fine. This rule was extended to all stolen articles.

**4–14. DAMAGE BY CATTLE OR FIRE, AND LAWS OF SAFE-KEEPING**

**4.** *eaten.* By cattle.

*let his beast loose.* Wilfully sending his cattle to graze in a field which did not belong to him. If they wandered there, without any culpable negligence on his part, he is not liable.

*of the best.* When estimating the damage, the best of the injured man's field is to be taken as the basis of calculation of the value of the whole.

**5.** *fire break out.* i.e. a man kindles a fire in his own field, and the wind carries sparks into a neighbouring field and a conflagration is caused.

**6.** *deliver.* A man asks his neighbour to take charge of valuables as a favour. He may wish to go on a journey, and in his own interest requests a person to safeguard his property.

*it be stolen.* i.e. the trustee affirms that there has been a theft.

**7.** *unto God.* As in xxi, 6. Having solemnly sworn that he had not embezzled what had been entrusted to him, the trustee is free from all obligation. In the event of his having perjured himself, his punishment would come from God Himself.

**8.** *trespass.* Here the equivalent of embezzlement.

*whereof one saith.* Either the owner or a witness comes forward and identifies something which is in the possession of the trustee or the thief as the lost property.

*this is it.* The thing lost.

# EXODUS XXII, 9     שמות משפטים כב

sheep, for raiment, or for any manner of lost thing, whereof one saith: 'This is it,' that cause of both parties shall come before God; he whom God shall condemn shall pay double unto his neighbour. ¶ 9. If a man deliver unto his neighbour an ass, or an ox, or a sheep, or any beast, to keep, and it die, or be hurt, or driven away, no man seeing it; 10. the oath of the LORD shall be between them both, to see whether he have not put his hand unto his neighbour's goods; and the owner thereof shall accept it, and he shall not make restitution. 11. But if it be stolen from him, he shall make restitution unto the owner thereof. 12. If it be torn in pieces, let him bring it for witness; he shall not make good that which was torn. ¶ 13. And if a man borrow aught of his neighbour, and it be hurt, or die, the owner thereof not being with it, he shall surely make restitution. 14. If the owner thereof be with it, he shall not make it good; if it be a hireling, he loseth his hire. ¶ 15. And if a man entice a virgin that is not betrothed, and lie with her, he shall surely pay a dowry for her to be his wife. 16. If her father utterly refuse to give her unto

---

*condemn.* Convict. If it is the trustee, he refunds the article and another of the same value. If the trustee is acquitted the witnesses who falsely accused him must pay him double the value of the lost article.

**9.** *be hurt.* By a fall, or an attack by another animal.

*driven away.* *i.e.* carried off by raiders.

**10.** *shall be between them both.* Shall decide between them. The trustee swears as to how the animal was hurt.

*put his hand.* To make an improper use of the animal, against the wishes of the owner, whereby it received its injury.

*accept it.* The oath, as fully acquitting the suspected trustee.

**11.** *stolen.* As distinct from its being carried off by a band of marauders, against whom he was powerless. In the case of theft, it was assumed that the trustee, who was paid to take care of the animal, had not done so sufficiently.

**12.** *bring it for witness.* Produce the torn flesh as evidence.

**13.** *aught.* An animal.

**14.** *be with it.* It is then the duty of the owner to take care of his animal.

*he loseth his hire.* Or, 'it is reckoned in its hire.' In accepting money for the use of the animal, the owner must take the risk.

## MORAL OFFENCES
### XXII, 15–XXIII, 9

#### 15, 16. SEDUCTION

**15.** *entice.* Induces her to be a consenting party. If he violates her against her will, he pays her father fifty shekels of silver and is obliged to marry her, without the possibility of a subsequent divorce (Deut. XXII, 28 f).

*not betrothed.* If the girl was betrothed, their crime is on a par with adultery, should the offence have taken place within a city. If it happened in a field, the man alone suffers capital punishment (Deut. XXII, 25). On betrothal, see note on Lev. XXI, 3.

*pay a dowry.* Or, 'endow her,' to be his wife. 'In this way virgins were shielded from permanent ignominy in consequence of a momentary crime' (Kalisch). The monetary payment prescribed in this verse would provide against the seducer escaping his obligations. Without it, he might demand her in marriage without paying the dowry (*mohar*), thinking that, in the circumstances, the father would be anxious to grant the request. Originally this *mohar* was paid to the father; cf. Gen. XXXIV, 12. In later times, it was received not by the father but by the bride, in order to enable her to enter with proper dignity into the house of her future husband.

**16.** *refuse.* According to the Rabbis, the same law applies if the girl declines to marry him.

*dowry of virgins.* Fifty shekels (Deut. XXII, 29).

EXODUS XXII, 17

him, he shall pay money according to the dowry of virgins. ¶ 17. Thou shalt not suffer a sorceress to live. ¶ 18. Whosoever lieth with a beast shall surely be put to death. ¶ 19. He that sacrificeth unto the gods, save unto the Lord only, shall be utterly destroyed. ¶ 20. And a stranger shalt thou not wrong, neither shalt thou oppress him; for ye were strangers in the land of Egypt.

שמות משפטים כב

מָאֵן יְמָאֵן אָבִיהָ לְתִתָּהּ לוֹ כֶּסֶף יִשְׁקֹל כְּמֹהַר הַבְּתוּלֹת׃
מְכַשֵּׁפָה לֹא תְחַיֶּה׃ כָּל־שֹׁכֵב עִם־בְּהֵמָה מוֹת יוּמָת׃
זֹבֵחַ לָאֱלֹהִים יָחֳרָם בִּלְתִּי לַיהוָה לְבַדּוֹ׃
וְגֵר לֹא־תוֹנֶה וְלֹא תִלְחָצֶנּוּ כִּי־גֵרִים הֱיִיתֶם בְּאֶרֶץ מִצְרָיִם׃

17 18
19
כ

### 17. WITCHCRAFT

**17.** *sorcerers to live.* Not because there was any reality in witchcraft, but because it was a negation of the unity of God and an abominable form of idolatry. It is noteworthy that the Septuagint translates the Heb. word for *sorceress* by 'poisoner'. Ancient witchcraft was steeped in crime, immorality and imposture; and it debased the populace by hideous practices and superstitions. Hence the place of this command in this chapter. It is preceded by provisions against sexual licence (*v.* 15) and followed by condemnation of unnatural vice and idolatry (*v.* 18 and 19). The wording of the command is in an unusual form. We should have expected, 'A sorcerer shall surely be put to death.' Some commentators, therefore, explain it as a prohibition of resorting to the sorceress, and thus enabling her to thrive in her nefarious avocation. The law applied to the sorcerer as well (Lev. XX, 27).

It is fashionable to trace all the horrors of the persecution of witches in medieval times to this verse. There is no justification for this. Witchcraft as a sinister danger in Jewish social life ceases to count long before the Destruction of the Second Temple. (The incident in connection with Simon ben Shetach is no proof to the contrary. Both Jewish and non-Jewish scholars —Derenbourg, *Essai*, 69; Israel Lévi, *Revue des Etudes Juives*, XXXV, 213; and Strack, *Einleitung*⁵, 118—have made it the subject of investigation, and are agreed that it is merely Haggadic). Later Jewish teachers (Samuel Ibn Chofni and Ibn Ezra) are among the earliest to deny the existence of demons or the efficacy of witchcraft. The hideous cruelties in the medieval trials of witches would have been impossible in Jewish judicial procedure. Torture to extort confession was unknown in Jewish law; and no confession on the part of the accused, that would have involved capital punishment, was allowable. 'No man can in law brand himself a criminal' (אין אדם משים עצמו רשע) is a principle in Jewish criminal law. Christianity, furthermore, which disregarded portions of the Decalogue (*e.g.* the Second Commandment, with respect to the prohibition of image-worship; and the Fourth Commandment, with respect to the Seventh day as the Sabbath) would certainly not have been guided in its attitude towards witchcraft by any single verse in the 'Old' Testament, if the New Testament had not been a demon-haunted book. Down to quite modern times the Church ascribed reality to the works of witches. In Germany alone, no less than 100,000 women and children are said to have suffered a cruel death during the horrible hunt for witches that disgraced the sixteenth century. So late as 1716, a woman and her daughter of nine years were hanged at Huntingdon for raising storms by witchcraft.

### 18. SODOMY

**18.** The law against witchcraft leads to the prohibition of kindred monstrous abominations, which formed part of many ancient heathen cults. See also Lev. XVIII, 23; XX, 15 f.; Deut. XXVII, 21.

### 19. POLYTHEISM

**19.** *sacrificeth.* 'As the offering of sacrifices was the chief part of divine service, all other branches of unlawful worship were contained therein' (Rosenmüller). The warning against sacrificing to other deities was for many ages, alas, not a superfluous one in Israel.

*the Lord only.* Not even to angels as His ministers, or to an intermediary between Him and man.

*utterly destroyed.* Or, 'devoted'; *i.e.* doomed to extirpation; see Lev. XXVII, 29.

### 20–23. OPPRESSION OF THE WEAK

**20.** *stranger.* Heb. *ger.* A resident alien; see XII, 19. He was not required to adopt the Jewish Faith, as little as the Israelites, with whose position in Egypt he is compared, were worshippers of Isis or Apis.

*shalt thou not wrong.* The Rabbis explain this term to mean that nothing must be done to injure or annoy him, or even by word to wound his feelings. The fact that a man is a stranger should in no way justify treatment other than that enjoyed by brethren in race. 'This law of shielding the alien from all wrong is of vital significance in the history of religion. With it alone true Religion begins. The alien was to be protected, not because he was a member of one's family, clan, religious community, or people; but because he was a human being. *In the alien, therefore, man discovered the idea of humanity*' (Hermann Cohen).

*for ye were strangers.* In the next chapter, *v.* 9, this phrase is preceded by the words, 'for ye know the heart of the stranger'; *i.e.* you know

# EXODUS XXII, 21     שמות משפטים כב

21. Ye shall not afflict any widow, or fatherless child. 22. If thou afflict them in any wise—for if they cry at all unto Me, I will surely hear their cry—23. My wrath shall wax hot, and I will kill you with the sword; and your wives shall be widows, and your children fatherless. ¶ 24. If thou lend money to any of My people, even to the poor with thee, thou shalt not be to him as a creditor; neither shall ye lay upon him interest. 25. If thou at all take thy neighbour's garment to pledge, thou shalt restore it unto him by that the sun goeth

כא כָּל־אַלְמָנָה וְיָתוֹם לֹא תְעַנּוּן: אִם־עַנֵּה תְעַנֶּה אֹתוֹ כִּי
כב
כג אִם־צָעֹק יִצְעַק אֵלַי שָׁמֹעַ אֶשְׁמַע צַעֲקָתוֹ: וְחָרָה אַפִּי
וְהָרַגְתִּי אֶתְכֶם בֶּחָרֶב וְהָיוּ נְשֵׁיכֶם אַלְמָנוֹת וּבְנֵיכֶם יְתֹמִים:פ
כד אִם־כֶּסֶף ׀ תַּלְוֶה אֶת־עַמִּי אֶת־הֶעָנִי עִמָּךְ לֹא־תִהְיֶה לוֹ
כה כְּנֹשֶׁה לֹא־תְשִׂימוּן עָלָיו נֶשֶׁךְ: אִם־חָבֹל תַּחְבֹּל שַׂלְמַת
כו רֵעֶךָ עַד־בֹּא הַשֶּׁמֶשׁ תְּשִׁיבֶנּוּ לוֹ: כִּי הִוא כְסוּתֹה לְבַדָּהּ

v. 22. חנון בצירי v. 24. סגול בס״פ v. 26. כסותו ק

from bitter experience what such a position means, and how it feels to be a stranger. Love of the alien is something unknown in ancient times. 'The Egyptians frankly hated strangers' (Holzinger); and the Greeks coined the infamous term 'barbarian' for all non-Greeks. The love of alien is still universally unheeded in modern times. Lev. XIX, 34, expressly demands in regard to the stranger, 'Thou shalt love him as thyself.' The Talmud mentions that the precept to love, or not to oppress, the stranger occurs thirty-six times in the Torah. The reason for this constantly-repeated exhortation is that those who have been downtrodden frequently prove to be the worst oppressors when they acquire power over anyone.

**21.** *widow, or fatherless child.* Who are bereft of their human protector and destitute of the physical force to defend their rights.

**22.** *thou afflict.* The verb is changed from the plural in the preceding verse to the singular in this verse; and Ibn Ezra makes the fine comment: if a single individual afflict the widow and orphan, and the community does not intervene to protect them, punishment will fall on all.

**23.** *My wrath shall wax hot.* The punishment of hard-heartedness against the weak is pronounced with extraordinary emphasis, and a severe 'measure for measure' is threatened (Kalisch).

### 24–26. LOANS AND PLEDGES

**24.** *if.* Better, *when*, as it is an obligation on an Israelite to assist his neighbour with a *free* loan (Mechilta).

*any of My people.* See comments on Lev. XXV, 35, and Deut. XXIII, 20 f.

*even to the poor.* A loan to prevent a poor man falling into destitution is considered one of man's most meritorious deeds, and among the greatest of lovingkindnesses that can be shown to the living. This feeling towards the poor has led to the Institution of a Free Loan (Gemillus Chasodim) Society in every well-organized Jewish community.

*creditor.* viz., by seizing the debtor's land, or selling him or his family into slavery, to recover payment; see II Kings IV, 1. 'If you know he cannot pay, do not press him and so put him to shame' (Rashi).

*interest.* All interest is forbidden on loans to the poor. 'In modern times money is commonly lent for *commercial* purposes, to enable the borrower to increase his capital and develop his business; and it is as natural and proper that a reasonable payment should be made for this accommodation, as that it should be made for the loan (*i.e.* the hire) of a house, or any other commodity. But this use of loans is a modern development: in ancient times money was commonly lent for the relief of poverty brought about by misfortune or debt; it partook thus of the nature of charity; to take interest on money thus lent was felt to be making gain out of a neighbour's need' (Driver).

**25.** *pledge.* In Deut. XXIV, 6, it is forbidden to take a handmill or a mill-stone as security, because it is an indispensable article in a house. It is precepts like these that caused Huxley to declare: 'There is no code of legislation, ancient or modern, at once so just and so merciful, so tender to the weak and poor, as the Jewish law.'

**26.** *I will hear.* Just as God hears the cry of the widow and orphan (*v.* 22). The chivalry to the poor ordained in these verses will appear even more striking when we recall the barbarous treatment of the debtor in ancient Rome. If the debtor was unable to make repayment within thirty days after the expiration of the term agreed upon, the Law of the Twelve Tables permitted the creditor to keep him in chains for 60 days, publicly exposing the debtor and proclaiming his debt. If no person came forward to pay the debt the creditor might sell him into slavery or put him to death. If there were several creditors they might cut him to pieces, and take their share of the body in proportion to their debt.

# EXODUS XXII, 26     שמות משפטים כב כג

down; 26. for that is his only covering, it is his garment for his skin; wherein shall he sleep? and it shall come to pass, when he crieth unto Me, that I will hear; for I am gracious.\* ¶ 27. Thou shalt not revile ¹God, nor curse a ruler of thy people. 28. Thou shalt not delay to offer of the fulness of thy harvest, and of the outflow of thy presses. The first-born of thy sons shalt thou give unto Me. 29. Likewise shalt thou do with thine oxen, and with thy sheep; seven days it shall be with its dam; on the eighth day thou shalt give it Me. 30. And ye shall be holy men unto Me; therefore ye shall not eat any flesh that is torn of beasts in the field; ye shall cast it to the dogs.

הוּא שִׂמְלָתוֹ לְעֹרוֹ בַּמֶּה יִשְׁכָּב וְהָיָה כִּי־יִצְעַק אֵלַי וְשָׁמַעְתִּי
כִּי־חַנּוּן אָנִי׃ ס   אֱלֹהִים לֹא תְקַלֵּל וְנָשִׂיא בְעַמְּךָ לֹא 27 רביעי
תָאֹר׃ מְלֵאָתְךָ וְדִמְעֲךָ לֹא תְאַחֵר בְּכוֹר בָּנֶיךָ תִּתֶּן־לִי׃ 28
כֵּן־תַּעֲשֶׂה לְשֹׁרְךָ לְצֹאנֶךָ שִׁבְעַת יָמִים יִהְיֶה עִם־אִמּוֹ בַּיּוֹם 29
הַשְּׁמִינִי תִּתְּנוֹ־לִי׃ וְאַנְשֵׁי־קֹדֶשׁ תִּהְיוּן לִי וּבָשָׂר בַּשָּׂדֶה ל
טְרֵפָה לֹא תֹאכֵלוּ לַכֶּלֶב תַּשְׁלִכוּן אֹתוֹ׃ ס

## CHAPTER XXIII     CAP. XXIII. כג

1. Thou shalt not utter a false report; put not thy hand with the wicked to be an

א לֹא תִשָּׂא שֵׁמַע שָׁוְא אַל־תָּשֶׁת יָדְךָ עִם־רָשָׁע לִהְיֹת עֵד

---
¹ That is, the judges.

כב׳. v. 26. קמץ בז״ק   v. 27. חצי הספר בפסוקים

---

### 27. RESPECT TOWARDS GOD AND RULERS

**27.** *thou shalt not revile God*. Some of the Rabbis interpreted this as referring to blasphemy, others understand *elohim* as 'judges' (cf. xxi, 6; xxii, 7). Josephus and Philo explain thus, 'Let no one blaspheme those gods which other citizens esteem as such'; *i.e.* do not speak disrespectfully of the religious beliefs of the followers of other faiths.

*a ruler*. The authorities of the State must be spoken of with respect. As to the connection of this with the preceding verse, Philippsohn remarks: 'The last verses treat of the poor. They are warned, even in their most desperate need, not to blaspheme God or entertain and give utterance to feelings of revolt against their rulers.'

### 28, 29. OFFERINGS OF FIRST-FRUITS

**28.** *fulness*. The law concerning firstlings is given more fully in Lev. xix; Num. xv, xviii; and Deut. xxvi.

*first-born*. For the sanctification of the first-born among men and beasts, see note on xiii, 2 f.

**29.** *seven days*. Maimonides explains that the animal is 'as if it had no vitality before the end of that period; and not until the eighth day can it be counted among those that enjoy the light of the world'.

### 30. UNLAWFUL MEAT

**30.** *holy men*. On the association of the idea of holiness with forbidden food, see on Lev. xi, 44. All the preceding laws, as well as those following, are in the singular: this verse alone is in the plural. The philosopher Moritz Lazarus calls attention to the fact that whenever the duty or ideal of holiness is spoken of in the Torah, the plural is invariably used (*e.g.* 'Ye shall be holy,' Lev. xix, 2), because mortal man can only attain to holiness when co-operating with others in the service of a great Cause or Ideal, as a member of a Community, Society, or 'Kingdom'. Of God alone can we say, the Holy One.

*torn of beasts*. Heb. *terefah*; which term originally was applied only to the meat of an animal torn by beasts in the field, but is now applied to any meats that are not ritually fit for Jewish consumption (kosher). The aim of Kashruth is the sanctification of life.

*to the dogs*. Such flesh is only fit to be eaten by dogs (Ibn Ezra).

### CHAPTER XXIII, 1–3. TRUTH IN JUSTICE

**1.** *utter a false report*. *i.e.* utter a groundless report; forbids originating a calumny. The Rabbis explain it as a warning not to listen to a calumny, or join others in spreading it. Slander, they say, kills three—the person slandered, the slanderer, and the person who takes up and passes on the slander. They also apply the words of the text to evidence given at a trial. Such evidence must not include a statement of which the witness is not absolutely certain. The Talmud, on the basis of this verse, rules that a litigant must not state his case to the Court in the absence of the other litigant.

*the wicked*. Better, *a guilty person*; the Heb. word denotes the party who is in the wrong.

*unrighteous witness*. lit. 'a witness of violence'. The meaning is, Do not make common cause with the guilty person to give evidence which will bring about his acquittal.

## EXODUS XXIII, 2

unrighteous witness. 2. Thou shalt not follow a multitude to do evil; neither shalt thou bear witness in a cause to turn aside after a multitude to pervert justice; 3. neither shalt thou favour a poor man in his cause. ¶ 4. If thou meet thine enemy's ox or his ass going astray, thou shalt surely bring it back to him again. ¶ 5. If thou see the ass of him that hateth thee lying under its burden, thou shalt forbear to pass by him: thou shalt surely release it with him.* v. ¶ 6. Thou shalt not wrest the judgment of thy poor in his cause. 7. Keep thee far from a false matter; and the in-

**2.** *a multitude.* This verse is a warning not to follow a majority blindly for evil purposes, especially to pervert justice. Because the majority of judges or witnesses are agreed on an opinion, which opinion he knows to be unjust, he should not abandon his own view in order to fall into line with the others. One, with God and the Right, are the true majority.

*bear witness.* For this use of the Heb. verb, see xx, 13.

*pervert justice.* The Rabbis disregarded the literal meaning of the last three Heb. words, and took them to imply that, except when it is 'to do evil', one should follow the majority.

**3.** *favour a poor man.* Out of false sympathy, or antipathy to the rich and powerful (Driver). The Biblical view of justice is remarkable for its unbending insistence on the strictest impartiality. If the matter in dispute is a question of money between a rich and a poor man, the judge is not to give a wrongful verdict in favour of the poor man on the plea that the rich man would not miss the sum involved. 'Sympathy and compassion are great virtues, but even these feelings must be silenced in the presence of Justice' (Geiger).

### 4, 5. LOVE OF ENEMY

**4.** *Thine enemy's ox.* Or any other animal belonging to him (Mechilta). This law is connected with the precepts concerning justice which immediately precede. Because your neighbour has done you an injury, so that you entertain a grievance against him, it is not right for you to allow it to influence your action when your duty towards him is clear. He has not ceased to be your fellowman, because he violates the law of neighbourly love towards you. Therefore, all envy or ill-will towards him is forbidden. No thought of vengeance (see on Lev. xix, 18) must be permitted to rise in your heart: *his* actions towards you must not be the standard of your conduct towards him. For the sake of your own human dignity there must be readiness to help him in his need, as in the typical instances adduced in the text.

Genuine, practical love of enemy is inculcated in this and following verse. As to the partisan statement in the New Testament, 'ye have heard that it was said, Thou shalt love thy neighbour *and hate thine enemy,*' that statement is absolutely baseless. 'Thou shalt hate thine enemy' is nowhere found in the Torah. C. G. Montefiore rightly observes that we cannot think very highly of the morality of that New Testament author in inventing a sentence unknown to the Torah in order to depreciate the Torah. Canon Rawlinson admits that '*hate thine enemy*' was no injunction of the Mosaic Law, but maintains that it is a conclusion which Rabbinical teachers unwarrantably drew from it. This charge against the Rabbis is utterly false. It is Christian teachers who rarely preached, and still more rarely practised, love of those whom they branded as 'enemies'. C. G. Montefiore has given an excellent summary of Jewish opinion on this matter: 'The adherents of no religion have hated their enemies more than Christians. The atrocities which they have committed in the name of religion, both inside and outside their own pale, are unexampled in the world's history. And even to-day it cannot be said that the various sects of Christians love one another, while anti-Semitism is a proof that they do not love those who are not Christians.'

**5.** *surely release it with him.* The general sense is clear. 'If you see the ass of a man who hates you lying helpless under its load, you must not leave it all to him, you must help him to release the animal' (Moffatt). This injunction has both the humanitarian motive towards the animal and the charitable motive towards the enemy. The greatest hero, say the Rabbis, is he who turns an enemy into a friend; and this can only be done by deeds of loving-kindness. 'If thine enemy be hungry, give him bread to eat, and if he be thirsty, give him water to drink . . . and the LORD will reward thee' (Prov. xxv, 21, 22).

### 6–9. IMPARTIALITY IN JUSTICE

**6.** *wrest the judgment.* 'As is well known, the maladministration of justice is, and always has been, a crying evil among Oriental nations' (Driver); but nowhere has there been such ringing denunciation of oppression of the poor and of denying justice to the victims of violence, as in Israel.

# EXODUS XXIII, 8

nocent and righteous slay thou not; for I will not justify the wicked. 8. And thou shalt take no gift; for a gift blindeth them that have sight, and perverteth the words of the righteous. 9. And a stranger shalt thou not oppress; for ye know the heart of a stranger, seeing ye were strangers in the land of Egypt. ¶ 10. And six years thou shalt sow thy land, and gather in the increase thereof; 11. but the seventh year thou shalt let it rest and lie fallow, that the poor of thy people may eat; and what they leave the beast of the field shall eat. In like manner thou shalt deal with thy vineyard, and with thy oliveyard. 12. Six days thou shalt do thy work, but on the seventh day thou shalt rest; that thine ox and thine ass may have rest, and the son of thy handmaid, and the stranger, may be refreshed. 13. And in all things that I have said unto you take ye heed; and make no mention of the name

8 כִּי לֹא־אַצְדִּיק רָשָׁע׃ וְשֹׁחַד לֹא תִקָּח כִּי הַשֹּׁחַד יְעַוֵּר
9 פִּקְחִים וִיסַלֵּף דִּבְרֵי צַדִּיקִים׃ וְגֵר לֹא תִלְחָץ וְאַתֶּם
יְדַעְתֶּם אֶת־נֶפֶשׁ הַגֵּר כִּי־גֵרִים הֱיִיתֶם בְּאֶרֶץ מִצְרָיִם׃
10 וְשֵׁשׁ שָׁנִים תִּזְרַע אֶת־אַרְצֶךָ וְאָסַפְתָּ אֶת־תְּבוּאָתָהּ׃
11 וְהַשְּׁבִיעִת תִּשְׁמְטֶנָּה וּנְטַשְׁתָּהּ וְאָכְלוּ אֶבְיֹנֵי עַמֶּךָ וְיִתְרָם
12 תֹּאכַל חַיַּת הַשָּׂדֶה כֵּן־תַּעֲשֶׂה לְכַרְמְךָ לְזֵיתֶךָ׃ שֵׁשֶׁת יָמִים
תַּעֲשֶׂה מַעֲשֶׂיךָ וּבַיּוֹם הַשְּׁבִיעִי תִּשְׁבֹּת לְמַעַן יָנוּחַ שׁוֹרְךָ
13 וַחֲמֹרֶךָ וְיִנָּפֵשׁ בֶּן־אֲמָתְךָ וְהַגֵּר׃ וּבְכֹל אֲשֶׁר־אָמַרְתִּי
אֲלֵיכֶם תִּשָּׁמֵרוּ וְשֵׁם אֱלֹהִים אֲחֵרִים לֹא תַזְכִּירוּ לֹא

**7.** *a false matter.* In the administration of justice; but this warning has the wider application as a rule of life of the highest importance.

*innocent and righteous.* Take every possible precaution so as not to condemn an innocent person to death. According to Talmudical law, a condemned man must have a re-trial whenever new evidence is forthcoming; but if there has been an acquittal, there cannot be a fresh hearing of the case.

*justify the wicked.* Better, *acquit a guilty person.* The guilty will not escape punishment at the hand of God, even if the human tribunal fails to inflict it.

**8.** *gift.* Better, *bribe.*

*blindeth.* A judge must not accept a gift even if he proposes to give a verdict in favour of the man who attempts to bribe him. A bribe has an insidious power; it will tend to shut the eyes of the judge to what he would otherwise have seen, and will inevitably corrupt him.

*perverteth.* Or, 'subverteth.' 'Destroys the case of a good man' (Moffatt).

**9.** *stranger.* See on XXII, 20-23. Like the poor, he was liable to become a victim of injustice. The alien was to receive the same treatment as the native Israelite; Deut. I, 16.

*ye were strangers.* See on XXII, 20.

### 10-12. THE SABBATH YEAR AND SABBATH DAY

The institution of the Sabbatical year is fully treated in Lev. XXV and Deut. XV. It is included here because, in one aspect, it reinforced the teaching of humanity to the poor and helpless (Ibn Ezra, Luzzatto).

**11.** *shalt let it rest.* Or, 'release it.' Heb. *shamat*, from which comes the name *shemittah* for the Sabbatical year, the Sabbath of the fields. 'The soil enjoyed a regular rest, doubly necessary in the imperfect state of agriculture of those ages, and calculated considerably to enhance its fertility in the other years' (Kalisch).

*may eat.* In an ordinary year, the poor could gather up the gleanings of the field, and also take from the 'corner' which had to be left unreaped (Lev. XIX, 9 f). In the Sabbatical year, there was no harvesting. Proprietor, servants, the poor and the stranger, all had equal rights to the produce (Lev. XXV, 6). Even the beats of the field are not forgotten.

**12.** 'Even though the entire year be one of "rest", the weekly Sabbath day must be observed' (Mechilta). And as with the Sabbatical year, so with the Sabbath day; the law is restated here in order to emphasize its humanitarian teaching of affording complete rest to the servant, the stranger and the domestic animals.

*be refreshed.* Equivalent to the colloquial 'catch their breath.' The word translated 're-freshed' (וינפש) is connected with the word נפש 'soul'; even the lowliest in Israel is to be reminded by the Sabbath day that he has a soul, that there is a higher life than mere drudgery; he is to receive spiritual refreshment on the Sabbath day.

**13.** *make no mention.* The Israelites could not serve God and any other deity at the same time; the very mention of the name of other gods is forbidden to them.

EXODUS XXIII, 14                     שמות משפטים כג

of other gods, neither let it be heard out of thy mouth. ¶ 14. Three times thou shalt keep a feast unto Me in the year. 15. The feast of unleavened bread shalt thou keep; seven days thou shalt eat unleavened bread, as I commanded thee, at the time appointed in the month of Abib—for in it thou camest out from Egypt; and none shall appear before Me empty; 16. and the feast of harvest, the first-fruits of thy labours, which thou sowest in the field; and the feast of ingathering, at the end of the year, when thou gatherest in thy labours out of the field. 17. Three times in the year all thy males shall appear before the Lord GOD. ¶ 18. Thou shalt not offer the blood of My sacrifice with leavened bread: neither shall the fat of My feast remain all night until the morning. 19. The choicest first-fruits of thy land thou shalt bring into the house of the LORD thy God. Thou shalt not seethe

14 יִשָּׁמַע עַל־פִּיךָ: שָׁלֹשׁ רְגָלִים תָּחֹג לִי בַּשָּׁנָה: אֶת חַג
טו הַמַּצּוֹת תִּשְׁמֹר שִׁבְעַת יָמִים תֹּאכַל מַצּוֹת כַּאֲשֶׁר צִוִּיתִךָ
לְמוֹעֵד חֹדֶשׁ הָאָבִיב כִּי־בוֹ יָצָאתָ מִמִּצְרָיִם וְלֹא־יֵרָאוּ
16 פָנַי רֵיקָם: וְחַג הַקָּצִיר בִּכּוּרֵי מַעֲשֶׂיךָ אֲשֶׁר תִּזְרַע בַּשָּׂדֶה
וְחַג הָאָסִף בְּצֵאת הַשָּׁנָה בְּאָסְפְּךָ אֶת־מַעֲשֶׂיךָ מִן־הַשָּׂדֶה:
17 שָׁלֹשׁ פְּעָמִים בַּשָּׁנָה יֵרָאֶה כָּל־זְכוּרְךָ אֶל־פְּנֵי הָאָדֹן |
18 יְהוָה: לֹא־תִזְבַּח עַל־חָמֵץ דַּם־זִבְחִי וְלֹא־יָלִין חֵלֶב־חַגִּי
19 עַד־בֹּקֶר: רֵאשִׁית בִּכּוּרֵי אַדְמָתְךָ תָּבִיא בֵּית יְהוָה
אֱלֹהֶיךָ לֹא־תְבַשֵּׁל גְּדִי בַּחֲלֵב אִמּוֹ:  ס   ששי

**14–18. THE THREE ANNUAL PILGRIM FESTIVALS**

The three pilgrimages which every adult Israelite had to make to the Sanctuary are more fully treated in Lev. XXIII and Deut. XVI.

**15.** *as I commanded thee.* In XII, 15.
*Abib.* lit. 'in the ear'; see IX, 31.
*empty.* This is explained in Deut. XVI, 17, 'every man shall give as he is able, according to the blessing of the LORD thy God which He hath given thee.' The pilgrim should bring with him offerings expressive of his gratitude for God's bounty.

**16.** *feast of harvest.* i.e. the feast of the first harvest. This is the festival of Pentecost. In Num. XXVIII, 26, it is called יום הבכורים, the day on which the first loaves made from the new corn were offered. In Deut. XVI, 10, it is called השבעות, the Feast of Weeks, because it is kept seven complete weeks after the first day of Passover. Jewish Tradition describes it as זמן מתן תורתנו, the anniversary of the Giving of the Torah, the revelation of the Decalogue having taken place on the sixth day of Sivan.
*feast of ingathering.* The Festival of Tabernacles; see Lev. XXIII, 34, 39 f.
*the end of the year.* i.e. of the agricultural year; see on Lev. XXIII, 34.

**17.** *all thy males.* i.e. adult males. Women are freed from all positive commandments depending on time, מצוות עשה שהזמן גרמא. Women could not be expected to leave their children unattended. Though it was not obligatory for them to do so, women were in the habit of accompanying their husbands to the Sanctuary; e.g. Elkanah and Hannah and Peninnah in I Sam. I; see further on XXXIV, 24.
*the LORD.* Heb. *adon*, master, overlord. These pilgrimages are marks of homage to the Sovereign of the land.

**18.** *leavened bread.* The Passover lamb was not to be slain until all the leaven had been removed.
*the fat.* This part of the sacrificial animal had to be burned on the altar (XXIX, 13).
*My feast.* Better, *My festival sacrifice*, i.e. the offering brought by the pilgrim.
*until the morning.* Cf. XII, 10.

**19.** *first-fruits.* The mode of presentation is described in Deut. XXVI, 2 f.
*thou shalt not seethe.* This command is repeated in XXXIV, 26, and Deut. XIV, 21. Upon these words, the Rabbis based the prohibition against eating meat and milk together in any way or form whatever. This prohibition was doubtless observed long before the age of the Rabbis; and in connecting it with this text, they merely sought a support in the Torah for an immemorial Jewish practice. Thus, Onkelos, who usually keeps close to the Hebrew text, renders, 'ye shall not eat flesh and milk.'
As to the original purpose of this law, opinions are divided. Some explain the commandment as levelled against idolatry and superstition (Maimonides); others state that it is a humanitarian ordinance intended to discourage a practice that would tend to harden the heart (Abarbanel, Luzzatto). 'We no longer know by what revolting sight this prohibition may have been called forth, but evidently that phrase became a kind of memorial by which Israel should always be reminded of that considerate humanity which was to distinguish it from the barbarous nations' (Ewald). Ibn Ezra writes: 'the reason of this prohibition is concealed from the eyes of even the wise.' Mendelssohn's comment on this law is, 'The benefit arising from the many inexplicable laws of God is in their practice, and not in the understanding of their motives.'

# EXODUS XXIII, 20

a kid in its mother's milk.*vi. ¶ 20. Behold, I send an angel before thee, to keep thee by the way, and to bring thee into the place which I have prepared. 21. Take heed of him, and hearken unto his voice; be not rebellious against him; for he will not pardon your transgression; for My name is in him. 22. But if thou shalt indeed hearken unto his voice, and do all that I speak; then I will be an enemy unto thine enemies, and an adversary unto thine adversaries. 23. For Mine angel shall go before thee, and bring thee in unto the Amorite, and the Hittite, and the Perizzite, and the Canaanite, the Hivite, and the Jebusite; and I will cut them off. 24. Thou shalt not bow down to their gods, nor serve them, nor do after their doings; but thou shalt utterly overthrow them, and break in pieces their pillars. 25. And ye shall serve the LORD your God, and He will bless thy bread, and thy water; and I will take sickness away from the midst of thee.* 111 26. None shall miscarry, nor be barren, in thy land; the number of thy days I will fulfil.

## 20–23. AN EXHORTATION

The summary of the entire Divine legislation—the Decalogue—has been followed by an outline of the most necessary moral, religious, and civil precepts. An exhortation is now added, as is usual throughout the Torah, faithfully to adhere to these laws, with the promise of the special Providential guidance to the Holy Land, and a happy existence in it, as rewards of such obedience.

**20.** *an angel*. The Heb. word does not of necessity imply a supernatural being. It denotes, as does also the English word in its original signification, a messenger; and it is evident that an actual person is meant. Consequently, it is most natural to understand the word as a reference to Moses, with whom God had spoken 'face to face', and who was able to communicate His will to the people (Ralbag and Luzzatto). Moses would only command what God had ordained; therefore, loyalty to him would mean obedience of God. The prophets and priests are also sometimes called God's 'angels'; cf. Mal. II, 7.

*the place*. The Promised Land.

**21.** *he will not pardon*. Because *he* cannot pardon. Although he may desire to be lenient with you and overlook your faults, God will punish disobedience.

*My name*. God's 'name', *i.e.* His Divine authority, was vested in His messenger; see on III, 13.

**22.** *I will be an enemy*. God would help them against their foes, who stood in the way of their taking possession of Canaan.

**23.** *Mine angel*. Not necessarily identical with the 'angel' of *v.* 20. In point of fact, it was Joshua who completed this task; but he, like Moses, was divinely appointed to the leadership (Deut. XXXI, 23).

*Amorite*. Cf. III, 17.

*I will cut them off*. God, and not the 'angel', will assure the victory to them. The Israelites were ever to remember to Whom alone they owed their success. Ehrlich connects *v.* 23 and 24 and translates, 'When mine angel shall go before thee ... and I cut them off, thou shalt not bow down to their gods.'

**24.** *do after their doings*. Construct images similar to those which the inhabitants had made (Ehrlich).

*overthrow them*. So long as idols remain, there will be temptation to worship them. Therefore, every trace of idolatry must be uprooted.

*pillars*. Either a natural boulder, or an artificial construction, which was considered to be the abode of a deity.

**25.** *bless thy bread and thy water*. God will secure for them the necessities of life; or, He will ensure that their food be a blessing to them; *i.e.* it will invigorate them.

*sickness*. Cf. xv, 26.

**26.** *I will fulfil*. God will allow the individual to reach old age and not come to a premature end. It is analogous to 'that thy days may be long' (xx, 12).

EXODUS XXIII, 27

27. I will send My terror before thee, and will discomfit all the people to whom thou shalt come, and I will make all thine enemies turn their backs unto thee. 28. And I will send the hornet before thee, which shall drive out the Hivite, the Canaanite, and the Hittite, from before thee. 29. I will not drive them out from before thee in one year, lest the land become desolate, and the beasts of the field multiply against thee. 30. By little and little will I drive them out from before thee, until thou be increased, and inherit the land. 31. And I will set thy border from the Red Sea even unto the sea of the Philistines, and from the wilderness unto [1] the River; for I will deliver the inhabitants of the land into your hand; and thou shalt drive them out before thee. 32. Thou shalt make no covenant with them, nor with their gods. 33. They shall not dwell in thy land—lest they make thee sin against Me, for thou wilt serve their gods—for they will be a snare unto thee.

**24**      CHAPTER XXIV

1. And unto Moses He said: 'Come up unto the LORD, thou, and Aaron, Nadab,

---
[1] That is, the Euphrates.

**27.** *My terror.* i.e. terror of Me. The nations, hearing that God is helping His people, will be panic-stricken at the approach of the Israelites. For historical instances, see Num. XXII, 2 f; Josh. IX, 3 f.

*turn their backs.* In flight.

**28.** *hornet.* Cf. Deut. VII, 20; Josh. XXIV, 12. The Israelites would be assisted in their campaign by a plague of stinging insects, which would harry and weaken the enemy. Some commentators take the Heb. word for 'hornet' as a reference to Egyptian invasions that would reduce the fighting power of the Canaanites. See on Deut. VII, 20.

**29.** *beasts of the field multiply.* The same thought occurs again in Deut. VII, 22. If the Canaanites had been swept from the land in a single, continuous campaign, the Israelites would not have been sufficiently numerous to inhabit the whole country. In consequence the large areas left desolate would swarm with wild beasts. Thus, after the deportation of the Ten Tribes to Assyria, lions infested the desolate district; see II Kings XVII, 25.

**30.** *by little and little.* The conquest of Canaan was not completed until the end of David's reign.

**31.** *Red Sea.* See on X, 19.

*sea of the Philistines.* i.e. the S.E. coast of the Mediterranean, which was the territory of the Philistines.

*wilderness.* At the south of Palestine, through which they were passing.

*the River.* Does not here mean the Nile, but the Euphrates. The boundaries extended to the Euphrates in the reigns of David and Solomon.

**32.** *no covenant.* The warning against forming an alliance with the inhabitants of Canaan, lest Israel be seduced by them into idolatry, is frequently repeated; and, as the whole later history of Israel proves, was sorely needed; cf. XXXIV, 12 f, and Deut. VII, 2 f.

**33.** *a snare.* A lure to destruction.

CHAPTER XXIV. RATIFICATION OF THE COVENANT

**1.** *And unto Moses He said.* After the Decalogue had been proclaimed in the hearing of the entire people, Moses again ascended the mountain (XX, 18), and received the commandments which form the Book of the Covenant (XX, 19–XXIII, 33). God commanded Moses to place these laws before the people, and then come to the mountain with Aaron, Nadab, and Abihu, and seventy elders (XXIV, 1) though he alone was to ascend the mountain (v. 2). Moses did so. He communicated to the people the words of God (v. 3) and after having ratified the covenant with a sacrifice, he went up with the men named (v. 9), when they were shown a Divine vision. Then Moses was commanded to ascend further with Joshua (v. 12 f) while the others stayed either

# EXODUS XXIV, 2     שמות משפטים כד

and Abihu, and seventy of the elders of Israel; and worship ye afar off; 2 and Moses alone shall come near unto the LORD; but they shall not come near; neither shall the people go up with him.' 3. And Moses came and told the people all the words of the LORD, and all the ordinances; and all the people answered with one voice, and said: 'All the words which the LORD hath spoken will we do.' 4. And Moses wrote all the words of the LORD, and rose up early in the morning, and builded an altar under the mount, and twelve pillars, according to the twelve tribes of Israel. 5. And he sent the young men of the children of Israel, who offered burnt-offerings, and sacrificed peace-offerings of oxen unto the LORD. 6. And Moses took half of the blood, and put it in basins; and half of the blood he dashed against the altar. 7. And he took the book of the covenant, and read in the hearing of the people; and they said: 'All that the LORD hath spoken will we do, and obey.' 8. And Moses took the blood, and sprinkled it on the people, and said: 'Be-

2 וְשִׁבְעִים מִזִּקְנֵי יִשְׂרָאֵל וְהִשְׁתַּחֲוִיתֶם מֵרָחֹק: וְנִגַּשׁ מֹשֶׁה
3 לְבַדּוֹ אֶל־יְהֹוָה וְהֵם לֹא יִגָּשׁוּ וְהָעָם לֹא יַעֲלוּ עִמּוֹ: וַיָּבֹא
מֹשֶׁה וַיְסַפֵּר לָעָם אֵת כָּל־דִּבְרֵי יְהֹוָה וְאֵת כָּל־הַמִּשְׁפָּטִים
וַיַּעַן כָּל־הָעָם קוֹל אֶחָד וַיֹּאמְרוּ כָּל־הַדְּבָרִים אֲשֶׁר־דִּבֶּר
4 יְהֹוָה נַעֲשֶׂה: וַיִּכְתֹּב מֹשֶׁה אֵת כָּל־דִּבְרֵי יְהֹוָה וַיַּשְׁכֵּם
בַּבֹּקֶר וַיִּבֶן מִזְבֵּחַ תַּחַת הָהָר וּשְׁתֵּים עֶשְׂרֵה מַצֵּבָה
5 לִשְׁנֵים עָשָׂר שִׁבְטֵי יִשְׂרָאֵל: וַיִּשְׁלַח אֶת־נַעֲרֵי בְּנֵי יִשְׂרָאֵל
6 וַיַּעֲלוּ עֹלֹת וַיִּזְבְּחוּ זְבָחִים שְׁלָמִים לַיהֹוָה פָּרִים: וַיִּקַּח
מֹשֶׁה חֲצִי הַדָּם וַיָּשֶׂם בָּאַגָּנֹת וַחֲצִי הַדָּם זָרַק עַל־
7 הַמִּזְבֵּחַ: וַיִּקַּח סֵפֶר הַבְּרִית וַיִּקְרָא בְּאָזְנֵי הָעָם וַיֹּאמְרוּ
8 כֹּל אֲשֶׁר־דִּבֶּר יְהֹוָה נַעֲשֶׂה וְנִשְׁמָע: וַיִּקַּח מֹשֶׁה אֶת־הַדָּם
וַיִּזְרֹק עַל־הָעָם וַיֹּאמֶר הִנֵּה דַם־הַבְּרִית אֲשֶׁר כָּרַת יְהֹוָה

---

where they were, or, more probably, returned to the camp; see the note on *v.* 14. After six days of waiting, during which the cloud covered the Mount, Moses alone was summoned to penetrate within the cloud (*v.* 16) and he remained there forty days (*v.* 18).

*come up.* This command was addressed to Moses as he was about to descend; and we are to supply before these words, 'Place my laws before the people and then.'

*Nadab, and Abihu.* Sons of Aaron.

*seventy of the elders.* Acting as representatives of the people.

*worship ye.* Prepare yourselves for the Divine vision which you are about to behold. (*v.* 10).

*afar off.* At a distance from the summit, which Moses alone was to reach.

**2.** *and Moses alone.* The abrupt change from the second to the third person is common in Hebrew; but its purpose here is to make it perfectly explicit that only Moses was to 'come near unto the Lord', *i.e.* go within the cloud (*v.* 15).

**3.** *and Moses came.* Ibn Ezra observes it is not mentioned that he descended the mountain, because there was no necessity to do so.

*words . . . ordinances.* As contained in the Book of the Covenant (*v.* 7).

*answered with one voice.* As in XIX, 8. 'The unanimity with which the Israelites here pledge themselves to the Divine worship partakes of the sublime; and we willingly forget for a moment how little they remained faithful to this promise even in the time immediately following' (Kalisch).

**4.** *pillars.* These were to serve as a symbol that the twelve tribes had accepted the Covenant; cf. Gen. XXXI, 45 f; Josh. XXIV, 27.

**5.** *the young men.* Onkelos renders, 'the firstborn', in agreement with the Talmudical statement that before the institution of the priesthood, the duty of offering sacrifice devolved upon the firstborn. 'Only the firstborn sons of the seventy elders can here be intended' (Ibn Ezra).

**6.** *half of the blood.* Was to be sprinkled upon the people, and the other half poured against the altar, which symbolized God. The two contracting parties to the Covenant were by this ceremony united by a solemn bond.

**7.** *book of the covenant.* According to Rashi, this means Genesis and the first half of Exodus. More probably it was the Decalogue and chapters XX, 19–XXIII, 33. They are the Torah in epitome.

*read.* Before sprinkling the blood, which would formally constitute the ratification of the Covenant, Moses read to the people what he had written, so that there could be no misunderstanding or doubt as to what they were undertaking.

*the people.* Not the elders only. Every Israelite was personally involved, and assumed individual responsibility.

*will we do, and obey.* Heb. נעשה ונשמע; instant and instinctive response to carry out the will of God. The Rabbis see in these words the utmost submission to God and self-consecration to His Covenant.

EXODUS XXIV, 9     שמות משפטים כד

hold the blood of the covenant, which the LORD hath made with you in agreement with all these words.' 9. Then went up Moses, and Aaron, Nadab, and Abihu, and seventy of the elders of Israel; 10. and they saw the God of Israel; and there was under His feet the like of a paved work of sapphire stone, and the like of the very heaven for clearness. 11. And upon the nobles of the children of Israel He laid not His hand; and they beheld God, and did eat and drink. ¶ 12. And the LORD said unto Moses: 'Come up to Me into the mount, and be there; and I will give thee the tables of stone, and the law and the commandment, which I have written, that thou mayest teach them.' 13. And Moses rose up, and Joshua his minister; and Moses went up into the mount of God. 14. And unto the elders he said: 'Tarry ye here for us, until we come back unto you; and, behold, Aaron and Hur are with you; whosoever hath a cause, let him come near unto them.' 15. And Moses went up into the mount, and the cloud covered the mount.*ᵐ· 16. And the glory of the LORD abode upon mount Sinai, and the cloud covered it six days; and the seventh day He called unto Moses out of the midst of the cloud. 17. And the appearance of the glory of the LORD was like devouring fire on the top of the mount in the eyes of the children of Israel. 18. And Moses entered into the midst of the cloud, and went up into the mount; and Moses was in the mount forty days and forty nights.

9 עִמָּכֶ֖ם עַ֥ל כָּל־הַדְּבָרִ֖ים הָאֵֽלֶּה׃ וַיַּ֥עַל מֹשֶׁ֖ה וְאַהֲרֹ֑ן נָדָב֙
10 וַאֲבִיה֔וּא וְשִׁבְעִ֖ים מִזִּקְנֵ֥י יִשְׂרָאֵֽל׃ וַֽיִּרְא֕וּ אֵ֖ת אֱלֹהֵ֣י יִשְׂרָאֵ֑ל
    וְתַ֣חַת רַגְלָ֗יו כְּמַעֲשֵׂה֙ לִבְנַ֣ת הַסַּפִּ֔יר וּכְעֶ֥צֶם הַשָּׁמַ֖יִם
11 לָטֹֽהַר׃ וְאֶל־אֲצִילֵי֙ בְּנֵ֣י יִשְׂרָאֵ֔ל לֹ֥א שָׁלַ֖ח יָד֑וֹ וַֽיֶּחֱזוּ֙ אֶת־
12 הָ֣אֱלֹהִ֔ים וַיֹּאכְל֖וּ וַיִּשְׁתּֽוּ׃ ס   וַיֹּ֨אמֶר יְהוָ֜ה אֶל־מֹשֶׁ֗ה
    עֲלֵ֥ה אֵלַ֛י הָהָ֖רָה וֶהְיֵה־שָׁ֑ם וְאֶתְּנָ֨ה לְךָ֜ אֶת־לֻחֹ֣ת הָאֶ֗בֶן
13 וְהַתּוֹרָה֙ וְהַמִּצְוָ֔ה אֲשֶׁ֥ר כָּתַ֖בְתִּי לְהוֹרֹתָֽם׃ וַיָּ֣קָם מֹשֶׁ֔ה
14 וִיהוֹשֻׁ֖עַ מְשָׁרְת֑וֹ וַיַּ֥עַל מֹשֶׁ֖ה אֶל־הַ֥ר הָאֱלֹהִֽים׃ וְאֶל־
(מפטיר  הַזְּקֵנִ֤ים אָמַר֙ שְׁבוּ־לָ֣נוּ בָזֶ֔ה עַ֥ד אֲשֶׁר־נָשׁ֖וּב אֲלֵיכֶ֑ם וְהִנֵּ֨ה
לספ׳)
15 אַהֲרֹ֤ן וְחוּר֙ עִמָּכֶ֔ם מִי־בַ֥עַל דְּבָרִ֖ים יִגַּ֥שׁ אֲלֵהֶֽם׃ וַיַּ֥עַל
מפטיר
16 מֹשֶׁ֖ה אֶל־הָהָ֑ר וַיְכַ֥ס הֶעָנָ֖ן אֶת־הָהָֽר׃ וַיִּשְׁכֹּ֤ן כְּבוֹד־יְהוָה֙
    עַל־הַ֣ר סִינַ֔י וַיְכַסֵּ֥הוּ הֶעָנָ֖ן שֵׁ֣שֶׁת יָמִ֑ים וַיִּקְרָ֧א אֶל־מֹשֶׁ֛ה
17 בַּיּ֥וֹם הַשְּׁבִיעִ֖י מִתּ֥וֹךְ הֶעָנָֽן׃ וּמַרְאֵה֙ כְּב֣וֹד יְהוָ֔ה כְּאֵ֥שׁ
18 אֹכֶ֖לֶת בְּרֹ֣אשׁ הָהָ֑ר לְעֵינֵ֖י בְּנֵ֥י יִשְׂרָאֵֽל׃ וַיָּבֹ֥א מֹשֶׁ֛ה
    בְּת֥וֹךְ הֶעָנָ֖ן וַיַּ֣עַל אֶל־הָהָ֑ר וַיְהִ֤י מֹשֶׁה֙ בָּהָ֔ר אַרְבָּעִ֣ים י֔וֹם
    וְאַרְבָּעִ֖ים לָֽיְלָה׃

**9–11.** Moses and Aaron, Nadab and Abihu, and seventy elders go up into the Mount, and are vouchsafed a mystic vision of the Divine Glory.

**10.** *and they saw.* 'And they beheld the majesty of the God of Israel, and beneath His majestic throne was work of precious stones, etc.' (Onkelos). What these men actually experienced is, of course, beyond human ken; but it is supposed that they fell into a trance in which this mystic vision was seen by them.

**11.** *nobles.* Moses, Aaron and his sons, and the seventy elders.

*laid not His hand.* They remained uninjured, because they were worthy to see the vision (Nachmanides).

*did eat and drink.* They brought with them the flesh of the peace-offerings, and consumed it as a sacred sacrificial meal, which formed part of the ceremony of ratification; see on Gen. xxxi, 46.

**12.** *come up to Me.* See on v. 1.

*tables of stone.* On which the Ten Commandments were inscribed.

*and the law.* Better, *even the law.* The Rabbis explain that the words, 'that thou mayest teach them,' refer to the Talmud. Every interpretation of the Law given by a universally recognized authority is regarded as given on Sinai; for every shade of meaning which Divinely inspired interpreters discover in the Law merely states *explicitly* what is implicitly and organically contained in it from the very beginning.

**13.** *Joshua.* See xvii, 9. He accompanied Moses from the camp and remained in the lower part of the Mount (Ibn Ezra).

**14.** *for us.* Moses and Joshua.

*Hur.* See on xvii, 10.

*hath a cause.* Moses had appointed magistrates to adjudicate disputes; but the difficult cases (xviii, 26), which would have been reserved for his decision, were, in the absence of Moses, to be referred to Aaron and Hur.

**15.** *the cloud.* A similar cloud had made its appearance before the revelation at Sinai (xix, 16).

**16.** *glory of the LORD.* See on xvi, 7, 10.

*seventh day.* The six days were apparently spent by Moses in preparing himself for communion with God.

**17.** *devouring fire.* Blazing fire. The people in the camp beheld flames of fire appearing above the cloud.

**18.** *into the mount.* To the top of the Mount.

*forty days.* Cf. xxxiv, 28; Deut. ix, 9.

# HAFTORAH MISHPATIM   הפטרת משפטים

### JEREMIAH XXXIV, 8–22, AND XXXIII, 25, 26

#### Chapter XXXIV

8. The word that came unto Jeremiah from the Lord, after that the king Zedekiah had made a covenant with all the people that were at Jerusalem, to proclaim liberty unto them; 9. that every man should let his man-servant, and every man his maid-servant, being a Hebrew man or a Hebrew woman, go free; that none should make bondmen of them, even of a Jew his brother; 10. and all the princes and all the people hearkened, that had entered into the covenant to let every one his man-servant, and every one hs maid-servant, go free, and not to make bondmen of them any more; they hearkened, and let them go; 11. but afterwards they turned, and caused the servants and the handmaids, whom they had let go free, to return, and brought them into subjection for servants and for handmaids; 12. therefore the word of the Lord came to Jeremiah from the Lord, saying: ¶ 13. Thus saith the Lord, the God of Israel: I made a covenant with your fathers in the day that I brought them forth out of the land of Egypt, out of the house of bondage, saying: 14. 'At the end of seven years ye shall let go every man his brother that is a Hebrew, that hath been sold unto thee, and hath served thee six years, thou shalt let him go free from thee'; but your fathers hearkened not unto Me, neither inclined their ear. 15. And ye were now turned, and had done that which is right in Mine eyes, in proclaiming liberty every man to his neighbour; and ye had

---

For the life and teachings of Jeremiah, see introduction to the Haftorah, p. 229.

The Sedrah opens with the enactment to free a Hebrew bondman after six years' service. The Haftorah records a grave breach of this regulation at a critical hour of Israel's history. In the face of the disaster threatening the Nation at the hands of the Babylonian besiegers, the last king of Judah had induced the ruling classes to bind themselves by oath to release their slaves, so that no Jew should any longer be a bondman to a fellow-Jew. They did so; but subsequently, when the danger had passed, they impiously broke their oath, and forced their emancipated brethren back into bondage. Jeremiah is outraged at this base conduct, and announces that the enemy will soon return; when fire, war, hunger and pestilence will rage in the city.

**8.** *with all the people*. With their representatives. Possibly, the Heb. term for 'all the people' stands for the National Assembly; see v. 19.

**9.** *of a Jew*. This is the earliest mention of the word *Yehudi* ('Jew') in Scripture.

**10.** *princes ... people hearkened*. Impending danger quickened their conscience into a course of action that might render them more worthy of deliverance.

**14.** *at the end of seven years ... and hath served thee six years*. In English we would say, 'at the end of six years' service' (Moffatt). A similar Heb. idiom says 'And on the *seventh* day God finished his work' (Gen. II, 2). Cf. the French 'quinze jours' for the English 'fourteen days'; or the German 'nach acht Tagen' for the English 'in a week's time'.

*hath been sold*. Or, 'hath sold himself.'

**16.** *ye turned and profaned My name*. The Holy One of Israel is sanctified *by justice*, and profaned *by inhumanity*.

*at their pleasure*. Better, *to be their own masters* (Biur).

### 17–22. The Punishment

**17.** *I proclaim for you a liberty*. *i.e.* from Me, from the Divine protection.

**18.** *cut the calf in twain*. A reference to the ancient method of ratifying a covenant, as in Gen. xv, 10.

323

## JEREMIAH XXXIV, 16

made a covenant before Me in the house whereon My name is called; 16. but ye turned and profaned My name, and caused every man his servant, and every man his handmaid, whom ye had let go free at their pleasure, to return; and ye brought them into subjection, to be unto you for servants and for handmaids. 17. Therefore thus saith the LORD: Ye have not hearkened unto Me, to proclaim liberty, every man to his brother, and every man to his neighbour; behold, I proclaim for you a liberty, saith the LORD, unto the sword, unto the pestilence, and unto the famine; and I will make you a horror unto all the kingdoms of the earth. 18. And I will give the men that have transgressed My covenant, that have not performed the words of the covenant which they made before Me, when they cut the calf in twain and passed between the parts thereof; 19. the princes of Judah, and the princes of Jerusalem, the officers, and the priests, and all the people of the land, that passed between the parts of the calf; 20. I will even give them into the hand of their enemies, and into the hand of them that seek their life; and their dead bodies shall be for food unto the fowls of the heaven, and to the beasts of the earth. 21. And Zedekiah king of Judah and his princes will I give into the hand of their enemies, and into the hand of them that seek their life, and into the hand of the king of Babylon's army, that are gone up from you. 22. Behold, I will command, saith the LORD, and cause them to return to this city; and they shall fight against it, and take it, and burn it with fire; and I will make the cities of Judah a desolation, without inhabitant.

### CHAPTER XXXIII

25. Thus saith the LORD: If My covenant be not with day and night, if I have not appointed the ordinances of heaven and earth; 26. then will I also cast away the seed of Jacob, and of David My servant, so that I will not take of his seed to be rulers over the seed of Abraham, Isaac, and Jacob; for I will cause their captivity to return, and will have compassion on them.

**19.** *all the people of the land.* Better, *the National Council*, who, with the rulers, were parties to the solemn covenant; cf. p. 80.

**20.** *dead bodies.* Shall remain unburied.

**21.** *that are gone up from you.* i.e. the Babylonian army, which had temporarily raised the siege. This led to premature rejoicing on the part of the princes and people, and was responsible for the gross breach of faith which is the subject of the prophet's denunciation.

**22.** *to return.* They have forced the slaves to return to bondage; therefore, the Babylonians shall return and be the instrument of the Divine punishment. Jerusalem was taken by them in 586, the Temple was burned, and the larger portion of the population carried away into exile.

### CHAPTER XXXIII, 25, 26

These verses foretell the Return from Babylonian captivity, and declare that this Divine promise of mercy is as sure as the ordinances of Nature.

# VII. TERUMAH

(Chapters XXV–XXVII, 19)

## THE SANCTUARY

With the exception of chaps. XXXII–XXXIV, which tell the story of the Golden Calf, the remainder of the Book of Exodus is concerned with the construction of the Sanctuary.

Israel had been redeemed from bondage, and God had proclaimed His laws unto them at Sinai. The communion of God with Moses and Israel was not, however, to cease with Israel's departure from Sinai. Moses is bidden to erect a Sanctuary that shall be a visible emblem to the people that God dwelleth among them.

In form, the Sanctuary was a portable structure, as it was to accompany the Israelites on their wanderings. It was primarily a tent, with a wooden frame-work to give it greater stability and security than ordinary tent-poles could give. The entire Sanctuary consisted of three parts:—

(1) There was the outer *Court*, enclosed by curtains supported on pillars. It was oblong in shape, 100 cubits by 50, and the entrance was on the eastern side.

(2) Within the Court, facing the entrance, was the *Altar of Sacrifice;* and behind it, towards the West, was the *Laver* for the Priests.

(3) In the western portion of the Court was the Sanctuary proper, the TABERNACLE. This was divided by a 'Veil', or hanging curtain, into two chambers. The first of these, which only the priests might enter, was the *Holy Place*, containing the Table, the Candlestick and the Altar of Incense. The second of the chambers was called the *Holy of Holies*, and contained the Ark of the Covenant. This was entered once a year by the High Priest on the Day of Atonement. Precious metals and finely woven coloured materials were employed in its construction. The nearer an object was to the Holy of Holies, the rarer and costlier the material; the objects further off being made of bronze and ordinary woven cloths.

The northern, western and southern sides of the Tabernacle were a wooden framework; the eastern side, *i.e.* the front, consisted of a screen. The entire Tabernacle was covered by a tent, and over the tent there were further coverings.

Practically all commentators are agreed that the Sanctuary was a symbol; and its purpose, to impress the children of men with spiritual teachings. What, however, were the spiritual teachings which the Tabernacle symbolized? This question offered full scope to the ingenuity of mystic interpreters, ancient and modern, Jewish and non-Jewish, who declared the Sanctuary to be an epitome of that which is presented on a larger scale in the Universe as a whole, and an emblem of Religion's profoundest teachings on Life and Eternity.

Their interpretations, however, are too remote from the spirit of the plain narrative to carry conviction. Much more helpful is the view of Maimonides, that the main purpose of the Sanctuary was to wean the Israelites from idolatrous worship and turn them towards God. The Sanctuary and its ritual occupy so large a place both in the Torah and in the life of ancient Israel, because they formed part of the Divine scheme in moulding the Chosen People for its spiritual mission. The Sanctuary re-inforced the laws which Moses had been commanded to set before the children of Israel. It kept before them the thought that God was in their midst; and their life, individually and collectively, had to be influenced by that knowledge. As God was holy and as the Sanctuary was holy, so must the Israelites make the sanctification of their lives the aim of all their endeavours. The Sanctuary thus embodies the principle which is the central thought of the whole of the Divine revelation to Moses.

# EXODUS XXV, 1 — שמות תרומה כה

## CHAPTER XXV

1. And the LORD spoke unto Moses, saying: 2. 'Speak unto the children of Israel, that they take for Me an offering; of every man whose heart maketh him willing ye shall take My offering. 3. And this is the offering which ye shall take of them: gold, and silver, and brass; 4. and blue, and purple, and scarlet, and fine linen, and goats' hair; 5. and rams' skins dyed red, and sealskins, and acacia-wood; 6. oil for the light, spices for the anointing oil, and for the sweet incense; 7. onyx stones, and stones to be set, for the ephod, and for the breastplate. 8. And let them make Me a sanctuary, that I may dwell among them. 9. According to all that I show thee, the pattern of the tabernacle, and the pattern of

CAP. XXV. כה

פ פ פ יט 19

2 וַיְדַבֵּר יְהֹוָה אֶל־מֹשֶׁה לֵּאמֹר: דַּבֵּר אֶל־בְּנֵי יִשְׂרָאֵל וְיִקְחוּ־לִי תְּרוּמָה מֵאֵת כָּל־אִישׁ אֲשֶׁר יִדְּבֶנּוּ לִבּוֹ תִּקְחוּ 3 אֶת־תְּרוּמָתִי: וְזֹאת הַתְּרוּמָה אֲשֶׁר תִּקְחוּ מֵאִתָּם זָהָב 4 וָכֶסֶף וּנְחֹשֶׁת: וּתְכֵלֶת וְאַרְגָּמָן וְתוֹלַעַת שָׁנִי וְשֵׁשׁ וְעִזִּים: 5 וְעֹרֹת אֵילִם מְאָדָּמִים וְעֹרֹת תְּחָשִׁים וַעֲצֵי שִׁטִּים: שֶׁמֶן 6 לַמָּאֹר בְּשָׂמִים לְשֶׁמֶן הַמִּשְׁחָה וְלִקְטֹרֶת הַסַּמִּים: אַבְנֵי־ 7 8 שֹׁהַם וְאַבְנֵי מִלֻּאִים לָאֵפֹד וְלַחֹשֶׁן: וְעָשׂוּ לִי מִקְדָּשׁ

## VII. TERUMAH

### (CHAPTERS XXV–XXVII, 19)

#### CHAPTER XXV

##### 2–7. MATERIALS FOR THE SANCTUARY

**2.** *an offering.* Heb. *terumah;* 'that which is lifted off', or separated; that which the Israelite sets apart from his possessions as a contribution to the requirements of the Sanctuary.

*maketh him willing.* Whosoever is stirred by a spontaneous desire to participate in the holy work. The beauty of the Tabernacle and the donation of material objects of value rendered necessary thereby called forth the spirit of self-sacrifice. The construction of the Tabernacle, with its demands for all treasures of the thought that invents and of the hand that labours; of wisdom and beauty; of wealth of wood and weight of stone; of the strength of iron, and the light of gold—thus became an external sign of love and gratitude and surrender to God's will (Ruskin).

**3.** *gold.* For the ark, the Cherubim, the table of showbread, the candlestick and the altar of incense.

*silver.* Was the only material not obtained by voluntary contribution, but by a levy of a half-shekel upon each adult Israelite; XXXVIII, 25.

*brass.* The Heb. means 'copper' or 'bronze', as is evident from Deut. VIII, 9, where the metal is said to be hewn out of mountains. This metal was used for the altar of burnt-offerings.

**4.** *blue.* i.e. threads dyed a very dark blue, perhaps violet, derived, according to the Rabbis, from the blood of a shell-fish found in the Mediterranean Sea.

*purple.* i.e. a reddish purple; a dye likewise obtained from a species of shell-fish (1 Macc. IV, 23).

*scarlet.* lit. 'worm of shining', from its brilliant hue. The worm referred to is the cochineal insect. The Arabs called it 'kirmiz', whence is derived the English word 'crimson'.

*fine linen.* 'A kind of linen which was only produced in Egypt' (Ibn Ezra), and worn by the royal family and the highest officials; see on Gen. XLI, 42.

*goats' hair.* This hair was woven by women into yarn (XXXV, 26), making a hard-wearing material most suitable as a tent-covering.

**5.** *rams' skins.* Dyed red, after they had been prepared.

*sealskins.* Or, 'badgers' skins.' Heb. *tachash;* possibly a species of sea-animal common in the Red Sea. Jewish legend explains it as a unique animal, which existed only in the time of Moses.

*acacia-wood.* lit. 'wood of Shittim', the Arabic name of the acacia tree. This tree grows abundantly in the Sinai Peninsula, but not farther north. It is a most durable wood.

**6.** *oil.* i.e. olive oil (XXVII, 20).
*spices.* See XXX, 22 f.
*sweet incense.* See XXX, 34 f.

**7.** *stones to be set.* See XXVIII, 17 f.
*ephod . . . breastplate.* See XXVIII, 6 f, and ibid., 14 f.

##### 8, 9. PURPOSE OF THE SANCTUARY

**8.** *make Me.* i.e. 'For My Name' (Rashi). It would only be a Sanctuary so long as it remained dedicated to the service of God.

*sanctuary.* Heb. *mikdash.* The same word occurs in the Song of Moses (XV, 17), and

EXODUS XXV, 10                                    שמות תרומה כה

all the furniture thereof, even so shall ye make it. ¶ 10. And they shall make an ark of acacia-wood: two cubits and a half shall be the length thereof, and a cubit and a half the breadth thereof, and a cubit and a half the height thereof. 11. And thou shalt overlay it with pure gold, within and without shalt thou overlay it, and shalt make upon it a crown of gold round about. 12. And thou shalt cast four rings of gold for it, and put them in the four feet thereof; and two rings shall be on the one side of it, and two rings on the other side of it. 13. And thou shalt make staves of acacia-wood, and overlay them with gold. 14. And thou shalt put the staves into the rings on the sides of the ark, wherewith to bear the ark. 15. The staves shall be in the rings of the ark;

9 וְשָׁכַנְתִּי בְּתוֹכָם: כְּכֹל אֲשֶׁר אֲנִי מַרְאֶה אוֹתְךָ אֵת תַּבְנִית
10 הַמִּשְׁכָּן וְאֵת תַּבְנִית כָּל־כֵּלָיו וְכֵן תַּעֲשׂוּ: ס וְעָשׂוּ
אֲרוֹן עֲצֵי שִׁטִּים אַמָּתַיִם וָחֵצִי אָרְכּוֹ וְאַמָּה וָחֵצִי רָחְבּוֹ
11 וְאַמָּה וָחֵצִי קֹמָתוֹ: וְצִפִּיתָ אֹתוֹ זָהָב טָהוֹר מִבַּיִת וּמִחוּץ
12 תְּצַפֶּנּוּ וְעָשִׂיתָ עָלָיו זֵר זָהָב סָבִיב: וְיָצַקְתָּ לּוֹ אַרְבַּע
טַבְּעֹת זָהָב וְנָתַתָּה עַל אַרְבַּע פַּעֲמֹתָיו וּשְׁתֵּי טַבָּעֹת עַל־
13 צַלְעוֹ הָאֶחָת וּשְׁתֵּי טַבָּעֹת עַל־צַלְעוֹ הַשֵּׁנִית: וְעָשִׂיתָ בַדֵּי
14 עֲצֵי שִׁטִּים וְצִפִּיתָ אֹתָם זָהָב: וְהֵבֵאתָ אֶת־הַבַּדִּים בַּטַּבָּעֹת
15 עַל צַלְעֹת הָאָרֹן לָשֵׂאת אֶת־הָאָרֹן בָּהֶם: בְּטַבְּעֹת הָאָרֹן

Ibn Ezra refers that verse and *v*. 13 ('Thou hast guided them ... to Thy holy habitation ... the sanctuary, O LORD, which Thy hands have established') to Mt. Sinai, which is indeed treated as a sanctuary in XIX and XX. 'God, who on Sinai dwelt in a Sanctuary which His hands have made, is now to dwell in a Sanctuary which Israel would make; and the Tabernacle would be a wandering Sinai' (B. Jacob).

*that I may dwell.* Heb. ושכנתי; the verb is the one from which *Shechinah*, the Rabbinic term for the Divine Presence, is derived.

*dwell among them.* Note that the Torah does not say, 'that I may dwell *in it*,' but '*among them*', *i.e.* in the midst of the people. The Sanctuary was not the dwelling-place of God; cf. I Kings VIII, 27. It was the symbol of that holiness which was to be the rule of life for the Israelites, if His Spirit was to abide with the community. They were to hold themselves aloof from everything that was defiling, because God was amongst them (Lev. xv, 31). The Sanctuary was, therefore, the fountain of holiness for the congregation of Israel.

**9.** *the pattern.* Moses was given detailed instructions in his Vision. He was shown a model, as it were, of the construction, from which he was not to deviate.

*tabernacle.* Better, *dwelling*. Heb. *mishkan*, the noun formed from the verb 'dwell' used in the preceding verse. The English word 'tabernacle' is the usual translation of the Heb. *ohel* ('tent'), and designates that part of the Sanctuary which was protected by a tent, *viz.* the Holy Place and the Holy of Holies.

*furniture.* All the articles, vessels and utensils in connection with the tabernacle.

**10–16. THE ARK**

The articles for the Holy of Holies are described first; and a beginning is made with the Ark, the most important article in the whole Sanctuary: the tabernacle was the edifice constructed to contain the Ark (see on *v*. 16).

**10.** *they shall make.* As in *v*. 8. The following verses have 'thou shalt'; *i.e.* Moses was to see that the command was duly carried out by others.

*an ark.* Also called, 'ark of the covenant', 'of the testimony', 'of God', and 'of the LORD'.

*cubit.* lit. 'the fore-arm', from the elbow to the tip of the middle finger—roughly eighteen inches; so that the Ark measured 3 feet 9 inches in length, and 2 feet 3 inches in width and depth.

**11.** *pure gold.* Only the purest and most precious metal was used in connection with the Holy of Holies. The Ark was overlaid with gold inside, where it was not visible to the eye, as well as outside where it was visible; to teach us that man must be as pure in mind and heart as he appears pure in outward manner and bearing. Especially is it the duty of a scholar, continue the Rabbis, to be inwardly what he pretends to be outwardly (תוכו כברו).

*upon it.* Running around the edge of the top surface.

*crown. i.e.* an ornamental rim or moulding.

**12.** *two rings.* For the purpose of transportation in the Israelites' wanderings in the Wilderness the Ark was provided with four rings at its four feet, two on each side, through which two gilded poles of acacia wood were passed.

**13.** *staves.* Poles, by means of which the Ark was carried.

*overlay them with gold.* May mean either gilding, an art well-known in Egypt, or plating.

EXODUS XXV, 16                                             שמות תרומה כה

they shall not be taken from it. 16. And thou shalt put into the ark the testimony which I shall give thee. \*11· 17. And thou shalt make an ark-cover of pure gold: two cubits and a half shall be the length thereof, and a cubit and a half the breadth thereof. 18. And thou shalt make two cherubim of gold; of beaten work shalt thou make them, at the two ends of the ark-cover. 19. And make one cherub at the one end, and one cherub at the other end; of one piece with the ark-cover shall ye make the cherubim of the two ends thereof. 20. And the cherubim shall spread out their wings on high, screening the ark-cover with their wings, with their faces one to another; toward the ark-cover shall the faces of the cherubim be. 21. And thou shalt put the ark-cover above upon the ark; and in the ark thou shalt put the testimony that I shall give thee. 22. And there I will meet with thee, and I will speak with thee from above the ark-cover, from between the two cherubim which are upon the ark of the testimony, of all things which I will give thee in commandment unto the children of Israel.

16 יִהְיוּ הַבַּדִּים לֹא יָסֻרוּ מִמֶּנּוּ: וְנָתַתָּ אֶל־הָאָרֹן אֵת הָעֵדֻת
שני
17 אֲשֶׁר אֶתֵּן אֵלֶיךָ: וְעָשִׂיתָ כַפֹּרֶת זָהָב טָהוֹר אַמָּתַיִם וָחֵצִי
18 אָרְכָּהּ וְאַמָּה וָחֵצִי רָחְבָּהּ: וְעָשִׂיתָ שְׁנַיִם כְּרֻבִים זָהָב
19 מִקְשָׁה תַּעֲשֶׂה אֹתָם מִשְּׁנֵי קְצוֹת הַכַּפֹּרֶת: וַעֲשֵׂה כְּרוּב
אֶחָד מִקָּצָה מִזֶּה וּכְרוּב־אֶחָד מִקָּצָה מִזֶּה מִן־הַכַּפֹּרֶת
כ תַּעֲשׂוּ אֶת־הַכְּרֻבִים עַל־שְׁנֵי קְצוֹתָיו: וְהָיוּ הַכְּרֻבִים
פֹּרְשֵׂי כְנָפַיִם לְמַעְלָה סֹכְכִים בְּכַנְפֵיהֶם עַל־הַכַּפֹּרֶת
וּפְנֵיהֶם אִישׁ אֶל־אָחִיו אֶל־הַכַּפֹּרֶת יִהְיוּ פְּנֵי הַכְּרֻבִים:
21 וְנָתַתָּ אֶת־הַכַּפֹּרֶת עַל־הָאָרֹן מִלְמָעְלָה וְאֶל־הָאָרֹן תִּתֵּן
22 אֶת־הָעֵדֻת אֲשֶׁר אֶתֵּן אֵלֶיךָ: וְנוֹעַדְתִּי לְךָ שָׁם וְדִבַּרְתִּי
אִתְּךָ מֵעַל הַכַּפֹּרֶת מִבֵּין שְׁנֵי הַכְּרֻבִים אֲשֶׁר עַל־אֲרֹן
הָעֵדֻת אֵת כָּל־אֲשֶׁר אֲצַוֶּה אוֹתְךָ אֶל־בְּנֵי יִשְׂרָאֵל: פ

**16.** *the testimony*. i.e. the two Tables of the Law which were evidence of the Divine Covenant concluded with Israel. Cf. I Kings VIII, 9, 'there was nothing in the ark save the two tables of stone.' The imageless inmost shrine was a continuous proclamation of the spirituality of God. The knowledge that in the holiest part of the Sanctuary was deposited nothing but the original Tables of the Law would ever impress the Israelites with the thought that the moral laws engraved on them constituted the conditions of that Covenant between God and Israel.

17–22. THE MERCY-SEAT AND CHERUBIM

**17.** *ark-cover*. RV has 'mercy-seat', first used by Tindale. Heb. *kapporeth*. It was a slab of gold, of the same dimensions as the top surface of the Ark, and was set upon it. According to the Talmud, it was a handbreadth in thickness. So much importance was attached to it that, in I Chron. XXVIII, 11, the Holy of Holies is called 'the house of the *kapporeth*'. The root of the word means not only 'to cover', but also 'to atone'. It is, therefore, doubtful whether the *kapporeth* served no other purpose than that of a cover to the Ark. It figures prominently in the ritual of the Day of Atonement (Lev. XVI, 2, 14 f).

**18.** *cherubim*. Apart from the mention of wings, there is no description offered of these emblematic figures. The Talmud, by a popular derivation of the Hebrew word, asserts that the cherubim had the faces of children. In Biblical poetry, the cherubim are an emblem of God's nearness to man. Thus the Psalmist speaks of God as 'enthroned upon the cherubim' (Ps. LXXX, 2), when he invokes Him to help his people: that is, He is not far off in the heavens, and not powerless to aid, but a very present Helper in the day of distress and trouble.

*beaten work*. i.e. hammered out of one piece.

**19.** *of one piece with*. Heb. is simply 'out of'. The figures were not made separately and fastened to the mercy-seat, but both were fashioned out of the same mass of gold (Rashi).

**20.** *screening the ark-cover*. The wings would thus veil the sight of the mercy-seat from the eyes of the High Priest when he entered the Holy of Holies on the Day of Atonement; and teach that no human being, even one who penetrated into the Holy of Holies, could attain to a full comprehension of God. There have been several mystical applications of the symbolism of the cherubim ('who had the faces of children') to educational problems. Children should be taught to aspire upwards ('spread out their wings on high'); to become protectors of the Ark of the Covenant ('covering the mercy-seat with their wings'); their faces towards their fellow-man ('their faces one to another'); and their eyes towards the mercy-seat of God.

**21.** See *v*. 16.

**22.** *I will meet with thee*. Heb. וְנוֹעַדְתִּי; hence the whole sanctuary is called אֹהֶל מוֹעֵד 'the Tent of Meeting', i.e. the place where God reveals His will, through Moses, to Israel.

# EXODUS XXV, 23

¶ 23. And thou shalt make a table of acacia-wood: two cubits shall be the length thereof, and a cubit the breadth thereof, and a cubit and a half the height thereof. 24. And thou shalt overlay it with pure gold, and make thereto a crown of gold round about. 25. And thou shalt make unto it a border of a handbreadth round about, and thou shalt make a golden crown to the border thereof round about. 26. And thou shalt make for it four rings of gold, and put the rings in the four corners that are on the four feet thereof. 27. Close by the border shall the rings be, for places for the staves to bear the table. 28. And thou shalt make the staves of acacia-wood, and overlay them with gold, that the table may be borne with them. 29. And thou shalt make the dishes thereof, and the pans thereof, and the jars thereof, and the bowls thereof, wherewith to pour out; of pure gold shalt thou make them. 30. And thou shalt set upon the table showbread before Me always.*ⁱⁱⁱˢ· ¶ 31. And thou shalt make a candlestick of pure gold: of beaten work shall the candlestick be made, even its base, and its shaft; its cups, its knops, and its flowers, shall be of one piece with it. 32. And there shall be six

23 וְעָשִׂיתָ שֻׁלְחָן עֲצֵי שִׁטִּים אַמָּתַיִם אָרְכּוֹ וְאַמָּה רָחְבּוֹ וְאַמָּה
24 וָחֵצִי קֹמָתוֹ: וְצִפִּיתָ אֹתוֹ זָהָב טָהוֹר וְעָשִׂיתָ לּוֹ זֵר זָהָב
כה סָבִיב: וְעָשִׂיתָ לּוֹ מִסְגֶּרֶת טֹפַח סָבִיב וְעָשִׂיתָ זֵר־זָהָב
26 לְמִסְגַּרְתּוֹ סָבִיב: וְעָשִׂיתָ לּוֹ אַרְבַּע טַבְּעֹת זָהָב וְנָתַתָּ
אֶת־הַטַּבָּעֹת עַל אַרְבַּע הַפֵּאֹת אֲשֶׁר לְאַרְבַּע רַגְלָיו: לְעֻמַּת
27 הַמִּסְגֶּרֶת תִּהְיֶיןָ הַטַּבָּעֹת לְבָתִּים לְבַדִּים לָשֵׂאת אֶת־
28 הַשֻּׁלְחָן: וְעָשִׂיתָ אֶת־הַבַּדִּים עֲצֵי שִׁטִּים וְצִפִּיתָ אֹתָם
29 זָהָב וְנִשָּׂא־בָם אֶת־הַשֻּׁלְחָן: וְעָשִׂיתָ קְּעָרֹתָיו וְכַפֹּתָיו
וּקְשׂוֹתָיו וּמְנַקִּיֹּתָיו אֲשֶׁר יֻסַּךְ בָּהֵן זָהָב טָהוֹר תַּעֲשֶׂה אֹתָם:
ל וְנָתַתָּ עַל־הַשֻּׁלְחָן לֶחֶם פָּנִים לְפָנַי תָּמִיד:* פ (שלישי
לספ׳)
31 וְעָשִׂיתָ מְנֹרַת זָהָב טָהוֹר מִקְשָׁה תֵּעָשֶׂה הַמְּנוֹרָה יְרֵכָהּ
32 וְקָנָהּ גְּבִיעֶיהָ כַּפְתֹּרֶיהָ וּפְרָחֶיהָ מִמֶּנָּה יִהְיוּ: וְשִׁשָּׁה
קָנִים יֹצְאִים מִצִּדֶּיהָ שְׁלֹשָׁה ׀ קְנֵי מְנֹרָה מִצִּדָּהּ הָאֶחָד

v. 29. ק׳ דגושה     v. 31. מלא יו״ד

### 23–30. THE TABLE OF SHOWBREAD

**23.** *table.* A representation of this table is on the Arch of Titus.

**24.** *a crown.* An ornamental moulding, as in v. 11.

**25.** *border.* Either on the top surface of the table or attached to the legs half-way down, so as to keep them together, like rungs of a chair. The illustration on the Arch of Titus favours the latter view.

*handbreadth.* i.e. the four fingers of the hand joined together; about three inches.

*crown.* Rashi makes this identical with the crown mentioned in the last verse, but on the Arch of Titus this central border has traces of decorative work.

**26.** *four rings.* For purposes of transportation, as in v. 12.

**29.** *dishes.* In which the loaves were brought to and from the table.

*pans.* Better, *cups*, for the frankincense which was set upon the two piles of loaves; see Lev. XXIV, 7.

*jars . . . bowls.* Jars and chalices used for the libation of wine which accompanied the burning of the incense. The former would be the large flagons in which the wine was stored; the latter, the bowls used in the actual libation.

**30.** *showbread.* lit. 'bread of the Presence'.

It is described in Lev. XXIV, 5–9, where it is said to have consisted of twelve loaves of wheaten flour, corresponding in number to the tribes of Israel. It was placed on the table on the Sabbath, arranged in two rows, and left there until the following Sabbath. When the loaves were removed, they were eaten by the priests. The symbolic meaning of the showbread is a matter of conjecture. Maimonides confesses, 'I do not know the object of the table with the bread upon it continually, and up to this day I have not been able to assign any reason to this commandment. Most commentators understand the Presence-bread as an expression of thankfulness and standing acknowledgment on the part of the children of Israel that God was the Giver of man's daily necessities.

**31.** *candlestick.* A lampstand. Among the spoils of the Temple depicted on the Arch of Titus the candlestick is conspicuous.

*beaten work.* See on v. 18.

*shaft.* The central stem.

*cups.* These were formed in the shape of an opened almond-blossom, the exterior being the 'knops', and the interior the 'flowers'; i.e. the outer and inner petals.

**32.** *six branches.* They curved to the same height as the central shaft, so that all the seven lamps were in a straight line. Seven represents the idea of completeness; and seven lamps therefore symbolize perfect life. See further on XXVII, 20 f.

## EXODUS XXV, 33

branches going out of the sides thereof: three branches of the candlestick out of the one side thereof, and three branches of the candlestick out of the other side thereof; 33. three cups made like almond-blossoms in one branch, a knop and a flower; and three cups made like almond-blossoms in the other branch, a knop and a flower; so for the six branches going out of the candlestick. 34. And in the candlestick four cups made like almond-blossoms, the knops thereof, and the flowers thereof. 35. And a knop under two branches of one piece with it, and a knop under two branches of one piece with it, and a knop under two branches of one piece with it, for the six branches going out of the candlestick. 36. Their knops and their branches shall be of one piece with it; the whole of it one beaten work of pure gold. 37. And thou shalt make the lamps thereof, seven; and they shall light the lamps thereof, to give light over against it. 38. And the tongs thereof, and the snuffdishes thereof, shall be of pure gold. 39. Of a talent of pure gold shall it be made, with all these vessels. 40. And see that thou make them after their pattern, which is being shown thee in the mount.* 111 a.

## 26
### CHAPTER XXVI

1. Moreover thou shalt make the tabernacle with ten curtains: of fine twined linen, and

---

**33.** *three cups.* Each branch was divided into three parts by having a 'cup' placed at the top end, and a third, and two-thirds of the way down towards the central shaft.

**34–36.** It is not quite certain from this description how these ornaments were arranged on the central shaft.

**37.** *lamps.* Receptacles for the oil and wick, probably shaped like elongated shells.
*over against it.* Or, 'in front of it.' According to Rashi, the lamps were so arranged that the wick-mouths from which the flame burned were directed towards the central shaft.

**38.** *tongs.* For drawing out the wick.
*snuffdishes.* Receptacles in which the burnt wicks are placed.

**39.** *talent of pure gold.* Josephus gives the weight as one hundred pounds, and that is approximately correct. The value would be about six thousand pounds sterling.

**40.** *which is being shown.* The Rabbis declare that Moses found it so difficult to grasp the verbal instruction in connection with the candlestick, that God constructed for him a model of fire. But from the text, it is not necessarily to be inferred that an actual model was shown to Moses. As Luzzatto remarks, the verb, 'to see,' may signify mental perception as well as ocular vision.

### CHAPTER XXVI

#### 1–6. THE CURTAINS OF THE TABERNACLE

**1.** *the tabernacle.* i.e. Holy Place and the Holy of Holies. The interior is to be covered with a fabric of curtains, supported upon a wooden framework.
*fine twined linen.* Linen of exceptional fineness, on which the figures of cherubim were worked in coloured threads.
*work of the skilful workman.* Or, 'work of a designer,' or 'pattern-weaver'; work requiring exceptional skill. The traditional explanation is that in this class of work a design appeared on both sides of the fabric.

EXODUS XXVI, 2

blue, and purple, and scarlet, with cherubim the work of the skilful workman shalt thou make them. 2. The length of each curtain shall be eight and twenty cubits, and the breadth of each curtain four cubits; all the curtains shall have one measure. 3. Five curtains shall be coupled together one to another; and the other five curtains shall be coupled one to another. 4. And thou shalt make loops of blue upon the edge of the one curtain that is outmost in the first set; and likewise shalt thou make in the edge of the curtain that is outmost in the second set. 5. Fifty loops shalt thou make in the one curtain, and fifty loops shalt thou make in the edge of the curtain that is in the second set; the loops shall be opposite one to another. 6 And thou shalt make fifty clasps of gold, and couple the curtains one to another with the clasps, that the tabernacle may be one whole. 7. And thou shalt make curtains of goats' hair for a tent over the tabernacle; eleven curtains shalt thou make them. 8. The length of each curtain shall be thirty cubits, and the breadth of each curtain four cubits; the eleven curtains shall have one measure. 9. And thou shalt couple five curtains by themselves, and six curtains by themselves, and shalt double over the sixth curtain in the forefront of the tent. 10. And thou shalt make fifty loops on the edge of the one curtain that is outmost in the first set, and fifty loops upon the edge of the curtain

אַרְבַּע בָּאַמָּה הַיְרִיעָה הָאֶחָת מִדָּה אַחַת לְכָל־הַיְרִיעֹת׃
3 חֲמֵשׁ הַיְרִיעֹת תִּהְיֶיןָ חֹבְרֹת אִשָּׁה אֶל־אֲחֹתָהּ וְחָמֵשׁ יְרִיעֹת
4 חֹבְרֹת אִשָּׁה אֶל־אֲחֹתָהּ׃ וְעָשִׂיתָ לֻלְאֹת תְּכֵלֶת עַל שְׂפַת
הַיְרִיעָה הָאֶחָת מִקָּצָה בַּחֹבָרֶת וְכֵן תַּעֲשֶׂה בִּשְׂפַת הַיְרִיעָה
5 הַקִּיצוֹנָה בַּמַּחְבֶּרֶת הַשֵּׁנִית׃ חֲמִשִּׁים לֻלָאֹת תַּעֲשֶׂה
בַּיְרִיעָה הָאֶחָת וַחֲמִשִּׁים לֻלָאֹת תַּעֲשֶׂה בִּקְצֵה הַיְרִיעָה
אֲשֶׁר בַּמַּחְבֶּרֶת הַשֵּׁנִית מַקְבִּילֹת הַלֻּלָאֹת אִשָּׁה אֶל־
6 אֲחֹתָהּ׃ וְעָשִׂיתָ חֲמִשִּׁים קַרְסֵי זָהָב וְחִבַּרְתָּ אֶת־הַיְרִיעֹת
7 אִשָּׁה אֶל־אֲחֹתָהּ בַּקְּרָסִים וְהָיָה הַמִּשְׁכָּן אֶחָד׃ וְעָשִׂיתָ
יְרִיעֹת עִזִּים לְאֹהֶל עַל־הַמִּשְׁכָּן עַשְׁתֵּי־עֶשְׂרֵה יְרִיעֹת
8 תַּעֲשֶׂה אֹתָם׃ אֹרֶךְ ׀ הַיְרִיעָה הָאַחַת שְׁלֹשִׁים בָּאַמָּה
וְרֹחַב אַרְבַּע בָּאַמָּה הַיְרִיעָה הָאֶחָת מִדָּה אַחַת לְעַשְׁתֵּי
9 עֶשְׂרֵה יְרִיעֹת׃ וְחִבַּרְתָּ אֶת־חֲמֵשׁ הַיְרִיעֹת לְבָד וְאֶת־
שֵׁשׁ הַיְרִיעֹת לְבָד וְכָפַלְתָּ אֶת־הַיְרִיעָה הַשִּׁשִּׁית אֶל־מוּל
י פְּנֵי הָאֹהֶל׃ וְעָשִׂיתָ חֲמִשִּׁים לֻלָאֹת עַל שְׂפַת הַיְרִיעָה
הָאֶחָת הַקִּיצֹנָה בַּחֹבָרֶת וַחֲמִשִּׁים לֻלָאֹת עַל שְׂפַת

v. 9. קמץ בז״ק

**2.** *length.* The curtains were arranged in two sets of five, each set being 28 cubits in length and 20 cubits in breadth. The Tabernacle was 30 cubits long and 10 cubits in width and height. Consequently, as Josephus declares, the curtains 'covered all the top and parts of the walls, on the sides and behind, so far as within one cubit of the ground'; because the two walls and top of the structure measured 30 cubits and the curtain only 28 cubits, leaving 2 cubits exposed. The length of the structure 30 cubits, and the western side, 10 cubits, would be exactly covered by the two sets of curtains, 20 cubits each in breadth. The eastern side, the entrance, was provided with a special screen; v. 36.

**4.** *loops.* Five curtains formed 'a set', and at the edge of each set there were to be fifty loops, so that they could be coupled together by means of clasps.

**6.** *that the tabernacle may be one.* They were formed of separate pieces, yet they were so arranged that when they formed the covering of the Tabernacle they were a single whole. Similarly the community of Israel, comprising different tribes and families, must be linked together in peace and solidarity (Ibn Ezra).

**7-14. THE CURTAINS AND COVERINGS OF THE TENT**

**7.** *of goats' hair.* To protect the finely-spun curtains of the Tabernacle from dust and rain, there was a tent erected as an outer covering, and the sides of the tent were made of goats' hair cloth. There were eleven of these curtains. Why an additional one was required is explained in v. 9.

**8.** *length.* The goats' hair curtains were of the same breadth as the linen, but were two cubits longer to make up the deficiency of a cubit on each side (see on 2 f.).

**9.** *double over.* Two cubits' length of the curtain was folded back at the entrance on the east side, so as to form a kind of portal above the entrance.

**10.** Similar to v. 4 f. It is not stated of what material the loops were to be made. They were probably of woven goats' hair. The clasps were of copper or bronze, because this outer covering was not part of the actual Tabernacle, like the curtains of linen, but only a protection against rain, dust and sun.

EXODUS XXVI, 11

which is outmost in the second set. 11. And thou shalt make fifty clasps of brass, and put the clasps into the loops, and couple the tent together, that it may be one. 12. And as for the overhanging part that remaineth of the curtains of the tent, the half curtain that remaineth over shall hang over the back of the tabernacle. 13. And the cubit on the one side, and the cubit on the other side, of that which remaineth over in the length of the curtains of the tent, shall hang over the sides of the tabernacle on this side and on that side, to cover it. 14. And thou shalt make a covering for the tent of rams' skins dyed red, and a covering of sealskins above.*iv. ¶ 15. And thou shalt make the boards for the tabernacle of acacia-wood, standing up. 16. Ten cubits shall be the length of a board, and a cubit and a half the breadth of each board. 17. Two tenons shall there be in each board, joined one to another; thus shalt thou make for all the boards of the tabernacle. 18. And thou shalt make the boards for the tabernacle, twenty boards for the south side southward. 19. And thou shalt make forty sockets of silver under the twenty boards: two sockets under one board for its two tenons, and two sockets under another board for its two tenons; 20. and for the second side of the tabernacle, on the north side, twenty boards. 21. And their forty sockets of silver: two sockets under one board, and two sockets under another

**12.** Since there were eleven hair curtains as against ten of linen, and two cubits of the eleventh curtain had been accounted for in v. 9, the remaining two cubits were allowed to trail on the ground at the back of the edifice, on the west side.

**13.** The hair curtains were two cubits longer than the linen, and this extra length provided for the cubit of the boards on either side which was left exposed by the other curtains (2 f.). The sides were thus completely protected by the outer curtains.

**14.** As a further protection to the precious fabrics of the Tabernacle, there were two additional coverings of skin spread over the roof, and hanging down at the sides. According to some Rabbis, there was only one additional covering of rams' skins, with patches of porpoise-skins.

**15-30. THE BOARDS OF THE TABERNACLE**

**15.** *boards.* Either solid boards, or, as some have suggested, 'frames'; i.e. two planks of wood joined by a cross-piece at the top and bottom.

*standing up.* The boards are to be placed vertically in position. The length of the board,

ten cubits (15 feet), represents the height of the Tabernacle.

**17.** *tenons. i.e.* projecting pegs, which fitted into sockets. These tenons were 'joined one to another', which may mean that they were fixed on to a plate of metal whereby they were held together.

**18.** *twenty boards.* Formed the length of the Tabernacle, each a cubit and a half in breadth. The total length was thus 30 cubits (45 feet).

*south side.* lit. 'towards the Negeb', i.e. the arid Southern part of Palestine. Likewise in v. 22, 'westward' is lit. 'sea-ward', as the Mediterranean formed the Western horizon in Palestine. Bible critics deduce from the use of such terms in this narrative that it was written after Israel had lived long enough in Canaan for the words to have acquired this sense. The argument is absurd; because it overlooks the fact that the Hebrew language did not originate in Egypt during the bondage, but that it had been in existence many, many centuries before the Children of Israel ever went down to Egypt.

**19.** *sockets.* To receive the tenons or projecting pegs. These sockets were on the bases or pedestals which kept the boards erect.

EXODUS XXVI, 22

שמות תרומה כו

22 הַקֶּרֶשׁ הָאֶחָד וּשְׁנֵי אֲדָנִים תַּחַת הַקֶּרֶשׁ הָאֶחָד: וּלְיַרְכְּתֵי
23 הַמִּשְׁכָּן יָמָּה תַּעֲשֶׂה שִׁשָּׁה קְרָשִׁים: וּשְׁנֵי קְרָשִׁים תַּעֲשֶׂה
24 לִמְקֻצְעֹת הַמִּשְׁכָּן בַּיַּרְכָתָיִם: וְיִהְיוּ תֹאֲמִם מִלְּמַטָּה וְיַחְדָּו
יִהְיוּ תַמִּים עַל־רֹאשׁוֹ אֶל־הַטַּבַּעַת הָאֶחָת כֵּן יִהְיֶה
כה לִשְׁנֵיהֶם לִשְׁנֵי הַמִּקְצֹעֹת יִהְיוּ: וְהָיוּ שְׁמֹנָה קְרָשִׁים
וְאַדְנֵיהֶם כֶּסֶף שִׁשָּׁה עָשָׂר אֲדָנִים שְׁנֵי אֲדָנִים תַּחַת
26 הַקֶּרֶשׁ הָאֶחָד וּשְׁנֵי אֲדָנִים תַּחַת הַקֶּרֶשׁ הָאֶחָד: וְעָשִׂיתָ
בְרִיחִם עֲצֵי שִׁטִּים חֲמִשָּׁה לְקַרְשֵׁי צֶלַע־הַמִּשְׁכָּן הָאֶחָד:
27 וַחֲמִשָּׁה בְרִיחִם לְקַרְשֵׁי צֶלַע־הַמִּשְׁכָּן הַשֵּׁנִית וַחֲמִשָּׁה
28 בְרִיחִם לְקַרְשֵׁי צֶלַע הַמִּשְׁכָּן לַיַּרְכָתַיִם יָמָּה: וְהַבְּרִיחַ
הַתִּיכֹן בְּתוֹךְ הַקְּרָשִׁים מַבְרִחַ מִן־הַקָּצֶה אֶל־הַקָּצֶה:
29 וְאֶת־הַקְּרָשִׁים תְּצַפֶּה זָהָב וְאֶת־טַבְּעֹתֵיהֶם תַּעֲשֶׂה זָהָב
ל בָּתִּים לַבְּרִיחִם וְצִפִּיתָ אֶת־הַבְּרִיחִם זָהָב: וַהֲקֵמֹתָ אֶת־
חמישי
31 הַמִּשְׁכָּן כְּמִשְׁפָּטוֹ אֲשֶׁר הָרְאֵיתָ בָּהָר: ס וְעָשִׂיתָ
פָרֹכֶת תְּכֵלֶת וְאַרְגָּמָן וְתוֹלַעַת שָׁנִי וְשֵׁשׁ מָשְׁזָר מַעֲשֵׂה
32 חֹשֵׁב יַעֲשֶׂה אֹתָהּ כְּרֻבִים: וְנָתַתָּה אֹתָהּ עַל־אַרְבָּעָה
עַמּוּדֵי שִׁטִּים מְצֻפִּים זָהָב וָוֵיהֶם זָהָב עַל־אַרְבָּעָה אַדְנֵי־
33 כָסֶף: וְנָתַתָּה אֶת־הַפָּרֹכֶת תַּחַת הַקְּרָסִים וְהֵבֵאתָ שָׁמָּה

v. 31. סבירין תעשה

board. 22. And for the hinder part of the tabernacle westward thou shalt make six boards. 23. And two boards shalt thou make for the corners of the tabernacle in the hinder part. 24. And they shall be double beneath, and in like manner they shall be complete unto the top thereof unto the first ring; thus shall it be for them both; they shall be for the two corners. 25. Thus there shall be eight boards, and their sockets of silver, sixteen sockets: two sockets under one board, and two sockets under another board. 26. And thou shalt make bars of acacia-wood: five for the boards of the one side of the tabernacle, 27. and five bars for the boards of the other side of the tabernacle, and five bars for the boards of the side of the tabernacle, for the hinder part westward; 28. and the middle bar in the midst of the boards, which shall pass through from end to end. 29. And thou shalt overlay the boards with gold, and make their rings of gold for holders for the bars; and thou shalt overlay the bars with gold. 30. And thou shalt rear up the tabernacle according to the fashion thereof which hath been shown thee in the mount.*v. ¶ 31. And thou shalt make a veil of blue, and purple, and scarlet, and fine twined linen; with cherubim the work of the skilful workman shall it be made. 32. And thou shalt hang it upon four pillars of acacia overlaid with gold, their hooks being of gold, upon four sockets of silver. 33. And thou shalt hang up the veil under the clasps, and shalt bring in thither within the veil the ark of the testimony; and the veil shall divide unto you between the holy

**22.** *westward.* There were only six boards to form the western wall, and these would occupy a space of nine cubits. It is certain that the width of the edifice was ten cubits, the same as the height. There is consequently still one cubit to be accounted for.

**24.** *double.* The remaining cubit (v. 22) was filled in by two boards, one fitted into each corner. These additional boards would naturally not protrude outside the building, but inside, and in this way they would be 'double', since they overlapped the last of the twenty boards on each side. They would serve as buttresses and strengthen the corners.

*the first ring.* See v. 29.

**26.** *bars.* Along each of the three walls of the Tabernacle bars were fixed in three rows. The central bar was the entire length of the structure; but on the top and bottom rows the bars were shorter.

**29.** *holders for the bars.* These bars fitted into rings. The rings and bars were to join the walls fast together, 'that the Tabernacle might not be shaken, either by the winds or by any other means, but that it might preserve itself quiet and immovable continually' (Josephus).

**30.** This verse (cf. xxv, 9, 40) perhaps implies that more detailed directions were given to Moses than are recorded in this Book; and this supplementary instruction filled in the gaps which occur in the written account, and explained its obscurities.

### 31–33. The Veil

**31.** *veil.* Its purpose was to form a partition between the Holy of Holies and the remaining part of the Tabernacle.

**32.** *pillars.* The veil was held up by four wooden posts with golden hooks. The posts fitted into silver sockets similar to those placed under the boards (v. 19).

**33.** *most holy.* The Holy of Holies formed a perfect cube, being 10 cubits in height, length and breadth.

*ark of the testimony. i.e.* the Ark containing the two tables of stone (xxv, 10 f).

EXODUS XXVI, 34

place and the most holy. 34. And thou shalt put the ark-cover upon the ark of the testimony in the most holy place. 35. And thou shalt set the table without the veil, and the candlestick over against the table on the side of the tabernacle toward the south; and thou shalt put the table on the north side. 36. And thou shalt make a screen for the door of the Tent, of blue, and purple, and scarlet, and fine twined linen, the work of the weaver in colours. 37. And thou shalt make for the screen five pillars of acacia, and overlay them with gold; their hooks shall be of gold; and thou shalt cast five sockets of brass for them.*vi.

## 27 CHAPTER XXVII

1. And thou shalt make the altar of acacia-wood, five cubits long, and five cubits broad; the altar shall be four-square; and the height thereof shall be three cubits. 2. And thou shalt make the horns of it upon the four corners thereof; the horns thereof shall be of one piece with it; and thou shalt overlay it with brass. 3. And thou shalt make its pots to take away its ashes, and its shovels, and its basins, and its flesh-hooks, and its fire-pans; all the vessels thereof

---

**35.** *thou shalt set.* Rashi gives the traditional account of the arrangement of the furniture in the Tabernacle. The table of showbread was set in the north, two and a half cubits from the wall; the candlestick in the south, an equal distance from the wall; and between the two was the golden altar of incense.

**36.** *screen.* Instead of the curtains, a special screen was made for the entrance. Its material was similar to the veil, except that no cherubim were embroidered thereon.

**37.** *five pillars.* The screen, unlike the veil, which had four pillars, was supported by five. It would require this additional support because of the frequency with which it would be drawn aside to allow the priests to enter.

### CHAPTER XXVII
#### 1–8. THE ALTAR OF BURNT-OFFERINGS

**1.** *altar.* The Rabbis explained the symbolism of the altar by making each letter of the Heb. name for altar (מזבח) the initial of a word, thus: מחילה 'forgiveness'—the altar was the channel whereby the Israelite could seek reconciliation with God, from Whom he had become estranged by sin; זכות 'merit'—gratitude, humility, contrition found an outlet on the altar, and by the exercise of these virtues, life was ennobled and 'merit' acquired; ברכה 'blessing'— by being true to the teachings that centred round

the altar, man earns the Divine blessings and himself becomes a blessing to his fellowmen; חיים 'life'—the altar points the way to the life everlasting, to the things that abide for evermore, truth, righteousness, holiness.

**2.** *horns.* There were projections at each of the four corners of the altar. The commonly accepted view is that they were pointed at the top. Josephus, describing the altar in the Second Temple, says, 'it had corners like horns.' The purpose of these horns can only be conjectured. The horn was the symbol of power, glory, salvation; and these horns no doubt typified to the worshipper the might of God and His ability to protect those who resorted to His altar. Consequently, a fugitive, unless he was a murderer, obtained safety by seizing hold of the altar-horns (see on XXI, 14).

*of one piece with it.* Cf. XXV, 19, 31.

*overlay it with brass.* Since fires would be constantly burning upon the altar.

**3.** *ashes.* Of the burnt animals and fuels.

*shovels.* To remove the ashes from the altar.

*basins.* Receptacles for the blood of the slain animals.

*flesh-hooks.* Forks for handling the flesh of the sacrifices.

*fire-pans.* In which burning coal was carried from the altar of burnt-offering to the altar of incense.

EXODUS XXVII, 4      שמות תרומה כז

thou shalt make of brass. 4. And thou shalt make for it a grating of network of brass; and upon the net shalt thou make four brazen rings in the four corners thereof. 5. And thou shalt put it under the ledge round the altar beneath, that the net may reach halfway up the altar. 6. And thou shalt make staves for the altar, staves of acacia-wood, and overlay them with brass. 7. And the staves thereof shall be put into the rings, and the staves shall be upon the two sides of the altar, in bearing it. 8. Hollow with planks shalt thou make it; as it hath been shown thee in the mount, so shall they make it.* vii. ¶ 9. And thou shalt make the court of the tabernacle: for the south side southward there shall be hangings for the court of fine twined linen a hundred cubits long for one side. 10. And the pillars thereof shall be twenty, and their sockets twenty, of brass; the hooks of the pillars and their fillets shall be of silver. 11. And likewise for the north side in length there shall be hangings a hundred cubits long, and the pillars thereof twenty, and their sockets twenty, of brass; the hooks of the pillars and their fillets of silver. 12. And for the breadth of the court on the west side shall be hangings of fifty cubits: their pillars ten, and their sockets ten. 13. And the breadth of the court on the east side eastward shall be fifty cubits. 14. The hangings for the one side [of the gate] shall be fifteen cubits: their pillars three, and their sockets three. 15. And for the other side shall be hangings of fifteen cubits: their pillars three, and their sockets three. 16. And for the gate of the court shall be a screen of twenty cubits, of blue, and purple, and scarlet, and fine twined linen, the work of the weaver in

4 וּמִזְלְגֹתָיו וּמַחְתֹּתָיו לְכָל־כֵּלָיו תַּעֲשֶׂה נְחֹשֶׁת: וְעָשִׂיתָ
לּוֹ מִכְבָּר מַעֲשֵׂה רֶשֶׁת נְחֹשֶׁת וְעָשִׂיתָ עַל־הָרֶשֶׁת אַרְבַּע
5 טַבְּעֹת נְחֹשֶׁת עַל אַרְבַּע קְצוֹתָיו: וְנָתַתָּה אֹתָהּ תַּחַת
כַּרְכֹּב הַמִּזְבֵּחַ מִלְּמָטָּה וְהָיְתָה הָרֶשֶׁת עַד חֲצִי הַמִּזְבֵּחַ:
6 וְעָשִׂיתָ בַדִּים לַמִּזְבֵּחַ בַּדֵּי עֲצֵי שִׁטִּים וְצִפִּיתָ אֹתָם נְחֹשֶׁת:
7 וְהוּבָא אֶת־בַּדָּיו בַּטַּבָּעֹת וְהָיוּ הַבַּדִּים עַל־שְׁתֵּי צַלְעֹת
8 הַמִּזְבֵּחַ בִּשְׂאֵת אֹתוֹ: נְבוּב לֻחֹת תַּעֲשֶׂה אֹתוֹ כַּאֲשֶׁר
הֶרְאָה אֹתְךָ בָּהָר כֵּן יַעֲשׂוּ: ס   וְעָשִׂיתָ אֵת חֲצַר   שביעי
9 הַמִּשְׁכָּן לִפְאַת נֶגֶב־תֵּימָנָה קְלָעִים לֶחָצֵר שֵׁשׁ מָשְׁזָר
10 מֵאָה בָאַמָּה אֹרֶךְ לַפֵּאָה הָאֶחָת: וְעַמֻּדָיו עֶשְׂרִים וְאַדְנֵיהֶם
11 עֶשְׂרִים נְחֹשֶׁת וָוֵי הָעַמֻּדִים וַחֲשֻׁקֵיהֶם כָּסֶף: וְכֵן לִפְאַת
צָפוֹן בָּאֹרֶךְ קְלָעִים מֵאָה אֹרֶךְ וְעַמְדוּ עֶשְׂרִים וְאַדְנֵיהֶם
12 עֶשְׂרִים נְחֹשֶׁת וָוֵי הָעַמֻּדִים וַחֲשֻׁקֵיהֶם כָּסֶף: וְרֹחַב הֶחָצֵר
לִפְאַת־יָם קְלָעִים חֲמִשִּׁים אַמָּה עַמֻּדֵיהֶם עֲשָׂרָה וְאַדְנֵיהֶם
13 עֲשָׂרָה: וְרֹחַב הֶחָצֵר לִפְאַת קֵדְמָה מִזְרָחָה חֲמִשִּׁים
14 אַמָּה: וַחֲמֵשׁ עֶשְׂרֵה אַמָּה קְלָעִים לַכָּתֵף עַמֻּדֵיהֶם
15 שְׁלֹשָׁה וְאַדְנֵיהֶם שְׁלֹשָׁה: וְלַכָּתֵף הַשֵּׁנִית חֲמֵשׁ עֶשְׂרֵה
16 קְלָעִים עַמֻּדֵיהֶם שְׁלֹשָׁה וְאַדְנֵיהֶם שְׁלֹשָׁה: וּלְשַׁעַר הֶחָצֵר
מָסָךְ ׀ עֶשְׂרִים אַמָּה תְּכֵלֶת וְאַרְגָּמָן וְתוֹלַעַת שָׁנִי וְשֵׁשׁ

v. 11. ועמדיו קרי

---

**5.** *ledge.* Half-way round the altar there ran a ledge, probably made of copper, and this rested upon a brazen grating, 2½ feet in height. According to Tradition, this ledge was a cubit in width, and seems to have been used by the priests to stand on. Attached to the grating were rings to enable the altar to be carried.

**8.** *hollow with planks.* The altar consisted of wooden planks covered with metal, so that the inside was hollow. Rashi explains that the command in xx, 21, 'an altar of earth thou shalt make unto Me,' signifies that a mound of earth, equal to the dimensions of the hollow of the altar, was heaped up, and the casing of the altar set over it.

**9-19.** THE COURT OF THE TABERNACLE

**9.** *court.* i.e. an enclosure, but without a roof. It marked off the limits of the Sanctuary-precincts. Any Israelite who was not ritually unclean could enter the court. The material used for the enclosure was 'fine twined linen' (see on xxvi, 1), and the length was 100 cubits (150 feet).

**10.** The hangings were supported by twenty pillars, set five cubits apart; and, since the height was five cubits (*v.* 18), the spaces created by the pillars were square.

*sockets.* See on xxvi, 19.

*fillets.* Narrow strips of binding material; binding-rods, connecting the pillars.

**12.** *breadth.* The court was twice as long as it was broad. There were twenty pillars along the length, and ten along the breadth.

**16.** *screen.* On the east side, there were hangings, as on the other three sides, but only for fifteen cubits from each corner. This left an open space in the middle, measuring twenty cubits, which was filled in by a screen. This screen was of the same fabric as that of the Tabernacle (xxvi, 36).

335

EXODUS XXVII, 17　　　　　　　　　שמות תרומה כז

colours: their pillars four, and their sockets four.*ᵐ· 17. All the pillars of the court round about shall be filleted with silver; their hooks of silver, and their sockets of brass. 18. The length of the court shall be a hundred cubits, and the breadth fifty every where, and the height five cubits, of fine twined linen, and their sockets of brass. 19. All the instruments of the tabernacle in all the service thereof, and all the pins thereof, and all the pins of the court, shall be of brass.

מפטיר מָשְׁזָר מַעֲשֵׂה רֹקֵם עַמֻּדֵיהֶם אַרְבָּעָה וְאַדְנֵיהֶם אַרְבָּעָה׃
17 כָּל־עַמּוּדֵי הֶחָצֵר סָבִיב מְחֻשָּׁקִים כֶּסֶף וָוֵיהֶם כָּסֶף
18 וְאַדְנֵיהֶם נְחֹשֶׁת׃ אֹרֶךְ הֶחָצֵר מֵאָה בָאַמָּה וְרֹחַב ׀ חֲמִשִּׁים
בַּחֲמִשִּׁים וְקֹמָה חָמֵשׁ אַמּוֹת שֵׁשׁ מָשְׁזָר וְאַדְנֵיהֶם נְחֹשֶׁת׃
19 לְכֹל כְּלֵי הַמִּשְׁכָּן בְּכֹל עֲבֹדָתוֹ וְכָל־יְתֵדֹתָיו וְכָל־יִתְדֹת
הֶחָצֵר נְחֹשֶׁת׃

**17.** *filleted.* i.e. bound round, as in v. 10.

**18.** *every where.* A difficult phrase. Its literal meaning is 'fifty by fifty', which the Talmud explains by supposing that on the East side the court was fifty cubits square.

**19.** *instruments.* Tools used in setting up the tabernacle; such as hammers for driving the pins into the ground.

*tabernacle.* The word is here used in its widest sense, to include the Court as well as the Holy Place and Holy of Holies.

*service thereof.* Its workmanship.

*pins.* Tent-pegs.

## HAFTORAH TERUMAH　　　　הפטרת תרומה

### I KINGS V, 26–VI, 13

#### CHAPTER V　　　　　　　　　　　CAP. V. ה

26. And the Lord gave Solomon wisdom, as He promised him; and there was peace between Hiram and Solomon; and they two made a league together. ¶27. And king Solomon raised a levy out of all Israel; and the levy was thirty thousand men. 28. And he sent them to Lebanon, ten thousand a month by courses: a month they were in Lebanon, and two months at home; and

26 וַיהֹוָה נָתַן חָכְמָה לִשְׁלֹמֹה כַּאֲשֶׁר דִּבֶּר־
לוֹ וַיְהִי שָׁלֹם בֵּין חִירָם וּבֵין שְׁלֹמֹה וַיִּכְרְתוּ בְרִית
27 שְׁנֵיהֶם׃ וַיַּעַל הַמֶּלֶךְ שְׁלֹמֹה מַס מִכָּל־יִשְׂרָאֵל וַיְהִי
28 הַמַּס שְׁלֹשִׁים אֶלֶף אִישׁ׃ וַיִּשְׁלָחֵם לְבָנוֹנָה עֲשֶׂרֶת אֲלָפִים

The Sedrah describes the Tabernacle in the wilderness. This is paralleled in the Haftorah by the description of the Temple of Solomon at Jerusalem.

It was King David's yearning desire to build a Temple unto God—a central Sanctuary that was to be the symbol of Israel's obedience to God's Law, of Israel's unity and Israel's peace. He was not destined to see his life-dream realized; but Solomon his son makes its fulfilment almost the first care of his reign.

**26.** *as He promised him.* See I Kings III, 12.

*Hiram.* King of Tyre, the principal city of Phœnicia, on the coast, north of Palestine. Hiram was a friend of David, and helped him to build his own house (II Sam. v, 11). He now agrees, at Solomon's request, to supply timber and skilled labour for the building of the Temple, in return for an annual payment of wheat and oil.

THE PREPARATION FOR THE WORK

**27.** *a levy.* Heb. *mas.* the same word as in Exod. I, 11, denoting a body of men set to forced labour for a definite time. 'It was perhaps from his Egyptian father-in-law that Solomon, to his own cost, learnt the secret of forced labour. In their Egyptian bondage the forefathers of Israel had been fatally familiar with the ugly word *mas*, the labour wrung from them by hard task-masters' (Farrar). See I Sam. VIII, 11–18. Discontent with this practice eventually rent Solomon's kingdom in twain. In contrast to this forced labour, the Tabernacle of old was the result of the free-will offerings of the entire People.

**28.** *to Lebanon.* To cut down the trees there. The mountain range of Lebanon, to the north of Palestine, is still noted for its magnificent cedar trees.

## I KINGS V, 29

Adoniram was over the levy. 29. And Solomon had threescore and ten thousand that bore burdens, and fourscore thousand that were hewers in the mountains; 30. besides Solomon's chief officers that were over the work, three thousand and three hundred, who bore rule over the people that wrought in the work. 31. And the king commanded, and they quarried great stones, costly stones, to lay the foundation of the house with hewn stone. 32. And Solomon's builders and Hiram's builders and the Gebalites did fashion them, and prepared the timber and the stones to build the house.

### Chapter VI

1. And it came to pass in the four hundred and eightieth year after the children of Israel were come out of the land of Egypt, in the fourth year of Solomon's reign over Israel, in the month of Ziv, which is the second month, that he began to build the house of the LORD. 2. And the house which king Solomon built for the LORD, the length thereof was threescore cubits, and the breadth thereof twenty cubits, and the height thereof thirty cubits. 3. And the porch before [1]the temple of the house, twenty cubits was the length thereof, according to the breadth of the house; and ten cubits was the breadth thereof before the house. 4. And for the house he made windows broad within, and narrow without. 5. And against the wall of the house he built a side-structure round about, against the walls of the house round about, both of the temple and of [2]the Sanctuary;

---
[1] That is, the holy place.
[2] Heb. *debir*, that is, the hindmost or innermost room, the most holy place.

*by courses.* i.e. in relays, or shifts. There were ten thousand at work each month; the others were resting in their homes for two months.

*Adoniram.* Was the overseer over the levy.

**29.** *hewers in the mountains.* i.e. sent to quarry stones in the hill-country of Palestine.

**30.** *bore rule.* As taskmasters.

**32.** *the Gebalites.* Inhabitants of Gebal, a maritime town north of Beyrout.

### Chapter VI. A General Description of the Temple

The Temple buildings stood within a large court in which the worshippers could assemble. The Temple proper was a rectangular hall 60 by 20 by 30 cubits. Its entrance, in the shape of a porch, was ten cubits long; and as it extended over the whole front, it was 20 cubits wide. On the three sides of the House were built a number of chambers in three stories. Within, the building was divided into two parts; the larger, to the East, being the Holy Place; and the smaller, the Most Holy Place.

**1.** *the month Ziv.* The ancient name of the second month, now called Iyyar.

**3.** *the temple of the house.* i.e. the Holy Place.

**4.** *broad within, and narrow without.* This translation follows the Targum. The Rabbis, however, explain that the windows were *narrow within* and cut obliquely through the wall, *widening towards the exterior*—teaching that the Sanctuary required no outward light, rather was its spiritual radiance to spread abroad and illumine the world outside.

**5.** *side-structure.* It enclosed the whole of three sides of the building; and within it, on different stories, he built the side-chambers mentioned below.

## I KINGS VI, 6

and he made side-chambers round about; 6. the nethermost story of the side-structure was five cubits broad, and the middle was six cubits broad, and the third was seven cubits broad; for on the outside he made rebatements in the wall of the house round about, that the beams should not have hold in the walls of the house.—7. For the house, when it was in building, was built of stone made ready at the quarry; and there was neither hammer nor axe nor any tool of iron heard in the house, while it was in building. —8. The door for the [1]lowest row of chambers was in the right side of the house; and they went up by winding stairs into the middle row, and out of the middle into the third. 9. So he built the house, and finished it; and he covered in the house with planks of cedar over beams. 10. And he built the stories of the side-structure against all the house, each five cubits high; and they rested on the house with timber of cedar. ¶11. And the word of the LORD came to Solomon, saying: 12. 'As for this house which thou art building, if thou wilt walk in My statutes, and execute Mine ordinances, and keep all My commandments to walk in them; then will I establish My word with thee, which I spoke unto David thy father; 13. in that I will dwell therein among the children of Israel, and will not forsake My people Israel.'

---

[1] Heb. *middle*.

---

*the sanctuary*. Heb. *debir*. That is, the Most Holy Place (RV Margin); the hindmost, or innermost room.

*side-chambers*. They were probably for the accommodation of the priests, and for storing the treasure of the Sanctuary.

**6.** *rebatements in the wall*. There were successive reductions in the thickness of the walls in the second and third story. The chambers thus *increased* somewhat in size in the upper stories, each of these resting on a recess, or rebatement, in the thick wall of the Temple.

*the beams should not have hold in the walls*. Thus the walls were not pierced in order to give support to the beams, and these were not fixed into the actual building of the Temple.

**7.** *at the quarry*. The stones were squared, dressed and finished at the quarries, before being sent to Jerusalem.

*neither hammer ... heard in the house*. The Temple rose *silently and peacefully*. Jewish Legend wove its magic web around this striking verse. If neither hammer nor axe was used in the building of the House, how then were the stones fitted together? the people asked. Solomon in his wisdom, was the answer, had come into possession of a wonderful worm, one of the marvels of creation, the *Shamir*, which, if placed upon the hardest stones, would instantly and noiselessly cleave them as desired. The great moral truth enshrined in this verse and legend is this: a Temple of the LORD cannot be where there is discord, violence or revolt.

**9.** *covered*. *i.e.* roofed it.

**10.** *the stories*. See *v.* 5.

### 11-13. CHARGE TO SOLOMON

**12.** *as for this house*. The erection of the Temple was only an external sign of the allegiance of Solomon and Israel to the LORD. To win Divine favour, they must submit their life and conduct to the guidance of the Divine Law.

## EXODUS XXVII, 20

**27** 20. And thou shalt command the children of Israel, that they bring unto thee pure olive oil beaten for the light, to cause a lamp to burn continually. 21. In the tent of meeting, without the veil which is before the testimony, Aaron and his sons shall set it in order, to burn from evening to morning before the LORD; it shall be a statute for ever throughout their generations on the behalf of the children of Israel.

**28** CHAPTER XXVIII

1. And bring thou near unto thee Aaron thy brother, and his sons with him, from among the children of Israel, that they may minister unto Me in the priest's office, even Aaron, Nadab and Abihu, Eleazar and Ithamar, Aaron's sons. 2. And thou shalt make holy garments for Aaron thy brother, for splendour and for beauty. 3. And thou

שמות תצוה כז כח

כז

20 ס ס ס כ

כ וְאַתָּה תְּצַוֶּה ׀ אֶת־בְּנֵי יִשְׂרָאֵל וְיִקְחוּ אֵלֶיךָ שֶׁמֶן זַיִת זָךְ

21 כָּתִית לַמָּאוֹר לְהַעֲלֹת נֵר תָּמִיד: בְּאֹהֶל מוֹעֵד מִחוּץ לַפָּרֹכֶת אֲשֶׁר עַל־הָעֵדֻת יַעֲרֹךְ אֹתוֹ אַהֲרֹן וּבָנָיו מֵעֶרֶב עַד־בֹּקֶר לִפְנֵי יְהֹוָה חֻקַּת עוֹלָם לְדֹרֹתָם מֵאֵת בְּנֵי יִשְׂרָאֵל: ס

CAP. XXVIII. כח

כח

א וְאַתָּה הַקְרֵב אֵלֶיךָ אֶת־אַהֲרֹן אָחִיךָ וְאֶת־בָּנָיו אִתּוֹ מִתּוֹךְ בְּנֵי יִשְׂרָאֵל לְכַהֲנוֹ־לִי אַהֲרֹן נָדָב וַאֲבִיהוּא אֶלְעָזָר וְאִיתָמָר

2 בְּנֵי אַהֲרֹן: וְעָשִׂיתָ בִגְדֵי־קֹדֶשׁ לְאַהֲרֹן אָחִיךָ לְכָבוֹד

3 וּלְתִפְאָרֶת: וְאַתָּה תְּדַבֵּר אֶל־כָּל־חַכְמֵי־לֵב אֲשֶׁר מִלֵּאתִיו

---

# VIII. TETZAVEH

### (CHAPTERS XXVII, 20–XXX, 10)

**20, 21. THE OIL FOR THE LAMP**

After the description of the Sanctuary, Scripture proceeds to deal with the requirements of those who were to minister therein.

**20.** *for the light.* That was to be kept burning in the Sanctuary every night.

*pure olive oil.* Used for all sacred purposes.

*beaten.* The olives were gently pounded in a mortar, and the first drops of oil obtained were of the purest quality.

*continually.* i.e. regularly, as a standing practice. Because no sunlight fell into the Sanctuary, there had always to be one light (cf. I Sam. III, 3). The lamp of the Sanctuary is represented in the Synagogue by the perpetual lamp burning before the Ark (the *Ner Tamid*). The Rabbis interpret the lamp as a symbol of Israel, whose mission it was to become 'a light of the nations' (Isa. XLII, 6).

**21.** *tent of meeting.* i.e. the Holy Place, not the Holy of Holies; see xxv, 22.

*without the veil.* Outside the veil.

*the testimony.* See xxv, 21.

*from evening to morning.* Cf. xxx, 7, where it is stated that it was Aaron's duty in the morning to remove the burnt wick, replace it with a fresh one and fill the lamp with oil. He was to light it in the evening.

**CHAPTER XXVIII.** THE VESTMENTS OF THE PRIESTS

After the instructions as to the building of the Sanctuary, Moses receives directions concerning the men who are to serve as priests. That sacred office was reserved for Aaron, his sons and their descendants. This chapter describes the garments which were to be worn by the priests when ministering in the Sanctuary. These garments distinguished the priest from the lay Israelite, and reminded him that even more than the layman he must make the idea of holiness the constant guide of his life. These vestments also added to the solemnity and awe of the service of the Sanctuary.

**1.** *that he may minister.* The verb is in the singular, referring to the principal person in the group, Aaron.

**2.** *holy garments.* i.e. garments to be worn by the priests when discharging their holy functions.

*for splendour and for beauty.* Or, 'for splendour and distinction.'

**3.** *wise-hearted.* In Bible psychology, the heart is the seat of intellect, not of feeling.

*whom I have filled.* Not that God had endowed certain men with extraordinary skill for this special occasion. Whatever gifts a man possesses are an endowment from God. Those, therefore, who are exceptionally skilful in craftsmanship are to offer their artistic skill for the making of the vestments.

*sanctify him.* The investiture in the priestly garments was part of the ceremony of induction into the priest's office, described in the next chapter.

## EXODUS XXVIII, 4

shalt speak unto all that are wise-hearted, whom I have filled with the spirit of wisdom, that they make Aaron's garments to sanctify him, that he may minister unto Me in the priest's office. 4. And these are the garments which they shall make: a breastplate, and an ephod, and a robe, and a tunic of chequer work, a mitre, and a girdle; and they shall make holy garments for Aaron thy brother, and his sons, that he may minister unto Me in the priest's office. 5. And they shall take the gold, and the blue, and the purple, and the scarlet, and the fine linen. ¶ 6. And they shall make the ephod of gold, of blue, and purple, scarlet, and fine twined linen, the work of the skilful workman. 7. It shall have two shoulder-pieces joined to the two ends thereof, that it may be joined together. 8. And the skilfully woven band, which is upon it, wherewith to gird it on, shall be like the work thereof and of the same piece: of gold, of blue, and purple, and scarlet, and fine twined linen. 9. And thou shalt take two onyx stones, and grave on them the names of the children of Israel: 10. six of their names on the one stone, and the names of the six that remain on the other stone, according to their birth. 11. With the work of an engraver in stone, like the engravings of a signet, shalt thou engrave the two stones, according to the names of the children of Israel; thou shalt make them to be inclosed in settings of gold. 12 And thou shalt put the two stones upon the shoulder-pieces of the ephod, to be stones of memorial for the children of Israel; and Aaron shall bear their names before the

שמות תצוה כח

רוּחַ חָכְמָה וְעָשׂוּ אֶת־בִּגְדֵי אַהֲרֹן לְקַדְּשׁוֹ לְכַהֲנוֹ־לִי:
4 וְאֵלֶּה הַבְּגָדִים אֲשֶׁר יַעֲשׂוּ חֹשֶׁן וְאֵפוֹד וּמְעִיל וּכְתֹנֶת
תַּשְׁבֵּץ מִצְנֶפֶת וְאַבְנֵט וְעָשׂוּ בִגְדֵי־קֹדֶשׁ לְאַהֲרֹן אָחִיךָ
5 וּלְבָנָיו לְכַהֲנוֹ־לִי: וְהֵם יִקְחוּ אֶת־הַזָּהָב וְאֶת־הַתְּכֵלֶת
וְאֶת־הָאַרְגָּמָן וְאֶת־תּוֹלַעַת הַשָּׁנִי וְאֶת־הַשֵּׁשׁ: פ
6 וְעָשׂוּ אֶת־הָאֵפֹד זָהָב תְּכֵלֶת וְאַרְגָּמָן תּוֹלַעַת שָׁנִי וְשֵׁשׁ
7 מָשְׁזָר מַעֲשֵׂה חֹשֵׁב: שְׁתֵּי כְתֵפֹת חֹבְרֹת יִהְיֶה־לּוֹ אֶל־
8 שְׁנֵי קְצוֹתָיו וְחֻבָּר: וְחֵשֶׁב אֲפֻדָּתוֹ אֲשֶׁר עָלָיו כְּמַעֲשֵׂהוּ
מִמֶּנּוּ יִהְיֶה זָהָב תְּכֵלֶת וְאַרְגָּמָן וְתוֹלַעַת שָׁנִי וְשֵׁשׁ
9 מָשְׁזָר: וְלָקַחְתָּ אֶת־שְׁתֵּי אַבְנֵי־שֹׁהַם וּפִתַּחְתָּ עֲלֵיהֶם
10 שְׁמוֹת בְּנֵי יִשְׂרָאֵל: שִׁשָּׁה מִשְּׁמֹתָם עַל הָאֶבֶן הָאֶחָת
וְאֶת־שְׁמוֹת הַשִּׁשָּׁה הַנּוֹתָרִים עַל־הָאֶבֶן הַשֵּׁנִית כְּתוֹלְדֹתָם:
11 מַעֲשֵׂה חָרַשׁ אֶבֶן פִּתּוּחֵי חֹתָם תְּפַתַּח אֶת־שְׁתֵּי הָאֲבָנִים
עַל־שְׁמֹת בְּנֵי יִשְׂרָאֵל מֻסַבֹּת מִשְׁבְּצוֹת זָהָב תַּעֲשֶׂה
12 אֹתָם: וְשַׂמְתָּ אֶת־שְׁתֵּי הָאֲבָנִים עַל כִּתְפֹת הָאֵפֹד אַבְנֵי
זִכָּרֹן לִבְנֵי יִשְׂרָאֵל וְנָשָׂא אַהֲרֹן אֶת־שְׁמוֹתָם לִפְנֵי יְהוָה

---

**4.** *breastplate*. This and the other garments of the High Priest, described later, were additional to the garments of the priests.

**5.** *they shall take*. i.e. the workmen shall receive the materials (xxv, 3) from those who give them.

### 6–12. THE EPHOD

**6.** *ephod*. A short close-fitting coat, worn round the body under the arms, and having straps over the shoulders to keep it in place.

*skilful workman*. See on xxvi, 1. The fabric of the ephod was the same as the curtains and veil of the Tabernacle, indicating the intimate connection between the High Priest and the Sanctuary. But in addition, there were gold threads woven into the material, probably as a symbol of royal power, because of the High Priest's position as the spiritual head of the community.

**8.** *band*. Around the waist, at the bottom of the ephod, was an artistically woven band, part of the ephod.

**9.** *onyx stones*. 'To fasten it, after the manner of buttons' (Josephus).

*children of Israel*. Better, '*sons of Israel*'; i.e. the twelve sons of Jacob, who gave their names to the tribes. The name of Joseph was used here instead of Manasseh and Ephraim.

**11.** *engraver*. Tut-an-khamen's Tomb, and the discoveries in regard to the goldsmith's art and precious jewellery at Ur, have shown that the art of engraving, such as here described, was common in the ancient world.

**12.** *stones of memorial*. To remind the children of Israel of their unity of descent, and unity of service to the God of Holiness.

*Aaron shall bear*. The names denoted in concrete form that the High Priest was the messenger and representative of the entire community.

EXODUS XXVIII, 13      שמות תצוה כח

LORD upon his two shoulders for a memorial.*¹¹· ¶ 13. And thou shalt make settings of gold; 14. and two chains of pure gold; of plaited thread shalt thou make them, of wreathen work; and thou shalt put the wreathen chains on the settings. ¶ 15. And thou shalt make a breastplate of judgment, the work of the skilful workman; like the work of the ephod thou shalt make it: of gold, of blue, and purple, and scarlet and fine twined linen, shalt thou make it. 16. Four-square it shall be and double: a span shall be the length thereof, and a span the breadth thereof. 17. And thou shalt set in it settings of stones, four rows of stones: a row of carnelian, topaz, and smaragd shall be the first row; 18. and the second row a carbuncle, a sapphire, and an emerald; 19. and the third row a jacinth, an agate, and an amethyst; 20. and the fourth row a beryl, and an onyx, and a jasper; they shall be inclosed in gold in their settings. 21. And the stones shall be according to the names of the children of Israel, twelve, according to their names; like the engravings of a signet, every one according to his name, they shall be for the twelve tribes. 22. And thou shalt make upon the breastplate plaited chains of wreathen work of pure gold. 23. And thou shalt make upon the breastplate two rings of gold, and shalt put the two rings on the two ends of the breastplate. 24. And thou shalt put the two wreathen chains of gold on the two rings at the ends of the breastplate. 25. And the other two ends of the two wreathen chains thou shalt put on the two settings, and put them on the shoulder-pieces of the

שני
13 עַל־שְׁתֵּי כְתֵפָיו לְזִכָּרֹן: ס וְעָשִׂיתָ מִשְׁבְּצֹת זָהָב:
14 וּשְׁתֵּי שַׁרְשְׁרֹת זָהָב טָהוֹר מִגְבָּלֹת תַּעֲשֶׂה אֹתָם מַעֲשֵׂה עֲבֹת וְנָתַתָּה אֶת־שַׁרְשְׁרֹת הָעֲבֹתֹת עַל־הַמִּשְׁבְּצֹת: ס
15 וְעָשִׂיתָ חֹשֶׁן מִשְׁפָּט מַעֲשֵׂה חֹשֵׁב כְּמַעֲשֵׂה אֵפֹד תַּעֲשֶׂנּוּ זָהָב תְּכֵלֶת וְאַרְגָּמָן וְתוֹלַעַת שָׁנִי וְשֵׁשׁ מָשְׁזָר תַּעֲשֶׂה
16 אֹתוֹ: רָבוּעַ יִהְיֶה כָּפוּל זֶרֶת אָרְכּוֹ וְזֶרֶת רָחְבּוֹ: וּמִלֵּאתָ
17 בוֹ מִלֻּאַת אֶבֶן אַרְבָּעָה טוּרִים אָבֶן טוּר אֹדֶם פִּטְדָה
18 וּבָרֶקֶת הַטּוּר הָאֶחָד: וְהַטּוּר הַשֵּׁנִי נֹפֶךְ סַפִּיר וְיָהֲלֹם:
19 וְהַטּוּר הַשְּׁלִישִׁי לֶשֶׁם שְׁבוֹ וְאַחְלָמָה: וְהַטּוּר הָרְבִיעִי
20 תַּרְשִׁישׁ וְשֹׁהַם וְיָשְׁפֵה מְשֻׁבָּצִים זָהָב יִהְיוּ בְּמִלּוּאֹתָם:
21 וְהָאֲבָנִים תִּהְיֶיןָ עַל־שְׁמֹת בְּנֵי־יִשְׂרָאֵל שְׁתֵּים עֶשְׂרֵה עַל־שְׁמֹתָם פִּתּוּחֵי חוֹתָם אִישׁ עַל־שְׁמוֹ תִּהְיֶיןָ לִשְׁנֵי עָשָׂר
22 שָׁבֶט: וְעָשִׂיתָ עַל־הַחֹשֶׁן שַׁרְשֹׁת גַּבְלֻת מַעֲשֵׂה עֲבֹת זָהָב
23 טָהוֹר: וְעָשִׂיתָ עַל־הַחֹשֶׁן שְׁתֵּי טַבְּעוֹת זָהָב וְנָתַתָּ אֶת־
24 שְׁתֵּי הַטַּבָּעוֹת עַל־שְׁנֵי קְצוֹת הַחֹשֶׁן: וְנָתַתָּה אֶת־שְׁתֵּי
כה עֲבֹתֹת הַזָּהָב עַל־שְׁתֵּי הַטַּבָּעֹת אֶל־קְצוֹת הַחֹשֶׁן: וְאֵת

### 13-30. THE BREASTPLATE

**14.** *pure gold.* The same metal as used in the Holy of Holies.

**15.** *breastplate.* The breastplate was double, open on all sides except the bottom. It is called 'the breastplate of judgment', because it was to contain the Urim and the Thummim, by means of which the High Priest was to seek the judgment of God on difficult questions affecting the welfare of the community (v. 30).

*like the work of the ephod.* i.e. of the same material as the ephod.

**16.** *double.* The piece of cloth was a cubit in length, and a half cubit in breadth; doubled over, so as to form a bag or pouch.

**17.** *settings of stones.* The distinguishing feature of the breastplate was that it was set with twelve precious stones, each engraved with the name of one of the tribes of Israel; the stones being arranged in gold settings in four rows, three stones in a row.

*carnelian.* Or, 'ruby.'

*topaz.* Its colour is yellowish green.

*smaragd.* Some authorities suggest the rock-crystal, a colourless stone used in ancient Egypt for engravings.

**18.** *carbuncle.* Or, 'red garnet.'

**19.** *jacinth.* A clear yellow stone.
*agate.* A red, opaque stone.

**20.** *beryl.* Or, 'chalcedony.' Its colour is green to yellow.
*jasper.* The colour is bright green.

**22.** The chains referred to in this verse are the same as those mentioned in *v.* 14.

**23.** *and shalt put.* i.e. and shall fasten.

**25.** *two ends.* i.e. the corners at the top of the breastplate.

# EXODUS XXVIII, 26

ephod, in the forepart thereof. 26. And thou shalt make two rings of gold, and thou shalt put them upon the two ends of the breastplate, upon the edge thereof, which is toward the side of the ephod inward. 27. And thou shalt make two rings of gold, and shalt put them on the two shoulder-pieces of the ephod underneath, in the forepart thereof, close by the coupling thereof, above the skilfully woven band of the ephod. 28. And they shall bind the breastplate by the rings thereof unto the rings of the ephod with a thread of blue, that it may be upon the skilfully woven band of the ephod, and that the breastplate be not loosed from the ephod. 29. And Aaron shall bear the names of the children of Israel in the breastplate of judgment upon his heart, when he goeth in unto the holy place, for a memorial before the LORD continually. 30. And thou shalt put in the breastplate of judgment the Urim and the Thummim; and they shall be upon Aaron's heart, when he goeth in before the LORD; and Aaron shall bear the judgment of the children of Israel upon his heart before the LORD continually.*ⁱⁱⁱ· ¶ 31. And thou shalt make the robe of the ephod all of blue. 32. And it shall have a hole for the head in the midst thereof; it shall

שְׁתֵּי קְצוֹת שְׁתֵּי הָעֲבֹתֹת תִּתֵּן עַל־שְׁתֵּי הַמִּשְׁבְּצוֹת וְנָתַתָּה
עַל־כִּתְפוֹת הָאֵפֹד אֶל־מוּל פָּנָיו: וְעָשִׂיתָ שְׁתֵּי טַבְּעוֹת זָהָב 26
וְשַׂמְתָּ אֹתָם עַל־שְׁנֵי קְצוֹת הַחֹשֶׁן עַל־שְׂפָתוֹ אֲשֶׁר אֶל־
עֵבֶר הָאֵפֹד בָּיְתָה: וְעָשִׂיתָ שְׁתֵּי טַבְּעוֹת זָהָב וְנָתַתָּה 27
אֹתָם עַל־שְׁתֵּי כִתְפוֹת הָאֵפוֹד מִלְמַטָּה מִמּוּל פָּנָיו לְעֻמַּת
מַחְבַּרְתּוֹ מִמַּעַל לְחֵשֶׁב הָאֵפוֹד: וְיִרְכְּסוּ אֶת־הַחֹשֶׁן 28
מִטַּבְּעֹתָו אֶל־טַבְּעֹת הָאֵפוֹד בִּפְתִיל תְּכֵלֶת לִהְיוֹת עַל־
חֵשֶׁב הָאֵפוֹד וְלֹא־יִזַּח הַחֹשֶׁן מֵעַל הָאֵפוֹד: וְנָשָׂא אַהֲרֹן 29
אֶת־שְׁמוֹת בְּנֵי־יִשְׂרָאֵל בְּחֹשֶׁן הַמִּשְׁפָּט עַל־לִבּוֹ בְּבֹאוֹ אֶל־
הַקֹּדֶשׁ לְזִכָּרֹן לִפְנֵי־יְהוָֹה תָּמִיד: וְנָתַתָּ אֶל־חֹשֶׁן הַמִּשְׁפָּט ל
אֶת־הָאוּרִים וְאֶת־הַתֻּמִּים וְהָיוּ עַל־לֵב אַהֲרֹן בְּבֹאוֹ לִפְנֵי
יְהוָֹה וְנָשָׂא אַהֲרֹן אֶת־מִשְׁפַּט בְּנֵי־יִשְׂרָאֵל עַל־לִבּוֹ לִפְנֵי שלישי
יְהוָֹה תָּמִיד: ס    וְעָשִׂיתָ אֶת־מְעִיל הָאֵפוֹד כְּלִיל תְּכֵלֶת: 31

v. 28. מטבעתיו ק׳

**26–28.** Two rings were to be attached to the inner lower corners of the breastplate. Two other rings were to be placed on the lower part of the shoulder-straps. Threads of blue passing through the rings tied them together. By these means the breastplate was kept firmly in its place on the breast of the High Priest.

**29.** *for a memorial*. 'The stones on his heart are Aaron's silent prayer to God on behalf of his entire people' (B. Jacob).

**30.** *the Urim and the Thummim*. lit. 'the Lights and the Perfections'; which may mean, in accordance with Heb. idiom, 'perfect lights.' Were the Urim and the Thummim identical with the breastplate and the twelve brilliant stones, or were they distinct from it? At first view, the wording of this verse, 'thou shalt put in the breastplate of judgment the Urim and the Thummim,' seems to favour the latter alternative; and many moderns think, 'they were two sacred lots, used for the purpose of ascertaining the Divine Will on questions of national importance' (Driver). Rashi, likewise, supposes that it was some material upon which the Name of God was engraven, which the High Priest carried in the breastplate. Against this opinion it is urged that in chap. XXXIX, where the making of the breastplate is given in detail, nothing is said in regard to the fashioning of the Urim and the Thummim. Thus, it seems that 'the Urim and the Thummim' was the term whereby the twelve stones were denoted. The fact that the breastplate is called 'the breastplate of judgment' indicates that the breastplate itself, and not something distinct from it, was the medium of the Divine communications. In Lev. VIII, 8, the Urim and the Thummim alone are mentioned, not the precious stones—a strong proof of the identity of both.

Scripture records that in times of doubt and national crisis during the earlier period of Israel's history, the people consulted the Urim and the Thummim for information and guidance (Num. XXVII, 21; I Sam. XXVIII, 6); but what the procedure was is nowhere explained. No recourse to the Urim and the Thummim is mentioned after the days of David. They remain one of the most obscure subjects connected with the High Priesthood.

## 31–35. THE ROBE

**31.** *robe*. A long garment worn by men of high rank. Whether the 'robe' was always sleeveless is uncertain, but that of the High Priest was so. It is called 'robe of the ephod', because the ephod was worn over it.

*all of blue*. The garment was woven of one kind of thread only; the colour *blue* was significant; cf. the thread of blue on the 'fringes' (Num. XV, 38).

EXODUS XXVIII, 33     שמות תצוה כח

have a binding of woven work round about the hole of it, as it were the hole of a coat of mail, that it be not rent. 33. And upon the skirts of it thou shalt make pomegranates of blue, and of purple, and of scarlet, round about the skirts thereof; and bells of gold between them round about: 34. a golden bell and a pomegranate, a golden bell and a pomegranate, upon the skirts of the robe round about. 35. And it shall be upon Aaron to minister; and the sound thereof shall be heard when he goeth in unto the holy place before the LORD, and when he cometh out, that he die not. ¶ 36. And thou shalt make a plate of pure gold, and engrave upon it, like the engravings of a signet: HOLY TO THE LORD. 37. And thou shalt put it on a thread of blue, and it shall be upon the mitre; upon the forefront of the mitre it shall be. 38. And it shall be upon Aaron's forehead, and Aaron shall bear the iniquity committed in the holy things, which the children of Israel shall hallow, even in all their holy gifts; and it shall be always upon his forehead, that they may be accepted before the LORD. 39. And thou shalt weave the tunic in chequer work

**32.** *for the head.* The robe had an opening only on top. It had, therefore, to be drawn over the head; and to prevent the material from tearing, the edge was strengthened by means of additional weaving.

**33–35.** The hem of the robe was adorned with balls of richly coloured material, of pomegranate shape. Between each pair of pomegranates was a golden bell. The Talmud states that there were 72 ornaments around the hem. The High Priest was on no account to officiate without donning his garments. The bells attached to the robe indicated to the congregation in the Court when he was performing his duties. Kalisch explains: 'The whole people gave themselves up to prayer and repentance, whilst the High Priest stepped into the Holy of Holies to officiate in their name. It was therefore most appropriate that they should all know the moment when he entered the Holy of Holies.'

36–43. THE PLATE, MITRE AND OTHER PRIESTLY GARMENTS

**36.** *plate of gold.* According to Tradition, it was two fingers in depth, and extended right across the forehead.

HOLY TO THE LORD. lit. 'Holiness to the LORD.' This inscription not only marked the dedication of the High Priest to the service of God, but also crystallized the aim and purpose of that service. It proclaimed the spiritual ideal of which the Sanctuary was the concrete emblem.

**37.** *thread of blue.* A thread of blue, attached to the extremities of the gold plate, kept it in position upon the forehead of the High Priest; but between the skin and the plate was the linen of the mitre (see *v.* 39).

**38.** *Aaron shall bear.* The meaning is probably this: What is presented to God must be without blemish, and the mode of presentation must be in agreement with the prescribed rites. Should there, however, be any imperfection in the sacrifice, or any error in the manner of offering, the High Priest assumes the responsibility. He is the custodian of the Sanctuary; and, by virtue of his sacred office, exemplified by the goldplate on his forehead, he can secure Divine acceptance of the offerings brought to the altar of God.

*always upon his forehead.* Whenever he officiates as High Priest.

**39.** *tunic.* 'This garment reached down to the feet, and was close to the body, and had sleeves that were tied fast to the arms' (Josephus).

*fine linen.* Or, 'silk'; the colour was no doubt white, the colour of purity and holiness.

*mitre.* This is a doubtful translation. The root signifies, 'to wind round'; and what is intended is possibly a kind of turban.

*girdle.* A sash.

# EXODUS XXVIII, 40

of fine linen, and thou shalt make a mitre of fine linen, and thou shalt make a girdle, the work of the weaver in colours. 40. And for Aaron's sons thou shalt make tunics, and thou shalt make for them girdles, and head-tires shalt thou make for them, for splendour and for beauty. 41. And thou shalt put them upon Aaron thy brother, and upon his sons with him; and shalt anoint them, and consecrate them, and sanctify them, that they may minister unto Me in the priest's office. 42. And thou shalt make them linen breeches to cover the flesh of their nakedness; from the loins even unto the thighs they shall reach. 43. And they shall be upon Aaron, and upon his sons, when they go in unto the tent of meeting, or when they come near unto the altar to minister in the holy place; that they bear not iniquity, and die; it shall be a statute for ever unto him and unto his seed after him.*<sup>iv.</sup>

## 29  CHAPTER XXIX

1. And this is the thing that thou shalt do unto them to hallow them, to minister unto Me in the priest's office: take one young bullock and two rams without blemish, 2. and unleavened bread, and cakes unleavened mingled with oil, and wafers unleavened spread with oil; of fine wheaten flour shalt thou make them. 3. And thou shalt put them into one basket, and bring them in the basket, with the bullock and the two rams. 4. And Aaron and his sons thou shalt bring unto the door of the tent of meeting, and shalt wash them with water. 5. And thou shalt take the garments, and

---

**40.** *Aaron's sons.* The ordinary priests were to have a coat and girdle, similar to the High Priest's. Instead of a mitre, they were to wear a cap on their heads.

**41.** *put them upon Aaron.* This ceremony of induction will be described in the next chapter.
*consecrate them.* lit. 'fill their hand' (with the first sacrifices)—the technical term for installing a priest in his office.

**42.** *breeches.* These reached to the knees. There is no mention of covering for the feet.

**43.** *altar.* Of burnt-offerings.
*holy place.* Here this phrase denotes the Sanctuary in general, including the Court.
*and die.* God ruthlessly punishes any desecration of the Tabernacle by its ministers; cf. the fate of Nadab and Abihu, Lev. x, 1 f.

### CHAPTER XXIX. CONSECRATION OF THE PRIESTHOOD

The fulfilment of the regulations here laid down is described more fully in Lev. VIII, with which this chapter should be compared.

**1.** *bullock.* Of the sin-offering (Lev. VIII, 2). The priests must themselves have undergone atonement for their transgressions before they could perform the ceremonies that would help others to gain purification from sin.
*two rams.* One served as a burnt-offering (v. 18), and the other was the 'ram of consecration' (v. 22).

**2.** *unleavened bread.* This, together with the cakes and wafers, constituted a 'meal offering' (see on Lev. II, 1).

**3.** *bring them.* To the court of the Sanctuary.

**4.** *shalt wash them.* See that they undergo ablution of the entire body. The moral symbolism of the act of washing, as the first stage in the ceremony of induction, is obvious. 'Clean hands and a pure heart,' according to the Psalmist (XXIV, 4), are an essential qualification in those who would draw near to God.

# EXODUS XXIX, 6

שמות תצוה כט

אֶת־הַכֻּתֹּנֶת וְאֵת מְעִיל הָאֵפֹד וְאֶת־הָאֵפֹד וְאֶת־הַחֹשֶׁן
וְאָפַדְתָּ לוֹ בְּחֵשֶׁב הָאֵפֹד: וְשַׂמְתָּ הַמִּצְנֶפֶת עַל־רֹאשׁוֹ וְנָתַתָּ 6
אֶת־נֵזֶר הַקֹּדֶשׁ עַל־הַמִּצְנָפֶת: וְלָקַחְתָּ אֶת־שֶׁמֶן הַמִּשְׁחָה 7
וְיָצַקְתָּ עַל־רֹאשׁוֹ וּמָשַׁחְתָּ אֹתוֹ: וְאֶת־בָּנָיו תַּקְרִיב 8
וְהִלְבַּשְׁתָּם כֻּתֳּנֹת: וְחָגַרְתָּ אֹתָם אַבְנֵט אַהֲרֹן וּבָנָיו 9
וְחָבַשְׁתָּ לָהֶם מִגְבָּעֹת וְהָיְתָה לָהֶם כְּהֻנָּה לְחֻקַּת עוֹלָם
וּמִלֵּאתָ יַד־אַהֲרֹן וְיַד־בָּנָיו: וְהִקְרַבְתָּ אֶת־הַפָּר לִפְנֵי אֹהֶל ׳
מוֹעֵד וְסָמַךְ אַהֲרֹן וּבָנָיו אֶת־יְדֵיהֶם עַל־רֹאשׁ הַפָּר:
וְשָׁחַטְתָּ אֶת־הַפָּר לִפְנֵי יְהוָה פֶּתַח אֹהֶל מוֹעֵד: וְלָקַחְתָּ 11
12
מִדַּם הַפָּר וְנָתַתָּה עַל־קַרְנֹת הַמִּזְבֵּחַ בְּאֶצְבָּעֶךָ וְאֶת־כָּל־
הַדָּם תִּשְׁפֹּךְ אֶל־יְסוֹד הַמִּזְבֵּחַ: וְלָקַחְתָּ אֶת־כָּל־הַחֵלֶב 13
הַמְכַסֶּה אֶת־הַקֶּרֶב וְאֵת הַיֹּתֶרֶת עַל־הַכָּבֵד וְאֵת שְׁתֵּי
הַכְּלָיֹת וְאֶת־הַחֵלֶב אֲשֶׁר עֲלֵיהֶן וְהִקְטַרְתָּ הַמִּזְבֵּחָה: וְאֶת־ 14
בְּשַׂר הַפָּר וְאֶת־עֹרוֹ וְאֶת־פִּרְשׁוֹ תִּשְׂרֹף בָּאֵשׁ מִחוּץ לַמַּחֲנֶה
חַטָּאת הוּא: וְאֶת־הָאַיִל הָאֶחָד תִּקָּח וְסָמְכוּ אַהֲרֹן וּבָנָיו טו

---

put upon Aaron the tunic, and the robe of the ephod, and the ephod, and the breastplate, and gird him with the skilfully woven band of the ephod. 6. And thou shalt set the mitre upon his head, and put the holy crown upon the mitre. 7. Then shalt thou take the anointing oil, and pour it upon his head, and anoint him. 8. And thou shalt bring his sons, and put tunics upon them. 9. And thou shalt gird them with girdles, Aaron and his sons, and bind head-tires on them; and they shall have the priesthood by a perpetual statute; and thou shalt consecrate Aaron and his sons. 10. And thou shalt bring the bullock before the tent of meeting; and Aaron and his sons shall lay their hands upon the head of the bullock. 11. And thou shalt kill the bullock before the LORD, at the door of the tent of meeting. 12. And thou shalt take of the blood of the bullock, and put it upon the horns of the altar with thy finger; and thou shalt pour out all the remaining blood at the base of the altar. 13. And thou shalt take all the fat that covereth the inwards, and the lobe above the liver, and the two kidneys, and the fat that is upon them, and make them smoke upon the altar. 14. But the flesh of the bullock, and its skin, and its dung, shalt thou burn with fire without the camp; it is a sin-offering. 15. Thou shalt also take the one ram; and Aaron and his sons shall lay their hands upon the head of

---

**5.** *put upon Aaron the tunic.* The clothing of Aaron, and his sons, invested them with the visible emblems of their holiness and their functions, and marked them as distinct from the rest of the nation. 'When the priests are clothed in their garments,' says the Talmud, 'their priesthood is upon them; when they are not clothed in their garments, their priesthood is not upon them.' This Rabbinic dictum teaches the important truth that the priests did not differ from the rest of Israel. Only when they functioned in the Sanctuary were they, for the time being, distinct from the remainder of the community.

**6.** *mitre.* Or, 'diadem'; the gold plate (XXVIII, 36).

**7.** *anointing oil.* Its composition is described in XXX, 22 f. The soothing effect of oil on the skin scorched by the burning sun in the Orient caused it to be regarded as a symbol of comfort and happiness. Hence its place in the ceremony of the anointing of kings and priests. It became synonymous with the imparting of the Divine blessing.

*pour it upon his head.* Only in the case of the High Priest. For an ordinary priest the oil was not poured, but smeared with the finger upon the head (see on Lev. VIII, 12).

**9.** *a perpetual statute.* The priesthood was for all time to be restricted to the house of Aaron.

**10–14.** The sin-offering of Aaron and his sons.

**10.** *lay their hands.* Each shall lay his hand to designate the animal as the representative of the person who brought the sacrifice; see on Lev. I, 4. Aaron and his sons no doubt make a confession of sins while their hands are upon the head of the animal.

**11.** *thou shalt kill.* The slaying of the sacrifice need not of necessity be done by a priest (see on Lev. I, 5).

**12.** The ritual which is now described is that which normally accompanied the sacrifice of a sin-offering (see Lev. IV, 4).

**13.** *make them smoke.* Heb. *hiktir*, the technical term for burning a sacrifice of incense.

**15.** *the one ram.* After the sin-offering, which brought purification from sin, there was the burnt-offering, which symbolized communion with God. The ritual of the burnt-offering is detailed in Lev. I and VIII, and will be explained in the notes on those chapters.

EXODUS XXIX, 16

the ram. 16. And thou shalt slay the ram, and thou shalt take its blood, and dash it round about against the altar. 17. And thou shalt cut the ram into its pieces, and wash its inwards, and its legs, and put them with its pieces, and with its head. 18. And thou shalt make the whole ram smoke upon the altar; it is a burnt-offering unto the Lord; it is a sweet savour, an offering made by fire unto the Lord.* 19. And thou shalt take the other ram; and Aaron and his sons shall lay their hands upon the head of the ram. 20. Then shalt thou kill the ram, and take of its blood, and put it upon the tip of the right ear of Aaron, and upon the tip of the right ear of his sons, and upon the thumb of their right hand, and upon the great toe of their right foot, and dash the blood against the altar round about. 21. And thou shalt take of the blood that is upon the altar, and of the anointing oil, and sprinkle it upon Aaron, and upon his garments, and upon his sons, and upon the garments of his sons with him; and he and his garments shall be hallowed, and his sons and his sons' garments with him. 22. Also thou shalt take of the ram the fat, and the fat tail, and the fat that covereth the inwards, and the lobe of the liver, and the two kidneys, and the fat that is upon them, and the right thigh; for it is a ram of consecration; 23. and one loaf of bread, and one cake of oiled bread, and one wafer, out of the basket of unleavened bread that is before the Lord. 24. And thou shalt put the whole upon the hands of Aaron, and upon the hands of his sons; and shalt wave them for a wave-offering before the Lord. 25. And thou shalt take them from their hands, and make them smoke on the altar upon the burnt-offering, for a sweet savour before the Lord; it is an offering made by fire unto the Lord. 26. And thou shalt take the breast of Aaron's ram of consecration, and wave it for a wave-offering before the Lord; and it shall be thy

**18.** *a sweet savour.* *i.e.* a savour agreeable to God. 'The burning of the offering is called "a sweet savour unto the Lord"; and so it undoubtedly is, since it serves to remove sinful thoughts from our hearts. The *effect of the offering upon the man* who sacrificed it, is pleasant upon the Lord' (Maimonides).

**19.** *the other ram.* For the consecration sacrifice. All that has preceded is only preparatory to the rites of induction.

**20.** *ear . . . thumb . . . toe.* The ear was touched with the blood, that it might be consecrated to hear the word of God; the hand, to perform the duties connected with the priesthood; and the foot, to walk in the path of righteousness. In a 'kingdom of priests', the consecration of ear, hand and foot should be extended to every member of that kingdom.

**21.** *sprinkle.* The double sprinkling of blood and soil typified the two main functions of the priesthood: to diffuse the light and joy of godliness, and impress upon the people the truth that atonement can be found for human wrong-doing.

**22–30.** Symbolized investiture of the priests with the authority to offer sacrifice. Typical offerings are to be placed upon their hands and waved before the altar, and finally burnt.

# EXODUS XXIX, 27

portion. 27. And thou shalt sanctify the breast of the wave-offering, and the thigh of the heave-offering, which is waved, and which is heaved up, of the ram of consecration, even of that which is Aaron's, and of that which is his sons'. 28. And it shall be for Aaron and his sons as a due for ever from the children of Israel; for it is a heave-offering; and it shall be a heave-offering from the children of Israel of their sacrifices of peace-offerings, even their heave-offering unto the LORD. 29. And the holy garments of Aaron shall be for his sons after him, to be anointed in them, and to be consecrated in them. 30. Seven days shall the son that is priest in his stead put them on, even he who cometh into the tent of meeting to minister in the holy place. 31. And thou shalt take the ram of consecration, and seethe its flesh in a holy place. 32. And Aaron and his sons shall eat the flesh of the ram, and the bread that is in the basket, at the door of the tent of meeting. 33. And they shall eat those things wherewith atonement was made, to consecrate and to sanctify them; but a stranger shall not eat thereof, because they are holy. 34. And if aught of the flesh of the consecration, or of the bread, remain unto the morning, then thou shalt burn the remainder with fire: it shall not be eaten, because it is holy. 35. And thus shalt thou do unto Aaron, and to his sons, according to all that I have commanded thee; seven days shalt thou consecrate them. 36. And every day shalt thou offer the bullock of sin-offering, beside the other offerings of

**24. wave them.** Turn the offering to all the four parts of heaven and earth, as a symbol that it was offered to the God of heaven and earth.

**26. the breast.** Was allowed to be retained by the officiating priests for food (Lev. VII, 34); hence it is allocated to Moses, who on this occasion filled the priest's office.

**27. sanctify.** Consecrate; *i.e.* set apart as the due of Aaron and his sons; see Lev. VII, 34 f.
*heave-offering.* Or, 'contribution,' by the worshipper to the priest.

**30. seven days.** See on *v.* 35 below.
*even he who cometh. i.e.* when he first cometh.

**31–34.** A continuation of *v.* 27, describing the sacrificial meal of Aaron and his sons in connection with their installation.

**32. shall eat.** A characteristic feature of the peace-offering was that it was a symbolic meal, in which, so to speak, God and the Israelite shared (see on XXIV, 11).

**33. atonement.** *i.e.* at-one-ment, setting at one, reconciliation.

*a stranger.* A non-priest.

**34. remain.** Cf. XII, 10. This law applied to all peace-offerings and sin-offerings.
*it is holy.* Sacred to God.

**35. seven days.** The rites of consecration were to be repeated daily for seven days.

**36. do the purification of the altar.** On the Day of Atonement, the High Priest purified the Sanctuary and its contents of any defilement which might have been contracted during the year (Lev. XVI, 19). Consequently, before the altar was used for the public offerings, a ceremony of purification was performed.

**37. whatsoever toucheth.** Or, 'whosoever toucheth'; anyone approaching the altar must be pure (Ibn Ezra, Rashbam). Most modern commentators explain the words to mean, Whatsoever touched the altar, became thereby 'holy'; *i.e.* the property of the Sanctuary, and had to be sacrificed.

EXODUS XXIX, 37

atonement; and thou shalt do the purification upon the altar when thou makest atonement for it; and thou shalt anoint it, to sanctify it. 37. Seven days thou shalt make atonement for the altar, and sanctify it; thus shall the altar be most holy; whatsoever toucheth the altar shall be holy.\* vi. ¶ 38. Now this is that which thou shalt offer upon the altar: two lambs of the first year day by day continually. 39. The one lamb thou shalt offer in the morning; and the other lamb thou shalt offer at dusk. 40. And with the one lamb a tenth part of an ephah of fine flour mingled with the fourth part of a hin of beaten oil; and the fourth part of a hin of wine for a drink-offering. 41. And the other lamb thou shalt offer at dusk, and shalt do thereto according to the meal-offering of the morning, and according to the drink-offering thereof, for a sweet savour, an offering made by fire unto the Lord. 42. It shall be a continual burnt-offering throughout your generations at the door of the tent of meeting before the Lord. where I will meet with you, to speak there unto thee. 43. And there I will meet with the children of Israel; and [the Tent] shall be sanctified by My glory. 44. And I will sanctify the tent of meeting, and the altar; Aaron also and his sons will I sanctify, to minister to Me in the priest's office. 45. And I will dwell among the children of Israel, and will be their God. 46. And they shall know that I am the Lord their God, that brought them forth out of the land of Egypt, that I may dwell among them. I am the Lord their God.\* vii.

## 30    Chapter XXX

1. And thou shalt make an altar to burn incense upon; of acacia-wood shalt thou make it. 2. A cubit shall be the length thereof, and a cubit the breadth thereof; four-square shall it be; and two cubits shall

---

38–42. The Daily Sacrifices

A summary of the daily sacrifices to be offered for the community as a whole, and the chief duty of the priests just consecrated; cf. Num. xxviii, 3–8.

**40.** *fine flour.* With the burnt-offering were to be brought a meal-offering and drink-offering.

**42.** *I will meet with you.* See xxv, 22.

43–46. The sacred purpose of the Sanctuary.

**43.** *with the children of Israel.* The Sanctuary is not the exclusive possession of the priests, nor will God manifest Himself there only to the High Priest.

*by My glory.* i.e. the Manifestation of God in the cloud; see xl, 34 f.

**44.** *I will sanctify.* God is the only source of holiness, and He alone can sanctify.

**45.** *dwell among.* Cf. xxv, 8.
*will be their God.* See vi, 7.

**46.** *and they shall know.* That the same God who rescued them from Egypt selected them as His people, and consecrated them to His service.

Chapter XXX, 1–10. The Altar of Incense

**1.** *altar.* No sacrifices were offered on it, and it was so called only because of its resemblance to the altar of burnt-offerings.

EXODUS XXX, 3

be the height thereof; the horns thereof shall be of one piece with it. 3. And thou shalt overlay it with pure gold, the top thereof, and the sides thereof round about, and the horns thereof; and thou shalt make unto it a crown of gold round about. 4. And two golden rings shalt thou make for it under the crown thereof, upon the two ribs thereof, upon the two sides of it shalt thou make them; and they shall be for places for staves wherewith to bear it. 5. And thou shalt make the staves of acacia-wood, and overlay them with gold. 6. And thou shalt put it before the veil that is by the ark of the testimony, before the ark-cover that is over the testimony, where I will meet with thee. 7. And Aaron shall burn thereon incense of sweet spices; every morning, when he dresseth the lamps, he shall burn it.*m. 8. And when Aaron lighteth the lamps at dusk, he shall burn it, a perpetual incense before the LORD throughout your generations. 9. Ye shall offer no strange incense thereon, nor burnt-offering, nor meal-offering; and ye shall pour no drink-offering thereon. 10. And Aaron shall make atonement upon the horns of it once in the year; with the blood of the sin-offering of atonement once in the year shall he make atonement for it throughout your generations; it is most holy unto the LORD.'

3. *pure gold.* Since the altar of incense was located in the Holy Place, and not in the Court with the altar of burnt-offering, the metal was gold; see p. 325.
*crown of gold.* See on xxv, 11.

4. *ribs.* Flanks. It has to have rings and acacia wood poles for transport, like the Ark, the table and the other altar.

6. *before the veil.* i.e. from the standpoint of one entering the Sanctuary. The altar of incense (or 'inner altar') was about half-way between the altar of burnt-offerings and the Holy of Holies.
*by the ark.* i.e. before the Ark.
*testimony.* See xxv, 16.
*where I will meet.* See xxv, 22.

7. *dresseth the lamps.* See XXVII, 21.
Incense had a symbolic significance, as is evident from Ps. CXLI, 2, 'Let my prayer be set forth as incense before Thee.' It became a metaphor for fervent and contrite Prayer. The Rabbis explained that the four letters of the Heb. word for incense, קטרת, stood for: קדושה, holiness; טהרה, purity; רחמים, pity; and תקוה, hope—a wonderful summary of the prerequisites of Prayer and of its spiritual results in the lives of men.

8. *at dusk.* Towards even.
*perpetual incense.* Better, *continual incense.*

9. *strange incense.* i.e. not prepared in the manner prescribed in *v.* 23, or offered in an irregular manner. This altar is to be reserved exclusively for incense.

10. *upon the horns.* By an application of the blood of the sin-offering (Lev. XVI, 18).
*once in the year.* On the Day of Atonement.
*for it.* To preserve it in its ideal holiness.

# HAFTORAH TETZAVEH

הפטרת תצוה

EZEKIEL XLIII, 10–27

CHAPTER XLIII

CAP. XLIII. מג

10. Thou, son of man, show the house to the house of Israel, that they may be ashamed of their iniquities; and let them measure accurately. 11. And if they be ashamed of all that they have done, make known unto them the form of the house, and the fashion thereof, and the goings out thereof, and the comings in thereof, and all the forms thereof, and all the ordinances thereof, and all the forms thereof, and all the laws thereof, and write it in their sight; that they may keep the whole form thereof, and all the ordinances thereof, and do them. ¶ 12. This is the law of the house: upon the top of the mountain the whole limit thereof round about shall be most holy. Behold, this is the law of the house. ¶ 13. And these are the measures of the altar by cubits—the cubit is a cubit and a handbreadth: the bottom shall be a cubit, and the breadth a cubit, and the border thereof by the edge thereof round about a span; and this shall be the base of the altar. 14. And from the bottom upon the ground to the lower settle shall be two cubits, and the breadth one cubit; and from the lesser settle to the

אַתָּה בֶן־אָדָם הַגֵּד אֶת־
בֵּית־יִשְׂרָאֵל אֶת־הַבַּיִת וְיִכָּלְמוּ מֵעֲוֺנוֹתֵיהֶם וּמָדְדוּ אֶת־
11 תָּכְנִית: וְאִם־נִכְלְמוּ מִכֹּל אֲשֶׁר־עָשׂוּ צוּרַת הַבַּיִת וּתְכוּנָתוֹ
וּמוֹצָאָיו וּמוֹבָאָיו וְכָל־צוּרֹתָו וְאֵת כָּל־חֻקֹּתָיו וְכָל־צוּרֹתָו
וְכָל־תּוֹרֹתָו הוֹדַע אוֹתָם וּכְתֹב לְעֵינֵיהֶם וְיִשְׁמְרוּ אֶת־כָּל־
12 צוּרָתוֹ וְאֶת־כָּל־חֻקֹּתָיו וְעָשׂוּ אוֹתָם: זֹאת תּוֹרַת הַבָּיִת
עַל־רֹאשׁ הָהָר כָּל־גְּבֻלוֹ סָבִיב ׀ סָבִיב קֹדֶשׁ קָדָשִׁים הִנֵּה־
13 זֹאת תּוֹרַת הַבָּיִת: וְאֵלֶּה מִדּוֹת הַמִּזְבֵּחַ בָּאַמּוֹת אַמָּה
אַמָּה וָטֹפַח וְחֵיק הָאַמָּה וְאַמָּה־רֹחַב וּגְבוּלָהּ אֶל־שְׂפָתָהּ
14 סָבִיב זֶרֶת הָאֶחָד וְזֶה גַּב הַמִּזְבֵּחַ: וּמֵחֵיק הָאָרֶץ עַד־
הָעֲזָרָה הַתַּחְתּוֹנָה שְׁתַּיִם אַמּוֹת וְרֹחַב אַמָּה אֶחָת

v. 11. צורתיו קרי ibid. תורתיו קרי

---

The Sedrah concludes with a description of the altar of incense. The Haftorah describes the altar of burnt-offering in the restored Temple of Ezekiel's vision, and its consecration. For Ezekiel's life and message, see pp. 178 and 244, and the introductory remarks to Haftorahs Parah and Hachodesh (see pp. 961 and 963).

The last portion of the Book of Ezekiel, chaps. XL–XLVIII, is a Vision of the New Jerusalem that is to arise when the Exile is over. In his vision the Prophet is in Palestine on Mount Zion, and he sees the Temple building arising and extending like a city. No detail is too small to be delineated with passionate care. Chapter XLIII describes God's return to the Temple and His directions as to the construction and dedication of the altar of burnt-offering. This new Temple was also to symbolize and embody in concrete form the teachings of Holiness and Purity preached by the Prophet in the preceding 39 chapters of his book. He therefore lays the greatest stress on correctness of Temple ritual and service. In this way alone can the aberrations and idolatries be prevented that so often disgraced the destroyed Temple. 'For Ezekiel the Law is the means of preserving religious freedom from contamination; without it, the prophetic ideas would hardly have survived. The real hope of the future for Ezekiel lies in perfect and willing obedience to the Law' (Lofthouse).

**10.** *son of man.* This expression is found almost exclusively in Ezekiel.

*show . . . ashamed of their iniquities.* The plan of the Holy House would awaken remorse for the past iniquities that had brought about the destruction of the Temple and the Exile, and implant a resolve to be worthy of a Restoration.

**11.** *if they be ashamed.* Then let them know the great future in store for them (Rashi).

*form of the house.* The picture of the Temple in its entirety.

*fashion thereof.* The courts and other parts of the Temple, showing their inter-connection.

*goings out . . . comings in.* The entrances and exits.

*and all the forms thereof.* The plans of the divisions of the Temple.

*the ordinances thereof.* The purpose of the different divisions.

**13–17. THE ALTAR OF BURNT-OFFERING**

The altar was to have a base, and upon it three square slabs of stone, one above the other, each decreasing in length, but increasing in thickness. The height of the altar, excluding the horns, would be 11 cubits (about 20 feet), and the top of the altar was to be reached by stairs on the east side (v. 17).

**13.** *the cubit is a cubit and an handbreadth.* i.e. one handbreadth longer than the common cubit (thus seven handbreadths in all).

**14.** *settle.* Or, 'ledge.'

## EZEKIEL XLIII, 15

greater settle shall be four cubits, and the breadth a cubit. 15. And the hearth shall be four cubits; and from the hearth and upward there shall be four horns. 16. And the hearth shall be twelve cubits long by twelve broad, square in the four sides thereof. 17. And the settle shall be fourteen cubits long by fourteen broad in the four sides thereof; and the border about it shall be half a cubit; and the bottom thereof shall be a cubit about; and the steps thereof shall look toward the east. ¶ 18. And He said unto me: 'Son of man, thus saith the Lord God: These are the ordinances of the altar in the day when they shall make it, to offer burnt-offerings thereon, and to dash blood against it. 19. Thou shalt give to the priests the Levites that are of the seed of Zadok, who are near unto Me, to minister unto Me, saith the Lord God, a young bullock for a sin-offering. 20. And thou shalt take of the blood thereof, and put it on the four horns of it, and on the four corners of the settle, and upon the border round about; thus shalt thou purify it and make atonement for it. 21. Thou shalt also take the bullock of the sin-offering, and it shall be burnt in the appointed place of the house, without the sanctuary. 22. And on the second day thou shalt offer a he-goat without blemish for a sin-offering; and they shall purify the altar, as they did purify it with the bullock. 23. When thou hast made an end of purifying it, thou shalt offer a young bullock without blemish, and a ram out of the flock without blemish. 24. And thou shalt present them before the Lord, and the priests shall cast salt upon them, and they shall offer them up for a burnt-offering unto the Lord. 25. Seven days shalt thou prepare every day a goat for a sin-offering; they shall also prepare a young bullock, and a ram out of the flock, without blemish. 26. Seven days shall they make atonement for the altar and cleanse it; so shall they consecrate it. 27. And when they have accomplished the days, it shall be that upon the eighth day, and forward, the priests shall make your burnt-offerings upon the altar, and your peace-offerings; and I will accept you, saith the Lord God.'

**15.** *the hearth.* The topmost stone, 4 cubits high, with a square surface of 12 square cubits.

*hearth.* Heb. *ariel* (see Isa. xxix, 1); lit. 'hearth of God.'

*four horns.* At the corners.

**17.** *the steps.* By which the priests ascend to the altar hearth.

**18–27.** The Consecration of the Altar

**18.** *and He said.* The angel who is God's spokesman to Ezekiel in his vision.

**19.** *the priests the Levites.* The priests, who were the tribe of Levi.

*Zadok.* A priest loyal to David during Absalom's rebellion. His descent is traced back to Aaron in I Chron. v. The high-priesthood remained in the hands of the descendants of Zadok till the times of the Maccabees.

351

# EXODUS XXX, 11

**30** 11. And the Lord spoke unto Moses, saying: 12. 'When thou takest the sum of the children of Israel, according to their number, then shall they give every man a ransom for his soul unto the Lord, when thou numberest them; that there be no plague among them, when thou numberest them. 13. This they shall give, every one that passeth among them that are numbered, half a shekel after the shekel of the sanctuary—the shekel is twenty gerahs—half a shekel for an offering to the Lord. 14. Every one that passeth among them that are numbered, from twenty years old and upward, shall give the offering of the Lord. 15. The rich shall not give more, and the poor shall not give less, than the

שמות כי תשא ל

פ פ פ כא 21

11 וַיְדַבֵּר יְהֹוָה אֶל־מֹשֶׁה לֵּאמֹר: כִּי תִשָּׂא אֶת־רֹאשׁ בְּנֵי־
12 יִשְׂרָאֵל לִפְקֻדֵיהֶם וְנָתְנוּ אִישׁ כֹּפֶר נַפְשׁוֹ לַיהֹוָה בִּפְקֹד
13 אֹתָם וְלֹא־יִהְיֶה בָהֶם נֶגֶף בִּפְקֹד אֹתָם: זֶה ׀ יִתְּנוּ כָּל־
הָעֹבֵר עַל־הַפְּקֻדִים מַחֲצִית הַשֶּׁקֶל בְּשֶׁקֶל הַקֹּדֶשׁ עֶשְׂרִים
14 גֵּרָה הַשֶּׁקֶל מַחֲצִית הַשֶּׁקֶל תְּרוּמָה לַיהֹוָה: כֹּל הָעֹבֵר
עַל־הַפְּקֻדִים מִבֶּן עֶשְׂרִים שָׁנָה וָמָעְלָה יִתֵּן תְּרוּמַת יְהֹוָה:
טו הֶעָשִׁיר לֹא־יַרְבֶּה וְהַדַּל לֹא יַמְעִיט מִמַּחֲצִית הַשָּׁקֶל

## IX. KI THISSA

(Chapters XXX, 11–XXXIV)

### Chapter XXX

#### 11–16. The Law of the Shekel

Whenever a census of the warriors was taken, every adult Israelite was to pay a half-shekel.

**12.** *their number.* Their mustering, as an army before going to war.

*a ransom.* Heb. כפר. This technical expression for 'ransom' occurs three times in the Torah, and each time it refers to the money paid by one who is guilty of taking human life in circumstances that do not constitute murder. Thus, the owner of the ox that had killed a man after the owner had received warning that the animal was dangerous, was charged with the death of a man; but as his crime was not intentional, he was permitted to pay a *ransom* (כפר). Such a ransom was forbidden in the case of deliberate murder. This is the conception that underlies the law of the half-shekel in this chapter. The soldier who is ready to march into battle is in the eyes of Heaven a potential taker of life, though not a deliberate murderer. Hence he requires 'a ransom for his life' (B. Jacob).

*when thou numberest them.* The soldier is to be impressed with the fact that, high as the aims for which he goes to battle may be, war remains a necessary *evil*. The ransom is, therefore, to be paid at the time of the mustering, long before the actual fighting begins.

*plague.* Heb. *negeph*. This word comes from the same root as the Heb. word for 'slaughter in battle'; and a noted Karaite commentator translates the phrase, 'that they suffer not defeat in battle.'

*when thou numberest them.* According to the above explanation, this phrase would begin v. 13.

**13.** *every one that passeth.* Before the officers mustering the forces for battle.

*shekel of the sanctuary.* The full-weight shekel used in connection with sacred things.

*offering to the Lord-.* Heb. *terumah*, 'contribution'; the same phrase is used in Num. XXXI, 52.

**14.** *twenty years.* The Israelite's military age.

**15.** *and the poor shall not give less.* All souls are of equal value in the eyes of God. Hence, all are to give the same ransom.

*to make atonement for your souls.* Heb. לכפר על נפשתיכם. This phrase is an amplification of כפר, and is repeated in the next verse. Even a rationalist commentator like Ehrlich rightly sees in the use of this last phrase one of the sublimest teachings of Scripture, unparalleled in any other sacred Book, ancient or modern. The same phrase is used in connection with the Midianite battle in Num. XXXI, 52. After signally defeating the Midianites, the victorious warriors come to the Tabernacle, bringing jewels and other valuable booty as an offering in order *to make atonement for their souls before the* Lord. 'Other peoples sing songs of triumph after a victory over their enemies; why then did these warriors offer sacrifices of atonement for their souls at such an hour?' asks Ehrlich; 'it is another indication of the horror of shedding human blood that the Torah inculcates. It is the same feeling that prompted the Jewish Sages to tell that the angels, when about to break forth in song over the Egyptian hosts drowning in the Red Sea, were silenced by God in the words, "My creatures are perishing, and ye are ready to sing!"'

**16.** *for the service.* The silver of the shekels

EXODUS XXX, 16

half shekel, when they give the offering of the LORD, to make atonement for your souls. 16. And thou shalt take the atonement money from the children of Israel, and shalt appoint it for the service of the tent of meeting, that it may be a memorial for the children of Israel before the LORD, to make atonement for your souls.' ¶ 17. And the LORD spoke unto Moses, saying: 18. 'Thou shalt also make a laver of brass, and the base thereof of brass, whereat to wash; and thou shalt put it between the tent of meeting and the altar, and thou shalt put water therein. 19. And Aaron and his sons shall wash their hands and their feet thereat; 20. when they go into the tent of meeting, they shall wash with water, that they die not; or when they come near to the altar to minister, to cause an offering made by fire to smoke unto the LORD; 21. so they shall wash their hands and their feet, that they die not; and it shall be a statute for ever to them, even to him and to his seed throughout their generations.' ¶ 22. Moreover the LORD spoke unto Moses,

16 לָתֵת אֶת־תְּרוּמַת יְהֹוָה לְכַפֵּר עַל־נַפְשֹׁתֵיכֶם: וְלָקַחְתָּ אֶת־כֶּסֶף הַכִּפֻּרִים מֵאֵת בְּנֵי יִשְׂרָאֵל וְנָתַתָּ אֹתוֹ עַל־עֲבֹדַת אֹהֶל מוֹעֵד וְהָיָה לִבְנֵי יִשְׂרָאֵל לְזִכָּרוֹן לִפְנֵי יְהֹוָה לְכַפֵּר עַל־נַפְשֹׁתֵיכֶם: פ

17 וַיְדַבֵּר יְהֹוָה אֶל־מֹשֶׁה לֵּאמֹר: וְעָשִׂיתָ כִּיּוֹר נְחֹשֶׁת וְכַנּוֹ
18 נְחֹשֶׁת לְרָחְצָה וְנָתַתָּ אֹתוֹ בֵּין־אֹהֶל מוֹעֵד וּבֵין הַמִּזְבֵּחַ
19 וְנָתַתָּ שָׁמָּה מָיִם: וְרָחֲצוּ אַהֲרֹן וּבָנָיו מִמֶּנּוּ אֶת־יְדֵיהֶם
כ וְאֶת־רַגְלֵיהֶם: בְּבֹאָם אֶל־אֹהֶל מוֹעֵד יִרְחֲצוּ־מַיִם וְלֹא יָמֻתוּ אוֹ בְגִשְׁתָּם אֶל־הַמִּזְבֵּחַ לְשָׁרֵת לְהַקְטִיר אִשֶּׁה
21 לַיהֹוָה: וְרָחֲצוּ יְדֵיהֶם וְרַגְלֵיהֶם וְלֹא יָמֻתוּ וְהָיְתָה לָהֶם חָק־עוֹלָם לוֹ וּלְזַרְעוֹ לְדֹרֹתָם: פ

22 וַיְדַבֵּר יְהֹוָה אֶל־מֹשֶׁה לֵּאמֹר: וְאַתָּה קַח־לְךָ בְּשָׂמִים
23

was used for the bases of the pillars of the Sanctuary, and also for the hooks to keep the boards together (XXXVIII, 27).

*a memorial. i.e.* that the Lord remember the children of Israel in grace, and grant them atonement for the blood shed in battle.

In later ages, the half-shekel became an annual tax devoted to maintaining the public services of the Temple; the daily worship was thus carried on by the entire People and not by the gifts of a few rich donors. The fact that the rich were not to give more, nor the poor less, than a half shekel taught that, 'weighed in the balance of the Sanctuary' (which is the lit. meaning of בשקל הקדש), differences of rank and wealth do not exist. The fact, furthermore, that only a *half*-shekel was to be paid, taught that an individual's contribution to the community was but a fragment. For any complete work to be achieved on behalf of the Sanctuary, the efforts of all, high and low, rich and poor alike, are required.

The Jews outside Palestine were, throughout the ancient world, as zealous in their contribution of this Temple tax as the inhabitants of Judea. Anti-Semites, in consequence, even raised the cry that the Jews 'were sending too much money out of the country'. One of the Roman Provincial Governors, who seized these offerings, was defended by Cicero in an anti-Jewish speech. After the destruction of the Temple, the Jews of the Empire were compelled to pay this contribution to the Temple of Jupiter at Rome! When this iniquitous tax was eventually abolished, the contribution from the Jews in the Diaspora was used for the support of the Rabbinical Academies in Palestine.

At the present day, the memory of the half-shekel is still kept alive by the reading of Exodus XXX, 11–16, on the Sabbath before the month of Adar, with a special Haftorah, Shekalim; and by donating half the value of a current silver coin to some worthy charitable cause on Purim. With the rise of the Jewish Nationalist Movement, the payment of the shekel, i.e. of an amount roughly equivalent to it in some modern currency, was revived as a token of sympathy with the aims of that movement.

17–21. THE LAVER

**18.** *base.* A pedestal.
*the altar.* Of burnt-offerings.

**20.** *that they die not.* To enter the Sanctuary with soiled hands and feet would have been a desecration of its holiness.
*to the altar.* Although the altar was situate in the Court and not in the Holy Sanctuary, the same penalty would be incurred.

**21.** *they shall wash.* The repetition of the preceding words is to stress that the ordinance was for ever.
*throughout their generations.* This rule has been observed by the pious in all ages, who wash their hands before beginning any of the statutory services, which the Rabbis declare to be the present-day equivalents of the sacrifices. Many synagogues arrange lavers at the entrance for such a ceremonial washing of the hands by the worshippers.

22–23. THE ANOINTING OIL

Olive oil was to be mixed with the essences of four aromatic herbs for use in the symbolic act of anointing; *i.e.* consecrating the Tent of Meeting and those that minister therein.

EXODUS XXX, 23

שמות כי תשא ל

saying: 23. 'Take thou also unto thee the chief spices, of flowing myrrh five hundred shekels, and of sweet cinnamon half so much, even two hundred and fifty, and of sweet calamus two hundred and fifty, 24. and of cassia five hundred, after the shekel of the sanctuary, and of olive oil a hin. 25. And thou shalt make it a holy anointing oil, a perfume compounded after the art of the perfumer; it shall be a holy anointing oil. 26. And thou shalt anoint therewith the tent of meeting, and the ark of the testimony, 27. and the table and all the vessels thereof, and the candlestick and the vessels thereof, and the altar of incense, 28. and the altar of burnt-offering with all the vessels thereof, and the laver and the base thereof. 29. And thou shalt sanctify them, that they may be most holy; whatsoever toucheth them shall be holy. 30. And thou shalt anoint Aaron and his sons, and sanctify them, that they may minister unto Me in the priest's office. 31. And thou shalt speak unto the children of Israel, saying: This shall be a holy anointing oil unto Me throughout your generations. 32. Upon the flesh of man shall it not be poured, neither shall ye make any like it, according to the composition thereof; it is holy, and it shall be holy unto you. 33. Whosoever com-

23. *chief spices.* lit. 'finest spices'.
*flowing myrrh.* Of the purest kind, which either exuded spontaneously from the plant or was obtained by tapping.
*five hundred shekels.* In weight; about sixteen pounds.

24. *cassia.* The inner bark of a species of cinnamon tree, peeled off and dried in the sun (Driver).
*a hin.* About ten pints.

25. *perfumer.* Great skill was required in obtaining the best compound of these ingredients. The work was therefore handed over to experts. In later times, certain 'sons of the priests' were trained for this work (I Chron. IX, 30).

29. *shall be holy.* Cf. XXIX, 37.

30. *anoint Aaron.* Cf. XXIX, 7, 29.

32. *man.* i.e. a non-priest. This holy oil was not to be utilized for secular purposes.
*neither shall ye make any like it.* For ordinary use.

33. *stranger.* One not authorized to be anointed with it.
*shall be cut off.* See on XII, 15.

34–38. THE HOLY INCENSE

Incense forms part of all forms of ancient ceremonial worship. On its symbolic significance see note on XXX, 7. The Jewish mystics declare, 'If men knew the sublime importance of the Holy Incense, they would set a crown of gold on each of the ingredients.' Incense possesses antiseptic properties; and it has a marked effect both on the nervous system and on the emotions of the worshippers. In the sayings of the Rabbis on the incense we can discern their recognition of these qualities.

34. *stacte.* A fragrant oil or resin. The Rabbis identified it with 'balm of Gilead'.
*onycha.* Obtained from certain shell-fish found in the Red Sea.
*galbanum.* Heb. חלבנה the gum of a shrub growing in Asia Minor and Persia. In contrast with the foregoing ingredients, it did not have an agreeable odour. Its inclusion was intentional, say the Rabbis. As the galbanum is an essential ingredient of the sacred incense, even so is the prayer of the Congregation of Israel most acceptable to God when it includes the prayers of sinners and transgressors.

35. *art of the perfumer.* Special skill was also demanded for the compounding of the incense, secrets which were transmitted from generation to generation in the family of Abtinas, who were entrusted with its manufacture.
*seasoned with salt.* Or, 'tempered together.'

EXODUS XXX, 34

poundeth any like it, or whosoever putteth any of it upon a stranger, he shall be cut off from his people.' ¶ 34. And the LORD said unto Moses: 'Take unto thee sweet spices, stacte, and onycha, and galbanum; sweet spices with pure frankincense; of each shall there be a like weight. 35. And thou shalt make of it incense, a perfume after the art of the perfumer, seasoned with salt, pure and holy. 36. And thou shalt beat some of it very small, and put of it before the testimony in the tent of meeting, where I will meet with thee; it shall be unto you most holy. 37. And the incense which thou shalt make, according to the composition thereof ye shall not make for yourselves; it shall be unto thee holy for the LORD. 38. Whosoever shall make like unto that, to smell thereof, he shall be cut off from his people.'

**31** CHAPTER XXXI

1. And the LORD spoke unto Moses, saying: 2. 'See, I have called by name Bezalel the son of Uri, the son of Hur, of the tribe of Judah; 3. and I have filled him with the spirit of God, in wisdom, and in understanding, and in knowledge, and in all manner of workmanship, 4. to devise skilful works, to work in gold, and in silver, and in brass, 5. and in cutting of stones for setting, and in carving of wood, to work in all manner of workmanship. 6. And I, behold, I have appointed with him Oholiab, the son of Ahisamach, of the tribe of Dan; and in the hearts of all that are wisehearted I have put wisdom, that they may make all that I have commanded thee: 7. the tent of meeting, and the ark of the testimony, and the ark-cover that is thereupon, and all the furniture of the Tent; 8. and the table and its vessels, and the pure candlestick with all its vessels, and the altar of incense; 9. and the altar of burnt-offering with all its vessels, and the laver and its base; 10. and the plaited garments, and the holy garments for Aaron the priest, and the garments of his sons, to minister in the priest's office; 11. and the anointing oil, and the incense of sweet spices for the holy place; according to all that I have commanded thee shall they do.' ¶ 12. And the LORD spoke unto Moses, saying: 13. 'Speak thou also unto the children of Israel,

**37.** *holy for the* LORD. Preparation of incense from similar ingredients and in similar proportions for private or profane use is forbidden.

CHAPTER XXXI

1–11. THE CHIEF ARTIFICERS AND THEIR TASK
See the commentary on xxxv, 30–xxxvi, 2.

13–17. THE SABBATH

**13.** *My sabbaths.* The work of constructing the Tabernacle that was now to commence was of the highest importance, and was work in the service of God; but it was not of greater importance than the Divinely-ordained Sabbath, and was not to be permitted to supersede it.

### EXODUS XXXI, 14

saying: Verily ye shall keep My sabbaths, for it is a sign between Me and you throughout your generations, that ye may know that I am the LORD who sanctify you. 14. Ye shall keep the sabbath therefore, for it is holy unto you; every one that profaneth it shall surely be put to death; for whosoever doeth any work therein, that soul shall be cut off from among his people. 15. Six days shall work be done; but on the seventh day is a sabbath of solemn rest, holy to the LORD; whosoever doeth any work in the sabbath day, he shall surely be put to death. 16. Wherefore the children of Israel shall keep the sabbath, to observe the sabbath throughout their generations, for a perpetual covenant. 17. It is a sign between Me and the children of Israel for ever; for in six days the LORD made heaven and earth, and on the seventh day He ceased from work and rested.'*ᵗᵗ· ¶ 18. And He gave unto Moses, when He had made an end of speaking with him upon mount Sinai, the two tables of the testimony, tables of stone, written with the finger of God.

## 32 CHAPTER XXXII

1. And when the people saw that Moses delayed to come down from the mount, the people gathered themselves together unto Aaron, and said unto him: 'Up, make us a

---

שמות כי תשא לא לב

לֵאמֹר אַךְ אֶת־שַׁבְּתֹתַי תִּשְׁמֹרוּ כִּי אוֹת הִוא בֵּינִי וּבֵינֵיכֶם
14 לְדֹרֹתֵיכֶם לָדַעַת כִּי אֲנִי יְהֹוָה מְקַדִּשְׁכֶם: וּשְׁמַרְתֶּם אֶת־
הַשַּׁבָּת כִּי קֹדֶשׁ הִוא לָכֶם מְחַלְלֶיהָ מוֹת יוּמָת כִּי כָּל־
הָעֹשֶׂה בָהּ מְלָאכָה וְנִכְרְתָה הַנֶּפֶשׁ הַהִוא מִקֶּרֶב עַמֶּיהָ:
טו שֵׁשֶׁת יָמִים יֵעָשֶׂה מְלָאכָה וּבַיּוֹם הַשְּׁבִיעִי שַׁבַּת שַׁבָּתוֹן
קֹדֶשׁ לַיהֹוָה כָּל־הָעֹשֶׂה מְלָאכָה בְּיוֹם הַשַּׁבָּת מוֹת יוּמָת:
16 וְשָׁמְרוּ בְנֵי־יִשְׂרָאֵל אֶת־הַשַּׁבָּת לַעֲשׂוֹת אֶת־הַשַּׁבָּת
17 לְדֹרֹתָם בְּרִית עוֹלָם: בֵּינִי וּבֵין בְּנֵי יִשְׂרָאֵל אוֹת הִוא
לְעֹלָם כִּי־שֵׁשֶׁת יָמִים עָשָׂה יְהֹוָה אֶת־הַשָּׁמַיִם וְאֶת־הָאָרֶץ
שני
18 וּבַיּוֹם הַשְּׁבִיעִי שָׁבַת וַיִּנָּפַשׁ: ס וַיִּתֵּן אֶל־מֹשֶׁה כְּכַלֹּתוֹ
לְדַבֵּר אִתּוֹ בְּהַר סִינַי שְׁנֵי לֻחֹת הָעֵדֻת לֻחֹת אֶבֶן כְּתֻבִים
בְּאֶצְבַּע אֱלֹהִים:

לב CAP. XXXII.

א וַיַּרְא הָעָם כִּי־בֹשֵׁשׁ מֹשֶׁה לָרֶדֶת מִן־הָהָר וַיִּקָּהֵל הָעָם

לא' v. 14. קמץ בז"ק

---

Hence the repetition of the law of the Sabbath; cf. xxxv, 2.

*a sign.* The Sabbath was more than a day of rest. Its observance by the Israelites was a constantly recurring acknowledgment of God as the Creator of the Universe. It would be an open denial of God for an Israelite to desecrate the Sabbath, even in the construction of the Tabernacle; as well as a contradiction of the essential purpose of the Sanctuary, the sanctification of Israel's life in the service of God.

*that ye may know.* lit. 'to know,' and the subject has to be supplied. Rashi and Maimonides explain it to mean 'that all nations shall know'. Similarly Driver comments: 'that all the world may recognize, by means of the Sabbath, that it is God Who sanctifies Israel, or provides it with the means of becoming a holy People.' The Sabbath was recognized throughout the ancient world as the peculiar and distinctive festival of the Jewish people.

**14.** *be put to death.* This extreme penalty was only to be inflicted if the culprit desecrated the Sabbath in the presence of two witnesses who had previously warned him of the punishment that awaited him.

**15.** *sabbath of solemn rest.* i.e. a complete cessation of work.

**16.** *a perpetual covenant.* The weekly hallowing of the Sabbath by the Israelites, being a proclamation of belief in God and obedience to His law, effects a perennial renewal of the covenant of God with the Patriarchs.

**17.** *in six days.* As in the fourth commandment (xx, 11).

#### 18. MOSES RECEIVES THE TABLES OF STONE

**18.** *tables of the testimony.* i.e. the Decalogue.
*finger of God.* An expression for the ineffable sanctity of the Tables, and for the Divine source of their Message to the children of men.

*v.* 18 connects this chapter with the narrative of the Golden Calf in the chapter following. XXXII, 15 relates that Moses had the Tablets in his hands, and this verse tells how he received them.

#### CHAPTER XXXII
#### THE GOLDEN CALF AND THE IDOLATRY OF THE PEOPLE

**1.** *delayed.* The Rabbis explain that the people expected Moses to return on the fortieth day, inclusive of the day of his ascent; but he remained forty clear days on Mount Sinai. When he did not appear on the day they expected him, the people concluded that he was dead, and a feeling of utter helplessness possessed them. They demanded a visible god.

## EXODUS XXXII, 2

god who shall go before us; for as for this Moses, the man that brought us up out of the land of Egypt, we know not what is become of him.' 2. And Aaron said unto them: 'Break off the golden rings, which are in the ears of your wives, of your sons, and of your daughters, and bring them unto me.' 3. And all the people broke off the golden rings which were in their ears, and brought them unto Aaron. 4. And he received it at their hand, and fashioned it with a graving tool, and made it a molten calf; and they said: 'This is thy god, O Israel, which brought thee up out of the land of Egypt.' 5. And when Aaron saw this, he built an altar before it; and Aaron made proclamation, and said: 'To-morrow shall be a feast to the LORD.' 6. And they rose up early on the morrow, and offered burnt-offerings, and brought peace-offerings; and the people sat down to eat and to drink, and rose up to make merry. ¶7. And the LORD spoke unto Moses: 'Go, get thee down; for thy people, that thou broughtest up out of the land of Egypt, have dealt corruptly; 8. they have turned

---

*unto Aaron*. When Moses departed from the camp, he left Aaron and Hur in charge (XXIV, 14). Why, then, is Aaron alone mentioned here? Tradition relates that Hur resisted the people's demand, and was put to death by them. Aaron, seeing the determination of the people, decided to work for gaining time till the arrival of Moses.

*who shall go before us*. The 'god' was to replace Moses as their leader.

**2.** *break off*. Aaron's intention may have been to cool their ardour, thinking they would hesitate to sacrifice their ornaments.

**3.** *broke off*. To Aaron's astonishment, the people at once complied with his request. 'What a fickle people!' say the Rabbis: 'one day they give their silver and gold for the Sanctuary of God; and on the morrow, they do the same for a Golden Calf.'

**4.** *fashioned it*. The golden articles were first melted, so that a mass of metal was formed, and this was shaped by Aaron into the semblance of a calf. The latter was the object of worship among Israel's Semitic kinsmen (see on I, 7).

**5.** *to-morrow*. The postponement, the Rabbis say, was due to Aaron's confident hope that Moses would appear by then, and the feast in honour of the calf would be changed into 'a feast to the LORD.' Yehudah Hallevi declares, 'the people did not intend to give up their allegiance to God.' They desired a *visible symbolic representation* of the God who brought them out of

Egypt. Their sin was not a breach of the First, but of the Second Commandment.

The conduct of Aaron throughout this incident is difficult to understand. There is, however, an explanation, though no excuse, for his behaviour. Tradition makes love of peace the outstanding trait of his nature. Always a lover of peace and a pursuer of peace, and thinking that resistance was futile, he acquiesced in the people's demand. There would doubtless have been many to side with him, but he feared division that might result in bloodshed.

**6.** *on the morrow*. After the altar had been erected.

*burnt offerings*. Cf. XX, 21.

*to eat and to drink*. Possibly a sacramental meal is intended (see on XXIV, 11).

*to make merry*. By dancing and singing (cf. *v*. 18 f), which usually figured in the religious celebrations of heathen peoples.

**7.** *thy people*. God disowns the sinful Israelites. He refuses to acknowledge them as His people. The Rabbis, on the other hand, understand '*thy* people which thou broughtest up out of the land of Egypt' as an allusion to the mixed multitude. It was not God who had brought these out of Egypt, but Moses had allowed them to accompany the Israelites.

**8.** *quickly*. It was less than six weeks since they had heard the Voice of God declaring, 'Thou shalt not make unto thee a graven image.'

EXODUS XXXII, 9

aside quickly out of the way which I commanded them; they have made them a molten calf, and have worshipped it, and have sacrificed unto it, and said: This is thy god, O Israel, which brought thee up out of the land of Egypt.' 9. And the LORD said unto Moses: 'I have seen this people, and, behold, it is a stiffnecked people. 10. Now therefore let Me alone, that My wrath may wax hot against them, and that I may consume them; and I will make of thee a great nation.' 11. And Moses besought the LORD his God, and said: 'LORD, why doth Thy wrath wax hot against Thy people, that Thou hast brought forth out of the land of Egypt with great power and with a mighty hand? 12. Wherefore should the Egyptians speak, saying: For evil did He bring them forth, to slay them in the mountains, and to consume them from the face of the earth? Turn from Thy fierce wrath, and repent of this evil against Thy people. 13. Remember Abraham, Isaac, and Israel, Thy servants, to whom Thou didst swear by Thine own self, and saidst unto them: I will multiply your seed as the stars of heaven, and all this land that I have spoken of will I give unto your seed, and they shall inherit it for ever.' 14. And the LORD repented of the evil which He said He would do unto His people. ¶ 15. And Moses turned, and went down from the mount, with the two tables of the testimony in his hand; tables that were written on both their sides; on the one side and on the other were they written. 16. And the tables were the work of God, and the writing was the writing of God, graven upon the tables. 17. And when Joshua heard the noise of the people as they shouted, he said unto Moses: 'There is a noise of war in the camp.' 18. And he said: 'It is not the voice of them that shout for mastery,

---

**9.** *stiffnecked.* Obstinate; here, persisting in its idolatry. The figure is taken from a stubborn ox that refuses to submit to the yoke.

**10.** *let Me alone.* The Rabbis explain this to mean that Moses understood from these Divine words that his intercession alone could save the Israelites from the extermination which threatened them.

**12.** *for evil.* With evil intent. Such would be the mockery of the Egyptians, if Israel were now to perish; cf. x, 10.

*the mountains.* Of the Peninsula of Sinai.

*repent.* Heb. idiom often attributes to God the feelings or emotions of man. God is thus said to 'repent', when, in consequence of a change in the character and conduct of men, He makes a corresponding change in the purpose towards them which He had previously announced (Driver).

**13.** *by Thine own self.* By the great Name which endures for all eternity.

15–20. MOSES RETURNS TO THE CAMP

**16.** *the work of God.* In his horror at the conduct of the Israelites Moses shattered the Tablets, although they were made by God Himself.

**17.** *Joshua.* Moses had left him on the lower slope of the mountain (XXIV, 13); and, consequently, Joshua was in ignorance of what had happened.

**18.** *sing.* i.e. answer in song; the answering voices of singers.

# EXODUS XXXII, 19

neither is it the voice of them that cry for being overcome, but the noise of them that sing do I hear.' 19. And it came to pass, as soon as he came nigh unto the camp, that he saw the calf and the dancing; and Moses' anger waxed hot, and he cast the tables out of his hands, and broke them beneath the mount. 20. And he took the calf which they had made, and burnt it with fire, and ground it to powder, and strewed it upon the water, and made the children of Israel drink of it. 21. And Moses said unto Aaron: 'What did this people unto thee, that thou hast brought a great sin upon them?' 22. And Aaron said: 'Let not the anger of my lord wax hot; thou knowest the people, that they are set on evil. 23. So they said unto me: Make us a god, which shall go before us; for as for this Moses, the man that brought us up out of the land of Egypt, we know not what is become of him. 24. And I said unto them: Whosoever hath any gold, let them break it off; so they gave it me; and I cast it into the fire, and there came out this calf.' 25. And when Moses saw that the people were broken loose—for Aaron had let them loose for a derision among their enemies—26. then Moses stood in the gate of the camp, and said: 'Whoso is on the LORD's side, let him come unto me.' And all the sons of Levi gathered themselves together unto him. 27. And he said unto

**19.** *Moses' anger waxed hot . . . and broke them.* The Heb. term translated by 'anger' covers both *anger* and *indignation*. Now, it was not *anger* that caused him to shatter the Tables. 'He who breaks anything in anger is as if he were an idolater,' say the Rabbis. Anger is selfish and blind, and a purely emotional reaction against an injury received. Thus, when a child hurts its foot against a stone, it is often so unreasonably angry as to strike the stone. Altogether different is the moral feeling of *indignation* that sweeps over us whenever we see a great wrong committed; not because it injures *us*, as is always the case in anger, but because the wrong is an outrage against justice and right. Such a feeling of righteous indignation filled Moses when he beheld a People that had been at Sinai, dancing before a golden calf! A mob guilty of such base and senseless ingratitude to God was, he felt, unworthy of the Divine Tables of the Law.

*beneath the mount.* At its foot.

**20.** *which they had made.* By contributing the gold, the Israelites were co-makers of the calf with Aaron.

*strewed it upon the water.* An emblem of perfect annihilation. In Deut. IX, 21, it is mentioned that a brook 'descended out of the mount'.

*made the children of Israel drink.* The Talmud compares this act with the ordeal imposed upon a suspected wife (Num. V); the drink harmfully affecting anyone who had been guilty, and leaving the innocent immune.

**21.** *brought a great sin upon them.* The participation of Aaron in such an offence fills Moses with amazement; and he demands an explanation.

**22.** *set on evil.* Aaron puts the whole blame on others.

**24.** *there came out this calf.* As if it happened by itself! Aaron's two pleas of compulsion and accident are the usual excuses in palliation of wrongdoing. His want of moral courage evoked the Divine displeasure; Deut. IX, 20.

**25.** *broken loose.* From their loyalty to God.
*a derision.* God's punishment of their sin would render them ignominious in the eyes of the neighbouring hostile peoples.

**26.** *whoso is on the LORD'S side.* By not having had any share in the idolatry.

**27.** *thus saith the LORD.* The Mechilta explains that Moses applied the law of XXII, 19. 'He that sacrificeth unto the gods, save unto the LORD only, shall be utterly destroyed.'

# EXODUS XXXII, 28

them: 'Thus saith the LORD, the God of Israel: Put ye every man his sword upon his thigh, and go to and fro from gate to gate throughout the camp, and slay every man his brother, and every man his companion, and every man his neighbour.' 28. And the sons of Levi did according to the word of Moses; and there fell of the people that day about three thousand men. 29. And Moses said: 'Consecrate yourselves to-day to the LORD, for every man hath been against his son and against his brother; that He may also bestow upon you a blessing this day.' 30. And it came to pass on the morrow, that Moses said unto the people: 'Ye have sinned a great sin; and now I will go up unto the LORD, peradventure I shall make atonement for your sin.' 31. And Moses returned unto the LORD, and said: 'Oh, this people have sinned a great sin, and have made them a god of gold. 32. Yet now, if Thou wilt forgive their sin—; and if not, blot me, I pray Thee, out of Thy book which Thou hast written.' 33. And the LORD said unto Moses: 'Whosoever hath sinned against Me, him will I blot out of My book. 34. And now go, lead the people unto the place of which I have spoken unto thee; behold, Mine angel shall go before thee; nevertheless in the day when I visit, I will visit their sin upon them.' 35. And the LORD smote the people, because they made the calf, which Aaron made.

*from gate to gate.* From one end of the camp to the other.

*his brother.* He summoned the Levites to kill the criminals with the sword, and not even to spare their nearest relatives if among the criminals. 'Brother' is often used in Heb. in the sense of 'relative'.

**29.** *consecrate yourselves to the LORD.* lit. 'fill your hand to the LORD,' see on XXVIII, 41; usually taken to mean that as a reward for fidelity and zeal, the tribe of Levi was to be given the charge of the Sanctuary.

*a blessing.* The privilege of being His servant.

**30.** *make atonement.* By intercession, win God's forgiveness for the people.

**32.** *if Thou wilt forgive.* Words such as 'I am content to live' must be supplied. This suppressing of part of a conditional sentence is not unusual in Hebrew.

*blot me.* Moses lived only for his people. If they were destroyed, he had no desire for life. 'This verse is one of the most beautiful and impressive in the whole of Scripture, strikingly depicting Moses' affection and self-devotion for his people' (Driver).

*Thy book.* In which the destinies of human beings are recorded; cf. Mal. III, 16, and Psalm CXXXIX, 16.

**33.** *him will I blot out of My book.* God will not permit Moses to suffer vicariously for others. Judaism recognizes neither vicarious punishment nor vicarious atonement. 'The soul that sinneth, it shall die'—unless by repentance and good deeds it gains the Divine forgiveness.

**34.** *Mine angel.* Not God Himself, because He cannot overlook what the people had done. For the 'angel', see on XXIII, 20.

*when I visit.* Moffatt, 'Yet when I am punishing, I will punish them for their sin.' The day of reckoning is only postponed; but, for the sake of Moses, the people shall, nevertheless, be led to the Land of Promise.

**35.** *smote.* A note confirming the words of the last sentence. Punishment was subsequently exacted from the people (Ibn Ezra).

# EXODUS XXXIII, 1

שמות כי תשא לג

## CHAPTER XXXIII

CAP. XXXIII. לג

1. And the LORD spoke unto Moses: 'Depart, go up hence, thou and the people that thou hast brought up out of the land of Egypt, unto the land of which I swore unto Abraham, to Isaac, and to Jacob, saying: Unto thy seed will I give it—2. and I will send an angel before thee; and I will drive out the Canaanite, the Amorite, and the Hittite, and the Perizzite, the Hivite, and the Jebusite—3. unto a land flowing with milk and honey; for I will not go up in the midst of thee; for thou art a stiffnecked people; lest I consume thee in the way.' 4. And when the people heard these evil tidings, they mourned; and no man did put on him his ornaments. 5. And the LORD said unto Moses: 'Say unto the children of Israel: Ye are a stiffnecked people; if I go up into the midst of thee for one moment, I shall consume thee; therefore now put off thy ornaments from thee, that I may know what to do unto thee.' 6. And the children of Israel stripped themselves of their ornaments from mount Horeb onward. ¶ 7. Now Moses used to take the tent and to pitch it without the camp, afar off from the camp; and he called it The tent of meeting. And it came to pass, that every one that sought the LORD went out unto the tent of meeting, which was without the camp. 8. And it came to pass, when Moses went out unto the Tent, that all the people rose up, and stood, every man at his tent door, and looked after Moses, until he was gone into the Tent. 9. And it came to pass, when Moses entered into the Tent, the pillar of cloud descended, and stood at the door of the Tent; and [the LORD] spoke

## CHAPTER XXXIII

### 1-6. THE CONTRITION OF THE PEOPLE

**1.** *thou and the people.* Not 'thy people', as in XXXII, 7. God no longer utterly repudiates them.

**2.** *before thee.* i.e. before Israel, to whom this message was to be delivered.

**3.** *consume thee.* Another act of treason on their part might well bring about their utter destruction.

**4.** *these evil tidings.* That God's spirit would not dwell with them. (Rashi).

**5.** *that I may know.* They had shown their remorse by stripping themselves of their ornaments. If they persevered in this chastened frame of mind, God would show mercy.

### 7-11. MOSES AND HIS TENT OF MEETING

**7.** *used to take.* From the time of the sin of the Golden Calf onwards (Rashi), until the Sanctuary had been erected.

*the tent.* Despite the use of the definite article, the allusion cannot be to the 'Tent of Meeting' mentioned in XXVII, 21, as that was not yet in existence. It may point back to Moses' tent, which is referred to in XVIII, 7, where Moses used to receive the people who came to him with their disputes.

*sought the* LORD. Through the medium of Moses.

*without the camp.* Because the camp had been defiled by the Golden Calf, and the sins of the people had removed the Divine Presence from their midst; but Moses, who was innocent of guilt, was not for that reason debarred from communion with God.

**8.** *rose up.* In reverence.

*looked after Moses.* Followed him reverently with their eyes.

**9.** *pillar of cloud.* The visible representation of the Shechinah (XIII, 21).

*stood.* i.e. remained.

*spoke.* The subject, 'the Lord,' is not stated; cf. Ezek. II, 1.

# EXODUS XXXIII, 10

with Moses. 10. And when all the people saw the pillar of cloud stand at the door of the Tent, all the people rose up and worshipped, every man at his tent door. 11. And the LORD spoke unto Moses face to face, as a man speaketh unto his friend. And he would return into the camp; but his minister Joshua, the son of Nun, a young man, departed not out of the Tent. *¶ 12. And Moses said unto the LORD: 'See, Thou sayest unto me: Bring up this people; and Thou hast not let me know whom Thou wilt send with me. Yet Thou hast said: I know thee by name, and thou hast also found grace in My sight. 13. Now therefore, I pray Thee, if I have found grace in Thy sight, show me now Thy ways, that I may know Thee, to the end that I may find grace in Thy sight; and consider that this nation is Thy people.' 14. And He said: 'My presence shall go with thee, and I will give thee rest.' 15. And he said unto Him: 'If Thy presence go not with me, carry us not up hence. 16. For wherein now shall

---

**10.** *worshipped.* Prostrated themselves to the ground.

**11.** *face to face.* i.e. not in obscure visions and dreams, nor in enigmatical allusions, but distinctly. 'As in a clear mirror was the Divine message reflected in Moses' mind,' say the Rabbis; see p. 402.

*he would return.* He only left them when it was essential to consult God, and then he would return to the camp.

*his minister.* His attendant; cf. xxiv, 13.

*a young man.* So called because he performed for Moses humble services, such as are generally given only by a youthful follower (Ibn Ezra). The Heb. term *naar* may also denote an unmarried man (Ehrlich); he was, therefore, able permanently to remain in charge of the tent. No children of Joshua are mentioned in the genealogical table in I Chron. VII, 27.

12–XXXIV, 7. MOSES' PRAYER, THE SECOND TABLES, AND THE THIRTEEN ATTRIBUTES OF GOD'S NATURE

After Israel had danced before the Golden Calf, and the Tables of the Law lay shattered at the foot of Sinai, Moses again ascended the mountain, and prostrated himself in prayer before God. After forty days, he returns unto Israel, when, in addition to new Tables of the Law, he brings a Heavenly commentary on that Law, the thirteen attributes of the Divine Nature, שלוש עשרה מדות, each a synonym of the everlasting mercy of God.

**12.** *whom Thou wilt send.* Moses, deprived of the assurance of God's Presence, feels that the task imposed upon him, 'Bring up this people,' is far too difficult to undertake. He therefore pleads for the Divine assistance.

*Thou hast said.* The Torah does not record the circumstances in which the words that follow were spoken by God: but they might well have been uttered when He desired to destroy the Israelites and make 'a great nation' of Moses (XXXII, 10).

*I know thee by name.* i.e. selected thee to fulfil My commission. Moses recalls these words of graciousness, for the purpose of contrasting them with the hopeless position in which he now finds himself.

**13.** *show me.* lit. 'make me to know.'

*Thy ways.* The Talmud understands Moses' request as a desire to know the principles on which God deals with human beings, granting prosperity to some and adversity to others; to understand God's nature, in order that he might lead and govern the people in accordance with the Divine will.

*this nation is Thy people.* And should not be left without the inspiration of God's Presence.

**14.** *My presence.* Heb. *panai.* The expression is synonymous with 'I' (cf. II Sam. XVII, 11). Onkelos renders by, 'My Shechinah.'

*give thee rest.* In the Promised Land. 'Thee' refers to the people, as in v. 2 f above.

**15.** *carry us not up hence.* Unless the Divine Presence be in their midst when they proceed on their journey, Moses begs that they stay at Sinai—a spot which had been hallowed by the Revelation.

EXODUS XXXIII, 17

it be known that I have found grace in Thy sight, I and Thy people? is it not in that Thou goest with us, so that we are distinguished, I and Thy people, from all the people that are upon the face of the earth?'*ᶦᵛ· ¶ 17. And the Lord said unto Moses: 'I will do this thing also that thou hast spoken, for thou hast found grace in My sight, and I know thee by name.' 18. And he said: 'Show me, I pray Thee, Thy glory.' 19. And He said: 'I will make all My goodness pass before thee, and will proclaim the name of the Lord before thee; and I will be gracious to whom I will be gracious, and will show mercy on whom I will show mercy.' 20. And He said: 'Thou canst not see My face, for man shall not see Me and live.' 21. And the Lord said: 'Behold, there is a place by Me, and thou shalt stand upon the rock. 22. And it shall come to pass, while My glory passeth by, that I will put thee in a cleft of the rock, and will cover thee with My hand until I have passed by. 23. And I will take away My hand, and thou shalt see My back; but My face shall not be seen.'*ᵛ·

**16.** *distinguished.* Israel's distinctiveness consisted solely in the Divine nearness to Israel.

**17.** *this thing also.* Better, *even this thing that thou hast spoken will I do.*

**18.** *Thy glory.* Emboldened by the success of his plea on behalf of the people, Moses begs the privilege of being acquainted with 'the glory of God', *i.e.* with His eternal qualities.

**19.** *My goodness.* God's moral attributes. The revelation of these Attributes of love and mercy is the source of the sublime principle of the *Imitation of God*, הדבקת במדותיו של הקב׳ה. This Jewish ideal, 'one of the most advanced triumphs of Religion,' goes back to the Divine demand in Lev. xix, 2. 'Ye shall be holy: for I the Lord your God am holy.' Israel is not only to serve God, but to imitate Him. Mortal man, however, cannot imitate God's infinity, omnipotence or eternity. That side of His nature, which is beyond human comprehension, is also beyond human imitation. But we *can* know His 'goodness', and we can follow *His ways of mercy and forgiveness.* Thus, pity is a Divine attribute; and man is never nearer to the Divine than in his compassionate moments. God's merciful qualities are, therefore, the most real links between God and Man. 'Even as I am merciful, be thou merciful; even as I am gracious, be thou gracious,' is the Rabbinic translation of the great commandment of the Imitation of God.

*proclaim the name of the* LORD. The term 'Name' has here the same significance as in III,

13 f, and denotes the Divine essence, nature and character.

*I will be gracious.* God will show mercy to those who deserve it. Who these are, is not expressly stated; but fallen and penitent Israel is intended (Driver). The Heb. idiom employed here is the same as in 'send by the hand of him whom Thou wilt send' (IV, 13).

**20.** *see My face.* Moses desires to know what no human being can fathom, what no human language can express. His request, however, is not due to curiosity, but in order to confirm the promise in *v.* 14.

*and live.* The expression that a mortal cannot see God and live is frequently found in Scripture.

**21.** *upon the rock.* Of Sinai.

**23.** *My face shall not be seen.* When God passes by, presumably in the form of fire (see XXIV, 17), Moses will be sheltered in 'a cleft of the rock'. He will thus not see 'the face', the full Manifestation of the Divine radiance; but only its afterglow, 'the back,' so to speak. It is, of course, quite impossible to penetrate the full mystery of these words, conveying sublime truths concerning the Divine nature in the ordinary language of man. Many interpreters deduce from this passage the teaching that no living being can see God's face, *i.e.* penetrate His eternal essence. It is only from the *rearward* that we can know Him. Even as a ship sails through the waters of ocean and leaves its wake behind, so God may be known by His Divine 'footprints' in human history, by His traces in the human soul.

# EXODUS XXXIV, 1

## CHAPTER XXXIV

1. And the LORD said unto Moses: 'Hew thee two tables of stone like unto the first; and I will write upon the tables the words that were on the first tables, which thou didst break. 2. And be ready by the morning, and come up in the morning unto mount Sinai, and present thyself there to Me on the top of the mount. 3. And no man shall come up with thee, neither let any man be seen throughout all the mount; neither let the flocks nor herds feed before that mount.' 4. And he hewed two tables of stone like unto the first; and Moses rose up early in the morning, and went up unto mount Sinai, as the LORD had commanded him, and took in his hand two tables of stone. 5. And the LORD descended in the cloud, and stood with him there, and proclaimed the name of the LORD. 6. And the LORD passed by before him, and proclaimed: 'The LORD, the LORD God, merciful and gracious, long-suffering, and abundant in goodness and truth; 7. keeping

## CHAPTER XXXIV

**1.** *hew thee two tables.* The vision of God which was now to be granted to Moses marks the re-establishment of the Covenant between God and Israel that had been annulled by the apostasy in connection with the Golden Calf. Therefore, the broken Tables of the Law are replaced by new Tables.

**2.** *be ready.* Even a man living a life so consecrated as Moses must 'prepare to meet his God' by self-purification; cf. XIX, 10.

*top of the mount.* From whence God had proclaimed the Ten Words (XIX, 20).

**3.** *no man.* Neither Aaron (XIX, 17) nor the elders (XXIV, 9) were to be with him on the mountain. Moses alone was this time to witness the Revelation. The Rabbis remark that the first Tables were given amid great pomp and upheaval, physical and psychic; and they were destroyed. The Second Revelation was given in silence, to one human soul alone in mystic communion with His Maker; and these Tables endured, for the salvation of Israel and mankind.

**4.** *went up.* Tradition relates that Moses ascended on the first day of Ellul, and after remaining on the Mount forty days, descended on the tenth of Tishri, the Day of Atonement, on which day he brought the tidings of God's perfect pardon unto the sinful people.

### 5–7. THE REVELATION OF GOD'S NATURE IN THE THIRTEEN ATTRIBUTES

God's 'ways' are now proclaimed unto Moses in the thirteen characteristic qualities of the Divine Nature, enumerated in *v.* 6 and 7. Judaism has been very chary of definitions of God. He is the *En sof*, the Infinite, the Undefinable. However, the Thirteen Attributes give us a definition of God in ethical terms. All schools of Jewish thought agree that these momentous and sublime attributes enshrine some of the most distinctive doctrines of Judaism. The Rabbis made *v.* 6 and 7, containing the Thirteen Attributes of Divine Mercy, the dominant refrain in all prayers of repentance.

**5.** *stood.* The subject is 'the LORD' (Ibn Ezra, Nachmanides).

**6.** *proclaimed.* God reveals the 'name of the LORD', *i.e.* His characteristic qualities, to Moses. The Rabbis held that there are thirteen distinct attributes in these two verses; though there are differences as to their precise enumeration. The enumeration in the following comments is in accordance with the views of Rabbenu Tam, Ibn Ezra, Mendelssohn and Reggio.

*the* LORD, *the* LORD. Heb. *Adonay, Adonay* (I and II). ADONAY denotes God in His attribute of mercy; and the repetition is explained in the Talmud as meaning, 'I am the merciful God before a man commits a sin, and I am the same merciful and forgiving God after a man has sinned. Whatever change has to be wrought, must be in the heart of the sinner; not in the nature of the Deity. He is the same after a man has sinned, as He was before a man has sinned.'

*God.* Heb. *el* (III). The all-mighty Lord of the Universe, Ruler of Nature and mankind.

*merciful.* Heb. *rachum* (IV); full of affectionate sympathy for the sufferings and miseries of human frailty.

*and gracious.* Heb. *ve-channun* (V); assisting

## EXODUS XXXIV, 8

שמות כי תשא לד

עַל־פָּנָיו וַיִּקְרָא יְהֹוָה ׀ יְהֹוָה אֵל רַחוּם וְחַנּוּן אֶרֶךְ אַפַּיִם
7 וְרַב־חֶסֶד וֶאֱמֶת: נֹצֵר חֶסֶד לָאֲלָפִים נֹשֵׂא עָוֹן וָפֶשַׁע
וְחַטָּאָה וְנַקֵּה לֹא יְנַקֶּה פֹּקֵד ׀ עֲוֹן אָבוֹת עַל־בָּנִים וְעַל־
8 בְּנֵי בָנִים עַל־שִׁלֵּשִׁים וְעַל־רִבֵּעִים: וַיְמַהֵר מֹשֶׁה וַיִּקֹּד
9 אַרְצָה וַיִּשְׁתָּחוּ: וַיֹּאמֶר אִם־נָא מָצָאתִי חֵן בְּעֵינֶיךָ אֲדֹנָי
ששי יֵלֶךְ־נָא אֲדֹנָי בְּקִרְבֵּנוּ כִּי עַם־קְשֵׁה־עֹרֶף הוּא וְסָלַחְתָּ
י לַעֲוֹנֵנוּ וּלְחַטָּאתֵנוּ וּנְחַלְתָּנוּ: וַיֹּאמֶר הִנֵּה אָנֹכִי כֹּרֵת

v. 7. נון רבתי

mercy unto the thousandth generation, forgiving iniquity and transgression and sin; and that will by no means clear the guilty; visiting the iniquity of the fathers upon the children, and upon the children's children, unto the third and unto the fourth generation.' 8. And Moses made haste, and bowed his head toward the earth, and worshipped. 9. And he said: 'If now I have found grace in Thy sight, O Lord, let the Lord, I pray Thee, go in the midst of us; for it is a stiffnecked people; and pardon our iniquity and our sin, and take us for Thine inheritance.'*ᵛⁱ· 10. And He said: 'Behold, I make a covenant; before all thy people I

and helping; consoling the afflicted and raising up the oppressed. 'In man these two qualities manifest themselves fitfully and temporarily; he is מרחם וחונן. It is otherwise with God: in Him, compassion and grace are permanent, inherent and necessary emanations of His nature. Hence, He alone can be spoken of as *rachun ve-channun*' (Mendelssohn).

*long-suffering.* Or, 'slow to anger.' Heb. *erech appayim* (vi); not hastening to punish the sinner, but affording him opportunities to retrace his evil courses.

*abundant in goodness.* Or, plenteous in mercy. Heb. *rav chesed* (vii); granting His gifts and blessings beyond the deserts of man.

*and truth.* Heb. *ve-emet* (viii); eternally true to Himself, pursuing His inscrutable plans for the salvation of mankind, and rewarding those who are obedient to His will. Note that '*chesed*', lovingkindness, precedes '*emet*,' truth, both here and generally throughout Scripture; as if to say, 'Speak the truth by all means; but be quite sure that you speak the truth *in love.*'

**7.** *keeping mercy unto the thousandth generation.* Heb. *notzer chesed la-alafim* (IX). Remembering the good deeds of the ancestors to the thousandth generation, and reserving reward and recompense to the remotest descendants.

*forgiving iniquity.* Heb. *noseh avon* (x); bearing with indulgence the failings of man, and by forgiveness restoring him to the original purity of his soul. The Heb. for 'iniquity' is *avon;* sins committed from evil disposition.

*transgression.* Heb. *pesha* (xi); evil deeds springing from malice and rebellion against the Divine.

*sin.* Heb. *chattaah* (xii); shortcomings due to heedlessness and error.

*will by no means clear the guilty. i.e.* He will not allow the guilty to pass unpunished. Heb. *venakkeh lo yenakkeh* (xiii). The Rabbis explain: *venakkeh* 'acquitting—the penitent; *lo yenakkeh,* but not acquitting—the impenitent.' He is merciful and gracious and forgiving; but He will never obliterate the eternal and unbridgeable distinction between light and darkness, between good and evil. God cannot leave repeated wickedness and obstinate persistence in evil entirely unpunished. His goodness cannot destroy His justice. The sinner must suffer the consequences of his misdeeds. The unfailing and impartial consequences of sin help man to perceive that there is no 'chance' in morals. The punishments of sin are thus not vindictive, but remedial.

*visiting . . . upon the children.* See xx, 5. This law relates only to the consequences of sin. Pardon is not the remission of the *penalty*, but the forgiveness of the guilt and the removal of the sinfulness. The misdeeds of those who are God's enemies are visited only to the third and fourth generation, whereas His mercy to those who love Him is unto a thousand generations.

### 8–9. Moses' Prayer

**8.** *made haste.* Upon learning the prominent place that mercy holds in the Divine Nature, Moses immediately supplicates God to exercise His quality of mercy in favour of Israel.

**9.** *our iniquity.* Moses identifies himself with his people. He speaks of 'our' iniquity. Similarly in the Liturgy of the Synagogue, especially in the Confession of the Day of Atonement, the prayers are composed in the plural ('we have sinned,' etc.); for the Rabbis exhort, 'The individual should associate himself with the Community in all his supplications.'

*for Thine inheritance. i.e.* by Thy presence in Israel's midst, acknowledge the people as Thine.

### 10–26. The Renewal and Conditions of the Covenant

**10.** *I make a covenant.* In answer to Moses' petition, God will go in the midst of Israel.

*thy people.* God will manifest wondrous deeds on their behalf, to convince them that He is desirous of leading them to their destination.

## EXODUS XXXIV, 11

will do marvels, such as have not been wrought in all the earth, nor in any nation; and all the people among which thou art shall see the work of the LORD that I am about to do with thee, that it is tremendous. 11. Observe thou that which I am commanding thee this day; behold, I am driving out before thee the Amorite, and the Canaanite, and the Hittite, and the Perizzite, and the Hivite, and the Jebusite. 12. Take heed to thyself, lest thou make a covenant with the inhabitants of the land whither thou goest, lest they be for a snare in the midst of thee. 13. But ye shall break down their altars, and dash in pieces their pillars, and ye shall cut down their Asherim. 14. For thou shalt bow down to no other god; for the LORD, whose name is Jealous, is a jealous God; 15. lest thou make a covenant with the inhabitants of the land, and they go astray after their gods, and do sacrifice unto their gods, and they call thee, and thou eat of their sacrifice; 16. and thou take of their daughters unto thy sons, and their daughters go astray after their gods, and make thy sons go astray after their gods. 17. Thou shalt make thee no molten gods. 18. The feast of unleavened bread shalt thou keep. Seven days thou shalt eat unleavened bread, as I commanded thee, at the time appointed in the month

---

**11.** *commanding thee.* i.e. Israel, as in XXXIII, 2 f.

**12.** *a snare.* Fraternization with the heathen would inevitably lead to idol-worship, and bring disaster upon the Israelites, as was proved abundantly in the time of the Judges.

**13.** *break down.* All forms of heathenish worship are to be obliterated.

*altars.* On which human sacrifice was not uncommon.

*pillars.* See on XXIII, 24. Wooden poles, around which immoral orgies were carried on.

*Asherim.* 'Probably wooden symbols of a goddess Ashera' (RV Margin), the Venus of the Phœnicians, Ashtoreth, Astarte. Immoral rites were practised at these shrines.

**14.** *name.* i.e. character (cf. XXXIII, 19).

*a jealous God.* See on XX, 5.

**15.** *call thee.* i.e. invite thee.

*eat of their sacrifice.* To partake of the flesh of a heathen sacrifice would be tantamount to apostasy, since religious ideas were associated with a sacrificial meal.

**16.** *take of their daughters.* The dangers of intermarriage from the spiritual point of view were recognized by the Patriarchs (Gen. XXIV and XXVIII). They are emphasized by Moses (Deut. VII, 3 f) and by Joshua (Josh. XXIII, 12). The danger, though of a different character, is just as real to-day. The training of every Jewish child should be such that he remain part of Israel, that he continue the work of Israel, and that he make the building of a home *in* Israel the ambition of his youth and manhood. Intermarriage would then be out of the question for any son or daughter of Israel. Unlike other peoples, Israel does not wage any wars; and rarely, therefore, does it require its children to lay down their lives in its defence; but Judaism expects that its sons and daughters should feel themselves bound, even though the duty involve the sacrifice of precious affections, to refrain from courses of conduct that undermine the stability of Israel. 'Every Jew who contemplates marriage outside the pale must regard himself as paving the way to a disruption which would be the final, as it would be the culminating, disaster in the history of his people' (M. Joseph).

**17.** *molten gods.* The 'pillars' and 'asherim' having been condemned as objects of worship, the warning against molten gods of silver and gold is repeated (XX, 20).

**18–26.** The commands in these verses concern exclusively the relation between God and man. For these verses speak of the Covenant which had been broken, not by any neglect of duties towards fellow-men, but by neglect of Israel's duty toward God.

EXODUS XXXIV, 19

Abib, for in the month Abib thou camest out from Egypt. 19. All that openeth the womb is Mine; and of all thy cattle thou shall sanctify the males, the firstlings of ox and sheep. 20. And the firstling of an ass thou shalt redeem with a lamb; and if thou wilt not redeem it, then thou shalt break its neck. All the first-born of thy sons thou shalt redeem. And none shall appear before Me empty. 21. Six days thou shalt work, but on the seventh day thou shalt rest; in plowing time and in harvest thou shalt rest. 22. And thou shalt observe the feast of weeks, even of the first-fruits of wheat harvest, and the feast of ingathering at the turn of the year. 23. Three times in the year shall all thy males appear before the Lord GOD, the God of Israel. 24. For I will cast out nations before thee, and enlarge thy borders; neither shall any man covet thy land, when thou goest up to appear before the LORD thy God three times in the year. 25. Thou shalt not offer the blood of My sacrifice with leavened bread; neither shall the sacrifice of the feast of the passover be left unto the morning. 26. The choicest first-fruits of thy land thou shalt bring unto the house of the LORD thy God. Thou shalt not seethe a kid in its mother's milk.'*vii.
¶27. And the LORD said unto Moses: 'Write thou these words, for after the tenor of these words I have made a covenant with thee and with Israel.' 28. And he was there

---

**18.** *feast of unleavened bread*. The reminder that Israel owes freedom and national existence to the redemptive power of God. Its due observance would prevent Israel's going astray after other gods.

**19.** *firstlings*. See XIII, 12 and XXII, 28 f. Ibn Ezra rightly explains that this law is mentioned here because it is connected with the Exodus from Egypt. The sparing of the firstborn of the Israelites (XII, 13) was commemorated by the dedication of the firstborn, human and animal, to God; see XIII, 2 f, 15.

**20.** *a lamb*. See XIII, 13.

*none shall appear*. Cf. XXIII, 15. These words are taken to refer to the Feast of Unleavened Bread, and also to the Feast of Weeks and of Ingathering (v. 22 f).

**21.** *seventh day*. See XX, 8, XXIII, 12. The observance of the Sabbath would likewise be a reminder of God, both as Creator of the Universe, and Deliverer of Israel from Egypt.

*in plowing time*. Even during the periods of the year when there is urgent pressure in the field, and the Israelite feels that his livelihood demands continuous work, without a break on the Sabbath, he must nevertheless not desecrate the holy day.

**22.** *feast of weeks*. See on XXIII, 16. This name is given also in Deut. XVI, 10, and the reason for it stated, 'seven weeks shalt thou number unto thee.'

*at the turn of the year*. The year being reckoned according to the agricultural seasons, the gathering of the harvest marks its end.

**24.** *covet thy land*. God will shield their homes against enemies who might seize such a favourable opportunity to attack the women and children.

**25.** *with leavened bread*. See XXIII, 18.

**26.** *seethe a kid*. See XXIII, 19.

#### 27, 28. THE SECOND TABLES

**27.** *these words*. The contents of v. 11–26, which were the conditions of the renewal of the Covenant.

**28.** *forty days*. This period is reckoned from his ascent mentioned in v. 4.

*the words of the covenant*. Better, *with the words of the covenant* (Ibn Ezra). Moses wrote

EXODUS XXXIV, 29

with the LORD forty days and forty nights; he did neither eat bread, nor drink water. And he wrote upon the tables the words of the covenant, the ten words. 29. And it came to pass, when Moses came down from mount Sinai with the two tables of the testimony in Moses' hand, when he came down from the mount, that Moses knew not that the skin of his face sent forth [1]beams while He talked with him. 30. And when Aaron and all the children of Israel saw Moses, behold, the skin of his face sent forth beams; and they were afraid to come nigh him. 31. And Moses called unto them; and Aaron and all the rulers of the congregation returned unto him; and Moses spoke to them. 32. And afterward all the children of Israel came nigh, and he gave them in commandment all that the LORD had spoken with him in mount Sinai. 33. And when Moses had done speaking with them, he put a veil on his face. 34. But when Moses went in before the LORD that He might speak with him, he took the veil off, until he came out; and he came out, and spoke unto the children of Israel that which he was commanded. 35. And the children of Israel saw the face of Moses, that the skin of Moses' face sent forth beams; and Moses put the veil back upon his face, until he went in to speak with Him.

[1] Heb. *horns*.

---

down all these commands, whilst God Himself inscribed the Decalogue upon the second Tables; see *v.* 1 and Deut. x, 1. The Heb. particle את here means 'with'; otherwise it would have been repeated before each of the two phrases.

Starting from this verse, the German poet Goethe conjectured in 1773 that the regulations in *v.* 14–26 could be grouped as ten laws, and these ten laws were the original Ten Commandments! In his later and riper years (*Wahrheit und Dichtung*, Book XII), he spoke of this alleged discovery of his as 'a freakish notion', due to his insufficient knowledge. Since his day, however, Wellhausen and other Bible Critics have revived the preposterous idea of the youthful poet as to a Second Decalogue, the 'moral' Decalogue as they call it, as distinct from the alleged 'ritual' Decalogue in this chapter. Leading Bible scholars, however, see the obvious intention of the narrative indicated in *v.* 1 ('I will write upon the tables the words which were upon the first tables, which thou didst break'). They furthermore recognize that it is only by arbitrary and baseless *guesswork* that the precepts in *v.* 14–26 can be arranged so as to make ten.

### 29–35. SHINING OF MOSES' FACE

**29.** *two tables of the testimony*. As in XXXI, 18.
*knew not*. Unconscious that the Divine lustre was reflected upon his face. The greatest are unconscious of their greatness.

*sent forth beams*. Of light. The Heb. קרן either means, 'a ray of light' or, more commonly, 'a horn.' The Latin translation of the Bible, the Vulgate, translates, 'his face sent out horns of light.' The medieval artists, therefore, including Michael Angelo, were thus misled into representing Moses as with horns protruding from his forehead!

*while He talked ... with him*. Communion with God illumines the soul with a Divine radiance.

**31.** *called*. To reassure them.
*returned*. The verb implies that they had retreated in terror.
*spoke to them*. He repeated to them what God had commanded him in the Mount.

**32.** *all that the LORD had spoken*. viz. the Covenant, upon the fulfilment of which His presence would accompany the people.

**33.** *veil*. The radiance was something that appertained to the Divine, and for that reason must not be put to a profane use.

**34.** *when Moses went in ... he took*. Better, *whenever Moses went in ... he would take ...*

**35.** *children of Israel saw*. The People were the more deeply impressed by his message when they beheld the radiance of his countenance.

# HAFTORAH KI THISSA

הפטרת כי תשא

I KINGS XVIII, 1–39

### Chapter XVIII

1. And it came to pass after many days, that the word of the Lord came to Elijah, in the third year, saying: 'Go, show thyself unto Ahab, and I will send rain upon the land.' 2. And Elijah went to show himself unto Ahab. ¶ And the famine was sore in Samaria. 3. And Ahab called Obadiah, who was over the household.—Now Obadiah feared the Lord greatly; 4. for it was so, when Jezebel cut off the prophets of the Lord, that Obadiah took a hundred prophets, and hid them fifty in a cave, and fed them with bread and water.—5. And Ahab said unto Obadiah: 'Go through the land, unto all the springs of water, and unto all the brooks; peradventure we may find grass and save the horses and mules alive, that we lose not all the beasts.' 6. So they divided the land between them to pass throughout it: Ahab went one way by himself, and Obadiah went another way by himself. ¶ 7. And as Obadiah was in the way, behold, Elijah met him; and he knew him, and fell on his face, and said: 'Is it thou, my lord Elijah?' 8. And he answered him: 'It is I; go, tell thy lord: Behold, Elijah is here.' 9. And he said: 'Wherein have I sinned, that thou wouldest deliver thy servant into the hand of Ahab, to slay me? 10. As the Lord thy God liveth, there is no nation or kingdom, whither my lord hath not sent to seek thee; and when they said: He is not here, he took an oath of the kingdom and nation, that they found thee

In the Sedrah, the people worship the Golden Calf. In the Haftorah, centuries later, their descendants in the time of King Ahab are wavering between God and Baal. Ahab was a generous ruler, but weak-willed and dominated by his Phœnician wife, who pursued the prophets with murderous cruelty. It was high treason to proclaim the God of Israel. Against this dark setting, the figure of Elijah stands out in all its greatness. He meets and confronts the king and queen, and fearlessly pronounces the doom that will follow upon their apostasy and their outrage of justice. On Mt. Carmel, though he is alone and defenceless, his titanic personality overawes the multitude at that historic scene. He brings the people back to God in an overwhelming act of surrender. Their confession: *Adonay, hu ha-elohim*, 'The Lord, He is God,' has become, alongside the declaration of the Unity, Israel's watchword. Elijah, the timeless and deathless Prophet, is the champion of Purity of Worship and Justice to fellow-man. He is a type of Israel.

**1.** *in the third year.* i.e. of the drought; see I Kings XVII, 1.

*Elijah.* To him the conflict between the worship of God and Baal was 'a conflict between two diametrically opposite religious principles which could not exist side by side; i.e. an immoral Nature-religion and the ethical Religion of Israel' (Skinner).

**2.** *Samaria.* The capital of the kingdom of Israel.

**4.** *Jezebel cut off.* Summarizes the persecution of the Prophets, i.e. members of the Prophetical schools, who aroused her murderous wrath because their activity was directed against her paganizing influence.

*hid them fifty.* In separate bands of 50 each, to save them from extermination by Jezebel.

*fed them with bread and water.* Water was scarce and more precious than gold during those days of drought; but he procured it for them at all costs—a striking testimony of his loyalty to the cause of God.

**7.** *fell on his face.* In reverence.

**9.** *to slay me.* He feared that, after Ahab had received the message, Elijah would vanish

I KINGS XVIII, 11

not. 11. And now thou sayest: Go, tell thy lord: Behold, Elijah is here. 12. And it will come to pass, as soon as I am gone from thee, that the spirit of the LORD will carry thee whither I know not; and so when I come and tell Ahab, and he cannot find thee, he will slay me; but I thy servant fear the LORD from my youth. 13. Was it not told my lord what I did when Jezebel slew the prophets of the LORD, how I hid a hundred men of the LORD's prophets by fifty in a cave, and fed them with bread and water? 14. And now thou sayest: Go, tell thy lord: Behold, Elijah is here; and he will slay me.' 15. And Elijah said: 'As the LORD of hosts liveth, before whom I stand, I will surely show myself unto him to-day.' ¶ 16. So Obadiah went to meet Ahab, and told him; and Ahab went to meet Elijah. 17. And it came to pass, when Ahab saw Elijah, that Ahab said unto him: 'Is it thou, thou troubler of Israel?' 18. And he answered: 'I have not troubled Israel; but thou, and thy father's house, in that ye have forsaken the commandments of the LORD, and thou hast followed the Baalim. 19. Now therefore send, and gather to me all Israel unto mount Carmel, and the prophets of Baal four hundred and fifty, and the prophets of the Asherah four hundred, that eat at Jezebel's table.' ¶ 20. And Ahab sent unto all the children of Israel, and gathered the prophets together unto mount Carmel. 21. And Elijah came near unto all the people, and said: 'How long halt ye between two opinions? if the LORD be God, follow Him; but if Baal, follow him.' And the people answered him not a word. 22. Then said Elijah unto the people: 'I, even I only, am left a prophet of the LORD; but Baal's prophets are four hundred and fifty men. 23. Let them therefore give us two bullocks; and let them choose one bullock for themselves, and cut it in pieces, and lay it on the wood, and put no fire under; and I will press the other bullock, and lay it on the

as suddenly as he now appeared, and that he (Obadiah) would have to meet the king's fierce anger.

**10.** *there is no nation.* The exaggeration of fear.

**12.** *whither I know not.* Elijah's movements had made them accustomed to sudden disappearances to localities unknown to them (Rashi).

**15.** *the LORD of hosts.* A solemn description of the universal character of God, *i.e.* LORD and Ruler of all men and nations and all the forces of existence.

**17.** *thou troubler of Israel.* Alluding to Elijah's prediction of the drought.

**18.** *Baalim.* The plural of Baal, the name of the principal god of the Canaanites.

**19.** *Asherah.* The female counterpart of Baal, the Astarte of the Phœnicians.

20–39. THE DAY OF DECISION: THE LORD OR BAAL?

**20.** *mount Carmel.* The only mountain on the Palestine coast, rising to nearly 1,800 ft. above the sea level.

**21.** *how long halt ye between two opinions?* lit. 'how long will ye go limping, resting now on one foot, now on another?' Or, 'hopping between two branches,' like birds; *i.e.* at one time serving Baal, at another, the LORD.

I KINGS XVIII, 24

wood and put no fire under. 24. And call ye on the name of your god, and I will call on the name of the LORD; and the God that answereth by fire, let him be God.' And all the people answered and said: 'It is well spoken.' ¶ 25. And Elijah said unto the prophets of Baal: 'Choose you one bullock for yourselves, and dress it first; for ye are many; and call on the name of your god, but put no fire under.' 26. And they took the bullock which was given them, and they dressed it, and called on the name of Baal from morning even until noon, saying: 'O Baal, answer us.' But there was no voice, nor any that answered. And they danced in halting wise about the altar which was made. 27. And it came to pass at noon, that Elijah mocked them, and said: 'Cry aloud; for he is a god; either he is musing, or he is gone aside, or he is in a journey, or peradventure he sleepeth, and must be awaked.' 28. And they cried aloud, and cut themselves after their manner with swords and lances, till the blood gushed out upon them. 29. And it was so, when midday was past, that they prophesied until the time of the offering of the evening offering; but there was neither voice, nor any to answer, nor any that regarded. ¶ 30. And Elijah said unto all the people: 'Come near unto me'; and all the people came near unto him. And he repaired the altar of the LORD that was thrown down. 31. And Elijah took twelve stones, according to the number of the tribes of the sons of Jacob, unto whom the word of the LORD came, saying: 'Israel shall be thy name.' 32. And with the stones he built an altar in the name of the LORD; and he made a trench about the altar, as great as would contain two measures of seed. 33. And he put the wood in order, and cut the bullock in pieces, and laid it on the wood. 34. And he said: 'Fill four jars with water, and pour it on the burnt-offering, and on the wood.' And he said: 'Do it the second

**22.** *am left a prophet of the* LORD. The other Prophets of the LORD were either killed, or in hiding.

**26.** *danced in halting wise.* Performed uncouth religious dances about the altar, as was customary in their ceremonies.

**27.** *for he is a god.* Spoken mockingly.

**28.** *cut themselves.* To excite the pity of their gods. Elijah's taunts stir them to a condition of frenzy.

**29.** *prophesied.* The word is used here in its original sense; meaning, they worked themselves into a frenzy by ecstatic cries and convulsive contortions.

**30.** *the altar.* It was the site of an altar in the days of Saul (Rashi).

**31.** *twelve stones.* Although the ten tribes of the kingdom of Israel had broken away from Judah, in the eyes of the Prophets the nation was an undivided unity.

**32.** *he built an altar.* To build an altar and offer sacrifices outside the Temple Mount, after the central Sanctuary at Jerusalem had been erected, was an action contrary to the Torah; but was permitted as an exceptional measure to meet an exceptional situation—*horaath shaah*.

# I KINGS XVIII, 35

מלכים א יח

time'; and they did it the second time. And he said: 'Do it the third time'; and they did it the third time. 35. And the water ran round about the altar; and he filled the trench also with water. 36. And it came to pass at the time of the offering of the evening offering, that Elijah the prophet came near, and said: 'O LORD, the God of Abraham, of Isaac, and of Israel, let it be known this day that Thou art God in Israel, and that I am Thy servant, and that I have done all these things at Thy word. 37. Hear me, O LORD, hear me, that this people may know that Thou, LORD, art God, for Thou didst turn their heart backward.' 38. Then the fire of the LORD fell, and consumed the burnt-offering, and the wood, and the stones, and the dust, and licked up the water that was in the trench. 39. And when all the people saw it, they fell on their faces; and they said: 'The LORD, He is God; the LORD, He is God.'

הָעֹלָה וְעַל־הָעֵצִים וַיֹּאמֶר שְׁנוּ וַיִּשְׁנוּ וַיֹּאמֶר שַׁלֵּשׁוּ
וַיְשַׁלֵּשׁוּ: וַיֵּלְכוּ הַמַּיִם סָבִיב לַמִּזְבֵּחַ וְגַם אֶת־הַתְּעָלָה
מִלֵּא־מָיִם: וַיְהִי ׀ בַּעֲלוֹת הַמִּנְחָה וַיִּגַּשׁ אֵלִיָּהוּ הַנָּבִיא
וַיֹּאמַר יְהֹוָה אֱלֹהֵי אַבְרָהָם יִצְחָק וְיִשְׂרָאֵל הַיּוֹם יִוָּדַע כִּי־
אַתָּה אֱלֹהִים בְּיִשְׂרָאֵל וַאֲנִי עַבְדֶּךָ וּבִדְבָרְךָ עָשִׂיתִי אֵת
כָּל־הַדְּבָרִים הָאֵלֶּה: עֲנֵנִי יְהֹוָה עֲנֵנִי וְיֵדְעוּ הָעָם הַזֶּה
כִּי־אַתָּה יְהֹוָה הָאֱלֹהִים וְאַתָּה הֲסִבֹּתָ אֶת־לִבָּם אֲחֹרַנִּית:
וַתִּפֹּל אֵשׁ־יְהֹוָה וַתֹּאכַל אֶת־הָעֹלָה וְאֶת־הָעֵצִים וְאֶת־
הָאֲבָנִים וְאֶת־הֶעָפָר וְאֶת־הַמַּיִם אֲשֶׁר־בַּתְּעָלָה לִחֵכָה:
וַיַּרְא כָּל־הָעָם וַיִּפְּלוּ עַל־פְּנֵיהֶם וַיֹּאמְרוּ יְהֹוָה הוּא
הָאֱלֹהִים יְהֹוָה הוּא הָאֱלֹהִים:

לה

36

37

38

39

v. 36. נ״א לישראל ibid. יתיר י'

**36.** *let it be known . . . at Thy word.* That all Elijah's actions, even his prophecy of drought, were in accordance with the will of God. His prayer is that the people shall recognize this, and be brought back to faith in God alone.

**39.** *the LORD, He is God.* Not Baal, or any other. These words form the conclusion of the Day of Atonement Service, and are the last words uttered by the dying Israelite.

The contest on Mt. Carmel is typical of every conflict in which opposite principles of conduct with vital consequences to the individual or the nation stand face to face; in which conflict prompt decision is both urgent and, as in the days of Elijah, can alone ensure the victory of Right (Dummelow).

## EXODUS XXXV, 1

### CHAPTER XXXV

1. And Moses assembled all the congregation of the children of Isreal, and said unto them: 'These are the words which the LORD hath commanded, that ye should do them. 2. Six days shall work be done, but on the seventh day there shall be to you a holy day, a sabbath of solemn rest to the LORD; whosoever doeth any work therein shall be put to death. 3. Ye shall kindle no fire throughout your habitations upon the sabbath day.' ¶ 4. And Moses spoke unto all the congregation of the children of Israel saying: 'This is the thing which the LORD commanded, saying: 5. Take ye from among you an offering unto the LORD, whosoever is of a willing heart, let him bring it, the LORD's offering: gold, and silver, and brass; 6. and blue, and purple, and scarlet, and fine linen, and goats' hair; 7. and rams' skins dyed red, and sealskins, and acacia-wood; 8. and oil for the light, and spices for the anointing oil, and for the sweet incense; 9. and onyx stones, and stones to be set, for the ephod, and for the breast-plate. 10. And let every wise-hearted man among you come, and make all that the LORD hath commanded: 11. the tabernacle, its tent, and its covering, its clasps, and its boards, its bars, its pillars, and its sockets; 12. the ark, and the staves thereof, the ark-cover, and the veil of the screen; 13. the

---

# X. VAYYAKHEL

### (CHAPTERS XXXV–XXXVIII, 20)

### CHAPTER XXXV

We now enter upon the final section of the Book of Exodus, dealing with the actual construction of the Sanctuary. Instead of giving a brief notice announcing the execution of the Divine command, Scripture describes in detail how every instruction was faithfully and lovingly carried out.

**1.** *assembled.* The Rabbis, assuming that Moses would lose no time in starting upon the work, declare that the assembly occurred on the 11th of Tishri, immediately after his descent from Sinai on the day which was to become the Day of Atonement (see on XXXIV, 4).

*all the congregation.* The Sanctuary was the concern of every individual in Israel.

### 2, 3. THE SABBATH

**2.** *a holy day.* lit. 'holiness.' The exhortation which God had given to Moses concerning the holiness of the Sabbath, which must not be violated even for the sacred purpose of building the Tabernacle (XXXI, 13 f), is repeated by Moses to the Congregation.

**3.** *kindle no fire.* This command has been understood by certain Jewish sects to prohibit even the *enjoyment* of light or fire on the Sabbath; the Rabbis, however, apply it only to cooking and baking. In connection with the Manna, it had already been pointed out that there must be no preparation of food by fire on the Sabbath (XVI, 23).

*your habitations.* This excludes the Sanctuary. Lamps and the fire on the altar were there attended to on the Sabbath.

*upon the sabbath day.* On Festivals (barring the Day of Atonement, which is the 'Sabbath of Sabbaths') kindling of fire is permitted.

**4.** *commanded, saying.* 'Saying' is not here the equivalent of 'namely', but of 'to say'; *i.e.* that I should say to you.

**5.** *from among you.* Better, *from you.*
*brass.* Better, *bronze.*

**6–9.** Corresponding to XXV, 4–7.

**10.** *wise-hearted.* See on XXVIII, 3.

**11.** *tabernacle.* See on XXVI, 1.
*covering.* See XXVI, 14.

EXODUS XXXV, 14

table, and its staves, and all its vessels, and the showbread; 14. the candlestick also for the light, and its vessels, and its lamps, and the oil for the light; 15. and the altar of incense, and its staves, and the anointing oil, and the sweet incense, and the screen for the door, at the door of the tabernacle; 16. The altar of burnt-offering, with its grating of brass, its staves, and all its vessels, the laver and its base; 17. the hangings of the court, the pillars thereof, and their sockets, and the screen for the gate of the court; 18. the pins of the tabernacle, and the pins of the court, and their cords; 19. the plaited garments, for ministering in the holy place, the holy garments for Aaron the priest, and the garments of his sons, to minister in the priest's office.' ¶ 20. And all the congregation of the children of Israel departed from the presence of Moses.\*ⁱⁱ· 21. And they came, every one whose heart stirred him up, and every one whom his spirit made willing, and brought the LORD'S offering, for the work of the tent of meeting, and for all the service thereof, and for the holy garments. 22. And they came, both men and women, as many as were willing-hearted, and brought nose-rings, and ear-rings, and signet-rings, and girdles, all jewels of gold; even every man that brought an offering of gold unto the LORD. 23. And every man, with whom was found blue, and purple, and scarlet, and fine linen, and goats' hair, and rams' skins dyed red, and sealskins, brought them. 24. Every one that did set apart an offering of silver and brass brought the LORD'S offering; and every man, with whom was found acacia-wood for any work of the service, brought it. 25. And all the women that were wise-hearted did spin with their hands, and brought that which they had spun, the blue,

**12.** ark. See xxv, 10–22.
veil of the screen. In front of the Holy of Holies (xxvi, 31).

**13.** table. See xxv, 23.
showbread. See xxv, 30.

**14.** candlestick. See xxv, 31.
oil. See xxvii, 20.

**15.** altar of incense. See xxx, 1.
anointing oil. See xxx, 23 f.
sweet incense. See xxx, 34 f.
screen. See xxvi, 36.

**16.** altar of burnt-offering. See xxvii, 1.
the laver. See xxx, 18.

**17.** hangings. See xxvii, 9.
screen for the gate. See xxvii, 16.

**18.** pins. See xxvii, 19.

cords. These were not specified in the earlier chapters, but the mention of 'pins' presupposes the use of cords to which they were fastened.

**19.** plaited garments. See xxxi, 10.
holy garments. See chap. xxviii.

20–29. THE RESPONSE OF THE PEOPLE

**20.** all the congregation. All were ready and eager to share in the erection of the Sanctuary.

**21.** whom his spirit made willing. Cf. xxv, 2. Moses depended upon the enthusiasm of the people for freewill offerings; he had no need to resort to a levy.

**22.** women. Although nothing was asked of them, they freely contributed their ornaments.
ear-rings. Or, 'bracelets' (Rashi).
girdles. The Heb. kumaz occurs again only in Num. xxxi, 50.

# EXODUS XXXV, 26

and the purple, the scarlet, and the fine linen. 26. And all the women whose heart stirred them up in wisdom spun the goats' hair. 27. And the rulers brought the onyx stones, and the stones to be set, for the ephod, and for the breastplate; 28. and the spice, and the oil, for the light, and for the anointing oil, and for the sweet incense. 29. The children of Israel brought a freewill-offering unto the LORD; every man and woman, whose heart made them willing to bring for all the work, which the LORD had commanded by the hand of Moses to be made.*¹¹¹(**¹¹). ¶ 30. And Moses said unto the children of Israel: 'See, the LORD hath called by name Bezalel the son of Uri, the son of Hur, of the tribe of Judah. 31. And He hath filled him with the spirit of God, in wisdom, in understanding, and in knowledge, and in all manner of workmanship. 32. And to devise skilful works, to work in gold, and in silver, and in brass, 33. and in cutting of stones for setting, and in carving of wood, to work in all manner of skilful workmanship. 34. And He hath put in his heart that he may teach, both he, and Oholiab, the son of Ahisamach, of the tribe of Dan. 35. Them hath He filled with

---

**27.** *rulers.* The leading men of the tribes.

### 30–XXXVI, 2

The appointment of the artificers of the Sanctuary. These sections are almost identical with XXXI, 1–6.

**30.** *the LORD hath called by name.* The artist is 'called'; *i.e.* specially endowed by native gift for his task; predestined, in a sense, for his artistic mission. The Rabbis explain the opening words, 'See, the LORD hath called, etc.' to mean that the nomination of Bezalel for his important task should be ratified by the community, as no leader may be set over a congregation without its approval.

*Hur.* The Rabbis identified him with the Hur of XVII, 10, XXIV, 14; and held that he was killed by the people for resisting their demand for the golden calf.

**31.** *the spirit of God.* Is regarded in Scripture as the source of any exceptional gift, power or activity of men; *e.g.*, Gen. XLI, 38, of administrative ability, and here of Bezalel's artistic capacity.

*in wisdom . . . understanding . . . knowledge.* *i.e.* displaying itself in artistic skill, whether that skill be the result of imitation, or the artist's own initiative and inspiration.

**32.** *to devise skilful works.* lit. 'to think

thoughts.' In all true art, there is a vital underlying *thought*, and artists have accordingly been among the great thinkers of mankind. An eminent painter of the nineteenth century has well expressed it: 'My intention has not been so much to paint pictures that will charm the eye as to suggest great thoughts that will appeal to the imagination and the heart, and kindle all that is best and noblest in humanity. I even think that, in the future, art may yet speak, as great poetry itself, with the solemn and majestic ring in which the Hebrew prophets spoke to the Jews of old, demanding noble aspirations, condemning in the most trenchant manner private vices, and warning us in deep tones against lapses from morals and duties' (F. W. Watts).

**33.** *skilful workmanship.* We are accustomed to limit Divine inspiration to thoughts expressed in words. This is not the Scriptural view. The worker in metals, the cutter of precious stones, and the carver of wood can likewise produce work that is inspired.

**34.** *that he may teach.* *i.e.* direct and train others. The true artist possesses the power to inspire others. A light that cannot kindle other lights is but a feeble flame. But להורת, 'to teach' has also a wider meaning. The core of art is its teaching and ennobling influence not only on other artists, but on humanity.

# EXODUS XXXVI, 1

wisdom of heart, to work all manner of workmanship, of the craftsman, and of the skilful workman, and of the weaver in colours, in blue, and in purple, in scarlet and in fine linen, and of the weaver, even of them that do any workmanship, and of those that devise skilful works.

## CHAPTER XXXVI

1. And Bezalel and Oholiab shall work, and every wise-hearted man, in whom the LORD hath put wisdom and understanding to know how to work all the work for the service of the sanctuary, according to all that the LORD hath commanded.' ¶ 2. And Moses called Bezalel and Oholiab, and every wise-hearted man, in whose heart the LORD had put wisdom, even every one whose heart stirred him up to come unto the work to do it. 3. And they received of Moses all the offering, which the children of Israel had brought for the work of the service of the sanctuary, wherewith to make it. And they brought yet unto him freewill-offerings every morning. 4. And

---

*tribe of Dan.* Bezalel belonged to Judah, the leading tribe: Oholiab, to one of the smaller tribes. The selection, declares the Midrash, was significant. In the service of God, the great and the small should be united.

Proper understanding and appreciation of these verses should modify current views on Judaism and its relation to Art. The opinion is often expressed that there is no art in Judaism; that the Jew lacks the æsthetic sense; and that this is largely due to the influence of the Second Commandment, which prohibited plastic art in Israel. Defenders of the Jew and Judaism usually reply that Judaism was determined to lift the God-idea above the sensual, and to represent the Divine as spirit only; that Art was not Israel's predestined province; that whereas the legacy of Greece was Beauty, the mission of Israel was Righteousness. Neither friend nor foe do full justice to the facts of the case. There is not such a clear-cut difference between the races as is generally assumed. Greek Art itself is now seen to be of Semitic origin; and Semites have produced many a monument of surpassing beauty in the world of Art. And is not poetry, too, a province of Art? Surely, the Books of Psalms, Isaiah and Job need fear no comparison with any literary product of man. And the above applies not merely to the Bible age. The Rabbis, too, had a passionate love of beauty. They prescribed a special Benediction at the sight of a beautiful tree or animal, as well as on beholding the first blossoms of spring (Authorized Prayer Book, p. 291). Some of them conceived the whole of Creation as a process of unfolding beauty; and spoke of God as the Incomparable Artist (אין צור כאלהינו—אין צייר כאלהינו). The highest artist, in the eyes of Jewish teachers of all generations, is not the greatest master in self-expression, but in self-control; he who fashions *himself* into a sanctuary. Such a view sounds strange in modern ears. One of the saddest phenomena of the age is the misuse of Art for the perversion of Youth. Art is a divine gift, and must be divinely used. 'When the Hebrew spirit prevails over the Greek, he strips it of its pagan sensuality, so that its beauty stands revealed untarnished by barbaric or ungodly association' (Solomon J. Solomon).

### CHAPTER XXXVI

**1.** *hath put wisdom.* 'God gives wisdom to him only who possesses wisdom,' is a paradoxical saying of the Rabbis. They were already wise-hearted; *i.e.* possessed of the necessary artistic aptitude, and God further endowed them with the requisite skill.

*the service. i.e.* the construction.

*according to all.* Better, '*with respect to all.*'

**2.** *to come unto.* lit. 'to draw near unto,' in order to participate in the construction.

#### 3–7. THE PEOPLE'S LIBERALITY

**3.** *of Moses.* lit. 'from before Moses.' The donations of the people are represented as lying in a heap before Moses, and the artificers took what they required.

**4.** *which they wrought.* More accurately, 'which they were doing.'

# EXODUS XXXVI, 5

all the wise men, that wrought all the work of the sanctuary, came every man from his work which they wrought. 5. And they spoke unto Moses, saying: 'The people bring much more than enough for the service of the work, which the LORD commanded to make.' 6. And Moses gave commandment, and they caused it to be proclaimed throughout the camp, saying: 'Let neither man nor woman make any more work for the offering of the sanctuary.' So the people were restrained from bringing. 7. For the stuff they had was sufficient for all the work to make it, and too much.\*iv.
¶ 8. And every wise-hearted man among them that wrought the work made the tabernacle with ten curtains: of fine twined linen, and blue, and purple, and scarlet, with cherubim the work of the skilful workman made he them. 9. The length of each curtain was eight and twenty cubits, and the breadth of each curtain four cubits; all the curtains had one measure. 10. And he coupled five curtains one to another; and the other five curtains he coupled one to another. 11. And he made loops of blue upon the edge of the one curtain that was outmost in the first set; likewise he made in the edge of the curtain that was outmost in the second set. 12. Fifty loops made he in the one curtain, and fifty loops made he in the edge of the curtain that was in the second set; the loops were opposite one to another. 13. And he made fifty clasps of gold, and coupled the curtains one to another with the clasps; so the tabernacle was one. ¶ 14. And he made curtains of goats' hair for a tent over the tabernacle; eleven curtains he made them. 15. The length of each curtain was thirty cubits, and four cubits the breadth of each curtain, the eleven curtains had one measure. 16. And he coupled five curtains by themselves, and six curtains by themselves. 17. And he made fifty loops on the edge of the curtain that was outmost in the first set, and fifty loops made he upon the edge of the curtain which was outmost in the second set. 18. And he made fifty clasps of brass to couple the tent together, that it might be one. 19. And he made a covering for the tent of rams' skins dyed red, and a covering of sealskins above.\*v. ¶ 20. And he made the boards for the tabernacle of acacia-wood, standing up. 21. Ten cubits was the length of a board, and a cubit and a half the breadth of each board. 22. Each board had two tenons, joined one to another. Thus did he make for all the

---

**7.** *sufficient . . . and too much.* Young and old, noble and commoner, were all aglow with holy enthusiasm, and cheerfully consecrated their diversity of gifts to the Sanctuary.

שמות ויקהל לו

ה אִישׁ מִמְּלַאכְתּוֹ אֲשֶׁר־הֵמָּה עֹשִׂים: וַיֹּאמְרוּ אֶל־מֹשֶׁה
לֵּאמֹר מַרְבִּים הָעָם לְהָבִיא מִדֵּי הָעֲבֹדָה לַמְּלָאכָה אֲשֶׁר־
6 צִוָּה יְהוָה לַעֲשֹׂת אֹתָהּ: וַיְצַו מֹשֶׁה וַיַּעֲבִירוּ קוֹל בַּמַּחֲנֶה
לֵאמֹר אִישׁ וְאִשָּׁה אַל־יַעֲשׂוּ־עוֹד מְלָאכָה לִתְרוּמַת הַקֹּדֶשׁ
7 וַיִּכָּלֵא הָעָם מֵהָבִיא: וְהַמְּלָאכָה הָיְתָה דַיָּם לְכָל־הַמְּלָאכָה
רביעי
8 לַעֲשׂוֹת אֹתָהּ וְהוֹתֵר: ס וַיַּעֲשׂוּ כָל־חֲכַם־לֵב בְּעֹשֵׂי
הַמְּלָאכָה אֶת־הַמִּשְׁכָּן עֶשֶׂר יְרִיעֹת שֵׁשׁ מָשְׁזָר וּתְכֵלֶת
וְאַרְגָּמָן וְתוֹלַעַת שָׁנִי כְּרֻבִים מַעֲשֵׂה חֹשֵׁב עָשָׂה אֹתָם:
9 אֹרֶךְ הַיְרִיעָה הָאַחַת שְׁמֹנֶה וְעֶשְׂרִים בָּאַמָּה וְרֹחַב אַרְבַּע
י בָּאַמָּה הַיְרִיעָה הָאֶחָת מִדָּה אַחַת לְכָל־הַיְרִיעֹת: וַיְחַבֵּר
אֶת־חֲמֵשׁ הַיְרִיעֹת אַחַת אֶל־אֶחָת וְחָמֵשׁ יְרִיעֹת חִבַּר אַחַת
11 אֶל־אֶחָת: וַיַּעַשׂ לֻלְאֹת תְּכֵלֶת עַל שְׂפַת הַיְרִיעָה הָאֶחָת
מִקָּצָה בַּמַּחְבָּרֶת כֵּן עָשָׂה בִּשְׂפַת הַיְרִיעָה הַקִּיצוֹנָה
12 בַּמַּחְבֶּרֶת הַשֵּׁנִית: חֲמִשִּׁים לֻלָאֹת עָשָׂה בַּיְרִיעָה הָאֶחָת
וַחֲמִשִּׁים לֻלָאֹת עָשָׂה בִּקְצֵה הַיְרִיעָה אֲשֶׁר בַּמַּחְבֶּרֶת
13 הַשֵּׁנִית מַקְבִּילֹת הַלֻּלָאֹת אַחַת אֶל־אֶחָת: וַיַּעַשׂ חֲמִשִּׁים
קַרְסֵי זָהָב וַיְחַבֵּר אֶת־הַיְרִיעֹת אַחַת אֶל־אַחַת בַּקְּרָסִים
וַיְהִי הַמִּשְׁכָּן אֶחָד: פ
14 וַיַּעַשׂ יְרִיעֹת עִזִּים לְאֹהֶל עַל־הַמִּשְׁכָּן עַשְׁתֵּי־עֶשְׂרֵה יְרִיעֹת
טו עָשָׂה אֹתָם: אֹרֶךְ הַיְרִיעָה הָאַחַת שְׁלֹשִׁים בָּאַמָּה וְאַרְבַּע
אַמּוֹת רֹחַב הַיְרִיעָה הָאֶחָת מִדָּה אַחַת לְעַשְׁתֵּי עֶשְׂרֵה
16 יְרִיעֹת: וַיְחַבֵּר אֶת־חֲמֵשׁ הַיְרִיעֹת לְבָד וְאֶת־שֵׁשׁ הַיְרִיעֹת
17 לְבָד: וַיַּעַשׂ לֻלָאֹת חֲמִשִּׁים עַל שְׂפַת הַיְרִיעָה הַקִּיצֹנָה
בַּמַּחְבָּרֶת וַחֲמִשִּׁים לֻלָאֹת עָשָׂה עַל־שְׂפַת הַיְרִיעָה הַחֹבֶרֶת
18 הַשֵּׁנִית: וַיַּעַשׂ קַרְסֵי נְחֹשֶׁת חֲמִשִּׁים לְחַבֵּר אֶת־הָאֹהֶל
19 לִהְיֹת אֶחָד: וַיַּעַשׂ מִכְסֶה לָאֹהֶל עֹרֹת אֵילִם מְאָדָּמִים
חמישי
כ וּמִכְסֵה עֹרֹת תְּחָשִׁים מִלְמָעְלָה: ס וַיַּעַשׂ אֶת־הַקְּרָשִׁים
21 לַמִּשְׁכָּן עֲצֵי שִׁטִּים עֹמְדִים: עֶשֶׂר אַמֹּת אֹרֶךְ הַקָּרֶשׁ
22 וְאַמָּה וַחֲצִי הָאַמָּה רֹחַב הַקֶּרֶשׁ הָאֶחָד: שְׁתֵּי יָדֹת לַקֶּרֶשׁ

---

v. 10. קמץ בז״ק

8–19. THE CURTAINS

Corresponding to XXVI, 1–11, 14.

## EXODUS XXXVI, 23     שמות ויקהל לו

boards of the tabernacle. 23. And he made the boards for the tabernacle; twenty boards for the south side southward. 24. And he made forty sockets of silver under the twenty boards; two sockets under one board for its two tenons, and two sockets under another board for its two tenons. 25. And for the second side of the tabernacle, on the north side, he made twenty boards, 26. and their forty sockets of silver: two sockets under one board, and two sockets under another board. 27. And for the hinder part of the tabernacle westward he made six boards. 28. And two boards made he for the corners of the tabernacle in the hinder part; 29. that they might be double beneath, and in like manner they should be complete unto the top thereof unto the first ring. Thus he did to both of them in the two corners. 30. And there were eight boards, and their sockets of silver, sixteen sockets: under every board two sockets. 31. And he made bars of acacia-wood: five for the boards of the one side of the tabernacle, 32. and five bars for the boards of the other side of the tabernacle, and five bars for the boards of the tabernacle for the hinder part westward. 33. And he made the middle bar to pass through in the midst of the boards from the one end to the other. 34. And he overlaid the boards with gold, and made their rings of gold for holders for the bars, and overlaid the bars with gold. ¶ 35. And he made the veil of blue, and purple, and scarlet, and fine twined linen; with cherubim the work of the skilful workman made he it. 36. And he made thereunto four pillars of acacia, and overlaid them with gold, their hooks being of gold; and he cast for them four sockets of silver. 37. And he made a screen for the door of the Tent, of blue, and purple, and scarlet, and fine twined linen, the work of the weaver in colours; 38. and the five pillars of it with their hooks; and he overlaid their capitals and their fillets with gold; and their five sockets were of brass.

---

20–34. THE WOODEN FRAMEWORK
Corresponding to XXVI, 15–29.

35–38. THE VEIL AND SCREEN
Corresponding to XXVI, 31 f, 36 f.

**38.** *their fillets.* Better, *their sockets.* In the parallel passage (XXVI, 37), it is, 'overlay them (*i.e.* the pillars) with gold.' In addition to the verbal instructions given on Sinai, Moses was granted a vision wherein he saw a pattern of what was required. Hence many of the directions are not given in full detail. We have, therefore, to assume that the word 'them' is used vaguely, and Moses understood that not the whole of the pillars, but only the tops, were to be overlaid with gold.

## EXODUS XXXVII, 1

### CHAPTER XXXVII

1 And Bezalel made the ark of acacia-wood: two cubits and a half was the length of it, and a cubit and a half the breadth of it, and a cubit and a half the height of it. 2. And he overlaid it with pure gold within and without, and made a crown of gold to it round about. 3. And he cast for it four rings of gold, in the four feet thereof: even two rings on the one side of it, and two rings on the other side of it. 4. And he made staves of acacia-wood, and overlaid them with gold. 5. And he put the staves into the rings on the sides of the ark, to bear the ark. 6. And he made an ark-cover of pure gold: two cubits and a half was the length thereof, and a cubit and a half the breadth thereof. 7. And he made two cherubim of gold: of beaten work made he them, at the two ends of the ark-cover: 8. one cherub at the one end, and one cherub at the other end; of one piece with the ark-cover made he the cherubim at the two ends thereof. 9. And the cherubim spread out their wings on high, screening the ark-cover with their wings, with their faces one to another; toward the ark-cover were the faces of the cherubim. ¶ 10. And he made the table of acacia-wood: two cubits was the length thereof, and a cubit the breadth thereof, and a cubit and a half the height thereof. 11. And he overlaid it with pure gold, and made thereto a crown of gold round about. 12. And he made unto it a border of a handbreadth round about, and made a golden crown to the border thereof round about. 13. And he cast for it four rings of gold, and put the rings in the four corners that were on the four feet thereof. 14. Close by the border were the rings, the holders for the staves to bear the table. 15. And he made the staves of acacia-wood, and overlaid them with gold, to bear the table. 16. And he made the vessels which were upon the table, the dishes thereof, and the pans thereof, and the bowls thereof, and the jars thereof, wherewith to pour out, of pure gold.*vi (**III). ¶ 17. And he made the candlestick of pure gold: of beaten work made he the candlestick, even its base, and its shaft; its cups, its knops, and its flowers, were of one piece with it. 18. And there were six branches going out of the sides thereof: three branches of the candlestick out of the one side thereof, and three branches of the

### CHAPTER XXXVII

**1–9. THE ARK**

Corresponding to xxv, 10–15, 18–20.

שמות ויקהל לז

## CAP. XXXVII. לז

א וַיַּעַשׂ בְּצַלְאֵל אֶת־הָאָרֹן עֲצֵי שִׁטִּים אַמָּתַיִם וָחֵצִי אָרְכּוֹ
2 וְאַמָּה וָחֵצִי רָחְבּוֹ וְאַמָּה וָחֵצִי קֹמָתוֹ: וַיְצַפֵּהוּ זָהָב טָהוֹר
3 מִבַּיִת וּמִחוּץ וַיַּעַשׂ לוֹ זֵר זָהָב סָבִיב: וַיִּצֹק לוֹ אַרְבַּע
טַבְּעֹת זָהָב עַל אַרְבַּע פַּעֲמֹתָיו וּשְׁתֵּי טַבָּעֹת עַל־צַלְעוֹ
4 הָאֶחָת וּשְׁתֵּי טַבָּעֹת עַל־צַלְעוֹ הַשֵּׁנִית: וַיַּעַשׂ בַּדֵּי עֲצֵי
ה שִׁטִּים וַיְצַף אֹתָם זָהָב: וַיָּבֵא אֶת־הַבַּדִּים בַּטַּבָּעֹת עַל
6 צַלְעֹת הָאָרֹן לָשֵׂאת אֶת־הָאָרֹן: וַיַּעַשׂ כַּפֹּרֶת זָהָב טָהוֹר
7 אַמָּתַיִם וָחֵצִי אָרְכָּהּ וְאַמָּה וָחֵצִי רָחְבָּהּ: וַיַּעַשׂ שְׁנֵי כְרֻבִים
8 זָהָב מִקְשָׁה עָשָׂה אֹתָם מִשְּׁנֵי קְצוֹת הַכַּפֹּרֶת: כְּרוּב־אֶחָד
מִקָּצָה מִזֶּה וּכְרוּב־אֶחָד מִקָּצָה מִזֶּה מִן־הַכַּפֹּרֶת עָשָׂה
9 אֶת־הַכְּרֻבִים מִשְּׁנֵי קצוותו: וַיִּהְיוּ הַכְּרֻבִים פֹּרְשֵׂי כְנָפַיִם
לְמַעְלָה סֹכְכִים בְּכַנְפֵיהֶם עַל־הַכַּפֹּרֶת וּפְנֵיהֶם אִישׁ אֶל־
אָחִיו אֶל־הַכַּפֹּרֶת הָיוּ פְּנֵי הַכְּרֻבִים: פ

י וַיַּעַשׂ אֶת־הַשֻּׁלְחָן עֲצֵי שִׁטִּים אַמָּתַיִם אָרְכּוֹ וְאַמָּה רָחְבּוֹ
11 וְאַמָּה וָחֵצִי קֹמָתוֹ: וַיְצַף אֹתוֹ זָהָב טָהוֹר וַיַּעַשׂ לוֹ זֵר זָהָב
12 סָבִיב: וַיַּעַשׂ לוֹ מִסְגֶּרֶת טֹפַח סָבִיב וַיַּעַשׂ זֵר־זָהָב
13 לְמִסְגַּרְתּוֹ סָבִיב: וַיִּצֹק לוֹ אַרְבַּע טַבְּעֹת זָהָב וַיִּתֵּן אֶת־
14 הַטַּבָּעֹת עַל אַרְבַּע הַפֵּאֹת אֲשֶׁר לְאַרְבַּע רַגְלָיו: לְעֻמַּת
הַמִּסְגֶּרֶת הָיוּ הַטַּבָּעֹת בָּתִּים לַבַּדִּים לָשֵׂאת אֶת־הַשֻּׁלְחָן:
טו וַיַּעַשׂ אֶת־הַבַּדִּים עֲצֵי שִׁטִּים וַיְצַף אֹתָם זָהָב לָשֵׂאת אֶת־
16 הַשֻּׁלְחָן: וַיַּעַשׂ אֶת־הַכֵּלִים ׀ אֲשֶׁר עַל־הַשֻּׁלְחָן אֶת־קְעָרֹתָיו
וְאֶת־כַּפֹּתָיו וְאֵת מְנַקִּיֹּתָיו וְאֶת־הַקְּשָׂוֹת אֲשֶׁר יֻסַּךְ בָּהֵן
זָהָב טָהוֹר: פ ששי (שלישי כשהן מחוב׳)

17 וַיַּעַשׂ אֶת־הַמְּנֹרָה זָהָב טָהוֹר מִקְשָׁה עָשָׂה אֶת־הַמְּנֹרָה
18 יְרֵכָהּ וְקָנָהּ גְּבִיעֶיהָ כַּפְתֹּרֶיהָ וּפְרָחֶיהָ מִמֶּנָּה הָיוּ: וְשִׁשָּׁה
קָנִים יֹצְאִים מִצִּדֶּיהָ שְׁלֹשָׁה ׀ קְנֵי מְנֹרָה מִצִּדָּהּ הָאֶחָד

v. 8. קצוותיו ק׳

**10–16. THE TABLE**

Corresponding to xxv, 23–29.

**17–24. THE CANDLESTICK**

Corresponding to xxv, 31–39.

379

## EXODUS XXXVII, 19

candlestick out of the other side thereof; 19. three cups made like almond-blossoms in one branch, a knop and a flower; and three cups made like almond-blossoms in the other branch, a knop and a flower. So for the six branches going out of the candlestick. 20. And in the candlestick were four cups made like almond-blossoms, the knops thereof, and the flowers thereof; 21. and a knop under two branches of one piece with it, and a knop under two branches of one piece with it, and a knop under two branches of one piece with it, for the six branches going out of it. 22. Their knops and their branches were of one piece with it; the whole of it was one beaten work of pure gold. 23. And he made the lamps thereof, seven, and the tongs thereof, and the snuffdishes thereof, of pure gold. 24. Of a talent of pure gold made he it, and all the vessels thereof. ¶ 25. And he made the altar of incense of acacia-wood: a cubit was the length thereof, and a cubit the breadth thereof, four-square; and two cubits was the height thereof; the horns thereof were of one piece with it. 26. And he overlaid it with pure gold, the top thereof, and the sides thereof round about, and the horns of it; and he made unto it a crown of gold round about. 27. And he made for it two golden rings under the crown thereof, upon the two ribs thereof, upon the two sides of it, for holders for staves wherewith to bear it. 28. And he made the staves of acacia-wood, and overlaid them with gold. 29. And he made the holy anointing oil, and the pure incense of sweet spices, after the art of the perfumer.* vii (** iv).

## 38 CHAPTER XXXVIII

1. And he made the altar of burnt-offering of acacia-wood: five cubits was the length thereof, and five cubits the breadth thereof, four-square, and three cubits the height thereof. 2. And he made the horns thereof upon the four corners of it; the horns thereof were of one piece with it; and he overlaid it with brass. 3. And he made all the vessels of the altar, the pots, and the shovels, and the basins, the flesh-hooks, and the fire-pans; all the vessels thereof made he of brass. 4. And he made for the altar a grating of network of brass, under the ledge round it beneath, reaching halfway up. 5. And he cast four rings for the four ends of the grating of brass, to be holders for the staves. 6. And he made the staves

25–27. THE ALTAR OF INCENSE AND ANOINTING OIL

Corresponding to xxx, 1–5.

CHAPTER XXXVIII

1–8. THE ALTAR OF BURNT-OFFERING AND LAVER

Corresponding to XXVII, 1–8, and xxx, 18–21.

EXODUS XXXVIII, 7

of acacia-wood, and overlaid them with brass. 7. And he put the staves into the rings on the sides of the altar, wherewith to bear it; he made it hollow with planks. ¶ 8. And he made the laver of brass, and the base thereof of brass, of the mirrors of the serving women that did service at the door of the tent of meeting. ¶ 9. And he made the court; for the south side southward the hangings of the court were of fine twined linen, a hundred cubits. 10. Their pillars were twenty, and their sockets twenty, of brass; the hooks of the pillars and their fillets were of silver. 11. And for the north side a hundred cubits, their pillars twenty, and their sockets twenty, of brass; the hooks of the pillars and their fillets of silver. 12. And for the west side were hangings of fifty cubits, their pillars ten, and their sockets ten; the hooks of the pillars and their fillets of silver. 13. And for the east side eastward fifty cubits. 14. The hangings for the one side [of the gate] were fifteen cubits; their pillars three, and their sockets three. 15. And so for the other side; on this hand and that hand by the gate of the court were hangings of fifteen cubits; their pillars three, and their sockets three. 16. All the hangings of the court round about were of fine twined linen. 17. And the sockets for the pillars were of brass; the hooks of the pillars and their fillets of silver; and the overlaying of their capitals of silver; and all the pillars of the court were filleted with silver.*ᵐ· 18. And the screen for the gate of the court was the work of the weaver in colours, of blue, and purple, and scarlet, and fine twined linen; and twenty cubits was the length, and the height in the breadth was five cubits, answerable to the hangings of the court. 19. And their pillars were four, and their sockets four, of brass; their hooks of silver, and the overlaying of their capitals and their fillets of silver. 20. And all the pins of the tabernacle, and of the court round about, were of brass.

---

**8.** *the mirrors.* These were made of burnished copper. According to a Rabbinic tradition, Moses at first wished to reject the offering of the mirrors because they ministered to feminine vanity; but God reminded him how the Israelite woman had shared the bitterness of her husband's bondage in Egypt and done her utmost to cheer him. Moses thereupon agreed to accept the mirrors, but utilized the metal for the laver, and not for the structure of the actual Tabernacle.

*did service.* Or, 'that come to pray' (Onkelos). A number of devout women, who yielded up their mirrors as a token of self-dedication to God, assembled at the entrance of the Tabernacle for prayer (Ibn Ezra).

*tent of meeting.* This may mean either the tent of Moses (xxxiii, 7) or the Sanctuary. If the latter, it is mentioned here by anticipation, since the Tent of Meeting had not yet been erected. They were the women who resolved to be in attendance there, and afterwards were.

9–20. THE COURT

Corresponding to xxvii, 9–19.

**18.** *answerable to.* i.e. *corresponding to.*

# HAFTORAH VAYYAKHEL (FOR ASHKENAZIM) הפטרת ויקהל לאשכנזים
# HAFTORAH PEKUDEY (FOR SEPHARDIM) הפטרת פקודי לספרדים
### I KINGS VII, 40–50

CAP. VII. ז

מ וַיַּ֣עַשׂ חִיר֔וֹם אֶת־הַכִּיֹּר֗וֹת
וְאֶת־הַיָּעִ֖ים וְאֶת־הַמִּזְרָק֑וֹת וַיְכַ֣ל חִיר֗וֹם לַעֲשׂוֹת֙ אֶת־כָּל־
41 הַמְּלָאכָ֔ה אֲשֶׁ֥ר עָשָׂ֛ה לַמֶּ֥לֶךְ שְׁלֹמֹ֖ה בֵּ֥ית יְהוָֽה׃ עַמֻּדִ֣ים
שְׁנַ֔יִם וְגֻלֹּ֧ת הַכֹּתָרֹ֛ת אֲשֶׁר־עַל־רֹ֥אשׁ הָעַמּוּדִ֖ים שְׁתָּ֑יִם
וְהַשְּׂבָכ֣וֹת שְׁתַּ֔יִם לְכַסּ֗וֹת אֶת־שְׁתֵּי֙ גֻּלֹּ֣ת הַכֹּתָרֹ֔ת אֲשֶׁ֖ר
42 עַל־רֹ֥אשׁ הָעַמּוּדִֽים׃ וְאֶת־הָרִמֹּנִ֛ים אַרְבַּ֥ע מֵא֖וֹת לִשְׁתֵּ֣י
הַשְּׂבָכ֑וֹת שְׁנֵֽי־טוּרִ֤ים רִמֹּנִים֙ לַשְּׂבָכָ֣ה הָֽאֶחָ֔ת לְכַסּ֗וֹת אֶת־
43 שְׁתֵּי֙ גֻּלֹּ֣ת הַכֹּֽתָרֹ֔ת אֲשֶׁ֖ר עַל־פְּנֵ֥י הָעַמּוּדִֽים׃ וְאֶת־הַמְּכֹנ֖וֹת
44 עָ֑שֶׂר וְאֶת־הַכִּיֹּרֹ֥ת עֲשָׂרָ֖ה עַל־הַמְּכֹנֽוֹת׃ וְאֶת־הַיָּ֥ם הָאֶחָ֖ד
מה וְאֶת־הַבָּקָ֥ר שְׁנֵים־עָשָׂ֖ר תַּ֥חַת הַיָּֽם׃ וְאֶת־הַסִּיר֨וֹת וְאֶת־
הַיָּעִ֜ים וְאֶת־הַמִּזְרָק֗וֹת וְאֵת֙ כָּל־הַכֵּלִ֣ים הָאֵ֔הֶל אֲשֶׁ֥ר עָשָׂ֛ה
46 חִירָ֥ם לַמֶּ֖לֶךְ שְׁלֹמֹ֑ה בֵּ֣ית יְהוָ֑ה נְחֹ֖שֶׁת מְמֹרָֽט׃ בְּכִכַּ֣ר
הַיַּרְדֵּ֗ן יְצָקָ֣ם הַמֶּ֔לֶךְ בְּמַעֲבֵ֖ה הָאֲדָמָ֑ה בֵּ֥ין סֻכּ֖וֹת וּבֵ֥ין
47 צָרְתָֽן׃ וַיַּנַּ֤ח שְׁלֹמֹה֙ אֶת־כָּל־הַכֵּלִ֔ים מֵרֹ֥ב מְאֹ֖ד מְאֹ֑ד לֹ֥א
48 נֶחְקַ֖ר מִשְׁקַ֥ל הַנְּחֹֽשֶׁת׃ וַיַּ֣עַשׂ שְׁלֹמֹ֔ה אֵ֥ת כָּל־הַכֵּלִ֔ים
אֲשֶׁ֖ר בֵּ֣ית יְהוָ֑ה אֵ֚ת מִזְבַּ֣ח הַזָּהָ֔ב וְאֶת־הַשֻּׁלְחָ֗ן אֲשֶׁ֥ר עָלָ֛יו
49 לֶ֥חֶם הַפָּנִ֖ים זָהָֽב׃ וְאֶת־הַמְּנֹר֗וֹת חָמֵ֤שׁ מִיָּמִין֙ וְחָמֵ֣שׁ מִשְּׂמֹ֔אל

v. 45. האלה קרי

---

## CHAPTER VII

40. And [1]Hiram made the pots, and the shovels, and the basins. ¶So Hiram made an end of doing all the work that he wrought for king Solomon in the house of the LORD: 41. the two pillars, and the two bowls of the capitals that were on the top of the pillars; and the two networks to cover the two bowls of the capitals that were on the top of the pillars; 42. and the four hundred pomegranates for the two networks, two rows of pomegranates for each network, to cover the two bowls of the capitals that were upon the top of the pillars; 43. and the ten bases, and the ten lavers on the bases; 44. and the one sea, and the twelve oxen under the sea. 45. and the pots, and the shovels, and the basins; even all these vessels, which Hiram made for king Solomon, in the house of the LORD, were of burnished brass. 46. In the plain of the Jordan did the king cast them, in the clay ground between Succoth and Zarethan. 47. And Solomon left all the vessels unweighed, because they were exceeding many; the weight of the brass could not be found out. 48. And Solomon made all the vessels that were in the house of the LORD: the golden altar, and the table whereupon the showbread was, of gold; 49. and the candlesticks, five on the right side, and five on the left, be-

[1] Heb. *Hirom*.

---

With the same care as in the Sedrah, we have in the Haftorah a description of the appurtenances for the Temple.

**40.** *Hiram*. A famous brass-worker, the son of a Tyrian father, who was also a skilled artist, and an Israelitish mother; see note on *v.* 14, p. 383.

**44.** *and the one sea*. An enormous circular vessel ten cubits (about 18 feet) in diameter and five cubits (about 9 feet) in depth. It was richly decorated, and was supported on the backs of twelve brazen oxen, three looking towards each of the cardinal points of the compass. See *v.* 23–26 of this chapter, p. 384.

**45.** *in the house of the* LORD. For use in the house of the LORD.

**46.** *between Succoth and Zarethan*. Succoth was on the other, the east side of the river, in Gad. Zarethan was on the west side of Jordan, about 24 miles north of the Dead Sea.

**47.** The amount of brass used was so great that no attempt was made to keep an account of it.

**48.** *the golden altar*. The altar of incense.

**49.** *the flowers*. The flower-like ornaments of the candlesticks.

To appreciate the significance of the Temple in the life of ancient Israel, we must continue reading the next chapter of the First Book of Kings, Solomon's Prayer of Dedication (set aside as the Haftorah for the first and eighth days of Tabernacles).

The Temple was the forum, the fortress, the 'university', as well as the Central Sanctuary, of Israel. The People *loved* it; the pomp and ceremony, the music and song of the Levites, the ministrations of the priests, the high priest as he stood and blessed the prostrate worshippers amid

# I KINGS VII, 50

fore the Sanctuary, of pure gold; and the flowers, and the lamps, and the tongs, of gold; 50. and the cups, and the snuffers, and the basins, and the pans, and the firepans, of pure gold; and the hinges, both for the doors of the inner house, the most holy place, and for the doors of the house, that is, of the temple, of gold.

---

profound silence on the Atonement Day. As for the choicer spirits, their passionate devotion found expression in words like those of the Psalmist (Ps. LXXXIV, 2–5):

'How lovely are Thy tabernacles,
    O LORD of Hosts!
'My soul yearneth, yea, even pineth for the
    courts of the LORD . . . .
'Happy are they that dwell in Thy house.'

The destruction of the Sanctuary could not drown Israel's undying love of its 'House of Holiness'. Throughout the ages down to this day, the sole relic of its ancient glory—the so-called Wailing Wall—has remained for millions of Jews the most sacred memento of their national sanctities, a 'Holy Place' from which the Shechinah has never departed.

---

## HAFTORAH VAYYAKHEL (FOR SEPHARDIM)

### I KINGS VII, 13–26

#### CHAPTER VII

13. And king Solomon sent and fetched Hiram out of Tyre. 14. He was the son of a widow of the tribe of Naphtali, and his father was a man of Tyre, a worker in brass; and he was filled with wisdom and understanding and skill, to work all works in brass. And he came to king Solomon, and wrought all his work. ¶ 15. Thus he fashioned the two pillars of brass, of eighteen cubits high each; and a line of twelve cubits did compass it about; [and so] the other pillar. 16. And he made two capitals of molten brass, to set upon the tops of the pillars; the height of the one capital was five cubits, and the height of the

---

The Sedrah continues the description of the skilled work lavished on the Tabernacle. Corresponding to this, the Haftorah describes the artistry of Hiram of Tyre on the pillars and the brass ornamental work in King Solomon's Temple.

**13.** *Solomon sent.* To the King of Tyre, for permission for his famous artist in brass and precious metals to assist in the work for the Temple.

**14.** *of Naphtali.* In II Chron. II, 13, his mother is called a daughter of Dan; and according to Jewish tradition, the father and not the mother (as might appear from the text) was of the tribe of Naphtali.

*his father was a man of Tyre.* i.e. he had settled in Tyre, though born in Israel.

**15.** *he fashioned.* i.e. he cast. Moulds were made in the earth, and the molten brass was poured into them.

*a line of twelve cubits.* i.e. they were 12 cubits (about 20 feet) in circumference. According to Jer. LII, 21, the pillars were hollow.

**16.** *capitals.* The upper parts of the columns. They were spherical in shape (v. 42).

# I KINGS VII, 17

other capital was five cubits. 17. He also made nets of checker-work, and wreaths of chain-work, for the capitals which were upon the top of the pillars: seven for the one capital, and seven for the other capital. 18. And he made the pillars; and there were two rows round about upon the one network, to cover the capitals that were upon the top of the pomegranates; and so did he for the other capital. 19. And the capitals that were upon the top of the pillars in the porch were of lily-work, four cubits. 20. And there were capitals above also upon the two pillars, close by the belly which was beside the network; and the pomegranates were two hundred, in rows round about upon each capital. 21. And he set up the pillars at the porch of the temple; and he set up the right pillar, and called the name thereof Jachin; and he set up the left pillar, and called the name thereof Boaz. 22. And upon the top of the pillars was lily-work; so was the work of the pillars finished. ¶23. And he made the molten sea of ten cubits from brim to brim, round the compass, and the height thereof was five cubits; and a line of thirty cubits did compass it round about. 24. And under the brim of it round about there were knops which did compass it, for ten cubits, compassing the sea round about; the knops were in two rows, cast when it was cast. 25. It stood upon twelve oxen, three looking toward the north, and three looking toward the west, and three looking toward the south, and three looking toward the east; and the sea was set upon them above, and all the hinder parts were inward. 26. And it was a handbreadth thick; and the brim thereof was wrought like the brim of a cup, like the flower of a lily; it held two thousand baths.

**17.** *nets . . . chain work.* The capitals were decorated with tracery.

**18.** *two rows.* Of pomegranates hung in festoons.

*to cover the capitals.* Referring to the network, which fitted closely to, and covered, the capitals.

**19.** *lily work.* The rim curving outwards. The capitals rested on a border of lily work on top of the pillars (see *v.* 22).

**21.** *the pillars.* They stood in the porchway, not supporting but clear of it. Detached pillars of this kind were a feature of temples in the East.

*Jachin.* That is, 'He shall establish,' *i.e.* the Temple, for ever.

*Boaz.* A union of two words: *bo* and *oz*; that is, 'In it is strength.' Through the services of the Temple, strength should come to Israel (Rashi).

**23.** *molten sea.* See on *v.* 44, p. 382.

*a line of thirty cubits.* Its circumference, about 52 feet.

**24.** *knops.* Egg-shaped (Targum); probably gourds which adorned the circumference of the bowl.

*ten cubits.* Ten in a cubit (Ralbag).

*cast when it was cast.* In the same mould as the basin.

**26.** *a handbreadth thick. i.e.* the casting, about 3 inches.

*two thousand baths.* A 'bath' was about 8 gallons.

## EXODUS XXXVIII, 21

**38** 21. These are the accounts of the tabernacle, even the tabernacle of the testimony, as they were rendered according to the commandment of Moses, through the service of the Levites, by the hand of Ithamar, the son of Aaron the priest.—22. And Bezalel the son of Uri, the son of Hur, of the tribe of Judah, made all that the LORD commanded Moses. 23. And with him was Oholiab, the son of Ahisamach, of the tribe of Dan, a craftsman, and a skilful workman, and a weaver in colours, in blue, and in purple, and in scarlet, and fine linen.—24. All the gold that was used for the work in all the work of the sanctuary, even the gold of the offering, was twenty and nine talents, and seven hundred and thirty shekels, after the shekel of the sanctuary. 25. And the silver of them that were numbered of the congregation was a hundred talents, and a thousand seven hundred and three-score and fifteen shekels, after the shekel of the sanctuary; 26. a beka a head, that is, half a shekel, after the shekel of the sanctuary, for every one that passed over to them that are numbered, from twenty years old and upward, for six hundred thousand and three thousand and five hundred and fifty men. 27. And the hundred talents of silver were for casting the sockets of the sanctuary, and the sockets of the veil: a hundred sockets for the hundred talents, a talent for a socket. 28. And of the thousand seven hundred seventy and five shekels he made hooks for the pillars, and overlaid their

---

## XI. PEKUDEY

(CHAPTERS XXXVIII, 21–XL)

With minute care these chapters of Exodus describe the concluding stages of the construction of the Sanctuary. *v.* 21–31 of this chapter give the total amount of the precious metals used.

**21.** *tabernacle of the testimony*. So called because of the Tables of the Decalogue that were deposited there; cf. XXV, 16.

*through the service of the Levites.* Or, 'being the work of the Levites, under the hand, etc.'

*Ithamar.* The superintendent of the Tabernacle (Num. IV, 28).

**22.** *Bezalel.* Tribute is paid in this and the following verse to the faithful manner in which the two principal architects executed their work.

**24.** *talents.* See on XXV, 39. A talent equalled 3,000 shekels.

*shekel of the sanctuary.* See on XXX, 13. It has been computed that the total quantity of gold was worth about £160,000.

**25.** *that were numbered.* Cf. XXX, 12 f. The silver weighed 301,775 shekels; and since each male adult contributed half a shekel, the census showed a total of 603,550; cf. Num. I, 46. This suggests that the computations recorded here were not made at this time, but after the erection of the Tabernacle.

**27.** *for casting the sockets.* See on XXVI, 19.

**29.** *brass of the offering.* The quantity of copper was about three tons.

EXODUS XXXVIII, 29

capitals, and made fillets for them. 29. And the brass of the offering was seventy talents, and two thousand and four hundred shekels. 30. And therewith he made the sockets to the door of the tent of meeting, and the brazen altar, and the brazen grating for it, and all the vessels of the altar, 31. and the sockets of the court round about, and the sockets of the gate of the court, and all the pins of the tabernacle, and all the pins of the court round about.

## 39     CHAPTER XXXIX

1. And of the blue, and purple, and scarlet, they made plaited garments, for ministering in the holy place, and made the holy garments for Aaron, as the LORD commanded Moses.\*11(\*\*v). ¶ 2. And he made the ephod of gold, blue, and purple, and scarlet, and fine twined linen. 3. And they did beat the gold into thin plates, and cut it into threads, to work it in the blue, and in the purple, and in the scarlet, and in the fine linen, the work of the skilful workman. 4. They made shoulder-pieces for it, joined together; at the two ends was it joined together. 5. And the skilfully woven band, that was upon it, wherewith to gird it on, was of the same piece and like the work thereof: of gold, of blue, and purple, and scarlet, and fine twined linen, as the LORD commanded Moses. ¶ 6. And they wrought the onyx stones, inclosed in settings of gold, graven with the engravings of a signet, according to the names of the children of Israel. 7. And he put them on the shoulder-pieces of the ephod, to be stones of memorial for the children of Israel, as the LORD commanded Moses. ¶ 8. And he made the breastplate, the work of the skilful workman, like the work of the ephod: of gold, of blue, and purple, and scarlet, and fine twined linen. 9. It was four-square; they made the breastplate double: a span was the length thereof, and a span the breadth thereof, being double. 10. And they set in it four rows of stones: a row of carnelian, topaz, and smaragd was the first row. 11. And the second row, a carbuncle, a sapphire, and an emerald. 12. And the third row, a jacinth, an agate, and an amethyst. 13. And the

---

**30.** *brazen altar*. There is no mention of the laver, which was likewise made of copper. The reason is that the material for this came from a special source; see *v.* 8 above.

### CHAPTER XXXIX
### 1–31. THE PRIESTS' VESTMENTS

### 2–7. THE EPHOD
Corresponding to xxviii, 6–12.

**3.** *beat the gold*. This verse does not occur in the parallel passage; it explains how the gold was utilized in making the vestments.

### 8–21. THE BREASTPLATE
Corresponding to xxviii, 15–28.

386

# EXODUS XXXIX, 14     שמות פקודי לט

fourth row, a beryl, an onyx, and a jasper; they were inclosed in fittings of gold in their settings. 14. And the stones were according to the names of the children of Israel, twelve, according to their names, like the engravings of a signet, every one according to his name, for the twelve tribes. 15. And they made upon the breastplate plaited chains, of wreathen work of pure gold. 16. And they made two settings of gold and two gold rings; and put the two rings on the two ends of the breastplate. 17. And they put the two wreathen chains of gold on the two rings at the ends of the breastplate. 18. And the other two ends of the two wreathen chains they put on the two settings, and put them on the shoulder-pieces of the ephod, in the forepart thereof. 19. And they made two rings of gold, and put them upon the two ends of the breastplate, upon the edge thereof, which was toward the side of the ephod inward. 20. And they made two rings of gold, and put them on the two shoulder-pieces of the ephod underneath, in the forepart thereof, close by the coupling thereof, above the skilfully woven band of the ephod. 21. And they did bind the breastplate by the rings thereof unto the rings of the ephod with a thread of blue, that it might be upon the skilfully woven band of the ephod, and that the breastplate might not be loosed from the ephod; as the LORD commanded Moses.\*iii(\*\*vi). ¶ 22. And he made the robe of the ephod of woven work, all of blue; 23. and the hole of the robe in the midst thereof, as the hole of a coat of mail, with a binding round about the hole of it, that it should not be rent. 24. And they made upon the skirts of the robe pomegranates of blue, and purple, and scarlet, and twined linen. 25. And they made bells of pure gold, and put the bells between the pomegranates upon the skirts of the robe round about, between the pomegrantes: 26. a bell and a pomegranate, a bell and a pomegranate, upon the skirts of the robe round about, to minister in; as the LORD commanded Moses. ¶ 27. And they made the tunics of fine linen of woven work for Aaron, and for his sons,

## 22–26. THE ROBE OF THE EPHOD
Corresponding to xxviii, 31–34.

## 27–29. THE TUNICS AND HEADGEAR
Corresponding to xxviii, 39–42.

**28.** *goodly headtires.* lit. 'ornaments of caps', *i.e.* ornamental caps. These were for the priests, whereas the mitre was for the High Priest.

## 30, 31. THE HOLY CROWN
Corresponding to xxviii, 36 f.

**30.** *holy crown.* Not mentioned in the parallel passage, but in xxix, 6. It is identical with the golden plate.

## 32–43. SUMMARY OF THE WORK

**33.** *brought . . . unto Moses.* The sectional pieces. The task of fitting them together, and

EXODUS XXXIX, 28

28. and the mitre of fine linen, and the goodly head-tires of fine linen, and the linen breeches of fine twined linen, 29. and the girdle of fine twined linen, and blue, and purple, and scarlet, the work of the weaver in colours; as the LORD commanded Moses. ¶ 30. And they made the plate of the holy crown of pure gold, and wrote upon it a writing, like the engravings of a signet: HOLY TO THE LORD. 31. And they tied unto it a thread of blue, to fasten it upon the mitre above; as the LORD commanded Moses. ¶32. Thus was finished all the work of the tabernacle of the tent of meeting; and the children of Israel did according to all that the LORD commanded Moses, so did they.*ⁱᵛ ¶ 33. And they brought the tabernacle unto Moses, the Tent, and all its furniture, its clasps, its boards, its bars, and its pillars, and its sockets; 34. and the covering of rams' skins dyed red, and the covering of sealskins, and the veil of the screen; 35. the ark of the testimony, and the staves thereof, and the ark-cover; 36. the table, all the vessels thereof, and the showbread; 37. the pure candlestick, the lamps thereof, even the lamps to be set in order, and all the vessels thereof, and the oil for the light; 38. and the golden altar, and the anointing oil, and the sweet incense, and the screen for the door of the Tent; 39. the brazen altar, and its grating of brass, its staves, and all its vessels, the laver and its base; 40. the hangings of the court, its pillars, and its sockets, and the screen for the gate of the court, the cords thereof, and the pins thereof, and all the instruments of the service of the tabernacle of the tent of meeting; 41. the plaited garments for ministering in the holy place; the holy garments for Aaron the priest, and the garments of his sons, to minister in the priest's office. 42. According to all that the LORD commanded Moses, so the children of Israel did all the work. 43. And Moses saw all the work, and, behold, they had done it; as the LORD had commanded, even so had they done it. And Moses blessed them.*ᵛ⁽**ᵛⁱⁱ⁾.

placing the articles of the Tabernacle in the right place, was to be carried out under the personal direction of Moses (XL, 1).

**37.** *lamps to be set in order.* i.e. to be arranged on it (Driver).

**40.** *all the instruments.* See on XXVII, 19.

**42.** *the children of Israel.* Credit is here given to the nameless donors and workers, who made the achievement of Bezalel and Oholiab possible.

**43.** *blessed them.* i.e. expressed his thanks by invoking a blessing upon them. The time had been short, the task great and arduous, but the labourers, fired by holy enthusiasm and zeal, had joyfully completed the work they had undertaken. Moses does not pronounce his blessing at the beginning of the sacred enterprise. Beginnings are easy; completions are as hard as they are rare. Tradition tells us that Moses composed Ps. XC, 'A Prayer of Moses,' for the occasion. Note its concluding words: 'Establish Thou also upon us the work of our hands; yea, the work of our hands establish Thou it.'

# EXODUS XL, 1

## CHAPTER XL

1. And the LORD spoke unto Moses, saying: 2. 'On the first day of the first month shalt thou rear up the tabernacle of the tent of meeting. 3. And thou shalt put therein the ark of the testimony, and thou shalt screen the ark with the veil. 4. And thou shalt bring in the table, and set in order the bread that is upon it; and thou shalt bring in the candelstick, and light the lamps thereof. 5. And thou shalt set the golden altar for incense before the ark of the testimony, and put the screen of the door to the tabernacle. 6. And thou shalt set the altar of burnt-offering before the door of the tabernacle of the tent of meeting. 7. And thou shalt set the laver between the tent of meeting and the altar, and shalt put water therein. 8. And thou shalt set up the court round about, and hang up the screen of the gate of the court. 9. And thou shalt take the anointing oil, and anoint the tabernacle, and all that is therein, and shalt hallow it, and all the furniture thereof; and it shall be holy. 10. And thou shalt anoint the altar of burnt-offering, and all its vessels, and sanctify the altar; and the altar shall be most holy. 11. And thou shalt anoint the laver and its base, and sanctify it. 12. And thou shalt bring Aaron and his sons unto the door of the tent of meeting, and shalt wash them with water. 13. And thou shalt put upon Aaron the holy garments; and thou shalt anoint him, and sanctify him, that he may minister unto Me in the priest's office. 14. And thou shalt bring his sons, and put tunics upon them. 15. And thou shalt anoint them, as thou didst anoint their father, that they may minister unto Me in the priest's office; and their anointing

## CHAPTER XL

### 1–33. THE SETTING UP OF THE SANCTUARY

**2.** *the first month.* In the second year after the Exodus from Egypt (*v.* 17). Nine months had elapsed since the people's arrival at Sinai (XIX, 1). The actual work of construction occupied about four months.

**3.** *screen the ark.* See XXVI, 33.

**4.** *set in order.* Lit. 'thou shalt arrange its arrangement'; see XXV, 30.

**5.** *golden altar.* For the location of the contents of the Holy Place, see on XXVI, 35.

**6.** *before the door of the tabernacle. i.e.* in the court.

**7.** *laver.* See XXX, 18.

**8.** *the court.* See XXVII, 9 f.

**9.** *anointing oil.* See XXX, 26–28.

**12.** *bring Aaron.* See XXIX, 4 f, XXX, 30.

**15.** *an everlasting priesthood.* It was to be hereditary in the family of Aaron.

*their anointing.* Only the High Priest had in every case to be anointed when inducted into his office. For the other priests, the anointing of the first priests, the sons of Aaron, was held to suffice; and the consecration of the ordinary descendant of the sons of Aaron consisted merely in being clothed in the priestly garments.

**16.** *thus did Moses.* The fulfilment of the command, so far as the erection of the Tabernacle was concerned, is described in the verses that follow. The induction of Aaron and his sons is narrated in Lev. VIII.

## EXODUS XL, 16

shall be to them for an everlasting priesthood throughout their generations.' 16. Thus did Moses; according to all that the LORD commanded him, so did he.*ᵛⁱ· ¶ 17. And it came to pass in the first month in the second year, on the first day of the month, that the tabernacle was reared up. 18. And Moses reared up the tabernacle, and laid its sockets, and set up the boards thereof, and put in the bars thereof, and reared up its pillars. 19. And he spread the tent over the tabernacle, and put the covering of the tent above upon it; as the LORD commanded Moses. ¶ 20. And he took and put the testimony into the ark, and set the staves on the ark, and put the ark-cover above upon the ark. 21. And he brought the ark into the tabernacle, and set up the veil of the screen, and screened the ark of the testimony; as the LORD commanded Moses. ¶ 22. And he put the table in the tent of meeting, upon the side of the tabernacle northward, without the veil. 23. And he set a row of bread in order upon it before the LORD; as the LORD commanded Moses. ¶ 24. And he put the candlestick in the tent of meeting, over against the table, on the side of the tabernacle southward. 25. And he lighted the lamps before the LORD; as the LORD commanded Moses. ¶ 26. And he put the golden altar in the tent of meeting before the veil; 27. and he burnt thereon incense of sweet spices; as the LORD commanded Moses.*ᵛⁱⁱ· ¶ 28. And he put the screen of the door to the tabernacle. 29. And the altar of burnt-offering he set at the door of the tabernacle of the tent of meeting, and offered upon it the burnt-offering and the meal-offering; as the LORD commanded Moses. ¶ 30. And he set the laver between the tent of meeting and the altar, and put water therein, wherewith to wash; 31. that Moses and Aaron and his sons might wash their hands and their feet thereat; 32. when they went into the tent of meeting, and when they came near unto the altar, they should wash; as the LORD commanded Moses. ¶ 33. And he reared up the court round about the tabernacle and the altar, and set up the screen of the gate of the court. So Moses finished the work.*ᵐ· ¶ 34. Then the cloud covered the tent of meeting, and the glory of the LORD filled the tabernacle.

**20.** *the testimony.* viz. the Tables of the Decalogue. Tradition declares that the broken pieces of the First Tables were also deposited in the Ark.

*set the staves on the ark.* From which they were not to be removed (xxv, 15).

**27.** *burnt thereon incense.* Moses performed this and other priestly duties during the week of consecration, until the priests were installed.

**34–38. THE CLOUD UPON THE TENT OF MEETING**

**34.** *the cloud.* As in XIII, 21, and XXIV, 15, a cloud screened the 'glory of the LORD', and was a visible symbol to the people of His Presence.

*glory of the LORD.* See XXIX, 43. Since God is not corporeal, this can only imply a spiritual manifestation of His presence in the tent of meeting; *i.e.* the Shechinah.

## EXODUS XL, 35     שמות פקודי מ

35. And Moses was not able to enter into the tent of meeting, because the cloud abode thereon, and the glory of the LORD filled the tabernacle.—36. And whenever the cloud was taken up from over the tabernacle, the children of Israel went onward, throughout all their journeys. 37. But if the cloud was not taken up, then they journeyed not till the day that it was taken up. 38. For the cloud of the LORD was upon the tabernacle by day, and there was fire therein by night, in the sight of all the house of Israel, throughout all their journeys.

לה הַמִּשְׁכָּן: וְלֹא־יָכֹל מֹשֶׁה לָבוֹא אֶל־אֹהֶל מוֹעֵד כִּי־
36 שָׁכַן עָלָיו הֶעָנָן וּכְבוֹד יְהֹוָה מָלֵא אֶת־הַמִּשְׁכָּן: וּבְהֵעָלוֹת
הֶעָנָן מֵעַל הַמִּשְׁכָּן יִסְעוּ בְּנֵי יִשְׂרָאֵל בְּכֹל מַסְעֵיהֶם:
37 וְאִם־לֹא יֵעָלֶה הֶעָנָן וְלֹא יִסְעוּ עַד־יוֹם הֵעָלֹתוֹ: כִּי עֲנַן
38 יְהֹוָה עַל־הַמִּשְׁכָּן יוֹמָם וְאֵשׁ תִּהְיֶה לַיְלָה בּוֹ לְעֵינֵי כָל־
בֵּית־יִשְׂרָאֵל בְּכָל־מַסְעֵיהֶם:

## חזק

סכום פסוקי דספר ואלה שמות אלף ומאתים ותשעה. אר״ט
סימן: וחציו אלהים לא תקלל: ופרשיותיו אחד עשר. אי זה
בית אשר תבנו לי סימן: וסדריו עשרים ותשעה. ולילה
ללילה יחוה דעת סימן: ופרקיו ארבעים. תורת אלהיו בלבו
סימן: מנין הפתוחות תשע וששים. והסתומות חמש ותשעים.
הכל מאה וששים וארבע פרשיות: ישלח עזרך מקדש
ומציון יסעדך סימן:

---

**35.** *filled the tabernacle.* The seal of His approval was thus set on the work that was now completed.

**36.** *went onward.* Still another purpose was served by the cloud: it was a signal for the People when to halt and when to proceed on their journey.

**38.** *fire therein. i.e.* with fire shining in the cloud by night (cf. Num. IX, 15 f). Without this fire, the cloud would not have been perceptible at night.

The Book of Exodus thus closes with the fulfilment of the promise in XXIX, 43, 45. Moses' appeal had been effective, and God's protecting and sanctifying Presence in the midst of His people would lead them to their appointed destination.

The Tabernacle, after it had accompanied the Israelites in their wanderings in the Wilderness, was most probably first set up in the Holy Land at Gilgal (Josh. IV, 19). Before the death of Joshua, it was erected at Shiloh (Josh. XVIII, 1). Here it remained as the national Sanctuary throughout the time of the Judges (Judg. XVIII, 31; I Sam. IV, 3). But its external construction was at this time somewhat changed, and doors seem to have taken the place of the entrance curtain (I Sam. III, 15). After the time of Eli, it was removed to Nob in the district of Benjamin, not far from Jerusalem (I Sam. XXI, 1–9). Thence, in the time of David, it was removed to Gibeon (I Kings III, 4). It was brought from Gibeon to Jerusalem by Solomon (I Kings VIII, 4). When the Temple of Solomon was built, the Tabernacle of the Wilderness had performed its work of protecting the Ark of the Covenant during all the migrations of Israel. The promise that the LORD would choose out a place for Himself in which His name should be preserved and His service should be maintained was then fulfilled.

\*    \*    \*    \*

According to Jewish custom, the completion of any of the Five Books of the Torah is marked in the Synagogue by the congregation exclaiming *Be strong, be strong, and let us strengthen one another*—an echo of the words of the ancient warrior, 'Be of good courage, and let us prove strong for our people, and for the cities of our God' (II Sam. X, 12). *Be strong, i.e.* to carry out the teaching contained in the Book just completed.

The Massoretic Note states the numbers of verses in Exodus to be 1,209; its Sedrahs (parshiyyoth), 11; its Sedarim, smaller divisions according to the Triennial Cycle, 29; and its Chapters, 40.

# HAFTORAH PEKUDEY (FOR ASHKENAZIM) הפטרת פקודי לאשכנזים

## I KINGS VII, 51–VIII, 21

### Chapter VII

51. Thus all the work that king Solomon wrought in the house of the LORD was finished. And Solomon brought in the things which David his father had dedicated, the silver, and the gold, and the vessels, and put them in the treasuries of the house of the LORD.

### Chapter VIII

1 Then Solomon assembled the elders of Israel, and all the heads of the tribes, the princes of the fathers' houses of the children of Israel, unto king Solomon in Jerusalem, to bring up the ark of the covenant of the LORD out of the city of David, which is Zion. 2. And all the men of Israel assembled themselves unto king Solomon at the feast, in the month Ethanim, which is the seventh month. 3. And all the elders of Israel came, and the priests took up the ark. 4. And they brought up the ark of the LORD, and the tent of meeting, and all the holy vessels that were in the Tent; even these did the priests and the Levites bring up. 5. And king Solomon and all the congregation of Israel, that were assembled unto him, were with him before the ark, sacrificing sheep and oxen, that could not be told nor numbered for multitude. 6. And the priests brought in the ark of the covenant of the LORD unto its place, into the Sanctuary of the house, to the most holy place, even under the wings of the cherubim. 7. For the cherubim spread forth their wings over the place of the ark, and the cherubim covered the ark and the staves thereof above. 8. And the staves were so long that the ends of the staves were seen from the holy place, even before the Sanctuary; but they could not be seen without; and there they are unto this day. 9. There was nothing in the ark save the two tables of stone which Moses put there at Horeb,

The Dedication of the Temple, and the first part of Solomon's Prayer of Consecration.

**51.** *and Solomon brought*. The Temple work completed, Solomon piously brings in the gifts his father David had given and consecrated for the House.

*in the treasuries*. Probably in the side-chambers referred to in I Kings VI, 5; see p. 338.

### Chapter VIII

**1.** *the city of David*. Where David had placed it after bringing it from the house of Obed-Edom (II Sam. VI, 12). The city of David was built on the site of the old Jebusite fort captured by David (II Sam. V, 9). The Temple was built on a higher slope of the hill.

*Zion*. The name was originally applied to the Temple hill and the city generally.

**2.** *the feast*. Of Tabernacles, the Feast of Ingatherings. The people were assembled prior to the Feast, for the purpose of the dedication and rejoicings thereat (seven days), and afterwards observed the Festival according to v. 65.

*Ethanim*. The month later named Tishri.

**4.** *tent of meeting*. The Tabernacle built by Moses in the Wilderness.

# I KINGS VIII, 10

when the LORD made a covenant with the children of Israel when they came out of the land of Egypt. 10. And it came to pass, when the priests were come out of the holy place, that the cloud filled the house of the LORD, 11. so that the priests could not stand to minister by reason of the cloud; for the glory of the LORD filled the house of the LORD. 12. Then spoke Solomon:
  The LORD hath said that He would dwell in the thick darkness.
  13 I have surely built Thee a house of habitation,
  A place for Thee to dwell in for ever.
14. And the king turned his face about, and blessed all the congregation of Israel; and all the congregation of Israel stood. 15. And he said: 'Blessed be the LORD, the God of Israel, who spoke with His mouth unto David my father, and hath with His hand fulfilled it, saying: 16. Since the day that I brought forth My people Israel out of Egypt, I chose no city out of all the tribes of Israel to build a house, that My name might be there; but I chose David to be over My people Israel. 17. Now it was in the heart of David my father to build a house for the name of the LORD, the God of Israel. 18. But the LORD said unto David my father: Whereas it was in thy heart to build a house for My name, thou didst well that it was in thy heart; 19. nevertheless thou shalt not build the house; but thy son that shall come forth out of thy loins, he shall build the house for My name. 20 And the LORD hath established His word that He spoke; for I am risen up in the room of David my father, and sit on the throne of Israel, as the LORD promised, and have built the house for the name of the LORD, the God of Israel. 21. And there have I set a place for the ark, wherein is the covenant of the LORD, which He made with our fathers, when He brought them out of the land of Egypt.'

---

**8.** *the staves.* The poles by which the Ark was carried protruded from the Holy of Holies into the Holy Place.

**9.** *there was nothing in the ark ... tables of stone.* The Ark contained no image or mystic appurtenance of pagan worship.

**12.** *in the thick darkness.* In the heavy cloud (see Exod. xx, 18) which now filled the Temple was the visible sign of the Shechinah (God's Presence).

**13.** *to dwell for ever.* The places where the Ark previously rested were only temporary Places of Worship until the Temple, Israel's permanent Sanctuary, was erected on the chosen site (Kimchi).

15–21. SOLOMON'S ADDRESS TO THE PEOPLE: THE CIRCUMSTANCES THAT LED TO HIS BUILDING THE TEMPLE

**17.** *in the heart of David.* To build the Temple was the cherished dream of David.

**18.** *the LORD said unto David.* Through the prophet Nathan; II Sam. VII, 8 f.
  *thou didst well that it was in thine heart.* Our own cherished high aims may not be fulfilled, but we are the better for striving for them.

**21.** *wherein is the covenant of the LORD.* The Tables of stone placed in the Ark.

# ADDITIONAL NOTES TO EXODUS

## A

### ISRAEL IN EGYPT: THE HISTORICAL PROBLEMS

#### I

#### WHAT LIGHT DOES EGYPTIAN HISTORY THROW ON ISRAEL IN EGYPT?

The history of ancient Egypt is usually divided into three periods. The earliest period is that of the Old Kingdom, which comprises the first ten dynasties of pyramid builders, ending 2500 B.C.E. The second period, the Middle Kingdom, from the eleventh to the seventeenth dynasty of rulers (2500–1587 B.C.E.), is one of great obscurity, and covers the age during which the Hyksos, Bedouin invaders from the Arabian desert, ruled Egypt. They were expelled by the founder of the eighteenth dynasty in 1587. He opens the third period, the New Kingdom, which continues to the end of the twentieth dynasty in 1100 B.C.E. After that date, the country successively came under Lybian, Persian, Macedonian, and Roman rule.

Biblical interest in Egypt begins during the Middle Kingdom. Joseph served one of the Hyksos kings. These invaders, 'princes of the desert,' as they called themselves, soon accommodated themselves to the system of Government they had found in Egypt; and their contribution to Egyptian culture was not inferior to that of the native kings. Their dominion was later described as one of desolation and ruin—which is quite untrue. The Hyksos kings restored and enlarged the temples, encouraged learning, and could not have destroyed any of the previous Egyptian monuments, seeing that these have come down to our own day. On the contrary, it is the native rulers who followed them that eradicated every trace of the Hyksos kings. This is responsible for the obscurity that overhangs the story of the whole Hyksos period, and the consequent uncertainty of so much of Egyptian chronology. Not long after the death of Joseph, the Hyksos were driven back into Asia; and a native ruler, the founder of the Eighteenth Dynasty, regained the throne.

The advent of this nationalist dynasty marked the turn of the tide in the fortunes of the descendants of Jacob. As friends of the overthrown Hyksos kings, they lost their favoured position, and their past services to the State were 'ignored'. From prosperous and honoured settlers in the Eastern Delta of the Nile, with freedom of movement and right of domicile throughout Egypt and her dominions, they were under the successive rulers of the Eighteenth Dynasty (1587–1350 B.C.E.) gradually reduced to a condition of serfdom. These rulers, as well as the kings of the Nineteenth Dynasty (1350–1200), were great architects and are famous for the number and magnificence of their monuments. That veritable frenzy for building which characterized all these rulers naturally called for vast levies of forced labour. The feared and hated Israelites seemed to these Pharaohs to be at hand for just such a purpose. The Israelites were now condemned to cruel slave labour as bricklayers and navvies, both the kind and conditions of their labour being utterly alien to the nature and the traditions of free and independent shepherd folk.

It is difficult to determine the name of the 'new king' who initiated the Oppression. Scripture does not give us the name of the ruler in question, *Pharaoh* being merely the royal title of the reigning monarch. The one aim of the Scripture story is to describe God's Providential guidance of His people. The narrative is 'theocentric'; and events are viewed under the aspect of eternity. Details, such as the exact names of the impious heathen oppressors, are passed over, and all the emphasis is placed on the religious truths with which the narrative throbs (Boehl). And as to the hieroglyphic monuments, their information on this whole subject is most meagre. Possibly this is due to the fact that as yet little excavation has taken place in Goshen, *i.e.* the Eastern Delta, which was the main domicile of the Israelites. But even when ancient Goshen is revealed to us, it will still be well to remember that the true-born Egyptian chronicler took little notice of the fortunes of an alien serf-class like the Israelites, whose original occupation—keeping sheep—was, in his eyes, that of outcasts (Gen. XLVI, 34).

There are, therefore, but few casual references on the monuments to the *Aperu* or *Apuriu*, which is the Egyptian form of the name 'Hebrews'. Thus, in a report addressed to an official of the reign of Rameses II, there occur the words: 'I have obeyed the message of my lord, in which he said, "Give corn to the native soldiers, and also to the Apuriu, who are bringing up stones for the great tower of Pa-Ramessu" ... I have given them their corn every month, according to the instructions of my lord.' In another report of the same age we read: 'I have hearkened to my lord's message, "Give provisions to the soldiers and to the *Aperu*, who bring up stones for Ra (the sun-god), viz. for Ra of Rameses, the beloved of Amon, in the southern quarter of Memphis."' So much for the nature of the few Egyptian references to the Hebrew serfs doing forced labour for the Pharaohs.

As to the exodus from Egypt, the Egyptian records pass it over in total silence—as was their invariable custom in connection with any defeat suffered by the ruler or nation. For instance, although the Hyksos conquest of Egypt is the most important political event in Egyptian history, yet almost no mention is made in the monuments of this catastrophe, which shook the whole social structure to its foundations. The Egyptian records confine themselves to the boastful recounting of victories. The Biblical writers alone, among all Oriental chroniclers, describe defeats of their king and armies; nay more, they arraign ruler and people alike whensoever these are unfaithful to the aims and ideals of the nation. This is one of the reasons why, of all Oriental chronicles, it is only the Biblical annals that deserve the name of history.

## II

WHO WAS THE PHARAOH OF THE OPPRESSION?

In view of the above, there are several candidates for the infamy of having been the 'Pharaoh of the Oppression', under whom the bondage of the Israelites ended in a systematic attempt at their extermination. The majority of scholars identify him with the splendour-loving and tyrannical Rameses II, whose dates are variously given as 1300–1234 B.C.E. (Petrie) and 1347–1280 (Mahler). 'He was a vain and boastful character, who wished to dazzle posterity by covering the land with constructions whereon his name was engraved thousands of times, and who prided himself in his inscriptions upon great conquests which he never made' (Naville). The Exodus itself is held to have taken place under his son, Merneptah, with whom the decline of Egypt began. Merneptah (or Menephtah) was an obstinate and vain despot. He too had the habit of claiming as his own the achievements of others. 'He was one of the most unconscionable usurpers (and defacers) of the monuments of his predecessors, including those of his own father, who had set him the example ... all due to a somewhat insane desire to perpetuate his own memory' (Prof. Griffith, *Encyclopædia Britannica*, 1929).

Some scholars, however, date the Oppression and the Exodus in the century preceding Rameses II, and connect it with the religious revolution of Amenophis IV, or Ikhnaton (1383–1365). This extraordinary personality abolished the multitudinous deities of the Egyptian Pantheon, and devoted himself exclusively to the worship of the Sun. These scholars hold that there was some relation between the faith of the Israelites and the solar monotheism of Ikhnaton, and that Israelite influence was partly responsible for this assault on the gross idolatry of Egypt. Ikhnaton was hated by the people as the 'heretic king', and his innovations were abandoned by his son-in-law Tut-an-khamen, who succeeded him, eventually to be altogether uprooted by Haremrab, the last Pharaoh of the Eighteenth Dynasty. When the native religion was restored—these scholars maintain—the Israelites suffered persecution and degradation; and the Oppression formed part of the extirpation of Ikhnaton's heresy.

Other Egyptologists go back still another century to Thotmes III (1503–1449), and declare him to have been the Pharaoh of the Oppression. They connect the Oppression and the departure of the Israelites from Egypt with the movements of the Habiri people in the Amarna age (see page 51, n. 13), and believe that the recently discovered inscriptions in the Sinai Peninsula likewise favour this theory.

One of the main reasons which induce both these groups of scholars to dissent from the general view that Rameses II was the Pharaoh of the Oppression, is the fact that the name 'Israel' is alleged to occur on an inscription of Merneptah. That Inscription (discovered in 1896) is a song of triumph of Merneptah describing in grandiloquent language his victories in Canaan; and, among other conquests, he boasts that 'Canaan is seized with every evil; Ashkelon is carried away; Gezer is taken; Yenoam is annihilated; *Ysiraal is desolated, its seed is not.*' From the phrase, 'Ysiraal is desolated,' these scholars deduce that the Israelites must in those days have been in possession of Canaan; and that, therefore, the Exodus must have taken place long before the time of Merneptah. However, it is not at all certain that the words, 'Ysiraal is desolated,' refer to Israel at all. Thus, Prof. Kennett takes the phrase as analogous to that concerning Ashkelon and Gezer; and therefore as merely stating that Merneptah had devastated the district of 'Jezreel.' And if 'Ysiraal' *does* mean Israel, then it refers to the settlements in Palestine by Israelites from Egypt before the Exodus (Jampel). From various notices in I Chronicles we see that, during the generations preceding the Oppression, the Israelites did not remain confined to Goshen or even to Egypt proper, but spread into the southern Palestinian territory, then under Egyptian control, and even engaged in skirmishes with the Philistines. When the bulk of the nation had left Egypt and was wandering in the Wilderness, these Israelite settlers had thrown off their Egyptian allegiance. And it is these settlements which Merneptah boasts of having devastated during his Canaanite campaign. There is, therefore, no cogent reason for dissenting from the current view that the Pharaoh of the Oppression was Rameses II, with his son Merneptah as the Pharaoh of the Exodus.

## III

THE 'INCONVENIENCE' OF BIBLICAL TRADITIONS

Little need be said in regard to the extreme and baseless scepticism, recently revived in Soviet anti-religious circles, that the Israelites never were in Egypt; and that, in consequence, there could not have been either an Oppression or an Exodus.

There is one conclusive answer to the doubts as to the historicity of the Exodus and other crucial events in Scriptural history; and that is, what has aptly been called *the 'inconvenience' of Biblical traditions*. One or two examples will both explain this argument and make clear its unanswerable force. The first example is taken from the story of Abraham. For centuries, the Hebrew tribes waged a life-and-death struggle with the native population for the possession of ancient Palestine. But instead of the Hebrews claiming that they too were natives of Canaan, or that they were the true aborigines of its soil, Bible Tradition concerning the beginnings of the Hebrew people is emphatic that its ancestors were *not* born in Canaan, but were nomads, immigrant shepherds, and had their origin in Ur of the Chaldees. Now, even the sceptical historian is forced to admit that such a tradition must be based on strict history, as no people would invent such an *inconvenient* tradition in regard to a matter of vital importance like its right and title to its national homeland. To take another example. The record of Genesis that Isaac and Jacob married Aramaean wives must be based on *fact*, and could not have arisen, as some Bible critics maintain, in the days of the Monarchy. For throughout the days of the Monarchy, Aram was the hereditary enemy of Israel, and was guilty of the most hideous barbarities in its continued attempts to annihilate Israel. It is clear that here too the tradition that the 'Mothers' of the Israelite people were Aramaean women was an *inconvenient* one—and cannot therefore be an invention of later legend (Cornill, Jirku).

All this applies with immeasurably greater force in regard to the historicity of the Oppression in Egypt. Compared with the Egyptian bondage and the deliverance therefrom, everything else in Bible history is of secondary importance. The memory of that bondage and deliverance is woven into the message of legislator, historian, psalmist, prophet and priest; and a large portion of Jewish life both in the Biblical and the post-Biblical ages is but a זכר ליציאת מצרים, an echo and reminder of that Divine event which meant the birth of Israel as a nation. Now, it is unthinkable that any nation, unless forced to do so by the overwhelming compulsion of unforgettable fact, would of its own account have wantonly affixed to its forefathers the stain and dishonour of slavery in a foreign country. No people has ever yet invented a *disgraceful* past for itself. The invention by a later age of a story so humiliating to national self-respect would be still more astounding in the case of Israel, when we consider that after the days of Menremptah the decline of Egypt began, and the invented national bondage would have been to a weak and waning Power. If, therefore, Israel's sojourn and bondage in Egypt were *merely* a fiction, such fiction would be quite inexplicable—in fact, a psychological miracle. Even a radical student of this question like Prof. Peet sums up his conclusions as follows: 'That Israel was in Egypt under one form or another no historian could possibly doubt; a legend of such tenacity, representing the early fortunes of a people under so unfavourable an aspect, could not have arisen save as a reflection of real occurrences.'

B

ISRAEL AND EGYPT: THE SPIRITUAL CONTRAST

Israel and Egypt represent two world-conceptions, two ways of looking on God and Man that are not merely in conflict, but mutually exclusive.

For ages Egypt was the Land of Wonder, and men spoke in awe of the wisdom of the Egyptians. We know now that they were indeed a wonderful people; but it is only in the arts and crafts, and especially in their colossal and titanic architecture, that they attained truly astonishing results.

The real tests of a nation's civilization, however, are far other than these. The supreme test is its vision of God. Now what were the objects of Egyptian worship? Stocks and stones, and, above all else, the beast. While there are traces, albeit faint traces, that the men of the Nile Valley were capable of learning both in religion and in conduct, they seem to have been quite incapable of *forgetting*. Egypt never discarded the low animism and savage fetishism of its prehistoric days, and remained always 'zoomorphic' in its conception of God: bulls, crocodiles, beetles, apes, cats, and goats—these were its gods. There were, it is true, stammerings of something nobler; glimpses of higher religious truth; but these remained only glimpses—like flashes of light for one brief moment in the night-time, leaving greater darkness, Egyptian darkness, behind. Once only was an attempt made by that remarkable man, Amenophis IV, to reform the barbarism of Egyptian worship and to put a kind of monotheism in its place. The sun was to be worshipped as the single deity under the name of Aton; and he changed his own name to Ikhnaton, 'Glory to the Sun.' But the reformation was a failure. He died amid the curses of his subjects, and the old confused polytheism returned stronger than ever. 'We have no grounds for holding the opinion,' says Prof. R. H. Hall, 'that the educated Egyptian priest, far less the man in the street, normally accepted any pious theories of a latent monotheism, underlying his blatant polytheism. Ikhnaton was branded as a criminal; and after his failure, we go back to the old spells and mumbo-jumbo again . . . till the death of the Egyptian religion in the days of Justinian. In religious matters, the Egyptians at all periods (except the educated at the end of the Eighteenth Dynasty) were in the mental condition of the blacks of the Gold Coast and Niger delta. They had "mysteries", of course, like the Ashantis or Ibos. It is a mistake, however, to think that these mysteries enshrined truth, and that there was an occult "faith" behind them. There is no more proof of it than in the case of the Ashantis or Ibos' (*Encyclopædia Britannica*, 1929).

Now where there is no vision of God there can be no vision of man. Hence the insignificance of man in the Egyptian world-conception. They bent the knee to the beast, but man throughout Egyptian history was in bondage. Human life had absolutely no value. The lives of vast multitudes of men were sacrificed in connection with the frenzied building schemes. Herodotus tells us that in the time of Pharaoh Necho II (609–588 B.C.E.), 120,000 labourers were worked to death in the construction of a canal connecting the Nile and the Red Sea. The pyramids, erected by the tyrant's unlimited command of human forces, remain everlasting monuments of human slavery—and of the national deification of reckless and irresponsible power.

In eternal contrast to Egypt, the whole story of Israel is one long protest against idolatry and inhumanity. A single incident in the life of a Jewish ruler will illustrate the world-wide difference between Israel and Egypt. King Jehoiakim, a contemporary of Pharaoh Necho II, tried to emulate his example, and built himself palaces by means of forced labour. In Egypt, such a thing was taken as a matter of course, as the unquestioned prerogative of the king. In Israel, that enterprise was deemed an outrage against reason and human decency. Jeremiah the Prophet arose and came to the door of Jehoiakim's palace, crying: 'Woe unto him that buildeth his house by unrighteousness, and his chambers by injustice; that useth his neighbour's service without wages, and giveth him not his hire.... Thine eyes and thy heart are not but for thy covetousness, and for shedding innocent blood, and for oppression, and for violence, to do it. Therefore thus saith the LORD concerning Jehoiakim, the son of Josiah, king of Judah: They shall not lament for him.... He shall be buried with the burial of an ass, drawn and cast forth beyond the gates of Jerusalem' (Jer. XXII, 13, 17–19). These words of Jeremiah are but a Prophetic echo of the Israelite's cry for freedom that pierced the heavens in the days of Moses: they are but the translation of the trumpet sounds of the Exodus and the Sinaitic Covenant, with their Divine and everlasting proclamation of the rights of man.

Another characteristic element in the religious life of Egypt was Worship of the dead. I give a brief summary of that worship, taken from W. Max Müller's article in the *Encyclopædia Biblica*. The huge pyramids alone, says Prof. Müller, would be sufficient to testify that the Egyptians devoted greater zeal than any nation on earth to the abodes of their dead, and to the sustenance of their souls by sacrifices. The Bible of the Egyptians is the so-called 'Book of the Dead'. It contains magic formulæ for the guidance of man after death, warning him of the dangers he might expect to meet, and providing him with powerful spells—previously placed on the coffins for this purpose—to guarantee his safety. When the dead man reached the great Judgment Hall of the god Osiris, his moral life was tested. In the course of that judgment, the deceased denied that he had ever committed any of the 42 cardinal sins. (R. H. Hall rightly says: The Egyptian was never a humble person, either genuinely or hypocritically. When he confessed he did not say, 'I am guilty'; he said, 'I am not guilty'; his confession was negative, and the *onus probandi* lay on his judges). Simultaneously with the doctrine just stated, there existed the conflicting belief that the departed souls lived in darkness and misery in the nether world, persecuted by evil spirits, so that it was best for the dead person to become, by witchcraft, one of these evil monsters himself.

No wonder that the influence of the Egyptian religion on the lives of men was not very profound. In every respect the morality of the Egyptians seems to have been lax. One example will suffice. The tombs were almost invariably broken into soon after burial, and no military protection could prevent even the royal tombs from being plundered.

When we compare the Egyptian attitude towards death with that of the Pentateuch, we see in the latter what appears to be a deliberate aim to wean the Israelites from Egyptian superstition. In this way alone can we explain the silence of Israel's Torah in regard to the Life after Death. On the one hand, there is not a word concerning immortality, or concerning reward and punishment in the Hereafter; and on the other hand, there is rigorous proscription of all magic and sorcery, of sacrificing to the dead, as well as every form of alleged intercourse with the world of spirits. Israel's Faith is a religion *of life*, not of death; a religion that declares man's humanity to man as the most acceptable form of adoration of the One God, the Creator of heaven and earth, Who is from everlasting to everlasting.

Israel while in Egypt was yet but a child, and was not strong enough to withstand Egypt *in* Egypt. Only *out* of Egypt could it grow, uncontaminated by noxious influences of a decadent civilization. Only when liberated from the contagion of a nation of mere childish stammerers in the things of the Spirit, could it flourish, and fill the earth with the glad tidings of a God of holiness and pity, and the message of Righteousness to men and nations.

## C

### DOES EXODUS VI, 3, SUPPORT THE HIGHER CRITICAL THEORY?

This query, as well as the answer to it, may have little meaning and no interest to the general reader. In that case, he will be well advised to skip the appropriate sections. There is, however, a good number of laymen who are aware of the crucial significance that is attached to Exodus VI, 3 in modern Biblical study. For them it is of utmost importance that the question which forms the title of this Note be dealt with in a thorough-going way. Even the man who is not possessed of technical knowledge will then see how feeble, how insubstantial, is the pillar on which so much of Bible Critical Theory rests.

I

Contrary to what we have seen to be the plain meaning of Exodus VI, 3, Bible Critics declare that, according to the author of this chapter, the Name Y H W H (Adonay) is here revealed for *the first time* to Moses. Therefore—they hold—all those chapters in Genesis and Exodus in which Adonay (or the LORD, in English) occurs, must have been written by another hand than Exodus VI, 3. They point to this verse as unanswerable proof of the alleged plurality of 'sources' in the Pentateuch (see p. 398); and Exodus VI, 3, is accordingly proclaimed in every learned and popular treatise on the Critical treatment of the Bible as *the* 'clue' to the various sources of the Pentateuch.

The current Critical explanation of this verse, however, rests on a total misunderstanding of Hebrew idiom. When Scripture states that Israel, or the nations, or Pharaoh, 'shall know that God is Adonay'—this does *not* mean that they shall be informed that His Name is Y H W H (Adonay), as the Critics would have it; but that they shall come to witness His power and comprehend those attributes of the Divine nature which that Name denotes. Thus, Jer. XVI, 21, 'I will cause them to know My hand and My might, and they shall know that My name is Adonay.' In Ezekiel the phrase, 'They shall know I am Adonay,' occurs more than sixty times. Nowhere does it mean, They will know Him by the four letters of His Name. Every time it means, They will know Him by His acts and the fulfilment of His promises (see *e.g.*, the Haftorah of Va-ayra).

If a new Name were indeed here announced for the first time, Hebrew idiom would require the use of the verb הגיד (cf. Gen. XXXII, 30; Judges XIII, 6); and the actual phrase would be ושמי ד' לא הגדתי להם. B. Jacob has shown that the revealing of a *new* name of God would have been announced somewhat in the following manner:

הנה לא ידעת עד כה את שמי וגם אל אברהם
אל יצחק ואל יעקב לא נודעתי כי אם בשם אל
שדי ושמי ד' לא הגדתי להם : ועתה הנני מודיעך
כי לא אל שדי יקרא עוד שמי כי אם ד' יהיה
שמי :

'Behold, thou hast not hitherto known my Name; and even unto Abraham, unto Isaac, and unto Jacob I was known only by my Name El Shaddai, but my Name Adonay I did not tell them. Now I make known unto thee that my Name shall no longer be called Shaddai, but Adonay shall my Name be.'

As it is, the writer of VI, 3 could not possibly have meant what the Critics attempt to read into his words. Furthermore, the Critics themselves furnish a most awkward obstacle to their own theory. This is the 'Redactor'. Think of it. After supposedly combining the story of the Patriarchs from documents constantly using the name Adonay, he now introduces a statement that the Patriarchs had never heard of this Name! By such a statement, that Redactor would have stultified himself completely—if he ever had any existence outside the imagination of modern Bible critics (W. H. Green).

One of these critics (Dr. J. Skinner) pleads that the Critical analysis of Scripture is a chain which is a good deal stronger than its weakest link. Whatever this may mean, no one will pretend that a chain can be stronger than its *strongest* link. And its strongest link—the alleged proof offered by Exodus VI, 3—consists not alone in disregarding the plain meaning of the text and attributing an absurdity to the Sacred Writer, but actually in sadly belittling the intelligence of the Critic's own creation, the 'Redactor'.

II

The so-called Analysis of Sources, with its series of non-existent authors and irresponsible 'Redactors', is unsupported by any external evidence whatsoever. None of these imaginary sources has come down to us in its original form, or in any form for that matter. 'The plurality of sources,' complains Naville, 'is *assumed* by the Critics as an indisputable fact. Unity of authorship is ruled out by them from the very first. They must at all costs discover diverse authors, in explanation of a perfectly simple narrative which unfolds itself in the most natural manner. It matters little that the text itself is altogether out of harmony with the conception of the Critics. The text must adjust itself to these conceptions. If it does not, what does it matter: *it* is at fault. They correct the text; with the result that it agrees with their theory.' Moreover, all this wanton tampering with the text leads nowhere. The varying use of the Divine Names does not indicate a difference of authorship, but is due to the different meanings of the Names, the choice of which is carefully considered in each case (see pp. 6, 199). Differences of style and treatment are called forth by differences in the nature of the subjects treated: *e.g.* in Exodus, the story of the Deliverance from Egypt demands a strong, energetic narrative, while the account of the building of the Tabernacle calls for technical details. All suggestions of repudiations and contradictions are merely due to an insufficient insight into the spirit and intention of Scripture on the part of the Higher Critics.

Instead of the misleading term 'Higher Criticism', its followers now prefer to speak of their school as that of Historical Criticism. This, however, is even more misleading: for *nothing is more characteristic of the Higher Critic than the way he refuses to revise his views, in the face of historical discovery which disproves those views.* One example will suffice. The Critical theory starts from the assumption that before the days of Solomon the Hebrews lived in a state of savagery. Thus, it was one of the 'finalities of scholarship' that the art of writing was unknown in ancient Israel. As recently as 1892, an eminent exponent of that theory asserted deliberately, 'The time, of which the pre-Mosaic narratives treat, is a sufficient proof of their legendary character. It was a time prior to all knowledge of writing.' Others said the same thing of the Mosaic age. Whereas to-day, Professor Sellin—a leading exegete, excavator, and historian—says: 'That the question should ever have been raised whether Moses could have known how to write, appears to us now absurd. Every petty Canaanitish "king" of a city-state had his scribe, who conducted his correspondence and kept the necessary lists.' But though the main assumption on which the Critical speculations are based has been proved false, the Higher Critics remain as imperturbable as ever. An unimpeachable witness like Prof. Kittel, the eminent historian, recently wrote: 'The facts themselves had rendered a large portion of Wellhausen's hypothesis untenable. One would have thought that Wellhausen would have taken note of this new knowledge. But he never retracted or modified any of his theories; and his followers continued writing, and building on his hypothesis, as if nothing had happened.' Wellhausen's devotees to-day still continue writing as if nothing had happened; and his speculations are still proclaimed as truths which it is heresy to question, by the popularizers, hacks, and journeymen of theological literature, especially in English-speaking countries.

The leaders, however, are not as confident as they used to be in regard to the criterion of the Divine Names for the supposed separateness of the 'sources'. Jewish and Christian scholars like Hoffmann and Wiener, Dahse and Eerdmans, W. H. Green and Naville have not laboured in vain; and the Critical structure begun in 1753, and completed with so much jubilation by Wellhausen, his forerunners and his disciples, is crumbling before our very eyes. Dr. B. Jacob recalls the fact that even as late as 1910, a Liberal-Jewish Critic had such an absolute faith in the Critical division of the Pentateuch according to the well-known symbols J, E, P, D, R, etc., that he permitted himself to declare: 'If one is to doubt the truth of the Critical analysis, one might just as well doubt the truth of Newton's law of gravitation!' In a statement of this nature, one sees mirrored the dogmatism of the entire school of Bible Criticism. Little did they dream of the Einsteins that were to arise, who, in the field of Physics, would restate the law of gravitation according to new categories of thought; and in the field of Bible study, shatter the foundations of the Wellhausen hypothesis, and definitely declare its assumptions to be both unscientific and obsolete.

D

## THE TEN PLAGUES

'Bible story is nowhere more vivid than in its picture of the Plagues of Egypt. Pharaoh is the incarnation of sullen force, yielding by inches, or for a single moment, only to harden his heart when the crisis is past. But it is human strength matching itself against the inexhaustible resources of nature, which Moses is permitted to wield. The river which is Egypt's pride runs with blood; from out its reed-grass, frogs invade the secret recesses of luxury; the dust of the ground takes life, to become loathsome vermin; indoors and outside, there is no escape from swarming flies and corruption. While all over the land of Egypt beasts are dying of murrain, in Israel's land of Goshen the cattle are intact. The royal magicians, seeking to compete with the wonders of Moses, become themselves victims to the plague of boils. Now the heavens begin to play their part, and rain down wasting hail; while, to enhance the wonder, fire winds about the hailstones and melts them not. The land of Egypt is one mass of desolation; but from outside, the east wind blows steadily until the swarming locusts hide the ground; at a sign from the champion of Israel, the western hurricane succeeds, and the locust hosts are swept into the Red Sea. Then the whole scene dissolves into darkness that might be felt; every man a solitary prisoner where he stands. At last, midnight reveals the slain firstborn and Pharaoh and his people thrust Israel forth' (R. G. Moulton).

*Who is the LORD, that I should hearken unto His voice to let Israel go? I know not the LORD, and moreover I will not let Israel go,* was the reply of Pharaoh to the message of the God of Righteousness, who demanded justice for Israel, His firstborn son. Pharaoh, too, is a child of God, but 'a rebellious son' (Deut. XXI, 18), who must be chastised before he will let his bondmen go free. The Plagues are disciplinary chastisements of God. Instead of annihilating the tyrant by one mighty stroke, God, in His Divine forbearance, inflicted ten successive plagues to break his pride. 'See how different are the ways of God from the ways of men,' say the Rabbis; 'when a mortal warrior would destroy his enemy, he attacks him by surprise; he spaces not out his blows; and when he has him beneath his feet, he makes an end of him. But God warned Pharaoh ten times, and ten times gave him respite to repent; and before punishing him, He ten times showed him His mercy.' For there is grace and merciful forgiveness for those who repent; but there is unsparing punishment for those who, hardening their hearts to the voice of God, continue to oppress their fellowmen.

The Ten Plagues form a symmetrical and regularly unfolding scheme. The first nine plagues consist of three series of three each: (*a*) blood, frogs, gnats; (*b*) fleas, murrain, boils; (*c*) hail, locusts, darkness. In each series the first plague is announced to Pharaoh beforehand at the brink of the Nile, the second is proclaimed by Moses at the Palace, and the third is sent without warning. Each series of plagues rises to a climax, the final series is the climax of all that preceded; and these are but the prelude to the tenth plague—the death of the firstborn, which seals the completeness of the whole. The first nine plagues, though often spoken of as wonders, are not fantastic miracles without any *basis* in natural phenomena. As everywhere else in Scripture, the supernatural is here interwoven with the natural; and the Plagues are but miraculously intensified forms of the diseases and other natural occurrences to which Egypt is more or less liable. Between June and August, the Nile usually turns to a dull red, owing to the presence of vegetable matter. Generally after this time, the slime of the river breeds a vast number of frogs; and the air is filled with swarms of tormenting insects. We can, therefore, understand that an *exceptional* defilement of the Nile would vastly increase the frogs which swarm in its waters; that the huge heaps of decaying frogs would inevitably breed great swarms of flies, which, in turn, would spread the disease-germs that attacked the animals and flocks in the pest-ridden region of the Nile. But, whether we place the greater emphasis on the natural or on the supernatural in the account of the Plagues, we must never forget the purpose for which they were recorded. As is true of every Scripture narrative, the purpose is not so much to give an exhaustive archæological or even historical chronicle, as it is moral and religious instruction. 'The story of the plagues is drawn with unfading colours, and its typical and didactic significance cannot be overrated. It depicts the impotence of man's strongest determination when it essays to contend with God, and the fruitlessness of all human efforts to frustrate His purposes' (Driver).

Moreover, the contest was far more than a dramatic humiliation of the unrepentant and infatuated tyrant. It was nothing less than a judgment on the gods of Egypt. The plagues fell on the principal divinities that were worshipped since times immemorial in the Nile Valley. The River was a god; it became loathsome to its worshippers. The frog was venerated as the sign of fruitfulness, and it was turned into a horror. The cattle—the sacred ram, the sacred goat, the sacred bull—were all smitten. The sacred beetle became a torment to those who put their trust in its divinity. When we add to these the plague of darkness, which showed the eclipse of Ra, the Sun-god, we see that we have here a contrast between the God of Israel, the Lord of the Universe, and the senseless idols of a senile civilization; as it is written (XII, 12), 'against all the gods of Egypt I will execute judgments: I am the LORD.'

E

## THE TEN COMMANDMENTS, OR THE DECALOGUE

No religious document has exercised a greater influence on the moral and social life of man than the Divine Proclamation of Human Duty, known as the Decalogue. These few brief commands—only 120 Hebrew words in all—cover the whole sphere of conduct, not only of outer actions, but also of the secret thoughts of the heart. In simple, unforgettable form, this unique code of codes lays down the fundamental rules of Worship and of Right for all time and for all men.

I

### THE DECALOGUE IN JUDAISM

From early times the basic importance of the Ten Commandments was duly recognized in Israel. The Teachers of the Talmud emphasized their eternal and universal significance by means of parable, metaphor, and all the rare poetic imagery of Rabbinic legend. The Tables on which the Ten Commandments were written, they said, were prepared at the eve of Creation—thus ante-dating humanity, and therefore independent of time or place or racial culture; and they were hewn from the sapphire Throne of Glory—and therefore of infinite worth and preciousness. The Revelation at Sinai, they taught, was given in desert territory, which belongs to no one nation exclusively; and it was heard not by Israel alone, but by the inhabitants of all the earth. The Divine Voice divided itself into the 70 tongues spoken on earth, so that all the children of men might understand its world-embracing and man-redeeming message. Each command, as it rang out from Sinai's top, filled the world with aroma. The dead in Sheol were revived, and betook themselves to Sinai; yea, even the souls of all the unborn generations in Israel were assembled there. As the Divine Commandments rang out from Sinai's height, no bird sang, no ox lowed, the ocean did not roar, and no creature stirred; all Nature was rapt in breathless silence at the sound of the Divine Voice asserting the supremacy of Conscience and Right in the Universe. The Rabbis held the sixth of Sivan, the day of the Revelation at Mount Sinai, to be as momentous as the day of Creation itself; for without the coming into existence of Moral Law, the creation of the material universe would have been incomplete, nay, meaningless. At the same time, the Teachers of the Talmud were most careful to emphasize that the Ten Commandments did not contain the Whole Duty of Man, as some Jewish sectaries in the days of the Second Temple contended. The Decalogue laid down the *foundations* of Religion and Morality, but was not in itself the entire structure of Human Duty.

The Rabbinic view of the Decalogue was shared by the religious teachers and philosophers in the Middle Ages, and is to-day held by the followers of all schools of Judaism. Saadyah and Yehudah Hallevi, Rashi and Abarbanel, the Karaites and the Cabalists, all agree in regarding the Ten Commandments as the Fundamentals of the Faith, as the Pillars of the Torah and its Roots. In modern times, various exponents of Judaism have shown that all the ritual observances prescribed in the Torah are visible embodiments of the general truths enshrined in the Decalogue; and that, in fact, the whole content of Judaism as Creed and Life can be arranged under the ten general headings of the Commandments.

## II

### The Decalogue outside Israel

It is interesting to note the place that the Decalogue held in the religious life of Humanity outside the Synagogue. One of the most renowned of the Church Fathers spoke of the Decalogue as 'the heart of the Law'; and this remained the opinion of Western Christendom for over 1,500 years. Luther's words—'Never will there be found a precept comparable or preferable to these commands, for they are so sublime that no man could attain to them by his own power'—are typical of thought in the Reformed Churches. The Humanists, the Deists and even the Freethinkers spoke in reverence of the Law of Sinai. Two generations ago, Renan wrote: 'The incomparable fortune which awaited this page of Exodus, namely, to become the code of universal ethics, was not unmerited. The Ten Words are for all peoples; and they will be, during all centuries, the commandments of God.' And historians of civilization are generally agreed that, low as the ethical standards of the world at present undoubtedly are, it is certain that they would be even lower, but for the supreme influence of the Ten Commandments.

Quite a different attitude towards the Decalogue began with the rise of Bible Criticism. Too often it has been one of undisguised hostility. This hostility is based on alleged historical and moral reasons. One example of each of these alleged reasons will suffice to show their groundlessness. Thus, during the greater part of the nineteenth century, Critics denied that the Decalogue was Mosaic, because of the prohibition of image-worship in the Second Commandment. The prevalence of image-worship during the period of the Judges and Monarchy, they maintained, proved that no prohibition of image-worship could have been promulgated in the days of Moses. Now it is quite true that the law against image-worship was for many centuries *disregarded* in large sections of ancient Israel; in the same way as throughout fourteen centuries after the rise of Christianity, the prohibition of image-worship was 'deliberately ignored by the entire Christian Church down to the Reformation, and is still treated as null and void by the major portion of Christendom' (Canon Charles). But it is never safe to argue that, because any law is openly broken or tacitly disregarded, such a law does not therefore exist. All experience, whether in ancient or modern societies, is against such an assumption. Eminent Bible Scholars fully recognize this; and men like Professors Burney and Sellin admit 'that no reasonable ground can be discovered against the Mosaic origin of the Decalogue'.

Not more convincing are the moral objections which Critics level against the Decalogue, *e.g.*, that it deals only with *outward* actions. They disregard the Tenth, the most inward of all the Commandments; or they deliberately deny that 'Thou shalt not covet' seeks to restrain the unlawful, inward desire for something that is another's. According to them, 'it emphasizes not so much the feelings, as the practical steps which might be taken to give effect to them' (Bennett). The reason for such an astounding explanation is given in the new Anglican Commentary as follows: 'A commandment which suggests so high a standard of morals as "Thou shalt not covet" is out of place in the Decalogue!' 'It is questionable,' adds the editor of that Commentary, 'whether the Decalogue should be so constantly and nakedly propounded as the summary of the Moral Law.' The motive behind this hostility of modernist ecclesiastics to the Decalogue, and to the whole of the Hebrew Scriptures, is a twofold one. In the first place, if the Tenth Commandment is given its right and honest interpretation, *wherein is the superiority of the Gospels over the Torah?* And this alleged superiority of Christianity to Judaism they are determined to maintain at all costs. And in the second place, they believe they will save the New Testament by discrediting the 'Old'. A vain hope. Rejection of the Decalogue leads to rejection of all morality and religion.

## III

### The Moral Chaos of our Times

Attacks on the Decalogue are singularly inopportune at the present day. For our age and generation stand in especial need of a Divine Confirmation of the Moral Law. The nineteenth century loved to speak of itself as the Age of Science. Now 'Science equips man, but does not guide him. It illuminates the world for him to the region of the most distant stars; but it leaves night in his heart. It is invincible; but indifferent, neutral, un-moral' (Darmesteter). That century widely heralded the discovery that man came from the beast; and very soon after that discovery, many of the literary and artistic leaders took it upon themselves to convince their contemporaries that it was only natural for man to return to the beast. A powerful Paganism began its assault against the ancient organized Morality. It dethroned God in the sphere of human conduct, derided all moral inhibitions, and declared instinct and inclination to be the true guides to human happiness. The twentieth century is bettering the instruction begun in the nineteenth. The so-called new Psychology preaches repression of instincts to be a danger to personality; and it regards as natural the unbridled gratification of impulses which civilized mankind has always been taught should be controlled or disciplined. A new ethic has arisen, as subversive as it is godless, which bids each man, woman or child do that which seems right in his or her own eyes. It teaches that *all* moral laws are man-made; and that *all* can, therefore, be unmade by man. There is, in consequence, on every side a questioning of the sacredness of human life, a scoffing at the holiness of purity, and an angry repudiation of the idea of property. In some lands, this has led to social and political upheavals, resulting in immemorial human institutions being torn up by the roots. Even in English-speaking countries there is to-day an impatience with moral authority; and men deny, or at any rate doubt, the reality of ethical distinctions. Things are tolerated, extenuated, nay encouraged—in fiction, on the stage, in everyday life—that only a generation ago would have been the subject of unqualified condemnation. The pilot's stars of moral guidance seem no longer to be fixed stars; and for the many voyagers over the ocean of life, the clouded heavens offer no guidance at all.

Amid this spiritual confusion and moral chaos, Judaism remains clear-eyed and unmoved. It clings unswervingly to the Divine origin of the Decalogue; and continues to proclaim that there is an everlasting distinction between right and wrong, an absolute 'Thou shalt' and 'Thou shalt not' in human life, a categorical imperative in religion—high above the promptings of passion, the peradventure of inclination, or the fashion of the hour. Weak and erring man needs an *authoritative* code in matters of right and wrong, laying down with unmistakable clearness the chief heads of duty, and denouncing the chief classes of sins. Such a Divine affirmation of the Moral Law was at all times a vital necessity for mankind, in order to set aside doubt, and to silence that perverse casuistry which is always ready to call good evil, and evil good. God is not only our Father. He is also our Law-giver; and in the Decalogue, He has made known to the children of men the foundations on which human welfare and happiness can be built.

## IV

### REVELATION AND THE DECALOGUE

Judaism stands or falls with its belief in the historic actuality of the Revelation at Sinai.

Revelation, in the first instance, means the unveiling of the character and will of God to the children of men. This is implied in the Theistic position. If we think of the Universe as merely an aggregate of blind forces, then there is, of course, no room for *communication* of any kind between God and man. But the moment we assert the existence of a Supreme Mind as the Fountain and Soul of all the infinite forms of matter and life, revelation, or communication between God and man, becomes a logical and ethical necessity. The exact *manner* of this supernatural communication between God and man will be conceived differently by different groups of believers. Some will follow the Biblical accounts of Revelation in their literal sense; others will accept the interpretation of these Biblical accounts by Rabbis of Talmudic days, Jewish philosophers of the Middle Ages, or Jewish religious thinkers of modern times. No interpretation, however, is valid or in consonance with the Jewish Theistic position, which makes human reason or the human personality the *source* of such revelation. A noted philosopher of religion has recently given expression to this truth in the words: '*All* Revelation is supernatural. There can be no such thing as a purely natural revelation. We cannot really know God except as He desires to be known and makes Himself apprehensible. No view of God that grew up "of itself" in the human mind, owing nothing to God's self-disclosing action, could have any value' (Wobbermin).

Revelation is thus but the obvious inference and corollary of the character of the Deity held by all who believe in a Personal God and Father in Heaven, in prayer to Whom, in worship of Whom, and in communion with Whom, the highest moments of our lives are passed and lived. This close spiritual relationship between God and man, this interplay of spiritual forces and energies, whereby the human soul responds to the Self-manifesting Life of all Worlds, attains in Israel's Prophets that overmastering *certainty* which enables them to declare, 'Thus saith the LORD.' Theirs is an absolute conviction that the thoughts which arose in their minds about Him and His will, and the commands and exhortations which they issued in His name, really came to them at His prompting and were invested with His authority. Maimonides compared revelation to illumination by lightning on a dark night. Some prophets were granted only one such lightning-flash from the Divine; in the case of others these lightning-flashes were oft repeated; whereas to Moses was accorded continuous, unintermittent Light. Not in dreams or visions or occasional flashes of Divine intuition was the manner of revelation in his case, but 'face to face'; *i.e.* in the form of self-luminous thought and complete self-consciousness. In his mind, the Rabbis say, the Divine Message was reflected as in a clear mirror (אספקלריה מאירה). The supreme revelation in the life of the Lawgiver, however, that of the Covenant at Mount Sinai, he shared with the whole of Israel. To all of them was then vouchsafed the psychic experience of a direct communion with God. Even as at the shores of the Red Sea, when, in the words of the Sages, an ordinary maidservant was able to perceive what an Ezekiel in his moments of ecstasy could not attain to—so at Sinai, a mystic Vision gripped the spirit of the awe-struck People, filling their souls with reverence and certitude and Light.

## V

### ISRAEL, THE PEOPLE OF REVELATION

A study of Israel's amazing story will strengthen any unbiased seeker of the Truth in the conviction that Israel's Vision of the Divine is different not only in degree *but in kind* from that of any other nation; and that, therefore, there has indeed been a unique impact of the Spirit of God upon the soul of Israel. In fact, from the very first there must have been a predisposition in the nature of the Jewish people to receive the Message of Sinai. The Rabbis point out that all the precepts of the Decalogue had been practised by the Patriarchs and had become the family tradition of their children. Before giving the Torah to Israel, Rabbinic legend furthermore tells us, God offered it to the other nations of the world; everyone of them, however, refused it for one reason or another. Thus, the children of Edom asked, 'What is written in this Torah?' When God named its principal commandment, *Thou shalt not kill*—their decisive answer was, 'We cannot accept it.' Other peoples objected to the seventh and eighth commandments—immorality and the appropriation of other men's possessions being the expression of their national bent. None of them, it seems, was against Religion as such, so long as Religion confined itself to general principles. What they all objected to was he definite, concrete 'do not's' of the Decalogue. 'We have no desire for the knowledge of Thy ways,' they exclaimed; 'give your Torah to Israel.' Then God came to Israel; and Israel's reply was, *All that the* LORD *hath spoken we will do and we will obey*.

So all-compelling has been the recognition of Israel's national genius for the Life of the Spirit that it has crystallized itself into the doctrine of the Election and Mission of Israel (I. Epstein). 'Israel is the People of Revelation,' says a modernist Jewish thinker. 'It must have had a native endowment to produce and rear the succession of Prophets. Hence we do not speak of the God of Moses, nor of the God of the Prophets, but of the God of Israel' (Geiger). 'Had there been no Israelites there would be no Torah,' said Yehudah Hallevi seven centuries before him. 'Israel's pre-eminence is not derived from Moses, it is Moses whose pre-eminence is due to Israel. The Divine love went out towards the descendants of the Patriarchs. Moses was merely the Divinely chosen instrument through whom God's Blessing was to be assured unto them.'

Medieval poet and modernist thinker alike agree that Israel was from its birth predestined to become a Kingdom of Priests. Its career as a Holy Nation dates from the historically actual, mystical experience at the foot of Sinai. *Without* the Covenant at Sinai, the Exodus would have had little meaning; the story of Israel, like that of other kindred Semitic tribes, would have lost itself in the sands of the desert. *With* the Covenant at Sinai, everlasting life was planted in Israel's soul; and the story of Israel issues in eternity.

## F

### IS THE CODE OF HAMMURABI THE SOURCE OF THE MOSAIC CIVIL LAW?

For nearly a century there has been continuous archæological rediscovery of ancient civilizations that had for ages vanished from earth. To take one example: we possess to-day the actual originals of the code of laws, administrative orders and official letters of King Hammurabi, who was a contemporary of Abraham, and is mentioned in the early chapters of the Book of Genesis. This code of laws is one of the landmarks in world history, and has important bearings on the civil legislation of the Torah.

*Mesopotamia*. The original inhabitants of the Euphrates Valley—the domain of King Hammurabi—are generally spoken of as Sumerians. Thousands of years before any other people, they built brick houses, devised a strong family organization, and grouped themselves into city-states. The first schools in the world were established by them; and the Sumerians were the pioneers in alphabetic writing, architecture, weights and measures, and scientific irrigation. Their division of the circle into 360 degrees, and of the hour into sixty minutes of sixty seconds, has remained to this day.

The extraordinary fertility of their land made it the goal of invaders from the desert countries to the east and west. The vastest of these invading hordes in historic times arrived about 2500 B.C.E. from the Arabian Peninsula. The invaders overwhelmed the country, and founded the city of Babylon in the year 2300—the city that was destined in time to become the emporium of the East and mistress of the world. The new population thoroughly assimilated, and immeasurably advanced, the religion and culture of the original Sumerians. The zenith of this

Babylonian civilization was reached under the sixth king of the Semitic dynasty, King Amraphel, better known as Hammurabi (1945–1902 B.C.E.), whose great achievement was the codification of Babylonian law. A generation ago this Code of Hammurabi was rediscovered for the modern world.

*Babylonian Society.* Nothing can give us such an insight into the cultural and social life of the Babylonians 3,900 years ago as this collection of laws. Society in ancient Babylonia consisted of certain definite castes; king, court and priests, men of gentle birth (aristocrats and officers), commoners and slaves. The differences between the social grades can be seen by various regulations; *e.g.* where capital punishment for theft was commuted for by payment, the thief had to pay thirtyfold if the theft was from the royal estate; tenfold, if from a gentleman; fivefold, if from a commoner. The commoner was a free man, but subject to *corvée*, or forced unpaid labour, and liable to be sold into slavery for debt or for crime.

The slave was merely a chattel, with his owner's name branded or tattooed on his arm, and could not go beyond the city gates without a written pass from his master. A strict fugitive slave law was in operation, which in some respects was as harsh as the American fugitive slave law of 'Uncle Tom' days. There were statutory rewards for the captor of the runaway slave; while anyone enticing a slave to escape was punished by death. Contrast with this the commandment in Deuteronomy XXIII, 16, 'Thou shalt not deliver unto his master a bondman that is escaped from his master unto thee.'

If a slave married a free woman, the children were free. If a free man married a slave woman, even as a second wife, the children were free, and the slave woman also became free on her master's death. The first wife had the right to punish insolence, but only by degradation. Ishmael, the son of a free man and a bond-servant, Hagar, is free. When Hagar is insolent to Sarah, the latter may punish her as harshly as Abraham would permit, but she could no longer sell her. The position of woman in Babylonian life was favourable. In marriage between different social grades, the wife maintained, and her children inherited, the higher status. On her marriage she brought a dowry to her husband, which remained tied to her for life. As wife, she could be witness, conduct business in her own name, and possess property which her husband's creditors could not take to pay any of his ante-nuptial debts.

*Land laws and commerce.* Land was private property, subject to an impost levied on the crop. Vast herds and flocks were owned. The shepherd gave a receipt for the animals entrusted to him, and was bound to return them with reasonable increase. He was allowed to use a certain number for food, and was not responsible for those killed by lion or lightning. Any loss due to his carelessness he had to repay tenfold. This illustrates Jacob's protest to Laban: 'These twenty years have I been with thee; thy ewes and thy she-goats have not cast their young, and the rams of thy flock have I not eaten. That which was torn of beasts I brought not unto thee; I bore the loss of it; of my hand didst thou require it, whether stolen by day or stolen by night' (Gen. XXXI, 38, 39).

In commerce, there was the all-pervading obligation of putting every business transaction in writing, signed, sealed, witnessed and in duplicate. There were detailed regulations for rent, lease and lease guarantees, administrators of property, safe-deposit, warehousing, partnership, commercial travellers and agents, transport and shipping. There were fixed tariffs for various classes of labourers, ox-drivers, harvesters, veterinary surgeons, ship-builders, boatmen and branders. The physician's fee was fixed according to the social grade of the patient, the builder's according to the size of the house.

The value placed on human life in this Code is slight. Horrible mutilations abound—of eyes, ears, tongue, and hand; and there are thirty-four crimes for which the death penalty is inflicted; among these every kind of theft, including receiving and buying from servants. It is well, however, to compare with this list, and the horrible forms of death prescribed, the exceedingly cruel modes of execution in European countries down to quite modern times. Even in England, pocket-picking was punishable by death till the year 1808, and sheep-stealing until 1832!

*Moses and Hammurabi.* Much more interesting than the examination of the detailed regulations of the Code is the question, What is the influence of this oldest code of laws in the world on the Mosaic civil law?

It is now admitted that some of the stories of the Patriarchs can only be fully understood in the light of Hammurabi family and shepherd law. This is so, as we have seen in the Sarah-Hagar incident; likewise, the complaint of Jacob against Laban is in strict conformity with sections 261 to 267 of the Code of Hammurabi. As for the legal portions of Exodus, Leviticus, and Deuteronomy, no feature can be definitely singled out as derived from the Hammurabi Code. There are, however, some twenty-four instances of *analogies* and *resemblances* between the two Codes—in regard to the laws of kidnapping, burglary, deposit, assault, and various others; and especially in the *lex talionis*, life for life, eye for eye, tooth for tooth. Now, it is argued, in view of the fact that the Mosaic law is at least 400 years the younger of the two, these resemblances constitute strong evidence that the Hammurabi Code is the immediate or the remote source of the Mosaic civil and criminal legislation.

Many scholars, however, challenge this inference. They say that common laws are often due to common human experience, which is much the same everywhere. The history of the Patriarchs, they agree, has a Babylonian background: but this is so because they were of Babylonian descent. Abraham came from Ur of the Chaldees, a favourite city of his contemporary Hammurabi. Abraham, Isaac and Jacob all lived in Canaan, which was then under Babylonian sway. The Mosaic Law, however, is in no way indebted to the Babylonian. For it would be absolutely inexplicable why there are no Babylonian loan-words in its terminology, if the Babylonian law were the source of the Pentateuchal legislation. A higher culture always forces its use of language upon a primitive people which adopts that culture. Again, laws, as the peculiar expression of a people's life, can only be imported where the habits of life of the two peoples are related, and where similar social and economic conditions exist. Now Israel is the least Babylonian of peoples, being nomadic, rural, primitive; whereas Babylon has an intricate, highly industrialized, commercial city-civilization. In Israel, the people is in possession of sovereign rights; the king is under the law. In Babylon, a limited monarchy would have been deemed a contradiction in terms. In Israel, the death penalty for property crimes is abolished; and whether the theft be from king, noble, commoner or slave, the fine is the same. The slave is considered a human being. He is to go free for the loss of an eye, or even a tooth, at the hands of his master. The Babylonian Code *closes* with the case of the slave whose ear is to be cut off for desiring freedom; whereas the Mosaic Civil law (Exodus XXI, 2–6) *opens* with the case of the slave whose ear is to be bored as a mark of disgrace for refusing to go free when his six years of servitude are at an end! There is not a trace of the Biblical ideal of personal holiness in the Babylonian Code, or of the beneficence and consideration for the poor and needy, which is so characteristic of the Mosaic legislation. Deeper still is the abyss between this Code and the Mosaic Law in their respective attitudes to human freedom. The words of Henry George, spoken fifty years ago, concerning the Mosaic Law, still hold good:

'The Hebrew commonwealth was based upon the individual—a commonwealth whose ideal it was that every man should sit under his own vine and fig-tree, with none to vex him or make him afraid; a commonwealth in which none should be condemned to ceaseless toil; in which for even the bond-slave there should be hope; in which for even the beast of burden there should be rest. It is not the protection of property, but the protection of humanity, that is the aim of the Mosaic Code. Its Sabbath day and Sabbath year secure, even to the lowliest, rest and leisure. With the blasts of the jubilee trumpets the slave goes free, and a re-division of the land secures again to the poorest his fair share in the bounty of the common Creator. The reaper must leave something for the gleaner; even the ox cannot be muzzled as he treadeth out the corn. Everywhere, in everything, the dominant idea is that of our homely phrase, "Live and let live."'

*'Eye for eye' in Mosaic Law.* Further, nothing can illustrate the fundamental difference of the legal systems of these two peoples better than their different application of the law of taliation, or the rule of 'measure for measure'. The enunciation of the principle of 'life for life, eye for eye, tooth for tooth', is to-day recognized as one of the most far-reaching steps in human progress. It means the substitution of legal punishment, and as far as possible the exact equivalent of the injury, in place of wild revenge. It is the spirit of equity. The Church Father, Augustine, was one of the first to declare that taliation was a law of justice, not of hatred; one eye, not two, for an eye; one tooth, not ten, for a tooth; one life, not a whole family, for a life. The founders of International Law—Hugo Grotius, Jean Bodin, and John Selden—all maintain that the rule 'eye for an eye' enjoins, on the one hand, that a fair and equitable relation must exist between the crime and the punishment; and, on the other hand, that all citizens are equal before the law, and that the injuries of *all* be valued according to the same standard. 'It is a law appropriate only for free peoples'—said one of the pioneers of modern Bible exegesis, John D. Michaelis—'in which the poorest inhabitant has the same rights as his most aristocratic assailant... It deems the tooth of the poorest peasant as valuable as that of the nobleman; strangely so, because the peasant must bite crust, while the nobleman eats cake.' Of course, in primitive society there was great danger of this principle becoming petrified into a hard and fast rule of terrible cruelty. In the Mosaic Law, however, monetary commutation had already begun. This is seen from the prohibition of accepting money-compensation for malicious murder: 'Ye shall take no ransom for the life of a murderer, that is guilty of death' (Numbers XXXV, 31). The literal application of 'eye for eye, tooth for tooth' was excluded in Rabbinic Law; and there is no instance in Jewish history of its literal application ever having been carried out.

*'Son for son, and daughter for daughter' in the Hammurabi Code.* Very different is the way in which this principle was applied in the Code of Hammurabi. The whole Code seems to be built on it; and instead of being merely a general maxim, as in Hebrew jurisprudence, it is taken literally and translated into cold prose; *e.g.* 'If a man has caused the tooth of a man who is his equal to fall out, one shall make his tooth to fall out'; and similarly in fourteen other cases. It is true that here likewise the beginning of money-compensation appears; but not for the aristocrat or free-born, only for slaves. Furthermore, the taliation principle is extended and carried to grotesque extremes. For example, if the jerry-builder, by his faulty constructing of a house, causes the death of the owner, the jerry-builder

is killed; but if he causes the death of the son or daughter of the owner, then not the jerry-builder but his son or his daughter is killed! This illumines a passage in the Mosaic civil code which no one could ever explain till the discovery of the Hammurabi Code. In Exodus, XXI, 28–31, we read:—

'If an ox gore a man or a woman, that they die, the ox shall surely be stoned . . . ; but the owner of the ox shall be quit. But if the ox was wont to gore in time past, and warning hath been given to its owner, and he hath not kept it in, but it hath killed a man or a woman; the ox shall be stoned, and its owner also shall be put to death. If there be laid on him a ransom, then he shall give for the redemption of his life whatsoever is laid upon him. Whether it has gored a son, or have gored a daughter, according to this judgement shall it be done unto him.'

Now, what is the meaning of the last clause? Prof. David Mueller, whose treatise on the Code (Die Gesetze Hammurabis und ihr Verhaeltniss zur mosaischen Gesetzgebung, Vienna, 1903) is by far the best and most scholarly, reminds us that in the pre-Mosaic age if a goring ox killed a man, the owner of the ox was killed; if, however, he killed a son or daughter, then not the owner of the ox, but his son or his daughter was killed. By this one unobtrusive clause, *Whether it have gored a son, or have gored a daughter, according to this judgment shall it be done unto him*—the Torah sweeps away an infamous caricature of human justice. And that the meaning of this clause be for ever unmistakable, it again declares elsewhere (Deuteronomy XXIV, 16), 'The fathers shall not be put to death for the children, neither shall the children be put to death for the fathers; every man shall be put to death for his own sin.'

*No direct relation between the Codes.* Now these differences certainly do away with the notion that the Hammurabi Code is the source of the Mosaic Civil Law. The best authoritative opinion indeed holds that these two systems are independent codifications of ancient Semitic Common Law. The resemblances in the two codes are due to the common usage of the Semitic ancestors of both Babylonians and Hebrews. This common element was in Babylon developed into the Code of Hammurabi; but in Israel it was, under Providence, sifted and transmuted in such a way as to include love of stranger, protection of slave, the Ten Commandments, and the law, 'Thou shalt love thy neighbour as thyself' (Leviticus XIX, 18, 34).

As to the influence of these Codes on the legislation of later ages, all trace of the Babylonian Code seems to have been lost with the passing of the Assyro-Babylonian Empire. It is far otherwise with Biblical Law. Woodrow Wilson called attention to the potent leaven of Judaic thought in the legislations of the Western peoples throughout the Christian era.

'It would be a mistake,' he writes, 'to ascribe to Roman legal conceptions an undivided sway over the development of law and institutions during the Middle Ages. The laws of Moses as well as the laws of Rome contributed suggestions and impulse to the men and institutions which were to prepare the modern world; and if we could but have the eyes to see the subtle elements of thought which constitute the gross substance of our present habit, both as regards the sphere of private life and as regards the action of the State, we should easily discover how very much besides religion we owe to the Jew.'

The discovery of the Hammurabi Code at the beginning of this century was most disturbing to Bible Critics. It had been to them one of the 'finalities of scholarship' that the Pentateuch came after the Prophets in time and was not, and could not have been, Mosaic. Now it was seen that as early as the days of Abraham there existed not only written laws, but a Code full of most remarkable detail which shed a new light on the Patriarchs and on the Torah. And though in Liberal Jewish circles the discovery of this Babylonian Code was hailed as 'a blow to Orthodoxy', because of its resemblances to the Mosaic Law, closer examination has made abundantly clear the everlasting difference between the two—in humanity, righteousness, and holiness.

That discovery, followed as it soon was by the finding of the Assyrian and Hittite Codes, has impressed a much-needed lesson on Bible Critics; and that is, Wisdom is not of yesterday! 'We must rid ourselves of the notion,' wrote the late Prof. Baentsch of Jena, one of the foremost Biblical scholars of our times, 'that the pre-Mosaic age in Israel was barbarous or semi-barbarous, with animistic tree, stone, and ancestor worship: with fetishism, totemism, witchcraft, and other such beautiful things. To-day, we know that the age of Abraham was the outcome of a religious development that goes back many thousands of years.' Verily, the horizon of human history has been widened by millennia; and the evolutionary view of history, the view which holds that progress is always in a straight line, is seen to be both fatalistic and false. There are ebb and flood-tides in the history of the human spirit; and periods of decline like the post-Homeric age in early Greece, or the barbarous period of the Judges in Israel, can no longer be used to disprove the existence of the Creative Epochs that preceded them. Once again we have seen that the words of the Psalmist, 'Truth shall spring from the earth,' have become literally fulfilled; and the very stones of the Euphrates and Tigris valleys have given their decisive testimony in vindication of the Torah.

ספר ויקרא

THE BOOK OF LEVITICUS

# ספר ויקרא

# THE BOOK OF LEVITICUS

NAME. The oldest name for the Third Book of Moses is תורת כהנים, 'The Law of the Priests,' *i.e.* the Book which describes the functions of the Priesthood and the duties of the priestly Nation. The Jewish name *Vayyikra* is from its opening Hebrew word. The current title, Leviticus, is derived from the Septuagint.

FUNDAMENTAL CONCEPTS. One half of the Book deals with sacrifice and the laws that safeguard the priestly character of Israel; and the other half with Holiness and the sanctification of human life.

I. SACRIFICE. The study of the origins of human worship has shown that animal sacrifice is an immemorial institution among virtually all races of men. It was therefore essential to raise this universal method of worship to a purely spiritual plane. (Maimonides). This is done in Leviticus. All magic and incantation are banished from the sacrificial cult, and everything idolatrous or unholy is rigorously proscribed. With very few exceptions (Lev. v, 1, 20–26), deliberate sins are excluded from the sphere of sacrifice: and in all cases, repentance and restitution of the wrong done must precede the sacrificial act. And thus, while there are resemblances between sacrifice in Israel and sacrifice among other peoples, there are also fundamental differences that transform sacrifice as ordained in the Pentateuch into a vehicle of lofty religious communion and truth. The *burnt-offering* expressed the individual's self-surrender to God's will; the *peace-offering*, gratitude for His bounties and mercies; the *sin-offering*, sorrow at having erred from the way of God and the firm resolve to be reconciled with Him. The *congregational sacrifices*, furthermore, taught the vital lesson of the interdependence of all members of the congregation as a sacred Brotherhood, and kept alive within the nation the consciousness of its mission.

II. HOLINESS. The other fundamental thought of the Book is Holiness, *i.e.* purity of life, purity of action, purity of thought, befitting a priestly Nation. All the precepts in Leviticus are merely a translation into terms of daily life of the Divine call, 'Ye shall be holy; for I the LORD your God am holy' (XIX, 2). Holiness is an active principle, shaping and regulating every sphere of human life and activity. In Chap. XIX, the demand, 'Ye shall be holy,' is included in a series of sublime ethical doctrines; in Chap. XI, it is embodied in the dietary laws. The rule of Holiness governs the body as well as the soul, since the body is the instrument through which alone the soul acts. The Holy People of the Holy God was to keep itself free not only from moral transgressions, but also from ceremonial defilement, which would weaken the barriers against the forces of heathenism and animalism that on all sides menaced Israel.

INFLUENCE. In ancient times, the Jewish child began the study of Scripture with Leviticus; 'because little children are pure and the sacrifices are pure, let those who are pure come and occupy themselves with pure things' (Midrash). And we may well judge this Book by its influence in the education of Israel. As a result of its stern legislation, Israel's sons and daughters were freed from the ignoble and the vile—from all brutality and bestiality. As a result of its sanctifying guidance, no people ever attained to a higher conception of God, or a saner appreciation of the vital significance of health and holiness in the life of men and nations.

DIVISIONS. Chaps. I–VII define the laws of sacrifice for the individual, for the congregation, and for the priests. Chaps. VIII–X describe the inauguration of worship in the completed Sanctuary. Chaps. XI–XVII deal with the laws of clean and unclean, of purity and purification, culminating in the institution of the Day of Atonement. Chaps. XVIII–XXVI legislate on marriage, personal and social ethics ('Thou shalt love thy neighbour as thyself'), the Sacred Festivals, land tenure, and conclude with a solemn exhortation on the connection between Religion and national welfare. Chap. XXVII is a supplementary chapter on vows and tithes.

# LEVITICUS I, 1

## Chapter I

1. And the Lord called unto Moses, and spoke unto him out of the tent of meeting, saying: 2. Speak unto the children of Israel, and say unto them: ¶When any man of you bringeth an offering unto the Lord, ye shall

ויקרא א

CAP. I. א

א וַיִּקְרָא אֶל־מֹשֶׁה וַיְדַבֵּר יְהֹוָה אֵלָיו מֵאֹהֶל מוֹעֵד לֵאמֹר׃
2 דַּבֵּר אֶל־בְּנֵי יִשְׂרָאֵל וְאָמַרְתָּ אֲלֵהֶם אָדָם כִּי־יַקְרִיב מִכֶּם

א' זעירא v. 1.

# I. VAYYIKRA

(Chapters I–V)

## The Laws of Sacrifice (Chapters I–VII)

### THE PRINCIPAL SACRIFICES

**Chapter I. The Burnt-Offering**

**1.** *And the* LORD. 'And' indicates the close connection between this and the preceding Book. Exodus, in its concluding chapter, records the completion of the Sanctuary. The opening of Leviticus, giving the commands concerning sacrifices and priestly functions to be performed in connection with the Sanctuary, continues the narrative of Exodus

*called.* According to an ancient regulation, the last letter of the word ויקרא is in miniature. The Sacred Text was in ancient times written in a continuous row of letters, without any division between the words. When the last letter of a word was the same as the first of the next, as is here the case, one character would often serve for both (Luzzatto). When at a later time both letters were written out, one of them was in smaller size to show that it did not originally occur in the Text—an illustration of the profound reverence with which the Sacred Text was guarded by the Scribes

*tent of meeting* The Tent of Revelation; see Exod. xxv, 22, 'and there I will meet with thee, and I will speak with thee.' Before the Tabernacle had been built, Moses had to ascend Mount Sinai to receive instruction.

**2.** *unto the children of Israel.* Chaps. I–V form a manual of the ritual of sacrifice for the use of the laity; and deal with *voluntary* private sacrifices, for expression of gratitude, prayer, spiritual communion or desire for expiation, on the part of the individual. v. 2 is a general introduction, containing some essential principles of sacrifice. These laws closely affected the life of all the children of Israel, and were not of exclusive interest to the priests. The Sanctuary was the property of the entire people, who had all of them, men and women, young and old, voluntarily and generously contributed the materials for its construction.

*any man.* Heb. *adam.* Even a heathen may bring an offering, if he is moved to do so. A man's faith, not the accident of birth, is regarded by God. An apostate is therefore denied the privilege of bringing an offering at Israel's Sanctuary (Sifra). God would accept the offering of a heathen who turned to Him (1 Kings VIII, 41 f), but not the sacrifice of a disloyal Israelite.

*bringeth an offering.* The custom of sacrifice is here pre-supposed, and is not introduced as something novel and hitherto unheard of. Otherwise, terms like 'burnt offering' (v. 3) and 'meal offering' (II, 1) would have been defined and their purpose stated, as was done in the case of the Passover sacrifice (Exod. XII), and of the sin and guilt-offerings in Chaps. IV and V. Nowhere in the Hebrew Scriptures 'is the significance of sacrificial ritual formally explained; it is treated as self-evident and familiar to everyone ... being the natural and, like prayer, universally current expression of religious homage' (Wellhausen). Sacrifice was thus an immemorial custom in Israel, and held to be coeval with mankind; Gen. IV, 3.

*an offering.* A voluntary sacrifice, as distinct from the obligatory sacrifice later to be described. The individual is left free, according to the occasion or according to his feelings, to decide the kind of prescribed sacrifice he wishes to bring. The Heb. word (*korban*) denotes 'that which is brought near' to God by presentation upon the Altar; but, 'alongside of this literal meaning, it likewise implies that the offering, if brought in the right spirit, is the medium whereby man attains to closer nearness to the Divine' (Abarbanel).

*unto the* LORD. A main purpose of the Levitical laws was to free the whole conception of sacrifice from all heathen associations (cf. XVII, 7). Hence, it was necessary clearly to indicate Who was to be the Israelite's sole object of devotion. The Name of God largely used in Leviticus is *Adonay*, the Deliverer and Guardian of Israel, and not *Elohim*, the term for 'God' used also by non-Israelites; cf. Exod. XXII, 19.

*herd ... flock.* Domestic animals only are to be used, as these alone represent a real *sacrifice* to him who offers any of them. Wild animals,

## LEVITICUS I, 3

bring your offering of the cattle, even of the herd or of the flock ¶ 3. If his offering be a burnt-offering of the herd, he shall offer it a male without blemish; he shall bring it to the door of the tent of meeting, that he may be accepted before the Lord. 4. And he shall lay his hand upon the head of the burnt-offering; and it shall be accepted for him to

ויקרא א

קָרְבַּן לַיהוָה מִן־הַבְּהֵמָה מִן־הַבָּקָר וּמִן־הַצֹּאן תַּקְרִיבוּ
3 אֶת־קָרְבַּנְכֶם: אִם־עֹלָה קָרְבָּנוֹ מִן־הַבָּקָר זָכָר תָּמִים
יַקְרִיבֶנּוּ אֶל־פֶּתַח אֹהֶל מוֹעֵד יַקְרִיב אֹתוֹ לִרְצֹנוֹ לִפְנֵי
4 יְהוָה: וְסָמַךְ יָדוֹ עַל רֹאשׁ הָעֹלָה וְנִרְצָה לוֹ לְכַפֵּר עָלָיו:

which cost nothing, are excluded; and the bringing of a stolen animal constituted a desecration (Isa. LXI, 8). Clean and domesticated animals, furthermore, neither prey on other creatures nor live by killing. Even as the use of iron was forbidden in the construction of the Sanctuary (Exod. xx, 22) because it was symbolic of the sword, so every animal that was associated with uncleanness or violence might not be offered on the Altar. A domestic animal that had mortally injured a human being was likewise declared by the Rabbis to be unfit as a sacrifice.

**3. burnt-offering.** Embodies the idea of the submission of the worshipper to the will of God in its most perfect form, as the entire animal was placed upon the Altar to be burnt. The Heb. name for burnt-offering, *olah*, signifies 'that which ascends', symbolizing the ascent of the soul in worship. 'By making the offering ascend to heaven, the one who offers it expresses his desire and intention to ascend himself to Heaven; *i.e.* to devote himself entirely to God and place his life in God's service' (Hoffmann). Some Semitic scholars derive עולה from עול, 'wrong,' and place it in the same class with חטאת and אשם, sin and guilt-offerings. Whatever its derivation, the burnt-offering is the oldest and commonest form of sacrifice for the community and individual, and it remained the chief spontaneous offering of the individual. It was brought whenever a man's conscience prompted him to do so from a feeling of estrangement from God, in expiation of evil thoughts or unwitting sins (Job I, 5) It was open to all men, even heathens from foreign countries (cf. Shekalim VII, 6, עכו״ם ששלח עולתו ממדינת הים), and was the most striking form of the Israelite's communion with God. But since communion with the Most High was impossible to anybody who was tainted with sin (cf. Isa. LIX, 2, 'your iniquities have separated between you and your God'), and since no man could be sure of being sinless, the rite of the burnt-offering first had an expiatory effect (see on next *v.*), before the worshipper's yearning for fellowship with God was fulfilled.

### 3–9. FROM THE HERD

**of the herd.** Burnt-offerings might also be taken from the flock (*v.* 10) or from fowls (*v.* 14). All alike are acceptable to God: He does not look to the quantity or cost of the sacrifice, but to the spirit in which it is offered (Talmud)

*without blemish.* As alone suitable for God's Altar.

*to the door.* lit. 'at the entrance'; in the Court, in front of the Sanctuary, where the Altar of sacrifice and the Laver were placed. In this way, centralization and unity of worship would be secured, and idolatrous rites rigorously banished. This injunction was, alas, too often disregarded in the course of Bible history, with calamitous spiritual and moral results. It is interesting to note that Plato likewise saw the danger of grave aberration if sacrifices and the erection of private temples were left to the caprice, or superstition, of every individual (Laws X).

*that he may be accepted.* Or, 'that it may be favourably received for him' (Leeser); see next *v.*

**4. lay his hand upon.** Press, or lean, his hands between the horns of the animal. By means of this act the animal was designated as the representative or substitute of the man who brought the sacrifice. This explanation is based on Num. XXVII, 18 and 23, where Moses placed his hands upon Joshua to denote that Joshua was to take the place of Moses as leader of the nation. Another explanation is that by laying his hands on the animal, the offerer indicates it to be his property, and hereby devotes it as *his* offering.

It does not seem probable that the sacrificial acts were ever performed altogether in silence. In Scripture, the Temple is spoken of as both 'a house of sacrifice' (II Chron. VII, 12) and 'a house of prayer' (Isa. LVI, 7). Prayer and confession accompanied the imposition of hands on the Day of Atonement (XVI, 21). There must, therefore, from the first have been prayer and confession in connection with every case of laying on of hands, such as have come down to us from the days of the Second Temple. To the Rabbis, sacrifice, without such prayer and confession, was devoid of all spiritual significance; and some applied to it the Scriptural verse, 'The sacrifice of the wicked is an abomination to the Lord' (Prov. XV, 8).

*accepted . . . to make atonement.* The Heb. word for 'atonement', usually derived from an Arabic root, meaning 'to cover' (the sin), is now connected with the Assyrian *kupparu*, 'to purge away sin.' In view of the yearning for God's favour manifested in the bringing of the offering, accompanied by confession and humble prayer, God would, as it were, wipe out the offence from

## LEVITICUS I, 5

make atonement for him. 5. And he shall kill the bullock before the LORD; and Aaron's sons, the priests, shall present the blood, and dash the blood round about against the altar that is at the door of the tent of meeting. 6. And he shall flay the burnt-offering, and cut it into its pieces. 7. And the sons of Aaron the priest shall put fire upon the altar, and lay wood in order upon the fire. 8. And Aaron's sons, the priests, shall lay the pieces, and the head, and the suet, in order upon the wood that is on the fire which is upon the altar; 9. but its inwards and its legs shall he wash with water; and the priest shall make the whole smoke on the altar, for a burnt-offering, an offering made by fire, of a sweet savour unto the LORD. ¶ 10. And if his offering be of the flock, whether of the sheep, or of the goats, for a burnt-offering, he shall offer it a male without blemish. 11. And he shall kill it on the side of the altar north-

ה וְשָׁחַט אֶת־בֶּן הַבָּקָר לִפְנֵי יְהֹוָה וְהִקְרִיבוּ בְּנֵי אַהֲרֹן הַכֹּהֲנִים אֶת־הַדָּם וְזָרְקוּ אֶת־הַדָּם עַל־הַמִּזְבֵּחַ סָבִיב
6 אֲשֶׁר־פֶּתַח אֹהֶל מוֹעֵד: וְהִפְשִׁיט אֶת־הָעֹלָה וְנִתַּח אֹתָהּ
7 לִנְתָחֶיהָ: וְנָתְנוּ בְּנֵי אַהֲרֹן הַכֹּהֵן אֵשׁ עַל־הַמִּזְבֵּחַ וְעָרְכוּ
8 עֵצִים עַל־הָאֵשׁ: וְעָרְכוּ בְּנֵי אַהֲרֹן הַכֹּהֲנִים אֵת הַנְּתָחִים אֶת־הָרֹאשׁ וְאֶת־הַפָּדֶר עַל־הָעֵצִים אֲשֶׁר עַל־הָאֵשׁ אֲשֶׁר
9 עַל־הַמִּזְבֵּחַ: וְקִרְבּוֹ וּכְרָעָיו יִרְחַץ בַּמָּיִם וְהִקְטִיר הַכֹּהֵן אֶת־הַכֹּל הַמִּזְבֵּחָה עֹלָה אִשֵּׁה רֵיחַ־נִיחוֹחַ לַיהֹוָה: ס
י וְאִם־מִן־הַצֹּאן קָרְבָּנוֹ מִן־הַכְּשָׂבִים אוֹ מִן־הָעִזִּים לְעֹלָה
11 זָכָר תָּמִים יַקְרִיבֶנּוּ: וְשָׁחַט אֹתוֹ עַל יֶרֶךְ הַמִּזְבֵּחַ צָפֹנָה

His sight. כפר thus means to reconcile; to restore by atonement that inward sense of close relationship with God which is lost through sin, evil desire, or constant brooding upon sinful things. In English, the word 'atone', which now means 'to make amends', originally meant 'to set at one, to reconcile, persons at variance'.

**5.** *he shall kill.* The subject is either the priest, or the offerer, or anyone deputed by them. The Heb. word used is not המית 'put to death', but ושחט 'slaughter', in the swift and painless way of *Shechitah*, which brings with it greatest effusion of blood and instant unconsciousness.

*before the LORD.* i.e. at the entrance of the Tent of Meeting.

*Aaron's sons, the priests.* Those of Aaron's sons who are officiating as priests. Only the slaughtering might be done by one who was not a priest.

*bring the blood.* The priests receive the blood in one of the service-vessels and bring it up to the Altar. 'The blood is regarded as the seat of life, and is given back to God, who is the author of life' (Driver).

*dash.* The blood was thrown against the northeast and south-west corners of the Altar. For the association of the blood with the idea of atonement, see note on XVII, 11.

**6.** *and he shall flay.* From II Chron. XXIX, 24, XXXV, 11 f, it appears that priests and Levites performed these duties. The hide was not part of the burnt-offering.

*cut it into its pieces.* The animal was to be dismembered, but the limbs were not to be broken. The flame would thus pass *between* the pieces, and symbolize the covenant established between God and the offerer; see Gen. XV, 10.

**7.** *put fire upon the altar.* The regulations concerning the fire upon the Altar are given in VI, 2 f. Since the flame on the Altar must never be allowed to be extinguished, some fresh pieces of wood must be added for each sacrifice. Others refer it to the occasion when the fire was kindled for the first time. Malbim takes this verse to refer to the period of the Wandering in the Wilderness, when, according to Sifra, the fire was put out whenever the Altar was transported.

**8.** *the head.* Is mentioned separately, because it would have been severed from the body before the latter was flayed.

**9.** *made by fire.* To the mind of the Israelite, the sight of the sacrifice consumed by the flames would exemplify the ascent of the soul Godward.

*a sweet savour.* Like the term 'food' (Chap III, 11), it is a survival in language of the early conception of sacrifice as affording physical pleasure to the deity But this stage is long passed in Scripture, and nowhere are such phrases understood literally. 'The burning of the offering is called *a sweet savour unto the LORD*; and so it undoubtedly is, since it serves to remove sinful thoughts from our hearts. The effect of the offering upon the man who sacrificed it is pleasant unto the LORD' (Maimonides).

### 10–13. FROM THE FLOCK

**10.** *and if.* This and the preceding paragraph are closely connected, and the regulations in them supplement each other; thus, the rite of imposition of hands is not mentioned again, although it equally applied to sheep and oxen.

**11.** *side of the altar.* Its rear; i.e. the north side, the south being the side from which the Altar was ascended.

*northward.* i.e. the space between the rear of the Altar and the north wall of the Court.

## LEVITICUS I, 12

ward before the Lord; and Aaron's sons, the priests, shall dash its blood against the altar round about. 12. And he shall cut it into its pieces; and the priest shall lay them, with its head and its suet, in order on the wood that is on the fire which is upon the altar. 13. But the inwards and the legs shall he wash with water; and the priest shall offer the whole, and make it smoke upon the altar; it is a burnt-offering, an offering made by fire, of a sweet savour unto the Lord.*¹¹· ¶ 14 And if his offering to the Lord be a burnt-offering of fowls, then he shall bring his offering of turtle-doves, or of young pigeons. 15. And the priest shall bring it unto the altar, and pinch off its head, and make it smoke on the altar; and the blood thereof shall be drained out on the side of the altar. 16. And he shall take away its crop with the feathers thereof, and cast it beside the altar on the east part, in the place of the ashes. 17. And he shall rend it by the wings thereof, but shall not divide it asunder; and the priest shall make it smoke upon the altar, upon the wood that is upon the fire; it is a burnt-offering, an offering made by fire, of a sweet savour unto the Lord.

## 2  CHAPTER II

1. And when any one bringeth a meal-offering unto the Lord, his offering shall be of fine flour; and he shall pour oil upon

### 14–17. Fowl as Sacrifice

**14.** *turtle-doves . . . young pigeons.* The regulation that the sacrifice must be a male and without blemish did not apply to fowl, except that no limb must be missing. Birds were the poor man's offering (v, 7; xii, 8), and the Torah did not wish to place an undue burden upon him. The dove is the most inoffensive of birds; and, though attacked by other birds, it never attacks in return. It is a symbol of Israel, say the Rabbis; and teaches the offerer that he should rather be of the persecuted than of those that persecute.

**15.** *the priest shall bring it.* There was no rite of imposition of the hands when a bird was offered. 'Possibly in order to enhance the importance of the poor man's offering, the whole ceremonial was performed by the priest' (Kalisch).

**16.** *crop with the feathers thereof.* Unlike the entrails of the animal, which are to be washed and offered on the Altar (v. 9, 13), those of the bird were to be thrown away 'The ox or sheep is fed by its owner; but the bird obtains its food wherever it can. The undigested food in its stomach may be stolen property, and must, therefore, have no place on God's Altar' (Midrash).

**17.** *a sweet savour.* The same expression is used in connection with fowl, herd, and flock. 'It matters not whether one offer much or little, so long as the worshipper directs his heart to Heaven' (Talmud).

### CHAPTER II. The Meal-Offering

Offerings of Flour, Wheat, or Barley, prepared with Oil and Frankincense.

### 1–3. Of Fine Flour

**1.** *any one.* Heb. *nefesh*, lit. 'soul'. 'Only a very poor man would bring a meal-offering instead of an animal or birds; and God views his sacrifice as though he had offered his very soul' (Talmud).

*meal-offering.* Heb. *minchah*; sacrifice, not involving the slaughter of an animal, but on that account not less ancient or important. Originally the term *minchah* was used in a wider sense and embraced any offering made to God, whether of animals or earth's produce; Gen. iv, 3. The two constituent parts of this offering—flour and oil—were the common articles of food. They are not natural products, but are obtained as the result of toil. The meal-offering typified the consecration of man's work to the service of God.

*pour oil.* Oil is used for sanctification.

*frankincense.* The emblem of devotion; Ps. cxli, 2.

## LEVITICUS II, 2

it, and put frankincense thereon. 2. And he shall bring it to Aaron's sons the priests; and he shall take thereout his handful of the fine flour hereof, and of the oil thereof, together with all the frankincense thereof; and the priest shall make the memorial-part thereof smoke upon the altar, an offering made by fire, of a sweet savour unto the LORD. 3. But that which is left of the meal-offering shall be Aaron's and his sons'; it is a thing most holy of the offerings of the LORD made by fire. ¶ 4. And when thou bringest a meal-offering baked in the oven, it shall be unleavened cakes of fine flour mingled with oil, or unleavened wafers spread with oil. ¶5. And if thy offering be a meal-offering baked on a griddle, it shall be of fine flour unleavened, mingled with oil. 6. Thou shalt break it in pieces, and pour oil thereon; it is a meal-offering.*¹¹¹· ¶7. And if thy offering be a meal-offering of the stewing-pan, it shall be made of fine flour with oil. 8. And thou shalt bring the meal-offering that is made of these things unto the LORD; and it shall be presented unto the priest, and he shall bring it unto the altar. 9. And the priest shall take off from the meal-offering the memorial-part thereof, and shall make it smoke upon the altar—an offering made by fire, of a sweet savour unto the LORD. 10. But that which is left of the meal-offering shall be Aaron's and his sons'; it is a thing most holy of he offerings of the LORD made by fire. 11 No meal-offering, which ye shall bring unto the LORD, shall be made with leaven; for ye shall make no leaven, nor any honey, smoke as an offering made by fire unto the LORD.

ויקרא ב

2 וְיָצַק עָלֶיהָ שֶׁמֶן וְנָתַן עָלֶיהָ לְבֹנָה: וֶהֱבִיאָהּ אֶל־בְּנֵי אַהֲרֹן הַכֹּהֲנִים וְקָמַץ מִשָּׁם מְלֹא קֻמְצוֹ מִסָּלְתָּהּ וּמִשַּׁמְנָהּ עַל כָּל־לְבֹנָתָהּ וְהִקְטִיר הַכֹּהֵן אֶת־אַזְכָּרָתָהּ הַמִּזְבֵּחָה
3 אִשֵּׁה רֵיחַ נִיחֹחַ לַיהוָה: וְהַנּוֹתֶרֶת מִן־הַמִּנְחָה לְאַהֲרֹן
4 וּלְבָנָיו קֹדֶשׁ קָדָשִׁים מֵאִשֵּׁי יְהוָה: ס וְכִי תַקְרִב קָרְבַּן מִנְחָה מַאֲפֵה תַנּוּר סֹלֶת חַלּוֹת מַצֹּת בְּלוּלֹת בַּשֶּׁמֶן
ה וּרְקִיקֵי מַצּוֹת מְשֻׁחִים בַּשָּׁמֶן: ס וְאִם־מִנְחָה עַל־
6 הַמַּחֲבַת קָרְבָּנֶךָ סֹלֶת בְּלוּלָה בַשֶּׁמֶן מַצָּה תִהְיֶה: פָּתוֹת
שלישי 7 אֹתָהּ פִּתִּים וְיָצַקְתָּ עָלֶיהָ שָׁמֶן מִנְחָה הִוא: ס וְאִם־
8 מִנְחַת מַרְחֶשֶׁת קָרְבָּנֶךָ סֹלֶת בַּשֶּׁמֶן תֵּעָשֶׂה: וְהֵבֵאתָ אֶת־הַמִּנְחָה אֲשֶׁר יֵעָשֶׂה מֵאֵלֶּה לַיהוָה וְהִקְרִיבָהּ אֶל־
9 הַכֹּהֵן וְהִגִּישָׁהּ אֶל־הַמִּזְבֵּחַ: וְהֵרִים הַכֹּהֵן מִן־הַמִּנְחָה אֶת־אַזְכָּרָתָהּ וְהִקְטִיר הַמִּזְבֵּחָה אִשֵּׁה רֵיחַ נִיחֹחַ לַיהוָה:
10 וְהַנּוֹתֶרֶת מִן־הַמִּנְחָה לְאַהֲרֹן וּלְבָנָיו קֹדֶשׁ קָדָשִׁים מֵאִשֵּׁי
11 יְהוָה: כָּל־הַמִּנְחָה אֲשֶׁר תַּקְרִיבוּ לַיהוָה לֹא תֵעָשֶׂה חָמֵץ כִּי כָל־שְׂאֹר וְכָל־דְּבַשׁ לֹא־תַקְטִירוּ מִמֶּנּוּ אִשֶּׁה

---

**2.** *and he shall take.* One of the priests shall take; the previous acts might be done by the offerer or another.

*the memorial-part thereof* The portion of the sacrifice which was actually used as an offering, as distinct from the part which became the property of the priests. It has been suggested that the Heb. *azkarah*, which is usually translated 'memorial', is an ancient Semitic sacrificial term, signifying the 'male', *i.e.* the best and finest, portion of the meal (Hommel).

**3.** *most holy.* The meal-offering would, therefore, be eaten only by the priests, and within the precincts of the Sanctuary; whereas ordinary 'holy things' (קדשים קלים) might be consumed by the priests and their households in any 'clean place'. In both cases it was necessary for the person who partook of that food to be ceremonially clean.

### 4–10. OF COOKED FLOUR

**4.** *unleavened wafers.* Similar to the unleavened bread used on Passover.

**6.** *break it in pieces.* The purpose of breaking up the cake may be the same as that of dissecting the animal of the burnt-offering; see on I, 6.

**8.** *of these things.* Enumerated in v. 4–7.

*and it shall be presented.* lit. 'and he (the offerer) shall bring it near'.

**9.** *the memorial-part thereof.* See *v.* 2. Although not here explicitly mentioned, incense accompanied every voluntary meal-offering.

### 11–13. LEAVEN, HONEY, AND SALT

**11.** *leaven . . . honey.* The prohibition extended only to their being burnt upon the Altar. Leaven was regarded as a symbol of fermentation and corruption; and man's tendency to sin was later viewed as a process of moral fermentation (שאור שבעיסה). Honey was deemed in heathen cults a favourite food of the gods, and its prohibition was intended to free the mind of the Israelite from any degrading notion that sacrifices might be the food of God (Maimonides, Hoffmann).

LEVITICUS II, 12

12. As an offering of first-fruits ye may bring them unto the LORD; but they shall not come up for a sweet savour on the altar. 13. And every meal-offering of thine shalt thou season with salt; neither shalt thou suffer the salt of the covenant of thy God to be lacking from thy meal-offering; with all thine offerings thou shalt offer salt. ¶14. And if thou bring a meal-offering of first-fruits unto the LORD, thou shalt bring for the meal-offering of thy first-fruits corn in the ear parched with fire, even groats of the fresh ear. 15. And thou shalt put oil upon it, and lay frankincense thereon; it is a meal-offering. 16. And the priest shall make the memorial-part of it smoke, even of the groats thereof, and of the oil thereof, with all the frankincense thereof; it is an offering made by fire unto the LORD.*ⁱᵛ

## 3

CHAPTER III

1. And if his offering be a sacrifice of peace-offerings: if he offer of the herd, whether male or female, he shall offer it without blemish before the LORD. 2. And he shall lay his hand upon the head of his offering, and kill it at the door of the tent of meeting; and Aaron's sons the priests shall dash the blood against the altar round about. 3. And he shall present of the sacrifice of peace-offerings an offering made by fire unto the LORD; the fat that covereth the inwards, and

ויקרא ב ג

12 לַיהוָה: קָרְבַּן רֵאשִׁית תַּקְרִיבוּ אֹתָם לַיהוָה וְאֶל־הַמִּזְבֵּחַ
13 לֹא־יַעֲלוּ לְרֵיחַ נִיחֹחַ: וְכָל־קָרְבַּן מִנְחָתְךָ בַּמֶּלַח תִּמְלָח וְלֹא תַשְׁבִּית מֶלַח בְּרִית אֱלֹהֶיךָ מֵעַל מִנְחָתֶךָ עַל כָּל־
14 קָרְבָּנְךָ תַּקְרִיב מֶלַח: ס וְאִם־תַּקְרִיב מִנְחַת בִּכּוּרִים לַיהוָה אָבִיב קָלוּי בָּאֵשׁ גֶּרֶשׂ כַּרְמֶל תַּקְרִיב אֵת מִנְחַת
15 בִּכּוּרֶיךָ: וְנָתַתָּ עָלֶיהָ שֶׁמֶן וְשַׂמְתָּ עָלֶיהָ לְבֹנָה מִנְחָה
16 הִוא: וְהִקְטִיר הַכֹּהֵן אֶת־אַזְכָּרָתָהּ מִגִּרְשָׂהּ וּמִשַּׁמְנָהּ עַל כָּל־לְבֹנָתָהּ אִשֶּׁה לַיהוָה: פ רביעי

CAP. III. ג

ג א וְאִם־זֶבַח שְׁלָמִים קָרְבָּנוֹ אִם מִן־הַבָּקָר הוּא מַקְרִיב אִם־
2 זָכָר אִם־נְקֵבָה תָּמִים יַקְרִיבֶנּוּ לִפְנֵי יְהוָה: וְסָמַךְ יָדוֹ עַל־רֹאשׁ קָרְבָּנוֹ וּשְׁחָטוֹ פֶּתַח אֹהֶל מוֹעֵד וְזָרְקוּ בְּנֵי
3 אַהֲרֹן הַכֹּהֲנִים אֶת־הַדָּם עַל־הַמִּזְבֵּחַ סָבִיב: וְהִקְרִיב מִזֶּבַח הַשְּׁלָמִים אִשֶּׁה לַיהוָה אֶת־הַחֵלֶב הַמְכַסֶּה אֶת־

**12.** *as an offering of first-fruits.* Cf. XXIII, 17. Leaven and honey might be presented at the Sanctuary, though not on the Altar as a sacrifice, as were the ordinary first-fruits (Deut. XXVI, 2).

**13.** *salt.* Was to be used with every cereal offering: leaven and honey with none. Salt prevents putrefaction, while leaven and honey produce it. Salt is a preservative, and typifies that which is abiding; cf. 'an everlasting covenant of salt' (Num. XVIII, 19). Among most ancient peoples it was a sign of friendship 'to eat salt together'.

*with all thine offerings.* Also with animal and bird offerings. And as, according to the Rabbis, a man's table has the sacredness of the Altar, this law led to the custom of dipping bread in salt for the Grace before meals.

### 14–16. OF FIRST-FRUITS

**14.** *meal-offering of first-fruits.* A further instance of the class of meal-offerings. 'Parched ears' were a common article of food among the poor. The Rabbis identify this offering with the bringing of the Omer (XXIII, 10 f).

### CHAPTER III. THE PEACE-OFFERING
### 1–5. FROM THE HERD

**1.** *peace-offerings.* Or, 'thank-offerings,' Heb. *zebach shelamim*, or merely *zebach* or *zebachim*,

sacrifice made in fulfilment of a vow, or in gratitude for benefits received or expected. It would thus be an occasion when man seeks and obtains peace with his Creator. In the peace-offering there was inherent a feeling of joyousness, either in celebrating a happy occasion in the people's life (I Sam. XI, 15), or some important event in connection with a family or individual (Gen. XXXI, 54). Unlike a burnt-offering, a peace-offering could be either male or female; and only a small part of the peace-offering was burnt on the Altar. All the rest, with the exception of portions reserved for the priests, was eaten by the offerer, his kinsmen and guests, at a solemn meal which followed the offering of the sacrifice. 'It promoted the feeling of solidarity in the nation or family, and also pointed to dependence upon God for protection and for all the blessings of life' (Chapmann-Streane).

**2.** *dash the blood.* To obtain atonement for the offerer, in case he has done anything that rendered him unworthy to partake of the sacrificial meal. It was a rite of purification.

**3.** *the fat.* That fat which is attached to the stomach and extends over the intestines is forbidden to Jews as food, and has to be removed from the animal by 'porging'. It is here commanded to be devoted to the Altar.

## LEVITICUS III, 4

ויקרא ג

all the fat that is upon the inwards, 4. and the two kidneys, and the fat that is on them, which is by the loins, and the lobe above the liver, which he shall take away hard by the kidneys. 5. And Aaron's sons shall make it smoke on the altar upon the burnt-offering, which is upon the wood that is on the fire; it is an offering made by fire, of a sweet savour unto the LORD. ¶ 6. And if his offering for a sacrifice of peace-offerings unto the LORD be of the flock, male or female, he shall offer it without blemish. 7. If he bring a lamb for his offering, then shall he present it before the LORD. 8. And he shall lay his hand upon the head of his offering, and kill it before the tent of meeting; and Aaron's sons shall dash the blood thereof against the altar round about. 9. And he shall present of the sacrifice of peace-offerings an offering made by fire unto the LORD; the fat thereof, the fat tail entire, which he shall take away hard by the rump-bone; and the fat that covereth the inwards, and all the fat that is upon the inwards, 10. and the two kidneys, and the fat that is upon them, which is by the loins, and the lobe above the liver, which he shall take away by the kidneys. 11. And the priest shall make it smoke upon the altar; it is the food of the offering made by fire unto the LORD. ¶ 12. And if his offering be a goat, then he shall present it before the LORD. 13. And he shall lay his hand upon the head of it, and kill it before the tent of meeting; and the sons of Aaron shall dash the blood thereof against the altar round about. 14. And he shall present thereof his offering, even an offering made by fire unto the LORD: the fat that covereth the inwards, and all the fat that is upon the inwards, 15. and the two kidneys, and the fat that is upon them, which is by the loins, and the lobe above the liver, which he shall take away by the kidneys. 16. And the priest shall make them smoke upon the altar; it is the food of the offering made

---

**4.** *the lobe*. Attaching the liver to the kidneys.

**5.** *make it smoke*. *i.e.* all that has been mentioned in the preceding verses.

### 6–17. FROM THE FLOCK

**9.** *the fat tail*. Of certain breeds of sheep in the Orient.

**11.** *food of the offering*. lit. 'bread of the offering'. The phrase is identical in meaning with the phrase in *v.* 16. The Heb. לחם, 'bread', has here its primitive Semitic meaning 'flesh'—another indication of the hoary age of the sacrificial system and its technical vocabulary.

**12.** *goat*. The treatment is the same as that of the lamb, with the exception of the fat tail. Birds were not accepted as a peace-offering, because they were not deemed sufficient to constitute a sacrificial meal

**17.** *a perpetual statute*. The Sifra explains the verse thus: 'a perpetual statute'—the prohibition of eating fat and blood applied not only whilst the Israelites were in the Wilderness, when the sacrificial fat was burnt on the Altar in the Tabernacle, but also during the period of the Temple. 'Throughout your generations'—the prohibition applies also to later times when

## LEVITICUS III, 17

by fire, for a sweet savour; all the fat is the LORD's. 17. It shall be a perpetual statute throughout your generations in all your dwellings, that ye shall eat neither fat nor blood.\*v.

### 4 CHAPTER IV

1. And the LORD spoke unto Moses, saying: 2. Speak unto the children of Israel, saying: ¶ If any one shall sin through error, in any of the things which the LORD hath commanded not to be done, and shall do any one of them: 3. if the anointed priest shall sin so as to bring guilt on the people, then let him offer for his sin, which he hath sinned, a young bullock without blemish unto the LORD for a sin-offering. 4. And he shall bring the bullock unto the door of the tent of meeting before the LORD; and he shall lay his hand upon the head of the bullock, and kill the bullock before the LORD; 5. And the anointed priest shall take of the blood of the bullock, and bring it to the tent of meeting. 6. And the priest shall dip his finger in the blood, and sprinkle of the blood seven times before the LORD, in front of the veil of the sanctuary. 7. And the priest shall put of the blood upon the horns of the altar of sweet incense before the LORD, which is in the tent of meeting; and all the remaining blood of the bullock shall he pour out at the base of the altar of burnt-offering, which is at the door of the tent of meeting. 8. And all the fat of the bullock of the sin-offering he shall take off from it: the fat

---

sacrifices were no longer offered; 'in all your dwellings'—and it applies to all lands, even those outside Palestine, where sacrifices could never be offered. See on XVII, 10.

#### CHAPTER IV, 1–V, 13. THE SIN-OFFERING

The animal sacrificed varied according to the rank of the offender, provision being made for simpler offerings on the part of the poor.

**2.** *sin*. This Heb. root חטא means in its simplest form, 'to miss the mark.' The sinner misses the true aim of human living.

*through error*. Or, 'unwittingly' (RV Text). The regulations here prescribed did not apply where the offence was committed deliberately; see, however, next chapter.

#### 3–12. OF THE HIGH PRIEST

Details are now given of those to whom the sin-offering applies.

**3.** *the anointed priest*. The High Priest. Upon his head alone anointing oil was poured at the ceremony of consecration (VIII, 12).

*so as to bring guilt*. By any involuntary offence. The High Priest was the teacher and leader of his community. Consequently any error he committed would tend 'to bring guilt on the people'.

*a sin-offering*. Heb. חטאת. Its real meaning is something that will purge, purify, and wash away the sin.

**6.** *the veil of the sanctuary*. i.e. the veil which separated the Holy Place from the Holy of Holies (Exod. XXVI, 33). The priest stood in the Holy Place and sprinkled the blood not on the veil, but in its direction.

**7.** *horns of the altar*. Of incense; see Exod. XXX, 2. They were corner-pieces rising upwards. Their significance lay in the fact that they pointed heavenward; and the application of the blood to these horns directed the thoughts of the sinner to God

**8.** *fat of the bullock*. Removal of fat applied to every sin-offering

417

# LEVITICUS IV, 9

that covereth the inwards, and all the fat that is upon the inwards, 9. and the two kidneys, and the fat that is upon them which is by the loins, and the lobe above the liver, which he shall take away by the kidneys, 10. as it is taken off from the ox of the sacrifice of peace-offerings; and the priest shall make them smoke upon the altar of burnt-offering. 11. But the skin of the bullock, and all its flesh, with its head, and with its legs, and its inwards, and its dung, 12. even the whole bullock shall he carry forth without the camp unto a clean place, where the ashes are poured out, and burn it on wood with fire; where the ashes are poured out shall it be burnt. ¶ 13. And if the whole congregation of Israel shall err, the thing being hid from the eyes of the assembly, and do any of the things which the LORD hath commanded not to be done, and are guilty: 14. when the sin wherein they have sinned is known, then the assembly shall offer a young bullock for a sin-offering, and bring it before the tent of meeting. 15. And the elders of the congregation shall lay their hands upon the head of the bullock before the LORD; and the bullock shall be killed before the LORD. 16. And the anointed priest shall bring of the blood of the bullock to the tent of meeting. 17. And the priest shall dip his finger in the blood, and sprinkle it seven times before the LORD, in front of the veil. 18. And he shall put of the blood upon the horns of the altar which is before the LORD, that is in the tent of meeting, and all the remaining blood shall he pour out at the base of the altar of burnt-offering, which is at the door of the tent of meeting. 19. And all the fat thereof shall he take off from it, and make it smoke upon the altar. 20. Thus shall he do with the bullock; as he did with the bullock of the sin-offering, so shall he do

**12.** *a clean place.* The sacrifice was not burnt on the Altar, lest the offerer imagine he was purchasing forgiveness from God by offering up the animal. It was removed outside the camp. The carcass had been used in the Sanctuary, and had to be treated reverently. The most appropriate place to which it could be removed was the ash-heap near the Sanctuary. Haupt and Ehrlich suggest that the phrase is a euphemism, and 'unclean place' is intended.

*shall it be burnt.* As the High Priest is himself one of those who have to be reconciled to God, he cannot, therefore, partake of the sacrifice. The holy meat must in consequence be destroyed by fire outside the camp, in a place free from ceremonial defilement.

### 13–21. OF THE COMMUNITY

**13.** *the whole congregation.* An error on the part of the High Priest could easily result in the entire community going astray.

*the eyes of the assembly.* Its leaders; *eye* being used in this sense in Rabbinic literature (Ehrlich).

**17.** *the veil.* Of the Inner Sanctuary; see *v.* 6.

**18.** *horns of the altar.* See *v.* 7.

**20.** *bullock of the sin-offering.* Of the High Priest, described in the first paragraph of this chapter.

*make atonement.* Or, 'make expiation for.'

*shall be forgiven.* Because God is plenteous in mercy, forgiving iniquity and transgression.

## LEVITICUS IV, 21

with this; and the priest shall make atonement for them, and they shall be forgiven. 21. And he shall carry forth the bullock without the camp, and burn it as he burned the first bullock; it is the sin-offering for the assembly. ¶ 22. When a ruler sinneth, and doeth through error any one of all the things which the LORD his God hath commanded not to be done, and is guilty: 23. if his sin, wherein he hath sinned, be known to him, he shall bring for his offering a goat, a male without blemish. 24. And he shall lay his hand upon the head of the goat, and kill it in the place where they kill the burnt-offering before the LORD; it is a sin-offering. 25. And the priest shall take of the blood of the sin-offering with his finger, and put it upon the horns of the altar of burnt-offering, and the remaining blood thereof shall he pour out at the base of the altar of burnt-offering. 26. And all the fat thereof shall he make smoke upon the altar, as the fat of the sacrifice of peace-offerings; and the priest shall make atonement for him as concerning his sin, and he shall be forgiven.\*<sup>vi.</sup> ¶ 27. And if any one of the common people sin through error, in doing any of the things which the LORD hath commanded not to be done, and be guilty: 28. if his sin, which he hath sinned, be known to him, then he shall bring for his offering a goat, a female without blemish, for his sin which he hath sinned. 29. And he shall lay his hand upon the head of the sin-offering, and kill the sin-offering in the place of burnt-offering. 30. And the priest shall take of the blood thereof with his finger, and put it upon the horns of the altar of burnt-offering, and all the remaining blood thereof shall he pour out at the base of the altar. 31. And all the fat thereof shall he take away, as the fat is taken away from off the sacrifice of peace-offerings; and the priest shall make it smoke upon the altar for a sweet savour unto the LORD; and the priest shall make atonement for him, and he shall be forgiven. ¶ 32. And if he bring a lamb as his offering for a sin-offering, he shall bring it a female without blemish. 33. And he shall lay his hand upon the head of the sin-offering, and kill

### 22–26. OF A RULER

**22.** *ruler.* Or, 'a prince of a tribe' (Ibn Ezra). 'Happy is the generation whose prince publicly confesses a sin committed by him in error, for how much more would he do so in case of a deliberate sin,' is the comment of the Rabbis.

*and is guilty.* Or, 'and become guilty' (Leeser).

**23.** *a goat.* As the sinner descends in status, so his offering decreases in cost.

**26.** *as concerning his sin.* The meaning of this verse can be expressed thus: 'The priest shall perform the rites of expiation on his behalf, and he shall be purged from his sin, and so made capable of receiving, as he shall receive, the Divine forgiveness' (Kennedy).

### 27–35. OF A COMMONER

**27.** *of the common people.* Heb. *am-ha-aretz.* It has been urged that in view of the fact that this case comes immediately after the ruler, *am-ha-aretz* might here be the technical term for the Council of the People; see p. 80. In that case, however, there would here be no provision for the unwitting transgression of the commoner.

## LEVITICUS IV, 34

it for a sin-offering in the place where they kill the burnt-offering. 34. And the priest shall take of the blood of the sin-offering with his finger, and put it upon the horns of the altar of burnt-offering, and all the remaining blood thereof shall he pour out at the base of the altar. 35. And all the fat thereof shall he take away, as the fat of the lamb is taken away from the sacrifice of peace-offerings; and the priest shall make them smoke on the altar, upon the offerings of the LORD made by fire; and the priest shall make atonement for him as touching his sin that he hath sinned, and he shall be forgiven.

## 5

### CHAPTER V

1. And if any one sin, in that he heareth the voice of adjuration, he being a witness, whether he hath seen or known, if he do not utter it, then he shall bear his iniquity; 2. or if any one touch any unclean thing, whether it be the carcass of an unclean beast, or the carcass of unclean cattle, or the carcass of unclean swarming things, and be guilty, it being hidden from him that he is unclean; 3. or if he touch the uncleanness of man, whatsoever his uncleanness be wherewith he is unclean, and it be hid from him; and, when he knoweth of it, be guilty; 4. or if any one swear clearly with his lips to do evil, or to do good, whatsoever it be that a man shall utter clearly with an oath, and it be hid from him; and, when he knoweth of it, be guilty in one of these things; 5. and it shall be, when he shall be guilty in one of these things, that he shall confess that wherein he hath sinned; 6. and he shall bring his forfeit unto the LORD for his sin which he

### CHAPTER V

#### 1–13. OTHERS WHO BRING A SIN-OFFERING

**1.** *if any one sin.* The Torah proceeds to describe special cases in which a sin-offering is required, viz. a witness who fails to give testimony (v. 1); one who contracts impurity (v. 2 and 3); one who omits to fulfil his vow (v. 4). No distinction is here made between 'wittingly' and 'unwittingly'; see IV, 2.

*heareth.* Better, *had heard*.

*adjuration.* Addressed to a person in possession of evidence to come forward and offer testimony. This adjuration was known as an אלה, 'curse,' probably because it was accompanied by the pronouncement of a curse upon the person should he maintain silence. Having interfered with the execution of justice, he required expiation through a sin-offering.

*bear his iniquity. i.e.* incur guilt.

**2.** *unclean thing.* The law on this subject is given in chap. XI, 24–43.

*be guilty.* According to the Rabbis, only if, forgetting his impurity, he partakes of sacrificial food or enters the Sanctuary.

*that he is unclean.* Better, *that he became unclean.*

**3.** *uncleanness. e.g.* the dead body conveying impurity to those who touch it.

**4.** *clearly with his lips.* In contrast to a silent oath (Rashi).

*to do evil, or to do good.* To his advantage or otherwise (cf. Ps. xv, 4). It may also mean 'to do anything whatever' (see note on Gen. III, 22; XXXI, 29).

*be hid from him. i.e.* he forgot his oath.

**5.** *one of these things. i.e.* the offences stated in v. 1–4.

*he shall confess.* Confession was obligatory in the case of a sin-offering.

## LEVITICUS V, 7

hath sinned, a female from the flock, a lamb or a goat, for a sin-offering; and the priest shall make atonement for him as concerning his sin. 7. And if his means suffice not for a lamb, then he shall bring his forfeit for that wherein he hath sinned, two turtle-doves, or two young pigeons, unto the LORD: one for a sin-offering, and the other for a burnt-offering. 8. And he shall bring them unto the priest, who shall offer that which is for the sin-offering first, and pinch off its head close by its neck, but shall not divide it asunder. 9. And he shall sprinkle of the blood of the sin-offering upon the side of the altar; and the rest of the blood shall be drained out at the base of the altar; it is a sin-offering. 10. And he shall prepare the second for a burnt-offering, according to the ordinance: and the priest shall make atonement for him as concerning his sin which he hath sinned, and he shall be forgiven.*vii. ¶ 11. But if his means suffice not for two turtle-doves, or two young pigeons, then he shall bring his offering for that wherein he hath sinned, the tenth part of an ephah of fine flour for a sin-offering; he shall put no oil upon it, neither shall he put any frankincense thereon; for it is a sin-offering. 12. And he shall bring it to the priest, and the priest shall take his handful of it as the memorial-part thereof, and make it smoke on the altar, upon the offerings of the LORD made by fire; it is a sin-offering. 13. And the priest shall make atonement for him as touching his sin that he hath sinned in any of these things, and he shall be forgiven; and the remnant shall be the priest's, as the meal-offering. ¶ 14. And the LORD spoke unto Moses, saying: 15. If any one commit a trespass, and sin through error, in the holy things of the LORD, then he shall bring his forfeit unto the LORD, a ram without

---

**8.** *for the sin-offering first.* The sin-offering must precede the burnt-offering. There must be reconciliation between God and the sinner, before the latter's gift could be acceptable.

**9.** *side of the altar.* See on I, 11.

**10.** *according to the ordinance.* Described in I, 14 f.

**12.** *upon the offerings.* Better, *after the manner of the offerings* (RV Margin).

**13.** *any of these things.* As in v. 4. The poor were allowed to bring fine flour as a sin-offering only for the offences described in the beginning of the chapter.

*as the meal-offering.* See II, 4.

### 14–19. THE GUILT-OFFERING

This section deals with him who causes loss to the Sanctuary by unintentionally appropriating to his own use some 'holy thing'. He is to restore the value of the article and be fined.

**15.** *a trespass.* Heb. מעילה, lit. 'a breach of faith'; here, misappropriation of property of the Sanctuary.

*the holy things of the LORD.* Gifts to the Sanctuary and portions due to the priests.

*according to thy valuation.* The suffix 'thy' is invariably added to the word 'estimation', *i.e.* valuation, in Leviticus; so also Num. XVIII, 16. That form had become the technical term reserved for sacred things.

*shekel of the sanctuary.* The shekel of full weight, twenty gerahs; Exod. xxx, 13.

## LEVITICUS V, 16   ויקרא ה

blemish out of the flock, according to thy valuation in silver by shekels, after the shekel of the sanctuary, for a guilt-offering. 16. And he shall make restitution for that which he hath done amiss in the holy thing, and shall add the fifth part thereto, and give it unto the priest; and the priest shall make atonement for him with the ram of the guilt-offering, and he shall be forgiven. ¶ 17. And if any one sin, and do any of the things which the LORD hath commanded not to be done, though he know it not, yet he is guilty, and shall bear his iniquity. 18. And he shall bring a ram without blemish out of the flock, according to thy valuation, for a guilt-offering, unto the priest; and the priest shall make atonement for him concerning the error which he committed, though he knew it not, and he shall be forgiven. 19. It is a guilt-offering—he is certainly guilty before the LORD. ¶ 20. And the LORD spoke unto Moses, saying: 21. If any one sin, and commit a trespass against the LORD, and deal falsely with his neighbour

16 בְּכֶסֶף־שְׁקָלִים בְּשֶׁקֶל־הַקֹּדֶשׁ לְאָשָׁם: וְאֵת אֲשֶׁר חָטָא
מִן־הַקֹּדֶשׁ יְשַׁלֵּם וְאֶת־חֲמִישִׁתוֹ יוֹסֵף עָלָיו וְנָתַן אֹתוֹ לַכֹּהֵן
וְהַכֹּהֵן יְכַפֵּר עָלָיו בְּאֵיל הָאָשָׁם וְנִסְלַח לוֹ: פ
17 וְאִם־נֶפֶשׁ כִּי תֶחֱטָא וְעָשְׂתָה אַחַת מִכָּל־מִצְוֹת יְהוָה אֲשֶׁר
18 לֹא תֵעָשֶׂינָה וְלֹא־יָדַע וְאָשֵׁם וְנָשָׂא עֲוֹנוֹ: וְהֵבִיא אַיִל
תָּמִים מִן־הַצֹּאן בְּעֶרְכְּךָ לְאָשָׁם אֶל־הַכֹּהֵן וְכִפֶּר עָלָיו הַכֹּהֵן
19 עַל שִׁגְגָתוֹ אֲשֶׁר־שָׁגָג וְהוּא לֹא־יָדַע וְנִסְלַח לוֹ: אָשָׁם הוּא
אָשֹׁם אָשַׁם לַיהוָה: פ
20 וַיְדַבֵּר יְהוָה אֶל־מֹשֶׁה לֵּאמֹר: נֶפֶשׁ כִּי תֶחֱטָא וּמָעֲלָה
21
מַעַל בַּיהוָה וְכִחֵשׁ בַּעֲמִיתוֹ בְּפִקָּדוֹן אוֹ־בִתְשׂוּמֶת יָד אוֹ

v. 18. קמץ בתביר

---

**16.** *add the fifth part.* One quarter of the original value, so that what he adds is a fifth of the repayment.

*and the priest.* Atonement could only be made *after* restitution.

**17.** *sin.* i.e. in error. Although these words are not added here, they occur in the next verse. This paragraph refers to what the Rabbis term אשם תלוי, the guilt-offering brought by one who is in doubt whether he has broken a law the infringement of which involves the bringing of a sin-offering.

**18.** *according to thy valuation.* As defined in v. 15.

*though he knew it not.* The meaning of the Hebrew phrase is, 'while not sure of it.' If at any time subsequently the offence is recollected, then there must be a sin-offering.

**19.** *he is certainly guilty before the LORD.* Render, *he hath made complete restitution to the LORD.* That is to say, even if eventually guilty, so long as he is not certain, the trespass-offering secures atonement for him.

20–26. GUILT-OFFERING FOR BREACH OF TRUST

**21.** *against the LORD.* Rabbi Akiba considered these seemingly superfluous words to be of great significance. They teach that the man who falsely denied that he possessed his neighbour's property denied God, who was witness to the deposit. Philo's comment on this phrase is similar: 'He who deposits anything with his neighbour depends upon the good faith alone of the man who receives it. There are no witnesses present except God, the most unerring and infallible witness who sees all the actions of men, whether they are willing that he should do so or not.'

*deal falsely.* A second class of מעילה, viz. embezzlement and misappropriation of property. The law here applies to cases which would not bring the offender within the jurisdiction of the civil courts. He had denied his guilt and sworn falsely. Later his awakened conscience caused him voluntarily to confess his wrongdoing. Though the Rabbis regarded a false oath as among the very gravest crimes, they accounted free confession of sin as a heroic moral act (Büchler).

*neighbour.* Fellow-man; see Additional Note D, p. 563.

*deposit.* He denies that any article had been deposited with him.

*pledge.* Security for a loan or the like. The rightful owner has no receipt to show that he had handed over the article. The accused, in the absence of witnesses, was only required to take an oath that he had not received the article, and then was exempt from repayment. Should he subsequently confess his guilt, the procedure described in this paragraph applies.

*robbery.* Includes theft. In the Prophets the word 'robbery' includes any injustice based on law, any legal pretext or trick by which the poor is deprived of what is his. The Rabbis gave an even wider application to the term 'robbery'. Thus, the owner of a field was not allowed to assign to his own poor relative the corner of the field that was to be left to all the poor, as he would thereby rob the other poor of their share.

## LEVITICUS V, 22 — ויקרא ה

in a matter of deposit, or of pledge, or of robbery, or have oppressed his neighbour; 22. or have found that which was lost, and deal falsely therein, and swear to a lie; in any of all these that a man doeth, sinning therein; 23. then it shall be, if he hath sinned, and is guilty, that he shall restore that which he took by robbery, or the thing which he hath gotten by oppression, or the deposit which was deposited with him, or the lost thing which he found, *ᵐ· 24. or any thing about which he hath sworn falsely, he shall even restore it in full, and shall add the fifth part more thereto; unto him to whom it appertaineth shall he give it, in the day of his being guilty. 25. And he shall bring his forfeit unto the LORD, a ram without blemish out of the flock, according to thy valuation, for a guilt-offering, unto the priest. 26. And the priest shall make atonement for him before the LORD, and he shall be forgiven, concerning whatsoever he doeth so as to be guilty thereby.

22 בְגָזֵל אוֹ עָשַׁק אֶת־עֲמִיתוֹ: אוֹ־מָצָא אֲבֵדָה וְכִחֶשׁ בָּהּ
וְנִשְׁבַּע עַל־שָׁקֶר עַל־אַחַת מִכֹּל אֲשֶׁר־יַעֲשֶׂה הָאָדָם לַחֲטֹא
23 בָהֵנָּה: וְהָיָה כִּי־יֶחֱטָא וְאָשֵׁם וְהֵשִׁיב אֶת־הַגְּזֵלָה אֲשֶׁר
גָּזָל אוֹ אֶת־הָעֹשֶׁק אֲשֶׁר עָשָׁק אוֹ אֶת־הַפִּקָּדוֹן אֲשֶׁר הָפְקַד מפטיר
24 אִתּוֹ אוֹ אֶת־הָאֲבֵדָה אֲשֶׁר מָצָא: ° אוֹ מִכֹּל אֲשֶׁר־יִשָּׁבַע
עָלָיו לַשֶּׁקֶר וְשִׁלַּם אֹתוֹ בְּרֹאשׁוֹ וַחֲמִשִׁתָיו יֹסֵף עָלָיו לַאֲשֶׁר
כה הוּא לוֹ יִתְּנֶנּוּ בְּיוֹם אַשְׁמָתוֹ: וְאֶת־אֲשָׁמוֹ יָבִיא לַיהוָה אַיִל
26 תָּמִים מִן־הַצֹּאן בְּעֶרְכְּךָ לְאָשָׁם אֶל־הַכֹּהֵן: וְכִפֶּר עָלָיו
הַכֹּהֵן לִפְנֵי יְהֹוָה וְנִסְלַח לוֹ עַל־אַחַת מִכֹּל אֲשֶׁר־יַעֲשֶׂה
לְאַשְׁמָה בָהּ:

v. 23. קמץ ברביע

*oppressed his neighbour.* The withholding, on any pretext, of money due. Thus, the hired servant accuses the master of not having paid him his wages, and the latter asserts that he has paid.

**23.** *if he hath sinned.* i.e. the accusation brought against him is true. He acknowledges his guilt.
*that which he took.* When this was not possible, the payment was in money.

**24.** *in the day of his being guilty.* i.e. on the day when he makes voluntary acknowledgment of his guilt, or, on the day of his guilt-offering. He is to repay what it was worth at the time he misappropriated it, plus a fifth.

**25.** *bring his forfeit.* But only *after* the misappropriated article had been restored.
When, on the destruction of the Second Temple, all atoning sacrifices ceased, and repentance, confession, and prayer in connection with the Day of Atonement took their place, Rabbi Eleazar ben Azaryah formulated the same principle: 'The Day of Atonement atones for sins between man and God, but does not atone for sins between man and his neighbour, until the sinner has made restitution to his neighbour and conciliated him.'

**26.** *shall make atonement.* After confession of the sin during the imposition of hands upon the animal.
*and he shall be forgiven.* When the atonement of the offender's grave sin against God and his fellow man had been secured by confession, by full restitution and payment of the fine, by sprinkling the blood and the performance of all the rites of the guilt-offering, the stain of the sin was washed away and the offender felt relieved of the burden of his transgression. Man, having cleansed himself, is thereupon completely purified by God's loving forgiveness, which turns the gravest sinner, if repentant, into a new man, free from all the transgressions of the past, at peace with man, at peace with his Father Who is in Heaven (Büchler).

# HAFTORAH VAYYIKRA הפטרת ויקרא

## ISAIAH XLIII, 21–XLIV, 23

CAP. XLIII. מג

#### CHAPTER XLIII

21. The people which I formed for Myself,
That they might tell of My praise.

22. Yet thou hast not called upon Me, O Jacob.
Neither hast thou wearied thyself about Me, O Israel.

23. Thou hast not brought Me the small cattle of thy burnt-offerings;
Neither hast thou honoured Me with thy sacrifices.

I have not burdened thee with a meal-offering,
Nor wearied thee with frankincense.

---

The Sedrah presents detailed instructions of service in the Tabernacle leading to obedience to God. The Haftorah deplores Israel's neglect of all worship. It is addressed to the Jews deported to Babylon after the first destruction of Jerusalem. Israel has been utterly careless of God: but He, for his own sake, forgives Israel's iniquities, redeems Jacob, and will glorify Himself in Israel.

#### CHAPTER XLIII

##### 21–25. THE MISSION OF ISRAEL

**21.** *the people which I formed for Myself.* Or, 'this people have I formed for myself' (Ibn Ezra; AV). Israel is an essential part of creation. By its life and history, Israel is to set forth the existence of spiritual values and a Divine purpose in the Universe: without which spiritual values, life would be meaningless; and without which Divine purpose, the material Universe would, morally speaking, be no better than primeval chaos, *tohu va-bohu*.

*that they might tell of My praise.* Through their righteousness, to which worship of God should lead them, and through the Divine purpose revealed in their history. The proclamation and advancement of God's honour is the sole reason of Israel's existence.

**22–25.** But Israel failed to serve God, and showed ingratitude instead of thankful praise. Not as a reward for the offerings it has brought, but in spite of sins punished and now freely forgiven, is God's mercy to be shown to Israel.

**22.** *not called upon Me.* They did not seek God in prayer. As in many modern circles to-day, there was then an alarming subsidence of the sense of worship. 'The statement is of course general, and is doubtless true of the majority of exiles; it does not exclude the existence of a believing minority which poured out its heart in prayer to God' (Cheyne).

*neither hast thou wearied thyself about Me.* As in the days of Micah (VI, 3) and Malachi (I, 13), Israel became weary of its Faith and Law. There are epochs in Jewish history when men's souls are parched and dry, when Israel forgets God, and a weariness of everything appertaining to Jewish Duty and destiny takes possession of Israel's spirit.

**23.** *the small cattle.* lit. 'the sheep'; the daily morning and evening sacrifice.

*I have not burdened thee with a meal-offering.* Though on Babylonian soil no sacrifice could be offered, yet the attitude of mind and heart of which the sacrifices were to be but the outward symbol is absent from the life of the people. This verse is often misunderstood. There is here no repudiation of sacrifice (Duhm); otherwise, it would destroy the whole sense of the Prophet's reproach (Marti). The Prophet addresses the people in Babylonian Exile, when the whole sacrificial system is suspended (Ibn Ezra). He tells them that the duty of calling on the Name of God is not less incumbent on them in that they are now unable to offer Him sacrifices. See Additional Note A, 'Do the Prophets Oppose Sacrifice?' p. 560.

*frankincense.* Generally accompanied meal-offerings; see Lev. II, 1.

# ISAIAH XLIII, 24

24. Thou hast bought Me no sweet cane with money,
Neither hast thou satisfied Me with the fat of sacrifices;
But thou hast burdened Me with thy sins,
Thou hast wearied Me with thine iniquities.

25. I, even I, am He that blotteth out thy transgressions for Mine own sake;
And thy sins I will not remember.

26. Put Me in remembrance, let us plead together;
Declare thou, that thou mayest be justified.

27. Thy first father sinned,
And thine intercessors have transgressed against Me.

28. Therefore I have profaned the princes of the sanctuary,
And I have given Jacob to condemnation,
And Israel to reviling.

## Chapter XLIV

1. Yet now hear, O Jacob My servant,
And Israel, whom I have chosen;

---

**24.** *sweet cane.* A scented reed, probably a constituent of the anointing oil (Exod. xxx, 23).
*satisfied Me with the fat.* See Lev. III, 3. A bold anthropomorphism.
*thou hast burdened Me with thy sins.* An even bolder anthropomorphism. Instead of loyal obedience, Israel not only took its whole duty to God lightly, but laid on Him the load of its aggravated guilt. He was compelled to mete out punishment when He yearned to scatter salvation.

**25.** *I, even I, am He that blotteth out thy transgressions.* I, against whom ye have sinned, will forgive you spontaneously, and *unsought for*. 'A verse of perfect tenderness, which reveals the tragedy of all sin. The pathos of the situation is that Israel has despised love, a love which forgave and will still forgive' (Skinner)
*for Mine own sake.* Because God is merciful and gracious, forgiving iniquity, transgression and sin (Exod. xxxiv, 6 f), God Himself takes the initiative in blotting out Israel's transgressions. 'For Mine own sake' may have the additional meaning, 'that My Name be not profaned.' God will restore Israel, not because Israel deserved restoration, but because God's Glory demanded it. This restoration will, however, be accompanied by spiritual renewal; see the Haftorah of Sabbath Parah.
*v.* 25 embodies the fundamental proclamation of Judaism that there is no other Saviour beyond God. R. Akiba deepened this teaching in the words: 'Happy are ye, O Israel! Before Whom do you purify yourselves and Who is it that purifieth you? Your father Who is in Heaven.'

**26–28.** GOD OFFERS ISRAEL A FREE PARDON: ISRAEL HESITATES TO ADMIT THE NEED OF IT

**26.** *put Me in remembrance.* A touch of irony.

'Remind me of aught in your favour I have overlooked. Set forth any argument to justify your conduct.'

**27.** *thy first father.* Adam; or, more probably, Jacob is meant (Hosea XII, 3 f).
*thine intercessors.* The Prophets and Teachers, the expounders of God's Word and Will; Jer. XXIII, 11 f; I Kings XXII, 10 f. If even patriarch and prophet have sinned, how much more the mass of the neople. From first to last, Israel had fully deserved the punishment that finally overwhelmed it.
*transgressed.* lit. 'played the rebels.' This is still Israel's spiritual tragedy to-day. The very men who should show forth to the world its truth and beauty are often in rebellion against Jewish Teaching and the whole Jewish Life.

**28.** *I have profaned.* Or, 'I will profane' (Targum, RV Text); cause them to lose their sacred dignity with the destruction of the Temple.
*the princes of the sanctuary.* Consecrated leaders, both princes and priests, who suffered such humiliation at the capture of Jerusalem.
*and Israel to reviling.* Among the nations (Kimchi).

## Chapter XLIV
### 1–5. Promise of Revival

Israel's weariness of God is only a passing phase in its history. Even as trees and plants, withered by drought, are restored and refreshed by rain, so will the Divine Spirit revive the parched soul of Israel, and awaken its children to the glory of belonging to Israel.

**1.** *now hear.* The good tidings of the Prophet.

## ISAIAH XLIV, 2

2. Thus saith the LORD that made thee,
And formed thee from the womb, who will help thee:
Fear not, O Jacob My servant,
And thou, Jeshurun, whom I have chosen.

3. For I will pour water upon the thirsty land,
And streams upon the dry ground;
I will pour My spirit upon thy seed,
And My blessing upon thine offspring;

4. And they shall spring up among the grass,
As willows by the watercourses.

5. One shall say: 'I am the LORD's';
And another shall call himself by the name of Jacob;
And another shall subscribe with his hand unto the LORD,
And surname himself by the name of Israel.

6. Thus saith the LORD, the King of Israel,
And his Redeemer the LORD of hosts:
I am the first, and I am the last,
And beside Me there is no God.

7. And who, as I, can proclaim—
Let him declare it, and set it in order for Me—
Since I appointed the ancient people?
And the things that are coming, and that shall come to pass, let them declare.

---

**2.** *from the womb.* From the time when the nation was born, at the Red Sea, the fire of true Religion had never been altogether extinct in Israel.

*fear not.* On account of past failure, or present inability to visualize the blessed future predicted.

*Jeshurun.* lit. 'The Upright One'. A poetic title of affection and honour for Israel (Deut. XXXII, 15).

**3.** *upon the thirsty land.* As the thirsty land is thus made fertile, so will I pour My spirit upon you and make you fruitful in righteousness and service.

*My spirit.* i.e. knowledge and fear of God; Isa. XI, 2, 3; Joel III, 1. 'Exile to the ancients meant national death. The life-giving spirit must first of all reawaken an Israelitish feeling, so that the thought of belonging to Jacob or Israel, and to Israel's God, is a source of pride and happiness' (Cheyne).

**4.** *they . . . as willows.* Israel's offspring shall be regenerated, even as the withered plants are restored by rain.

**5.** *I am the LORD'S.* Showing sacred pride in Israel and the God of Israel.

*shall call himself by the name of Jacob.* Priding himself on belonging to the Holy People (Ibn Ezra).

*another shall subscribe with his hand.* A sign of public self-dedication to the service of the true God.

*surname himself.* Or, 'use for a title' (Cheyne). The name *Israelite* will be deemed the highest and most flattering of human titles.

**6–23. GOD'S GREATNESS AND SUPREMACY ARE BEYOND CHALLENGE**

**6.** *first, and . . . last.* There is no God before Him and none after Him. 'Grander than even His pre-eminence in space is His pre-eminence in time' (Duhm).

**7.** *who, as I, can proclaim.* He is the First and the Last, the God presiding over all history; He who from the first knew all future times and events, and summons each to appear at its right moment. He can therefore proclaim, i.e. foretell, them, which none of the lifeless idols can do.

*ancient people.* Heb. עם עולם; either to be translated, 'the everlasting People'—a fine and poetical description of Israel (Ewald), here used in reference to the impending fall of the idolatrous nations; or, 'the people of antiquity', the first inhabitants of the world (Ibn Ezra). According to the first translation, prophecy is stated to have been continuous since Israel was formed into a nation; according to the latter, the succession of prophets goes back to the creation of man.

## ISAIAH XLIV, 8

8. Fear ye not, neither be afraid;
Have I not announced unto thee of old, and declared it?
And ye are My witnesses.
Is there a God beside Me?
Yea, there is no Rock; I know not any.

9. They that fashion a graven image are all of them vanity,
And their delectable things shall not profit;
And their own witnesses see not, nor know;
That they may be ashamed.
10. Who hath fashioned a god, or molten an image
That is profitable for nothing?
11. Behold, all the fellows thereof shall be ashamed;
And the craftsmen skilled above men;
Let them all be gathered together, let them stand up;
They shall fear, they shall be ashamed together.
12. The smith maketh an axe,
And worketh in the coals, and fashioneth it with hammers,
And worketh it with his strong arm;
Yea, he is hungry, and his strength faileth;
He drinketh no water, and is faint.

13. The carpenter stretcheth out a line;
He marketh it out with a pencil;
He fitteth it with planes,
And he marketh it out with the compasses,
And maketh it after the figure of a man,
According to the beauty of a man, to dwell in the house.
14. He heweth him down cedars,
And taketh the ilex and the oak,
And strengtheneth for himself one among the trees of the forest;
He planteth a bay-tree, and the rain doth nourish it.

---

**8.** *Rock.* Striking figure for God as Refuge and Shelter; cf. Isa. xxvi, 4.

### 9–20. THE ABSURDITY OF IDOL-MAKING

The prophet repeatedly returns to this theme because, it seems, idolatry had not yet altogether ceased among the exiles; or, readiness 'to come to terms' with idolatry 'began to make itself felt among the younger generation born in Babylon'.

**9.** *vanity.* Or, 'confusion.' They that fashion idols are faltering, confused men.
*delectable things.* i.e. the idols in which they delight.
*shall not profit.* Are of no avail.
*their own witnesses.* Their devotees.
*that they may be ashamed.* i.e. the idol-worshippers. The consequence of their folly is sarcastically stated as if it was the aim and object of their blind unintelligence (Skinner).

**11.** *all the fellows.* That join themselves in idol-worship.

*let them all be gathered together.* An ironical exhortation to unite for a combined effort.

**12–17.** The details of idol-manufacture. It is the description of an eye-witness of the activity in an idol-workshop.

**12.** *he is hungry.* The idol is produced by one who himself grows faint of hunger and thirst in making it!

**13.** *stretcheth out a line.* To mark off its dimensions on the block of wood.
*marketh it out.* Draws the outlines of the idol.
*to dwell in the house.* In a temple or in a private shrine.

**14–17.** The Prophet now traces the history of the idol back to the choosing of the wood. The workman uses part of the tree to make a fire, to warm himself and cook his meals, and with the remainder he makes a god!

**14.** *strengtheneth.* Reareth.

## ISAIAH XLIV, 15

15. Then a man useth it for fuel;
And he taketh thereof, and warmeth himself;
Yea, he kindleth it, and baketh bread;
Yea, he maketh a god, and worshippeth it;
He maketh it a graven image, and falleth down thereto.

16. He burneth the half thereof in the fire;
With the half thereof he eateth flesh;
He roasteth roast, and is satisfied;
Yea, he warmeth himself, and saith:
'Aha,
I am warm, I have seen the fire';

17. And the residue thereof he maketh a god, even his graven image;
He falleth down unto it and worshippeth, and prayeth unto it,
And saith: 'Deliver me, for thou art my god.'

18. They know not, neither do they understand;
For their eyes are bedaubed, that they cannot see,
And their hearts, that they cannot understand.

19. And none considereth in his heart,
Neither is there knowledge nor understanding to say:
'I have burned the half of it in the fire;
Yea, also I have baked bread upon the coals thereof;
I have roasted flesh and eaten it;
And shall I make the residue thereof an abomination?
Shall I fall down to the stock of a tree?'

20. He striveth after ashes,
A deceived heart hath turned him aside,
That he cannot deliver his soul, nor say:
'Is there not a lie in my right hand?'

21. Remember these things, O Jacob,
And Israel, for thou art My servant;
I have formed thee, thou art Mine own servant;
O Israel, thou shouldest not forget Me.

22. I have blotted out, as a thick cloud, thy transgressions,
And, as a cloud, thy sins;
Return unto Me, for I have redeemed thee.

23. Sing, O ye heavens, for the LORD hath done it;
Shout, ye lowest parts of the earth;
Break forth into singing, ye mountains,
O forest, and every tree therein;
For the LORD hath redeemed Jacob,
And doth glorify Himself in Israel.

טו נָטַע אֹרֶן וְגֶשֶׁם יְגַדֵּל: וְהָיָה לְאָדָם לְבָעֵר וַיִּקַּח מֵהֶם וַיָּחָם אַף־יַשִּׂיק וְאָפָה לָחֶם אַף־יִפְעַל־אֵל וַיִּשְׁתָּחוּ עָשָׂהוּ
16 פֶסֶל וַיִּסְגָּד־לָמוֹ: חֶצְיוֹ שָׂרַף בְּמוֹ־אֵשׁ עַל־חֶצְיוֹ בָּשָׂר יֹאכֵל יִצְלֶה צָלִי וְיִשְׂבָּע אַף־יָחֹם וְיֹאמַר הֶאָח חַמּוֹתִי
17 רָאִיתִי אוּר: וּשְׁאֵרִיתוֹ לְאֵל עָשָׂה לְפִסְלוֹ יִסְגָּד־לוֹ
18 וְיִשְׁתַּחוּ וְיִתְפַּלֵּל אֵלָיו וְיֹאמַר הַצִּילֵנִי כִּי אֵלִי אָתָּה: לֹא יָדְעוּ וְלֹא יָבִינוּ כִּי טַח מֵרְאוֹת עֵינֵיהֶם מֵהַשְׂכִּיל לִבֹּתָם:
19 וְלֹא־יָשִׁיב אֶל־לִבּוֹ וְלֹא דַעַת וְלֹא־תְבוּנָה לֵאמֹר חֶצְיוֹ שָׂרַפְתִּי בְמוֹ־אֵשׁ וְאַף אָפִיתִי עַל־גֶּחָלָיו לֶחֶם אֶצְלֶה בָשָׂר וְאֹכֵל וְיִתְרוֹ לְתוֹעֵבָה אֶעֱשֶׂה לְבוּל עֵץ אֶסְגּוֹד:
כ רֹעֶה אֵפֶר לֵב הוּתַל הִטָּהוּ וְלֹא־יַצִּיל אֶת־נַפְשׁוֹ וְלֹא
21 יֹאמַר הֲלוֹא שֶׁקֶר בִּימִינִי: זְכָר־אֵלֶּה יַעֲקֹב וְיִשְׂרָאֵל כִּי עַבְדִּי־אָתָּה יְצַרְתִּיךָ עֶבֶד־לִי אַתָּה יִשְׂרָאֵל לֹא תִנָּשֵׁנִי:
22 מָחִיתִי כָעָב פְּשָׁעֶיךָ וְכֶעָנָן חַטֹּאותֶיךָ שׁוּבָה אֵלַי כִּי גְאַלְתִּיךָ:
23 רָנּוּ שָׁמַיִם כִּי־עָשָׂה יְהוָה הָרִיעוּ תַּחְתִּיּוֹת אָרֶץ פִּצְחוּ הָרִים רִנָּה יַעַר וְכָל־עֵץ בּוֹ כִּי־גָאַל יְהוָה יַעֲקֹב וּבְיִשְׂרָאֵל יִתְפָּאָר:

v. 14. נון זעירא  v. 15. קמץ בז״ק  v. 17. יתיר ו'  v. 23. קמץ בז״ק

---

**18.** *their eyes are bedaubed.* Only total intellectual blindness can account for such folly.

**19.** *abomination.* The contemptuous word for 'idol'.

**20.** *he striveth after ashes.* Or, 'feeding on ashes, a deceived heart, etc.' (Driver) Feeding on ashes is a proverbial phrase for resting content with what is essentially unreal, disappointing.
*hath turned him aside.* i.e. hath led him astray.
*deliver his soul.* Free himself from his error.

**21–23.** CONCLUSION

**21.** *these things.* The facts just enunciated, and the sublime words of v. 6–8, that God is Israel's Redeemer, and that there is none beside Him.

**22.** *as a thick cloud.* Which soon passes away because of winds and sun. Israel need only turn to God and become conscious of His unconditional, redeeming love.
*I have redeemed thee.* The redemption is already accomplished in the decree of God.

**23.** *sing.* The redemption of Israel is of such profound meaning in the religious history of mankind that all creation utters a jubilant cry over it.
*lowest parts.* The abysses of earth.
*doth glorify Himself.* Israel shall become a crown of glory in His hands.

## LEVITICUS VI, 1

### CHAPTER VI

1. And the LORD spoke unto Moses, saying:
2. Command Aaron and his sons, saying:
¶ This is the law of the burnt-offering: It is that which goeth up on its firewood upon the altar all night unto the morning; and the fire of the altar shall be kept burning thereby. 3. And the priest shall put on his linen garment, and his linen breeches shall he put upon his flesh; and he shall take up the ashes whereto the fire hath consumed the burnt-offering on the altar, and he shall put them beside the altar. 4. And he shall put off his garments, and put on other garments, and carry forth the ashes without the camp unto a clean place. 5. And the fire upon the altar shall be kept burning thereby, it shall not go out; and the priest shall kindle wood on it every morning; and he shall lay the burnt-offering in order upon it, and shall make smoke thereon the fat of the peace-offerings.

ויקרא צו ו

CAP. VI. ו

פ פ פ כה 25

2 וַיְדַבֵּר יְהֹוָה אֶל־מֹשֶׁה לֵּאמֹר: צַו אֶת־אַהֲרֹן וְאֶת־בָּנָיו לֵאמֹר זֹאת תּוֹרַת הָעֹלָה הִוא הָעֹלָה עַל מוֹקְדָה עַל־הַמִּזְבֵּחַ כָּל־הַלַּיְלָה עַד־הַבֹּקֶר וְאֵשׁ הַמִּזְבֵּחַ תּוּקַד בּוֹ:
3 וְלָבַשׁ הַכֹּהֵן מִדּוֹ בַד וּמִכְנְסֵי־בַד יִלְבַּשׁ עַל־בְּשָׂרוֹ וְהֵרִים אֶת־הַדֶּשֶׁן אֲשֶׁר תֹּאכַל הָאֵשׁ אֶת־הָעֹלָה עַל־
4 הַמִּזְבֵּחַ וְשָׂמוֹ אֵצֶל הַמִּזְבֵּחַ: וּפָשַׁט אֶת־בְּגָדָיו וְלָבַשׁ בְּגָדִים אֲחֵרִים וְהוֹצִיא אֶת־הַדֶּשֶׁן אֶל־מִחוּץ לַמַּחֲנֶה אֶל־
5 מָקוֹם טָהוֹר: וְהָאֵשׁ עַל־הַמִּזְבֵּחַ תּוּקַד־בּוֹ לֹא תִכְבֶּה וּבִעֵר עָלֶיהָ הַכֹּהֵן עֵצִים בַּבֹּקֶר בַּבֹּקֶר וְעָרַךְ עָלֶיהָ הָעֹלָה

v. 2. מ' זעירא

## II. TZAV

### (CHAPTERS VI–VIII)

### DIRECTIONS TO THE PRIESTS

#### CHAPTER VI, 1–6. FIRE FOR THE DAILY BURNT-OFFERING

**2. Aaron and his sons.** The first five chapters were addressed to 'the children of Israel', and concerned the whole people. Chapters VI and VII form a manual of sacrifice addressed to the priests.

*law.* Heb. *torah*; lit. 'direction, instruction'. The phrase, 'this is the *torah* of,' frequently heads a section in Lev. concerning a special law or group of allied laws.

*burnt-offering.* The sacrifice described in Chap. I is a free-will offering of an individual. Here the burnt-offering is the continual sacrifice brought every morning and evening in the name of the community (Exod. xxix, 38–42). Hence its name *tamid*, the perpetual offering. The evening sacrifice is to be kept burning through the night until the flames can be used to kindle the wood for the morning burnt-offering.

In later times, this burnt-offering was regarded as an atoning sacrifice for the community, and hence a national institution. The Pharisees, therefore, insisted that the whole Jewish people, and not merely a few wealthy donors, should share in the privilege of defraying its cost. They furthermore arranged for direct spiritual participation of the entire nation in the actual offering of these daily sacrifices. For this purpose, Palestine Jewry was divided in 24 'Watches' (משמרות) of priests and Levites, each in turn to present itself for Temple service for one week. With each priestly Watch, there was also a corresponding delegation (מעמד) of Israelites, part of which stood by the priests, reciting prayers during the performance of the sacrificial rites. The remainder of the delegation would gather in their local synagogues and read the portions of the Torah relating to the sacrifice. 'Thus the spiritual danger that public and perpetual offerings would be looked upon as automatically securing atonement was averted' (Büchler).

*thereby.* By the firewood and sacrifice.

**3.** *shall he put upon his flesh.* The garments are described in Exod. XXVIII, 39, 42.

*the ashes.* Their removal (תרומת הדשן) completed the sacrifice of the preceding day, and therefore priestly garments were required.

*beside the altar.* The ashes of the burnt-offering were, according to Tradition, deposited daily on the east side of the incline leading to the Altar. When they accumulated they were carried forth outside the camp; see next v.

**4.** *other garments.* The holy priestly garments could be worn only in the Sanctuary.

*a clean place.* See on IV, 12.

**5.** *it shall not go out.* During the day also. Even on the Sabbath, fuel was to be placed on the Altar. The law, 'ye shall kindle no fire throughout your habitations upon the Sabbath day' (Exod. XXXV, 3) did not apply to the Sanctuary.

*peace-offerings.* Mentioned only as an example.

## LEVITICUS VI, 6

6. Fire shall be kept burning upon the altar continually; it shall not go out. ¶ 7. And this is the law of the meal-offering: the sons of Aaron shall offer it before the LORD, in front of the altar. 8. And he shall take up therefrom his handful, of the fine flour of the meal-offering, and of the oil thereof, and all the frankincense which is upon the meal-offering, and shall make the memorial-part thereof smoke upon the altar for a sweet savour unto the LORD. 9. And that which is left thereof shall Aaron and his sons eat; it shall be eaten without leaven in a holy place; in the court of the tent of meeting they shall eat it. 10. It shall not be baked with leaven. I have given it as their portion of My offerings made by fire; it is most holy, as the sin-offering, and as the guilt-offering. 11. Every male among the children of Aaron may eat of it, as a due for ever throughout your generations, from the offerings of the LORD made by fire; whatsoever toucheth them shall be holy.\*¹¹· ¶ 12. And the LORD

---

**6.** *continually.* By means of the two daily burnt-offerings a perpetual fire was kept burning on the Altar. A continuous fire was also maintained on some heathen altars. Their fire, however, was looked upon as either the symbol of the deity or as identical with it; whereas, on the Hebrew Altar, the perpetual fire, like the *Ner Tamid* (Exod. XXVII, 20), was but a witness of Israel's unremitting zeal in the service of God and typified its Religion, which embraces the whole of life and is not limited to certain special times or places. This principle, fundamental in Judaism, is translated by the Rabbinic codes into terms of everyday duty.

In the time of the Second Temple, there was a special day set apart 'when it was customary for everyone to bring wood for the Altar, that there might never be a want of fuel for that fire which was unquenchable and always burning' (Josephus). This is confirmed in the Talmud.

**7–11.** FURTHER DIRECTIONS CONCERNING THE MEAL-OFFERING

These verses repeat and supplement the regulations in Chap. II, having specially in view the daily meal-offering accompanying the *tamid* (Exod. XXIX, 41 f).

**8.** *his handful.* Not a fixed measure; because each priest's handful varied slightly.

*memorial-part thereof.* See on II, 2.

**9.** The priests were to eat it, and they could not dispose of it in any other way

*without leaven.* Better, *as unleavened bread*

**10.** *their portion.* Leaven was prohibited in the part of the meal-offering burnt on the Altar (II, 4, 11), and likewise in the portion eaten by the priests.

*most holy.* See on II, 3. It could therefore be eaten only by the male descendants of Aaron.

**11.** *every male.* Even those disqualified by reason of a blemish; see XXI.

*a due.* Heb. חק; usually 'statute', but here as in Gen. XLVII, 22, meaning, 'portion,' 'due.'

*whatsoever . . . shall be holy.* As ritual impurity was infectious, even so could ritual holiness be conveyed from one thing to another. Any food coming in contact with holy food itself becomes 'holy', and is subject to all the regulations of קדשים קלים or קדשי קדשים (II, 3) as the case may be. Many modern commentators take the phrase 'shall be holy' to imply some form of consecration to the Sanctuary or obligation to do service at it. In that case, however, the Text should have been יתקדש, as in Exod, XIX, 22, instead of יקדש (Wessely).

**12–16.** THE HIGH PRIEST'S DAILY MEAL-OFFERING

**13.** *in the day when he is anointed.* This Heb. phrase (as again in VII, 36) may mean, 'from the day when he is anointed onwards' (Ibn Ezra). After his ordination Aaron was to bring a daily meal-offering at his own expense, not on his behalf alone but for the priesthood as well (*minchath chabittim*). Likewise every priest, but only at the commencement of his ministry, offered a meal-offering (*minchath chinnuch*, 'the meal-offering of initiation').

## LEVITICUS VI, 13

spoke unto Moses, saying: 13. This is the offering of Aaron and of his sons, which they shall offer unto the LORD in the day when he is anointed: the tenth part of an ephah of fine flour for a meal-offering perpetually, half of it in the morning, and half thereof in the evening. 14. On a griddle it shall be made with oil; when it is soaked, thou shalt bring it in; in broken pieces shalt thou offer the meal-offering for a sweet savour unto the LORD. ¶ 15. And the anointed priest that shall be in his stead from among his sons shall offer it, it is a due for ever; it shall be wholly made to smoke unto the LORD. 16. And every meal-offering of the priest shall be wholly made to smoke; it shall not be eaten. ¶ 17. And the LORD spoke unto Moses, saying: 18. Speak unto Aaron and to his sons, saying: ¶ This is the law of the sin-offering: in the place where the burnt-offering is killed shall the sin-offering be killed before the LORD; it is most holy. 19. The priest that offereth it for sin shall eat it; in a holy place shall it be eaten, in the court of the tent of meeting. 20. Whatsoever shall touch the flesh thereof shall be holy; and when there is sprinkled of the blood thereof upon any garment, thou shalt wash that whereon it was sprinkled in a holy place. 21. But the earthen vessel wherein it is sodden shall be broken; and if it be sodden in a brazen vessel, it shall be scoured, and rinsed in water. 22. Every male among the priests may eat thereof; it is most holy. 23. And no sin-offering, whereof any of the blood is brought into the tent of meeting to make atonement in the holy place, shall be eaten; it shall be burnt with fire.

## 7 CHAPTER VII

1. And this is the law of the guilt-offering; it is most holy. 2. In the place where they

---

**14.** *soaked.* lit. 'well mixed.'

*in broken pieces.* 'The meaning of the Hebrew word is uncertain' (RV Margin).

**16.** *every meal-offering.* i.e. not only that prescribed here by the Torah; but also when a priest voluntarily brought a meal-offering it was wholly consumed upon the Altar.

**17–23.** Holiness of the sin-offering (cf. IV–V, 13).

**19.** *shall eat it.* i.e. the portion left after the burning of the prescribed parts was to be eaten by the officiating priest and his fellows (see v. 22).

**21.** *shall be broken.* An earthen vessel would absorb and retain some of the contents, even after scouring and cleansing (see XI, 33).

**23.** *sin-offering.* As described in Chap. IV.

### CHAPTER VII, 1–10. THE GUILT-OFFERING
(cf. v, 14–26)

**1.** *guilt-offering.* Unlike the sin-offering, it did not bring complete expiation. It was brought either as penalty for a 'trespass' (see v, 14–16, 20–26), when it had to be offered besides the restitution; or in doubtful cases (see v, 17–19), where its purpose was to suspend the effects of sin.

*most holy.* See on II, 3.

**2.** *in the place where.* See I, 11.

*shall be dashed.* The blood of the sin-offering was sprinkled in the direction of the base of the Altar or applied to its horns (IV, 6 f) as a rite of complete expiation. But the guilt-offering served no such purpose, see on v. 1; hence the blood was simply dashed round the sides of the Altar.

## LEVITICUS VII, 3

kill the burnt-offering shall they kill the guilt-offering; and the blood thereof shall be dashed against the altar round about. 3. And he shall offer of it all the fat thereof: the fat tail, and the fat that covereth the inwards, 4. and the two kidneys, and the fat that is on them, which is by the loins, and the lobe above the liver, which he shall take away by the kidneys. 5. And the priest shall make them smoke upon the altar for an offering made by fire unto the LORD; it is a guilt-offering. 6. Every male among the priests may eat thereof; it shall be eaten in a holy place; it is most holy. 7. As is the sin-offering, so is the guilt-offering; there is one law for them; the priest that maketh atonement therewith, he shall have it. 8. And the priest that offereth any man's burnt-offering, even the priest shall have to himself the skin of the burnt-offering which he hath offered. 9. And every meal-offering that is baked in the oven, and all that is dressed in the stewing-pan, and on the griddle, shall be the priest's that offereth it. 10. And every meal-offering, mingled with oil, or dry, shall all the sons of Aaron have, one as well as another. *¹¹¹. ¶ 11. And this is the law of the sacrifice of peace-offerings, which one may offer unto the LORD. 12. If he offer it for a thanksgiving, then he shall offer with the sacrifice of thanksgiving unleavened cake mingled with oil, and unleavened wafers spread with oil, and cakes mingled with oil, of fine flour soaked. 13. With cakes of leavened bread he shall present his offering with the sacrifice of his peace-offerings for thanksgiving. 14. And of it he shall present one out of each offering for a gift unto the LORD; it shall be the priest's that dasheth the blood of

---

**7.** *that maketh atonement.* The officiating priest.

**8.** *skin.* The burnt-offering was to be flayed (I, 6).

**10.** *or dry.* Without oil; being the sin-offering of the poor man who brought fine flour instead of an animal (v, 11); see, however, Num. v, 15.

**11–21. PEACE-OFFERING AND THANK-OFFERING**
(cf. Chap. III)

**11.** *peace-offerings.* See on III, 1. This class falls into three divisions: (1) thanksgiving-offerings for deliverance from sickness or danger (Ps. CVII); (2) those in fulfilment of a vow made in time of distress (Ps. CXVI); and (3) free-will offerings, when the heart is moved at the remembrance of God's tender mercies (Ps. CIII, 1–5).

**12.** *thanksgiving.* The Rabbis regarded the thank-offering as a supreme type of sacrifice; and they declare that, in the Messianic era, all sacrifices will have completed their educational mission—all save the one inculcating the duty of gratitude. That sacrifice is to continue for ever. The Prophets rank ingratitude as a sin that reduces man below the level of a dumb animal (Isa. I, 3). Since the cessation of sacrifices, the Jew instead pronounces Benedictions of thanksgiving. Persons who have been in peril of life during journeys by sea or land, in captivity or sickness, upon their deliverance or recovery, publicly utter the *Gomel*-blessing (Authorised Prayer Book, p. 148) when called to the Reading of the Law.

*unleavened cakes.* See on II, 4.

*soaked.* See on VI, 14.

**13.** *leavened bread.* The accompaniment of an ordinary meal, and also of a sacrificial meal; it was not, of course, offered upon the Altar (see II, 11).

**14.** *one out of each offering.* One cake of each sort.

*a gift.* 'As a select portion' (Moffatt).

# LEVITICUS VII, 15

the peace-offerings against the altar. 15. And the flesh of the sacrifice of his peace-offerings for thanksgiving shall be eaten on the day of his offering; he shall not leave any of it until the morning. 16. But if the sacrifice of his offering be a vow, or a freewill-offering, it shall be eaten on the day that he offereth his sacrifice; and on the morrow that which remaineth of it may be eaten. 17. But that which remaineth of the flesh of the sacrifice on the third day shall be burnt with fire. 18. And if any of the flesh of the sacrifice of his peace-offerings be at all eaten on the third day, it shall not be accepted, neither shall it be imputed unto him that offereth it; it shall be an abhorred thing, and the soul that eateth of it shall bear his iniquity. 19. And the flesh that toucheth any unclean thing shall not be eaten; it shall be burnt with fire. And as for the flesh, every one that is clean may eat thereof. 20. But the soul that eateth of the flesh of the sacrifice of peace-offerings, that pertain unto the LORD, having his uncleanness upon him, that soul shall be cut off from his people. 21. And when any one shall touch any unclean thing, whether it be the uncleanness of man, or an unclean beast, or any unclean detestable thing, and eat of the flesh of the sacrifice of peace-offerings, which pertain unto the LORD, that soul shall be cut off from his people. ¶ 22. And the LORD spoke unto Moses, saying: 23. Speak unto the children of Israel,

תְּרוּמָה לַיהוָה לַכֹּהֵן הַזֹּרֵק אֶת־דַּם הַשְּׁלָמִים לוֹ יִהְיֶה׃
טו וּבְשַׂר זֶבַח תּוֹדַת שְׁלָמָיו בְּיוֹם קָרְבָּנוֹ יֵאָכֵל לֹא־יַנִּיחַ
16 מִמֶּנּוּ עַד־בֹּקֶר׃ וְאִם־נֶדֶר ׀ אוֹ נְדָבָה זֶבַח קָרְבָּנוֹ בְּיוֹם
הַקְרִיבוֹ אֶת־זִבְחוֹ יֵאָכֵל וּמִמָּחֳרָת וְהַנּוֹתָר מִמֶּנּוּ יֵאָכֵל׃
17 וְהַנּוֹתָר מִבְּשַׂר הַזָּבַח בַּיּוֹם הַשְּׁלִישִׁי בָּאֵשׁ יִשָּׂרֵף׃ וְאִם
18 הֵאָכֹל יֵאָכֵל מִבְּשַׂר־זֶבַח שְׁלָמָיו בַּיּוֹם הַשְּׁלִישִׁי לֹא
יֵרָצֶה הַמַּקְרִיב אֹתוֹ לֹא יֵחָשֵׁב לוֹ פִּגּוּל יִהְיֶה וְהַנֶּפֶשׁ
19 הָאֹכֶלֶת מִמֶּנּוּ עֲוֺנָהּ תִּשָּׂא׃ וְהַבָּשָׂר אֲשֶׁר־יִגַּע בְּכָל־טָמֵא
לֹא יֵאָכֵל בָּאֵשׁ יִשָּׂרֵף וְהַבָּשָׂר כָּל־טָהוֹר יֹאכַל בָּשָׂר׃
כ וְהַנֶּפֶשׁ אֲשֶׁר־תֹּאכַל בָּשָׂר מִזֶּבַח הַשְּׁלָמִים אֲשֶׁר לַיהוָה
21 וְטֻמְאָתוֹ עָלָיו וְנִכְרְתָה הַנֶּפֶשׁ הַהִוא מֵעַמֶּיהָ׃ וְנֶפֶשׁ כִּי־
תִגַּע בְּכָל־טָמֵא בְּטֻמְאַת אָדָם אוֹ ׀ בִּבְהֵמָה טְמֵאָה אוֹ
בְּכָל־שֶׁקֶץ טָמֵא וְאָכַל מִבְּשַׂר־זֶבַח הַשְּׁלָמִים אֲשֶׁר לַיהוָה
22 וְנִכְרְתָה הַנֶּפֶשׁ הַהִוא מֵעַמֶּיהָ׃ וַיְדַבֵּר יְהוָה אֶל־מֹשֶׁה
23 לֵּאמֹר׃ דַּבֵּר אֶל־בְּנֵי יִשְׂרָאֵל לֵאמֹר כָּל־חֵלֶב שׁוֹר וְכֶשֶׂב

---

**15.** *on the day of his offering.* Cf. VIII, 32, 'that which remaineth of the flesh and of the bread shall ye burn with fire.'

**16.** *vow, or a freewill-offering.* When a man says, 'I take upon myself to bring an offering,' without specifying the animal, it is a 'vow'; a 'freewill' offering is when he says, 'This animal shall be an offering' (Talmud).

*on the morrow.* They were more frequently brought than the thank-offerings; and if the same law had applied to offerings for a vow as to peace-offerings, much of the flesh would have been wasted.

**18.** *neither shall it be imputed. i.e.* the sacrifice becomes null and void.

*an abhorred thing.* Heb. *piggul;* the technical term for stale sacrificial flesh.

*bear his iniquity.* Stated in XIX, 8, 'that soul shall be cut off from his people.' 'Death through Divine agency is meant, not punishment inflicted at the hands of the community' (Driver). Certain heinous offences, both moral and ceremonial, carried the sentence of כרת, 'excision,' as their penalty. In some cases, however, כרת seems to be equivalent to outlawry. The man who refused to enter the covenant (Gen. XVII, 14), or the man who would not join in the celebration of the Passover—the Nation's birth-festival (Exod. XII, 15)—was looked upon as a traitor, and exile was not too severe a punishment for him (Sulzberger).

**19.** *and the flesh.* viz. of the peace-offerings.

**20.** *his uncleanness.* This refers to impurity due to physical causes in the man himself, such as those enumerated in XI–XV.

**21.** *uncleanness of man.* See v, 2 f.

*detestable thing.* Heb. *sheketz;* a creeping creature forbidden as food. It is here described as 'unclean', which means that it is dead.

### 22–27. PROHIBITION OF FAT AND BLOOD

**23.** *no fat.* The general law had been given in III, 17. Here the subject is treated in more detail.

*ox, or sheep, or goat.* The three sacrificial animals; their fat, called חלב, is forbidden, except when such fat is covered with flesh, when it does not come within the prohibition. The fat of other 'clean' animals is spoken of as שומן, and is permitted.

## LEVITICUS VII, 24

saying: ¶ Ye shall eat no fat, of ox, or sheep, or goat. 24. And the fat of that which dieth of itself, and the fat of that which is torn of beasts, may be used for any other service; but ye shall in no wise eat of it. 25. For whosoever eateth the fat of the beast, of which men present an offering made by fire unto the LORD, even the soul that eateth it shall be cut off from his people. 26. And ye shall eat no manner of blood, whether it be of fowl or of beast, in any of your dwellings. 27. Whosoever it be that eateth any blood, that soul shall be cut off from his people. ¶ 28. And the LORD spoke unto Moses, saying: ¶ 29. Speak unto the children of Israel, saying: ¶ He that offereth his sacrifice of peace-offerings unto the LORD shall bring his offering unto the LORD out of his sacrifice of peace-offerings. 30. His own hands shall bring the offerings of the LORD made by fire: the fat with the breast shall he bring, that the breast may be waved for a wave-offering before the LORD. 31. And the priest shall make the fat smoke upon the altar; but the breast shall be Aaron's and his sons'. 32. And the right thigh shall ye give unto the priest for a heave-offering out of your sacrifices of peace-offerings. 33. He among the sons of Aaron, that offereth the blood of the peace-offerings, and the fat, shall have the right thigh for a portion. 34. For the breast of waving and the thigh of heaving have I taken of the children of Israel out of their sacrifices of peace-offerings, and have given them unto Aaron the priest and unto his sons as a due for ever from the children of Israel. ¶ 35. This is the consecrated portion of Aaron, and the consecrated portion of his sons, out of the offerings of the LORD made by fire, in the day when they were presented to minister

---

**24.** *dieth of itself.* Heb. *nevelah;* is also the technical term for an animal that has not been correctly slaughtered.

**26.** *fowl or of beast.* Since the two species alone are named, the Rabbis deduced that the law did not apply to fish. Therefore the process of ritual *salting*, which is used for the purpose of extracting the blood, is unnecessary with the latter.

**27.** *eateth any blood.* See on XVII, 10.

28–34. PRIESTS' SHARE OF THE PEACE-OFFERINGS

**30.** *wave-offering.* The prescribed part of the offering being laid upon the offerer's hands, the priest placed his own hands beneath those of the offerer, and moved them first forward and backward, and then upward and downward—symbolizing the consecration of the gift to God, the Ruler of heaven and earth.

**31.** *the breast.* The fat only was for the Altar, the breast being the portion of the priests.

**32.** *right thigh.* Considered one of the best parts of the animal, it was reserved for the most distinguished guest (I Sam. IX, 24).

**34.** *breast of waving . . . thigh of heaving.* The breast that is waved and the thigh that is 'heaved', *i.e.* set apart.

35–38. CONCLUDING SECTION ON OFFERINGS

**35.** *in the day when. i.e.* on the day and afterwards; cf. on VI, 13.

# LEVITICUS VII, 36

unto the LORD in the priest's office; 36. which the LORD commanded to be given them of the children of Israel, in the day that they were anointed. It is a due for ever throughout their generations. ¶ 37. This is the law of the burnt-offering, of the meal-offering, and of the sin-offering, and of the guilt-offering, and of the consecration-offering, and of the sacrifice of peace-offerings; 38. which the LORD commanded Moses in mount Sinai, in the day that he commanded the children of Israel to present their offerings unto the LORD, in the wilderness of Sinai.*ᶦᵛ

## 8 CHAPTER VIII

1. And the LORD spoke unto Moses, saying: 2. 'Take Aaron and his sons with him, and the garments, and the anointing oil, and the bullock of the sin-offering, and the two rams, and the basket of unleavened bread; 3. and assemble thou all the congregation at the door of the tent of meeting.' 4. And Moses did as the LORD commanded him; and the congregation was assembled at the door of the tent of meeting. 5. And Moses said unto the congregation: 'This is the thing which the LORD hath commanded to be done.' 6. And Moses brought Aaron and his sons, and washed them with water. 7. And he put upon him the tunic, and girded him with the girdle, and clothed him

---

**37.** *consecration.* lit. 'filling.' The Heb. idiom for appointing to an office is 'to fill the hand'; probably alluding to the offerings placed in the hand, authorizing him to officiate as priest. This offering is described in Exod. XXIX.

**38.** *in the day.* 'At the time.'

CHAPTERS VIII–X. INAUGURATION OF THE SANCTUARY-SERVICE

CHAPTER VIII. CONSECRATION OF AARON AND HIS SONS

The appointment of Aaron and his sons to the priesthood is commanded in Exod. XXVIII; and directions are given in Exod. XXIX and XL as to their vestments and installation into their sacred office. The Torah first describes the different classes of offerings before recounting in Leviticus the institution of the Sanctuary-service and the consecration of the priesthood.

**2.** *basket of unleavened bread.* See Exod. XXIX, 2.

**3.** *all the congregation.* Some commentators (*e.g.* Ibn Ezra) understand the phrase to mean merely the heads of tribes and the elders; others, that every man was summoned. The vast majority would have had to stand outside, probably upon the slope of Mount Sinai, at the foot of which they were encamped.

**5.** *this is the thing.* The consecration which is to commence is by the expressed will of God. The purpose of the general assembly witnessing the consecration was, likewise, to avoid a revolt against the privileges of Aaron and his sons. An attempt to foment one was made later by Korah (Num. XVI).

**6.** *Moses brought.* i.e. to the entrance of the Tent of Meeting, where the Laver was placed.

*washed.* i.e. he commanded them to wash their hands and feet (Ibn Ezra). According to the Sifra, the priests were also to bathe first the entire body, as the High Priest did on the Day of Atonement (XVI, 4). Ordinarily they washed only the hands and feet on entering the Sanctuary (Exod. XXX, 19); but on the day of consecration complete immersion was required. The spiritual significance of the act of immersion, as the first stage of their consecration, is obvious.

**7.** *upon him.* Upon Aaron. The garments of Aaron and his sons are described in Exod. XXVIII, and the investment of the priests in Exod. XXIX. The clothing of Aaron and his sons was the next step in the actual induction into their sacred offices; it invested them with the visible emblems of their holiness and their functions; see p. 345.

435

with the robe, and put the ephod upon him, and he girded him with the skilfully woven band of the ephod, and bound it unto him therewith. 8. And he placed the breast-plate upon him; and in the breast-plate he put the Urim and the Thummim. 9. And he set the mitre upon his head; and upon the mitre, in front, did he set the golden plate, the holy crown; as the LORD commanded Moses. 10. And Moses took the anointing oil, and anointed the tabernacle and all that was therein, and sanctified them. 11. And he sprinkled thereof upon the altar seven times, and anointed the altar and all its vessels, and the laver and its base, to sanctify them. 12. And he poured of the anointing oil upon Aaron's head, and anointed him, to sanctify him. 13. And Moses brought Aaron's sons, and clothed them with tunics, and girded them with girdles, and bound head-tires upon them; as the LORD commanded Moses. *v. 14. And the bullock of the sin-offering was brought; and Aaron and his sons laid their hands upon the head of the bullock of the sin-offering. 15. And when it was slain, Moses took the blood, and put it upon the horns of the altar round about with his finger, and purified the altar, and poured out the remaining blood at the base of the altar, and sanctified it, to make atonement for it. 16. And he took all the fat that was upon the inwards, and the lobe of the liver, and the two kidneys, and their fat, and Moses made it smoke upon the altar. 17. But the bullock, and its skin, and its flesh, and its dung, were burnt with fire without the camp; as the LORD commanded Moses. 18. And the ram of the burnt-offering was presented; and Aaron and his sons laid their hands upon the head of the ram. 19. And when it was killed, Moses dashed

---

**8.** *Urim and Thummim.* See on Exod. XXVIII. 30.

**10.** *anointing oil.* Its components are described in Exod. xxx, 23-24. The soothing effect of oil on skin scorched by the burning sun made it symbolize comfort and happiness; while its use for illumination suggested light and life.

**11.** *seven times.* The sanctification of the Altar was appointed for seven days, on each of which the Altar was to be anointed; Exod. XXIX, 36.

**12.** *he poured of the anointing oil.* In other passages (Exod. XXVIII, 41; XL, 15; Lev. VII, 36; X, 7) all the priests are referred to as having been anointed. Though Aaron and his sons alike were *sprinkled* with oil, the High Priest alone had oil *poured* upon his head.

**13.** *as the LORD commanded.* See Exod. XXIX, 8 f.

**14.** *sin-offering.* The first sacrifice to be offered was to cleanse the priests of any transgressions which they might have committed. They themselves must obtain atonement before they could help to secure it for others.

*laid their hands.* Making confession of their sins while doing so; see on I, 4.

**15.** *when it was slain.* By Moses. The procedure was that which normally followed the sin-offering (Chap IV).

*to make atonement for it.* Better, *by making atonement for it.*

**17.** *as the LORD commanded.* See IV, 12.

**18.** *the ram.* After the sin-offering, they next brought a burnt-offering (see Exod. XXIX, 15 f) as an expression of whole-hearted submission to the will of God and desire for fellowship with Him. The usual procedure of the burnt-offering (Chap. I) was followed.

# LEVITICUS VIII, 20

the blood against the altar round about. 20. And when the ram was cut into its pieces, Moses made the head, and the pieces, and the suet smoke. 21. And when the inwards and the legs were washed with water, Moses made the whole ram smoke upon the altar; it was a burnt-offering for a sweet savour; it was an offering made by fire unto the LORD; as the LORD commanded Moses.*vi. 22. And the other ram was presented, the ram of consecration, and Aaron and his sons laid their hands upon the head of the ram. 23. And when it was slain, Moses took of the blood thereof, and put it upon the tip of Aaron's right ear, and upon the thumb of his right hand, and upon the great toe of his right foot. 24. And Aaron's sons were brought, and Moses put of the blood upon the tip of their right ear, and upon the thumb of their right hand, and upon the great toe of their right foot; and Moses dashed the blood against the altar round about. 25. And he took the fat, and the fat tail, and all the fat that was upon the inwards, and the lobe of the liver, and the two kidneys, and their fat, and the right thigh. 26. And out of the basket of unleavened bread, that was before the LORD, he took one unleavened cake, and one cake of oiled bread, and one wafer, and placed them on the fat, and upon the right thigh. 27. And he put the whole upon the hands of Aaron, and upon the hands of his sons, and waved them for a wave-offering before the LORD. 28. And Moses took them from off their hands, and made them smoke on the altar upon the burnt-offering; they were a consecration-offering for a sweet savour; it was an offering made by fire unto the LORD. 29. And Moses took the breast, and waved it for a wave-offering before the LORD; it was Moses' portion of the ram of consecration; as the LORD commanded Moses.*vii. 30. And Moses took of

ויקרא צו ח

כ הַדָּם עַל־הַמִּזְבֵּחַ סָבִיב: וְאֶת־הָאַיִל נִתַּח לִנְתָחָיו וַיַּקְטֵר
21 מֹשֶׁה אֶת־הָרֹאשׁ וְאֶת־הַנְּתָחִים וְאֶת־הַפָּדֶר: וְאֶת־הַקֶּרֶב
וְאֶת־הַכְּרָעַיִם רָחַץ בַּמָּיִם וַיַּקְטֵר מֹשֶׁה אֶת־כָּל־הָאַיִל
הַמִּזְבֵּחָה עֹלָה הוּא לְרֵיחַ־נִיחֹחַ אִשֶּׁה הוּא לַיהוָֹה
22 כַּאֲשֶׁר צִוָּה יְהוָֹה אֶת־מֹשֶׁה: וַיַּקְרֵב אֶת־הָאַיִל הַשֵּׁנִי
אֵיל הַמִּלֻּאִים וַיִּסְמְכוּ אַהֲרֹן וּבָנָיו אֶת־יְדֵיהֶם עַל־רֹאשׁ
23 הָאָיִל: וַיִּשְׁחָט ׀ וַיִּקַּח מֹשֶׁה מִדָּמוֹ וַיִּתֵּן עַל־תְּנוּךְ אֹזֶן
אַהֲרֹן הַיְמָנִית וְעַל־בֹּהֶן יָדוֹ הַיְמָנִית וְעַל־בֹּהֶן רַגְלוֹ
24 הַיְמָנִית: וַיַּקְרֵב אֶת־בְּנֵי אַהֲרֹן וַיִּתֵּן מֹשֶׁה מִן־הַדָּם עַל־
תְּנוּךְ אָזְנָם הַיְמָנִית וְעַל־בֹּהֶן יָדָם הַיְמָנִית וְעַל־בֹּהֶן רַגְלָם
25 הַיְמָנִית וַיִּזְרֹק מֹשֶׁה אֶת־הַדָּם עַל־הַמִּזְבֵּחַ סָבִיב: וַיִּקַּח
אֶת־הַחֵלֶב וְאֶת־הָאַלְיָה וְאֶת־כָּל־הַחֵלֶב אֲשֶׁר עַל־הַקֶּרֶב
וְאֵת יֹתֶרֶת הַכָּבֵד וְאֶת־שְׁתֵּי הַכְּלָיֹת וְאֶת־חֶלְבְּהֶן וְאֵת
26 שׁוֹק הַיָּמִין: וּמִסַּל הַמַּצּוֹת אֲשֶׁר ׀ לִפְנֵי יְהוָֹה לָקַח חַלַּת
מַצָּה אַחַת וְחַלַּת לֶחֶם שֶׁמֶן אַחַת וְרָקִיק אֶחָד וַיָּשֶׂם
27 עַל־הַחֲלָבִים וְעַל שׁוֹק הַיָּמִין: וַיִּתֵּן אֶת־הַכֹּל עַל כַּפֵּי
28 אַהֲרֹן וְעַל כַּפֵּי בָנָיו וַיָּנֶף אֹתָם תְּנוּפָה לִפְנֵי יְהוָֹה: וַיִּקַּח
מֹשֶׁה אֹתָם מֵעַל כַּפֵּיהֶם וַיַּקְטֵר הַמִּזְבֵּחָה עַל־הָעֹלָה
29 מִלֻּאִים הֵם לְרֵיחַ נִיחֹחַ אִשֶּׁה הוּא לַיהוָֹה: וַיִּקַּח מֹשֶׁה
אֶת־הֶחָזֶה וַיְנִיפֵהוּ תְנוּפָה לִפְנֵי יְהוָֹה מֵאֵיל הַמִּלֻּאִים
30 לְמֹשֶׁה הָיָה לְמָנָה כַּאֲשֶׁר צִוָּה יְהוָֹה אֶת־מֹשֶׁה: וַיִּקַּח

ח' ו. 23. קמוצה

---

**22.** *ram of consecration.* This last sacrifice was the offering special to the consecration (Exod. XXIX, 19 f); see next *v*.

**23.** *ear . . . hand . . . foot.* Symbolic; representing consecration of the whole body. The priest must have consecrated ears ever to be attentive to the commands of God; consecrated hands at all times to do His will; and consecrated feet to walk evermore in holy ways (Dillmann); see Exod. XXIX, 20.

**24.** *Aaron's sons were brought.* This is not mentioned in Aaron's case, because he doubtless stood at the side of Moses throughout the ceremony.

**25.** *right thigh.* See on VII, 32.

**27.** *put the whole.* These parts of the different sacrifices were laid upon the priests' hands, reminding them of their trust on behalf of the people for the service of the Altar, and of their sacred obligation faithfully to discharge that trust.

*waved them.* See on VII, 30.

**29.** *Moses' portion.* Because he had temporarily filled the priestly office.

**30.** *of the anointing oil, and of the blood.* This act was the crowning point of the consecration ceremony; the double sprinkling 'sanctified' the

## LEVITICUS VIII, 31

the anointing oil, and of the blood which was upon the altar, and sprinkled it upon Aaron, and upon his garments, and upon his sons, and upon his sons' garments with him, and sanctified Aaron, and his garments, and his sons, and his sons' garments with him. 31. And Moses said unto Aaron and to his sons: 'Boil the flesh at the door of the tent of meeting; and there eat it and the bread that is in the basket of consecration, as I commanded, saying: Aaron and his sons shall eat it. 32. And that which remaineth of the flesh and of the bread shall ye burn with fire.*[m.] 33. And ye shall not go out from the door of the tent of meeting seven days, until the days of your consecration be fulfilled; for He shall consecrate you seven days. 34. As hath been done this day, so the LORD hath commanded to do, to make atonement for you. 35. And at the door of the tent of meeting shall ye abide day and night seven days, and keep the charge of the LORD, that ye die not; for so I am commanded.' 36. And Aaron and his sons did all the things which the LORD commanded by the hand of Moses.

---

priests and their garments, and typified the two main duties of the priesthood—to diffuse the light of godliness, and proclaim the truth that God grants atonement for human wrong-doing.

*upon his sons.* See on v. 12.

**31.** *there eat it.* This meal sealed the covenant of the priests with God. For the custom of ratifying an agreement by means of a sacrificial meal, see Gen. XXXI, 46.

*as I commanded.* We must understand the subject to be God. Onkelos and Septuagint render the Heb. 'as I was commanded.' It involves no change of consonants in the Hebrew Text.

**32.** *remaineth.* Until the morning.

**33.** *ye shall not go out.* A precaution against contracting impurity, and to prevent their diversion by worldly matters. Throughout the week of consecration, mind and heart were to be concentrated upon the solemnity and importance of the office they were entering.

**34.** *as hath been done this day.* The rites performed on the first day were to be repeated on each of the seven days (Exod. XXIX, 35 f).

**35.** *that ye die not.* The warning was frequently given to the priests that any breaking of the Divine regulations involved them in the greatest danger.

**36.** *Aaron and his sons did.* Voluntarily underwent the consecration, testifying their readiness to enter upon the service of the Most High.

# HAFTORAH TZAV    הפטרת צו

### JEREMIAH VII, 21–VIII, 3; IX, 22, 23

#### CHAPTER VII

21. Thus saith the LORD of hosts, the God of Israel: Add your burnt-offerings unto your sacrifices, and eat ye flesh. 22. For I spoke not unto your fathers, nor commanded them in the day that I brought them out of the land of Egypt, concerning burnt-offerings or sacrifices; 23. but this thing I commanded them, saying: 'Hearken unto My voice, and I will be your God, and ye shall be My people; and walk ye in all the way that I command you, that it may be well with you.' 24. But they hearkened not, nor inclined their ear, but walked in their own counsels, even in the stubborn-

#### CAP. VII. ז

21 כֹּה אָמַר יְהֹוָה צְבָאוֹת אֱלֹהֵי יִשְׂרָאֵל
22 עֹלוֹתֵיכֶם סְפוּ עַל־זִבְחֵיכֶם וְאִכְלוּ בָשָׂר: כִּי לֹא־דִבַּרְתִּי אֶת־אֲבוֹתֵיכֶם וְלֹא צִוִּיתִים בְּיוֹם הוֹצִיא אוֹתָם מֵאֶרֶץ
23 מִצְרָיִם עַל־דִּבְרֵי עוֹלָה וָזָבַח: כִּי אִם־אֶת־הַדָּבָר הַזֶּה צִוִּיתִי אוֹתָם לֵאמֹר שִׁמְעוּ בְקוֹלִי וְהָיִיתִי לָכֶם לֵאלֹהִים וְאַתֶּם תִּהְיוּ־לִי לְעָם וַהֲלַכְתֶּם בְּכָל־הַדֶּרֶךְ אֲשֶׁר אֲצַוֶּה
24 אֶתְכֶם לְמַעַן יִיטַב לָכֶם: וְלֹא שָׁמְעוּ וְלֹא־הִטּוּ אֶת־אָזְנָם

v. 22. הוציאי קרי

For the life of Jeremiah, see p. 229.

The Sedrah continues the laws regulating sacrifice: the Haftorah reveals the object of sacrifice and of all outward worship; *i.e.* to deepen the inward sense of religion and to stimulate to a holy life. It proclaims the uselessness of worship when combined with unholiness and unrighteousness.

It was spoken by Jeremiah in the year 608 B.C.E. to some solemn gathering of the people in the Temple-area. His denunciation of mere mechanical performance of acts of worship; of the superstition that the Temple ritual could be a guarantee of security, while the people were divorced from obedience to the Moral Law; and his prediction of national disaster, which only whole-hearted repentance could avert, infuriated both priests and people, and placed him in imminent risk of death (see Jer. XXVI).

#### CHAPTER VII

**21–28.** God ever demanded obedience rather than sacrifice, but Israel has not taken to heart this teaching.

**21.** *add your burnt-offerings . . . and eat ye flesh.* Burnt-offerings were wholly consumed in the flames of the Altar and were not to be eaten by the worshipper (Lev. I, 9). The Prophet bids the people treat them as if, like peace-offerings, they could be eaten by the worshipper. 'For all God cares'—he in effect says to them—'you may eat the one along with the other, because both burnt-offerings and peace-offerings, when offered by guilty hands, have no value in His eyes!' They are then merely so much 'flesh', having no sacred significance whatsoever.

**22.** *I spoke not . . . concerning burnt-offerings.* The Prophet clearly and literally refers to Exod. XIX, 5, and wishes to say: At that moment I did not ask for sacrifices as a condition of my choice—I did not utter a single word about them —but only for the moral obedience towards Me and the Commandments which I was then to announce to you. Have you kept them?

The commandments that God gave to Israel at the Going out of Egypt were the laws at Sinai; and the laws of sacrifice are not among the laws of primary importance that constitute the Decalogue. עיקר המצוה לא היתה על דברי עולה וזבח אלא שמעו בקולי והייתם לי לעם (Kimchi). Others regard this verse as merely an extreme antithetical expression of the truth that 'to obey is better than sacrifice' (I Sam. XV, 22). The Prophet proclaims that sacrifice can be no substitute for justice and mercy, and that compared with the latter, it is altogether of minor importance. But Jeremiah by no means opposed sacrifice brought in the right spirit. In his picture of the Restoration (Jer. XXXIII, 18), due place is given to Temple worship and priestly sacrifices. See Additional Note, p. 561.

Jeremiah's passionate conviction that the moral laws should have precedence over ceremonial law was at no time altogether lost sight of in Israel. This is recognized even by some Christian commentators. 'In general it may be said the obedience to the Moral Law always ranked first, and sacrifices were, as is here taught, wholly worthless when offered by the immoral. The Jews read in their Services this portion of Jeremiah as the Lesson from the Prophets in connection with Lev. VI–VIII, thus supporting the view that sacrifices are but secondary' (Streane).

**23.** *hearken . . . well with you.* A free paraphrase of Exod. XIX, 3–6; Deut. V, 16.

**24.** *but they hearkened not.* Does not necessarily refer to the generation that went out of Egypt, whose lovingkindness the Prophet praises in Jer. II, 2.

*backward and not forward.* To desert the path of faithfulness and righteousness, no matter under what new or attractive name, is always *to go backward.*

## JEREMIAH VII, 25

ness of their evil heart, and went backward and not forward, 25. even since the day that your fathers came forth out of the land of Egypt unto this day; and though I have sent unto you all My servants the prophets, sending them daily betimes and often, 26. yet they hearkened not unto Me, nor inclined their ear, but made their neck stiff; they did worse than their fathers. ¶ 27. And thou shalt speak all these words unto them, but they will not hearken to thee; thou shalt also call unto them, but they will not answer thee. 28. Therefore thou shalt say unto them:

> This is the nation that hath not hearkened
> To the voice of the LORD their God,
> Nor received correction;
> Faithfulness is perished,
> And is cut off from their mouth.

29. Cut off thy hair, and cast it away,
And take up a lamentation on the high hills;
For the LORD hath rejected and forsaken the generation of His wrath.

30. For the children of Judah have done that which is evil in My sight, saith the LORD; they have set their detestable things in the house whereon My name is called, to defile it. 31. And they have built the high places of Topheth, which is in the valley of the son of Hinnom, to burn their sons and their daughters in the fire; which I commanded not, neither came it into My mind.

וַיֵּלְכוּ בְּמֹעֵצוֹת בִּשְׁרִרוּת לִבָּם הָרָע וַיִּהְיוּ לְאָחוֹר וְלֹא
כה לְפָנִים: לְמִן־הַיּוֹם אֲשֶׁר יָצְאוּ אֲבוֹתֵיכֶם מֵאֶרֶץ מִצְרַיִם
עַד הַיּוֹם הַזֶּה וָאֶשְׁלַח אֲלֵיכֶם אֶת־כָּל־עֲבָדַי הַנְּבִיאִים
26 יוֹם הַשְׁכֵּם וְשָׁלֹחַ: וְלוֹא שָׁמְעוּ אֵלַי וְלֹא הִטּוּ אֶת־אָזְנָם
27 וַיַּקְשׁוּ אֶת־עָרְפָּם הֵרֵעוּ מֵאֲבוֹתָם: וְדִבַּרְתָּ אֲלֵיהֶם אֶת־
כָּל־הַדְּבָרִים הָאֵלֶּה וְלֹא יִשְׁמְעוּ אֵלֶיךָ וְקָרָאתָ אֲלֵיהֶם
28 וְלֹא יַעֲנוּכָה: וְאָמַרְתָּ אֲלֵיהֶם זֶה הַגּוֹי אֲשֶׁר לוֹא־שָׁמְעוּ
בְּקוֹל יְהוָה אֱלֹהָיו וְלֹא לָקְחוּ מוּסָר אָבְדָה הָאֱמוּנָה
29 וְנִכְרְתָה מִפִּיהֶם: גָּזִּי נִזְרֵךְ וְהַשְׁלִיכִי וּשְׂאִי עַל־
ל שְׁפָיִם קִינָה כִּי מָאַס יְהוָה וַיִּטֹּשׁ אֶת־דּוֹר עֶבְרָתוֹ: כִּי־
עָשׂוּ בְנֵי־יְהוּדָה הָרַע בְּעֵינַי נְאֻם־יְהוָה שָׂמוּ שִׁקּוּצֵיהֶם
31 בַּבַּיִת אֲשֶׁר־נִקְרָא שְׁמִי־עָלָיו לְטַמְּאוֹ: וּבָנוּ בָּמוֹת הַתֹּפֶת
אֲשֶׁר בְּגֵיא בֶן־הִנֹּם לִשְׂרֹף אֶת־בְּנֵיהֶם וְאֶת־בְּנֹתֵיהֶם בָּאֵשׁ
32 אֲשֶׁר לֹא צִוִּיתִי וְלֹא עָלְתָה עַל־לִבִּי: לָכֵן הִנֵּה־יָמִים
בָּאִים נְאֻם־יְהוָה וְלֹא־יֵאָמֵר עוֹד הַתֹּפֶת וְגֵיא בֶן־הִנֹּם

---

**25.** *sending them daily betimes.* Better, '*sending them early every day*' (Friedlander); 'daily in good time and often' (Rashi, Kimchi).

**28.** *from their mouth.* So hardened have they become that faithfulness not only is dead in their hearts, but they do not even make pretence to it in their speech (Kimchi). Hypocrisy is the tribute of vice to virtue; they do not recognize the necessity of even lip-homage to truth.

**29–VIII, 3.** The nation's hideous sin and its impending doom—destruction of the living and desecration of the dead.

**29.** *cut off thy hair.* As a sign of mourning.
*generation of His wrath.* Upon which His wrath is destined to be poured out.

**30.** *their detestable things.* The idols set up in the Temple by Manasseh (II Kings XXI, 3–7, XXIII, 4–12). During the long reign of that king, heathendom became the established religion in Jerusalem. All the foul impurities, gruesome rites, and unspeakable practices of ancient idolatry were fostered; the laws and precepts of Israel alone were proscribed. Shameful images were erected in the Temple itself.

**31.** *the high places of Topheth.* Where hideous cults with human sacrifices, especially of children, were carried on.
*valley of the son of Hinnom.* Heb. *Ge-Hinnom*. So called after a former owner. By reason of its evil repute as the place of human sacrifice, and later as the receptacle and burning-place of the refuse of the city, the name Ge-Hinnom (afterwards Gehenna) became the term for the later conception of 'hell'.
*to burn their sons.* Moloch-worship was introduced. The fact that the neighbouring nations—Phœnicians and Moabites—sacrificed their first-born to their gods, was sufficient reason for Manasseh and the worldly-minded among the Israelites to imitate the horrors of religious savagery.
*neither came it into My mind.* It seems that the 'Progressives' of that day even quoted Scripture for their purpose, and distorted the ancient command concerning the first-born in order to support their hideous innovations.

# JEREMIAH VII, 32

32. Therefore, behold, the days come, saith the LORD, that it shall no more be called Topheth, nor The valley of the son of Hinnom, but The valley of slaughter; for they shall bury in Topheth, for lack of room. 33. And the carcasses of this people shall be food for the fowls of the heaven, and for the beasts of the earth; and none shall frighten them away. 34. Then will I cause to cease from the cities of Judah, and from the streets of Jerusalem, the voice of mirth and the voice of gladness, the voice of the bridegroom and the voice of the bride; for the land shall be desolate.

## CHAPTER VIII

1. At that time, saith the LORD, they shall bring out the bones of the kings of Judah, and the bones of his princes, and the bones of the priests, and the bones of the prophets, and the bones of the inhabitants of Jerusalem, out of their graves; 2. and they shall spread them before the sun, and the moon, and all the host of heaven, whom they have loved, and whom they have served, and after whom they have walked, and whom they have sought, and whom they have worshipped; they shall not be gathered, nor be buried, they shall be for dung upon the face of the earth. 3. And death shall be chosen rather than life by all the residue that remain of this evil family, that remain in all the places whither I have driven them, saith the LORD of hosts.

## CHAPTER IX

22. Thus saith the LORD:
Let not the wise man glory in his wisdom,
Neither let the mighty man glory in his might,
Let not the rich man glory in his riches;

**32.** *the valley of slaughter.* The place where they slaughtered their innocent children shall be the scene of their own slaughter.
*for lack of room.* The bodies will lie unburied.

**33.** *frighten.* The corpses will lie untended on the ground with none to scare away the birds.

### CHAPTER VIII

**1.** *they shall bring out.* The enemies of Israel, who are the instruments of the coming Divine punishment. The enemy will even open the tombs of the kings, not for the treasure buried with them, but to desecrate the bones of the dead rulers.
*the bones of the priests.* Of Baal.

**2.** *host of heaven.* The worship of sun, moon and stars was another Babylonian cult introduced by Manasseh.

*whom they have loved.* To regard as gods (Altschul). The heavenly hosts look down in cold indifference and powerlessness on the insults heaped upon their former worshippers!

**3.** *and death shall be chosen.* So great will be the misery of the generation that is exiled. Fortunately, the Prophet's worst apprehensions were not realized. Time softened the utter despair of the first exiles. Jeremiah himself was yet to advise them to build houses and rear families; Jer. XXIX, 5 f.
*family.* Poetically used for 'people'.

### CHAPTER IX, 22, 23

In order that the Haftorah may close on a note of encouragement, these verses are added, which give the practical conclusion drawn from God's righteous dealings with His people. The people have been trusting in false values. It is not the

## JEREMIAH IX, 23

23. But let him that glorieth glory in this,
That he understandeth, and knoweth Me,
That I am the LORD who exercise mercy,
Justice, and righteousness, in the earth;
For in these things I delight,
Saith the LORD.

כִּי אִם־בְּזֹאת יִתְהַלֵּל הַמִּתְהַלֵּל הַשְׂכֵּל וְיָדֹעַ אוֹתִי כִּי אֲנִי יְהֹוָה עֹשֶׂה חֶסֶד מִשְׁפָּט וּצְדָקָה בָּאָרֶץ כִּי־בְאֵלֶּה חָפַצְתִּי נְאֻם־יְהֹוָה: 23 בִּגְבוּרָתוֹ אַל־יִתְהַלֵּל עָשִׁיר בְּעָשְׁרוֹ:

v. 23. למדנחאי ומשפט

wiles of statecraft, strong battalions, or vast wealth that are the real and permanent foundations of a national life; as little as worldly wisdom, power, and riches are in themselves the guarantors of happiness or peace in the life of the individual.

**23.** *let him that glorieth glory in this.* If one must glory, one should at least glory not in ephemeral things, but in things that are of eternal worth. Higher than all worldly wisdom and power is true knowledge of God, as the Fountain of Lovingkindness and Justice.

*mercy.* Precedes 'judgment and righteousness'. Elsewhere in Scriptures it even precedes 'truth' (חסד ואמת). Truth, justice and righteousness must all be spoken and acted in *lovingkindness*; otherwise, they cease to be truth, justice and righteousness.

*for in these things I delight.* God's delight is in those who train their hearts to imitate the Divine Attributes of Lovingkindness, Justice and Righteousness.

## LEVITICUS IX, 1

### CHAPTER IX

1. And it came to pass on the eighth day, that Moses called Aaron and his sons, and the elders of Israel; 2. and he said unto Aaron: 'Take thee a bull-calf for a sin-offering, and a ram for a burnt-offering, without blemish, and offer them before the LORD. 3. And unto the children of Israel thou shalt speak, saying: Take ye a he-goat for a sin-offering; and a calf and a lamb, both of the first year, without blemish, for a burnt-offering; 4. and an ox and a ram for peace-offerings, to sacrifice before the LORD; and a meal-offering mingled with oil; for to-day the LORD appeareth unto you.' 5. And they brought that which Moses commanded before the tent of meeting; and all the congregation drew near and stood before the LORD. 6. And Moses said: 'This is the thing which the LORD commanded that ye should do; that the glory of the LORD may appear unto you.' 7. And Moses said unto Aaron: 'Draw near unto the altar, and offer thy sin-offering, and thy burnt-offering, and make atonement for thyself, and for the people; and present the offering of the people, and make atonement for them; as the LORD commanded.' 8. So Aaron drew near unto the altar, and slew the calf of the sin-offering, which was for himself. 9. And the sons of Aaron presented the blood unto him; and he dipped his finger in the blood, and put it upon the horns of the altar, and poured out the blood at

## III. SHEMINI

(CHAPTERS IX–XI)

CHAPTER IX. THE PRIESTS ENTER UPON THEIR OFFICE

**1.** *the eighth day.* The day after the seven days of consecration of the priests (VIII, 33).

**2.** *a bull-calf.* A two-year-old animal.
*a sin-offering.* The newly-installed High Priest began his duties by sacrificing a sin-offering for himself and on behalf of his sons.

**3–4.** The offering brought for the people was of a comprehensive character, and included the principal types of sacrifices. The simplicity of this ceremony is in contrast with the holocausts which King Solomon slaughtered when he dedicated the Temple (I Kings VIII, 63). God does not require of His people more than they can bear.

**3.** *unto the children of Israel.* i.e. to the assembled elders as representatives of the community.

**4.** *appeareth.* The Heb. is in the perfect tense; the action is pictured as done, because it is sure to take place.

**5.** *before the LORD.* In His presence, as they were assembled before the Tent of Meeting.

**6.** *that ye should do.* Until the priests and the people had been purified, God would not manifest His approval of the Sanctuary.

*glory of the LORD.* They would not behold God Himself, only a manifestation of His Presence (v. 24).

**7.** *draw near.* Aaron was diffident and fearful of approaching the Altar; and therefore Moses had to reassure him (Sifra). Aaron did not enter upon his sacred duties with a feeling of self-exaltation or pride.

*for thyself, and for the people.* The High Priest's purity involved and reflected the purity of the nation.

**9.** *sons of Aaron.* Since Aaron himself did the slaughtering, he would require the assistance of

LEVITICUS IX, 10

the base of the altar. 10. But the fat, and the kidneys, and the lobe of the liver of the sin-offering, he made smoke upon the altar; as the LORD commanded Moses. 11. And the flesh and the skin were burnt with fire without the camp. 12. And he slew the burnt-offering; and Aaron's sons delivered unto him the blood, and he dashed it against the altar round about. 13. And they delivered the burnt-offering unto him, piece by piece, and the head; and he made them smoke upon the altar. 14. And he washed the inwards and the legs, and made them smoke upon the burnt-offering on the altar. 15. And the people's offering was presented; and he took the goat of the sin-offering which was for the people, and slew it, and offered it for sin, as the first. 16. And the burnt-offering was presented; and he offered it according to the ordinance.*¹¹· 17. And the meal-offering was presented; and he filled his hand therefrom, and made it smoke upon the altar, besides the burnt-offering of the morning. 18. He slew also the ox and the ram, the sacrifice of peace-offerings, which was for the people; and Aaron's sons delivered unto him the blood, and he dashed it against the altar round about, 19. and the fat of the ox, and of the ram, the fat tail, and that which covereth the inwards, and the kidneys, and the lobe of the liver. 20. And they put the fat upon the breasts, and he made the fat smoke upon the altar. 21. And the breasts and the right thigh Aaron waved for a wave-offering before the LORD; as Moses commanded. 22. And Aaron lifted up his hands toward the people, and blessed them; and he came down from offering his sons in the performance of the attendant rites.

*horns of the altar.* Of burnt-offering.

**10.** *of the sin-offering.* See IV, 8 f.

**11.** *and the flesh and the skin.* See IV, 12.

**13.** *piece by piece.* See I, 6.

**15.** *offered . . . as the first.* The purgation, i.e. the sprinkling of blood, was performed in the same manner as Aaron's own sin-offering, v. 8 f.

**21.** *waved.* Better, *had waved;* i.e. before the fat was burnt on the Altar. For the ceremony of waving, see on VII, 30. The order of the sacrifices described had religious significance. First there came the sin-offering, denoting purification; then the burnt-offering, indicating self-surrender to God; then the meal-offering, notifying consecration of labour; and finally the peace-offering, symbolizing fellowship with God. Let the people rid themselves of sin, let them submit their will to the Divine will, let them consecrate their daily toil to His service, and they would enjoy that Divine communion which is the supreme experience of man.

**22.** *lifted up his hands.* In blessing.
*blessed them.* According to the Rabbinic explanation, he used the words of the Priestly Blessing, Num. VI, 22 f.

**23.** *blessed the people.* This phrase probably means, 'greeted the people,' with the joyful news that the priesthood was now able to discharge its sacred functions for the spiritual welfare of the community.

444

# LEVITICUS IX, 23

the sin-offering, and the burnt-offering, and the peace-offerings. 23. And Moses and Aaron went into the tent of meeting, and came out, and blessed the people; and the glory of the LORD appeared unto all the people.*iii. 24. And there came forth fire from before the LORD, and consumed upon the altar the burnt-offering and the fat; and when all the people saw it, they shouted, and fell on their faces.

## CHAPTER X

1. And Nadab and Abihu, the sons of Aaron, took each of them his censer, and put fire therein, and laid incense thereon, and offered strange fire before the LORD, which He had not commanded them. 2. And there came forth fire from before the LORD, and devoured them, and they died before the LORD. 3. Then Moses said unto Aaron: 'This is it that the LORD spoke, saying: Through them that are nigh unto Me I will be sanctified, and before all the people I will be glorified.'

---

**24.** *came forth fire.* Portions of sacrificial flesh still upon the Altar-hearth were suddenly consumed by Divine fire—a sign that the sacrifice and what it denoted found favour in the sight of God; cf. 1 Kings XVIII, 38.

*shouted.* They broke into joyful song; 'they praised' (Targum).

*fell on their faces.* In gratitude and worship; cf. Gen. XXIV, 26, 52.

### CHAPTER X
### 1–5. DEATH OF NADAB AND ABIHU

**1.** *Nadab and Abihu.* Aaron's eldest sons. Their death points the moral, 'Boast not thyself of to-morrow for thou knowest not what a day may bring forth!' That day promised to be the happiest in Aaron's life. As he, the High Priest, was moving about in his magnificent robes and performing the solemn duties of his exalted office, how elated he must have been! Yet soon his two sons were lying dead at his feet.

*censer.* A pan for carrying live coal.

*strange fire.* Unconsecrated fire, not from the Divinely kindled flames on the Altar. On the very day of the consecration of the Sanctuary they ventured to change an essential of the Service in obedience to a momentary whim. In the circumstances, and in view of their office, it constituted an unpardonable offence. The Rabbis, observing that the narrative is followed by an injunction that the priests were not to drink intoxicating liquor before performing their duties (v. 8 f), state that Nadab and Abihu had dared to enter the Sanctuary under the influence of drink. Another suggestion is that they had consulted neither Moses nor Aaron in taking the step they did; and that this deliberate disregard of their elders sprang from unfilial jealousy. They asked themselves,

'When will these old men die? How long must we wait to lead the congregation?' It was an impious ambition that led them to commit the unhallowed deed which called down terrible retribution upon them.

**2.** *devoured them.* Mysteriously—the Rabbis explain—only their souls were consumed; their bodies remained untouched. It is probable that the fire took the form of a lightning flash, killing them without destroying their garments.

**3.** *then Moses said.* To help the bereaved father understand the significance of what had happened.

*this is it.* The words which follow do not occur literally elsewhere, but their teaching is implied in such passages as Exod. XIX, 22, and XXIX, 1, 44, setting forth the duty of sanctification for the priesthood.

*Through them that are nigh unto Me I will be sanctified.* In sharp contrast to the common view that highly-placed or gifted men may disregard the laws of morality, Judaism teaches that the greater a man's knowledge or position, the stricter the standard by which he is to be judged, and the greater the consequent guilt and punishment, if there is a falling away from that standard (S. R. Hirsch). 'With the righteous, God is exacting even to a hair's breadth' (Talmud).

*and before . . . glorified.* Or, 'that before all the people I may be glorified.' When He is sanctified by those who are near to Him, the effect will be that He is glorified by the people, who look to the priests for guidance and example.

*held his peace.* He found no answer to Moses' argument; or, he resigned himself to the just sentence which God had imposed upon his sons: cf. Ps. XXXIX, 10. 'I am dumb, I open not my mouth; because thou hast done it'.

# LEVITICUS X, 4

And Aaron held his peace. 4. And Moses called Mishael and Elzaphan, the sons of Uzziel the uncle of Aaron, and said unto them: 'Draw near, carry your brethren from before the sanctuary out of the camp.' 5. So they drew near, and carried them in their tunics out of the camp, as Moses had said. 6. And Moses said unto Aaron, and unto Eleazar and unto Ithamar, his sons: 'Let not the hair of your heads go loose, neither rend your clothes, that ye die not, and that He be not wroth with all the congregation; but let your brethren, the whole house of Israel, bewail the burning which the LORD hath kindled. 7. And ye shall not go out from the door of the tent of meeting, lest ye die; for the anointing oil of the LORD is upon you.' And they did according to the word of Moses. ¶ 8. And the LORD spoke unto Aaron, saying: 9. 'Drink no wine nor strong drink, thou, nor thy sons with thee, when ye go into the tent of meeting, that ye die not; it shall be a statute for ever throughout your generations. 10. And that ye may put difference between the holy and the common, and between the unclean and the clean;

**4.** *Mishael and Elzaphan.* Aaron's first cousins, and the next-of-kin who were not priests. If the body had been touched by any of the priests, they would have become ritually defiled and unable to officiate in the Tabernacle.

*brethren.* Kinsfolk.

*out of the camp.* To bury them. Since the grave defiled whoever came in contact with it, the dead were buried outside the Israelite encampment.

**5.** *tunics.* See on Ex. XXVIII, 39.

### 6–7. THE PRIESTS NOT TO MOURN

**6.** *rend your clothes.* The commonest sign of grief (Gen. XXXVII, 29; XLIV, 13). Jews still rend the garment (*Keriah*) on hearing of the death of a near relative.

*that ye die not.* As the consequence of condoning the desecration of the Sanctuary of which the dead had been guilty.

*be not wroth.* An ancient Rabbinic interpretation connects the words 'be not wroth', with what follows. We should then render: 'And that he be not wroth with all the congregation, seeing that all your brethren, the whole house of Israel, will bewail, etc.' The meaning is: If the priests show signs of grief, the rest of the community will also lament the occurrence, and perhaps declaim against God for the calamity that marred the festivities of that day. His anger would then be roused against them.

**7.** *not go out.* Cf. VIII, 33, and XXI, 12.

### 8–11. PRIESTS WARNED AGAINST INTOXICANTS

**9.** *wine nor strong drink.* As stated above, the Rabbis connected the incident of Nadab and Abihu with this injunction against intoxicating liquors before officiating in the Sanctuary. Mourners were encouraged to drink. ('Give wine unto the bitter in soul; let him drink . . . and remember his misery no more,' Prov. XXXI, 6 f). The prohibition against bewailing the dead is, therefore, followed by a further command against resorting to wine.

*when ye go into the tent.* Wine is a beneficent gift of God, when enjoyed in moderation. The priests need not abstain from it, except when discharging their sacred function as priests or teachers. In those circumstances, the prohibition is made permanent.

**10.** *put difference.* As they would be called upon to decide questions affecting the life of the people, theirs must never be irresolute or confused guidance. 'They reel in vision, they totter in judgment,' is the terrible charge which Isaiah brings against the drunken spiritual guides of Judah; see p. 227.

*the holy and the common.* This has a wider than a merely levitical or ritual application. It is the sacred function of the priest to teach the children of men the everlasting distinction between holy and unholy, between light and darkness, between clean and unclean, between right and wrong; Deut. XXIV, 8.

## LEVITICUS X, 11

11. and that ye may teach the children of Israel all the statutes which the LORD hath spoken unto them by the hand of Moses.'\*ⁱᵛ· ¶ 12. And Moses spoke unto Aaron, and unto Eleazar and unto Ithamar, his sons that were left: 'Take the meal-offering that remaineth of the offerings of the LORD made by fire, and eat it without leaven beside the altar; for it is most holy. 13. And ye shall eat it in a holy place, because it is thy due, and thy sons' due, of the offerings of the LORD made by fire; for so I am commanded. 14. And the breast of waving and the thigh of heaving shall ye eat in a clean place; thou, and thy sons, and thy daughters with thee; for they are given as thy due, and thy sons' due, out of the sacrifices of the peace-offerings of the children of Israel. 15. The thigh of heaving and the breast of waving shall they bring with the offerings of the fat made by fire, to wave it for a wave-offering before the LORD, and it shall be thine, and thy sons' with thee, as a due for ever; as the LORD hath commanded.'\*ᵛ· ¶16. And Moses diligently inquired for the goat of the sin-offering, and, behold, it was burnt; and he was angry with Eleazar and with Ithamar, the sons of Aaron that were left, saying: 17. 'Wherefore have ye not eaten the sin-offering in the place of the sanctuary, seeing it is most holy, and He hath given it you to bear the iniquity of the congregation, to make atonement for them before the LORD? 18. Behold, the blood of it was not brought into the sanctuary within; ye should certainly have eaten it in the sanctuary, as I commanded.' 19. And Aaron spoke unto Moses: 'Behold, this day have they offered their sin-offering

**11.** *ye may teach.* This duty of the priesthood is impressively formulated by the Prophet, 'For the priest's lips should keep knowledge, and they should seek the law at his mouth: for he is the messenger of the LORD of hosts' (Mal. II, 7).

12–19. DISPOSAL OF THE INITIATORY OFFERINGS

This paragraph continues Chap. IX.

**12.** *meal-offering that remaineth.* See IX, 4.

**13.** *for so I am commanded.* These words seem to refer to the special circumstances which were here involved. The priests were to eat their share of the meal-offering, although they were mourners.

**14.** *and thy daughters.* As the peace-offerings were not of the 'most holy' class, the portions could be eaten in any 'clean' place within the camp of Israel. The daughters were thus able to have a share.

**16.** *the goat of the sin-offering.* See IX, 15.
*Eleazar and Ithamar.* In IX, 15 it is stated that Aaron had sacrificed this offering. Moses, however, addresses himself to the sons, in order to uphold the dignity of the High Priest's office (Rashi).

**17.** *in the place of the sanctuary.* Better, *in the holy place;* for the law regulating the sin-offering, see VI, 19.
*to bear the iniquity.* lit. 'to carry away the iniquity.' The Targum paraphrases, 'to obtain pardon.'

**18.** *as I commanded.* In VI, 19. We must understand, 'in the name of the LORD,' being implied here.

**19.** *Aaron spoke.* Although the rebuke had been addressed to the sons, it had been intended for him (see on *v.* 16). As on this day the priests had had to secure atonement for themselves, they

## LEVITICUS X, 20

and their burnt-offering before the LORD, and there have befallen me such things as these; and if I had eaten the sin-offering to-day, would it have been well-pleasing in the sight of the LORD?' 20. And when Moses heard that, it was well-pleasing in his sight. *vi.

חַטָּאתָם וְאֶת־עֹלָתָם לִפְנֵי יְהוָֹה וַתִּקְרֶאנָה אֹתִי כָּאֵלֶּה
כ וְאָכַלְתִּי חַטָּאת הַיּוֹם הַיִּיטַב בְּעֵינֵי יְהוָֹה: וַיִּשְׁמַע מֹשֶׁה
וַיִּיטַב בְּעֵינָיו: פ ששי

did not deem themselves in a state of purity to share in the solemn rite of eating the people's sin-offering. That feeling of imperfection became intensified when 'such things as these'—the death of Nadab and Abihu—had befallen them.

**20.** *it was well-pleasing.* He was convinced that the priests had acted as they did from praiseworthy motives.

### CHAPTERS XI–XVI. THE LAWS OF PURITY

The first ten chapters of Leviticus contain The Law of the Sanctuary, in the stricter sense of the term. With the exception of paragraphs here and there, the remainder of the Book deals with matters other than priests and sacrifices, with what might be described as The Law of Daily Life. The Torah takes the whole of human life as its province; in the eyes of the Torah nothing human is secular. It penetrates into the home of the Israelite, and aims at controlling even the most intimate relations of his domestic existence. It is of the utmost importance to grasp this characteristic feature of the Torah. 'The Law of God embraces the whole of life with all its actions; and as none of these actions can be withdrawn from the unity of life, so can the Law be excluded from none of them' (Hermann Cohen). Many things, therefore, that affect only the physical life come under the purview of that Law. A healthy soul in a healthy body is clearly its ideal. The regulations prescribed in these chapters are means towards the attainment of that end, and have therefore a spiritual purpose and eternal worth.

### CHAPTER XI. DIETARY LAWS

Among the laws of purity, first place is given to the subject of food, because the daily diet intimately affects man's whole being. The subscription to this chapter, *v.* 43 f, clearly reveals the object of the Dietary Laws. God brought Israel out of Egypt to be a 'holy people', a consecrated people, 'a people apart, distinguished from all others by outward rites which in themselves helped to constitute Holiness. Outward consecration was symbolically to express an inner sanctity.' This thought of being a 'holy people'— a light supernaturally kindled, lest darkness should become complete—a witness to God's sovereignty and purity, lest He become utterly unacknowledged in the world He had made— a 'kingdom of priests', sanctified in themselves, and sanctified for the rest of the world's sake— this sublime thought would be daily impressed on their minds by these Commandments which separated them from other nations. These would, furthermore, prevent that close and intimate association with heathens which would result in complete absorption. Indeed, the Dietary Laws have proved an important factor in the preservation of the Jewish race in the past, and are, in more than one respect, an irreplaceable agency for maintaining Jewish identity in the present. An illustrious Jewish scientist wrote: 'It may appear a minute matter to pronounce the Hebrew blessing over bread, and to accustom one's children to do so. Yet if a Jew, at the time of partaking of food, remembers the identical words used by his fellow Jews since time immemorial and the world over, he revives in himself, wherever he be at the moment, communion with his imperishable race. In contrast to not a few of our co-religionists, who have no occasion for weeks and months together to bestow a thought on their Creed or their People, the Jew who keeps *Kashrus* has to think of his religious and communal allegiance on the occasion of every meal; and on every such occasion the observance of those laws constitutes a renewal of acquiescence in the fact that he *is* a Jew, and a deliberate acknowledgment of that fact' (Haffkine).

The Rabbis were content to say that these laws belong to the class called חוקים, 'statutes,' which must be obeyed, although the reason for them transcend human understanding, and although they provoke the derision of heathens, Jewish and non-Jewish. There have, however, at all times been those who have seen a hygienic purpose in these prohibitions, and have held that the forbidden meats were not prohibited arbitrarily, but were unwholesome and repulsive in themselves. Modern research, too, recognizes that certain animals harbour parasites that are both disease-creating and disease-spreading. Their flesh is consequently harmful to man. Such animals are excluded from the Hebrew dietary. Furthermore, as it is in the blood that the germs or spores of infectious disease circulate, the flesh of all animals must be thoroughly drained of blood before serving for food. This is most effectively done by the Jewish method of Shechitah, and especially by the Traditional koshering of the meat before it is prepared for food. Statistical investigation has demonstrated

# LEVITICUS XI, 1

## CHAPTER XI

1. And the LORD spoke unto Moses and to Aaron, saying unto them: 2. Speak unto the children of Israel, saying: ¶ These are the living things which ye may eat among all the beasts that are on the earth. 3. Whatsoever parteth the hoof, and is wholly cloven-footed, and cheweth the cud, among the beasts, that may ye eat. 4. Nevertheless these shall ye not eat of them that only chew the cud, or of them that only part the hoof: the camel, because he cheweth the cud but parteth not the hoof, he is unclean unto you. 5. And the rock-badger, because he cheweth the cud but parteth not the hoof, he is unclean unto

## CAP. XI. יא

2 וַיְדַבֵּר יְהֹוָה אֶל־מֹשֶׁה וְאֶל־אַהֲרֹן לֵאמֹר אֲלֵהֶם: דַּבְּרוּ אֶל־בְּנֵי יִשְׂרָאֵל לֵאמֹר זֹאת הַחַיָּה אֲשֶׁר תֹּאכְלוּ מִכָּל־
3 הַבְּהֵמָה אֲשֶׁר עַל־הָאָרֶץ: כֹּל ׀ מַפְרֶסֶת פַּרְסָה וְשֹׁסַעַת
4 שֶׁסַע פְּרָסֹת מַעֲלַת גֵּרָה בַּבְּהֵמָה אֹתָהּ תֹּאכֵלוּ: אַךְ אֶת־זֶה לֹא תֹאכְלוּ מִמַּעֲלֵי הַגֵּרָה וּמִמַּפְרִסֵי הַפַּרְסָה אֶת־הַגָּמָל כִּי־מַעֲלֵה גֵרָה הוּא וּפַרְסָה אֵינֶנּוּ מַפְרִיס טָמֵא הוּא
5 לָכֶם: וְאֶת־הַשָּׁפָן כִּי־מַעֲלֵה גֵרָה הוּא וּפַרְסָה לֹא יַפְרִיס

---

that Jews as a class are immune from, or less susceptible to, certain diseases; and their life-duration is frequently longer than that of their neighbours. Competent authorities have not hesitated to attribute these healthy characteristics to the influence of the Dietary Laws. In the Middle Ages, when epidemics devastated many a country, the Jews were far less affected than the rest of the population; and this immunity gave rise to the malicious accusation that the Jews had caused the plague by poisoning the wells! Although much remains to be discovered to explain in every detail the food-laws in Leviticus, sufficient is known to warrant the conviction that their observance produces beneficial effects upon the human body; cf. XVIII, 5.

The supreme motive, however, of the Dietary Laws remains Holiness, not as an abstract idea, but as a regulating principle in the everyday lives of men, women, and children. 'The Dietary Laws train us in the mastery over our appetites; they accustom us to restrain both the growth of desire and the disposition to consider pleasure of eating and drinking as the end of man's existence' (Maimonides). Whosoever eats forbidden foods becomes imbued with the spirit of impurity, and is cast out of the realm of Divine Holiness (Zohar). Rejection of the Dietary Laws has at various times been considered as equivalent to apostasy. The Maccabean martyrs died rather than transgress them. At the present day, the great majority of Jews continue to abstain from forbidden food, not only from personal aversion, but because 'our Father in Heaven has decreed that we should abstain from it' (Sifra). These laws constitute an invaluable training in self-mastery. 'Is there not something spiritually attractive in the idea of the Jew of this age voluntarily submitting to restrictions on his appetites for the sake of duty—forming one of a religious guild, whose special characteristic is its self-control? It ought to be the pride of the modern Jew and every child should be taught to feel it—that his religion demands from him a self-abnegation from which other religionists are absolved; that the price to be paid for the privilege of belonging to the hierarchy of Israel is continuous and conscious self-sacrifice. The Dietary Laws foster this spirit of self-surrender. Respect for them teaches and helps the Jew, in Rabbinic language, to abase his desires before the will of his Father in Heaven' (M. Joseph).

1–8. CLEAN AND UNCLEAN QUADRUPEDS

**1.** *and to Aaron.* It was the duty of the priests to 'put difference between the holy and the common, and between the unclean and the clean' (X, 10).

**2.** *speak unto the children of Israel.* The subject matter of this chapter is repeated in Deut. XIV. For the variations between the two accounts, see the commentary on Deuteronomy. A distinction between clean and unclean animals goes back to the earliest period of Biblical history; but whether the criteria were then the same as are indicated in this chapter is not known.

*earth.* Land; in contrast to v. 9, where the creatures that live in water are mentioned.

**3.** *whatsoever parteth the hoof.* Instead of enumerating the animals which may be eaten, as is done in Deut., the general rule is here given by which the individual species could be tested. The animal must possess three characteristics: (*a*) it must divide the hoof; (*b*) it must be wholly cloven-footed; and (*c*) it must chew the cud. It is probable that the three characteristics—divided hoof, cloven-footed, and chewing the cud—are named because they broadly demarcate beasts of prey and animals of obnoxious habits from those suitable for human consumption.

**4.** *camel.* At the bottom of the camel's hoof there is an elastic pad or cushion on which the camel gets its foothold in the sand. This pad prevents the hoof from being wholly divided.

**5.** *rock-badger.* Or, 'coney.' This animal, and likewise the hare, have the habit of working the jaws as though they were masticating food.

## LEVITICUS XI, 6

you. 6. And the hare, because she cheweth the cud but parteth not the hoof, she is unclean unto you. 7. And the swine, because he parteth the hoof, and is cloven-footed, but cheweth not the cud, he is unclean unto you. 8. Of their flesh ye shall not eat, and their carcasses ye shall not touch; they are unclean unto you. ¶ 9. These may ye eat of all that are in the waters: whatsoever hath fins and scales in the waters, in the seas, and in the rivers, them may ye eat. 10. And all that have not fins and scales in the seas, and in the rivers, of all that swarm in the waters, and of all the living creatures that are in the waters, they are a detestable thing unto you, 11. and they shall be a detestable thing unto you; ye shall not eat of their flesh, and their carcasses ye shall have in detestation. 12. Whatsoever hath no fins nor scales in the waters, that is a detestable thing unto you. ¶ 13. And these ye shall have in detestation among the fowls; they shall not be eaten, they are a detestable thing: the great vulture, and the bearded vulture, and the ospray; 14. and the kite, and the falcon after its kinds; 15. every raven after its kinds; 16. and the ostrich, and the night-hawk, and the sea-mew, and the hawk after its kinds; 17. and the little

**7. swine.** The aversion to the pig is not confined to Israel. The primary abhorrence was caused, in all probability, by its loathsome appearance and mode of living.

**8. *their carcasses*.** The carcass of a *clean* animal which had been slaughtered by the Traditional method did not communicate defilement.

### 9-12. CLEAN AND UNCLEAN FISH

**9. *in the waters*.** 'The characteristics given in the Law of the permitted animals, *viz.* chewing the cud and divided hoofs for cattle, and fins and scales for fish, are in themselves neither the cause of the permission when they are present, nor of the prohibition when they are absent; but merely signs by which the recommended species of animals can be discerned from those that are forbidden' (Maimonides). In general, the Torah forbids every kind of shell-fish—which is disease-breeding, especially in hot countries.

**10. *living creatures that are in the waters*.** This alludes to the sea animals which do not come under the category of fish, such as seals and whales.

*detestable thing.* In the first paragraph, the forbidden species are described as 'unclean'; *i.e.* not only uneatable, but the touch of their carcass is defiling. With fish it was otherwise. They were 'detestable' and disallowed as food, but they were not defiling by touch.

**12. *fins nor scales in the waters*.** As long as they have the fins and scales *when in the water*, they are edible. The Rabbis were of the opinion that every fish which has scales also has fins, although these may be of a very rudimentary kind and not discernible to the eye. Therefore in actual practice they permit fish with scales only, but not fish with fins only.

### 13-19. UNCLEAN BIRDS

The birds prohibited all belong to the class denoted as birds of prey, and also those that live in dark ruins or marshy land. But since the Torah adds the words 'after its kind', the Rabbis enumerated various criteria by which a clean bird may be distinguished.

**13. *in detestation*.** See on *v.* 10.

*great vulture.* The Heb. word is often translated 'eagle', but it is very probable that the griffon-vulture is intended. It is the most powerful of the birds of prey; see Deut. XXXII, 11.

*ospray.* Possibly the sea-eagle is intended.

**15. *raven*.** The species including the crow, jackdaw, and rook.

**16. *ostrich*.** lit. 'daughter of wailing'. This bird is represented in the Bible as living in dreary ruins (Isa. XIII, 21) and constantly wailing (Micah I, 8).

*night-hawk.* Or, 'owl'; the meaning of the Heb. word is uncertain.

*sea-mew.* Or, 'sea-gull.'

## LEVITICUS XI, 18

owl, and the cormorant, and the great owl; 18. and the horned owl, and the pelican, and the carrion-vulture; 19. and the stork, and the heron after its kinds, and the hoopoe, and the bat. ¶ 20. All winged swarming things that go upon all fours are a detestable thing unto you. 21. Yet these may ye eat of all winged swarming things that go upon all fours, which have jointed legs above their feet, wherewith to leap upon the earth; 22. even these of them ye may eat: the locust after its kinds, and the bald locust after its kinds, and the cricket after its kinds, and the grasshopper after its kinds. 23. But all winged swarming things, which have four feet, are a detestable thing unto you. ¶ 24. And by these ye shall become unclean; whosoever toucheth the carcass of them shall be unclean until the even. 25. And whosoever beareth aught of the carcass of them shall wash his clothes, and be unclean until the even. 26. Every beast which parteth the hoof, but is not cloven-footed, nor cheweth the cud, is unclean unto you; every one that toucheth them shall be unclean. 27. And whatsoever goeth upon its paws, among all beasts that go on all fours, they are unclean unto you; whoso toucheth their carcass shall be unclean until the even. 28. And he that beareth the carcass of them shall wash his clothes, and be unclean until

---

**17.** *little owl*. Mentioned in Ps. CII, 7, as dwelling amidst ruins.

*cormorant*. lit. 'the hurler'; *i.e.* the bird which hurls itself from a height and snatches fish from the water.

*great owl*. The Heb. probably means, 'the bird which dwells in twilight,' an inhabiter of ruined places (Isa. XXXIV, 11).

**18.** *horned owl*. Or, 'swan.'

*pelican*. Mentioned several times in Scripture as leading a solitary life in desert places (Ps. CII, 7).

**19.** *stork*. The Heb. signifies a bird which is 'kind and affectionate' to its young.

*heron*. Or, 'ibis.'

*hoopoe*. An uncertain word. The Rabbis understood it to be a species of grouse.

*bat*. Named together with moles as being a creature which prefers dark places (Isa. II, 20).

### 20–23. WINGED SWARMING THINGS

**20.** *winged swarming things*. Insects that multiply rapidly and become a pest to man.

*go upon all fours*. The phrase used here cannot be taken to mean that the insects were possessed of only four legs. The words probably refer to their method of locomotion, and signify, 'that move like quadrupeds.'

**21.** *jointed legs*. Bending hind legs, higher than their other legs.

**22.** *locust*. None of the four kinds of locusts mentioned is certainly known (RV Margin). For this reason also, later Jewish authorities, realizing that it is impossible to avoid errors being made, declare every species of locust to be forbidden.

**23.** *which have four feet*. *i.e.* without the 'bending legs'.

### 24–28. DEFILEMENT THROUGH CONTACT

**24.** *and by these*. The Sifra (and so Rashi) makes this paragraph a preface to *v.* 26 f.

*shall be unclean*. *i.e.* incapable of taking part in Sanctuary worship, or of touching 'holy' food.

*until the even*. When he had to bathe his body.

**25.** *beareth*. Carrying from one place to another. The impurity is passed on to the garments, and these also had to be purified.

## LEVITICUS XI, 29

the even; they are unclean unto you. ¶ 29. And these are they which are unclean unto you among the swarming things that swarm upon the earth: the weasel, and the mouse, and the great lizard after its kinds, 30. and the gecko, and the land-crocodile, and the lizard, and the sand-lizard, and the chameleon. 31. These are they which are unclean to you among all that swarm; whosoever doth touch them, when they are dead, shall be unclean until the even. 32. And upon whatsoever any of them, when they are dead, doth fall, it shall be unclean; whether it be any vessel of wood, or raiment, or skin, or sack, whatsoever vessel it be, wherewith any work is done, it must be put into water, and it shall be unclean until the even; then shall it be clean.\* vii. 33. And every earthen vessel, whereinto any of them falleth, whatsoever is in it shall be unclean, and it ye shall break. 34. All food therein which may be eaten, that on which water cometh, shall be unclean; and all drink in every such vessel that may be drunk shall be unclean. 35. And every thing whereupon any part of their carcass falleth shall be unclean; whether oven, or range for pots, it shall be broken in pieces; they are unclean, and shall be unclean unto you. 36. Nevertheless a fountain or a cistern wherein is a gathering of water shall be clean; but he who toucheth their carcass shall be unclean. 37. And

### 29–43. UNCLEAN CREEPING THINGS

**29.** *unclean.* Prohibited as food, and whose dead bodies are defiling.

**30.** *gecko.* This and the succeeding three names are of uncertain meaning, probably denoting species of lizards.

**31.** *when they are dead.* Unclean creatures do not therefore defile by contact while alive.

**32.** *any vessel.* These creatures, which come in close contact with filth and when dead are covered with parasites, needed to be particularly guarded against.

**33.** *earthen vessel.* This is evidence that the concept of 'impurity' coincided to some extent with 'infection', and that different grades of impurity were different degrees of liability to infection; as otherwise the distinction between metal or glazed ware and earthenware would have no meaning. In the latter case, the infection could not be removed by washing; hence it had to be broken.

**34.** *all food therein.* The meaning is: If a dead creature fall into an earthen vessel wherein is food, the food becomes unclean only if it had at one time been moistened; the occasional moisture becoming a conductor of impurity for all times (cf. *v.* 38).

**35.** *oven, or range for pots.* The latter denotes a vessel in two compartments to receive two pots, the Heb. being in the dual. They were alike, usually made of earthenware; therefore they had to be broken if rendered unclean.

**36.** *a fountain.* This verse states the exceptional case where the carcass has no defiling effect. When it falls into water of a well, spring, or a large cistern in which the water is collected in a natural manner (*i.e.* not drawn by a vessel), then it does not render the water unclean. Such 'natural' waters are alone to be used for ritual purification. The minimum quantity for a ritual bath (Mikvah) is 24 cubic feet, so as to permit complete immersion.

*but he who toucheth.* Although it does not defile the water, it does affect anybody who touches it, even whilst it is in the cistern or pool.

**37.** *sowing seed. i.e.* seed to be planted. This does not contract impurity.

452

## LEVITICUS XI, 38

if aught of their carcass fall upon any sowing seed which is to be sown, it is clean. 38. But if water be put upon the seed, and aught of their carcass fall thereon, it is unclean unto you. ¶ 39. And if any beast, of which ye may eat, die, he that toucheth the carcass thereof shall be unclean until the even. 40. And he that eateth of the carcass of it shall wash his clothes, and be unclean until the even; he also that beareth the carcass of it shall wash his clothes, and be unclean until the even. ¶ 41. And every swarming thing that swarmeth upon the earth is a detestable thing; it shall not be eaten. 42. Whatsoever goeth upon the belly, and whatsoever goeth upon all fours, or whatsoever hath many feet, even all swarming things that swarm upon the earth, them ye shall not eat; for they are a detestable thing. 43. Ye shall not make yourselves detestable with any swarming thing that swarmeth, neither shall ye make yourselves unclean with them, that ye should be defiled thereby. 44. For I am the LORD your God; sanctify yourselves therefore, and be ye holy; for I am holy;

ויקרא שמיני יא

38 הוּא: וְכִי יֻתַּן־מַיִם עַל־זֶרַע וְנָפַל מִנִּבְלָתָם עָלָיו טָמֵא
39 הוּא לָכֶם: ס וְכִי יָמוּת מִן־הַבְּהֵמָה אֲשֶׁר־הִיא לָכֶם
מ לְאָכְלָה הַנֹּגֵעַ בְּנִבְלָתָהּ יִטְמָא עַד־הָעָרֶב: וְהָאֹכֵל מִנִּבְלָתָהּ
יְכַבֵּס בְּגָדָיו וְטָמֵא עַד־הָעָרֶב וְהַנֹּשֵׂא אֶת־נִבְלָתָהּ יְכַבֵּס
41 בְּגָדָיו וְטָמֵא עַד־הָעָרֶב: וְכָל־הַשֶּׁרֶץ הַשֹּׁרֵץ עַל־הָאָרֶץ
42 שֶׁקֶץ הוּא לֹא יֵאָכֵל: כֹּל הוֹלֵךְ עַל־גָּחוֹן וְכֹל ׀ הוֹלֵךְ
עַל־אַרְבַּע עַד כָּל־מַרְבֵּה רַגְלַיִם לְכָל־הַשֶּׁרֶץ הַשֹּׁרֵץ עַל־
43 הָאָרֶץ לֹא תֹאכְלוּם כִּי־שֶׁקֶץ הֵם: אַל־תְּשַׁקְּצוּ אֶת־
נַפְשֹׁתֵיכֶם בְּכָל־הַשֶּׁרֶץ הַשֹּׁרֵץ וְלֹא תִטַּמְּאוּ בָּהֶם וְנִטְמֵתֶם
44 בָּם: כִּי אֲנִי יְהֹוָה אֱלֹהֵיכֶם וְהִתְקַדִּשְׁתֶּם וִהְיִיתֶם קְדֹשִׁים
כִּי קָדוֹשׁ אָנִי וְלֹא תְטַמְּאוּ אֶת־נַפְשֹׁתֵיכֶם בְּכָל־הַשֶּׁרֶץ

v. 42. ו' רבתי והיא חצי התורה באותיות. v. 43. חסר א'

---

**38.** *be put upon the seed.* Better, *be poured upon seed;* i.e. grain stored for food.

**39.** *die.* A natural death. The carcass of even a clean beast causes uncleanness. *Touching* the carcass infects the person; but *carrying* it necessitates also the washing of clothes.

**40.** *eateth of the carcass.* Forbidden in Deut. XIV, 21.

**41.** *swarming thing.* This verse continues the exposition of the Dietary Laws which had been interrupted by the regulations concerning defilement. It follows on v. 23, which dealt with the larger class of 'swarming things', and refers to the smaller insects, like worms and slugs.

**42.** *belly.* The third letter of the word גחון is written in large character to make it stand out more boldly. It is the middle letter of the Pentateuch.
*upon all fours.* i.e. snake-like creatures which have legs, like the scorpion.
*whatsoever hath many feet.* e.g. spiders, caterpillars, centipedes.

**43.** *not make yourselves detestable.* By eating any of the forbidden things. The Rabbis widened this warning into a prohibition of any action or habit which is calculated to provoke disgust, such as eating from unclean plates or taking one's food with unwashed hands.

**44-47.** SPIRITUAL PURPOSE OF THE LAWS

**44.** *sanctify yourselves therefore, and be ye holy.* lit. 'strive after holiness and ye shall be holy'; i.e. the mere striving after holiness in itself sanctifies (Hermann Cohen).
Israel is bidden to be holy. This demand has two aspects—one positive and the other negative. The positive aspect may be called the Imitation of God; see on XIX, 2. The negative aspect means the withdrawal from things impure and abominable. Even as nothing that suggested the least taint could be associated with God, so it was the duty of the Israelites to strive, so far as it was attainable by man, to avoid whatever would defile them, whether physically or spiritually. Wherever men and women honestly strive after holy living, such striving carries its own fulfilment with it. Rabbi Pinchas ben Yair said: 'Heedfulness leads to cleanness; cleanness to purity; purity to holiness; holiness to humility; humility to dread of sin; dread of sin to saintliness (chassiduth); saintliness to the possession of the Holy Spirit (רוח הקודש).'
The Rabbis, translating as ever general principles of religion into terms of life, based the precept of Washing the hands before Meals on והתקדשתם ('sanctify yourselves').
*for I am holy.* 'This constitutes the basis for your duty to sanctify yourselves, as well as the guarantee of your capacity to attain sanctification of life. Holiness is the very essence of the Divine being; and, in breathing His spirit into you, He made you the partaker of His Divine nature, and endowed you with the power to attain to holiness. "Because I am holy, you *shall* be holy, and you *can* be holy"' (S. R. Hirsch).

## LEVITICUS XI, 45

neither shall ye defile yourselves with any manner of swarming thing that moveth upon the earth.*ᵐ·* 45. For I am the LORD that brought you up out of the land of Egypt, to be your God; ye shall therefore be holy, for I am holy. ¶ 46. This is the law of the beast, and of the fowl, and of every living creature that moveth in the waters, and of every creature that swarmeth upon the earth; 47. to make a difference between the unclean and the clean, and between the living thing that may be eaten and the living thing that may not be eaten.

**45.** *that brought you up out of the land of Egypt.* To Him the Israelites owe their freedom; therefore, He has the authority to dictate His will to them. The verse also indicates that the purpose God had in delivering them from bondage was to bring them to His sanctifying service.

**46-47.** These verses form the epilogue to the chapter.

A brief résumé of the Dietary Laws and the rules of koshering are found in Dayan Lazarus, *The Ways of Her Household*, Part I, 1-37; and M. Friedländer, *The Jewish Religion*, 455-466.

---

## HAFTORAH SHEMINI

### II SAMUEL VI, 1–VII, 17

#### CHAPTER VI

1. And David again gathered together all the chosen men of Israel, thirty thousand. 2. And David arose, and went with all the people that were with him, from Baale-judah, to bring up from thence the ark of God, whereupon is called the Name, even the name of the LORD of hosts that sitteth

After restoring the unity of the nation, David consolidated it by establishing a capital, Jerusalem. But that impregnable natural fastness was destined to be far more than the royal residence of Judah and the political centre of the tribes of Israel. 'She was to be the City of God; and this sacred character, which has been hers ever since, was stamped upon her by David himself. His vision went beyond the immediate foundation to the issues that lay in time to come' (Marx-Margolis). It was his first care to bring back the sacred Ark from the out-of-the-way country town to which, a generation earlier, the Philistine conquerors had taken it, and to install it in his newly acquired capital.

The Sedrah describes the consecration of the Tabernacle in the Wilderness; the Haftorah tells of the transportation of the Ark of the Covenant. An untoward and tragic incident marks both Sedrah and Haftorah. The death of Nadab and Abihu in the Sedrah is a warning that no kind of caprice can be tolerated in the service of God.

The same lesson is enforced in the Haftorah by the death of Uzzah, who was guilty of irreverence towards God's Majesty.

#### CHAPTER VI

**1.** *again.* Refers to the assembly at Hebron that was convened for David's coronation, described in II Sam. v, 1.

*all the chosen men.* David wished to interest the leading men of Israel in his sacred enterprise; cf. I Chron. XIII, 1 f.

**2.** *from Baale-judah.* The phrase is an abbreviated one, meaning, 'They went from Baale-judah, whither they had come to bring thence the Ark' (Kimchi). Baale-judah is another name for Kirjath-jearim (*i.e.* the City of Forests), about half-way between Jerusalem and Ashdod near the Mediterranean coast.

*to bring up.* Jerusalem is on higher ground than Kirjath-jearim.

*sitteth upon the cherubim.* See Exod. xxv, 22.

## II SAMUEL VI, 3

upon the cherubim. 3. And they set the ark of God upon a new cart, and brought it out of the house of Abinadab that was in the hill; and Uzzah and Ahio, the sons of Abinadab, drove the new cart. 4. And they brought it out of the house of Abinadab, which was in the hill, with the ark of God, and Ahio went before the ark. 5. And David and all the house of Israel played before the LORD with all manner of instruments made of cypress-wood, and with harps, and with psalteries, and with timbrels, and with sistra, and with cymbals. ¶ 6. And when they came to the threshing-floor of Nacon, Uzzah put forth his hand to the ark of God, and took hold of it; for the oxen stumbled. 7. And the anger of the LORD was kindled against Uzzah; and God smote him there for his error; and there he died by the ark of God. 8. And David was displeased, because the LORD had broken forth upon Uzzah; and that place was called ¹Perez-uzzah, unto this day. 9. And David was afraid of the LORD that day; and he said: 'How shall the ark of the LORD come unto me?' 10. So David would not remove the ark of the LORD unto him into the city of David; but David carried it aside into the house of Obed-edom the Gittite. 11. And the ark of the LORD remained in the house of Obed-edom the Gittite three months; and the LORD blessed Obed-edom, and all his house. ¶ 12. And it was told king David, saying: 'The LORD hath blessed the house of Obed-edom, and all that pertaineth unto him, because of the ark of God.' And David went and brought up the ark of God from the house of Obed-edom into the city of David with joy. 13. And it was so, that when they that bore the

---

¹ That is, *The breach of Uzzah.*

**3.** *a new cart.* The first attempt to bring the Ark to Mount Zion failed through want of reverence on the part of those transporting it. It should not have been carried in a common way on a waggon. It should have been borne on the shoulders of Levites (Num. III, 29 f).

*in the hill.* Better, *on the hill;* in or near the town of Kirjath-jearim.

**7.** *and God smote him there.* For this act of undue familiarity. The regulations surrounding Tabernacle and Temple were to deepen the sense of God's Holiness and of reverence for Him. The Ark was in especial degree the sign of His Presence. 'It has been surmised that Uzzah was crushed by a sudden and violent movement of the waggon bearing the Ark' (Ottley).

**8.** *and David was displeased.* Unlike Aaron, who submitted to God's will in silence, David resented the judgment which God had inflicted, and in a petulant spirit abandoned the enterprise.

**10.** *the Gittite.* So called because he probably came from Gath-Rimmon, a Levitical city (Josh. XXI, 25).

**13.** *when they that bore the ark.* With staves on the shoulders of the Levites; see I Chron. XV, 15. The requirements of the Law were now observed.

*he sacrificed an ox.* Because he saw his action now did not incur Divine displeasure. All were again swayed by religious joy. David himself flung aside all the ordinary restraints of royalty.

**14-19.** In a great popular celebration, in which the king himself takes a leading part, the Ark is brought to Jerusalem. Many are of opinion that the words of Psalm XXIV, 7:

Lift up your heads, O ye gates;
And be ye lifted up, ye everlasting doors:
That the King of glory may come in,

were composed and sung on the occasion of that great celebration.

## II SAMUEL VI, 14

ark of the LORD had gone six paces, he sacrificed an ox and a fatling. 14. And David danced before the LORD with all his might; and David was girded with a linen ephod. 15. So David and all the house of Israel brought up the ark of the LORD with shouting, and with the sound of the horn. ¶ 16. And it was so, as the ark of the LORD came into the city of David, that Michal the daughter of Saul looked out at the window, and saw king David leaping and dancing before the LORD; and she despised him in her heart. 17. And they brought in the ark of the LORD, and set it in its place, in the midst of the tent that David had pitched for it; and David offered burnt-offerings and peace-offerings before the LORD. 18. And when David had made an end of offering the burnt-offering and the peace-offerings, he blessed the people in the name of the LORD of hosts. 19. And he dealt among all the people, even among the whole multitude of Israel, both to men and women, to every one a cake of bread, and a cake made in a pan, and a sweet cake. So all the people departed every one to his house. ¶ 20. Then David returned to bless his household. And Michal the daughter of Saul came out to meet David, and said: 'How did the king of Israel get him honour to-day, who uncovered himself to-day in the eyes of the handmaids of his servants, as one of the vain fellows shamelessly uncovereth himself!' 21. And David said unto Michal: 'Before the LORD, who chose me above thy father, and above all his house, to appoint me prince over the people of the LORD, over Israel, before the LORD will I make merry. 22. And I will be yet more vile than thus, and will be base in mine own sight; and with the handmaids whom thou hast spoken of, with them will I get me honour.' 23. And Michal the daughter of Saul had no child unto the day of her death.

---

**14.** *with a linen ephod.* Not in his royal robes, but in the dress of a priest ministering before the Ark.

**16.** *Michal.* The only discordant note is the contemptuous greeting of his wife, the haughty daughter of Saul, who condemns his enthusiastic demeanour.

*she despised him in her heart.* Her pride revolted against the unseemliness, as she thought it, of a king breaking through conventional decorum to dance in front of a religious procession.

**19.** *dealt among all the people.* Divided among those who accompanied the Ark to its destination.

**20.** *to bless his household.* Or, 'to greet his family' (Moffatt).

*vain fellows.* Worthless fellows. She had the folly to despise, and the cruelty to ridicule, him.

**21–22.** David retorts that, for the sake of the Lord who had elevated him above her father's house, he would find honour in still humbler abasement.

**23.** *had no child.* The greatest cause of sorrow to an Eastern woman. Perhaps an explanation of her coldness and heartlessness.

## II SAMUEL VII, 1

### CHAPTER VII

1. And it came to pass, when the king dwelt in his house, and the LORD had given him rest from all his enemies round about, 2. that the king said unto Nathan the prophet: 'See now, I dwell in a house of cedar, but the ark of God dwelleth within curtains.' 3. And Nathan said to the king: 'Go, do all that is in thy heart; for the LORD is with thee.' 4. And it came to pass the same night, that the word of the LORD came unto Nathan, saying: 5. 'Go and tell My servant David: Thus saith the LORD: Shalt thou build Me a house for Me to dwell in? 6. for I have not dwelt in a house since the day that I brought up the children of Israel out of Egypt, even to this day, but have walked in a tent and in a tabernacle. 7. In all places wherein I have walked among all the children of Israel, spoke I a word with any of the tribes of Israel, whom I commanded to feed My people Israel, saying: 'Why have ye not built Me a house of cedar? 8. Now therefore thus shalt thou say unto My servant David: Thus saith the LORD of hosts: I took thee from the sheepcote, from following the sheep, that thou shouldest be prince over My people, over Israel. 9. And I have been with thee whithersoever thou didst go, and have cut off all thine enemies from before thee; and I will make thee a great name, like unto the name of the great ones that are in the earth. 10. And I will appoint a place for My people Israel, and will plant them, that they may dwell in their own place, and be disquieted no more; neither shall the children of wickedness afflict them any more, as at the first, 11. even from the day that I commanded judges to be over My people Israel; and I will cause thee to rest from all

### שמואל ב ז
### CAP. VII. ז

א וַיְהִ֕י כִּי־יָשַׁ֥ב הַמֶּ֖לֶךְ בְּבֵית֑וֹ וַֽיהוָ֛ה הֵנִֽיחַ־ל֥וֹ מִסָּבִ֖יב מִכָּל־
2 אֹיְבָֽיו: וַיֹּ֤אמֶר הַמֶּ֙לֶךְ֙ אֶל־נָתָ֣ן הַנָּבִ֔יא רְאֵ֣ה נָ֔א אָנֹכִ֥י
יוֹשֵׁ֖ב בְּבֵ֣ית אֲרָזִ֑ים וַֽאֲרוֹן֙ הָֽאֱלֹהִ֔ים יֹשֵׁ֖ב בְּת֥וֹךְ הַיְרִיעָֽה:
3 וַיֹּ֤אמֶר נָתָן֙ אֶל־הַמֶּ֔לֶךְ כֹּ֛ל אֲשֶׁ֥ר בִּֽלְבָבְךָ֖ לֵ֣ךְ עֲשֵׂ֑ה כִּ֥י
4 יְהוָ֖ה עִמָּֽךְ: וַֽיְהִ֖י בַּלַּ֣יְלָה הַה֑וּא ׃ וַיְהִי֙ דְּבַר־
ה יְהוָ֔ה אֶל־נָתָ֖ן לֵאמֹֽר: לֵ֤ךְ וְאָֽמַרְתָּ֙ אֶל־עַבְדִּ֣י אֶל־דָּוִ֔ד
6 כֹּ֖ה אָמַ֣ר יְהוָ֑ה הַֽאַתָּ֛ה תִּבְנֶה־לִּ֥י בַ֖יִת לְשִׁבְתִּֽי: כִּ֣י לֹ֤א
יָשַׁ֙בְתִּי֙ בְּבַ֔יִת לְמִיּ֞וֹם הַעֲלֹתִ֤י אֶת־בְּנֵ֣י יִשְׂרָאֵל֙ מִמִּצְרַ֔יִם
7 וְעַ֖ד הַיּ֣וֹם הַזֶּ֑ה וָאֶֽהְיֶה֙ מִתְהַלֵּ֔ךְ בְּאֹ֖הֶל וּבְמִשְׁכָּֽן: בְּכֹ֥ל
אֲשֶׁר־הִתְהַלַּ֘כְתִּי֮ בְּכָל־בְּנֵ֣י יִשְׂרָאֵל֒ הֲדָבָ֣ר דִּבַּ֗רְתִּי אֶת־אַחַ֞ד
שִׁבְטֵ֤י יִשְׂרָאֵל֙ אֲשֶׁ֣ר צִוִּ֔יתִי לִרְע֖וֹת אֶת־עַמִּ֣י אֶת־יִשְׂרָאֵ֑ל
8 לֵאמֹ֕ר לָ֛מָּה לֹֽא־בְנִיתֶ֥ם לִ֖י בֵּ֥ית אֲרָזִֽים: וְ֠עַתָּ֠ה כֹּֽה־תֹאמַ֞ר
לְעַבְדִּ֣י לְדָוִ֗ד כֹּ֤ה אָמַר֙ יְהוָ֣ה צְבָא֔וֹת אֲנִ֤י לְקַחְתִּ֙יךָ֙ מִן־
הַנָּוֶ֔ה מֵאַחַ֖ר הַצֹּ֑אן לִֽהְי֣וֹת נָגִ֔יד עַל־עַמִּ֖י עַל־יִשְׂרָאֵֽל:
9 וָאֶהְיֶ֣ה עִמְּךָ֗ בְּכֹל֙ אֲשֶׁ֣ר הָלַ֔כְתָּ וָאַכְרִ֥תָה אֶת־כָּל־אֹיְבֶ֖יךָ
מִפָּנֶ֑יךָ וְעָשִׂ֤תִֽי לְךָ֙ שֵׁ֣ם גָּד֔וֹל כְּשֵׁ֥ם הַגְּדֹלִ֖ים אֲשֶׁ֥ר בָּאָֽרֶץ:
י וְשַׂמְתִּ֣י מָק֡וֹם לְעַמִּי֩ לְיִשְׂרָאֵ֨ל וּנְטַעְתִּ֜יו וְשָׁכַ֤ן תַּחְתָּיו֙ וְלֹ֣א
יִרְגַּ֣ז ע֔וֹד וְלֹֽא־יֹסִ֤יפוּ בְנֵֽי־עַוְלָה֙ לְעַנּוֹת֔וֹ כַּאֲשֶׁ֖ר בָּרִאשׁוֹנָֽה:
11 וּלְמִן־הַיּ֗וֹם אֲשֶׁ֨ר צִוִּ֤יתִי שֹֽׁפְטִים֙ עַל־עַמִּ֣י יִשְׂרָאֵ֔ל וַהֲנִיחֹ֥תִי

v. 4. פסקא באמצע פסוק

---

### CHAPTER VII

David's desire to build a Temple. The Prophet's message is that not David shall build a house unto God, but God shall build a 'house' (*i.e.* a dynasty) for David.

**1.** *had given him rest.* Recalling words in Deut. XII, 10–11. David felt that the duty now fell on him to build a permanent Central Sanctuary.

**2.** *Nathan the prophet.* The fearless prophet who played such an important part in the lives of both David and Solomon.

*within curtains. i.e.* in a tent. He is struck by the contrast of his own palace of cedar with the simple tent which contained the Ark.

**3.** *go, do all that is in thine heart.* Nathan speaks here as a courtier, as one who saw that David was filled with a worthy desire to honour God. That same night he receives the Divine message to David.

**5.** *shalt thou build? i.e.* thou shalt not build. He was not the man to build; he had been, perforce, too much engaged in warfare, had shed too much human blood; I Chron. XXII, 8. Moreover, in spite of appearances, the kingdom was not yet sufficiently safe from hostile efforts to overthrow it, to justify the great undertaking of building a worthy national Temple.

**8.** *the sheepcote.* lit. 'the habitation,' *i.e.* of the sheep, and therefore the sheep-pen. But more likely the habitation of the shepherd, the shepherd's hut, is intended.

457

II SAMUEL VII, 12

thine enemies. Moreover the LORD telleth thee that the LORD will make thee a house. 12. When thy days are fulfilled, and thou shalt sleep with thy fathers, I will set up thy seed after thee, that shall proceed out of thy body, and I will establish his kingdom. 13. He shall build a house for my name, and I will establish the throne of his kingdom for ever. 14. I will be to him for a father, and he shall be to Me for a son; if he commit iniquity, I will chasten him with the rod of men, and with the stripes of the children of men; 15. but My mercy shall not depart from him, as I took it from Saul, whom I put away before thee. 16. And thy house and thy kingdom shall be made sure for ever before thee; thy throne shall be established for ever.' 17. According to all these words, and according to all this vision, so did Nathan speak unto David.

**10.** *I will appoint a place.* Better, *I have appointed . . . have planted . . . and they dwell in their own place.*

*be disquieted no more.* Better, *shall not be moved any more.*

**11.** *make thee a house.* Establish your family as a dynasty.

**12.** *thy seed.* This Divine promise was especially welcome in view of the insecurity of dynasties in Eastern countries, and the fearful tragedies that were often perpetrated to get rid of the old king's family (Blaikie).

**13.** *he shall build a house.* The word *he* is emphatic, and of course refers to Solomon.

**14.** *with the rod of men.* i.e. such chastisement as men inflict upon their children to correct and reclaim them, not to destroy them (Speaker's Bible).

**16.** *shall be made sure.* i.e. permanently established. The Davidic family reigned without interruption for 347 years. It was restored to rulership after the Exile, and continued to the end of the Maccabean dynasty. In the days of the Roman Empire and well into the Middle Ages, the 'Patriarchs' of Palestine and Exilarchs of Babylonia prided themselves on their Davidic descent.

'David is the most luminous figure and the most gifted personage in Israelitish history, surpassed in ethical greatness and general historical importance only by Moses, the man of God. He is one of those phenomenal men such as Providence gives but once to a people, in whom a whole nation and its history reaches once for all its climax. True, the picture of David does not lack the traits of human frailty, which Israelitish tradition, with a truly admirable sincerity, has neither suppressed nor palliated; but the charm which this personality exercised over all contemporaries without exception has not yet faded for us of later day. The king who did more for the worldly greatness and earthly power of Israel than any one else, was a genuine Israelite in that he appreciated also Israel's religious destiny; he was no soldier-king, no conqueror of common stamp, no ruler like any one of a hundred others, but he is the truest incorporation of the distinctive character of Israel—a unique personality in the history of the world' (Cornill).

# THAZRIA

## Laws of Purification (Chapters XII–XV)

Food laws were dealt with in the last chapter. We now have laws of purification in regard to (a) child-birth (XII); (b) leprosy (XIII, XIV); (c) bodily secretions (XV). (Another rite of purification, after contact with a human corpse, is expounded in Num. XIX.) There is abundant evidence that the laws of purity and impurity were from the earliest times faithfully observed in Israel. These laws, however, underwent various amplifications in the course of centuries; and not long after the Destruction of the Second Temple, disappeared, for the greater part, from Jewish life, even in Palestine. Only such comments as are essential to the understanding of the general meaning of the Text will here be given. The detailed exposition of this complex subject, with its successive expansions (the 'institutions' of Ezra, the modifications of the early Scribes and the Pharisees, and the deviating practice among later sects), must be sought for in specialist works, or in commentaries for the learned.

There are two distinct views in regard to the laws of purity and impurity: one, that they are hygienic; the other, that they are 'levitical', *i.e.* purely religious. Advocates of the hygienic view hold that the sources of impurity in Scripture—disease or death, the disintegrating corpse of man or beast, skin-diseases, and disorders in connection with sex-life—are in the main physical. In all these cases—they hold—impurity is equivalent to infection or the danger of infection; the rules of separation are intended to prevent the spread of infection; and the prescribed purification, whether by water or fire, is really *disinfection*. The procedure of purification bears out the character of disinfection. At no stage is there prescribed any prayer or formula to be recited; and the sacrifice, which invariably takes place *after* purification, is merely the token of re-admission into the camp (Katzenelsohn). The sanitary interpretation of the laws of purity is, however, contested by other authorities, who, on their side, would rule out the hygienic motive altogether. They point to the Scripture passages which over and over again state that the supreme end of these laws is to lead men to holiness, and preserve them from anything that is defiling or that would exclude them from the Sanctuary. Strong arguments can thus be marshalled in favour of either view. However, while neither the hygienic nor the levitical motive can by itself account for all the facts, the two views are not mutually exclusive. Thus, in regard to Sabbath observance, Scripture assigns both a religious motive (Exod. XX, 11) and a social motive (Deut. V, 14). In the same manner, the eating of flesh of an animal torn in the fields is in one place forbidden for reasons of holiness (Exod. XXII, 30), and in another place plainly for reasons of hygiene (Lev. XI, 39, 40).

It is to be noted that most laws of purity and impurity apply only in reference to the Sanctuary and the holy objects connected with it. They did not apply in ordinary life, or to persons who did not intend to enter the Sanctuary.

### Chapter XII. Purification after Child-birth

After the birth of a child, the mother brought a burnt-offering and a sin-offering at the Sanctuary, and thereby became ritually clean. Many non-Jewish commentators connect the regulation with the doom pronounced on Eve (Gen. III, 16). Life and death are in this way associated with the idea of the first sin in the Garden of Eden. Motherhood would thus in itself be a sinful thing, and its occurrence require purification and atonement. Such a thought, however, is utterly foreign to the general teaching of Scripture. 'Be fruitful and multiply, and replenish the earth' (Gen. I, 28), is the first command in the Torah; and childlessness was regarded as the worst calamity.

The more acceptable view is that the Law deals solely with the physical secretions attendant on child-birth. The mother becomes unclean through conditions attendant on parturition, but not the child. If impurity were associated with child-birth as a fact in nature, the child, who is the cause of the mother's defilement, would itself have been unclean.

## LEVITICUS XII, 1

### CHAPTER XII

1. And the LORD spoke unto Moses, saying: 2. Speak unto the children of Israel, saying: ¶ If a woman be delivered, and bear a man-child, then she shall be unclean seven days; as in the days of the impurity of her sickness shall she be unclean. 3. And in the eighth day the flesh of his foreskin shall be circumcised. 4. And she shall continue in the blood of purification three and thirty days; she shall touch no hallowed thing, nor come into the sanctuary, until the days of her purification be fulfilled. 5. But if she bear a maid-child, then she shall be unclean two weeks, as in her impurity; and she shall continue in the blood of purification threescore and six days. 6. And when the days of her purification are fulfilled, for a son, or for a daughter, she shall bring a lamb of the first year for a burnt-offering, and a young pigeon, or a turtle-dove, for a sin-offering, unto the door of the tent of meeting, unto the priest. 7. And he shall offer it before the LORD, and make atonement for her; and she shall be cleansed from the fountain of her blood. This is the law for her that beareth, whether a male or a female. 8. And if her means suffice not for a lamb, then she shall take two turtle-doves, or two young pigeons:

---

## IV. THAZRIA

### (CHAPTERS XII AND XIII)

### CHAPTER XII. PURIFICATION AFTER CHILDBIRTH (Continued)

**2.** *seven days.* Her uncleanness is of the same strict degree as that during menstruation (XVIII, 19). Seven days after that period, the ritual bath of purification is taken. During the remainder of the forty (or eighty) days she is only unclean as regards the Sanctuary (see v. 4).

**3.** *circumcised.* See Gen. XVII. This proves that the purification of the mother was solely from her physical condition. The circumcision is not a means of purifying the child; because in that case, we should have expected a ceremony of purification for a female child. The Rabbis deduced from the words 'the eighth *day*' that the rite must be performed on that day, even if it be the Sabbath; and during the daytime, not at night.

**5.** *two weeks.* There is no satisfactory explanation why the period is doubled when a female child is born. It cannot be because a female was regarded as more defiling than a male, since the mother's purification was the same for either sex.

**6.** *burnt-offering . . . sin-offering.* They are not here given in the usual order, which prescribes the sin-offering before the burnt-offering. The sin-offering was here merely a purgation offering, as with other cases of uncleanness (cf. xv, 30), where no sin had been committed (Sifra). The burnt-offering symbolized rededication to God, after the period of abstention from the Sanctuary.

*unto the door.* As it was only after the offerings had been sacrificed that she was again clean, she could not bring the animals beyond the entrance of the Tent of Meeting.

**7.** *he shall offer it.* i.e. each one of the two offerings.

*make atonement.* See on I, 4. The meaning is here that by virtue of the offerings, the cause which had made it impossible for her to come to the Sanctuary was *obliterated*.

## LEVITICUS XIII, 1

the one for a burnt-offering, and the other for a sin-offering; and the priest shall make atonement for her, and she shall be clean.

## 13 CHAPTER XIII

1. And the LORD spoke unto Moses and unto Aaron, saying: ¶ 2. When a man shall have in the skin of his flesh a rising, or a scab, or a bright spot, and it become in the skin of his flesh the plague of leprosy, then he shall be brought unto Aaron the priest, or unto one of his sons the priests. 3. And the priest shall look on the plague in the skin of the flesh; and if the hair in the plague be turned white, and the appearance of the plague be deeper than the skin of his flesh, it is the plague of leprosy; and the priest shall look on him, and pronounce him unclean. 4. And if the bright spot be white in the skin of his

ויקרא תזריע יב יג

יָדָהּ דֵּי שֶׂה וְלָקְחָה שְׁתֵּי־תֹרִים אוֹ שְׁנֵי בְּנֵי יוֹנָה אֶחָד לְעֹלָה וְאֶחָד לְחַטָּאת וְכִפֶּר עָלֶיהָ הַכֹּהֵן וְטָהֵרָה׃ פ

CAP. XIII. יג

2 וַיְדַבֵּר יְהוָֹה אֶל־מֹשֶׁה וְאֶל־אַהֲרֹן לֵאמֹר׃ אָדָם כִּי־יִהְיֶה בְעוֹר־בְּשָׂרוֹ שְׂאֵת אוֹ־סַפַּחַת אוֹ בַהֶרֶת וְהָיָה בְעוֹר־בְּשָׂרוֹ לְנֶגַע צָרָעַת וְהוּבָא אֶל־אַהֲרֹן הַכֹּהֵן אוֹ אֶל־אַחַד מִבָּנָיו 3 הַכֹּהֲנִים׃ וְרָאָה הַכֹּהֵן אֶת־הַנֶּגַע בְּעוֹר־הַבָּשָׂר וְשֵׂעָר בַּנֶּגַע הָפַךְ לָבָן וּמַרְאֵה הַנֶּגַע עָמֹק מֵעוֹר בְּשָׂרוֹ נֶגַע צָרַעַת 4 הוּא וְרָאָהוּ הַכֹּהֵן וְטִמֵּא אֹתוֹ׃ וְאִם־בַּהֶרֶת לְבָנָה הִוא

---

**8.** *two young pigeons.* As with the sin-offering of the poor in v. 7.

In our days, the mother visits the synagogue as soon as convalescence and circumstances permit, in order to render thanks for her recovery, and to offer prayer on behalf of the new-born child (Authorised Prayer Book, p. 312).

### CHAPTERS XIII–XIV
### THE LAW OF LEPROSY

The prominence given to this subject must be due to the prevalence of this class of malady in the Near East; and this explanation is confirmed by the frequent reference to leprosy in the Bible.

As stated in the last chapter, many authorities regard these regulations as based only on sanitary principles. A suspected person was isolated for a period of time until the diagnosis became more certain; and when he was found to be afflicted, he was compelled to reside outside the camp.

It is to the ceremony of purification that we have to turn for the idea which underlies the treatment of the leper. That ceremony can bear only one interpretation; viz. the leper suffered from a *physical* impurity which debarred him from fulfilling his duty as an Israelite towards the Sanctuary. In the same manner that a priest who suffered from a bodily blemish could not officiate in the Sanctuary, so an Israelite who was hideously disfigured was disqualified from membership in 'a kingdom of priests'. During his leprosy, he was accounted as dead; when he recovered, he had to be formally rededicated as an Israelite to the service of God.

The Rabbis regard leprosy as a Providential affliction in punishment for slander or tale bearing (מצורע מוציא שם רע); thus teaching that the slanderer is a moral leper, and should find no place in the camp of Israel.

### CHAPTER XIII
#### 2–8. EARLY SYMPTOMS OF THE DISEASE

**1.** *and unto Aaron.* To diagnose the disease was one of the functions of the priesthood.

**2.** *the skin of his flesh.* Possibly a technical term for the cuticle; see on *v.* 5.

*rising.* A tumor.

*scab.* A scurf which can fall off or be peeled away.

*bright spot.* A glossy patch.

*the plague of leprosy.* Lit. 'a stroke of leprosy'. It has been questioned whether the word צרעת corresponds to the English term 'leprosy'. In the latter, the most notable features are the swelling of organs and the rotting of the limbs. Nothing is here mentioned of these disfigurements. Moreover, leprosy is normally an incurable disease, whereas צרעת is deemed curable. In some of the paragraphs in this chapter a form of leprosy known as elephantiasis seems to be meant.

*he shall be brought.* Or, 'it (viz. the matter of the infection) shall be brought' (Ehrlich), to determine whether the malady was of such a character, or had so developed, as to make it necessary for the person to leave the camp.

**3.** *pronounce him unclean.* i.e. ritually defiled and unfit to enter the Sanctuary.

**4.** *shut up him.* The purpose of the period of isolation was to prevent him, during the time of doubt, from defiling others by contact, should he really be infected.

*seven days.* What is now called leprosy is a slowly developing disease, and very little difference would be discernible in the space of a week.

# LEVITICUS XIII, 5

flesh, and the appearance thereof be not deeper than the skin, and the hair thereof be not turned white, then the priest shall shut up him that hath the plague seven days. 5. And the priest shall look on him the seventh day; and, behold, if the plague stay in its appearance, and the plague be not spread in the skin, then the priest shall shut him up seven days more.\* ¹¹· 6. And the priest shall look on him again the seventh day; and, behold, if the plague be dim, and the plague be not spread in the skin, then the priest shall pronounce him clean: it is a scab; and he shall wash his clothes, and be clean. 7. But if the scab spread abroad in the skin, after that he hath shown himself to the priest for his cleansing, he shall show himself to the priest again. 8. And the priest shall look, and, behold, if the scab be spread in the skin, then the priest shall pronounce him unclean: it is leprosy. ¶ 9. When the plague of leprosy is in a man, then he shall be brought unto the priest. 10. And the priest shall look, and, behold, if there be a white rising in the skin, and it have turned the hair white, and there be quick raw flesh in the rising, 11. it is an old leprosy in the skin of his flesh, and the priest shall pronounce him unclean; he shall not shut him up; for he is unclean. 12. And if the leprosy break out abroad in the skin, and the leprosy cover all the skin of him that hath the plague from his head even to his feet, as far as appeareth to the priest; 13. then the priest shall look; and, behold, if the leprosy have covered all his flesh, he shall pronounce him clean that hath the plague;

---

**5.** *stay.* There has been no alteration for better or worse.

*spread in the skin.* i.e. deeper into the skin, attacking the cutis as well as the cuticle.

**6.** *dim.* i.e. fainter in appearance, and therefore giving evidence of passing away (Ibn Ezra).

*wash his clothes.* An outward symbol that he was freed from suspicion, and could now associate with his brethen and join in the life of the Community. Several Jewish authorities, however, are of opinion that wherever Scripture enjoins washing of the garments, bathing the body is to be also understood.

**7.** *spread abroad in the skin.* Better, *spread into the skin.*

### 9–17. DIAGNOSING THE DISEASE

This paragraph deals with the person who is suddenly attacked by the disease, or in whom it has developed rapidly, without the preliminary symptoms described above.

**9.** *he shall be brought.* See on v. 2.

**10.** *a white rising.* In the disease of elephantiasis one of the early manifestations is the growth of vesicles of a glistening white hue, which burst and discharge a whitish fluid.

*in the skin.* As in v. 5; the disease had penetrated to the cutis.

*quick raw flesh.* i.e. it is an open sore.

**11.** *old leprosy.* Confirmed leprosy; the malady is definitely established as rooted in the system by the presence of quick raw flesh and white hair. No preliminary isolation is necessary; it is a clear case of uncleanness.

**12–17.** These verses apparently refer to common white leprosy. It is less serious than elephantiasis or leprosy proper. The health of the person remains normal during the time the malady persists, and it generally passes off after a while. There is only discoloration of the skin in this milder form of infection.

462

## LEVITICUS XIII, 14

it is all turned white: he is clean. 14. But whensoever raw flesh appeareth in him, he shall be unclean. 15. And the priest shall look on the raw flesh, and pronounce him unclean; the raw flesh is unclean: it is leprosy. 16. But if the raw flesh again be turned into white, then he shall come unto the priest; 17. and the priest shall look on him; and, behold, if the plague be turned into white, then the priest shall pronounce him clean that hath the plague: he is clean.* iii.

¶ 18. And when the flesh hath in the skin thereof a boil, and it is healed, 19. and in the place of the boil there is a white rising, or a bright spot, reddish-white, then it shall be shown to the priest. 20. And the priest shall look; and, behold, if the appearance thereof be lower than the skin, and the hair thereof be turned white, then the priest shall pronounce him unclean: it is the plague of leprosy, it hath broken out in the boil. 21. But if the priest look on it, and, behold, there be no white hairs therein, and it be not lower than the skin, but be dim, then the priest shall shut him up seven days. 22. And if it spread abroad in the skin, then the priest shall pronounce him unclean: it is a plague. 23. But if the bright spot stay in its place, and be not spread, it is the scar of the boil; and the priest shall pronounce him clean.* iv (** ii).

¶ 24. Or when the flesh hath in the skin thereof a burning by fire, and the quick flesh of the burning become a bright spot, reddish-white, or white; 25. then the priest shall look upon it; and, behold, if the hair in the bright spot be turned white, and the appearance thereof be deeper than the skin, it is leprosy, it hath broken out in the burning; and the priest shall pronounce him unclean: it is the plague of leprosy. 26. But if the priest look on it, and, behold, there be no white hair in the bright spot, and it be no lower than the skin, but be dim; then the priest shall shut him up seven days. 27. And the priest shall look upon him the seventh day; if it spread abroad in the skin, then the priest shall pronounce him unclean: it is the plague of leprosy. 28. And if the bright spot stay in its place, and be not spread in the skin, but be dim, it is the rising of the burning, and the priest shall pronounce him clean; for it is the scar of the burning.* v.

¶ 29. And when a man or woman hath a plague upon the head or upon the beard, 30. then the priest shall look on the plague;

---

**18–28. Special Symptoms of Leprosy**
**18.** *boil.* Probably a form of ulcer.
**23.** *scar.* Or, 'inflammation.'

**29–44. Leprosy on Head and Face**
**29.** *plague.* Here, a form of elephantiasis.
**30.** *scall.* The Heb. denotes, 'what one is inclined to scratch or tear away.'

## LEVITICUS XIII, 31

and, behold, if the appearance thereof be deeper than the skin, and there be in it yellow thin hair, then the priest shall pronounce him unclean: it is a scall, it is leprosy of the head or of the beard. 31. And if the priest look on the plague of the scall, and, behold, the appearance thereof be not deeper than the skin, and there be no black hair in it, then the priest shall shut up him that hath the plague of the scall seven days. 32. And in the seventh day the priest shall look on the plague; and, behold, if the scall be not spread, and there be in it no yellow hair, and the appearance of the scall be not deeper than the skin, 33. then he shall be shaven, but the scall shall he not shave; and the priest shall shut up him that hath the scall seven days more. 34. And in the seventh day the priest shall look on the scall; and, behold, if the scall be not spread in the skin, and the appearance thereof be not deeper than the skin, then the priest shall pronounce him clean; and he shall wash his clothes, and be clean. 35. But if the scall spread abroad in the skin after his cleansing, 36. then the priest shall look on him; and, behold, if the scall be spread in the skin, the priest shall not seek for the yellow hair: he is unclean. 37. But if the scall stay in its appearance, and black hair be grown up therein; the scall is healed, he is clean; and the priest shall pronounce him clean. ¶ 38. And if a man or a woman have in the skin of their flesh bright spots, even white bright spots; 39. then the priest shall look; and, behold, if the bright spots in the skin of their flesh be of a dull white, it is a tetter, it hath broken out in the skin: he is clean.*vi(**iii). ¶ 40. And if a man's hair be fallen off his head, he is bald; yet is he clean. 41. And if his hair be fallen off from the front part of his head, he is forehead-bald; yet is he clean. 42. But if there be in the bald head, or the bald forehead, a reddish-white plague, it is leprosy breaking out in his bald head, or his bald forehead. 43. Then the priest shall look upon him; and, behold, if the rising of the plague be reddish-white in his bald head, or in his bald forehead,

**31.** *no black hair.* So long as there was black hair on the infected spot, or it grew black hair (see *v.* 37), the man was not to be regarded as a leper.

**38.** *bright spots.* See *v.* 2.

**39.** *tetter.* Old English for, 'freckled spot,' a skin disease which is not leprous.

**40.** *fallen off.* The falling away of the hair was one of the symptoms that accompanied elephantiasis (see on *v.* 29); but in itself it was not a feature that rendered a person unclean, even if the head were left entirely bald.

**42.** *bald head.* Baldness from the crown backwards to the neck.

**43.** *in the skin of the flesh.* i.e. when the disease occurs in any other part of the body.

# LEVITICUS XIII, 44

as the appearance of leprosy in the skin of the flesh, 44. he is a leprous man, he is unclean; the priest shall surely pronounce him unclean: his plague is in his head. ¶ 45. And the leper in whom the plague is, his clothes shall be rent, and the hair of his head shall go loose, and he shall cover his upper lip, and shall cry: 'Unclean, unclean.' 46. All the days wherein the plague is in him he shall be unclean; he is unclean; he shall dwell alone; without the camp shall his dwelling be. ¶ 47. And when the plague of leprosy is in a garment, whether it be a woollen garment, or a linen garment; 48. or in the warp, or in the woof, whether they be of linen, or of wool; or in a skin, or in any thing made of skin: 49. if the plague be greenish or reddish in the garment, or in the skin, or in the warp, or in the woof, or in any thing of skin, it is the plague of leprosy, and shall be shown unto the priest. 50. And the priest shall look upon the plague, and shut up that which hath the plague seven days. 51. And he shall look on the plague on the seventh day: if the plague be spread in the garment, or in the warp, or in the woof, or in the skin, whatever service skin is used for, the plague is a malignant leprosy: it is unclean. 52. And he shall burn the garment, or the warp, or the woof, whether it be of wool or of linen, or any thing of skin, wherein the plague is; for it is a malignant leprosy; it shall be burnt in the fire. 53. And if the priest shall look, and, behold, the plague be not spread in the garment, or in the warp, or in the woof, or in any thing of skin; 54. then the priest shall command that they wash the thing wherein the plague is, and he shall shut it up seven days more.*vii (**iv) 55. And the priest shall look, after that the plague is washed; and, behold, if the plague have not changed its colour, and the plague be not spread, it is unclean;

### 45–46. TREATMENT OF THE LEPER

**45.** *the leper.* The word is in the masculine; the female sufferer also left the camp and lived apart, but was not required to tear her garments and uncover her head (Sifra).

*his clothes.* The customs of the leper are those of a mourner. He was to regard himself as one upon whom death had laid its hand. His was a living death, not only in the physical sense, as suffering from a loathsome and lingering disease; but also in the spiritual sense, as cut off from the life of the Community of Israel.

*unclean, unclean.* To warn people from touching them. In later times, lepers wore a bell for the same purpose.

**46.** *alone.* Better, *apart*.

### 47–59. LEPROSY OF GARMENTS

The materials could have become infected with the disease through contact with a leper or his sores. Some explain the spots on the garments as caused by mildew, or by some parasitic infection, analogous in its effects to leprosy of the body.

**47.** *garment.* The Heb. can refer to any cloth material, not necessarily an article of apparel.

**48.** *in the warp, or in the woof.* Or, 'woven or knitted stuff.'

## LEVITICUS XIII, 56

thou shalt burn it in the fire; it is a fret, whether the bareness be within or without. 56. And if the priest look, and, behold, the plague be dim after the washing thereof, then he shall rend it out of the garment, or out of the skin, or out of the warp, or out of the woof.*m· 57. And if it appear still in the garment, or in the warp, or in the woof, or in any thing of skin, it is breaking out, thou shalt burn that wherein the plague is with fire. 58. And the garment, or the warp, or the woof, or whatsoever thing of skin it be, which thou shalt wash, if the plague be departed from them, then it shall be washed the second time, and shall be clean. 59. This is the law of the plague of leprosy in a garment of wool or linen, or in the warp, or in the woof, or in any thing of skin, to pronounce it clean, or to pronounce it unclean.

**55.** *it is a fret.* It has eaten into the cloth.
*whether the bareness be within or without.* lit. 'in its front-baldness or its back-baldness'; whether the threadbare appearance be on the right or on the reverse side.

**59.** *this is the law.* The purpose of this regulation is the same as that of the leprous body, viz. to remove from the camp of Israel everything which was unclean.

## HAFTORAH THAZRIA

### II KINGS IV, 42–V, 19

#### CHAPTER IV

42. And there came a man from Baal-shalishah, and brought the man of God bread of the first-fruits, twenty loaves of barley, and fresh ears of corn in his sack. And he said: 'Give unto the people, that they may eat.' 43. And his servant said: 'How should I set this before a hundred men?' But he said: 'Give the people, that they may eat; for thus saith the LORD: They shall eat, and shall leave thereof.'

The Haftorahs of this and of the succeeding Sedrah relate incidents from the cycle of tales describing the activities of the Prophet Elisha. There is little resemblance between him and the sublime, storm-compelling personality of his great Master. Unlike Elijah, 'he was the friend and counsellor of kings. His deeds were not of wild terror, but of gracious, soothing, homely beneficence, bound up with the ordinary tenor of human life' (Stanley). Many of these tales give us interesting glimpses into the social life of Israel in his day; *e.g.* the stories that form the Haftorah of Vayyera, see p. 76. Our Haftorah tells two stories—one in which, during the great famine, the scanty bread of a poor man's offering is multiplied, so that Elisha is enabled to feed a hundred of the 'sons of the prophets'; and the other, the story of the captain of Syria's host, who is cured of his leprosy by Elisha. This incident connects with the Sedrah, which deals with the diagnosis and treatment of that disease.

#### CHAPTER IV

**42.** *Baal-shalishah.* In the country of Ephraim, to the north of Bethel. Fruits ripened there earlier than elsewhere in Palestine.
*give unto the people.* i.e. to the disciples, the 'sons of the prophets', who were with him (v. 38).
**43.** *should I set this.* i.e. is it not too little for them?

II KINGS IV, 44

44. So he set it before them, and they did eat, and left thereof, according to the word of the LORD.

## CHAPTER V

1. Now Naaman, captain of the host of the king of Aram, was a great man with his master, and held in esteem, because by him the LORD had given victory unto Aram; he was also a mighty man of valour, but he was a leper. 2. And the Arameans had gone out in bands, and had brought away captive out of the land of Israel a little maid; and she waited on Naaman's wife. 3. And she said unto her mistress: 'Would that my lord were with the prophet that is in Samaria! then would he recover him of his leprosy.' 4. And he went in, and told his lord, saying: 'Thus and thus said the maid that is of the land of Israel.' 5. And the king of Aram said: 'Go now, and I will send a letter unto the king of Israel.' And he departed, and took with him ten talents of silver, and six thousand pieces of gold, and ten changes of raiment. 6. And he brought the letter to the king of Israel, saying: 'And now when this letter is come unto thee, behold, I have sent Naaman my servant to thee, that thou mayest recover him of his leprosy.' 7. And it came to pass, when the king of Israel had read the letter, that he rent his clothes, and said: 'Am I God, to kill and to make alive, that this man doth send unto me to recover a man of his leprosy? but consider, I pray you, and see how he seeketh an occasion against me.' ¶ 8. And it was so, when Elisha the man of God heard that the king of Israel had rent his clothes, that he sent to the king, saying: 'Wherefore hast thou rent thy clothes? let him come now to me, and he shall know that there is a prophet in Israel.' 9. So Naaman came with his horses and with his chariots, and stood at the door of the house of Elisha. 10. And Elisha sent a messenger unto him, saying: 'Go and wash in the Jordan seven

## CHAPTER V. THE HEALING OF NAAMAN

**1.** *but he was a leper.* A famous general, great and honoured in the land, but a leper; the *but*'s of life can be even more grim and heart-breaking than its *if*'s.

**2.** *in bands.* In marauding bands, raiding the territory of Israel even when no formal war existed between the two peoples. Since the death of Solomon, Syria had become a persistent and implacable foe to Israel.

**3.** *recover.* Cure; lit. 'receive him back'—as the cured leper was received back into the camp and city life from which he had been excluded (Kimchi).

**5.** *took with him.* As a gift to the Prophet, who, as we learn later, would receive nothing at his hands.

*ten talents of silver.* A very large sum.

**6.** *recover him of his leprosy.* By using his influence with the Prophet. Only the main point of the letter is quoted. The king of Israel is addressed as a vassal.

**7.** *rent his clothes.* As at the receipt of bad news. The king trembles at the Syrian's demand, and thinks he is seeking a pretext for war.

## II KINGS V, 11

times, and thy flesh shall come back to thee, and thou shalt be clean.' 11. But Naaman was wroth, and went away, and said: 'Behold, I thought: He will surely come out to me, and stand, and call on the name of the LORD his God, and wave his hand over the place, and recover the leper. 12. Are not Amanah and Pharpar, the rivers of Damascus, better than all the waters of Israel? may I not wash in them, and be clean?' So he turned, and went away in a rage. 13. And his servants came near, and spoke unto him, and said: 'My father, if the prophet had bid thee do some great thing, wouldest thou not have done it? how much rather then, when he saith to thee: Wash, and be clean?' 14. Then went he down, and dipped himself seven times in the Jordan, according to the saying of the man of God; and his flesh came back like unto the flesh of a little child, and he was clean. ¶ 15. And he returned to the man of God, he and all his company, and came, and stood before him; and he said: 'Behold now, I know that there is no God in all the earth, but in Israel; now therefore, I pray thee, take a present of thy servant.' 16. But he said: 'As the LORD liveth, before whom I stand, I will receive none.' And he urged him to take it; but he refused. 17. And Naaman said: 'If not, yet I pray thee let there be given to thy servant two mules' burden of earth; for thy servant will

**11.** *Naaman was wroth*. Elisha did not come out to him, and Naaman was enraged that the Prophet was no respecter of persons—in his case. He was especially annoyed at the *simplicity* of the remedy: he expected the Prophet to come out and play the wonder-worker.

**12.** *Amanah and Pharpar*. His patriotic pride is wounded: why was he bidden to wash in that wretched, turbid, tortuous stream—the Jordan —rather than in the pure and flowing waters of his own native Amanah and Pharpar?

The Prophet's bidding has a wider meaning than the ephemeral counsel to the ancient Syrian general. Whenever mankind seeks to be cured of moral leprosy, it can gain that cure only in Jordan, only in rivers of Jewish inspiration and teaching. The waters of India and Greece, of Italy and Germany, may be far greater, stronger, clearer; but they cannot restore moral health to the ailing soul of man. In the crises of life, whether of the individual or of humanity, we turn not to the Vedas or Homer, nor to Dante or Goethe, but to the Book of Psalms.

**15.** *he returned*. Naaman was grateful. 'It is difficult to conceive the transport of a man cured of this most loathsome and humiliating of all earthly afflictions' (Farrar).

*take a present*. Accustomed to the ways of heathen priests, he could not imagine that so great a service would be rendered to a wealthy applicant without monetary reward.

**16.** *I will receive none*. Like Abraham, who would not take even a 'shoe-latchet' from the people he befriended (Gen. XIV, 23).

**17.** *two mules' burden of earth*. i.e. of the Holy Land, for constructing an altar to the God of Israel in Syria. Naaman held the heathen view that a deity was only powerful in the country which recognized him; and therefore that outside Palestine, God could only be worshipped on *soil* from Israel's land!

II KINGS V, 18

henceforth offer neither burnt-offering nor sacrifice unto other gods, but unto the LORD. 18. In this thing the LORD pardon thy servant: when my master goeth into the house of Rimmon to worship there, and he leaneth on my hand, and I prostrate myself in the house of Rimmon, when I prostrate myself in the house of Rimmon, the LORD pardon thy servant in this thing.' 19. And he said unto him: 'Go in peace.' So he departed from him some way.

18 לֵאלֹהִים אֲחֵרִים כִּי אִם־לַיהוָה: לַדָּבָר הַזֶּה יִסְלַח יְהוָה לְעַבְדֶּךָ בְּבוֹא אֲדֹנִי בֵית־רִמּוֹן לְהִשְׁתַּחֲוֺת שָׁמָּה וְהוּא ׀ נִשְׁעָן עַל־יָדִי וְהִשְׁתַּחֲוֵיתִי בֵּית רִמֹּן בְּהִשְׁתַּחֲוָיָתִי 19 בֵּית רִמֹּן יִסְלַח־נא יְהוָה לְעַבְדְּךָ בַּדָּבָר הַזֶּה: וַיֹּאמֶר לוֹ לֵךְ לְשָׁלוֹם וַיֵּלֶךְ מֵאִתּוֹ כִּבְרַת אָרֶץ:

v. 18. כתיב ולא ק׳

**18.** *prostrate myself.* Or, 'bow myself.' Though he knows that the Lord God of Israel is the only living God, he must accompany his master on state occasions to the temple of *his* god Rimmon. The phrase, *to bow in the house of Rimmon*, has thus become proverbial to indicate unwilling and perfunctory homage, or dangerous and dishonest compromise.

**19.** *go in peace.* Elisha neither approves nor disapproves. Probably he did not wish to place too great a strain upon the devotion of the new convert. The phrase, 'go in peace' means lit. 'go *towards* peace.' In the ideology of our Sages the whole of life is a journey towards Peace; only when life is completed has man reached life's goal and entered into real peace. Hence the formula when the mortal remains are committed to the grave: 'May he come to his place *in* peace.'

# LEVITICUS XIV, 1

## Chapter XIV

1. And the Lord spoke unto Moses, saying: ¶ 2. This shall be the law of the leper in the day of his cleansing: he shall be brought unto the priest. 3. And the priest shall go forth out of the camp; and the priest shall look, and, behold, if the plague of leprosy be healed in the leper; 4. then shall the priest command to take for him that is to be cleansed two living clean birds, and cedar-wood, and scarlet, and hyssop. 5. And the priest shall command to kill one of the birds in an earthen vessel over running water. 6. As for the living bird, he shall take it, and the cedar-wood, and the scarlet, and the hyssop, and shall dip them and the living bird in the blood of the bird that was killed over the running water. 7. And he shall sprinkle upon him that is to be cleansed from the leprosy seven times, and shall pronounce him clean, and shall let go the living bird into the open field. 8. And he that is to be cleansed shall wash his clothes, and shave off all his hair, and bathe himself in water, and he shall

ויקרא מצרע יד

Cap. XIV. יד

פ פ פ פ כח 28

2 וַיְדַבֵּר יְהוָה אֶל־מֹשֶׁה לֵּאמֹר: זֹאת תִּהְיֶה תּוֹרַת הַמְּצֹרָע
3 בְּיוֹם טָהֳרָתוֹ וְהוּבָא אֶל־הַכֹּהֵן: וְיָצָא הַכֹּהֵן אֶל־מִחוּץ לַמַּחֲנֶה וְרָאָה הַכֹּהֵן וְהִנֵּה נִרְפָּא נֶגַע־הַצָּרַעַת מִן־הַצָּרוּעַ:
4 וְצִוָּה הַכֹּהֵן וְלָקַח לַמִּטַּהֵר שְׁתֵּי־צִפֳּרִים חַיּוֹת טְהֹרוֹת
5 וְעֵץ אֶרֶז וּשְׁנִי תוֹלַעַת וְאֵזֹב: וְצִוָּה הַכֹּהֵן וְשָׁחַט אֶת־
6 הַצִּפּוֹר הָאֶחָת אֶל־כְּלִי־חֶרֶשׂ עַל־מַיִם חַיִּים: אֶת־הַצִּפֹּר הַחַיָּה יִקַּח אֹתָהּ וְאֶת־עֵץ הָאֶרֶז וְאֶת־שְׁנִי הַתּוֹלַעַת וְאֶת־הָאֵזֹב וְטָבַל אוֹתָם וְאֵת הַצִּפֹּר הַחַיָּה בְּדַם הַצִּפֹּר הַשְּׁחֻטָה
7 עַל הַמַּיִם הַחַיִּים: וְהִזָּה עַל הַמִּטַּהֵר מִן־הַצָּרַעַת שֶׁבַע פְּעָמִים וְטִהֲרוֹ וְשִׁלַּח אֶת־הַצִּפֹּר הַחַיָּה עַל־פְּנֵי הַשָּׂדֶה:

## V. METZORA

### (Chapters XIV–XV)

### Chapter XIV, 1–32. Purification of a Leper

**2. day.** The Rabbis took this phrase literally, and ruled that the purification could not take place at night.

*he shall be brought.* To an appointed place outside the camp. Or, 'it (the news of the leper's recovery) shall be brought (*i.e.* reported) to the priest' (Ehrlich); see on XIII, 2.

**3. out of the camp.** To the leper.

*shall look.* The priest had to satisfy himself that the disease had completely passed away, before commencing the ceremony of purification.

**4. command to take.** The birds and articles required for the ceremony were not necessarily provided by the leper himself. This fact disposes of the idea that the birds were intended as a sacrifice. And further, no portion of the birds was placed on the Altar. The first part of the ceremony must be interpreted as a symbolic representation of the leper's restoration to life and his re-admission to the camp of Israel.

*cedar-wood.* The most durable of woods, with the strongest resisting power to decay; and therefore symbolical of the cured leper who had overcome the putrefying effects of his disease. Maimonides, however, declares, 'I do not know at present the reason of any of these things'; viz., the cedarwood, hyssop and scarlet.

*scarlet.* According to Rabbinic tradition, a band of wool, dipped in scarlet, was used.

*hyssop.* See on Exod. XII, 22; it was a convenient instrument for sprinkling, as its leaves readily absorb the liquid and freely give it out when shaken. It was used in ceremonies of purification where sprinkling was included (Num. XIX, 6, 18), and therefore became later associated with the idea of cleanliness (Ps. LI, 9).

**5. kill one of the birds.** For the blood required in the ceremony; as a contrast to the other bird, which was allowed to live, thus representing the state of death from which the leper has escaped and the new life to which he can now look forward.

*running water.* lit. 'living water'; *i.e.* water fresh from a spring, or a stream; the natural symbol for life, freshness, and purity. The blood flowed into the vessel which contained the water.

**7. pronounce him clean.** He could now rejoin his brethen, although a further ceremony was necessary before he was permitted to approach the Sanctuary.

*let go the living bird.* In like manner, the leper had been spared from death, and was free to enter the camp.

**8. shave.** This is part of the rites of purification, since the disease specially attacked the hair; see next *v.*

# LEVITICUS XIV, 9 ויקרא מצרע יד

be clean; and after that he may come into the camp, but shall dwell outside his tent seven days. 9. And it shall be on the seventh day, that he shall shave all his hair off his head and his beard and his eyebrows, even all his hair he shall shave off; and he shall wash his clothes, and he shall bathe his flesh in water, and he shall be clean. 10. And on the eighth day he shall take two he-lambs without blemish, and one ewe-lamb of the first year without blemish, and three tenth parts of an ephah of fine flour for a meal-offering, mingled with oil, and one log of oil. 11. And the priest that cleanseth him shall set the man that is to be cleansed, and those things, before the Lord, at the door of the tent of meeting. 12. And the priest shall take one of the he-lambs, and offer him for a guilt-offering, and the log of oil, and wave them for a wave-offering before the Lord.* 13. And he shall kill the he-lamb in the place where they kill the sin-offering and the burnt-offering, in the place of the sanctuary; for as the sin-offering is the priest's, so is the guilt-offering; it is most holy. 14. And the priest shall take of the blood of the guilt-offering, and the priest shall put it upon the tip of the right ear of him that is to be cleansed, and upon the thumb of his right hand, and upon the great toe of his right foot. 15. And the priest shall take of the log of oil, and pour it into the palm of his own left hand. 16. And the priest shall dip his right finger in

---

*outside his tent seven days.* An intermediate stage between his complete isolation and his complete liberty, which was to restore to him his religious privileges, and with them his full social rights (Kalisch).

**9.** *shave.* No longer to purify him of his former defilement, but to prepare him for the rite of consecration, even as the Levites should be shaven (Num. VIII, 7) before their induction to the service of the Sanctuary.

*wash his clothes.* Cf. the preparation of the Levites prior to their consecration (Num. VIII, 7).

**10.** *ephah.* Approximately a bushel.
*log.* About one pint.

**11.** *at the door of.* See on XII, 6. In the time of the Second Temple, he was brought to what was known as Nicanor's Gate, which divided the Women's Court from the Court of the Israelites. The latter Court, but not the former, was regarded as part of the Sanctuary.

**12.** *guilt-offering.* This was the first of the three offerings sacrificed on behalf of the cleansed leper. He had been completely cut off from his people, and therefore his first act was to renew his covenant, as an Israelite, with God. It was explained on VII, 1 that the guilt-offering was not an expiatory sacrifice, but a forfeit which was offered when a man had made restitution. By his severance from the life of the community, the leper had failed to bring his dues to the Sanctuary, and so took the earliest opportunity to place his forfeit on the Altar.

*wave-offering.* See on VII, 30; and Num. VIII, 11. The act of waving had the additional significance of dedicating the bringer of the sacrifice to the service of the Most High.

**13.** *is the priest's.* See VII, 6 f.

**14.** *ear . . . hand . . . foot.* This ceremony was identical with that of the consecration of the priests, and had the same significance; see on VIII, 23.

**15.** *of the log of oil.* i.e. some of the additional log, mentioned in v. 10. This was different from the anointing of the High Priest, upon whose head the oil was poured (VIII, 12). Here the priest only 'put' it on the person's head.

## LEVITICUS XIV, 17

the oil that is in his left hand, and shall sprinkle of the oil with his finger seven times before the LORD. 17. And of the rest of the oil that is in his hand shall the priest put upon the tip of the right ear of him that is to be cleansed, and upon the thumb of his right hand, and upon the great toe of his right foot, upon the blood of the guilt-offering. 18. And the rest of the oil that is in the priest's hand he shall put upon the head of him that is to be cleansed; and the priest shall make atonement for him before the LORD. 19. And the priest shall offer the sin-offering, and make atonement for him that is to be cleansed because of his uncleanness; and afterward he shall kill the burnt-offering. 20. And the priest shall offer the burnt-offering and the meal-offering upon the altar; and the priest shall make atonement for him, and he shall be clean.* ¹¹¹ (** v). ¶ 21. And if he be poor, and his means suffice not, then he shall take one he-lamb for a guilt-offering to be waved, to make atonement for him, and one tenth part of an ephah of fine flour mingled with oil for a meal-offering, and a log of oil; 22. and two turtle-doves, or two young pigeons, such as his means suffice for; and the one shall be a sin-offering, and the other a burnt-offering. 23. And on the eighth day he shall bring them for his cleansing unto the priest, unto the door of the tent of meeting, before the LORD. 24. And the priest shall take the lamb of the guilt-offering, and the log of oil, and the priest shall wave them for a wave-offering before the LORD. 25. And he shall kill the lamb of the guilt-offering, and the priest shall take of the blood of the guilt-offering, and put it upon the tip of the right ear of him that is to be cleansed, and upon the thumb of his right hand, and upon the great toe of his right foot. 26. And the priest shall pour of the oil into the palm of his own left hand. 27. And the priest shall sprinkle with his right finger some of the oil that is in his left hand seven times before the LORD. 28. And the priest shall put of the oil that is in his hand upon the tip of the right ear of him that is to be cleansed, and upon the thumb of his right hand, and upon the great toe of his right foot, upon the place of the blood of the guilt-offering. 29. And the rest of the oil that is in the

**19.** *sin-offering.* viz. the ewe-lamb mentioned in *v*. 10. The sin-offering was, in this case, nothing more than a medium of purification; see on XII, 6.

**20.** *meal-offering.* The flour and the oil (see *v*. 10). This final sacrifice expressed the gratitude of the former leper.

**21.–32.** In the case of poverty, the demand for the guilt-offering remains, but the other two

## LEVITICUS XIV, 30

priest's hand he shall put upon the head of him that is to be cleansed, to make atonement for him before the LORD. 30. And he shall offer one of the turtle-doves, or of the young pigeons, such as his means suffice for; 31. even such as his means suffice for, the one for a sin-offering, and the other for a burnt-offering, with the meal-offering; and the priest shall make atonement for him that is to be cleansed before the LORD. 32. This is the law of him in whom is the plague of leprosy, whose means suffice not for that which pertaineth to his cleansing.*¹ᵛ(**ᵛⁱ). ¶ 33. And the LORD spoke unto Moses and unto Aaron, saying: ¶ 34. When ye are come into the land of Canaan, which I give to you for a possession, and I put the plague of leprosy in a house of the land of your possession; 35. then he that owneth the house shall come and tell the priest, saying: 'There seemeth to me to be as it were a plague in the house.' 36. And the priest shall command that they empty the house, before the priest go in to see the plague, that all that is in the house be not made unclean; and afterward the priest shall go in to see the house. 37. And he shall look on the plague, and, behold, if the plague be in the walls of the house with hollow streaks, greenish or reddish, and the appearance thereof be lower than the wall; 38. then the priest shall go out of the house to the door of the house, and shut up the house seven days. 39. And the priest shall come again the seventh day, and shall look; and, behold, if the plague be spread in the walls of the house; 40. then the priest shall command that they take out the stones in which the plague is, and cast them into an unclean place without the city. 41. And he shall cause the house to be scraped within round about, and they shall pour out the mortar that they scrape off without the city into an unclean place. 42. And

animal sacrifices are replaced by turtle-doves or young pigeons, as in XII, 8.

### 33–53. LEPROSY IN A HOUSE

Caused by some fungus akin to that which produces dry rot. Others suppose that parasitic insects had nested in the house, or a nitrous incrustation had formed in the walls.

**33.** *saying.* We must understand some such words as, 'Speak unto the children of Israel.'

**34.** *when ye are come.* The Torah here legislates for the time when the Israelites shall have settled in their land and inhabit houses.

*I put.* This form of speech is used, because all phenomena are ultimately the consequence of the Divine will.

**36.** *empty the house.* Until the priest formally pronounced the house infected, its contents were not unclean. Similarly, a man was not leprous until the priest passed the verdict upon him. All the furniture was removed before the inspection, to save it from being defiled, should the house be condemned.

**37.** *streaks. i.e.* the plague had eaten into the material of the wall.

**40.** *take out the stones.* This is analogous to cutting out the infected part of a garment (XIII, 56).

*unclean place. i.e.* a place known to be unclean and used for such a purpose.

## LEVITICUS XIV, 43

they shall take other stones, and put them in the place of those stones; and he shall take other mortar, and shall plaster the house. 43. And if the plague come again, and break out in the house, after that the stones have been taken out, and after the house hath been scraped, and after it is plastered; 44. then the priest shall come in and look; and, behold, if the plague be spread in the house, it is a malignant leprosy in the house: it is unclean. 45. And he shall break down the house, the stones of it, and the timber thereof, and all the mortar of the house; and he shall carry them forth out of the city into an unclean place. 46. Moreover he that goeth into the house all the while that it is shut up shall be unclean until the even. 47. And he that lieth in the house shall wash his clothes; and he that eateth in the house shall wash his clothes. 48. And if the priest shall come in, and look, and, behold, the plague hath not spread in the house, after the house was plastered; then the priest shall pronounce the house clean, because the plague is healed. 49. And he shall take to cleanse the house two birds, and cedar-wood, and scarlet, and hyssop. 50. And he shall kill one of the birds in an earthen vessel over running water. 51. And he shall take the cedar-wood, and the hyssop, and the scarlet, and the living bird, and dip them in the blood of the slain bird, and in the running water, and sprinkle the house seven times. 52. And he shall cleanse the house with the blood of the bird, and with the running water, and with the living bird, and with the cedar-wood, and with the hyssop, and with the scarlet. 53. But he shall let go the living bird out of the city into the open field; so shall he make atonement for the house; and it shall be clean.\* ¶ 54. This is the law for all manner of plague of leprosy, and for a scall; 55. and for the leprosy of a garment, and for a house; 56. and for a rising, and for a scab, and for a bright spot; 57. to teach when it is unclean, and when it is clean; this is the law of leprosy.

**43–45.** The reappearance of the plague in the house was analogous to the recurrence of the malady in a leper (XIII, 7 f) and demanded measures of the utmost stringency.

**47.** *lieth in the house.* This presupposes a longer stay in the house, and therefore the garments are likewise defiled.

**48.** *shall come in.* After the house had been in quarantine for a week, or at the end of the second week.

**53.** *make atonement for the house.* Only purification is implied; cf. Exod. XXIX, 36, where the priests are told to make atonement for the Altar.

**54.** *this is the law.* These four concluding verses summarize the contents of the section, chaps. XIII–XIV.

**57.** *to teach.* The word is to be connected with, 'This is the law' (v. 54) and properly signifies 'to give a decision'. The meaning is: 'This is instruction concerning all manner . . . to decide when it is unclean.'

# 15

## LEVITICUS XV, 1

### CHAPTER XV

1. And the LORD spoke unto Moses and to Aaron, saying: 2. Speak unto the children of Israel, and say unto them: ¶ When any man hath an issue out of his flesh, his issue is unclean. 3. And this shall be his uncleanness in his issue: whether his flesh run with his issue, or his flesh be stopped from his issue, it is his uncleanness. 4. Every bed whereon he that hath the issue lieth shall be unclean; and every thing whereon he sitteth shall be unclean. 5. And whosoever toucheth his bed shall wash his clothes, and bathe himself in water, and be unclean until the even. 6. And he that sitteth on any thing whereon he that hath the issue sat shall wash his clothes, and bathe himself in water, and be unclean until the even. 7. And he that toucheth the flesh of him that hath the issue shall wash his clothes, and bathe himself in water, and be unclean until the even. 8. And if he that hath the issue spit upon him that is clean, then he shall wash his clothes, and bathe himself in water, and be unclean until the even. 9. And what saddle soever he that hath the issue rideth upon shall be unclean. 10. And whosoever toucheth any thing that was under him shall be unclean until the even; and he that beareth those things shall wash his clothes, and bathe himself in water, and be unclean until the even. 11. And whomsoever he that hath the issue toucheth, without having rinsed his hands in water, he shall wash his clothes, and bathe himself in water, and be unclean until the even. 12. And the earthen vessel, which he that hath the issue toucheth, shall be broken; and every vessel of wood shall be rinsed in water. 13. And when he that hath an issue is cleansed of his issue, then he shall number to himself seven days for his cleansing, and wash his clothes; and he shall bathe his flesh in running water, and shall be clean. 14. And on the eighth

## CHAPTER XV, 1–30. IMPURITY OF ISSUES

This chapter treats of physical secretions which render a person unclean, precluding him from coming into contact with anything appertaining to the Sanctuary. The gentile was excluded from these regulations, since he was exempt from all obligations in respect to the Holy Place. In *v.* 2 the reference is to a chronic discharge. The person thus is regarded as a source of ritual, no less than physical, infection. The uncleanness described in *v.* 16–18 did not apply to laymen. It involved merely absence from the 'camp', which in Rabbinic exegesis was taken to mean the Sanctuary proper and the Levite encampment around the Sanctuary. It also involved abstention from sacrificial food (*terumah* and *maaser*). If the prescribed priestly ablutions had been taken, the prohibition ceased in regard to the Levite encampment and *maaser*.

A provision, ascribed to Ezra, to make *v.* 16–18 apply also outside the Sanctuary in the case of laymen reading in the Law, was in time disregarded; see Maimonides, *Yad* II, 1, 4.

*v.* 19–30 deal with menstruation; on which see XVIII, 19.

475

# LEVITICUS XV, 15

day he shall take to him two turtle-doves, or two young pigeons, and come before the LORD unto the door of the tent of meeting, and give them unto the priest. 15. And the priest shall offer them, the one for a sin-offering, and the other for a burnt-offering; and the priest shall make atonement for him before the LORD for his issue.*vi (**vii). ¶16. And if the flow of seed go out from a man, then he shall bathe all his flesh in water, and be unclean until the even. 17. And every garment, and every skin, whereon is the flow of seed, shall be washed with water, and be unclean until the even. 18. The woman also with whom a man shall lie carnally, they shall both bathe themselves in water, and be unclean until the even. ¶ 19. And if a woman have an issue, and her issue in her flesh be blood, she shall be in her impurity seven days; and whosoever toucheth her shall be unclean until the even. 20. And every thing that she lieth upon in her impurity shall be unclean; every thing also that she sitteth upon shall be unclean. 21. And whosoever toucheth her bed shall wash his clothes, and bathe himself in water, and be unclean until the even. 22. And whosoever toucheth any thing that she sitteth upon shall wash his clothes, and bathe himself in water, and be unclean until the even. 23. And if he be on the bed, or on any thing whereon she sitteth, when he toucheth it, he shall be unclean until the even. 24. And if any man lie with her, and her impurity be upon him, he shall be unclean seven days; and every bed whereon he lieth shall be unclean. ¶ 25. And if a woman have an issue of her blood many days not in the time of her impurity, or if she have an issue beyond the time of her impurity; all the days of the issue of her uncleanness she shall be as in the days of her impurity: she is unclean. 26. Every bed whereon she lieth all the days of her issue shall be unto her as the bed of her impurity; and every thing whereon she sitteth shall be unclean, as the uncleanness of her impurity. 27. And whosoever toucheth those things shall be unclean, and shall wash his clothes, and bathe himself in water, and be unclean until the even. 28. But if she be cleansed of her issue, then she shall number to herself seven days, and after that she shall be clean.* vii. 29. And on the eighth day she shall take unto her two turtle-doves, or two young pigeons, and bring them unto the priest, to the door of the tent of meeting. 30. And the priest shall offer the one for a sin-offering, and

**31-33. CONCLUDING ADMONITION**
**31.** *ye separate.* Or, 'ye warn.' The subject is Moses and Aaron, to whom these regulations had been addressed.

## LEVITICUS XV, 31

the other for a burnt-offering; and the priest shall make atonement for her before the LORD for the issue of her uncleanness.* ᵐ· ¶ 31. Thus shall ye separate the children of Israel from their uncleanness; that they die not in their uncleanness, when they defile My tabernacle that is in the midst of them. ¶ 32. This is the law of him that hath an issue, and of him from whom the flow of seed goeth out, so that he is unclean thereby; 33. and of her that is sick with her impurity, and of them that have an issue, whether it be a man, or a woman; and of him that lieth with her that is unclean.

*defile My tabernacle.* These words are the basis for the deduction of the Rabbis that these laws applied only to one about to enter the Sanctuary, or to come in contact with, or partake of, sacred things.

## HAFTORAH METZORA

### II KINGS VII, 3–20

#### CHAPTER VII

3. Now there were four leprous men at the entrance of the gate; and they said one to another: 'Why sit we here until we die? 4. If we say: We will enter into the city, then the famine is in the city, and we shall die there; and if we sit still here, we die also. Now therefore come, and let us fall unto the host of the Arameans; if they save us alive, we shall live; and if they kill us, we shall but die.' 5. And they rose up in the twilight, to go unto the camp of the

The theme of this Haftorah is again an incident in the life of Elisha during the siege of Samaria by the Syrians. It tells of four lepers who were facing death in that time of horror. All available food had been consumed, and even the refuse of the streets was sold at famine prices. The inhabitants were in the last stages of despair, and the king learns of women who had arranged to use their children for food! He blames the Prophet Elisha for all these calamities, as the Prophet no doubt encouraged the people to continue the resistance, and the king is determined to put him to death. However, when faced by the Prophet, he is overawed. Elisha then makes the astonishing announcement that the very next day God would send relief, and the famine would be at an end. A courtier standing by breaks out in mockery at the prediction. Signal punishment is announced to overtake him for this act of unbelief.

#### CHAPTER VII

3. *at the entrance of the gate.* Lepers were not permitted to live in the city. In the circumstances, they would naturally keep as near the entrance as possible.

4. *fall unto.* Desert to.
*if they save us alive.* If the Syrians killed them they would be no worse off; but the Syrians might spare their lives.

6. *the noise of a great host.* Thinking that mighty hosts were advancing against them. 'It was the result of one of those sudden unaccountable panics to which huge, unwieldy, heterogeneous Eastern armies, which have no organized system of sentries and no trained discipline, are constantly liable' (Farrar). The cradle of the Hittite power was in N. Syria, and Egypt was in the South. Accordingly the Syrians thought they were entrapped, and fled in confusion.

II KINGS VII, 6

Arameans; and when they were come to the outermost part of the camp of the Arameans, behold, there was no man there. 6. For the LORD had made the host of the Arameans to hear a noise of chariots, and a noise of horses, even the noise of a great host; and they said one to another: 'Lo, the king of Israel hath hired against us the kings of the Hittites, and the kings of the Egyptians, to come upon us.' 7. Wherefore they arose and fled in the twilight, and left their tents, and their horses, and their asses, even the camp as it was, and fled for their life. 8. And when these lepers came to the outermost part of the camp, they went into one tent, and did eat and drink, and carried thence silver, and gold, and raiment, and went and hid it; and they came back, and entered into another tent, and carried thence also, and went and hid it. ¶ 9. Then they said one to another: 'We do not well; this day is a day of good tidings, and we hold our peace; if we tarry till the morning light, punishment will overtake us; now therefore come, let us go and tell the king's household.' 10. So they came and called unto the porters of the city; and they told them, saying: 'We came to the camp of the Arameans, and, behold, there was no man there, neither voice of man, but the horses tied, and the asses tied, and the tents as they were.' 11. And the porters called, and they told it to the king's household within. 12. And the king arose in the night, and said unto his servants: 'I will now tell you what the Arameans have done to us. They know that we are hungry; therefore are they gone out of the camp to hide themselves in the field, saying: When they come out of the city, we shall take them alive, and get into the city.' 13. And one of his servants answered and said: 'Let some take, I pray thee, five of the horses that remain, which are left in the city—behold, they are as all the multitude of Israel that are left in it; behold, they are as all the multitude of Israel that are consumed—and let us send and see.' 14. They took therefore two chariots with horses; and the king sent after the host of the Arameans, saying: 'Go and see.' 15. And they went after

**9.** *punishment will overtake us.* lit. 'guilt will find us,' for having delayed to bring the good news to their starving brethren in the city. The Heb. word *iniquity* (עָוֹן) connotes also *punishment* for iniquity.

**10.** *the porters.* The keepers of the city gate.

**11.** *the porters called.* The guardians of the city gate called the guardians of the king's gate who told the news within the royal household (Ralbag).

**12.** *we shall take them alive.* The king suspects a stratagem on the part of the Syrians to lure him and his army out of the city and capture them.

**13.** *behold . . . left in it; behold . . . consumed.* Whether they share the fate of those who are still alive in the city or those who have already perished, they are all destined to the same end—death by starvation. The few horses may, therefore, well be risked in the enterprise.

## II KINGS VII, 16

them unto the Jordan; and, lo, all the way was full of garments and vessels, which the Arameans had cast away in their haste. And the messengers returned, and told the king. ¶ 16. And the people went out, and spoiled the camp of the Arameans. So a measure of fine flour was sold for a shekel, and two measures of barley for a shekel, according to the word of the LORD. 17. And the king appointed the captain on whose hand he leaned to have the charge of the gate; and the people trod upon him in the gate, and he died as the man of God had said, who spoke when the king came down to him. 18. And it came to pass, as the man of God had spoken to the king, saying: 'Two measures of barley for a shekel, and a measure of fine flour for a shekel, shall be to-morrow about this time in the gate of Samaria'; 19. and that captain answered the man of God, and said: 'Now, behold, if the LORD should make windows in heaven, might such a thing be?' and he said: 'Behold, thou shalt see it with thine eyes, but shalt not eat thereof'; 20. it came to pass even so unto him; for the people trod upon him in the gate, and he died.

**16.** *according to the word of the LORD.* See v. 1 and 2 of this chapter.

**17–20.** The fulfilment of Elisha's prophecy against the king's officer and his punishment for the scoffing spirit in which he received the Prophet's hopeful words. Scoffing at matters sacred was always regarded by the Jewish Teachers as a heinous offence. 'Four classes shall not see God—the scoffer, the liar, the slanderer and the hypocrite' (Talmud).

**17.** *on whose hand he leaned.* The king's confidential counsellor.

**19.** *behold, if the LORD . . . thing be?* Better, *Behold, the LORD is about to make windows in heaven! Can this thing be?* The first utterance is a mocking assertion; the second, an unbelieving question.

**20.** *for the people trod upon him.* He was knocked down and trampled to death in the rush of the people, who were maddened by famine, and hastening to the Syrian camp for food.

## LEVITICUS XVI, 1

### CHAPTER XVI

1. And the LORD spoke unto Moses, after the death of the two sons of Aaron, when they drew near before the LORD, and died; 2. and the LORD said unto Moses: 'Speak unto Aaron thy brother, that he come not at all times into the holy place within the veil, before the ark-cover which is upon the ark; that he die not; for I appear in the cloud upon the ark-cover. 3. Herewith shall Aaron come into the holy place: with a young bullock for a sin-offering, and a ram for a burnt-offering. 4. He shall put on the holy linen tunic, and he shall have the linen breeches upon his flesh, and shall be girdled with the linen girdle, and with

ויקרא אחרי מות טז

CAP. XVI. טז

א וַיְדַבֵּר יְהֹוָה אֶל־מֹשֶׁה אַחֲרֵי מוֹת שְׁנֵי בְּנֵי אַהֲרֹן בְּקָרְבָתָם
לִפְנֵי־יְהֹוָה וַיָּמֻתוּ: וַיֹּאמֶר יְהֹוָה אֶל־מֹשֶׁה דַּבֵּר אֶל־אַהֲרֹן
אָחִיךָ וְאַל־יָבֹא בְכָל־עֵת אֶל־הַקֹּדֶשׁ מִבֵּית לַפָּרֹכֶת אֶל־
פְּנֵי הַכַּפֹּרֶת אֲשֶׁר עַל־הָאָרֹן וְלֹא יָמוּת כִּי בֶּעָנָן אֵרָאֶה
עַל־הַכַּפֹּרֶת: בְּזֹאת יָבֹא אַהֲרֹן אֶל־הַקֹּדֶשׁ בְּפַר בֶּן־
בָּקָר לְחַטָּאת וְאַיִל לְעֹלָה: כְּתֹנֶת־בַּד קֹדֶשׁ יִלְבָּשׁ וּמִכְנְסֵי־

v. 4. קמץ ברביע

## VI. ACHAREY MOS

(CHAPTERS XVI–XVIII)

### THE DAY OF ATONEMENT

CHAPTER XVI, 1–28. THE RITUAL OF THE ANNUAL CEREMONY OF PURIFICATION IN THE SANCTUARY

**1.** *after the death.* The unfortunate incident narrated in x, 1–3 gave occasion for instructions as to the time and manner in which the High Priest might enter the Holy Place. The death of Aaron's sons was a solemn warning addressed to the High Priest, that any desecration, whether it be on the part of the High Priest, or an ordinary priest, or the laity (see xv, 31), would be severely punished. See comment on x, 1 as to the reasons for the death of Aaron's sons—intoxication, unholy ambition, arbitrary tampering with the service, and introducing 'strange fire' into the Sanctuary. The story of Nadab and Abihu is a parable for Young Israel in every generation. 'He who is affected to tears while reading this portion of the Torah, taking its teaching to heart, will win forgiveness for his own sins and the blessing of old age for his children' (Zohar).

**2.** *that he come not at all times.* Only once a year, on the Day of Atonement, and with a due observance of prescribed rites.

*the veil.* Heb. *parocheth*, which separates the Holy Place from the Holy of Holies.

*ark-cover.* The solid gold plate which formed the cover for the Ark, on which the cherubim were fixed; see on Exod. xxv, 17.

*the cloud.* In which God manifests His presence; Exod. XL, 35; Isa. VI, 4.

3–10. HOW AARON IS TO COME INTO THE HOLY PLACE, HIS ATTIRE, AND THE OFFERING HE IS TO BRING

**3.** *herewith.* With the offerings and ceremonies set forth in the following verses. In later times the High Priest began to prepare himself for his functions seven days before the Sacred Day. During that time, he lived apart in a special portion of the Temple, and the elders read and expounded to him the ordinances of this chapter. The night prior to the Sacred Day he would pass sleepless, and be kept awake by readings from Job, Ezra, Chronicles and Daniel.

*holy place.* Not that he is to take the animals into the Holy Place, but their sacrifice is part of the prerequisite ceremony for entering there.

*bullock . . . ram.* These offerings are personal to the High Priest, and must be his own property. The atonement for his own sins was his first act on the Great Day. Only when purged of his own sin, was he fitted to secure forgiveness for the sins of others.

**4.** *holy garments.* In the Holy of Holies, he was not to be attired in his golden vestments, which on all other occasions he was to wear for 'splendour and distinction', but in simple garments of white linen—emblems of the lowliness and purity of thought demanded by the Sacred Day. For the same reason, white linen garments were for many centuries worn, and in some communities are still worn, by worshippers on the Day of Atonement. The Rabbis gave an additional reason for this custom. 'When men are summoned before an earthly ruler to defend themselves against some charge, they appear downcast and dressed in black like mourners. Israel appears before God arrayed in white, as if going to a feast, confident that all who return penitently to their Maker will receive not condemnation but pardon at His hands.'

# LEVITICUS XVI, 5

the linen mitre shall he be attired; they are the holy garments; and he shall bathe his flesh in water, and put them on. 5. And he shall take of the congregation of the children of Israel two he-goats for a sin-offering, and one ram for a burnt-offering. 6. And Aaron shall present the bullock of the sin-offering, which is for himself, and make atonement for himself, and for his house. 7. And he shall take the two goats, and set them before the LORD at the door of the tent of meeting. 8. And Aaron shall cast lots upon the two goats: one lot for the LORD, and the other lot for Azazel. 9. And Aaron shall present the goat upon which the lot fell for the LORD, and offer him for a sin-offering. 10. But the goat, on which the lot fell for Azazel, shall be set alive before the LORD, to make atonement over him, to send him

---

**5.** *of the congregation.* Rites of purification were to be performed for the community as a body, and each individual was to regard himself as essentially a unit in the Brotherhood of Israel. The Confession on the Atonement Day is in the plural: '*We* have transgressed, *we* have dealt treacherously, etc.'; see on XXIII, 27.

**6.** *shall present.* The presentation is that alluded to in I, 3 f—at the entrance of the Tent of Meeting.

*his house.* The order of priests, who were sons of Aaron. The Rabbis, however, understood 'his house' to mean his wife; and the High Priest was not allowed to officiate on the Day of Atonement unless his wife was living at the time. In the traditional account of the rites of the Day of Atonement, preserved in the Mishnah, the High Priest made this confession: 'O God, I have sinned, I have committed iniquity, I have transgressed against Thee, I and my household. I beseech Thee by Thy Name, grant Thou atonement for the sins, and for the iniquities, and for the transgressions wherein I have sinned, and committed iniquity and transgressed against Thee, I and my household.' In his confession, the High Priest used the ineffable Name of God, the Tetragrammaton, in its true pronunciation; whereupon the assembled priests and people in the Court prostrated themselves to the ground, and exclaimed, 'Blessed be His Name, Whose glorious kingdom is for ever and ever.'

**8.** *lots.* By taking from an urn tablets, alike in size and shape, describing the destination of each animal (Mishnah).

*Azazel.* Better, *dismissal.* In the Septuagint this mysterious Hebrew word is rendered, 'the one to be sent away'; which agrees with the term used in the Mishnah. The Authorised Version, following the Vulgate, has 'scapegoat'; *i.e.* the goat driven, or escaping, into the wilderness. The Heb. *Azazel,* however, is not a proper name, but a rare Hebrew noun (עזלזל contracted to עזאל) meaning, 'dismissal' or, 'entire removal' (RV Margin, Gesenius, Hoffmann, and the Oxford Hebrew Dictionary). It is the ancient technical term for the entire removal of the sin and guilt of the community, that was symbolized by the sending away of the goat into the wilderness.

In the Talmud, *Azazel* was translated by 'steep mountain', and was applied to the rock in the wilderness from which in later times the animal was hurled.

At an early period, however, the word עזאזל became personified, just as were the Hebrew words for the Underworld (*Sheol*) and Destruction (*Abaddon*). Thereupon, the strangest theories and legends grew up in connection with '*Azazel*'. In certain Jewish traditions, for example, *Azazel,* or *Azalzel,* is foremost among the Fallen Angels who taught unrighteousness to the children of men (Book of Enoch). This view that the word *Azazel* is the name of a demon in the wilderness was shared by Ibn Ezra and Nachmanides, and is to-day adopted by most Bible critics. But it is quite untenable. The offering of sacrifices to 'satyrs' is spoken of as a heinous crime in the very next chapter, XVII, 7; homage to a demon of the wilderness cannot, therefore, be associated with the holiest of the Temple-rites in the chapter immediately preceding.

**9.** *offer him.* lit. 'make it,' *i.e.* appoint it. The offering of this goat is not mentioned until *v.* 15. The High Priest exclaimed over it, 'for the LORD, a sin offering' (Sifra).

**10.** *over him.* Refers to the confession of sins over the head of the animal.

## LEVITICUS XVI, 11

away for Azazel into the wilderness. 11. And Aaron shall present the bullock of the sin-offering, which is for himself, and shall make atonement for himself, and for his house, and shall kill the bullock of the sin-offering which is for himself. 12. And he shall take a censer full of coals of fire from off the altar before the Lord, and his hands full of sweet incense beaten small, and bring it within the veil. 13. And he shall put the incense upon the fire before the Lord, that the cloud of the incense may cover the ark-cover that is upon the testimony, that he die not. 14. And he shall take of the blood of the bullock, and sprinkle it with his finger upon the ark-cover on the east; and before the ark-cover shall he sprinkle of the blood with his finger seven times. 15. Then shall he kill the goat of the sin-offering, that is for the people, and bring his blood within the veil, and do with his blood as he did with the blood of the bullock, and sprinkle it upon the ark-cover, and before the ark-cover. 16. And he shall make atonement for the holy place, because of the uncleannesses of the children of Israel, and because of their transgressions, even all their sins; and so shall he do for the tent of meeting, that dwelleth with them in the midst of their uncleannesses. 17. And there shall be no man in the tent of meeting when he goeth in to make atonement in the holy place, until he come out, and have made

11 הַמִּדְבָּֽרָה׃ וְהִקְרִיב אַהֲרֹן אֶת־פַּר הַחַטָּאת אֲשֶׁר־לוֹ
וְכִפֶּר בַּעֲדוֹ וּבְעַד בֵּיתוֹ וְשָׁחַט אֶת־פַּר הַחַטָּאת אֲשֶׁר־לוֹ׃
12 וְלָקַח מְלֹא־הַמַּחְתָּה גַּֽחֲלֵי־אֵשׁ מֵעַל הַמִּזְבֵּחַ מִלִּפְנֵי יְהֹוָה
וּמְלֹא חָפְנָיו קְטֹרֶת סַמִּים דַּקָּה וְהֵבִיא מִבֵּית לַפָּרֹֽכֶת׃
13 וְנָתַן אֶת־הַקְּטֹרֶת עַל־הָאֵשׁ לִפְנֵי יְהֹוָה וְכִסָּה ׀ עֲנַן הַקְּטֹרֶת
14 אֶת־הַכַּפֹּרֶת אֲשֶׁר עַל־הָעֵדוּת וְלֹא יָמוּת׃ וְלָקַח מִדַּם
הַפָּר וְהִזָּה בְאֶצְבָּעוֹ עַל־פְּנֵי הַכַּפֹּרֶת קֵדְמָה וְלִפְנֵי הַכַּפֹּרֶת
טו יַזֶּה שֶֽׁבַע־פְּעָמִים מִן־הַדָּם בְּאֶצְבָּעֽוֹ׃ וְשָׁחַט אֶת־שְׂעִיר
הַחַטָּאת אֲשֶׁר לָעָם וְהֵבִיא אֶת־דָּמוֹ אֶל־מִבֵּית לַפָּרֹכֶת
וְעָשָׂה אֶת־דָּמוֹ כַּאֲשֶׁר עָשָׂה לְדַם הַפָּר וְהִזָּה אֹתוֹ עַל־
16 הַכַּפֹּרֶת וְלִפְנֵי הַכַּפֹּֽרֶת׃ וְכִפֶּר עַל־הַקֹּדֶשׁ מִטֻּמְאֹת בְּנֵי
יִשְׂרָאֵל וּמִפִּשְׁעֵיהֶם לְכָל־חַטֹּאתָם וְכֵן יַעֲשֶׂה לְאֹהֶל מוֹעֵד
17 הַשֹּׁכֵן אִתָּם בְּתוֹךְ טֻמְאֹתָֽם׃ וְכָל־אָדָם לֹא־יִהְיֶה ׀ בְּאֹהֶל
מוֹעֵד בְּבֹאוֹ לְכַפֵּר בַּקֹּדֶשׁ עַד־צֵאתוֹ וְכִפֶּר בַּעֲדוֹ וּבְעַד

---

**11–28. Detailed Account of the Ceremonial of Purification**

**11.** *present.* lit. 'bring it near,' to the Altar to be slain.

*and for his house.* According to the Rabbis, 'house' here refers to the order of priests; and the High Priest repeated his confession (as in *v.* 6), adding after 'my household' the words, 'and the sons of Aaron, Thy holy people.'

**12.** *a censer.* Heb. 'the censer'; a censer made of gold was, according to the Mishnah, used on this day.

*the altar.* The brazen Altar in the Fore-court.

*befor the Lord.* See on I, 5.

*within the veil.* This is the first entrance of the High Priest into the innermost part of the Holy of Holies.

**13.** *cloud of the incense.* The purpose of the incense-smoke was to create a screen which would prevent the High Priest from gazing upon the Holy Presence.

On returning from the Holy of Holies, the High Priest in later times offered the following prayer: 'May it please Thee, O Lord our God, that this year may be a year of rain. Let there not be wanting a ruler belonging to the House of Judah. Let not Thy people Israel be in want, so that one Israelite may not be forced to beg his sustenance from another or from strangers; and hearken not to the prayer of travellers'—since they pray for rainless weather, which is a calamity in the Holy Land (Talmud).

**14.** *sprinkle . . . upon the ark-cover.* This act constituted the rite of expiation for the High Priest and the priestly order.

**15.** *then shall he kill.* The goat which had been designated by lot 'for the Lord' (*v.* 9).

**16.** *uncleannesses.* Besides the annual rite of atonement for the Community, there was also once a year a ceremonial cleansing of the Sanctuary from defilement through the presence of Israelites who were ritually unclean.

*transgressions.* This is defined by the Rabbis as alluding to the wilful entering of the holy precincts by a person who knew himself to be defiled. By 'sins' is meant those who entered without the knowledge that they were unclean.

**17.** *no man.* Not even the priests were to remain in the Tent while the ceremony of atonement was being performed. The awe of the occasion would be increased by the High Priest being quite alone in the Sanctuary.

## LEVITICUS XVI, 18

atonement for himself, and for his household, and for all the assembly of Israel. 18. And he shall go out unto the altar that is before the LORD, and make atonement for it; and shall take of the blood of the bullock, and of the blood of the goat, and put it upon the horns of the altar round about. 19. And he shall sprinkle of the blood upon it with his finger seven times, and cleanse it, and hallow it from the uncleannesses of the children of Israel. 20. And when he hath made an end of atoning for the holy place, and the tent of meeting, and the altar, he shall present the live goat. 21. And Aaron shall lay both his hands upon the head of the live goat, and confess over him all the iniquities of the children of Israel, and all their transgressions, even all their sins; and he shall put them upon the head of the goat, and shall send him away by the hand of an appointed man into the wilderness. 22. And the goat shall bear upon him all their iniquities unto a land which is cut off; and he shall let go the goat in the wilderness. 23. And Aaron shall come into the tent of meeting, and shall put off the linen garments, which he put on when he went into the holy place, and shall leave them there. 24. And he shall bathe his flesh in water in a holy place, and put on

ויקרא אחרי מות טז

שני 18 בֵּיתוֹ וּבְעַד כָּל־קְהַל יִשְׂרָאֵל: וְיָצָא אֶל־הַמִּזְבֵּחַ אֲשֶׁר
לִפְנֵי־יְהוָה וְכִפֶּר עָלָיו וְלָקַח מִדַּם הַפָּר וּמִדַּם הַשָּׂעִיר
19 וְנָתַן עַל־קַרְנוֹת הַמִּזְבֵּחַ סָבִיב: וְהִזָּה עָלָיו מִן־הַדָּם
בְּאֶצְבָּעוֹ שֶׁבַע פְּעָמִים וְטִהֲרוֹ וְקִדְּשׁוֹ מִטֻּמְאֹת בְּנֵי יִשְׂרָאֵל:
כ וְכִלָּה מִכַּפֵּר אֶת־הַקֹּדֶשׁ וְאֶת־אֹהֶל מוֹעֵד וְאֶת־הַמִּזְבֵּחַ
21 וְהִקְרִיב אֶת־הַשָּׂעִיר הֶחָי: וְסָמַךְ אַהֲרֹן אֶת־שְׁתֵּי יָדוֹ עַל־
רֹאשׁ הַשָּׂעִיר הַחַי וְהִתְוַדָּה עָלָיו אֶת־כָּל־עֲוֹנֹת בְּנֵי יִשְׂרָאֵל
וְאֶת־כָּל־פִּשְׁעֵיהֶם לְכָל־חַטֹּאתָם וְנָתַן אֹתָם עַל־רֹאשׁ
22 הַשָּׂעִיר וְשִׁלַּח בְּיַד־אִישׁ עִתִּי הַמִּדְבָּרָה: וְנָשָׂא הַשָּׂעִיר
עָלָיו אֶת־כָּל־עֲוֹנֹתָם אֶל־אֶרֶץ גְּזֵרָה וְשִׁלַּח אֶת־הַשָּׂעִיר
23 בַּמִּדְבָּר: וּבָא אַהֲרֹן אֶל־אֹהֶל מוֹעֵד וּפָשַׁט אֶת־בִּגְדֵי
24 הַבָּד אֲשֶׁר לָבַשׁ בְּבֹאוֹ אֶל־הַקֹּדֶשׁ וְהִנִּיחָם שָׁם: וְרָחַץ
אֶת־בְּשָׂרוֹ בַמַּיִם בְּמָקוֹם קָדוֹשׁ וְלָבַשׁ אֶת־בְּגָדָיו וְיָצָא

v. 21. ידיו קרי

---

**18.** *shall go out.* i.e. he shall go in the direction of the exit, towards the golden Altar of Incense.

**19.** *cleanse it.* From the defilement of the past year.
*hallow it.* Reconsecrate it for sacred use in the coming year.

**20.** *and the altar.* The golden Altar.
*he shall present.* Better, *he brings near to himself.* The ceremony of the 'scapegoat' took place in the Court.

**21.** *confess.* The High Priest placed his two hands on the goat to be sent away, and thereby, having confessed, symbolically transferred the people's sins to the head of the animal. The form of confession, as given in the Mishnah, was: 'O God, Thy people, the House of Israel, have sinned, they have committed iniquity, and they have transgressed against Thee.'
*iniquities.* The Heb. עון lit. means 'crookedness' and denotes a wilful departure from the law of God. Unlike the ordinary sacrifices, which were limited in their expiatory power to *involuntary* transgressions, the Day of Atonement and its sacrifices purged away wilful iniquities as well as errors and involuntary sins.
*transgressions.* The Heb. פשע is stronger than 'transgression'; its lit. translation is 'rebellion'.

*sins.* The Heb. חטא denotes an unintentional deviation from the right path.
*appointed.* Or, 'in readiness' for that purpose.

**22.** *a land which is cut off.* A district effectually cut off from the encampment of Israel, so that the animal could not wander back. In later times the animal was cast down a precipice (see on *v.* 8), as it was no longer possible to send the goat to a place whence it would not return to inhabited parts. This chapter narrates the primitive custom in accordance with conditions in the Mosaic age, and is evidence of the antiquity of what is here described.
*he shall let go.* With this symbolic carrying away of the people's sins, cf. Micah VII, 19, 'Thou wilt cast all their sins into the depths of the sea.' These Prophetic words led to the institution of a similar rite—*Tashlich*—in connection with the New Year.

**23.** *Aaron shall come.* According to the Talmud, this verse refers to what happened after the sacrifice of the burnt-offerings described in *v.* 24 f.

**24.** *in a holy place.* A special chamber in the Court for the purpose.
*his burnt-offering.* The ram of the High Priest (*v.* 3) and the ram of the people (*v.* 5).

# LEVITICUS XVI, 25 ויקרא אחרי מות טז

his other vestments, and come forth, and offer his burnt-offering and the burnt-offering of the people, and make atonement for himself and for the people.\*¦¦¦(\*\*¦¦). 25. And the fat of the sin-offering shall he make smoke upon the altar. 26. And he that letteth go the goat for Azazel shall wash his clothes, and bathe his flesh in water, and afterward he may come into the camp. 27. And the bullock of the sin-offering, and the goat of the sin-offering, whose blood was brought in to make atonement in the holy place, shall be carried forth without the camp; and they shall burn in the fire their skins, and their flesh, and their dung. 28. And he that burneth them shall wash his clothes, and bathe his flesh in water, and afterward he may come into the camp. ¶ 29. And it shall be a statute for ever unto you: in the seventh month, on the tenth day of the month, ye shall afflict your souls, and shall do no manner of work, the home-born, or the stranger that sojourneth among you. 30. For on this day shall atonement be made for you, to cleanse you; from all your sins shall ye

שְׁלִישִׁי (שֵׁנִי
בְּשֶׁהֵן מְחוּבָּר) וְעָשָׂה אֶת־עֹלָתוֹ וְאֶת־עֹלַת הָעָם וְכִפֶּר בַּעֲדוֹ וּבְעַד הָעָם׃
26 כה וְאֵת חֵלֶב הַחַטָּאת יַקְטִיר הַמִּזְבֵּחָה׃ וְהַמְשַׁלֵּחַ אֶת־
הַשָּׂעִיר לַעֲזָאזֵל יְכַבֵּס בְּגָדָיו וְרָחַץ אֶת־בְּשָׂרוֹ בַּמָּיִם
27 וְאַחֲרֵי־כֵן יָבוֹא אֶל־הַמַּחֲנֶה׃ וְאֵת פַּר הַחַטָּאת וְאֵת ׀
שְׂעִיר הַחַטָּאת אֲשֶׁר הוּבָא אֶת־דָּמָם לְכַפֵּר בַּקֹּדֶשׁ יוֹצִיא
אֶל־מִחוּץ לַמַּחֲנֶה וְשָׂרְפוּ בָאֵשׁ אֶת־עֹרֹתָם וְאֶת־בְּשָׂרָם
28 וְאֶת־פִּרְשָׁם׃ וְהַשֹּׂרֵף אֹתָם יְכַבֵּס בְּגָדָיו וְרָחַץ אֶת־בְּשָׂרוֹ
29 בַּמָּיִם וְאַחֲרֵי־כֵן יָבוֹא אֶל־הַמַּחֲנֶה׃ וְהָיְתָה לָכֶם לְחֻקַּת
עוֹלָם בַּחֹדֶשׁ הַשְּׁבִיעִי בֶּעָשׂוֹר לַחֹדֶשׁ תְּעַנּוּ אֶת־נַפְשֹׁתֵיכֶם
וְכָל־מְלָאכָה לֹא תַעֲשׂוּ הָאֶזְרָח וְהַגֵּר הַגָּר בְּתוֹכְכֶם׃
ל כִּי־בַיּוֹם הַזֶּה יְכַפֵּר עֲלֵיכֶם לְטַהֵר אֶתְכֶם מִכֹּל חַטֹּאתֵיכֶם
31 לִפְנֵי יְהֹוָה תִּטְהָרוּ׃ שַׁבַּת שַׁבָּתוֹן הִיא לָכֶם וְעִנִּיתֶם

---

**26.** *wash his clothes.* Since the 'scapegoat' bore upon itself the sins of the community, the man who had been in contact with it necessarily became defiled.

### 29–34. INSTITUTING THE DAY OF ATONEMENT

**29.** *it shall be.* Refers to what follows. Atonement is not automatically secured as a result of the ceremonies allotted to the High Priest. The people, too, had their part to perform in obtaining forgiveness.

*seventh month.* Cf. XXIII, 27 f.

*afflict your souls.* This Heb. phrase well indicated the spiritual aim of fasting. As the principal source of sin is the gratification of bodily appetites, the Fast is to demonstrate to the sinner that man can conquer all physical cravings, that the spirit can always master the body. The abstention from all food and from gratification of other bodily desires, however, must be accompanied by deep remorse at having fallen short of what it was in our power to be and to do as members of the House of Israel. Without such contrite confession, accompanied by the solemn resolve to abandon the way of evil, fasting in itself is not the fulfilment of the Divine command and purpose of the Day of Atonement. תשובה תפלה וצדקה—Repentance, Prayer and Beneficence—these can change the whole current of a man's life and destiny, and lead to perfect atonement. 'Let the wicked forsake his way, and the man of iniquity his thoughts; and let him return unto the LORD, and He will have compassion upon him, and to our God, for He will abundantly pardon' (Isaiah LV, 7).

*the stranger.* Ibn Ezra points out that it is only work that the stranger is forbidden to do. He is not compelled to 'afflict his soul'.

**30.** *on this day.* Called in the Talmud יומא, *the* Day; see also on Exod. XXXIV, 4. For the name *Yom ha-kippurim*, see on XXIII, 27.

*shall atonement be made for you.* Heb. יכפר עליכם. As the preceding and following verses describe the duties of the people on the Day, the subject of יכפר עליכם cannot be the High Priest; otherwise, he would have been specially mentioned. Rabbi Akiba held the subject to be God. 'Happy Israel—he exclaimed—before Whom do ye purify yourselves, and Who is it that purifieth you? Your Father Who is in Heaven; as it is said (Ezek. XXXVI, 25) "I will sprinkle clean water upon you, and ye shall be clean".' Note that the initiative in atonement is with the sinner. He cleanses himself on the Day of Atonement by fearless self-examination, open confession, and the resolve not to repeat the transgressions of the past year. When our Heavenly Father sees the abasement of the penitent sinner, He—and not the High Priest or any other Mediator—sprinkles, as it were, the clean waters of pardon and forgiveness upon him. 'The whole philosophy of monotheism is contained in this rallying-cry of Rabbi Akiba' (Hermann Cohen).

*all your sins.* Not only involuntary transgressions; see the Confession, Authorised Prayer

LEVITICUS XVI, 31

be clean before the LORD. 31. It is a sabbath of solemn rest unto you, and ye shall afflict your souls; it is a statute for ever. 32. And the priest, who shall be anointed and who shall be consecrated to be priest in his father's stead, shall make the atonement, and shall put on the linen garments, even the holy garments. 33. And he shall make atonement for the most holy place, and he shall make atonement for the tent of meeting and for the altar; and he shall make atonement for the priests and for all the people of the assembly. 34. And this shall be an everlasting statute unto you, to make atonement for the children of Israel because of all their sins once in the year.' And he did as the LORD commanded Moses.*iv.

## 17    CHAPTER XVII

1. And the LORD spoke unto Moses, saying: 2. Speak unto Aaron, and unto his sons,

---

Book, p. 258b and 259. Repentance can give rebellious sins the character of 'errors'; *i.e.* by his penitence, the sinner shows that his wilful sins were largely due to ignorance, and hence are treated by God as if they were 'errors'. גדולה תשובה שזדונות נעשות כשגגות. A modern philosopher of religion finds the keynote of the Day in Num. xv, 26 ('And all the congregation of the children of Israel shall be forgiven, and the stranger that sojourneth among them; for in respect of all the people it was done *in error*')—the verse recited before the opening of the evening service on Kol Nidré night.

*before the* LORD. From Whom alone, and not from the priest or the Altar, man is to seek atonement.

The order of the Heb. words is: 'from all your sins before the LORD shall ye be clean.' Thereon Rabbi Eleazar ben Azaryah founded the sublime teaching: 'For transgressions of man against God, the Day of Atonement atones (given repentance on the part of the sinner); but for transgressions against a fellow-man the Day of Atonement does not atone, unless and until he has conciliated his fellow-man and redressed the wrong he had done him.' The Confession (וידוי) deals almost exclusively with moral trespasses against our fellowmen. Especially numerous are the terms denoting sins committed with the tongue—falsehood, slander, frivolous and unclean speech. The Rabbis, who certainly did not underrate ritual offences, deemed moral shortcomings to be infinitely graver, and hence confined the Confession to them.

**31–34.** These verses explain that the ceremonies of the Day of Atonement are for all time. Although the Torah has been naming 'Aaron' as the atoning priest, whoever had been duly consecrated after him to the High Priest's office was eligible to perform the sacred functions prescribed in this chapter.

**31.** *sabbath of solemn rest.* The repetition is to impress the fact that cessation from labour and fasting must continue even when there are no longer priestly ceremonies (Wessely).

**34.** *everlasting statute.* The Day of Atonement survived the High Priesthood; nay, it gained in inwardness and spiritual power with the passing of the sacrificial system. 'The fasting and humiliation before God, the confession of sins and contrition for them, and fervent prayer for forgiveness, were even before the destruction of the Temple the reality in regard to the Day of Atonement, of which the rites in the Temple were but a dramatic symbol' (Moore). The Rabbis had stressed the Prophetic teaching that without repentance no sacrificial rites were of any avail. With the cessation of sacrifices, therefore, repentance was left as the sole condition of the remission of sins. 'In our time when there is no Temple and no Altar for atonement, there is repentance. Repentance atones for all iniquities' (Maimonides). The Day of Atonement, the Rabbis further declare, will never pass away, even if all other Festivals should pass away. And indeed as long as Israel does not lose its soul, so long shall the Day of Atonement remain. See also on XXIII, 27–32.

*he did.* The subject is Aaron.

### CHAPTER XVII. HOLINESS IN MEAT FOODS

This chapter may be looked upon as supplementary to the first part of Leviticus. It ordains that meat-foods must be free from idolatrous taint. This taint assumed two forms: sacrificing to 'satyrs' (*v.* 7), and eating the blood (10–14).

485

## LEVITICUS XVII, 3

and unto all the children of Israel, and say unto them: This is the thing which the LORD hath commanded, saying: ¶ 3. What man soever there be of the house of Israel, that killeth an ox, or lamb, or goat, in the camp, or that killeth it without the camp, 4. and hath not brought it unto the door of the tent of meeting, to present it as an offering unto the LORD before the tabernacle of the LORD, blood shall be imputed unto that man; he hath shed blood; and that man shall be cut off from among his people. 5. To the end that the children of Israel may bring their sacrifices, which they sacrifice in the open field, even that they may bring them unto the LORD, unto the door of the tent of meeting, unto the priest, and sacrifice them for sacrifices of peace-offerings unto the LORD. 6. And the priest shall dash the blood against the altar of the LORD at the door of the tent of meeting, and make the fat smoke for a sweet savour unto the LORD. 7. And they shall no more sacrifice their sacrifices unto the satyrs, after whom they go astray. This shall be a statute for ever unto them throughout their generations.*v(**iii). ¶ 8. And thou shalt say unto them: Whatsoever man there be of

### 3–7. ON SLAYING ANIMALS FOR FOOD

**3.** *killeth an ox.* Evidently refers to a time when the slaughtering of animals for food was rare, and only at a family festivity or other formal gathering was meat consumed. During the wandering in the Wilderness the people lived on manna; and only exceptionally would it happen that an animal was slaughtered for consumption. Every such slaughtering had to be a sacrificial act; it had to take place at the Sanctuary; and it was deemed a peace-offering. In Deut. XII, 20 f, the law is modified in anticipation of the fact that Israel would soon be spread over a large area; for the requirement that every animal killed for food should be brought to the Sanctuary could apply only when the entire Community lived in the closest proximity to it.

According to the Rabbis this section refers only to animals intended as sacrifices—that they must not be offered except at the door of the Tabernacle.

**4.** *an offering.* A peace-offering is meant; see next *v.*

*before the tabernacle.* On the Altar.

*blood shall be imputed.* 'Blood' is here used in the sense of 'the guilt of blood', as in Deut. XXI, 8. He is regarded as though he had shed blood, and thereby incurs a severe penalty.

*be cut off.* The offender was not to be punished by an earthly tribunal. The penalty was what the Rabbis term 'death by the hand of Heaven'.

**5.** *which they sacrifice.* i.e. which they had up to now sacrificed upon 'high places' in the open field.

*peace-offerings.* See on III, 1. In peace-offerings the offerer had a share of the sacrifice.

**7.** *satyrs.* lit. 'goats.' They were deemed to be sylvan gods or demons who inhabited waste places (Isa. XIII, 21; XXXIV, 14). The worship of the goat, accompanied by the foulest rites, prevailed in Lower Egypt. This was familiar to the Israelites, and God desired to wean them from it (cf. Josh. XXIV, 14; Ezek. XX, 7).

Some commentators point to this verse as giving a main purpose of the sacrificial system in the Torah; *viz.* gradually to wean Israel away from primitive ideas and idolatrous practices. The *manner* of worship in use among the peoples of antiquity was retained, but that worship was now directed towards the One and Holy God. 'By this Divine plan, idolatry was eradicated, and the vital principle of our Faith, the existence and unity of God, was firmly established—without confusing the minds of the people by the abolition of sacrificial worship, to which they were accustomed' (Maimonides).

*for ever.* That offerings to 'satyrs' are forbidden.

**8–9.** The actual offering of the sacrifice as well as its slaughtering must on no account be performed at any place except at that Sanctuary. This prohibition applies not only to Israelites, but also to those strangers (גרי צדק) who had been completely incorporated in Israel.

## LEVITICUS XVII, 9

the house of Israel, or of the strangers that sojourn among them, that offereth a burnt-offering or sacrifice, 9. and bringeth it not unto the door of the tent of meeting, to sacrifice it unto the LORD, even that man shall be cut off from his people. ¶ 10. And whatsoever man there be of the house of Israel, or of the strangers that sojourn among them, that eateth any manner of blood, I will set My face against that soul that eateth blood, and will cut him off from among his people. 11. For the life of the flesh is in the blood; and I have given it to you upon the altar to make atonement for your souls; for it is the blood that maketh atonement by reason of the life. 12. Therefore I said unto the children of Israel: No soul of you shall eat blood, neither shall any stranger that sojourneth among you eat blood. ¶ 13. And whatsoever man there be of the children of Israel, or of the strangers that sojourn

ויקרא אחרי מות יז

9 הַגֵּר אֲשֶׁר־יָגוּר בְּתוֹכֲכֶם אֲשֶׁר־יַעֲלֶה עֹלָה אוֹ־זָבַח: וְאֶל־פֶּתַח אֹהֶל מוֹעֵד לֹא יְבִיאֶנּוּ לַעֲשׂוֹת אֹתוֹ לַיהוָה וְנִכְרַת הָאִישׁ הַהוּא מֵעַמָּיו: וְאִישׁ אִישׁ מִבֵּית יִשְׂרָאֵל וּמִן־10 הַגֵּר הַגָּר בְּתוֹכָם אֲשֶׁר יֹאכַל כָּל־דָּם וְנָתַתִּי פָנַי בַּנֶּפֶשׁ 11 הָאֹכֶלֶת אֶת־הַדָּם וְהִכְרַתִּי אֹתָהּ מִקֶּרֶב עַמָּהּ: כִּי־נֶפֶשׁ הַבָּשָׂר בַּדָּם הִוא וַאֲנִי נְתַתִּיו לָכֶם עַל־הַמִּזְבֵּחַ 12 לְכַפֵּר עַל־נַפְשֹׁתֵיכֶם כִּי־הַדָּם הוּא בַּנֶּפֶשׁ יְכַפֵּר: עַל־כֵּן אָמַרְתִּי לִבְנֵי יִשְׂרָאֵל כָּל־נֶפֶשׁ מִכֶּם לֹא־תֹאכַל דָּם וְהַגֵּר 13 הַגָּר בְּתוֹכְכֶם לֹא־יֹאכַל דָּם: וְאִישׁ אִישׁ מִבְּנֵי יִשְׂרָאֵל וּמִן־הַגֵּר הַגָּר בְּתוֹכָם אֲשֶׁר יָצוּד צֵיד חַיָּה אוֹ־עוֹף אֲשֶׁר

### 10–14. BLOOD NOT TO BE EATEN

**10. eateth any manner of blood.** The prohibition, which included the eating of flesh containing blood, has been stated in general terms in Lev. III, 17; VII, 26 f.

The reason for these repeated solemn injunctions is not given. The purpose may be to tame man's instincts of violence by weaning him from blood, and implanting within him a horror of all bloodshed. The slaying of animals for food was in time taken away altogether from the ordinary Israelite, and was relegated to a body of pious and specially trained men, *Shochetim*. These injunctions have undoubtedly contributed to render the Israelites a humane people. 'Consider the one circumstance that no Jewish mother ever killed a chicken with her own hand, and you will understand why homicide is rarer among Jews than among any other human group' (A. Leroy Beaulieu).

The Jewish method of slaughter (*Shechitah*) causes the maximum effusion of blood in the animal; and the remaining blood is extracted by means of the washing and salting of the meat. For the prescribed regulations, see Dayan Lazarus, *The Ways of Her Household*, Part I.

In regard to the terms *nevelah* and *terefah* in v. 15, the flesh of an animal that died of itself (*nevelah*), or was torn by beasts (*terefah*), is emphatically forbidden. The latter term (*terefah*) includes flesh of all animals ritually slaughtered but found to contain injuries or organic diseases, whether patent or determined by inspection of the animal after Shechitah. Animals not killed strictly in the prescribed Jewish manner are technically also termed *nevelah*. The flesh of animals which are not found on Rabbinic inspection to be sound is forbidden food.

**11. life of the flesh.** The vital principle of the animal was in the blood. While life and blood are not quite identical, the blood is the principal carrier of life. With heavy loss of blood, vital powers dwindle; and if the loss continues, they cease altogether. Blood is therefore something sacred. It is withdrawn from ordinary use as an article of food, and reserved for a sacred symbolic purpose.

*I have given it to you.* i.e. I have appointed it to be placed on the Altar on *your* behalf. These words effectually dispose of any idea that the life of the animal presented to God was intended as a bribe. The blood on the Altar was for the spiritual welfare of the worshipper, not for the gratification of God.

*maketh atonement by reason of the life.* Which it contains. The use of blood, representing life, in the rites of atonement symbolized the complete yielding up of the worshipper's life to God, and conveyed the thought that the surrender of a man to the will of God carried with it the assurance of Divine pardon.

**12. therefore I said.** i.e. because the life resides in the blood, for that reason is its consumption prohibited.

**13. cover it with dust.** The blood being the symbol of life, it had to be treated in a reverent manner, in the same way that a corpse must not be left exposed. The covering with dust was the equivalent of burial in the case of a dead body. According to Hoffmann, the exhortation to act reverently in regard to the blood of an animal was not liable to be forgotten in connection with animals that were admitted as sacrifices, but some reminder was necessary in the case of those other animals that could not be brought as sacrifices; hence the command to cover the blood.

## LEVITICUS XVII, 14

among them, that taketh in hunting any beast or fowl that may be eaten, he shall pour out the blood thereof, and cover it with dust. 14. For as to the life of all flesh, the blood thereof is all one with the life thereof; therefore I said unto the children of Israel: Ye shall eat the blood of no manner of flesh; for the life of all flesh is the blood thereof; whosoever eateth it shall be cut off. 15. And every soul that eateth that which dieth of itself, or that which is torn of beasts, whether he be home-born or a stranger, he shall wash his clothes, and bathe himself in water, and be unclean until the even; then shall he be clean. 16. But if he wash them not, nor bathe his flesh, then he shall bear his iniquity.

## 18  CHAPTER XVIII

1. And the LORD spoke unto Moses, saying: 2. Speak unto the children of Israel, and say unto them: ¶ I am the LORD your God.

---

**15–16. CARCASS WHICH CAUSES DEFILEMENT**
15. Cf. XI, 39 f.
*a stranger.* A full proselyte, גר צדק (Sifra); otherwise, he was not debarred from eating it; see Deut. XIV, 21.
**16.** *he shall bear his iniquity.* Should he enter the Sanctuary, or partake of sacred food.

### CHAPTER XVIII
### PROHIBITION OF UNLAWFUL MARRIAGES, UNCHASTITY AND MOLECH WORSHIP

Chapters XI–XVII, the subject of which is ritual uncleanness and its purification, are now followed by chapters XVIII–XX, dealing with moral uncleanness and its punishment. The laws and precepts contained in XVIII–XX lie at the very root of the life of purity and righteousness, and form the foundation principles of social morality. The first place among these is given to the institution of marriage (XVIII). Marriage, the cornerstone of all human society, is here conceived in a purely ethical spirit; and any violation of the sacred character of marriage is deemed a heinous offence, calling down the punishment of Heaven upon both the offender and the society that condones the offence. Impurity in marriage, incestuous promiscuity among near relations, and other abominations are unpardonable sins, blighting the land and its inhabitants with defilement. 'In graphic brevity and comeliness, Lev. XVIII surpasses all other passages of similar import; more delicately and at the same time more seriously, such matters cannot be spoken about' (Ewald).

If the cultural condition of any people can be measured by the purity of its home life, then Israel's is the primacy in moral culture among the peoples. In Israel, marriage is regarded as a Divine institution, under whose shadow alone there can be true reverence for the mystery, dignity, and sacredness of life. Marriage is a primary religious duty. He who has no wife— say the Rabbis—lives without comfort, help, joy, blessing, atonement (*i.e.* true religious communion with God). The Jewish husband—they declare—loves his wife as himself, and honours her more than himself. 'I will work for thee, I will honour thee, I will support thee, even as it beseemeth a Jewish husband to do,' is to this day the husband's vow in the Jewish marriage-contract. The affectionate consideration shown to the Jewish wife, however, as well as the domestic purity and devotion that are the glory of Jewish womanhood, are both largely the fruit of the laws and warnings in these chapters of Leviticus. They effectively prevented the submergence of Israel in the sea of heathen impurity that covered the whole ancient world. These laws proved the ramparts for a new human ideal —that of the Holiness of Home—an ideal that became one of the distinguishing features of the Jewish people throughout the ages.

Chapter XVIII forms one of the Readings of the Day of Atonement. 'The selection was no doubt prompted by the desire to inculcate on the most solemn day in the Calendar the paramount duty of purity and self-control. And there is but little doubt that obedience to these behests has been, by Divine Providence, one of the most potent factors in the preservation of Israel' (Hermann Adler).

**1–5. INTRODUCTORY EXHORTATION**
**2.** *I am the LORD your God.* These words proclaim the Source from which the precepts emanate, as well as the Power who will not brook the wanton violation of these fundamental laws.

# LEVITICUS XVIII, 3      ויקרא אחרי מות יח

3. After the doings of the land of Egypt, wherein ye dwelt, shall ye not do; and after the doings of the land of Canaan, whither I bring you, shall ye not do; neither shall ye walk in their statutes. 4. Mine ordinances shall ye do, and My statutes shall ye keep, to walk therein: I am the LORD your God. 5. Ye shall therefore keep My statutes, and Mine ordinances, which if a man do, he shall live by them: I am the LORD.*vi· ¶ 6. None of you shall approach to any that is near of kin to him, to uncover their naked-

---

**3.** *doings ... Egypt ... Canaan.* Neither the immoral practices of the land they left, nor the abominations of the land they were going to, should influence their religious life.

*statutes.* lit. 'laws engraven,' denotes the ordinances which control the life of the nation. The vicious practices of paganism, especially of Egypt and Canaan, were sanctioned by their national laws. 'Both the practices and the laws were contrary to Reason, Conscience, and the Divine Will' (Wogue).

**4.** *ordinances.* Israel was receiving a new code of laws that was to take the place of what they had seen in force in Egypt and would find in Canaan. *Judgments* are laws dictated by the moral sense, like the prohibition of theft: *statutes* are distinctive precepts addressed to the Israelite, like the prohibition of swine's flesh; see on Gen. XXVI, 5.

*do ... keep.* The two verbs are complementary. *Do* is the mechanical performance; *keep* includes the idea of study and understanding of the principle underlying the command. Only where there is *intelligent* conformity to the letter of the Torah, does its spirit become a transforming power in the lives of men.

*to walk therein.* This phrase occurs only in two other places in the Torah (XX, 23; XXVI, 3). It means not merely to obey the behests of Religion once or twice, but to *walk* in them, to order life in accordance with them.

*I am the LORD.* i.e. I who command these precepts am the LORD your God. The refrain—'I am the LORD' gives peculiar solemnity to the demands which it accompanies in these chapters. Man must obey, because it is God who commands. 'The Divine imperative is its own self-sufficient motive' (Moore).

**5.** *if a man do.* The Rabbis emphasize the word *man*. Rabbi Meir used to say, 'Whence do we know that even a heathen, if he obeys the law of God, will thereby attain to the same spiritual communion with God as the High Priest? Scripture says, "which if a *man* do, he shall live by them"—not priest, Levite, or Israelite, but *man*' (Talmud).

*he shall live by them.* He will gain the life eternal in the world to come (Onkelos, Targum Jonathan, Rashi); yea, through it alone can he gain true life in this world, as the life of the wicked is not really Life (Hoffmann). The plain meaning is, that by adhering to the precepts of God, a man will enjoy well-being and length of days; cf. 'that your days may be multiplied, (Deut. XI, 21). 'No country was ever prosperous and strong in which the sanctity of family life and the value of personal purity were not upheld and practised' (W. R. Inge).

The Rabbis take the words 'he shall live by them' to mean that God's commandments are to be a means of life and not of destruction to His children, וחי בהם ולא שימות בהם. With the exception of three prohibitions, all commandments of the Law are, therefore, in abeyance whenever life is endangered. No man, however, is to save his life at the price of public idolatry, murder, or adultery. This was the decision of the Rabbis in the war of extermination which the Roman Emperor Hadrian waged against Judaism; see on XXII, 32.

### 6–18. FORBIDDEN MARRIAGES

All unions between the sexes that are repellent to the finer feelings of man, or would taint the natural affection between near relations, are sternly prohibited. Primary prohibited marriages are:— (*a*) blood-relations — mother, sister, daughter, grand-daughter, father's sister and mother's sister; and (*b*) cases of affinity—the wives of blood-relations and of the wife's blood-relations. All unions—whether temporary or permanent—between persons belonging to these groups are classed as 'incestuous' (עריות). They have no binding force whatsoever in Jewish Law and can in no circumstance be deemed a 'marriage'; hence, no divorce (*Get*) is required for their dissolution. The issue are illegitimate (*mamzerim*).

The Rabbis have expanded the primary Prohibited Degrees in the ascending and descending line. These expansions are known as 'secondary Prohibited Marriages, שניות'; *e.g.* as the mother is forbidden, so is the grandmother and great-

## LEVITICUS XVIII, 7

ness: I am the LORD. ¶ 7 The nakedness of thy father, and the nakedness of thy mother, shalt thou not uncover: she is thy mother; thou shalt not uncover her nakedness. ¶ 8. The nakedness of thy father's wife shalt thou not uncover: it is thy father's nakedness. ¶ 9. The nakedness of thy sister, the daughter of thy father, or the daughter of thy mother, whether born at home, or born abroad, even their nakedness thou shalt not uncover. ¶ 10. The nakedness of thy son's daughter, or of thy daughter's daughter, even their nakedness thou shalt not uncover; for theirs is thine own naked-

ויקרא אחרי מות יח

7 אֶל־כָּל־שְׁאֵר בְּשָׂרוֹ לֹא תִקְרְבוּ לְגַלּוֹת עֶרְוָה אֲנִי יְהוָֹה׃ ס עֶרְוַת אָבִיךָ וְעֶרְוַת אִמְּךָ לֹא תְגַלֵּה אִמְּךָ הִוא לֹא

8 תְגַלֶּה עֶרְוָתָהּ׃ ס עֶרְוַת אֵשֶׁת־אָבִיךָ לֹא תְגַלֵּה

9 עֶרְוַת אָבִיךָ הִוא׃ ס עֶרְוַת אֲחוֹתְךָ בַת־אָבִיךָ אוֹ בַת־אִמֶּךָ מוֹלֶדֶת בַּיִת אוֹ מוֹלֶדֶת חוּץ לֹא תְגַלֶּה עֶרְוָתָן׃

10 ס עֶרְוַת בַּת־בִּנְךָ אוֹ בַת־בִּתְּךָ לֹא תְגַלֶּה עֶרְוָתָן כִּי

grandmother; as the step-mother so is the grandfather's wife; as the daughter-in-law, so is the grandson's wife. Marriages of the secondary Prohibited Degrees must be dissolved by a divorce, and the children are legitimate.

The above Prohibited Degrees of marriage, whether Biblical or Rabbinical, are based on instinctive abhorrence and natural decorum. Jewish sectaries, however, as well as various Christian Churches, largely under the influence of Roman Law, greatly extended these prohibitions, until even an alliance between the great-grand-children of two brothers and sisters was by them deemed forbidden. The Church introduced further prohibitions in connection with 'spiritual kinship'; e.g. a godfather could not marry the child at whose baptism he was sponsor. The hardship resulting from such unbounded extension of Prohibited Degrees by the Roman Law and Church, was to some extent mitigated by *dispensation*, which the Church granted in certain circumstances; but this led to great abuses. Both dispensation and 'spiritual kinship' are, of course, unknown in Judaism.

The Rabbis explain that prior to the Revelation at Sinai, only the following marriages were prohibited: *viz.* mother, father's wife, married woman, and sister on mother's side. Hence Abraham was permitted to marry his half-sister; and Jacob, two sisters.

**6.** *none of you . . . nakedness.* No one shall contract a marriage with a blood-relation. The broad principle (כלל) is here stated, and then particulars are given in *v.* 7–18.

There was dire need for the legislation in this chapter. Many of the incestuous marriages herein mentioned were common among contemporary peoples, and were recognized in parts of the Roman world as late as the early Middle Ages. In Egypt, marriage with a sister was quite usual, especially in royal families. The Greeks countenanced marriage with a half-sister. Among the Persians, marriages with mother, sisters, and daughters were expressly recommended as meritorious and as most pleasing to the gods. Such were the usages, not of barbarous and reckless tribes unused to moral restrictions, but of the cultured nations of antiquity. 'It is evident that Mosaism brought the world a new message in the matter of marriage' (Dillmann). When we think of the influence of this Chapter on the Western and Near Eastern peoples, we realise that Judaism is indeed a religious civilization!

*near of kin.* lit. 'flesh of his flesh'; his flesh and blood. Within a certain degree of consanguinity two relatives are regarded as one flesh, and one person.

*uncover their nakedness.* Used for, 'to take to wife' in alliances which can never be regarded as 'marriage'. It is employed here, instead of the usual phrase, in order to bring out more strikingly the moral hideousness and animality of the transgression (S. R. Hirsch).

**7.** *of thy father.* Forbids a union between mother and son, as a dishonour both to father and mother.

**8.** *father's wife.* Forbids union with a step-mother. As marriage makes man and wife one (Gen. II, 24), a step-mother was regarded as a blood-relation of the nearest kind.

It was a practice among Eastern heirs-apparent to take possession of the father's wives, as an assertion of their right to the throne, that action identifying them with the late ruler's personality in the eyes of the people. This explains Reuben's conduct in Gen. XXXV, 22, and Absalom's in II Sam. XVI, 20–22.

**9.** *born at home.* A half-sister born of a legal marriage; see XX, 17.

*born abroad.* A half-sister born either of an illegal marriage or out of wedlock (Ibn Ezra).

**10.** *thy son's daughter.* As marriage with a step-grand-daughter is forbidden in *v.* 17, this verse seems superfluous. The Rabbis, however, understood it as referring to the daughter of an illegitimate son or daughter.

Marriage with a daughter is not expressly forbidden; because, in view of this prohibition of the grand-daughter, it is self-evident.

*thine own nakedness.* 'They are part of yourself' (Moffatt).

## LEVITICUS XVIII, 11

ness. ¶ 11. The nakedness of thy father's wife's daughter, begotten of thy father, she is thy sister, thou shalt not uncover her nakedness. ¶ 12. Thou shalt not uncover the nakedness of thy father's sister: she is thy father's near kinswoman. ¶ 13. Thou shalt not uncover the nakedness of thy mother's sister; for she is thy mother's near kinswoman. ¶ 14. Though shalt not uncover the nakedness of thy father's brother, thou shalt not approach to his wife: she is thine aunt. ¶ 15. Thou shalt not uncover the nakedness of thy daughter-in-law: she is thy son's wife; thou shalt not uncover her nakedness. ¶ 16. Thou shalt not uncover the nakedness of thy brother's wife: it is thy brother's nakedness. 17. Thou shalt not uncover the nakedness of a woman and her daughter; thou shalt not take her son's daughter, or her daughter's daughter, to uncover her nakedness: they are near kinswomen; it is lewdness. 18. And thou shalt not take a woman to her sister, to be a rival to her, to uncover her nakedness, beside the other in her life-time. 19. And thou shalt not approach unto a woman to uncover her

11 עֶרְוַת בַּת־אֵשֶׁת אָבִיךָ מוֹלֶדֶת ס עֶרְוָתָהּ הֵנָּה׃
12 אָבִיךָ אֲחוֹתְךָ הִוא לֹא תְגַלֶּה עֶרְוָתָהּ׃ ס עֶרְוַת
13 אֲחוֹת־אָבִיךָ לֹא תְגַלֶּה שְׁאֵר אָבִיךָ הִוא׃ ס עֶרְוַת
14 אֲחוֹת־אִמְּךָ לֹא תְגַלֶּה כִּי־שְׁאֵר אִמְּךָ הִוא׃ ס עֶרְוַת
אֲחִי־אָבִיךָ לֹא תְגַלֶּה אֶל־אִשְׁתּוֹ לֹא תִקְרָב דֹּדָתְךָ הִוא׃
15 ס עֶרְוַת כַּלָּתְךָ לֹא תְגַלֶּה אֵשֶׁת בִּנְךָ הִוא לֹא תְגַלֶּה
16 עֶרְוָתָהּ׃ ס עֶרְוַת אֵשֶׁת־אָחִיךָ לֹא תְגַלֶּה עֶרְוַת
17 אָחִיךָ הִוא׃ ס עֶרְוַת אִשָּׁה וּבִתָּהּ לֹא תְגַלֵּה אֶת־
בַּת־בְּנָהּ וְאֶת־בַּת־בִּתָּהּ לֹא תִקַּח לְגַלּוֹת עֶרְוָתָהּ שַׁאֲרָה
18 הֵנָּה זִמָּה הִוא׃ וְאִשָּׁה אֶל־אֲחֹתָהּ לֹא תִקָּח לִצְרֹר לְגַלּוֹת
19 עֶרְוָתָהּ עָלֶיהָ בְּחַיֶּיהָ׃ וְאֶל־אִשָּׁה בְּנִדַּת טֻמְאָתָהּ לֹא תִקְרַב

v. 14. קמץ בז״ק

**11. thy father's wife's daughter.** Descent from the same mother was long deemed a closer degree of relationship than descent from the same father (Gen. xx, 12). Consequently, v. 9 might have been misunderstood to apply to either 'thy sister (viz. of the same mother) who is the daughter of thy father,' i.e. a full sister; or, to 'the daughter of thy mother', i.e. a half-sister from the same mother but different father. Union with a half-sister from the same father but different mother might thus have been thought permissible. Hence the need of a clear prohibition of the daughter from the same father by another mother, as is here given (Hoffmann).

**12. thy father's sister.** This prohibition, too, was new to Israelites and contrary to their former usage (Exod. VI, 20).

**14. thy father's brother.** Union with the wife of a father's brother is an offence against two persons whom marriage had made 'one flesh' (see v. 8). For that reason, her nephew could not marry her after his uncle's death. The Rabbis declare marriage with the wife of a mother's brother equally illegal.

**15–18.** Cases of affinity by marriage.

**15. daughter-in-law.** Forbids marriage between a man and his daughter-in-law after divorce or the husband's death. It was deemed a foul offence, almost on a plane with 'marriage' with a daughter.

**16. brother's wife.** An exception to this rule is given in Deut. xxv, 5 f, where the obligation is placed upon a man to marry his brother's widow, should his brother have died without issue.

**17. lewdness.** lit. 'harlotry'. The union of a man with both a woman and her daughter or grand-daughter, whether at the same time or after the death of one, is considered an execrable action, an 'enormity' (RV Margin).

**18. to be a rival to her.** Better, *as a fellow-wife*. Sisterly love would thereby turn to rivalry and hatred.

*in her life-time.* During the first wife's life-time, even if he had divorced her, he could not marry her sister. After her death it was permitted, and was even deemed by the Rabbis a praiseworthy thing to do, as no other woman would show the same affection to the orphaned children of the deceased sister.

**19–23. IMMORAL PRACTICES FORBIDDEN**

**19. impure.** In xv, 24, the same matter had been dealt with from the point of view of the ritual defilement that is thereby incurred. Here the practice is denounced as contrary to the principles of moral purity; see also xx, 18.

While recognizing the sacred nature of the estate of wedlock, Judaism prescribes continence even in marriage. 'The Jewish ideal of holiness is not confined to the avoidance of the illicit; its ideal includes the hallowing of the licit' (Moore). It categorically demands reserve, self-control, and moral freedom in the most intimate relations of life. It ordains the utmost consideration for the wife not only throughout the monthly period of separation (*niddah*), but also during the seven following days of convalescence and recovery (*taharah*), which are terminated by ritual purification through total immersion either in a fountain,

## LEVITICUS XVIII, 20

nakedness, as long as she is impure by her uncleanness. 20. And thou shalt not lie carnally with thy neighbour's wife, to defile thyself with her. 21. And thou shalt not give any of thy seed to set them apart to Molech, neither shalt thou profane the name of thy God: I am the LORD.*vii(**iv). 22. Thou shalt not lie with mankind, as with womankind; it is abomination. 23. And thou shalt not lie with any beast to defile thyself therewith; neither shall any woman stand before a beast, to lie down thereto; it is perversion. ¶ 24. Defile not ye yourselves

---

or a 'gathering of living water' (*mikweh*, in later Hebrew, *mikvah*; see on XI, 36). By the reverent guidance in these vital matters which these laws afford, Jewish men have been taught respect for womanhood, moral discipline, and ethical culture. As for Jewish women, they were, on the one hand, given protection from uncurbed passion; and, on the other hand, taught to view marital life under the aspect of holiness (קדושה).

Even apart from their purely religious side, the importance of these regulations, scrupulously observed throughout the generations in Israel, cannot be over-estimated. They have fostered racial sanity and well-being, and have proved as favourable to hygiene as to morals. The overwhelming majority of Jewish women still live, thank God, under the 'yoke' of these laws—to their own good and the biologic good of the Jewish people. Striking testimony has been given by scientists to the fact that, though health is not put forward as the primary purpose of these regulations, yet such is their indubitable result. These laws of marital continence are now held by some scientists to accord with the fundamental rhythm in woman's nature. While medical opinion is not unanimous on this difficult subject, there can be no doubt as to the significance of statistics like the following: an investigation, conducted over a number of years at Mount Sinai Hospital, New York, in connection with 80,000 Jewish women who observe *niddah* and *taharah* laws, showed that the proportion of those suffering from uterine cancer was one to fifteen of non-Jewish women of corresponding social and economic status. Even more noteworthy is the difference in the proportion of a certain form of cancer among Jewish and non-Jewish men respectively (Sorsby, *Cancer and Race*, 1931). 'The Mosaic Code again stands out as an astonishing example of inspired wisdom and foresight which should appeal with redoubled force to the enlightened minds of to-day. Discipline and self-restraint are perhaps the lessons most needed for the present times' (Lieut.-Col. F. E. Freemantle, Chairman, International Cancer Conference, London, July, 1928).

For a brief account of the traditional laws of *niddah* and *taharah*, see Dayan Lazarus, *The Ways of Her Household*, Part II (Myers and Co., 1923). See also Rabbi David Miller, *The Secret of the Jew; his Life—his Family* (Oakland, Calif.).

**20.** *thy neighbour's wife.* This prohibition is so vital to human society that it is included in the Ten Commandments, immediately after the protection of life, as being of equal importance with it (Ewald); see also note on XX, 10.

**21.** *set them apart.* Or *pass through the fire.* We have here the first mention in the Bible of the dreadful practice of child-sacrifice to a deity of the surrounding heathen Semites. Israel's Teachers shudder at this hideous aberration of man's sense of worship, and they do not rest till all Israel shares their horror of it.

Sexual impurity, especially when it is allied with, or elevated into, a form of worship, as it was in the cults of Baal and Astarte, dehumanizes, and leads to the deadening of the holiest human instincts.

*neither shalt thou profane.* Better, *that thou profane not;* such savage idolatry being an infamous travesty of all religion or adoration of God.

**22.** *with mankind.* Discloses the abyss of depravity from which the Torah saved the Israelite. This unnatural vice was also prevalent in Greece and Rome.

**23.** *perversion.* 'A violation of nature and of the Divine order' (Dillmann); cf. Exod. XXII, 18; Lev. XX, 15 f.

The almost incredible bestialities, revealing the hideous possibilities of corrupt human nature, enumerated in *v*. 21–23, are but too well attested in laws, customs, and legends of the ancient and medieval world. They are not unknown in modern societies. Nowhere in literature is there such an uncompromising condemnation of these offences as in XVIII and XX. It led to their extirpation in the midst of Israel, and eventually to their moral outlawry among all peoples that came under the sway of the Hebrew Scriptures.

**24–30.** An exhortation to lay to heart the fate of the Canaanites, whose loathsome customs, disruptive of social morality, would bring about their annihilation.

# LEVITICUS XVIII, 25

ויקרא אחרי מות יח

כה אֲשֶׁר־אֲנִי מְשַׁלֵּחַ מִפְּנֵיכֶם: וַתִּטְמָא הָאָרֶץ וָאֶפְקֹד עֲוֺנָהּ
26 עָלֶיהָ וַתָּקִא הָאָרֶץ אֶת־יֹשְׁבֶיהָ: וּשְׁמַרְתֶּם אַתֶּם אֶת־חֻקֹּתַי
וְאֶת־מִשְׁפָּטַי וְלֹא תַעֲשׂוּ מִכֹּל הַתּוֹעֵבֹת הָאֵלֶּה הָאֶזְרָח
27 וְהַגֵּר הַגָּר בְּתוֹכְכֶם: כִּי אֶת־כָּל־הַתּוֹעֵבֹת הָאֵל עָשׂוּ אַנְשֵׁי־
28 הָאָרֶץ אֲשֶׁר לִפְנֵיכֶם וַתִּטְמָא הָאָרֶץ:* וְלֹא־תָקִיא הָאָרֶץ
אֶתְכֶם בְּטַמַּאֲכֶם אֹתָהּ כַּאֲשֶׁר קָאָה אֶת־הַגּוֹי אֲשֶׁר
29 לִפְנֵיכֶם: כִּי כָּל־אֲשֶׁר יַעֲשֶׂה מִכֹּל הַתּוֹעֵבֹת הָאֵלֶּה וְנִכְרְתוּ
ל הַנְּפָשׁוֹת הָעֹשֹׂת מִקֶּרֶב עַמָּם: וּשְׁמַרְתֶּם אֶת־מִשְׁמַרְתִּי
לְבִלְתִּי עֲשׂוֹת מֵחֻקּוֹת הַתּוֹעֵבֹת אֲשֶׁר נַעֲשׂוּ לִפְנֵיכֶם וְלֹא
תִטַּמְּאוּ בָּהֶם אֲנִי יְהֹוָה אֱלֹהֵיכֶם:

מפטיר
מפטיר
לסמ״(

v. 27. סבירין האלה

in any of these things; for in all these the nations are defiled, which I cast out from before you. 25. And the land was defiled, therefore I did visit the iniquity thereof upon it, and the land vomited out her inhabitants. 26. Ye therefore shall keep My statutes and Mine ordinances, and shall not do any of these abominations; neither the home-born, nor the stranger that sojourneth among you—*ᵐᵃ·27. for all these abominations have the men of the land done, that were before you, and the land is defiled—*ᵐ ˢ· 28. that the land vomit not you out also, when ye defile it, as it vomited out the nation that was before you. 29. For whosoever shall do any of these abominations, even the souls that do them shall be cut off from among their people. 30. Therefore shall ye keep My charge, that ye do not any of these abominable customs, which were done before you, and that ye defile not yourselves therein: I am the LORD your God.

**24.** *defile not ye yourselves.* Whenever sex is withdrawn from its place in marriage and separated from its function as the expression of reverent and lawful wedded love (whereby its quality is completely changed), the person concerned is defiled. The Rabbis deem sexual immorality the strongest of defilements (טומאה), cutting man off from God.

*any of these things.* The words refer to all the foregoing—the forbidden marriages, the neglect of marital restrictions, as well as unnatural abominations.

**25.** *the land was defiled.* Only moral offences, and not ceremonial transgressions, are said to defile the land. Every 'enormity' first defiles the person who commits it, be he a Canaanite or an Israelite, and he in turn defiles the land (Büchler).

*I did visit the iniquity thereof.* The land (*i.e.* its inhabitants) is punished. Through pestilence and drought, its inhabitants are vomited out in the same manner as the human system rejects food which is disagreeable to it. The verbs in this verse visualize the future as though it had actually come into being.

**29.** *shall be cut off.* In most of the offences mentioned, the penalty prescribed is death. With the remainder, the culprits were expelled from the Community and presumably from the country, since their presence contaminated the land.

**30.** *keep My charge.* The Rabbis understood this phrase in the sense of 'guard My charge'; *i.e.* it is the duty of the Religious Authorities to make a 'fence round the Law', in order to keep men far from sin, and to warn and instruct the people as to the seriousness and sacredness of these prohibitions.

*I am the LORD your God.* The former inhabitants indulged in unnatural vices because the worship of their gods was demoralizing. It is otherwise with Israel. The Lord is their God, and His service is elevating and spiritualizing. Hence there is here a natural transition to the next chapter with its opening command, 'Ye shall be holy; for I the LORD your God am holy.'

# HAFTORAH ACHAREY MOS
הפטרת אחרי מות

## EZEKIEL XXII, 1–19

### CHAPTER XXII

1. Moreover the word of the LORD came unto me, saying: 2. 'Now, thou, son of man, wilt thou judge, wilt thou judge the bloody city? then cause her to know all her abominations. 3. And thou shalt say: Thus saith the Lord GOD: O city that sheddest blood in the midst of thee, that thy time may come, and that makest idols unto thyself to defile thee; 4. thou art become guilty in thy blood that thou hast shed, and art defiled in thine idols which thou hast

### CAP. XXII. כב

2 א וַיְהִ֥י דְבַר־יְהֹוָ֖ה אֵלַ֥י לֵאמֹֽר׃ וְאַתָּ֣ה בֶן־אָדָ֔ם הֲתִשְׁפֹּ֥ט הֲתִשְׁפֹּ֖ט אֶת־עִ֣יר הַדָּמִ֑ים וְה֣וֹדַעְתָּ֔הּ אֵ֖ת כָּל־תּוֹעֲבוֹתֶֽיהָ׃
3 וְאָמַרְתָּ֗ כֹּ֤ה אָמַר֙ אֲדֹנָ֣י יְהֹוִ֔ה עִ֣יר שֹׁפֶ֥כֶת דָּ֖ם בְּתוֹכָ֑הּ
4 לָב֣וֹא עִתָּ֑הּ וְעָשְׂתָ֧ה גִלּוּלִ֛ים עָלֶ֖יהָ לְטָמְאָ֑ה בְּדָמֵ֤ךְ אֲשֶׁר־

For Ezekiel's life and message, see pp. 178, 244, and 350; and the introductions to Haftorahs Parah and Hachodesh at the end of this volume.

The Sedrah ordains strict regulations for assuring the religious and moral purity of Israel; while the Haftorah is a terrible indictment of Jerusalem for callous violation of these regulations and prohibitions. 'The sins mentioned in Lev. XVIII were those which disgraced the heathen inhabitants of Canaan whom the Israelites were to cast out. The commission of like sins would ensure like judgment' (Speaker's Bible). This Haftorah forms part of a prophecy delivered in 590 B.C.E. Four years later, the Jewish State fell, Jerusalem was captured, the Temple burnt, and the larger portion of the People carried into Babylonian exile.

Ezekiel's role in those times that tried men's souls was a manifold one. He began as the denouncer of Israel, and ended as Israel's comforter. It was his task to utter a cry of doom, unrelenting and fierce, against Jerusalem and its inhabitants. With the destruction of the Temple, however, he opens wide the gates of hope, and prophesies an outpouring of the Divine Spirit that would lead to contrition and penitence, and the consequent resurrection of Israel in the Holy Land.

The Fall of Jerusalem and the Destruction of the Temple had left Israel spiritually stunned. Were the Israelites of that generation so morally degenerate—they asked—so especially godless as to have deserved nothing less than national annihilation and all the horrors of siege and exile? 'The way of the LORD is not equal,' many were saying to themselves (Ezek. XVIII, 25). Israel was overwhelmed by doubt as to the existence of a Righteous Ruler of the Universe.

First of all, therefore, Ezekiel deemed it necessary to vindicate the ways of God with Israel. He passes in review the entire past of Israel; and, unlike the other Prophets, he declares it to have been one long chain of ingratitude and sin. The reason for the Prophet's pitiless vehemence is plain: it is only when Israel is *sincerely repentant* of its apostasies and abominations, it is only when Israel sees that its sufferings are the just chastisement of a holy God, that its redemption and resurrection can begin.

A great danger faces the Prophet; he may succeed too well in his denunciation of his people and condemnation of its entire past (Cornill). He may end in planting despair in the hearts of the exiles, and make them exclaim, 'If such has been Israel's past, Israel never deserved to live; and now that it is a valley of dry bones, Israel's story is at an end (Ezek. XXXVII, 11). "Our hope is lost, we are clean cut off".' He meets that danger by striking two notes; one is that God desires not the destruction, but the repentance, of Israel. 'Say unto them, As I live, saith the LORD God, I have no pleasure in the death of the wicked; but that the wicked turn from his way and live: turn ye, turn ye from your evil ways; for why will ye die, O house of Israel?" And the other note is, that God's glory is bound up with the resurrection of Israel. God will restore them, not because Israel deserves restoration, but because God's glory demands it; see Haftorah Parah at the end of this volume.

The terrible earnestness of this great Preacher of Repentance wrought a wondrous change in Israel. The result of his ministry is, as C. G. Montefiore rightly says, unique in the history of humanity. A fragment of a small people, forcibly transplanted to an enemy's land, remains there for half-a-century without disintegrating or coalescing with its environment, and returns unimpaired to its own soil and resumes its own life, with national and religious identity heightened and strengthened!

### CHAPTER XXII
#### 1–12. THE SINS OF JERUSALEM

**2.** *wilt thou judge.* To rehearse the history of the fathers is to hold up the mirror to themselves (Davidson).

*bloody city.* Because of perversion of justice, murderous partisan conflicts, and chiefly the child-sacrifices during the reign of Manasseh.

**3.** *sheddest blood . . . makest idols.* Bloodshed and idolatry are the outstanding sins of the city.

*that thy time may come.* Her sins hasten the time of her destruction (Kimchi). She seems to be courting retribution.

*unto thyself.* Her idols are her real foes; crying out, as it were, for her punishment.

EZEKIEL XXII, 5

made; and thou hast caused thy days to draw near, and art come even unto thy years; therefore have I made thee a reproach unto the nations, and a mocking to all the countries? 5. Those that are near, and those that are far from thee, shall mock thee, thou defiled of name and full of tumult. ¶ 6. Behold, the princes of Israel, every one according to his might, have been in thee to shed blood. 7. In thee have they made light of father and mother; in the midst of thee have they dealt by oppression with the stranger; in thee have they wronged the fatherless and the widow. 8. Thou hast despised My holy things, and hast profaned My sabbaths. 9. In thee have been talebearers to shed blood; and in thee they have eaten upon the mountains; in the midst of thee they have committed lewdness. 10. In thee have they uncovered their fathers' nakedness; in thee have they humbled her that was unclean in her impurity. 11. And each hath committed abomination with his neighbour's wife;

שָׁפַכְתְּ אָשֵׁמְתְּ וּבְגִלּוּלַיִךְ אֲשֶׁר־עָשִׂית טָמֵאת וַתַּקְרִיבִי יָמַיִךְ וַתָּבוֹא עַד־שְׁנוֹתָיִךְ עַל־כֵּן נְתַתִּיךְ חֶרְפָּה לַגּוֹיִם ה וְקַלָּסָה לְכָל־הָאֲרָצוֹת: הַקְּרֹבוֹת וְהָרְחֹקוֹת מִמֵּךְ יִתְקַלְּסוּ־ 6 בָךְ טְמֵאַת הַשֵּׁם רַבַּת הַמְּהוּמָה: הִנֵּה נְשִׂיאֵי יִשְׂרָאֵל 7 אִישׁ לִזְרֹעוֹ הָיוּ בָךְ לְמַעַן שְׁפָךְ־דָּם: אָב וָאֵם הֵקַלּוּ בָךְ 8 לַגֵּר עָשׂוּ בַעֹשֶׁק בְּתוֹכֵךְ יָתוֹם וְאַלְמָנָה הוֹנוּ בָךְ: קָדָשַׁי 9 בָּזִית וְאֶת־שַׁבְּתֹתַי חִלָּלְתְּ: אַנְשֵׁי רָכִיל הָיוּ בָךְ לְמַעַן י שְׁפָךְ־דָּם וְאֶל־הֶהָרִים אָכְלוּ בָךְ זִמָּה עָשׂוּ בְתוֹכֵךְ: עֶרְוַת־ 11 אָב גִּלָּה־בָךְ טְמֵאַת הַנִּדָּה עִנּוּ־בָךְ: וְאִישׁ ׀ אֶת־אֵשֶׁת רֵעֵהוּ עָשָׂה תּוֹעֵבָה וְאִישׁ אֶת־כַּלָּתוֹ טִמֵּא בְזִמָּה וְאִישׁ

v. 4. למדנחאי עת כתיב עד ק׳ ibid. נ״א בגוים

**4.** *thy days.* Of judgment.
*thy years.* Of punishment and destruction.
*therefore have I made.* The judgment is as certain as though it had already taken place (Streane)—the Prophetic perfect tense.

**5.** *tumult.* Turbulence and disorder.

**6.** *princes of Israel.* Those to whom the people would look for an example of right living abandon themselves to evil. Everything most sacred in the Jewish life, and all that is the basis of human society, have been outraged—filial duty, justice, love of the stranger, compassion towards orphan and widow, observance of the Sabbath; and sins most sternly prohibited and regarded with utmost horror—usury and impure relationships—have been committed.
*according to his might.* They recognize no law but might.
*to shed blood.* By form of law; see I Kings XXI. These crimes were the order of the day among other ancient peoples, and were looked upon as part of the normal course of human events. In Israel alone did there arise teachers of religion who were dumbfounded at human ferocity, as at something against nature and reason; and whose cry of indignation at these inhumanities re-echoed the wrath of the Deity. 'Greece and Rome had their rich and poor, just as Israel had, and the various classes continued to slaughter one another for centuries; but no voice of justice and pity arose from the fierce tumult. Therefore, the words of the Prophets have more vitality at the present time, and answer better to the needs of modern souls, than all the classic masterpieces of antiquity' (Darmesteter).

**7.** *in thee.* In the Holy City.

**8.** *thou.* Jerusalem.

**9.** *talebearers.* Informers and false witnesses, the instruments of judicial murder.
*in thee they have eaten upon the mountains.* 'High places' were the seat of heathen and impure rites. Participation in such Bacchanalian orgies is open idolatry.

**10.** *uncovered.* Marriage with the father's wife, though common among the surrounding heathens, was a heinous crime; Lev. XVIII, 7.
*unclean.* See Lev. XVIII, 19; XX, 18.

**11.** *defiled.* Idolatry, then as now, means sexual licence and the throwing overboard of all laws of holiness such as are given in Lev. XVIII.

**12.** *taken gifts . . . oppression.* These crimes have darkened Eastern societies since times immemorial; but Israel 'should have known better'.
*hast forgotten Me.* All their degeneracy is summed up in this crowning sin, 'They have forgotten Me, saith the LORD.' This was the root of their evil doing. Forgetting Him, they returned to the lower moral standards of heathenism—something that is seen over and over again in Jewish history.

# EZEKIEL XXII, 12

and each hath lewdly defiled his daughter-in-law; and each in thee hath humbled his sister, his father's daughter. 12. In thee have they taken gifts to shed blood; thou hast taken interest and increase, and thou hast greedily gained of thy neighbours by oppression, and hast forgotten Me, saith the Lord GOD. ¶ 13. Behold, therefore, I have smitten My hand at thy dishonest gain which thou hast made, and at thy blood which hath been in the midst of thee. 14. Can thy heart endure, or can thy hands be strong, in the days that I shall deal with thee? I the LORD have spoken it, and will do it. 15. And I will scatter thee among the nations, and disperse thee through the countries; and I will consume thy filthiness out of thee. 16. And thou shalt be profaned in thyself, in the sight of the nations; and thou shalt know that I am the LORD.' ¶ 17. And the word of the LORD came unto me, saying: 18. 'Son of man, the house of Israel is become dross unto Me; all of them are brass and tin and iron and lead, in the midst of the furnace; they are the dross of silver. 19. Therefore thus saith the Lord GOD: Because ye are all become dross, therefore, behold, I will gather you into the midst of Jerusalem.'

12 אֶת־אֲחֹתוֹ בַת־אָבִיו עִנָּה־בָךְ׃ שֹׁחַד לָקְחוּ־בָךְ לְמַעַן שְׁפָךְ־דָּם נֶשֶׁךְ וְתַרְבִּית לָקַחַתְּ וַתְּבַצְּעִי רֵעַיִךְ בַּעֹשֶׁק וְאֹתִי
13 שָׁכַחַתְּ נְאֻם אֲדֹנָי יֱהֹוִה׃ וְהִנֵּה הִכֵּיתִי כַפִּי אֶל־בִּצְעֵךְ
14 אֲשֶׁר עָשִׂית וְעַל־דָּמֵךְ אֲשֶׁר הָיוּ בְּתוֹכֵךְ׃ הֲיַעֲמֹד לִבֵּךְ אִם־תֶּחֱזַקְנָה יָדַיִךְ לַיָּמִים אֲשֶׁר אֲנִי עֹשֶׂה אוֹתָךְ אֲנִי
טו יְהֹוָה דִּבַּרְתִּי וְעָשִׂיתִי׃ וַהֲפִיצוֹתִי אֹתָךְ בַּגּוֹיִם וְזֵרִיתִיךְ
16 בָּאֲרָצוֹת וַהֲתִמֹּתִי טֻמְאָתֵךְ מִמֵּךְ׃ וְנִחַלְתְּ בָּךְ לְעֵינֵי גוֹיִם
17 וְיָדַעַתְּ כִּי־אֲנִי יְהֹוָה׃ ס וַיְהִי דְבַר־יְהֹוָה אֵלַי לֵאמֹר׃
18 בֶּן־אָדָם הָיוּ־לִי בֵית־יִשְׂרָאֵל לְסִיג כֻּלָּם נְחֹשֶׁת וּבְדִיל
19 וּבַרְזֶל וְעוֹפֶרֶת בְּתוֹךְ כּוּר סִגִים כֶּסֶף הָיוּ׃ לָכֵן כֹּה אָמַר אֲדֹנָי יֱהֹוִה יַעַן הֱיוֹת כֻּלְּכֶם לְסִגִים לָכֵן הִנְנִי קֹבֵץ אֶתְכֶם אֶל־תּוֹךְ יְרוּשָׁלָ͏ִם׃

*כאן מסיימין הספרדים v. 18. לסיג ק'

### 13–19. THE PUNISHMENT

**13.** *I have smitten My hand.* In grief.

**14.** *can thy heart endure.* The suffering that will result from thy transgressions.

**15.** *consume thy filthiness out of thee.* The chastisements of God are not vindictive, but intended to purge the nation of its sin.

**16.** *thou shalt be profaned in thyself.* Or, 'thou shalt take thine inheritance' (AV; Kimchi), *i.e.* of punishment and shame.
*and thou shalt know that I am the LORD.* Punishment will purify you, and lead you to acknowledge Him as the God of Justice and Holiness.

**18.** *dross.* The people are to be tried in the furnace of affliction. Jerusalem, and all that it contains, will be subject to the fire of God's wrath. Only the dross will be burnt away. The purified remnant shall survive the fire.

**19.** *I will gather you.* The certainty of the siege approaches, and the people from the surrounding country take refuge within the walls of Jerusalem (Lofthouse). In brief, the end is at hand.

# LEVITICUS XIX, 1

**CHAPTER XIX**

1. And the LORD spoke unto Moses, saying:
2. Speak unto all the congregation of the children of Israel, and say unto them: ¶ Ye shall be holy; for I the LORD your God am

ויקרא קדשים יט

**CAP. XIX.** יט

פ פ פ פ ל 30

2 וַיְדַבֵּר יְהוָֹה אֶל־מֹשֶׁה לֵּאמֹר: דַּבֵּר אֶל־כָּל־עֲדַת בְּנֵי־ א

## VII. KEDOSHIM

(CHAPTERS XIX–XX)

CHAPTER XIX. A MANUAL OF MORAL INSTRUCTION

This remarkable chapter occupies the central position in Leviticus, and therefore in the Pentateuch. The Rabbis rightly regarded it as the kernel of the Law and declared that 'the essentials of the Torah (רוב גופי תורה) are summarized therein' (Sifra). This chapter has in fact been looked upon as a counterpart of the Decalogue itself, the Ten Commandments being in essence repeated in its verses (I and II in *v.* 4; III in *v.* 12; IV and V in *v.* 3; VI in *v.* 16; VII in *v.* 29; VIII and IX in *v.* 11–16; and X in *v.* 18). The precepts contained in the chapter may, at first sight, appear a medley of the spiritual and ceremonial—fundamental maxims and principles of justice and morality alongside of ritual laws and observances. The Torah, however, regards human life as an indivisible whole, and declines to exclude any phase thereof from its purview; see introductory note to chapters XI–XVI.

2. HOLINESS AND THE IMITATION OF GOD

As the command, 'ye shall be holy, for I the LORD your God am holy,' dominates not only this chapter but the whole ethical legislation in Leviticus, it is necessary to have a clear understanding of the word *holy* (קדוש) in its ethical, as distinct from its ritual, signification. First, it denotes the sublime exaltedness and overpowering majesty of God: in the presence of that Divine holiness, mortal man feels 'but dust and ashes' and is crushed by the sense of his unworthiness (Isa. VI, 5). Secondly, *holy* expresses God's complete freedom from everything that makes men imperfect, and His recoil from everything impure and unrighteous; in the words of the Prophet, 'Thou art of eyes too pure to behold evil, and canst not look on mischief' (Hab. I, 13). Thirdly, *holy* stands for the fulness of God's ethical qualities—for more than goodness (טוב), more than purity (טהור), more than righteousness (צדיק); it *embraces* all these in their ideal completeness. 'The Holy One, blessed be He!' (הקדוש ברוך הוא) is the most common name for God in Rabbinical literature, as well as on the lips of the Jewish masses. In its ritual usage, the word 'holy' is applied to persons and things connected with the Sanctuary, or consecrated for religious purposes.

2. *all the congregation*. The Torah and its message of holiness is the heritage of the *congregation* of Israel. There was not to be a small class of 'specialists' in religion who dwelt apart, while the people were sunk in ignorance and superstition. Israel was to form a spiritual democracy; Deut. XXXIV; see note on Exod. XXII, 30.

*ye shall be holy: for I the* LORD *your God am holy*. Man is not only to worship God, but to imitate Him. By his deeds he must reveal the Divine that is implanted in him; and make manifest, by the purity and righteousness of his actions, that he is of God. Mortal man cannot imitate God's infinite majesty or His eternity; but he *can* strive towards a purity that is Divine, by keeping aloof from everything loathsome and defiling (XI, 44); and especially can he imitate God's merciful qualities. This 'imitation of God' is held forth by the Rabbis as the highest human ideal. 'Be like God; as He is merciful and gracious, so be thou merciful and gracious. Scripture commands, *Walk ye after the* LORD *your God*. But the LORD is a consuming fire; how can men walk after Him? But the meaning is, by being as He is—merciful, loving, long-suffering. Mark how, on the first page of the Torah, God clothed the naked—Adam; and on the last, He buried the dead—Moses. He heals the sick, frees the captives, does good even to His enemies, and is merciful both to the living and the dead' (Talmud). These merciful qualities, therefore, are real links between God and man; and man is never nearer the Divine than in his compassionate moments. Dr. Schechter has pointed out that the Imitation of God is confined by the Rabbis to His attributes of mercy and graciousness. 'The whole Rabbinic literature might be searched in vain for a single instance of the sterner Biblical attributes of God being set up as a model for a man to copy' (Abrahams).

Holiness is thus not so much an abstract or a mystic idea, as a regulative principle in the everyday lives of men and women. The words, 'ye shall be holy,' are the keynote of the *whole* chapter, and must be read in connection with its various precepts; reverence for parents, consideration for the needy, prompt wages for reasonable hours, honourable dealing, no talebearing or malice, love of one's neighbour and

## LEVITICUS XIX, 3

holy. 3. Ye shall fear every man his mother, and his father, and ye shall keep My sabbaths: I am the LORD your God. 4. Turn ye not unto the idols, nor make to yourselves molten gods: I am the LORD your God. ¶ 5. And when ye offer a sacrifice of peace-offerings unto the LORD, ye shall offer it that ye may be accepted. 6. It shall be eaten the same day ye offer it, and on the morrow; and if aught remain until the third day, it shall be burnt with

ויקרא קדשים יט

יִשְׂרָאֵל וְאָמַרְתָּ אֲלֵהֶם קְדֹשִׁים תִּהְיוּ כִּי קָדוֹשׁ אֲנִי יְהֹוָה
3 אֱלֹהֵיכֶם: אִישׁ אִמּוֹ וְאָבִיו תִּירָאוּ וְאֶת־שַׁבְּתֹתַי תִּשְׁמֹרוּ
4 אֲנִי יְהֹוָה אֱלֹהֵיכֶם: אַל־תִּפְנוּ אֶל־הָאֱלִילִם וֵאלֹהֵי מַסֵּכָה
5 לֹא תַעֲשׂוּ לָכֶם אֲנִי יְהֹוָה אֱלֹהֵיכֶם: וְכִי תִזְבְּחוּ זֶבַח
6 שְׁלָמִים לַיהֹוָה לִרְצֹנְכֶם תִּזְבָּחֻהוּ: בְּיוֹם זִבְחֲכֶם יֵאָכֵל

cordiality to the alien, equal justice to rich and poor, just measures and balances—together with abhorrence of everything unclean, irrational, or heathen. Holiness is thus attained not by flight from the world, nor by monk-like renunciation of human relationships of family or station, but by the spirit in which we fulfil the obligations of life in its simplest and commonest details: in this way—by doing justly, loving mercy, and walking humbly with our God—is everyday life transfigured. See also p. 315.

### 3–4. FUNDAMENTAL MORAL LAWS

**3.** *ye shall fear . . . his father.* The first precept stressed is reverence for parents. Neglect of filial duty vitiates a man's whole attitude to life, and places the ideal of holiness out of his reach; see p. 298. 'If we have failed in our duty towards our parents, we are not likely to succeed in our relations towards others' (Foerster).

*fear . . . his mother.* lit 'stand in awe of . . . his mother'. In the Decalogue the father is mentioned before the mother, and the word used is *honour* instead of *fear*. The Rabbis suggest the following reason for the difference: the father is the parent who disciplines the child; the mother is richer in manifestations of affection and kindliness. The child would consequently have 'love' for the mother, but 'stand in awe' before the father. Therefore, the Torah insists on the child showing love and reverence to both. The term 'fear' in this verse is that used in reference to God. 'Dear to God is the honouring of father and mother, for Scripture employs the same expressions about honouring and revering parents as about honouring and revering Himself' (Talmud). For the child, his father and mother are more than ordinary mortals; and, in fact, the Fifth Commandment is in the Decalogue the connecting link between our duties towards God and our fellowmen. Many are the beautiful sayings in Rabbinical literature in regard to this Commandment, but none more beautiful than the story of Dama. Dama, a heathen dealer in jewels in Ascalon, had a stone such as was required to replace one of the precious stones in the High Priest's breastplate. A deputation from Jerusalem came to him to negotiate for its purchase; and he agreed to sell it for one hundred *dinars*, but when he went into an inner room to fetch the stone, he found that his father was asleep in that room. Dama came back, and said he could not after all sell the stone. The deputation offered two hundred dinars, three hundred, a thousand dinars—but in vain. Soon after, his father having waked, Dama ran after the Temple emissaries with the jewel; but he refused to take more than the original one hundred dinars of the first offer. 'I will not make any profit from the honour which I paid to my father,' he said. Filial reverence, the Rabbis held, was a dictate of Natural Religion, and therefore of universal application; and it is characteristic of their broad humanity that they selected the action of a contemporary heathen as a perfect example of filial piety.

*ye shall keep My sabbaths.* The connection of these two precepts is significant. Even as honouring of parents stands foremost among human duties, the sanctification of the Sabbath is the first step towards holiness in man's spiritual life. For the Sabbath is not only a day of cessation from work, but the weekly opportunity for communal worship and spiritual growth; see p. 297. These two commands are placed side by side in order to teach that the fear of parents must not exceed the fear of God. Should they demand anything that contravenes God's law, then the child must place his duty to God before that to his parents (Talmud).

*I am the LORD your God.* This phrase (often in the shorter form, *I am the LORD*) occurs sixteen times in this Chapter. It is the Divine seal set to the enactments of the law. It 'points to God at once as the Holy One and as the Judge; it is meant both to encourage and to awe; both to exhort to vigilance and to menace with punishment' (Kalisch).

**4.** *idols.* lit 'things of nought, non-entities'; *i.e.* things that have no real existence; see Jer. XIV, 14.

### 5–8. RITUAL LAWS

**5.** *when ye offer.* Or 'if ye offer'. See III, 1 and VII, 15–20. Note that the form used is not the imperative—'ye shall offer'; sacrifices are voluntary (Kimchi). The main concern of Scripture seems to be not so much *that* a sacrifice shall be brought, as, if brought, *how* it shall be brought; *i.e.* that it be offered in strict accordance with the regulations prescribed for avoiding heathen associations.

# LEVITICUS XIX, 7

ויקרא קדשים יט

7 וְאִם הֵאָכֹל יֵאָכֵל בַּיּוֹם הַשְּׁלִישִׁי פִּגּוּל הוּא לֹא יֵרָצֶה: 8 וְאֹכְלָיו עֲוֺנוֹ יִשָּׂא כִּי־אֶת־קֹדֶשׁ יְהֹוָה חִלֵּל וְנִכְרְתָה הַנֶּפֶשׁ הַהִוא מֵעַמֶּיהָ: 9 וּבְקֻצְרְכֶם אֶת־קְצִיר אַרְצְכֶם לֹא תְכַלֶּה פְּאַת שָׂדְךָ לִקְצֹר וְלֶקֶט קְצִירְךָ לֹא תְלַקֵּט: 10 וְכַרְמְךָ לֹא תְעוֹלֵל וּפֶרֶט כַּרְמְךָ לֹא תְלַקֵּט לֶעָנִי וְלַגֵּר תַּעֲזֹב אֹתָם אֲנִי יְהֹוָה

fire. 7. And if it be eaten at all on the third day, it is a vile thing; it shall not be accepted. 8. But every one that eateth it shall bear his iniquity, because he hath profaned the holy thing of the LORD; and that soul shall be cut off from his people. ¶ 9. And when ye reap the harvest of your land, thou shalt not wholly reap the corner of thy field, neither shalt thou gather the gleaning of thy harvest. 10. And thou shalt not glean thy vineyard, neither shalt thou gather the fallen fruit of thy vineyard; thou shalt leave them for the poor and for the

### 9-10. CONSIDERATION FOR THE POOR

**9. corner of thy field.** What is here commanded is a statutory charge on one's harvest, to which the English poor rate is analogous. It does not exclude private and voluntary assistance, according to the generous impulse of the giver.

Consideration for the poor distinguishes the Mosaic Law from all other ancient legislations, such as the Roman Law. The object of the latter seems to be primarily to safeguard the rights of the possessing classes. In the Torah, the poor man is a *brother*, and when in need he is to be relieved ungrudgingly not only with an open hand but with an open heart. In his noble self-defence, Job (XXXI, 17-20) protests:

Never have I eaten my morsel alone,
Without sharing it with the fatherless;
Never saw I any perish for want of clothing
But I warmed him with fleece from my lambs,
And his loins gave me their blessing.

The Rabbis continued this doctrine, and declared pity to be a distinguishing trait of the Jewish character. If a Jew—they held—shows himself lacking in consideration for a fellowman in distress or suffering, we may well doubt the purity of his Jewish descent. 'There is no ethical quality more characteristic of Rabbinic Judaism than Rachmonuth—pity. The beggar whose point of view is that you are to thank him for allowing him to give you the opportunity for showing Rachmonuth, is a characteristically Jewish figure' (Montefiore).

**gleaning.** The ears of corn which fall to the ground at the time of reaping.

### 11-16. DUTIES TOWARDS OUR FELLOWMEN

These precepts restate the fundamental rules of life in human society that are contained in the Second Table of the Decalogue. These moral principles were expanded by the Rabbis and applied to every phase of civil and criminal law.

**11.** *ye shall not steal.* 'Even as a practical joke; or, in order to enable another to profit by the four- or five-fold restitution which thou shalt have to make; or, to reclaim by stealth thine own stolen property, lest thou seem a thief' (Sifra). Everything that has the appearance of stealing is strictly forbidden, lest a man become habituated to the act of stealing (Shulchan Aruch). Especially reprehensible is 'stealing the good opinion of others' (גניבת דעת)—by any manner of misrepresentation, 'publicity,' or flattery deceiving others into having a better opinion of him or his doings than he deserves. ראשון שבגנבים גונב דעת הבריות (Mechilta, Mishpatim). 'Let a man earn the good opinion of his fellowmen, but let him not steal it' (S. R. Hirsch). A classical example is afforded by Absalom's manner of ingratiating himself with all who felt discontent at 'the law's delay', suggesting that if *he* were king, things would be very different. 'And Absalom used to rise up early, and stand beside the way of the gate: and it was so, that when any man had a suit which should come to the king for judgment, then Absalom called unto him and said, . . . See, thy matters are good and right; but there is no man deputed of the king to hear thee. Absalom said moreover, Oh that I were made judge in the land, that every man which hath any suit or cause might come unto me, and I would do him justice! . . . So Absalom *stole the hearts* of the men of Israel' (II Sam. xv, 2-6).

**deal falsely.** lit. 'falsely deny'.

**nor lie.** 'Let your Yes be righteous, and your No be righteous. He who exacted retribution from the generation of the Flood will exact it of the man who does not stand by his word. Truth is one of the pillars of the Universe; it is God's own seal. The liar is an outcast from the Divine fellowship. Men too punish him, for he is not believed even when he speaks the truth. The good man is he who is what he seems' (Talmud). The truth, however, must be spoken *in love*. Truthfulness must be moral: it ceases to be truthfulness and becomes an abominable form of lying when it is used as a tool of revenge or malice in order to ruin another or for putting him to open shame.

'A truth that's told with bad intent
Beats all the lies you can invent' (Blake).

# LEVITICUS XIX, 11

stranger: I am the LORD your God. 11. Ye shall not steal; neither shall ye deal falsely, nor lie one to another. 12. And ye shall not swear by My name falsely, so that thou profane the name of thy God: I am the LORD. 13. Thou shalt not oppress thy neighbour, nor rob him; the wages of a hired servant shall not abide with thee all night until the morning. 14. Thou shalt not curse the deaf, nor put a stumbling-block before the blind, but thou shalt fear thy God: I am the LORD.*ˡˡ⁽**ᵛ⁾. 15. Ye shall do no unrighteousness in judgment; thou shalt not respect the person of the poor,

---

**12.** *and ye shall not swear.* *And* indicates that the verse is to be closely associated with the preceding one. 'If thou hast stolen, thou wilt end by falsely denying, lying, and swearing by My Name to a falsehood' (Sifra)—profaning the Name of God for the purpose of deceit and fraud.

**13.** *oppress.* 'Defraud' (Moffatt). In Deut. XXIV, 14, 'a hired servant' is substituted for 'thy neighbour'. 'Oppressing' a hired servant means taking advantage of his helplessness and paying him less than his due for his work.

*rob him.* By withholding from him that which is his.

*abide with thee.* If the labourer is hired by the day, his wages must be paid to him immediately after the day's work is done. The poor man lives from hand to mouth.

**14.** *curse the deaf.* Defame the deaf, or anyone who cannot hear, and so cannot vindicate his own character.

*nor put a stumbling-block before the blind.* 'Trip up a blind man' (Moffatt), either in sport or malice. Alas for the prevalence of human callousness and cruelty that render the formulation of such a precept necessary.

'Deaf' and 'blind' are typical figures of all misfortune, inexperience, and moral weakness. This verse is a warning against leading the young and morally weak into sin, or provoking them to commit irretrievable mistakes. The following are typical violations of this ethical precept: he who gives disingenuous advice to the inexperienced; he who tempts the Nazirite to break his oath not to drink wine; he who sells lethal weapons to weak or dangerous characters—all these transgress the command 'Thou shalt not put a stumbling-block before the blind'. Equally so does the man who administers corporal punishment to a grown-up son: it may make that son forgetful of filial duty, and in blind anger commit an unpardonable offence (Talmud).

*fear thy God.* Who is the avenger of the helpless; of the deaf or absent man who cannot protect himself from the reviling which he has not heard; of the 'blind' man who cannot avoid the stumbling-block of which he is not aware.

Furthermore, the man who deliberately gives harmful advice may allege the noblest of intentions. But Scripture exhorts him to 'fear God', who searches the innermost recesses of the human heart and knows its secret thoughts. See the note on Exod. I, 17, showing that *fearing God* means natural piety and fundamental humanity.

**15.** *respect the person of the poor.* 'You shall not be partial to a poor man' (Moffatt). With all its sympathy for the poor and helpless, the Torah fears that justice might be outraged in favour of the poor man when he is in the wrong. Even sympathy and compassion must be silenced in the presence of Justice. In this Scriptural command, as in Exod. XXIII, 3 (Thou shalt not favour a poor man in his cause) 'there is a sublimity of moral view, which compels the reverence of all' (Geiger).

*nor favour.* The judge must not say, 'This man is rich and well connected; how can I put him to shame by deciding against him?' (Sifra).

*in righteousness.* There is to be neither prejudice in favour of the poor, nor dread of offending the great, but *justice;* see on Exod. XXIII, 3. Thus, one of the litigants is not to be permitted to state his case at length, and the other bidden 'to cut it short'. One litigant must not be allowed to be seated in court, and the other kept standing (Sifra). 'The judge should feel as though a sword were suspended above his head throughout the time he sits in judgment' (Talmud).

Another authoritative explanation of *in righteousness shalt thou judge thy neighbour* is, 'Judge every man in the scale of merit (לכף זכות); refuse to condemn by appearances, but put the best construction on the deeds of your fellowmen' (Talmud).

The teaching of this and the preceding verses is thus restated by the Prophet: 'Speak ye every man the truth with his neighbour; execute the judgment of truth and peace in your gates; and let none of you devise evil in your hearts against his neighbour; and love no false oath; for all these are things that I hate, saith the LORD' (Zech. VIII, 16, 17).

LEVITICUS XIX, 16     ויקרא קדשים יט

16 בְּצֶ֥דֶק תִּשְׁפֹּ֖ט עֲמִיתֶֽךָ׃ לֹא־תֵלֵ֤ךְ רָכִיל֙ בְּעַמֶּ֔יךָ לֹ֥א תַעֲמֹ֖ד
17 עַל־דַּ֣ם רֵעֶ֑ךָ אֲנִ֖י יְהוָֽה׃ לֹֽא־תִשְׂנָ֥א אֶת־אָחִ֖יךָ בִּלְבָבֶ֑ךָ
18 הוֹכֵ֤חַ תּוֹכִ֙יחַ֙ אֶת־עֲמִיתֶ֔ךָ וְלֹא־תִשָּׂ֥א עָלָ֖יו חֵֽטְא׃ לֹֽא־
תִקֹּ֤ם וְלֹֽא־תִטֹּר֙ אֶת־בְּנֵ֣י עַמֶּ֔ךָ וְאָֽהַבְתָּ֥ לְרֵעֲךָ֖ כָּמ֑וֹךָ אֲנִ֖י

nor favour the person of the mighty; but in righteousness shalt thou judge thy neighbour. 16. Thou shalt not go up and down as a talebearer among thy people; neither shalt thou stand idly by the blood of thy neighbour: I am the LORD. 17. Thou shalt not hate thy brother in thy heart; thou shalt surely rebuke thy neighbour, and not bear sin because of him. 18.

**16.** *go up and down as a talebearer.* lit. 'go up and down as a pedlar'. This expressive idiom is here applied to a person who travels about dealing in scandal and malicious hearsay, getting the secrets of people and *retailing* them wherever he goes (Rashi). A mischievous business, even if the report is true and told without malice (Maimonides). 'A more despicable character exists not; such a person is a pest to society, and should be exiled from the habitation of men' (Adam Clarke). Injurious gossip may often do as much harm as slanderous defamation. Hence the prayer, three times daily, 'O my God, guard my tongue from evil and my lips from speaking guile' (Authorised Prayer Book, p. 54). The slanderer, the man of the evil tongue (לשון הרע), the calumniator, is worse than a murderer, since he destroys a man's reputation, which is more precious than his life (Talmud). Hence the informer (*moser*) was deemed the most abandoned creature among all evil-doers to their kind.

*Stand idly by the blood of thy neighbour.* i.e. when his life is in danger. Do not stand idly by, watching with indifference thy fellowman in mortal danger through drowning, or attacked by wild animals, or robbers, without hastening to his rescue (Talmud). In protecting the life of another, it is permitted to take the life of the assailant, even as in self-defence. The Sifra gives a further application to this verse: if thy fellowman is accused of a crime, and evidence that would clear him of it is in thy possession, thou art not at liberty to keep silent.

17–18. PROHIBITION OF HATRED AND VENGEANCE: LOVE OF NEIGHBOUR

**17.** *hate thy brother in thine heart.* Nursing your grievance against your fellowman. Most of the hating in the world is quite unjustified, groundless hating for its own sake (שנאת חנם). 'Thou shalt not hate thy brother *in thine heart.* Our Rabbis taught that if Scripture had merely said, "Thou shalt not hate thy brother," this precept might be explained to mean only that you must not injure him, nor insult him, nor vex him; and so the words "in thine heart" are added to forbid us even to feel hatred in our heart without giving it outward expression. Causeless hatred ranks with the three cardinal sins: Idolatry, Immorality, and Murder. The Second Temple, although in its time study of the Law and good works flourished and God's commandments were obeyed, was destroyed because of causeless hatred' (Achai Gaon). When it is fed by racial rivalry or religious bigotry, causeless hatred petrifies the heart and becomes organized malice. None has suffered, and is still suffering, from causeless hatred more than the Jewish People. The Talmud instances the Emperor Hadrian's conduct as typical of men swayed by such hatred. One day on Hadrian's journey in the East, a Jew passed the Imperial train and saluted the Emperor. Hadrian was beside himself with rage. 'You, a Jew, dare to greet the Emperor! You shall pay for this with your life.' In the course of the same day, another Jew passed him, and, warned by example, he did not greet Hadrian. 'You, a Jew, dare to pass the Emperor without a greeting,' he angrily exclaimed. 'You have forfeited your life.' To his astonished courtiers he replied: 'I hate the Jews. Whatever they do, I find intolerable. I therefore make use of any pretext to destroy them.' So are all anti-Semites; so are all slaves of 'causeless hatred'.

*rebuke thy neighbour.* A precept extremely difficult of fulfilment; it is as difficult to administer reproof with delicacy and tact, as it is to receive reproof. Reproof must, of course, be offered in all kindness, otherwise it fails of its purpose; and if it entails putting a man to shame in public, it is mortal sin. No matter how much learning and good works the man who commits such a sin may possess, he has no share in the world to come—says a great Mishnah teacher.

*sin because of him.* Unless there is a frank statement from the aggrieved party, the hatred or dislike smouldering in his heart may lead him into sin.

**18.** *thou shalt not take vengeance.* Forbids repaying evil with evil. 'If a man finds both a friend and an enemy in distress, he should first assist his enemy, in order to subdue his evil inclination,' i.e. man's inborn passion for revenge (Talmud). Scripture inculcates this virtue both by precept and illustrious example. Joseph's conduct to his brethren, and David's to Saul, are among the noblest instances of forgiveness to be found in literature. Such examples are not confined to the Biblical period. Samuel ibn Nagrela was a Spanish-Jewish poet of the eleventh century, who was vizier to the king of Granada. He was one

## LEVITICUS XIX, 19

Thou shalt not take vengeance, nor bear any grudge against the children of thy people, but thou shalt love thy neighbour as thyself: I am the LORD. 19. Ye shall keep My statutes. Thou shalt not let thy cattle gender with a diverse kind; thou shalt not sow thy field with two kinds of seed; neither shall there come upon thee a garment of two kinds of stuff mingled together. 20. And whosoever lieth carnally with a woman, that is a bondmaid, desig-

19 יְהוָֽה׃ אֶת־חֻקֹּתַי֮ תִּשְׁמֹרוּ֒ בְּהֶמְתְּךָ֙ לֹא־תַרְבִּ֣יעַ כִּלְאַ֔יִם שָׂדְךָ֖ לֹא־תִזְרַ֣ע כִּלְאָ֑יִם וּבֶ֧גֶד כִּלְאַ֛יִם שַֽׁעַטְנֵ֖ז לֹ֥א יַעֲלֶ֖ה
20 עָלֶֽיךָ׃ וְ֠אִישׁ כִּֽי־יִשְׁכַּ֨ב אֶת־אִשָּׁ֜ה שִׁכְבַת־זֶ֗רַע וְהִ֤וא שִׁפְחָה֙ נֶחֱרֶ֣פֶת לְאִ֔ישׁ וְהָפְדֵּה֙ לֹ֣א נִפְדָּ֔תָה א֥וֹ חֻפְשָׁ֖ה לֹ֣א נִתַּן־
21 לָ֑הּ בִּקֹּ֧רֶת תִּהְיֶ֛ה לֹ֥א יוּמְת֖וּ כִּי־לֹ֥א חֻפָּֽשָׁה׃ וְהֵבִ֤יא אֶת־

day cursed in the presence of the king, who commanded Samuel to punish the offender by cutting out his tongue. The Jewish vizier, however, treated his enemy kindly, whereupon the curses became blessings. When the king next noticed the offender, he was astonished that Samuel had not carried out his command. Samuel replied, 'I have torn out his angry tongue, and given him instead a kind one.' The Rabbis rightly declare, 'Who is mighty? He who makes his enemy his friend.'

The Jew is not 'a good hater'. Shylock is 'the Jew that Shakespeare drew'. He is not the Jew of real life, even in the Middle Ages, stained as their story is with the hot tears—nay, the very heart's blood—of the martyred race. The medieval Jew did not take vengeance on his cruel foes. The Jews hunted out of Spain in 1492 were in turn cruelly expelled from Portugal. Some took refuge on the African coast. Eighty years later the descendants of the men who had thus inhumanly treated their Jewish fellowmen were defeated in Africa, whither they had been led by their king, Dom Sebastian. Those who were not slain were offered as slaves at Fez to the descendants of the Jewish exiles from Portugal. 'The humbled Portuguese nobles,' the historian narrates, 'were comforted when their purchasers proved to be Jews, for they knew that they had humane hearts' (M. Joseph).

*nor bear any grudge.* Waiting for an opportunity to repay evil with evil. The Rabbis give the following explanation of these two phrases: 'If a man says, I will not lend you the tool you require, because you did not lend it me when I asked for it—that is vengeance. If a man says, I will lend you the tool, although you refused to lend it when I asked for it—that is bearing grudge.' In an ancient Jewish book, that has come down to us probably from Maccabean times, known as *The Testaments of the Twelve Patriarchs*, we read: 'Love ye one another from the heart; and if a man sin against thee, cast forth the poison of hate and speak peaceably to him. If he confess and repent, forgive him. But if he be shameless and persist in his wrongdoing, even so forgive him from the heart, and leave to God the avenging. Beware of hatred; for it works lawlessness even against the Lord Himself. For it will not hear the words of the Commandments concerning the loving of one's neighbour. Love would quicken even the dead, and would call back them that are condemned to die; but hatred would slay the living.' The Rabbis declare, 'He who has a forgiving spirit is himself forgiven. Whosoever does not persecute them that persecute him, whosoever suffers wrong in silence and requites it not, they are deemed the *friends of God*.'

*thou shalt love thy neighbour as thyself.* Heb. ואהבת לרעך כמוך ; *i.e.* let the honour and property of thy fellowman be as dear to thee as thine own. These three Heb. words were early recognized as the most comprehensive rule of conduct, as containing the essence of religion and applicable in every human relation and towards all men. Even the criminal condemned to die, say the Rabbis, has a claim on our brotherly love, and we must spare him unnecessary suffering. Hillel paraphrased this rule into 'Whatever is hateful unto thee do it not unto thy fellow'; and declared it to be the whole Law, the remainder being but a commentary on this fundamental principle of the Torah. See Additional Note 'Thou Shalt Love Thy Neighbour As Thyself', p. 563.

### 19–26. MISCELLANEOUS PRECEPTS

**19.** *statutes.* Laws for which the reason has not been revealed to us. However, the word may here mean as in Jer. XXXIII, 25, fixed laws which God had instituted for the government of the physical universe. The purpose of the following regulations would then be: man must not deviate from the appointed order of things, nor go against the eternal laws of nature as established by Divine Wisdom. What God has ordained to be kept apart, man must not seek to mix together.

*diverse kind.* Josephus suggested as the reason for the prohibition of mixed breeding the fear that such unnatural union in the animal world might lead to moral perversion among human beings.

*two kinds of seed.* See Deut. XXII, 9

*mingled together.* Heb. *shaatnez.* See Deut. XXII, 11, where the law is more explicitly stated: 'mingled stuff, wool and linen.' 'Nature does not rejoice in the union of things that are not in their nature alike' (Josephus).

**20.** *bondmaid.* Here we have an example of 'prohibited mixture in the sphere of moral relationship'—the union with a heathen bondmaid betrothed to a Hebrew slave. The offence is not as serious as in the case of a betrothed

# LEVITICUS XIX, 21 — ויקרא קדשים יט

nated for a man, and not at all redeemed, nor was freedom given her; there shall be inquisition; they shall not be put to death, because she was not free. 21. And he shall bring his forfeit unto the LORD, unto the door of the tent of meeting, even a ram for a guilt-offering. 22. And the priest shall make atonement for him with the ram of the guilt-offering before the LORD for his sin which he hath sinned; and he shall be forgiven for his sin which he hath sinned.*iii. ¶23. And when ye shall come into the land, and shall have planted all manner of trees for food, then ye shall count the fruit thereof as forbidden; three years shall it be as forbidden unto you; it shall not be eaten. 24. And in the fourth year all the fruit thereof shall be holy, for giving praise unto the LORD. 25. But in the fifth year may ye eat of the fruit thereof, that it may yield unto you more richly the increase thereof: I am the LORD your God. 26. Ye shall not eat with the blood; neither shall ye practise divination nor soothsaying. 27. Ye shall not round the corners of your heads, neither shalt thou mar the corners of thy beard. 28. Ye shall not make any cuttings in your flesh for the dead, nor imprint any marks upon you: I am the LORD. 29. Profane not thy daugh-

22 אֲשָׁמוֹ לַיהוָה אֶל־פֶּתַח אֹהֶל מוֹעֵד אֵיל אָשָׁם: וְכִפֶּר
עָלָיו הַכֹּהֵן בְּאֵיל הָאָשָׁם לִפְנֵי יְהוָה עַל־חַטָּאתוֹ אֲשֶׁר
חָטָא וְנִסְלַח לוֹ מֵחַטָּאתוֹ אֲשֶׁר חָטָא: פ שלישי
23 וְכִי־תָבֹאוּ אֶל־הָאָרֶץ וּנְטַעְתֶּם כָּל־עֵץ מַאֲכָל וַעֲרַלְתֶּם
עָרְלָתוֹ אֶת־פִּרְיוֹ שָׁלֹשׁ שָׁנִים יִהְיֶה לָכֶם עֲרֵלִים לֹא יֵאָכֵל:
24 וּבַשָּׁנָה הָרְבִיעִת יִהְיֶה כָּל־פִּרְיוֹ קֹדֶשׁ הִלּוּלִים לַיהוָה:
כה וּבַשָּׁנָה הַחֲמִישִׁת תֹּאכְלוּ אֶת־פִּרְיוֹ לְהוֹסִיף לָכֶם תְּבוּאָתוֹ
26 אֲנִי יְהוָה אֱלֹהֵיכֶם: לֹא תֹאכְלוּ עַל־הַדָּם לֹא תְנַחֲשׁוּ
27 וְלֹא תְעוֹנֵנוּ: לֹא תַקִּפוּ פְּאַת רֹאשְׁכֶם וְלֹא תַשְׁחִית אֶת
28 פְּאַת זְקָנֶךָ: וְשֶׂרֶט לָנֶפֶשׁ לֹא תִתְּנוּ בִּבְשַׂרְכֶם וּכְתֹבֶת
29 קַעֲקַע לֹא תִתְּנוּ בָּכֶם אֲנִי יְהוָה: אַל־תְּחַלֵּל אֶת־בִּתְּךָ
ל לְהַזְנוֹתָהּ וְלֹא־תִזְנֶה הָאָרֶץ וּמָלְאָה הָאָרֶץ זִמָּה: אֶרֶת־

freewoman; nevertheless, the act is branded as immoral and one to be punished.

*There shall be inquisition.* Better, 'there shall be a lashing,' or corporal punishment. The Heb. בקרת means a lash made of ox-hide (Ibn Ezra).

**23.** *forbidden.* lit. you shall regard its fruit as defective. The fruit tree in its first three years is to be regarded as a male infant during his first eight days; *i.e.* as unconsecrated (Dillmann). Its fruit was then stunted in its growth and unfit as a first-fruit offering to God; and hence forbidden for human use.

**25.** *more richly.* The trees become more productive if they are stripped of the blossoms in the early years.

**26-31. PROHIBITION OF CANAANITE CUSTOMS**

The context suggests that the allusion is to a heathenish rite of divination, well-known to the Israelites.

**26.** *with the blood.* 'They killed a beast, received the blood in a vessel or pot, and ate of the flesh of that beast, whilst sitting round the blood. They imagined that in this manner, the spirits would come to partake of the blood which was their food; brotherhood and friendship would be established with the spirits' (Maimonides). It is, however, taken by the Rabbis both in a literal sense ('do not eat flesh from an animal whose blood is yet in it', *i.e.* whose life has not yet departed), and as an ethical injunction ('the members of a Court whose decree of capital punishment has been carried out shall on that day abstain from all food').

*divination.* Charms and incantations. Ancient life, whether in Egypt, Canaan, or Mesopotamia, was crushed under an intolerable weight of enchantment, magic, and demonology. The Israelite was freed from the incubus of superstition by these prohibitions, which constitute one of the great negations of Judaism; cf. Num. XXIII, 23.

*soothsaying.* Or, 'divination' by observing times and seasons and declaring one day 'lucky' and another 'unlucky'—a common practice among heathens.

**27.** *round the corners.* In this and the following verse, various mourning customs connected with the heathen worship of the dead are forbidden, as unbecoming the dignity of God's people and incompatible with loyalty to a God of holiness.

**28.** *cuttings . . . for the dead.* See on Deut. XIV, 1. Eastern peoples, in their excessive demonstration of grief at a bereavement, often gashed and mutilated themselves. The shedding of blood was also believed to have a sacrificial value for the dead person. Even apart from the prohibition of this idolatrous practice, the Torah inculcates reverence for the human body, as the work of God.

*imprint any marks.* By means of writing that sinks into the flesh. What is here forbidden is the custom of tattooing some part of the body. Often this was a representation of the deity worshipped by the bearer of that mark.

503

# LEVITICUS XIX, 30 ויקרא קדשים יט

31 שַׁבְּתֹתַי תִּשְׁמֹרוּ וּמִקְדָּשִׁי תִּירָאוּ אֲנִי יְהוָֹה: אַל־תִּפְנוּ
אֶל־הָאֹבֹת וְאֶל־הַיִּדְּעֹנִים אַל־תְּבַקְשׁוּ לְטָמְאָה בָהֶם אֲנִי
32 יְהוָֹה אֱלֹהֵיכֶם: מִפְּנֵי שֵׂיבָה תָּקוּם וְהָדַרְתָּ פְּנֵי זָקֵן וְיָרֵאתָ
33 מֵאֱלֹהֶיךָ אֲנִי יְהוָֹה: ס וְכִי־יָגוּר אִתְּךָ גֵּר בְּאַרְצְכֶם לֹא
34 תוֹנוּ אֹתוֹ: כְּאֶזְרָח מִכֶּם יִהְיֶה לָכֶם הַגֵּר הַגָּר אִתְּכֶם
וְאָהַבְתָּ לוֹ כָּמוֹךָ כִּי־גֵרִים הֱיִיתֶם בְּאֶרֶץ מִצְרָיִם אֲנִי יְהוָֹה

ter, to make her a harlot, lest the land fall into harlotry, and the land become full of lewdness. 30. Ye shall keep My sabbaths, and reverence My sanctuary: I am the LORD. 31. Turn ye not unto the ghosts, nor unto familiar spirits; seek them not out, to be defiled by them: I am the LORD your God. 32. Thou shalt rise up before the hoary head, and honour the face of the old man, and thou shalt fear thy God: I am the LORD.*iv(**vi). 33. And if a stranger sojourn with thee in your land, ye shall not do him wrong. 34. The stranger that sojourneth with you shall be unto you as the home-

---

**29.** *profane not thy daughter.* A prohibition for a father to hand over his daughter to a man without the previous rites of 'sanctification'—i.e. without a legal marriage; as well as prohibition for a woman of her own free will to consort with a man without such legal marriage (Sifra). The use of the word *profane* is noteworthy. It presupposes the sacredness of womanhood; and it brands such an action as a profanation and a desecration of the sacred personality of a human being.

*the land.* i.e. its inhabitants, as in XVIII, 25.

*fall into harlotry.* Looking upon the 'demand' for harlotry as a normal condition of things, and tolerating the consequent 'supply' of human beings for such life of shame.

**30.** *sabbaths ... sanctuary.* The parenthetical insertion of this injunction may be intended to impress upon the Israelite that reverence for Sabbath and Sanctuary will keep him from the heathenish rites and immoralities mentioned in the preceding verses and that following.

**31.** *familiar spirits.* The English word 'familiar' here means 'attendant'. The wizard professes to know through the spirit attendant upon him, or residing within him, what is hidden from the ordinary person.

*to be defiled.* Physically, by coming into contact with the dead bones which were part of the paraphernalia of the wizard; and spiritually, by sinking into the mire of superstition inseparable from witchcraft and necromancy; see on xx, 6.

### 32–37. ETHICAL INJUNCTIONS

**32.** *rise up before the hoary head.* 'Hoary,' white with age. The ethical sublimity of this exhortation is not diminished by the fact that parallels exist among other ancient peoples, and that in the Orient reverence for old age is or was the rule until the present day.

*honour the face of the old man.* 'Honour the person of an old man' (Moffatt). The Rabbis enlarged the connotation of the word 'old' and made it include anyone who had acquired wisdom (זקן, זה שקנה חכמה). But even where there is no book-learning, there may be the matured wisdom of experience. A famous rabbi would stand up even before an aged heathen peasant, saying, 'What storms of fortune has this old man weathered in his life-time.'

*thou shalt fear.* Cf. on *v.* 14. Here, too, the inner motives of a man are involved, not only his outward acts.

**33.** *a stranger.* The duty of loving the stranger is stressed thirty-six times in Scripture and is placed on the same level as the duty of kindness to, and protection of, the widow and the orphan. 'The alien was to be protected, although he was not a member of one's family, clan, religious community, or people; simply *because he was a human being.* In the alien, therefore, man discovered the idea of humanity' (Hermann Cohen). See the comments on Exod. XXII, 20.

*not do him wrong.* Heb. לא תונו. Not only oppression by unrighteous deeds, such as taking advantage of his ignorance to overreach him. The Rabbis take the word in sense of 'offend', and they emphasize the peculiar heinousness of wounding the alien's feelings by insulting speech (אונאת דברים). Few modern peoples, alas, can truthfully be said to have learned this ethical precept.

**34.** *as the home-born.* There was to be one law only, the same for home-born and alien alike (XXIV, 22; Num. xv, 16); see p. 260. The stranger is to share in the corners of the field, the forgotten sheaf, and every form of poor relief. The tremendous seriousness with which justice to the stranger is inculcated is seen from the fact that, among the covenant admonitions at Mount Ebal, we read 'Cursed be he that perverteth the justice due to the stranger' (Deut. XXVII, 19). Israel was not permitted to hate even the Egyptian, the people that enslaved him. It was to transform those memories of bitter oppression into feelings of compassion to all the friendless and downtrodden. In other ancient codes, the stranger was

# LEVITICUS XIX, 35

born among you, and thou shalt love him as thyself; for ye were strangers in the land of Egypt: I am the LORD your God. 35. Ye shall do no unrighteousness in judgment, in meteyard, in weight, or in measure. 36. Just balances, just weights, a just ephah, and a just hin, shall ye have: I am the LORD your God, who brought you out of the land of Egypt. 37. And ye shall observe all My statutes, and all Mine ordinances, and do them: I am the LORD.*v.

## CHAPTER XX

1. And the LORD spoke unto Moses, saying: 2. Moreover, thou shalt say to the children of Israel: ¶ Whosoever he be of the children of Israel, or of the strangers that sojourn in Israel, that giveth of his seed unto Molech; he shall surely be put to death; the people of the land shall stone him with stones. 3. I also will set My face against that man, and will cut him off from among his people, because he hath given of his seed unto Molech, to defile My sanctuary.

---

rightless. Thus, the Romans had originally one word, 'hostis' for both stranger and enemy. According to Germanic Law the stranger was 'rechtsunfähig'. See on XXIV, 22.

*thou shalt love him as thyself.* Do to him what you would wish others to do unto you, if you were a stranger in a strange land. See Additional Note, 'Thou Shalt Love Thy Neighbour As Thyself,' p. 563.

**35.** *in judgment.* Not an unnecessary repetition of the same phrase in v. 15. God abhors unrighteousness, *i.e.* dishonesty, in business. 'For all that do such things are an abomination unto the LORD' (Deut. xxv, 16).

**36.** *ephah.* The standard dry measure; somewhat larger than a bushel.

*hin.* A measure for liquids; a sixth of the ephah, about 1¼–1½ gallons.

*brought you out.* God had delivered the Israelites from a land where they had suffered from injustice; let them not practise injustice in their dealings with one another.

**37.** *I am the LORD.* Thus this remarkable series of precepts ends on the exalted note with which it opened; v. 2.

### CHAPTER XX. PENALTIES FOR UNLAWFUL MARRIAGES, MOLECH WORSHIP AND NECROMANCY

This chapter is a natural pendant to XVIII and XIX, and enumerates the acts that would debase Israel's life, and altogether destroy its ideal of Holiness. In an organized society, it is essential to institute penalties for the violation of enactments that are vital to its existence. Ruthless measures were indispensable against the abominable vices and hideous practices which Israel was in danger of transplanting into its own life from its Canaanite and Egyptian neighbours. Flaming jealousy for Israel's mission of Holiness, and gigantic energy on the part of its ethical guides and religious teachers, could alone have overcome the bestialities of heathendom.

Unsparing condemnation of the crimes did not, however, invariably lead to the unsparing punishment of everyone suspected of them. In Jewish Law, the presumption of innocence is given to the accused, and capital punishment requires two eye-witnesses to the *premeditated* commission of the crime. This alone rendered actual conviction in such cases a rare thing.

### 1–5. PENALTIES FOR MOLECH WORSHIP

**2.** *strangers.* Such horrors should not be permitted even to resident strangers on any false idea of toleration, or on the ground that it was no concern of the community what 'aliens' did.

*Molech.* See on XVIII, 21.

*people of the land.* Heb. *am ha-aretz.* Here again it is better to translate, *the National Council; i.e.* the national representatives, acting on behalf of the nation, shall stamp out this hideous idolatry.

*stone him.* Stoning goes back to hoary Semitic antiquity, and was prescribed for crimes that demanded punishments with a deterrent effect upon the people. In later ages, the original method was modified to render it more humane. The Talmud tells that, in capital offences, delinquents were drugged in order to deaden the senses before execution.

**3.** *set My face.* See XVII, 10.

*will cut him off.* This verse refers to the case of a man who performs the atrocity in private, so

LEVITICUS XX, 4

and to profane My holy name. 4. And if the people of the land do at all hide their eyes from that man, when he giveth of his seed unto Molech, and put him not to death; 5. then I will set My face against that man, and against his family, and will cut him off, and all that go astray after him, to go astray after Molech, from among their people. 6. And the soul that turneth unto the ghosts, and unto the familiar spirits, to go astray after them, I will even set My face against that soul, and will cut him off from among his people. 7. Sanctify yourselves therefore, and be ye holy; for I am the LORD your God.*vi(**vii). 8. And keep ye My statutes, and do them: I am the LORD who sanctify you. 9. For whatsoever man there be that curseth his father or his mother shall surely be put to death; he hath cursed his father or his mother; his blood shall be upon him. 10. And the man that committeth adultery

כִּי מִזַּרְעוֹ נָתַן לַמֹּלֶךְ לְמַעַן טַמֵּא אֶת־מִקְדָּשִׁי וּלְחַלֵּל אֶת־
שֵׁם קָדְשִׁי: וְאִם הַעְלֵם יַעְלִימוּ עַם הָאָרֶץ אֶת־עֵינֵיהֶם 4
מִן־הָאִישׁ הַהוּא בְּתִתּוֹ מִזַּרְעוֹ לַמֹּלֶךְ לְבִלְתִּי הָמִית אֹתוֹ:
וְשַׂמְתִּי אֲנִי אֶת־פָּנַי בָּאִישׁ הַהוּא וּבְמִשְׁפַּחְתּוֹ וְהִכְרַתִּי 5
אֹתוֹ וְאֵת ׀ כָּל־הַזֹּנִים אַחֲרָיו לִזְנוֹת אַחֲרֵי הַמֹּלֶךְ מִקֶּרֶב
עַמָּם: וְהַנֶּפֶשׁ אֲשֶׁר תִּפְנֶה אֶל־הָאֹבֹת וְאֶל־הַיִּדְּעֹנִים 6
לִזְנוֹת אַחֲרֵיהֶם וְנָתַתִּי אֶת־פָּנַי בַּנֶּפֶשׁ הַהִוא וְהִכְרַתִּי אֹתוֹ
מִקֶּרֶב עַמּוֹ: וְהִתְקַדִּשְׁתֶּם וִהְיִיתֶם קְדֹשִׁים כִּי אֲנִי יְהֹוָה 7
אֱלֹהֵיכֶם: וּשְׁמַרְתֶּם אֶת־חֻקֹּתַי וַעֲשִׂיתֶם אֹתָם אֲנִי יְהֹוָה 8
מְקַדִּשְׁכֶם: כִּי־אִישׁ אִישׁ אֲשֶׁר יְקַלֵּל אֶת־אָבִיו וְאֶת־אִמּוֹ 9

ששי (שביעי כשהן מחוברות)

that there are no witnesses of the act. In that event, God will Himself punish the evil-doer.

*to defile My sanctuary.* 'The community of Israel which is sanctified to God' (Rashi); or the soil would be defiled by such an enormity (XVIII, 27), and the defilement conveyed to the Sanctuary established upon it.

*to profane My holy name.* See XVIII, 21.

**4.** *hide their eyes. i.e.* overlook it. For such an offence to be connived at and condoned by the authorities and nation is evidence of both religious demoralization and social decay. It furthermore proves that they too are on the threshold of succumbing to Molech worship (Strack).

**5.** *his family. i.e.* his sympathizers or accomplices. Ibn Ezra quotes an explanation which refers 'his family' to *am ha-aretz* in the preceding verse. They hide their eyes from his crime because they are of his family. Targum Jonathan renders this verse: 'And I shall choose My own time to attend to that man and to the members of the family who take him under their protection, and shall chasten them with painful trials; but the man himself I shall destroy.'

**6.** *familiar spirits.* See on XIX, 31. The punishment is left in the hands of God; but as for the necromancer himself, the penalty is death by stoning (*v.* 27 below), since to cause others to sin is worse than sinning. Here, too, ruthlessness—social surgery—was required, if true and ethical religion was not to perish from the earth. 'Not to realize the vital necessity of these laws concerning witchcraft and the vital duty of its extirpation, is to fall a victim to the superstition that witchcraft was mere harmless make-believe

that did not call for any drastic punishment. At the bottom of this sceptical attitude towards the laws of witchcraft is indifference towards the unique value of monotheism. In a conflict of this nature—witchcraft *versus* monotheism—there can be no hesitancy or mutual tolerance of opposite points of view. It is a question of To be or not to be for the ethical life' (Hermann Cohen).

7-21. LAWS BEARING ON IMMORALITY

**7.** *sanctify yourselves.* This and the following verses are introductory to the laws which follow. The first section deals with idolatry and heathenish superstition. The motive that should guide the life of the Israelite and restrain him from wrong actions is solemnly repeated; cf. XI, 44.

**8.** *sanctify you.* By electing you from all the nations to be My people, and by giving you laws and institutions designed to lead to a holy life. Before the performance of any religious precept, the Israelite repeats the Blessing: 'Blessed art thou, O Lord our God, King of the universe, who hast *sanctified* us by thy commandments and hast commanded us . . .'

**9.** *curseth.* See Exod. XXI, 15, 17; Prov. XX, 20 ('Whoso curseth his father or his mother, his lamp shall be put out in the blackest darkness'). It was a capital offence; but the Rabbis, though they shared the horror with which the moral hideousness of such an action was viewed, endeavoured in various ways to render the carrying out of the penalty as rare as possible.

*his blood shall be upon him. i.e.* 'He has brought it upon himself that he should be killed' (Rashi). Some see in these Heb. words the formula used in pronouncing the condemnation.

# LEVITICUS XX, 11

with another man's wife, even he that committeth adultery with his neighbour's wife, both the adulterer and the adulteress shall surely be put to death. 11. And the man that lieth with his father's wife—he hath uncovered his father's nakedness—both of them shall surely be put to death; their blood shall be upon them. 12. And if a man lie with his daughter-in-law, both of them shall surely be put to death; they have wrought corruption; their blood shall be upon them. 13. And if a man lie with mankind, as with womankind, both of them have committed abomination: they shall surely be put to death; their blood shall be upon them. 14. And if a man take with his wife also her mother, it is wickedness: they shall be burnt with fire, both he and they; that there be no wickedness among you. 15. And if a man lie with a beast, he shall surely be put to death; and ye shall slay the beast. 16. And if a woman approach unto any beast, and lie down thereto, thou shalt kill the woman, and the beast: they shall surely be put to death; their blood shall be upon them. 17. And if a man shall take his sister, his father's daughter, or his mother's daughter, and see her nakedness, and she see his nakedness: it is a shameful thing; and they shall be cut off in the sight of the children of their people: he hath uncovered his sister's nakedness; he shall bear his iniquity. 18. And if a man shall lie with a woman having her sickness, and shall uncover her nakedness—he hath made naked her fountain, and she hath uncovered the fountain of her blood—both of them shall be cut off from among their people. 19. And thou shalt not uncover

**10.** *committeth adultery.* The repetition of the phrase and the substitution of *neighbour's wife* for *another man's wife* stress the heinousness of the offence. The consent of the husband is quite immaterial. Marriage is not merely a 'contract'; it is consecration, and adultery is far more than merely an offence against one of the parties to a contract. It is an offence against the Divine Command proclaimed at Sinai, and constitutes the annihilation of holiness in marriage (Z. Frankel).

**11.** *father's wife.* Stepmother; see XVIII, 7 f.

**13.** *mankind.* See XVIII, 22.

**14.** *wife also her mother.* Cf. XVIII, 17; brands as 'wickedness' (or 'enormity') the union with the two women at the same time.

**15.** *beast.* See XVIII, 23. Because it was the cause of the person's downfall, and would be a reminder to others of what had taken place.

**17.** *see.* Has the same meaning as 'uncover' in XVIII, 9, 11.

*shameful thing.* Or, 'impiousness,' unholiness. The Heb. term is an expression of strongest moral detestation. The vehement condemnation of this crime may be due to the fact that, in early times, marriage with a half-sister was deemed unobjectionable, a custom that lingered on for centuries after its proscription at Sinai.

*cut off in the sight.* The words signify that there was a public ceremony of excommunication.

*he shall bear his iniquity.* Ibn Ezra understands the second half of the verse to refer to the case where the sister was seduced against her will. He alone is then punished. According to Hoffmann, the repetition of the phrase is to indicate that his is a double turpitude, as it is a brother's part to defend his sister's honour.

**18.** *she hath uncovered.* See XVIII, 19.

**19.** *thy mother's sister.* See XVIII, 12 f.

## LEVITICUS XX, 20

the nakedness of thy mother's sister, nor of thy father's sister; for he hath made naked his near kin; they shall bear their iniquity. 20. And if a man shall lie with his uncle's wife—he hath uncovered his uncle's nakedness—they shall bear their sin; they shall die childless. 21. And if a man shall take his brother's wife, it is impurity: he hath uncovered his brother's nakedness; they shall be childless. ¶ 22. Ye shall therefore keep all My statutes, and all Mine ordinances, and do them, that the land, whither I bring you to dwell therein, vomit you not out.*ᵛⁱⁱ· 23. And ye shall not walk in the customs of the nation, which I am casting out before you; for they did all these things, and therefore I abhorred them. 24. But I have said unto you: 'Ye shall inherit their land, and I will give it unto you to possess it, a land flowing with milk and honey.' I am the LORD your God, who have set you apart from the peoples.*ᵐ· 25. Ye shall therefore separate between the clean beast and the unclean, and between the unclean fowl and the clean; and ye shall not make your souls detestable by beast, or by fowl, or by any thing wherewith the ground teemeth, which I have set apart for you to hold unclean. 26. And ye shall be holy unto Me; for I the LORD am holy, and have set you apart from the peoples, that ye should be Mine. ¶ 27. A man also or a woman that divineth by a ghost or a familiar spirit, shall surely be put to death; they shall stone them with stones; their blood shall be upon them.

---

**20.** *shall die childless.* See XVIII, 14. Childlessness was regarded as little less calamitous than death. 'It is evidently meant as a heavenly and supernatural retribution' (Kalisch).

**21.** *brother's wife.* See XVIII, 16.

### 22–26. EXHORTATION

From here to the end of the Chapter is the concluding exhortation of the Law of Holiness (XVIII–XX), or possibly of the whole section beginning with Chap. XI (cf. *v.* 25 below). This paragraph may be compared with XVIII, 24–30.

**22.** *vomit.* See XVIII, 25.

**23.** *customs of the nation.* Cf. XVIII, 3. Heb. *chukoth ha-goy.* In later times, these Heb. words gave the name to the important principle in accordance with which Jewish life was jealously guarded against adopting the religious customs of surrounding nations.

**24.** *set you apart.* By means of distinctive laws and precepts.

**25.** *clean . . . unclean.* The inclusion of this verse is significant. It is a reminder, still required by the Jewish people, that the ideal of holiness for the Israelite consists in more than moral purity. The dietary laws have likewise their essential place in the scheme of the Torah, and form a necessary aid in the pursuit of the goal set by God.

**26.** *ye shall be holy.* Sums up the whole end and aim of the preceding laws. The people whom a holy God has chosen for His own must, like Him, be holy.

*unto Me.* 'If ye be separated from the heathen nations, then ye belong to Me; but if not, ye belong to Nebuchadnezzar and his colleagues,' *i.e.* you shall go into exile, become assimilated among the nations and lose your distinctive identity (Sifra).

**27.** *familiar spirit.* The position of this verse, after the exhortation, is intended as a final warning against superstition that was deadly to all higher religion. Unlike *v.* 6 the subject here is the person with 'the familiar spirit', and not he who consults the wizard.

# HAFTORAH KEDOSHIM (FOR ASHKENAZIM)   הפטרת קדשים לאשכנזים

## AMOS IX, 7–15

### CHAPTER IX

7. Are ye not as the children of the Ethiopians unto Me,
O children of Israel? saith the LORD.
Have not I brought up Israel out of the land of Egypt,
And the Philistines from Caphtor,
And Aram from Kir?

8. Behold, the eyes of the Lord GOD
Are upon the sinful kingdom,
And I will destroy it from off the face of the earth;
Saving that I will not utterly destroy the house of Jacob,
Saith the LORD.

9. For, lo, I will command, and I will sift the house of Israel among all the nations,
Like as corn is sifted in a sieve,
Yet shall not the least grain fall upon the earth.

10. All the sinners of My people shall die by the sword,
That say: 'The evil shall not overtake nor confront us.'

### CAP. IX. ט

7 הֲלוֹא כִבְנֵי כֻשִׁיִּים אַתֶּם לִי בְּנֵי יִשְׂרָאֵל נְאֻם־יְהֹוָה הֲלוֹא אֶת־יִשְׂרָאֵל הֶעֱלֵיתִי מֵאֶרֶץ מִצְרַיִם וּפְלִשְׁתִּיִּים
8 מִכַּפְתּוֹר וַאֲרָם מִקִּיר: הִנֵּה עֵינֵי ׀ אֲדֹנָי יְהֹוִה בַּמַּמְלָכָה הַחַטָּאָה וְהִשְׁמַדְתִּי אֹתָהּ מֵעַל פְּנֵי הָאֲדָמָה אֶפֶס כִּי לֹא
9 הַשְׁמֵיד אַשְׁמִיד אֶת־בֵּית יַעֲקֹב נְאֻם־יְהֹוָה: כִּי־הִנֵּה אָנֹכִי מְצַוֶּה וַהֲנִעוֹתִי בְכָל־הַגּוֹיִם אֶת־בֵּית יִשְׂרָאֵל כַּאֲשֶׁר יִנּוֹעַ
10 בַּכְּבָרָה וְלֹא־יִפּוֹל צְרוֹר אָרֶץ: בַּחֶרֶב יָמוּתוּ כֹּל חַטָּאֵי
11 עַמִּי הָאֹמְרִים לֹא־תַגִּישׁ וְתַקְדִּים בַּעֲדֵינוּ הָרָעָה: בַּיּוֹם הַהוּא אָקִים אֶת־סֻכַּת דָּוִיד הַנֹּפֶלֶת וְגָדַרְתִּי אֶת־פִּרְצֵיהֶן

11. In that day will I raise up
The tabernacle of David that is fallen,
And close up the breaches thereof,
And I will raise up his ruins,
And I will build it as in the days of old;

---

Amos lived in the days of King Jeroboam II, about 750 B.C.E. The master-word of existence to Amos is Righteousness, which to him, as to his successors, means holiness of life in the individual and the triumph of right in the world. In His dealings with men and nations, he proclaims: God has but one test—their loyalty to the laws of righteousness; and He judges them accordingly. See p. 152.

The opening of the Sedrah strikes the note of consecration in the individual life; and the Haftorah in its earlier verses is an oracle against those who have rejected that high Jewish ideal, and thereby bring about the downfall of the Kingdom. But Israel will yet be true to its high and holy ideal, and worthy of the blessings that follow in the wake of such loyalty.

**7.** *as the children of the Ethiopians.* Two great teachings are here enunciated. The first is: God has guided other nations as well as the Israelites. All races are equally dear to Him; and the hand of Providence is seen not only in the migration of Israel, but in every historical movement. The second teaching is, God's special relationship to Israel rests on moral foundations. Degenerate Israel is no more to God than the despised inhabitants of distant Ethiopia, the descendants of Ham.

*Caphtor.* Probably the island of Crete.
*Kir.* A place in the remote North; II Kings XVI, 9.

**8.** *the sinful kingdom.* The Kingdom of Israel (*i.e.* that of the Ten Tribes), sinful in its royal house from beginning to end, will be destroyed.
*the house of Jacob.* A faithful and worthy 'Remnant' will survive the catastrophe, and form the nucleus of a purer community in the future. This thought, implicit in this verse, was adopted afterwards by Isaiah (I, 26–28) and became one of the most characteristic elements of his teaching (Driver).

**9.** *I will sift.* The whole nation will be subjected to a winnowing process, yet no good grain will be lost. Only the sinners will disappear (*v.* 10).

**10.** *confront.* Old English for 'meet' or 'come up to', 'catch'.

**11.** *in that day.* The day of Redemption which shall follow those other happenings of disaster.

AMOS IX, 12          עמום ט

12. That they may possess the remnant of Edom,
And all the nations, upon whom My name is called,
Saith the LORD that doeth this.

13. Behold, the days come, saith the LORD,
That the plowman shall overtake the reaper,
And the treader of grapes him that soweth seed;
And the mountains shall drop sweet wine,
And all the hills shall melt.

14. And I will turn the captivity of My people Israel,
And they shall build the waste cities, and inhabit them;
And they shall plant vineyards, and drink the wine thereof;
They shall also make gardens, and eat the fruit of them.

12 וַהֲרִסֹתָיו֙ אָקִ֔ים וּבְנִיתִ֖יהָ כִּימֵ֣י עוֹלָֽם׃ לְמַ֨עַן יִֽירְשׁ֜וּ אֶת־שְׁאֵרִ֣ית אֱד֗וֹם וְכָל־הַגּוֹיִ֔ם אֲשֶׁר־נִקְרָ֥א שְׁמִ֖י עֲלֵיהֶ֑ם נְאֻם־יְהוָ֖ה עֹ֥שֶׂה זֹּֽאת׃

13 הִנֵּ֨ה יָמִ֤ים בָּאִים֙ נְאֻם־יְהוָ֔ה וְנִגַּ֤שׁ חוֹרֵשׁ֙ בַּקֹּצֵ֔ר וְדֹרֵ֥ךְ עֲנָבִ֖ים בְּמֹשֵׁ֣ךְ הַזָּ֑רַע וְהִטִּ֤יפוּ הֶֽהָרִים֙

14 עָסִ֔יס וְכָל־הַגְּבָע֖וֹת תִּתְמוֹגַֽגְנָה׃ וְשַׁבְתִּי֙ אֶת־שְׁב֣וּת עַמִּ֣י יִשְׂרָאֵ֗ל וּבָנ֞וּ עָרִ֤ים נְשַׁמּוֹת֙ וְיָשָׁ֔בוּ וְנָטְע֣וּ כְרָמִ֔ים וְשָׁת֖וּ אֶת־

15 יֵינָ֑ם וְעָשׂ֣וּ גַנּ֔וֹת וְאָכְל֖וּ אֶת־פְּרִיהֶֽם׃ וּנְטַעְתִּ֖ים עַל־אַדְמָתָ֑ם וְלֹ֨א יִנָּתְשׁ֜וּ ע֗וֹד מֵעַ֤ל אַדְמָתָם֙ אֲשֶׁ֣ר נָתַ֣תִּי לָהֶ֔ם אָמַ֖ר יְהוָ֥ה אֱלֹהֶֽיךָ׃

15. And I will plant them upon their land,
And they shall no more be plucked up
Out of their land which I have given them,
Saith the LORD thy God.

v. 14. קמץ בז״ק

*will I raise up the tabernacle of David.* The House of David, and revive the glories of the golden age of the Monarchy.

**12.** *possess the remnant of Edom.* That the empire of David may be restored to its former limits.

*upon whom My name has been called.* In token of ownership. Through their subjugation by David, they were deemed a part of Israel.

**13–15.** God's mercy will prevail, and will find a way of bringing back His banished ones to a state of prosperity as well as of purity. In these verses, 'the rigour relaxes, the voice softens, and the promise of restoration and blessing struggles up like a late winter dawn' (Horton).

**13.** *the plowman shall overtake the reaper . . . seed.* So fruitful will be the soil that the seasons will run into one another. Before they have ceased ploughing, the harvest will be ready for gathering in; cf. Lev. XXVI, 5, 10.

*sweet wine.* The newly pressed juice of the grape.

*hills shall melt.* As though the hills dissolved themselves in the rich streams which they poured down.

**14.** *turn the captivity.* Foretells the homecoming of the exiled Israelites. They shall rebuild the waste places for the fulfilment of their destined vocation in the uplifting of humanity. This promise is again being literally fulfilled in the New Judea that has come to life during our own time.

Many Bible Critics maintain that the prophecy of Amos ends with the words, ' I will destroy it from off the face of the earth' (*v.* 8), and deem the remainder of the book to be from a later hand. This view fails to do justice to the idea of prophecy or of the prophet's office. 'For a prophet to close the entire volume of his prophecies without a single gleam of hope for a happier future, is very much opposed to the analogy of prophecy. Jeremiah and Ezekiel, for instance, blame Judah not less unsparingly than Amos blames Israel; but both nevertheless draw ideal pictures of the restored nation's future felicity' (Driver). 'If Amos had altogether despaired of Israel's future, he would not have had what to prophesy, nor to whom to prophesy. One does not moralize to the dead. Every preacher believes in the possibility of betterment, if the sinner repent; and he hopes that his words will lead to such repentance and consequent betterment. Thus also Amos' (Klausner).

# HAFTORAH KEDOSHIM (FOR SEPHARDIM)  הפטרת קדשים לספרדים

### EZEKIEL XX, 2–20

#### CHAPTER XX

2. And the word of the LORD came unto me, saying: 3. 'Son of man, speak unto the elders of Israel, and say unto them: Thus saith the Lord GOD: Are ye come to inquire of Me? As I live, saith the Lord GOD, I will not be inquired of by you. 4. Wilt thou judge them, son of man, wilt thou judge them? cause them to know the abominations of their fathers; 5. and say unto them: Thus saith the Lord GOD: In the day when I chose Israel, and lifted up My hand unto the seed of the house of Jacob, and made Myself known unto them in the land of Egypt, when I lifted up My hand unto them, saying: I am the LORD your God; 6. in that day I lifted up My hand unto them, to bring them forth out of the land of Egypt into a land that I had sought out for them, flowing with milk and honey, which is the beauty of all lands; 7. and I said unto them: Cast ye away every man the detestable things of his eyes, and defile not yourselves with the idols of Egypt; I am the LORD your God. 8. But they rebelled against Me, and would not hearken unto Me; they did not every man cast away the

---

This retrospect of the early history of Israel in the Wilderness is the opening portion of the same prophecy from which the Haftorah of the preceding Sedrah is taken. It was spoken to the exiles who had been deported ten years earlier to Babylon, after the first capture of Jerusalem in 597 B.C.E. The impending destruction of the City is declared by the Prophet to be the wages for disloyalty to the 'statutes and judgments' of which the 19th chapter of Leviticus in the Sedrah is so outstanding a summary; see p. 494.

**3.** *son of man.* In the presence of the awful majesty of God, Ezekiel is ever conscious of his mortality. This phrase occurs nearly 100 times in Ezekiel.
*to inquire of Me.* To consult Him through His prophet; probably in 589 B.C.E., about three years before the fall of the Jewish State. The anxiety of the exiles was deepening over the ultimate fate of Judea and their own chance of returning to the Holy Land.
*will not be inquired of by you.* Because their act of inquiry was insincere, as the elders were themselves in secret sympathy with those of the exiles who were willing to become 'good Babylonians' and give up the Jewish Life and Faith. In *v.* 32 f of this same chapter, the Prophet exclaims: 'And that which cometh into your mind shall not be at all; in that ye say, We will be as the nations, as the families of the countries, to serve wood and stone. As I live, saith the LORD GOD, surely with a mighty hand . . . will I be king over you.'

**4.** *judge them.* Rehearsing the sins of the past with their consequences, as the people are still one in spirit and conduct with Israel in the past.

**5–9.** The iniquities in Egypt.

**5.** *lifted up My hand.* 'Sware.'
*made Myself known.* Through Moses.

**6.** *in that day.* At that period.
*the beauty of all lands.* See Jer. III, 19.

**7.** *detestable things.* Idols; many of the Israelites in Egypt adopted in time Egyptian religious practices.

**8.** *in the midst . . . Egypt.* The history of the Exodus is silent on the internal struggles in Israel itself. The efforts of Moses in educating the people are entirely passed over in the history (Davidson); see p. 206.

**9.** *but I wrought for My name's sake.* That the Divine nature—His justice, mercy and faithfulness—should be fully understood by Israel as well as the world.

## EZEKIEL XX, 9

detestable things of their eyes, neither did they forsake the idols of Egypt; then I said I would pour out My fury upon them, to spend My anger upon them in the midst of the land of Egypt. 9. But I wrought for My name's sake, that it should not be profaned in the sight of the nations, among whom they were, in whose sight I made Myself known unto them, so as to bring them forth out of the land of Egypt. 10. So I caused them to go forth out of the land of Egypt, and brought them into the wilderness. 11. And I gave them My statutes, and taught them Mine ordinances, which if a man do, he shall live by them. 12. Moreover also I gave them My sabbaths, to be a sign between Me and them, that they might know that I am the LORD that sanctify them. 13. But the house of Israel rebelled against Me in the wilderness; they walked not in My statutes, and they rejected Mine ordinances, which if a man do, he shall live by them, and My sabbaths they greatly profaned; then I said I would pour out My fury upon them in the wilderness, to consume them. 14. But I wrought for My name's sake, that it should not be profaned in the sight of the nations, in whose sight I brought them out. 15. Yet also I lifted up My hand unto them in the wilderness, that I would not bring them into the land which I had given them, flowing with milk and honey, which is the beauty of all lands; 16. because they rejected Mine ordinances, and walked not in My statutes, and profaned My sabbaths—for their heart went after their idols. 17. Nevertheless Mine eye spared them from destroying them, neither did I make a full end of them in the wilderness. 18. And I said unto their children in the wilderness: Walk ye not in the statutes of your fathers, neither observe their ordinances, nor defile yourselves with their idols; 19. I am the LORD your God; walk in My statutes, and keep Mine ordinances, and do them; 20. and hallow My sabbaths, and they shall be a sign between Me and you, that ye may know that I am the LORD your God.

**10–20.** The Generation in the Wilderness.

**11.** *he shall live by them.* As those laws are the foundations of all social life. Obedience to them ensures prosperity and stability in life; Lev. XVIII, 5; Deut. IV, 40.

**12.** *to be a sign.* The special sign of God's covenant with Israel (Exod. XXXI, 17). Since the observance of the Sabbath was not confined to Judea, its importance deepened in the eyes of the exiles, deprived of Temple and sacrifice.

**14.** *but I wrought for My name's sake.* See on v. 9. A sudden judgment upon Israel would have been misunderstood by the heathen.

**17.** *Mine eye spared them.* Another motive of God's long-suffering towards Israel—pity for the sinners; Ps. LXXVIII, 38 ('But He, being full of compassion, forgiveth their iniquity and destroyeth not; yea, many a time doth He turn His anger away').

**20.** *a sign.* Ezekiel again and again emphasizes the Sabbath as a constantly recurring reminder to Israel of their special relationship to God.

## LEVITICUS, XXI, 1

### CHAPTER XXI

1. And the LORD said unto Moses: Speak unto the priests the sons of Aaron, and say unto them: ¶ There shall none defile himself for the dead among his people; 2. except for his kin, that is near unto him, for his mother, and for his father, and for his son, and for his daughter, and for his brother; 3. and for his sister a virgin, that is near unto him, that hath had no husband, for her may he defile himself. 4. He shall not defile himself, being a chief man among his people, to profane himself. 5. They shall not make baldness upon their head, neither shall they shave off the corners of their beard, nor make any cuttings in their flesh. 6. They shall be holy unto their God, and not profane the name of their God; for the offerings of the LORD made

### CAP. XXI. כא

ויקרא אמר כא

פ פ פ לא 31 כא

א וַיֹּאמֶר יְהוָה אֶל־מֹשֶׁה אֱמֹר אֶל־הַכֹּהֲנִים בְּנֵי אַהֲרֹן
2 וְאָמַרְתָּ אֲלֵהֶם לְנֶפֶשׁ לֹא־יִטַּמָּא בְּעַמָּיו: כִּי אִם־לִשְׁאֵרוֹ
3 הַקָּרֹב אֵלָיו לְאִמּוֹ וּלְאָבִיו וְלִבְנוֹ וּלְבִתּוֹ וּלְאָחִיו: וְלַאֲחֹתוֹ
הַבְּתוּלָה הַקְּרוֹבָה אֵלָיו אֲשֶׁר לֹא־הָיְתָה לְאִישׁ לָהּ יִטַּמָּא:
4 לֹא יִטַּמָּא בַּעַל בְּעַמָּיו לְהֵחַלּוֹ: לֹא־יִקְרְחוּ קָרְחָה בְּרֹאשָׁם
ה וּפְאַת זְקָנָם לֹא יְגַלֵּחוּ וּבִבְשָׂרָם לֹא יִשְׂרְטוּ שָׂרָטֶת:
6 קְדֹשִׁים יִהְיוּ לֵאלֹהֵיהֶם וְלֹא יְחַלְּלוּ שֵׁם אֱלֹהֵיהֶם כִּי

v. 5. יקרחו ק׳

---

## VIII. EMOR

(CHAPTERS XXI–XXIV)

### REGULATIONS CONCERNING PRIESTS AND SANCTUARY

#### CHAPTER XXI

##### 1–9. THE ORDINARY PRIEST

Whatever comes near, or is presented, to God must be perfect of its kind. Priests, therefore, must be free from physical defects or ceremonial impurity (XXI), and sacrifices must be without blemish (XXII).

The ideal of holiness, as expounded in the previous chapters, was intended for the whole Community of Israel. But since the priests were closely and constantly associated with the ritual of the Sanctuary, special laws were instituted for them and a higher standard was demanded.

**1.** *unto the priests.* To those performing sacerdotal functions, and not to such a one as had been rendered unfit for the priesthood on account of his father having contracted a marriage forbidden to a priest (see *v*. 7). The daughters of priestly families were not subject to these laws.

*defile himself for the dead.* Contact with the dead defiles (Num. XIX) and, for the time being, renders a priest unfit to perform his duties. The law only held good when the dead person was 'among his people'; *i.e.* if there were others who were not priests able and willing to attend to the burial (Sifra). In the case of an unattended dead body of a friendless man (מת מצוה), everyone, even a High Priest or a Nazirite, had to busy himself with the last rites.

**2.** *except for his kin.* A concession to the natural feelings of the priest as man. The word for 'kin' denotes the closest possible bond of relationship. The wife is not mentioned because, as throughout the Torah, man and wife are regarded as 'one flesh' (Gen. II, 24), and 'his wife' is here understood of itself. The mother is named before the father, because there is usually a deeper attachment between her and the son (see on XIX, 3), and the desire to be with her at the last would be more intense.

**3.** *sister . . . near unto him.* The Rabbis explain this to include a sister who is betrothed. Although betrothal was considered almost as close a bond as marriage (Deut. XXII, 23 f), the priest may attend to the body in the event of her death. On her marriage, she became part of her husband; and in the same way that a priest was not allowed to defile himself for his brother-in-law, he was similarly forbidden to do so for his brother-in-law's wife, though she be his sister.

**4.** *being a chief man.* The translation is based on Onkelos. The reason why the priest is subjected to these special laws is that he is 'a chief man among his people'; his is an honour which carries with it peculiar obligations. Instead of 'chief man', Sifra translates 'as a husband' (so also RV Margin) and takes it to mean that he is forbidden to attend to his dead wife, if she belonged to any of the classes named in *v*. 7.

*to profane himself.* To render himself unfit for the service of the Sanctuary.

**5.** *baldness . . . cuttings.* See on X, 6 f and XIX, 27 f.

**6.** *they shall be holy.* The motive for the special laws of the priests is the same as the motive for the laws of the Community (xx, 26). The sole reason why the restrictions on the priests were heavier was that they had the additional privilege of offering the sacrifices to God.

*the bread of their God.* See on III, 11.

LEVITICUS XXI, 7

by fire, the bread of their God, they do offer; therefore they shall be holy. 7. They shall not take a woman that is a harlot, or profaned; neither shall they take a woman put away from her husband; for he is holy unto his God. 8. Thou shalt sanctify him therefore; for he offereth the bread of thy God; he shall be holy unto thee; for I the LORD, who sanctify you, am holy. 9. And the daughter of any priest, if she profane herself by playing the harlot, she profaneth her father: she shall be burnt with fire. ¶ 10. And the priest that is highest among his brethren, upon whose head the anointing oil is poured, and that is consecrated to put on the garments, shall not let the hair of his head go loose, nor rend his clothes; 11. neither shall he go in to any dead body, nor defile himself for his father, or for his mother; 12. neither shall he go out of the sanctuary, nor profane the sanctuary of his God; for the consecration of the anointing oil of his God is upon him: I am the LORD. 13. And he shall take a wife in her virginity. 14. A widow, or one divorced, or a profaned woman, or a harlot, these shall he not take; but a virgin of his own people shall he take to wife. 15. And he shall not profane his seed among his people; for I am the LORD who sanctify him.*ⁱⁱ. ¶ 16. And the LORD spoke unto Moses, saying: 17. Speak unto Aaron, saying: ¶ Whosoever he be of thy seed

---

**7.** *profaned.* Or, 'polluted' (RV Margin), 'dishonoured' (Driver). The Rabbis understand it as 'profaned'—the daughter of a forbidden marriage contracted by a priest, or a woman who had already entered into a marriage forbidden to a priest (*i.e.* a divorced woman whose previous husband, a priest, ought not to have married her).

*put away.* Better, *divorced.* There is no mention of a widow among the women whom a priest may not marry; see on Ezek. XLIV, 22, p. 529.

**8.** *thou shalt sanctify.* The Community as a body is addressed. The Israelites are to consider the priests as consecrated to God, and pay them the honour which is due to them. It is from this verse that the custom arose to give the *Kohen* precedence in such matters as the Reading of the Law.

**9.** *burnt with fire.* The Talmud maintains that the penalty of burning (see on XX, 14) was inflicted only if the priest's daughter became unchaste when betrothed or married—a crime which was in all cases considered a capital offence.

10–15. INCREASED RESTRICTIONS FOR THE HIGH PRIEST

**10.** *anointing oil.* See VIII, 12.

*consecrated . . . garments.* Or, 'consecrated by donning the vestments' (cf. XVI, 32). Nobody but a High Priest could wear the special garments; and his investiture in them was part of his consecration to his exalted office.

*hair . . . go loose.* See on X, 6.

**11.** *for his father.* Even for his father. But, according to the Rabbis, he must do so for the unattended body of a friendless man (see on *v.* 1).

**12.** *out of the sanctuary.* Cf. X, 7. He was dispensed from following even the funeral procession of his father or mother. It is probable that the High Priest had permanent quarters in the Temple-precincts (see I Sam. III, 2 f).

*I am the LORD.* These words are added to increase the solemnity of the warning.

**14.** *of his own people.* lit. 'of his kinsfolk'. The Septuagint and Philo limit his choice to the priestly families.

**15.** *profane his seed.* Impair the pure descent of the Aaronic family by an improper marriage.

16–24. PHYSICAL BLEMISHES IN A PRIEST

A physical defect in a priest disqualified him from officiating in the Sanctuary.

## LEVITICUS XXI, 18

throughout their generations that hath a blemish, let him not approach to offer the bread of his God. 18. For whatsoever man he be that hath a blemish, he shall not approach: a blind man, or a lame, or he that hath any thing maimed, or any thing too long, 19, or a man that is broken-footed, or broken-handed, 20. or crook-backed, or a dwarf, or that hath his eye overspread, or is scabbed, or scurvy, or hath his stones crushed; 21. no man of the seed of Aaron the priest, that hath a blemish, shall come nigh to offer the offerings of the LORD made by fire; he hath a blemish; he shall not come nigh to offer the bread of his God. 22. He may eat the bread of his God, both of the most holy, and of the holy. 23. Only he shall not go in unto the veil, nor come nigh unto the altar, because he hath a blemish; that he profane not My holy places; for I am the LORD who sanctify them. ¶ 24. So Moses spoke unto Aaron, and to his sons, and unto all the children of Israel.

## 22 CHAPTER XXII

1. And the LORD spoke unto Moses, saying: 2. Speak unto Aaron and to his sons, that they separate themselves from the holy things of the children of Israel, which they hallow unto Me, and that they profane not My holy name: I am the LORD. 3. Say unto them: ¶ Whosoever he be of all your seed throughout your generations, that approacheth unto the holy things,

---

**20.** *dwarf.* He was not to blame for being a dwarf, but only men without blemish and who had the full measure of manly power were permitted to exercise the functions of that holy office. Even so in the higher realms of the soul, a spiritual dwarf cannot offer the bread of his God to his fellows.

*eye overspread.* Probably, the white and black parts of the eye are not properly defined.

**21.** *that hath a blemish.* Any blemish not restricted to those just enumerated.

**22.** *he may eat.* Though he may not officiate, he is still a priest by birth; and he is, therefore, entitled to his share of the sacrificial dues.

*most holy.* e.g. the flesh of the sin-offering, which could be eaten by male priests alone.

**24.** *all the children of Israel.* These laws, although they were the peculiar concern of the priests, were also addressed to the Community as a whole. The people must insist upon their being honoured.

## CHAPTER XXII. HOLINESS OF THE SANCTUARY

### 1–9. REGULATIONS FOR PRIESTS WHO SHARE IN A SACRIFICIAL FEAST

The last Chapter dealt with the bodily defects that disqualify the priest from officiating in the Sanctuary: this section insists on physical purity as the condition in which alone he could handle the offerings.

**2.** *that they separate themselves.* The sacred foods may be eaten only by priests and the members of their family, and then only if they are ritually clean. We must add words like, 'in the time of impurity,' which are implied in the context.

*holy things of.* A comprehensive expression for all offerings presented at the Altar. Even the offerings which the priests themselves bring to the Altar on their own behalf must not be sacrificed or eaten by them when they are ritually unclean (Rashi).

**3.** *approacheth.* To participate in the offering of the sacrifices or in the sharing of the sacred dues.

*uncleanness.* The term is defined in the next verses.

*shall be cut off.* Some understand this to mean

LEVITICUS XXII, 4          ויקרא אמר כב

which the children of Israel hallow unto the LORD, having his uncleanness upon him, that soul shall be cut off from before Me: I am the LORD. 4. What man soever of the seed of Aaron is a leper, or hath an issue, he shall not eat of the holy things, until he be clean. And whoso toucheth any one that is unclean by the dead; or from whomsoever the flow of seed goeth out; 5. or whosoever toucheth any swarming thing, whereby he may be made unclean, or a man of whom he may take uncleanness, whatsoever uncleanness he hath; 6. the soul that toucheth any such shall be unclean until the even, and shall not eat of the holy things, unless he bathe his flesh in water. 7. And when the sun is down, he shall be clean; and afterward he may eat of the holy things, because it is his bread. 8. That which dieth of itself, or is torn of beasts, he shall not eat to defile himself therewith: I am the LORD. 9. They shall therefore keep My charge, lest they bear sin for it, and die therein, if they profane it: I am the LORD who sanctify them. 10. There shall no ¹common man eat of the holy thing; a tenant of a priest, or a hired servant, shall not eat of the holy thing. 11. But if a priest buy any soul, the purchase of his money, he may eat of it; and such as are born in his house, they may eat of his bread. 12. And if a priest's daughter be married unto a common man, she shall not eat of that which is set apart from the holy things. 13. But if a priest's daughter be a widow, or divorced, and have no child,

¹ That is, one who is not a priest.

---

exclusion from the priestly service. It is, however, more likely that a sterner punishment is intended; see v. 9, and chap. x.

**4.** *unclean by the dead.* See Num. XIX. For the various forms of uncleanness and the manner of purification, see XI–XV.

*whose seed.* See XV, 16.

**5.** *swarming thing.* i.e. a dead insect or reptile; XI, 24, 29 f.

*a man ... uncleanness.* See XV, 5, 7, 19.

**6.** *the soul.* Heb. idiom for 'the person'.

**7.** *bread.* Or, 'food.' Certain portions of the sacrifices were the prescriptive right of the priests, and they depended upon them for their sustenance (cf. x, 12 f).

**8.** *or is torn of beasts.* This prohibition is repeated here for the special warning of the priests, since the impurity thereby caused would incapacitate them for service at the Sanctuary (Ibn Ezra); see also Ezek. XLIV, 31, p. 530.

**9.** *for it.* Either for the Sanctuary (Ibn Ezra), or for the 'food' in v. 7, since the context speaks of the eating of the flesh of the sacrifices.

*die therein.* The Rabbis explain this as 'death by the hand of Heaven'.

**10–16.** No layman was to eat a sanctified thing; with a list of the exceptions to that rule.

**10.** *common man.* Not a priest; a layman.

*tenant.* One who dwells with the priest, or is his guest; or the Hebrew slave who refused his freedom in the seventh year and remained in his service.

*hired servant.* As distinct from a non-Israelite slave, who was considered a member of the household (see next v.). The Torah does not mention that the priest's wife may eat of the portion, as husband and wife were deemed one person; see note on XXI, 2.

**11.** *the purchase of his money.* The non-Israelite slave purchased by a priest became part of the family, and was allowed to share in the sacrificial portion.

**12.** *priest's daughter.* On marrying a layman, she no longer belonged to the priestly family (see on XXI, 3).

LEVITICUS XXII, 14

and is returned unto her father's house, as in her youth, she may eat of her father's bread; but there shall no common man eat thereof. 14. And if a man eat of the holy thing through error, then he shall put the fifth part thereof unto it, and shall give unto the priest the holy thing. 15. And they shall not profane the holy things of the children of Israel, which they set apart unto the LORD; 16. and so cause them to bear the iniquity that bringeth guilt, when they eat their holy things; for I am the LORD who sanctify them.*iii. ¶ 17. And the LORD spoke unto Moses, saying: 18. Speak unto Aaron, and to his sons, and unto all the children of Israel, and say unto them: ¶ Whosoever he be of the house of Israel, or of the strangers in Israel, that bringeth his offering, whether it be any of their vows, or any of their freewill-offerings, which are brought unto the LORD for a burnt-offering; 19. that ye may be accepted, ye shall offer a male without blemish, of the beeves, of the sheep, or of the goats. 20. But whatsoever hath a blemish, that shall ye not bring; for it shall not be acceptable for you. 21. And whosoever bringeth a sacrifice of peace-offerings unto the LORD in fulfilment of a vow clearly uttered, or for a freewill-offering, of the herd or of the flock, it shall be perfect to be accepted; there shall be no blemish therein. 22. Blind, or broken, or maimed, or having a wen, or scabbed, or scurvy, ye shall not offer these unto the LORD, nor make an offering by fire of them upon the altar unto the LORD. 23. Either a bullock or a lamb that hath any thing too long or too short, that mayest thou

**13.** *have no child.* If there is issue of the marriage, she is still regarded as attached to her husband's family. If, however, the issue of the marriage died, she regained her former status as a priest's daughter.
*bread.* Food, as in v. 7 above.

**14.** *through error.* Cf. chap. v, 14–16.
*the holy thing. i.e.* its equivalent.

**15.** *they shall not profane.* The subject is the priests, and the profanation is the admission of unqualified persons to partake of the sacred dues (Rashi).

17–25. QUALITY OF OFFERINGS

After laws concerning the purity of the priesthood and the holiness of the sacrifices, there follow regulations concerning the faultlessness of the offerings. Jewish tradition demands of the Israelite such faultlessness in the case of any gift or offering set apart for sacred purposes, whether in the sphere of religion or of charity.

**18.** *the strangers.* Aliens who were residing in their midst; see on 1, 2.

**19.** *male without blemish.* See on 1, 3.
*beeves.* The same Heb. word is rendered 'herd' in 1, 3.

**20.** *shall ye not bring.* The Rabbis extended the scope of this law and insisted that the oil, wine, flour and wood offered and used in the Temple must likewise be of the best quality. Even the wood to be burnt on the Altar was to be carefully selected so as to contain no worm-eaten pieces.

**22.** *blind . . . scabbed.* The blemishes which disqualify the animal as an offering are very similar to those which render the priest unfit for service (XXI, 18 f).
*wen.* A running sore, an ulcer.

**23.** *mayest thou offer.* According to the Rabbinic interpretation, this means that the imperfect animal may not be sacrificed upon the Altar, but it may be donated to the Temple for working purposes.

# LEVITICUS XXII, 24

offer for a freewill-offering; but for a vow it shall not be accepted. 24. That which hath its stones bruised, or crushed, or torn, or cut, ye shall not offer unto the LORD; neither shall ye do thus in your land. 25. Neither from the hand of a foreigner shall ye offer the bread of your God of any of these, because their corruption is in them, there is a blemish in them; they shall not be accepted for you. ¶ 26. And the LORD spoke unto Moses, saying: ¶ 27. When a bullock, or a sheep, or a goat, is brought forth, then it shall be seven days under the dam; but from the eighth day and thenceforth it may be accepted for an offering made by fire unto the LORD. 28. And whether it be cow or ewe, ye shall not kill it and its young both in one day. 29. And when ye sacrifice a sacrifice of thanksgiving unto the LORD, ye sacrifice it that ye may be accepted. 30. On the same day it shall be eaten; ye shall leave none of it until the morning: I am the LORD. 31. And ye shall keep My commandments, and do them: I am the LORD. 32. And ye shall not profane My holy name; but I will be hallowed among the children of Israel: I am the LORD who hallow you, 33. that brought you out of the land of Egypt, to be your God: I am the LORD.*iv.

---

**24.** *ye do thus.* The Heb. can bear two interpretations. It can mean, 'Ye shall not offer such mutilated animals'; or it may be taken, according to the Rabbis, as a general prohibition of emasculation in men and animals.

**25.** *foreigner.* Blemished animals are unacceptable even from a non-Israelite who 'comes out of a far country for Thy name's sake' (I Kings VIII, 41). The priest was not to think that he need not be so strict in such a case.

*their corruption is in them.* 'They are faulty' (Moffatt).

*accepted for you.* Who offer these animals on behalf of the foreigner.

26–33. FURTHER DIRECTIONS IN REGARD TO SACRIFICIAL ANIMALS

**27.** *eighth day.* See on Exod. XXII, 29.

**28.** *not kill it and its young.* Not only for sacrificial purposes, but also for ordinary consumption.

*in one day.* 'It is prohibited to kill an animal with its young on the same day, in order that people should be restrained and prevented from killing the two together in such a manner that the young is slain in the sight of the mother; for the pain of the animals under such circumstances is very great. There is no difference in this case between the pain of man and the pain of other living beings, since the love and the tenderness of the mother for her young ones is not produced by reasoning but by feeling, and this faculty exists not only in man but in most living things' (Maimonides); cf. the similar prohibition of the mother-bird being taken with her young (Deut. XXII, 6 f).

**30.** *on the same day.* See on VII, 15.

## CHILLUL HASHEM AND KIDDUSH HASHEM

**32.** *ye shall not . . . Israel.* This verse has been called 'Israel's Bible in little' (Jellinek). It contains the solemn warning against the Profanation of the Divine Name (*Chillul Hashem*), and the positive injunction to every Israelite to hallow the Name of God (*Kiddush Hashem*) by his life and, if need be, by his death. Although spoken in reference to the priests as the appointed guardians of the Sanctuary, this commandment, both in its positive and negative forms, was early applied to the whole of Israel.

*ye shall not profane My holy name.* Be ye exceedingly guarded in your actions, say the Rabbis, so that ye do nothing that tarnishes the

## LEVITICUS XXIII, 1

### CHAPTER XXIII

1. And the LORD spoke unto Moses, saying:
2. Speak unto the children of Israel, and say unto them: ¶ The appointed seasons of the LORD, which ye shall proclaim to be holy convocations, even these are My

וַיְדַבֵּר יְהֹוָה אֶל־מֹשֶׁה לֵּאמֹר: דַּבֵּר אֶל־בְּנֵי יִשְׂרָאֵל 2 א
וְאָמַרְתָּ אֲלֵהֶם מוֹעֲדֵי יְהֹוָה אֲשֶׁר־תִּקְרְאוּ אֹתָם מִקְרָאֵי

---

honour of Judaism or of the Jew. Especially do they warn against any misdeed towards a non-Jew as an unpardonable sin, because it gives a false impression of the moral standard of Judaism. The Jew should remember that the glory of God is, as it were, entrusted to his care; and that *every Israelite holds the honour of his Faith and of his entire People in his hands.* A single Jew's offence can bring shame on the whole House of Israel. This has been the fate of Israel in all the ages; and nothing, it seems, will ever break the world of its habit of putting down the crimes, vices, or failings of a Jew, no matter how estranged from his people or his people's Faith he may be, to his Jewishness, and of fathering them upon the entire Jewish race. The Rabbis say: 'Wild beasts visit and afflict the world because of the profanation of the Divine Name' (Ethics of the Fathers, v, 11). And, indeed, wherever Jews are guilty of conduct unworthy of their Faith, there the wild beast in man—blind prejudice and causeless hatred—is unchained against Israel. No student of Jewish history will question the truth of this judgment. The Rabbis, in a striking apologue, picture a boat at sea, full of men. One of them begins to bore a hole in the bottom of the boat and, on being remonstrated with, urges that he is only boring under his own seat. 'Yes,' say his comrades, 'but when the sea rushes in we shall be drowned with you.' So it is with Israel. Its weal or its woe is in the hands of every one of its children.

*I will be hallowed.* Not to commit Chillul Hashem is only a negative virtue. Far more is required of the Israelite. He is bidden so to live as to shed lustre on the Divine Name and the Torah by his deeds and influence. Rabbi Simon ben Shetach one day commissioned his disciples to buy him a camel from an Arab. When they brought the animal, they gleefully announced that they had found a precious stone in its collar. 'Did the seller know of this gem?' asked the Master. On being answered in the negative, he called out angrily, 'Do you think me a barbarian that I should take advantage of the letter of the law by which the gem is mine together with the camel? Return the gem to the Arab immediately.' When the heathen received it back he exclaimed: 'Blessed be the God of Simon ben Shetach! Blessed be the God of Israel!'

The highest form of hallowing God is martyrdom; and Jewish Law demands of every Israelite to surrender his life, rather than by public apostasy desecrate the Name of God (Shulchan Aruch, Yore Deah, CLVII). When, during the war of annihilation which the Emperor Hadrian waged against Judaism, the readiness for martyrdom on the part of young and old began to imperil the existence of the Jewish nation, the Rabbis decreed that only with regard to three fundamental laws—idolatry, incest, and murder—should death be preferred to transgression. See also p. 201, on the Akedah, and the ideal of martyrdom in Jewish history. 'The Jewish martyrs of olden days, who bore witness to their God at the stake, are described as having yielded up their lives for the "sanctification of the Divine Name". Such testimony is within the power, and constitutes the duty, of the Jew in these times also. If he is not called upon to die for the sanctification of the Name, he has at least to live for it. His life must give glory to God, vindicate his God-given religion' (M. Joseph).

*among the children of Israel.* If it is a sacred duty to hallow the Name of God and Israel before the nations, it is even a more sacred duty to do so '*among* the children of Israel'. Moses could make Pharaoh fear God; the dukes of Edom, the mighty men of Moab, and the peoples of Canaan trembled before him; but he was far from uniformly successful in making his own people do so. Therefore he was to see the promised Land afar off, but he was not to enter it. 'Get thee up unto Mount Nebo, and die in the mount as Aaron thy brother died on Mount Hor, because ye sanctified me not *in the midst* of the children of Israel' (Deut. XXXII, 49–52). It is important to make non-Jews respect Judaism, but even more so to make Jews respect Judaism.

### CHAPTER XXIII
### THE HOLY DAYS

This chapter gives a comprehensive description of the sacred seasons in the Jewish year. There is no mention of the New Moon, because it was not necessarily a day of cessation from work, and was not ranked as one of the 'holy convocations'. The sacrifices for each Festival are given in Num. XXVIII.

**2.** *appointed seasons.* Or, 'appointed (or fixed) seasons.'

*holy convocations.* An assembly 'convoked', or called together, for worship at the Sanctuary. The calling together was done by means of sounding two silver trumpets (Num. x, 1–10). Although it was only on the three Pilgrimage Festivals that the Israelites were to appear before the Lord at the Sanctuary, many would no doubt also come for the Days of Memorial and Atonement.

## LEVITICUS XXIII, 3

appointed seasons. 3. Six days shall work be done; but on the seventh day is a sabbath of solemn rest, a holy convocation; ye shall do no manner of work; it is a sabbath unto the Lord in all your dwellings. ¶ 4. These are the appointed seasons of the Lord, even holy convocations, which ye shall proclaim in their appointed season. 5. In the first month, on the fourteenth day of the month at dusk, is the Lord's passover. 6. And on the fifteenth day of the same month is the feast of unleavened bread unto the Lord; seven days ye shall eat unleavened bread. 7. In the first day ye shall have a holy convocation; ye shall do no manner of servile work. 8. And ye shall bring an offering made by fire unto the Lord seven days; in the seventh day is a holy concovation; ye shall do no manner of servile work. ¶ 9. And the Lord spoke unto Moses, saying: 10. Speak unto the children of Israel, and say unto them: ¶ When ye are come into the land which I give unto you, and shall reap the harvest thereof, then ye shall bring the sheaf of the first-fruits of your harvest unto the priest. 11. And he shall wave the sheaf before the Lord, to be accepted for you; on the morrow after the sabbath the priest shall wave it. 12. And in the day when ye wave the sheaf, ye shall offer a he-lamb without blemish of the first year for a

---

**3.** *sabbath of solemn rest*. The reference to the Sabbath in this connection is, according to the Rabbis, to emphasize the fact that the seventh day of the week must always be 'a sabbath of solemn rest'—even when it coincides with a Festival, on which day, otherwise, only manual labour is prohibited, but not such as is necessary for the preparation of meals.

*all your dwellings*. See on III, 17.

### 5–8. THE PASSOVER

For the meaning and observance of this Festival, see on Exod. XII, 1–28.

**5.** *first month*. See on Exod. XII, 2.

*at dusk is the LORD'S passover*. Better, *towards even is a passover unto the LORD* (Friedländer); *i.e.* a paschal offering in honour of the Lord.

**6.** *feast of unleavened bread*. Only the 15th day of the month is 'the *feast* of unleavened bread', so called because the partaking of *matzah* (מצה של מצה) is obligatory on the eve thereof, although unleavened bread is eaten for seven days and the seventh day is a 'holy convocation'.

**7.** *servile work*. lit. 'work of labour', the usual work which one does on an ordinary week day. It implies a less strict abstinence from labour than was demanded for the Sabbath (*v.* 3) and the Day of Atonement (*v.* 28), and does not include the prohibition of preparing food.

**8.** *offering*. This is defined in detail in Num. XXVIII, 19 f.

### 9–14. THE OMER

At the beginning of the barley harvest—barley ripens two or three weeks before the wheat—the first sheaf was presented at the Sanctuary; see Deut. XXVI, 2.

**10.** *when ye are come*. When the Israelites had begun to till the soil of their land.

**11.** *on the morrow after the sabbath*. Better, *on the morrow after the day of rest;* Heb. ממחרת השבת. The interpretation of this phrase was the subject of heated controversy in early Rabbinic times between the Pharisees and Sadducees. The latter took the word 'sabbath' in its usual sense, and maintained that the Omer was to be brought on the morrow of the first Saturday in Passover. The Pharisees argued that 'sabbath' (השבת) here means, 'the day of cessation from work'; and the context shows that the Feast of Unleavened Bread is intended: therefore, the Omer was to be brought on the 16th of Nisan. This is supported by the Septuagint, which renders 'on the morrow of the first day', and by Josephus. 'The offerings of the sheaf took place on the 16th, the first busy work-day of the harvest, in relation to which the preceding day might well be called a *Sabbath* or rest-day,

## LEVITICUS XXIII, 13

burnt-offering unto the LORD. 13. And the meal-offering thereof shall be two tenth parts of an ephah of fine flour mingled with oil, an offering made by fire unto the LORD for a sweet savour; and the drink-offering thereof shall be of wine, the fourth part of a hin. 14. And ye shall eat neither bread, nor parched corn, nor fresh ears, until this selfsame day, until ye have brought the offering of your God; it is a statute for ever throughout your generations in all your dwellings. ¶ 15. And ye shall count unto you from the morrow after the ¹day of rest, from the day that ye brought the sheaf of the waving; seven weeks shall there be complete; 16. even unto the morrow after the seventh week shall ye number fifty days; and ye shall present a new meal-offering unto the LORD. 17. Ye shall bring out of your dwellings two wave-loaves of two tenth parts of an ephah;

¹ Heb. *sabbath*.

---

though not all labour was prohibited. This is alone compatible with the context, and is free from the objections to which all the other opinions are open' (Kalisch).

**12.** *ye shall offer*. The offering in connection with the bringing of the Omer is here specified, as it finds no mention in Num. XXVIII.

**13.** *ephah . . . hin*. See on XIX, 36.

**14.** *neither bread . . . day*. Josh. V, 11 contains a historical reference to this regulation.

### 15–21. FEAST OF WEEKS—SHAVUOS

One of the three agricultural festivals, the feast of the first harvest יום הבכורים. Jewish tradition, however, connects it with the Covenant on Mount Sinai, and speaks of the festival as זמן מתן תורתנו 'the Season of Giving of our Torah'. The Israelites arrived at Sinai on the New Moon. On the second of the month, Moses ascended the mountain; on the third, he received the people's reply; on the fourth, he made the second ascent and was commanded to institute three days of preparation, at the conclusion of which the Revelation took place. Hence its association with the Feast of Weeks, which became the Festival of Revelation.

**15.** *and ye shall count*. The paragraph dealing with the Feast of Weeks has no introductory formula, 'The Lord spake unto Moses', such as we find in connection with the other Festivals, because it was conceived as the complement of the Passover, and not something independent of it. Its name in Talmudic literature is not *Shavuos*, but almost invariably עצרת, 'the concluding festival' to Passover. 'We count the days that pass since the preceding Festival, just as one who expects his most intimate friend on a certain day counts the days and even the hours. This is the reason why we count the days that pass since the offering of the Omer, between the anniversary of our departure from Egypt and the anniversary of the Law-giving. The latter was the aim and object of the exodus from Egypt' (Maimonides). In other words, the Deliverance from bondage was not an end in itself; it was the prelude to Sinai (Exod. III, 12). Liberty without law is a doubtful boon, whether to men or nations.

*unto you*. From this addition, the Rabbis deduce that each Israelite had the duty of counting for himself; hence the 'counting of the days of the Omer' even after the Omer itself was no longer brought to the Temple. The season between Passover and Shavuos (or Pentecost, which in Greek means 'the fiftieth day' after the first day of Passover) is known as *Sephirah*, Period of Counting. It is a period of semi-mourning, because repeatedly dire calamities befell the Jewish people at this time.

*day of rest*. This is a departure from the RV which translates 'sabbath'; see on *v*. 11.

*seven weeks*. lit. 'seven sabbaths'. It is evident that here and in XXV, 8, the Heb. *shabbath* signifies 'week'. Hence the most common name for the Festival, חג השבועות, the Feast of Weeks; Deut. XVI, 10.

**16.** *seventh week*. Instead of, 'seventh sabbath' (RV).

*new meal-offering*. The cereal offering of the produce of the new wheat harvest; see next *v*.

'With the destruction of the Second Temple, the agricultural aspect of the Festival receded, and Shavuos became primarily the Feast of Revelation. An echo of nature, however, still lingers in the present custom of adorning the Synagogue with flowers' (H. M. Adler).

## LEVITICUS XXIII, 18

they shall be of fine flour, they shall be baked with leaven, for first-fruits unto the LORD. 18. And ye shall present with the bread seven lambs without blemish of the first year, and one young bullock, and two rams; they shall be a burnt-offering unto the LORD, with their meal-offering, and their drink-offerings, even an offering made by fire, of a sweet savour unto the LORD. 19. And ye shall offer one he-goat for a sin-offering, and two he-lambs of the first year for a sacrifice of peace-offerings. 20. And the priest shall wave them with the bread of the first-fruits for a wave-offering before the LORD, with the two lambs; they shall be holy to the LORD for the priest. 21. And ye shall make proclamation on the selfsame day; there shall be a holy convocation unto you; ye shall do no manner of servile work; it is a statute for ever in all your dwellings throughout your generations. ¶ 22. And when ye reap the harvest of your land, thou shalt not wholly reap the corner of thy field, neither shalt thou gather the gleaning of thy harvest; thou shalt leave them for the poor, and for the stranger: I am the LORD your God.*v. ¶ 23. And the

---

**17.** *your dwellings.* The Rabbis explain this as meaning that the corn must have grown in the Holy Land.

*baked with leaven.* The loaves were made to represent the common food of the people, and symbolically mark their gratitude to the Provider of their sustenance. They were not offered upon the Altar (II, 11), but only 'waved'; they belonged to the priest.

**19.** *ye shall offer.* These offerings are additional to those mentioned in Num. XXVIII, 27.

**20.** *to the LORD for the priest.* *i.e.* they are devoted to God by being eaten by the priest; cf. Num. V, 8, for a similar usage.

**22.** *when ye reap.* A repetition of XIX, 9 f. A significant reminder to the Israelite that his thankfulness to God for the wheat-harvest was to be demonstrated by more than an offering on the Altar. If he failed to share God's bounty with the poor, his observance of the Festival would be unacceptable.

### 24–25. DAY OF MEMORIAL—ROSH HASHANAH

As the seventh day in the week was a holy day, so the seventh month was the holy month in the year. Each New Moon was made the occasion for additional offerings (Num. XXVIII, 11 f.) It is, therefore, not surprising that the New Moon of the seventh month should be a Festival of special solemnity. In later times, it was known as *Rosh Hashanah*, New Year's Day. But unlike the New Year celebrations of many ancient and modern nations, the Jewish New Year is not a time of revelry, but an occasion of the deepest religious import.

**24.** *a memorial.* In Num. XXIX, 1, the occasion is called 'a day of blowing the horn', *i.e.* Shofar, the ram's horn; Josh. VI, 4. This act must be differentiated from the sounding of the 'trumpet' (*not* the Shofar) which took place while the offerings were brought on all the Festivals and New Moons (Num. X, 10). The blowing of the Shofar had consequently quite a different significance, and was more awe-inspiring (see Amos III, 6) than the blowing of the silver trumpets, which generally was a joyous sound. The sound of Shofar, consisting, as handed down by Tradition, of three distinctive Shofar-notes—tekiah, shevarim, teruah—has been looked upon from time immemorial as a call to contrition and penitence, as a reminder of the Shofar-sound of Sinai; and the Day of Memorial, the beginning of the Ten Days of Repentance (עשרת ימי תשובה), which culminate in the Day of Atonement, as a time of self-examination and humble petition for forgiveness. 'The Scriptural injunction of the Shofar for the New Year's Day has a profound meaning. It says: Awake, ye sleepers, and ponder over your deeds; remember your Creator and go back to Him in penitence. Be not of those who miss

## LEVITICUS XXIII, 24

ויקרא אמר כג

LORD spoke unto Moses, saying: 24. Speak unto the children of Israel, saying: ¶ In the seventh month, in the first day of the month, shall be a solemn rest unto you, a memorial proclaimed with the blast of horns, a holy concovation. 25. Ye shall do no manner of servile work; and ye shall bring an offering made by fire unto the LORD. ¶ 26. And the LORD spoke unto Moses, saying: ¶ 27. Howbeit on the tenth day of this seventh month is the day of atonement; there shall be a holy convocation unto you, and ye shall afflict your souls; and ye shall bring an offering made by fire unto the LORD. 28. And ye shall do no manner of work in that same day; for it is a day of atonement, to make atonement for you before the LORD your God. 29. For whatsoever soul it be that shall not be afflicted in that same day, he shall be cut off from his people. 30. And whatsoever soul it be that doeth any manner of work in that same day, that soul will I destroy from among his people. 31. Ye shall do no manner of work; it is a statute for ever throughout your generations in all your

לֵאמֹר בַּחֹדֶשׁ הַשְּׁבִיעִי בְּאֶחָד לַחֹדֶשׁ יִהְיֶה לָכֶם שַׁבָּתוֹן
כה זִכְרוֹן תְּרוּעָה מִקְרָא־קֹדֶשׁ: כָּל־מְלֶאכֶת עֲבֹדָה לֹא תַעֲשׂוּ
26 וְהִקְרַבְתֶּם אִשֶּׁה לַיהוָה: ס וַיְדַבֵּר יְהוָה אֶל־מֹשֶׁה
27 לֵּאמֹר: אַךְ בֶּעָשׂוֹר לַחֹדֶשׁ הַשְּׁבִיעִי הַזֶּה יוֹם הַכִּפֻּרִים
הוּא מִקְרָא־קֹדֶשׁ יִהְיֶה לָכֶם וְעִנִּיתֶם אֶת־נַפְשֹׁתֵיכֶם
28 וְהִקְרַבְתֶּם אִשֶּׁה לַיהוָה: וְכָל־מְלָאכָה לֹא תַעֲשׂוּ בְּעֶצֶם
הַיּוֹם הַזֶּה כִּי יוֹם כִּפֻּרִים הוּא לְכַפֵּר עֲלֵיכֶם לִפְנֵי יְהוָה
29 אֱלֹהֵיכֶם: כִּי כָל־הַנֶּפֶשׁ אֲשֶׁר לֹא־תְעֻנֶּה בְּעֶצֶם הַיּוֹם
ל הַזֶּה וְנִכְרְתָה מֵעַמֶּיהָ: וְכָל־הַנֶּפֶשׁ אֲשֶׁר תַּעֲשֶׂה כָּל־
מְלָאכָה בְּעֶצֶם הַיּוֹם הַזֶּה וְהַאֲבַדְתִּי אֶת־הַנֶּפֶשׁ הַהִוא
31 מִקֶּרֶב עַמָּהּ: כָּל־מְלָאכָה לֹא תַעֲשׂוּ חֻקַּת עוֹלָם

---

realities in their pursuit of shadows and waste their years in seeking after vain things which cannot profit or deliver. Look well to your souls and consider your acts; forsake each of you his evil ways and thoughts, and return to God so that He may have mercy upon you' (Maimonides).

**25.** *an offering.* Described in Num. XXIX, 2 f.

### 26–32. DAY OF ATONEMENT

On the subject of this the most solemn day in the Jewish year, see the commentary on XVI, 29–34. No other nation, ancient or modern, has an institution approaching the Day of Atonement in religious depth—'a day of purification and of turning from sins, for which forgiveness is granted through the grace of the merciful God, who holds penitence in as high an esteem as guiltlessness' (Philo).

**27.** *day of atonement.* Heb. *yom kippurim.* lit. 'Day of Atonements'. The name of this most sacred of Festivals is in the plural, 'because it represents two streams of love. As soon as the desire for reconciliation has awakened in the sinner's soul, and wings its way Heavenward, God's grace comes down to meet it, calming his breast with the assurance of Divine pardon and forgiveness' (Zohar).

*afflict your souls.* See on XVI, 29; this Day, set aside for penitence and moral regeneration, is the only one for which the Torah prescribes fasting —which is the intensest form of devotion and contrition. 'On that Day,' the Rabbis state, 'the Israelites resemble the angels, without human wants, without sins, and linked together in love and peace.' It is the only day of the year—they add—on which the accuser Satan is silenced before the Throne of Glory, and even becomes the defender of Israel. Confession of sin is the most essential and characteristic element in the services of the Day of Atonement; 'every one entreating pardon for his sins and hoping for God's mercy, not because of his own merits but through the compassionate nature of that Being who will have forgiveness rather than punishment' (Philo). The Confession is made by the whole Community collectively; and those who have not themselves committed the sins mentioned in the confession regret that they were unable to prevent them from being committed by others (Friedländer).

*an offering.* See Num. XXIX, 7 f.

**28.** *no manner of work.* The phrase is not qualified by the addition of the word 'servile'. With regard to work, the Day of Atonement is of the same strictness as the Sabbath (Exod. XX, 10), with similar exceptions where life might be endangered.

*to make atonement for you.* 'As I live, saith the Lord God, I have no pleasure in the death of the wicked, but that the wicked turn from his way and live; turn ye, turn ye from your evil ways' (Ezek. XXXIII, 11).

**30.** *will I destroy.* Synonymous with 'shall be cut off', showing that the punishment is not by a human Court.

**31.** *it is a statute.* As in III, 17.

523

## LEVITICUS XXIII, 32

dwellings. 32. It shall be unto you a sabbath of solemn rest, and ye shall afflict your souls; in the ninth day of the month at even, from even unto even, shall ye keep your sabbath.*vi. ¶ 33. And the LORD spoke unto Moses, saying: ¶ 34. Speak unto the children of Israel, saying: ¶ On the fifteenth day of this seventh month is the feast of tabernacles for seven days unto the LORD. 35. On the first day shall be a holy convocation; ye shall do no manner of servile work. 36. Seven days ye shall bring an offering made by fire unto the LORD; on the eighth day shall be a holy convocation unto you; and ye shall bring an offering made by fire unto the LORD; it is a day of solemn assembly; ye shall do no manner of servile work. ¶ 37. These are the appointed seasons of the LORD, which ye shall proclaim to be holy convocations, to bring an offering made by fire unto the LORD, a burnt-offering, and a meal-offering, a sacrifice, and drink-offerings, each on its own day; 38. beside the sabbaths of the LORD, and beside your gifts, and beside all your vows, and beside all your freewill-offerings, which ye give unto the LORD. ¶ 39. Howbeit on the fifteenth day of the seventh month, when ye have gathered in the fruits of the land, ye shall keep the feast of the LORD seven days; on the first day shall be a solemn rest, and on the eighth day shall be a solemn rest. 40.

**32.** *in the ninth day.* The Day commencing with the preceding eve (Gen. I, 5). Both the opening and closing evenings are marked by services (Kol Nidré and Neilah) of special solemnity. The Neilah Amidah is one of the most masterly products of Israel's religious genius. It begins: 'Thou givest a hand to transgressors, and Thy right hand is stretched out to receive the penitent. Thou hast taught us, O LORD our God, to make confession unto Thee of all our sins, in order that we may cease from the violence of our hands and may return unto Thee who delightest in the repentance of the wicked.' These words contain what has been called 'the Jewish doctrine of salvation.'

### 33–43. FEAST OF TABERNACLES

**34.** *fifteenth day.* Like the Passover, this Feast commenced at full moon.

*tabernacles.* Heb. *Succoth.* lit. 'booths'. In Exod. XXIII, 16, it is called 'the Feast of Ingathering'. In Rabbinic literature, it is known as 'the Feast', because, as the time of harvest, it would naturally be a period of rejoicing and holiday-making. It really consists of two groups: the first seven days, Tabernacles proper; and the eighth day, Atzeres. The seventh day of Tabernacles became in later times an echo of the Day of Atonement and was known as *Hoshanah Rabbah;* and the 'second day' of Atzeres assumed the nature of a separate Festival under the name of *Simchas Torah*, Rejoicing of the Law, the day on which the annual reading of the Torah was completed and restarted.

**36.** *an offering.* See Num. XXIX.

*solemn assembly.* Or, 'closing festival'. Heb. *atzereth*, the concluding day of a festival season, applied to the seventh day of Passover (Deut. XVI, 8), and, in Rabbinic literature, to the Feast of Weeks (see on *v.* 15). Maimonides explains the purpose of this eighth day to be, 'in order to complete our rejoicings, which cannot be perfect in booths, but in well-built houses.'

**38.** *the sabbaths. i.e.* the additional sacrifices offered on the Sabbaths (Num. XXVIII, 9 f).

*gifts.* The voluntary offerings that accompanied the Israelite on his pilgrimage to the Temple, when he was bidden not to appear before the LORD 'empty' (Deut. XVI, 16 f).

*vows.* See on VII, 16.

**39–43.** Additional directions in regard to Tabernacles for the time when, after the settlement in Canaan, the people would be tilling the soil and reaping the harvest.

**39.** *eighth day.* Which is deemed a Festival on its own account, distinct from the Feast of Tabernacles.

## LEVITICUS XXIII, 41

And ye shall take you on the first day the fruit of goodly trees, branches of palm-trees, and boughs of thick trees, and willows of the brook, and ye shall rejoice before the LORD your God seven days. 41. And ye shall keep it a feast unto the LORD seven days in the year; it is a statute for ever in your generations; ye shall keep it in the seventh month. 42. Ye shall dwell in booths seven days; all that are home-born in Israel shall dwell in booths; 43. that your generations may know that I made the children of Israel to dwell in booths, when I brought them out of the land of Egypt: I am the LORD your God. ¶ 44. And Moses declared unto the children of Israel the appointed seasons of the LORD.\*vii

## CHAPTER XXIV

1. And the LORD spoke unto Moses, saying: 2. 'Command the children of Israel, that they bring unto thee pure olive oil beaten for the light, to cause a lamp to burn continually. 3. Without the veil of the testimony, in the tent of meeting, shall Aaron order it from evening to morning

---

**40.** *fruit of goodly trees.* Tradition holds that this is the *ethrog*, the citron.

*thick trees.* Better, *thick-leaved trees;* myrtle branches. These traditional explanations are supported by the testimony of Josephus, who writes: 'On this Festival we carry in our hands a branch of myrtle, and willow, and a bough of the palm-tree, with the addition of the citron.'

*and ye shall rejoice before the LORD.* This phrase was closely linked with the preceding, and gave rise to the joyous processions in the Temple. The pilgrims held the *lulav* and *esrog* in their hands and sang Psalms of praise to God.

**42.** *booths.* The Heb. *sukkah* represents a hastily-constructed and unsubstantial edifice, such as the Israelites must have set up during the wanderings in the Wilderness. In addition to its historical associations, reminding the Israelite of the Divine protection during the desert-journey, the command to dwell in booths has also a religious signification. 'Man ought to remember his evil days in his days of prosperity. He will thereby be induced to thank God repeatedly, to lead a modest and humble life. We, therefore, on Tabernacles leave our houses in order to dwell in booths. We shall thereby remember that this has once been our condition' (Maimonides). The Book of Ecclesiastes is aptly set aside for special reading during Tabernacles or Atzeres.

**44.** *Moses declared.* Cf. XXI, 24. Not only did he communicate the contents of the chapter to the people, but, as each Festival occurred, he took the opportunity of repeating the commands so that they were properly observed (Sifra).

## CHAPTER XXIV

### 1–9. THE LAMPS AND THE SHEWBREAD

The Torah, before leaving the subject of the Sanctuary, alludes to the constant duty of the priests to see that the lamp is kept perpetually alight and the shewbread regularly arranged. These are outstanding obligations of priesthood, which must not be relaxed even at the special seasons of the year, when the attention and energies of the Temple-servants were otherwise taxed to the full.

**2.** *pure olive oil.* See on Exod. XXVII, 20 f.

**3.** *shall Aaron order it.* In Exod. the phrase 'and his sons' is added after 'Aaron'. In the first instance, the lamp was kindled by Aaron (Num. VIII, 3).

**4.** *the pure candlestick.* So called either because made of pure gold (Exod. XXV, 31 f), or because it was to be cleansed each time that the lamps are arranged upon it.

*before the LORD.* It must on no account be removed from the Sanctuary.

525

## LEVITICUS XXIV, 4

before the LORD continually; it shall be a statute for ever throughout your generations. 4. He shall order the lamps upon the pure candlestick before the LORD continually. ¶ 5. And thou shalt take fine flour, and bake twelve cakes thereof: two tenth parts of an ephah shall be in one cake. 6. And thou shalt set them in two rows, six in a row, upon the pure table before the LORD. 7. And thou shalt put pure frankincense with each row, that it may be to the bread for a memorial-part, even an offering made by fire unto the LORD. 8. Every sabbath day he shall set it in order before the LORD continually; it is from the children of Israel, an everlasting covenant. 9. And it shall be for Aaron and his sons; and they shall eat it in a holy place; for it is most holy unto him of the offerings of the LORD made by fire, a perpetual due.' ¶ 10. And the son of an Israelitish woman, whose father was an Egyptian, went out among the children of Israel; and the son of the Israelitish woman and a man of Israel strove together in the camp. 11. And the son of the Israelitish woman blasphemed the Name, and cursed; and they brought him unto Moses. And his mother's name was Shelomith, the daughter of Dibri, of the tribe of Dan. 12. And they put him in ward, that it might be declared unto them at the mouth of the LORD. ¶ 13. And the LORD spoke unto Moses, saying: 14. 'Bring forth him that hath cursed without the camp; and let all that heard him lay

---

**5.** *twelve cakes.* See on Exod. xxv, 30; see also *v.* 8.

**6.** *rows.* Or, 'piles.'

*pure table.* *i.e.* overlaid with pure gold (Exod. xxv, 24).

**7.** *memorial-part.* See on II, 2. The incense was put in two small golden cups, and one placed near each row of cakes. It symbolized prayer, and thus gave expression to the petition that God continue to grant food to the people of His covenant (Koenig).

**8.** *every sabbath day.* The bread remained on the table for a week, and was renewed each Sabbath.

*an everlasting covenant.* This phrase is applied to the Sabbath itself (Exod. xxxi, 16); and this weekly offering from the Children of Israel typified the regular renewal of the covenant between God and His people, of which the Sabbath was 'a sign'.

**9.** *holy place.* See II, 3.

### 10–23. THE PENALTY OF BLASPHEMY

The sole aim of all that is enjoined in the Book of Leviticus is to sanctify Israel, individually and collectively. When, therefore, anyone presumes to desecrate the Divine Name, the penalty must be ruthless.

**10.** *went out.* Or, 'had come forth' from Egypt, among the children of Israel (Ehrlich). The cause of the quarrel is not stated, because it is not of material importance. Note that the blasphemer is not 'an Israelite' but the 'son of the Israelitish woman'. Only one of the mixed multitude (Exod. XII, 38) could be guilty of so heinous an offence.

**11.** *blasphemed.* lit. 'to indicate by name', here with unholy contempt and dishonour.

*the Name.* The Divine Name of the four letters, Y H W H, which is never pronounced, but read as Adonay.

*his mother's name.* Rashi remarks that his genealogy is recorded to impress upon the Israelite that a man's life is not his own to do with as he pleases. His disgrace is also that of his parents, of his tribe, of his people.

**12.** *that it might be declared.* The Torah had ordained, 'Thou shalt not revile God' (Exod. XXII, 27); but no penalty had been mentioned in that connection.

## LEVITICUS XXIV, 15

their hands upon his head, and let all the congregation stone him. 15. And thou shalt speak unto the children of Israel, saying: Whosoever curseth his God shall bear his sin. 16. And he that blasphemeth the name of the LORD, he shall surely be put to death; all the congregation shall certainly stone him; as well the stranger, as the home-born, when he blasphemeth the Name, shall be put to death. 17. And he that smiteth any man mortally shall surely be put to death. 18. And he that smiteth a beast mortally shall make it good: life for life. 19. And if a man maim his neighbour; as he hath done, so shall it be done to him: 20. breach for breach, eye for eye, tooth for tooth; as he hath maimed a man, so shall it be rendered unto him.*m. 21. And he that killeth a beast shall make it good; and he that killeth a man shall be put to death. 22. Ye shall have one manner of law, as

---

**14.** *without the camp.* Where all executions took place, so as not to defile its holiness.

*lay their hands.* They thereby signified that they were personally concerned in the offence, inasmuch as the blasphemous words had fallen upon their ears. They were, therefore, discharging their duty by bringing the culprit to justice.

*stone him.* See on xx, 2.

**15.** *and thou shalt speak.* The incident became the opportunity of presenting to the Israelites a law on this and kindred offences.

**16.** *the stranger.* Although he is not subject to the precepts of the Torah and is to be allowed a large degree of tolerance, he yet may not be permitted to desecrate the holiness of the camp. If he does not wish to worship the God of Israel, he is not to be compelled to do so; but should he publicly revile the Holy Name, the offence is as serious with him as with the Israelite.

**18.** *life for life.* This phrase is a legal term equivalent to 'fair compensation'; for it cannot mean that anyone who slew an animal should forfeit his own life in return! In the same way, the phrase, 'as he hath done, so shall it be done to him' in *v.* 19, and 'eye for eye' and 'tooth for tooth' in *v.* 20, are merely technical phrases for the demand that adequate and equitable compensation, after due and judicial appraisement of the injury inflicted, is to be paid for the injury. There is in Jewish history no instance of the law of retaliation ever having been carried out *literally*—eye for an eye, tooth for a tooth. To the Talmudists the Biblical words *eye for eye* had become a mere expression of the law of equality. 'None of the later [Rabbinic] law books even suggest retaliation as a proper remedy, the example of contemporary European and Asiatic systems of jurisprudence to the contrary notwithstanding' (D. W. Amram). The last clause reminds us of one of the paradoxes of history. On the one hand, Judaism, the so-called religion of 'strict justice', rejected the literal application of the law of retaliation, and knew neither torture in legal procedure nor mutilation as a legal punishment. In Christian lands, on the other hand, mutilation and torture are well-nigh the indispensable accompaniments of justice from the middle of the thirteenth century down to the end of the eighteenth, and in some countries to the middle of the nineteenth century and beyond. See also pp. 309 and 405.

**22.** *ye shall have one manner of law . . . homeborn.* One of the great texts of Scripture; cf. XIX, 33 f. Though in this connection the application of the law may be, so to speak, disadvantageous to the alien, the general principle of equality between alien and native is only strengthened thereby. In no other code was there one and the same law for native-born and alien alike. Even in Roman law, every alien was originally classed as an enemy, and therefore devoid of any rights. Only gradually was the protection of the law in a limited degree extended to him. It is not so very long ago that aliens in European states were incapable of owning landed property. In many countries, the denial by the dominant race of civic and political rights to 'aliens', though these may have lived for generations in the land of their sojourn, is a matter of contemporary history; see p. 260.

*for I am the LORD your God.* The reason given is noteworthy: show equal justice to all men, for I am your God, the God of Israel, the Father of all mankind. Once again, monotheism is the

## LEVITICUS XXIV, 23

well for the stranger, as for the home-born; for I am the LORD your God.' 23. And Moses spoke to the children of Israel, and they brought forth him that had cursed out of the camp, and stoned him with stones. And the children of Israel did as the LORD commanded Moses.

יְהֹוָה אֱלֹהֵיכֶם: וַיְדַבֵּר מֹשֶׁה אֶל־בְּנֵי יִשְׂרָאֵל וַיּוֹצִיאוּ 23
אֶת־הַמְקַלֵּל אֶל־מִחוּץ לַמַּחֲנֶה וַיִּרְגְּמוּ אֹתוֹ אָבֶן וּבְנֵי־
יִשְׂרָאֵל עָשׂוּ כַּאֲשֶׁר צִוָּה יְהֹוָה אֶת־מֹשֶׁה:

basis for the brotherhood of man (Hermann Cohen).

**23.** *stoned him.* For a later historical applica-tion of the law of blasphemy, see the story of Naboth in I Kings XXI.

## HAFTORAH EMOR    הפטרת אמר

### EZEKIEL XLIV, 15–31

CHAPTER XLIV

15. But the priests the Levites, the sons of Zadok, that kept the charge of My sanc-tuary when the children of Israel went astray from Me, they shall come near to Me to minister unto Me; and they shall stand before Me to offer unto Me the fat and the blood, saith the Lord GOD; 16. they shall enter into My sanctuary, and they shall come near to My table, to minister unto Me, and they shall keep My charge. 17. And it shall be that when they enter in at the gates of the inner court, they shall be clothed with linen garments; and no wool shall come upon them, while they minister in the gates of the inner court, and within.

CAP. XLIV. מד

וְהַכֹּהֲנִים טו
הַלְוִיִּם בְּנֵי צָדוֹק אֲשֶׁר שָׁמְרוּ אֶת־מִשְׁמֶרֶת מִקְדָּשִׁי בִּתְעוֹת
בְּנֵי־יִשְׂרָאֵל מֵעָלַי הֵמָּה יִקְרְבוּ אֵלַי לְשָׁרְתֵנִי וְעָמְדוּ לְפָנַי
לְהַקְרִיב לִי חֵלֶב וָדָם נְאֻם אֲדֹנָי יֱהֹוִה: הֵמָּה יָבֹאוּ אֶל־ 16
מִקְדָּשִׁי וְהֵמָּה יִקְרְבוּ אֶל־שֻׁלְחָנִי לְשָׁרְתֵנִי וְשָׁמְרוּ אֶת־
מִשְׁמַרְתִּי: וְהָיָה בְּבוֹאָם אֶל־שַׁעֲרֵי הֶחָצֵר הַפְּנִימִית בִּגְדֵי 17
פִשְׁתִּים יִלְבָּשׁוּ וְלֹא־יַעֲלֶה עֲלֵיהֶם צֶמֶר בְּשָׁרְתָם בְּשַׁעֲרֵי

The Haftorah is taken from the last portion of the Book of Ezekiel (XL–XLVIII), which is a Vision of the New Jerusalem and the New Temple that are to arise when the Captivity is over. If, however, the new Temple is to be the embodiment in concrete form of Israel's ideals of Holiness and Purity, those that shall minister in the House of God must not, as in the past, permit any violations of those ideals. Therefore, only descendants of the loyal family of Zadok shall be the priests of the future. In this Haftorah, Ezekiel undertakes to define their duties and ministrations; and thus connects with the Sedrah which regulates the life and work of the priests.

**15.** *sons of Zadok.* The high priest appointed to that office by King Solomon (I Kings II, 35). Ezekiel was himself a priest, and in all probability spent his childhood and youth within the precincts of the Temple in Jerusalem. He therefore had a first-hand and sympathetic understanding of the better elements of the priestly class.

*to minister unto Me.* In contrast to the Levites mentioned in preceding verses, who had been unfaithful.

**16.** *come near to My table.* i.e. the Table of shewbread (Targum). The sacrifices named in the previous verses were offered in the outer Court. The service at the Table of shewbread was conducted in the Sanctuary, *i.e.* the inner Court.

*they shall keep My charge.* In all the remaining spheres of priestly service (Altschul).

**17.** *enter . . . the inner court.* i.e. on the Day of Atonement.

*linen garments.* The reason is given in the next verse: sweat was regarded as a form of unclean-ness.

EZEKIEL XLIV, 18

18. They shall have linen tires upon their heads, and shall have linen breeches upon their loins; they shall not gird themselves with any thing that causeth sweat. 19. And when they go forth into the outer court, even into the outer court to the people, they shall put off their garments wherein they minister, and lay them in the holy chambers, and they shall put on other garments, that they sanctify not the people with their garments. 20. Neither shall they shave their heads, nor suffer their locks to grow long; they shall only poll their heads. 21. Neither shall any priest drink wine, when they enter into the inner court. 22. Neither shall they take for their wives a widow, nor her that is put away; but they shall take virgins of the seed of the house of Israel, or a widow that is the widow of a priest. 23. And they shall teach My people the difference between the holy and the common, and cause them to discern between the unclean and the clean. 24. And in a controversy they shall stand to judge; according to Mine ordinances shall they judge it; and they shall keep My laws and My statutes in all My appointed seasons, and they shall hallow My sabbaths. 25. And they shall come near no dead person to defile themselves; but for father, or for mother, or for son, or for daughter, for brother, or for sister that hath had no husband, they may defile themselves. 26. And after he is cleansed, they shall reckon unto him seven days. 27. And in the day that he goeth into the sanctuary, into the inner court, to minister in the sanctuary, he shall offer his sin-offering,

18. *linen tires upon their heads.* Worn for ornament (Kimchi).

19. *sanctify not the people.* A precaution against confusion of the sacred and the common. They are not to mingle with the people in their sacred garments (Targum), lest the thoughtless among the people might consider themselves qualified to perform duties of the Temple Service.

20. *shave ... grow long.* Both prohibitions in this verse are protests against customs of heathen worship that prevailed in one cult or another of the time.

*poll their heads.* i.e. keep it at a moderate and even length all round.

22. *neither shall they take ... a widow.* In the Sedrah (Lev. XXI, 14) the prohibition is restricted to the High Priest. Although this is only a more stringent application of the principle underlying the original law—possibly in that decadent age, when the moral standards had lowered, it was found necessary to do so in order to protect the purity of the priestly families—it is one of Ezekiel's apparent divergencies from the Torah, and it raised doubts in the early Rabbinic period as to whether his Book should remain in the Canon of Scripture.

23. *teach.* Instruction, teaching the people the eternal difference between right and wrong, holy and unholy, 'Jewish' and heathen, has always been the main function and mission of priest, prophet, sage, rabbi or teacher in Judaism.

24. *to judge.* Cf. Deut. XVII, 8 f, on the judicial power given to the priests.

25. *but for father.* As in the Sedrah (XXI, 1–3) there is no mention of the wife, it being self-evident; cf. Ezek. XXIV, 15 f.

26. *and after he is cleansed.* The period before his cleansing seems likewise to have been seven days; Num. XIX, 11.

27. *he shall offer his sin-offering.* Contact with the dead was a technical, *i.e.* ritual, sin; the reference is not to any moral lapse.

## EZEKIEL XLIV, 28

saith the Lord GOD. 28. And it shall be unto them for an inheritance: I am their inheritance; and ye shall give them no possession in Israel: I am their possession. 29. The meal-offering, and the sin-offering, and the guilt-offering, they, even they, shall eat; and every devoted thing in Israel shall be theirs. 30. And the first of all the first-fruits of every thing, and every heave-offering of every thing, of all your offerings, shall be for the priests; ye shall also give unto the priest the first of your dough, to cause a blessing to rest on thy house. 31. The priests shall not eat of any thing that dieth of itself, or is torn, whether it be fowl or beast.

יחזקאל מד

28 אֲדֹנָי יֱהֹוִה: וְהָיְתָה לָהֶם לְנַחֲלָה אֲנִי נַחֲלָתָם וַאֲחֻזָּה
29 לֹא־תִתְּנוּ לָהֶם בְּיִשְׂרָאֵל אֲנִי אֲחֻזָּתָם: הַמִּנְחָה וְהַחַטָּאת
וְהָאָשָׁם הֵמָּה יֹאכְלוּם וְכָל־חֵרֶם בְּיִשְׂרָאֵל לָהֶם יִהְיֶה:
ל וְרֵאשִׁית כָּל־בִּכּוּרֵי כֹל וְכָל־תְּרוּמַת כֹּל מִכֹּל תְּרוּמוֹתֵיכֶם
לַכֹּהֲנִים יִהְיֶה וְרֵאשִׁית עֲרִסוֹתֵיכֶם תִּתְּנוּ לַכֹּהֵן לְהָנִיחַ
31 בְּרָכָה אֶל־בֵּיתֶךָ: כָּל־נְבֵלָה וּטְרֵפָה מִן־הָעוֹף וּמִן־
הַבְּהֵמָה לֹא יֹאכְלוּ הַכֹּהֲנִים:

**28–31.** Enumerate the dues for the maintenance of the priests. They had no possession in Israel—in contrast to the priests of the Babylonian temples, who, besides stated tariffs for their services, often had large private estates (like medieval abbeys) and did much banking business (Lofthouse).

**28.** *I am their inheritance.* The priest's inheritance is a spiritual, not a material one.

**29.** *devoted thing.* Everything on which a ban had been placed; Lev. XXVII, 28.

**30.** *heave-offering.* Heb. *terumah*, 'contribution.'

**31.** *shall not eat.* The Rabbis explain that repetition of this law was required in the case of the priests, as the manner of the slaying (*e.g.* מליקה) of those sacrifices, of which the priests were permitted to partake, did not altogether coincide with the laws of Shechitah outside the Sanctuary.

In connection with this verse and *v.* 22, it is well to remember that this Haftorah is part of a half-ideal and half-allegorical programme of the New Jerusalem that is to follow the Captivity. The Prophet's symbolic picture was probably never intended for, and certainly never received, literal realization. A deeper study of his Vision shows that the account of the Temple, the City, the Prince, and the divisions of the land are as ideal as his vision of the stream that issues from under the threshold of the Temple and flows through the desert of southern Judea into the Dead Sea, fertilizing the one and transforming the other into a fresh-water lake swarming with life and surrounded by noble trees that bear fruit every month (XLVII, 1–12). Where all else is ideal, actuality is not to be affixed to the regulations alone concerning priests and their offerings. The Rabbis were therefore guided by highest spiritual wisdom (רוח הקודש) when, disregarding the apparent or real divergencies from the Torah which these chapters contain, they permitted the Book to remain part of Holy Scripture.

## LEVITICUS XXV, 1

### CHAPTER XXV

1. And the LORD spoke unto Moses in mount Sinai, saying: 2. Speak unto the children of Israel, and say unto them: ¶ When ye come into the land which I give you, then shall the land keep a sabbath unto the LORD. 3. Six years thou shalt sow thy field, and six years thou shalt prune thy vineyard, and gather in the produce thereof. 4. But in the seventh year shall be a sabbath of solemn rest for the land, a sabbath unto the LORD; thou shalt neither sow thy field, nor prune thy vineyard. 5. That which groweth of itself of thy harvest thou shalt not reap, and the grapes of thy undressed vine thou shalt not gather; it shall be a

ויקרא בהר כה

CAP. XXV. כה

פ פ פ לב 32

2 וַיְדַבֵּ֤ר יְהֹוָה֙ אֶל־מֹשֶׁ֔ה בְּהַ֥ר סִינַ֖י לֵאמֹֽר׃ דַּבֵּ֞ר אֶל־בְּנֵ֤י יִשְׂרָאֵל֙ וְאָמַרְתָּ֣ אֲלֵהֶ֔ם כִּ֤י תָבֹ֙אוּ֙ אֶל־הָאָ֔רֶץ אֲשֶׁ֥ר אֲנִ֖י

3 נֹתֵ֣ן לָכֶ֑ם וְשָׁבְתָ֣ה הָאָ֔רֶץ שַׁבָּ֖ת לַיהֹוָֽה׃ שֵׁ֤שׁ שָׁנִים֙ תִּזְרַ֣ע שָׂדֶ֔ךָ וְשֵׁ֥שׁ שָׁנִ֖ים תִּזְמֹ֣ר כַּרְמֶ֑ךָ וְאָסַפְתָּ֖ אֶת־תְּבוּאָתָֽהּ׃

4 וּבַשָּׁנָ֣ה הַשְּׁבִיעִ֗ת שַׁבַּ֤ת שַׁבָּתוֹן֙ יִהְיֶ֣ה לָאָ֔רֶץ שַׁבָּ֖ת לַיהֹוָ֑ה

ה שָׂדְךָ֙ לֹ֣א תִזְרָ֔ע וְכַרְמְךָ֖ לֹ֥א תִזְמֹֽר׃ אֵ֣ת סְפִ֤יחַ קְצִֽירְךָ֙

v. 4. קמץ בז״ק

## IX. BEHAR

### (CHAPTERS XXV–XXVI, 2)

#### CHAPTER XXV. THE SABBATICAL YEAR AND THE YEAR OF JUBILEE

The cycle of sacred seasons begun in XXIII is here continued, and the system of sabbaths—the Sabbath at the end of the week; Pentecost at the end of seven weeks; the Seventh month, as the sacred month studded with Festivals—is here completed by the Sabbatical year and by the Jubilee, which came after a 'week' of Sabbatical years.

During the Sabbath-year the land was to lie fallow (Exod. XXIII, 10 f) and was to be 'released' from cultivation. The land is not the absolute possession of man; it belongs to God, and is to be held in trust for His purposes. The Sabbath-year does not seem to have been regularly observed in pre-exilic times, and, according to the Mishnah, the Sabbath-year was fully enforced only in Palestine. A promise to observe it in the future formed part of the covenant on the Return from Babylon; Neh. x, 32. Alexander the Great remitted to the Jews the tribute in every seventh year 'because then they did not sow their fields' (Josephus). Julius Caesar acted in the same manner.

Heathens did not trouble to understand the meaning of this unique law, which, among other things, saved the soil from the danger of exhaustion. Thus, the Roman historian Tacitus attributes the Jews' observance of it to indolence.

**1.** *spoke unto Moses.* Better, *had spoken unto Moses.* As these laws are intended to meet the social problems that would arise in the Israelitish Commonwealth, they bring the legal part of Leviticus to an appropriate conclusion.

**2.** *the land keep a sabbath.* The land is personified. It should rest in the seventh year, as man rests on the seventh day. The Israelite may not during that year till it himself or allow anyone to do so on his behalf. 'Just as the freedom of the individual was a fundamental principle of the Torah, so was the freedom of the land from the absolute ownership of man' (F. Perles).

*unto the LORD.* As the Sabbath was more than a cessation of labour, and was a day dedicated to God—similarly during the Sabbatical year, the soil was to be devoted to Him by being placed at the service of the poor and the animal creation (Exod. XXIII, 10, 11). In Deut. XXXI, 10 f, we learn that the seventh year was, furthermore, to be utilized for national educational ends, and special measures were to be taken to acquaint the men and the women, the children as well as the resident aliens, with the teachings and duties of the Torah. Josephus rightly claims that while the best knowledge of olden times was usually treated as a secret doctrine, and confined to the few, it was the glory of Moses that he made it current coin. 'To place within the reach of the English worker, once in every seven years, a year's course at a University in science and law and literature and theology, would be something like the modern equivalent for one of the advantages which the Sabbath-year offered to the ancient Hebrew' (F. Verinder in *My Neighbour's Landmark*, Short Studies in Bible Land Laws, 1911).

**4.** *in the seventh year.* In the seventh month of that year, after the gathering of the harvest, the year of rest began.

*sabbath of solemn rest.* A Sabbath of the strictest kind. The same phrase is used of the Day of Atonement (XXIII, 32), as well as of the Sabbath day (XXIII, 3).

**5.** *undressed vine.* The Heb. is the word for a Nazirite whose hair was to remain unshorn (Num. VI, 5). Like him, the vines were not to be trimmed during the Sabbatical year. There was to be neither planting, pruning, nor gathering.

# LEVITICUS XXV, 6      ויקרא בהר כה

year of solemn rest for the land. 6. And the sabbath-produce of the land shall be for food for you: for thee, and for thy servant and for thy maid, and for thy hired servant and for the settler by thy side that sojourn with thee; 7. and for thy cattle, and for the beasts that are in thy land, shall all the increase thereof be for food. ¶ 8. And thou shalt number seven sabbaths of years unto thee, seven times seven years; and there shall be unto thee the days of seven sabbaths of years, even forty and nine years. 9. Then shalt thou make proclamation with the blast of the horn on the tenth day of the seventh month; in the day of atonement shall ye make

לֹא תִקְצוֹר וְאֶת־עִנְּבֵי נְזִירֶךָ לֹא תִבְצֹר שְׁנַת שַׁבָּתוֹן יִהְיֶה
6 לָאָרֶץ: וְהָיְתָה שַׁבַּת הָאָרֶץ לָכֶם לְאָכְלָה לְךָ וּלְעַבְדְּךָ
7 וְלַאֲמָתֶךָ וְלִשְׂכִירְךָ וּלְתוֹשָׁבְךָ הַגָּרִים עִמָּךְ: וְלִבְהֶמְתְּךָ
וְלַחַיָּה אֲשֶׁר בְּאַרְצֶךָ תִּהְיֶה כָל־תְּבוּאָתָהּ לֶאֱכֹל: ס
8 וְסָפַרְתָּ לְךָ שֶׁבַע שַׁבְּתֹת שָׁנִים שֶׁבַע שָׁנִים שֶׁבַע פְּעָמִים
וְהָיוּ לְךָ יְמֵי שֶׁבַע שַׁבְּתֹת הַשָּׁנִים תֵּשַׁע וְאַרְבָּעִים שָׁנָה:
9 וְהַעֲבַרְתָּ שׁוֹפַר תְּרוּעָה בַּחֹדֶשׁ הַשְּׁבִעִי בֶּעָשׂוֹר לַחֹדֶשׁ

**6.** *the sabbath-produce of the land.* A poetic term for the chance, spontaneous produce during the Sabbath-year.

*for you.* The plural is used to comprehend all those that are to benefit by this provision. The fruit and grain which grew of itself in the Sabbatical year might be plucked and eaten, but not stored. Grain growing of itself—*i.e.* without regular ploughing and sowing—is not uncommon in Palestine; see on *v.* 22.

*hired servant ... settler.* Non-Israelites are included (Sifra); see XIX, 10.

**7.** *cattle.* Heb. בהמה; domestic animals.

*beasts.* Heb. חיה; free beasts of the field or forest; sometimes used in contrast to חיה רעה 'evil beast' (XXVI, 6). The Divine promise in this verse is in accordance with the uniformly tender regard for animals throughout Scripture. They were part of God's creation, and as such were comprehended in His pity and love; see the concluding verse of Jonah. 'A righteous man regardeth the life of his beast' (Prov. XII, 10).

### 8–55. THE JUBILEE

In the fiftieth year, the Hebrew slaves with their families are emancipated, and property, except house property in a walled city, reverts to its original owner. The Jubilee institution was a marvellous safeguard against deadening poverty. By it, houses and lands were kept from accumulating in the hands of the few, pauperism was prevented, and a race of independent freeholders assured. It represented such a rare and striking introduction of morals into economics, that many have been inclined to question whether this wonderful institution was ever in actual force. However, 'nothing is more certain than that the Jubilee was once for centuries a reality in the national life of Israel' (Ewald). Ezekiel speaks of its non-observance as one of the signs that 'the end is come' upon the nation for its misdoings; and he mentions (see p. 966) 'the year of liberty', when a gift of land must return to the original owner. 'It is impossible to think that, as has sometimes been supposed, the institution of the Jubilee is a mere paper-law; at least as far as concerns the *land* (for the periodical redistribution of which there are analogies in other nations), it must date from ancient times in Israel' (Driver). According to the Talmud, the law of the Jubilee was observed as long as the entire territory of the Holy Land was inhabited by Israelites. When a portion of the tribes went into exile, the law lapsed.

**8.** *the days of.* Equivalent to 'the time of', as in Gen. XXV, 7; XLVII, 8 f.

**9.** *Horn.* Heb. *Shofar.*

*in the day of atonement.* Although the year commenced on the first of Tishri, Rosh Hashanah, it was not until the tenth of the month, Yom Kippur, that the proclamation of the Jubilee was made. The Day of Atonement and the Jubilee had much in common. The message of both was a 'new birth'. The Day of Atonement freed man from slavery to sin and enabled him to start life anew, at one with God and with his fellow men. The Jubilee had for its aim the emancipation of the individual from the shackles of poverty, and the readjustment of the various strata in the commonwealth in accordance with social justice. No more appropriate day, therefore, for inaugurating such a year of rectification —as well as to attune the hearts of all to the sacrifices demanded by such rectification—than the day of Atonement; and no more suitable signal to inaugurate it than the blowing of the Shofar. Isa. LVIII, which forms the Haftorah for the Day of Atonement, seems to have been spoken on a Yom Kippur inaugurating a Jubilee year.

**10.** *the fiftieth year.* Some have held that the forty-ninth year itself was the Jubilee, as otherwise there would be two consecutive Sabbath-years. This opinion is not the traditional view,

## LEVITICUS XXV, 10

ויקרא בהר כה

10 בְּיוֹם הַכִּפֻּרִים תַּעֲבִירוּ שׁוֹפָר בְּכָל־אַרְצְכֶם: וְקִדַּשְׁתֶּם אֵת שְׁנַת הַחֲמִשִּׁים שָׁנָה וּקְרָאתֶם דְּרוֹר בָּאָרֶץ לְכָל־יֹשְׁבֶיהָ יוֹבֵל הִוא תִּהְיֶה לָכֶם וְשַׁבְתֶּם אִישׁ אֶל־אֲחֻזָּתוֹ
11 וְאִישׁ אֶל־מִשְׁפַּחְתּוֹ תָּשֻׁבוּ: יוֹבֵל הִוא שְׁנַת הַחֲמִשִּׁים שָׁנָה תִּהְיֶה לָכֶם לֹא תִזְרָעוּ וְלֹא תִקְצְרוּ אֶת־סְפִיחֶיהָ
12 וְלֹא תִבְצְרוּ אֶת־נְזִרֶיהָ: כִּי יוֹבֵל הִוא קֹדֶשׁ תִּהְיֶה לָכֶם
13 מִן־הַשָּׂדֶה תֹּאכְלוּ אֶת־תְּבוּאָתָהּ: בִּשְׁנַת הַיּוֹבֵל הַזֹּאת
14 תָּשֻׁבוּ אִישׁ אֶל־אֲחֻזָּתוֹ: וְכִי־תִמְכְּרוּ מִמְכָּר לַעֲמִיתֶךָ
15 אוֹ קָנֹה מִיַּד עֲמִיתֶךָ אַל־תּוֹנוּ אִישׁ אֶת־אָחִיו: בְּמִסְפַּר שָׁנִים אַחַר הַיּוֹבֵל תִּקְנֶה מֵאֵת עֲמִיתֶךָ בְּמִסְפַּר שְׁנֵי־
16 תְבוּאֹת יִמְכָּר־לָךְ: לְפִי ׀ רֹב הַשָּׁנִים תַּרְבֶּה מִקְנָתוֹ וּלְפִי

v. 11. קמץ בז״ק

---

proclamation with the horn throughout all your land. 10. And ye shall hallow the fiftieth year, and proclaim liberty throughout the land unto all the inhabitants thereof; it shall be a jubilee unto you; and ye shall return every man unto his possession, and ye shall return every man unto his family. 11. A jubilee shall that fiftieth year be unto you; ye shall not sow, neither reap that which groweth of itself in it, nor gather the grapes in it of the undressed vines. 12. For it is a jubilee; it shall be holy unto you; ye shall eat the increase thereof out of the field. 13. In this year of jubilee ye shall return every man unto his possession.\*ii. 14. And if thou sell aught unto thy neighbour, or buy of thy neighbour's hand, ye shall not wrong one another. 15. According to the number of years after the jubilee thou shalt buy of thy neighbour, and according unto the number of years of the crops he shall sell unto thee. 16. According to the multitude of the years thou shalt increase the price thereof, and according to the fewness of the years thou shalt diminish the price of

though it finds some support in Heb. idiom; see p. 323 (on Jer. XXXIV, 14).

*proclaim liberty.* The emancipation of the slaves, and the release of landed property from mortgage.

*all the inhabitants thereof.* Even to the man who had been sold into slavery and had refused to go out in the seventh year (Exod. XXI, 5).

*a jubilee.* Or, 'a year of jubilee'; the year is so named from the blast (Heb. *yobel;* lit. 'a ram's horn') by which it was announced.

*every man unto his possession.* In this way the original equal division of the land was restored. The permanent accumulation of land in the hands of a few was prevented, and those whom fault or misfortune had thrown into poverty were given a 'second chance'.

According to Scripture 'the earth is the LORD's'; and all the land was, as it were, held from God on lease (*v.* 23). The Israelite who voluntarily or through some compulsion sold his land to another, sold not the ownership of the land, but the remainder of the lease—till the next year of Jubilee, when all the leases fell in simultaneously. The land then came back to his family, all contracts of sale to the contrary notwithstanding. His children thus enjoyed the same advantage of a 'fair start' as their father had had before them (Verinder). Heine rightly remarks that the Torah does not aim at the impossible—the abolition of property, but at the *moralization* of property, striving to bring it into harmony with equity and the true law of Reason by means of the Jubilee-year. This institution forms a most striking contrast to 'prescription' among the Romans, according to which the possessor of a piece of land could not, after the lapse of a certain period, be compelled to restore it to its real owner, so long as the latter was unable to show that he had during that period demanded restitution in due form. Far other is the spirit that we find in the Law of Moses. 'It is not the protection of property, but the protection of humanity, that is the aim of the Mosaic Code. Its Sabbath day and Sabbath year secure even to the lowliest, rest and leisure. With the blast of the jubilee trumpets the slave goes free, and a redivision of the land secures again to the poorest his fair share in the bounty of the common Creator' (Henry George).

**11.** *ye shall not sow.* The Jubilee year shares the features of the Sabbatical year.

**12.** *out of the field.* The Israelite may not store any of the produce, but whenever he requires corn or fruit, he may go out into the field and gather it.

**13.** *unto his possession.* This repetition of *v.* 10 serves as an introduction to the exposition of the law of land-tenure.

**14.** *ye shall not wrong.* There is to be no rack-renting.

**15.** *according to the number of years.* What is really conveyed to the purchaser is *not the land*, but the number of harvests which the incoming tenant would enjoy.

**16.** *the number of the crops.* As the land itself belonged to God (*v.* 23), only the produce could be a matter of sale.

533

# LEVITICUS XXV, 17

it; for the number of crops doth he sell unto thee. 17. And ye shall not wrong one another; but thou shalt fear thy God; for I am the LORD your God. 18, Wherefore ye shall do My statutes, and keep Mine ordinances and do them; and ye shall dwell in the land in safety.*iii (**ii). 19. And the land shall yield her fruit, and ye shall eat until ye have enough, and dwell therein in safety. 20. And if ye shall say: 'What shall we eat the seventh year? behold, we may not sow, nor gather in our increase'; 21. then I will command My blessing upon you in the sixth year, and it shall bring forth produce for the three years. 22. And ye shall sow the eighth year, and eat of the produce, the old store; until the ninth year, until her produce come in, ye shall eat the old store. 23. And the land shall not be sold in perpetuity; for the land is Mine; for ye are strangers and settlers with Me. 24. And in all the land of your possession ye shall grant a redemption for the land.*iv. ¶ 25. If thy brother be waxen poor, and sell some of his possession, then shall his kinsman that is next unto him come, and shall redeem that which his brother hath sold. 26. And if a man have no one to redeem it, and he be waxen rich and find sufficient means to redeem it; 27. then let him count the

---

**17.** *wrong.* Overreach; see on XIX, 33.

*fear thy God.* This principle of a fair deal in the leasing of landed property was to be acted upon in all relations between man and man. Hence the addition of 'thou shalt fear thy God'; see on *v.* 43 and XIX, 14.

### 18–23. EXHORTATION

**18.** *dwell in . . . safety.* What follows must be understood of both the Sabbatical and Jubilee years. If the enactments are conscientiously carried out, the people, far from suffering because of the 'Sabbath' allowed to the land, would dwell in safety; *i.e.* secure from the perils of drought and famine (cf. XXVI, 5).

**21.** *for the three years.* The exceptional fertility in the sixth year might be compared with the double portion of manna which was to be gathered on the sixth day (Exod. XVI, 22).

**22.** *ninth year.* Until the Feast of Tabernacles; for then the produce of the eighth year is gathered in and stored (Rashi). 'The experience of the present day in Syria shows that, after lying fallow for a year, a field requires several ploughings before it can be sown. The consequence is that sowing cannot be begun till the following spring —the eighth year of *v.* 22—and the crop is not available till late autumn, when the ninth year has begun' (Kennedy).

**23.** *the land is Mine.* This verse enunciates the basic principle upon which all these enactments rest. 'The earth is the LORD's' (Ps. XXIV, 1), and His people hold their lands in fee from Him. The ground itself, then, was not a proper object of sale, but only the result of man's labour on the ground.

### 24–28. REDEMPTION OF LAND

**25.** *be waxen poor.* Only dire poverty would induce an Israelite to part with his family heritage. When Ahab asks Naboth to sell his vineyard, he answers the king, 'The LORD forbid it me, that I should give the inheritance of my fathers unto thee' (I Kings XXI, 3).

*his kinsman.* Heb. *goel*, lit. 'redeemer'; the technical term for him whose duty it was to avenge the person of his next-of-kin, or redeem his property that had been leased away. See Jer. XXXII, 8–12, the Haftorah to the Sedrah.

*shall redeem.* The next-of-kin is not under compulsion to do this; it is a moral obligation upon him, if his circumstances permit, to see that the property reverts to the family at the earliest opportunity. In that case, the purchaser cannot refuse to accept a just offer of repayment and return the land.

**26.** *waxen rich . . . redeem it.* 'Becomes rich enough to buy it back himself' (Moffatt).

## LEVITICUS XXV, 28

years of the sale thereof, and restore the overplus unto the man to whom he sold it; and he shall return unto his possession. 28. But if he have not sufficient means to get it back for himself, then that which he hath sold shall remain in the hand of him that hath bought it until the year of jubilee; and in the jubilee it shall go out, and he shall return unto his possession. \*v(\*\*iii). ¶ 29. And if a man sell a dwelling-house in a walled city, then he may redeem it within a whole year after it is sold; for a full year shall he have the right of redemption. 30. And if it be not redeemed within the space of a full year, then the house that is in the walled city shall be made sure in perpetuity to him that bought it, throughout his generations; it shall not go out in the jubilee. 31. But the houses of the villages which have no wall round about them shall be reckoned with the fields of the country; they may be redeemed, and they shall go out in the jubilee. 32. But as for the cities of the Levites, the houses of the cities of their possession, the Levites shall have a perpetual right of redemption. 33. And if a man purchase of the Levites, then the house that was sold in the city of his possession, shall go out in the jubilee; for the houses of the cities of the Levites are their possession

---

**27.** *the overplus.* The amount by which the purchase money of the field exceeded the value of the crops reaped by the purchaser. In Rabbinic law, if the purchaser had resold the land to a second buyer, then the owner treats with the first purchaser, if he had sold it at a higher price than he paid; and with the second, if the price had been smaller. The purpose of this regulation was to give the advantage to the original owner, and also to discourage speculation in land values.

**28.** *it shall go out.* Into freedom. According to the testimony of Josephus, there was due recognition of tenants' improvements. 'When the Jubilee is come, he that sold the land, and he that bought it, meet together, and make an estimate, on the one hand, of the fruits gathered; and, on the other hand, of the expenses laid out upon it. If the fruits gathered come to more than the expenses laid out, he that sold it takes the land again; but if the expenses prove more than the fruits, the present possessor receives of the former owner the difference that was wanting, and leaves the land to him; and if the fruits received and the expenses laid out prove equal to one another, the present possessor relinquishes it to the former owner.'

### 29–34. REDEMPTION OF HOUSES

**29.** *a dwelling-house.* A house in a walled city could be disposed of in perpetuity; but the owner had the right of re-purchase during the first year of the sale.

*a walled city.* In contrast to villages; see on v. 31.

**30.** *walled city.* The Written Text (Kethib) really is 'unwalled city.' The Rabbis explain this anomalous reading of the text to indicate that this law applies also to a city that was originally walled in, but is no longer so.

*be made sure.* That is, a house in the town could be sold 'out and out'; but not houses in the open country; see next v.

**31.** *reckoned with the fields.* Being indispensable to the man who had to work the land.

**32.** *Levites.* While Aaron and his sons were chosen for the priestly office, the menial services at the Sanctuary and Temple were assigned to the Levites—the rest of the tribe. In the Wilderness, they bore the furniture of the Sanctuary during the wanderings. At the Settlement in Canaan, the tribe of Levi received no definite domain, but scattered cities were assigned to them in territory belonging to other tribes. In these cities (see Num. xxxv, 2 f) the vendor has a perpetual right of redemption.

**33.** *if a man purchase of the Levites.* If one purchases a house in one of the Levitical cities, even if it be a walled city, the law of v. 30 does not apply; in the Jubilee, it reverts to the owner.

535

## LEVITICUS XXV, 34

among the children of Israel. 34, But the fields of the open land about their cities may not be sold; for that is their perpetual possession. ¶ 35. And if thy brother be waxen poor, and his means fail with thee; then thou shalt uphold him: as a stranger and a settler shall he live with thee. 36. Take thou no interest of him or increase; but fear thy God; that thy brother may live with thee. 37. Thou shalt not give him thy money upon interest, nor give him thy victuals for increase. 38. I am the LORD your God, who brought you forth out of the land of Egypt, to give you the land of Canaan, to be your God.* vi(**iv). ¶ 39. And if thy brother be waxen poor with thee, and sell himself unto thee, thou shalt not make him to serve as a bondservant. 40. As a hired servant, and as a settler, he shall be with thee; he shall serve with thee unto the year of jubilee. 41. Then shall he go out from thee, he and his children with him, and shall return unto his own family, and unto the possession

ויקרא בהר כה

אֲחֻזָּתוֹ בְּיֹבֵל כִּי בָתֵּי עָרֵי הַלְוִיִּם הִוא אֲחֻזָּתָם בְּתוֹךְ
34 בְּנֵי יִשְׂרָאֵל: וּשְׂדֵה מִגְרַשׁ עָרֵיהֶם לֹא יִמָּכֵר כִּי־אֲחֻזַּת
לה עוֹלָם הוּא לָהֶם: ס וְכִי־יָמוּךְ אָחִיךָ וּמָטָה יָדוֹ עִמָּךְ
36 וְהֶחֱזַקְתָּ בּוֹ גֵּר וְתוֹשָׁב וָחַי עִמָּךְ: אַל־תִּקַּח מֵאִתּוֹ נֶשֶׁךְ
37 וְתַרְבִּית וְיָרֵאתָ מֵאֱלֹהֶיךָ וְחֵי אָחִיךָ עִמָּךְ: אֶת־כַּסְפְּךָ
38 לֹא־תִתֵּן לוֹ בְּנֶשֶׁךְ וּבְמַרְבִּית לֹא־תִתֵּן אָכְלֶךָ: אֲנִי יְהוָה
שני (רביעי אֱלֹהֵיכֶם אֲשֶׁר־הוֹצֵאתִי אֶתְכֶם מֵאֶרֶץ מִצְרָיִם לָתֵת לָכֶם
כשהן מחוב׳) אֶת־אֶרֶץ כְּנַעַן לִהְיוֹת לָכֶם לֵאלֹהִים: ס וְכִי־יָמוּךְ
39
אָחִיךָ עִמָּךְ וְנִמְכַּר־לָךְ לֹא־תַעֲבֹד בּוֹ עֲבֹדַת עָבֶד:
מ כְּשָׂכִיר כְּתוֹשָׁב יִהְיֶה עִמָּךְ עַד־שְׁנַת הַיֹּבֵל יַעֲבֹד עִמָּךְ:

### 35–38. PRACTICAL LOVE OF NEIGHBOUR

**35.** *if thy brother be waxen poor.* He still remains thy brother, and is to be treated in a brotherly and considerate manner. This is in strongest contrast to the treatment of the impoverished debtor in ancient Rome. The creditor could imprison him in his own private dungeon, chain him to a block, sell him into slavery, or even put him to death. If the debtor had several creditors, the Roman Law of the Twelve Tables ordained that they could hew him in pieces; and although one of them took a part of his body larger in proportion than his claim, the other creditors had no redress!

*uphold him.* Or, 'relieve him.' Do not suffer him to come down into the depths of misery, for then it is difficult to raise him; but come to his support at the time when his means *begin* to fail (Rashi).

*as a stranger and a settler shall he live.* Better, *yea though he be a stranger, or a sojourner; that he may live* (AV, Zunz, Benisch—following Rashi and Ibn Ezra). The great principle of 'Thou shalt love thy neighbour as thyself' must be a reality in Israelite life. The stranger and alien settler are explicitly included in the term *thy brother*, and are to be helped by timely loans, free of interest.

*shall he live with thee.* These words can be understood quite literally: it is the Israelite's *duty* to see to it that his fellowman does not die of starvation. It was centuries, millennia even, before the world outside Israel learned this elementary duty. Constantine in 315 is the first European ruler to have effected poor relief legislation, only to be repealed by Justinian two centuries later. It was not till the days of Queen Elizabeth that poor relief came to be recognized as a duty of the State. Other States followed England's example in the nineteenth century.

**36.** *interest.* This prohibition led to the establishment in every organized Jewish community of a *Gemillus Chassodim* Society, for advancing loans free of interest to the poor; see also on Deut. XXIII, 20.

*fear thy God.* To take advantage of the dire need of the poor is contrary to all decent human feeling; for the Heb. idiom see on Exod. I, 17.

**37.** *victuals for increase.* Interest on foodstuffs, seed, and the like, which was paid in kind.

**38.** *brought . . . Egypt.* The Israelites, in their prosperity, were to remember the days when they were in bondage and needed the help that God had vouchsafed to them. Let them follow the Divine example, and not imitate the callousness of their Egyptian masters, but deal with their fellowmen in a spirit of brotherhood and justice.

### 39–46. NO PERMANENT SERVITUDE FOR ANY ISRAELITE

When a man's ill fortune forces him to sell himself into bondage, his Hebrew master had definite obligations towards one who is of the same flesh and blood as himself. These regulations are unique in the respect for labour they inculcate and the manner in which the dignity of the labourer is safeguarded.

**40.** *as a hired servant.* He was not to be given any menial or degrading work, but only agricultural tasks or skilled labour, such as would be performed by a free labourer who is hired for a season.

## LEVITICUS XXV, 42

of his fathers shall he return. 42. For they are My servants, whom I brought forth out of the land of Egypt; they shall not be sold as bondmen. 43, Thou shalt not rule over him with rigour; but shalt fear thy God. 44. And as for thy bondmen, and thy bondmaids, whom thou mayest have: of the nations that are round about you, of them shall ye buy bondmen and bondmaids. 45. Moreover of the children of the strangers that do sojourn among you, of them may ye buy, and of their families that are with you, which they have begotten in your land; and they may be your possession. 46, And ye may make them an inheritance for your children after you, to hold for a possession: of them may ye take your bondmen for ever; but over your brethren the children of Israel

41 וְיָצָא מֵעִמָּךְ הוּא וּבָנָיו עִמּוֹ וְשָׁב אֶל־מִשְׁפַּחְתּוֹ וְאֶל־
42 אֲחֻזַּת אֲבֹתָיו יָשׁוּב: כִּי־עֲבָדַי הֵם אֲשֶׁר־הוֹצֵאתִי אֹתָם
43 מֵאֶרֶץ מִצְרָיִם לֹא יִמָּכְרוּ מִמְכֶּרֶת עָבֶד: לֹא־תִרְדֶּה בוֹ
44 בְּפָרֶךְ וְיָרֵאתָ מֵאֱלֹהֶיךָ: וְעַבְדְּךָ וַאֲמָתְךָ אֲשֶׁר יִהְיוּ־לָךְ
מֵאֵת הַגּוֹיִם אֲשֶׁר סְבִיבֹתֵיכֶם מֵהֶם תִּקְנוּ עֶבֶד וְאָמָה:
מה וְגַם מִבְּנֵי הַתּוֹשָׁבִים הַגָּרִים עִמָּכֶם מֵהֶם תִּקְנוּ וּמִמִּשְׁפַּחְתָּם
אֲשֶׁר עִמָּכֶם אֲשֶׁר הוֹלִידוּ בְּאַרְצְכֶם וְהָיוּ לָכֶם לַאֲחֻזָּה:
46 וְהִתְנַחַלְתֶּם אֹתָם לִבְנֵיכֶם אַחֲרֵיכֶם לָרֶשֶׁת אֲחֻזָּה לְעֹלָם

*unto the year of jubilee.* This must be understood in connection with Exod. XXI, 2 f, and Deut. XV, 12 f, which ordain that the Hebrew who sells himself into slavery serves his master for six years, and goes free in the seventh. Should the Jubilee occur before his six years of service are over, the servant regains his personal freedom at the same time that his inheritance returns to him, in the year of Jubilee.

**41.** *his children.* Should the Hebrew be the father of a family when he sells himself into slavery, the master has to take the children into his care and maintain them.

*his own family.* The Rabbis taught that the freed slave must be received with cordiality and friendliness by his relatives, and no slight shown to him because of his former servitude.

**42.** *for they are My servants.* An Israelite therefore can never be more than nominally a slave to any human master.

*they shall not be sold as bondmen.* lit. 'they shall not be sold the sale of a slave'. The Rabbis ruled that a Hebrew is not to be sold publicly in the slave-market, but the sale is to be privately arranged.

**43.** *with rigour.* The same word is used to describe the hardship of Israel's bondage in Egypt (Exod. I, 13). In Rabbinic law, the rules that should regulate the relationship between a master and his Hebrew slave are given in great detail, and are based on the principle that master and man are kinsmen; *e.g.* the slave must not be given inferior food or accommodation to that of the master. Kindliness and chivalry are to characterize the bearing of the Israelite towards his less fortunate brother.

*but shalt fear thy God.* 'Whenever this phrase is used it refers to matters that are part of heart-religion,' דבר מסור ללב (Sifra); *i.e.* part of natural piety and fundamental humanity in our dealings with our fellowmen.

**46.** *of them may ye take your bondmen.* Better, *you may hold them to service* (Leeser); Heb. בהם תעבדו. 'You may hold them to service, but only to service, nothing more' (Sifra).

### XXV, 46. SLAVERY

The system of slavery which is tolerated by the Torah was fundamentally different from the cruel systems of the ancient world, and even of Western countries down to the middle of the last century. The Code of Hammurabi has penalties only for the master who destroys the tooth or eye of *another man*'s slave. It orders that a slave's ear be cut off, if he desires freedom; while to harbour a runaway slave was considered a capital offence. As to Greece, a slave was deemed 'an animated tool', and he could claim no more rights in his relationship to his master than a beast of burden. Agricultural labourers were chained. If at any time it was thought that there were too many slaves, they were exterminated, as wild beasts would be. Athens was an important slave market, and the State profited from it by a tax on the sales. So much for 'the glory that was Greece'. The 'grandeur that was Rome' was even more detestable. The slave was denied all human rights, and sentenced to horrible mutilation and even crucifixion at the whim of his master. Sick slaves were exposed to die of starvation, and there was *corporate* responsibility for slaves: Tacitus records that as late as the Empire the 400 slaves of one household were all put to death because they had been under their master's roof when he was murdered. Worlds asunder from these inhumanities and barbarities was the treatment accorded to the Hebrew slave. The position of Eliezer in Abraham's household (Gen. XXIV) enables us to realize the nature of servitude in the ancient Hebrew home. Kidnapping a man or selling him as a slave was a

## LEVITICUS XXV, 47

ye shall not rule, one over another, with rigour.*vii. ¶ 47. And if a stranger who is a settler with thee be waxen rich, and thy brother be waxen poor beside him, and sell himself unto the stranger who is a settler with thee, or to the offshoot of a stranger's family, 48. after that he is sold he may be redeemed; one of his brethren may redeem him; 49, or his uncle, or his uncle's son, may redeem him, or any that is nigh of kin unto him of his family may redeem him; or if he be waxen rich, he may redeem himself. 50. And he shall reckon with him that bought him from the year that he sold himself to him unto the year of jubilee; and the price of his sale shall be according unto the number of years; according to the time of a hired servant shall he be with him. 51. If there be yet many years, according unto them he shall give back the price of his redemption out of the money that he was bought for. 52. And if there remain but few years unto the year of jubilee, then he shall reckon with him; according unto his years shall he give back the price of his redemption. 53. As a servant hired year by year shall he be with him; he shall not rule with rigour over him in thy sight. 54. And if he be not redeemed by any of these means, then he shall go out in the year of jubilee,

וִיקְרָא בְּהַר כה

שביעי
47 בָּהֶם תַּעֲבֹדוּ וּבְאַחֵיכֶם בְּנֵי־יִשְׂרָאֵל אִישׁ בְּאָחִיו לֹא־תִרְדֶּה בוֹ בְּפָרֶךְ: ס וְכִי תַשִּׂיג יַד גֵּר וְתוֹשָׁב עִמָּךְ וּמָךְ אָחִיךָ עִמּוֹ וְנִמְכַּר לְגֵר תּוֹשָׁב עִמָּךְ אוֹ לְעֵקֶר
48 מִשְׁפַּחַת גֵּר: אַחֲרֵי נִמְכַּר גְּאֻלָּה תִּהְיֶה־לּוֹ אֶחָד מֵאֶחָיו
49 יִגְאָלֶנּוּ: אוֹ־דֹדוֹ אוֹ בֶן־דֹּדוֹ יִגְאָלֶנּוּ אוֹ־מִשְּׁאֵר בְּשָׂרוֹ מִמִּשְׁפַּחְתּוֹ יִגְאָלֶנּוּ אוֹ־הִשִּׂיגָה יָדוֹ וְנִגְאָל: וְחִשַּׁב עִם־קֹנֵהוּ מִשְּׁנַת הִמָּכְרוֹ לוֹ עַד שְׁנַת הַיֹּבֵל וְהָיָה כֶּסֶף מִמְכָּרוֹ
51 בְּמִסְפַּר שָׁנִים כִּימֵי שָׂכִיר יִהְיֶה עִמּוֹ: אִם־עוֹד רַבּוֹת
52 בַּשָּׁנִים לְפִיהֶן יָשִׁיב גְּאֻלָּתוֹ מִכֶּסֶף מִקְנָתוֹ: וְאִם־מְעַט נִשְׁאַר בַּשָּׁנִים עַד־שְׁנַת הַיֹּבֵל וְחִשַּׁב־לוֹ כְּפִי שָׁנָיו יָשִׁיב
53 אֶת־גְּאֻלָּתוֹ: כִּשְׂכִיר שָׁנָה בְּשָׁנָה יִהְיֶה עִמּוֹ לֹא־יִרְדֶּנּוּ
54 בְּפֶרֶךְ לְעֵינֶיךָ: וְאִם־לֹא יִגָּאֵל בְּאֵלֶּה וְיָצָא בִּשְׁנַת הַיֹּבֵל
מפטיר
נה הוּא וּבָנָיו עִמּוֹ: כִּי־לִי בְנֵי־יִשְׂרָאֵל עֲבָדִים עֲבָדַי הֵם

capital offence. Cruelty on the part of the master that resulted in injury to an organ of the body secured the slave's freedom (Exod. XXI, 26 f); and if a slave ran away, he must not be surrendered to his master (Deut. XXIII, 16 f). A Fugitive Slave Law, such as existed in America, with the tracking of runaway slaves by blood hounds, would have been unthinkable to the Israelite of old.

47–55. ISRAELITES WHO ARE SLAVES OF ALIENS

**47.** *offshoot.* Children of alien settlers would frequently join the Israelitish community; but the case dealt with here is that of a Hebrew selling himself into the service of an alien who remained aloof from the community.

**48.** *may be redeemed.* Forthwith.
*may redeem him.* For *may* substitute *shall*, here and in the next verse.

**49.** *if he be waxen rich.* lit. 'if he attaineth to power' (or 'means').

**50.** *unto the year of jubilee.* Hence it is to be deduced that, unlike the Hebrew slave who sells himself to a Hebrew master, his service does not automatically cease at the end of six years (Exod. XXI, 2). It is presupposed here that the man sold himself for an indefinite period, and unless redeemed would continue in bondage until the Jubilee.
*a hired servant.* The calculation is to be based on the assumption that the total sum paid was for a definite number of years till the Jubilee. This total sum is to be divided by the number of years, and it was to be considered that he had hired himself for the resulting amount per year (Rashi).

**51.** *yet many years.* To the Jubilee, and the amount required for the redemption accordingly high.

**53.** *servant.* He was to be treated like a workman hired by the year who belonged to a higher grade of labour.
*in thy sight.* If you see the alien master ill-treating him, you must intervene; but you have no right to enter his house to make investigation as to how he treats his slave (Sifra).

**54.** *by any of these means.* Lit. 'by those' which may refer to the kinsmen mentioned in *v.* 48, or to the method of regaining his freedom, described in *v.* 50 f.
*and his children.* See on *v.* 41 above.

**55.** *My servants.* Cf. *v.* 42.

LEVITICUS XXV, 55

he, and his children with him.* m. 55. For unto Me the children of Israel are servants; they are My servants whom I brought forth out of the land of Egypt; I am the LORD your God.

## 26 CHAPTER XXVI

1. Ye shall make you no idols, neither shall ye rear you up a graven image, or a pillar, neither shall ye place any figured stone in your land, to bow down unto it; for I am the LORD your God. 2. Ye shall keep My sabbaths, and reverence My sanctuary: I am the LORD.

### CHAPTER XXVI

The traditional Hebrew division of the Bible Text attaches the first two verses of this chapter to the preceding. The association of ideas is explained by the Sifra in this way: at the end of the last chapter, the Torah had treated of the case of an Israelite who had sold himself as a slave to a heathen master, and who might be tempted to follow the worship of his heathen master. Therefore, the warning of these verses is uttered. The words may, however, have a wider application. These two verses give 'the quintessence of the foregoing legislation' (Baentsch).

1-2. IDOLATRY FORBIDDEN, AND THE SABBATH TO BE OBSERVED

1. **idols**. See on XIX, 4.

*pillar*. Heb. *matzebah*. A memorial stone, as in Gen. XXVIII, 18, Exod. XXIV, 4; and also a stone or carved obelisk used for idolatrous worship (Exod. XXIII, 24, Deut. VII, 5).

*figured stone*. With some idolatrous representation carved on it.

*unto it*. Better, *thereon*.

2. *sabbaths . . . sanctuary*. Cf. XIX, 30. Not only have the Israelites to refrain from idol-worship, but God demands from them the due observance of 'Sabbaths'—which here includes the festive occasions as well as the Sabbatical years—and also the fulfilment of all obligations connected with the Sanctuary.


# HAFTORAH BEHAR

### JEREMIAH XXXII, 6-27

#### CHAPTER XXXII

6. And Jeremiah said: 'The word of the LORD came unto me, saying: 7. Behold, Hanamel, the son of Shallum thine uncle, shall come unto thee, saying: Buy thee my field that is in Anathoth; for the right of redemption is thine to buy it.' 8. So Hanamel mine uncle's son came to me in the court of the guard according to the word of the LORD, and said unto me: 'Buy my field, I pray thee, that is in Anathoth, which is

For a brief characterization of the life and message of Jeremiah see p. 229.

The Sedrah deals with the redemption of a family inheritance; and the Haftorah furnishes a striking instance of its observance at a great crisis in Israel's history. It was in the year 587, during the siege of Jerusalem, when Jeremiah was

in prison because of his outspoken foretelling of the inevitable capture and destruction of the City by the Babylonians. At that dark hour, the Prophet 'redeemed' a piece of land, so that it should not pass out of his family.

He looks beyond the storm of judgment to the hope of a brighter day. In the offer of redemp-

## JEREMIAH XXXII, 9

in the land of Benjamin; for the right of inheritance is thine, and the redemption is thine; buy it for thyself.' Then I knew that this was the word of the LORD. 9. And I bought the field that was in Anathoth of Hanamel mine uncle's son, and weighed him the money, even seventeen shekels of silver. 10. And I subscribed the deed, and sealed it, and called witnesses, and weighed him the money in the balances. 11. So I took the deed of the purchase, both that which was sealed, containing the terms and conditions, and that which was open; 12. and I delivered the deed of the purchase unto Baruch the son of Neriah, the son of Mahseiah, in the presence of Hanamel mine uncle['s son], and in the presence of the witnesses that subscribed the deed of the purchase, before all the Jews that sat in the court of the guard. 13. And I charged Baruch before them, saying: 14. 'Thus saith the LORD of hosts, the God of Israel: Take these deeds, this deed of the purchase, both that which is sealed, and this deed which is open, and put them in an earthen vessel; that they may continue many days. 15. For thus saith the LORD of hosts, the God of Israel: Houses and fields and vineyards shall yet again be bought in this land.'
¶ 16. Now after I had delivered the deed of

בֶּן־דֹּדִי כִּדְבַר־יְהוָה אֶל־חֲצַר הַמַּטָּרָה וַיֹּאמֶר אֵלַי קְנֵה
נָא אֶת־שָׂדִי אֲשֶׁר־בַּעֲנָתוֹת אֲשֶׁר ׀ בְּאֶרֶץ בִּנְיָמִין כִּי־לְךָ
מִשְׁפַּט הַיְרֻשָּׁה וּלְךָ הַגְּאֻלָּה קְנֵה־לָךְ וָאֵדַע כִּי דְבַר־
9 יְהוָה הוּא: וָאֶקְנֶה אֶת־הַשָּׂדֶה מֵאֵת חֲנַמְאֵל בֶּן־דֹּדִי
אֲשֶׁר בַּעֲנָתוֹת וָאֶשְׁקֲלָה־לּוֹ אֶת־הַכֶּסֶף שִׁבְעָה שְׁקָלִים
10 וַעֲשָׂרָה הַכָּסֶף: וָאֶכְתֹּב בַּסֵּפֶר וָאֶחְתֹּם וָאָעֵד עֵדִים
11 וָאֶשְׁקֹל הַכֶּסֶף בְּמֹאזְנָיִם: וָאֶקַּח אֶת־סֵפֶר הַמִּקְנָה אֶת־
12 הֶחָתוּם הַמִּצְוָה וְהַחֻקִּים וְאֶת־הַגָּלוּי: וָאֶתֵּן אֶת־הַסֵּפֶר
הַמִּקְנָה אֶל־בָּרוּךְ בֶּן־נֵרִיָּה בֶּן־מַחְסֵיָה לְעֵינֵי חֲנַמְאֵל דֹּדִי
וּלְעֵינֵי הָעֵדִים הַכֹּתְבִים בְּסֵפֶר הַמִּקְנָה לְעֵינֵי כָּל־הַיְּהוּדִים
13 הַיֹּשְׁבִים בַּחֲצַר הַמַּטָּרָה: וָאֲצַוֶּה אֶת־בָּרוּךְ לְעֵינֵיהֶם
14 לֵאמֹר: כֹּה־אָמַר יְהוָה צְבָאוֹת אֱלֹהֵי יִשְׂרָאֵל לָקוֹחַ אֶת־
הַסְּפָרִים הָאֵלֶּה אֵת סֵפֶר הַמִּקְנָה הַזֶּה וְאֵת הֶחָתוּם וְאֵת
סֵפֶר הַגָּלוּי הַזֶּה וּנְתַתָּם בִּכְלִי־חָרֶשׂ לְמַעַן יַעַמְדוּ יָמִים
15 רַבִּים: כִּי כֹה אָמַר יְהוָה צְבָאוֹת אֱלֹהֵי יִשְׂרָאֵל

---

tion that is made to him by a kinsman, he sees a God-sent opportunity to show forth to his brethren a Divine pledge that the night of Captivity will be followed by the morn of Return, when houses and lands will once again be freely bought and sold. His action finds a parallel during Hannibal's invasion of Italy, when a Roman purchased, at full price in public auction, the ground on which the enemy's army was encamped.

**7.** *Anathoth.* Jeremiah's birthplace.

*right of redemption.* As next-of-kin, Jeremiah has the right of pre-emption to his relative's land, so that it shall not pass out of the family; Lev. xxv, 24 f.

**8.** *court of the guard.* A part of the court surrounding the Palace, railed off to guard prisoners whom it was not desired to throw into the common dungeon (Driver).

*then I knew that this was the word of the LORD.* He had previously (v. 7) had a mysterious premonition of the visit and of its purpose; but now he is convinced that God had inspired the visit. The purchase would illustrate in a most striking manner the certainty of Israel's restoration (see v. 15).

**9–11.** He bought the field, and sealed the purchase with all the legal formalities. The Jews had been vassals of Assyria and Babylon for about a century; and, it seems, transference of land was now performed according to the legal procedure of the Sovereign Power. As in all Babylonian documents of that nature, the deed was written on clay, and enclosed in a clay envelope, which was sealed up. A copy of the contract was inscribed on the envelope: this is referred to in v. 14 as the 'open' deed. Only in case of the writing on the envelope becoming obliterated, or of suspicion that it had been tampered with, was the envelope broken and the text itself examined.

**12.** *Baruch.* Jeremiah's faithful secretary who, at the Prophet's dictation, wrote down his addresses (see Chap. xxxvi). It is to him that we owe the preservation of the Prophet's utterances.

**14.** *in an earthen vessel.* Similarly bottles are used nowadays to preserve documents placed in the memorial stones of public buildings (Bennett).

*that they may continue many days.* Though it would be a long time before the deed would be needed, yet the prophecy of which it is a sign would be fulfilled.

**15.** *houses . . . again be bought.* He who had been denounced as a deserter and traitor is now their best comforter and counsellor.

**16–27.** A wave of doubt surges over Jeremiah. He is himself overwhelmed by the darkness that is enveloping his People. From the court of the guard, he could see the works of the besiegers; and, within the City, famine and pestilence were

# JEREMIAH XXXII, 17

the purchase unto Baruch the son of Neriah, I prayed unto the LORD, saying: 17. 'Ah Lord GOD! behold, Thou hast made the heaven and the earth by Thy great power and by Thy outstretched arm; there is nothing too hard for Thee; 18. who showest mercy unto thousands, and recompensest the iniquity of the fathers into the bosom of their children after them; the great, the mighty God, the LORD of hosts is His name; 19. great in counsel, and mighty in work; whose eyes are open upon all the ways of the sons of men, to give every one according to his ways, and according to the fruit of his doings; 20. who didst set signs and wonders in the land of Egypt, even unto this day, and in Israel and among other men; and madest Thee a name, as at this day; 21. and didst bring forth Thy people Israel out of the land of Egypt with signs, and with wonders, and with a strong hand, and with an outstretched arm, and with great terror; 22. and gavest them this land, which Thou didst swear to their fathers to give them, a land flowing with milk and honey; 23. and they came in, and possessed it; but they hearkened not to Thy voice, neither walked in Thy law; they have done nothing of all that Thou commandedst them to do; therefore Thou hast caused all this evil to befall them; 24. behold the mounds, they are come unto the city to take it; and the city is given into the hand of the Chaldeans that fight against it, because of the sword, and of the famine, and of the pestilence; and what Thou hast spoken is come to pass; and, behold, Thou seest it. 25. Yet Thou hast said unto me, O Lord GOD: Buy thee the field for money, and call witnesses; whereas the city is given into the hand of the Chaldeans.' ¶ 26. Then came the word of the LORD unto Jeremiah, saying: 27. 'Behold, I am the LORD, the God of all flesh; is there any thing too hard for Me?

ירמיה לב

עוֹד יִקָּנוּ בָתִּים וְשָׂדוֹת וּכְרָמִים בָּאָרֶץ הַזֹּאת:
16 וָאֶתְפַּלֵּל אֶל־יְהוָה אַחֲרֵי תִתִּי אֶת־סֵפֶר הַמִּקְנָה אֶל־בָּרוּךְ
17 בֶּן־נֵרִיָּה לֵאמֹר: אֲהָהּ אֲדֹנָי יְהוִה הִנֵּה ׀ אַתָּה עָשִׂיתָ
אֶת־הַשָּׁמַיִם וְאֶת־הָאָרֶץ בְּכֹחֲךָ הַגָּדוֹל וּבִזְרֹעֲךָ הַנְּטוּיָה
18 לֹא־יִפָּלֵא מִמְּךָ כָּל־דָּבָר: עֹשֶׂה חֶסֶד לַאֲלָפִים וּמְשַׁלֵּם
עֲוֹן אָבוֹת אֶל־חֵיק בְּנֵיהֶם אַחֲרֵיהֶם הָאֵל הַגָּדוֹל הַגִּבּוֹר
19 יְהוָה צְבָאוֹת שְׁמוֹ: גְּדֹל הָעֵצָה וְרַב הָעֲלִילִיָּה אֲשֶׁר־
עֵינֶיךָ פְקֻחוֹת עַל־כָּל־דַּרְכֵי בְּנֵי אָדָם לָתֵת לְאִישׁ כִּדְרָכָיו
כ וְכִפְרִי מַעֲלָלָיו: אֲשֶׁר־שַׂמְתָּ אֹתוֹת וּמֹפְתִים בְּאֶרֶץ־מִצְרַיִם
עַד־הַיּוֹם הַזֶּה וּבְיִשְׂרָאֵל וּבָאָדָם וַתַּעֲשֶׂה־לְּךָ שֵׁם כַּיּוֹם
21 הַזֶּה: וַתֹּצֵא אֶת־עַמְּךָ אֶת־יִשְׂרָאֵל מֵאֶרֶץ מִצְרָיִם בְּאֹתוֹת
וּבְמוֹפְתִים וּבְיָד חֲזָקָה וּבְאֶזְרוֹעַ נְטוּיָה וּבְמוֹרָא גָּדוֹל:
22 וַתִּתֵּן לָהֶם אֶת־הָאָרֶץ הַזֹּאת אֲשֶׁר־נִשְׁבַּעְתָּ לַאֲבוֹתָם לָתֵת
23 לָהֶם אֶרֶץ זָבַת חָלָב וּדְבָשׁ: וַיָּבֹאוּ וַיִּרְשׁוּ אֹתָהּ וְלֹא־
שָׁמְעוּ בְקוֹלֶךָ וּבְתוֹרָתְךָ לֹא־הָלָכוּ אֵת כָּל־אֲשֶׁר צִוִּיתָה
לָהֶם לַעֲשׂוֹת לֹא עָשׂוּ וַתַּקְרֵא אֹתָם אֵת כָּל־הָרָעָה
24 הַזֹּאת: הִנֵּה הַסֹּלְלוֹת בָּאוּ הָעִיר לְלָכְדָהּ וְהָעִיר נִתְּנָה
בְּיַד הַכַּשְׂדִּים הַנִּלְחָמִים עָלֶיהָ מִפְּנֵי הַחֶרֶב וְהָרָעָב וְהַדָּבֶר
כה וַאֲשֶׁר דִּבַּרְתָּ הָיָה וְהִנְּךָ רֹאֶה: וְאַתָּה אָמַרְתָּ אֵלַי אֲדֹנָי
יְהוִה קְנֵה־לְךָ הַשָּׂדֶה בַּכֶּסֶף וְהָעֵד עֵדִים וְהָעִיר נִתְּנָה
26 בְּיַד הַכַּשְׂדִּים: וַיְהִי דְּבַר־יְהוָה אֶל־יִרְמְיָהוּ לֵאמֹר:
27 הִנֵּה אֲנִי יְהוָה אֱלֹהֵי כָּל־בָּשָׂר הֲמִמֶּנִּי יִפָּלֵא כָּל־דָּבָר:

v. 23. ibid. קמץ בז״ק ובתורתך קרי.

---

raging. He therefore turns to God and seeks assurance for the faith and confidence which he has sought to implant in others by his symbolic action of purchase.

**17-19.** Jeremiah begins his prayer by declaring God's power in creation and history, and His righteous government of humanity.

**18.** *the iniquity of the fathers.* Recalling the words of the Second Commandment; Exod. xx, 5, 6.

**20-23.** He remembers the wonders of God wrought for Israel in Egypt, and the bounties bestowed on them after the Exodus.

**20.** *unto this day.* They are known and remembered to this day (Kimchi).

**21.** *great terror.* Struck into Egypt by the wonders He wrought at the Exodus.

**24.** *the mounds.* Embankments against the City walls, for the attacking soldiers to make their assaults.

*Chaldeans.* Chaldea at that time included the whole of Babylonia.

**27.** *Is there any thing too hard for me?* One of the great answers—and facts of history; cf. Gen. XVIII, 14. God gives back to Jeremiah his own words 'There is nothing too hard for Thee' (v. 17). He had come to God with the best thoughts about Him, and God gives him the answer that his thoughts are true.

LEVITICUS XXVI, 3

3. If ye walk in My statutes, and keep My commandments, and do them; 4. then I will give your rains in their season, and the land shall yield her produce, and the trees of the field shall yield their fruit. 5. And your threshing shall reach unto the vintage, and the vintage shall reach unto the sowing time; and ye shall eat your bread until ye have enough, and dwell in your land safely. * ii. 6. And I will give peace in the land, and ye shall lie down, and none shall make you afraid; and I will cause evil beasts

3 אִם־בְּחֻקֹּתַי תֵּלֵכוּ וְאֶת־מִצְוֹתַי תִּשְׁמְרוּ וַעֲשִׂיתֶם אֹתָם:
4 וְנָתַתִּי גִשְׁמֵיכֶם בְּעִתָּם וְנָתְנָה הָאָרֶץ יְבוּלָהּ וְעֵץ הַשָּׂדֶה
ה יִתֵּן פִּרְיוֹ: וְהִשִּׂיג לָכֶם דַּיִשׁ אֶת־בָּצִיר וּבָצִיר יַשִּׂיג אֶת־
שני זָרַע וַאֲכַלְתֶּם לַחְמְכֶם לָשֹׂבַע וִישַׁבְתֶּם לָבֶטַח בְּאַרְצְכֶם:
6 וְנָתַתִּי שָׁלוֹם בָּאָרֶץ וּשְׁכַבְתֶּם וְאֵין מַחֲרִיד וְהִשְׁבַּתִּי חַיָּה

## X. BECHUKOSAI

(CHAPTERS XXVI, 3–XXVII)

### CONCLUDING ADMONITION

The Book of Leviticus has its sacerdotal chapters, its ceremonial parts, its ethical section; and, in its concluding portion, it strikes the note of Prophetic admonition and warning. This is not to be wondered at when we recall the fact that Moses is 'the Father of the Prophets'. The Jewish name for this chapter from *v.* 14–45 (as well as for the parallel section in Deut. XXVIII) is *Tochacha*, תוכחה; lit. 'Warning', 'Admonition'.

After having declared the higher law and rooted all human duty, both to God and man, in the Holiness-ideal—'Ye shall be holy, for I the LORD your God am holy'—the Lawgiver endeavours to enlist man's natural fear and hope as allies of that sublime principle. In startling and indeed in terrifying form, he contrasts the blessings, in the event of faithfulness to God, with the dire calamities, if the people prove disloyal to Him. This fundamental thought, viz. that God rewards the righteous and punishes the wicked, is an essential doctrine of Judaism as of every higher religion. They may differ as to the nature and form of Divine retribution, but the belief that right is rewarded and wrong punished is part of an ethical faith, a belief vindicated and confirmed by the experience of humanity. 'One lesson, and only one, history may be said to repeat with distinctness, that the world is built somehow on moral foundations; that in the long run it is well with the good; in the long run it is ill with the wicked' (Froude). But, while there is general agreement with this truth underlying the Admonition, there has always been discontent with the manner in which it is presented in this chapter. 'Why,' it is asked, 'does Scripture enter into such dreadful details concerning the consequences of disobedience?' Two observations must be made in regard to this form of appeal. The first is, that it is a language which the people to whom this homiletic discourse on the Wages of Disobedience was originally addressed, could clearly understand. 'A wealth of bliss may be depicted in two or three concise phrases, but to cause the primitive mind to realize the awful consequences of sin and transgression, the words of denunciation must come swift and powerful as hammer blows, and must picture to their last terrible results the dreadful devastation wrought by human perversity' (Drachmann). The second is that the *Tochacha*, though it may sound harsh, is true; and truth in its nakedness is not always pleasant. The promises and, alas, also the warnings in this chapter have abundantly been borne out by Jewish history. 'As a survey of the worldly blessings and tribulations employed by God in His education of Israel in Canaan, this chapter is fairly exhaustive, and is in line with what Prophecy proclaimed, and historical experience taught, in the course of the centuries' (Dillmann); see also on Deut. XXVIII.

3–13. BLESSINGS IN THE WAKE OF OBEDIENCE

**3.** *if ye walk in My statutes.* Heb. אם בחקתי תלכו; Sifra translates: 'Would that you walked in my statutes!'

*statutes.* See on XVIII, 4.

**4.** *rains.* The rainfall is of supreme importance in the Holy Land. If it fails, the result is famine. Consequently, it comes first among the blessings.

**5.** *threshing.* Cf. Amos IX, 13. There will be so much corn to thresh, that the work will continue throughout the season until it is time to cut the vines.

*safely.* Without fear of famine; as in XXV, 19.

**6.** *I will give peace in the land.* Prosperity is valueless unless it can be enjoyed in tranquillity, without the dread of assault, robbery or devastation of war.

*evil beasts.* In the time of warfare, when the land is desolated, wild beasts multiply; cf. Exod. XXIII, 29; Isa. XXXV, 9.

*sword.* The symbol of an invading army; cf. Ezek. XIV, 17.

# LEVITICUS XXVI, 7

ויקרא בחקתי כו

to cease out of the land, neither shall the sword go through your land. 7. And ye shall chase your enemies, and they shall fall before you by the sword. 8. And five of you shall chase a hundred, and a hundred of you shall chase ten thousand; and your enemies shall fall before you by the sword. 9. And I will have respect unto you, and make you fruitful, and multiply you; and will establish My covenant with you.*iii(**v). 10. And ye shall eat old store long kept, and ye shall bring forth the old from before the new. 11. And I will set My tabernacle among you, and My soul shall not abhor you. 12. And I will walk among you, and will be your God, and ye shall be My people. 13. I am the LORD your God, who brought you forth out of the land of Egypt, that ye should not be their bondmen; and I have broken the bars of your yoke, and made you go upright. ¶ 14. But if ye will not hearken unto Me, and will not do all these commandments; 15. and if ye shall reject My statutes, and if your soul abhor Mine ordinances, so that ye will not do all My commandments, but break My covenant; 16. I also will do this unto you: I will appoint terror over you, even consumption and fever, that shall make the eyes to fail, and the soul to languish; and ye shall sow your seed in vain, for your enemies shall eat it. 17.

---

**7.** *ye shall chase.* Should they attempt to attack you.

**8.** *five . . . hundred.* These are round numbers, not to be taken literally. They express the idea that the Israelites, with God as their helper, will be able to overcome vastly superior forces; *e.g.* the victories of the Maccabees over armies of great numerical superiority.

**9.** *respect unto you.* lit. 'turn unto you'; *i.e.* be gracious, favourably inclined towards you.
  *establish.* Carry out.

**10.** *the old. i.e.* of the previous years; cf. xxv, 22.

**11.** *My tabernacle.* Better, *My abiding presence* (cf. Exod. xxv, 8); God will be manifestly with His people, as evidenced by their extraordinary happiness.
  *abhor you.* Withdraw My favour so as to expose you to misfortune; cf. Jer. xiv, 19.

**12.** *walk among you.* A forcible image to describe how intimately God will associate with Israel.

**13.** *brought you forth.* That God is able to fulfil His promises is proved by His mighty acts in overthrowing the power of Egypt and setting Israel free.

*bars.* With which the yoke was fastened to the animal's neck.

### 14–39. THE WAGES OF DISOBEDIENCE

In dealing with the consequences of faithfulness, the Torah speaks in general terms; but in regard to the wages of disobedience, this Prophetical warning describes in much detail the penalties and horrors that would befall the sinful people. These are arranged in a series of five groups of increasing severity—sickness and defeat, famine, wild beasts, siege and exile.

### 16–18. SICKNESS AND DEFEAT

**16.** *terror. i.e.* terrible things, defined by what follows. The diseases which are mentioned are such as would strike terror in the heart of a person afflicted with any of them; cf. Deut. xxviii, 22.
  *consumption.* Any disease which causes a wasting of the body.
  *fever.* lit. 'a burning', internally.
  *sow your seed in vain.* Toiling without enjoying the fruits of their labour is frequently given as a punishment for faithlessness; cf. Deut. xxviii, 30.

**17.** *set My face.* See xvii, 10; xx, 3, 6.
  *ye shall flee.* They will be so demoralized that panic will seize them without cause; cf. *v.* 36 below.

543

## LEVITICUS XXVI, 18

And I will set My face against you, and ye shall be smitten before your enemies; they that hate you shall rule over you; and ye shall flee when none pursueth you. 18. And if ye will not yet for these things hearken unto Me, then I will chastise you seven times more for your sins. 19. And I will break the pride of your power; and I will make your heaven as iron, and your earth as brass. 20. And your strength shall be spent in vain; for your land shall not yield her produce, neither shall the trees of the land yield their fruit. 21. And if ye walk contrary unto Me, and will not hearken unto Me; I will bring seven times more plagues upon you according to your sins. 22. And I will send the beast of the field among you, which shall rob you of your children, and destroy your cattle, and make you few in number; and your ways shall become desolate. 23. And if in spite of these things ye will not be corrected unto Me, but will walk contrary unto Me; 24. then will I also walk contrary unto you; and I will smite you, even I, seven times for your sins. 25. And I will bring a sword upon you, that shall execute the vengeance of the covenant; and ye shall be gathered together within your cities; and I will send the pestilence among you; and ye shall be delivered into the hand of the enemy. 26. When I break your staff of bread, ten women shall bake your bread in one oven, and they shall deliver your bread again by weight; and ye shall eat, and not be satisfied. ¶ 27. And if ye will not for all this hearken unto Me, but walk contrary unto Me; 28. then I will

---

**18.** *seven times.* A round number, meaning 'very much more.'

### 19–22. Famine and Wild Beasts

**19.** *pride of your power.* The power which is the cause of your pride. By 'power' is to be understood the feeling of independence that results from prosperity; cf. Deut. VIII, 11–18.

*heaven as iron.* A cloudless heaven in the rainy season and an unproductive soil would quickly humble the pride of the people, and make them realize their helplessness.

**21.** *contrary unto Me.* Heb. קרי, acting perversely, and wilfully doing the opposite of what God wishes. The Heb. also means 'accident'. In defiant opposition to God, they would despise God's laws, and act as if *accident* ruled the moral and spiritual universe (S. R. Hirsch).

*plagues.* Strokes, smitings.

### 23–26. The Horrors of Siege

**23.** *corrected unto Me.* The purpose of God's chastisements is the moral discipline of His people.

**25.** *vengeance of the covenant.* i.e. retribution for disregarding My covenant with you.

*within your cities.* You will flee from the enemy and take refuge behind the fortifications of your cities (cf. Jer. IV, 5); but even there punishments, in the form of epidemics, will overtake you and weaken your powers of resistance.

**26.** *break your staff of bread.* An expression denoting the cutting off of the food-supply. Food being that upon which life is supported, it is symbolized as a staff; Isa. III, 1.

*ten women.* A round number. Although each household has its own oven, ten families will require the use of only one oven.

*by weight.* Food is so scarce that it is doled out by measure.

### 27–39. National Destruction and Exile

**28.** *in fury.* The continued stubbornness of the people will lead to direr and direr punishment. The warnings now reach the climax of horror.

## LEVITICUS XXVI, 29

walk contrary unto you in fury; and I also will chastise you seven times for your sins. 29. And ye shall eat the flesh of your sons, and the flesh of your daughters shall ye eat. 30. And I will destroy your high places, and cut down your sun-pillars, and cast your carcasses upon the carcasses of your idols; and My soul shall abhor you. 31. And I will make your cities a waste, and will bring your sanctuaries unto desolation, and I will not smell the savour of your sweet odours. 32. And I will bring the land into desolation; and your enemies that dwell therein shall be astonished at it. 33. And you will I scatter among the nations, and I will draw out the sword after you; and your land shall be a desolation, and your cities shall be a waste. 34. Then shall the land be paid her sabbaths, as long as it lieth desolate, and ye are in your enemies' land; even then shall the land rest, and repay her sabbaths. 35. As long as it lieth desolate it shall have rest; even the rest which it had not in your sabbaths, when ye dwelt upon it. 36. And as for them that are left of you, I will send a faintness into their heart in the lands of their enemies; and the sound of

---

**30.** *high places.* Heb. *bamoth;* the altars on the hilltops, or mounds, built by the Canaanites and taken over by idolatrous Israelites.

*sun-pillars.* Or 'images of the sun-god.'

*cast your carcasses.* See II Kings XXIII, 14, 20, for a historical instance.

*abhor you.* In contrast to what was stated in v. 15.

**31.** *your sanctuaries.* God will not associate Himself with such a Temple; hence 'your sanctuaries', not 'My sanctuary' as in v. 2. The plural may refer to the different divisions of the Sanctuary.

*I will not smell.* Cf. Amos v, 21. Since the incense symbolized prayer (see on II, 1), the phrase means, 'I will ignore your petitions.' Sanctuary and sacrifice are valueless, if unaccompanied by moral obedience.

**32.** *astonished.* Amazement will seize them at the appalling desolation, and they will perceive that it is due to superhuman agency.

**33.** *you will I scatter among the nations.* 'There is a marvellous and grand display of the greatness of God in the fact that He holds out before the people whom He has just delivered from the hands of the heathen the prospect of being scattered again among the heathen, and that even before the land is taken by the Israelites, He predicts its return to desolation. These could only be spoken of by One who has the future really before His mind, who can destroy His own work, yet attain His end, certain of victory notwithstanding all opposing difficulties' (quoted in Keil-Delitzsch).

*the sword after you.* An expression for the hot pursuit of fugitives; cf. Ezek. XXI, 8–11. Malbim explains these words as an essential qualification of the first part of the verse, *scatter among the nations.* 'Israel's dispersion is not a curse in itself: it is a means of fulfilling God's purpose of spreading His word among the nations. The tragedy lies in being scattered because of the sword.'

**34.** *be paid her sabbaths.* Better, *satisfy its sabbaths; i.e.* make compensation for the years of release which the Israelites did not observe according to the dictates of the Law (Leeser). Driver explains that the Heb. word rendered 'be paid' is the technical term in connection with the settlement of an account. When the people are exiled, the land, here personified, will receive payment of an overdue account in the long Sabbath-rest which it will then enjoy; see next v.

**36.** *left of you.* The two preceding verses are a parenthesis, describing the 'rest' which the land would have, when its inhabitants had been carried into captivity. This verse resumes v. 33, and alludes to the fate, with its resulting cowardice and 'spiritual slavery', that would be in store for those who escaped. 'The author possessed the imagination of a poet as well as the eloquence of an orator' (Kennedy).

## LEVITICUS XXVI, 37

a driven leaf shall chase them; and they shall flee, as one fleeth from the sword; and they shall fall when none pursueth. 37. And they shall stumble one upon another, as it were before the sword, when none pursueth; and ye shall have no power to stand before your enemies. 38. And ye shall perish among the nations, and the land of your enemies shall eat you up. 39. And they that are left of you shall pine away in their iniquity in your enemies' lands; and also in the iniquities of their fathers shall they pine away with them. 40. And they shall confess their iniquity, and the iniquity of their fathers, in their treachery which they committed against Me, and also that they have walked contrary unto Me. 41. I also will walk contrary unto them, and bring them into the land of their enemies; if then perchance their uncircumcised heart be humbled, and they then be paid the punishment of their iniquity; 42. then will I remember My covenant with Jacob, and also My covenant with Isaac, and also My covenant with Abraham will I remember; and I will remember the land. 43. For the land shall lie forsaken without them, and shall be paid her sabbaths, while she lieth desolate without them; and they shall be paid the punishment of their iniquity; because, even because they rejected Mine ordinances, and their soul abhorred My statutes. 44. And yet for all that, when they are in the

**37.** *stumble.* In their panic, caused by demoralization and not by a real enemy, they would forget the need for mutual help; and each would endeavour to escape, even at the cost of sacrificing his brother—true psychology of the Golus.

**38.** *eat you up.* For the image of a land consuming those who dwell upon its soil, see Num. XIII, 32.

**39.** *in their iniquity.* From the consequences of their guilt; *i.e.* their punishment. To this guilt (and punishment) their fathers have contributed.

*with them.* Refers to the fathers. There will be an added agony to the wretched lot of the sinful parents, that they will behold their children, who had followed their evil example, experiencing the hard fate which was so bitter to themselves. This explanation is supported by the Traditional accentuation of the words.

### 40–45. REPENTANCE SHALL BRING RESTORATION

**40.** *confess.* God desireth not the death of the sinner; and, therefore, every threat of punishment for disobedience is followed by a promise of mercy, if there is repentance and amendment. Divine discipline is for moral ends; and in truth the Exile proved a purifying furnace unto Israel.

*treachery.* Implying that faithlessness to the Covenant is a wrong committed directly against God; cf. *v.* 15.

**41.** *I also will walk.* Better, *I also walk.* They will acknowledge that the calamities which had overtaken them were God's method of humbling their arrogance.

*uncircumcised.* Unconsecrated, unclean; closed to the Divine call or appeal; cf. on XIX, 23.

*be paid.* Acknowledge that the punishment was deserved; see, however, *v.* 35 and 43.

**42.** *Jacob . . . Isaac . . . Abraham.* God is stirred to mercy by recalling the noble ancestors of Israel and the Covenant He entered into with each. In retrospect, the last comes first to mind.

*the land.* Which was itself a symbol of the Covenant with the Patriarchs, and prominently figured in the promises which God had made to them.

**43.** *shall lie forsaken without them.* Because the Israelites had failed to observe the Sabbatical year, they had wronged the soil of the Holy Land, and that wrong had to be expiated before they could return and resettle there; see XVIII, 25.

## LEVITICUS XXVI, 45

land of their enemies, I will not reject them, neither will I abhor them, to destroy them utterly, and to break My covenant with them; for I am the LORD their God. 45. But I will for their sakes remember the covenant of their ancestors, whom I brought forth out of the land of Egypt in the sight of the nations, that I might be their God: I am the LORD. ¶ 46. These are the statutes and ordinances and laws, which the LORD made between Him and the children of Israel in mount Sinai by the hand of Moses.*ⁱᵛ⁽**ᵛⁱ⁾

מה בְּרִיתִי אִתָּם כִּי אֲנִי יְהוָֹה אֱלֹהֵיהֶם: וְזָכַרְתִּי לָהֶם בְּרִית רִאשֹׁנִים אֲשֶׁר הוֹצֵאתִי־אֹתָם מֵאֶרֶץ מִצְרַיִם לְעֵינֵי הַגּוֹיִם 46 לִהְיֹת לָהֶם לֵאלֹהִים אֲנִי יְהוָֹה: אֵלֶּה הַחֻקִּים וְהַמִּשְׁפָּטִים וְהַתּוֹרֹת אֲשֶׁר נָתַן יְהוָֹה בֵּינוֹ וּבֵין בְּנֵי יִשְׂרָאֵל בְּהַר סִינַי בְּיַד־מֹשֶׁה:*

פ רביעי (שׁשׁי כשׁהן מחוב׳)

## 27

### CHAPTER XXVII

1. And the LORD spoke unto Moses, saying: 2. Speak unto the children of Israel, and say unto them: ¶ When a man shall clearly utter a vow of persons unto the LORD, according to thy valuation, 3. then thy valuation shall be for the male from twenty years old even unto sixty years old, even thy valuation shall be fifty shekels of silver, after the shekel of the sanctuary. 4. And if it be a female, then thy valuation shall be thirty shekels. 5. And if it be from five years old even unto twenty years old, then thy valuation shall be for the male twenty shekels, and for the female ten shekels. 6. And if it be from a month old even unto five years old, then thy valuation shall be for the male five shekels of silver, and for the female thy valuation shall be three shekels of silver. 7. And if it be from sixty years old and upward:

### CAP. XXVII. כז

כז

2 א וַיְדַבֵּר יְהוָֹה אֶל־מֹשֶׁה לֵּאמֹר: דַּבֵּר אֶל־בְּנֵי יִשְׂרָאֵל וְאָמַרְתָּ אֲלֵהֶם אִישׁ כִּי יַפְלִא נֶדֶר בְּעֶרְכְּךָ נְפָשֹׁת לַיהוָֹה:
3 וְהָיָה עֶרְכְּךָ הַזָּכָר מִבֶּן עֶשְׂרִים שָׁנָה וְעַד בֶּן־שִׁשִּׁים שָׁנָה
4 וְהָיָה עֶרְכְּךָ חֲמִשִּׁים שֶׁקֶל כֶּסֶף בְּשֶׁקֶל הַקֹּדֶשׁ: וְאִם־
5 נְקֵבָה הִוא וְהָיָה עֶרְכְּךָ שְׁלֹשִׁים שָׁקֶל: וְאִם מִבֶּן־חָמֵשׁ שָׁנִים וְעַד בֶּן־עֶשְׂרִים שָׁנָה וְהָיָה עֶרְכְּךָ הַזָּכָר עֶשְׂרִים
6 שְׁקָלִים וְלַנְּקֵבָה עֲשֶׂרֶת שְׁקָלִים: וְאִם מִבֶּן־חֹדֶשׁ וְעַד בֶּן־חָמֵשׁ שָׁנִים וְהָיָה עֶרְכְּךָ הַזָּכָר חֲמִשָּׁה שְׁקָלִים כָּסֶף
7 וְלַנְּקֵבָה עֶרְכְּךָ שְׁלֹשֶׁת שְׁקָלִים כָּסֶף: וְאִם מִבֶּן־שִׁשִּׁים

---

**44.** *yet for all that.* The chapter ends characteristically on a note of hope. God's anger may be severe, but it is not everlasting. He will grant His people every opportunity to renew the ancient Covenant. Israel—'a people who have been overthrown, crushed, scattered; who have been ground, as it were, to very dust, and flung to the four winds of heaven; yet who, though thrones have fallen, and empires have perished, and creeds have changed, and living tongues have become dead, still exist with a vitality seemingly unimpaired' (Henry George).

**45.** *their ancestors.* lit. 'the first' generations. It alludes not only to the Patriarchs, but to the founders of the Twelve Tribes and their descendants who left Egypt; cf. Deut. XIX, 14; Isa. LXI, 4.

**46.** *these are the statutes.* This verse is the subscription not only to chaps. XVII–XXVI, but to the whole of Leviticus, the following chapter being an appendix to the Book.

### CHAPTER XXVII

#### REDEMPTION OF VOWS AND TITHES

The Book of Leviticus concludes, as it opened, with a chapter of Sanctuary-regulations—voluntary contributions to the upkeep of the Sanctuary, such offerings being a true expression of devotion to the House of God.

#### 2–8. VOWING AND VALUATION OF A PERSON

**2.** *clearly utter a vow.* By setting a valuation upon himself or any of his family, the money being paid into the treasury of the Sanctuary.

**3.** *fifty shekels.* The equivalent of £7 of our money, but the true value in purchasing power is many times that sum (Kennedy). The form, *thy* estimation, is archaic. See on Exod. xxx, 13.

**4.** *thirty shekels.* The valuation seems to have been made on the basis of what might be called the market value of the individual's labour. A woman, not possessing the physical strength of a man, had a lower valuation set upon her.

**6.** *from a month old.* No valuation is placed in regard to a child under a month old. In Jewish law there are no mourning rites to be observed for a child who dies within a month of birth.

## LEVITICUS XXVII, 8

if it be a male, then thy valuation shall be fifteen shekels, and for the female ten shekels. 8. But if he be too poor for thy valuation, then he shall be set before the priest, and the priest shall value him; according to the means of him that vowed shall the priest value him. ¶ 9. And if it be a beast, whereof men bring an offering unto the LORD, all that any man giveth of such unto the LORD shall be holy. 10. He shall not alter it, nor change it, a good for a bad, or a bad for a good; and if he shall at all change beast for beast, then both it and that for which it is changed shall be holy. 11. And if it be any unclean beast, of which they may not bring an offering unto the LORD, then he shall set the beast before the priest. 12. And the priest shall value it, whether it be good or bad; as thou the priest valuest it, so shall it be. 13. But if he will indeed redeem it, then he shall add the fifth part thereof unto thy valuation. ¶ 14. And when a man shall sanctify his house to be holy unto the LORD, then the priest shall value it, whether it be good or bad; as the priest shall value it, so shall it stand. 15. And if he that sanctified it will redeem his house, then he shall add the fifth part of the money of thy valuation unto it, and it shall be his.*v(**vii). ¶ 16. And if a man shall sanctify unto the LORD part of the field of his possession, then thy valuation shall be according to the sowing thereof; the sowing of a homer of barley shall be valued at fifty shekels of silver. 17. If he sanctify

ויקרא בחקתי כז

שָׁנָה וָמַעְלָה אֶרְכְּךָ וְהָיָה עֶרְכְּךָ חֲמִשָּׁה עָשָׂר שָׁקֶל
8 וְלַנְּקֵבָה עֲשֶׂרֶת שְׁקָלִים: וְאִם־מָךְ הוּא מֵעֶרְכֶּךָ וְהֶעֱמִידוֹ
לִפְנֵי הַכֹּהֵן וְהֶעֱרִיךְ אֹתוֹ הַכֹּהֵן עַל־פִּי אֲשֶׁר תַּשִּׂיג יַד הַנֹּדֵר
9 יַעֲרִיכֶנּוּ הַכֹּהֵן: ס וְאִם־בְּהֵמָה אֲשֶׁר יַקְרִיבוּ מִמֶּנָּה
10 קָרְבָּן לַיהוָה כֹּל אֲשֶׁר יִתֵּן מִמֶּנּוּ לַיהוָה יִהְיֶה־קֹּדֶשׁ: לֹא
יַחֲלִיפֶנּוּ וְלֹא־יָמִיר אֹתוֹ טוֹב בְּרָע אוֹ־רַע בְּטוֹב וְאִם־הָמֵר
יָמִיר בְּהֵמָה בִּבְהֵמָה וְהָיָה־הוּא וּתְמוּרָתוֹ יִהְיֶה־קֹּדֶשׁ:
11 וְאִם כָּל־בְּהֵמָה טְמֵאָה אֲשֶׁר לֹא־יַקְרִיבוּ מִמֶּנָּה קָרְבָּן
12 לַיהוָה וְהֶעֱמִיד אֶת־הַבְּהֵמָה לִפְנֵי הַכֹּהֵן: וְהֶעֱרִיךְ הַכֹּהֵן
13 אֹתָהּ בֵּין טוֹב וּבֵין רָע כְּעֶרְכְּךָ הַכֹּהֵן כֵּן יִהְיֶה: וְאִם־
14 גָּאֹל יִגְאָלֶנָּה וְיָסַף חֲמִישִׁתוֹ עַל־עֶרְכֶּךָ: וְאִישׁ כִּי־יַקְדִּשׁ
אֶת־בֵּיתוֹ קֹדֶשׁ לַיהוָה וְהֶעֱרִיכוֹ הַכֹּהֵן בֵּין טוֹב וּבֵין רָע
15 כַּאֲשֶׁר יַעֲרִיךְ אֹתוֹ הַכֹּהֵן כֵּן יָקוּם: וְאִם־הַמַּקְדִּישׁ יִגְאַל
16 אֶת־בֵּיתוֹ וְיָסַף חֲמִישִׁית כֶּסֶף־עֶרְכְּךָ עָלָיו וְהָיָה לוֹ: וְאִם
מִשְּׂדֵה אֲחֻזָּתוֹ יַקְדִּישׁ אִישׁ לַיהוָה וְהָיָה עֶרְכְּךָ לְפִי זַרְעוֹ

v. 9. סבירין ממנה v. 10. קמץ בטרחא

**8.** *according to the means.* 'If he (the person making the vow) be too poor to pay the valuation, then he shall set him (the person vowed) before the priest, and the priest shall value him.' The priest, in forming his estimate of what he could pay, must leave him sufficient means for his necessities (Talmud).

### 9–13. REDEMPTION OF AN ANIMAL

**9.** *if it be a beast.* If a 'clean' animal, that and none other had to be presented.

*shall be holy.* It became the property of the Sanctuary, and all profane use of it was interdicted.

**10.** *not alter it.* Even for one of greater value. *Alter* is to replace one species by another, *e.g.* a bull for a sheep; *change* refers to different members of the same species.

**12.** *good or bad. i.e.* whether it be of much value or little.

**13.** *fifth part.* See on *v.* 16.

### 14–15. REDEMPTION OF A HOUSE

**14.** *sanctify.* Dedicate.

**15.** *redeem.* As in *v.* 13. The law of xxv, 29 f applied to this case where the redeemer was not the owner. If the house was in a walled city, it could be redeemed by the owner within a year; and if not redeemed, it remained for ever in the possession of the buyer. In the case of a house situated in a village, the Jubilee-year brought its restitution to the owner.

### 16–25. REDEMPTION OF LAND

**16.** *possession.* An inherited field, as contrasted with a piece of land which he had bought (*v.* 22).

*the sowing thereof.* The value of the land was estimated by the quantity of seed required to sow it. For each *homer* of seed used in sowing barley, the valuation was placed at fifty shekels for the whole period of forty-nine years. A *homer* was ten ephahs (see on XIX, 36), and nearly six bushels in capacity.

**17.** *from the year of jubilee.* From the conclusion of the year.

*it shall stand.* At the valuation of fifty shekels for each *homer* of seed.

**18.** *an abatement.* A proportionate reduction in the price; cf. xxv, 50 f.

## LEVITICUS XXVII, 18

his field from the year of jubilee, according to thy valuation it shall stand. 18. But if he sanctify his field after the jubilee, then the priest shall reckon unto him the money according to the years that remain unto the year of jubilee, and an abatement shall be made from thy valuation. 19. And if he that sanctified the field will indeed redeem it, then he shall add the fifth part of the money of thy valuation unto it, and it shall be assured to him. 20. And if he will not redeem the field, or if he have sold the field to another man, it shall not be redeemed any more. 21. But the field, when it goeth out in the jubilee, shall be holy unto the LORD, as a field devoted; the possession thereof shall be the priest's.\*vi. 22. And if he sanctify unto the LORD a field which he hath bought, which is not of the field of his possession; 23. then the priest shall reckon unto him the worth of thy valuation unto the year of jubilee; and he shall give thy valuation in that day, as a holy thing unto the LORD. 24. In the year of jubilee the field shall return unto him of whom it was bought, even to him to whom the possession of the land belongeth. 25. And all thy valuations shall be according to the shekel of the sanctuary; twenty gerahs shall be the shekel. ¶ 26. Howbeit the firstling among beasts, which is born as a firstling to the LORD, no man shall sanctify it; whether it be ox or sheep, it is the LORD's. 27. And if it be an unclean beast, then he shall ransom it according to thy valuation, and shall add unto it the fifth part thereof; or if it be not redeemed, then it shall be sold according to thy valuation. ¶ 28. Notwithstanding, no devoted thing, that a man may devote

---

**20.** *if he will not redeem.* If the redeemer of the field is not the owner, the Sanctuary becomes the *de jure* owner of the field, which at the next Jubilee becomes the inalienable property of the Sanctuary.

**21.** *field devoted.* See on *v.* 28.

**22.** *bought.* Since he bought the field until the Jubilee only, it is clear that his gift to the Sanctuary is only temporary.

**23.** *in that day.* The price had to be paid in one sum and in full-weight shekels (see on Exod. xxx, 13).

### 26–27. REDEMPTION OF A FIRSTLING

**26.** *to the* LORD. As a firstling, it *ipso facto* belonged to God; see Exod. XIII, 2. Therefore, the owner cannot vow it again as a gift to the Sanctuary; it was not his to give away.

*shall sanctify.* *i.e.* devote, as a voluntary offering.

**27.** *an unclean beast.* *i.e.* a dedicated clean animal that became blemished; in which case the proceeds of the sale were to be used for Temple repair (Rashi).

### 28–29. LAW OF THE BAN

**28.** *devoted thing.* lit. 'cut-off, excluded', irrevocably given up. There were three varieties of the ban, of differing degrees of stringency: the war ban, the justice ban, and the private ban. This verse deals with the last-named. The 'devoting' of anything to the Temple was a more solemn act than a mere presentation. The human being, animal, or field became 'most holy', *i.e.* remained the inalienable property of the Sanctuary, and passed into the possession of the priests.

*field of his possession.* Only an inheritance could be 'devoted', not a purchased field, since the latter only belonged to the owner temporarily, and passed out of his possession in the Jubilee. In the same manner, a Hebrew slave

# LEVITICUS XXVII, 29

unto the LORD of all that he hath, whether of man or beast, or of the field of his possession, shall be sold or redeemed; every devoted thing is most holy unto the LORD.*vii. 29. None devoted, that may be devoted of men, shall be ransomed; he shall surely be put to death. ¶ 30. And all the tithe of the land, whether of the seed of the land, or of the fruit of the tree, is the LORD's; it is holy unto the LORD. 31. And if a man will redeem aught of his tithe, he shall add unto it the fifth part thereof.*m. 32. And all the tithe of the herd or the flock, whatsoever passeth under the rod, the tenth shall be holy unto the LORD. 3. He shall not inquire whether it be good or bad, neither shall he change it; and if he change it at all, then both it and that for which it is changed shall be holy; it shall not be redeemed. ¶ 34. These are the commandments, which the LORD commanded Moses for the children of Israel in mount Sinai.

אֲשֶׁר־ל֣וֹ מֵאָדָ֤ם וּבְהֵמָה֙ וּמִשְּׂדֵ֣ה אֲחֻזָּת֔וֹ לֹ֥א יִמָּכֵ֖ר וְלֹ֣א שביעי
29 יִגָּאֵ֑ל כׇּל־חֵ֕רֶם קֹֽדֶשׁ־קׇֽדָשִׁ֥ים ה֖וּא לַיהֹוָֽה׃ כׇּל־חֵ֗רֶם אֲשֶׁ֧ר
ל יׇֽחֳרַ֛ם מִן־הָאָדָ֖ם לֹ֣א יִפָּדֶ֑ה מ֖וֹת יוּמָֽת׃ וְכׇל־מַעְשַׂ֨ר הָאָ֜רֶץ
31 מִזֶּ֤רַע הָאָ֙רֶץ֙ מִפְּרִ֣י הָעֵ֔ץ לַיהֹוָ֖ה ה֑וּא קֹ֖דֶשׁ לַֽיהֹוָֽה׃ וְאִם־ מפטיר
32 גָּאֹ֥ל יִגְאַ֛ל אִ֖ישׁ מִמַּֽעַשְׂר֑וֹ חֲמִשִׁית֖וֹ יֹסֵ֥ף עָלָֽיו׃ וְכׇל־מַעְשַׂ֤ר
בָּקָר֙ וָצֹ֔אן כֹּ֥ל אֲשֶׁר־יַעֲבֹ֖ר תַּ֣חַת הַשָּׁ֑בֶט הָֽעֲשִׂירִ֕י יִֽהְיֶה־
33 קֹּ֖דֶשׁ לַיהֹוָֽה׃ לֹ֧א יְבַקֵּ֛ר בֵּֽין־ט֥וֹב לָרַ֖ע וְלֹ֣א יְמִירֶ֑נּוּ וְאִם־
הָמֵ֣ר יְמִירֶ֔נּוּ וְהָֽיָה־ה֧וּא וּתְמוּרָת֛וֹ יִֽהְיֶה־קֹ֖דֶשׁ לֹ֥א יִגָּאֵֽל׃
34 אֵ֣לֶּה הַמִּצְוֺ֗ת אֲשֶׁ֨ר צִוָּ֧ה יְהֹוָ֛ה אֶת־מֹשֶׁ֖ה אֶל־בְּנֵ֣י יִשְׂרָאֵ֑ל
בְּהַ֖ר סִינָֽי׃

## חזק

סכום פסוקי דספר ויקרא שמונה מאות וחמשים ותשעה. נטף
סימן: וחציו והנגע בבשר הזב: ופרשיותיו עשרה. בא נד סימן:
וסדריו שלשה ועשרים. וכתורתו יהגה יומם ולילה סימן:
ופרקיו שבעה ועשרים. ואהיה עמך ואברכך סימן: מניין
הפתוחות שתים וחמשים. והסתומות ששה וארבעים. הכל
שמנה ותשעים פרשיות. דודי צח ואדום סימן:

could not be 'devoted' because he regained his freedom in the seventh year.
*sold.* To another person.
*redeemed.* By the owner.

**29.** *devoted.* i.e. doomed.
*of men.* 'The reference here is to the justice-ban; in other words, to the judicial sentence by the proper authorities on such malefactors as the idolater (see Exod. XXII, 19), and the blasphemer' (Kennedy). The individual was not permitted to carry out such a ban. Deut. XII, 31, forbids human sacrifice, and the putting to death of a slave is forbidden in Exod. XXI, 20.

### 30–33. REDEMPTION OF THE TITHE

**30.** *tithe of the land.* This so-called 'second tithe', described in Deut. XIV, 22 f, was analogous to the firstling of sacrificial animals, and the same law of redemption applied.
*is the LORD'S.* Tithes belong to God as the real owner of the land; see on XXV, 23. They are a kind of rent paid by the people as His tenants. Being already God's, they cannot be made the subject of vows (Dummelow).

**32.** *tithe of the herd.* Every tenth animal born of the herd or flock had to be treated like the tenth of the produce of the field. The animals were sacrificed and the flesh consumed in Jerusalem.
*passeth under the rod.* The Mishnah thus describes the procedure: The new-born animals were herded in a pen with one narrow exit, through which they could only pass in single file. As they came out, each tenth animal was touched on the back with a rod coated with red paint, and in this manner distinguished for the tithe.

**33.** *he shall not inquire.* The owner could not select which animals should form part of the tithe. If he substituted one of the designated animals for another, whether of better or inferior quality, he forfeited both.

**34.** *these are the commandments.* Cf. XXVI, 46. This verse seems to be the subscription of the concluding chapter only.

The Massoretic Note states the number of verses in Leviticus to be 859; its Sedrahs (parshiyoth) 10; its Sedarim, smaller divisions according to the Triennial Cycle, 23; and its Chapters 27.

# HAFTORAH BECHUKOSAI
## הפטרת בחקתי
### JEREMIAH XVI, 19–XVII, 14

### Chapter XVI

19. O Lord, my strength, and my stronghold,
And my refuge, in the day of affliction,
Unto Thee shall the nations come
From the ends of the earth, and shall say:
'Our fathers have inherited nought but lies,
Vanity and things wherein there is no profit.'
20. Shall a man make unto himself gods,
And they are no gods?
21. Therefore, behold, I will cause them to know,
This once will I cause them to know
My hand and My might;
And they shall know that My name is the Lord.

### Chapter XVII

1. The sin of Judah is written
With a pen of iron, and with the point of a diamond;
It is graven upon the tablet of their heart,
And upon the horns of your altars.

---

The Sedrah proclaims the happy result of national faithfulness, and the inevitable and disastrous consequences of national faithlessness to the Divine Law. The Haftorah is the utterance of the Prophet who witnessed the destruction of the Temple and State through the religious and moral degeneracy of the nation. His words, especially in the verses preceding this section, are thus an echo of the prophecy of Moses. But Jeremiah's message here is one of great hope. Even heathen nations shall acknowledge that truth and moral sanity are only to be found in the Revelation given to Israel. Let Israel trust—as he does—in God, the faithful Physician, who will heal them, and establish them on an eternal foundation.

**19.** *have inherited nought but lies.* The Prophet foresees the time when the heathen from the utmost ends of the earth will realize the vanity and falsehood of their hereditary gods, and come to acknowledge God's glorious Name.

That all mankind will at last grope their way out of the night of traditional ignorance towards the Truth, is a fundamental conviction of the Jewish spirit. This has found expression in the *Oleynu* prayer, with its culminating aspiration, taken from the Prophet (Zech. xiv, 9), *The Lord shall be King over all the earth; in that day shall the Lord be One, and His name one* (Authorised Prayer Book, p. 77), and in the ויאתיו hymn of the New Year liturgy, dating from the early Middle Ages:—

'All the world shall come to serve Thee,
And bless Thy glorious Name,
And Thy righteousness triumphant
The islands shall acclaim.
And the peoples shall go seeking
Who knew thee not before;
And all the ends of the earth shall praise Thee,
And tell Thy greatness o'er.

They shall build for Thee their altars,
Their idols overthrown;
And their graven gods shall shame them,
As they turn to Thee alone.
They shall worship Thee at sunrise
And feel Thy Kingdom's might,
And impart their understanding
To those astray in night.'

(Trans. I Zangwill.)

**21.** *that My name is the Lord.* They shall understand all that is implied in the Name *Adonay*—One God, who rules universally and eternally and fulfils His word (Rashi); see p. 232.

### Chapter XVII

The action of the heathens only deepens the sin and folly of Israel, for resisting Divine teaching and sinking into the bog of the impure idolatry of Canaan.

**1.** *with a pen of iron, and with the point of a diamond.* Instruments used for cutting into hard substances; here, on the heart hardened by sin. Sin is indelibly ingrained in their nature, and their guilt is patent to all.

*of your altars.* A swift and effective change from the indirect (*their* heart) to the direct form of address (*your* altars). Other instances in the Scriptures are numerous (Kimchi).

## JEREMIAH XVII, 2

2. Like the symbols of their sons are their altars.
And their Asherim are by the leafy trees, Upon the high hills.
3. O thou that sittest upon the mountain in the field,
I will give thy substance and all thy treasures for a spoil,
And thy high places, because of sin, throughout all thy borders.
4. And thou, even of thyself, shalt discontinue from thy heritage
That I gave thee;
And I will cause thee to serve thine enemies
In the land which thou knowest not;
For ye have kindled a fire in My nostril, Which shall burn for ever.

5. Thus saith the LORD:
Cursed is the man that trusteth in man, And maketh flesh his arm,
And whose heart departeth from the LORD.
6. For he shall be like a tamarisk in the desert,
And shall not see when good cometh;
But shall inhabit the parched places in the wilderness,
A salt land and not inhabited.
7. Blessed is the man that trusteth in the LORD,
And whose trust the LORD is,
8. For he shall be as a tree planted by the waters,
And that spreadeth out its roots by the river,
And shall not see when heat cometh,

2 עַל־לוּחַ לִבָּם וּלְקַרְנוֹת מִזְבְּחוֹתֵיכֶם: כִּזְכֹּר בְּנֵיהֶם
מִזְבְּחוֹתָם וַאֲשֵׁרֵיהֶם עַל־עֵץ רַעֲנָן עַל גְּבָעוֹת הַגְּבֹהוֹת:
3 הֲרָרִי בַּשָּׂדֶה חֵילְךָ כָל־אוֹצְרוֹתֶיךָ לָבַז אֶתֵּן בָּמֹתֶיךָ
4 בְּחַטָּאת בְּכָל־גְּבוּלֶיךָ: וְשָׁמַטְתָּה וּבְךָ מִנַּחֲלָתְךָ אֲשֶׁר
נָתַתִּי לָךְ וְהַעֲבַדְתִּיךָ אֶת־אֹיְבֶיךָ בָּאָרֶץ אֲשֶׁר לֹא־יָדָעְתָּ
5 כִּי־אֵשׁ קְדַחְתֶּם בְּאַפִּי עַד־עוֹלָם תּוּקָד: כֹּה ׀ אָמַר
יְהֹוָה אָרוּר הַגֶּבֶר אֲשֶׁר יִבְטַח בָּאָדָם וְשָׂם בָּשָׂר זְרֹעוֹ
6 וּמִן־יְהֹוָה יָסוּר לִבּוֹ: וְהָיָה כְּעַרְעָר בָּעֲרָבָה וְלֹא יִרְאֶה
כִּי־יָבוֹא טוֹב וְשָׁכַן חֲרֵרִים בַּמִּדְבָּר אֶרֶץ מְלֵחָה וְלֹא
7 תֵשֵׁב: בָּרוּךְ הַגֶּבֶר אֲשֶׁר יִבְטַח בַּיהֹוָה וְהָיָה
8 יְהֹוָה מִבְטַחוֹ: וְהָיָה כְּעֵץ ׀ שָׁתוּל עַל־מַיִם וְעַל־יוּבַל
יְשַׁלַּח שָׁרָשָׁיו וְלֹא יִרְאֶה כִּי־יָבֹא חֹם וְהָיָה עָלֵהוּ רַעֲנָן

But its foliage shall be luxuriant;
And shall not be anxious in the year of drought,
Neither shall cease from yielding fruit.

v. 8. יראה קרי

---

**2.** *like the symbols of their sons.* Following Ehrlich, who sees in these words a reference to the symbols of their immoral rites, symbols that correspond to the wooden poles of Asherah-worship.

*Asherim.* See Exod. XXXIV, 13. Poles set up near an altar for idol worship, generally for the worship of Astarte.

**3.** *O thou that sittest upon the mountain in the field.* Jerusalem, which was built on a hill, high above the surrounding plain or field (Rashi).

**4.** *shalt discontinue from thy heritage.* Shalt cease to retain thy land and be driven forth to foreign soil.
*for ever.* For a long time (Altschul); a frequent use of the phrase לעולם; cf. p. 305.

**5-14.** Passages of great beauty—on the Two Paths of life; the mystery and intricacy of the human heart; the fleetingness of ill-gotten gains; and God our Hope and our Physician.

**5-8.** The Two Paths—an epitome of the Blessings and Warnings of the Sedrah. These verses explain the doom just predicted.

**5.** *his arm.* i.e. his strength. Relies on flesh and blood with its inherent weakness for his help. Judah was looking to Egypt and Assyria for help in its troubles; hence this utterance (Kimchi).

**6.** *shall be like a tamarisk.* A small juniper tree, starved and stunted, and deprived of vivifying water, just hanging on to a miserable life. Such are those who rely entirely on human aid.
*and shall not see when good cometh.* Good, i.e. rain; the rain that refreshes other trees shall remain unknown to it.

**8.** *planted by the waters.* The tree planted by

## JEREMIAH XVII, 9

9. The heart is deceitful above all things,
And it is exceeding weak—who can know it?

10. I the Lord search the heart,
I try the reins,
Even to give every man according to his ways,
According to the fruit of his doings.

11. As the partridge that broodeth over young which she hath not brought forth,
So is he that getteth riches, and not by right;
In the midst of his days he shall leave them,
And at his end he shall be a fool.

12. Thou throne of glory, on high from the beginning,
Thou place of our sanctuary,

13. Thou hope of Israel, the Lord.
All that forsake Thee shall be ashamed;
They that depart from Thee shall be written in the earth,
Because they have forsaken the Lord,
The fountain of living waters.

14. Heal me, O Lord, and I shall be healed;
Save me, and I shall be saved;
For Thou art my praise.

---

the watercourse shall not perceive or feel the heat—a picture of the undisturbed heart and mind of him whose trust is in the Lord, the Fountain of Living Waters.

*not be anxious.* Because it is not dependent on rain.

**9–10.** The mystery of the human heart.

**9.** *deceitful.* Or, 'intricate.' Perhaps the ideal in the previous verse causes the Prophet to realize that his own heart has not always been true to that ideal. The Prophet recoils in amazement and dread at the sinful possibilities of human nature.

*exceeding weak.* AV renders 'And desperately wicked'. The Heb. אנש, however, means 'weak'; or, perhaps 'human', from אנוש man: 'the heart is deceitful above all things, and so very human!'

**10.** *I the LORD.* Answers the question in the preceding verse, 'Who can know it?' (*i.e.* the heart). The intricacies, windings, and subtleties of the human heart are all open to God.

*reins.* The seat of feeling in Bible psychology.

*fruit of his doings.* Good intentions are not sufficient. Man is judged by the outcome and unforeseen results of his actions.

**11.** Ill-gotten gains.

*as the partridge...forth.* It was a popular belief of the day that the partridge took possession of another bird's nest, and that the young which are thus nurtured afterwards desert their false mother. So does wealth its unlawful possessor.

*he shall be a fool.* In the moral sense; he will be recognized by all as a 'wicked man', colour-blind in matters of religion and duty. A life of slavery to Mammon is essentially irrational. Some see in this verse a reference to King Jehoiakim; see p. 397.

**12–14.** God our Hope and our Physician.

**12.** *Thou throne of glory...hope of Israel.* It is an invocation to God. From the vanity of earthly thrones, the Prophet lifts his eyes to Him who is from everlasting.

*the place of our sanctuary.* These terms are used of God as we use the words 'the Throne', 'the Court', 'the Crown' for the actual ruler.

**13.** *written in the earth.* Unlike those engraved in some enduring material, they will be blotted out.

**14.** *heal me.* This petition has been taken over into the daily litany, the Shemoneh Esreh (Authorised Prayer Book, p. 47).

*my praise.* My boast and my glory.

# ADDITIONAL NOTES TO LEVITICUS

## A

### THE BOOK OF LEVITICUS

#### Its Antiquity and Mosaic Authorship

Both the antiquity and the Mosaic authorship of the Book of Leviticus are denied by Bible Critics. They declare Leviticus to be part of that section of the Pentateuch which they call the 'Priestly code' and usually designate by the letter P. This 'Priestly code,' or P, is supposed to include, besides Leviticus, some portions of Genesis and Exodus (especially the chapters on the Tabernacle) and twenty-eight chapters of Numbers. They maintain that while some portions of P may be earlier than others, they were all edited, or written, by Ezra and his School and made an integral part of the Law of Moses in the year 444 before the Christian era, or very shortly thereafter.

It must be clearly understood that this idea of a 'Priestly code' and of its late origin is nothing more than pure hypothesis, and there is not a shred of evidence to show that it ever constituted a separate work. In fact, the whole Documentary theory as propounded by Julius Wellhausen and his followers—*i.e.* that the Pentateuch consists of separate 'documents' of different date and authorship—rests on unproved assumptions. It is easy to make any theory look plausible, if the facts are selected or trimmed judiciously; and Bible Critics are most judicious both in selecting the facts and in trimming them to suit their purpose. When the facts are against their theory, the facts are altered or pronounced to be a later gloss in the passage in which they occur, or the Critics declare the whole passage to be sheer forgery. Irreconcilable differences between the 'documents' are created, leading to a complete reversal of Israel's story. And the principal support for such a topsyturvy presentation of Bible history and religion is the alleged existence of these irreconcilable differences between the 'documents'. It is all reasoning in a vicious circle.

Outstanding scholars, like Prof. Sayce, have from the first pronounced the Documentary theory of the Pentateuch to be a 'baseless fabric of subjective imagination'. Others have come to share his view, realizing more and more the insuperable objections to the theory of the late origin of the Levitical legislation. The whole Critical theory is to-day being questioned on fundamental issues. Nevertheless, the popularizers of theological literature ignore altogether the existence of any other opinion than that of the Critics, and they continue to write as if the lateness of Leviticus were indeed one of the 'finalities of scholarship'. That nothing could be further from the truth will be plain to any student who will take the trouble to consult the following books:—

J. Robertson, *The Early Religion of Israel* (William Blackwood)—the first critical investigation of the Wellhausen hypothesis in English;

James Orr, *The Problem of the Old Testament* (James Nisbet)—gives a comprehensive survey of the weaknesses of the Critical position;

W. L. Baxter, *Sanctuary and Sacrifice* (Eyre and Spottiswoode)—demolishes the foundation pillars of Wellhausen's structure;

H. M. Wiener, *Essays in Pentateuchal Criticism* (Elliot Stock)—is a lawyer's examination of the Critical claims; and

D. Hoffmann, *Die Wichtigsten Instanzen gegen die Graf-Wellhausensche Hypothese* (Poppelauer, Berlin)—written over a generation ago, but still unanswered because unanswerable.

### I

#### The Internal Evidence Against the Critical Theory

Leviticus merely continues the story of the departure from Egypt and of the Children of Israel in the Wilderness. The few incidents in Leviticus, as well as its legislation, point to a sojourn in the Desert of the Sinai Peninsula prior to the occupation of Canaan. A verse such as 'After the doings of the land of Egypt, wherein ye dwelt, shall ye not do; and after the doings of the land of Canaan, whither I bring you, shall ye not do' (XVIII, 3), is in itself decisive in favour of the Mosaic date.

In many passages of the Book, the going forth from Egypt, and the manifestation of God's protecting power in the release, are spoken of as events of recent occurrence, fresh in the memory of those who had *experienced* the Divine mercy.

Israel is contemplated as living in tents, and the conditions of life which are presupposed are those of a *camp* (see on Lev. XVII, 3). The Sanctuary is depicted as a temporary structure of a portable nature, such as would be required while the people were wandering in the Wilderness. Leviticus assumes the people to be within reach of the religious centre, and in a position to attend the Sanctuary during the pilgrimage Festivals: in Ezra's time, this was impossible, as the bulk of the people was in Babylon, and another portion had drifted back to Egypt. The ritual of *Azazel* on the Day of Atonement is patently archaic, and had to be modified to meet the conditions of later times; see commentary on Lev. XVI, 21, p. 483.

The priests are always denoted as 'Aaron and his sons.' Their initial consecration to the priestly office is described (Lev. VIII), to which ceremony 'all the congregation' was summoned (ibid. *v*. 3). This is meaningless on the supposition of the late origin of the Book. Furthermore, P exalts the High Priest. In Ezra's age, the High

Priests were not worthy of honour, and seem to have been among those that attempted to thwart the work of religious reformation.

Similarly, the story of the blasphemer in Leviticus (xxiv, 10–12) is inexplicable on the Critical theory. A son of an Israelitish woman blasphemes, he is put in ward, but no one knows what punishment is to be meted out for that offence. Compare with this the story of Naboth and his judicial murder for alleged blasphemy in I Kings xxi, which chapter the Critics declare to be centuries older than Leviticus. When Jezebel, by means of perjured witnesses, convicts Naboth of that grave offence, there is not the slightest doubt in the mind of the judges and the people—as little as in Jezebel's own mind—what his punishment is to be. Now, if we were to admit that the narrative of the blasphemer was indeed written, or even 'edited', for the benefit of the post-Exilic community, is it reasonable to assume that in those days there would be doubt as to the penalty for blasphemy?

The evidence of the *language* of Leviticus precludes a late date of composition. Reihn, Delitzsch, Dillmann, and Hoffmann have demonstrated that it cannot truthfully be said to show traces of Exilic or post-Exilic times. The technical terms of the sacrificial regulations point to hoary antiquity, and are linguistically derived from ancient Arabic and Minæan (Hommel). There is in Leviticus an entire absence of neo-Babylonian or Persian loan-words that would reflect the age of the Exile. Of course, the language, vocabulary, and style differ considerably from that of the historical parts of the Pentateuch. But this is due to the nature of the subjects treated in Leviticus; *e.g.* sacrifices, leprosy, land laws, as against stories of family life, national history, and moral admonition in the other books. One hundred years ago, Macaulay drafted the Penal Code for India. In that work, his whole manner of writing—vocabulary, sentence-formation, and style—is different from that used by him in his History, Essays, Speeches, or Ballads. Yet, would anyone question Macaulay's authorship of the Indian Code, or would anyone advance the hypothesis of the existence of five separate Macaulays—one each for the History, Essays, Speeches, Ballads, and Code—and living centuries apart from one another?

Bible Critics point to the *Tochacha*, the Admonition in Lev. xxvi, as proof that at any rate that chapter must have been written at a late date, because the punishments foreshadowed in that chapter (v. 14–45) were clearly realized in the time of the Babylonian Exile. Those who do not eliminate the Divine from history or from human life regard the *Tochacha* as belonging to that unique mass of Bible predictions that have been fulfilled to the letter, and that are wholly inexplicable except on the Providential view of human history. But even quite apart from the predictive element in prophecy, there is no reason to doubt the Mosaic authorship of this chapter.

Hoffmann has drawn attention to a parallel of the *Tochacha* in the far older code of Hammurabi. One thousand years before Moses, that code concludes with the promise of blessings of the god Shamash for obedience to his law, and with a detailed account of the calamities that would overtake those who are faithless to them. Leviticus xxvi is thus merely another instance of the principle דברה תורה כלשון בני אדם, which the Jewish exegetes of the Middle Ages translated to mean—Scripture chooses those forms of literary expression that would be most effective with the hearers to whom they are addressed.

One more striking circumstance. The Ten Commandments are given on Mt. Sinai, and the promulgation of the other laws takes place in the Wilderness and the plains of Moab. How came they to be attributed to lands *outside* the Holy Land, territories that had no sacred associations for the men of Ezra's age, or for that matter even for the heroes of the Patriarchal age? Surely such a strange, 'inconvenient,' unnatural tradition is not likely to have been *invented*, but is based on fact. And if so, the events associated with that tradition could only have taken place in Mosaic times.

II

IMPROBABILITY OF THE CRITICAL THEORY

It is evident that if the Critical account of the origin and promulgation of the so-called Priestly code is accepted, it is necessary to attribute deliberate fraud to Ezra. The Critics do not feel this moral difficulty, because the avowed object of many of the Critics has for a long time been to 'deprive Israel of its halo', and to degrade its saints and heroes. But even those who do not recoil from attributing fraud to the sacred writers should weigh the sheer *improbability* of the introduction of a new code in the manner put forward by the Critical theory.

'It is utterly out of the question, that a body of laws, never before heard of, could be imposed upon the people as though they had been given by Moses centuries before; and that they could have been accepted and obeyed by them, notwithstanding the fact that these laws imposed new and serious burdens, set aside established usages to which the people were devotedly attached, and conflicted with the interests of powerful classes of the people' (W. H. Green).

Thus, on the theory of the Critics, tithes of corn, oil, and cattle for the support of the Levitical order had never before been heard of; yet the people submit to the new burdens without dissent. The Book of Nehemiah shows that there was a strongly disaffected party and a religiously faithless party in Jerusalem; yet no one raises a doubt. The Book of Deuteronomy was in the hands of at least the priests; yet even the hostile members of that body do not attempt to ward off the alleged new legislation by appealing to Deuteronomy XIII, 1, 'All this word which I command you, that shall ye observe to do; *thou shalt not add thereto*, nor diminish from it.' Even the Samaritans—then the bitterest enemies of Ezra and the Jews—are supposed to receive 'Ezra's Torah' as the undoubted work of Moses, and seem to keep on changing and enlarging it, as the followers of Ezra—on the assumption of the Critics—keep on making new additions to it for at least a century after his death!

The improbability of Ezra attempting to pass off his work as the work of Moses, or of his succeeding in such a hypothetical attempt, will be considerably increased, when we realize the lack of agreement between the 'Priestly code' and the conditions that confronted Ezra and his generation. P brings many things that could have been only of archæological interest. Its largest section deals with the portable Sanctuary in the Wilderness; but in Ezra's time, the Tabernacle, the Ark, the Urim and Thummim had long ceased to exist. The tithe-laws as given in P are intended for a large body of Levites and a small number of priests, in the proportion of ten Levites to one priest. But the Books of Ezra and Nehemiah tell us that in the community under Ezra's spiritual guidance there were, on the contrary, twelve *priests* to one Levite! And yet Ezra is alleged by the Critics to have spent fourteen years, from 458–444, in the adaptation of the older legal enactments to the conditions of the community in Palestine (Oxford Hexateuch, I, 137).

Even more strange, on the theory of the Critics, is the absence of *all* reference in the 'Priestly code' to the burning religious problems of the returned exiles, such as intermarriage. Ezra is crushed by grief and despair when he realizes the extent of the evil in the new community. 'And when I heard this thing, I rent my garments and my mantle, and plucked off the hair of my head and of my beard, and sat down. . . . I fell upon my knees and spread out my hands unto the LORD my God.' He then set about the work of reformation; he called upon the nobles and people to put away their strange wives. They answer with a loud voice, 'As thou hast said, so must we do'; and they enter upon the covenant, so fateful for the future of Israel and of monotheism. But to all this matter of intermarriage, which was of vital concern to Ezra and his School, there is not the slightest reference in the very legislation which, we are asked to believe, was produced for the salvaging of the community from the mortal danger of absorption among the heathens. No less than two chapters in the 'Priestly code' (Lev. XVIII and XX) are devoted to the subject of prohibited marriages; but not a word to the question which shook the post-Exilic community to its foundations. Surely an unaccountable omission—if the Critics are right.

There is, furthermore, no provision in P for the singers, porters, Nethinim, and Levites of Ezra's day. 'The musical services of the Temple are as much beyond its line of vision as the worship of the Synagogue.' In view of the minute way in which Leviticus regulated worship for the Mosaic generation, is it conceivable that, if Leviticus were a product of Ezra's age, there would be in it nothing directly bearing on the manner of contemporary worship?

III

THE ARGUMENT FROM SILENCE

A favourite argument against the early date of Leviticus is the so-called argument from silence. It is somewhat as follows: Throughout the period of the Judges and Kings, we find that the precepts of the Book of Leviticus were violated; hence, they could not then have existed. Furthermore, it is alleged that there is no explicit reference to them in the historical books of Judges, Samuel, and Kings—another supposed proof that they could not have been known.

As to the first consideration, even cases of flagrant violation do not disprove the existence of the law as laid down in Leviticus. Neither a Jewish law, nor any other law, necessarily presupposes universal compliance with its terms. All historical experience is against it. It is unnecessary to point to modern laws of incontestable and universally acknowledged existence that are accompanied by open and organized violation. And the same is true of ancient laws, even of those believed to have Divine sanction. Take the prohibition of image-worship in the Ten Commandments. Canon Charles has aptly pointed out that for fifteen centuries the whole of Christendom disregarded it, and half of the Christian Church is still disregarding it. If violation of a law were proof of its non-existence, then the Second Commandment has to this day not yet been given! In fact, the Critics themselves note that the existence and the disregard of a law-book may very well go together. Deuteronomy became known—they hold—in the year 620, during the reign of king Josiah. It was observed during his lifetime; but immediately after his death, it was totally disregarded. The attitude of the Critics is therefore as follows:—non-observance of the Law in the ages after Moses is proof absolute that no such Law was ever promulgated in the days of Moses; but non-observance of the Law after the death of Josiah does not prove the non-existence of the Law in Josiah's time. In other words, 'witnesses are reliable when they testify in favour of the Critics; but their veracity is promptly impeached, if their testimony is on the other side' (Baxter). For departures from statutory law in exceptional circumstances, see p. 371.

And as for the second consideration, viz, the silence of the Historical books, that is an even feebler support for the Critical position. A few examples will illustrate its feebleness. Thus, none of the Prophets speaks of the Ten Commandments, and there are exceeding few references to Sabbath, New Moon, or circumcision outside the Pentateuch; and yet no responsible historian doubts the existence of these institutions in ancient Israel. As for the Day of Atonement, the first clear and unmistakable mention of it after the Pentateuch is in Roman times by Josephus! Furthermore, all Critics admit that the Passover and the Feast of Weeks existed in Israel since the earliest days. The Feast of Weeks, however, is nowhere named in the Historical books of the Bible; and Passover only twice, and then only in connection with exceptional conditions. An examination of the passages in which Passover is alluded to (Josh. v and II Kings XXIII) shows conclusively that, but for these exceptional conditions, viz. that the Festival had for a long time fallen into neglect, there would have been no record of its celebration. Would, in that case, the silence of the Bible have been valid evidence that Passover was unknown until after the Exile? Similarly, wherever the Sabbath is referred to outside the Pentateuch, it is nearly always in passages where the Israelites are rebuked for desecrating the holy day. Had the Sabbath been duly observed by the Israelites, none of the Prophets would have had occasion to mention it. The fact, then, that the Day of Atonement is never alluded to in the Historical books is really *evidence in favour of its regular observance*.

Critics dwell on the fact that the Day of Atonement is not mentioned in I Kings VIII, 65, which describes the celebration of the dedication of Solomon's Temple. That celebration lasted a fortnight, during which period the tenth of the seventh month occurred, and there is no record that the festivities were suspended for that day. But neither is there in that chapter any indication that the popular rejoicings were moderated on the Sabbath day. Are we to argue that the Sabbath was unknown? We have here but another instance that, in regard to the feasts and fasts, Scripture does not record what is usual and normal, but only what is unusual and abnormal. This also explains Nehemiah VIII. That chapter describes the unusual events in the seventh month of the year 444, among them the observance of the Feast of Tabernacles on the 15th, 'for since the days of Joshua the son of Nun unto that day had not the children of Israel done so' (v. 17). It is silent in regard to the Day of Atonement, because evidently there had been no interruption in its observance, as it is quite unlikely that the priests ever allowed their supreme function in the Temple service on that day to fall into abeyance. The fast described in Nehemiah IX was not a substitute for the Day of Atonement. It was a special fast for special evils. It was a day of prayer and contrition, on which the people confessed the 'iniquities of their fathers' as well as their own. There is not the slightest analogy to the Day of Atonement. It was a fast supplementary to it, called forth by the uniqueness of the circumstances.

What we can deduce from the Biblical data is that past history is repeating itself at the present time. Just as many modern Jews who neglect the Sabbath and Festivals adhere to Yom Kippur, so in the periods of religious decadence in the past, the Israelites seem to have hallowed the Day of Atonement while ignoring the other Festivals.

IV

'EVOLUTION' IN SACRIFICE

'Those who advocate revolutionary ideas, either in government, in scholarship, or in religion, must show good cause and their arguments must possess overwhelming force. The proof must be clear, strong, and conclusive, without a shadow of suspicion in its reality or its sufficiency.' None can gainsay the reasonableness of this demand, put forward by an impartial judge of the Critical views, nor the lamentable failure of those views to meet this reasonable demand. 'But,' it is said, 'these new views are in line with the principle of Evolution. In ritual, as in everything else, the more developed must be later than the less developed, out of which, on the principle of Evolution, it has gradually grown. As the Priestly code (Leviticus and Numbers) shows the most ramified sacrificial enactments, it must be the latest of all the documents of the Pentateuch.' We are even told that there is a clear evolution from the simple to the complex in sacrifice, a straight line of development from the Prophetic document (JE) to Deuteronomy (D), from Deuteronomy (D) to Ezekiel, and from Ezekiel to the Priestly Code (P).

If there ever was an instance when the saying was true that 'theories are vast soap-bubbles with which the grown-up children of Learning amuse themselves, while the ignorant public stand gazing on and dignify these vagaries by the name of Science', that instance is Evolution in sacrifice. In the first place, the straight line of evolution—JE, D, Ezekiel, and P—turns out to be anything but straight. It is now generally admitted by the Critics that the 'Priestly code'—or at any rate its most important constituent, the Holiness chapters—is far from being the latest of the series. Instead of being the culmination of the chain, it is the *source* of Ezekiel. Ezekiel is saturated with the phraseology of Leviticus XVII–XXVI, and he takes for granted an acquaintance therewith on the part of his Babylonian hearers. But Leviticus is not only older than Ezekiel's half-ideal and half-allegorical vision of the constitution of the New Jerusalem, it is older than Deuteronomy; for the law of leprosy in Lev. XIII is the basis of Deuteronomy XXIV, 8, and Deuteronomy XII presupposes Lev. XVII.

In the second place, the whole idea of evolution *does not apply to a field of human history like the institution of sacrifice.* In the realm of language, for example, it is not true to say that, on the one hand, the more simple the language, the more primitive it is; nor, on the other hand, the more complex it is, the later is its appearance in the life of any ethnic group. Thus, Anglo-Saxon, with its five cases and eight declensions of the noun, is immeasurably more complicated than its direct lineal descendant, modern English; even as Latin is far more complex than Italian. The same holds true in the development of ritual laws. Besides, the statement that Leviticus must be the latest sacrificial legislation, because its ritual laws are the most elaborate, is quite against the evidence of primitive cultures. 'It does not appear that very simple systems of law and observance do belong to very primitive societies, but rather the contrary' (Rawlinson).

The case for 'evolution' in Biblical sacrifice is furthermore based by its advocates on a series of dogmatic assumptions which are not only not borne out by the facts, but are in direct contradiction to the facts. Among those unwarranted assumptions are the following: that in ancient Israel *every* slaughter for food was an act of sacrificial worship; that originally there was unlimited freedom of altar-building; that early sacrifices were all joyful feasts, with a total absence of any underlying reference to sin; and that sin- and guilt-offerings are late inventions, the fruit of the 'monotonous seriousness' of the so-called Priestly code.

Hoffmann, Wiener, and especially Baxter in his masterly *Sanctuary and Sacrifice*, have subjected these assumptions to an annihilating examination and shown their utter falsity.

As to sacrifice and slaughter being absolutely synonymous terms, Wiener refers to Exod. XXI, 37 ('If a man steal an ox, or a sheep, and kill it'), and he asks, Does the Legislator contemplate the *sacrifice* of stolen animals and of places made holy as the result? To ask the question is to reveal the utter absurdity of the Critical contention on this point.

To proceed to the next assumption of the Critics. The statement that there was unrestricted altar-building, and consequent multiplicity of sanctuaries, in ancient Israel rest, upon a mistranslation of Exodus XX, 24. בכל המקום does not mean 'in every place', but 'in whatever place' (Graetz). That is, in whatever place God would designate for worship—Shiloh, Gibeon, Jerusalem—an altar might be erected, and sacrificial worship would there be considered legitimate. Such permission of *successive* places of worship, till the building of the Central Sanctuary in Jerusalem, is something quite different from a recognition of *simultaneous* sanctuaries in different places.

The charge that the strict regulations concerning the sacrificial cult killed all the spontaneous joy which characterized ancient Israelite worship, implies a partiality on the part of the Critics for the lawless licence, foul sensuality, and unrestrained jollity of the heathen merry-makings —half-sacrifices, half-picnics—that were not infrequent in times of national apostasy. For nothing is further from the truth than to say that the Torah did, or does, kill joy. One commandment alone—that concerning Tabernacles, and found in the so-called Priestly code—would be sufficient to refute this. 'And ye shall take you on the first day the fruit of goodly trees, branches of palm trees, and boughs of thick trees, and willows of the brook, *and ye shall rejoice before the LORD your God seven days*' (Lev. XXIII, 40). The very men whom the Critics would turn into the makers of the 'Priestly code' soothe the people when weeping over their sins on that historic New Year's Day (Nehemiah VIII) with the words: 'This day is holy unto the LORD your God; mourn not, nor weep. Go your way, eat the fat, and drink the sweet, and send portions unto him for whom nothing is prepared; *for the joy of the LORD is your strength.*'

Even more astounding is the statement, in effect, that the sense of sin was unknown in Israel before the days of Ezra! It is sufficient to point to the agonized cry in Micah VI, 6 and 7—

'Wherewith shall I come before the LORD . . .
Shall I give my first-born for my transgression,
The fruit of my body for the sin of my soul?'

Surely, if the semi-heathen worshipper of whom Micah speaks felt such a sense of guilt, the loyal Israelite did not have to wait for Ezra to invent sin- and guilt-offerings to ease his soul. And were not penitential psalms written in Babylon some two thousand years before Ezra's date? So far from sin- and guilt-offerings being of quite late date, they are distinctly mentioned in pre-Exilic times (*e.g.* II Kings XII, 17); and, for that matter, are never mentioned in any post-Exilic Prophet. There is no truth whatsoever in the statements that P assigns 'an enormous importance' to the sin offering, or that peace offerings were in post-Exilic times practically banished. In the most exhaustive sacrificial catalogue in the 'Priestly Code' (Numbers VII), the other sacrifices outnumber sin offerings in the proportion of seventeen to one!

Probably the strangest argument of all for the lateness of P is, that Ezekiel and his circle wrote down from memory the pre-existent Temple usage; for 'so long as the cult lasted, no sacrificial code was needed'. This is contrary both to reason and historical analogy. It is contrary to reason to maintain 'that the laws of sacrificial worship were first written down, or even invented, during the Exile in Babylon, when there was no longer any sacrificial worship' (Dillmann). It is also contrary to historical analogy. Written regulations for the existing sacrificial cult existed in Egypt, Babylonia, and Phœnicia.

One concluding consideration. The Critics themselves tell us that sacrifice was of old the natural and universal expression of religious homage; that religion without sacrificial cult was unthinkable throughout antiquity; and they admit that 'heathen sacrificial worship was a constant menace to morals and monotheism' (Wellhausen). If, therefore, there was any Divine choice of Israel at all, is it not of all things the most natural that Israel's manner of Divine Service should be freed from everything foul, cruel, immoral, and idolatrous? (Baxter). But for such regulation at the hand of Moses, banishing everything debasing either to morals or monotheism from what is admitted by all to have been the universal expression of religious homage, his mission would assuredly have failed, and his work would have disappeared.

## B

## TABLE OF PROHIBITED MARRIAGES

IN FORCE AMONG JEWS TO-DAY

*A man may not marry :—*

(*a*) His mother, grandmother, and ascendants; the mother of his grandfather; his stepmother, the wife of his paternal grandfather, and of his ascendants; and the wife of his maternal grandfather.

(*b*) His daughter, grand-daughter, great-granddaughter and her descendants; his daughter-in-law; the wife of his son's son, and descendants; and the wife of his daughter's son.

(*c*) His wife's mother or grandmother; the mother of his father-in-law, and ascendants.

(*d*) His wife's daughter or her grand-daughter, and descendants.

(*e*) His sister, half-sister, his full- or half-brother's wife (divorced or widow; see, however, on Deut. xxv, 5, 9); and the full- or half-sister of his divorced wife in her lifetime.

(*f*) His aunt, and uncle's wife (divorced or widow), whether the uncle be the full- or half-brother of his father or mother.

(*g*) A married woman, unless Get has been given; and his divorced wife after her remarriage (her second husband having died or divorced her).

(*h*) Anyone who is not a member of the Jewish Faith; the issue of an incestuous union (*mamzereth*); the married woman guilty of adultery with him; and the widow whose husband died childless, until Chalitzah has been performed. A *Kohen* may not marry a divorced woman, a Chalitzah widow, or a proselyte.

[*A man may thus marry* :—

(*a*) His stepsister, his stepfather's wife (divorced or widow), his [1]niece; and his full- or half-brother's or sister's daughter-in-law.

(*b*) His cousin; his stepson's wife (divorced or widow); and his deceased wife's sister.]

*A woman may not marry* :—

(*a*) Her father, grandfather, and ascendants; her stepfather; and the husband of her grandmother, and of her ascendants.

(*b*) Her son, grandson, great-grandson; her son-in-law, and the husband of her grand-daughter and descendants.

(*c*) Her husband's father, or grandfather, and the father of her father-in-law—and ascendants; and the father of her mother-in-law.

(*d*) Her husband's son or grandson, and descendants.

(*e*) Her brother; half-brother; her full- or half-sister's divorced husband in her sister's lifetime; and her husband's brother and her nephew.

(*g*) A married man, unless Get has been given; and her divorced husband after the death or divorce of her second husband.

(*h*) Anyone who is not a member of the Jewish Faith; the issue of an incestuous union (*mamzer*); and the man guilty of adultery with her as a married woman.

[*A woman may thus marry* :—

(*a*) Her stepbrother; and her stepmother's former husband.

(*b*) Her cousin; and her deceased sister's husband, whether of a full- or half-sister.

(*c*) Her [1]uncle.]

---

[1] *In English law a man may marry the daughter of his wife's brother or his wife's sister; but not the daughter of his brother or sister.*

## C

## THE SACRIFICIAL CULT

### I. Sacrifice: Hebrew and Heathen

According to Bible and Talmud, the institution of sacrifice is as old as the human race. The study of primitive man, likewise, traces its origins back to the very beginnings of human society, and declares sacrificial worship to be both an elementary and a universal fact in the history of Religion.

Apart from various unconvincing theories as to the rise of sacrifice, there are two simple explanations as to the fundamental meaning of sacrifice.

The first of these takes sacrifice to be an act of homage and submission to the Heavenly Ruler, or of thankfulness for God's bounties; even as the suppliant expresses his submissiveness and his gratitude to an earthly ruler by gifts. The other declares that sacrifice arose from primitive man's yearning for reconciliation with the Deity. If for some reason the worshipper feared that he had forfeited Divine favour, he sought to propitiate it; and the giving up of things dearest to him—his first-born, his cattle, his possessions—was intended to effect this propitiation.

The existence of animal sacrifice as a virtually universal custom of mankind from times immemorial proves that the expression of religious feeling in this form is an element of man's nature and, therefore, implanted in him by his Creator. To spiritualize this form of worship, free it from cruel practices and unholy associations, and so regulate the sacrificial cult that it makes for a life of righteousness and holiness, was the task of monotheism. In heathen Semitic religions, sacrificial worship was cruel, often requiring human victims. It was foul—licentious rites being an essential element in many kinds of sacrifice. It was immoral—covering crimes and deliberate iniquities against fellow-men. It was irrational—steeped in demonology and magic. In absolute contrast to this degrading heathenism, the Torah banishes everything cruel, foul and unholy from the sacrificial cult. Moreover, the sphere of the efficacy of sacrifice is strictly limited; and, with a few specified exceptions (Lev. v, 1–6, 20–26), sacrifice atones only for sins committed unwittingly, if no human being suffers by them; viz., if restitution precedes the sacrifice. 'A deliberate moral obliquity is not to be obliterated by sacrifice. It must be punished under the penal law or forgiven by repentance, and for the individual there is no other means of atonement' (Montefiore).

Moderns do not always realize the genuine hold that the sacrificial service had upon the affections of the people in ancient Israel. It was for ages the main outward manifestation of religion, as well as the vehicle of supreme spiritual communion. The Central Sanctuary was the axis round which the national life revolved. The Temple was the forum, the fortress, the 'university' and, in the highest sense, the spiritual home of ancient Israel. The people *loved* the Temple, its pomp and ceremony, the music and song of the Levites and the ministrations of the priests, the High Priest as he stood and blessed the prostrate worshippers amid profound silence on the Atonement Day. As for the choicer spirits, their passionate devotion found expression in words like those of the Psalmist:—

'How lovely are Thy tabernacles, O Lord of hosts,
My soul longeth, yea, fainteth for the courts of the Lord. . . .
Happy are they that dwell in Thy house.'

'As the hart panteth after the water brooks,
So panteth my soul after Thee, O God.
My soul thirsteth for God, for the living God:
When shall I come and appear before God?'

'O send out Thy light and Thy truth; let them lead me;
Let them bring me unto Thy holy mountain, and to Thy dwelling-places;
Then will I go unto the altar of God, unto God, my exceeding joy.'

Religious ecstasy has rarely found nobler expression than in these lines of the Psalmist; and that words like these reflected the sincere and earnest faith of god-fearing men is beyond question. However, 'bad men also confided in sacrifice as an effective means of placating God, just as a gift might serve to corrupt a judge. This confidence in the efficacy of sacrifice involved an immoral idea of God and Religion. Against it, therefore, the Prophets direct their attack' (Moore).

### II. Do the Prophets oppose Sacrifice?

Widespread misunderstanding exists in regard to the attitude of the Prophets to the sacrificial cult, which attitude is often represented as an uncompromisingly hostile one. This is far from being the case.

The Prophets do not seek to alter or abolish the externals of religion as such. They are not so unreasonable as to demand that men should worship without aid of any outward symbolism. What they protested against was the fatal tendency to make these outward symbols the whole of religion; the superstitious *over-estimate* of sacrifice as compared with justice, pity and purity; and especially the monstrous wickedness with which the offering of sacrifices was often accompanied.

Thus, Amos denounces the people for their oppressions and impurities, warning them that as long as these are adhered to, the multiplication of sacrifices will not avert God's threatened judgments.

'I hate, I despise your feasts, and I will take no delight in your solemn assemblies. Yea, though you offer me burnt-offerings and your meal-offerings, I will not accept them, neither will I regard the peace-offerings of your fat beasts. Take thou away from Me the noise of thy song; and let Me not hear the melody of thy psalteries. But let justice well up as waters, and righteousness as a mighty stream' (v, 21–24).

God would not be the God of Holiness if He did not 'hate' and 'despise' sacrifices, hymns and songs of praise on the part of unholy and dishonourable worshippers. But there is no intimation that sacrifice, prayer and praise will continue to be 'hated', if the worshippers cast away their vile and oppressive deeds. In the same exhortation, he pleads :—

'Hate the evil, and love the good, and establish justice in the gate; it may be that the LORD, the God of hosts, will be gracious unto the remnant of Joseph' (v, 15).

Isaiah declares that the most elaborate ritual, if unaccompanied by righteous conduct, is both futile and blasphemous. In his opening arraignment of contemporary Israel, he proclaims :—

'Ah sinful nation, a people laden with iniquity....

'To what purpose is the multitude of your sacrifices unto Me? saith the LORD: I am full of the burnt-offerings of rams, and the fat of fed beasts ...

'When ye come to appear before Me, who hath required this at your hand, to trample My courts?

'Bring no more vain oblations; it is an offering of abomination unto me; new moon and sabbath, the holding of convocations—I cannot endure iniquity along with the solemn assembly.

'Your new moons and your appointed seasons my soul hateth; they are a burden unto Me; I am weary to bear them.

'And when ye spread forth your hands, I will hide Mine eyes from you: yea, when ye make many prayers, I will not hear: your hands are full of blood ...

'Put away the evil of your doings from before Mine eyes; cease to do evil; learn to do well; seek justice, relieve the oppressed, judge the fatherless, plead for the widow' (Isa. I, 4, 11–17).

If this is to be taken as an absolute condemnation by Isaiah of all sacrifice, then that absolute condemnation must also include Sabbaths and Festivals; solemn Assemblies, *i.e.*, public gatherings for worship, and the appearing before the LORD in the Temple : for all these are classed by him with 'blood of bullocks' and 'fat of fed beasts'. But, of course, to Isaiah, prayers and Sabbaths and solemn assemblies and Temple were noble and sacred institutions, indispensable to religious life, and it was only their intolerable *abuse* which he condemned. The same thing applies to his view of sacrifices. The Prophet's call is not, Give up your sacrifices, but, Give up your evil-doing.

A fair examination of the above words of Amos, the first of the literary Prophets, and of Isaiah, who utters what is taken to be the most sustained condemnation of sacrifice, bears out the considered opinion that 'there was use, a seemly and beneficial use, of sacrifice, but there was also an abuse, a vile and God-dishonouring abuse. The Prophets made war upon the latter, but it does not follow that they objected to the former' (Baxter).

The Prophets were orators, and made occasional use of hyperbole, in order to drive home upon the conscience of their hearers a vital aspect of truth which those hearers were ignoring. And when they were confronted by the pernicious belief that God desired nothing but sacrifice, and saw sacrifice being held to excuse iniquity, heartlessness and impurity—they gave expression to their burning indignation in the impassioned language of vehement emotion (see on Jeremiah VII, 22, p. 439).

The lesson which the Prophets laboured to impress upon the soul of Israel was nevermore forgotten. It is repeated by the sacred singers to whom we owe the Book of Psalms, 'the hymnbook of the second Temple'; by the Sages, who teach that 'the sacrifice of the wicked is an abomination to the LORD' (Prov. xv, 8), that offerings made of goods wrung by extortion from the poor are like murder (Ecclesiasticus XXXIV, 20); as well as by the Rabbis, who declare that obedience to God and love of men are greater than sacrifice.

### III. THE RABBIS AND THE SACRIFICIAL CULT

To the Rabbis, the institution of sacrifice is a mark of the Divine love unto Israel. Its purpose is to bring peace to the world. Nevertheless, the sacrificial cult is not to them of pre-eminent importance, but is co-ordinated with the knowledge and study of the Torah, with Prayer, and with the performance of good deeds. To the details of the sacrificial requirements they give symbolical meanings, and draw from them deep ethical and spiritual teachings. Thus, the sacrificial ordinances prove that God is with the persecuted. Cattle are chased by lions; goats, by panthers; sheep, by wolves; but God commanded, 'Not them that persecute, but them that are persecuted, offer ye up to Me.' In similar manner, Philo taught that 'the perfection of the victims indicates that the offerers should be irreproachable; that the Israelites should never bring with them to the altar weakness or evil passion in the soul, but should endeavour to make it wholly pure and clean; so that God may not turn away with aversion from the sight of it. The tribunal of God is inaccessible to bribes; it rejects the guilty, though they offer daily 100 oxen, and receives the guiltless though they offer no sacrifices at all. God delights in fireless altars, round which virtues form the choral dance.'

The Rabbis proclaim the cardinal importance, wellnigh the omnipotence, of Repentance in the spiritual life of man. 'Men asked Wisdom, "If a man sin what shall his punishment be?" Wisdom answered, "Evil pursueth the evil-doer." Men then asked Prophecy, the Torah, and God, "If a man sin what shall his punishment be?" Prophecy answered, "The soul that sinneth, it shall die." The Torah answered, "Let him bring a guilt-offering, and his sin shall be forgiven him." God answered, "Let him repent and it shall be forgiven him." ' Henceforth, Repentance becomes the sole condition of all expiation and Divine forgiveness of sins: 'Neither the sin-offering, nor trespass-offering, nor the Day of Atonement is of any avail, unless accompanied by Repentance.' With the cessation of sacrifices, study of the Torah, Prayer and Beneficence definitely take the place of the Temple Service. It is for this reason that the disappearance of the Temple did not in any way cripple Judaism. When the Temple fell, there still remained the Synagogue—with reading and exposition of the Torah, and congregational worship without priest or sacrificial ritual. The Temple was only in Jerusalem, while the Synagogue was in every village, the expression of the Jew's religion day by day and week by week. 'The Temple was the altar, the Synagogue was the hearth, and the sacred fire burned on each of them. With the fall of the Temple, the fire was quenched on the altar, stamped out under the heel of the conqueror; but it still glowed on the hearth.... In all their long history, the Jewish people have done scarcely anything more wonderful than to create the Synagogue. No human institution has a longer continuous history, and none has done more for the uplifting of the human race' (Herford).

IV. JEWISH INTERPRETATIONS OF SACRIFICE

Rabbinical Judaism accepted the law of sacrifices without presuming to find a satisfactory explanation of its details. 'The sacrificial institutions were an integral part of revealed religion, and had the obligation of statutory law. It was of no practical concern to inquire why the divine Lawgiver had ordained thus and not otherwise. It was enough that he had enjoined upon Israel the observance of them' (Moore). Sometimes, the Rabbis resorted to symbolism, though to a far lesser extent than Philo. Their attitude towards sacrifices has remained that of the main body of Jews in all generations, and has found eloquent expression in the writings of Yehudah Hallevi during the Middle Ages, and of S. R. Hirsch and D. Hoffmann in modern times. According to the last-named, sacrifices are symbols of man's gratitude to God and his dependence on Him; of the absolute devotion man owes to God, as well as of man's confidence in Him.

Alongside the symbolic interpretation of sacrifice is the so-called juridical. It is advocated by Ibn Ezra and to some extent by Nachmanides. Its essence is: As a sinner, the offender's life is forfeit to God; but by a gracious provision he is permitted to substitute a faultless victim, to which his guilt is, as it were, transferred by the imposition of hands. Many Christian exegetes adopted this interpretation, and built the whole theological foundation of their Church upon it.

Quite otherwise is the rationalist view of sacrifice held by Maimonides and Abarbanel. Maimonides declares that the sacrificial cult was ordained as an accommodation to the conceptions of a primitive people, and for the purpose of weaning them away from the debased religious rites of their idolatrous neighbours. (See on Lev. XVII, 7.) Hence the restriction of the sacrifices to one locality, by which means God kept this particular kind of service within bounds. By a circuitous road, Israel was thus to be led slowly and gradually up to a perception of the highest kind of service, which is spiritual. Abarbanel finds support for Maimonides' view in a striking parable of Rabbi Levi recorded in the Midrash. 'A king noticed that his son was wont to eat of the meat of animals that had died of themselves, or that had been torn by beasts. So the king said, "Let him eat constantly at my table, and he will rid himself of that gross habit." So it was with the Israelites, who were sunk in Egyptian idolatry, and were wont to offer their sacrifices on the high places to the demons, and punishment used to come upon them. Thereupon the Holy One, blessed be He, said, "Let them at all times offer their sacrifices before Me in the Tabernacle, and they will be weaned from idolatry, and thus be saved." '

Notwithstanding these views, the Rabbis and such thinkers as Maimonides and Abarbanel did not cease to look forward to a restoration of the sacrificial cult in Messianic times. 'Even those laws which have been enacted by human authority remain in force till they are repealed in a regular and legal manner. Whether any of these laws of the Torah will ever be abrogated we do not know, but we are sure that in case of such abrogation taking place, it will be done by a revelation as convincing as that on Mount Sinai. On the other hand, the revival of the sacrificial Service must, likewise, be sanctioned by the divine voice of a prophet' (M. Friedländer).

The Rabbis, however, hoped that with the progress of time, human conduct would advance to higher standards, so that there would no longer be any need for expiatory sacrifices. Only the feeling of gratitude to God would remain. 'In the Messianic era, all offerings will cease, except the thanksgiving offering, which will continue forever' (Midrash).

## D

### THOU SHALT LOVE THY NEIGHBOUR AS THYSELF

#### LEVITICUS XIX, 18

*The 'Golden Rule' in Judaism.* The world at large is unaware of the fact that this comprehensive maxim of morality—the golden rule of human conduct—was first taught by Judaism. No less a thinker than John Stuart Mill expressed his surprise that it came from the Pentateuch. Not only is it Jewish in origin, but, long before the rise of Christianity, Israel's religious teachers quoted Leviticus XIX, 18, either verbally or in paraphrase, as expressing the essence of the moral life. Thus, Ben Sira says, 'Honour thy neighbour as thyself.' In the Testaments of the Twelve Patriarchs we read: 'A man should not do to his neighbour what a man does not desire for himself.' Tobit admonishes his son in the words, 'What is displeasing to thyself, that do not unto any other.' Philo and Josephus have sayings similar to the above. As to the Rabbis, there is the well-known story of Hillel and the heathen scoffer who asked Hillel to condense for him the whole Law in briefest possible form. Hillel's answer is, 'Whatever is hateful unto thee, do it not unto thy fellow: this is the whole Torah; the rest is explanation.' Targum Jonathan adds to its translation of Lev. XIX, 18 a paraphrase in words almost identical with those of Hillel. In the generation after the Destruction of the Temple, Rabbi Akiba declares ' "Thou shalt love they neighbour as thyself" is a fundamental rule in the Torah.' His contemporary Ben Azzai agrees that this law of love is such a fundamental rule, provided it is read in conjunction with Gen. V, 1 ('This is the book of the generations of man. In the day that God created man, in the likeness of God made He him'); for this latter verse teaches reverence for the Divine image in man, and proclaims the vital truth of the unity of mankind, and the consequent doctrine of the brotherhood of man. All men are created in the Divine image, says Ben Azzai; and, therefore, all are our fellow-men and entitled to human love.

And the command of Lev. XIX, 18 applies to classes and nations as well as to individuals. The Prophets in their day, on the one hand, arraigned the rich for their oppression of the poor; and, on the other hand, pilloried the nations that were guilty of inhumanity and breach of faith towards one another. Their sublime conception of international morality has found wonderful expression in the words of Judah the Pious, a medieval Jewish mystic, who said: 'On the Judgment Day, the Holy One, blessed be He, will call the nations to account for every violation of the command "Thou shalt love thy neighbour as thyself" of which they have been guilty in their dealings with one another.'

*Modernist Depreciation of Lev.* XIX, 18, 34. Though the Founder of Christianity quotes 'Thou shalt love thy neighbour as thyself' as the old Biblical command of recognized central importance, many Christian theologians maintain that the Heb. word for 'neighbour' (*rea*) in this verse refers only to the fellow-Israelite. Its morality therefore is only tribal. But the translation of the Heb. word *rea* by 'fellow-Israelite' is incorrect. One need not be a Hebrew scholar to convince oneself of the fact that *rea* means neighbour of whatever race or creed. Thus in Exodus XI, 2—'Let them ask every man of his neighbour, and every woman of her neighbour, jewels of silver, etc.'—the Heb. word for *neighbour* cannot possibly mean 'fellow-Israelite', but distinctly refers to the Egyptians. As in all the moral precepts of Scripture, the word *neighbour* in Lev. XIX, 18, is equivalent to 'fellow-man', and it includes in its range every human being by virtue of his humanity.

In order to prevent any possible misunderstanding, the command of love of neighbour is in *v.* 34 of this same nineteenth chapter of Leviticus extended to include the homeless alien.

'The stranger (*ger*) that sojourneth with you shall be unto you as the home-born among you, and thou shalt love him as thyself; for ye were strangers (*gerim*) in the land of Egypt.'

But even this marvellous law, that is absolutely without parellel in any ancient or modern code of civil law, is cavilled at by modernist theologians and decried as 'narrow'. The Heb. word *ger*, they hold, denotes only an alien who had become a fellow-worshipper of the God of Israel. This is contrary to fact. The Israelites in Egypt are in this very verse spoken of as *gerim*: but they did not as a body adopt the worship of Isis or Apis; they were hated, suspected and enslaved 'strangers'. It is evident, therefore, that Lev. XIX, 34 likewise refers to the friendless and homeless foreigner. He was throughout antiquity the victim of injustice and oppression, as were the Israelites in Egypt; in Israel alone he was not obliged to struggle for recognition as a human being. (See further on love of alien and of enemy, pp. 313 and 316.)

*The 'Negative' Golden Rule.* There is one other argument that is resorted to in order to prove that the true Golden Rule was first promulgated by Christianity. The greatest stress is laid on the fact that both Tobit and Hillel paraphrase Lev. XIX, 18 in a negative way—'Whatever is hateful unto thee, do it not unto thy fellow.' This is contrasted, and unfavourably so, with the positive paraphrase in the New Testament, 'All things whatsoever ye would that men should do unto you, even so do ye unto them.' It is claimed that the former is only negative morality; and that in its positive restatement alone, as formulated in the Gospels, is the Rule a great imperative of moral enthusiasm.

This argument is now seen to be illusory. 'The delicate difference which has been thought to exist between the negative and positive form is due to modern reflection on the subject, and was quite unapparent to the men of antiquity' (G. Kittel). In the oldest Christian literature the two forms are recorded indiscriminately; and the negative Golden Rule occurs in the Western texts of Acts xv, 20, Romans xIII, 10, the Teaching of the Twelve Apostles, and the Apostolical Constitutions. And positive forms of the Rule have had a place in Judaism. Thus Hillel says, 'Love thy fellow-creatures'; and Eleazar ben Arach, 'Let the honour of thy neighbour be as dear to thee as thine own.' But the mere fact that Lev. xIX, 18 is positive, itself renders all talk of a negative Jewish morality in connection with the Golden Rule fatuous.

It is time that the attempt to rob Judaism of its title to having given the Golden Rule to humanity, as well as the dispute as to the superiority of the positive over the negative form, came to an end.

*As thyself.* 'Thou shalt love thy neighbour *as thyself*.' Regard for self has its legitimate place in the life of man. Unlimited self-surrender is impossible; and a sound morality takes account of our own interests equally with those of others. In the luminous words of Hillel: 'If I am not for myself, who will be for me? And if I am only for myself, what am I?' The Sifra, the oldest Rabbinic commentary on Leviticus, records the following: 'Two men are in the desert with a little water in possession of one of them. If the one drinks it, he will reach civilization; but if the two of them share it, both will die. Ben Petura said, Let the two of them drink, though both will die. Rabbi Akiba held that, in such a case, your own life has precedence over the life of your fellow-man.' Rabbi Akiba could not agree that two should perish where death demands but one as its toll. And, indeed, if the Torah had meant that a man must love his neighbour to the extent of sacrificing his life for him in all circumstances, it would have said: 'Thou shalt love thy neighbour *more than* thyself.'

There are those, both in ancient and in modern times, who do not agree with Rabbi Akiba, and who deem the view of Ben Petura the more altruistic, the more heroic. Such would have preferred that the words *as thyself* had not occurred in the Golden Rule. Others again preach the annihilation of self, or at any rate its total submergence, as the basic principle of human conduct. New formulations of the whole duty of man have in consequence been proposed by various thinkers. We need examine but one of these formulations—*Live for others*. Were such a rule seriously translated into practice, it would lead to absurdity. For *Live for others* necessarily entails that others live for you. You are to attend to everybody else's concerns, and everybody else is to attend to your concerns—except yourself. A moment's examination of this or any other proposed substitute for 'Thou shalt love thy neighbour as thyself' only brings out the more clearly the fundamental sanity of Judaism.

www.ingramcontent.com/pod-product-compliance
Lightning Source LLC
Chambersburg PA
CBHW060307240426
43661CB00059B/2682